Books by C. L. Sulzberger

An Age of Mediocrity

AN AGE OF MEDIOCRITY

Memoirs and Diaries

1963-1972

C. L. SULZBERGER

MACMILLAN PUBLISHING CO., INC.

New York

Macmillan Publishing Co., Inc.
866 Third Avenue, New York, N.Y. 10022
Collier-Macmillan Canada Ltd., Toronto, Ontario

Library of Congress Catalog Card Number: 73–2746

FIRST PRINTING 1973

Printed in the United States of America

For Adrian,

my son-in-law,
with respect and affection

ACKNOWLEDGMENTS

I WISH to thank the honorable Walworth Barbour for permission to quote from two letters to me dated January 20, 1966 and July 5, 1966; Margaret Truman Daniel for permission to quote from her father's letter to me of December 1, 1969; The Office of the President for permission to quote from President Nixon's letter to me of April 7, 1970; Harcourt Brace Jovanovich, Inc., for permission to quote four lines from C. P. Cavafy's "Candles," from *The Complete Poems of Cavafy,* translated by Rae Dalven; and the *New York Times* for permission to republish my 1971 interview with President Nixon.

I also wish to thank Miss Isabel Bass for her assistance in the preparation of the manuscript and for her invaluable help in the editing.

CLS

Contents

The diaries cited in this book cover the period between December 1963 and the end of 1971. Certain passages quoted in the first five chapters pertain either to earlier conversations already published in *A Long Row of Candles* and *The Last of the Giants,* or to later discussions in 1972. The 1972 material represents only partial extracts of talks I have decided not yet to print *in extenso.*

C L S

I

THE MEDIOCRE SHALL
INHERIT THE EARTH

Webster's New International Dictionary informs us that the word mediocre means "Of a middle quality; of but a moderate or low degree of excellence; indifferent; ordinary" and that mediocrity means the "Quality or state of being mediocre; a middle, intermediate or mean state, degree or quality; moderate mental capacity, ability, skill, etc." It is my contention that this is an Age of Mediocrity in the various senses defined by the great American lexicographer.

There were giants in the earth during earlier days of this century. But now, at this moment in time, most of them have already stumbled off to eternity. They leave behind, in the period covered by this book, but a few grand, vestigial figures—men like Mao Tse-tung or Charles de Gaulle.

How can the spectator like myself, living so close in time to those whose significance he would analyze, dare distinguish between the greater and the lesser figures of his era? All, as it were, achieved great rank as president, king, emperor, minister, or tyrant. Which among them approaches liminal grandeur?

Perhaps the advice of Isocrates is best heeded: "Listen to what men say about each other and try to discern at the same time the character of those who speak and of those about whom they speak." Such words are this book's raw material.

Before commencing to shape and elaborate this raw material, however, I wish to stress one theorem. This is simply that, although without question the period I have covered is little marked by giants and much featured by mediocrities, the latter, when taken in Noah Webster's sense "of a middle quality" will be seen to carry with it political benefits. For the political giants are produced by crises—or produce them. The men of the "moderate degree" of excellence are tailored better to the normal if sometimes unexciting needs of peace. I urge the reader to contemplate this proposition as he turns the ensuing pages.

Late in 1970, the year before his death, Dean Acheson complained to me at his Maryland farm: "We are now in a period where there are mediocre men everywhere. People have opinions but no knowledge and leaders are made in the image of the masses. Democracy is only tolerable because no other governmental system is."

In a sense Acheson's gloomy observations parallel those of Oswald Spengler. Spengler pointed out in 1914 in *The Decline of the West* that the English had only one Pitt in over two hundred years, but that their tradition enabled them to survive subsequent mediocrities. And even if this very tradition, as the pessimistic German could not know, was still to nourish in Churchill a greater man than Pitt, what mark did even this glorious moment leave on the history of the gallant British people? Georges Pompidou, then prime minister and soon to be president of France observed to me (January 23, 1968): "The British simply don't work hard enough, and for years they have been living above their means. They have become accustomed to a wealth they no longer have, and at the root of all their trouble are the labor unions which insist on imposing too many workers on every conceivable kind of enterprise."

And so the British empire disintegrated, confirmation of Spengler, who wrote:

> I lay it down that Imperialism, of which petrifacts such as the Egyptian empire, the Roman, the Chinese, the Indian, may continue to exist for hundreds and thousands of years—dead bodies, amorphous and dispirited masses of men, scrap-material from a great history—is to be taken as the typical symbol of the end.

It is almost as if Karl Marx, whose vision Spengler disliked, had written these very words. But Marx himself did not know how his own theory would be distorted. Russia, the first state seeking to build itself in his image, succeeded only in distorting that image beyond but the dimmest recognition.

Our age of mediocrity is marked not only by an absence of outstanding men, but also by an absence of vigorous new ideas. Religion based on the concepts of either God or man is foundering. And those who invented God to explain man to himself, as if proclaiming a shattering discovery, now announce God is dead.

From Ireland to Tibet the priestly profession is slowly sickening for lack of applicants to fill death's immutable roster. And Marxism, the most successful substitute devised for deism, is crumbling into two major rival faiths, like the old Roman and Greek churches, and a host of subsidiary protestant sects. Perhaps as good an explanation for this latter phenomenon as any I have read comes from Robert Ardrey, anthropologist and ethologist, who wrote in his essay on "Four Dimensional Man":

> Not the vices or virtues but the failures of Marxism concern me. Why, after over half a century of social experiment, have post-Revolutionary states emphatically failed to "wither away," classless societies obstinately refused to come into being, and the suppression of private property been accomplished only through the persuasions of unimaginable numbers of policemen?

Deeply rational, if poetic, Milovan Djilas, once a Marxist, observed of the communist world (May 17, 1968): "Mao was treated as a godlike figure, like Stalin. But there were major differences. Mao was the first Marxist to say that the classless society must be educated and developed in a period of centuries, not decades. . . . And Mao has understood that what has come about in Russia now is the development of a new privileged class. He is trying to prevent the same thing from happening in China; but he will succeed only during his own lifetime, as long as he lives. After he dies everything will change."

Even the right-wing fanatics, who have produced since time began their own kind of greatness—Alexander, Napoleon—are today a confused and seedy lot. Fat neo-Nazis fumble in the land of that dreadful dogma's birth; prattling actors still intermittently seek to strut the stage of Caesar's —and Mussolini's—Rome.

Following his third prison term for ideological heresy (one under the prewar monarchy, which incarcerated him as a communist; two under Tito, who jailed him as an anticommunist), Djilas said to me (May 17, 1968): "We are moving toward the death of all ideologies; not ideas, ideologies. Religion was the first ideology but it lacked a social outlook; it was only moral. The first truly complete ideology was Marxism. But now we are going toward the death of all isms. Hegel produced the last great philosophical system but he was not a great philosopher.

"I am not a religious man but I know that a human being must have conscience and morality. I agree with religion that a man must believe in something, but not in God. All versions of communism are becoming decadent. They must inevitably change into a new democratic society. This is absolutely inevitable. Communism is a combative warrior's concept and organization and society cannot bear to live indefinitely in such a tense atmosphere. . . ."

Without isms or credos to guide them, men must look even more to inspirational leadership, a characteristic that now seems lacking. What, aside from inherited characteristics like hunger, sex, or Ardrey's much-debated "territorial imperative," is there to guide mankind at this moment?

Once I discussed this with de Gaulle (July 1, 1965). I recalled that Stalin named fear as the principal force motivating men. Others cited religion, nationality, family. What did the General think was the primary influence governing men in their actions? Without a moment of hesitation he answered:

"One must draw a distinction between the individual and the collective masses. For the individual, it is ambition and a taste for adventure. I think the real motivation, the primordial motivating force for the individual, is ambition, but for the masses it is fear. There Stalin was right. And this applies to the masses of all countries."

Ideology moves fewer and fewer people. Pompidou, de Gaulle's pragmatic successor, concludes: "There are no profound differences except for ideology dividing Moscow and Washington, and ideology is losing its importance. After all, when the Russians have automobiles, what will be the difference?"

With men, alas, as with ideas, it is not the meek who shall inherit the earth, it seems, but the mediocre who have already done so. And one quality they lack is meekness. In January 1972, André Malraux, extraordinarily gifted writer, revolutionist, and warrior, who abandoned his left-wing credo to become *metteur en scène* of de Gaulle's Fifth Republic, complained one day at lunch:

"This is a sadly barren era: there are no great men in any field—politics, art, writing, etc. None in America, in Europe. There is no Hemingway, no Kipling, no Tolstoi. Solzhenitsyn is a brave and noble man in his personal behavior, but this doesn't make him a great novelist."

To some degree Malraux attributed this to the shifting locus of power and civilization. He said: "The capital fact is the death of Europe. When I was twenty years old the United States was approximately in the position of Japan today in terms of world importance. Europe was at the heart of things and the great superpower was the British empire. But now all dominating forces in today's world are foreign to Europe. The great power in the world is the United States and, to the side, there is the Soviet Union. Europe has virtually disappeared as a factor and it took astonishingly little time for this change to come about. Two centuries ago the United States was not even a nation; now it is a colossus."

Nor did he think Europe could be reborn as a community emerging from the Common Market. "The idea of a European community is not a serious major force," he said. "You can't create a United States of Europe the way the various American states drew together as a United States of America. After all, they had a common enemy, the redskins. If China invaded Europe—speaking theoretically—Europe could perhaps become a united force in face of such a common enemy. But that is the only way this is possible."

And even China, without a giant, might founder, Malraux continued. No one knew what would happen to China when Mao died. Chou had no ambition to succeed him; he only wanted to be foreign minister. There might be a civil war of succession; almost surely some bloodshed. Who could predict the outcome? After all, who could have foreseen Khrushchev sitting in Stalin's office? To the mind of the old poet-revolutionary: "If it is not a revolution that we are living through, then indeed it is our death agony that is beginning." And he has no doubt it is the latter.

Over another long lunch (July 11, 1969), Malraux remarked that the new, post-de Gaulle French government was "a triumph of mediocrity" and thought this was in line with an apparent tendency throughout the world. He spoke of France's new president Pompidou as another Louis-Philippe, the pudgy French king who reigned between two revolutions. Pompidou's program, he said, was simply another version of Louis-Philippe's "*enrichissez-vous.*"

With the nostalgia of a romantic, he spoke (January 12, 1972) of de Gaulle, Churchill, and Mao Tse-tung as the three dominating figures he had met, as "the giants." He added that Stalin had been a devil "but a great devil."

As for the successors? Chou En-lai, despite his cultivation, was not a great man. He was "very secondary."

When unable to satisfy their strange penchant for "giants" and for dominating leadership, the French are obsessed with the fear of being dominated by other nations. Pompidou confessed to me (January 23, 1968): "We here in Europe—and I especially refer to France—must keep from being absorbed by the U.S.A. As a matter of fact, little by little I think this is bound to come about anyway."

The French have a particularly strange complex about the menace of America. For them it resembles what St. Augustine once called "the great western Babylon," which "endeavors to communicate her language to all the lands she has subdued, to procure a fuller society." Thus Maurice Couve de Murville, an indifferent prime minister but a great foreign minister, transfers to Americans a psychological problem elaborated by French Cartesian logic. He says:

"You are discovering how powerful you are militarily. And you are irritated that you can be opposed despite this. You are obsessed by your strength. . . . No nation has ever had such a power for destruction as the power you hold today. You want to be the gendarmes of the world. You don't admit it but this is a fact. And, while you can destroy the world, you cannot conquer it. For example, you could destroy China, or a large part of it, but you cannot conquer China. We think this is the real question, the real issue today.

"And we also think this poses a deep-seated problem in your country. You are caught between this new pressure, represented by your military people, and your tradition and instinct, which is opposed to such a trend

—your tradition and instinct to be tolerant and liberal and friendly with everyone. This whole matter plays a very important role not only in French public opinion but also throughout Europe and you should realize it."

Fearing its own ability to be led by mediocrities, France fears even more the threat of other nations similarly led. Maybe the French are particularly pessimistic when there is no great man on the horizon because, by nature anti-Marxist, they are inherently ungovernable except by giants. As David Ben-Gurion once commented to me (July 24, 1968): "All Frenchmen are Bonapartists." Even of the murdered John F. Kennedy, Hervé Alphand, a former French envoy to Washington, who knew Kennedy well, sadly quoted the words of Stendhal: *"Il n'est qu'un brillant peut-être."* This was December 21, 1963, just weeks after Kennedy's assassination.

An aspect of greatness never found in mediocre men is style. Mediocrity seems usually to be accompanied by a total absence of charisma and often by a total absence of taste. Consider even the contrasting methods of departure: de Gaulle to his Merovingian forest in France's gloomy eastern marches, investing in philanthropy the profits of his fabulous literary success; or the dilapidated Churchill, still *grand seigneur* of his estate at Chartwell. And then, the roistering *nouveau riche* cattleman, Lyndon Johnson, at home in the gimcrackery of his Texas ranch, swollen by profits not wholly unconnected with his political success.

Johnson was a man who had great dreams, but not the quality to achieve them. He used to say at his Texas ranch: "This is the tree I expect to be buried under and when my grandchildren see this tree I want them to think of me as the man who saved Asia and Vietnam and who did something for the Negroes in this country." Yet even he seemed at times to doubt his abilities.

". . . there are some people [he said] in this country, those Fulbrights, who only want a Fortress America, maybe supporting a Little White Europe. Those Fulbrights say about Asia—they are not our kind of people. Well I don't share that view. I am preserving the brown man, not warring on him. Somebody has got to protect the two and a half billion people in Asia. I am interested in those people and their education and their food and their health and that's what I am always saying. Why I tell Ho Chi Minh, if you will just lay down your pistol I'll help you."

A few days after he succeeded the slaughtered Kennedy, Johnson was already saying: "I don't think this country is ready for a president from Texas. I just don't think the east is going to accept me. I am sure that in this respect I am doomed to fail."

It was not his geographical or social origin that doomed Johnson in a country that has honored and esteemed Truman, Eisenhower, and others of modest western background. It was simply the fact that democracy could detect in its leader that "mean state, degree, or quality" defined by Webster and therefore could not be aroused or guided by him.

A Frenchman, who once served in Washington as ambassador, knew Johnson's successor. Richard Nixon was, he said: "a mediocrity. He lacks education and culture, is *un primaire*. Perhaps he has some charm but he is a definite second-rater." When discussing the current talk of a "New Nixon," the envoy sniffed with quiet sarcasm (October 6, 1968): "I suppose that means the rich Nixon. He has money now, doesn't he?"

Not only the French see the political horizon cumbered with nothing but squat, unimpressive figures. Adenauer, a large-hewn man made by a carpenter, was confident that no one within his ken could emerge at the German helm. How true this has proven. The succession: Ludwig Erhard, the acme of mediocrity in means and manner; Kurt Kiesinger, the smooth Teutonic version of Britain's Macmillan, himself no great man; and Willy Brandt, more noble in form than in content.

Small men, indeed, are governed by the conviction that their predecessors were incompetents and their successors only schemers. They are not impressed by grandeur and deliberately scoff at its rare portents. Witness Dean Rusk, for example, on de Gaulle (December 15, 1963): "Remember he is not twelve feet tall. He is only six and a half feet tall."

This is not the time of great innovations and great innovators. It is more an ingathering of the "middle quality" and of but "a moderate degree of excellence." Even the old ideas that but so recently made music in men's ears, excited visions, turned human morality starward, are tarnished, worn, and dead.

They haven't been even remotely replaced by those whose only accomplishment is the use of home-made explosives to produce intellectual and physical nihilism on a leaden scene. The giants are now *in*, not *on* the earth, save for a scantling of surviving images outliving their own past. Mao, the archetype, represents his own erstwhile glory. Like the stiff corpse of El Cid, he is bound to his horse to lead, unconsciously, a final charge against the enemy.

When Henry Kissinger accompanied President Nixon in a formal call on Mao he was impressed by the old magnifico. Kissinger told me (April 3, 1972): "He was grossly overweight but he had a remarkable capacity to dominate things around him. Physically he exuded will power. De Gaulle dominated any room in which he stood because of his sheer character. Adenauer dominated by his serenity. Mao dominated equally—by this feeling of will.

"We only talked for a little over an hour and I have no way of knowing if Mao has more than an hour or two of effective mental force during a day. But he did convey this impressive atmosphere of tremendous power. Very recently I reviewed the transcript of our conversation and I found it like the overture of a Wagnerian opera. Every single thing we discussed in the subsequent conversations with Chou En-lai was previously mentioned in that single talk with Mao."

Maybe Kissinger was influenced by the Mao legend. Or maybe the faltering giant, like Churchill in his latter years, still had moments of illumination. But other evidence suggests the Chinese revolutionary has lost his active power, even with those around him. A recent French visitor to Mao was horrified to find Chou En-lai sitting near Mao reading a newspaper. "Imagine anyone reading a paper next to de Gaulle," he protested with due reverence.

Even journalism, my own trade, has been marked by mediocrity's leveling influence. A métier that once produced distinguished writers like Rudyard Kipling, Stephen Crane, and Ernest Hemingway, as well as audacious reportorial craftsmen such as Frederick Birchall, Richard Harding Davis, Henry Morton Stanley, and "Bull Run" Russell, is now served by instant analysts. Prejudice has replaced pride as inspiration, emotion substitutes for intellect, passion for honesty.

Where today can one find the kind of thoughtful lucubration of a man like Walter Lippmann who, even when wrong (which was not infrequent), thought deeply and expressed himself in lucid prose. Such calm consideration is replaced by savage bias or by the felicitous neat platitude considered profound because it is aimed a half inch above the level of the middle-brow.

No vast human shadows seem capable of dominating today's historical horizon, but who can ever discern tomorrow's giants? Who, in 1939, knew that an unsuccessful politician named Churchill would be Britain's greatest statesman since Pitt, that an obscure and retired provincial mayor named Adenauer would be Germany's greatest leader since Bismarck, and that an aloof colonel named de Gaulle would be France's greatest hero since Napoleon? The observation is not new. Max Weber, echoing Nietzsche, wrote long ago:

> No one knows who will live in this building. No one knows whether, at the end of this formidable transformation, entirely new prophets will arise, whether old ideas and ideals of yesterday will assume a new vigor, or whether, on the contrary, a mechanical rigidity embellished by a kind of fossilized self-importance will gain the day. In the latter event it would be true of the "final men" of this evolution of culture that they would be mindless specialists, heartless men of pleasure. These nullities would boast of having climbed to a never previously reached peak of humanity.

2

THE SECOND OLDEST

PROFESSION

THOMAS JEFFERSON, WHO WAS NOTABLY PREJUDICED ON THE subject, wrote of royal rule, then still a common practice:

> Take any race of animals, confine them in idleness and inaction, whether in a stye, a stable or a stateroom, pamper them with high diet, gratify all their sexual appetites, immerse them in sensualities, nourish their passions, let everything bend before them, and banish whatever might lead them to think, and in a few generations they become all body and no mind. . . . Such is the regimen in raising Kings, and in this way they have gone on for centuries.

Today the profession of kingship is far more restricted. Its surviving practitioners have, for the most part, learned how to adjust their conceptions, their habits, and their family educational systems to an era of popular government. Even their mode of breeding has changed, if only because so few of their peers remain.

Jefferson objected that "the practice of Kings marrying only in the families of Kings, has been that of Europe for some centuries." Yet today some of the most successful monarchs come from short-lived, rudely vigorous dynasties: Haile Selassie's, established by ruse and force in this century despite its titular boasts; Shah Mohammad Reza's, created by his father, an ambitious cavalry sergeant; and that of the twentieth-century Saudi sovereigns of Arabia, who first had to make a country in order to rule it.

In many lands, like socialist Scandinavia or democratic Britain, monarchy is largely a matter of symbolism and ritual. Of all titles conceived by man for man—transcending in arrogance even those like King of Kings,

Shahinshah, Ilkhan, or The Conquering Lion of Judah—the most magnificent in its pretentiousness is that of First Sea Lord, conceived when Britannia ruled the waves. How sad that during those brief days when little Spitfires and Hurricanes were racketing through the skies to save freedom, the British never appointed a First Lord of the Air.

There is something pathetically splendid about the glamor that nations deliberately attach to the titular trappings of their chieftains, even to those lesser lordlings: the Wali of Swat, the Imam of Yemen, the McGillicuddy of the Reeks, the Jamsahib of Las Bela, the Knight of Glin, the Fakir of Ipi, the O'Connor Don, or the Nono of Spiti. By clothing mere mortals in such ornate verbal dress, the excuse is provided for voluntary abasement to their power.

But save in odd and eccentric corners of history, save as vestigial remnants of an antique past, *Ces Princes Qui Nous Gouvernent* (to steal the title of a political tract once written by French Prime Minister Michel Debré) have departed from the active scene. The prince is used at best as a token of national continuity, as a kind of confidential counselor to his statesmen. With rare exceptions, few surviving princes can pretend to any true ruling function nowadays.

The sovereign's function today resembles Martial's description of the office: "Tis the chief virtue of a Prince to know the people about him." Or, as the acknowledged expert on the subject, Niccolo Machiavelli, wrote: "If he listen to a multitude of advisers, the Prince who is not wise will never have consistent counsels, nor will he know of himself how to reconcile them. Each of his counselors will study his own advantage, and the Prince will be unable to detect or correct them. Nor could it well be otherwise, for men will always grow rogues on your hands unless they find themselves under a necessity to be honest."

This function was understood by that modest, upright king of Norway, Haakon VII, who led his country during World War II and helped cleanse its soul from the stain of Quisling. Haakon, an eminently constitutional and unassuming sovereign, used to say: "I'm just the hat placed on a chair to show it's occupied."

In 1945, some months after his return to Oslo from England, he told me he habitually advised his government not to be irked because small nations were not invited to make international decisions. "I tell them," he said, "it is just like in school and they shouldn't get complexes. In school the senior boys make all the decisions and then tell the younger boys. The younger boys may complain and they may have very sensible ideas. But the senior boys say it's too bad, all the decisions have been made and it will be done accordingly."

Such homespun logic shows an effective modern view of the atavistic royal tradition. Haakon had a useful concept of the continuity of his advisory role. He told me (June 1949) that he had personally urged his government to join the North Atlantic pact. He wanted to make clear to all who their real friends were—and to do so in peacetime, so they could never again be fooled during war as the Norwegians were by Germany in 1940. He was trying to consider all questions in terms of a fifty-year period.

This is a modest and useful theory of kingship and suited to the gathering Age of Mediocrity, which well before its inception had largely discarded royalty. In this century there have been few monarchs who played any major part in influencing destiny.

At various times I have observed this dwindling status in rulers of twenty-six peoples. Some were active; some were cast upon the exile's scrapheap, and some aspired to return. These have been sovereigns or pretenders in Japan, Belgium, Britain, Saudi Arabia, Swat, Iran, Morocco, Egypt, Holland, Bahrain, Greece, Iraq, Ethiopia, Italy, Vietnam, Sweden, Rumania, Jordan, Norway, Jaipur, Spain, Albania, Italy, Afghanistan, Jugoslavia, and the Vashawasha branch of Rhodesia's Mashonas.

Among these sheikhs, sultans, maharajahs, princes, kings, and emperors, I found some efficacious men—Haile Selassie, Hussein of Jordan, solemn Baudouin of Belgium, Reza Pahlevi of Iran—and one woman, Holland's Juliana. But there was only one true giant: King Abdul Aziz Ibn Abdur Rahman Al Feisal Al Saud of Saudi Arabia, whose guest I was at a tent city outside Mecca in 1946.

In 1900 Ibn Saud, a refugee chieftain in Kuwait, mounted an attack in the heart of the desert area from which his ancestors came and captured its main town, Riyadh, in a surprise night raid, climbing the walls with ladders and overpowering the guards. The aged king told me of this exploit, which started his conquest of a vast land, pointing successively to his numerous wounds as we dined with his sons and brothers or talked in a lean-to tent, surrounded by a semicircle of squatting guards, the silver filigree on their pistols, rifles, and swords, their teeth and the whites of their eyes all glittering in the moonlight.

But one wound he did not mention. Later, the Emir Bin Jiluwi, who took part in that famous raid, told me the story. Bin Jiluwi had been among the handful of loyal followers who stormed out of Kuwait with Ibn Saud and across the desert on their camels. While the fighting raged atop the wall of Riyadh, Ibn Saud was dangerously wounded in his privates, and Bin Jiluwi said to him sorrowfully: "Ah, Abdul Aziz, you have gained a city but you have lost something more precious."

To prove that nothing vital had happened to him, Ibn Saud ordered a soldier to bring in a woman during the battle. Then he proceeded to demonstrate he was not impaired.

Indeed, he sired an enormous family with his various wives and concubines, formally honoring with the royal prerogative only the male offspring of legal spouses. These never exceeded four at any one time because of his strict fundamentalist interpretation of Islam; but they constantly shifted in personnel. He showed me a family tree of the resulting princes. To the best of my recollection, they exceeded fifty in number and spanned some fifty years in age.

The king, as I have previously written (*A Long Row of Candles*), resembled some grand Old Testament chieftain. He liked to speak in parables. Referring to Germany, then recently defeated, he related to me the following tale, which his official interpreter translated from the archaic desert Arabic:

"Once there was an old sheikh. A tiny serpent came to him and said, 'There is a wolf hunting me and I crave protection.' The sheikh put the serpent in his bosom but the serpent said he did not feel safe there because the wolf might reach up and scratch him. Therefore he asked to be put in the sheikh's mouth, and the wolf went away. Then the serpent said to the sheikh, 'Now I will reward you for your kindness. I am going to bite you. But I shall offer you a choice as to whether I bite you in the tongue or on the palate.' That is the way of an enemy. It is the way of Germany and one must take care."

The quality of kings—and their role—had elsewhere long since dwindled. Haile Selassie, a diminutive, well-made little man with strikingly aristocratic features, did indeed bring some kind of political unity to the newly liberated states of Africa by sponsoring their UN regional organization. Shah Mohammad Reza accomplished the unusual feat of launching a revolution by decree in order to force reactionary landlords to install modern methods in Iran. Baudouin and Juliana have worked hard and earnestly at difficult tasks. But, in general, both the character of monarchs and their importance has faded. As a species they become even rarer than whooping cranes.

Yet the late King Paul of Greece contended (January 25, 1957) that kingship was still viable in the space age. He argued: "A king should influence his people and his government in the right direction. In very few countries does the king have an active role in affairs of state. For example, I have the right to dissolve parliament, to choose prime ministers, to grant pardons, and to give decorations. That's about all. Of course, I'm considered the head of the armed forces. But I can't act there without my government and my staffs.

"Immediate contact with the people is what is essential. My wife and I travel about the country constantly and we try and figure out ways of helping the particular traits of this people. I have done something which should have a great effect owing to the peculiarities of this country. I've started a committee to give dowries to the poorest girls. There is now a special wicket in each bank for the dowry fund so that it can be accumulated and distributed. Some of these girls can thus set aside enough to buy a small house when they get married.

"The most important thing for a king is to know the feeling of his people. And he must remember also that there is something in the theory of kingship that makes people look up to a king—if he is a decent person—not like Carol [of Rumania], of course. People tend to place their best hopes and feelings on the person of a king and, if he doesn't live up to this, they feel let down. My grandfather [King George I] had an excellent motto: 'My strength is the love of my people.' I think that is the best motto in kingship, don't you?"

He thought there was more need for royal leadership in a poor country like Greece than in richer, better educated lands like Scandinavia. Of the latter, he said, "They have a higher level. Therefore there is less room for the initiative of a king. Here one has to build up everything constantly.

"There is still plenty of room," he added, "for behind-the-scenes maneuvers and endeavors even if there are strict limits on the king's actual authority." He was amused by the fact that Queen Elizabeth of England had been challenged by the parliamentary opposition for selecting Harold Macmillan as prime minister, although he had not yet been chosen head of the Tory party. "Just exactly like me and Prime Minister Caramanlis," he chuckled.

Once when I lunched with Paul at his summer palace in Corfu he told me that he thought the technique of kingship was changing, and he was trying to bring his son up with a practical and democratic background to face the new requirements.

He foresaw that a king would no longer be able to command armed forces; how could he keep up with military evolution? Military science was too complicated; no king could know the problems of all services. And kings, he thought, would not need more specialized knowledge of economics or foreign affairs.

The basic need for a king was common sense. The next generation of kings would have to take more active decisions, as the need for decision-making increased. A strong man was useful at the head of any democracy, although in the ideal democracy, like Switzerland, nobody even knew the president's name.

The method of ruling had become more democratic, but the role of king was just as necessary as in earlier days. People needed a symbol which was also responsible. It was impossible to establish the same kind of affectionate relationship between the public and a president because presidents changed too fast. Also a king could serve as a repository of knowledge as he gained experience with time. A king was a nonpolitical figure who could even work with a socialist government if necessary—although it was impossible to work with communists.

Notwithstanding, Prince Paul of Jugoslavia, an ex-ruler then living in Paris, later commented that despite the Greek sovereign's good intentions he was making a mess of young Constantine's education. He told me that under the influence of Queen Frederika, Greece's Paul was preparing Constantine badly for kingship.

He was giving him an old-fashioned education which "is no good nowadays." A prince, to have any chance as king, should be "stuffed with knowledge" and should mix with all kinds of people to know what they are like and what they want.

Young Constantine, indeed, did have little luck when he succeeded to the throne. As recounted later—in Constantine's own words—he was sucked into the political vortex, a process that ended in a military *coup d'état* against him and against constitutional government. When, eight months later, he sought to reverse the coup, Constantine failed dismally and fled to Rome.

The poor fellow had gambled all or nothing on the advice of his principal general. The general was wrong; Constantine lost his job. Had he won his bet, history might have regarded him as the savior of his nation. Yet nothing fails like failure—as is known by many decrowned kings.

I asked Japan's tiny, gentle-voiced Emperor Hirohito how he envisioned the profession of sovereign which, I pointed out, was probably the second oldest profession in the world.

As translated by the court's visibly awed interpreter, Hirohito claimed that emperorship has shown an ability to keep up with the changes brought about by time and politics. One of its main functions, he said, was to modernize itself.

I asked if, because of evolving requirements, he thought it desirable to educate an emperor differently today than when he himself was young, for example stressing physics and other sciences. He acknowledged this was desirable; science was very important.

But he went out of his way to stress the moral qualities of the job. For him, too, the most important aspect was the link between the emperor and his people; this must be kept alive as social development came about. He seemed to think this moral core was primordial. (Afterward, the Grand Master of the Ceremony, who was present, observed that both the crown prince and his son attended regular schools rather than being privately tutored as had been the case with Hirohito.)

The emperor, then already seventy, said he had had to make two most momentous decisions. One was assumption of governing responsibility on February 26, 1936, at the time of a military coup. The 1936 incident occurred when it was widely believed that, as a result of the coup, Prime Minister Keisuke Okada had been assassinated, although in fact he was only hiding. The emperor felt it incumbent on himself to preside over a cabinet meeting during the crisis.

The second decision was to terminate World War II by accepting

Allied surrender terms. In August 1945, a cabinet headed by Prime Minister Kantaro Suzuki was unwilling to assume responsibility and asked the emperor to make the decision on stopping hostilities.

In each case, 1936 and 1945, Hirohito was used as a last administrative recourse when normal governmental machinery broke down. Circumstances forced him to take two crucial initiatives.

The postwar Imperial Rescript, imposed by the United States, states that sovereign power rests on the will of the people. It limits, at least by inference, an imperial power that previously claimed divine origin. Hirohito acknowledged it was a momentous development in Japanese history. But he insisted there has "always been a great love of the emperor for his people," and thought there was precedent for his diminished authority. He said, referring back to the Meiji Era, there had been the "Five Articles" (Go-Ka-Jo Go-Seimon) which presaged the emperor's status as reflected in the Rescript.

It is interesting that Hirohito told me the man who had most influenced him was Genpachi Mitsukuri, a historian who lived from 1862 to 1919 and specialized in European studies. He more or less introduced Western historical thought to Japan. Professor Mitsukuri, according to Hirohito, interpreted democracy in a way not previously understood in Japan. This had contributed to the changed status of the emperor.

Rulers may accept diminishment of their power, but it is rare for them to give it up completely and voluntarily. Edward VIII of England was one who did. His love story transcended his monarchic or political talents. Yet there is no doubt that he lived up to the royal tradition of indomitable courage.

The last time (January 1972) I saw the Duke of Windsor (as Edward had been called since his abdication) before his death, I felt deeply sympathetic regarding his ravaged face, once the idol of young girls the world around. He had had cancer of the throat for months and had endured more than forty exceedingly painful cobalt treatments. He looked frail; his left eye was almost closed, aggravating a condition he had long suffered and which, I suspect, resulted from a stroke. A small man at best, he couldn't have weighed more than a hundred pounds and was barely able to hobble with a stick. But he was spry and talkative.

He spoke of kingship and his own decision to abandon the profession. I raised the matter because Lord Boothby had declared on the BBC that Edward VIII resigned because he was fed up with the royal routine rather than because of his love for Wallis Simpson, the lovely Marylander for whom he yielded a crown.

"Boothby is a . . . fool," said Windsor testily. "He shouldn't shoot his trap off about things he doesn't know. The point was simply that I felt I couldn't handle the job of being king all alone. I had to have the woman I loved at my side. That was the agonizing decision and I took it. That was all." I believed him entirely; one could see how much the two lovers still adored each other.

Leopold of Belgium also left his throne. But he left it against his will, partly because of his marriage to a striking brunette who became Princess de Réthy. Leopold, a handsome restless man, admitted to me once: "The chief duty of a king is to see that the constitution is observed."

He was succeeded by his son, Baudouin, an earnest young man whom I had known slightly since his boyhood when I watched his father solemnly correct his homework and charge him to do better. Baudouin, like Leopold, adored golf and had distinct talent for it. Yet he told me in the gloomy Brussels palace (February 10, 1971) that he had given up the game and thought he would only resume when he retired. He added: "Just when that will be is hard to calculate because kings are normally in office for life."

Not charismatic and surely tinged with sadness, Baudouin, a tall, slender man, obviously took kingship as a serious responsibility. Throughout one long talk he jotted notes on his pad, reversing the usual roles of monarch and journalist.

He showed himself an earnest practitioner of his trade and by no means lacking in vision. He was deeply impressed by the Common Market, from which he thought Belgium had already benefited immensely; he did not think there would be the slightest difficulty between monarchies and republics when member countries eventually federated under one supranational assembly. He even hoped Belgium's angry language dispute might ultimately dissolve within the concept of a broader "Europe." A principal function of that "Europe" and its "proper role in history," he believed, would be to help backward countries. A worthy and generous conception.

Moreover, he seemed to regard himself as a symbol capable of testing the political atmosphere for his subjects' benefit. Thus, he was planning to visit Germany with Queen Fabiola; this would enable his nation to judge whether the suffering imposed by the Germans during two world wars had been washed away by time.

Queen Juliana of Holland, a wise and winsome woman, has a very up-to-date understanding of the modern function of a ruler. I asked (June 16, 1972) what her philosophy of monarchy was, and why she thought it had survived in a world that had changed so much.

She replied: "I suppose it's harder for me to answer that than any other person. There are such differences in monarchies, aren't there? But even in countries like Ethiopia or Iran they're trying to use the parliamentary system. I suppose there is a value of symbolism to monarchy. It makes it easier to face transitions from time to time."

She thought it difficult to analyze just how children should be brought up nowadays for the specialized trade of kingship. Certainly her own children had been educated differently from herself and she from her mother.

But she expected the generation gap and the education gap were not very different from those in other families.

She continued: "What generation has been the same as that of its parents? Come to think of it, I was horrified at the way my mother [Queen Wilhelmina] told me she had been brought up. And our generation thought we had brand new ideas and we were confident and certain there would never be another war. We did such things as marathon dances. We couldn't imagine another disaster was coming."

Juliana's view is warmly human and clearly she practices what she preaches; her children are modern, open-minded. Years earlier (in 1961) I had lunched with Crown Princess Beatrix, an exceedingly nice, forward-looking girl. She was indignant with Greece's Queen Frederika's refusal to go hear Maria Callas because Callas had twice let the audience down by refusing to sing. Beatrix insisted: "But she gives everything to art. She is a great artist. Once you hear her you forget everything."

Juliana, deeply democratic both by instinct and education, ought to practice autocracy with one respect—shooting all photographers who have ever taken her picture. They record her as a rather unattractive ogress. In fact, she is a sweet-looking, demure woman with pink and white complexion and very feminine manner.

Moreover, both she and Holland should thank their blessings in having as the royal consort Prince Bernhard, a remarkable representative of the lesser German nobility. He is an athlete, sportsman, pilot, military expert, businessman, champion of ecology and wildlife preservation, talented organizer of international conferences among statesmen and intellectuals, and, withal, a man of singular charm.

With respect to one interest of this versatile man—hunting—Juliana said with a smile: "I don't shoot but I must admit that all people who kill animals seem also to be most concerned about preserving them. Like my husband with his World Wildlife. I only object that they so *enjoy* killing them."

These observations brought her to the doleful subject of man killing man. She saw justice in popular manifestations against Hirohito's European journey in 1971. There had been ugly and hostile demonstrations in Holland. But she could understand how people felt since "he was the same man who led them in the war, after all." She merely felt it would have been more dignified had the Dutch people simply stayed at home. The Queen then asked: "Did you ever see the film *Tora, Tora, Tora?*" When I replied affirmatively she observed with a twinkle: "They never got to Washington as their navy said they would."

Yet she showed no vindictiveness. She said President Heinemann of the German Federal Republic had been well received in Holland: "After all, he was in the opposition, he was against Hitler. And he behaved very tactfully. He was very good about honoring the Jews here." With reference to Hitler, she found it fortunate that conquerors were almost always insane and overreached themselves and thus were destroyed. Nevertheless, for her the most important thing was that they conquered at all—not that they didn't hold their gains for long.

But despite the presence of six monarchs like Hussein, Haakon, Baudouin, Juliana, Haile Selassie, and Shah Mohammad Reza, broadly speaking, the quality of kingship during the dotage of this form of rule is singularly unimpressive. The first sovereign I ever met, Zog of Albania, had seized his throne in 1928 with a small invading force of Gheg chieftains and unemployed emigré tsarist officers. He was at various times in the pay of the Jugoslavs, Italians, and British. A disappointed Jugoslav diplomat showed me copies of his IOUs for foreign bribes. When Mussolini invaded his country he fled with the national gold reserve and other valuables, including his family, leaving a rearguard to protect his flight.

Emperor Bao Dai of Vietnam proved his personal courage by cave-shooting tigers: a hardy sport requiring the hunter to crawl in with a torch attached to his headgear and firing at the glittering eyes. Only one shot is possible. Despite this audacity, he failed to do anything to help his people in their struggle against either the French or communists. He preferred to invest in French real estate and retire to the Riviera. Don Juan, whose claim to the Spanish throne was superseded by his son's, told me: "The only good things ever done in Spain were done by the kings of Spain."

Kingship is not a happy profession. Hussein is convinced he knows how he will die: shot in the back by an officer wearing the Jordanian army uniform. (He is unlikely to be shot from in front; he packs a gun and few men are braver.) Hussein was spattered with his grandfather's blood when that sage sovereign, Emir Abdullah, was murdered in Jerusalem.

Nor has kingship any alternative to success. The deposed monarch is usually striking proof of the old adage: exile is a bad counselor. Cairo, London, Rome, and Estoril have given recent testimonial to this fact. The saddest confirmation may be seen in the sordid decay of Peter II, last king of Jugoslavia, who was placed on his throne in March 1941, by a British-sponsored military coup.

Peter's first proclamation was forged and read on the radio by an officer. He was driven from his homeland by Hitler's myrmidons before he had ruled a fortnight. He spent the rest of his life in emigration, becoming an alcoholic, after his country was taken over by Tito, a man of sterner and more brilliant stuff.

I knew Peter in Cairo, London, Paris, and attended the christening of his son in Westminster Abbey when England's King George VI carried the hollering baby around the fount as it was splashed with holy water by the Serbian patriarch.

The Jugoslav monarch's mother-in-law used to mix Peter dry martinis from an improvised bar in a hotel closet. Alas, the habit became self-sustaining. When he died on November 3, 1970, at a hospital in Denver, Colorado, the medical certificate stated the cause as cirrhosis of the liver.

Jefferson unjustly failed to recognize the debt of the young United States to its great French friend, Louis XVI, who subsequently lost his head. Louis, by sending fleets, admirals, and generals to help the American rebels, contributed far more to their cause than Lafayette. Yet Jefferson called Louis "a fool, of my own knowledge," and wrote: "No race of kings has ever presented above one man of common sense in twenty generations."

Jefferson described various rulers of his time as "a fool," "an idiot," "a mere hog in body as well as in mind," "really crazy." He added: "These animals had become without mind and powerless; and so will every hereditary monarch be after a few generations . . . And so endeth the book of Kings.

Strong words, these, for there is a curious persistence of human respect for royalty just as men still yearn to worship an Earth Mother goddess, vestigially hinted at in contemporary religions. Yet, in but few cases on today's political horizon are sovereigns more than relics of the past; and several of the surviving thrones are doomed by inherent circumstances to disappear. Who, however, is replacing them? My text is not relics but mediocrities, in the sense of those with "moderate" capacities, and whether it is bad that they should govern us.

3

LONG LIVE

REVOLUTIONARY

MODESTY

THE USUAL MEANS OF OVERTHROWING KINGS OR ALTERING THE political status quo is by what is known as revolution. Yet most would-be revolutionists forget that the first upheaval called by this label was England's Glorious Revolution of 1688. This merely restored Protestantism, by now the traditional popular faith.

Revolution then meant what counter-revolution means today. It was a way of returning to what was considered normal. The political term derives from Renaissance astronomy, which had proved that the earth revolved around the sun, always returning to its starting point.

As this odd political misconception was accepted and then as revolution came to imply something new rather than old, it assumed profound significance. Terrible as were the events of the French revolutions and the 1870 Commune, they were committed in the name of beneficent change for mankind. The Soviet revolution in 1917 was made in the name of peace and of an end to autocracy. China's revolution sought true equality and the resurrection of national pride.

Modern revolutions are almost always conceived under the label of socialism. Either directly or inferentially they proclaim themselves linked to Marx. But despite the brilliance of that sponsor and his intellectual twin, Engels, Marxism over the decades, like every other human organism, has shown that it contained within itself the seeds of its own destruction. We are living in an era when those seeds have sprouted.

Where, today, with the single exception of doddering old Mao, do we find the faintest hint of any man or any idea that can with validity hope to remake the world? Where is the magnificent organizational talent and single-mindedness of a Lenin, the inspirational dynamism of a Trotsky?

Over the entire globe Marxism has been featured by its dropouts. Tito, a phenomenally influential man who saved his nation—at least for a while —is more indicative of change away from rather than toward revolution, more seventeenth than twentieth century in that sense. This change, perhaps by seeking to humanize and democratize Marxism, may explain Tito's extensive influence in Eastern Europe. Less land is state-owned in present-day Jugoslavia than under the prewar monarchy.

A school of pragmatists has replaced the dogmatists who strove for violent change. Houari Boumedienne in Algeria, Gamal Abdel Nasser in Egypt, even Chile's Salvador Allende, stressed practical limitations of their goals. The first two, at least, emphasized their differences with Marxist theory. Ho Chi Minh, a singularly brave and resolute national leader, contributed less to the science of government than to the art of mass manipulation.

In Russia itself, matrix of modern revolutionary thought, Marxism has become a lifeless Byzantine parody. State capitalism waxes; sitting in the seat of Lenin, once the great god Stalin died, unmourned, has been a succession of second-raters.

The new governing class has come to profess the worst type of embourgeoisement. Who can say Brezhnev has revolutionary fire in his bowels? When Willy Brandt visited Brezhnev on the Black Sea, he was taken for a yacht ride by his host. Imagine Lenin in a yacht! When Brezhnev made a state trip to France, among the things he most wanted to do was to taste the pleasures of "gay Paree."

The kind of mindless populism represented in revolts of malcontents throughout the noncommunist world implies a sense of maladjustment more than fundamental desire to improve the social system. Parroting distorted and often misunderstood platitudes, processions of students have manifested in the United States, France, Egypt, West Germany, England, Italy, and even Spain, often bearing anarchy's black flag instead of the red banner of the Marxists. In the absence of intellectual inspiration and disciplinary order, society, feeling itself unthreatened, comfortably recalls the old French saying that every generation has its moment on the barricades.

Molotov (with Mikoyan the last of the old Leninist band) perhaps was one of a handful of loyalists who did keep a certain restrained and dignified link to his Bolshevik origins. He insisted (January 1956) that "basically the two systems [capitalism and communism] are contradictory. Capitalism is founded upon a system of exploitation of one people by another people, one class by another class, and one person by another person. Communism rejects the theory of such exploitation of one man by another man. In that sense the two systems are incompatible. But the change-over depends upon historic conditions. We should like the change-over to communism to be as painless as possible."

Khrushchev, too young for membership in the Lenin patrol, had a certain charisma and the courage to think more of man than of Marx. He told me (September 5, 1961): "Soviet people, who are mostly not religious, although we do have our religious people, love earthly life and have no desire to get to paradise in heaven. They want paradise on earth. They want to live and work and enjoy the fruits of their labor, and we are quite successful in that.

"In forty-four years since the revolution we have achieved great successes and now our road into a real, a communist, paradise is paved by the draft of our party's new program and we shall spare no effort to have this program implemented and make it come true. With the implementation of this program, we shall have crossed the threshold and will build communism." This sounds like evolutionary capitalism—which is perhaps one reason why his colleagues ousted him.

The East European satellite leaders, originally selected for loyalty to Moscow, were and remain a dreary lot; only Tito and Rumania's Ceausescu established their intellectual and political independence. Bierut, Gottwald, Zapotocky, Georgiu-Dej, Rákosi, Kadar, Zhivkov—all had the historical impact of pebbles dropped in the sea. Zhivkov said earnestly (October 11, 1965): "We feel the life of anyone, regardless of origin, is all right if it is in a socialist republic." As for Kadar, the last time I saw him in Budapest (November 6, 1969) I noted: "He seems a tough but irresolute man, the kind who might watch you sadly while you drowned."

Tito, who fought down Hitler and faced down Stalin, gives a far stronger human impression. "My outstanding success," he told me (May 16, 1968), "was winning the battle to defeat Hitler here alone and to make of the Jugoslavs, torn by internal conflicts, a sound federation. As for my failures, there have been many both small and big. I remember them still but I prefer to look back on the successes."

Oddly enough one of the most objective analyses of Tito comes from his bitter enemy and former friend, Milovan Djilas. Djilas said (May 17, 1968): "I loved Tito in the past. He is a great man, although I don't agree with him. He is historically great and he did two magnificent things —the revolution and victory during the war, and the 1948 victory over the [Stalinist] Cominform. In 1948 he was no more resolute than I and the other members of the Central Committee. Yet without him there would have been only confusion.

"Politically he is a fine leader, very courageous. Militarily he was not a good leader during the war. He is more a politician than a military man. After all, our war was only a war of small units without a master-strategy. But as a political leader in the army and in the nation during the war he was wonderful. His mistakes were only military, never political. Like Churchill. Churchill made many mistakes when he mixed in military operations."

Ceausescu had no such glamorous past as Tito in the smithy of revolutionary violence. Nevertheless, he too developed an independent line of thought to wean his country away from satellite dependence on Russia. "Of course," he told me (October 30, 1968), "the philosophy created by Marx and later developed by others cannot be claimed as the 'property' of any single man or group. For, as in every other field of activity, social science requires continuous development; it does not remain static." He referred to "those theoreticians [meaning Brezhnev] who claim the right to pass final judgements," and then added: "It is quite another thing to apply this philosophy to the particular problems of different countries."

Ceausescu also manifested no ideological bigotry. I was interested to hear his views of Nixon, whom he had met. Although the Republican president is conventionally regarded by his American opponents as extremely conservative if not reactionary, the Rumanian communist said: "He impressed me. He showed a real understanding of international problems and of our own situation. I found that we agreed very substantially on China. We both thought there could be no solid basis for world peace until China was brought into it. We also agreed on disarmament. He impressed me as being an experienced and knowledgeable man."

For European communism, Eastern or Western, the old messianic spirit has departed. The attitude of Waldeck Rochet, France's party leader, indicates how far its body and spirit have separated. Rochet, a Burgundian peasant who took over from that old Stalinist boss, Maurice Thorez, told me (April 20, 1967), when I asked if he considered his party "revolutionary," that this depended on definitions. "If by 'revolutionary' you mean trying to take power by force or violence, then in that sense we are no longer revolutionary, but we wish to transform society into a just society. Revolution means economic transformation, not violent methods. We want a peaceful road to socialism in France."

It was during Rochet's tenure of office that hapless French students, when they staged their pitiful mock insurrection, largely abandoned communism's red flag for the black banner of anarchy. No wonder! His successor, Georges Marchais, confirmed the gradualist line (February 8, 1971): "We certainly don't reject the parliamentary road to power." He added that he was in favor of a plurality of political parties, thus putting period to Stalin's old thesis of the unique (Communist) party.

Africa has been the area where non-Marxist socialist revolution has been most productive, and it is a brand influenced far more by pragmatic needs than by dogmatic considerations. Nasser, who more or less invented the term "Arab Socialism" (although the Syrian Ba'ath also lays claim to the term), accordingly explained his ideology (February 26, 1969):

> We don't describe it as socialist democracy but as a "socialist community." People base their lives on socialism. Democracy, according

to our charter, is freedom for the community and freedom for the individual, but it ends exploitation of the individual. . . . This is, of course, my dream. I want to see this country without servants before my death. Now it is difficult for people to find servants. And this always-increasing problem about getting servants means an increasing standard of living.

This is a reasonable approach and revolutionary only when compared to Egypt's unhappy, undeveloped past, a lamentable memory for the world's oldest nation-state. And the revolutionists who served Nasser as models? Marx? "I was influenced by Mohammed and also by Jesus. I believe in both of them. I believe in God."

The other successful, moderate, and non-Marxist revolution in the Arab world was developed if not invented by Algeria. President Houari Boumedienne explained his ideology in this way to me (February 23, 1971):

Socialism in its essence is the same. It means avoiding the exploitation of one class by another class. But conditions differ in different lands. We have very special conditions here in Algeria. We were colonized for a century and a quarter. This meant we were exploited and held back. . . .

Of course, we are against exploitation. So one of our aims is to completely free the Algerian people from any vestigial exploitation from abroad or any remnants of the exploitation system that existed here. . . . We want everyone to have a job. And we want to insure that no class or category can exploit any other. But we must be realistic.

We have chosen realism as our method and progress requires time. We must move step by step. We don't want to go too fast. . . . And although we press for economic advance, we want no forced marches. . . . We are not at all dogmatic. We are pragmatic. The world goes too fast for theories. We can't take the risk of tying ourselves to theories that will be bypassed soon by events. This is no longer 1917 (the year of the Soviet revolution). This is a time when men are going to other planets. . . .

Our official ideology is that we wish to build a socialist society, adjusted to realities and suitable to our own traditions. Thus, for example, it cannot be an atheist ideology because we are religious Moslems. And we will not impose socialism by force. Our peasants must voluntarily desire it. They must participate.

Moreover, we wish to keep certain private sectors even though we wish to eliminate foreign privilege. We are nationalizing banks, insurance companies and strategic heavy industries. But there is still a private sector in light industry. And we want foreign capital where it will help Algeria.

On another occasion (July 25, 1972—not fully reported in this volume) Boumedienne elaborated:

> We stick to the requirements imposed by reality. It is not a question of great ideologies and the ideas elaborated in other lands. This is a different kind of world today. Ideas are evolving at a dizzying pace. Communications are instantaneous and they carry ideas all over.

> The real purpose of our socialism is to achieve happiness for our nation, our national entity. The means of production are all controlled by the state. We have liquidated the last vestiges of colonial dependence. The great masses of Algeria have been freed. But it takes time to alter the disparity between different regions and different groups of society. It takes time to spread education equally everywhere. Nevertheless, the old exploiting class has been ended and minimal standards for everyone have been created.

If one considers the background from which the Algerian revolution emerged, Boumedienne's ideas seem sensible and temperate if not blazingly original. English socialism and de Gaulle's concept of *participation* are mixed in with the dictatorship and single-party system that every evolving African state finds necessary to impose because of the lack of mass political experience. By comparison with the traditional revolutionary movements that seized power in Europe and Asia, the socialist methodology of Nasser and Boumedienne is modest and, on the whole, restrained.

Sheikh Mujibur Rahman, first prime minister of Bangladesh, leader of the Bengali nationalist revolution, is likewise the mildest kind of anti-ideologue. He sums up his philosophy accordingly (February 14, 1972): "A man can suffer for a cause. I suffered for my people, my Bangladesh. My people love me and I knew it. This gave me the strength to suffer. If a man is ready to die, how can you kill him?

"I am not a philosopher; I am a practical man. I believe in God. We call him Allah. He helped me to endure my suffering. Allah is great. And my ideology? First I am a nationalist. Then I am a democrat. Then I am for secularism. And then I am a socialist. But it is my own socialism, not imported from abroad."

In recent years, by way of contrast, the most original if by no means wholly successful revolutionary movements claiming some debt to Marx have occurred in Latin America. There, perhaps less theatrical and more efficient uprisings are still needed to rectify a stagnant social and economic system.

Despite the bitterly romantic death of Ché Guevara in the jungles of Bolivia, and despite the flamboyant tightrope walk of Salvador Allende across the chasm of Chilean democracy, it is Castroism that gives its generic name to the contemporary Marxist trend south of the United States.

And yet, also, despite his own boasts and the fulminations of his enemies, I doubt if Castro is or was ever seriously a full-fledged communist.

I discussed this with him for six long hours throughout the night of October 30, 1964. He was indignant at my suggestion that he wasn't what he claimed to be. My argument was simply that when, according to his own statements, he had already become one, Khrushchev told me Castro wasn't a communist. Surely, I insisted, the "pope" of your movement should know who is orthodox.

Castro argued: "Before becoming a communist I was a Utopian idealist. I began to study political economics at the university. There I began to form ideas about a different form of organization, of society, then capitalism—even though I was studying capitalistic forms at the university. Later on, as a more advanced student, I first read the *Communist Manifesto* and was strongly impressed. Why? I already had many social and economic impressions and opinions of my own.

"But I was especially struck by the eloquence and clear logic of this document. Above all, this made up for the unclear works I had previously read and it had great polemic force. One phrase struck me especially— that the bourgeoisie accuses the communists of trying to abolish private property but private property was already beyond the reach of nine-tenths of the population. I understood this myself because I had been raised in a property-owning family surrounded by those who were landless." (His father, a Spaniard from Galicia, had become a very rich farmer in Cuba.)

"Naturally," Castro continued, "one document doesn't make a communist. The primary thing in a revolutionary is the sensitiveness of a man toward contemporary events, his capacity for feeling the sufferings of others. Naturally abstract ideas have a great importance but the coming together of a man who himself has revolutionary feelings with a revolutionary abstract idea completes a revolution. This is not an abrupt event like a revelation. It is a long process and it took a long time with me."

I expressed the opinion that Cuba's Communist party had joined him, not vice versa. He conceded: "In my final student stage at university I had come a long way in reading Marx and Engels, but I couldn't call myself a communist. I was an individual seeking the truth. I did not belong to the Communist party. I was not ready to join a Marxist party. My analysis was basically idealistic. I did not conceive of methods of action in the classical Marxist fashion. But I did not realize that you could not change a society without holding power. Therefore I began contemplating methods of attaining power by revolutionary means based on popular support."

Castro, when pinned down, said he had become a true Marxist-Leninist during the winter of 1960–61. He made plain that he felt the act was consummated following the ill-fated Bay of Pigs invasion sponsored by the Kennedy administration. He added: "We announced the socialist nature of our revolution after the attacks by CIA planes bearing Cuban markings

—on the eve of the Bay of Pigs. . . . This is more or less the way it came about. But already, as early as my university days, the communists and the persecutions they suffered called to my mind the first Christians and their persecution."

Personally, I like Castro and sympathize with his dreams. But I have less admiration for the way he has sought to apply them in Cuba itself, and am astounded by the exaggerated scope of his ambitions as a leader or example for all Latin America. He is a talkative, intelligent, interesting, restless man with some of the kinetic energy of Bolívar but with perhaps less understanding of contemporary opportunities offered to his cause.

I asked Castro if he was really dogmatic enough to be the communist he called himself. I told him that Nasser called himself a pragmatist, not a dogmatist. Castro replied: "I am neither pragmatic nor dogmatic; I am dialectical. Dialecticism is the negation of dogmatism. Nothing is permanent but everything changes. As Heraclitus said, nobody bathes twice in the same river." He went on: "We desire to strengthen our ties with Russia and, if circumstances require it for our security, the possibility of an alliance would not be excluded."

Perhaps the reason for Castro's appeal abroad, which endured for a considerable time, was the fact that his somewhat confused analysis of Marxism showed more of a hankering for Bakunin's anarchistic ideas than for the stern discipline of Lenin. He insisted that communism's aim was to have less and less government until there was finally none, a goal that becomes increasingly distant in all communist countries, including Cuba. I said this confirmed my suspicions of his innate anarchism because communism the world around had proven that it produced more and more government and bureaucracy, rather than the reverse.

Salvador Allende, president of Chile at this writing, is a socialist who thinks of himself as both a Marxist and a democrat. He is attempting an entirely different type of revolution than is Castro—a ballot-box revolution. Moreover, he insists he has no interest in making of his experiment a pilot project for other South American countries—unlike Castro who dreams of subverting a whole continent by force.

According to the bespectacled, quick-moving, little Chilean, who is a pure political animal, he hopes to change his nation's social structure—but to do this gradually, by constitutional means. This interesting endeavor is already starting to encounter almost as much hostility from Chile's extreme Left as from its Right. Allende told me (March 23, 1971):

"The Popular Unity government [ruling coalition] wants to transform the capitalistic system entirely, to change it totally. . . . In our Popular Unity government the socialists, communists, and other left-wing groups hold equal roles. . . . [But] the Chilean Communist party is sufficiently realistic to know that any policy that might subject Chilean interests to those of another country [Russia] would have disastrous effects here. . . .

"It could be possible that the dynamic of events might eventually create a revolutionary party, one party of the revolution. The dynamic I refer to —and which certainly does not exist now—would be a profound harmony of thinking in Chile and a homogeneity of views on the best tactical approach to our problems. But this is not possible for the imminent future and I shall certainly not press for it. Don't forget that Karl Marx foresaw a time when there would be no governments at all. But when would that be? It hasn't come yet."

He told me he foresaw a multiparty system in Chile for at least a decade. He described himself as "a scientific Marxist-socialist" essentially because "I am a Marxist in my tactics. But the strategy of socialism must depend on the realities of any country where it is attempted. To be a socialist is obviously not the same thing as being a communist. Evidently they must be different because, after all, the socialists and the communists are two different parties even if they have the same interpretation of history. . . .

"Our purpose is not at all to serve as an example to others. We have to base our program and our methods on our own experience. To have a Popular Unity government means that you have to have political parties, a parliament, viable trade unions. And this is not a very common combination in South America."

Allende pledges: "No matter how extensive our economic and social reform will be, we will not only respect human rights but actually increase them." (Among these rights he specifically referred to free press, free speech, free movement, free worship.) Moreover, he guaranteed to me: "If we are defeated, another party would certainly [be allowed to] take over." And he recalled: "When I visited the United States more than thirty years ago, when I was minister of health, I heard some of Roosevelt's enemies say things about him that were as bad as what some of my enemies today say about me."

Certainly he is right in this respect and, if he sticks to his restrained promises to let the people choose, history may some day compare his program to FDR's New Deal. The Allende disclosed to the world so far is no revolutionary firebrand. His emphasis is on socialism, not communism, on a multiparty system, on human rights and freedoms, and on eschewing any desire to ignite similar movements elsewhere.

The other main symbol of contemporary Latin revolution is more flamboyant than Castro and less successful than Allende. Ché Guevara, as a youth in northern Argentina, aspired to be a twentieth-century San Martín (another Argentinian and a liberator of much of the southern continent). Guevara became a pursuer of lost causes after breaking with Castro, although they remained ideological colleagues to the end.

Ché sought to carry the fight for freedom into Africa and became hopelessly mired in the confusion of tribal rivalries, so he sent friends elsewhere to scout favorable terrain for uprisings. As a result, he took his banner of revolt to the jungle lowlands of Andean Bolivia where he was hunted down and slain.

He failed, but there was something infinitely dashing and romantic about him. He turned many a woman's heart. In thinking of Guevara vis-à-vis Castro, one is minded of a comparison Malraux makes between Napoleon and the great eighteenth-century soldier, Maréchal de Saxe. In heaven Saxe could reproach Napoleon with Waterloo: "You lost a battle." But Napoleon could answer: "You never made women dream."

Although I never met Guevara I did meet several of his friends and admirers including young Régis Debray, the French intellectual, who joined Ché's tiny force of guerrillas in the fatal Bolivian revolt. Debray was captured, sentenced to prison, and only released after much suffering and the persistent intervention of France. He is one of the few youthful revolutionaries I have encountered with a considered, serious purpose. Audacious enough to put his money where his mouth is, he is not content simply to organize demonstrations.

He told me that at the age of twenty he first became interested in Latin America as a consequence of studies in Spanish revolutionary thought acquired from his reading on the Spanish civil war and above all the works of Alejo Carpentier, the Cuban writer. Debray came from a well-connected, prosperous Parisian family.

The result of his intellectual passion is well known. He spent considerable time in Cuba and managed to become an intimate of both Castro and Guevara. After his desperate experience in Bolivia, where he acknowledges that his life was really saved by de Gaulle's active interest, he returned to Paris following a long sojourn in Chile where he had joined the entourage of Allende.

Debray considers that Guevara, despite his premature death, made an important mark on history and was a significant figure. He admitted to me (July 10, 1971) that after a difficult clandestine journey it was terribly disappointing to arrive in Bolivia and find oneself faced by the bleakly hostile stares of the Tibetan-looking Quechua Indians, descendants of the Incas, who mistrusted all white men, regardless of their politics.

But Debray insists that after Guevara's death and the collapse of his uprising, the Indians came to understand what the revolt sought and have since created a genuine revolutionary movement. He holds this to be a concrete and tangible result of Guevara's insurrection. He describes Ché as perhaps romantic in his strategic vision but as a very cold, hard man in his tactical actions.

On November 1, 1971, I invited Debray to lunch to meet Malraux, a man with somewhat similar youthful experiences two generations earlier. When Malraux inquired: "What were your objectives in Bolivia?" the young leftist answered coolly: "The establishment of revolutionary centers as a base for all Latin America." He implied that part of the reason for total failure was treason in Guevara's ranks. "Tania," an East German girl fighting in the small guerrilla band, had been a Soviet agent.

Malraux argued with Debray's ideological concepts, which mirrored those of Ché. "The right no longer exists," the old writer insisted, "and today everybody is on the left, which means the left no longer exists." This provoked Debray to ask whom or what he considered the primordial enemy. Malraux bristled: "There is no enemy; there is no single enemy. There are just many, and these are all symbolic." When Debray mentioned capitalism, Malraux said: "The matter is no longer important. One asks oneself if one is good or bad, charitable or egoist, brave or cowardly—but not, am I a capitalist?"

Debray, a sensitive but titanium-hard young man, symbolizes what is best in the younger half of revolution's generation gap. He at least knows where he wants to go and how he wants to get there. He has written treatises on his methodology and is more interested in his aims than in personal ambition.

Where else among the loud-mouthed, breast-beating young Left of our time (so emotionally applauded by a posturing middle-aged Left) can one find the voice of logic and the willingness to risk all? Who are the other youthful revolutionaries, apart from the South Americans—the Uruguayan Tupamaros, the followers of Marighella in Brazil? Surely not turgid old Professor Herbert Marcuse, the demigod that failed. Not slapdash Dany le Rouge who incited French students to march in 1968 and boasted that his mistress was a minister's daughter. Not Red Rudi Dutschke in West Germany. These are not even historical footnotes.

As for the offshoot revolutions, seeking only national independence in the most old-fashioned sense, they have contributed nothing to the intellectual growth of social doctrine. When I visited an EOKA underground headquarters in Cyprus (September 1955) I was told by the leaders of that nationalist guerrilla outfit: "We will never compromise with communism. We mistrust the communists and won't let any communist into our organization for fear of penetration."

In July 1972 I talked with leaders of both branches of the Irish Republican Army, the more moderate "Provisionals" and the revolutionary "Officials." David O'Connell of the first faction said the principal tacticians studied by his group had been those of the Cypriot EOKA and Israel's terroristic Irgun Zva Leumi, but the eventual unification of Ireland must be produced by peaceful means. More violent tendencies, such as those of Ché Guevara, were "too academic." And Mairin de Burca, a small, taut young woman leader of the "Officials" confessed that she was a "good Christian" although not a Catholic, and that although Marx, Lenin, and Castro were admirable models for Irish revolutionists, Mao Tse-tung and Tito were "not relevant"!

The old world of revolution has been shattered during the past quarter century and it has not yet been succeeded by a new one. The crisscross and conflict of ideas have been interred. Djilas, who suffered even more than young Debray for his revolutionary ideas in the nineteen-thirties and nineteen-forties and then for his effort to adjust them in the nineteen-sixties, observed to me in 1968:

"Ultimately there must be an understanding between China and the United States. The United States is infinitely the greatest economic power; and the second greatest power is the United States in Europe, the American economic empire in Europe. There is a strange phenomenon today, the expansion of American technology, not of American military force. The only modern empire today is that of the United States. The Russian empire is old-fashioned, continental, not global, world-wide and modern. America is a great military force, has a great military power, but it is not a military empire, only a technical empire."

Thus it is the technicians who have shoved the ideologues aside. Old ideas such as nationality and geographical contiguity reassert themselves. Once (July 1, 1965) I asked de Gaulle what he had meant by constant reference to a Europe "from the Atlantic to the Urals." Did he not accept that this implied partition of the Soviet Union? He replied:

"I recognize that this phrase irritates the Russians, but that is their affair, not mine. The real Russia stops at the Urals. All the rest—Turkistan, Siberia, parts of Mongolia—these are all colonies, colonies colonized by the Russians. And probably, almost surely, in the future they will become a part of China. China has 700 million people. It is not a great power today. But in twenty years it will be a great power and in fifty years it will be an enormous power.

"The Russians know this well—and so do the Chinese. This is the inner basis of their quarrel. Of course, being communists, they always put everything on an ideological basis. But the truth is the opposition between Russia and China has national origins."

Indeed, one might say nationalism, the state and its power rather than the people and its well-being, seem to be the hallmarks of recent revolutions as they are actually carried out, regardless of ideological dreams they may profess. Contemporary revolutionists, if they are not truly serious, appear content with simple manifestations, like the rash of student revolts. And if they are serious, power itself rather than the power to reform, becomes the goal.

But its seizure alone is not enough. Typical of this kind of stalemated, would-be revolution is that which Papadopoulos and his colonels have achieved in Greece, a movement whose peccadilloes and tracasseries are etched in further pages of this book. Revolution as the mere achievement of dictatorship is as idle an exercise in human growth as revolution by parade.

It is not enough simply to march beneath banners advertising a search for change. It is necessary to know how to reach the end of the road, what will be found there, and why it is better for mankind to make the journey.

Ideas are what make men move, even when their leaders are of unimpressive stature. But what are the new ideas to inspire this generation? When I visited Algeria after it had been seized by revolution, I read the legend on a banner hung above the entrance to a recently collectivized farm: "Long Live Revolutionary Modesty." Imagine a modest revolution making the world turn faster!

4

OF PRIDE, PREJUDICE, HEROES, SAINTS, AND DEATH

IT IS DIFFICULT TO CLASSIFY PEOPLE'S ABILITIES BEFORE THEIR DAY in the sun is over and when, unlike those blazing figures, Churchill and de Gaulle, they have not been tested by unusual crises. The myopia with which one views contemporaries tends to level them in the common ruck only farsighted history can measure.

Are the lesser men of our era only lesser in appearance—or in fact? And can one avoid personal prejudice in seeking to make such judgments? Can one be objective about one's ideology?

My own prejudices are perhaps not easy to describe. In the hagiography of the Eastern Orthodox church, to which my Greek-born wife belongs, Saint Marina is always depicted with a small devil crouching somewhat to her left. Since January 21, 1942, I have been that tamed fiend for my Marina. Her private ideology endorses a special movement, the Extreme Center. I am somewhat to her left, like her name-saint's devil.

Having long since passed fifty, I know now it is hardly ever worth talking to anyone over that age, since by then they are either sclerotic or senile. But I also know that only the very young and the very old are truly independent because neither is afraid of life. The first has nothing to regret and the second realizes nothing is so remote as regret.

I have sought, as a journalist, to maintain loyalty to truth. Like Plato's *idea*, it can only be approached and never attained. This search has caused me to be labeled at times a communist or fellow-traveler: for example when I wrote in 1942 that, contrary to the U.S. War Department, Hitler would never conquer Russia, or that Tito was a nationalist revolutionary who controlled most of occupied wartime Jugoslavia. At other times I have been condemned as a fascist or reactionary because I wrote that Greece remained our ally, nasty as its regime might be; or that, with all its miserable putrefaction, life was freer in South Vietnam than in North Vietnam.

To produce this book, I have larded these pages with the ideas of honest thinkers more capable than I; yet what journalist is not forced into such shady practice? In the last analysis, after all, journalism concerns people and what they do or say about each other and themselves. It is only by considering the boastful or contradictory views of people that one can judge their actions.

What have been their influences on history? What, for example, was the effect upon U.S. foreign policy produced by the fact that Henry Kissinger experienced Hitler's oppression during his youthful days as a Jew in Germany? Did this fact in one or another way influence his views on the Middle East or on anti-Semitic Russia, or did it even inspire conjectures about new prejudice engulfing the United States? Could the sadness of his boyhood have stimulated in this brilliant statesman a fondness for being photographed in the company of society beauties? And, if this was perhaps the case, what induced in his predecessor, Walt Rostow of the Johnson era, a preference for being snapped in tennis togs with generals? One dreamed of the salon, the other of the sports field, both aspects of American civilization.

What was it in John F. Kennedy that caused him to lean so heavily on quick, computer minds like that of the cold intellectual, McGeorge Bundy, or Robert McNamara, a kind of modern centaur—half human, half data-bank—and perhaps our most disastrous secretary of defense since Louis Johnson?

In memoirs one discloses indiscreet things; a journalist learns indiscreet things. Revealing these occurrences is not only tactless but immodest. Yet, as my old friend, John L. Lewis, the redoubtable labor leader, used to say: "He who tooteth not his own horn, that same horn shall not be tooted."

And now that I have attained an age when polite youngsters rise in honor of my white hair, I find vanity more amusing than important and certainly indiscretion seasons a book of recollections. What is the manna for journalism if not the indiscretions of the great? All this despite Chairman Mao's warning: "Do not talk behind people's backs."

Long ago in 1938, Mussolini's chief subversion agent in Albania showed me over a bottle of gin his list of the tribal chiefs already in Italian pay. A few weeks later, the Duce's proconsul in the south took me on an aerial tour to point out landing fields where Italy's forces planned to land —which they did a few months later.

When the security agents of NATO had failed to discover the source for secret alliance reports being slipped to me, Lord Ismay, first secretary-general, wisely invited me to lunch and asked me to stop publishing them —which I did.

A charming French girl handed me an entire stack of classified Big Three documents to read during the 1947 Moscow conference. Fourteen years later Khrushchev gave me a message for Kennedy which he considered so confidential that he enjoined me against showing it to the U.S. envoy. Likewise, our ambassador in Paris asked me to interpret at a lunch *à trois* with Georges Pompidou; he didn't want anyone in his embassy to know the substance of the conversation.

John F. Kennedy asked me for a memo on de Gaulle before he met the General; Nixon requested an analysis of Chile and where it was heading under the Allende government. And Lyndon Johnson, cruising one evening on his Potomac yacht, disclosed how he had used the "hot line" to the Kremlin to warn the Russians off Israel during the 1967 Six-Day War.

More than most aging men in other times, my life spans the end of one era and the beginning of another. What has passed is the cycle that saw primary inventions like the wheel, the match, the telephone, the gun, dynamite, and the airplane. What has come is the discovery of new life inside the atom and perhaps some day in outer space. The infinity of both smallness and largeness is explored.

I have seen Greek soldiers march off to war with flowers in their rifles, and Russian sleighs, drawn by horses through snowy forests, bearing jerrycans of gasoline for tanks. Scientific knowledge has since exploded. I did not, in those days, realize that I was witnessing the last global conflict in which humans actually counted.

I have followed the first men to the moon from a Florida cape and a Texas space center. But this is also the era of electronic conversation and canned thought. Imagine approaching de Gaulle or Churchill with a tape recorder to take down conversation. Or imagine believing that either man did not, in fact, write his own speeches or books but, like Nixon or Kennedy, bought the best available ghosts.

In reviewing the diaries that span this period I find I have never asked myself questions I most frequently ask others—for example, who has influenced you (me) and your (my) life most. For Eisenhower it was an obscure general named Fox Conner. For Adenauer it was a little-known Rhineland schoolteacher with the French name of Petit. For de Gaulle it was his father—and his subsequent enemy, Pétain. For Nixon it was the Indian football coach of tiny Whittier College.

I suppose, with respect to myself, I don't know the answer. I could pretend it was T. S. Eliot, for whose critical estimates above all I entertained such vast respect: or Eduard Beneš, because of the happy advice he gave me in 1938 to go to the Balkans as World War II was simmering; the Balkans, an area where I found adventure, my métier, and my wife. But it would be pretentious to summon these impressive counselors. Luck and the American Calvinist tradition of hard work (a tradition that embraces even Jewish atheists) were the only steadfast guides.

And what of the influence of Jewishness itself? What impress does it have on an American whose forebears first came to this continent three centuries ago? What is it, anyway? Is it a religion? I am an atheist, devoutly if such is possible. Is it a nationality? I bow to no one as a better American. Is it a race? The anthropologists unanimously say no.

In Israel, according to the law, a Jew is someone whose mother was Jewish and who feels himself to be a Jew. But what of the mothers of converts like Sammy Davis or Elizabeth Taylor?

Jewishness is a feeling—even for those who don't accept its theological tenets. I have raised my children on the credo that they should consider themselves Jewish so long as that label can in any way be considered unpopular or disadvantageous; that is all.

Old David Ben-Gurion, the patriarch of Israel whose own daughter-in-law was a convert and therefore technically not Jewish according to the country's rabbinical law, once defined Jewishness for me (July 24, 1968): "The Greeks were the most civilized people of the ancient world and, among them, the most civilized were the Athenians. And the greatest Athenian, I think, was Plato. Plato lived in the midst of the war with Sparta and he exhorted the Greek tribes not to make war against each other. He said war was only permissible against the non-Greeks, the barbarians. But Isaiah taught, in the Bible, that there would be no war at all. This is the essence of the Jewish religion." (Odd, coming from the Middle-Eastern Sparta!)

He continued: "Moses taught the Jews that they had to excel, to be the best, in order to survive, a small people surrounded by mighty Egypt and Babylon. And they learned this lesson; for otherwise how could they have survived? . . . It is this moral factor that counts. This is the essence of the question."

As mysterious to me as the unanswerable question of "what is a Jew?" is the insidious tradition of anti-Semitism. That psychological malady dates back at least twenty-six centuries. The burden of the wandering Jew has been to bring anti-Semitism with him.

Humans, I have found, are really contemptible creatures of a far lower order than, for example, beagles. They are addicted to inexplicable pre-judice against what appears to be different. So long as there are humans, there will be Jews and anti-Jews; and there will be humans on this earth until another Noah exports them to another planet in the face of another catastrophe.

The question for me has been complicated by the creation of Israel, popular as an underdog but not as an overdog. As much of the world becomes disenchanted with that doughty little state one can see this atti-tude reflected in its views toward Jews as Jews, whatever their nationality. Right-wing anti-Semitism is often endorsed by left-wing propaganda except perhaps in the United States where, it has been written, "the American Jew is, in many ways, the tolerated jester of a WASP society."

The moral quality mentioned by Ben-Gurion remains an all-important force in any vigorous society. It is, I find, notable by its absence in such recently more dynamic systems as those of the United States and Russia. Cynical old Dean Acheson observed in the last year of his life (September 17, 1970): "Adenauer said he couldn't understand our policy and asked me to explain it. I only told the chancellor: 'Faith moves mountains.'" Put another and less sardonic way, Milovan Djilas admitted to me (May 17, 1968): "I learned during my last prison term [for political heresy] that a man may fight against reality—and even win."

Another theme that has consistently fascinated me is to contemplate what great men, of whom there are so few, leave behind them. Bonaparte left the *Code Napoléon*—but also a wreckage. Churchill bequeathed the glory of victory but also the reality of defeat for an England no longer capable of sustaining triumph. De Gaulle's testimony was a brief and evanescent dream of grandeur.

So often, I have concluded, all the ambition, drive, verbal fluency, imagination, conviction of rightness, and resistance to conformity that mark the political giant combine to produce only a fleeting memory as if written upon sand. A remarkably moving recognition of this evanescence was confided by de Gaulle to West German Chancellor Kiesinger. The General said: "You [Germans] and we [French] have gone through much together. We have gone through jungles swarming with wild beasts and through heavy storms, looking for hidden treasure—and all that remains is friendship."

I have always remarked that creative artists who have held or been close to power and the political giants who wield it are puzzled and fascinated by the phenomenon. Djilas's interpretation was: "I never really liked power but I held it from 1945 to 1954. Power engenders suspicion in a man's psychology. He becomes unable to live without power. It corrupts him. In the end it didn't succeed in corrupting me. But it corrupts."

Malraux was also fascinated by the question, and was intellectually obsessed by what power represented. Great men were his passion. He did not think Chou En-lai a great man; despite his cultivation he was very secondary. Nor, said Malraux (January 12, 1972—a conversation not fully recorded in this book) was Nehru truly great; nor his daughter, Mrs. Gandhi. In fact (a strange observation), he had never met any woman who impressed him enormously—except those in the realm of religion, "and they don't truly belong to this world." Malraux believed that John Kennedy's role in history had been assured by the fact of his assassination but that he would never rank among the giants.

Although lesser men were ennobled by political murder, the dominating figures he had met were de Gaulle, Churchill, and Mao Tse-tung. He found Mao convinced that whatever had to be done in China had to be done by himself. Malraux recounted this to de Gaulle on returning to Paris and the General was fascinated.

I told him de Gaulle once remarked to me that Churchill was a great man only during World War II, neither before nor afterwards. Malraux thought the General was "most unjust" in this. After all, it was Churchill who had the vision of what the Soviet Union meant as a threat to the West. He concluded: "Churchill was a very great man."

But Malraux could acknowledge the evanescence of such a great man's importance. He quoted Mao (December 5, 1966) as having told him: "We, people like de Gaulle and myself, have no successors."

Religion and ideology are only two among several diverse factors affecting men's actions. "You know," said Archbishop Makarios (July 26, 1968), first president of Cyprus, "people admire two kinds of personalities—the hero and the saint. Most people prefer the hero type, but I believe the saint is greater."

Another ecclesiastic, the huge Orthodox Patriarch, Athenagoras, bearded like Michelangelo's *Moses*, was also of this opinion. He had enormous respect for the combination of saintly and worldly qualities he saw in Orthodoxy's ancient opponent, the Pope

Speaking of Paul VI, he said approvingly: "The Pope is a great man. A great leader. I respect him. He had to follow his gospel. I am close to him and I know. He left the door open to evolution." Incidentally, the late patriarch, who once lived in the United States, insisted (August 6, 1968): "America has a secret destiny. Nothing can stop it from fulfilling this secret destiny. Vietnam? Pooh!"

Djilas, although he was without religion, inclined increasingly to a religious approach in life, perhaps because he suffered such grievous disappointments. During World War II, as a Jugoslav partisan leader, he held no regular command. He was generally sent to take up especially desperate causes. "I almost always lost them," he once confessed with a grin.

After Djilas's political disgrace, Marshal Tito said to me: "He will never play any political role. Of course he can write what he wants [although his books weren't published in his native land] but usually writers are rather bad politicians. If they are out of politics they can write more and better." An acid observation.

Djilas liked Churchill as a "romantic." Yet he acknowledged that Stalin, despite his brutality, was the greatest man he had ever met. "He had complete control of himself. He knew how to use power. And he had great charm when he wanted to use it, horrible as he was. He was brilliant but he killed as many men as Hitler. Hitler also was brilliant but mad and a fanatic. Stalin was cold and clear."

In 1951 when Djilas called on Churchill, then leader of the opposition, the Englishman asked: "If you were a member of the Russian Politburo would you attack Europe now?" "No," said Djilas.

"I would," Churchill said, adding: "Europe is weak. Russia could go right across, perhaps right up to England. Only the American atomic bomb could stop them." Then he sat up in bed—he was ill—and imitated with his hands the dropping and exploding of A-bombs. He asked his visitor, still the Number Two to Tito, if the Jugoslavs had been upset by the attack on them in his famous Fulton, Missouri, speech which formally opened the cold war. "No," Djilas replied. "We were pleased. It was a form of recognition." "It was a mistake," said Churchill. "But I have made many mistakes."

Most leaders of note are as fully conscious of their errors as of their triumphs. De Gaulle once talked to me about his own failures and successes (December 13, 1966). After telling me that even the chief of collaborationist Vichy, Marshal Pétain, had secretly sent him a message in 1944 by a certain Admiral Auphan: "You must take over; you must lead France," he wondered: "How do you define success or failure? Only history itself can define these terms. In reality, life and action are always made up of a series of successes and checks.

"Life is a combat and therefore each one of its phases includes both successes and failures. And you cannot really say which event was a success and which event was a failure. Success contains within it the germs of failure and the reverse is also true. . . . France has been notably reestablished both in its own eyes and in the eyes of the world. How far that will continue into the future, of course, we cannot foresee. But the comparison between France in 1940 and France in 1966 is very evident, very striking. That was a success for France and I think I have participated in this success, but no one can foresee where it will all lead."

Perhaps the most successful of de Gaulle's attributes was his gift of prophecy. This helped him lay the groundwork for French policy in the Middle East but it showed itself falsely based with respect to the French-speaking citizens of Canada. On the first he told me (January 22, 1968) long before Egypt forced the Soviet withdrawal:

"It is not a good idea to leave the Russians alone with the Arabs. The Soviets are very interested in the Arab world with all its petroleum and with the Suez Canal. After all, if the Soviets want to send a ship to India, it must go by way of Suez. We should not leave the Arabs alone with the Soviets. France can have a useful influence with the Arabs, just as it has had in the past. But this is of course not a monopoly. This does not prevent other countries from coming in. We don't want to be the only representative of the West. Nor do the Arabs; and the Arabs certainly don't want to be alone with the Soviets."

That proved in a few years' time, as emotions faded, to be a soundly-based view. However, the General's vision of Canada seems strikingly askew. He explained the latter to me as follows: "The people of Quebec are French living under foreign rule. England took Canada and the Canadian French when France was preoccupied with other parts of the world. The French people of Canada are under foreign domination. *In the whole world this is the only people subjected to foreign domination with the possible exception of the Arabs in Palestine and the Tibetans in China."* (My italics.)

All men make mistakes, which is perhaps the lesson of de Gaulle's Quebec policy. The last time I saw Eisenhower (July 11, 1967), he was still amazed at the way Britain had conducted the Suez war in which it took the lead. "I told the British," he said, "that for God's sake, if they determined to go to the battlefield—and they certainly knew my views in advance—they should be sure to have the proper basis to go on with the full understanding and support of their public opinion.

"They knew exactly what we were going to do and I talked to Anthony Eden time after time, and then the damn fools, when they decided in spite of us to act as they did, they did it very badly. Their operation was a mess. I like Anthony and I still write to him. We have always been friendly. The British attitude then was understandable in terms of their resentment. But they did it all wrong."

The old general-statesman made some rather striking observations on a subsequent conflict, the Six-Day War of 1967. "I don't know what they [the Israelis] could have done," he said, "except that, with all those Arab armies on their borders and Nasser talking of a total war to drive Israel into the sea. . . . Try and make an analogy for this country. Supposing I had been president and some combination of enemies, much bigger than us, had been gathered on the seas and in Canada and Mexico promising our extinction. If I hadn't attacked first while I had the chance I would have been tried for treason. . . .

"But I will tell you that as a professional military man I am amazed that the Egyptians could be caught that way after bragging so much about what they were going to do. I was surprised that they could be caught tactically like that with their planes parked all together on airfields and not even any revetments. But that sure was some harvest the Israelis got. I never had a harvest like that in World War II—340 planes in one night."

Yet, in a sense, how strange. Consider: Ben-Gurion told me the following year that he had talked to General Walter Bedell Smith, Eisenhower's former chief of staff, former ambassador to Moscow, and former head of the CIA, long after the Suez campaign. Smith assured him: "Of course, I never believed there was any collusion between Israel and the British and French on Suez." Said the astonished Ben-Gurion: "Imagine the head of your intelligence service believing that!"

Killing, alas, has been a massive influence in our time. No longer the organized holocaust of the great powers, become so dangerous that perhaps it is now outmoded; "small-scale" wars have flamed across the earth. A so-called peaceful era is marked by slaughter in southeast Asia, the Indian subcontinent, southwest Asia, east-central Africa, Kashmir, Kurdistan, the entire Palestine region, Sudan, Chad, Nigeria, Uganda, Congo, Mozambique. The roll is endless.

And during these decades, peoples not famed for centuries as warriors, have again been forged on the anvil of Mars. Prior to 1947 the Jews were considered a peaceful, unbelligerent people. And I recall visiting, in 1940, the famed Weygand *Armée du Levant* in Syria. There I was shown timid little Annamites, assigned to stretcher-bearing and menial duties because they were held unfit to carry arms. Today they are known as Vietnamese!

De Gaulle once said to me (July 1, 1965): "I remember a very characteristic phrase of Chou En-lai. Someone had asked him if he did not think everything must be done to avoid the suffering caused by war. He replied that, on the contrary, it was by war that big things were achieved. He said China had become what it is today as a result of invasion, destruction, and suffering. This philosophical attitude is very impressive and I am afraid it remains a factor in Chinese policy."

War and its outcome, death, are to me subjects of fascination and fear. The manner of dying or its timing, as in the case of Kennedy, may have relative importance; not death itself. Death has the unequaled quality of rendering almost all men mediocre, by obliterating them, as if they had never even existed. And its methodology provides insight into national behavior. As Djilas says: "The Russian will kill you—and then weep. The Serb will just kill you."

When de Gaulle grew older, although he feared only the indignity of old age which he regarded as "a shipwreck," he thought much about death. He developed an increasing passion for his grandchildren and for dogs, explaining to his friend Malraux, "they are not afraid of me." He also showed increasing interest in woodworkers, paying keen attention to the foresters and carpenters around his gloomy estate in Colombey-les-Deux-Églises. Malraux contended that most men have an affinity either for wood or for metal that psychologists can't explain. He said de Gaulle had immense interest in carpentry but none in locksmiths or plumbers.

As with the style of living, de Gaulle gave much thought to the style of his dying. I asked him after he attended Churchill's funeral, a tremendous historical spectacle, whether its pomp and circumstance had incited him to make similar plans for himself.

No, the General answered. It was indeed important and he had thought about it a good deal. But his funeral would be the opposite of Churchill's. There would be no spectacle. "There will be no spectacle for de Gaulle," he concluded. This, as it transpired and as, indeed, he must have foreseen, was not the case.

Tito, who at this moment of writing is over eighty but very much alive, also contemplated the anonymity of death. In 1968 he told me: "Death depends on how one lives. If you have done something useful it will survive you. . . . Much depends on what one has contributed to a country or a people. History is a long process. People never forget what was positive in the contribution of any leader. They will always remember what was good in his achievements. There is a proverb: 'Happy is the man who lives forever.' What this means is that he has done something good."

Two months later, I discussed death with the even older Ben-Gurion. He was already in retirement, leading a life of heartbreaking simplicity on a kibbutz in the barren Negev desert. Yet, somewhat like Tito who aged amid Roman imperial splendor, Israel's creator said: "The purpose of life is to enjoy it, to make it pleasanter for every human being. We don't know of another world so we must concentrate on this one.

"People," he continued, fingering the twin horns of thistledown hair thrusting thinly from his skull, "should be just and decent and loving. There is no mention in our Bible [the Old Testament] of an afterlife. Death is what it seems to be. But I don't know. Nobody knows.

"Once I talked about this to Einstein and he said: 'The more we progress in science, the more we realize what we don't know. Our ignorance increases; the riddle grows.' I asked him: 'Is there life after death?' He said: 'I wish I knew.' But remember, in his will he left orders that his body should be burned. He didn't think he would come back again. Remember, there is no word in the Torah that concerns any other life."

Turning to considerations of style in dying, I recalled what de Gaulle had told me of his funerary plans after returning from the Churchill service in London. "I was there," Ben-Gurion blurted. Very well, I inquired, had he prepared his own funeral instructions?

He said he had but that, as with de Gaulle, there would be no spectacle. (I suspect his grateful countrymen will insure that there is.) When I asked about posthumous arrangements, Ben-Gurion only said: "I have ordered that my remains should stay here at Sde Boker beside my wife."

Konrad Adenauer, a wise and philosophically simple man, offered this comment on death (July 22, 1963): "No human knows that answer. If I could tell you that—but no one can. It is perhaps a gift of God that I myself have little if any fear. I think of death with equanimity.

"I cannot imagine that the soul, which is our life, could fade to nothing when death comes. Somehow it must continue to exist. Man is not permitted to know how—but it must. Because the origin of life, life itself, is as much a mystery as death and we are unable to explain either phenomenon. The highest commandment has always been that which others hand on to us—to do one's duty."

How fascinating to compare the essence of what three old men said on this subject: Tito, the Slavic communist, "If you have done something useful it will survive you"; Ben-Gurion, the Jew, "People should be just and decent and loving"; and the devoutly Catholic Adenauer, "do one's duty."

The Biblical Hebrews whom Ben-Gurion resembled were deeply conscious of their mediocre role in the concept of infinity. Consequently, they cherished harsh respect for death which they knew to be synonymous with eternity. In the gospel that became Ecclesiastes they warned that out of nothing came man and thence he would return:

> Vanity of vanities, saith the Preacher, vanity of vanities; all is vanity. What profit hath a man of all his labor which he taketh under the sun? One generation passeth away, and another generation cometh: but the earth abideth forever. . . . [Man and beast], All go unto one place; all are of the dust, and all turn to dust again.

Such is the ultimate for the giant, the dwarf, and the mediocre: all unto one place, dust.

5

MEN OF MAN'S

DIMENSIONS

I N THE FOOTSTEPS OF THE GIANTS WE FIND THE TECHNICIANS, A competent but uninspiring lot. The splendid days are gone. With Juvenal, we say:

> So farewell, Rome, I leave you
> To sanitary engineers and municipal architects. . . .

Aided by the immensely complicated machines that these technicians have perfected, man is enabled to soar aloft, tentatively feeling the borders of infinity. This is a magnificent age of science and, for some, adventure, delving into the microcosm of the atom and the macrocosm of the universe.

But the terrestrial talents of man in the usual ways he has expressed himself seem for the moment moribund. It is Wernher von Braun, not Einstein, who leads inquiry of the intellect. Andy Warhol walks in the footsteps of Picasso and Braque. Even if Solzhenitsyn's literary talent is correctly assessed by Malraux, where are his peers?

Historic eras, like ethnic frontiers, overlap; mediocrities coexist with giants; Harold Wilson coexisted in time with Mao. But where are the leaders to guide us down the highways being opened into space?

Is it the exuberant self-confidence of today's youth that will set us on the glory road? Commenting on the famous French student uprisings of 1968, which many people mistook for serious revolution, Malraux said sadly: "They had no serious or meaningful philosophy to follow. Ché Guevara and Régis Debray have nothing to impart. In fact the reason for French intellectual interest in Cuba is that Cuba is so light and meaningless." (When I invited Debray to meet Malraux at lunch, de Gaulle's old friend said on leaving: "That young man has much to learn.")

How many societies of our time can echo the boast of Pericles: "The claim of excellence is also recognized; and when a citizen is in any way distinguished, he is preferred to the public service, not as a matter of privilege, but as the reward of merit." Today the state is increasingly disregarded—at least in the democratic world—as an institution worthy of respect or capable of working.

President Johnson once remarked to me (September 14, 1967): "It would be a sad country if we couldn't depend on the local citizen following his city or state laws. Certainly it would be a very difficult thing for the federal government to interfere with all local violations. If we can't depend on city and state law, we can't depend on very much." Well said. But Johnson was no Pericles and the U.S.A., despite its power, is no longer the glory that was Greece.

Who are the men who lead the world at this particular time? Let us take a few random examples. Zulfikar Ali Bhutto, president of Pakistan. Following the venerable politician's law (my predecessor was an incompetent, my successor is a schemer), he told me (February 7, 1972) that General Yahya Khan, whom he replaced, was "an Ivan the Terrible, a drunken, irresponsible man." He added: "I am a student of history, and the military genius who most fascinated me was Genghis Khan." He told me he used to like shooting but got a complex because his brother was a much better shot—so he threw his gun away.

South Vietnam's President Nguyen Van Thieu (February 23, 1972): "I am confident that not more than 5 percent of the North Vietnamese support their government and I hope that some day they will revolt against it."

B. J. Vorster, who sits in the seat of grand old Field Marshal Smuts as prime minister of South Africa: "Thirteen is my lucky number; it guides my life." And Egyptian President El Sadat, who told me (October 21, 1970), after acknowledging the enormous influence upon him of that mediocre American writer, Lloyd Douglas: "This man started as a doctor and then became a priest. He only began to write after the age of forty. He has great power. He gives faith and confidence."

Eminence of origin is mercifully not helpful nowadays in gaining preeminent position. Brezhnev, Nixon, Heath, Pompidou, Brandt were all of simple background as were, it may be added, Stalin, Bevin, Adenauer, Andrew Jackson, and Abe Lincoln. The luxurious heritage of a Roosevelt or a Churchill or a Kennedy is a distinct exception in the contemporary realm of politics.

It takes quality to climb the ladder of success. President Makarios of the tiny republic of Cyprus was a shepherd in the mountains above Paphos, where Aphrodite emerged amid flecks of foam, but he never saw the nearby sea himself until he was ten. Djilas saw his first train when, at eighteen, he boarded one in Montenegro to take him off to university in Belgrade. To rise above the common ruck, above all in the messy world of politics, one needs either driving ambition—like that of Lyndon Johnson or Harold Wilson—or else some outstanding quality like what Malraux called de Gaulle's "geological courage."

Of Wilson, a once and perhaps future British prime minister, I am tempted to append an incident. Once I wrote a column after seeing him and described him as having the face of a halibut with the eyes of a shark. I received many outraged letters of protest from English readers. Not one objected that I had insulted a great man's reputation, only that sharks don't have blue eyes. I assigned two girls to interview ichthyologists and compile the Latin names of species with blue, grey, or green eyes.

A feature of the Age of Mediocrity, one might adduce, is the low quality of its diplomats. From Dean Acheson and John Foster Dulles through Dean Rusk to William Rogers, the U.S. State Department steadily lost influence. Once (December 15, 1965) I discussed the problem with Dean Rusk, who, if no Talleyrand, is a fine, moral, upright man. Inadvertently, he put his finger on an important point: "Dulles was a lone wolf who always liked to get things done alone. He was a wonderful negotiator as he proved in the Japanese treaty. But he was a lawyer and he always wanted to win a case."

I pointed out that François de Callières, the great eighteenth-century expert on diplomacy, said the most dangerous profession from which to draw diplomats was the law. Rusk smiled bitterly. He recalled that only seven of our secretaries of state had not been lawyers.

If one contemplates the roster of foreign ministers at the moment this is written, one cannot escape a feeling of depression. Andrei Gromyko, by virtue of long years of subservience to a variety of Soviet masters, is undoubtedly the dean, and was even made a Politburo member in 1973. Yet Khrushchev used to mock him, claiming among other things that he didn't even know which end of a gun went off. Brezhnev assured a gathering of Frenchmen that Gromyko was a cuckold. Walter Scheel, in West Germany, doesn't make policy. No one any longer even knows the name of the diplomatic chiefs in Japan, India, China, or Italy. Nor, one may say, has any foreign minister of France's Fifth Republic *made* foreign policy, although all have been intelligent, respected men.

Rusk confessed to me that "Politics is a very important aspect of policy-making in the United States. Acheson never understood this but Truman, his president, did." Certainly politics has been permitted to water the value of American ambassadorial appointments. Some of the dreary businessmen and narrow-minded skinheads named by Nixon to represent him abroad were quite appalling, far from the Periclean theorem that a citizen "is preferred to the public service not as a matter of privilege, but as the reward of merit." Fat campaign contributions do not constitute expertise on, shall we say, Spain or France.

There is already sufficient real reason for the decline of diplomatic practice as it once was known. The world has become so swiftly accessible through instant satellite communications and almost-instant jet travel that more and more governments have developed the habit of virtually ignoring their missions in foreign capitals. Indeed, Denmark seriously studied whether it might not be wise to do away with this traditional concept in all but a very few cases, substituting committees of experts on various aspects of international affairs who would fly to the lands where problems posed themselves.

Henry Kissinger, certainly the era's outstanding roving envoy, concluded (April 3, 1972—not fully reported): "All modern governments have seen foreign policy move from the ministries of foreign affairs to the office of the prime minister or president—in France, West Germany, Britain, China, and Russia." He acknowledged that this was clearly happening in the United States and added: "It is part of the same process." And one reason for this evident centralization of policy-making authority was the need "to drive the bureaucracy against its inclinations."

As he perceptively discerned, the "process" was valid, regardless of the brilliance or lack of brilliance of the head of any particular government. Just as Nixon has his Kissinger, Prime Minister Heath had his Trend and Armstrong, President Pompidou his Jobert, Chancellor Brandt his Egon Bahr, and Brezhnev his Aleksandrov; the little-known people (except in Kissinger's case) who enable their bosses to run the world.

In an era when "hot lines" and frequent encounters allow leaders to know—and even, we may hope, to understand—each other, all this may lead us slowly to an age of rationality. And in such a period giants are no longer necessary; they are, perhaps, not at all to be desired.

For giants, like de Gaulle, are rather in the line of what Tocqueville described in his "Recollections": "Looking for what is ingenious and new rather than for what is true, being fonder of what makes an interesting picture than what serves a purpose, being very appreciative of good acting and fine speaking without reference to the play's results." Or, to quote another Frenchman, Molière: "Good sense views all extremes with detestation, and bids us to be noble in moderation."

The American leaders, since Eisenhower left the scene and Kennedy was cut down, are of strikingly different types. Johnson had the kind of dynamic energy possessed by an earlier frontiersman, Andrew Jackson, and the homespun, coarse humor of a Lincoln, if without the latter's subtlety. But the vulgarity of Johnson's taste, the lack of self-assurance concealed by a dominating manner and his cheap streak of jealousy—above all for the Kennedy clan and "east-coast intellectuals"—relegated him to the "mean state" of mediocrity despite his touching dreams of glory.

Nixon is of a different stripe. He has showed, among other things, a remarkable capacity to grow and an assured willingness to assume the responsibility for which he had fought. He has less gaudy visions than his predecessor and a certain dreariness of language that indicates a need for new ghost-writers. But he possesses first-class talents of application—above all in foreign affairs—and a careful way of preparing for the future: as, for example, monetary reform.

Yet, as Watergate proved, he tended to surround himself with intellectual second-raters and moral third-raters.

Externally, he had the wisdom to choose Kissinger as his diplomatic right arm, and also to heed his counsel on occasion. And, in a way, he had the same sense of useful gimmickry as Kennedy, who invited Leonard Bernstein to his White House Camelot. Nixon asked Malraux to counsel him on China, before proceeding to Peking—but painstakingly avoided following the old romanticist's advice.

Heath is in many ways a strikingly similar type, although, perhaps because of his European surroundings, more cultivated in the arts and letters. He too acknowledges an influence from Churchill, but also from Eden and Macmillan, which sounds like a political application of Gresham's law. He likes to read, walk, occasionally play golf. He enjoys wine, ballet, theater, and attending the opera.

He knows music well enough to conduct as a gifted amateur and is so fine an organist that he might have made a professional career of it. He loves to drive fast cars until, when prime minister, the security people put a stop to that. He is interested in architecture. He is a passionate yachtsman. Once he told me (December 8, 1970): "I like to think I am an all-around character and therefore subject to many influences—mountains, music, people, the sea."

But his personal history and, indeed, his manner are Nixonian. He came of a background that was particularly modest in terms of Tory leadership tradition, low in the complex hierarchy of England's middle class. He showed himself, like Nixon, eminently practical and ready to tack according to the winds of political possibility. While aiming as steersman to transform his country's economy and place in the world, he continually modified his method of overcoming unexpected hazards and abandoned many principles he had once proclaimed. Also like Nixon, he was more a doer than a thinker and had an extraordinary will to succeed.

During a subsequent interview (January 10, 1973) with Heath, I observed that so-called "giants" among statesmen were either produced by crises or produced crises and that maybe it was healthier for the peace of mankind to have as leaders men who were more of man's dimensions. He said: "Superficially this is a very attractive thesis. It is an interesting philosophical idea. In your definition of crises are you talking only of wars?"

I said no and cited the case of Roosevelt facing the great depression in 1933. He agreed and said after all neither Gladstone nor Disraeli had been produced by crises. "They just seem to have been there all the time." He added:

"Asquith in his way was a towering figure in 1906 but he wasn't produced by a crisis. Yet I am prepared to admit that there are those who do come in by crisis. I don't know if Churchill and de Gaulle were produced by crises. They simply existed already and benefitted from the crises. I suppose in a way we could say that Churchill helped produce his own crisis by the fiasco in Norway in the spring of 1940 when he was at the Admiralty. Two days later he became prime minister.

"Possibly if there had been no World War II he would have gone down in history as a great writer and as the statesman who tried to keep Edward VIII king.

"I wonder if you can recognize the characteristics of a giant. The real secret is to pick out the best who will grow and those who won't and to know how far they will get and to make use of them if you can."

Pompidou, another of this pragmatic group, had the unusual disadvantage of immediately succeeding a giant, Charles de Gaulle. Thus, while acting in the name of Gaullism and its tenets, he had at the same time to modify many of its methods and bring them in line with the reality of French capacities, which he was shrewd enough to know were far below the visionary compass of the General's dream. The art of being both Gaullist and non-Gaullist (a quality discerned in him by de Gaulle himself) was his special contribution to bringing France back to modest reality.

He too was of humble antecedents. His grandfather had been a peasant in the poor province of Auvergne. His father mounted the social ladder to the rank of teacher, highly esteemed in France. Pompidou had a simple boyhood during which he learned such amusements as trout-tickling in the purling streams. Yet he went on to high intellectual attainments as a student of literature and a connoisseur of the arts. De Gaulle, not Churchill, was his idol and the man who made his career; and de Gaulle was also his *monstre sacré*. His dream was far less grandiose than the General's: to put France on a pay-as-you-go basis and to limit its ambitions for influence abroad to contiguous areas like Europe and the Mediterranean.

In a recent conversation (December 14, 1972) Pompidou acknowledged to me: "Gaullism doesn't have a precise code. It is based upon the conception of the independence of France. And other people than General de Gaulle must now define the problems as they arise and the necessary means of solving them. One can't just sit back and imagine what General de Gaulle would have done under this or that circumstance. That would certainly drive one mad." And so: *sic transit gloria. . . .*

As for Willy Brandt, fourth of these contemporary Western chiefs, handsomest among them and the only socialist, he told me (November 16,

1972): "Great leaders derive from chaos but it is a good thing that we do not have chaos in our part of the world. This doesn't, of course, preclude the existence of leaders with great influence. It doesn't mean that everything must move toward mediocrity."

The historical worth of these four leaders, on the whole commonsensical and of ordinary stature, has been to blow the dust off the clock, and to recognize that they and their nations, after all, belong first and foremost to humanity and can, in the end, have no excessive pretensions, imperial or otherwise. It is a pattern for our times.

Brandt, for example, is no Adenauer, but has seen things—including the existence of East Germany, a new, separate Prussia—for what they were; he built policy on erasure of past illusions. Likewise, Nixon calmly dropped imaginings of an "American century," which, as vice president, he had wholeheartedly endorsed. Heath discarded vestigial hankerings for empire and welded Britain to an amputated Europe; Pompidou shrank the Fifth Republic down to a size acceptable to other Frenchmen.

When I was young, a famous professor of history at my college, a man with a powerful voice and the naked head of a dinosaur egg, used to thunder at us: "War makes kings and kings make war." What he meant, of course, was that cataclysm produces dynamic leaders and vice versa. This is not Marxist historical theory, and it certainly oversimplifies; but there is essential truth to it.

General de Gaulle once told me: "It is only in times of crisis that nations throw up giants. They don't need them in normal times. When the situation is grave, the giants come nearer to a return."

Giants make good subject matter for journalists and historians, but lesser men may make for better government—and peace. The giants bring with them their overweening sense of domination and also their inherent leanings toward authoritarian decisions. As Aristophanes wrote so very long ago: "It is preferable not to rear a lion within your city but, if you do, then you must humor all his moods."

The giant is more impatient and also less tolerant. He may admire humanity as a subject but not as a collection of individuals. De Gaulle loved France but not the French. The mediocrity, the man "of a middle quality," is more likely to understand the exquisite meaning of compassion. He is suited to normal times. There is value to the leader of less grandiose ambitions inhabiting an era of common sense.

Robert Ardrey, the ethologist, says in his essay, "Four Dimensional Man," that "the classic definition of fitness, just a bit circular in its quality, has stated that the fittest is that which best fits the existing environment." Surely the existing environment on planet Earth—if not in the heavens around it—tends toward the mediocre in its search to escape disaster. And the mediocrity, not the giant, is a suitable leader. Concluding with Ardrey's percipient remark: "The survival of the fittest, then, refers to those who are fit for today *and* tomorrow."

Are not such men as Nixon, Heath, Brandt, and Pompidou fit men for this age of technocrats? Efficient, competent, none is genuinely popular or charismatic in the least. Nixon was smudged by events, and none is a superman, a giant, but each got things done. They are men of man's dimensions.

6

A DIABOLICAL SENSE

OF MISCHIEF

LUNCHED TODAY WITH GEORGES GALICHON, DIRECTEUR DU CABINET OF President de Gaulle, primarily charged with the organization of de Gaulle's personal and political (in the French internal sense) life, also security. Galichon knows that no matter what happens, de Gaulle will be back from lunch at 2:40 P.M. and will finish his day at 7:55 P.M. He is remarkably well-organized.

Galichon said that no matter what de Gaulle had accomplished or had not accomplished, France today was different from the France of five years ago. He said that if de Gaulle leaves in one or two years—after six or seven years of Gaullism—France will have been totally changed. I made no indiscreet inquiries, but I was struck by the fact that he would not talk about ten or fourteen years of de Gaulle.

Yesterday evening I had a long and excellent talk with Dean Rusk at the American embassy residence. Ambassador Chip Bohlen very discreetly left us alone in front of the fireplace of his downstairs study, merely sending in a servant with drinks. Rusk accepted a big slug of whisky on the rocks. Toward the end of our conversation he had so warmed up that he took his jacket off and sat in his shirtsleeves.

"What does de Gaulle mean when he talks of a trip-wire strategy and immediate use of nuclear weapons?" Rusk asked rhetorically. "Does this mean that France would use its atomic weapons immediately if Russia attacked Norway or Turkey? I rather doubt that. And the French say Berlin is a special case. But this special case cannot be pushed aside. After all, Berlin is the principal point where armed conflict could begin.

"The strategy argument doesn't affect force goals for the alliance. These force goals were adopted originally on the thesis that war would mean nuclear war and they are the minimal contingents necessary for a nuclear war. You would need larger commitments if you were working for a real conventional pause. Therefore the practical gap is really not very great.

"There has been too much controversy about the word 'pause.' Everybody is so nervous about it that it should be called 'menopause.' This idea of a pause doesn't originate with the Kennedy administration anyway but was conceived by General Lauris Norstad under the Eisenhower administration. And we can't assume that such a pause would last more than five minutes.

"There are those, including de Gaulle, who are ready to bet one hundred percent on the capacity of a deterrent to deter and who are unwilling to think of any exception to this theory. The Germans fear the possibility of a conventional action by Russia, such as the seizure of Hamburg, and think this needs a nuclear response. But if the deterrent doesn't deter, if it isn't a one hundred percent guarantee, under what conditions do you incinerate your country? This is the problem, as it must be considered.

"Why should one go to nuclear war over a trivial incident on the autobahn? We cannot take a one hundred percent gamble on deterring. Those who advocate that we should don't really believe it. This attitude they express is not credible and therefore it fails to deter. A combination of an overwhelming nuclear force and a substantial conventional force is a much stronger deterrent because it makes clear not only that you say you are willing to fight but that you can fight.

"What difference does it make? No other ally agrees with de Gaulle. This is not a practical difference of views. When it comes down to discussing targeting, de Gaulle will find out just how many Soviet missiles are aimed at France and he will have to think about that. And he won't delegate to anyone, including any other Frenchman, any automatic course of action in accordance with the strategy he claims to advocate. At that moment he will reserve the decision to himself and, when put to it, he might not fire his atomic weapons. Maybe we agree with de Gaulle on the kind of response necessary in case of all-out atomic war. The real question is Berlin.

"What are the real differences? There is no difference on the MLF [multilateral nuclear force]. The French merely won't join. As for atomic aid, de Gaulle is quite right in saying that he never asked for it. And we never said to him that France should not have a *force de frappe*. As far as strategy is concerned, the only differences are semantics.

"The only one point of disagreement is that de Gaulle has worked for a special position in Europe which the rest of Europe won't accept and which we won't help him obtain. This was the essence of his *'directoire'* proposal. If Eisenhower had accepted it, all the rest of the argument would have fallen into place. But this is an issue between France and Europe, not between France and the U.S.

"Maybe de Gaulle feels the pressure of his own isolation. Just look at de Gaulle's approach and the rest of the world. He has a very low opinion of everybody else including other Frenchmen. Therefore there is no one he can talk to. He has no exchanges of ideas or discussions of positions to find out qualified opinion on what might be right and what might be wrong. It is difficult to make calculations based on fact with this approach."

Rusk then said sadly that he thought de Gaulle was drawing to a bitter, isolated end and "this will probably turn out to be the final chapter of a very great man. Personally I deeply sympathize with any patriotic Frenchman who saw the experiences suffered by his country during all these years and who lived through these experiences himself. And I can understand de Gaulle's deep desire to restore all the prestige of France. He fought against the dry rot in this country not only during World War II but before it. But he hasn't got the strength available in France to build up prestige to the immense degree he seems to think the country requires. He has taken France down a road where he is increasingly alone.

"Had he thrown France into the leadership of an authentic European movement with full cooperation with the other side of the Atlantic, French prestige would be soaring. But the trend he has chosen may turn out to be tragic, especially for the dream he has himself desired to accomplish."

I asked him what we would do in Italy if the Opening to the Left should fail. I recalled that we had once had a policy of flatly refusing to let Italy go communist by any means, even peaceful elections, and it was clear we would have intervened. Was this still the case?

Rusk said: "The alternative isn't a communist take-over. And anyway all NATO would oppose such a communist take-over, not just the United States. A few years ago when the U.S. did have that policy there was no Europe and no NATO; now they exist. I think the alternative would be a shift to the Right rather than the Left and a communist take-over.

"Furthermore the new Pope [Paul VI] will have a much more positive effect than Pope John XXIII. John's actions allowed the wives of communists, who had hitherto been afraid of Catholic censure, to vote for the communists. I estimate that 500,000 women shifted their votes to the Left because they now thought it was respectable to do so."

He put down his drink and started fumbling for his jacket, but then sat down again to add these final comments: "If another crisis came in Cuba or Berlin we would all come together again and France would be right with the U.S.A. The problems we now have are problems we can afford. Unfortunately I won't discuss matters of substance like this with de Gaulle on Monday. I am sure we won't exchange ideas like this. But remember, he is not twelve feet tall. He is only six and one-half feet tall."

PARIS, *December 17, 1963*

Interesting talk with Defense Secretary McNamara, who is here for the NATO meeting—on his way to South Vietnam. Before I could get started on my own questions, he hauled me into a corner and began pumping me about de Gaulle. I had published in yesterday's paper a column on de Gaulle's views on strategy.

McNamara quickly summarized his impression of de Gaulle's strategic views and then proceeded to knock down the thesis he had just built up. He said de Gaulle quite obviously had to emphasize what McNamara calls his *force de frappe* for reasons of internal politics, including previous army uneasiness and the struggle with inflation. Now he has to stress its alleged value not just because of pride but because so much money has been put into it that he has to proclaim for it a *raison d'être*.

"But what use is this force strategically and what, in fact, does de Gaulle mean when he says he intends to use nuclear weapons instantly if war starts?" asked McNamara. "Even de Gaulle says that Berlin is an exception, a special case. And how would he respond if some sort of armed incident began around Berlin, the exceptional case? The French do recognize that Berlin deserves another response than a nuclear response. Well, if there is an exception there, where are the other exceptions?

"The French have admitted that if Norway were invaded they would not try to reply with an atomic strike because they don't consider this in French interest. If the Russians were to try and seize Hamburg perhaps the French would reply with nuclear weapons. Perhaps. We don't know. And that is no strategy.

"The United States *does* have a strategy. We will use the necessary means required to reply to any kind of military attack." (By this McNamara was referring to our concept of graduated deterrent.) "We have a strategy, but de Gaulle's public statements on strategy are hollow. I doubt if de Gaulle himself believes his own statements. And what he says about not giving the Germans any nuclear arms or seeing any reason to do so is just plain nonsense.

"The British and the French cannot keep repeating that it is a mark of sovereignty to have an independent nuclear force, and expect the Germans to remain silent on this issue. You cannot treat the Germans that way. They are a strong, vigorous, rich, dynamic, proud nation and when de Gaulle talks that way he is sowing the seeds of trouble.

"Our theory is that the military response must be appropriate to the military aggression and with sufficient power to show the Russians that you have control of the possibilities of escalation at any and all points. This is the issue at odds between de Gaulle's strategy and ours.

"But the difficulty is that you have to develop a different force structure if you are going to pursue the kind of strategy we want. And de Gaulle isn't even consistent in this respect. Why does he keep a fleet with his strategy? He doesn't need it. If he is going to let go right away with atomic weapons there is no point having a fleet.

"Probably in a war our responses would be very much the same as France's except those of the United States would be stronger. The real difference is in the preparation for the future. De Gaulle's strategy would lead to the dissolution of all forces except for a small strategic air command, as far as France is concerned. He no longer has a real army. Apart from the two divisions in Germany he is building the equivalent of a gendarmerie force in France with the idea of placing one regiment in each *département* in order to fight a kind of guerrilla warfare.

"The danger of de Gaulle's strategy is not so much the argument on the kind of response, but that it leads to the dissolution of his force, which we would like to have available for our strategy. It is not so vital that all his divisions should be committed to NATO in peacetime, so long as we can count on having them available in case of war.

"You should ask de Gaulle why the Soviets maintain a large and costly military establishment in addition to their nuclear missile force, if de Gaulle's own theory has merit. If his ideas should be valid, they would be valid on both sides. But the Russians don't seem to think so. I am convinced de Gaulle doesn't believe his own strategy but is using it only for internal reasons and also, as I pointed out, to apply pressure against the allies in order to increase French political ascendancy. This is a very dangerous game, especially as it is applied to Germany with its strength, energy, and will power. The Germans won't accept that.

"There is nothing we can do to force the Russians to change their defense budget," he said. "They can continue as they are, decline, or increase. Maybe we can encourage them to decline by cutting down on our own expenditures, but this is only a subsidiary benefit. The real fact is that there is a finite limit to the amount of nuclear power we need and we are *at* that point. We no longer need any more."

PARIS, *December 25, 1963*

Dined last night at a rather intellectual gathering, including Mary McCarthy, George Orwell's widow Sonia, and Max Ernst, the surrealist painter. Ernst is a frisky, white-haired old German from Cologne who looks like a refugee from Dublin's Abbey Theater. He is clearly a mischievous, humorous old devil.

He said that until nine years ago (when he was sixty-four) he had no financial success with his painting, although since he came to Paris in 1922, encouraged by Paul Eluard, he has had a critical following. He used to know Salvador Dali and Luis Buñuel around 1927 when they did their *Chien Andalou* which he thinks is a first-class movie. He thought they were nice, attractive kids. Dali had always had a tendency to be a phony but didn't become a real phony until 1937—and he had great talent.

For years Ernst had various kinds of odd jobs to support himself in Paris on a bare subsistence level, doing things like making those little tourist gimmicks such as miniature Eiffel Towers. He lived in one bare room and also painted there. It was a very hard thing to find enough food to eat. Sometimes he and his first wife would go down to the south of France for a few months. I asked him what he did during those days for relaxation when he just felt he could not paint. He said he used to go swimming, play chess, and "I have a pretty wife."

PARIS, *December 30, 1963*

Lunched with Manlio Brosio, Italian ambassador to France, an ambitious and interesting man. He is very eager to succeed Dirk Stikker as NATO secretary-general and, brother, he is working hard at the job.

Brosio says de Gaulle is a "noble" man but not a "good" man. He is the opposite of a "good" man. Brosio doesn't think a statesman should be "good"; to be "good" is a great handicap in politics and a man must shed it.

It is not Italian policy to try and improve relations between Spain and Russia. In the early summer of 1962 Count Motrico (Spanish ambassador to France) asked him whether he knew Sergei Vinogradov (the Soviet envoy to France) well. Brosio said he did because Vinogradov had been head of the European section of the foreign office in Moscow when Brosio was ambassador there. Brosio said to Motrico, "Why, do you want to meet him?" Motrico said yes. Brosio invited them both for lunch in early July 1962.

Apparently Vinogradov and Motrico then saw something of each other. Last July Motrico invited Brosio and Vinogradov and their wives to lunch with him at the Spanish embassy, together with Motrico's counselor and his wife. Vinogradov now seems to be pushing the idea of establishing diplomatic relations between Moscow and Madrid.

PARIS, *December 31, 1963*

Lunched today with Hervé Alphand (French ambassador to Washington). We were discussing how Kennedy would be regarded by history. He came up with a quote from one of Stendhal's lesser known novels: *"Ce n'est qu'un brilliant peut-être."*

Hervé said he dined at the White House about three weeks before the assassination and Kennedy told him he intended to give de Gaulle a parade when he came over to America in early 1964. Alphand said he didn't think the General would want that because it was planned as a working visit. Kennedy replied that he intended this honor because America felt that de Gaulle was the greatest of the Allied statesmen and wished to demonstrate its feeling.

In May 1961, when de Gaulle saw Kennedy, Alphand thought things were going to go very well between the U.S.A. and France. But even then he thought it was a mistake for Kennedy to go on to Vienna to see Khrushchev.

Alphand blamed Franco-American misunderstandings on skillful British propaganda. He is very bitter on this subject. He claims that all kinds of fake slogans, like "An Inward-Looking Europe," were made up in England and then slyly distributed around the U.S.A.

Hervé thinks it is a foolish mistake for the U.S. to back Russia in its quarrel with China. We would do much better to stay out of the mess.

PARIS, *January 3, 1964*

Lunched with Motrico. He suggests the U.S.A. would be well advised to try and patch up its relations with Cuba, or at least to explore the situation through Spain. He points out that Castro comes from a Gallego family, as does Franco, and the Gallegos always stick together like Irishmen. This explains Franco's oddly tolerant view of Castro despite his communism.

Motrico told me the story of his negotiations with Vinogradov. In December 1936 the Spanish Republic sent its large gold reserves, totalling 650 tons, from Madrid to Alicante and from there to Odessa. The gold was deposited in a Soviet state bank after all the ingots had been counted and receipts for them were given to Juan Negrin. When Negrin died a refugee in France, he instructed his son to send these receipts to Madrid so the Franco regime could lay a claim to Spain's gold.

When Count Casa Rojas was here in Paris as ambassador, prior to Motrico, he sent photostats of these documents to Vinogradov in 1957 or 1958, laying a claim. The Russians replied that the gold had been entirely used up in the account of the Spanish Republic. Casa Rojas wanted to pursue conversations with Vinogradov, but Spain then took the attitude that the gold claim must first be settled, and the Russians refused.

Spain tried unsuccessfully to make its claim through the World Bank. But Russia is not a member of the World Bank and Eugene Black did not want to get involved. Spain also considered putting its claim to the World Court but this maneuver didn't materialize.

Motrico came here in 1960, and in 1961 he met Vinogradov through a luncheon given by Brosio. They continued these contacts afterwards. Vinogradov suggested they should discuss establishing commercial, cultural, and sports relations between their two countries.

Two high commercial experts from Spain and two from Russia met in Paris to discuss this in 1962. However, in April 1963 the Spanish communist Julian Grimau was executed despite formal protest by Khrushchev to Franco to commute his sentence. Bilateral conversations stopped.

In June 1963 the Russians circularized all Mediterranean countries, proposing the region should be denuclearized. Vinogradov personally gave Motrico his note addressed to "His Excellency, Generalissimo Franco, Chief of State," thus for the first time officially acknowledging this fact. Spain sent a note in reply addressed to Khrushchev as Chief of Government. These were the first diplomatic notes exchanged between Franco Spain and Soviet Russia.

Motrico and Vinogradov met for the first time after Christmas at the Élysée diplomatic reception given by de Gaulle on January 1. Vinogradov proposed a private toast saying, "I hope that this is the year when we will start relations."

Paris, *January 9, 1964*

We gave a dinner party last night. [Charles E.] Chip Bohlen recalled a fascinating aspect of Stalin's character. During the many conferences he attended with Stalin the Soviet dictator always doodled on a pad with a pencil or crayon. The doodle was always the same—heads of wolves.

Paris, *January 16, 1964*

Talked with Bohlen this morning. The shit has hit the electric fan. France has recognized China—and we are boiling mad.

I must say, de Gaulle has a diabolical sense of mischief. He took pains to invite Chip and Avis [Mrs. Bohlen] to lunch on Tuesday, January 14—the first anniversary of his famous press conference when he vetoed British admission to the Common Market. It was a very cordial luncheon. Absolutely nothing was said having to do with serious matters.

The day afterward, yesterday, Couve de Murville asked Chip to call upon him at the *Quai* and told him that, as France had promised to do, we were being notified in advance that Paris had decided to recognize Peking. Chip went through all the old formula of pointing out what a grave and difficult situation this would produce, but Couve was politely unruffled.

Afterward, as soon as Washington had received Chip's urgent flash, Averell Harriman (Dean Rusk was out of town) summoned French

Ambassador Hervé Alphand. Alphand protested that this was not really a very significant or important step. Harriman brutally said: "I have known you for many years as an intelligent and experienced diplomat so there isn't any use repeating such twaddle."

He asked me when I wrote about this to refer to the column I sent on October 15 stating that France was contemplating recognition of China. "After all," he said, "you got that one from Couve. So then, if they complain of any leakage from me because they know we are friends, I can point out the original leak came from Couve."

I forecast to Chip that de Gaulle would go all out to say nice things about America in his press conference because he always likes to pat a dog after he has kicked it.

PARIS, *January 17, 1964*

John Bennett came for lunch on his way to Bujumbura, the capital of Burundi, where he has just been named British ambassador. John says the Chinese are very active and seem to be financing certain rebel groups. The Chinese have a relatively large embassy in Burundi, but their central point of agitation is Dar es Salaam, Tanzania. John isn't terribly worried about the Russians who are also represented in Burundi. He claims that if the natives rise up they are quite incapable of distinguishing between a Russian and an Englishman. He believes the Russians are fully aware of the personal risk they run. He thinks he had better start a propaganda campaign as soon as he arrives, proclaiming to all the natives: "Don't forget, the Chinese are also white men."

PARIS, *January 22, 1964*

Agreeable talk this afternoon with Vinogradov, the Soviet ambassador. Vinogradov was exceptionally friendly and served scotch and soda and American commissary biscuits.

He told me he had been a professor of modern Russian history at the University of Leningrad when in 1940 he was suddenly sent to Ankara as counselor of embassy. Four months later he was made ambassador and has been a diplomat ever since.

He thinks de Gaulle is a very great man—even greater than Churchill. At the time of the French referendum in 1961 he asked de Gaulle if he planned to run again and de Gaulle said no, that he wished to retire after having restored stability to France. However, in December Vinogradov posed the question once more. De Gaulle said he considered it a duty to his country to guide it along the right path, and made the point that Adenauer had started his political career at the age of seventy-three, while it was still some months before his own seventy-third birthday.

He was very curious as to where I got my information for my column on Spanish and Russian recognition and wondered if the Spanish were serious about the negotiations and what the American view was. I told him I could not disclose my source and he laughed, saying, *"Je vous ai compris"* (de Gaulle's phrase, famous in France).

Russia's view was of course consistent in wanting China in the UN and wanting all countries to recognize China, so therefore Moscow was content with de Gaulle's recognition of Peking. But from there on he launched himself on a vivid attack against the Chinese. He said Mao Tse-tung was a far worse despot "even than Stalin" and that if anybody raised his voice to criticize the government "his head was knocked off." The Chinese lived in misery and economically the country was a shambles. The Chinese were racists and hated every white man. He added that it was not just a legend but that—although he could not reveal his source—he knew it for a fact that Mao had said he wasn't worried about another war because three hundred million Chinese could survive and rule the world.

I asked if he was concerned about the possibility that France might give technical aid or assistance to China in developing nuclear weapons. He admitted that Russia was very concerned about this, "just like the United States." He said Russia had no intention of giving China any aid on nuclear weapons, and then wanted to know if I thought the French had a thermonuclear weapon. I said I didn't think they would for eighteen months.

He said that much as the Chinese hated us, they seemed to dislike the Russians even more for not helping them enough.

PARIS, *January 24, 1964*

Today I asked Jean Laloy (the brilliant French diplomat) if he thought de Gaulle was influenced on recognizing China by a desire to protect French commercial interests in southeast Asia. He said: "Don't be foolish; de Gaulle simply believes that Mao, Ho, and Prince Sihanouk and all the others are Gaullists." They are Gaullist nationalists and in the end will respect the ambitions and influence of nationalism because it is the be-all and end-all of political projection.

Jean was desperately worried about Johnson and thought he was really dangerous because he didn't know a thing about the world. He went on to say that Kennedy was an enormously overrated president. He could understand the emotional reaction when this attractive young man had been shot but Kennedy was not a real intellectual, merely a catalyst, meaning he was not as serious about international relationships as his posthumous reputation now indicates.

PARIS, *January 27, 1964*

This afternoon I spent a very interesting hour at the *Quai d'Orsay* with Maurice Couve de Murville (foreign minister). I asked whether he thought France, by its new policy, was developing the possibilities of a "two Chinas" formula. He answered: "No, we never thought of this. This is not our business. It is not for us to decide the future of the Chinese people. We are merely establishing diplomatic relations with *the* government of China and we are not in so doing indicating whether we think this is a bad government or a good government."

I asked Couve what he thought would be the implications of this policy vis-à-vis southeast Asia. He said that depended on both sides—the communists and the U.S.A.—in the Vietnamese and Laotian civil wars. He continued:

> France thinks that for the time being the least bad direction would be a neutral regime in South Vietnam; South Vietnam alone, not North Vietnam. I say this hesitantly, but so long as the unification of Vietnam as a concept is based on neutrality, this is the least disagreeable step. Naturally neutrality excludes a communist regime in North Vietnam, but for the present there is no way of changing this.

> I don't know if this would be discussed in any conferences on the status of Cambodia but at any rate we may hope for some kind of international guarantees in South Vietnam and pray that the situation in North Vietnam will change. I admit that this is a very dangerous policy and I am not convinced it is good. But the alternative is even worse; and I see no third choice.

> The difficulty in South Vietnam is that there is no government, there is no national feeling. The Diem regime *was* a government, even if it was unpopular. It *had* a policy and it *ruled*. But now there is nothing, there is nothing except a deep longing for peace.

> There is really only one other possibility and that is to carry the war to North Vietnam, but that is not to be recommended. It might produce the same result as Korea.

I then moved on and asked him if he thought there could be repercussions in Europe of the decision on China, above all in terms of some sort of settlement on Germany between the East and the West. Couve said this was out of the question and the two areas were unrelated.

He added: "If you look for the last analysis in all of this, it is a manifestation of an end of the existence of two ideological blocs. That system of two blocs is finished. This is not a deduction; it is a fact. The world is now back to national policies instead of bloc policies. Germany is divided, not because of ideology but because the Russians decided as Russians that Germany should not be reunified. That is all. This is a national policy. It has nothing to do with communism. And that won't change. Above everything else, Russia is frightened most of all by the prospect of a unified Germany. This has to do with national, not ideological views."

Lunched with Raymond Aron (professor at the Sorbonne and a brilliant writer). As usual he was provocative and clear-minded, even where I did not agree with him.

To my astonishment he told me that as a young man his great ambition was to be a tennis champion and that for some years he was ranked in the *Deuxième Série* of French tennis players.

He thinks de Gaulle will run again for president. He doesn't believe he can have a real successor any more than he had a real predecessor.

Couve de Murville and [General Lyman L.] Lemnitzer came for dinner last night. Couve, who was most relaxed and agreeable, was saying that the British had created the Cyprus mess unnecessarily. As soon as the war ended in 1945 they should have given Cyprus to Greece the way the Dodecanese Islands were awarded at that time. There would have been no argument from Turkey.

Dirk Stikker [NATO secretary-general] invited me to lunch.

The Multilateral Force is now regarded as dead and Stikker has tried out an alternative plan on Rusk and McNamara. In the meantime (as I predicted) the Germans are trying a new approach on getting atomic weapons. They privately acknowledge that the MLF is a dead turkey and Heinrich Krone came to Paris last month to ask de Gaulle for secret collaboration between the Germans and the French on nuclear weapons. He was specifically charged with this mission by Erhard (who would prefer to have Britain in on the deal but knows it is impossible) *and*—I emphasize this word—Adenauer.

Stikker thinks there is going to be a war between Greece and Turkey. He just doesn't see any way of preventing this. Arms are being sent to the Greek and Turkish Cypriots from Greece and Turkey and nobody is stopping this.

He recalled that, as Dutch foreign minister, he had opposed the admission of Greece and Turkey to NATO, and that he thought if a war came it would permanently wreck the alliance. The Russians at the moment were backing the Greeks but if they thought it convenient they would switch sides.

PARIS, *February 23, 1964*

Golfed and lunched today with Couve de Murville, Bohlen, and Olivier Wormser of the *Quai d'Orsay* (later Governor of the Bank of France). Couve said that when he finishes as foreign minister he wants to retire and get a money-making job in private life.

Couve's family originally was called Couve de Murville and then, after the revolution, dropped the de Murville and was plain Couve. His father, a judge, took back the de Murville. The family had lived in the Ile de France (now called Mauritius) until 1802 when the British captured it. They then went to Bordeaux and his ancestor married a Protestant girl, whence his own Protestantism. But the Catholic branch stayed in Mauritius and he has a distant cousin who is now an English Jesuit in the United Kingdom. Couve himself was born in Reims where his father was a judge.

ROME, *February 25, 1964*

Lunched alone at the German embassy with Herbert Blankenhorn, now ambassador here. He fascinates me: a strong admirer of Adenauer, then Strauss, he is now a great Erhard booster.

Adenauer, he says, is still in remarkable shape for a man of eighty-eight and his mind is good, but his memory is failing. He is writing his memoirs with no notes of his own and no ghost, merely masses of official documents and memoranda he extracted from the Schaumburg. Everyone is frightened he will get everything balled up.

De Gaulle quite plainly wants to keep Germany divided and fears 70 million Germans united on his border or a Europe dominated by Germany in a supranational bloc. He pretends to take a strong Berlin line to win German popularity, but in fact his policy is against Germany's interests.

The world should never forget the danger of German nationalism. It sleeps now but would awaken strongly in an economic crisis. The new generation has no complexes about a guilt it did not share. If the MLF fails, nationalism would revive, fostered by Strauss.

Blankenhorn thinks there is "almost fascism" in France but Gaullism, without de Gaulle, is weak and has neither a program nor able leaders.

De Gaulle told Erhard frankly that France supported the Oder-Neisse frontier because it had old ties of friendship with Poland it wished to preserve.

ROME, *February 26, 1964*

Dined last night at the Reinhardts (Fred is U.S. ambassador here). Talked at length with Admiral Ernesto Giuriati, chief of staff at the ministry of the navy. Giuriati says the long-term armistice imposed in 1943 was modified at Italy's expense, which is why Badoglio prevented the publication of the modified terms. Some clauses have never been published—including those that gave a battleship, two cruisers, and other warships to the Russians.

ROME, *February 27, 1964*

Good talk with Giuseppe Saragat, now foreign minister (later Italian president). He said there were three forces in Italian foreign policy-making; the prime minister, himself, and Pietro Nenni, the socialist leader. Not long ago Nenni had been under Soviet influence but now the British Labor party was the main force.

Saragat, who has just returned from an official visit with President Antonio Segni to Paris, says de Gaulle is a fair man who wants France to be greater than it is. He finds that his [de Gaulle's] toughness with the U.S.A. tends to make him popular with Americans "while we, your friends, aren't even noticed."

Saragat was surprised when I asked if Brosio was the official candidate for NATO secretary-general, saying this was secret. I said I'd written about it. He then said that Rome wanted the job for an Italian.

He wanted to know all about Lyndon Johnson, urged that the U.S. should get tough on Vietnam, and said Italian public opinion would understand. Nenni would publicly complain and privately be pleased.

Cyprus was dangerous but less important than we thought. If Greece and Turkey forced us to choose, the U.S.A. would choose Turkey. The best way to handle Makarios would be to send a Roman Catholic priest to set up a rival show.

CAIRO, *February 28, 1964*

Had drinks with Harold Beeley, the British ambassador. He says Nasser is backing Makarios in the hopes he will win, expel British Cyprus bases and break relations with Israel. Nasser also started the antibase campaign in Libya where there is trouble, riots favoring a Nasserist former premier, and indications the king (Idris) is ailing. When Idris goes, the place will probably fall under Nasserist sway.

In recent months there has been a hiatus in U.S.-UAR relations. Beeley says there are too many Johnsons and the Egyptians can't keep them apart. Eric Johnston made the Arab-Israeli water-sharing plan. Joe Johnston had secret talks on refugees. Alexis Johnson made a speech just after the Arab Summit warning them against war. And Lyndon Johnson made a speech at the Weizmann Institute dinner saying we would help Israel use nuclear energy to desalinize water.

United States Ambassador John Badeau told me John Foster Dulles reneged on the High Dam in 1956 for these reasons: (1) Under Senator

Walter George, Congress had gone on record that aid funds should not be used on the dam because it would increase a rival cotton output— although only five percent of the new lands would be for cotton; (2) the U.S.A. feared the UAR had mortgaged its cotton crop to the hilt against Soviet arms and economically it would not be a sound deal; (3) we felt Nasser was playing us against Moscow, always warning they would do more if we didn't help and we disliked this; (4) there was not yet a riparian agreement with the Sudan so the "title" to the project wasn't clear; (5) the economic planning for the project was incomplete.

But Dulles employed methods that particularly irked the UAR. He deliberately cut Nasser down to size. Our "foreign policy" was not to help on the dam but our "diplomacy" was so rough it upset our policy objectives.

Badeau says Nasser didn't complain about the murder of Arabs in Zanzibar because they were the rich "reactionaries," because Kenya and Tanganyika backed the new regime, because it had achieved a *fait accompli* and nothing could be changed, because Zanzibar is nonaligned, because he did not want to seem an Arab "imperialist" in Arab eyes.

ADDIS ABABA, ETHIOPIA, *March 5, 1964*

Haile Selassie accomplished one great thing. He transformed the geography of his nation from a unique Middle-Eastern anachronism into a committed *African* power.

Haile Selassie did this for the following reason: 1956 was a key year because of the Suez war. It reconfirmed Nasser as the head of a dynamic Arab movement. Also at approximately this time the British made clear that Ghana would get its independence.

The Ghana decision signaled that Africa faced a great change—the end of colonialism. This meant that a great upheaval would be coming and that Africa was fated to take over its own destiny. Haile Selassie saw that the UN was interested in Africa and intended to create an economic commission for Africa (ECA). Haile Selassie lobbied to bring ECA headquarters here, on the grounds that Ethiopia was the oldest independent state. He financed the building with $2 million.

Having done this, he went to the United States and asked for jet airliners to facilitate international travel to the new headquarters. In 1960 he got a pledge for this purpose. He then obtained an Export-Import Bank loan in 1961 to purchase jets.

When all this progress was well in hand, Haile Selassie announced in May 1962 that he was convoking an African summit conference for May 1963. He started building roads, hotels, etc., for this purpose.

The Russians wish to improve their position along the Red Sea. They backed Nasser with arms and the dam. They are in the Yemen. They hammer away at colonial vestiges in Aden and French Somaliland which control the straits of Bab el Mandab. The Russians want an east African base to push toward Mozambique and Madagascar. Somalia is a good base from which to send African students or communist agents.

ADDIS ABABA, ETHIOPIA, *March 6, 1964*

Dined last night with Prime Minister Tsahafe Taezaz Aklilou Abte Wold. Aklilou is a short, dark, energetic man. His father was a country priest, but he was a bright boy, and French missionaries sent him to study in Marseille and Paris, where he got a good education and married a French girl.

He was Haile Selassie's assistant at Geneva and representative in Paris after the Italian conquest. When the Germans occupied France, he was helped by Admiral [William D.] Leahy to get to Lisbon, and finally returned to Ethiopia. He was foreign minister before becoming prime minister.

Aklilou is obsessed with the Somalia question. He says that Ernest Bevin as British foreign minister submitted a plan for a greater Somalia in 1946. This would have included both the former British and Italian colonies as well as French and the Ethiopian province of Ogaden. At the time of the Paris peace conference in 1946 Ethiopia firmly turned this down.

This afternoon I had a long talk with Robert Gardiner, head of the UN's Economic Commission for Africa (ECA) in Africa Hall, a rather splendid new building set aside for this purpose by the emperor. Gardiner is a Ghanaian of exceptional intelligence and a rather quiet, humorous charm. He is very dark with Negroid features and a calm, quiet, sad voice.

He said that although Africa as a continent was still in a very confused and early stage of economic development with different corners bound to non-African areas, the concept of treating Africa as a basic unit would be favorable. This continent which today has a population of about 260 million, would in twenty years have a population of about 400 million.

The economic infrastructure of Africa was at present very rudimentary and confused. Most African countries produced primary commodities now and had a limited foreign trade which often was duplicative between one country and another. But this could and would change. It was necessary for the self-sustained growth of the continent to have an industrial program.

ADDIS ABABA, ETHIOPIA, *March 7, 1964*

I dined last night with British Ambassador Sir John and Aliki Russell. John produced some interesting little facets about Ethiopia.

The church here is the only church in the world that preaches that the earth is flat and canonizes Pontius Pilate.

There are only 25 qualified Ethiopian doctors, whereas there are 150 thousand priests.

In 1895, at the time of the Berlin Congress on Africa, only approximately ten percent of this continent was occupied by Europeans. Fifty years later, only ten percent was not occupied by Europeans. Now we are back to the 1895 figure. Colonialist domination was of relatively short duration.

The Ethiopian army until last year had the extremely odd system of conscripting its officers but accepting only volunteer troops. In one high school the headmaster complained to John that his graduating class was conscripted each year as officer material. Both conscript officers and volunteer other ranks are in the army for life; until last year they could not get out.

About ninety percent of the country—and this is only a guess—is illiterate. Even in the priesthood about seventy percent is illiterate.

The Maria Theresa dollar is still currency in many regions and in parts of the interior salt bars serve as money.

Ed Korry, United States ambassador (with whom we're staying), told me Khrushchev sent a long letter which was delivered three days ago to the emperor. This accused the Americans and British of wishing to establish bases in Somalia and of trying to dominate Ethiopia. Khrushchev is offering the Ethiopians, in effect, Soviet mediation with Somalia and a virtually limitless military aid program.

ADDIS ABABA, ETHIOPIA, *March 9, 1964*

This morning I saw Haile Selassie in his "office palace," guarded by Imperial Guardsmen in natty tan uniforms and by two lazy tethered lions. He received me in a comfortable office, covered with oriental rugs and a yellow bearskin, sitting on a stiff-backed throne-armchair with an embossed seal in the back. He wore a tan summer uniform stiff with ribbon decorations. His little Pekingese dog leapt up beside him as we talked. We spoke directly in French. He was apparently ready to chat forever. But he uttered so many platitudes that after forty-five minutes I begged off.

I asked him how Africa could keep itself isolated from the cold war and he said, obliquely, that the continent needed many things and was divided into blocs such as the Francophone and Anglophone. "Liberty produces difficulties," he continued vaguely, "and to erase these troubles is difficult. It requires the help of the former colonizers. I told all the African chiefs of state we must live with the old colonizers and that they had done good things as well as bad; that the good things must not be forgotten. I hope little by little we can escape from our difficulties and find a unity of purpose based on friendship with the old colonial powers and secure their aid."

The continent cannot follow any single system. "Each African country has its own problems and there are big regional differences. De Gaulle has done much in France that was good and could be followed but he was not the sole useful model."

Addis Ababa was the capital of Ethiopia, which in turn wanted to help African unity. In time, perhaps, this could then become an African Geneva (in League of Nation days); but not right away. Ethiopia with its mixed peoples and religions was a kind of African Switzerland. (!)

He said: "The colonialists left us many things, including frontiers that had been delimited. These should be continued because otherwise there would be a danger of war. We are all in favor of keeping existing borders in Africa."

Haile Selassie said the Russians had promised to arm twenty thousand Somalians and he hoped Moscow would reconsider this. He had protested and hoped Russia understood.

He said Sweden or England provided models for the kind of constitutional monarchy he sought for Ethiopia. "That is our goal; and it will come in a very few years. But time is needed. That is why I am working so hard to expand our school program and send students abroad to learn about democracy."

NAIROBI, KENYA, *March 10, 1964*

Talked with Bill Attwood this afternoon. He just arrived as the first United States ambassador to independent Kenya (which became fully free only in December).

U.S. basic policy, he says, is to press for federation of Kenya, Uganda, Tanganyika, and Zanzibar to make them more viable, keep communism out, then eventually to work for a confederation with Nyasaland, Northern Rhodesia, Rwanda-Burundi. Such a regional bloc would make it far easier for sensible regional planning.

Kenyatta is regarded by everyone as a Grand Old Man. He has far greater stature than Nyerere, who lost immense face by timidity during the Tanganyika coup. Kenyatta is seventy-three but remarkably strong and healthy.

Russia and China are seeking instability here and have a joint interest in that. But once there is chaos, each will work for its own purposes. Each wants control. They would like then to press from east Africa down to southwest Africa, Southern Rhodesia, Mozambique, and South Africa— their great goal. They have agents in the Liberation Movements headquartered in Dar es Salaam and Castro is built up as an ideal.

The communists would like to make a showpiece of little Zanzibar with its three hundred thousand population, to create inexpensively a kind of "Potemkin village" of African success. And they also want to bring collapse on the mainland by scaring foreign capital and merchants out of east Africa. China and Russia each reckon that in about ten years South Africa will explode, and they each want to be ready to move in. But they are working together in phase one of this effort.

NAIROBI, KENYA, March 11, 1964

Lunched today with Mike Dunford. I first knew Mike as a captain in the British army in 1942. He settled here in 1947, married a pretty, intelligent Greek girl, and established his own very successful public relations business in 1954. When I last saw him here in late 1952, early 1953, he and Cleo always were armed and he wore a Home Guard uniform; it was the height of the Mau Mau terror. But he is now happily adjusted to an independent Kenya, has a nice house in Nairobi, a prosperous farm in the Masai country, and is optimistic and doing well. We lunched at the Nairobi Club.

It was much the same as in the old colonial days. The relations between servants and the whites seemed unchanged. I asked Mike about what he thought of the white man's life and future, and this is his account.

> Independence creates conditions for development on a much greater scale than under a colonial regime. Under a colonial regime the majority of a country's population is against the government. But nowadays, under independence, your own staff has a desire to work. We have already seen this clearly. There is a spirit of "*Harambee*"— which is Swahili for "let's pull together," this is the biggest difference. It is not any more just for the sake of working to earn money for oneself but for the country as a whole.
>
> However, on the negative side a bout of lawlessness has set in. There are land squatters, stock thefts, illegal stock movements which spread cattle disease, and theft of wire fences. In the cities there is an increase of crime. Everyone has a desire to possess and at the same time there is more unemployment because investment has dried up.
>
> It is more pleasurable to do business with African civil servants than with colonial civil servants. The European was too preoccupied with routine but the African smiles. He is eager and interested in what you have to say.
>
> The African likes to take decisions, even if they are wrong. The European was afraid to take decisions because this might prejudice his pension rights. Sometimes the decisions taken nowadays are cockeyed but nevertheless something does happen and it happens quickly.

Personally, I feel activated by a desire to take part in this tremendous change. I decided to stay here because I wanted myself and my family to participate in making a nation. This is a fascinating experience because there is no other former colonial nation that has come to independence with a mixture of minorities, European, Asian, and Arab. This made me want to stay.

But I would want my son to be very careful of the consequences if he were to think of marrying an African girl. No, I think I feel even stronger than that: I would do everything to prevent it. But I realize this sort of thing is bound to happen because there is much more social intercourse between the whites and blacks. The women are much tougher on this, however.

Some people say that Britain held the empire by originally keeping women at home and letting the administrators sleep with the natives and learn something. The women came later. After the Jinja bridge was opened from Uganda, people said—first came the white fathers, then the white ants, then the white women; the country was finished.

The African is very much more courteous than the European. I do not really understand the African. We all think we do but we don't. I can't pretend that I have any close African friends. It is still a bit early yet. And there is a big legacy of racial suppression which is now manifesting itself in the reverse. Today the European has to prove himself a decent fellow. They judge you on your ability to laugh with them.

It is essential to have a sense of humor because the majority values it. You must avoid impatience. If you lose your temper through impatience you lose your sense of humor and then you are licked.

In West Africa they have a saying "Wawa," when you are confronted with a completely frustrating situation. The old hands say to this "*Wawa*"—West Africa wins again. Relax and take it. Now *Eawa* is starting here you cannot afford to lose your temper.

Had tea and a talk at State House this afternoon with Malcolm MacDonald, new governor general (chief of state and representative of the Queen) for independent Kenya. A nice man, I saw him last in Singapore, bright, sympathetic, with a heart.

MacDonald says that the basic British policy is this:

The first step, independence, has been achieved. Secondly we would like to see federation although we cannot support this because it would look like an imperial plan; nevertheless, we are ready to help. Thirdly, federated or not, we want these countries to have governments of free people, not communist-run.

I don't think the British parliamentary form of government is suitable to African states. I doubt if a two-party system is needed. We don't want two parties done away with as in Ghana or even in Tanganyika, just gradual maturation.

With federation, the danger of communism is less. The majority against communism is very strong in Kenya and Uganda and even in Tanganyika. The chances of communism slipping in would be less with federation.

MacDonald said the movement of black against white was not entirely over. But nearly all black states are now independent and "the fight against white colonialists is over. However, it continues in its filthiest and purely racial form in the Union of South Africa. All the independent black governments are bitterly opposed to the white supremacy of the white South African and they are prepared to overthrow it by war if necessary. The longer apartheid stays the worse its echos will be, and this may land all Africa in a mess.

"The Chinese have no sense of responsibility and they are very racist in their propaganda. They accuse the Russians of being white and they have got it across that they themselves are not white. The Peking radio gets into parts of Africa where no other radio is heard and it broadcasts in African languages."

NAIROBI, KENYA, *March 12, 1964*

This afternoon I saw Tom Mboya, minister of justice and constitutional affairs, and perhaps the outstanding man in the government, after [Jomo] Kenyatta. He is a stocky, medium-sized man, a Luo, very dark, with a smooth, flat face, rather thin lips, pug nose that is not exceptionally broad, wide head.

He said: "Some aspects of tribalism should be preserved. A people cannot be a people without some deeply integrated foundations that give them a feeling that there are things in life of value. You cannot substitute for this foreign ideas and knowledge acquired elsewhere. That is the positive side of the fact.

"The negative side is that which expresses itself in looking down on persons from other tribes. This must be ended. It provides an area that can be exploited by reckless politicians.

"The economic and industrial revolutions bring people together and move them from their tribal homes. This produces the habit of working with other people from other tribes. Within the trade unions people have to learn to respect each other and understand each other. Also in the schools. Children learn how to get on together and this creates a new atmosphere.

"Many African leaders from different tribes and areas have established even closer relations with each other than those in Europe. They shared common experiences in universities in Europe and the U.S.A.

"Time will take care of this problem. You cannot legislate *for* unity—only against discrimination on a tribal or racial basis."

I then asked if he saw a threat of black racism. He replied: "Don't forget, you are dealing with a human society. There is a background in which the European was the master for a long time. He wielded a power far beyond his desserts and he did this contemptuously. The Africans suffered at the hands of the Europeans and the unscrupulous Asian businessmen.

"The ordinary man in the street feels resentful and arrogant now that he has taken power. He may try to pay back for what he suffered. But this problem can be solved by the resolution of African leadership."

DAR ES SALAAM, TANGANYIKA, *March 17, 1964*

This morning I talked with Amir Jamal, minister for communications, power, and works, the only Asian member of the cabinet. I noticed that the toilets in the Tancot (Tanganyika Cotton) Building where his ministry has offices are still marked Ladies (E) and Ladies (A), etc., (European and African), more than two years after independence.

Jamal is a very nice, intelligent man with a good, handsome face, fine features and slightly greying black hair. He speaks extremely well. The atmosphere was, as everywhere here, informal, and he received me in shirtsleeves, puffing a pipe.

I asked Jamal about the role of the Asian. He started out rather diffidently, saying: "There is a great danger in emphasizing racial separateness. The very use of the word Asian or European is self-defeating. The more you talk about their special role, the more dangerous, for these distinctions can boomerang. And the use of the word Asian has connotations with China, India, Pakistan, Indonesia, and all their problems.

"What you are really saying is that you mean a brown-skinned chap who made his home here. And the more you associate him with the Asian label, the less likely you are to graft him on to local society. But the question remains, how can you achieve a fully integrated society? It is best to minimize and understate these labels, Asian and European. Economics will have to solve the problem ultimately. Racial divisions now existing are coexistent with economic divisions.

"Until only recently the African, whether in town or country, was content to live in an unchanging atmosphere and never thought of improvement or the future. There was a master-servant relationship in which the African was never called on for initiative or responsibility. He had the habit of remaining static and not thinking of the future.

"Only sixty or seventy of the twenty-five thousand Europeans have taken out citizenship. The great bulk are simply not loyal to the state. Most Europeans are civil servants, technicians, or agents of companies working on behalf of external interests. This, for the moment, is mutually convenient for them and the state. The economy needs them so long as Africans are untrained.

"As for the Asians—about twelve thousand have registered as citizens and others don't have to register. About thirty thousand are now citizens; but two-thirds are not."

DAR ES SALAAM, TANGANYIKA, *March 18, 1964*

This morning I went to State House to see President Julius Nyerere. The rains have started and it was a hot, humid day with lowering clouds.

Nyerere received me behind his large desk which faces out toward the harbor. He is a slender, slight man with a high forehead, a head that slopes suddenly backward, a small Chaplin moustache, rather high but pleasant voice, a bright manner and agreeable way of speaking excellent English.

He was wearing white trousers and a dark green half-sleeved open shirt. Behind him on the wall were a few spears and tribal shields. Beside his desk on a small table and on the desk were no less than seven telephones, two of them white. The air was heavy and flies buzzed; a small ant kept crawling over my notebook which I had laid out on the glass of his desk.

I started by asking who had influenced him most, which person, alive or dead. He said: "It is very difficult to tell. To some extent, perhaps, I can name people. Certainly the Indian leaders, Gandhi and Nehru. I never saw Gandhi and I only met Nehru once. But also Abraham Lincoln. It is just possible that I have read all of Lincoln's speeches."

I asked if, because of his name and also because he had translated Shakespeare's *Julius Caesar* into Swahili, he was particularly fascinated by the character of Caesar. He said:

"No. No particular fascination. My translation of Caesar was accidental. It happened to be the set book for the Edinburgh University exams when I went in and I had to study it fairly thoroughly. Actually, I have read little about the historical Julius Caesar. Shakespeare makes him into a rather arrogant old man and he doesn't appeal to me much. The character in the play for whom I have got respect is Brutus—a man of great principle."

I then asked, apropos of his own brochure, *Second Scramble for Africa*, whether he had any formula for keeping Tanganyika and Africa out of the cold war. He said:

"No, there isn't any formula. We can but struggle all the time and it isn't an easy thing. The big powers are anxious to get us involved. And whether or not we take sides, we are still involved. Were there a formula to stay out, all the African countries would have applied it."

I asked him if he thought that for a fixed period Africa's existing frontiers should be frozen, in order to get started on a peaceful road of cooperation. He said:

"Certainly they should be frozen for a fixed period. They should be frozen for good. I don't see how now or in the future we can play with these borders. That would bring Balkanization. The answer to Africa's problems is unity, not revision of boundaries, either now or in the future. I know of no instance in history where there has been a peaceful revision of frontiers. Unity is the only answer."

I asked him if, in view of the legacy of racial hatred left by colonialism, he thought his concept of a multiracial society in Tanganyika stood a good chance of success. He said:

"One can only work for this because it is the only possible good. In this world we are all multiracial countries. There is no monoracial country in the world. Our racial groups in Tanganyika are more visibly different because they came in recently. But what chance have we got if people don't learn to live together in a multiracial world? What is the alternative? Extermination. There simply is no alternative to a genuine attempt to live together.

"You can't have racial laws, laws eliminating prejudice. I can't wipe prejudice from the minds of people. That is a medical, a psychiatric problem. I'm not a doctor. But I can erase legal distinctions between races. And if we don't succeed? We must succeed. The world, after all, is nonracial."

Excellent talk with Bill Leonhart, United States ambassador. The moment for any form of intervention in the recent Zanzibar crisis (when the ruler was ousted) has ended. In February, when the British still had an aircraft carrier in these waters, there was still a chance; now none. It had been hoped that by now [Julius] Nyerere, [Jomo] Kenyatta, and [Milton] Obote would have a joint meeting to discuss the problem; they haven't. We have missed about three chances on Zanzibar; will we get any more? The U.S.A. is poor on islands—look at Cuba. Our greatest success on Quemoy in recent years was getting it out of the news. Odd for the world's greatest naval power.

Everything went wrong in Zanzibar. The British walked away and left the sultan in control—the second time they have walked out and left a minority government; the first time was South Africa. The British had previously run Zanzibar as a preclusive little domain.

There was the Hobson's choice between the old feudal, obsolete, pro-British regime or an African regime which leaned to the communists.

United States errors on this whole issue have been fundamental. (1) We assume Britain has the lead in east Africa; it has, only because we do even less. (2) We reckon there are no good or bad groups so long as they are black, that it is too early to choose sides, that today's friends may be tomorrow's enemies.

In the end the Zanzibar incident may be more disastrous for U.S. interests than Cuba.

There are three basic propositions to steer by in Africa:

(1) This generation of African leaders is the best leadership likely to emerge in this century. They are responsible, have thought patterns formed in molds we can understand, and concepts of law, order, and politics familiar to the West.

(2) Of all the real issues here, the primary one is the search for dignity. And the way to get dignity, it is felt, is by modernization. In the end the racial question dominates everything. There is an important antagonism between Asia and Africa; and it is worse in Kenya where one must add more Europeans. All you need to judge African politics is an isobar chart. Wherever the climate is good, the whites come in in numbers and the chances of true independence diminish—as in South Africa. Climate and water set the pattern.

(3) The stakes in black Africa are still to be won. Washington is bemused by the multitude of new African governments.

BUJUMBURA, BURUNDI, *March 24, 1964*

Rwanda-Burundi holds about five million people along the backbone of Africa on its watershed, flowing into the Congo and Nile: eighty-four percent Hutu, fifteen percent Tutsi. The Tutsi—tall, shrewd, cruel, proud; the Hutu—patient, cheerful, hard-working, irascible, short; the Twa—obedient, greedy, uninhibited, brave, dwarfish.

The Belgians abolished domestic slavery here only in 1923. Mwami (King) Mwambutsa has reigned since 1915 when he ascended at the age of three.

There is a racial resentment against whites. The Mwami is criticized for having a white mistress.

BUJUMBURA, BURUNDI, *March 25, 1964*

Last night British Ambassador John Bennett, our host, gave a dinner party. Among those present were United States Ambassador Dumont (with his pied-noir wife); French Ambassador Barbey; [Peers] Carter, British foreign office inspector; Belgian Ambassador Col. Hennequiau and his dark, Congolese wife.

Quite a crisis. The Mwami and his French doll, dubbed the Tutsi Roll, were invited. In the afternoon the palace calmly called up and said they weren't coming. John protested to the doll, on palace advice, and she said keep two places in case the Mwami changed his mind. He didn't. His *chef de cabinet*, a tall Tutsi, showed up (without wife) and left promptly after dinner.

KAMPALA, UGANDA, *March 29, 1964*

Thursday, March 27, we drove up to Kigali, Rwanda, with Bennett, Peers Carter, and Paul Fabian, of Bennett's embassy.

Near Gitarama we left the main road for a British (Anglican) mission which has been having trouble. The mission runs a school for Tutsi and Hutu boys. They claim the Tutsis are much brighter and therefore do better—both in school and in later life, which is why they had all the cushy jobs. After the recent troubles many of the Tutsi boys' families had been slaughtered. The boys in school have split up and throw rocks at each other.

Rwanda is a paradisical place, green, wooded, lovely flowers. But the missionaries say occasional killings still take place in the vicinity and that a Tutsi was laid out on a hill nearby just a few days ago and had his hands and feet chopped off by Hutus. This is all hearsay and Bennett, alas, couldn't pin them down on any provable fact.

Easter holiday was coming up and twelve Tutsi boys had asked the missionaries for advice. Should they go home for holiday? (Some no longer had homes.) If they went, they might be killed en route. If they stayed, they might be killed. (The mission's only arm was a .22 rifle to kill mad dogs.) If they stayed next term to get their diplomas they might be killed. (All boys between sixteen and eighteen.) One said: "I know I'm going to die; I only hope it's a bullet, not a spear."

Bennett counseled the missionaries to tell the boys to stay. It would be hard for them to make their way to the Burundi border and cross the rivers where Hutu soldiers guard the bridges. They should tell the local prefecture they were staying and demand protection.

From this grim bunch of pleasant-looking missionaries in shorts and shirts, looking like scoutmasters, in their simple little houses with calico-clad wives, blond babies, and little puppies, we drove on through the magnificently lovely land of Rwanda.

At one point two huge crested cranes, with fuzzy feather halos, picked their way through green, swampy fields studded with orchids, hopping forward in a love-dance before taking off, slowly folding up their legs and flapping great white, black-rimmed wings.

Dined with Dudley Withers, U.S. ambassador, a pleasant man with huge walrus moustache. He is an avid photographer, carpenter, and wood-sculptor. His wife paints and plays a tiny portable electric organ. Thus they keep sane in Kigali, which has five thousand people.

Withers argues there is no *continent* of Africa. There is Arab North Africa; there is Middle Africa; and there is a bloc of South Africa, the Rhodesias, and Katanga.

Friday, March 27, I saw Rwanda's President Gregoire Kayibanda in his office, a little reddish stucco building protected by two stupid-looking guards with helmets and tommy guns. Kayibanda is a small Hutu (about five feet, three inches), skinny, with a small head and intent expression. I'm told he is far above his colleagues.

He described the Tutsi situation as "tranquil for the present, but that depends on the actions of the Nyenzi" (the Cockroaches who lead the Tutsi refugees and who, according to the missionaries, are preparing a new invasion for April).

Kayibanda says the fact that the Cockroaches have automatic arms proves they receive financial aid. He does not know for sure from whom this comes but he claims it is "not the communists"; he blames "the church —above all the Protestants."

Kayibanda says, "The missionaries interfere to a certain extent in internal affairs. With some individual exceptions, this is not true of the Catholics but of the Protestants. Of course, I am a Catholic, you know."

Afterward, Frey, the Swiss adviser to Kayibanda, called on me. His government assigned him here on a one-year loan. He hates it. On the advice of the Belgian who is military adviser, he sleeps with a cocked tommy gun beside him each night. So does the Belgian.

Ed Lillis, a six-feet, five-inch young American vice consul (he is twenty-six; it is his first post and he is called "the white Tutsi" by the natives, because of his size), drove us northward in his Volkswagen.

We went by herds of beautiful Tutsi cattle (now herded by Hutus) with horns more than a yard wide, gleaming with beauty. (They are tokens of wealth, rarely butchered, and provide hardly any milk.) There were droves of dove and francolin and guinea fowl. In some thorn trees hung hollowed-out logs, put there for bees to collect in hives. Banana and coffee clumps grew in the green fields and hillsides. There were dots of round, thatched mud huts with smoke oozing out through the roofs. These people have never figured out the value of a chimney—or a window.

We spent the night at the Gabiro lodge in the game park, run by an Irish couple who had had a large coffee plantation in the Congo and were driven out broke. Then we motored north past herds of zebra to the broad Kagera River that flows between Rwanda and Tanganyika and into Uganda's Lake Victoria, eventually the Nile: thick, turbulent, bordered by papyrus clumps. We crossed the frontier into Uganda over a steep gorge. Passed the little rest house of an Italian woman named Toni Nuti, who has built on an island in the rushing Kagera where she fishes and listens to the hippopotami. You get to her by a windlass-operated cable car. She refuses to serve blacks.

It was pouring rain; this is the season. We whizzed past hundreds of little round thatched mud Tutsi refugee huts in camps, near the border, and finally reached Mbarara, capital of Ankole, one of the kingdoms that make up Uganda. There we lunched at an Indian-run hotel and saw the poor Anglican bishop who still talks, vainly, of going to Rwanda which has refused him a visa.

Long talk with Milton Obote, prime minister and chief of government in Uganda.

Obote is very dark, with flat nose, high forehead, angular, intelligent face. He is so thin and well-dressed in closely cut suit that he looks tall, although I suspect he is two inches shorter than I. He speaks very good English (with African accent), has a sedate, grave manner which clearly masks a very passionate internal personality.

I asked if Obote thought the security situation was now safe. He said: "No country is ever satisfied with its security situation—not even yours. But my difficulties in January were not really very difficult. The main part of the Uganda army [two slim battalions] was all right. It was just a question of trouble with the headquarters company of one battalion which wanted to take a leaf out of the Tanganyikan book. They had seen people get away with it in Tanganyika and wanted to get away with it here. But they did not take up arms or leave their barracks. The three hundred of them simply went on a sit-down strike. I sent the minister of interior to them and within two hours they were back in their barracks (which he said they had never left). But I had already asked for British troops from Kenya. It wasn't a bad situation—except that a sit-down strike in the army is bad enough."

I asked if he was worried about communist activities and propaganda. He said: "I think that is inescapable. Propaganda is evident but other activity is less open. They are more interested in pamphlets and circulating papers. They are trying to cultivate friends and agents as a first step. This refers to both Russia and China but people are more worried about China. Chinese propaganda is especially anti-Western and antiwhite, which also hits the Russians."

I asked Obote if he was working for a multiracial society. He said: "I can only work for liberty, the liberty of individuals residing in Uganda. This is regardless of race. There should be a square deal for everyone and this idea is popularly accepted. There are, of course, small inter-racial quarrels. But the broad masses want peace and tolerance."

Was Uganda having any trouble with missionaries? Obote said: "We could have trouble with them here although most of us have been reared in their schools. One thing they don't realize is the need for a separation between church and state. They would really like a say in governmental decisions. Sometimes they openly support candidates in elections.

"We haven't reached the level of trouble of Sudan or Rwanda. But we would like to avoid trouble by having more African clergymen. We don't even like the word 'missionary.' They did good work in the past but the era of missionary work is now over. The church here should be more a Ugandan movement. The missionaries still are an aspect of the nineteenth century."

7

OCCASIONAL CHUFF

OF LIONS

MASINDI, UGANDA, *April 1, 1964*

DAVE WILLIAMS, OUR WHITE HUNTER, SAYS THE KABAKA (KING) OF Buganda is a nice fellow but a bad shot. Dave lined up a lion for him at eighty yards, standing placidly on the other side of a tree with his whole chest and neck exposed on one side and his rear on the other. The Kabaka hit the tree and the lion roared up filled with splinters.

Here are some impressions of the area between Masindi and Murchison Falls, where Lake Victoria bursts out into the Upper Nile: mahogany trees, rubber trees girdled with orchids, huge crested hornbills, monkeys, herds of tan-pink elephants, orange lizards, large dark brown and black ant hills higher than a man . . . Murchison with its steaming, fetid hippo pool, quiet elephants which can be murdered by smashing the brain pan with the same skill and risk as shooting squirrels . . . Lake Albert with hollowed log pirogues, banana groves, flocks of pelicans, herds of sounding, blowing hippos.

The deceptive African calm and sudden unexpected violence which overturns boats with crazy, invisible gusts of wind. This afternoon a storm on Lake Albert sweeps abruptly across to the Congo Mountains. Pelicans and cormorants hunt leaping minnows in the waves and millions of dragonflies flicker above the water. Calm returns. Perfectly arched rainbows form overhead and touch the ground at both ends. Africans hurl hand-lines at leaping fish in the shallows by a tumble-down village where high waters have ruined the shoreline and eaten into the houses and jetty installation in the port of Butiaba. The large, abandoned river steamer

Robert Coryndon rusts, empty and desolate at anchor. Spear-bearers run into the bush, frightened by our Land Rover.

Drove through the disturbed areas, where the kings of Buganda and Toro are quarreling, to Fort Portal below the Ruwenzoris, and past tea plantations. Black boys from the Scottish Mission School called "Fort Portal Scottish" wander by in red sweaters and socks and tan kilts with fake sporrans, causing our two black hunters to roar with laughter. Two Norwegian policewomen from the new Norwegian Peace Corps stop beside us for gas and say they are helping to create a Ugandan corps of police-women. On the slopes below the Ruwenzoris we see small, black, thin-tusked elephants called Congo rats.

SEMLIKI, UGANDA, *April 4, 1964*

Dined with a bunch of "old boys," former British officers who should be memorialized by Somerset Maugham. Colonel "Bombo" T.: a white, bald, strong superintendent of national parks, named for the town where his battalion of the old King's African Rifles was headquartered.

T. tells of how hyenas attack newborn elephants by continually circling the herd and finally snatching the helpless creature while it is still tied by its umbilical cord. Packs of wild dogs hunt down antelope bucks, each one tearing off a piece of flesh. T. saw one buck still loping along when he had no more flesh and hardly any muscle. He once saw a buffalo kill a lion who missed in his first leap to break the buffalo's neck. Lions hunt in pairs. The male roars and tries to terrify the prey while the female sneaks up behind and does the killing. The male eats first.

SEMLIKI, UGANDA, *April 5, 1964*

The night is silent except for the occasional chuff of lions. Then with the dawn comes the hum of insects, the chatter of birds, and the yowl of hyenas and other animals.

I shot a kob and trailed it with the two black hunters by spots of blood from its broken leg and bubbling gut shot. At the very end, as it hobbles past a buck kob with his does (they come successively to the buck to be served), the wounded intruder is attacked as an interloper.

The hippos blow in a small, swampy lake while elephant families trudge by unconcerned. Lesser bustards leap heavily into the air and a pair of plovers fight and eventually frighten off a huge eagle coming too close to their nest. A great pack of mongooses rushes silently out of a bush where I am chasing a guinea fowl. Two hartebeests fight, booting each other, as the Ruwenzoris are suddenly unveiled by clouds, exposing the snow gla-ciers below their peaks.

SEMLIKI, UGANDA, *April 6, 1964*

Obscene little pygmies just inside the beginning of the vast Ituri forest, standing there with evil eyes and smiling faces, clutching their miniature bows and steel-tipped poison arrows which look like toys but can kill an elephant. Williams discovers that his two black hunters, members of the Waliangulu tribe on the Kenya coast, have been collecting vulture feathers. This is what they make a special glue with to hold the poison for their arrows.

SEMLIKI, UGANDA, *April 7, 1964*

A huge bull hippo suddenly rises near our boat while fishing on Lake Albert, and Williams shoots us away at full speed when he dives threateningly. I chase a guinea fowl into the bush trying to rise him, not seeing an elephant looking menacingly out of the brush thirty yards away. Murderers from Congo, Kenya, Tanganyika, and Uganda congregate in the stinking little fishing village by Lake Albert where stark naked babies, ducks, and chickens scramble among rotting fish guts by the bamboo frames where clean fish dry in the sun. Crowds of idle men guzzle banana beer in the local bars.

NAIROBI, KENYA, *April 7, 1964*

Mr. Samuel, our affable black guide in the game park, drives us up to a pride of lions sleeping in the sunshine. "Squeaky," a castrated lion, huge and maneless, ambles up. Looking at Squeaky, Mr. Samuel says: "What are you doing? What are you doing? Gentleman, what are you doing?"

NAIROBI, KENYA, *April 10, 1964*

Cleo Dunford was in Leopoldville just before and just after Congolese independence. She tells a story of one extraordinary racket. Witch doctors and other phonies sold great big boxes sealed tight and wrapped in ribbons marked "To be opened on Independence Day." They cost more than $20 each. When they were opened, they proved to contain nothing.

RABAT, MOROCCO, *April 20, 1964*

This morning I saw Mehdi Benouna, who now runs *Mapresse* (Moroccan news agency). We had drinks on the terrace of the Tour Hassan. In 1954–55 Ahmed Ben Bella stayed in Mehdi's fine old family house in Tetuan. Mehdi gave him a separate apartment with a special set of keys and a Yale lock in addition to the immense old front door key.

One day Mehdi discovered a pile of plastics and detonators. He protested, saying they should store such things in a safe place, that he had his mother, wife, and children there, and if the explosives blew up, they would wreck most of Tetuan. Ben Bella was furious, threw the large key at him, said, "We are at war, even your mother and children; what does it matter where we die?"

He thinks little of Ben Bella as an emotional ignorant fool. But the real force, who holds potential power, is Boumedienne, who prefers to act behind Ben Bella's facade.

RABAT, MOROCCO, *April 21, 1964*

Late this afternoon I was received by King Hassan II in his palace offices, where his father had received me five years ago. Prince Alaoui, who interpreted for me in 1959 when Mohammed V preferred to speak Arabic, was there.

The door opened and Alaoui prostrated himself. I followed, standing up, and shook hands with Hassan, a short, trim man with rather dark, not especially Arabic features, very well dressed in a grey suit. He reminded me in appearance and courteous manner (as well as his repute for outdoor life) of Hussein of Jordan. He waved me to a seat before his desk. A servant appeared with orange juice and mint tea.

At the very end of our conversation Hassan said in beautiful French: "I understand you like to shoot and fish." We talked about this a bit and he boasted of the trout, mouflon, wild boar, partridge, and ducks. He asked "When can you come and hunt with me?" I said not before October. He said: "That's fine. The season will just have opened. We can fish too." I asked about the trout season. "Don't worry," he said. "They're *my* streams. There is no season. You'll like it."

Our conversation started on territorial claims. He said that, vis-à-vis Algeria "the big problem is to make the Algerians realize this is a question for the future, not now."

Hassan, apropos of Spain, said: "There is a process of African liberation which Spain must admit. We have explained that the example of creating states from nothing doesn't work" (a clear reference to both Mauretania and, perhaps, Rio de Oro). "Our rights to the south are solid."

I asked if de Gaulle had ever formally brought up the subject of a Mediterranean pact with Morocco. He said not in that form but, last year when Hassan visited Paris, de Gaulle spoke to him of the need for a Franco-Spanish-Moroccan "Axis" of the three north-south countries bordering the Atlantic and the Mediterranean.

I asked what he thought Algeria was after in Morocco, when it started last autumn's war. He said: "I think the Algerians were deceived by some of their friends who told them the Moroccan monarchy was feeble and could be crumbled by just a small frontier incident. After all, Boumedienne said in Cairo that had Nasser confined his revolution to the valley of the Nile, it wouldn't have lived; it needed to expand. And likewise the Algerian revolution had to spread to survive."

I asked about the prospects of Maghreb (north African) unity. He said: "Our concept of socialism is different. We want to enrich the poor whereas Algeria wants to impoverish the rich. I am a socialist also, but I want to be positive.

"My father adored his family and his children but when the moment of choice came, he sacrificed them for his country. This was his big lesson for me, to have a passion for my country. You must love your country more than anything; this is primordial for a chief of state."

Hassan thought monarchy was a sound governmental philosophy and added: "In Africa there are many monarchies without kings—where dictators have more power than any king."

ALGIERS, *April 26, 1964*

Spent the day at and near Blida, lunching at the home in Blida of M'Hamed Yazid and then driving around the Mitidja visiting cooperative farms and those under *Comités de Gestion* (abandoned French lands).

Yazid is from Blida where his family has lived for generations. His grandfather, father, and brother were career officers in the French army. Another brother was killed by the French during the war. He studied at Blida, then went to the Sorbonne to study law. There he became involved in politics and joined the *Étoile*, a group that linked the Algerian, Tunisian and Moroccan nationalists in Paris.

During 1952–54, under nine extremist leaders, an organization was created to fight an independence war and it was to be launched November 3, 1954. But the French got wind of the plot, so the uprising was moved up two days to November 1. Revolution was proclaimed with simultaneous incidents all over the country. Yazid was among the first to join. He went to Cairo where he joined Ben Bella.

Yazid is now a deputy and also a special roving envoy assigned by Ben Bella to particular missions like the Moroccan affair, Tunis, or a trip to see Kennedy during the Moroccan crisis.

After lunch two young revolutionary officials from Blida took us on a tour of factories and farms in the Mitidja area. I was struck by one among many exhortatory posters: "Long Live Revolutionary Modesty."

ALGIERS, *April 27, 1964*

Dined last night at the home of General Jean-Louis de Rougemont at Alger Plage, about twenty-five kilometers out of town, eastward, on the beach. He commands the twentieth division which, at one time, had all eastern Algeria under its administration. It is now pulling out.

The only sensible French decisions vis-à-vis Algeria, says he, were those of Charles X in 1830 to invade and end piracy, and that of Charles de Gaulle to grant independence; everything in between was folly. The French *colons* tried to sway French policy in between. They were disagreeable, tough, unsympathetic people. The army resented them and sought, in its last years, to protect the Moslems from them and raise their standards, but it was too late.

Jean-Louis says Algeria won't go communist although it may develop an even worse system of its own. But it will be less dangerous to the West, avoiding alliance with the Soviet bloc.

Had a long talk with (U.S. ambassador) Bill Porter today. He says the U.S.A. is feeding more than a third of the Algerian population still. The government does not advertise this much but the Algerian people know it and are grateful.

Algeria will be extremely unsettled for the next two or three years. There is a lack of brains and experience at the top because so much administrative talent has been discarded. Algerian economic policy frightens away many American investors who would otherwise be pleased to come in. The country is still going down. The government is trying to fit a French-type economy into a loose socialist framework of a disjointed and amorphous sort.

Ben Bella keeps talking about destroying Western and capitalist influences here. He himself is influenced by a mixed-up Marxist team that moved in from the Congo and Tunisia. Many of these people are quite unorthodox. These include Raptis, a Greek who fought as "General Pablo" for the Spanish Republicans; Serge Michel, a Trotskyist and former Lumumba supporter; and a French leftist named Simon.

Ben Bella is heading for lots of trouble unless he acquires some administrative talent around him. He wants to consolidate his power. Then he hopes he will be in a position to personally lead the country to order, stability, and prosperity. He aspires to a kind of agrarian-plus-industrial socialism which would eliminate excessive differences between high and low living standards. His socialism follows Nasser's in spirit and Tito's in technique. And he admires Castro for resisting a great power.

Ben Bella's greatest talent is his ability to balance opposition elements against each other and then to reduce all these divided factions. He has a cunning sense of maneuver and an innate stubbornness. He has managed to make himself indispensable. Personally he feels very close to Nasser, whom he admires. He is a big-boned peasant boy with powerful hands, great stamina, and a devotion to his job.

This is a war-weary country that wants food and work. The people have never been asked if they want socialism.

PARIS, *May 3, 1964*

Lunched with Stikker. Stikker went to Cyprus last week because he feared Turkey was about to invade the island and Greece would then respond with war. This is the third time Turkey has been on the verge of invasion.

The French are obstructing NATO in every way. They are balking on moving two divisions east because they have a "backward" strategy. They refuse to accept the NADGE (Air Defense) arrangement. Russia has twenty-eight NADGE-type stations in East Germany and area. We plan to have fourteen on our side of the line. But we only have two so far. This is why U.S. planes have been lost on the other side of the curtain. Senior French naval and military officers had accepted a plan for French cooperation on NATO naval relations. But before he went to the hospital, de Gaulle received the plan and physically tore it up.

PARIS, *May 4, 1964*

Lunched with André de Staercke (Belgian ambassador to NATO). André said many leaders are not really as important as they think. Churchill had told him: "Montgomery was indispensable to the world for two weeks. The trouble is that this experience made him think he was indispensable forever."

Churchill also told him: "If a military man explains something to you and you don't understand, it is he who is stupid, not you."

PARIS, *May 5, 1964*

Lunched today at (former premier) Edgar Faure's. Faure said that in early 1961 he saw de Gaulle, who brought up the subject of China. Faure thought there was nothing that could be done at that time. It would be foolish to emulate the British and end up with only a *chargé d'affaires* and incomplete recognition. De Gaulle agreed and the matter was dropped.

In July 1963 Faure was taking a vacation with his wife in Ischia. He kept reading in the newspapers about the Sino-Soviet quarrel, became very restless and said: "I must do something; I must see what is going on." He went to Switzerland and through the French embassy he contacted the Chinese envoy in Bern who said to him: "Why don't you come and see us again?" Faure had been to China in 1957. He said he was quite prepared to make a new visit, and a visa was granted.

One day in August he received a telephone call from the Élysée saying that de Gaulle wanted to see him. De Gaulle asked Faure why he didn't look into the situation in China since he had already been there once.

Faure said he was already planning to do this and had his visa. De Gaulle authorized Faure to say, when he was in China, that he spoke with the General's approval.

He says Chou is now the real boss and he is the absolute boss in foreign policy. Mao is a kind of fossilized, tired symbol who speaks for the party but no longer runs things. Chou even read a newspaper while they were talking to Mao. Faure said: "Imagine reading a newspaper in the presence of General de Gaulle!"

He said it was clear from the very first conversation that Chou wished to exchange recognition with France and was in a position to more or less make the decision although he had to refer it as a matter of form to Mao. Mao has never traveled and is very naive about the world.

Faure thinks that if the United States would make a settlement with China world peace would be assured for decades. He says France can play no role between China and Russia, although it could conceivably develop contacts between China and the U.S.A.

Faure thinks Johnson should send some unofficial envoy to China to start exploratory talks. At this juncture the United States cannot afford to say it will get out of Formosa, and China cannot afford to demand that we get out of Formosa. But these matters must be put on ice while other things are discussed. The Chinese once loved us and now they hate us, but this is a real love-hate relationship and they could very swiftly start to love us again.

Faure said that until this year he had not been in Russia since 1956 and that he had found a profound change. "For the first time we saw women," he observed. "Before you saw only bundles and sacks. When I was there last, a foreigner was a noteworthy object. Even his shoes caused astonishment. Now that has all changed."

THE HAGUE, NETHERLANDS, *May 12, 1964*

Spent a couple of hours strolling and sitting at a cafe this afternoon with Senator Fulbright, who is spending one day here, not as a delegate but in a wind-up of his trip (London, Athens, Ankara, Copenhagen, The Hague).

Fulbright said he has no interest in being secretary of state. He wouldn't take it if offered. But he did admit he would consider it if great pressure were applied. He says he's getting old (fifty-nine), has seniority in the senate, doesn't even know how long he wants to stay on there. Says two cabinet ministers resigned to run for the senate but he never heard of a senator resigning to join the cabinet. He thinks Rusk an excellent secretary.

He said the president, Rusk, and McNamara are very leery about extending the Vietnam war and starting something that can't be finished. This idea is mostly propounded by lower level people or legislators not of the top rank. It would be impossible to negotiate from the present chaos.

THE HAGUE, NETHERLANDS, *May 13, 1964*

Drink and chat with Dean Rusk today. I asked him if he would stay on as secretary. He said: "I am the fifty-fourth secretary of state and someday there will be a fifty-fifth. I serve at the pleasure of the president. But I may point out that only twenty-two of the secretaries of state have served as long as one presidential term. Hull was there longest—thirteen years— but there has been a constitutional change since and that record will never be equaled.

"You know the problem is financial. When I have no more money, when I am down to zero, I shall have to quit." I remarked it was too bad he couldn't have a good investment counselor, but that, alas, was against the law. "There isn't anything to invest," he said.

Rusk admitted we had not done well on our Aswan policy. He thought Russia had benefited by being able to build large projects like Aswan or the Bokara steel mill in India. They had cut in on us. Congress had been opposed to the Indian project.

Our aid program was generally more interested in fundamentals, like education, technical training, etc. We did few things for straight effect, like the Russians, who put up a stadium in Djakarta. But we have helped on important national projects, although not so dramatic as Aswan in scale.

Shifting to Vietnam, I said it seemed to me that logic dictated that ulti- mately we would have to accept either a de Gaulle (neutralization and abandonment) or Nixon (northward attack) policy. Rusk said neither he nor McNamara was yet prepared to concede this, that South Vietnam, with our help, cannot win the war. There is not as yet "any objective reason to conclude this.

"The French tell us you can't do with fifteen thousand men what we couldn't do with two hundred and fifty thousand. But things are different. In general the people of South Vietnam don't want a Vietcong [com- munist] solution. Sure, they're tired of twenty years of fighting. And the countryside is largely apolitical. When people are terrorized by the Viet- cong at night they won't cooperate with the government in the daytime. They're scared. Security is an indispensable problem.

"But you must look at things province by province. Much of the north and center needs only police action; they have been largely pacified. In one or another province, of course, three hundred or four hundred Viet- congs can cause a lot of trouble. But the real problem, the serious problem, is in the delta, and both the government and the Vietcongs are concentrat- ing there.

"We don't believe we have to make a choice between the extremes you mention."

Talking about the role of secretary of state, Rusk said: "The U.S. con- stitutional system provides that when a secretary of state goes abroad he acts, in effect, as an ambassador. A minister in our government acts on the instructions of the president. There is no independent portfolio of foreign affairs as there is in some other governments.

"Marshall took the view, which I share, that when a secretary of state travels his seal of office remains at home. The acting secretary then becomes responsible for issuing instructions. When he goes abroad, the secretary doesn't take the State Department with him.

"Dulles didn't wholly accept this theory and he took very large delegations abroad with him. But I've cut these down to the minimum. I take only the people needed to do the scheduled job. If any other questions arise, I send to Washington for instructions."

I asked Rusk who, what man, had most influenced his career. He said: "In terms of the person who had a tremendous influence on my attitudes toward public service—Marshall. In many, many ways. The things he set as standards for himself and his colleagues. These caught my fancy closely."

PARIS, *May 17, 1964*

Played golf with Couve and then a long chat over late lunch. He thinks the Franco-British Suez expedition was a tremendous mistake. France and Britain should either have invaded right away without waiting, or they should have done nothing in terms of force but tried to settle at the UN. And the U.S. should certainly have not interfered when the Franco-British expedition started.

Couve says Dulles was so emphatic in the way he chose to break off our offer to help on the Aswan dam because he was afraid of being cramped in his policy by a congressional alliance including representatives of the southern cotton-growing states, states with large Jewish populations, and right-wingers who were furious with Nasser for recognizing China.

Five or six years ago when Ben-Gurion came here on an official visit, he stated to Couve: "I understand you opposed Suez." Couve said this was true because he was in principle opposed to failures. Ben-Gurion said: "It wasn't a failure for us."

He thinks [Paul-Henri] Spaak is terribly vain and unrealistic and wants to tell the great powers what to do. Couve has little respect for Belgium, which he says isn't even a country and has never solved its own nationalities problem the way, for example, Switzerland has.

PARIS, *May 25, 1964*

An hour with Couve de Murville at the *Quai d'Orsay*. I asked him at what point France thought the U.S.A. should encourage the prospect of negotiations over South Vietnam.

Couve said:

It really is very difficult to answer this. The U.S. is not the only one involved. I discussed this at length with Rusk and I said that, after all, in Algeria we had had a kind of guerrilla war that was no more pleasant than the one in South Vietnam. We knew that it was a losing affair and that in the end there would have to be a political settlement. We therefore decided that the Algerian people would have to choose and this meant independence.

And it is very hard to start negotiations even after we had made our basic decision. When negotiations really began they lasted for at least two years during which time we continued to fight. Everybody, even the army, knew that we were both negotiating and fighting at the same time. This is a very difficult procedure and many feared that it would destroy army morale, but we had to take that risk and we succeeded.

Of course the situation in Vietnam is by no means just the same. But thinking of taking a political road or seeking a negotiation does not mean you have to abandon everything and stop fighting immediately.

The big difference in Vietnam is that, contrary to the situation in Algeria, things are deteriorating all the time from a military point of view. In Algeria the military situation was much better in 1962 than in 1959, although we granted independence in 1962. In South Vietnam time is not running for the West, for the U.S.A. or for General Khanh.

To establish some kind of stable military situation is theoretically the correct approach but I am not sure that what is theoretically right is practicable or possible. There are many ways to start a negotiation. The normal way is simply to explore, to explore the possibility through other countries and with other countries. I really doubt if I can say any more about this.

France would like to get South Vietnam established as a neutral and independent country, as envisioned ten years ago. Obviously the question of North Vietnam remains for the future because we cannot hope to neutralize it now. We must take our chances. But surely it is better to have a neutral South Vietnam than to continue with the present situation.

We cannot foresee the future after that, after the neutralization of South Vietnam. It is very hard to forecast eventual relations between China and North Vietnam and the trend is unclear.

But the longer the war goes on, the more North Vietnam will depend totally on China. This is perfectly obvious. And the threat of U.S. military action against North Vietnam makes North Vietnam tie itself even more closely to China. If you enlarge the war and attack North Vietnam, it is obvious that North Vietnam will be occupied by China.

I then turned to Germany. I asked Couve if he thought it would be better to leave the German and Berlin situations precisely where they now are or to take the opportunity of worsening Soviet-Chinese troubles in order to seek a settlement.

Couve replied: "It is obvious that the approaches to the Russian problem and to the Chinese problem are different on both sides of the Atlantic. All the same, what you did not say is that the long term and profound national interests of the U.S.A. and Europe are *not* different. You Americans may be more directly interested in Asian affairs than we Europeans are. But the countries of Europe and the U.S. are made up of the same people and the same civilization. They really depend upon each other. If Europe were to disappear, you would be left alone in the world with countries like Cuba.

"Asia is of course very important strategically. But Asia is made up of countries of a thoroughly different nature than those of the West. The Asian countries can never be your real allies and you can never really bind them in the same sense as Europe. If, for example, the countries of southeast Asia were to be submerged by Russia and China, it would be very unpleasant for you; but still you would not be left alone in the world. You would still have Europe and you would still be in the best position." (Meaning, I inferred, vis-à-vis Russia.)

"I have said in the past that we would fight for Berlin but not for South Vietnam. Some people interpret this as meaning that we are not interested in Asia. But quite frankly I don't think we differ too much from one another on this. You Americans can consider Berlin and central Europe questions of life and death for you as well as for us. But I am not really sure you feel the same way about southeast Asia.

"So, getting back to your original question about Germany, all I can say is that the best thing is not to take sides in the Sino-Soviet debate. The Russians are big enough to fight China if they want to—without your help. Let's just leave both sides alone and see what will happen.

"What would really be silly would be to concede anything to the Russians just because they are in trouble—in this case with China."

I asked him if France still considered itself bound to Israel by any "special" relationship. He said no. At the time of Suez, France and Israel were allies although there was no formal alliance.

With a smile, he continued: "There was no treaty, only a plot. And of course France has been selling arms to Israel for years. Even before Suez we were selling Israel arms. We started that at least in 1954 and everyone knows that in recent years we have been sending a number of Mirages to Israel. There is no change in this policy. It is not a policy; it is simply business. If Egypt wanted to buy Mirages and could pay for them, I think we would sell them to Egypt."

PARIS, *May 26, 1964*

This noon I had a very pleasant talk with Prime Minister Pompidou. As usual he was informal, agreeable, and friendly. He has gotten a bit thinner since his days at the Rothschild Bank. He waved me over to a table by the window overlooking the lovely Matignon garden. I note he now smokes king-size Pall Malls instead of those rather foul, strong, black tobacco cigarettes of the past.

Pompidou said: "We consider that our nuclear force is now operational. If there were a war we would launch nuclear explosives. It is a mystery to no one that during the rest of 1964 and part of 1965 we will complete the first phase of our nuclear weapons program based upon the Mystère IV."

I asked him if inflation had been checked in France. He answered: "No. Things are getting better and we are on a good road but the problem certainly still remains. You need several preconditions to prevent inflation. In France we took moderate measures against inflation because we did not want to stop the tendency toward industrial expansion."

I asked him what France would do if Algeria nationalized petroleum and natural gas—and I had had the impression in Algeria that this is what they intended to do.

Pompidou said: "Of course, they promised they would not nationalize but I don't believe an Arab ever. I am sure that as soon as they think they can grab things without ruining themselves they will try to do it. But this is their problem. The Russians can't help them. The Russians are having plenty of trouble. Their foreign aid program is really relatively small and even though they are capable of giving aid to Algeria they can't buy Algerian oil."

I asked if he thought de Gaulle would seek reelection in 1965. He said: "I think that his recent (prostate) operation has increased his chances for running again. He now feels that he has rid himself of something that had been threatening him. It is not a case like that of Eisenhower who ran for a second term following an illness in his first term. This is a different situation and de Gaulle does not have to prove himself to himself. Of course he is old. He would be seventy-five if he were to present himself again. We all remember that Adenauer started his career at that age but that was a very phenomenal exception. Seventy-five is very old."

I told Pompidou that I had always had the impression that de Gaulle was obsessed with a fear of growing old in the public eye, recalling his remark that "*la vieillesse est un naufrage.*" Pompidou agreed and said that de Gaulle felt this very strongly. He said he was sure that de Gaulle doesn't really know what he plans to do and that he certainly changes his mind from one day to the next and from one month to the next. Moreover, he did not think de Gaulle would publicly intimate his decision until the very last minute.

I asked whether de Gaulle had ever given him any hint or indication that he considered Pompídou as his *dauphin* or successor. He grinned and said: "That is a rather embarrassing question." I repeated it. He said then: "If de Gaulle does not run for a second term, I will. And I will run with his blessing." I then asked if he thought de Gaulle would actively back him or would take a rather stand-off attitude like that shown by Eisenhower toward Republican candidates. Pompidou said: "I am sure he will help me; I know he will help me.

"Of course, de Gaulle will probably run again. If not, I shall certainly be the candidate. It is still difficult to foresee just what would happen."

PARIS, *May 27, 1964*

Lunched with Tom Finletter (U.S. ambassador to NATO). Tom thinks McNamara is up among the front runners seeking the vice-presidential nomination but he is likely to come a cropper very soon over Vietnam. He has been most foolishly associating himself with an over-optimistic picture of Vietnam and now the time of reckoning has come.

Finletter agrees that there are only two solutions: de Gaulle's and Nixon's. He thinks they are both bad for us but our hand may be forced by another—and this time neutralist—*coup d'état* in Saigon. That would really push us out.

Finletter had the feeling that the greatest culprit in the failure of MLF to get ahead was the U.S.A. Kennedy talked a lot about it but never did anything. Kennedy was an intellectual and a talker but not a man of action. The only action he ever took was in Cuba in 1962 and he could not dodge that one because of the Bay of Pigs.

PARIS, *June 2, 1964*

Had drinks and dinner last night with Bill Benton who has just come back from a whirlwind trip to Moscow, where he saw Khrushchev. Khrushchev attacked the presence of U.S. troops in South Korea and South Vietnam. He said: "South Vietnam is aflame and you are in a morass. U.S. policy is doomed. The same is true in Korea except that American troops can walk the streets of the cities without trouble.

"Why do you always ally yourselves with the reactionary forces? You call any revolution communistic even though there may be no communist party in the country involved and the leaders may never even have heard of Marx and Lenin."

Khrushchev said he and Kennedy had agreed in Vienna (June 1961) that neither the U.S.A. nor the Soviet Union would attempt to change the national borders of other countries. They agreed there should be no outside interference. But Kennedy interpreted this differently from Khrushchev and "this is the question of questions that divides us."

Khrushchev explained that he thought people were entitled to revolt against tyranny and a rotten society and this did not constitute outside interference. He added: "Can you expect us not to be sympathetic with oppressed people when they revolt?"

PARIS, *June 5, 1964*

Lunched with Jean Laloy, one of the most brilliant *Quai d'Orsay* officials. Laloy believes the U.S. position in the world is getting worse and worse. We have become the symbol of protection for reactionary regimes, kings, and generals. If we were to bomb North Vietnam in order to protect our interests in South Vietnam we would just look like an old-fashioned imperialist power blowing up the natives.

Incidentally, Laloy said on the subject of Indochina that when General [Philippe] Leclerc went there in 1945 as the first Frenchman in charge of the liberated area, he promptly recommended to the Paris government that France should pull out of Indochina, as it had no future there. Unfortunately, the next year Admiral Thierry d'Argenlieu was sent there shortly before de Gaulle's departure, and the trouble started with a change in policy.

PARIS, *June 8, 1964*

Yesterday I played golf with Couve de Murville. We then lunched together and sat around gassing.

Couve told me the private envoy sent by President Johnson to General de Gaulle was Bob Anderson, the Texas Republican who used to be Eisenhower's secretary of the treasury. This is most secret. The meeting had been arranged by a letter from Johnson to de Gaulle which was transmitted by cable through the French embassy in Washington.

It was really incorrect of the press to report that France and the U.S.A. had agreed on objectives but disagreed on methods. They did not agree on objectives. The words used were the same but the meaning was different. France thinks of a neutral South Vietnam as a truly nonaligned state. The French idea is to get back to the theory of the 1954 Geneva agreement. But the U.S.A. thinks of a pro-Western version of neutralism.

Furthermore, on methods, while the French would very much like to see a military victory prior to a negotiated settlement, they see absolutely no chance of this. They think we should start diplomatic contacts now. The French think it would be a terrible mistake for the U.S.A. to escalate the war by attacking North Vietnam. We would accomplish nothing by bombing North Vietnam except to bring China into that country.

The U.S.A. has immense military power and could surely fight a war against China and maybe kill one hundred million Chinese. But what would that accomplish? The U.S.A. could not occupy China, and after the slaughter the entire world would be against America.

And this, of course, has nothing to do with the very real danger that Russia might feel forced to defend China and thus start World War III.

The U.S.A. was undoubtedly in a better position to take such risks during Korea and yet we did not believe them worthwhile taking then. It would be ridiculous to take them now.

The U.S.A. must realize that it can't win the South Vietnam war by bombing Hanoi or China and that the last chance for that sort of approach was in Korea.

Southeast Asia and the entire Asian mainland are lost to the West. No form of Western occupation will be tolerated anywhere on the Asian mainland. But the U.S.A. does not recognize this fact yet. It feels that its borders are entirely up against China and this makes it very nervous because of its views of the Pacific as an American lake.

But Europe feels its borders are right up against Russia and is more concerned with Russia. For Western Europe the Sino-Soviet rift makes freedom possible and this is the true explanation of the new stir in the satellites.

The U.S.A. must reconcile itself to withdrawing from the Asian mainland to the island chain, in which the Philippines are particularly important.

Couve says the United States has been very foolish in its Cuban policy. We were foolish to exaggerate the dangers and importance of Castro. Kennedy handled the 1962 Cuban confrontation only fairly well. He should have followed through and insisted that the Russians get out entirely. They would have done so because the U.S.A. had Khrushchev on the run. It was a great mistake not to carry out a complete victory.

The French are just about to rent a residence in Peking for their new ambassador and the very first batch of people they will send there is a team of experts to look for hidden microphones. "Guess where the team is now," Couve said with an amused grin. "Washington," I replied. "You're right," he said.

PARIS, *June 12, 1964*

Last night at dinner the Duke of Windsor kept insisting that Barry Goldwater (whom he referred to as Barry) was a great man. He would add: "I was against Dewey, but I am for Barry." This is a rather odd statement for a former king of England.

He said his happiest days were when he was in the navy before he went to Oxford, but he found Oxford quite agreeable "because we were drunk all the time."

I made a speech today, then answered questions and had lunch with the NATO Defense College. After lunch the commandant, General Wolf von

Baudissin, asked me in for a chat. Baudissin was Rommel's G-2 in the Western desert until he was captured. He liked Rommel but claims he had no idea of the political and civilian world. Rommel was absolutely brilliant in handling an armored division, but that was his extreme limit of talent.

NEW YORK, *June 26, 1964*

This morning I went to see Prime Minister Ismet Inonu of Turkey at his suite on the thirty-sixth floor of the Waldorf Towers. He has been over here for several days at President Johnson's invitation to discuss Cyprus. It was apparent that no progress has been made toward a solution.

Inonu looks as frail and as old as ever but is always as indestructibly spry. Despite his hearing aid he is really quite deaf. We drank orange juice and chatted. He started off with a long harangue about the "irresponsible" forces that had brought about the crisis.

He said the United States seemed to have no formula for settlement. Johnson had presented none. The U.S. merely wants to "manage" its two allies who find themselves on the brink of war. American policy was obviously to prevent such a war and to keep the alliance alive. The question was how to accomplish this.

Inonu said that the phrase "self-determination" was now being used by the Greeks instead of *enosis* but it means exactly the same thing. All Turkey would accept would be a "double *enosis*," which means partition.

The Russians were of course pleased to see NATO cracking on its eastern flank. But they opposed *enosis*. They preferred to see an independent island under control of the Greek Cypriots so that they could communize it.

This afternoon I went to see Andreas Papandreou, son of the Greek prime minister, and his principal cabinet member, an *éminence grise*. Papandreou is very American after years as a professor in California and at Harvard. He was an American citizen until last year.

I started by asking Andreas who sent (General George) Grivas to Cyprus and why. He admitted that Grivas had gone on the initiative of Athens. In other words, just as he was sent to command the EOKA insurrection in 1955 by the then prime minister, Alexander Papagos, he has been sent in June 1964 as military commander by Prime Minister Papandreou. Andreas also said quite blandly that the Greek government has "guaranteed" the safety of the Turkish minority. This acknowledges obviously that Greece has begun to act as if it already owned Cyprus.

I asked him if President Johnson had produced any formula for solution. He answered with a categorical no. Johnson had emphasized that if a war came the U.S. would cut off all aid to both countries.

NEW YORK, *June 28, 1964*

Last night I went to a dinner in his country house in Rye given by Spyros Skouras for Papandreou, the Greek prime minister.

Clare Luce was there. She is a remarkably well-preserved woman—still lovely at sixty or so—and incredibly pleased with herself.

She is convinced Italy will go communist as soon as the U.S.A. is militarily engaged in Asia. I think she is wrong.

NEW YORK, *June 30, 1964*

Z., of the CIA, says our intelligence estimate is that, should the U.S. become militarily engaged with China because of the southeast Asia crisis, Russia would not aid China unless it felt its own vital interests were affected.

When the Russian scientists pulled out of China in 1960 they took with them all the blueprints for the gaseous diffusion plant under construction. Nuclear advances were delayed for about three years.

There has not yet been a definite decision by the U.S.A. on whether to expand the Vietnam war. We fear that if we were to bomb North Vietnam it might provoke Ho Chi Minh to launch an all-out, one-shot attack on the southern border with expanded guerrilla operations and a direct invasion with his regular army. We must be sure that South Vietnamese and Laotian bases are strong enough before such a risk can be contemplated.

Israel has probably attained the capability of manufacturing two small nuclear warheads per annum. Under the original arrangements, in which the French helped the Israelis build the Dimona reactor, a core was provided by France for the reactor but it was always sent back to France to extract plutonium, in order to prevent Israel from making weapons materials. Now the Israelis have bought uranium from South Africa and mined some themselves and probably have the material for a very small scale weapons program. They deny that they intend this, but it is obvious that their strategic situation is ultimately very dismal vis-à-vis the Arab world and they must have some means of striking back if there is an explosion.

NEW YORK, *July 20, 1964*

Dined last night with the Norstads [General Lauris Norstad, former NATO commander]. Larry said that on October 27, 1962 (just before Khrushchev knuckled under in the Cuban crisis), Kennedy called him in Paris and asked him what he thought of Khrushchev's (then latest) offer. This was to trade Russian withdrawal of missiles from Cuba against U.S. withdrawal of missiles from Turkey. Norstad said he thought this was a very dangerous idea.

Norstad says that, although there is no record of any commitment by Kennedy to withdraw the missiles from Turkey in exchange for Khru - shchev's Cuba withdrawal, historians will undoubtedly conclude that there was some kind of a private deal to that effect.

WASHINGTON, *July 21, 1964*

We have been staying with the Harrimans. Averell likes Tshombe and thinks he is probably the best bet although he is undoubtedly going to fail also. He thinks the only big mistake in our Congo policy was that we wasted four years and $500 million to keep Tshombe away.

Harriman admits Tshombe is called an "Uncle Tom" by all other Africans but he says: "Let's make him our Uncle Tom anyway."

WASHINGTON, *July 22, 1964*

We went out for dinner last night on the *Sequoia*, which used to be the presidential yacht and which is now assigned to the secretary of the navy for entertaining purposes. The party was given by Bill Bundy, now assistant secretary of state for the Far East, in honor of General and Mrs. Paul Harkins. Until a few weeks ago Harkins was our commander in South Vietnam and he is retiring next week.

Harkins kept explaining how difficult it was to accomplish the minutiae of training the Vietnamese. We had introduced pills against beriberi, but they refused to take them because they were brown and there is some superstition about eating your enemy's ordure. When we changed them to blue the little girls kept them to play with. Shotguns had to be distributed to villages to ward off crows because if a crow settles on the roof of a house while it is being built nobody can live in it. The Vietnamese refused to have three-man patrols because they insisted on four for special cere- monial reasons.

Incidentally, Harriman told me Eisenhower got his wartime command of the Allies by sheer luck. General Marshall told Harriman that he intended to appoint General Andrews as allied commander but Andrews was killed in an airplane crash in Iceland.

Long talk with McNamara this morning. Rather to my surprise, at one point, he opened a ledger on his desk and showed me the figures for the number of nuclear bombers and missiles on an instant alert basis. These were frighteningly impressive.

McNamara was sitting behind his desk in his enormous office in shirt- sleeves. I noticed his reading has changed. Last time he had just de Gaulle's memoirs on the table behind him. They were gone.

I asked whether we had elaborated any kind of doctrine to oppose revolutionary warfare and, if so, were there any books or papers prepared on this for our war colleges? McNamara said we had no such doctrine because "this is not primarily a military operation. It is political and economic and only uses military operations as a subsidiary tool."

I found his observations on this subject both naive and uninformed, and this frightens me. I don't think he understands what Revolutionary War is.

McNamara sees the whole question only in terms of southeast Asia and not in terms of the global implications of Revolutionary War. He said: "We are evolving a doctrine of our own and we are learning how to carry on such operations. First of all there is the problem of information. We must learn how to educate and indoctrinate the peasants on what their government can offer. And we must establish the physical organisms for distributing information and propaganda."

The U.S.A. had discovered that most Vietnamese had no access to radios and there are no daily papers outside of Saigon. Therefore we are now dotting the country with transistor sets and one hundred thousand have been ordered from Japan. We had already placed several thousand transmitters around the country so they could call for military help in case of attack.

The transmitter program was started two years ago, yet obviously the security situation is much worse.

I asked McNamara if he wasn't alarmed by the recent statement of General Nguyen Cao Ky (of the air force) demanding a direct attack on North Vietnam. McNamara said he didn't know why Ky had made such aggressive statements. General Ky "had better shut up or they will find themselves with a new air force commander." (This doesn't sound precisely like a U.S. policy of "advising" the Vietnamese on how to fight the war, but not intervening.)

I observed that it was rather paradoxical that the Republicans were shaping up their campaign with the intention of emphasizing exactly the same things that had been emphasized four years ago by the Democrats: prestige and the missile gap. McNamara said there was a big difference. He added: "Kennedy and the Democrats did *not* create the idea of a missile gap. This was then the belief of all of our independent analysts and therefore the issue was used by the Democrats but not created by them. But the Goldwater approach is something else. He is actually distorting the facts. Why, we have spent $30 billion more on defense than if we had continued under the Eisenhower administration's schedule, and this has brought a tremendous increment of power which allowed us to respond effectively in Berlin, Cuba, and southeast Asia."

Lunched with Averell Harriman at his office. Harriman is convinced that Khrushchev will continue to talk forever about communizing the world but he is acting in favor of coexistence. That is to say, he has in no sense abandoned his desire to spread the Soviet system but he has abandoned all thought of violence to do so.

Likewise we will continue indefinitely to talk of freeing the captive nations. But we will take no violent action to do so.

Averell is very concerned about the alarm abroad caused by Goldwater's nomination. He thinks it is necessary and desirable to encourage distinguished moderate Republicans, who are well-known abroad, to travel this summer making speeches and perhaps talking with allied statesmen. He doesn't think there is much use in having them talk with communist statesmen. The latter—like Khrushchev and Gomulka—are being very foolish in attacking Goldwater because it only helps the senator.

But a man like Jack McCloy should go to Europe and give some public speeches as soon as the commission on Kennedy's assassination (of which he is a member) publishes its report at the end of this month. Harriman asked me to urge the president tomorrow to pay more attention to the overseas repercussions of the Goldwater phenomenon.

Averell was irked by a column I had published today calling for greater emphasis on career diplomats in ambassadorial posts. He claims our foreign service is still tarnished by McCarthyism and fear of taking independent action.

After lunch [Undersecretary of State] George Ball talked about Vietnam. Ball says the (Maxwell) Taylor-(Alexis) Johnson-(Bill) Sullivan team we have sent to Saigon is the best team we could field, and it should have a good run under the present policy before we consider whether it is necessary to change it.

We have lost much time during the dislocation produced by *coups d'état*, and the government position has been seriously undermined. Nevertheless the U.S.A. still hopes and believes the situation can be handled within the frontiers of South Vietnam. If not, we still must face the decision of whether to discourage Ho Chi Minh by direct means. "We are prepared to do this if necessary," said Ball.

I asked Ball what he thought of the French idea that it was not necessary to achieve a battlefield victory before beginning diplomatic negotiations, citing the instance of Algeria. Ball said that if you negotiate while you are fighting you destroy the will to resistance of South Vietnam. He added: "They would quit if there were even a whisper that we were negotiating with Hanoi."

WASHINGTON, *July 23, 1964*

This morning I had a forty-five-minute talk with President Johnson. He could not have been more friendly but the experience did not make me very happy. Obviously Johnson is an expert politician, as is shown by his great success in getting bills through Congress. But he is not an impressive man; he surely is not an intellectual; and there is something about his face I don't quite trust. Maybe his eyes are a little too narrow and close together.

He talks willingly but does not stick to the subject and, of course, right now he is obsessed with American politics, so whenever we started talking about something else he brought the conversation back to local affairs.

He spoke in a very low voice. When I was waved into his office—ten minutes early—he was on the telephone and, even with my good ear turned toward him, I found it difficult to understand him. He was in the process of bawling out somebody about what he called six major misstatements in today's press and television reports concerning himself.

Another thing that distressed me was that he did not look well. He has thickened around the middle; he walked heavily; his face seemed greyish and drawn. I do hope he chooses a good vice-presidential candidate.

When he had finished his telephone conversation, he came over and sat beside me. He said he remembered well our conversation in Paris and that he had made time to see me on this very busy day because he wanted to benefit from my knowledge. This was just good political blarney.

Then he asked: "How are you planning to handle this conversation? You know, I have 1,500 of you fellows around here and I don't find the time to see very many. I have a letter from the managing editor of the *Washington Post* right now asking to see me and I can't do it. I hope you won't quote me directly but just say something like 'the president believes' or 'friends of the president say.' "

I started off by saying I was very concerned about the effect during the next one hundred days of the Goldwater campaign on both our friends and our adversaries overseas. All the experts said that Goldwater stood no chance of winning the election, but the mere fact of his candidacy was disruptive and seemed to be disuniting our allies and uniting our enemies. I feared that there would be new support for the Gaullist theory that the U.S.A. could not be depended on indefinitely and also for the Maoist drive to foment anti-Western racism. Wasn't there some way of counteracting these effects right now?

Johnson said: "I am concerned by this problem of the effect of Goldwater's position not only overseas but also at home. But we always have problems in American election years. Remember that Wilson campaigned on a platform to keep us out of war and Roosevelt promised that he would not bring us into war—despite the signs of the times that they could very well see.

"The farther you are from the central scene the more likely you are to be concerned, but the American people have a way of infiltrating a candidate and getting him on balance and we all hope for that in this case. There is no question but that the views of some of the Goldwater people are very curious. There is this talk about the effect of fallout on the milk of children producing sterility when they grow up, or two-headed babies.

"You should not worry too much about things. Nixon had one out of two of all the independent voters behind him, but Goldwater has only one out of four. Nixon had 92 percent of the Republicans behind him, but according to the very latest polls which I received this morning, Goldwater has only 62 percent of the Republicans."

If these notes stray from subject to subject, it is a faithful rendering of the conversation. Johnson kept talking with absolutely no interruption or pause but there were continual sharp switches in subject matter.

He said: "If we had given the military a free run in Vietnam we would have been at war and bombing China all over the place long ago. Even the military didn't want a free run. They like a little check themselves.

"But the polls are running very well for me. The latest poll in Kansas, which is a rock-ribbed Republican state, has things going two to one for me. All this may soften Goldwater up. And it may catch some of the rich, financial quarters who will bring influence to bear and that will help.

"Nevertheless, what you say is true and at present our enemies are being encouraged and our friends discouraged.

"I would not want you to write this in any way, so please keep it completely off the record, but I thought that Scranton would be harder to beat than Goldwater and Mac [McGeorge] Bundy agreed with me. But it would have been a better campaign from the viewpoint of the national interest.

"There are a lot of nasty things going on that remind me of the situation in Europe when I first came to Washington thirty-three years ago. I have positive information listing the names and the amounts of contributors to Goldwater in January 1963, and those people are primarily southern racists and northern labor baiters. I saw the list this morning. We got a hold of a list enumerating these people and some of the contributors gave as much as $25,000. Don't forget that this was in January 1963 and they were a bad group of people. It makes me think of the dangerous period in Europe. It is frightening. It was frightening to see old man Hunt [H. L. Hunt] roaming around in San Francisco. There is a revival of McCarthyism right now and I am afraid it must run its course.

"Nevertheless, as things are, the most recent Gallup poll favors me by seven to three after the convention. Roosevelt had only 62 percent when he won every state in the union but Maine and Vermont. The Gallup poll gives me 68 percent to Goldwater's 32 percent.

"In order to win, Goldwater must keep all the Republicans, the majority of the independents, and gain a substantial number of Democrats."

I mentioned that in talking with Harriman, the latter had suggested it might be helpful to the country if moderate Republicans who were well-known abroad could travel this summer and make some speeches and perhaps see a few foreign statesmen in order to reassure the world. He said he thought this would be a very good idea.

I said it seemed strange that the Republicans should choose foreign policy as the main issue. Imitating the Democrats in 1960, they selected "prestige" and a "weapons gap" to emphasize. Johnson replied: "He will get off of that. But Goldwater wants us to get in trouble in Vietnam so it can help him. He also wants race riots in this country so it can help him. He has said this on TV himself.

"But this arms business is nonsense. We have spent $30 billion more on national defense during the last four years than we would have spent if we had followed Eisenhower's rate. We have been spending a year $7,500 million more than Eisenhower. We were dangerously weak at the start of 1961. You know, I think that if we had gone on into the Bay of Pigs it might have been very difficult for us to stand up in a real crisis. Of course, Ike is now saying that we have been spending too much.

"The American people want prudence. They will fight to save freedom but they don't want any unnecessary dangers.

"And don't forget that these have been the most prosperous years in America's peacetime history, unmarred by recessions. There were three recessions during the Eisenhower administration, during 1952 and 1960. But for the first peacetime period of four years in a century we have gone on under this administration without any recession."

Johnson then buzzed Jack Valenti, his appointments secretary and one of the "Texas Mafia." The president had been reading from a piece of paper. When Valenti came in, Johnson said: "Take out this business of 'the Kennedy-Johnson administration.' Just make it read: 'the four years from 1961.' Take out all reference to 'the Kennedy-Johnson administration.'" I gathered that this was going to be in a speech. Obviously what Johnson was doing was inferentially building himself up by omitting references to Kennedy. But he turned to me with a knowing look as Valenti left the room and said: "I am trying to take all politics out of this." Baloney!

I asked if he had any plans for a meeting with de Gaulle after the elections. He answered with a categorical no. Did [Ambassador Robert] Anderson's meeting with de Gaulle have anything to do with such a possible meeting. He said: "No, that is nonsense. There was nothing at all in that. Chip Bohlen was sore at me about this but he was even sorer at you. Why, that was a laughable and unimportant matter. Chip should not be sore at you. What happened was that Anderson had brought a very good friend of de Gaulle's to see me. I gave him ten minutes. Why, I am going to give you almost an hour. So when Anderson went to Paris de Gaulle's friend took him to see the General. He didn't get anything out of it, and the only thing I authorized him to do was to say that he had seen me. Chip has no right to be so irritated at this sort of thing. Why, it is as if Rusk got angry with me today because I am seeing you. It is like my two girls; one of them gets jealous if I talk too much to the other.

"That is all there is to that. I have told de Gaulle I understand his viewpoint. I don't think it adds to his luster to try and break up our relations with Germany. We are not trying to break his relations with Germany. In fact, I think it is a very good idea for him to have close relations with the Germans. But such relations need not be an exclusive operation.

"De Gaulle gives us our problems—above all in Vietnam. We would be glad to move out of there if anyone could guarantee its independence. But I tell this to Chip and he goes and asks de Gaulle for his blueprints on how he is going to do this—and there aren't any.

"But I understand de Gaulle and I know, just like in Cuba, that he is with us when the chips are down.

"I don't have any plans to see him as of now. But after the elections, when there is a vice president and I can travel, I am not averse to meeting anyone, anywhere, older or younger than I. But many people are alarmed whenever I walk across the street. You can't take any chances with the thought of a man like [Speaker of the House John] McCormack moving into the White House."

Much to my surprise then, the president went into a long business about my yesterday's column in which I said that career diplomats should be favored as U.S. ambassadors. He had taken this up with Mac Bundy and Dean Rusk. He and Rusk had drawn up a list of the appointments that he had made since he became president and they were almost all career men, with the exception of one woman who had been named and whose father had been an ambassador, so she had spent a lot of her youth in diplomatic surroundings.

I asked Johnson, apropos of his remarks on career diplomats, if he intended to stress the appointment of career men after the elections when he names new ambassadors. He said he certainly intended to do this. He added:

"I have been doing this all along and I was really rather shocked by your article. I can't think of two political people I have named. I have put in non-career people like the man from the University of Pennsylvania whom I sent to Colombia because he was an expert on Latin America; but I am certainly going to stress quality in my future appointments."

I then asked who had influenced Johnson most in his life, anyone living or dead. He looked rather sad and surprised by the question, thought for about two minutes and then came out with the profound sentiment: "My mother." He thought some more and then he really began to talk. "Next my wife. In public life perhaps President Roosevelt because he was the first president I knew intimately. I have been associated with all presidents since him and even in a way have been influenced from Hoover on down. None of these presidents has been a weak sister and all of them have influenced me.

"And I was also influenced by Senator Vandenberg whom I greatly admired. I used to sit next to him and I was thrilled when he changed his views on foreign policy. And I came up under the kind hand of Mr. Rayburn who was a great internationalist. And then there were all kinds of people: Lovett, Patterson, Harriman, and Harry Hopkins during the war. And Fulbright is a close friend. Why, I am going to his house on Sunday."

I asked him what political philosopher of the past had influenced him. "Oh," he said, "I thought you meant people since I came to Washington. I guess I am a great Jefferson man and I admire Woodrow Wilson."

Johnson was in no hurry. He started some more soft-soaping about how he read my column with enormous interest and it was very good and thorough. He said: "You serve your country very well, far better than I am able to do."

NEW YORK, *September 9, 1964*

Dined last night at the Norstads'. Present were Amory Houghton [ex-ambassador to Paris] and his wife, Fritz [Frederick] Nolting and his wife. Nolting used to be ambassador in Saigon.

Nolting says the United States really should not be in South Vietnam, in a military way, but now that it is there it cannot get out. Our only chance was to deal with a real government and try to build up political, economic, and social unity and reform. That chance was ended when we decided to dump Diem and there has never been a government since.

Norstad complains—and Nolting agrees—that at no time has there ever been a decision that helping South Vietnam might require an ultimate war with China. In fact the subject has never officially been discussed. Nolting says that there have been contingency plans drawn up involving China but never a decision on whether under any circumstances they might be implemented.

Nolting concedes that if the U.S.A. now resolved to put five divisions in South Vietnam in order to hunt down and squeeze out all the Vietcong guerrillas, we would end up by having the entire Vietnamese population unleashed against us on a national and anticolonial basis.

Neither Norstad nor Nolting advocates spreading the war into North Vietnam, and Nolting adds that the South Vietnamese people likewise oppose this alternative. Norstad says he thinks it would be advisable for Washington to start playing down more and more our military role in South Vietnam while advertising more and more our economic role.

Nolting, again and again, said that the greatest mistake of U.S. southeast Asian policy—and we must consider the area as a whole, not just South Vietnam—was to dump Diem and all possibility of a Saigon government.

NEW YORK, *September 17, 1964*

Cabot Lodge, at lunch, expressed the hope and also the prediction that Goldwater would suffer a tremendous defeat. I asked him what the definition of that would be, and he said something like Landon in 1936. Only then can the intelligent, liberal leadership of the Republican party pick up the pieces.

On Vietnam he professed a restrained, long-range optimism. He says that we are spending $1.1 million a day but this is less than the cost of a new aircraft carrier. We are losing fewer casualties than the number of uniformed Americans killed in traffic accidents each year. And the stakes are immense. If we lose South Vietnam this will reaffirm the success of China's rough, tough methods and make Russia adopt a similar line. The Philippines, Malaya, and Thailand would go. Then there would be nothing to restrain Indonesia, and Australia fears it would be swallowed up. Our prestige in the whole underdeveloped world would be deeply wounded. The NATO countries would begin to lose their ability to honor their overseas commitments.

He agreed that Washington has constantly erred in taking an overoptimistic line in its public statements on Vietnam. He thinks it was a great mistake to neutralize Laos instead of partitioning it but points out that he was not in the administration at the time.

Kennedy's instructions to him when he went to Vietnam were that he should not do anything to "thwart" an attempt to overthrow Diem. Lodge thinks that the ideal solution would have been to throw out his brother Nhu —who was impossible—and to reform and keep the Diem administration. But things had gone too far and the secret police were already brutalizing the population.

NEW YORK, *September 18, 1964*

Dined last night at Ham Armstrong's, in honor of the maharajah of Sikkim and Princess Hope, his young American wife. Others present were Adlai Stevenson and Marietta Tree.

The maharajah is a Tibetan-looking man of good size, pleasant and earnest, given to a twitch or occasional stutter. He seems to resent the control India has over him and is afraid of China. He said China has built a parallel road network on the other side of the Himalayas, which is obviously designed for military purposes as there is no economic reason for such a network. He recently rounded up a Chinese espionage group in Sikkim.

Princess Hope is very young (in her twenties) and Seldon Chapin's niece. She met the maharajah when she was traveling in India with her grandmother. They fell in love at Darjeeling. Soothsayers persuaded the maharajah to put off the wedding for three years. She not only dresses in native costume now but speaks English in a singsong Indian accent and has such an Oriental posture that I thought she had something wrong with her back. She is a very intelligent young woman and knows a great deal about her country.

Stevenson assured me he had never really wanted to be president but that he was very anxious to be secretary of state. He thought it was most unlikely that he could be considered because he was far too committed on too many subjects and he didn't think there was a chance.

NEW YORK, *September 24, 1964*

Dined last night with Adlai Stevenson. Stevenson told me Humphrey is backing him strongly as secretary of state.

He complained bitterly about our French policy. Adlai said that while Kennedy was still running for the presidency in the fall of 1960, he had recommended that we give nuclear aid to France—and Kennedy was so angry that they almost split.

He thinks the UN has an enormous use for the U.S.A. as a repository of hopeless causes and he doesn't know what is going to happen if this ends. The day may come when we are forced to use a veto. So far the Russians have used 102 vetoes and we have never exercised our veto right. But the Congress will never accept decisions that are contrary to our interests or imposed by the UN where the Afro-Asian majority can outvote us on anything.

NEW YORK, *September 29, 1964*

Talk with Nixon. He was very sensible, presenting his position with calm and logic and making the best of a rather bad case. If he were the Republican candidate this year I might very well be inclined to support him. He has grown a great deal in modesty, humanity, wisdom, and stature in the four years since he was defeated.

Nixon regrets that foreign policy has not been properly discussed in the campaign and thinks the only issue that has been brought up has been the nuclear one—and that in a confused and unsatisfactory way. The real question is not how nuclear weapons should be used but how to apply policy in such a way that they will never be used.

He considers Johnson dangerously egocentric and power-hungry and that it is imperative to have enough Republicans in Congress to keep the president from being corrupted by his own power. Nixon has no illusions about the outcome of the election.

Nixon expresses admiration for Johnson's political techniques but doesn't like the moral tenor of his administration. He thinks Johnson is wise not to engage in debates with Goldwater, and that he has been mistaken both in mentioning Goldwater too much and in using members of his cabinet in the political campaign. Johnson has a bad television personality and it would help Goldwater a great deal if he put his own attractive personality on television more.

Nixon thinks the situation in Vietnam is drifting more and more and that if we don't come out with some kind of a policy we are going to lose it within a year or two or have no chance to influence the outcome. Then, through Indonesia, communism would threaten the frontiers of the Philippines and Australia.

He says Goldwater never asked him before announcing that he would name Nixon his secretary of state and that he had learned himself four years ago that it is "counter-productive" to talk of cabinet appointments before election.

PARIS, *October 9, 1964*

Dined last night alone with Manlio Brosio, my first encounter since he became NATO secretary-general on August 1.

It is quite untrue that he received a special and unprecedented briefing from President Johnson when he was in the States last month. This was just a political stunt by Johnson who had his press people put out information to that effect in order to demonstrate that he, Johnson, was more interested in supporting NATO than Goldwater. "Johnson is one thousand percent politician," said Brosio.

Brosio only had one decent talk—for about an hour—with the president and that was during their airplane ride back east. The president showed an interest in NATO, MLF, and other things, but also showed very little knowledge and understanding. On the way out he insisted on setting up charts showing the president's status in the electoral campaign on a state-by-state basis, concentrating (for the benefit of his Italian-NATO visitor) on the current situation in doubtful states. He explained to Brosio that such charts were submitted to him every day.

Brosio said he had recently read a report from an intelligent young Italian ambassador whom he did not identify. It said that the new lands of Africa were weak and backward not because they had been colonies; they had been colonized because they were weak and backward.

Breakfast today with Dirk Stikker, former NATO secretary-general. Last July, when he was still at NATO, he saw [Pierre] Messmer, French minister of defense. Messmer told him that shortly after he had taken office under de Gaulle in January 1960, [Franz-Josef] Strauss, who was then German minister of defense in Adenauer's government, had asked him to implement the secret French-German agreement on nuclear weapons.

Messmer was startled and said he knew of no such agreement. Strauss then told him that he and Jacques Chaban-Delmas, minister of defense in the Fourth Republic government of Felix Gaillard from November 1957 until April 1958, had made a secret accord under which Germany agreed to help finance and manufacture nuclear weapons to be kept in storage on French soil, some of them allotted to German ownership and control. (The Western European Union Treaty stipulates that Germany cannot "manufacture" such weapons but does not precisely ban assistance in fabricating them outside the country.) Messmer told Stikker that he had said to Strauss that France could do nothing about such an undertaking. It was not the policy of France to give Germany nuclear arms.

Kai-Uwe von Hassel, present German defense minister, told him later in the summer that it was not German policy to request aid in obtaining a national atomic arms stockpile. Stikker asked for assurance that this represented the policy of the Erhard government and asked von Hassel to ask Erhard. On October 1, von Hassel telegraphed Stikker giving him such an assurance.

Stikker also asked Adenauer this summer if he knew anything concerning this agreement between Strauss and Chaban-Delmas. Adenauer said he had heard something about it but had deliberately avoided making further inquiries because he did not wish to become involved: an extraordinary statement for a man who had then been chief of government.

LONDON, *October 13, 1964*

Lunched with [Ambassador] David Bruce. He says that if Labor wins, Wilson will start out by being virtually a one-man government, seeking to control all the principal ministries himself.

A Labor government would try to do two things at once: to try and become a kind of honest broker between Moscow and Washington; and to tighten London's special relation with Washington.

Another Tory government would inevitably make a new try at linking Britain to the Common Market. Wilson will definitely *not* do this; he is not a "European."

Wilson is personally unsure of himself, caught in the middle of the class structure, unwilling to allow himself to have close friends. He was always jealous of [Hugh] Gaitskell's snob friends who had "wine cellars." There is *no* inner, kitchen cabinet. Wilson even goes home and writes all his own speeches—which is why he makes many snide remarks about Eldon Griffiths, Sir Alec Douglas-Home's ghost.

LONDON, *October 15, 1964*

Dined last night at the Bruces. David told me General Marshall had persuaded Truman to offer the post of ambassador to France to Mrs. Roosevelt. Very wisely she turned it down and said she thought it would be most "unsuitable."

8

SACRIFICE THE HORSE

ARRIVED LAST NIGHT AND WAS STRUCK AT THE AIRPORT BY THE resemblance, in uniforms, mixed-blood appearance, enthusiasm, red tape, and confusion, to Algeria nowadays.

To succeed, a revolution in a small country or a weak country, requires external sustenance or pressure (Poland), internal wealth (Indonesia or Algeria), or skilled diplomacy (UAR or Jugoslavia). Cuba has none of these, although it believes it has (1) and (3).

I went to Hemingway's house, Finca Vigia (Outpost Farm), at the village of San Francisco de Paulo. Lovely rambling old Spanish house on a hilltop, once a fortress, with a three-story tower built next door for Hemingway to write. Mary used the roof for sunbaths and Ernest read military history in his writing room, but never wrote there. He said he missed the "house noises" of his own room.

A couple of lovely tree-filled, garden-filled acres. We were shown around by a charming, quiet *mestizo* guide who had lived with Ernest twelve years and said Ernest regarded him as his "Cuban son." The basement of the tower used to be tenanted by cats which Ernest adored. He also had eleven dogs. He kept eleven servants always on the payroll, whether he was there or not, and spent lots each year on regular wreaths to the graves of dead former villagers.

The house sprawls: large, comfortable rooms. I saw the sitting room. One armchair was used only by Ernest. If anyone sat in it by mistake he wouldn't sit down until it was vacated. Books all over the place (including my own *My Brother Death*), drink tray still filled with bottles and glasses by Ernest's chair. Mounted African (and one U.S. elk) heads all over. The first two lion-skin trophies, aged and motheaten. Photos, including one of David Bruce with Ernest's son and daughter-in-law; dining room with table set with three places ready for Ernest's favorite Chinese food, which Mary cooked, and candles in sticks.

His bed made in his bedroom, with sheet turned up as he liked it to expose his feet. His portable typewriter open on his bookcase where he used to type, a pad with page of penciled manuscript beside it. Desk covered with pictures of Mary and war correspondent insignia and war souvenirs like German insignia. His bifocal glasses on the desk. I tried them and found he used the same lens as I for reading and was a bit less nearsighted for distance.

Collections of knives, bayonets, and rifles. Bathroom with scale. Bookcases jammed in every room. In tower basement fishing rods (including broken one from record marlin), spoons, reels, swords of fish, hunting hats, many pairs of boots. Telescope on top room of tower. He would look at ships in the harbor; she was an amateur astronomer. Charming, comfortable, and cozy. Everyone in the village and our guide knew him only as "Papa." The house is now a museum. I looked through the visitors' book—which I signed. Most of the recent tourists were Russians or East Germans.

HAVANA, CUBA, *October 24, 1964*

The Bay of Pigs in 1961 justifiably gave Castro a superiority complex (which he didn't need) vis-à-vis the U.S.A. And this has not by any means been wholly removed by the October 1962 showdown.

Castro's future seems in the hands of the Soviet bloc, if there is a bloc. If Moscow wants to purchase good relations with Washington, it can cease buying Cuban sugar. An easy price can be paid in Latin America which is not, like Berlin, a primary zone of Soviet interest.

It is silly to blame Castro for promising one revolution and producing another. They all do—Tito, Nasser, Sukarno, Nkrumah.

The military complex is interesting. Stenographers and clerks put on uniforms and weapons once a week to do guard duty at their offices—like the pretty secretary of the minister in the foreign office, who says she is better with a pistol than the heavy rifle she lugs around, and who once lived in Brooklyn (which she adored) during junior high school days and was a great fan of the Dodgers; or like Major Faustino Perez, now head of the hydraulic projects, once chief of the Havana underground, who wears uniform, sidearms, and ammunition in his office.

There is a jealousy between the bearded rebel army veterans and the shaven underground veterans, between the young in power and the old out.

This morning I went about fifty miles (in the snappy Cadillac placed at my disposal by the foreign ministry) to the Abraham Lincoln Sugar Central in Andorra, Province of Pinar del Rio. There was a mass meeting of Central workers with their managers and big shots from Havana to discuss production problems and explain the role of this important cane grinding and refining center to the 1970 goal of 10 million tons per annum. (The best so far was 7 million.) The meeting room, a modest wooden building, was hung with paper Cuban and Soviet flags and slogans like "Long Live Socialist Emulation" as well as a sign put up last summer warning against the dangers of possible U.S.A. attack.

When Juan de Onis (the *New York Times* correspondent) and I entered and showed our documents there were *vivas* and applause and we were asked (we declined) to sit on the dais with the officials. One speaker explained: "We like Americans but not their government." In the audience workers, smoking cigars, wearing dirty shirts and trousers, straw-brimmed hats, and army caps with visors, grinned at us and clapped. They were mostly in their deep middle-age, a mixture of faces: Spanish, *mestizo*, Negro. Only one mulatto face was among the dozen on the dais.

The Havana big boss explained (beneath pictures of Fidel and other heroes) that it might be difficult to meet the 1970 goal because of the shortage of qualified engineers. Sticky, languid flies floated through the warm, humid air.

Cuba has diabetes: too much sugar in its blood stream and no economic or political insulin has yet been invented.

Like all revolutions, this one is convinced in its heart that *it* is really the very first. Yesterday I went to the revolutionary museum in the Martí monument, filled with gruesome photos of Batista tortures, slaughters, etc.; homemade or primitive weapons including a bulldozer-tank; bloody uniforms, and even a shot-down U.S. U-2. My guide was appalled when I said it was almost exactly like the IRA museum in Dublin, which has an anti-Black and Tan display.

HAVANA, CUBA, *October 25, 1964*

Last night called Celia Sanchez, Castro's closest woman friend, to inquire about my appointment. A recorded announcement replied: "After seven o'clock in the evening, don't call. If it is not an urgent matter, don't call. If you are calling to discuss personal matters, relating to housing, expropriated lands, a house on the beach, furniture, refrigerators, automobiles, automobile parts, scholarships, exit visas, or prisoners, address yourself to the proper organism. I do not work in any of those departments."

The announcement is repeated twice. Initiates merely hang on to the phone and then Celia or someone else eventually answers.

HAVANA, CUBA, *October 26, 1964*

Castro is a stunning example of the nuclear-age political paradox. In preatomic times it is virtually sure the U.S.A. would have invaded and upset him. But because of weapons he doesn't have—whether they are sited on Cuban or European soil—the U.S.A. it leery because of a Russian-sponsored threat of holocaust.

I walked at length last night after leaving the Havana Libre hotel where Castro made a long speech on economics. There is very little traffic and a huge proportion of the cars limp along, quite run-down, on badly patched tires.

Lunched yesterday at the Floridita, where Hemingway used to hang out. A fancy, luxurious place off a charming square downtown, famed for its daiquiris (which it no longer makes according to formula because of a lack of grenadine). The headwaiter pointed out the bust erected above the end of the bar where Hemingway used to stand and drink when he was alone; we were at the table where he sat when he was with someone. Headwaiter: "One day he was standing there drinking when an American at the bar began to use vulgar language. Papa leaned forward and told him to shut up. The American told him to go to hell. Papa put down his drink, came around and knocked him flat. Then he announced: 'Cubans can use any language they please in this bar. But I have something to say about how Americans speak.' "

The bartender said he had two children but had put them on the plane for Miami and sent them off. There were no relatives in the U.S.A. "but, even if the plane had crashed in the sea I would have preferred that to seeing them brought up here."

This morning I drove around town with Everardo Janez, the twenty-one-year-old foreign ministry press official assigned to me, visiting the cathedral and the museum in the old governor's palace, both quite lovely and of mild interest. Lunched with Janez and Xavier Varona, another official, taking them to a place called 1830 where a moderately good lunch set me back $70.

Among the current jokes they told me: Khrushchev and Johnson are playing a chess game to settle the fate of the world. Khrushchev is astonished to find what a good player Johnson is and gets into a pickle. He calls time, gets on the phone and telephones Mikhail Botvinnik, world champion. He explains the board position and asks what to do. "Sacrifice the horse," says Botvinnik. (Horse is one of the nicknames for Fidel and also is what the piece we know as the knight is called in Spanish.)

Another: Fidel goes to a Chinese restaurant and orders dinner. "I'd like some prawns to start," he says. "So sorry," says the owner, "we have no fish." Fidel then orders sweet and sour pork. "So sorry," says the owner, "we have no meat." Then he orders chicken chop suey. "So sorry," says the owner, "no chicken today." "Never mind," says Fidel, "soon we will have everything: fish, meat, and chicken." "Are you planning to quit?" asks the Chinaman.

HAVANA, CUBA, *October 28, 1964*

Yesterday was my birthday and I spent most of it in bed, having first visited a dentist with a bad sore throat and swollen jaw. He said I had an abcess and prescribed antibiotics. Went to the drugstore he recommended; they had none. Finally got some out of the British embassy on the promise I would send the same drugs back.

Things operate with appalling inefficiency. Celia's telephone recording is an example. This morning she was still asleep at 11:00 A.M., having been up until dawn. Fidel wanders about, has no office but his car. At a reception he told one ambassador he wanted to see him: "Ride back to the hotel with me while I make one call, then we'll get together." The ambassador and his wife had to sit in Fidel's car until 6:00 A.M. while he gassed with his pal in the hotel.

HAVANA, CUBA, *October 30, 1964*

Just before midnight Fidel Castro showed up in the Hotel Riviera and came to my room for a conversation which, before it had ended, lasted six hours. He would have been ready to go on indefinitely but I had to catch my airplane to Mexico.

Yesterday evening Ramiro del Rio, chief of the foreign ministry press section, said the interview would definitely come off sometime during the night. Ramiro arrived at the hotel himself at 11:30 P.M. and Juan de Onis, stationed here for the moment, went down to greet him. A few minutes before midnight there was a knock on the door. Before I could open it (the key was in the latch) it swung in and Castro and his crony, Dr. Vallejo (a veteran of the Sierra Maestra campaign), strode in, followed by del Rio and de Onis. Outside, in the quiet hallway I saw uniformed guards, some with rifles and some with tommy guns.

Del Rio was wearing an ordinary civilian suit and necktie (rare in shirtsleeved Havana) but Castro and Vallejo were in full uniform with paratrooper boots and sidearms in holsters and ammunition pouches. They each wore military caps. They shook hands, without removing their hats, and I waved Castro to an armchair where he sat, slightly ill at ease. He only removed his cap after several minutes. Then Vallejo took his off.

Vallejo and del Rio perched on the ends of the twin beds. De Onis sat in a chair near Castro from which he interpreted and I took the other armchair. Castro lit a huge cigar and we served cognac, a bottle of which I had brought to de Onis from Paris. Castro drank very little. As he smoked, he allowed his cigar ashes to fall all over the carpet around him.

He is a big man though not so tall as I had expected. Without para-trooper boots I would say he was a bare fraction over six feet. He is heavily built and getting thick around the middle. He has very broad hips. His skin is pale and clear, both on the face and hands, which are small, above all for a man who likes to fancy himself as a baseball pitcher. His wrists are unusually slender. His face is broad but this is counteracted by his scraggly beard which makes him look a bit, from an angle, like a Hasidic rabbi. From other angles he looks like a football guard in fancy dress. He has a straight nose, flat cheekbones, and a broad but not espe-cially high forehead. He moves with considerable grace and gestures gracefully as he talks, using both hands and arms.

I remarked that Castro followed a most curious schedule and I won-dered how he stayed in his apparently good physical condition. He said although his bedtime is irregular he always sleeps six hours and then tries to take a nap after lunch.

He says he eats only twice a day and generally tries to do this at 11:00 A.M. and at 7:00 or 8:00 P.M. He tries to keep fit by doing physical exercises, taking hikes in the mountains, skin-diving, and occasionally playing baseball (which he apparently does in the same army uniform and boots). With juvenile pride he told me: "You know, I am a better pitcher now than I was at the university. I have a better curve and more control," he continued, making a pitcher's motion with his cigar. I could not help but wonder if opposing batters tried to hit him as hard as when he pitched rather unsuccessfully for Havana University.

I remarked that Franco had told me he took up golf shortly after Eisenhower was elected president, but he had to give it up because he was so terrible. I would deem it indicative of a more pro-American policy when Castro took up golf. He said he actually did try a few times. Once he went out to play with Ché Guevara, who had been a caddy in Argentina. Cuban caddies had shown Fidel how to hold the club. Photographers took pictures of Castro and Guevara which were published in the Havana press. Fidel quipped that he intended to play Eisenhower (who was still president) and Ché would play the president of the United Fruit Com-pany.

I began our serious conversation by asking Castro what man, alive or dead, had most influenced him. He thought for a while, rubbing his beard. He leaned forward in the chair pondering and puffing his cigar. He said: "That is one of the most difficult questions I have ever been asked. I have never thought about this before. I don't suppose there is any single living man who has had a particular influence on me. But in my youth I sup-pose it was mainly the influence of Cubans who had fought for our inde-pendence. I read much by and about José Martí and was devoted to him as a revolutionary, an intellectual, and a human being. I also had much admiration for General Antonio Maceo as a warrior. But if I ask myself I can't think of any single person who really influenced me."

I observed that he had had the opportunity to meet many prominent world leaders since coming to power; who among them would he consider the greatest? He answered: "There aren't many. Of course, among them, I had most of my dealings with Khrushchev but perhaps this is not an opportune moment to answer you about Khrushchev and to give you my views on him. But I will answer anyway. Khrushchev was certainly a very intelligent man. [He had just lost power in Moscow.]

"Ben Bella also made a strong impression on me. And I would like to add something that has nothing to do with current problems. This is that when I talk of Khrushchev I am making a personal and not a political judgment.

"I also know Sukarno as well as Sekou Touré but in fact I have not had too many personal dealings with them. And I should not forget Nasser. I have great respect for Nasser."

I asked when he first became an outright communist and why. This touched off a long, hand-waving, and confused speech.

Castro said:

> Before becoming a communist I was a Utopian idealist. I began to study political economics at the university. There I began to form ideas about a different form of organization, of society, than capitalism, even though I was studying capitalistic forms at the university.
>
> Later on, as a more advanced student, I first read the *Communist Manifesto* and was strongly impressed. Why? I already had many social and economic impressions and opinions of my own. But I was especially struck by the eloquence and clear logic of this document.
>
> Above all, this made up for the unclear works I had previously read and it had great polemic force. One phrase struck me especially —that the bourgeoisie accuses the communists of trying to abolish private property, but private property was already beyond the reach of nine-tenths of the population. I understood this myself because I had been raised in a property-owning family surrounded by those who were landless.
>
> Naturally one document doesn't make a communist. The primary thing in a revolutionary is the sensitiveness of a man toward contemporary events, his capacity for feeling the sufferings of others. Naturally abstract ideas have a great importance, but the coming together of a man who himself has revolutionary feelings with a revolutionary abstract idea completes a revolution. This is not an abrupt event like a revelation. It is a long process and it took a long time with me.
>
> I had been reading other interpretations of history but none of these had convinced me. I then began to read more Marx and I was impressed by his *French Civil War* and *Eighteenth Brumaire of Napoleon Bonaparte*. Then, while I was still in university, I read some Engels and some Lenin.

Before this I had principally been influenced by Martí and, as a romantic revolutionary, I had read several histories of the French revolution and Lamartine, even before entering the university. I also read a history of the Spartacus rebellion. But as a student I did not pursue philosophical literature that preceded Marxism such as Hegel or Feuerbach.

I was much more attracted by the concrete aspects of political action than by pure philosophy. But my two years in prison, after the Moncada Barracks fight, allowed me to read much history and to start a more systematic approach. I tried to amplify my knowledge. I read Plato and I read Kant, whom I found very difficult. But I was more interested in political literature—Plutarch, Suetonius, Livy, Demosthenes, Cicero.

Whenever I had to choose between reading history and philosophy, I chose history. I read Machiavelli's *The Prince* with Napoleon's notes. I also read biographies. I read the biographies by Zweig and Ludwig. I read a biography of Bolívar.

Ninety-five percent of the books I now read are technical, primarily on agriculture, chemistry, and botany. I am planning to study bio-chemistry and mathematics in order to help me prepare for my work.

For a year and a half I have been reading almost only agricultural treatises, although every now and then I read some history. Like now I am reading Carl Sandburg's *Lincoln*. I have been reading a history of the Mexican revolution by a Mexican writer named Silva Herzog. I read a historical view of the conquistadors' triumph over the Indians called *A Vision of the Vanquished*. And I recently read that book about the CIA called *The Invisible Government*. I also read a book on the Bay of Pigs and a Mexican novel by Martín Guzmán called *The Shadow of the Caudillo*. And I read that book about migratory workers, what's it called?

Dr. Vallejo, who was beginning to nod, perched uncomfortably at the end of a bed, supplied the answer—Steinbeck's *Grapes of Wrath*.

I went back to the business of when Castro had formally decided he was a communist. His answer was immensely long-winded. In my own mind I had the impression he never really became a communist in the usual sense and I remarked to him that I thought the Communist party of Cuba had joined him, not vice versa (an observation he received with no enthusiasm). Nevertheless he said:

In my final student stage at university I had come a long way reading Marx and Engels but I couldn't call myself a communist. I was an individual seeking the truth. I did not belong to the Communist party. My analysis was basically idealistic. I did not conceive of methods of action in the classical Marxist fashion. But I did realize that you could not change a society without holding power. Therefore I began conceiving methods of attaining power by revolutionary means based on popular support. I recognized the simple logic that a revolution had to be made for the people and by the people. And I had decreasing faith in the chances of solving Cuba's problems by peaceful methods such as elections. The powerful vested interests that ran the country were supported by a professional army.

These were still very personal ideas but in accordance with them I began to act. There was then, at that time, a political movement with considerable popular support which criticized corruption and the existing state of affairs in Cuba. This was the Party of the Cuban People, directed by Senator Eduardo Chivas and I had relations with its leaders.

My mental process was moving forward. I could distinguish between social revolution and a movement merely seeking to improve conditions within the existing framework. I progressively became more separated ideologically from the merely reformist program. I became convinced it was simply fooling the people just to promise a better life if the basic circumstances hindering their progress were not removed. Then, in 1951, Chivas died and his party fell into the hands of incompetents.

From that time on I struck out along my own road. I wanted to lead the party into a more revolutionary attitude. But then the Batista coup came along. At first I hoped there would be a united front by all elements to overthrow Batista and I talked with the different opposition leaders and told them I was willing to fight with them, under their leadership, as a soldier in the ranks. But time passed and the leaders divided and their forces broke up. I lost all hope and, with no resources, no party, barely known by the people, I decided to form a revolutionary organization myself. That was at the end of 1952.

As you can see from my methods, not being a member of a Marxist party at the time, I nevertheless interpreted things in a Marxist fashion and recognized the importance of the masses. I had good relationships with some of the communists in the university and it was the communists who often loaned me Marxist books.

By then I clearly understood that a revolution could only be carried out by the exploited and against the exploiting classes. But it could not be said that I was yet a communist. I was primarily preoccupied with formulating a strategy and gathering together the means to do away with the Batista regime. It was then that we organized our first plan, the attack on the Moncada Barracks in 1953, in order to seize a strong point and from there to gain control of a province and summon the people to overthrow the regime.

Castro went on to describe the Moncada abortive coup and his defense speech after his capture. He added that he had deliberately eschewed legal counsel and defended himself, in order better to advertise his revolutionary program, and this was gradually disseminated around the country by his supporters. And when he was a prisoner on the Isle of Pines, he used to write secret messages in lemon juice on the paper of innocuous pen-and-ink letters and he included some of his famous Moncada speech ("History Will Absolve Me") in these letters. They were put together and distributed in pamphlets by the underground. Castro continued:

> But even then, I could not be called a communist although, at the trial, I had spoken out clearly against the essence of the capitalistic system. Perhaps at that time my ideas did not have the full extent they came to have later, but nevertheless at the time of Moncada we proclaimed a radical, social revolutionary program.
>
> During my years in prison I evolved my concepts more profoundly and elaborated a new plan of attack. I developed a plan of guerrilla warfare and three years later we began this in Oriente after training in Mexico for the Granma landing. But I was not yet a communist although we had come back to Cuba determined to carry out a social revolution. We could not yet say how far that revolution would go but we were already working with the peasants and the workers not only against the regime but against the social structure.
>
> I was still too idealist to be a Marxist-Leninist. I thought it was enough for things to be just and that if they were just everyone would understand us. By then I had read Lenin on imperialism but I had not yet come to realize in full just what the problem was.
>
> I thought the United States would respect this attitude and would respect us. At that time, perhaps because our actual war, or military operations, was the immediate task, I did not clearly see that a social revolution would collide directly with the United States and that the antagonism arising from this would produce the concrete events of later years.
>
> But we were determined to carry out the revolution at any cost. If I had then understood the meaning of international problems and the imperialism phenomenon, then I would truly have become a Marxist-Leninist. But to reach that point I had to have two years of armed conflict during which I saw United States planes and U.S. bombs being used to attack the defenseless population, doing enormous damage and causing measureless suffering, before my final evolution. A year of revolutionary government would have to pass before we reached the real experience which would make of us genuine revolutionaries and Marxist-Leninists in the full sense.

At this point I pinned Castro down and asked him precisely what was the date when in that full sense he became a Marxist-Leninist. He said he thought it was fair to call it the winter of 1960–61.

"We announced the socialist nature of our revolution," he continued, "after the attacks by CIA planes bearing Cuban markings—on the eve of the Bay of Pigs [April 1961]. We contributed to the formation of a revolutionary movement and we opened new revolutionary roads on which all the revolutionary forces in Cuba joined together.

"This is more or less the way it came about. But already, as early as my university days, the communists and the persecutions they suffered called to my mind the first Christians and their persecution."

Castro explained that as a young man he initially found it "very difficult to register in any opposition party. I was sent to a Catholic school. I went to mass every day. I did everything the others did."

I asked him what he was today—a lapsed Catholic, an agnostic, or an atheist. He said: "In a religious way I reject all the explanations I was originally taught about nature and the development of life. I am convinced that science is the only way to understand things and science excludes divinity. It is interesting to see how science today explains many things that were not understood in the past. I am an atheist but I respect any man's religious belief. And I can see how men don't understand many things that science has not yet been able to answer. And therefore they believe in God."

I was much struck by his unusually disorganized personal schedule and asked why he had no office or permanent home which he was accustomed to use. He said:

In the first place, I am very opposed to bureaucratic forms of work and I am absolutely convinced that bureaucracy is one of the most pernicious aspects in any ideological system. I do not underestimate the importance of organization and the need for office and officials. But I fight tenaciously against the spread of bureaucracy and I recognize that this will be one of the most difficult battles for me to win. This and the agricultural problem are my main battles.

When I became prime minister I found that the office was costing a million pesos a year [one peso equals one dollar] and was fulfilling no useful function so I decided to suppress it. I reduced the prime minister's office to a very small bureau where we receive and answer mail with a few secretaries. The state has plenty of offices I can use when I need them. When I have military problems to discuss, I discuss them in the armed forces ministry. When I have educational problems, I discuss them in the ministry of education. When I have argicultural problems, I discuss them in the ministry of agriculture.

I have discovered several things since we took power. At the start I tried to work in the prime minister's office just like any other prime minister and I received everyone there. But I rapidly learned that I had no interest in seeing ninety percent of the people who were interested in seeing me. And I saved an enormous amount of time on matters of pure courtesy and protocol so I decided to adopt a method enabling me to see those people it was necessary to see or interesting to see without being bothered by the others.

As I see it, the prime minister's job here is not administrative but political. Perhaps thanks to this conception I have been able to establish a very wide contact with the people and with the countryside because I am incessantly visiting different places and talking with different people. To sum up, I am a determined enemy of organized bureaucracy.

I then said I understood Castro's closest family attachment was to his son and asked where the boy was and whether he often saw him. He said: "My boy is here in Cuba and I visit him frequently." He did not elucidate.

I was struck by the fact that Cuba had turned Hemingway's former house into a national museum, although Hemingway was an American and an anticommunist. Castro said: "Shakespeare was not a communist. Nor was Cervantes. Nor was Michelangelo. They were all admired for their genius.

"Hemingway wrote certain works which influenced me, like *For Whom the Bell Tolls.* This opened my eyes to many possibilities of guerrilla warfare. And then there was his story about a Cuban fisherman [*The Old Man and the Sea*] which is an extremely moving human story. I knew Hemingway and I liked him. He was a legendary figure. He was not a communist but he was far from being an imperialist or a reactionary."

I asked him how well he knew Hemingway. He said: "I talked with him first at the time of the fishing derby where he gave a prize which I won with a marlin. That was in 1959 and he personally awarded me the prize. I felt great sympathy for him."

I said Castro must forgive a question that might seem embarrassing and impertinent but nevertheless I considered it important. Why did his sister, Juana, leave Cuba and openly start to fight him? He hunched over in his chair, made a gesture as if washing his face with both hands, mumbled, and then began a long answer in fits and starts. He became very emotional during the course of this. At one point he was clearly on the verge of tears. This is what he said:

"Whatever I say on this might seem to be based on rancor. Juanita acted by her own lights as a member of the social class to which she belongs and which she defends. It is difficult to judge the actions of individuals and I prefer to judge symptoms. And the CIA played a role in all this which shows the brutal and horrible lack of scruples of the CIA. [Here Castro became patently furious.] We know that the CIA played a role. A CIA official in Mexico and she had an interview with one of our Cubans and tried to urge him to defect. It is disgusting for the CIA to do things of that sort.

"My brother Raúl and I could only have avoided this problem with our sister by being derelict in our duties and by practicing nepotism. This sister of ours is a girl who lacks a cultural foundation. She didn't even finish high school and has no political qualities. The differences between us arose precisely because she wanted to use the influence of her connection with us for business deals. Also, our revolutionary laws affected the possessions of our family. My father was a prosperous man and our family had about 12,000 hectares of land, but the agricultural reform reduced this property to 400 hectares.

"When our mother died I firmly opposed the family distribution of her property for both moral and legal reasons. Morally, I and my brothers were the only boys of that region who were well clothed and fed, while there were hundreds of youngsters of our age who were never able to go to school. If I was privileged to study it was because my parents could pay for my education, and they could pay for it thanks to the fact that there were hundreds of poor workers employed on our farm. I had received a great privilege and in this sense all my brothers and sisters had the same privilege. None of them needed the property my mother left because they had jobs which paid them incomes. My sister Juana had a relatively high salary. Yet, only a few hours after my mother's death—and this hurt me a great deal—the discussion started on how to divide the inheritance.

"I didn't want to act in arbitrary fashion. My mother had left some money in the bank and 180 hectares of land. Raúl and I agreed when the problem arose with Juanita, because she wanted the land, on how we should behave. Juanita went to the property and she wanted to sell the cattle and everything else without consulting anyone. So then the problem arose and we agreed to divide the estate, excluding myself and Raúl, letting the land itself become state property."

Castro was fumbling for words but pushed on. "And there was a legal argument. My father died after acquiring a large debt to a sugar enterprise to which he sold cane; he had been unsuccessful in business during his last seven years. When the sugar enterprise was nationalized, the state became the creditor. My father's farm was mortgaged and no one had a right to it. My decision on this was based on legal grounds. And anyway, I am strongly opposed to inheritance. It always foments unnatural family quarrels. There are many young people who just wait to inherit from their elders.

"Communists are often accused of not having family ties but this is nonsense and we feel very close to each other. Nevertheless, in this case our enemies could not have given a greater demonstration of lack of scruples, for purely political reasons, than by trying to use one member of a family against the others. I don't like to speak of this; it is very distasteful to me; but you raised the subject and I must answer."

I asked Castro if he considered *Fidelismo* a symbol or a movement. He sniffed: "It is just a word. It is used to synthesize an idea. It is an expression of confidence—but I don't feel that it exists."

I asked him if he was really dogmatic enough to be a communist, as he called himself, or if he was not in fact just pragmatic. I told him that Nasser called himself a pragmatist, not a dogmatist. Castro replied: "I am neither pragmatic nor dogmatic; I am dialectical. Dialecticism is the negation of dogmatism. Nothing is permanent but everything changes. As Heraclitus said, nobody bathes twice in the same river."

I then asked whom he would delegate to take over leadership in case of an emergency such as his own assassination. He said: "I have no right to name my successor because we now have a party and a government and this would be their task and naturally if I were dead I would not be around to influence them. But I have given this problem thought. In the first stages of our revolution there was always the possibility of an accident to me and this could have created great difficulties then, but that preoccupation no longer exists. My role in the first days of the revolution was much more important than it is now. Now there is an organization and a whole team to make decisions and carry them out.

"At that time, in the early days, there was talk of assassination attempts but I said even then that this would not hamper the revolution. But after we gained power, at a mass meeting of nearly a million people, I proposed that in the case of my death Raúl should take over. I did not really have to say this because it responded to national sentiment. Raúl has played a very important role in all our revolutionary history, starting with the Moncada Barracks affair and going on through jail, exile and the Granma expedition. He has great prestige and authority both through his government and party and his military positions. Many people consider him more radical than I and, in revolutions, people have sympathy always toward the radical position. But now such a succession would have to be decided by the national directorate of the party [PURS]."

I turned to more precise subjects. I asked Castro why he gave up non-alignment as a policy by becoming a communist. I pointed out that Ben Bella in Algeria maintained relations with both ideological blocs and that Nasser in Egypt had expressed to me an admiration for Tito, who had shown him how to get help from both sides without joining either. Castro said:

Each country must develop its own policy on the basis of its own problems. I respect anyone else's position and I feel that Nasser is an intelligent, capable man. But it is not fair to say that he is non-aligned. He is aligned against imperialism and colonialism and in that sense we too are aligned. The so-called nonaligned countries have similar positions on a whole series of international problems, as was shown at the recent Cairo meeting.

But we now receive aid from only one side for the simple reason that there is only one side to help us. It is practically impossible that the U.S.A. should help us because the U.S.A. would demand ideological concessions and we will never be prepared to make concessions of that sort. The U.S.A. has helped some countries without demanding concessions but it would never do this in the case of Cuba, which affects the United States much more directly and more intimately than revolutions in North Africa. That decision was not taken by us but by the United States.

The concept of nonalignment is not an ideological concept. The idea of nonalignment merely means nonentanglement with blocs, the absence of commitments to military pacts. All the countries that participated in the recent Cairo meeting of nonaligned states felt that Cuba had a right to be there and supported our position. We found great sympathy.

I asked if, despite such pretended nonalignment, Cuba desired to strengthen its formal ties with Moscow by a military alliance on a bilateral basis or by membership in the Warsaw Pact. He said: "We desire to strengthen our ties with Russia and, if circumstances require it for our security, the possibility of an alliance would not be excluded."

I pointed out that inside the world of communism there were now various doctrines, and asked if he felt closer to that of Moscow, that of Peking, or that of Belgrade. He said: "Our line is that of unity in the socialist camp. I believe that conditions now exist that permit the camp to overcome present internal misunderstandings. Revolutions develop differently in different countries. There are factors of national character. But they have a common philosophy. Therefore I feel that existing differences between Russia and China are transitory and they can find common points to overcome their divergencies."

I asked him how he interpreted the fall of Khrushchev both ideologically and in terms of world communism. This was his answer:

"In my opinion the political change in the Soviet Union creates the opportunity to make a serious effort to overcome the difficulties between Russia and China. It is already apparent that both parties have lately been demonstrating symptoms which favor that possibility. The leaders of both will surely take advantage of this in a responsible and intelligent manner, and other communist parties in other lands should work for this goal in order to strengthen the socialist camp. That would increase the security of smaller socialist countries like our own."

I said that when I had been in east Africa earlier this year I heard a lot of rumors that Cuba had played a role in the Zanzibar revolution, but I was inclined to discount them. What was the truth? He said:

"Cuba played no important role in that revolution. There were some young people in it who sympathized with us and perhaps the example of our revolution had some influence, but we deserve no credit for that revolution in Zanzibar.

"Our position on revolutionary movements is that we made public in Cairo: we support movements of national liberation just like the other nonaligned countries."

I asked how it happened that his own avowedly communist regime had such close relations with the avowedly anticommunist regime of Franco in Spain and wondered if it was because both Castro and Franco were Gallegos (both Franco's and Castro's fathers came from Spanish Galicia) and felt some clannish bond. He replied:

"Being a Gallego has nothing to do with this. The important factor is Cuba's Spanish origin and history and, as we have always had over the years, good commercial exchanges benefit us both. When any government resists United States pressures and defends its political sovereignty by impeding the illegitimate American blockade, as Spain does, naturally we are pleased. No country has the right to strangle another. This is against international law. Spain's trade with Cuba does not hurt Spain; it only hurts the U.S."

I asked what were the relationships between state and church in Cuba and whether there were any negotiations with the Vatican to arrange a concordat. He said: "There has never been a question of a concordat and there was no concordat before the revolution. But relations with the Catholic Church have gradually been improving and the revolution is inspired with the respect for everyone's freedom of belief."

I then turned to Latin America. Did Castro foresee any revolutions in the near future elsewhere in Latin America and if so where? He replied:

Of course I cannot prophesy. But one can see from statistics that in many Latin American countries there is a growing impoverishment, that the population is increasing faster than production and that consumption is declining. This inevitably leads to revolution and there is no way of stopping it.

Already we can see a virtual civil war in Bolivia. Divisions are increasing manifestly in Brazil, Colombia, Venezuela, and Argentina. There is progressive impoverishment everywhere except in Venezuela, which is an exception because of its huge oil exports. But even in Venezuela there is great restlessness. The Venezuelan people have a strong revolutionary conscience and nationalist sentiment.

And there is a similar situation in Central America. There is a fear that the U.S.A. will dump its cotton surplus and restrict sugar imports. The miracle that might save these countries from revolution is not apparent.

How and where was Cuba helping revolutionary movements in Latin America? He said: "We help by our example but the greatest assistance revolutionary movements there receive is from the United States itself. U.S. commercial policies are accelerating revolution because of your low prices for raw material imports and your high charge for manufactured U.S. exports. The United States extracts more money from Latin America than the amount it sends in through the Alliance for Progress. And the United States supports right-wing governments, oligarchies, and *coups d'état*.

"Why, the United States won dozens of medals at the Olympic Games and Latin America won none. That shows the difference in the level of development [a rather strange observation]. The Alliance for Progress is an alliance between one millionaire and many beggars. There is only one country in the Organization of American States that has a stable political and economic system and that is Mexico—because Mexico had a revolution."

I then moved the conversation directly to relations between Havana and Washington. I started off by observing that although Ben Bella had been at war with France he had made up with the French; why didn't Castro make up with the United States with which he had not been at war? He said:

French policy is more intelligent than that of the U.S.A. France offered economic cooperation to Algeria but the United States only offered a blockade to Cuba. European countries are more experienced than you are, although I must admit that we share in the blame for the deterioration of relations with you. Nevertheless, it is mostly your fault.

I think it will require many years before diplomatic relations are restored. I don't think conditions exist in the United States that permit positive steps. I believe an improvement of relations must be regarded as a long-term affair. After all, one must be realistic.

We want relations to improve among all the countries of the world. The relations between Cuba and the United States can improve only when the relations of all socialist countries with the United States improve. [Obviously the innuendo here is addressed to China.] We are much more interested in the unity of the socialist camp than in improving relations with the United States for our own sake. We would not want to improve relationships with the United States while your intervention continues in Vietnam. We wouldn't want peace for ourselves alone. This question depends on the relations of the United States with *all* socialist countries and we are not interested in improving relationships for ourselves alone.

I asked if, after Kennedy's assassination, he had ordered any serious investigation of Lee Oswald's strange Cuban connections. Castro said:

"When we first heard the report of Oswald's trip to Mexico to seek a Cuban visa we asked for a full report. We found that Oswald had applied for a transit visa and had filled out a form. He was told to wait for an official reply. Then he was informed that he could have no transit visa to Cuba without first producing a visa for the country of his ultimate destination."

I then went into the delicate field of military affairs and Soviet arms aid. I said he seemed to have given contradictory statements about who initiated the Soviet military deal. Who proposed it first and when, who took the initiative? Castro said: "Cuba took the responsibility for the presence of the missiles here. It is not easy to clarify the details for security reasons, but both Russia and Cuba participated. We aspired to get an effective guarantee to warn off the possibility of a U.S. attack on Cuba and to make it evident that any such attack would provoke a nuclear world war and Russia had its own position. Each country had its own position."

Was it true that Khrushchev had urged Castro not to use the surface-to-air missiles, provided by the USSR, to shoot down American U-2s? Castro answered: "We are absolutely opposed to U-2 flights. We have never felt that we could tolerate such flights. But for a long time the SAMs were not under our control. We did not have the personnel trained to use them.

"However, when our forces took over control of the SAMs the arrangement carried with it an obligation not to proceed unilaterally in shooting at U-2 flights. The commitment we assumed was that all legal means to put an end to U-2 flights should first be exhausted, but this is not a commitment for an indefinite period. The SAMs are now under Cuban control."

I asked if the crews at SAM sites were entirely Cuban, and when Cuba took control. He dodged this. I then inquired how many Soviet military personnel were left in Cuba and what they were doing, whether any were combat troops. He said: "There are a number of technicians left and we shall certainly continue their presence as long as the U.S.A. continues an aggressive policy toward us."

I repeated the inquiry as to whether these were combat troops. He said: "They are certainly not military tourists. All military technicians have a military capability and would fight in case of an aggression. The function of the Russians here is as technical advisors, but if Cuba were attacked they would serve as combat forces.

"When I say 'if Cuba were attacked' I don't mean something like the Bay of Pigs. I mean an actual invasion by the United States or by some such other country instigated by the United States or by the armed forces of the United States."

I asked how large a combat force the Russians comprised. He answered: "Enough are left to form a solid combat force." I then asked if there were any other military personnel here from any other foreign nation and he said no.

I inquired how many Russian military men had been here at the peak. He said: "That figure is still secret but I can tell you it was much larger than the figures published." [The figures published said 22,000.]

I asked if Cuba had held a veto power over Russia's right to fire the Soviet missiles stationed in Cuba. He said:

> That is a theoretical question because circumstances would have made it impossible to have a disagreement. There would have had to be a general war in which Cuba was naturally involved.
>
> Such missiles could not have been used independently of the use of Soviet nuclear missiles on a global basis. Had a conflict arisen elsewhere, as in Berlin, somewhere outside of Cuba, naturally there would have been a general war and these missiles would have been used.
>
> The presence here of both technical and strategic weapons was conceived in terms of a possible aggression against Cuba. The agreement under which the missiles came here was tied to the possibility of an act of aggression against Cuba.
>
> Nothing was said about the use of the missiles if a conflict arose elsewhere in the world in which case their use would have been determined by specific circumstances.
>
> But it is obvious they would have come into play in any general war. The accord with Moscow on the MRBMs in Cuba contained the understanding that they would be used in defense of Cuban territory in the event of aggression against Cuba and through agreement between the two contracting parties.
>
> But in total war all strategic arms would obviously be used by both sides independently of where they were located.

I said Castro kept complaining about our U-2 flights. Nevertheless, I inquired how the United States could be assured beyond any doubt that all missiles and nuclear warheads had been removed from Cuban territory and that none had since been sent back. He became quite agitated and squatted down on his legs among the cigar ashes he had scattered on the carpet around him.

He said: "The first element of security for you is obviously that Cuba cannot produce such weapons. Secondly, you could be reassured if the United States removed any cause for the presence here of such arms by ceasing its aggressive policy.

"Cuba has no obligation to give the United States a guarantee that the missiles and warheads are out, are gone. We do not accept the right of the United States to inspect or control what arms Cuba has."

I remarked that this was a rather arrogant and short-sighted attitude. He resented our U-2 flights but refused to arrange for any other guarantee. The United States had every right, in its own security interests, to be positive on this point. It seemed necessary to me to arrange some formula that could reassure us if, indeed, there was ever to be a thought of ending the U-2 flights. Otherwise a situation might develop that could lead to an unintentional and undesired war by accident or, at the very least, a repetition of the October 1962 crisis.

Castro asked if I could suggest any such formula. I said this was difficult to do but possibly the United Nations could devise a machinery. After all, the International Red Cross had helped on inspection during the 1962 crisis.

Castro said Cuba had to be assured that no offensive expedition was being mounted from the United States or elsewhere against Cuba. I said that it seemed at least theoretically possible that some kind of UN inspection device could conceivably be arranged to satisfy the security requirements of both Cuba and the United States, although naturally it would be a very difficult thing to work out. He said he would deliberate on the idea.

By now I had finished my questions. It was 4:30 A.M. Vallejo and del Rio were somnolently balanced on the ends of their twin beds but Castro was full of vigor. He came over beside me and squatted on the floor. He borrowed a pad to sketch out the bureaucratic organization he was seeking to diminish. He said he hoped to freeze the existing limits of bureau - cracy and then gradually put useless bureaucrats to other work.

I then turned back to Russia. He said: "I know both Brezhnev and Kosygin. I have met them. Brezhnev especially impresses me. As to Khrushchev's removal—this is an internal problem for the Soviet Union. Cuba's relations are with the Soviet state and the Soviet Communist party. They are not relations between individuals. And the change can have positive results for the socialist camp. But as a person I had great liking and respect for Khrushchev."

I remarked to Castro that on September 5, 1961, months after Castro's formal conversion to communism, Khrushchev had said to me he didn't think Castro was a communist.

(A later check of the full notes on my Khrushchev conversation shows that he said: "As far as we know Castro is not a member of the Communist party. He is just a revolutionary and a patriot of his country. If he were to join the Communist party I should welcome him; he would make a fine addition to the ranks of the communists. But this is for him to decide.")

I thought he was too undisciplined and romantic to be an orthodox communist and I had known many. He seemed to be more of an anarchist, closer to Bakunin than to Lenin.

This produced an inchoate discussion. Castro insisted the aim of communism was to have less and less government until there was finally none. I said this confirmed my suspicions of his innate anarchism because communism the world around had proven that it produced more and more government—more bureaucracy—rather than the reverse.

At this point, as our discussion was revolving like a squirrel in a cage, Castro proposed we go down and have some coffee and take a tour around sleeping Havana. We got up. Vallejo and del Rio blinked and followed us. We filed down to the elevator and, circled by Castro's guard, downstairs.

The porter led us through the bowels of the hotel to the kitchen where a cook gave us tiny cups of sweet thick Cuban coffee. Then we piled into several cars. Castro got into the front seat of a modest Oldsmobile and Juan and I got in back. The driver was a soldier. The other cars followed us and we drove around the port while Castro pointed out the sights and jabbered about his ideas.

He told me the car had a regular police radio so that he could be contacted quite quickly. When he takes hikes in the mountains there is generally a helicopter hovering overhead which can contact him in times of crisis.

I said that in a sense he was lucky to have his historical importance at this time when the really great powers like the U.S.A. and Russia were so strong that they became weak. Their possibilities of action were almost paralyzed by the terrible potential of their weapons and this allowed more freedom of action to smaller countries. Cuba would have had a much more difficult time in an earlier period. Castro agreed. He also agreed that the impact of Woodrow Wilson in terms of encouraging the idea of self-determination, an idea which had spread to many continents although originally conceived for Europe alone, had produced perhaps a greater force than Leninism.

I said to Castro: "You are now thirty-eight. Twenty years ago, when you were only eighteen, what was your ambition, what did you want to be?" With great delight he swiveled round in the front seat and said: "I wanted to be doing exactly what I am doing now."

He told me that his father, who had been born in Spain, was a big farmer who had only a general and vague interest in politics. His father had come to Cuba as a soldier in the Spanish army during the independence war and then had returned after being demobilized. I asked him if it was true, as I had been told, that his father got his first break by winning a state lottery which allowed him to purchase a good-sized farm. Castro said this was not true.

We drove round by the fishing port of Havana, where a dry dock towed from the Soviet Union has been placed in position. It can repair vessels of a size up to 3,000 tons. Castro told me that the Russians will make this a base for part of their fishing fleet.

At one point I noticed that he put on glasses—the first time during the talk—to gaze out into the distance. He must be either mildly nearsighted or astigmatic.

By 5:45 A.M. I was a bit nervous about catching my plane so we drove back to the hotel—incidentally always at a reasonable speed. Apparently Castro is very opposed to reckless driving for fear of reducing Cuba's limited supply of automobiles. At the entrance of the hotel, at 6:00 A.M., we all got out and Castro bade me a warm farewell. He did not look in the least bit tired. He asked when I would come back and promised to take me fishing.

I said I really couldn't tell but that I would like to see him again. Nevertheless, I reminded him, it had taken me over two years to get my present visa. With evident satisfaction he commented: "It's easier to see me than to get here." For the third time he shook my hand and then the whole cavalcade whizzed off into the dawn.

PARIS, *November 9, 1964*

Talked with Prime Minister Pompidou this afternoon. He is very worried about the situation. There are two basic points. The most important one is the quarrel with the U.S. over MLF. The second one is the quarrel with Germany over grain prices in the Common Market.

De Gaulle feels that the U.S. has changed its policy that once supported the idea of an independent European partner and now wants a subservient Europe. Without even intending to, the U.S. is producing a form of economic imperialism, and if the trend is not checked the gap between powerful, rich U.S. and Europe will widen. Already the only calculating machines and electronic devices of that sort in the West are made by IBM and General Electric. Now the French electronics industry is entirely in U.S. hands.

(Compagnie des Machines Bull is the most important French manufacturer of electronic calculators. General Electric sought to buy them at the rate of twenty percent of Bull's capital last year but de Gaulle, Giscard d'Estaing, and others opposed this American participation. It now turns out that the entire enterprise has been taken over through three independent companies, in which the American part is approximately fifty percent, and Bull, to all intents and purposes, is under complete American control.)

He claims that de Gaulle is the most European of Europe's leaders and despite his distaste for international organizations, he wants to establish a Europe that is politically, economically, and militarily viable. Like all Gaullists, he is obsessed with strategic problems. He outlines the following possibilities as a hypothesis:

An East German invasion of West Germany begins, backed by Russia. NATO quite probably probes their intentions with an armored division. We find it is really serious and we have to use nuclear weapons. With that we destroy Poland, Czechoslovakia, and maybe Hungary. In the process Germany is destroyed and possibly even France. But Russia and the U.S. are untouched and finally decide to make a peace. What good would even a fine peace do to all the European dead?

I asked Pompidou if he objected to seeing Germany with nuclear weapons, whether there was a counter-project to our MLF, and if de Gaulle would offer to share in the European nuclear force. I pointed out that Strauss had made a deal with Chaban-Delmas under the Fourth Republic and that de Gaulle had refused to implement it. Pompidou nodded and said: "Yes, that is true, and you have put your finger on a weak point of our policy, because we have no alternative plan."

The French are now wondering whether Johnson (and at this point Pompidou thanked God that Johnson had defeated Goldwater) will have a foreign policy of his own the way Kennedy had. He said that Kennedy had a "Kennedy policy" which France could recognize even if she didn't agree with all of it. But he wondered if Johnson will have a "Johnson policy" or whether Johnson will have a bureaucratic policy, depending to a great measure on cabinet members and functionaries for advice.

Pompidou insists that a country—above all an enormously powerful country as the U.S.A.—must have an identifiable policy associated with a leader. Even Germany and Italy today have an Erhard and Moro policy, such as they are. Nothing but complete chaos can result if Johnson simply takes refuge in bureaucracy to decide his position. The position of the U.S. is so paramount that it must be clear.

Pompidou strongly indicated the feeling that the MLF is developing into an effort to isolate France. When it was originally conceived in the last Eisenhower years and under Kennedy, it was developed as a way of enticing France from the proclaimed intention of building a nuclear force. But now France has a nuclear force and we are pushing MLF harder than ever.

Europe must have its own means of defense even if that is conflicting with that of the U.S. France likewise feels it must have the industrial know-how, especially in the field of electronics, to continue scientific research in the future and that it is a sacrifice, but necessary if she is to refuse the idea of giving up her national industry. France must make an effort so as not to allow the U.S. to have total control of European defense as it would have under the MLF. France wants to be able to push its own button and protect its own interests if need be.

PARIS, *November 16, 1964*

Played poker last night at Chip Bohlen's. The game was arranged in honor of "Tommy" [Ambassador Llewellyn E.] Thompson, who won. Dean Rusk played with us for about three hours. I am glad to report that he (Rusk) is a shrewd, bland poker player.

PARIS, *November 18, 1964*

An hour's talk with Couve de Murville at the foreign ministry. I started off by asking why France had not by now drawn up at least a tentative plan for NATO reform, since it doesn't like MLF and yet refused to offer any suggestion of its own. Couve said France had failed to offer such a formal plan or proposal for three reasons:

"(1) There is no use discussing reform of NATO so long as there is no agreement on the direction NATO should take. France wants less integration; everyone else wants more. Therefore the argument is hopeless from the beginning.

"(2) Also we have taken several moves already on our part which show which direction we want NATO to take. We have reduced our force commitments and at the same time have stressed our plan for an atomic force. We have therefore reformed NATO ourselves to the extent that we could. We have disintegrated as much as we could without danger.

"(3) But the atomic affair is the most important. We have rearranged the French army without taking account of NATO's view. We have reduced the size of our conventional forces in order to be able to spend more on our atomic force."

I could not understand why France did not at least offer a reform blueprint as a basis for discussion. He answered:

"What would be the point? No one in NATO, apart from France, dares to speak up to the U.S.A. And really, apart from France, Britain, and Germany, the rest of the allies think the best thing to do is to leave everything to Uncle Sam and spend the least possible amount on defense."

The big question was: "Who will decide when NATO should go to nuclear war? Ninety-nine percent of the West's strategic weapons are under the U.S.A. and the American president will alone decide when these should be used. Likewise the head of the British and French governments must ultimately decide when British and French strategic weapons are used.

"There are tactical weapons in Germany and these could someday be used on a different basis but even here the question is not clear. The weapons assigned to non-American units are under U.S. control and it must be decided by the U.S. government and the government of the troops on a bilateral basis when these tactical weapons should be fired.

And there are even weapons that I suppose you might call neither strategic nor tactical. These are very complicated matters.

"When we concluded the North Atlantic Alliance, we didn't have the organization of NATO. Nevertheless, we considered ourselves allied. The Alliance is not, however, an unconditional commitment to accept everything.

"The military organization of NATO was created at the time of the Korean war when all of us reckoned there was a real danger of war with Russia and we put the Alliance on a virtual war footing. But today France sees no reason to keep it that way.

"We must get rid of *all* integration. We should distinguish between peacetime and wartime organization. The so-called NATO army is continually being altered as individual countries wish and as Alliance members are forced to draw out troops for use in Algeria and Indonesia and the Congo. The NATO army isn't really practicable."

I asked if France was now making a real effort to draw closer to the Arab world and whether this was not having a repercussion in cooling off the previously warm relations and virtual alliance with Israel. Couve said: "We are normalizing relations with the Arabs and therefore we are obviously normalizing relations with Israel." I asked if he meant by this that France was less allied to Israel and he nodded affirmatively.

Couve then talked for some time about the Franco-German alliance. He said there were really three parties involved—Germany, France, and the U.S.A. He could never understand why the U.S.A. was so opposed to Franco-German *entente.* Yet it was evident we were doing everything possible against it. America seemed to think the alliance is directed against it. Nevertheless the future of Franco-German cooperation depended on the U.S.A., which unfortunately was working against Franco-German friendship.

PARIS, *November 19, 1964*

Lunched with Y. He says Lucien Paye, French ambassador in Peking, has sent strange reports that indicate from conversations with Mao that Mao is at the very best senile nowadays. Mao, for example, told Paye that Hitler had been nothing but a paper tiger as events proved because "where is Hitler today?" Y. commented wryly, "It took several million lives and several million tons of steel to make that paper tiger."

Y. knew all about the Strauss and Chaban-Delmas incident and says I was slightly wrong in my facts. He says that Strauss and Chaban-Delmas discussed this in December 1957—at the initiative of Chaban. (The Félix Gaillard government, in which Chaban-Delmas was minister of defense, came to office on November 6, 1957, and left office on April 16, 1958.) No documents were signed. Chaban merely asked Strauss for German support on the French nuclear force in exchange for access to weapons, and Strauss agreed.

Y. continued that in July 1958, shortly after de Gaulle had come back to power, Strauss raised the matter with de Gaulle's first defense minister, Pierre Guillaumat, not later on with Messmer, as I had written. Guillaumat, according to Y., was fully *au courant* and turned the idea down bluntly, rather offending Strauss. A French mission went to see Strauss in November 1958 to explain to him in more delicate terms why France could not embark on a secret and bilateral nuclear project with Germany, and that this would only infuriate the U.S.A. and poison German relations with Washington as well as those of France. He said that Strauss was very understanding.

PARIS, *November 20, 1964*

Had dinner last night with the Burin des Roziers [secretary-general of the Élysée]. Étienne told me there is a strong bond between de Gaulle and Malraux. It may sound curiously naive but the principal link is the same romantic patriotism. They share the same feeling for France. Malraux really had two careers—one as lover of the proletariat, one as lover of France. He still feels the proletarian pull.

De Gaulle is very vain. He doesn't like to wear glasses if he can help it. He just quickly glances at something with glasses and then takes them off. Another form of vanity shows on trips like that to South America, when he was conscientiously giving from his repertoire a few memorized speeches. He inserted into these Spanish phrases which he had meticulously learned.

PARIS, *November 23, 1964*

I spent yesterday with Couve de Murville playing golf and then lunching. On Saturday Couve lunched with Jean Monnet who said that all Britain was trying to do now was to keep its nuclear deterrent and have the U.S. pay for it. The future of sterling is a world problem because so much trade depends upon it and Couve doesn't see any escape from devaluation, although the ultimate results are hard to forecast.

Couve was very opposed to the Suez expedition from the start. He was ambassador in Bonn at the time of Suez. In 1959 he received Ben-Gurion at the *Quai d'Orsay.* Ben-Gurion said to him he understood that Couve had opposed Suez. Couve replied: "I am always opposed to failures." Ben-Gurion answered: "But it was not a failure; for Israel it was a success." Couve replied: "Yes, but it was a failure for France."

Couve says that de Gaulle thought the British were genuinely interested in coming into "Europe" at the time of the Champs meeting with Macmillan (June 1962). He thought something could be arranged to gain

British support in European defense. Couve says he himself never had any illusions but that de Gaulle was finally deceived at his Rambouillet meeting (in January 1963) with Macmillan and by the ensuing Nassau meeting.

When the British were talking about "joining Europe," they froze their policy for some time in the hope that de Gaulle would lose the French provincial elections but they were deceived.

Couve says he was not in the least surprised when Pope Paul VI refused to yield any power to the Ecumenical Council, causing a crisis this week. He says the Catholic Church must remain an autocracy or disappear. It was ridiculous to think of Pope Paul as a liberal. He also said that it was silly to think the church was well informed on world affairs; it is very badly informed.

Couve says the Nassau pact signaled a U.S. effort to grab control of the Royal Air Force and eventually of the French air force. The MLF is an attempt to insure U.S. control of France's nuclear force after de Gaulle disappears.

I asked Couve how he had learned to speak such impeccable English. He said he had had a Scottish governess and that afterward he had studied English at school and had spent two months in England *au pair* with Harold Nicolson. He says he knows English so well he can think in it.

PARIS, *December 3, 1964*

Had a good talk with [Undersecretary of State] George Ball today. He has been attending OECD [Organization for Economic Cooperation and Development] meetings but also had a long conversation with Couve yesterday. "There would be no difficulties in talking to Hanoi if they have something to say," Ball said. "There are plenty of open channels through which Hanoi can communicate."

He says a negotiated solution has always been contemplated by Washington but we must be sure that we can get something useful and pick the right moment for contacts.

He acknowledged that the threat of escalation was our primary trump. Hanoi clearly feared having its economy blown up and at the same time disliked the idea of a potential Chinese occupation.

Ball says that the Pentagon would definitely like to take the risk of escalation because, if the Chinese intervene at all, we could blow up their nuclear plant of Sinkiang.

I asked if we had ever discussed the question of the Chinese nuclear bomb with the Russians even in indirect or informal diplomatic talks. He said: "This has entered into casual conversations over a long period of time but obviously the Russians are not ready to talk with us about this for perfectly clear reasons, not any more than we would be prepared to talk to them about France's nuclear capacity."

Couve made it clear to Ball that France didn't want the Germans to have nuclear weapons in any form—above all so long as there is a divided Germany. (The implication is that Bonn might wish to use the weapons for reunification purposes.) France is determined to keep the Germans out of any form of nuclear club. We think this is a wrong approach and that it would generate complexes in Germany. We remember that between the two world wars nobody was able to keep the Germans from rearming.

The fundamental of de Gaulle's policy is that he wants France to be the only continental, West-European nation with atomic weapons. That would serve as symbol of French leadership.

PARIS, *December 11, 1964*

Lunched at Lucas Carton with Olivier Guichard. There is a strike of electricity and gas and of most public services like subways, taxis, and the post office. The *plats du jour* were prepared last night and kept warm today in their wood stoves. The place was lit by candles and kerosene lanterns.

Guichard is in charge of money-raising for the UNR (the so-called Gaullist party) and is also in charge of the political fortunes of Pompidou. He says it will require a minimum of six months—with de Gaulle's active participation in the country and on the television—to make Pompidou a successful candidate if de Gaulle decides not to run for reelection next year. Therefore he thinks de Gaulle will have to make up his mind by April. But nobody, including de Gaulle, has a clue yet as to what the decision will be.

De Gaulle's regular doctor is dead and his new physician has much less influence on him. Madame de Gaulle is opposed to his running again but she opposed his reentering politics after 1946. The Boissieus and the Vendroux, his son-in-law's and brother-in-law's families, are very much in favor of his running again. Madame Boissieu, de Gaulle's daughter, has a big influence on her papa but none of these matters are discussed in the family directly and nobody else has any close contacts with de Gaulle except Malraux, with whom he has long cultural but nonpolitical discussions.

PARIS, *December 15, 1964*

This afternoon I went over to see Dr. Martin Luther King on his way back to New York from Oslo where he received the Nobel Peace Prize. He is short and a warm brown, not black, with a moustache and a calm resonant voice. He was in shirtsleeves, most informal and cordial as we sat and chatted. He talks like most preachers. Once he begins to say something he rolls on and on, clearly fascinated by the sound of his own voice.

I asked King if he didn't think the American Negro community should contribute more to Africa financially, technically, culturally, and by personal volunteer service. I pointed out that the Irish-American, Italo-American, and Jewish-American communities had all in one or another way contributed as separate American communities to help Ireland, Italy, and Israel at various periods. It seemed to me that it was thus in accordance with the traditions of America's mixed society and mixed origins for the Negro community to play a more useful role in helping the new nations of Africa.

King replied that he certainly agreed. He said:

> The American Negro has not contributed enough of his resources to Africa in the effort to aid Africa in its struggle for a better and higher life. But there is more conscious support in their field than ever before. There is an awareness on our part of the paucity of our support to date.

> Just recently the civil rights leaders in the U.S.A. came together in what was known as civil rights leaders conferences on Africa. The first was in 1963 and there was another last September in which civil rights leaders met with leaders of other Negro community organizations to discuss ways of lending support to the whole of Africa. There is a growing realization that something more must be done and that we have many resources that could be most helpful.

> There has been a slowness to act along these lines for two reasons. The first is that for so many years the Negro in America was so ashamed of his heritage that he didn't want to identify himself with Africa. He wanted to forget anything that reminded him of his past. His thinking was negative and misinformed both on Africa and on its history. The second reason is that we have been so involved in our own struggle for racial justice and dignity in the U.S.A. that we have tended to forget our brothers and sisters in Africa.

> But it is obvious that until the problems of Africa are solved our problems will not be solved. This is due to the oneness of humanity and the fact that injustice anywhere means injustice everywhere. We can't live as an isolated island cut off from the mainstream. The forces of history compel us to do more.

> Certainly we can do something more financially, although by far the large financial support for Africa should come from the federal government. There should be a massive movement to urge more federal aid because there is a real need for a Marshall Plan for Africa.

> Until now the federal government has given much more support to Asia than to Africa and there is need for a far greater U.S. contribution to Africa. Our civil rights movement should urge such increased aid.

But there are certain things the Negroes can do in terms of private charity and private financial support. This must be developed on a much larger scale than the missionary channels used in the past in which the Negroes themselves through their churches have helped.

It is also important to get young people and trained older technicians from our community to go to Africa. One way to do this is through established channels like the Peace Corps. There should be more Negroes in the Peace Corps where they can contribute their skills to the development of Africa.

It is inevitable that there will be a much more structural arrangement for American Negro support, financial and technical, for the new African nations. And the African leaders welcome this. They want it.

PARIS, *December 17, 1964*

Lunched with Walter Eytan, Israeli ambassador here since 1960. He is a bright, attractive man in younger middle-age, quiet, serious but with a sense of humor.

I asked if it wasn't true that France, in the process of "normalizing" relations with the Arab world, was not also "normalizing" relations with Israel by downgrading it from the status of alliance. He said that when Prime Minister Eshkol came here last July he was worried about how he would be received; Eytan went with him to see de Gaulle.

The General started off the conversation before Eshkol had had a chance to say a single word by expressing his pleasure at receiving the prime minister of Israel, which France considered both a friend and an ally. Eytan said that you could almost hear Eshkol's sigh of relief.

When King Hussein was received by de Gaulle the General told him France would never tolerate an attack by Israel on Jordan or another Arab state; but France also would never tolerate an attack by Jordan or another Arab state on Israel. Hussein, of course, had no objection whatsoever to this and the word was passed on to Israel—which was delighted.

PARIS, *December 21, 1964*

I lunched with Gaston Palewski, minister of state in charge of scientific research and atomic and space questions. He gave me an excellent lunch, tête-à-tête, in the dining room of his office in the ministry of marine looking out on the Place de la Concorde. I wonder if the French navy eats like that. We were served by sailors: *rouget, pintade* with a compote of prunes, salad of endives and fresh almonds, cheese and a half pineapple filled with fruit, whipped cream, and liqueur, plus two wines.

Palewski admits the cost of the Pierrelatte nuclear establishment has exceeded original estimates by fifteen percent but this rise had been foreseen in budgets and caused absolutely no trouble. The French and Germans are working together on special weapons at St. Louis and at one point Gaston admitted that they included nuclear devices. He said that the Germans are determined some day to have their own nuclear weapons but France is standing by Bonn's treaty commitment not to manufacture or possess them on German soil.

He said a very responsible German had told him that Bonn's policy is as follows: some day U.S. troops will be withdrawn and Russian troops will be withdrawn from East Germany. Then Bonn will foment a *coup d'état* in East Germany and reunify. At this point Germany will depend on the U.S. nuclear umbrella to prevent Russia from spoiling the game. Gaston is very worried.

He says Israel has confided to France its suspicion that Egypt is manufacturing a radiation "garbage bomb" but has said nothing about Indian aid. He says that Israel hopes to make its own nuclear weapons but it is a difficult thing and they are running into trouble.

Palewski says there is no way to prevent other countries from making nuclear weapons—above all, once laser developments provide a shortcut to fusion. No one can tell when this will happen, either in a few days or in thirty-five years. But it is probable that it will come before too long because the scientific revolution is speeding up so much. Once there is a shortcut to fusion weapons it is almost impossible that we can prevent the destruction of the earth.

9

IN INDOCHINA
THE GROUND IS ROTTEN

I SPENT AN HOUR WITH DE GAULLE THIS AFTERNOON. HE WAS IN A marvelous mood: brisk, chipper, funny, sarcastic. I ran out of questions and finally felt somewhat embarrassedly that I really ought to wish him a Merry Christmas, get up and go, which is exactly what happened. I think perhaps this was a mistake because he seemed ready to gas on.

I came early in order to see Georges Galichon and say hello. I was immediately ushered in to the aide-de-camp's room instead of being made to wait in the antechamber as usual. The aide-de-camp, a young naval commander with hair *en brosse*, asked if I would mind coming into the cabinet room. It was explained that there was someone with the General next door and they didn't want anybody to see me.

The cabinet room is, I should guess, about forty feet by twenty-five feet in size, dominated by a large oval table covered with an orange-brown baize cloth. On top of this in the center is a long strip of green and gold brocade. There are fourteen chairs plus two armchairs around the table. These are of dark maroon velvet with gilded wood. In the center is an ormolu clock facing what must be de Gaulle's armchair—it has its back to the fireplace. The walls are of green and gold brocade and the doors to the room are all painted a rather pleasant light green. In addition to tapestry there are two bad paintings by Robert and Bidault, eighteenth- and nineteenth-century French painters. In the fireplace are real logs but clearly it is never used. On the mantelpiece are two hideous black-winged angels bearing candelabras filled with real candles. There were large, leather-covered blotters in front of de Gaulle's and the other armchair, which I presume is Pompidou's. On the table in a corner, where I assume a stenographer sits, were piles of pads and individual blotters.

Galichon came in to see me and told me if de Gaulle asked if I was going away I should tell him I was going immediately because Galichon had insisted he should see me now because of my impending departure. Galichon also told me to be absolutely sure not to tell anybody I was seeing de Gaulle today. There seemed to be something particularly mysterious about the procedure.

The naval officer came back and beckoned me into the General's office.

As usual, de Gaulle got up, shook hands, waved me to a seat across from him at his desk and said, "Naturally," when I said I wanted to ask him some questions. He looked pale and had a shrewd if not wicked gleam in his eyes behind his spectacles. He was wearing a dark grey flannel, double-breasted suit. I spread out my notes on my side of the desk, hauled out my notebook and pencil, and dove right in.

I started by asking him what he foresaw for 1969 when the North Atlantic Treaty expires. Did he foresee a new kind of treaty organization? Or a renewed general alliance? Or some other kind of agreement?

Obviously he loved this subject. It was terribly hard for me to ever get him off it. He said: "Another organization, of course. There is an alliance and that should be conserved. The alliance is necessary. Obviously a certain number of states, such as the U.S.A. and France, should commit themselves to help each other in case of war. But the organization that has been based upon the North Atlantic Treaty, NATO, will not be maintained. We must make a simpler and different arrangement, not an integration. It is not necessary to have the kind of machinery that now exists, a pyramid of staffs and budgeteers. That is useless.

"The organization ends in 1969 and before then we must decide on another kind of organization to replace it or there will be none. France will not agree to keep NATO."

I asked if it were true there was a plan drawn up by his staff envisaging some kind of Western European treaty organization connected with NATO. He said: "It is not impossible that one might be brought about but certainly not now. First, we must have a political organization of Europe. We are on our way to make an economic organization of the Common Market. But this has not yet been made.

"In reality the Common Market is merely a miniature commercial treaty of six states. These six states have ended internal custom duties between them or are ending them and are adopting a common policy toward other states but that is all. Not even this has been made yet although I believe now that it will lead to something.

"But there is no political organization in Europe and I don't know if one will be made. Certainly not yet. And for a European defense organization you would need some kind of a political organization. And by that I don't mean such strange ideas as the MLF, which the Germans recommended.

"Maybe someday there will be a European organization and then a European defense arrangement. But there is no political organization yet. Two years ago we proposed something and even that was very elementary —the Fouchet plan. But for various reasons the others didn't want this. England was not included and there were still other reasons which made this start displeasing to others. They didn't feel the defense aspect depended sufficiently on NATO. But it remains as a project if it is wanted —even though it is very elementary.

"The idea of any common organization in Europe is not yet very vigorous. After all, in order to have a European policy there must first be agreement among European countries on what one policy they want—especially for themselves. It is very difficult to make a political organization if you don't have a policy. But everywhere there is disagreement. For example, not one country is politically in accord on Germany.

"Dulles had a German policy. You could identify his policy. He wanted a big strong NATO that was very integrated. And then he wanted to threaten Russia so that it would draw back and accept the unity of Germany. But the Russians didn't draw back. They rearmed instead. So the problem remains.

"At present the misfortune of German partition is not really a very serious concern. A reunited Germany would be very dangerous because the East would never accept it. There would be an immediate risk of war. Reunification is out of the question."

Throughout our conversation I found de Gaulle harping upon the German menace and insisting that German unity was completely *hors de question*.

I asked if it were true that relations between France and the U.S.A. were easier now as a result of the NATO meeting, his talks with Rusk, our announced willingness to share intelligence information on Soviet defenses, and agreement in principle to discuss joint targeting in defense plans. De Gaulle didn't seem impressed, rather to my surprise. He said: "Why is there more understanding now? I have always explained my viewpoint. I have never made any secret of it.

"But until now U.S. policy toward Europe has been one of integration, of domination—naturally *à la manière démocratique*. I recognize that since World War II this was a natural development, because of the immense power of the U.S.A. after the war and because of the direct menace of Russia to Europe. I recognize the effort you put into such projects as the Marshall Plan. It was natural that the U.S.A. should wish to exercise a hegemony over Europe.

"But it is no longer natural that this should continue. Now such hegemony is becoming artificial. The Soviet menace is now much less.

And the European countries have resumed, have restored, a stability—not power but stability. Above all this is economic. Germany and France have an economic stability." (De Gaulle kept using the word *"consistence"* but the best definition I can get out of the dictionary really means "stability" or "firmness.")

"Now the American protectorate is less justified. Nevertheless, the possibility of a war remains. This is inescapable. Therefore we must preserve an alliance between Europe and the U.S.A., above all between France and the U.S.A. But we want an alliance, not a protectorate. A protectorate is impossible. Little by little the U.S.A. will see that this change has come. It is in no one's interest to impose a system that simply will not work anymore.

"The U.S.A. will recognize the changed circumstances and will change its attitude, above all vis-à-vis France. It will accept France as independent. But independence does not prevent friendship, or alliance. This is what the U.S.A. will realize. If France wants to make nuclear weapons it *will*.

"We must not exaggerate things. At this time France is only starting its atomic force. It is just starting. It is still almost nothing. It will only be relatively important in four or five years.

"But at that time, if the U.S.A. and France are still allied—which I hope—and allied in a normal way, then the two general staffs, or better yet the two governments, will work together and will draw up arrangements so that they can help each other in case of any war *in which they are both involved*, and will decide how to divide up possible targets.

"This is the normal method among allies. But it is not integration. France will not accept integration. It is a question of the coordination of two policies—if the two governments want to work it out together."

In terms of the long-range future, at what time approximately did he think Europe would be strong enough to defend itself and would not have to depend on U.S. protection? He answered, "I don't see that for years and years to come. For years and years the alliance will be needed. We must be explicitly allied. This is necessary because the Soviet menace remains even if it is less than it has been in the past.

"Russia is not now preparing to attack us and the U.S.A. is not preparing to attack Russia, but no one can tell what the situation will be in ten years. Who even knows what Russia will be then? We have seen great changes, you and I, even though you are younger than I. We have seen the Weimar Republic and then it was replaced by Hitler's Germany. We have seen great changes in Russia.

"Certainly the alliance as an alliance and not as an organization must continue for years. It is very useful. But do not forget the East is changing. [By the East he means the USSR and its satellites.] Externally it is changing toward peace and *détente* and internally it is changing toward liberty.

It is good to encourage contacts and peaceful arrangements and it is possible to imagine some distant day when an alliance may no longer be necessary. But that day cannot be imagined soon.

"However, the question of the organization of an alliance is a different thing and this must be it. It is not necessary to think that the U.S. forces stationed in Europe will be needed very much longer. The U.S.A.'s power is not represented by its divisions in Germany. It is represented by its nuclear strength and that is in the U.S.A.

"Such nuclear strength as you have in Europe now is only here because you have U.S. divisions here. But one day these divisions will go and then your nuclear weapons will go. We must look ahead to the future."

I then asked the General if he didn't think the moment propitious for a meeting with President Johnson at some time relatively early in 1965. He raised his eyebrows, looked sceptical, spread his long arms, shrugged his shoulders, and said, "That depends. What do you expect? Would it only be a contact between chiefs of state to talk together amiably or to explain to each other their views and aims as between friends and allies? That would be very useful. President Kennedy's visit to Paris was very useful, although at the moment perhaps he did not see this. If President Kennedy had not been assassinated, if he had lived, that contact between us would have been shown to be more and more useful. You know there had been arrangements for me to see him. I was going to see him last March for a new talk. In such conditions personal discussions are very useful. But there must be enough time. And one must not look for spectacular changes, miracles, or altered policies. If that is the case, no. Nothing can be arranged in such a meeting. If President Johnson wants to come he will be very well received by me. No, not by me, he will be very well received by France, just as President Kennedy was very well received by France."

Would France accept financial or technical aid from any other European country—such as Germany—to help build its nuclear force? "No," he replied categorically. "We will give our bombs to no one and we will accept aid from no one."

I asked if France envisaged the possibility of German reunification so long as Moscow retains any form of satellite control over Eastern Europe. Again quite categorically he said, "No, that would mean war. Germany can only be reunified in the foreseeable future by war. Neither Russia nor its satellites, the Poles, the Czechs, or the Rumanians, will ever accept German unification under anything resembling present conditions. That would lead to the abyss.

"Europe remembers all too well the danger of Germany. This memory remains in the popular mind. And people are stronger than regimes. If the tsars still ruled in Russia they would oppose German reunification just as the communists do. The same is true of Poland. This fear of Germany and German reunification holds the Eastern countries together. And we French also suffered enormously from the Germans. We will not accept any terms for German unification that are not also acceptable to the East. German unification can only come some day when a European equilibrium is assured and built around it. There is no question of this now. Perhaps some day. But who can foresee the future?"

I asked de Gaulle if he still considered valid his earlier phrase about a Europe from the Atlantic to the Urals. He said he did and that as the "Eastern regimes change and liberalize their internal policy while applying an external policy of peace such a development would gradually permit an East-West arrangement covering all Europe."

I asked if he thought there was any value in the idea of a nonaggression pact between NATO and the Warsaw Alliance. He said, "This has no interest. Pacts mean nothing. I don't see enough change yet in Europe to give any value to the idea of such a pact. After all, we must remember that Russia has signed many pacts in the past—and then denounced them. For Russia and for the Eastern countries a pact under present conditions is meaningless. It is all right to do business, to trade, make exchanges, but not pacts. One cannot make pacts now or under present conditions."

I asked de Gaulle if France had offered its good offices to the U.S.A. to settle the Vietnam crisis. He said, "Yes, of course. We proposed what we could. We proposed to organize a conference that would discuss all the problems involved. This would seek to neutralize all of southeast Asia. But we have made no other proposal since.

"We told the Americans—you cannot succeed in Indochina. The ground is rotten [*le terrain est pourri*]. It is impossible. We in France know. We failed and you will fail.

"Naturally, you can continue the present system. A strong rich power can stay in by one or another way, using one or another general as your leader in South Vietnam; but that doesn't help. Things continue to get worse and worse.

"Or you can make war. You can make war on North Vietnam. Or you can make war on China. You can even start a world war. But is it worth it? Is it even worth it just in North Vietnam alone? Why would it be worth it? To continue the system that now exists in South Vietnam? That would not be a good policy.

"The best thing would be to have a conference as we suggested, a conference including China. This at least could neutralize Laos, Cambodia, and Vietnam—and then we could see what would happen next."

I then asked him what he thought about the Congo situation. He answered, "Do you consider it dangerous?" I said I thought it was very dangerous. He interjected: "dangerous for the Congo."

"There was a U.S. and Belgian intervention to save the white people there. I don't disapprove of this. But it doesn't settle the situation. It just helped the hostages. And surely they are better off in Belgium than they were in the Congo.

"France is very reserved on this affair. Our idea is that it is the very nature of the Congo to be anarchic and this nature will not change. The Congolese can change themselves someday perhaps and we should help them change. We should help them find the means to exist, to organize an administration. We French can help in this respect. You know Tshombe came to see me and he asked administrative help. We have sent him some.

"But as for politics—no. We must not interfere in the Congo. The Congolese must settle the question themselves and it will take a long, long time.

"There won't be any more direct Chinese or Soviet intervention in the Congo than direct U.S. intervention. But there is bound to be a continued indirect intervention by both sides. It is inevitable in an anarchy.

"But these interventions won't go too far. There is no pressure or danger in a global sense. Certainly things are not pretty in the Congo but what do we want?

"The world has learned to live with such problems. For centuries there have been similar situations. There have been revolts in China, famines in India, revolutions in Latin America, but the world has survived. And we cannot intervene everywhere. I repeat, France is very reserved on the Congo."

By this time almost an hour had passed and I was afraid he might want to ease me out but he was very relaxed and seemed to want to talk more. I asked him if he had enjoyed his Latin American trip and he said very much indeed. He said, "You know, I didn't know Latin America. Before I had only been to Guiana. There are many Latin Americas. It is a very diversified area with many regions that differ strongly. The thing that really struck me most was the diversity of the continent. And there is very little liaison between the different regions. I understand the difficulties of your country in trying to help the area develop. It is so huge and disorganized and yet it has vast resources such as oil, minerals, fertile land, timber. But very few of the countries are organized and most have no conception of organization."

I told de Gaulle I had recently seen Castro and he asked me a few questions about him. He said Castro wasn't really a communist and that the U.S.A. should show more calm and reserve about Cuba. "Don't get all excited," he said.

He then continued in a kind of "thinking aloud monologue." He said: "The principal thing is that no one wants war. There is no Hitler now. There are many differences among the countries but I don't see any evil figure who wants to start a war. Not even in China. The Chinese don't want a war now.

"Of course we can't tell what will be the case in ten or twenty years. Maybe China or maybe Russia or maybe even the U.S.A. might someday want a war. But not now and not for a long time to come.

"Therefore in such conditions, people shouldn't get excited. We must stay calm.

"There is no point in suggesting difficult and provocative formulas such as the MLF. That does no good. There was no point to the MLF.

"France is not trying to dominate any situation. We stick to our own road and we are not offering any dangerous or provocative proposals.

"We make our bombs—yes. But these are not for export and they are not for attack. They are for our independence—only that."

At approximately that point de Gaulle looked at me with a glint in his eyes and said, "You know, I read all your articles. I read the *New York Times* every day. Of course I don't read the New York edition but I read the International Edition of the *New York Times* and the *New York Herald Tribune*; also the *London Daily Telegraph*. I asked him what he thought of the *New York Times*. He said, "It is very malicious toward me. It is malicious toward France. [He used the word *malveillant*.] All through 1964 it has been malicious toward me and France although now it is getting a little better.

"But I am used to that. All the French press is just the same. It is also malicious. It doesn't bother me, I assure you it doesn't bother me."

PARIS, *January 3, 1965*

Spent the New Year's weekend with the (General Pierre) Billottes at Pont-Sainte-Maxence. Billotte says Guy Mollet made a final and firm decision that France should manufacture nuclear weapons in late 1956 after the Suez disaster. Originally, the project had been voted as a tentative decision in 1954 by the Mendès-France government but it was dropped in 1955 under Edgar Faure. Mollet revived it.

Billotte told me his mother, who was then in Cannes, received two telegrams at the same moment in May 1940, both from General Weygand. One announced Pierre's promotion in the *Légion d'Honneur*; the other announced his father's death. His father was one of the best-known generals in France and might have ended up as commander-in-chief had he lived.

Sybil Billotte was first married to an Italian fascist from Florence who had taken part in the march on Rome. She was completely innocent of politics when she arrived in Italy. Her mother-in-law said she must join the Fascist party. "What's that?" she asked. "Why it's Mussolini's party," was the answer. "Who's he?" Sybil asked.

She says that every day in the spring and summer she and other Roman society women would lunch on the beach with Dino Alfieri and other fascist leaders. The government bosses would stay there until 4:00 P.M. and then go home to take a nap. They went to their offices just long enough to check in before changing for dinner at 8:00. "No wonder they couldn't run the country," says Sybil. Alfieri used to tap the telephones of all the women to know what they were saying about other women and him, and then would tease them about it.

PARIS, *January 6, 1965*

Drinks yesterday evening with Averell Harriman who came into town yesterday and is leaving this afternoon for London. He must be almost seventy-four now and he doesn't look a day over sixty. His only concession to age is a little transistor hearing aid.

Averell says a heavy amount of communist and Egyptian armaments have been sent to the Congo rebels now. Furthermore the French are having trouble with their own Congo (Brazzaville) regime. It is too bad de Gaulle didn't feel able to pull another Gabon coup in Brazzaville.

Whatever happens, Harriman insists it is necessary that Tshombe keep his white mercenaries.

Averell is convinced that Alexandr Nikolaevich Shelepin is going to win the power struggle in Moscow and will end up as the next real boss.

ROME, *January 9, 1965*

Tea with Herbert Blankenhorn, German ambassador. Blankenhorn blames everything wrong on de Gaulle. He says it's his fault that there is a vibrant new nationalism in Germany. This is headed by young reserve officers and students who are pro-Gaullist in the sense of "If he can do it, why can't we?" Germany will swing loose from integrated allied ties, become neutralist, and make its own deal with Russia to get unity and Eastern markets.

We then talked about Italy and Blankenhorn was gloomy. There is probably no way to stop a take-over, before another year, by a popular front, followed by the legal gain of control by the communists. Italy is in its worst political crisis since 1948.

The "Opening to the Left" has flopped as a strategy—unless one wants to include the communists! There is no future for a left-oriented government without communist support—and the communists' demands will rise as a price. Because there is a less perceptible Soviet menace, there is no longer a U.S. policy to intervene to keep Italy from going communist.

ROME, *January 10, 1965*

Last night Luigi Barzini gave us a dinner party at his farm outside Rome. Luigi started things off by saying the Christian Democratic party is like a dead whale washed up on the beach and stinking up the atmosphere.

Italy has all the problems of a developed country—big cities, inadequate planning—and also of an underdeveloped country. Its two fundamental conditions are poverty and illiteracy—cabinet ministers who don't read books, an illiterate elite.

How can this be fought? The only thing the Italians should do is reconstruct the state and make whatever state they think would satisfy current needs: a rule of law, an honest bureaucracy. This would rid Italy of the communist menace, which is the product of poverty, illiteracy, an Ottoman bureaucracy, and a shambles state.

The Christian Democrats *can't* reconstruct the state—they can't even make it function. The church believes that it can prosper more in a decaying, weak state than in a strong state. It is wrong—as can be seen from the way it flourishes in the U.S.A. But it has nevertheless had this belief for centuries.

ROME, *January 11, 1965*

Dined last night with Jozsef Szall, the Hungarian ambassador here. He and his wife (a rather pretty young photographer who earns almost as much as he—from the Hungarian Telegraphic Agency) took us to the Osteria del Orso, the most lavish and expensive restaurant in Rome.

He is a good communist but with a strong nationalist tinge, above all when the word Rumania is mentioned. Her communism seems skin-deep. She denounced the former dictator, Mátyás Rákosi, strongly and says Jozsef still defends him because he simply didn't know what Rákosi was doing. And she says Rumanian persecution of the Hungarian minority and the Jews is now worse than it was under the royalists or fascists in Bucharest.

Jozsef knows Kadar well. Janos Kadar was in the interior ministry at the time of the Rajk trial. He was arrested in the latter days of Stalin when "national" communists were being rounded up. Kadar had been in Hungary during the war, was not a "Muscovite." He was terribly tortured while in jail but doesn't show it externally.

Jozsef told me this joke: At an international conference there is a shortage of accommodation and the Soviet and English foreign ministers have to share the same hotel room. The Russian commits suicide so the Englishman is interrogated. He says, "When we arrived at the airport we were advised we would have to share a room. I nodded politely, as is our custom, and the Russian looked unhappy, as is their custom.

"We were invited to a reception so I put on a dinner jacket, as is our custom, and the Russian put on his yellow shoes, blue suit, and red tie, as is their custom.

"When we came home to retire, I put on pyjamas, as is our custom, and he stripped to his underpants, as is their custom.

"Just as we were going to sleep there was a knock on the door. 'It's the police,' said a voice. So I went to the door and opened it and invited them to come in, as is our custom. But the Russian went to the window and jumped, as is their custom."

ROME, *January 12, 1965*

Armand Bérard, the French ambassador, says the French notion of a state with a centralized regime has existed since King Francis I, but there is no such notion here [in Italy]. The central government is not the ultimate factor and one cannot apply Cartesian logic as in France.

Italy is like a cat—when you throw it out of the window it isn't killed, it lands on its feet. The people are enormously intelligent. And having had no central administration of an efficient sort, they know how to scramble. In other countries, when things get very bad, the state must intervene; not here. The parliament is comic, ridiculous, with all its games and conspiracies.

In Umbria or Tuscany the situation is like in Poland; the population is largely anticommunist, but everything is run by the communists: the unions, cooperatives, municipalities, commerce, stores, hotels, cafes. The party earns money from this; and any youngster seeking to get ahead must join the party. Nevertheless, the tottering Rome government will continue.

In every Italian village there are only two forces—the Communist party and the church. The church must pursue a slightly leftist policy but not that of John XXIII, who went too far toward the Russians, thus helping the communists here.

PARIS, *February 3, 1965*

Lunched with Chip Bohlen. Chip says de Gaulle is going to try to undercut the dollar as a world currency and in effect try to return the world to a pure gold standard represented by some new symbolic currency as yet unnamed. De Gaulle's idea, stimulated by Jacques Rueff, is to have a group of the wealthiest nations agree to make gold deposits in Basel to support this concept.

BONN, *February 5, 1965*

Excellent and very friendly talk with former Chancellor Adenauer in the office that is provided him as a courtesy in the Bundesrat Building. Adenauer, who is now eighty-nine, looked remarkably well. He is just a tiny bit thinner and paler and a suspicion shorter than when I last saw him. He walked with great agility, getting up to pick things off his desk and bring them back. He had a firm handshake and I noticed that his large hands are unusually youthful for a man of his age. He was humorous, alert, and full of twinkle.

I asked what he thought of the policy of President Johnson. He said: "One interesting aspect of your political system is that the president is elected by the people but is not answerable to them. He is both chief of state and chief of government. Your press is therefore called upon to play a more important role than in other democratic countries. The president often deals with matters through the press, whereas a prime minister in another country would answer questions in parliament.

"Thinking over the past few years it occurs to me how relatively short a time there has been to have so many changes in the personality of your president. You have had Eisenhower, Kennedy, and Johnson—all inside of twelve years. I feel that sometimes this change in personalities is reflected in U.S. policy. After all, these three men—Eisenhower, Kennedy, and Johnson—are all completely different in type. Let me explain why I now have a mistrust for U.S. policy.

"While Kennedy was still president, our military leaders thought no European defense would be possible without medium range rockets [MRBMs]. The United States was hesitant in its position on this. You people did not want the MRBM. But when I paid my first call on President Kennedy he discussed this at length and I suggested that he should instruct General [Maxwell D.] Taylor, who was then chairman of your joint chiefs of staff, to talk over the matter with General Adolf Heusinger, who was then in Washington representing us on the NATO military committee.

"Taylor and Heusinger studied the matter and they came up with an agreement on the necessity of MRBMs. The next meeting I had with President Kennedy, I told him General Heusinger had reported to me that he and Taylor agreed on the necessity of these weapons in Europe. Kennedy confirmed that General Taylor had told him the same thing. We both, therefore, agreed that MRBMs were needed for European defense.

"Nevertheless, nothing was ever done about this. Your government never took any action. There was never even a serious effort to build the weapons we had decided were necessary. Although I had come back to Bonn reassured by what President Kennedy told me, nothing happened. And now—as a result—Europe is defenseless. If Russia wants, their tanks can roll to the Atlantic Ocean through Germany and France. You can see why there are reasons for the scepticism I have developed."

He then said: "The United States administration doesn't seem to be aware that the greatest danger to the United States remains in Western Europe, not elsewhere. Washington pays far too little attention to this fact. You are the biggest and most powerful country. You should take the lead in fixing up NATO and in making certain of the defenses of the West.

But nothing happens. Of course there is an unpleasant situation in South Vietnam and, unfortunately, I am sure it will get worse. But this is an area of secondary importance to you.

"Look at Western Europe as it must appear from Moscow and through Soviet eyes. The day will come when de Gaulle will no longer be here. And the communists are clearly preparing to install a popular front in France. Since 1946 the Communist party has been the biggest and best organized party in France.

"In Moscow it is perfectly clear that the Russians figure that the day will come when communism—or a communist control group—will take over in France. And on that day, what can Germany do, sandwiched between a popular front government in France and the Russians?

"Do you believe that simply because the Communist party has been outlawed here, there are no communists? Why there are at least twenty thousand agents who have come across into Western Germany from the Soviet Zone. And Italy is clearly swinging to the Left. The danger of a popular front is strong in Italy.

"If France, Italy, and Germany all fall behind Soviet policy, it would be the end for the United States. The Soviet Union would be the strongest nation in the world. I don't mean that these three countries would become satellites but they would follow Russian policy."

I asked Adenauer what he would recommend that we should do, if he saw things in such a gloomy way? Adenauer replied: "The first thing is to show a greater interest in Western Europe and a greater interest in NATO. What is it worth even if you should be able to hold on in Vietnam if you risk losing Western Europe while you do so? There is a lack of American interest and of American leadership now. Some people claim that America tried to assert leadership in the whole MLF affair. But I never believed it was possible to accomplish anything with the MLF."

I asked what he thought Germany had gained in a concrete sense by its treaty of special alliance with France. He answered: "In defense policy the interest of neighboring states are identical. If Germany survives a war, France will. And vice versa. This is the main reason for our community of interests. Without an agreement between France and Germany, no European union would ever be possible.

"De Gaulle told me often that if we Germans were attacked, France would be at our side from the start with all its might because, de Gaulle insisted, France must be defended in Germany. Nevertheless we never deceived ourselves. Even with French nuclear capacity and a German conventional capacity, the two of us alone could never withstand a Soviet attack. We are too weak. But we would hope that in such a conflict the United States would be compelled to throw in its nuclear capacity immediately on our behalf."

He continued: "My policy has always been based upon the two following ideas. The relationship between Russia and China would develop in such a way that Russia would be pleased to have no enemies in the West and would therefore feel free to turn its attention increasingly toward the East. Secondly I felt it was quite obvious that the Soviet Union was having increasing economic difficulties. I thought it would be folly to help Russia solve these economic difficulties unless the Russians made concessions on their side.

"Unfortunately the democracies have not taken advantage of the latter situation. First the British Conservative government sent supplies to the Russians. Then the Americans sent their wheat, asking for no counter-concessions. This was a capital folly on the part of the British and the Americans. It makes it much easier for a dictatorship to produce a foreign policy in such circumstances. A dictatorship can avoid internal economic pressure. But the businessmen in a democracy want to make money and that is dominant. Then they put pressure on their government. First this happened in Britain, then in America, then in France. Now the same thing is being repeated as our own industry exerts pressure on our government.

"Don't make any mistake. I don't want the Russians to starve. But I see no reason to send them factories unless they make concessions to us in exchange.

"When President Kennedy was still alive I told de Gaulle: 'You simply must go to Washington. The situation has changed and you must go and talk to Kennedy. You must stay at least a week and you must bring Madame de Gaulle along with you.' After thinking for a few moments about what I had said, de Gaulle agreed. But unfortunately President Kennedy was murdered.

"Then, later on, de Gaulle invited President Johnson to meet him at Martinique. But Johnson, quite rudely, said no. He said he could not leave the country. He made no other explanations. He offered no counter-proposal.

"De Gaulle is a highly intelligent man. He is just as well aware as I am of the fact that without the United States Europe would be lost. And I repeat to you what I said earlier, it is in Western Europe that the United States has its Achilles heel."

He continued: "Why have the Russians kept their hold so obstinately on the East Zone [of Germany]? It is for no reason except as bait to attract the Federal Republic. If France were to go communist, to fall to a popular front, and West Germany were between France and Russia, what should we do if the Russians offered some kind of false terms for unification with that East Zone bait?

"Certainly up to now the danger of right-wing extremists among German people has been insignificant. Nevertheless, you can never forget that over the last several decades the German people have not been mentally well balanced. Therefore their reactions are unpredictable. After all, we have lost two great wars. There was the Weimar Republic, which was not particularly excellent. And then came the Nazi terror followed by the ghastly second war which left this country destroyed and partitioned. And now, remarkably, we have regained prosperity. There has been too much change accomplished in too short a time."

Adenauer went on: "When a nation is forced to fight a very distant war, as you are doing in Vietnam, there are certain psychological limits easily reached. People get fed up. And if you people get fed up because of your Vietnam war that will mean a return to isolationism.

"My only hope is that the American people awaken in time to the real danger here and become more concerned. This is not the danger of today —but of the day after tomorrow."

I asked him who was the greatest man he had encountered. Without hesitation, he got up and went over to his desk. He picked up a photograph of John Foster Dulles descending from the ramp of an airplane on his last visit here in 1959, with Adenauer standing at the bottom of the ramp to greet him. He handed me the picture. "There," he said. I then asked "Why was he the greatest?" Adenauer replied: "He thought clearly. He thought ahead, with visions of what was coming; and he kept his word. He kept his promises."

BONN, *February 8, 1965*

Today I spent two and a half hours with Franz-Josef Strauss, former minister of defense and head of the Bavarian branch of the Catholic party, the CSU.

After chatting in his office, we went out to a Chinese restaurant where Strauss devoured huge amounts of rice and a very poor lobster curry.

He said: "We have a feeling that now again there are some contacts between the United States and France—and maybe the United Kingdom— to establish a kind of a *directoire* along the lines that de Gaulle originally wanted. And de Gaulle emphasized very strongly to Erhard at Rambouillet that he will never abandon the U.S. nuclear guarantee. He considers his *force de frappe* [France's nuclear weapon program] as an additional psychological deterrent. We agree that it is a good thing to add this incalculable element as a further deterrent."

I asked if he favored de Gaulle's idea of "Europeanizing" the question of the German reunification. Strauss answered: "This is the only possible approach under prevailing conditions. I do not feel particularly optimistic about it, but there isn't any other choice. There is no possibility of using force to achieve reunification."

Strauss said: "A long time ago the Western powers ceased pressing Russia to fulfill its commitments. Look at the Geneva conference of 1955.

Bulganin and Khrushchev went to Geneva in order to find out whether the United States was ready to take a risk on the subject of Berlin and Germany. They found out that America was not prepared to take such a risk. In Berlin, the Russians blandly ignored the Geneva communiqué. By autumn 1955, at the foreign ministers' conference, it became clear that the Russians regarded this as a dead letter. And the Hungarian events in 1956 proved the rightness of the Soviet conclusions.

"We feel and fear that Washington is planning a progressive demilitarization of the European continent. This would seem to envision the withdrawal from Europe of U.S. nuclear delivery systems and the conversion of aircraft to purely conventional purposes."

Strauss said the first defense agreement between Israel and Germany had been completed before he left the defense ministry in January 1963. This concerned training Israelis, the dispatch of small arms and giving general military advice. The more recent agreement under which U.S. tanks were being sent from Germany to Israel was the third agreement. "After all, Israel cannot be expected to defend itself on words alone. This is part of our restitution—in a practical sense."

Dinner tonight with military leaders. General Heusinger, now retired; Brigadier General Wolfgang Köstlin, head of the Department of Internal Leadership (*Innere Führung*) on the *Bundeswehr* staff; and Richard Balken, foreign minister, Gerhard Schroeder's liaison with both the cabinet and parliament.

Heusinger said several groups of people—but above all the British— were pushing the idea of gradually removing missiles from Europe as a sort of disengagement. This favored the concept of a missile fleet.

He said de Gaulle's conception was ridiculous because France could not force the U.S.A. to use strategic nuclear weapons merely by pulling the trigger of the *force de frappe*. If de Gaulle were to strike at Russia, the Russians could immediately announce that they would use their nuclear missiles not against the U.S. but only against France. That would leave us in the position of having to make the initial decision to strike Russia.

He tended to reckon that if de Gaulle dies, the *force de frappe* would also die. The French were having a very difficult time financing this endeavor. The French calculate the only deterrent is the threat of massive retaliation. This is wrong. The Russians know that real massive retaliation —from the United States—would only be employed by Washington as a last resort, never at the very start. Furthermore Heusinger said it was impossible for a military man to give his political leaders only one option for strategy in case of war. There must be at least three options: a conventional reply, a conventional reply plus a limited atomic reply, and an all-out strategic reply.

In July 1914 the Kaiser told his chief of staff, [Helmuth] von Moltke, he thought German forces in east Prussia were too weak and he wanted to send six more divisions there. Moltke answered him: "Majesty, I am not prepared for such a situation. If you demand six divisions in east Prussia, I will not be able to carry out my plan in eastern France." A general can never be wholly committed to a single plan without any possible alternative.

Heusinger said: "I think it is not impossible that a war could start and then at the very beginning the Soviets would declare they would use only conventional weapons. What would the West do under such circumstances? That is why I so strongly support development of conventional weapons." Heusinger said France has a backward strategy. France cannot rebuild its divisions, pledged to both its own and NATO's defense, until 1969. France had pledged seven divisions to NATO. But all it has is two weak divisions in Germany.

The Russians would immediately be able to distinguish between a U.S. or a French nuclear strike. The path of missiles can easily be traced. Secondly there would be a tremendous difference between a French strike and a U.S. strike, even when the French have gotten to the stage of having missiles of their own. Any U.S. strike would be infinitely larger.

I talked at some length with General Köstlin about the *Innere Führung*, or internal leadership program in the army. I asked how the whole question of divided loyalties as in the July 20, 1944, anti-Hitler plot was now handled in his teaching to the armed forces. Köstlin said: "We acknowledge that every officer must decide what he should defend and that this was the case in 1944. Did he owe allegiance to the government or did he owe a greater allegiance to humanity? A good deal of this depended on how much information the individual had. We know that most officers and soldiers placed in a difficult situation like this know too little to be able to judge for themselves."

BONN, *February 9, 1965*

This morning I spent an hour with Chancellor [Ludwig] Erhard. He has a turgid and tedious way of expressing himself.

I asked Erhard exactly what he and de Gaulle had discussed in terms of elaborating a common defense policy. Erhard replied: "De Gaulle made it clear he recognizes that only the nuclear power of the United States insures the protection and freedom of Western Europe. Furthermore, he told me he considered vital for Germany that United States troops should be kept here.

"Of course we do not think of any new organization outside NATO. But we would like to develop Europe's own views inside NATO. And there are other aspects to a common defense program such as the development of common arms manufacture systems."

I asked whether any German regime at any time had offered to accept the Oder-Neisse line as a permanent eastern frontier in exchange for reunification on the basis of free self-determination of East Germany.

Erhard answered: "No German government could be expected to make such an offer. The East Zone has always stated that any talks on the subject of reunification can only be on the basis that the two states are first recognized as independent sovereign countries. They want this first. This is their precondition. They have also stated that reunification can only be on the basis of the East being a communist state."

Long talk with Berthold Beitz, managing director of Krupp. Krupp is entirely owned by Alfried Krupp von Bohlen and Halbach, but Beitz is boss; he has *pleins pouvoirs* to do anything he wants.

Beitz was brought up in Stettin, which is now Polish. He worked for Shell Oil and was sent to occupied Poland by the Germans and stayed there four years on oil business. He has a splendid record for having helped Poles to escape the threat of concentration camps, etc.

I asked if Krupp was trying to do in Poland approximately what American companies are trying to do in Europe—that is to say, to establish new plants that could benefit from cheap labor as well as new markets. Beitz said that in essence there was something in this.

He said: "The Poles want to work with us. They want Western training and know-how. They want cheaper production. My political idea, however, is point number one in the project. I think it is a good idea for us with the name of Krupp to do everything in a country that suffered from German aggression.

"It is necessary to erase the bad picture of West Germany, to change its image. And Krupp, with its strange name, symbolizes everything that is bad in their memory. Think of the word Krupp, Krupp, Krupp, Krupp: It sounds like a gun going off."

He said that after he left war criminals' prison Alfried Krupp swore he would never go back to the arms business. He refused when the German government started to remilitarize. Krupp makes trucks but won't sell them to the armed forces.

PARIS, *February 15, 1965*

Chat with Couve de Murville at Morfontaine. Very gloomy. He thinks at least a limited war is now inevitable in the Far East. He ventured the extraordinary opinion that perhaps the only thing that could prevent war is if Moscow joins Peking in a categorical promise to intervene if the U.S.A. escalates the conflict against North Vietnam. "After all," he remarked with a gloomy smile, "that would constitute a real deterrent."

I asked Couve if he felt the war he foresees inevitably means World War III. Again he made a strange remark. "No," he said, "not all of us would be involved." This doesn't sound much like the Cuba spirit of 1962, when France was among the first to stand up and be counted.

PARIS, *February 23, 1965*

Lunched with Jean-Marie Soutou [French diplomat]: as usual penetrating and brilliant. Soutou says China's most dangerous role in Africa is not merely that it gives aid to left-wing nationalist and racist movements. The Chinese are unable to export much military or financial help. But they act as a catalytic agent and incite the Russians to do what Moscow doesn't want to do. The Russians did not wish to provide airplanes for Algerian and Egyptian help to the Congo rebels. But the Chinese keep saying that Russia has no interest in quick liberation in Africa and Moscow feels forced to do something.

PARIS, *February 25, 1965*

Long talk with Chip Bohlen who came back at midnight from several days in Washington during the visit of Couve de Murville to Johnson and Rusk.

The first time Chip saw Johnson, the president leaned over, patted him on the knee, and said: "Chip, I am glad you're in government. I want you to know that you can stay in Paris as long as I'm in the White House."

At an official dinner party, Representative Hale Boggs of Louisiana complained to Couve: "You French are more popular in Louisiana than anywhere else in this country, but we can't understand the trouble you are making for us on gold, NATO, and Indochina." Boggs thought France should pay its World War I debts if it was going to try to attack the U.S. financial position. Couve replied that in such a case France would have to claim compensation for its aid to America during its revolution—and the interest rates would be very high.

Chip urged me not to leave for the Far East because he said, "You would be foolish to be away. Things may get hot around here. We may come to the point of stating officially that we think the French are behaving in an unfriendly fashion."

PARIS, *February 28, 1965*

Last night at dinner (we were spending the weekend at Alain de Rothschild's) Chip Bohlen said it is perfectly clear that we have now made a policy decision in Washington to bomb North Vietnam if, when, and where we please, unrelated to Vietcong actions in the south—except for the Hanoi-Haiphong complex which, for the present, we are leaving alone.

Chip said that at the Washington meeting President Johnson told Couve de Murville we objected to the French talking so much in public about their ideas for a conference to neutralize South Vietnam. If they really wanted to work for a conference, why didn't they proceed more diplomatically and in private?

PARIS, *March 1, 1965*

Played golf yesterday and lunched with Couve de Murville and Bohlen. Couve said what France really wants in terms of fiscal reform is to double the price of gold. But France doesn't dare to say this openly because it would have an unsettling effect. Nevertheless, if gold were revalued to $70 an ounce, the United States would automatically end the problem of its leaking reserves. England would be in much better financial shape. There would be enough gold available to finance international commercial exchanges. I asked if this didn't provide too much help to Russia and South Africa. Couve scoffed at this and said all it would do is to steam up their gold production.

Lunched with Étienne Manac'h, Head of Asia at the *Quai d'Orsay*. Manac'h was French consul general in Bratislava at the time Zorin engineered the communist *coup d'état* for Stalin. "He was expelled from Czechoslovakia in 1951—accused of being chief of *all* Western espionage services and especially of conspiring with Vladimir Clementis, the foreign minister who was later hanged.

Manac'h simply cannot understand why the Russians decided to send Zorin here to replace Vinogradov. He says with a shrug: "Now both the Chinese and the Russians will have ambassadors in Paris who don't speak a word of French. Imagine the reaction on the General."

The French are convinced there are two Chinese policies. Ideologically China is pushing in all directions and trying to establish its communist preeminence through propaganda and subversion. But, as a nation, China is much more prudent and it wishes to avoid a war.

North Vietnam is in a sandwich between the danger of Chinese occupation and American bombardment. Kosygin went to Hanoi to exploit the situation. The Russians would like to have a peace conference and a genuine neutralization of South Vietnam which would also strengthen the hand of North Vietnam vis-à-vis Peking by gradually removing pressure. Unfortunately, the Americans chose to bomb North Vietnam while Kosygin was there. This forced the Russians closer—in public—to the Chinese position and made them promise more aid than they had intended to Ho Chi Minh.

The Chinese have made clear to the French that they would like to have a peace conference in Vietnam but they can't say so now, while the United States opposes a conference and also shortly after the United States bombings of North Vietnam. The French believe the Russians and Chinese agree on one precondition to a conference—namely that U.S. bombings of the north should cease. The Russians tell the French that they do *not* insist that U.S. troops should leave South Vietnam before a conference—only after a settlement.

PARIS, *March 5, 1965*

I applied today for a North Vietnamese visa at the North Vietnamese Trade Delegation. The Vietnamese were very friendly and promised to telegraph my request to Hanoi and ask for a telegraphed response. I told this to Chip Bohlen who wired Secretary Dean Rusk asking if a waiver could be granted permitting me—despite the bar—to visit North Vietnam.

PARIS, *March 6, 1965*

Dined and played bridge with Couve de Murville last night. Couve says he expects China to react to American bombing of North Vietnam by striking at two points where we fancy our influence is secure in Asia: Thailand and the Philippines. Trouble is already shaping up in Thailand and it will come later in the Philippines.

SAIGON, *March 11, 1965*

Talked for an hour and a quarter this afternoon with General Max Taylor, our ambassador here. He feels Johnson lags behind Kennedy on "counter-insurgency" in general and Vietnam in particular.

He indicated it had been discussed as long ago as 1961 whether North Vietnam should be bombed. He (Taylor) had only come around to the decision a year ago: since then (until February) the delay was Johnson's. The bombing would be slowly and selectively stepped up and moved northward to frighten Ho Chi Minh into calling off his dogs.

He admitted that the country was cut in half at the north—by a combination of last autumn's floods and the Vietcong. The floods had knocked out bridges that the Vietcong prevents us from rebuilding.

I asked if he thought the "falling dominoes" theory still tenable. He said: "No, I suppose not. There is nothing inevitable in this area. It is perhaps a 'tilting domino.' We could establish a Mekong barrier. We could hold Thailand and Malaysia. The pressure might also shift elsewhere. But things would certainly be much more bleak if we lost South Vietnam."

Taylor said that apart from any political or diplomatic value, our program of selectively bombing the north was "a sound operation militarily speaking. The aim is to affect the *will* of the opponent."

He said: "My main job here is to get a government. That's our basic problem. You must remember this has never been a nation with a government that could assert its authority all over. How do you establish the juridical basis for such a government?

"The military can throw out any government if it wishes to. All you really need here is two men—an honest, able prime minister and a loyal commander-in-chief. That would be the answer. But where are they?"

Taylor said that undoubtedly the end of [Ngo Dinh] Diem was a "great disaster." No alternative solid regime has developed.

I remarked that bringing in the 3,500 U.S. marines implied that we wished to release Vietnamese forces to do other jobs, and wondered if their presence didn't encourage communist antiwhite racist propaganda— talking of "white" Americans and trying to unite all "Asians" against them.

Taylor said the marines helped ease the shortage. Government military strength, all told, was about 600,000 while the Vietcong had 34,000 hard-core regulars plus another 70,000 to 80,000 "local guerrillas." All recent successful counter-insurgency operations had shown that, even when there are no foreign sanctuaries for the guerrillas, you need from ten to twenty to one manpower superiority.

"We are trying to get tension to rise," he said. "Neither Peking nor Moscow wants to get into this thing directly. Therefore we are most interested in Ho's reaction. He worked hard to build up, during ten years, such an industrialization program as he has been able to establish. Will he be willing to sacrifice this for an uncertain South Vietnam and/ or the possibility of Chinese occupation? And don't forget, the Soviets are showing signs of unhappiness."

I then said: "Ultimately, it seems to me, your biggest problem is race. What do you do about it? How can you convince a yellow-skinned Buddhist peasant who wants peace and knows no ideology that we—not the yellow-skinned Vietcong—are his friends?" Taylor replied: "I don't think you can persuade him. The only thing is to give him security. That is the first requisite."

Taylor admitted that in the summer of 1963, when Diem was still in power, he and McNamara had both forecast that within two years (from then) the war here could be turned into a police action. It has gone way downhill since.

SAIGON, *March 12, 1965*

This morning I had a talk with André Mattei, the French chargé d'affaires: a dark, short, nervous-looking, saturnine man who had been arrested by Nasser during his last foreign mission, in Cairo. He said there is less sign of visible war today than during the French-Vietminh war; not just in the cities but also in the countryside. The schools work; there are few patrols, just village guards. But suddenly, the next day, a killing patrol can emerge.

The real difficulty lies not in any major operations but in the steady expansion of the Vietcong's civilian authority, the parallel hierarchies. They are moving constantly into larger areas, establishing their tax-paying and administrative arms. And both money and people from the more prosperous classes are fleeing at an ever-growing rate. The whole country wants peace—almost at any price.

What is most needed is a true regime to lead an administration that can fight back throughout the country against the parallel hierarchies. But this does not exist. There is *no* state. There is *no* army, only generals. There is *no* nation, only factions, religious sects, tribes.

SAIGON, March 15, 1965

An exceedingly interesting day yesterday, flying up to Hué with General William E. De Puy and then afterwards to Danang. All told about six or seven hours in airplanes or helicopters. In the evening I dined with De Puy and General Richard Stillwell, chief of staff.

De Puy says the pacification program has certainly gone down the drain for the moment. The Vietcong has moved in a few new battalions. It has begun to intimidate local forces.

U.S. airstrikes are primarily a diplomatic weapon. The strikes on barracks north of the seventeenth parallel probably killed a number of North Vietnamese soldiers. For the rest they are of minor importance.

There is no way to cut off the supply of manpower from the north to the Vietcong unless Hanoi can be forced to decide to cut off the supply.

If the U.S.A. can keep the heat on for two years the VC troubles will be much greater than ours. This is just the start of a new phase.

A VC company commander who was recently taken prisoner said: "If the war ends now, we will win. If it drags on for two years, you will win."

The brother of "Big" Minh, the ARVN commander in chief, is a VC general. He is in northern Tay Ninh province. That is where the Central Committee headquarters are. It is on the Cambodian border in a village area. The central office of South Vietnam (which is the headquarters of the National Liberation Front) is there.

Until very recently the United States made the assumption that the Vietnamese could win this war by themselves. But events have proved this wrong. We have now resolved that we now need a much bigger ARVN and an overwhelming U.S. air force and basic involvement.

I asked how long the U.S. was willing to stay on here. He said as long as two political conditions were met: that the American public supports the commitments; that the Vietnamese government does not put in a neutralist government through a *coup d'état* or a "peace" government through communist-front movements.

We arrived at an airport outside Hué. A helicopter was waiting for us to take us into Hué itself. Two gunners manned their guns.

Hué is a lovely sleepy town which was the early nineteenth-century capital of Annam and was built as an imperial city on the model of Peking. It lies along the Perfume River. Like Saigon, it seems a peaceable normal bustling town. However, the American mission area is very heavily protected and cars are searched when they come in to be sure there are no bombs attached to them by VC agents.

I met three university students: frail young men, all twenty-five years old but looking about sixteen. Two came from Hanoi and one was born in Hué. One said he was a Confucian, one said that he was a Deist, and the third said he was a Catholic.

One said: "Many people think the Americans are fighting here for their own interest only. The common people think the United States manipulate events. We appreciate your help. But you should help us to help ourselves without intervening in our domestic affairs. We think the Americans want a strong man in power. But we need a strong government, not a strong man."

None of them had done their military service yet, and although they talk like vivid patriots they don't seem eager to join the army.

The first said: "If you don't improve the situation here soon, morale will become very bad. The Vietcong continues to infiltrate everywhere."

They approved of U.S. air raids in the north but at this point the second student, the one from Hué, changed his mind and said: "No. Most of the North Vietnamese people are true Vietnamese and not communists. We don't want to see the Americans kill them."

At the officers' mess, a timid but pleasant American captain sat at our table. He is district adviser a bit north of Hué, near the North Vietnamese border, the only American in a very unsteady area. The Vietcong was more or less in control of every hamlet. The captain gave 200 piastres (about $2 at the black market rate) reward for every Vietcong killed. He pays this out of his own pocket. De Puy complained he should know there are intelligence funds available for use in buying information. The captain said: "What's the use? You can't buy loyalty."

We were whisked back to the airfield by our helicopter, and took off immediately for Danang. I had last been in Danang fifteen years ago when the French were fighting the Vietminh. In those days it was called Tourane and the *lingua franca* was German because there were two Foreign Legion battalions stationed there and they were about ninety percent German. Now the *lingua franca* is English because of the air base and the marines.

I was driven to the headquarters of the (recently arrived) U.S. marine unit that has moved up on a mountain a few miles from the air field to guard against Vietcong attacks. They have dug themselves in pretty well and very quickly.

On the flight home from Danang, De Puy told me North Vietnam has recently held special maneuvers showing how to infiltrate an entire division a distance of 150 miles. A unit is melted in the population and then reformed and concentrated in a different area.

At dinner that night De Puy insisted that we would have to "do something" about Sihanoukville, the south Cambodian port from which the VC is drawing logistical support. Stillwell went even further and discussed the possibility that Sihanouk might have to be overthrown in Cambodia.

SAIGON, *March 16, 1965*

Talk with U. Alexis Johnson, deputy ambassador. He said Hanoi felt cheated in 1954 when, with victory in its grasp, South Vietnam was taken away from it. Hanoi would feel the same thing now vis-à-vis a peace conference.

Hanoi, in addition to being communist, is nationalist. It wants to restore the empire of the Tonkinese of the north over the south. Likewise in the south there is a desire to avoid domination from the north.

The Vietcong can take big losses with little effect on morale because it can continue to get its ranks replenished by recruits from North Vietnam. As things are now most VC material comes by sea and most of the men by land, primarily through Laos.

War is a way of life here. Draftees being conscripted into the army today were born while the war was on. To survive, people have adopted the habit of never committing themselves too far. We must give them some kind of a sense of light at the end of the tunnel. The Vietnamese are not yet convinced that the United States is willing to see this thing through.

BANGKOK, *March 19, 1965*

Staying with the Sir Anthony and Felicity Rumbolds (British ambassador). I discovered that my old friend Bob Jantzen is chief spook here. He says Thailand's northeast region had been entirely neglected by Bangkok. The people in the northeast began to slip to the other side simply by default. The communists were coming over from Laos and recruiting.

In 1960 Marshal Sarit became alarmed. He created mobile development units, including army and civilian elements, to help open roads, dig wells, improve health, and establish a governmental presence. The communists are trying to tear this down.

There have been unconfirmed reports that Chinese factories near the southern border are being moved to safe areas. Two months ago the Chinese bought $1 million of Thai baht in Hong Kong and have stepped up a Thai language program in Peking, and opened a new school in Canton. In January Chen Yi, the foreign minister, said in a speech Thailand would be the next liberation target.

We have built about two hundred air strips in Laos where Air America, a CIA charter outfit, lands its planes. Thai pilots help out and also train

Lao pilots. Souvanna Phouma, the neutralist prime minister, is fed up with the communists and has become strong and helpful. He applauds the U.S. raids against North Vietnam.

BANGKOK, *March 20, 1965*

Good talk with Graham Martin, U.S. ambassador, at one time U.S. aid coordinator in Paris. He is a soft-spoken, serious-looking, rather diffident, bespectacled man, but very hard-nosed.

Martin said it was significant that, next to English, Thai had become the most active foreign language in Peking. The Chinese were hunting up all their Thai experts. They took a decision to make a push here some time ago and now they are pushing it hard.

Hanoi still believes the U.S. bombing in North Vietnam represents the last thrashing about of a dying policy. We must show willingness to persist calmly and gradually. This will reestablish credibility in our determination and force a gradual Vietcong withdrawal. It won't happen overnight.

For the first time in our history we haven't totally abdicated to the military in a war. In a sense we have the most sensible war aims ever, but for these limited aims we must make our unlimited means credible.

BANGKOK, *March 21, 1965*

Long talk with Thanat Khoman, foreign minister of Thailand. An impressive man: small, a bit plump, bland solemn face and glasses, very self-composed. He speaks excellent English and perfect French.

He said: "This is not an internal rebellion in South Vietnam. It is not even a civil war. It is an attempt by an outside power to encroach upon a free and independent country. It is a deliberate effort by North Vietnam to put South Vietnam under its control.

"We also know that North Vietnam has designs on Laos and Cambodia. It wants to fill France's shoes in Indochina. Therefore, since this is not an internal matter and violates the Geneva agreement, South Vietnam has every right to call for help—and the United States is helping.

"If the United States had not taken that step, most people in southeast Asia would lose hope and would become doubtful whether South Vietnam—and all of southeast Asia—could resist their downfall."

I then asked what he thought China would do in response to our bombing. Thanat replied: "If you look deeper at realities, China doesn't want North Vietnam to become too strong. We know for a fact that the Vietnamese and the Chinese are like oil and water. They don't mix.

"If the Chinese found themselves in direct confrontation with the United States, they wouldn't risk destruction of their military installations. We can safely presume there will be no worthwhile reaction from China."

BANGKOK, *March 22, 1965*

Last night Tony Rumbold told a fascinating story. X., an important French political figure, was on a parliamentary delegation visiting England. They lunched at the House of Commons. After lunch they were taken to look at the session in the chamber and the head of the English delegation guiding them couldn't find X. He went back to the dining room and saw him standing there held by two policemen. One politely explained: "Sir, he was stealing the silver." They had noticed X. taking something off the table and frisked him, pulling a valuable salt cellar out of his pocket. X. explained that he had kept it as a souvenir.

COLOMBO, CEYLON, *March 25, 1965*

This afternoon I went over to see Dudley Senanayke. Senanayke just asked to form a government following Monday's elections. He is not impressive: a bit overweight, fairly large for a Ceylonese, was wearing a sloppy, rather sweaty white suit and a very sweaty green shirt; a fishlike character with a fishlike handshake.

He said there would be no essential change in foreign policy. However, in the past, Ceylon had been leaning heavily toward the communist bloc. He meant his policy to be truly nonaligned, showing friendship to everybody.

NEW DELHI, *March 28, 1965*

Dined with Ambassador Chester Bowles and some of his aides. Bowles was exuberantly over-optimistic, in strange contrast to his own reports which I had read in the morning. I remarked on this to Chet but, while admitting that everything was not perfect, he plunged on trying to sell me on India's great success. He was only partially successful. Says he: "There are more gains here than in any country in the world, and more remains to be done also."

Bowles acknowledges the following bad things: the population problem is a worry although India could raise four or five times the amount of present food by proper means. There are not yet enough teachers, housing, doctors, radios, clothes. Overgrown cities like Calcutta produce an emotional problem.

There is an outdated economic approach among the older leaders who were brought up on the economics of Fabian socialism and worry more about division than increasing production. Nehru had no interest in economics. There is a lack of confidence and feeling of mistrust for the government.

Bowles thinks it's a fifty-fifty chance India will work out well. If not, the army would reluctantly take over to forestall the Left—although the generals don't want this.

India will do anything to keep Russia and China apart. Nehru has believed China wouldn't be aggressive for twenty years but, like Stalinist Russia, would concentrate on internal problems.

NEW DELHI, *March 31, 1965*

Yesterday evening I saw Prime Minister Shastri in his official office at 10 Jan Path, a large and perfectly comfortable house which adjoins Shastri's "bungalow." A covered passage has been built between. Shastri preferred not to live in the splendid governor general's palace where Nehru resided.

Shastri is unusually small—about four feet, eleven inches. He has a pleasant, square, tan face. He was wearing a white cap and the traditional brown homespun coat. He spoke to me in very good English, learned here in India.

I asked if it was not frustrating to suddenly be called upon to fill the shoes of a very big man. He said: "It is a difficult task indeed—especially coming after Mr. Nehru who dominated the scene for fourteen years as prime minister and before that also as a great freedom fighter and liberator.

"We are a young country. Since independence, there has been a new urge toward different languages and different cultures. These sometimes create difficulties. But by and large there is a sense of unity and whenever there is any emergency people do work shoulder to shoulder and stand for the country as a whole."

I asked if he had any hope of ever settling the Pakistan problem. He said: "We can only settle it if both countries are reasonable and show a genuine desire to settle it. We will do our best on our side to draw the two nations together. But, in fact, I must admit during the last few months things have not been so happy."

He said: "It is obvious relations between Russia and China are very unsatisfactory. That does not hurt us. China is becoming more isolated. This shows that there is something wrong with China. Russia had tried its level best to remove the misunderstanding with China and they are both communist countries after all."

Dinner again with Bowles and his wife. Chet admitted the Russians have begun to put in their surface-to-air missile sites and that there is a team of thirty Russians here helping the Indians. One set of SAM-2 missiles has been installed.

Bowles insists that all the equipment we sell to India is useful only in the Himalayan region against China and not against Pakistan. On the contrary, he says all equipment including heavy tanks that we give to the Pakistanis is designed primarily to fight on the Indian plains.

In 1952 or 1953 when he was here for six months, the Chinese had managed to put a tap on his telephone. One night he had Kim Roosevelt in for a long, long talk, and the whole thing was recorded by the Chinese. When they discovered the tap they found the wire ran over to the Chinese military attaché's house nearby.

If we cannot get U.S. F-5 aircraft for the Indians our entire arms program here is going to peter out. He is doing his level best to help out on these all-weather planes which can be used at night and are of particular value up near the Chinese border.

Bowles says the Indians asked Britain to give them some kind of nuclear guarantee against attack but the British turned the idea down. Bowles thinks this was a mistake.

NEW DELHI, *April 1, 1965*

I saw today a secret report from Bowles to the secretary of state on Soviet efforts in India and how to counter them. It was dated May 21, 1964. Some points: the Russians are trying to persuade leftists to unite in a front (Popular Front) with rightist elements to weaken the moderate government and destroy U.S. influence. (Nehru died six days after this report but I'm told the situation remains substantially the same.)

The Russians managed to induce India to shelve its May 1963 agreement to let us build a Voice of America transmitter near Calcutta. This had first been requested by India. It was to be a million-watt transmitter to transmit to China and southeast Asia. The Indians would run it and let us have two hours a day to broadcast in east Asia—but not in India or in Indian languages.

The Russians claimed our Seventh Fleet "intruded" on Indian non-alignment. Russia emphasizes its guarantee against Pakistan which it claims the U.S.A. backs. It says there are no strings on Soviet military equipment sent here which can be used against Pakistan.

PARIS, *April 9, 1965*

Dined last night at Alain de Rothschild's. Bertrand Goldschmidt said: "India will most certainly have manufactured an atomic bomb within three years at the latest." Bertrand, who is one of the top dogs in the French nuclear program, says it is perfectly apparent the Indians are working on this from the questions he is asked whenever he sees Dr. Homi Bhabha, their best physicist. Bertrand believes the Indians won't test their bomb; they will merely announce when they have one. Eight years ago Bhabha told Bertrand he asked Nehru whether to go ahead and make a bomb. Nehru did not answer him; he merely said, "Tell me when you have one."

PARIS, *April 14, 1965*

Lunched today with Manac'h. He told me there are now 125 Russian technicians in North Vietnam. The Chinese had been telling all neutralists and socialists that Russia was not serious in offering to help North Vietnam. The Russians were so enraged that they passed the word around to everyone, including the French Communist party, that China was blocking Soviet attempts to send help to Hanoi.

Moscow is trying both to strengthen Ho Chi Minh's regime and the Soviet position in North Vietnam. China, on the other hand, is trying to build up the Vietcong and its political expression, the FLN. Russia is working on a government-to-government basis and China is working on a people-to-people basis.

The Chinese fear that if Russia is able to send modern weapons which require trained experts to handle them to North Vietnam, they will end up by bringing so many people to Hanoi that they can assert a political control and enter into a direct negotiation with the U.S. on North Vietnam, just the way they did on Cuba in 1962—paying no more attention to Ho Chi Minh's desires than they paid to Castro's.

Russia fears that if it doesn't get into the southeast Asian problem actively, the entire area will become a happy hunting ground for China.

There is great pressure in the Pentagon for escalating the Vietnamese war into a U.S. aerial attack on Chinese industrial and nuclear installations. The Chinese could not prevent this but would reply by massive ground assaults in southeast Asia. Then the United States would be in the soup.

PARIS, *April 15, 1965*

Lunched with Bertrand Goldschmidt. He said that in December 1957, Eisenhower had promised American help to any NATO ally wanting to build atomic submarines. Only Holland and France showed any interest and Holland soon backed out. However, France persevered. In late 1958 the U.S.A. reneged on its offer.

Another complication in the nuclear problem is in the field of computers. It was only thanks to good computers that the French were able to save a good deal of time and make remarkably accurate forecasts when they began their nuclear weapons program. Now they need more advanced computers. They tried to get one from Control Data Corporation for their military-nuclear program. Two had already been sold with Washington's approval to Sud-Aviation and to a French statistical firm, but Washington refused to sell another one to the French government (the *Haut Commissariat*). This placed the *Haut Commissariat* in the strange position of being refused a computer of its own, although it could rent or borrow the same apparatus from a private French company.

PARIS, *April 16, 1965*

Lunched with Chip Bohlen. He said there has been an official policy decision that France should continue to be treated by the U.S.A. as an ally and a friend but the Pentagon, including McNamara, doesn't like this. Bohlen has been trying to help the French purchasing requests and the Pentagon has been trying to block him.

ROCQUENCOURT, FRANCE, *April 22, 1965*

I had a talk with General Lemnitzer today. He said that when the North Atlantic Alliance was formed in 1949, the north African coast afforded it bases and training areas from Alexandria to Morocco. Now, apart from facilities at Wheelus Air Force Base in Libya, the only base in the region left to a NATO country was France's toehold at Mers el Kebir in Algeria.

The question of aligning the global interests of some allies with the European interests of others is very complex.

Even in the Alliance area there are difficulties. For example, NATO has a major headquarters in Malta, which is now independent, but not a member of NATO. Cyprus was also in NATO as a British colony in 1949 but is now independent, although Britain still maintains two national bases there.

I O

"YOU ARE LOOKING

AT THE GUY

WHO MOST WANTS

TO NEGOTIATE"

WASHINGTON, *May 5, 1965*

G OOD TALK WITH SECRETARY OF STATE RUSK. I ASKED IF WE HAD any concrete evidence on whether Russia and China are still split on Vietnam. He said the split continues. Peking claims Russia is conspiring with the United States to sell out Hanoi. Peking and Moscow are vying with each other to support North Vietnam and this does not necessarily make our position any easier.

We have evidence that Vietcong morale is continuing to slip. Defections are increasing. Prisoners tell us of shortages of food and medicine. Also they are complaining about having to move around all the time because of our bombardments.

The United States has plainly conveyed to North Vietnam that our bombing of the north will stop if they on their part stop other things. We have left it open—as far as the "other things" are concerned.

I asked if the United States would object—in any peace conference—to the presence of Vietcong representatives as members of the North Vietnamese delegation. Rusk said that it was entirely up to Hanoi to choose its delegates. Thus, in a sense, Hanoi could name Vietcong members and have them sitting at the table.

Rusk says France is increasingly isolating itself. It is only an observer now in SEATO. It is playing no role in disarmament discussions. It is playing scarcely any role in NATO. No one is concerned at all about France's views on Asia—not even the communist powers.

Lunched with Walt Rostow. He was nice, brisk, and friendly, but I must say he is about the most conceited man I have ever met. He uses the word "I" more than anyone I know. Everything was "I, I, I."

Rostow assured me that a television broadcast he had made in Japan was considered so important that they were going to take pains to see that it was heard by every Japanese with a TV set. He told me "I" urged Kennedy to bomb North Vietnam since 1961.

Talk with Eugene Black, former president of the World Bank, now President Johnson's special representative on our Mekong River Valley economic development plan.

Black says some things can be done in terms of positive southeast Asian development even though a war is still going on. Johnson has the same theory as Eisenhower that if the cost of armament can be cut, the money saved should be used for economic development.

One project is to establish an Asian development bank. The theory behind this project is that if you have a bank established for a particular region a better understanding is created for that area's particular problems.

WASHINGTON, *May 6, 1965*

I was taking a bath when I received a call telling me to get over to the White House right away, first to see McGeorge Bundy and then the president. Mac received me in his cellar office, a depressing, relatively modest room with ceiling light.

He hauled a bottle out of his desk drawer and we had a couple of drinks: very informal and agreeable.

He said the British Tories did not honor the Nassau agreement Macmillan made with Kennedy but the U.S. had not held a knife to them to force them to honor it. Had we gotten tough they probably would have honored the agreement "but President Kennedy didn't wish to act that way."

Bundy said there had been from time to time a theoretical plan for a mixed manned Latin American force, and this has now been dusted off. It would primarily be used for antisubmarine patrols and surveillance. But it would probably be much harder to use battalions of mixed nationalities quickly enough to act in any Latin American crisis.

We shifted to southeast Asia. Mac says the Vietcong is waiting for the monsoons, but we are not yet positive whether, when the rains come, the communists will make a serious offensive or just lie low and allow the war to drag on while nobody can hit them.

China thinks that, win or lose, intransigence is the right policy. Then if eventually there are negotiations, Peking can blame any compromise on others. Nationally speaking, Russia is in a good position by seeing Chinese communism embarrassed in the Far East, but ideologically Russia is in a bind and sees left-wing revolutionary leadership slipping away.

At this point we got a call to come up to the president's office—the oval room where I saw Kennedy last and where I saw Johnson last summer. He took me into a tiny study next door which is called the "think tank."

Johnson had quite a sunburn, which I imagine he gets from a sun lamp, but he didn't look well. He is too heavy. He was tired and yawned several times. His eyes twitched occasionally. He fiddled with a pencil and kept tapping his fingers.

Lady Bird is away and there is no doubt that the president gets very lonely when his wife is out of town. Also she has a restraining and calming influence on him, and her absence may cause some of his fatigue and fidgetiness.

At the entrance to Johnson's office was the little Japanese-American photographer Yoichi Okamoto, who seems to record the president's various meetings. While Johnson was talking, "Oki," as he is called, snapped several photos. He then came into the "think tank" with us and continued for about five minutes, during which time a colored servant brought me some coffee and brought Johnson a drink—an opaque tall glass whose contents I could not ascertain.

I asked Johnson how he managed to relax under the strain, and he said he takes a nap every afternoon, walks whenever possible, and manages to sleep well at night. I doubt the latter.

Bundy told me the president has a new telephone system with buttons linking him directly to all his assistants and it is a very complicated apparatus which he uses all the time. He seems to feel more intimate and at ease on the telephone than in actual conversation. He calls various people at all hours of the night, which doesn't indicate that he sleeps well.

Johnson did not indicate that he reads to amuse himself, but he said, "I like to listen to music. I turned the music off here when you came because I thought it might bother you. Shall we turn some music on now?" "Why not." I replied, eager to see what kind of music he would choose. He got up and played with some switches, but nothing happened, so he abandoned the project, returned to his armchair across from me and started fiddling with a pencil.

I asked him a question I had asked him before just to see if he would give me the same answer—and he did not. The question was who had influenced him most among people he had met or great historical figures of the past. He had answered me the first time: "My mother." This time he hesitated a moment and then said: "My father." He waited a few seconds and added: "The president of my school, Dr. C. E. Evans. And Senator A. J. Wirtz. And my wife. And Mr. [Sam] Rayburn, of course, during thirty-five years in politics."

At this point the conversation began to ramble. We started to talk about the Dominican business and Johnson said: "We will benefit enor-mously if an OAS force comes out of this affair. We have been waiting for one for years but it has taken much persuading and shouting. We're in a funny position. It is just as if I am the eldest in my family. That's no reason why I should have to support everybody and also be cussed by them. It is much better for a family to go together and share responsibili-ties equally.

"We had two things we had to do quickly and we did these with phenomenal success. Between Saturday and Wednesday [April 24 and April 28] fifteen hundred people were dead in the streets. They were killed by savages. And then they threatened to kill our people, so that within two hours we got in there and not one of our civilians was killed. Who could estimate the value of saving those lives?

"And a great benefit could come out of this by demonstrating the necessity for evolving a doctrine that will give collective security for the hemisphere. Even Costa Rica has agreed to send ten or twenty policemen to such a collective force.

"We must prove that this is not a 'barbarious' [that is the way he pronounced it] world. But things threaten to get just like when those people in the Congo were killing and eating each other. Everyone saw when they were cutting a major's stomach open to kill him. And we sent planes into the Congo and got those people out.

"Likewise we couldn't let the streets run blood in the Dominican Republic after the authorities there said they couldn't protect anyone any-more. Poor [W. Tapley] Bennett, our ambassador there. He's as good as we've got and he has a Phi Beta Kappa. He's an expert in the field. First he said no troops were needed, but a few hours later he said you'd better send them now because things are getting out of hand."

Johnson said he was "very strongly" backed in Congress on Vietnam and there had been only three votes "against us" in the Senate, seven in the House. He thought some of public opinion on the subject of Vietnam was coming around, and "if the *New York Times* and [Walter] Lippmann would let up I would have ninety percent with me. All those so-called intellectuals read the *Times*."

Johnson then said: "Everybody says negotiate. But you must have two to negotiate. We have had four to six channels open to the communists all the time but they tell us to go to hell. You are looking at the guy in the U.S.A. who most wants to negotiate."

He thought the Vietnamese situation was getting a bit better every day. He said the Congo has definitely gotten a lot better. He said, "Since you and I talked last there have been bad moments in the Congo, Cyprus, Guantanamo, and Panama. But the main thing is now Vietnam."

Johnson thought that "if we get by this week" the Dominican situation will be a lot better and the OAS will be in. Then Vietnam will be the principal problem.

His conversation roved. Several times I made as if to rise and go, but he waved me back, adding: "I have got all the time in the world for you and you just stay as long as you want."

He said France was the only problem in Western Europe and it was better to leave things as they are. He added, with reference to de Gaulle: "I see no point in feuding with an old man. He has his pride and his nationalism and I am glad that France now has some of that. It is a lot better than when they used to have elections every two weeks. And I will never forget when he came right in with us on Cuba. In seventeen months he hasn't bothered me. If he throws his fast ball, I just step aside and go on with my business. I am prepared to smile and turn the other cheek."

By this time it was almost half past eight and I made another move to go, but Johnson again practically pushed me back into my seat and said: "You have closer ideas to mine than almost anyone and you are entitled to time." So I sat.

Johnson was anxious to ease tension with Russia "but Vietnam has made them tense. I told [Ambassador Anatoli] Dobrynin I wanted him to come down to Texas for a few days. I see their problem on Vietnam and their necessity to denounce us. But we will have to learn how to live together, and the quicker the better.

"Things like the Dominican mess are not a holocaust, and we can progress in the field of human relations. I don't think Gromyko went to Paris to see de Gaulle in order to needle us. That was de Gaulle trying to needle us, not Russia. And Erhard has now told de Gaulle to go to hell.

"My relations with Russia have been all right. I have said that I want to see the Russians here and that I am ready to go there. The more they see of our country, the better. Khrushchev was never the same after he visited an Iowa farm. Now the Russians should see some of our laboratories and then they will learn they can't catch us for another hundred years.

"We can work together with the Russians. We have been working together on desalinizing water, on space and other things. The more we work together, the less likely we are to fight together.

"And we have got to bring the Germans together. Erhard is a much more flexible man than Adenauer, and Adenauer was always scared to death of communism. I have told Erhard, 'You must check out what you have to give in order to get what you must have' on unifying Germany. I told Erhard that was a two-way thing."

Johnson said that some real good may come out of the Dominican mess and if there is an inter-American defense force it will be wonderful for both U.S. and hemispheric security.

He described Undersecretary of State Mann as "Tom Mann, the ablest, strongest man I have got around me." Then he went on with paeans of praise for [Ellsworth] Bunker, adding: "I wanted to send Bunker to Indonesia as ambassador, but everyone here said we couldn't spare him from Washington. We all agree that Bunker is a wonderful man—a patient, sweet diplomat who looks so soft but is really hard. He is seventy-two years old and he has lost his wife and brother, but he just keeps on working."

Johnson ruminated: "We are doing well. The world is not caving in on us. Our economy is booming. There are one million four hundred thousand more people working and revenue is one billion dollars up on our estimates. Castro is behaving in Guantanamo. Panama is going well. The Congo has improved. The Italians are happy and I had wonderful talks with [Aldo] Moro. [Paul-Henri] Spaak was helpful. And I won't get into a quarrel with de Gaulle. I've got more give than he has, and I will just smile and turn the other cheek. But if he insists on running me out of Paris I will go reluctantly but I will take two hundred million dollars with me. But he has done a lot for France and he has made it strong and proud. And just remember, he is a lot older than I am and I am going to outlive him."

At this point it was a quarter to nine. I was forty-five minutes late to a dinner party given in our honor and I didn't have time to dress. In fact I arrived an hour and a quarter late. Johnson urged me again to stay, but I didn't see how. So he got up with me and pointed on the wall to pictures of five presidents he had grouped in one frame. He then took me to the door, saying: "Come and see me any time you want, but just give me two or three days notice. I wish you would spend more time in this country."

WASHINGTON, *May 10, 1965*

Dined with the Harrimans. Averell, as expected, gave the usual line about the urgent need to act in Santo Domingo. Claims the OAS states now realize subversion is as important as overt aggression.

Harriman would like to take a tough stand against de Gaulle and tell him if he doesn't behave we'll make him pay. But has no precise idea how to back up these threats. He also wants to go to Moscow where, says he, he is an old pal of Kosygin. The state department won't let him go to either Paris or Moscow, which he resents. He is loyal to Johnson and Rusk, says the president is a fine strong man with lots of guts.

WASHINGTON, *May 11, 1965*

Good talk with Vice President Humphrey. I asked what his role was in the making and application of foreign policy. The point of my question was to satisfy myself that he really knew what was going on. If anything were to happen to Johnson, Humphrey would get dumped into the middle of a bag of crises.

Humphrey talked easily, modestly, and, on the whole, with a certain air of excitement at being able to deal with fascinating overseas problems of diplomacy, strategy, and intelligence.

"The first thing is to keep informed. At 7:30 every morning a man in my office comes out to my home with briefing papers and state department and CIA cables and situation reports. These keep me fully up to date. Thus, just this morning I had a CIA report that China has exploded its second nuclear bomb; but this was highly qualified and we don't know yet whether it is true.

"I meet with the joint chiefs on problems of the moment and also on the general line of strategy. I also meet with the CIA people and get briefings in depth. The USIA regularly sends me a weekly report on its activities. "On all these matters when I think I have something to contribute I make my own suggestions.

"I have almost daily meetings with the state department—with Rusk or George Ball or Tom Mann. Sometimes I will have breakfast with one of them. I work particularly closely with the Middle East and Latin American sections of the state department.

"The president has insisted that I should be kept as well informed as he is and all the services made available to him are made available to me. I spend a great deal of time on this and I try to relay back suggestions that I may have. I do this normally informally in chats or by telephone. I often have talks with Mac Bundy across the street, but I try not to bother the president too much personally, although I occasionally send him memoranda directly and have meetings with him.

"I sit in on all meetings of the national security council and also on all major discussions with important foreign visitors. When a foreign visitor comes through I not only participate in the general formalities, but I have my own personal visit with him.

"On my staff I have a foreign affairs man who was with the state department for a long time and also one who serves as my specialist on CIA and defense matters.

"But I want to stress that I don't consider myself a decision maker. I am more of an aide, adviser, and observer, although I do try from time to time to present helpful suggestions.

"Above all I try to keep myself informed. I am the first vice president to be totally incorporated into the information system of the president. He made it that way. I have become a member of the innermost team of the president on foreign affairs."

At this point Humphrey went over and got a briefcase off a sofa. He opened it and pulled out a batch of top-secret documents from CIA and state to show me the kind of stuff he saw every day. For example, he showed me that day's battle map from Vietnam so that I could see how the battle around Song Be was going.

Humphrey said Johnson "rides herd on foreign policy. He likes it. He has a total involvement in it." So does Humphrey, it was quite evident. He said with considerable pride, as a former senator: "No senator except an occasional committee chairman gets the kind of information I get."

NEW YORK, *May 14, 1965*

The Chinese announced that they had exploded their second bomb today.

Dined last night with Roger Seydoux, French ambassador to the UN Edgar Faure had assured him that the basic reason for Khrushchev's dismissal was the fear by both the Soviet Communist party hierarchy and the Chinese Communist party hierarchy that Khrushchev wanted an outright split between China and Russia. Both were prepared for a separation but not for a divorce.

PARIS, *May 30, 1965*

Last night I dined with Chip Bohlen. Chip told me that when he went to see de Gaulle three weeks ago, my book was on the General's desk, which surprised him (and now surprises me).

Chip says de Gaulle was entirely "negative" on everything they discussed. He is positive the General will try to squeeze SHAPE and NATO out of France in 1966 after he is reelected, and that he will definitely run for reelection. Furthermore, he is convinced de Gaulle will denounce the North Atlantic Treaty in either 1968 or 1969.

Chip says the embassy has now gotten its hands on written concrete evidence showing that de Gaulle is sending anti-U.S.A. instructions to his cabinet ministers. Even Couve admits things are getting pretty bad between our countries.

PARIS, *June 2, 1965*

Lunch with Edgar Faure, twice a Radical prime minister of France and now an ardent Gaullist. He called for toothpicks at the restaurant (Lucas Carton) and feverishly picked his teeth throughout the meal, with much noise, skill, and gusto. He eats with great enthusiasm.

Faure says nobody in the cabinet ever speaks up to de Gaulle. Pompidou sees de Gaulle every day but never disagrees with him. Couve de Murville is primarily responsible for introducing the ideas of Rueff on gold revaluation to de Gaulle. Faure thinks these are essentially nonsense and that nobody could benefit from them.

He was disturbed by the reputation he had acquired as being "anti-American." He was going to tell his friends around here that, rather than being anti-American, he had lunched with me today and was lunching with Walter Lippmann tomorrow. I said this wouldn't do him any good because the two of us were known as the only surviving American "Gaullists." Faure smiled and said, "I guess I am the only surviving French Gaullist."

He thinks the best solution we could hope for in Vietnam would be to have a long period of battle and a final stalemate months, or even years, from now along the seventeenth parallel fixed by Geneva. Gradually American bombardments of North Vietnam would dwindle to almost nothing and American casualties would dwindle to almost nothing. Fighting would virtually cease. There would be no negotiation but there would be a kind of stalemate and eventually the whole thing would slip off the front pages. It is absolutely impossible for the communists, above all Oriental communists, to even imagine the idea of a negotiation as long as the "escalation" is going on. Yet he understands that the United States must stand and fight because this is a contest of will which affects the whole world.

PARIS, *June 3, 1965*

Lunched with [Étienne] Burin des Roziers [secretary-general of the Élysée]. It is blatantly obvious that he has had prepared for de Gaulle a memorandum on Latin America.

Burin said that the Monroe Doctrine began as a result of the Polignac convention in 1823. Polignac (at that time French ambassador to the Court of St. James) had proposed a general sharing-out among the European powers in Latin America.

Essentially, Polignac wanted to squash the new liberal nationalist governments that had achieved Latin American independence of Spain. Étienne continued that Monroe had reacted to this scheme; that his doctrine had been amended by Teddy Roosevelt, permitting U.S. intrusion into Latin America; and that France was very worried now that Johnson was following up on Teddy Roosevelt's theory by proclaiming the right of military intervention on ideological excuses.

PARIS, *June 4, 1965*

Thierry de Clermont-Tonnere went to see de Gaulle recently, as his publisher, to discuss literary plans and to ask him if he was working on the fourth volume of his memoirs. De Gaulle said that he was not, that he did not intend to and that there would be no fourth volume.

PARIS, *June 8, 1965*

Excellent talk with Couve de Murville. He regretted that the United States had gotten dirt on its face in the Dominican Republic operation because when the United States was smudged, France also was. France did not like to see its ally get into trouble. But he thought we had messed things up. France could understand and appreciate Johnson's action in sending the marines initially to save American—"and French," Couve added—lives. But then they should have gotten out.

I shifted by asking Couve: "If there is no change in the NATO organization by 1969, will France denounce the North Atlantic Treaty?" He answered: "It is hard to answer that hypothetically because the question is based on a hypothesis. Nobody knows who will be governing France or who will be running other governments or what their policies will be four years from now. But certainly we want to change the structure of NATO before 1969. Now it is a question of choosing the proper moment. We are not seeking a sudden decision. We have been saying what we want, expressing our views, since 1958."

I asked if France ultimately preferred—instead of NATO—to have bilateral alliances or multilateral alliances with other Western countries. He said there was no question that France still preferred the multilateral alliance system. There was nothing wrong with that. Therefore there was no need to change the treaty itself, only the organization that had been built upon the treaty. New military arrangements were required. The organization that had been erected by NATO was not required by the treaty. And it represented too heavy a burden for peacetime purposes.

I asked if France contemplated requesting that either SHAPE headquarters at Rocquencourt or NATO headquarters in Paris should move from French soil. He said undoubtedly SHAPE represented an important part of the organization to which France objected. This French frame of mind had been increasing with the years. But this kind of logic did not apply to NATO as a political set-up or to the NATO council headquarters, only SHAPE. Nevertheless France had no real plan yet and no blueprint of its own ideas concerning the reform of the NATO organization.

Was France drawing up any plan of its own suggesting a reform of NATO? He said: "There is no French plan. If you have a blueprint for a plan it comes out immediately. It is leaked. And we don't want any such plan to be leaked until we have prepared it. It is therefore better to discuss this problem for a while first."

Couve went on to question whether it was indeed wise, in peacetime, to have a military organization such as NATO. It was justified only in terms of a war and that would mean a general war with the Soviet Union. But it was costly and also interfered with the gradual normalization of the political relationships to have the kind of integrated NATO organization that now existed.

He realized there had been a considerable growth of anti-French feeling in the United States and this was bad for Franco-American relations. It was regrettable. Nevertheless it was not a danger from the general viewpoint. The reality remained that France and the United States were together in this world.

He thought "what irritates the United States is not the French attitude on NATO but when France does not agree with the United States on foreign policy matters it does things in the world which Washington considers anti-American." He referred specifically to Vietnam and the attitude on Santo Domingo. The principal reason for the new wave of anti-French feeling in the U.S.A. was the French attitude on gold and the U.S. dollar. France's view on this had nothing to do with any desire to injure the dollar but was based on reality and logic.

There was a deep-seated psychological problem which was at the root of everything. He added: "You are discovering how powerful you are militarily. And you are irritated that you can be opposed despite this. You are obsessed by your strength—and your military leaders want to use that strength. Therefore there is a very dangerous trend in the United States and this worries us a considerable amount.

"No nation has ever had such a power for destruction as the power you hold today. You want to be the gendarmes of the world. You don't admit it but this is a fact. And, while you can destroy the world, you cannot conquer it. For example you could destroy China, or a large part of it, but you cannot conquer China. We think this is the real question, the real issue today. And we also think this poses a deep-seated problem in your country.

"You are caught between this new pressure, represented by your military people, and your tradition and instinct which is opposed to such a trend, your tradition and instinct to be tolerant and liberal and friendly with everyone. This whole matter plays a very important role not only in French public opinion but also throughout Europe and you should realize it."

PARIS, *June 9, 1965*

Lunched with Costa Caramanlis [former Greek prime minister]. He says Greece is cursed with its own history which always leads to periods of chaos or dictatorship. The late King Paul told C. once that C. would be his choice for dictator if that became necessary. C. said that dictatorship was impossible in Greece because it would give Bulgaria, Jugoslavia, and Albania an excuse to intervene in the name of "democracy," and public opinion among Greece's allies would prevent allied intervention because "democracy" had been violated. Several times C. turned down decorations offered by the king and said, "You can give them to me when I am dead, not before."

PARIS, *June 14, 1965*

Played golf and lunched yesterday with Couve. Couve says de Gaulle, who never forgets anything, has a strange habit of using the expressions of his childhood like, *"Vous me la baillez belle."* ["You're trying to delude me."]

He says Greece is getting back to its normal state—chaos. Couve admires Caramanlis as a tough, able man, but makes the strange observation: "He is not Greek—he is Macedonian."

At dinner last night I sat next to the lovely Louise de Vilmorin. She says she hates writing and only does it to make money. The things she depends on most are servants and clean sheets, and this needs money. She is firmly convinced of an afterlife that will be much more interesting and amusing than her present existence.

She used to be married to an American silver king, and lived in Las Vegas when it was just a desert dump. Every Saturday night in Las Vegas Louise would go into town with her French maid on the pretense of posting a letter and waltz through the bars just to hear the miners say "Hello, gorgeous."

PARIS, *June 21, 1965*

Lunched with (retired) General Pierre Gallois, who is wrongly regarded in America as de Gaulle's great nuclear adviser. Gallois says there are too many contradictions in U.S. policy. In 1963 McNamara promised that things were going so well American troops would be out of Vietnam by Christmas. And only two months ago Rusk assured the country that eventually our troops would pull out.

This kind of talk totally undermines our position with the South Vietnamese, who are scared, who know they couldn't last two hours without us, and who therefore make their own private accommodation. At the same time, by our bombing program we encourage the Vietcong to stick only to guerrilla operations and that is the one kind of operation the U.S.A. cannot defeat.

The U.S.A. has shown the world that Asian alliances are meaningless. Hanoi and Peking are bound by both military and doctrinal alliances but there has been no real reaction to Washington's policy from Peking—despite the fact that the Eastern world is united by its race complex and supposed to be more coherent than the Western world.

Gallois insists that the U.S.A. *must* be present on the mainland of Asia because, now that China is a nuclear power, it would be able to blackmail every Asian country. We have to stay in Asia wherever we feel we have national interests.

Probably the outcome in Vietnam will be that the U.S.A. will be strong enough to achieve a military stalemate, but all the Vietnamese will wind up in a nationalist movement against us.

American policy is cockeyed. For ten years, says Gallois, U.S. experts assured Europe that a surface fleet could be wiped out by nuclear weapons. Then it came up with the MLF to protect Europe. McNamara told the French for years that a *force de frappe* was useless because it was aimed against cities and therefore it means suicide. But the MLF was only good against cities—who is going to waste a two-megaton bomb against a single installation. The U.S. told France the Mirage was no good because airplanes were outmoded and then it ordered one thousand F-111s and at the same time insisted that the complicated NADGE system be effective in the 1970s—which is only useful against aircraft.

Chip Bohlen told me about Vice President Humphrey's conversation with de Gaulle. The atmosphere was remarkably friendly. It was quite a contrast to de Gaulle's meeting with Johnson in 1961 when the latter was vice president. The General had received Johnson for twenty minutes and started off: "What are you here to learn?"

PARIS, *June 25, 1965*

Dined last night at the Windsors. The duke said about Rudyard Kipling that he was a journalist, that he was Stanley Baldwin's cousin, and that he died on the same day as King George V. I told him about T. S. Eliot's comments in 1933 comparing Hemingway to Kipling. He asked me if Hemingway was a classmate of mine at college. Then he asked who Eliot was. After I told him he said: "Oh yes, the chap who wrote prose plays."

He told me he had played six holes of golf yesterday, all alone. A sad end for a once-glamorous king.

PARIS, *July 1, 1965*

This afternoon I saw de Gaulle. Something strange has happened to his face. It seems to have shrunk vertically and to protrude more, horizontally. He was also a bit pink but it didn't look like a natural pink.

I said that when I had last talked to him, he had indicated that France would denounce the NATO treaty in 1969 and would seek to negotiate bilateral treaties with several allies. But since then I had been informed France was content to let the treaty continue without denunciation so long as the organization set up by NATO was changed. Which was correct?

He said the treaty itself could be accepted as a "basis." There was nothing in the idea of the treaty that could not serve as a basis for bilateral French alliances with other countries such as the United States, Britain, and "maybe Germany." But, he continued, "the organization of NATO is not acceptable and must be replaced—if possible by bilateral conventions with other nations. This could be done on the basis of the principles expressed in the treaty."

I asked if he intended to ask SHAPE headquarters to quit French soil by 1969. He replied: "In any bilateral arrangements we may make to replace the treaty, evidently France cannot accept foreign forces on French soil except under French command. And the SHAPE headquarters is part of the integration which France cannot accept. It is an integrated headquarters." It was perfectly plain that he intends to ask SHAPE to get out.

I then asked: "Even if France demands withdrawal of SHAPE headquarters, would it permit NATO council headquarters to stay since after all they are political?" Again he was negative. He said: "The council would not be anything without integration and I see no need for its presence."

I inquired whether he saw any value in a summit meeting with President Johnson this year. He replied: "I don't know what President Johnson wants. If he should come to Europe I should be very happy to see him. But frankly I don't know whether such a meeting would be useful. It is not France which is involved in difficult projects now, it is the United States. And the United States must make its decisions. We have nothing to request.

"In these affairs, these summits, I don't see any purpose as nothing positive can be achieved. I have always thought that no good can come out of such visits to the summit—if you don't know ahead of time certain possible results that can be achieved. You will see what I mean if you remember Khrushchev's visit to the United States or Khrushchev's visit to Paris at the time of the four-nation summit meeting. Nothing resulted from these meetings and it is really better not to have them. A great deal of attention is paid to them in the press and there is much disappointment when they fail.

"Of course, when Prime Minister [Harold] Wilson came here to see me it was a valuable visit because we had much concrete business to do. We accomplished many things such as an agreement on the Concorde airplane and the beginning of an agreement on military aviation. Furthermore we had a lot to discuss about the pound sterling. But what could President Johnson come to say here? I don't know what he might have in his mind. It is not for me to say. But France has nothing to ask."

I remarked that four Republican congressmen had recommended that Johnson seek a meeting with de Gaulle now. The General sniffed and said: "That is meaningless, that is politics."

I asked if France intended to denounce the SEATO treaty. He said, "No, I don't like SEATO but it is insignificant."

In view of the new Saigon government's decision to break relations with Paris, did he intend to recognize North Vietnam? He said: "French policy does not depend on Saigon. That is not a government. It simply does not exist. Now, as for Hanoi, that *is* a government. It is not a satisfactory government but it governs. Nevertheless we have not recognized it although it is not impossible that we will do so one day. But the question is not current now."

I asked if he thought a Cambodian conference would be useful to try to get some kind of preliminary negotiations going on Vietnam. He replied: "Certainly it would be very useful but I don't see how such a conference can be brought about. Cambodia would like it very much but the Vietcong must be there. The real government of South Vietnam is the Vietcong. But it would be very difficult for the United States to come to such a meeting and negotiate with the Vietcong. Here again I do not think the idea of such a conference is '*actuelle*' now."

De Gaulle went on to say that quite obviously, the Chinese and the North Vietnamese are opposed to the thought of negotiations at this time. There was a distinct possibility that a big war could break out in the Far East and "every day this becomes more likely.

"Nor does this disturb the Chinese. Of course they would lose a great deal in such a war and if the United States were to use nuclear weapons it would bring vast destructions. But the Chinese don't care. On the contrary I wonder if they would not like to have the United States become involved in a large war.

"I remember a very characteristic phrase of Chou En-lai. Someone had asked him if he did not think everything must be done to avoid the suffering caused by war. He replied that on the contrary, it was by war that big things were achieved. He said China had become what it is today as a result of invasion, destruction, and suffering. This philosophical attitude is very impressive and I am afraid it remains a factor in Chinese policy."

I asked him if he envisaged any kind of new bilateral accord with Russia. He said: "We already have several economic accords. We have trade agreements and agreements on color television. And there will be more, for example, an agreement on tourism. But political accords—that I don't envision. Certainly not now. That depends on the degree of evolution in Russia."

Did he still feel that gold was the necessary basis for world currency and trade? He talked about this quite eagerly and said: "I think that in reality the necessary base for regulating payment balances, the base for an international monetary system must necessarily be gold. All other bases are fictional.

"So long as the United States had most of the world's gold it faced no embarrassment because it could pay its debts in either dollars or gold. They were virtually equivalent. But today this is no longer the case. The United States has much less gold and does not like to pay out in gold. It would not have enough. The dollar is no longer the equivalent of gold.

"We must change our concept and find a new basis. I believe that gold is the only such basis and that its value must be changed. As there is not enough gold for liquidity under a gold standard, theoreticians like M. [Jacques] Rueff say that the value of gold should be doubled. I think—and naturally I don't speak as a specialist—that one day or another, maybe after serious crises, we will have to accept gold as the basis for international currency. The value given to gold and the method of using it internationally is something that is up to the technicians. Of course some people say this would help the Russians because they have much gold. But that is foolish. They already make payments abroad in gold because the ruble has no value. So what difference would it make?"

I recalled to the General that in his last press conference he had suggested that Germany's neighbors must be brought into discussions on reunification, and asked if he thought there would be any value in having a conference on the subject, at least a conference of neighbors. He answered: "Not now; there is no point in such a conference now because Germany cannot be reunited now. Russia would not accept that East Germany should join West Germany. This is only an election question for the Germans at this moment; it is not a world diplomatic question. One day, I agree, we should perhaps try and unify Germany but we cannot do this until all Germany's neighbors agree. The idea of unification naturally is strong in the German mind. But this cannot come about by peaceful methods for a long, long time. And it would come about by war but we won't do that. We won't fight a war—above all to unite Germany."

I then asked him if he thought any purpose would be served by French recognition of East Germany. He replied in the negative: "No," he said, "that would be bad. East Germany is an artificial country. There is no reason to recognize it. It was made by the Russians and it was made by completely artificial measures."

I said that I had always been puzzled by his reference to a Europe "from the Atlantic to the Urals." I recognized that the Urals were the conventional geographical boundary between Europe and Asia but what did he mean politically since this concept partitioned Russia?

He replied: "I recognize that this phrase irritates the Russians but that is their affair, not mine. The real Russia stops at the Urals. All the rest —Turkistan, Siberia, parts of Mongolia—these are all colonies. Colonies colonized by the Russians.

"And probably, almost surely, in the future they will become a part of China. China has 700 million people. It is not a great power today. But in twenty years it will be a great power and in fifty years it will be an enormous power. The Russians know this well—and so do the Chinese. This is the inner basis of their quarrel. Of course, being communists, they always put everything on an ideological basis. But the truth is the opposition between Russia and China has national origins."

I asked if France had decided to proceed with the Channel tunnel to England. He assured me definitely yes and said: "We have always endorsed this project in principle. Now the only remaining questions are financial. We need capital for this enterprise and private capital in England as well as in France wants state guaranties. This takes time to straighten out but I think we will certainly go ahead and make the tunnel because there is no objection to it."

I asked if he believed changes in the regime in Algiers required any changes in French policy, especially concerning French oil and nuclear installation rights. He said: "There will be no changes in our policy. Our policy did not depend on Ben Bella although we were not against him. He didn't do badly—at least for that country." He continued with a haughty sniff: "If they wanted to change their regime that is their affair. But Algeria is always there. Algeria remains and we want to cooperate in its development. We want to develop the oil to their benefit."

French newspapers said he intended to make public his decision to stand for reelection in October and asked if it was true. He replied: "I don't know when I will make the decision but five months remain between now and the elections and there is no reason for me to say now what I intend to do."

I wanted to ask a philosophical question. Stalin had said the principal force motivating men was fear. Others cited religion, nationality, family. What did he think was the primary force governing men in their actions? Without a moment of hesitation he answered: "One must draw a distinction between the individual and the collective masses.

"For the individual it is ambition and a taste for adventure. I think the real motivation, the primordial motivating force for the individual is ambition, but for the masses it is fear. There Stalin was right. And this applies to masses of all countries."

I also wished to pose an indiscreet question which was a bit philosophical. He had attended Churchill's funeral and had seen what a tremendous historical spectacle it was. Because of his own sense of history he must have been impressed by such a spectacle and by the fact that Churchill had planned it. Had this incited him to make similar plans for himself because of his own well-known interest in history and his own role therein? I admitted the question was lugubrious and perhaps impertinent.

"No," de Gaulle answered. "It is indeed important and I have thought about it a good deal. But my funeral will be the opposite of Churchill's. There will be no spectacle. There will be no spectacle for de Gaulle."

At this point I folded up my notebook and was ready to go but de Gaulle wanted to ramble on a bit. He said: "The American press has been a little less disagreeable toward me recently. Just a little less, but I hope this will continue." He said he had never met Humphrey before and then rather mischievously observed: "I saw him at the time of President Kennedy's funeral but did not speak to him. I believe he was supposed to go to London for Churchill's funeral but I did not see him there." (Of course Johnson did not send Humphrey, which de Gaulle knew.)

He said then: "You know, in our conversation Vice President Humphrey and I were in agreement on this point—our two countries, the United States and France, have often been in disagreement over the last two centuries. Certainly we were not in agreement over Mexico one hundred years ago. And from 1914 to 1917 the United States had relations with Germany while we were at war. After the Versailles treaty, the United States failed to join in the League of Nations and opposed reparations for France. In 1940 the United States was not ready to go to war to protect France and England.

"We have often been in disagreement and Vice President Humphrey shared my view that it doesn't matter. Despite our differences, our two nations have always remained friends, naturally and spontaneously. I see no reason this should not continue."

At the end, when I was already half way out of my chair de Gaulle said he was positive the Chinese would not negotiate on South Vietnam; nor would Hanoi. Furthermore, it was clear the United States were not prepared to negotiate. Therefore, such ideas as Harold Wilson's commonwealth mission were foolish and meaningless.

BUDAPEST, *July 8, 1965*

This morning I was received by Janos Kadar, Hungary's boss. I spent two and a quarter hours with him and I liked him: serious, friendly, modest but no foolishness; he is an ardent communist and makes no pretenses of coddling up to the West despite the fact that he has considerably liberalized the regime.

Kadar is moderately short, slender but strongly built, with a good strong face, a firm, cleft chin, brown hair, pale skin, and rather kindly blue eyes. He has large strong hands with perfectly formed fingernails, belying the report they were torn out when he was tortured by Rákosi's police. The only sign of nervous strain left over from torture was an occasional but marked twitch of the right eye.

He received me in his office in party headquarters, overlooking the Danube: Bright sunlight filled the room and shone on several potted rubber plants. On one wall was a painting of Lenin regarding a chess board. In the antechamber were shelves lined with Hungarian and Russian Marxist books.

He said of peaceful coexistence:

> Countries can proceed in the field of bilateral relations along the line of peaceful coexistence. It is more difficult to find spheres of co-operation between groups of countries: at least experience has tended to show this up to the present time.

> [Palmiro] Togliatti, who was a deeply educated Marxist thinker and very conscious of what he was saying, enunciated something which was sensible. However, the way it is being interpreted in the West, and what Togliatti meant by polycentrism is quite another matter.

I can tell you the way I see polycentrism. Among us communists there is a rule that each party is independent and has no superior authority. So if anyone anywhere comes across a stand taken by a Communist party, he must realize that the decision emanated from the Central Committee of the Communist party in question.

The countries grouped in the Warsaw Pact are independent. I would not say that there wasn't among these countries a system of manifold and complex relationships. There is such a system among them and there is also an interdependence in certain respects. All thinking people realize this. If, for instance, I bought a lighter from you, and you would also be my only source of flint as well, I would already depend on you, even if in a small way.

We, for instance, have very good relations with the Soviet Communist party as well as with the Italian Communist party. The reason is that these three parties, in matters of decisive importance and mutual interest, have an identical attitude. But this agreement does not extend to the hundreds of problems encountered by any of these three parties day by day, problems to which each has to respond. So the agreement between them does not mean an identity of views right down to the most minute problems.

If there is no imminent war conflict between the camps, then they coexist peacefully—and, if that is so, there are continuous sets of contracts. I see the future of peaceful coexistence in the form which it has assumed in these days. If events take a trend toward lasting peace, sooner or later a situation must arise where the Warsaw pact and NATO agree about something, and later still these groupings would be simultaneously wound up (in sense of winding up their operations). At that juncture, bilateral relations will continue to be decisive.

I think what you call Titoism came about in actual practice when a conflict, a particular situation arose—without any theory to it. The theory was elaborated later, and on both sides. Titoism—may I be permitted to say so—was elaborated by us. When the conflict arose over certain problems, and in a certain logical sequence, we had—based on fictional and assumptive grounds—laid a whole theory at the doors of the Jugoslavs which in reality—looking back at it now—had never existed. I think the Jugoslavs themselves in that given situation became isolated . . . they had to exist some way or another and so elaborated some practical rules and even set up a theory. This is the way I see it.

Social systems have some fundamental features which are unchangeable: for instance, the public, or private, ownership of the means of production. There is no possible third solution in this field. What is the actual situation? In principle I can believe—I don't know practices in the United States well enough, but I can see such things in the practice of the European capitalist countries—that, for instance, the social insurance system develops, that workers are being drawn in some indirect manner into some kind of factory council, and other such changes occur.

A long time ago—now almost 120 years—when Marx and Engels were still active in word and writing (they were both colleagues of yours, as in a certain period of their lives they worked as professional journalists), they too carried on discussions about this subject. They said, very satirically and bitingly, that anyone who mistook "a public lavatory free of charge" for socialism would be very wrong, because the two are entirely unconnected—even if the public lavatory is not privately owned. Of course, in a capitalist society there are—very consciously run—communal sewage systems and other public utilities run by cities, etc.—but that does not constitute socialism. I don't want to say that it is indifferent to a working man in a given capitalist country whether there is a system of social insurance or not. It is not an indifferent matter. It is better if there is such a system, but still such matters have nothing to do with socialism.

I asked why Hungarian-American diplomatic relations hadn't been restored yet. He said:

"I am sure you have experienced yourself that the death of Kennedy, the circumstances around it, and the manner of this death have aroused certain doubts vis-à-vis the United States in many countries. At least, a certain reserve has developed; the simple question arose: what is going to happen next, where is the United States heading?

"Another exterior problem, a set of problems of even wider significance internationally, was set off by the attack against Vietnam by the U.S.A. and all that was entailed by it in the whole field of international life."

I inquired: "What is the underlying cause of Russian-Chinese differences?" He said: "For some years, a dispute has been going on in the international Communist movement. There are certain Chinese theses which are not accepted and are held incorrect by many parties.

"Let me tell you what I am thinking of. When we in Hungary say that we want to overtake a capitalist country in some field, say in ten to fifteen years, this is a realistic aim on our part and it refers to the foreseeable future. But to say, and implement, such things in a country like China is quite another matter. It is quite another matter in a country of the size of China to industrialize, or to build up an educational system like the one in Hungary at present. I would not wish to imply here that it is the fault of the Chinese leaders or that it was the merit of the Hungarian leaders that matters stand as they do. Certain historical circumstances have shaped things this way."

Talking of Hungary, he said: "I would like to point to the spring, and not the autumn, of 1956. There were various, very serious difficulties and there was no clear way out. Three standpoints could be clearly made out, in party circles as well as in wider circles. There was one marked by the name of Rákosi; this trend had a ready-made answer for everything, namely that everything was all right as it was. Another was marked by the name of Imre Nagy. This was an extremist trend inside the party which called for some kind of radical upheaval. Besides, there was a third, clear-cut standpoint and attitude in the party whose essence was that practices must be changed in party life, public life, economic building. I would like to call attention to the fact that the last-mentioned standpoint I myself adopted with many other people.

"Then the events of October and of later months ensued. After that, a certain stage of development began whose progress is internationally known. What is being seen are somewhat more elastic, livelier economic policies, greater resilience in contacts with Western countries, the observance of legality in dealing with the citizens, a generally extended freedom of discussion."

Kadar said: "If you ask me, for instance, who was the person with whom I was pleased to spend some time, I would name Khrushchev. He had different conditions of life, a different nationality and mentality, and we even disagreed about a number of questions. But on a human plane we got on well and I was pleased to be with him."

C.L.S.: "This is not exactly a 'popular' moment for saying so."

K.: "We have mentioned here Kennedy, Johnson, Goldwater, etc.—I knew none of them personally and I only know as much about them, as human beings, as anyone who pays attention to what the world's press is writing. Based on such impressions, I would say something to you: It seems to me, as a communist, that the most dangerous opponent was Kennedy, and the least dangerous would have been Goldwater. I don't want to go into details why this is so, as I am sure you understand why."

BUDAPEST, *July 9, 1965*

Long talk with Elim O'Shaughnessy, U.S. chargé d'affaires. Our conversation was difficult because of a constant hammering. Workers have been sent over here by the state department to repair the legation and insure its security. Hidden microphones have been found in the walls.

On February 13 an Afro-Asian mob of students wrecked the legation with the blessing of the police. Actually some well-known police agents in their leather jackets were spotted among the crowd. The thing was allowed to continue until the crowd broke into the legation building. Then the rioters were sent home.

O'Shaughnessy came here in November. In all the time he has been here he has never been received by either the foreign minister or Kadar. The highest he has gotten is the vice minister of foreign affairs.

It was odd thinking that as I talked with Elim, in the office next to his secretary lived Cardinal Mindszenty. He has been here since 1956. He has one huge room and then a little tiny bedroom with a cot in it and a bathroom across from a pantry where he has an icebox. This would have been the suite of the chief of mission.

Mindszenty has it furnished in usual routine U.S. embassy furniture—a big round table, two leather sofas, two leather chairs, a large standard desk. He occasionally sees his sister, and a confessor, a Hungarian priest, comes in once a month. Every day Mindszenty says mass on a little altar he has set up on a table with white cloth.

The American legation staff takes turns in escorting him on walks around the courtyard around 6:00 P.M., after the office hours so that nobody will see him. He walks around as long as he wishes. He is now almost seventy-four but very spry although he wears glasses. Some of the legation staff attend his Sunday masses. Nobody except foreign service officers or code clerks are allowed to go in to see Mindszenty or take him on his walks.

He primarily speaks about his hatred of communism, his dislike of Kadar, and the Rumanian treatment of the Hungarian minority in Transylvania. He seems to live in a past world.

The state department is so rigid about the terms of his asylum that even President Kennedy's sisters when they were here could not talk with him although allowed to attend mass. Mindszenty recently calculated that he has been in prison twenty-four percent of the time since he became a priest fifty years ago and eighty percent of the time since he became an archbishop cardinal. He was imprisoned by the Nazis as an antifascist Hungarian, by the Hungarians in 1948 as a conspirator, and then he has been in asylum in the U.S. legation since 1956. The U.S.A. was very reluctant to accept him in asylum because we don't like that idea on account of our position in Latin America where asylum is very much the mode.

Mindszenty is fed through the legation cafeteria (which is really a snack bar). His meals are brought up to the third floor by an ordinary servant and then taken in to him on a tray by the duty officer. Occasionally he has beer or wine.

The only visitors he has had apart from an occasional doctor or his sisters and the American legation staff have been Cardinal Koenig of Vienna, who came here earlier in the year on his fiftieth anniversary as a priest, bearing a gift from the Pope; and Monsignor Casaroli, a Vatican official, who has been negotiating with the Hungarian government.

Mindszenty takes himself very seriously not only as a Catholic but as primate of Hungary with all the princely privileges of that old medieval title. He is a tremendous Hungarian nationalist.

BUDAPEST, *July 10, 1965*

This morning I had a long talk with Janos Peter, Hungarian foreign minister. Until 1956 he was a bishop of the Calvinist church. His title was Bishop of Debrecen. He was ordained a priest in 1933.

He refused to discuss his past although at the very end he said that he enjoyed very much being foreign minister and the only other thing he thought was of equal interest was being a bishop. I don't know how religious he is now. He told me he had studied in Paris, Glasgow, and Berlin. He speaks very workable English despite his accent.

He is a large man—abut six feet tall and about two hundred pounds. He has grey hair and glasses. He was conservatively dressed in a dark suit and smoked American cigarettes.

I asked why United States-Hungarian relations were not improving. He said there were many complicated factors but primarily these were connected with the deteriorating world situation caused by the crisis in southeast Asia. "This crisis in Asia is beginning to overshadow European questions and socialist relations with the United States."

All questions remaining open between the U.S.A. and Hungary could be easily negotiated. Even the crown of St. Stephen is not an outstanding issue. The United States has recognized that the crown belongs to Hungary and also acknowledges that it is in the United States at the moment.

Although Hungary demands an end to our bombing of North Vietnam, Peter said that he would personally favor exchanging ambassadors right away, regardless of what we did in Vietnam, if we agreed. But nevertheless the Vietnamese question does intrude on our relations.

VIENNA, *July 13, 1965*

Came to Vienna by car. I noted with curiosity that the Hungarian foreign ministry car which went as far as the border had Swiss diplomatic plates on it.

The villages and countryside in Hungary looked relatively well-off and I saw quite a few television antennae in the villages. But there is a big difference when you cross over to Austria—cheaper gas, better roads, more goods in shop windows, even in the villages, and more televisions. Also a great many more cars.

My Austrian driver pointed out to me that the barbed wire entanglements that line the border on the Hungarian side are still there, just as in the old Iron Curtain days, with a high wooden watch-tower every five hundred meters. He told me that a new bunch of mines had been laid in between the two strands of wire. I can't understand this with all the talk of freer travel.

VIENNA, *July 16, 1965*

Lunch with Bruno Kreisky, the red-headed socialist who has been foreign minister of Austria for more than six years. Kreisky came from a very wealthy family but became a socialist before the war and was imprisoned by the conservatives during the civil war here. He is a Jew, the first Jewish foreign minister in a Germanic state since Rathenau in Germany.

Kreisky said the Rumanians are not halfway between Paris and Moscow, as some people think, but halfway between Moscow and Peking. Kreisky is struck by the gradual disentanglement of Eastern European countries from their Russian ties.

All of these countries are trying to become as nationalist as possible and to liberalize themselves as far as possible without running into trouble. The difficulty is that in all of them except Czechoslovakia there is no alternative to communism that has any possible chance. They had right-wing fascist predecessors. Czechoslovakia was the only country which had a viable democratic system before the communists took over. Also in many of these countries the only opposition within the party is a Stalinist and reactionary opposition. So the present leaders don't want to go too far in their liberalization quest and end up by inspiring a Stalinist takeover.

The East European countries are now freer to make their own foreign policy so long as it fits within the overall Soviet pattern. Thus Hungary is concentrating on coexistence with Jugoslavia and Austria. Bulgaria is concentrating on coexistence with Jugoslavia, Greece, and Turkey. Czechoslovakia is in a difficult position because it is faced by a divided Germany and, as far as Austria is concerned, the Czechs have not yet agreed to pay off settlements of Austrian claims.

PARIS, *July 19, 1965*

Lunched with General Paul Stehlin, French air force boss, who was as usual most interesting. We talked about the various military conspiracies against de Gaulle. Stehlin says he never made any secret of the fact that he personally was "*Algérie Française*" but loyalty is the prior necessity.

Stehlin says de Gaulle never has a policy on a long-term basis, "only for tomorrow." He is a tactician, not a strategist. Stehlin once heard de Gaulle assure a small group of French officers: "France will never forsake Algeria." But Stehlin thinks that with all his cynicism, de Gaulle is a brilliant and great man.

He says the French nuclear force is meaningless and doesn't even have a trigger value because the United States could let Russia know within two minutes that it was not responsible if France blew up some Soviet city; and Russia could confirm this scientifically. They would then proceed to blow up France and give the whole world a lesson.

Stehlin is convinced Russia and America are content to have a stand-off in which they know nobody else can start trouble and that they probably exchange information telling each other what they have got. But de Gaulle's nuclear force has a political value. When he assures the French people that because of the *force de frappe* France is truly independent, can take care of itself and can make its own policy, even if well-informed persons know this is poppycock the masses believe de Gaulle.

PARIS, *July 20, 1965*

I gave a small dinner last night for Gene Black and the Bohlens. Afterward Alex of Lucas Carton took us through his *cave*. Following this delicious inspection Black observed: "Why, this place makes Twenty-One look like a ten-cent store."

I I

"THERE ARE

LOTS OF ARMS

AROUND HERE"

KASTRI, GREECE, *July 27, 1965*

I DROVE OUT TO THIS LITTLE SUBURB ABOUT TEN MILES FROM Athens on this hot morning to spend an hour and a half with former Prime Minister George Papandreou. His house was surrounded by agitated politicians and there were many more inside, all jabbering away. The old man looked exceptionally well for seventy-seven —full of beans and very healthy. I am told he likes to dance in the evenings.

Papandreou said: "In the end, the present crisis must be settled by general elections. There is one big difference between dictatorship and democracy. Dictatorship has an entrance but no exit. The exit from democracy is elections.

"The present crisis results only from the king's intervention. He can only create a fictitious government of the moment based on a lack of any real material support. We need elections as soon as possible. That is imperative.

"Some people talk about the danger of a popular front. But elections would split that danger. The masses would only gather together in a popular front during a fight, a crisis, not in an election. In an election, the Extreme Left would back its candidates and the moderates would back their candidates.

"If the king refuses to have elections that will mean he wants an antidemocratic solution and he will be responsible. It is the king's choice whether we shall have elections or a dictatorship. I exclude a dictatorship.

"We will *never* recognize the right of the king to choose our leaders, party leaders, or the prime minister. That is not democracy. That is a provocation and an arrogance."

I asked the old man how he thought the Greek people would vote in a plebiscite on the monarchy if it were ever proposed. He said: "The Greek people still want royal democracy. This regime is better for us. But it must function in a really democratic spirit. We do not want any change in the constitution. No revision is necessary.

"But we feel that the king must reign, the people should govern. The king advises, the government decides. The leaders of the government and the parties are chosen through the people and not through the favor of the king."

ATHENS, *July 28, 1965*

This morning I went to the headquarters of the ERE (conservative) party on Bucharest Street, a modest and rather tranquil little place as compared with Papandreou's offices, to see Panayotis Canellopoulos, uncle of Mrs. Caramanlis and center party chief since Caramanlis chose exile in Paris.

He complains that Papandreou "has transformed Greek democracy into mobocracy." He says the king can try two or three times to find a stop-gap prime minister. If he then fails, there will have to be another national election. Canellopoulos hopes not; there have been too many elections. They cost too much and parliament requires a minimal stability.

I had a most interesting lunch with Andreas Papandreou. Andreas told me he had started out at Harvard in 1940 although he did not have a degree from Athens University. He got an M.A. and a Ph.D. Then he was an instructor at Harvard until he was offered a post as associate professor at the University of Minnesota. He was made full professor and head of the economics department at the University of California.

He has considerable charm and talks well but has a shady look about him because his eyes are too close together. He glanced around furtively (we were sitting at a corner table) and then said: "I do not see any traitors."

Andreas said the nearest base to Cyprus for Greek planes was in Crete. But this was so far away they only had about one minute of flying time left over Cyprus before they had to turn around and go home. This had posed a special problem when Archbishop Makarios demanded Greek protection at the time of the Turkish air raids. He warned that if he could not get such protection he would have to buy defensive armament, perhaps from the communist bloc.

KYP (the Greek Central Intelligence Service) is enormously tied to American CIA. They have the common job of counter-espionage in the area to the north of Greece. CIA gave KYP 10 million drachmas annually.

Andreas says this should be paid directly to the Greek government and not directly to KYP.

Andreas said there had been a fundamental issue since the first day of the Papandreou government. The palace considered the army its personal property. After Paul died, King Constantine sent an envoy to George Papandreou saying that he was sure they could get on very well together so long as Papandreou left the army alone.

Andreas says Constantine is young, intelligent, and a stronger personality than his father. But, he added: "He has no Western culture. He grew up in a small circle in Greece. And he believes he is the head of the Orthodox church just in the same way that a Byzantine emperor was. He believes the army is his own and he won't yield control. And he sees the Communist party as a gang, not a political movement. He feels this very strongly.

"This is at the root of the problem. We had an army problem and we partly won the elections on the slogan 'Take politics out of the army.' My father from the very start sensed a palace resistance to any thought of change in the armed forces.

"But you know about Plan Pericles? This was an army plan for winning the elections for Caramanlis. It started in 1958 after the communists got a twenty-five percent vote. It was put into effect in the 1961 elections but we only got hard evidence of it in 1965. My father brought out this evidence in parliament and there was a real shock."

Andreas told me: "I would like to be a prime minister, but I won't violate my principles to be one. There have been various offers by businessmen to buy me off. I have been offered up to $200,000 for one deal. But I won't do it. I have insisted on standing by our promises on social justice, economic and foreign policy. My father loves me as a son but my unbending tendencies have caused him trouble. I am a tough nut. He felt I was going overboard. He has not supported me politically as his successor. In fact, he has gone overboard the other way.

"If I had needed a military organization to help me politically, why would I have gone to captains as they charge in the Aspida case?* Generals and admirals visit me all the time. If I wanted to stage a *coup d'état* I knew the top bosses.

"I have a very wide popular base today. After George Papandreou, I have the widest popular base in Greece. I do not need George Papandreou [his father]."

Andreas claims there are only two issues today—the king's power and the role of the army. He asked: "Are we a crown democracy or a constitutional monarchy?" He said the king must have the confidence of the people but he has no substantive power. He said both the king and the Center

---

* An alleged plot to organize an antiroyalist *coup d'état*.

Party say that the army should be out of politics but the king means that the army should be his.

Andreas says Cyprus is in a sense Greece's Vietnam, because it has to act independently of NATO in Cyprus the way the U.S.A. acts independently of NATO in Vietnam.

He added: "My father has only traitors around him except for me. They are all traitors, save for his son."

He said Mitsotakis (a dissenter) had collected two hundred gunmen to force his way into the party meeting tomorrow. Andreas added: "We have at least as many gunmen—and we won't let him in." He said Mitsotakis had armed bodyguards with him and then added, "But I have two myself. There are lots of arms around now."

ATHENS, *July 29, 1965*

Last night I had a long talk and drinks with young King Constantine. In the past, I had seen him when I visited his father and mother, during his childhood and as a youth. Then he seemed a rather brash playboy, not serious, not very bright, interested in sailing.

This time, my impression has entirely changed. I had the feeling he was a very grown-up young man; he is now twenty-five. He is tough, bright, and self-confident; perhaps even over-confident. He said he liked his job and felt prepared for it. I stayed with him, talking and drinking highballs, until 10:00 P.M.

We sat in comfortable armchairs facing each other across a table by the fireplace. It was a pleasant bourgeois room—which I had not seen since I talked with his father there—lined with books and pictures of family royalty upon the bookcases. There was a gold model of a sailboat on a table—presumably the vessel he sailed to victory when he won Greece's only gold medal in modern Olympic Games.

The king speaks rapidly and extremely fluently although with a slight accent. A favorite phrase he uses both in conversation and telephone talk is "tic-tic-tic." He will say, for example, "and then so-and-so said tic-tic-tic and. . . ."

He began by reminding me that this was a very secret meeting. He said: "Maybe this is a sign of how well our democracy works. *I* am not *allowed* to be quoted."

Constantine continued: "I came into this business pretty young. Anybody else in Greece can say what he wants. An ex-prime minister [meaning Papandreou], for example, can say whatever he wishes. And often I must confess I would like to be able to speak up.

"You know, I got on well enough with the old boy, Papandreou, until this crisis broke. I told him from the start that he was first-class on giving confidence to the armed forces and that I much appreciated this. But when the Cyprus thing began to get more peaceful and there was less of an atmosphere of danger, a period began when he started to look around. His policy commenced to shift and he started to ask for changes in the armed forces."

The king leaned forward in his chair: "I want to tell you how this all began to happen, from the very start. Is that all right with you?" I nodded. He continued.

"Then the old boy let me know his plan to fire his defense minister over the telephone and through a third person. I told him that he should talk it all over with me first. It was too much for a seventy-seven-year-old man to discuss a question of this sort in a three-minute telephone conversation.

"At this point his press launched a lying campaign about me. It complained that I had refused three times to see him and charged me with breaking the constitution. It said that this was an issue of democracy versus monarchy. But I had not even seen his report on the question yet, and he hadn't requested an audience.

"He sent me a message and I told him that I would be glad to see him. But it was clear that he was planning a showdown. It was at that point that I sent him my first letter, which I know you have seen, the letter dated July 8 from Corfu. He replied to this with a decree discharging the defense minister.

"The next day I called him at seven o'clock in the morning to announce the birth of my child. We had a very friendly discussion. Then he came to Corfu. I must admit that he did not even congratulate me on the birth of my child. While he was in Corfu, I sent him my second letter, dated July 10. The old boy, when he saw me, said it was an absolutely 'perfect' letter, 'the best he had ever received.' He then told me his case.

"Papandreou admitted to me that it had been a mistake of him not to talk the matter over with me first before firing the minister. When I mentioned the attacks on me in his press, Papandreou said: 'But I am attacked by my own press also. I do not control it.' I replied to him: 'But you can talk back to your press, I cannot. I am constitutionally forbidden.'

"I told the old boy that the last time he had asked to see me was in February. I suggested that he should have called me in between for a serious conversation.

"Then the old boy said to me: 'You know, Your Majesty, I am the breakwater against the Communist party. I can bring its vote down in any election to ten percent.' I said: 'Yes, they will all vote for you.'

"Papandreou insisted he was a firm democrat, but I reminded him that he had collaborated with [Field Marshal Alexander] Papagos and the right in 1952 and then had collaborated with the communists in 1956. I said this contradicted his statement and he did not deny it.

"Papandreou then said he wanted to take over the defense ministry himself. I recommended very strongly against this. I said a very delicate question was posed concerning the conspiracy his son was alleged to be involved with. [What the king obviously meant was the Aspida conspiracy of which one now hears so much.] I said I did not know about these charges but I thought it was better to leave the question of his taking the ministry until this issue had been investigated and settled.

"I said to him: 'We are discussing this question as adults. Why don't you get someone else in your party to take over the job? That would be the sensible thing to do.'

"He agreed with the wisdom of this and he also promised me, in response to a demand of mine, that he would issue a statement saying that I as king was honoring the constitution. But then he put out a denunciatory statement afterward in which he claimed that I was bitterly against him and the democratic press.

"Then I summoned the old boy and he walked in, right here and sat where you are sitting now. Our conference lasted only four minutes. I asked him to reconsider the issue and pointed out my desire to keep the army out of politics and to avoid any implication that he might be covering up an alleged conspiracy involving his son. I said to him: 'After all, what will it look like if you become defense minister, if the father is taking over the one job that could shield his son?' I said it would look immoral. I urged him to try and find a way out.

"He replied that he could not go down in history as the prime minister who was forbidden to take over the portfolio of defense minister. I replied that he could take it over—one month later.

"At this point he said to me that he would have to resign if I was adamant on the issue. He said he had a right to demand national elections —but he would not ask for them. He would leave that until later. I was aghast when he even mentioned the subject because I knew he knew his deputies would not stand with him in an election coming from such an issue.

"He then continued by saying that he would resign the next day. All this went tic-tic-tic. It was fast, just like that. I knew what he was up to. I figured that if I let him go until tomorrow he would get a hold of the radio and get his crowds out into the street.

"So I said to him: 'I will accept your resignation as of now. Now I am free to make my choice.'

"He said: 'Your Majesty, I understand.'

"At this point he started to leave. It did not look as if he was going to shake hands with me but I stopped him and said: 'You know, we have worked well together for eighteen months and we have had good relations. I want you to know that whatever happens our personal feelings won't change.' At this point the old boy turned around and we shook hands."

The king took a deep breath and a swallow of his drink. Then he said, "You know, I can fight this one out. I am twenty-five and I have a pretty wife and a nice baby. He is seventy-seven. I can fight this out; but that is not my job. I feel that the old boy is much too old to want to plot in politics. But nevertheless it seems he is also too old to stop.

"Our army had to be slowly brought back into a position of real capacity after the defeat in the war against the Axis and after the communist war. My father brought it back into a normal position after a long struggle. The army is loyal to me, myself, but it is also loyal to the crown as a continuity. The king's job is to keep the army and the crown out of any political party squabbles and out of any possible civil wars.

"But the fact of the matter is that they—the old boy and his people— want to grab control of the army and some day to make a dictatorship.

"When the old boy left me the last time, I had to find out who could get the most votes inside his party. I wanted to keep his party intact but I had to get a new prime minister. Now I have a government of twenty-one ministers who are doing a splendid job.

"I am going to get this country out of this mess. We must fight it out in parliament. Not in the streets. This is a political argument that belongs in parliament, and not with the mob. That is the way I am going to play this game.

"My father gave me a damned good piece of advice. He told me never to play any dirty tricks. I am going to play this straight down the line. My policy is a clear-cut policy."

The king began to talk about Andreas, Papandreou's son. He said Andreas once told him that his father had requested Andreas to keep contact with the communists. He then added: "I told this to the old boy and he seemed very startled when I said it. But I do believe that Andy is in constant contact with him. It was Andy who put in the head of the labor unions and organized a series of strikes and demonstrations by the left in favor of his father.

"I do not want to fight. But on the other hand I know that most of the people in his own party no longer want the old boy. I just do not see how he can ever come back. When my father died and I took over I told the old boy that I thought everything was working very well. I said I agreed with what he had told my father, which was that the king has the right and the duty to say what goes on the armed forces. And Papandreou agreed.

"The constitution provides for change. The king and the prime minister must work together to bring this about. It should not be done by slogans and street fighting. I said to Papandreou that he knew me. Did he think I wanted to spend my time being a kaiser? Papandreou nodded. But I hate spending my time dealing with lies."

Papandreou had ordered the Greek air force to protect Cyprus after the Turkish bombing in 1964. The king said he was in bed when he heard this but within minutes he had the prime minister on the phone and said to him: "'Are you mad? It takes two hours for our planes to get there from

Crete and all they have is five minutes before they have to go back for fuel. Do you mean to say you want to lose ten planes just to please Makarios?' He called the operation off."

When Makarios came to Athens on a visit last year Papandreou had persuaded Constantine to receive the archbishop. He told Makarios: "Greece does not want to unite with Cyprus; Cyprus wants to unite with Greece." It was for this reason, he told Papandreou, that he had requested the Greek air force operation be called off. Constantine said he had assured Makarios that NATO "could do no harm if it had a base in Cyprus." Makarios agreed and said that he would accept such a base, contrary to what he had previously told Papandreou. The king said he assured Makarios that he would try to arrange a NATO base which included the Turks and the Americans but would not be dominated by either of them, and in August 1964, Makarios agreed to this formula.

When the king told this to Papandreou, Papandreou was enthusiastic. On this basis, Constantine wrote to President Johnson about his formula and also told U.S. Ambassador Labouisse. He had been deeply distressed because it took Johnson between ten days and two weeks to answer, and then he only received a meaningless, platonic reply.

He bitterly criticized Papandreou for "keeping the people in the streets" but nevertheless he felt increasingly confident. He thought the failure of the previous day's general strike had been a tremendous defeat for Papandreou. If a showdown came, "the old boy won't have a leg to stand on, but nevertheless I don't want to get into a popularity contest with him."

I asked if he liked his job. Rather enthusiastically, young Constantine looked me squarely in the eye and said: "Yes. I was born into this job. It has terrible responsibilities, but I am ready to accept them. But I must admit that every now and then I feel terribly alone. Nevertheless, I have a feeling that it is my duty to steer my country into history."

The king walked to the door with me and said: "Do not tell anyone about this. I am ready to continue this conversation whenever you want."

ATHENS, *July 30, 1965*

Evangelos Averoff, foreign minister under Caramanlis, dropped in. Evangelos told me the reason for the king not permitting Papandreou a twenty-four-hour delay before accepting his resignation was as follows:

He had taken a secret survey of the loyalty of military units stationed around Athens. The commandos were one hundred percent pro-king but the tanks were fifty percent pro-Papandreou. The king feared that if Papandreou were given twenty-four hours he would get up on the radio and make some kind of a demagogic speech and then the EDA or somebody else would summon the tanks into action.

ATHENS, *August 9, 1965*

This morning I spent another hour with the king, again going through the back door. Again we sat down in the two chairs by the fireplace. I offered him one of my cigarettes but today he preferred a pipe, taking one from a stand beside him.

Constantine seemed astonishingly optimistic about the chances that Stefanos Stefanopoulos, Papandreou's former deputy prime minister and now splitting off from the old man, would be able to form a government. I was surprised and said that it seemed like trying to build the Parthenon out of wet macaroni. But the king said he was quite hopeful.

The king gave me a rundown on his conversations during the last few days with the political leaders. He saw Papandreou first on Thursday, August 5—the first time he had seen him since the old man resigned July 15. Papandreou made it very clear that what he mainly wanted was new elections. Constantine told me he had said: "Elections would be very unwise now because of the explosive atmosphere that has developed."

He had received Papandreou again yesterday. The first meeting had been long—about an hour—and was rather relaxed. Yesterday's was short, only a few moments, and, said Constantine: "Not a bit agreeable." He had told Papandreou: "It would be both unwise and unsafe to hold elections now. I have found through my conversations with other political leaders that they are opposed to the idea of elections at this time and they do not feel that the general atmosphere would be good for such a move.

"In 1961, you strongly urged my father not to hold elections at that time although in 1963 you wanted them. When you won in 1963 you did not, however, gain the majority of 151 seats, so you asked my father for another election although this was unusually soon for a second round. My father had not hesitated to give you the prime ministry in 1963 even before the speaker of parliament was elected. [The king explained to me that the speaker is elected by secret ballot and that therefore sometimes a different proportion in party strength appears.]

"You told my father that you could not get either conservative or communist (EDA) support and did not have a majority through your own party and therefore you requested another election in two months. My father granted your request although it really was rather peculiar. You won fifty-three percent of the vote and a real majority, but now look what a state of affairs we have."

Papandreou listened quietly and did not say a word. Constantine told Papandreou that there was not really much point to his second request, that he receive the mandate to form a government, because: "If I gave you the mandate, you yourself said you would go to your party and they would ask for elections." It was obvious he could only form a government with the support of the Left.

He told Papandreou: "You tell me you do not want communist backing in order to form a government. That means of course that you have to have an election if I give you the mandate. But I have told you why I think it is a bad idea to have elections."

According to Constantine, Papandreou then said: "I see that my requests have been refused. I hope that God will enlighten you and help you to find a solution."

Constantine answered: "I also hope so. And I hope that you will help me."

Papandreou answered: "I cannot."

Constantine then looked at me with a certain amount of despair and asked the rhetorical question: "Why don't they go to the parliament building for their party caucus and avoid the screaming crowds?"

Of course the answer to that is obvious. Old Papandreou bullies his deputies inside the Liberal Club and the mob formed by Andreas threatens them outside.

I then asked him how he regarded his role as king, philosophically speaking.

He said: "I am trying to do what my father did, to seek harmony and peace inside the country, to avoid national squabbles, and to work for national progress. I have to work constitutionally and I need competent understanding from my ministers because I must speak through my prime ministers and what I do should be on the advice of my prime ministers. Surely it should be easy for a prime minister and a king to work together. But that depends on good faith and you cannot have lying. Papandreou has been lying to me all along.

"The communists now—that is to say EDA—would like it if I named a government of personalities. The communists like the present situation and a deadlock which permits them to have mass demonstrations.

"Sooner or later a stable government must come into power and see to it that organized minorities do not dominate our political life. But there is no evidence now that the communists are preparing for violence or bloodshed. I do not get the impression that they are accumulating arms."

According to the king, he told Papandreou: "You have been speaking to the people and telling them untruths. You have been telling them that this is a question as to whether the king or the people should rule. The proof that democracy exists in Greece is that you are able to go and freely tell such tales. You talk to the press, the Greek press, and the foreign press. But I cannot. You spurred on Andreas and Margaret [his wife] and she wrote letters urging that the United States should intervene on your behalf. I have read those letters which urge Americans to protect democracy in Greece because it is supposed to be in danger. She wrote there was going to be a clash between you and me, even before it happened. How did she know?"

Papandreou swore he knew nothing of the letters when they were sent. Constantine said: "I am prepared to take your word for that but I am not prepared to take your word that Andreas did not know. And what kind of a family do you run, anyway?"

He told Papandreou: "Your people are calling on the crowds to demonstrate. I could have gone to the radio and demanded that the Greek people assemble in the streets to protect me because I am being menaced. But I do not intend to do that. I want your party to hold together and not to crack up. If the center party splits up, part of it will go to the Left. I have not forgotten that the president of EDA said to you in parliament: 'We put you in power.' "

Constantine told me that, when he received a successive group of politicians, his conversation with Ioannis Passalides, the old (communist) boss of EDA, had been "marvelous." Passalides was over eighty and had once been a Menshevik in Russia during Lenin's day. He was a Greek from Russia and still speaks with a heavy accent. He addressed the king in the familiar form so that the king used the same form of address for him and they had a really good talk. Constantine laughed heartily as he told me about their conversation.

He said: "I told him 'before you start talking to me about bringing the country back to constitutionalism, let me tell you the details of my conversation with Papandreou and what really happened.' Passalides said: 'I am not interested in details. I hate politicians and parties.' " Constantine answered: "Ah, here we agree."

He then told Passalides that the constitution had not been violated; the only thing that could be maintained by Passalides was that parliamentary custom had been violated. Old Passalides laughed at this. He then told Constantine: "You should be like those kings in Scandinavia, who have socialists running their governments." Constantine replied: "We have no socialists. We only have EDA on the Left. Why not be honest, you would prefer that I should not be king, isn't that so?"

Passalides replied: "No, I am not one of those. I am quite happy."

Passalides then complained rather mildly to the king that the real communist leaders (not EDA) were out of the country because they were banned, and he said that the king should bring them back. Constantine replied: "But you yourself are breaking the constitution when you suggest that you are telling the king to bring back a party that is legally banned."

He said Passalides had complained to him that the constitution was not very good. Constantine told him: "You know, I was not born when it was written and I was still a schoolboy when it was amended. But I have sworn an oath to support it—and so have you."

At the end of their talk Passalides was so tired that the king had to go across and haul him out of his chair. Then he supported the old man as he got him to the door. He said to him, as he was leaving: "That's right, you should lean on your king and all will go well."

ATHENS, *October 4, 1965*

Long talk with King Constantine. I have just returned to Athens, having finished my holiday. He seemed rather relieved that the whole damned crisis is over—at any rate, as he said, "I hope it is over but it all depends on how this government does."

I asked Constantine what factors had actually broken the crisis. He said: "The biggest problem was when the Aspida conspiracy came into the open and the wheels started to turn.

"Papandreou had intended to make a clean sweep of high-ranking military officers, according to what I hear. I had sent him a message asking him to discuss this with me. I told him I thought he should tell me which officers were bad and why, and that he had no right just to chuck all of those he opposed out. As a matter of fact, I think that he and I could have had an understanding, but the people around him egged him on. I must confess to you that I rather liked the old man.

"But when he was egged on, his group started a press campaign against me. He came up to see me in Corfu. That was the first time I had a chance of seeing how his machine operates to bring his followers around him. Corfu is a small place and I was close enough to see how he brought buses of people along with him from the mainland and the islands. I told him I thought it was undesirable to take over the defense ministry as he wished."

The king went on for quite some time along these lines. Finally, when he stopped to light a cigarette, I asked if he thought measures were needed to protect the deputies in parliament from threats and blackmail such as those they had received during the crisis.

He said: "I do not think so. Not unless the whole procedure is changed. But maybe changes are indeed required. Is it necessary to have so many deputies? And no qualifications are required for them; should not the deputies be required to have special qualifications? Maybe it would be a good idea to have the government in a position to administer without always depending on its deputies?

"These are some vague ideas I am thinking of with respect to the future. Maybe it would be a good idea to have a system in which parliament makes the laws and then the government administers. The prime minister should have a free hand to appoint his ministers without always depending on the approval of the deputies."

I asked him what this crisis had taught him concerning the role of a king in contemporary times. He said that if he put the clock back now to May 1965, "I would do the whole thing the same way. I have no regrets about what I have done.

"But one certainly has learned. To be quite frank, this has increased my belief that politicians are damned shocking liars. That is what exhausted me—lies, lies, lies. I have now found out how complicated a thing this is. If you do nothing, you're dumb. If you do do something, someone will get hurt and begin to scream. And I have no right under the law to explain and justify myself to the public. I can't talk about politics although I would love to. I would love to but I cannot and I think this is wrong. That is the biggest drawback to being a head of state."

Constantine said that the security forces of Greece need to be looked at now and morale certainly needed boosting, but the army was in good shape and untarnished by the crisis.

I asked if there had been any indications of arms being sent in to the communists. He said that some had come in and that also the communists had purchased a lot of hunting weapons but this was not very important. The most dangerous thing had been the return to Greece of communists from abroad—including exiles living in Tashkent.

"They are propagandizing freely under our democracy and sometimes I think, as my father used to say, democracy is becoming demo-crazy."

It was unfortunately not clear just who were the legitimate interpreters of the constitution and the royal prerogatives permitted by the constitution. For example, he had asked his professor of constitutional law how many times he was permitted under the constitution to appoint prime ministers who were then spurned by parliament. The professor answered: "Not too many." Constantine said: "That is not very precise, is it?"

He is convinced Prince Peter is trying to oust him from the throne and to take it for himself. Peter would like to have himself declared regent of Greece, with Prince Michael as his successor. He is going to write a letter to Peter in the very near future telling him what he thinks of him. He says Peter is "in the wrong hands" by which he plainly means Irene, his wife.

By this time it was long after one o'clock. I had a long-distance call waiting for me from Paris. When we said goodbye he asked me rather diffidently: "If I get to Paris one of these days, do you mind if I call you up?" I said certainly not, that I would be delighted. The poor boy; I am quite sure that he would like nothing better than to be able to shrug his royal atmosphere and have a cozy dinner.

SOFIA, *October 7, 1965*

I rode up from Athens by train. There was no diner but I grabbed some bread, *kiofte*, and red wine at Stanko Dimitrov station where we stopped twenty minutes. There were a few Greek families on the train and I was struck by the way at station after station other Greeks, obviously alerted ahead of time, came to greet them and jabbered away in Greek, with emotional embraces and shouts of *"Patera, patera.* [Father, father.]"

SOFIA, *October 8, 1965*

Chatted at length with Nat Davis, U.S. minister, a nice young man, bright, speaks Russian and Bulgarian.

In December 1963 a Bulgarian diplomat at the UN named Asim Georgiev was tried, convicted, and executed on charges of being a liaison with the CIA. That December 1963 there was a mob assault on the U.S. legation, hurling rocks and wrecking cars. A freeze followed in our relations.

The U.S.A. wants to normalize things on a reasonable basis; to achieve about the same status here as France or Italy. We are not trying to wean Bulgaria away from Russia. This is an underdeveloped land which with massive Soviet aid has had some success in catching up.

But the big brake on any search for real improvement remains Vietnam which hangs over everything.

I talked at length with Ivan Bashev, the foreign minister. He is a tall, well set-up, youthful man with a tough friendly face. He was trained as a lawyer and is evidently pleased to be foreign minister. He said the Chinese didn't much care for Bulgaria's pro-Soviet attitude but relations were correct.

Bulgaria was prepared to make fifty-fifty deals on factories here with Western concerns, and an agreement with the French on an oil refinery is being elaborated. Bulgaria is prepared to let Westerners rent land for 99 years, guaranteed against expropriation, for seaside villas, taking each case separately as applications are received.

SOFIA, *October 11, 1965*

Took a trip yesterday with Nat Davis and his young wife, Elizabeth. At forty Nat is the youngest U.S. chief of mission.

We drove off on a fine autumn day to Rila Monastery. There seems to be a good deal of electrification in the countryside, but little running water. People drawing at wells or carrying buckets are commonplace. Old-fashioned peasant costumes are now rare. Lovely hillsides and woods; herds of sheep and some cattle; rooting swine; occasional farmers with shotguns and batches of partridge tied to their belts.

Rila Monastery was built on its present site in the fourteenth century and rebuilt in the early nineteenth, after being damaged by the Turks. It is surrounded by a fortress-like structure and contains an ancient stone tower and newer church in the courtyard. The monastery must have once housed hundreds of monks who defended themselves militarily. Now it is a hostel; no monks. The church is filled, outside and inside, with gaily colored frescoes, very much like Rumanian churches, with scenes from hell and devils to the left of the portal, paradise to the right.

Gossip: Davis says the Diplomatic Club is slowly reviving after a period of doldrums. The then president, ambassador of the UAR, fired a terrible waiter after the latter had spilled food all over him. The waiter objected: "You can't fire me; I'm a lieutenant colonel in the security forces." He was bounced anyway and the Club was immediately restricted.

I have a television set—quite splendid—in my room. It doesn't work. The only thing that does is a huge, hideous rubber plant. The clock outside my room is permanently at five-twenty o'clock. All but one of the hotel clocks I've seen are stopped; the one that works is wrong.

This afternoon I spent an hour and a half with Todor Zhivkov, present boss of Bulgaria; prime minister and first secretary of the Communist party. He received me in his office in party headquarters, a huge square room with ugly, comfortable furniture. Behind his desk are two big pictures of Marx and Lenin; opposite, a picture of Georgi Dimitrov, the erstwhile Comintern boss.

Zhivkov is shortish, squat, fat, almost bald. He has a long nose, large ears, mobile mouth, cunning brown eyes. He was very friendly, indeed ingratiating, but gave the impression of being unsure of himself.

As a token of friendship he showered me with gifts when I left. Shortly after I got back to my hotel a young man arrived bearing three volumes of books which turned out to be Z.'s collected speeches in English, inscribed to me; an envelope with an autographed photograph; and three boxes. I opened these and they contained: ceramics, a red table cloth, rose attar, Bulgarian cigarettes, Euxinograd white wine, Euxinograd *slivova.*

I asked if Zhivkov had any claims on Jugoslav Macedonia or considered there was a Bulgarian minority in that province. He said, rather idiotically: "We're Marxists. [I didn't remind him of Marx's writings on the South Slavs as 'Balkan trash.'] The most important question is whether there is collectivism or not. We feel the life of anyone, regardless of origin, is all right if it is in a socialist republic. [This is kind of silly since Greece and Turkey, with Bulgarian minorities, aren't 'socialist' and most of Jugoslavia's land is not collectivized.] We only are concerned with whether or not they are building revolution.

"The Macedonian problem doesn't exist now except in the minds of historians and extreme nationalists. We are developing the friendliest relations with Jugoslavia and with neighboring countries and socialist countries."

I asked what he hoped for on U.S. relations and how he viewed President Johnson's policy of building "bridges" to the East. He said: "We haven't felt the effect of any such bridges yet. There are no basic problems to overcome—except you must eliminate discrimination against imports from Bulgaria."

Why were VOA [Voice of America] broadcasts still jammed here? He said with a self-satisfied and cunning smile: "We'll jam until the U.S.A. stops discriminating." I asked if, putting it bluntly, what he meant was simply a flat deal—Bulgaria becomes a "most-favored nation" and simultaneously stops jamming. "Precisely," he said, delighted. "That's just what I mean. We can stop our jamming very fast."

I tried to explain that most-favored-nation status, now accorded only to Poland and Jugoslavia among communists, is a matter of law and Congress, not of presidential fiat. Z. didn't understand at all. He thinks all LBJ has to do is sign a paper.

He complained: "The United States considers Bulgaria the most intimate satellite of the Soviet Union. China also says the same thing." Then, rather to my surprise, he naively continued: "Of course, we are Russia's most confident ally so in a way perhaps this is true. The question is on how you define what a satellite is."

I asked if he considered our obvious differences on Vietnam a barrier to improved relations. He said: "Of course U.S. policy on Vietnam is an important factor and a negative influence on East-West relations. Nevertheless, our relations with you can improve even despite that difficulty, if there is good will in Washington."

I asked him just what was the significance of the antiregime plot last April. He tried to laugh it off. He said: "Why, the Western press named so many generals as having been killed at the time that we simply don't have so large a number of generals."

I asked him if they were really pro-Chinese (in fact they were rather pro-Titoist). He said stupidly: "I wasn't at their trial so I don't know the details about their real ideology. But they were not pro-Chinese. I don't think they themselves knew what their own ideology was."

PARIS, *October 17, 1965*

Spent the day with Couve de Murville playing golf, lunching, and riding to and from Paris. Couve says de Gaulle's family has been rooted in Lille for many generations and is of Flemish origin. It is a Flemish name and the "de" is a definite article—"the."

Couve is not impressed by the improvement of our military situation in Vietnam. He says this can continue for as long as the United States is willing to spend the money and make the military effort. But the minute we cease, the guerrillas will filter back and whatever flimsy regime exists in Saigon will promptly collapse. Since this is a military conflict which cannot be "won" by either side, it must eventually be solved by a political negotiation.

Couve wonders how long even a wealthy country like the United States can continue to aid foreign countries on the present scale. He reckons we are giving India $1 billion a year and that we will very shortly make a new food deal giving Egypt $150 million.

He says France spends about $100 million a year on its cultural program abroad. This is entirely operated by the *Quai d'Orsay*. When the project is debated in the assembly, the assembly generally wants the *Quai* to spend even more, not less, in this sphere. There are about 45,000

French teachers and professors abroad. Not quite half of these are in Algeria, Morocco, and Tunisia. The normal method of payment is for the host government to pay at the local salary rate and for France to make up the difference. The French think this is a very important project.

I asked Couve what foreign minister in history had been in office longer than he. He said only Vergennes, who died in 1786 after thirteen years in office. Vergennes, of course, was the French statesman most responsible for helping America become independent.

Couve complains it is impossible to talk confidentially with either the Americans or the British. They immediately leak the substance of every talk to all the other allied capitals. A few months ago Couve had a long and very confidential talk with Bohlen and two days later it was published in the press. If the French request that special care by kept to safeguard secrecy, reports of such conversations are merely labeled "top secret" instead of "secret" when they are circulated to the allies. This makes it hard to deal with the "Anglo-Saxons" and France feels it must talk seriously with the United States in early 1966 about NATO; yet it doesn't know how to do this because of this total indiscretion.

He is appalled by the indiscreet memoirs published in the United States by people associated with Kennedy; of course this comes about because of the enormous price offered by publishing houses. Such indiscretions would be for the most part banned in France and what was not legally banned would be considered improper.

Couve says there is not the slightest doubt that Germany wants actual ownership and possession of nuclear weapons on a national basis. Foreign Minister Gerhard Schroeder has been very forthright on this recently. The French have been generous toward Germany and have wished to forgive and forget, but they will change rapidly if the Germans get atomic weapons.

Couve made the odd observation that U.S. foreign aid often created more problems than it solved. Thus our food aid to India prevents a famine which might force the Indians to solve their over-population problem. Our forthcoming resumption of aid to Egypt enabled Nasser to dodge the consequences of his slaphappy ignorance of economics.

PARIS, *October 18, 1965*

Lunched with [NATO Secretary-General Manlio] Brosio. De Gaulle won't last forever. And if he doesn't provoke any new crises, there is no reason why the SHAPE military headquarters should not remain in their present temporary installations. Of course, if de Gaulle does get nasty and pull out the remnants of French cooperation with NATO, SHAPE can easily move to Holland, Belgium, or Luxembourg. There are contingency plans for everything.

There has been a big change during the last eighteen months in de Gaulle's policy. Once he really wanted a "Europe"—although along his own lines. Now it's clear he doesn't want any "Europe" at all. Once he was the strongest defender of Germany against any Soviet threat. Now he threatens the Germans with hints of a Franco-Soviet accord. Brosio is convinced that de Gaulle wants to freeze all European developments and to seek a world—not a European—role for France.

He said one of the big concerns of NATO was the fear of a Soviet-United States deal. It was traditional that small countries should always be alarmed by the prospect of deals over their heads of large countries.

PARIS, *October 21, 1965*

[Prime Minister Georges] Pompidou invited me for lunch—en tête-à-tête. He couldn't have been nicer, more informal, or more forthright.

A beautiful well-muscled but extremely thin black greyhound went upstairs with me like a member of the family and sat on a sofa in Pompidou's outer office, placing its head on my hands. It was a very French atmosphere.

There was a vase of flowers on a bureau and three modern paintings. A butler entered and gave me a whisky and soda while I waited.

At 1:30 Pompidou came in. I complimented him on his *bonne mine* and he on mine. I said the difference was that I didn't have any great secret to hide. He grinned and took a glass of tomato juice.

I asked him how it happened that all the French newspapers about ten days ago had put out simultaneous stories to the effect that de Gaulle had decided to run again. He said he wasn't sure just how this started.

He said he had heard two accounts. One was that Chaban-Delmas had seen de Gaulle and received *"l'impression"* that the General had made up his mind, and had decided to leak his own impression. The other was that Burin des Roziers had lunched with several newspaper editors and put out the story.

I then asked: "Okay, these are rumors and speculations—what are the facts?" He said it was perfectly evident that de Gaulle had made up his mind to run again. At various times during our conversation he referred to aspects of this decision but there was never even one-hundredth of one percent of doubt. De Gaulle had had a medical check-up some time since August and everything was fixed. But he also said quite frankly that de Gaulle clearly had no thought of remaining in office for the next seven years. The impression left by Pompidou was that when de Gaulle resigns the torch would be handed on to him.

Rather to my surprise Pompidou himself brought up the subject of a possible incapacity of de Gaulle during his second term and he mentioned first of all the possibility that de Gaulle might become insane (*devient fou*) rather than die or suffer a stroke. I asked what would happen in such a case.

He said everything had been arranged for a governmental decision when the president would be declared no longer able to fulfill his duties. Under the present law this would mean that the president of the senate would succeed him temporarily and then a new president would be elected. But Pompidou made it very clear that one of the first things that would be done during de Gaulle's second term would be to change that law and provide for a new succession. He was not eager to discuss the details of this project.

Pompidou waved me into his little private dining room, à coté, and we were served with an excellent lunch: fresh caviar, ice-cold vodka, small steaks, delicious vegetables, a fine claret, cheese, and fruit.

He admitted it was ridiculous to think that Europe could be defended by anything except the United States nuclear strategic force for a long time to come. But it was evident that, whether or not there was an alliance, the United States would have to defend West Europe with its strategic force in case of a showdown. Therefore in a sense there was a certain United States policy that had nothing to do with the alliance.

Furthermore, the United States would never allow any other country to control the use of its strategic nuclear force or any important part of it. De Gaulle understands this and if he were in a similar position he would follow a similar policy.

So far France had not presented its own views on how NATO should be reformed. But it was perfectly clear these would be ready by the spring of 1966. These dealt with three major problems: organization, use of atomic weapons, Germany.

France felt that in peacetime it was illogical to expect the supranational integration of NATO. However there was no argument about the need for such supranational organization the minute war came. Furthermore, such theoretical arguments about headquarters could continue in peacetime, but actual commands of units must be separated within the Alliance during peacetime. The latter question would not be answered by giving NATO commands to French officers on French soil.

The big issue involved both the atom and Germany. As long as Germany was partitioned, it was quite impossible to give Germany any kind of a voice in Allied nuclear matters, because some German government might be tempted to use atomic blackmail to achieve either reunification or frontier revision. After all, said Pompidou, neither the United States nor any West European country wants anything in a national sense from Russia; but Germany does. Therefore it is impossible to give the Germans any nuclear say so long as they are not reunited and have not renounced frontier claims.

Pompidou said it was obvious that some day France and Britain should have a kind of pool and use their nuclear force for the sake of Europe, but this was a difficult thing to arrange and the British had missed their opportunity.

He admitted that France was not in a very good position at the moment because it had not yet formulated its own ideas on NATO reforms, but this would certainly come.

Pompidou said that the most important problem in the West—more important than NATO—was economic. He also admitted that this problem had never been discussed in a frank way with Washington.

It was ridiculous to see a system under which the United States, France, and Canada, for example, paid huge bonuses to their farmers to grow wheat and sell it cheap to rich countries like Germany and England and Russia—at subnormal prices. The producing countries must get together and handle this kind of phony support and let prices find their own level in world markets.

The trouble was that the United States tended to regard all French views as de Gaulle's private views and therefore hostile to the U.S.A. It would certainly be wrong to consider himself, Pompidou, pro-American in a propaganda sense but he was certainly not anti-American, rather the contrary. After all there was some justice in the attacks he received from the left as a "Rothschild banker."

But he also felt strongly that there must be some kind of arrangement to prevent over-investment by U.S. companies in France. After all, he said, if General Motors wanted to really buy out French industry, it could. France must protect itself and if the threat became too great, France would protect itself by *étatisme* which would throw it more toward the Soviet Union.

Yet, it was absolutely out of the question that France should wish to negotiate a new Franco-Soviet pact. France was with the West and the bonds linking the West were very strong despite many differences.

We talked about politics a while. I asked him what he thought of [François] Mitterand. He looked at me quizzically and then he said: "Well, strictly between us, I think he is cold and ambitious. I mistrust him."

Incidentally, Pompidou said he very much regretted the legacy of suspicion between our two countries. For example, Britain had recognized China long ago but nobody complained in Washington. Britain long ago had indicated its desire to continue controlling its own nuclear weapons, and nobody seemed to mind in the United States. It was only when France made similar claims that they were resented.

PARIS, *October 30, 1965*

Yesterday afternoon I called on Ezra Pound, in Paris for the first time since 1924, to celebrate his eightieth birthday. He is staying with Dominique de Roux, a young French literary editor. I was greeted by de Roux and introduced to an elderly woman with a sweet face, Olga Rudge.

She disappeared and I heard her calling "Ezra?" A few minutes later he emerged in an open shirt and sweater, a thin, bewildered man with bedraggled beard and glasses. I believe he was once tall, well built, and strong but now he has withered.

He kept regarding me suspiciously with his strange blue eyes and saying absolutely nothing. I have a feeling he is definitely senile. After about four minutes looking at me he murmured in a quavering, thin voice something like: "I think I'll take the train."

Everybody stood around and talked to Pound and about other things as if he were behaving in a perfectly normal way. Finally after ten embarrassed minutes I suggested to Mrs. Rudge that maybe I could come back on another day when he was feeling stronger. She thought that would be wise. He shook hands doubtfully and I left.

PARIS, *November 1, 1965*

Lunched with Harlan Cleveland, our new ambassador to NATO. He is a calm, cool, thoughtful, unexcitable intellectual. I have a feeling that he is one of the "power" boys of the administration, that he looks at everything in terms of strength.

Cleveland sniffs at the French *force de frappe* as unimportant and as costing France too much. Likewise, he says France simply doesn't have the influence in the world to which it aspires, so there is no reality to de Gaulle's policy.

Cleveland is obviously a "tough" envoy and believes in getting things done. He thinks we should not permit the French to hold up alliance planning and should even be prepared, if the French were to remain neutral or hostile in any war with Russia, to seize such installations as we require on French soil even if briefly this was tantamount to "fighting a two-front war."

PARIS, *November 6, 1965*

Last night I gave a small dinner *à quatre* to Étienne and Jane Burin des Roziers. Étienne said Stanislaw Gajewski, who was Polish ambassador here for many years, went to see de Gaulle at Colombey in the autumn of 1956 after Gomulka had taken power in Warsaw. He said to de Gaulle: "At last we have our independence." De Gaulle merely sniffed and observed wryly: "But you never told me that you weren't independent before now."

PARIS, *November 8, 1965*

Unusually agreeable luncheon today with Lemnitzer. He came down to Lucas Carton—a good half hour from his headquarters—in full uniform with ribbons all the way from his Adam's apple to his navel.

Alex Allegrier, the owner of the restaurant, came over and invited us down to his cellar. Rather to my surprise, Lemnitzer accepted with alacrity. Alex opened up a little padlocked section in one of the *caves* and said he wished to share with us something he never shared with anyone outside of his family. This proved to be an 1884 cognac in a magnum, covered with dust. Rather to the horror of Lemnitzer he first made us hold out our hands and wash them in some of this priceless grape juice.

Then we drank a toast proposed by Alex to "America—without whom in 1914–1918 or in 1939–1945, I would not be a Frenchman." Lemnitzer was very touched, above all because I had told him of de Gaulle's relationship with Alex, who owns the hotel where the General used to stay. Alex showed us through the *cave* and then insisted we have another handwash and throat-swallow of 1900 marc de Bourgogne which, again to my astonishment, Lemnitzer accepted with alacrity.

Alex then told Lemnitzer (I translated) some of the tales of this restaurant but said he would never write them—despite the offers of French publishers—because he preferred to go to his grave with his own memories. With Lemnitzer's eyes popping out, he told how Joffre, Lord French, and Pershing had agreed to the 1918 armistice in his restaurant —and informed Alex. He recounted the story of the Gestapo agent who came to spy on the 1937 royal visit of King George VI and came back in 1940, when Alex refused to give him the table he wished. He told him how Laval came to Lucas Carton on June 22, 1941, and told Alex, just after Germany had attacked Russia, "At last we have won the war." He swears Laval was not a traitor and he should have gone to Spain for six months to get over the hysteria of revenge in France.

Finally, he said that General von Choltitz had his last dinner in Paris there with Taittinger, mayor of Paris under the Germans, and had toasted "Paris—a city which belongs to the world." Alex claims Choltitz was mistreated by the French and that Taittinger never should have been arrested as a collaborator. But Alex said history had its revenge when Taittinger's son was later elected mayor of Paris.

Lemnitzer himself had an anniversary. Twenty-three years ago today "Torch" (the Anglo-American landing in north Africa) took place while Lemnitzer, the deputy chief of planning for that operation, was in Eisenhower's headquarters in Gibraltar waiting to see whether or not Spain and/or Germany would react.

I asked if it was correct that General Charles Ailleret, French armed forces chief of staff, had notified Lemnitzer France would not participate in Fallex, an exercise held every two years involving all the NATO powers. He told me this was correct. In June the French government through diplomatic channels had advised the permanent NATO council of this. In July Ailleret spelled it out to Lemnitzer.

French operational units, including the two divisions assigned to NATO, will not participate in these maneuvers in the autumn of 1966. This means that French operational units and French officers in SHAPE who are involved in operational planning will not take part. It would be inconvenient but not impossible to work out European defense without France participating, but he had never thought of giving France an equivalent role vis-à-vis the U.S.A. to that now held by Spain.

If France broke with NATO it would be expensive but easy to shift SHAPE and NATO headquarters elsewhere, and it would be possible to reduce reliance on lines of communication going across France by building up stockpiles in forward areas (meaning Germany).

PARIS, *November 11, 1965*

Lunched with Baron Adolph "Dolf" Bentinck, the Dutch ambassador, whom I have known since Cairo days during World War II. He saw de Gaulle October 18 and had quite an interesting conversation.

At the end of his formal, planned conversation the General indicated he had a few more minutes. At this point Dolf said to him: "You told my friend Cy Sulzberger that you believed Russia was bounded on the East by the Urals and that Soviet territory, in Asia, would someday return to China." I asked if de Gaulle had shown irritation to this reference to what he had told me. He said that on the contrary, de Gaulle had seemed very pleased and merrily talked on, confirming everything I had written.

Bentinck was specially interested because, during the summer, he had asked Soviet ambassador Zorin for his reactions on my column concerning this point and the Soviet ambassador had scoffed at it saying: "This is merely part of Sulzberger's typical wishful thinking."

PARIS, *November 12, 1965*

This morning I had a good long talk with Pierre Chatenet, president of EURATOM, Gaullist, and minister of the interior from May 1959 until his resignation in May 1961.

Everybody realizes that it is quite easy for a technically skilled country to develop military nucleonics from peaceful nucleonics. Yet we are against disseminating the former and actually encourage disseminating the latter.

If you send reactors to a highly developed country with laboratories, technicians, scientists, and a high industrial level, it is quite different from sending these to some underdeveloped African state. Thus, in fact, you are disseminating the potential of nuclear weapons while opposing the dissemination of the weapons.

If one had wished to prevent the development in Germany of *any* atomic military potential then installation of peaceful atomic reactors should have been barred. After all, Germany has a remarkable infrastructure of scientists, techniques, and industries. And today Germany is undoubtedly industrially and technologically able, should it so decide, to start making an atomic bomb.

Let us be realistic. The Germans have not so far refrained from this because of the ABC weapons ban, but because they are "good" and responsible democrats. Should they stop being "good," they could start immediately making A-bombs. They are in a position to do so when they wish and they could probably do it quite rapidly.

The only barrier today for the Germans is moral and political—not technical. In the long run, we just depend on Germany's good will. They have the industrial capacity to make anything and we all know that world scientists publish practically all secrets except for technological gimmicks that can facilitate and speed up one or another process.

One cannot sell Germany peaceful atomic equipment without risking the chance that some day they will make military atomic equipment. The important thing is that countries like the United States and France should *know* the risk they are taking and not delude themselves.

PARIS, *November 24, 1965*

Toshikazu Kase, former Japanese ambassador to the UN, dropped in this morning. He is acting as diplomatic adviser to his prime minister.

Kase was with the prime minister when they went to Washington in January 1965 and discussed world affairs with Johnson. In the joint communiqué then published, three new words were included with respect to the Japanese-U.S. security treaty. This new phrase stressed that it was valid "against any attack," a very important implication. What it really means is that the treaty, which was originally negotiated to protect Japan against Russia, has now changed its emphasis and is aimed primarily against China.

PARIS, *December 1, 1965*

Lunch with Jacques de Beaumarchais, now Number Three man in the *Quai d'Orsay* [later French ambassador to London].

Beaumarchais was interesting on his recent Russian trip when he accompanied Couve de Murville. He was struck by the informality prevailing among Russian leaders in their Black Sea villas. Mikoyan said: "The day Hitler attacked us Molotov put on boots instead of ordinary shoes and he wore them right through the war. This was *his* contribution to the war effort."

Mikoyan also told a sadly amusing story about Churchill's visit to Moscow in 1942. He said that when Churchill's plane was due to arrive all the principal Soviet leaders except Stalin rushed around to get white shirts, neckties, and respectable-looking suits to greet the famous Western aristocrat in suitable fashion (Stalin, of course, continued to wear his uniform). To the horror of Mikoyan and the others, Churchill descended from his airplane "looking like a mechanic." He was of course wearing his famous "teddy-bear suit."

PARIS, *December 4, 1965*

Dined last night at the Windsors. I distinguished myself by asking one lady whether it was true that General Weygand had been the bastard son of Empress Carlotta. She looked a bit flabbergasted, nudged me and whispered that my other neighbor was Weygand's daughter-in-law.

PARIS, *December 15, 1965*

Last night I spent more than two hours talking and drinking with Dean Rusk. I started by asking whether he thought there was any means of satisfying West Germany's nuclear defense desires without at the same time ruining chances of an antiproliferation treaty with Russia. Rusk said this is a false comparison and the two things should not be joined in "counterpoint."

He added: "We oppose proliferation more strongly than anyone. But the Russians have not been so consistent. After all, they helped China until about 1959. We are more virginal than Russia on this question. But the Russians are raising the issue because they don't know what we have in mind for Germany and also they don't like NATO or any attempts to strengthen it."

I asked Rusk if we intend to ask France if it has any specific ideas for a NATO reform and, if so, when we planned to pose the question. He said: "We have been asking this question for three years and they have never put any ideas forward. The last time I saw Couve in New York we had dinner together and I was determined not to raise the question of NATO, not even to mention it because we had brought it up so often. Couve didn't mention it either. And then, when he briefed the French press, he expressed regret that I hadn't brought it up because he claimed he had some interesting new ideas. What the hell. You can't win.

"We have been pressing the French for years to define exactly what they mean and want. The French won't say. What do they mean when they talk about neutralizing southeast Asia? Which countries are involved and how is neutralization defined? The French won't say."

I asked if France denounced the North Atlantic Treaty in 1969 and requested a bilateral defense treaty with the U.S.A., would we be willing to negotiate? "There is no chance at all of that," said Rusk. "Not a prayer."

Rusk made the interesting point that if the French forced SHAPE and NATO headquarters to move and close down existing lines of communication, they would have to break many contracts. This would subject them to legal penalties of a financial sort.

I asked if the U.S.A. was prepared to endorse Spanish membership in NATO. He said: "We would favor it," and that the big majority of the Allies would favor it but certain "socialist governments" would not and such a question requires unanimity.

Rusk does *not* think the Soviet line on Vietnam is hardening. He implied that some Russians have been killed in our bombing of the North Vietnam missile sites but neither we nor the Russians wanted to talk about it.

Toward midnight I volunteered to go, especially since I have an incipient grippe and only half a voice. But Rusk urged me to join him in another drink. We talked about Arthur Schlesinger's book on Kennedy. I told him I was being bombarded by indignant letters from Arthur, complaining that I had written in a column that he may have been sticking his knife into Rusk's back because Rusk refused to put out information in front of Schlesinger for fear it would be promptly published in a book. Rusk said I was absolutely right.

Rusk said anybody working for the state department had to sign a statement on leaving, pledging themselves not to take away or make use of official papers—classified or unclassified. He admitted that Secretary of State Byrnes violated this but he could think of no one else in the postwar period. Generally state department papers are locked up for twenty-two or twenty-three years before they are made available to the public. But some papers are locked up forever. This can be a presidential decision. CIA or FBI papers are permanently out of the public domain.

We had a long discussion about de Gaulle. Rusk revealed an alarming tendency to oversimplify his analysis of the General. "Let's talk really off the record," Rusk said. "Do you think de Gaulle is the Cross of Lorraine or Pétain?"

I said I didn't have a clue as to what he meant. I gathered from the subsequent conversation that Rusk wished to know whether I thought de Gaulle would lead France to war beside the U.S.A. if we became involved in a conflict—in other words, whether France would fight or "collaborate."

I said I thought de Gaulle was an honorable man and he would fight. Rusk was more than sceptical. He also asked if I thought de Gaulle really understood the implication of nuclear weapons. I said I certainly thought he did and that we were the ones who didn't understand what de Gaulle was after.

I said de Gaulle had obviously built the *force de frappe* as a political weapon against his allies, and not as a military weapon against his enemies. For this reason he had decided on a cheap, high-level version of the Mirage IV instead of a much more expensive low-level version, because de Gaulle had no intention of using it as a weapon. This was an important distinction the United States failed to make.

Rusk sniffed at de Gaulle's Asiatic policy and said France didn't have a single trump in the game and just wanted to pick up any crumbs left behind by China. He has a cynical analysis of de Gaulle. He concedes that de Gaulle stood up loyally for the count during the Cuban confrontation but thinks the General realized the implication of his alliance commitments then and they might mean the incineration of France.

He wonders if de Gaulle could be counted on in a new crisis. He said: "I understand his problem. If I were in his position I might also worry about it. But I am not the president of France. I'm the United States secretary of state and I have to worry about these problems from our angle."

Rusk asked if I thought de Gaulle's policy would change after the elections. I said categorically no, neither the policy nor the means of applying it. Rusk said: "I agree."

Rusk thinks the Chinese are essentially realistic people and that eventually common sense will influence their present southeast Asian policy. We therefore wish to avoid pressing China into a corner where it must take a "cosmic decision."

Rusk said de Gaulle should realize that if he gets out of NATO, France might conceivably face destruction without our help. I said this was crazy because of France's position. He said: "De Gaulle exaggerates the importance of France's geographical position."

Rusk said he had been an old friend of Dulles, who brought him into the Rockefeller Foundation. Dulles was a lone wolf who always liked to get things done alone. He was a wonderful negotiator, as he proved in the Japanese treaty. But he was a lawyer and he always wanted to win a case. To achieve a reasonable settlement sometimes you have to tell the other fellow when he doesn't seem to understand things plainly. I pointed out that François de Callières, the eighteenth-century diplomatic expert, had said the most dangerous profession from which to draw diplomats was the law. Rusk smiled bitterly and said that only seven of our secretaries of state had not been lawyers.

Rusk said he will never write his memoirs. He seems mildly optimistic that we will eventually get a Vietnamese settlement and, "then, once that is over, everything is now going our way."

Politics is a very important aspect of policy making in the U.S.A. Acheson never understood this. Truman did. Acheson was furious when Truman asked Dulles as a Republican to negotiate the Japanese peace treaty—after Dulles had fought a vicious campaign for the senate against Lehman in New York. Truman smiled and said: "Naturally Dulles will be a Republican every two years but the rest of the time he will work as an American." Acheson was on the Yale board of governors with Senator Taft. When Mrs. Taft fell ill, Acheson sent her flowers and Taft wrote him a very nice letter. The next day Taft got up on the floor of the senate and demanded Acheson's resignation. Acheson never got over that.

Rusk looked very well. I asked him how he did it. He said: "I do one thing at a time and I never suffer insomnia."

PARIS, *December 30, 1965*

Lunched with Jean Chauvel, the retired French ambassador who recently took a trip to China and North Vietnam.

Chou says the Chinese regard the U.S.A. and Russia with equal hostility. Chauvel reminded Chou that the U.S.A. and France were allies. "Yes," said Chou, "like Russia is ours."

Chou made it plain that China considers the Vietnam war as only a small part of a struggle for world hegemony between China on the one hand and the U.S.A. and the USSR on the other. China is convinced that Russia and America want to partition the world and have made a deal to do so, sees our parallel policies in India as proof. China will not consider halting the Vietnam war under *any* conditions. China anticipates escalation which will first involve Laos and Cambodia, then Thailand, and then China itself. Chou foresees the possibility that the U.S.A. could destroy everything China has accomplished in the last fifteen years, but he adds: "If they invade our territory, none of them will leave alive."

The outlook in Hanoi is different. The Americans are not talked about as wicked devils but as idiotic fools.

PARIS, *January 4, 1966*

Lunched today with Jacques de Beaumarchais, now chief of the political section of the *Quai d'Orsay*. Jacques says the only country that can conceivably help the U.S.A. out of its Vietnam impasse is Russia. But the U.S.A. must make concessions to Russia in exchange. These concessions cannot come in Germany because the Germans won't accept them. Therefore they must come in Asia. The Russians must first gain control in Hanoi by magnifying their arms shipments—and the Americans must accept this.

PARIS, *January 10, 1966*

Dinner last night with Louis Joxe who professes keen amusement at the new cabinet. He says de Gaulle has tied up three cats in a bag—Pompidou, Debré, and Faure. He is going to let them fight it out—"and the only winner will be de Gaulle." Joxe says there is no "dauphin." The dauphin will be the man who is in power when de Gaulle dies or has to quit. By putting Debré in the cabinet in a strong position de Gaulle did the equivalent of the Esso advertisement "put a tiger in your tank."

PARIS, *January 11, 1966*

Lunched with Raymond Aron. He has an extraordinary facility for answering you instantly in brilliant phrases, and the order of his logic is impeccable.

He doesn't think much of Walter Lippmann. When Lippmann had his seventy-fifth birthday and a book of tributes was published, Aron wrote one of these. Prior to so doing, he reread a lot of Lippmann's books. He was fascinated to discover that Lippmann has been consistently wrong on almost every important issue for the last forty years—and nevertheless retains a reputation as a prophet. Lippmann was wrong on Germany before the war, on England during the war, and on Russia after the war. He thought the cold war had ended—just three weeks before the (1948) rape of Czechoslovakia. He has always been convinced that nineteenth-century ideas of spheres of interest should govern the world, but this has been outmoded for a quarter of a century.

Raymond thinks that when Moscow broke with Peking, Moscow had the choice of going either to the left or to the right of China. It rapidly found out that it would not be enough to go to the left in terms of words alone, but such a political slant would also have to be accompanied by actions. Therefore Russia made the deliberate decision to accept China's communist opposition from the left, the way Stalin accepted a Trotskyite opposition from the left.

The conflict between Russia and China is primordial in Soviet thinking. Relations with the U.S.A. are secondary to this. Furthermore, it is perfectly apparent that Washington accepts this approach. The important fundamental of U.S.-Soviet relations is that they must be tacit, in terms of their common purpose. The conflict between the U.S.A. and the USSR must remain explicit; and the agreement between them must remain implicit.

Simultaneously the U.S.A. and the USSR must remain both allies and enemies. This is a very complex relationship.

PARIS, *February 8, 1966*

The CIA is increasingly concerned about a scandalous problem which it is now investigating: the black market in South Vietnam. Chinese merchants from Cholon (the Chinese quarter of Saigon) traditionally bank in France. They are now transferring to France considerably more than 100 million dollars a year on profits from the black market on U.S. goods. This provides France with an enormous dollar surplus—far larger than any surplus in foreign trade—with which to buy gold from the United States. Thus, as a result of the American black market in Saigon, France is given a weapon with which to deliberately weaken the U.S. dollar.

PARIS, *February 11, 1966*

Lunched with Chip Bohlen. He thinks we should make as the basic point of our propaganda concerning our objectives in Vietnam the pledge that all we are fighting for is free elections in South Vietnam and that we are ready to abide by the outcome, whatever it may be. He claims the communists have won only a single free election in history; the 1917 Vladivostok city vote.

The great danger in dealing with communists is to try to obtain objectives by force. Bombing North Vietnam will probably produce an effect opposite to the desired one of pressing the communists to the negotiation table. If one analyzes communist methods in history, one finds that it is only by indirect persuasion that goals can be achieved. Thus in Korea it was the implied threat that the conflict might escalate into atomic war that finally produced its end. Direct threats such as bombing North Vietnam are unlikely to work.

I spent an hour this morning at the *Quai d'Orsay* with Maurice Couve de Murville, the foreign minister. It is clear the gap between Paris and Washington is widening steadily.

PARIS, *February 17, 1966*

Couve said France felt the United States could enter into a Vietnam negotiation if it were ready to put aside the problem of a military decision. Both sides would first have to agree that no military victory was possible.

Furthermore, there must be a consensus on the ultimate objectives for Vietnam. The French definition of such objectives is: (1) both North and South Vietnam should be independent, (2) there should be no intervention of any sort from outside, (3) both countries should have a completely free choice on deciding their future and their form of government, and (4) because of the need to prevent outside intervention the two halves of Vietnam must be neutral or noncommitted.

France did not believe the United States was ready to acknowledge such aims. Nobody has yet satisfactorily explained the U.S. official position except in "meaningless generalities." Likewise, Couve says there has been no change in Hanoi's position. He adds:

"No negotiation is possible until we know what United States policy really is. Does the U.S.A. really want an independent South Vietnam or does it only want a South Vietnam under a government approved by Washington? Your government is not clear on this."

Couve said Moscow agrees entirely with the French point of view and "obviously Hanoi cannot disagree." But he said Peking's view was different. China is not actively participating in the war and therefore its attitude was different from Hanoi's. China is in no hurry for peace. Indeed, it likes the war to continue. Couve commented wryly: "I have always told your people that you are playing into the Chinese hand."

Couve said the Saigon government of Marshal Ky was not a representative government and clearly could not represent South Vietnam in negotiations. I had a feeling that French policy opposes any representative from South Vietnam except for the Vietcong Liberation Committee.

Couve said: "One of the basic differences between the United States and France is that you believe there is a government in South Vietnam and the trouble is caused by foreign intervention: that you are fighting communism. We believe this is not the case. We believe you are fighting the population of South Vietnam helped by others—particularly by North Vietnam. The people of South Vietnam are fighting you. That is the basis of the present situation. Someday the United States must accept the idea that you are fighting the Vietnamese people."

I said France's foreign policy seemed aimed at becoming the leader of a kind of political, not geographical, third force. He said: "In a way this is true. We are basing our policy on the independence of states and on the view that ideological blocs are bad things in themselves. This accords with world trends that show that such blocs are disintegrating. The concept of blocs is vanishing. Therefore, it is no accident that our policy is deliberately pursuing such a goal."

WASHINGTON, *February 26, 1966*

Lunched with Averell Harriman today. Averell said he liked and admired Mrs. Johnson, but confessed he didn't like the president although he respected him. But Averell appears in thorough accord on the Vietnam policy. Thinks we must be tough.

Harriman says Kosygin last July refused to intervene in Vietnam when Harriman saw him and was quite nasty; said we should contact Hanoi. We got Tito, Shastri, and Nasser to ask Kosygin; and they got the same answer.

Harriman thinks Russia tried to get Hanoi to negotiate when Shelepin was there, but we have little definite information. Russia is worried about China. China accuses Russia of not striking at the West in Europe, especially Berlin, and of not sending materiel by sea to North Vietnam (where there would be a maritime confrontation with the U.S.A.).

Harriman is bewildered by the foolish Bobby Kennedy statement on including communists in the Saigon government. Is irked at Lippmann and the *New York Times* approach. Complains that photographers in Vietnam refuse to take pictures of Vietcong atrocities.

WASHINGTON, *February 27, 1966*

Went to a ball last night honoring the Mac Bundys. (He leaves Washington and the White House tomorrow to head the Ford Foundation.)

Dined at Mrs. [Alice] Longworth's, where Larry O'Brien, now postmaster general, made the point that the Irish became a powerful political element here because, like all minorities, they organized to care for each other, but they were the only minority to speak English on arriving.

At the party Bobby Kennedy came over and sat with me for over an hour. Complained my column dismissed his Vietnam idea in one curt sentence. I told him I'd read his entire seven-page speech and it made sense neither read backwards nor forwards. He was not pleased. I mistrust him but he is a skillful dialectician; lays down a heavy smoke screen and shoots suddenly from behind it; pretends innocence and naiveté that isn't there.

WASHINGTON, *February 28, 1966*

Good talk with McNamara at the Pentagon. The Chinese have sent construction battalions (about twenty thousand men) to North Vietnam to repair and build roads and railroads; no fighting troops. There have also been some new airfields built in south China.

Soviet supplies to North Vietnam are mostly going there by land across China. The Chinese have placed some obstacles in the way of such Soviet shipments but hardly anything goes by sea.

We have made no sensational break-through in counter-guerrilla weapons although there have been useful improvements. The 257-mm. rocket has been adjusted to helicopters. The 40-mm. grenade is now air-launched. Infrared equipment has been most usefully developed for locating an enemy. The M-16 rifle has proven very useful in guerrilla combat—greater fire rate, and lighter than the M-14.

But these don't greatly affect the military balance. The most important thing has been the vastly improved application of mobility and the rate of fire power. Ninety percent or more of our wounded are taken out to casualty stations by helicopter now as against ten percent in Korea.

McNamara insists it has not been hard to elaborate the concepts of counter-insurgency, but it is hard to administer them, just as the same has been true for guerrillas.

It is hard to cut supply shipments on the Ho Chi Minh trail on the ground but only twelve to thirty tons a day get through and then are distributed to units. Pressure from the air increases the difficulties and cost of these supplies.

We believe the Vietcong violate Cambodian territory but we have no evidence that this is with Sihanouk's complicity. It isn't a fundamental in the war anyway, not even Sihanoukville. Nor is Haiphong's role as a North Vietnam port fundamental.

I 2

"THINK BACK TO WHEN

WE ASSASSINATED

DIEM"

I SPENT THE BETTER PART OF TODAY WITH THE TWO TOP PEOPLE OF our government, and I came away with mixed feelings. The day started badly for me with an abcessed tooth which I had to have removed in a fairly major operation. I was still feeling kind of rocky when I was taken to see Johnson at 12:30 by Bill Moyers, White House press chief. We sat in the little room just off of Johnson's office, a room widely called the "think tank." I didn't get out of the White House until 4:00 P.M.

I am somewhat bewildered by the present U.S. leadership. McNamara yesterday impressed me again as having a remarkable machine-like mind but very little sensitivity to human relationships. Rusk again struck me as being unusually decent, but I don't have a feeling he is profound or subtle. The most interesting and most bothersome man is the president himself.

Incidentally, he said Senator Bobby Kennedy had conceived of his much-debated idea of forming a coalition government in Saigon after a private meeting at Bobby's Washington house (Hickory Hill) with certain unnamed members of the State Department whom Johnson described as "stupid and low-level."

Johnson is obsessed with opinion polls and political statistics. He is shrewd but he doesn't impress me as being nice, wise, or possibly even strong—massive as he is physically and competitive as he is by nature. If Johnson succeeds in Vietnam he will almost certainly be regarded as a very great president. If he fails he may go down in history on a par with Andrew Johnson.

Our conversation was very informal (indeed, it ended in the barber shop). He sprawled in an armchair and I sat on a sofa. He drank Coca-

Cola and I had coffee. In his usual somewhat heavy-handed way, Johnson was very flattering and recalled a meeting we had had some years ago in Paris where he said I had given him excellent advice. He told me he thought that even on the rare occasions when he didn't agree with me I always sought to be honest and objective. This was, of course, blarney.

Johnson looked better physically than when I saw him last. He is perceptibly thinner. At one point he mentioned that he weighs 200 pounds. I suspect the figure is actually somewhat higher because he is a large man, but when he took off his jacket in the barber shop his paunch was far less pendulant. He was well dressed in a dark grey suit, white shirt, and conservative necktie. He stretched out in the armchair, his long legs sprawling as he slumped.

He began talking about the efforts of Senator Morse today to repeal the 1964 congressional resolution endorsing any actions he might wish to take after the Gulf of Tonkin incident. He said: "Anyone who wants to handicap the president should vote with Morse on this. Our policy is to support SEATO and to respond to an armed attack as carried out by the present aggressors. Those members of Congress who believe this should vote with me and the rest should vote with Morse. I want this thoroughly clear and I will not have the Gulf of Tonkin resolution diluted. That resolution, which was approved on October 10, 1964, specifically stated that it would not expire until the president determined that peace and security of the area affected had been reasonably assured or until the resolution was specifically terminated by Congress."

He said that last year we had had more than three hundred contacts of a diplomatic sort seeking to explore the chances of a negotiation and two pauses in bombing during which we suggested to everybody interested that the Vietnamese question could be settled by negotiation. But nothing had come of this. The Russians had been the first to suggest that there should be a bombing pause of from twelve to twenty days. Ambassador Dobrynin put forth this idea in separate conversations with Fulbright, Morse, Bobby Kennedy, and Mac Bundy. He had indicated that if such a pause came there might be a peace negotiation.

"Why, Shastri wrote to me a day before he died—on this subject. And I think the Russians did try. I think Shelepin tried hard in Hanoi to get a negotiation started. But he failed.

"Nevertheless, there have been decided gains as a result of our effort. One hundred and fifteen nations genuinely responded to the American offer. Everyone except Hanoi and Peking. We hunkered down for thirty-seven days and didn't do any bombing and we suffered the consequences, and this was obviously pleasing to many people—those in the Eastern European camp like Poland, Hungary, and Russia, and also the countries of Latin America, as well as Canada and Britain. But the other fellows just weren't interested.

"Anyway that certainly put an end to propaganda talk that this is a colonialist war. That taint was erased. The world reaction was good. Why, the Pope's reaction was very generous. De Gaulle had doubts about the efficacy of the bombing pause—as I did. But I tried to go the last mile. I didn't think this would do the trick, but I thought it was necessary to satisfy all those who doubt us. Now we can see that it doesn't work.

"Look at all we have done. Think back to when we assassinated Diem [I was startled to have him use that phrase], when we removed General [Paul D.] Harkins because he was supposed to be too warlike, when we moved Ambassador [Frederick] Nolting because he was supposed to be too close to Diem. None of those things did the trick. But people now know in their hearts—like Goldwater said, in their hearts—that we would negotiate if we could and that we are strong enough and determined enough to be unafraid of negotiations.

"Some people think that if you have one bombing pause and then another bombing pause it hurts. But it doesn't really change opinion substantially. I have looked at all the polls. Before the pause and the televised senate hearings the poll takers said that ten percent of the people were doves. After the bombing pause and the TV hearings there were still ten percent. There has been a shift up and down in the numbers who support me—all the way between forty and seventy percent. It goes up when we take strong action like the Tonkin Gulf. But that's a kind of inflation.

"You can get enormous support when you get tough, but I don't like that kind of inflation. After the bombing pause and the TV hearings those who supported me declined from sixty-three to forty-nine percent. But the shift didn't go to the doves. It went to the hawks. That's what worries me and that's what people should know. The figure for the doves stays unchanged.

"Did you know that during the last sixty days the enemy has had thirty thousand casualties? The people of this country just don't know this yet. Not even [General Vo-Nguyen] Giap knows it. They're hurting.

"But the hearings have not built up the doves. They have only served to pull down the number of those supporting a moderate policy."

I remarked that while it was perfectly clear to Americans that we weren't engaged in any kind of colonial war, this was far less clear overseas. Many people suspected us of fighting another imperialist war with racist overtones—the white man against the Asian. I thought it was necessary to make more of an effort to eliminate this impression.

Johnson: "The best way to refute that charge of colonialism is two hundred years of history. All our experiences have shown that this isn't true. Look at the case of the Philippines. I have said time and time again we are not fighting for any territory and we don't intend to hold any bases in that area. We would pull out tomorrow if the other fellow would just get behind his parallel.

"Of course there are some people in this country, those Fulbrights, who only want a Fortress America, maybe supporting a Little White Europe. Those Fulbrights say about Asia—they are not our kind of people. Well, I don't share that view. I am preserving the brown man, not warring on him. Somebody has got to protect the 2½ billion people in Asia. I am interested in those people and their education and their food and their health, and that's what I am always saying. Why, I tell Ho Chi Minh—if you will just lay down your pistol I'll help you. I am ready to let them join in all our efforts to build up southeast Asia—if they will only make peace.

"Of course there are people who think the Asians are not worth saving —not as worth saving as the Europeans. Well, I am not one of those people who went to Oxford and thinks that way. I think they are worth saving whatever color they are.

"Do you know, Cy, I find there is a little racial overtone in those who oppose us. Don't you forget—Fulbright was against civil rights and he's always been against civil rights. Well I'm for civil rights and for TVA and for wages and hours. But he just wants a sweatshop and racism."

I asked him why we had never declared war in Vietnam, apart from the obvious problem that it would be hard to decide against whom we should declare war. He answered: "Why should we? I think we would stand to lose a lot. For example we don't know what treaties Hanoi has got with Peking or the others. We don't know what kind of a SEATO they have in their part of the world—in secret. They may even have a secret deal with de Gaulle. If we declared war on them we might spring all the agreements they have.

"The SEATO treaty says we are going to prevent anybody from coming into our area if they ask for help—as South Vietnam did—and we don't need any declaration of war. Everything is clear on this for the members of SEATO and the protocol states. We are simply defending ourselves. And just look: we are not bombing Hanoi or Haiphong. We are not bombing Peking or landing paratroopers up there. We are just standing where we are, like Joe Robinson used to say." Here he got into a rambling, aimless reminiscence of the late Senator Joseph T. Robinson (Democrat, Arkansas).

Johnson then resumed: "We don't want this war. We would rather show Hanoi how to grow better rice and how to let its people learn how to read and get happy and they can do all that the day they stop fighting. We are not declaring war; we are declaring peace."

Johnson said that until Dulles began the first of our commitments in Asia, "we were damn near slipping under and into slavery." Dulles was the first to recognize that we had to save Asia the way we had already saved Europe with the Marshall Plan and NATO. Again Johnson began to ramble and to proclaim that "without Churchill we'd have all been slaves" in World War II and that Dulles had likewise seen the need to keep Asia from being conquered by communism. But he complained that "those God-damned Oxford-educated people like Fulbright don't believe in defending any part of the world that isn't white."

Johnson said Dulles had recognized on the basis of recent U.S. experience, including the sudden communist attack in Korea, that it was necessary for us to make plain where we would stand up. It was the absence of such advance proclamations that helped bring about both World War II and the attack in Korea. Johnson continued: "It was Dulles who decided that we should serve notice in Asia of where we stood—Asia, where two and a half billion people live. We had never really seen the importance of Asia. I was out in Asia during World War II. I was there. And I saw how our armed forces in the Asian theater of war were regarded as second-class citizens.

"Dulles took the decision that we must say—this is the wall and don't tread on me. Anyone who tries to swallow up southeast Asia now knows that any country there can call on eight friends in that SEATO alliance and we are all obliged to respond with all our power. Dulles hoped that making this plain might prevent aggression. But if that didn't work at least it gave us the force to act. And the senate ratified that SEATO treaty eighty-two to one.

"From 1954 to 1960 the communists didn't do much out there. Why they didn't even form that National Liberation Front until December 1960. But then they saw that we were getting weak. They looked around and saw what Castro did and they saw that young man sit in here in the White House. And when Khrushchev talked like war to Kennedy in Vienna we just didn't do very much. We called up the reserves but that didn't scare Khrushchev. He put his missiles in Cuba and all that young fellow here did was to say to Khrushchev: 'Please, sir, take your missiles out and we won't trouble you any more. Yes, you can go ahead and propagate communism in Cuba and we won't touch you if you will just take those missiles out.'

"China and Hanoi concluded we were soft and that there wasn't going to be any massive retaliation no matter what they did. They figured they would have a little repeat performance of their own. Their propaganda began to stress that Diem was corrupt and no good. They said we will just talk those Americans into assassinating Diem and we will get them to remove Nolting and Harkins and we will call them colonialists and racists. And that's what happened."

Johnson continued: "My people told me that we would either have to surrender and tear up the alliance and come home or I would have to permit them to stop those fellows from bringing in supplies to the VC and I would have to put in enough forces to stop their aggression. And that's what I did. From 1961 until 1965 I didn't bomb. They would have taken over the whole place in 1965 as they planned to if we had torn up the alliance and come home and they would have turned the Pacific into a red sea. But I determined I was not going to let them do that.

"You hear all this talk about escalation. Well the quickest way to escalate in Asia is just to give the Chinese Vietnam. Why [Henry Cabot] Lodge told our ambassadors yesterday [our Asian ambassadors were meeting in the Philippines] that the most escalating act he could imagine would be for us to get out of Vietnam.

"The other fellow is paying very heavily now. Because we are there to stay. I don't know what [General] Westmoreland wants but whatever he wants he is going to get it. There are probably forty or fifty thousand more men going out to support him now and if he needs more he can have it. I am going ahead in a measured, moderate way. I am not going to spit in China's face. China knows what she would get if she spit in our face. And what I am doing is a prudent, moderate thing, and even the Chinese know that."

Then Johnson went on: "No small nation anywhere would be safe if we got out of Vietnam."

I asked if the Vietnamese conflict had in any sense altered his basic approach toward Russia and Eastern Europe. He had told me about ten months ago that he was determined—despite the Vietnam issue—to keep working for closer contacts with Eastern Europe and improved relations. He said now "there has been a change on their side but not on ours. Our policy has not changed and we are hopeful. We hope to continue exchanging ideas. We want to have them live up to their cultural exchanges with us and vice versa. But they are afraid to go on with all this because of China and complaints from China. I understand their position. Nevertheless I am pushing this as best I can."

I asked about our efforts to build up the East Asia Bank and an economic aid project for southeast Asia. He said this was going along and "Gene [Eugene] Black has just been to see me. The whole thing is going very well in Congress and Gene will be going back out there as soon as Congress has finished endorsing the project and making it law. The majority in favor of all this is already there in both houses and you can regard it already as a *fait accompli*."

At this point I left—not because I wanted to and quite obviously not because Johnson wanted me to. But Bill Moyers, who is a very young, earnest, impressive fellow, told the president he simply had to get on with his schedule and he was already an hour and a half behind.

I chatted a while with Moyers and then, as I was walking to the room where I had left my hat and coat, who should appear but Lyndon B. Johnson. When he spotted me he grabbed me in his overpowering way and took me into the little one-room barber shop with him, asking if I didn't want to chat. I had no intention of missing the chance. The whole room is about eight by eight feet with one barber chair in the center. The president took off his jacket and sat in the chair, putting out his hand to a jaded elderly manicurist while the barber started to trim the sides of his skull.

Johnson never stopped talking. I was a bit horrified by the feeling that he was being indiscreet and that possibly the manicurist and barber were not the best audience for his confidences. He seemed to enjoy these peculiar circumstances. Here are some of the things Johnson said:

According to a White House study there have been 162 interventions of a military sort by the United States president, acting as commander-in-chief, without any declaration of war or congressional assent. Thus, in 1798 a three-year naval war against France was begun in this way. Johnson said the conception of congressional resolutions endorsing military acts by the president as the commander-in-chief became part of our constitutional process as a consequence of political conditions after World War II.

Truman had tried very strongly to continue the World War II idea of a bipartisan foreign policy and made a great effort to play up to Senator Arthur Vandenberg. Vandenberg changed his basic concepts and did his best to support Truman by "going international." But Senator Taft never accepted this approach and went after Vandenberg. Johnson said wryly: "Your own *New York Times* made a great thing out of Vandenberg and built him up as an intellectual leader . . . because he stopped being completely stupid. But after all Vandenberg believed that national politics should stop at the water's edge."

Johnson said Taft agreed with Vandenberg that Truman should go ahead with U.S. commitments overseas, but Taft maintained Truman should have requested prior congressional approval through a resolution —for example, in Korea. Johnson acknowledged that Congress has a particular power by being able to finance wars, and Vandenberg, in order to improve cooperation between the branches of the government, got the concession that the White House would ask congressional approval through resolutions.

"But Eisenhower didn't want to have the legislature usurp any authority and he called me down to ask me for a resolution to condemn the Soviets for breaking their international agreements." (I am not quite sure just what Johnson meant at this point because it was after the Berlin and Korean crises. But he was sitting back in the barber's chair with his eyes half closed while the barber was applying lather above his enormous ears and the manicurist was polishing his fingernails.) Musing aloud, Johnson said: "I agreed to get the foreign relations committee to do so—to condemn the Russians. But Taft, as majority leader, demurred. I took the ball and I ran with it when Taft was fumbling. This made Taft mad. As a result Taft never let the other members of the committee report this project out of the foreign relations committee. This is the kind of thing they are trying to do to me now.

"Then the Formosa business came along. I am not the man for resolutions the way Eisenhower was. I came to Eisenhower and I said 'You don't need a resolution on this from Congress. If they start fighting you, you fight back. There is no time for a legislative poll on all this. But if you do want a resolution out of Congress, I can get it for you.'

"He said he did want a resolution, so I got it and we passed it. The same was true on the Lebanon.

"Now you look at the kind of thing we are in now. There was Kennedy in Vienna. Khrushchev scared the poor little fellow dead. Kennedy called out the reserves. He got a resolution. He said he was going to get Congress in on the take-offs as well as the landings and that's why he wanted that resolution.

"We tried to push for social reforms in Vietnam in 1964. That is when I came in. My ambassadors—first I brought in Lodge and then he wanted to run for the presidency and I brought in [Maxwell] Taylor—worked hard on that. Taylor was a good man and he was a general, but he didn't seem as bellicose as the other generals so he was useful. Also he was Bobby's [Robert F. Kennedy's] selection—and President Kennedy's.

"My ambassadors and my generals, they said to me that unless we were willing to stop this aggression in Vietnam and to extend a fly-line to the north so they couldn't bring their stuff in, all the king's horses and all the king's men couldn't save South Vietnam. So we started bombing the north. And we started to give them all the equipment and manpower they needed. Why they increased their forces up to 790,000.

"But to avoid being driven into the sea we needed our own manpower. By last July I had agreed to send in 125,000 and we're going to send in everything that's necessary. But before I did this I reminded those people in Congress, I said to Congress—I don't need you to approve this. I am the commander-in-chief. Nevertheless, if you are going to be in on the landings I want you in on the take-offs.

"Now when the going gets tough this pays off. I see these stories that the war over there is going to last three to seven years, although I don't know where these stories come from. I don't know where these stories come from but there are some pretty horrible things going on like the way those communists kill the teachers. So I am glad that Congress came into this act and they passed my resolution five hundred and four to two.

"Dulles wanted SEATO to build a line and to give advice to everybody that any aggression against this line was at the other fellow's risk and they shouldn't be blind to the consequences. I don't know what the president will have to use to stop this aggression—whether it will be a kid's slingshot or an A-bomb—but we're gonna do the job."

At this moment Jack Valenti came into the barber shop—small, worried, and a bit embarrassed. He conferred on the current status of the senate argument concerning [Senator Wayne] Morse's proposal to rescind the 1964 [Tonkin Gulf] resolution. Johnson insisted there was not to be the slightest tolerance of any change. Valenti dutifully nodded and went out.

The president took up the conversation again and again started talking insistently about Bobby Kennedy's idea of including communists in the Saigon government. Johnson blamed it—as earlier reported—on Bobby's meeting with "those low-level state department people" at Hickory Hill. Johnson got exercised about presidential authority as commander-in-chief and the fact that he doesn't have to depend on congressional approval. He said: "I did it in the Dominican Republic. There wasn't any resolution there. I did it in Guantanamo—when Castro cut off the water and I warned him what was going to happen. I ordered my general in Panama to do so—to shoot—and he did."

(I was a little scared by this continual referring to I, I, I—like Napoleon or de Gaulle.)

Johnson had suddenly leaned forward in the barber chair, much to the dismay of the barber himself, and said: "Cy, you can write this but don't write it as coming from me. You can just say that Lyndon Johnson told this to two or three hundred congressmen the other day." He then embarked on a long and rambling story of the pre-Roosevelt period when there was a contest for Speaker of the House after the death of Nicholas Longworth. The hero of the tale appeared to be "old Martin Dies, Sr., who was a great jokester." The burden was that to be a congressman you had to be twenty-five years old and to be a senator you had to be thirty years old and in each case you had to be able to read and therefore you should know what you were voting on; but this was not in every case true.

With great satisfaction this brought Johnson back to a phrase now becoming too familiar in these notes when he claimed he told Congress a few days ago: "Boys, I will take you in at both ends with me, on the take-off as well as the landing."

He then digressed about the [General James M.] Gavin theory that in Vietnam we should lock ourselves up in enclaves. He said: "We can't just hunker down like a jackass in a hailstorm. We must seek the enemy out and deter him. I don't think there is much sense to that Gavin theory but at any rate there *is* a *Gavin* theory. Morse doesn't even have a theory. He just wants to pull out. And then there are the folks who simply want to take out the primary China targets by bombing."

This gave the president pause. And all of a sudden he started mournfully to recall how many teachers were being murdered by the Vietcong in the south and how they were "amputating those kids."

He got into a long session of worrying about India. He was deeply concerned about the food problem. He said, "Cy, did you know that we are sending more food to India this year than the U.S.A. consumes in a year. Yet more people are going to die in India than there are alive in Vietnam."

This, I must confess, is a singularly gloomy thought. Nevertheless, the president had been duly trimmed by this time and I was on the verge of being late for his secretary of state, so when he got out of the barber chair and started to put on his jacket I fled.

I walked over to the state department from the White House. Rusk was distressed that our press in Vietnam seemed to write almost entirely about U.S. military actions and very little about those of the South Vietnamese army or the Korean and other allied units such as the Australians.

There had been a very definite change in the military situation as a result of our increasing pressure. The VC weren't able to maintain a battalion or regiment in contact for twenty-four or more hours. Such units could not stand the fire power that was swiftly mustered against them. Rusk thought there would be no attempt by Giap to expand into massed operations.

He said there are a great many misleading statistics put out concerning the amount of territory and population in VC control. He said there are forty-three provinces in South Vietnam and the forty-three capitals of these provinces were all controlled by the government. There were 240 districts in South Vietnam and all but eight of their capitals were in government hands.

The key factors involved in the war—factors he suggested I keep a special eye out for when I get to Saigon—were these: (1) Hanoi is relying on military victory; (2) a collapse of resistance in South Vietnam; (3) a build-up of international opinion opposing Saigon; (4) internal differences within the United States. Rusk says (anent point 4) that Hanoi bets we are going to react just like the French, who collapsed at home.

I asked what the United States was doing about blocking French flights across American territory of planes that were bringing material to the Tahiti testing ground, and also whether it was possible to close off the Panama Canal, an international waterway, against such shipments by sea. Rusk said so far there was no problem. We were accepting French statements that they were not moving test material through the U.S.

I asked if we had made a direct request to Moscow asking for Soviet help in producing a Vietnamese peace negotiation. He said: "Moscow has made it clear to us that it is not a messenger for anyone, either for Washington or for Hanoi. Moscow is not prepared to act as an intermediary or even to take an initiative as co-chairman of the Geneva conference."

De Gaulle had told us, Rusk went on, that he was prepared to help when the time comes but he doesn't see that moment yet. The French community in Saigon is now much more helpful in its attitude toward us than the Paris government.

As for Cambodia, we are glad to have the French continue reasonable contacts there. This is particularly helpful because of our exclusion. Prince [Norodom] Sihanouk still fears China, which he seems to regard as the wave of the future, but Rusk is confident that his attitude will change as this conviction about China's destiny fades.

He recalled that de Gaulle had told Kennedy in 1961 that there would never again be French soldiers in southeast Asia. "The fact is that de Gaulle resigned from SEATO right then," Rusk concluded.

I brought up the subject I had discussed with the president about whether there could possibly be any advantage to a formal declaration of war in Vietnam. Rusk strongly opposed the idea and said: "A declaration of war would make it more difficult for both sides to control the situation. It would pose a major challenge on the matter of doctrine. After all, since the UN charter was adopted there has never been a declaration of war by anyone.

"The last country on which the United States made an open declaration of war in advance—not just the device of recognizing that a state of war exists—was Mexico in the middle of the last century.

"As a matter of policy we want the whole *casus belli* concept to wither away. There have been numerous instances during the last twenty years of what would normally have been considered a *casus belli*—like Russia's blockade of Berlin or the invasion of Korea.

"A declaration of war suggests the maximum commitment of a U.S. force to bring about a result. This would challenge the other side to a maximum commitment also and an orgasm of decision-making would result. We wish if possible to avoid any greater confrontation."

Rusk said he was not disturbed about the reaction in either Japan or India toward our Vietnamese policy. Both governments had an obvious public opinion problem, but the leadership in each case was very careful and we were satisfied. The only government in Asia that has been outright in its support of the communists has been that of Sukarno in Indonesia, and his influence has been sharply cut. Even Sihanouk has wavered and wobbled.

HONOLULU, *March 7, 1966*

This afternoon I went to Pacific Command Headquarters above Pearl Harbor, and first had a briefing on Vietnam, then a talk with Admiral U. S. Grant Sharp, the commander-in-chief of this combined headquarters.

Pacific Command covers everything from Japan down. Its mission is to defend the United States against an attack through the Pacific and to maintain "a forward strategy on the periphery of the Sino-Soviet bloc in the western Pacific." Also to check communist subversion. I am interested to note the continued use of NATO's term "forward strategy," the outmoded phrase "Sino-Soviet bloc," and the "holy war" reference to communist subversion.

Admiral Sharp is a small, trim, kindly-looking man with grey-white hair and a pleasant smile. Out of his four-star uniform it would be hard to guess his profession. Some of the things he said:

It would be most dangerous if the British carried out their recent proposals for a new East-of-Suez defense plan, but Sharp is convinced they won't. (God knows why he is so convinced.) He is certain the British won't be kicked out of Malaysia and they will also manage to stay in Singapore. Australia simply won't accept the British cuts envisioned and they have no interest in a new British base in Australia; they want that British base to stay in Singapore.

Japan depends heavily on free access to the Straits of Malacca through which most of its oil (from the Middle East) passes. Were the Malacca and Sunda straits blocked, Japan would be in a fix. But Japan, although its principal officers realize this, will do nothing about playing an active Pacific defense role.

PAPEETE, TAHITI, *March 9, 1966*

Flew in early this morning via Pago Pago, Samoa, which was in the midst of a late-night tropical rainstorm. A tawdry Samoan orchestra of two men and a woman, wearing leis and strumming guitars, whined Polynesian songs as we sank sweating into chairs at Pago Pago and waited interminably for take-off.

Here we were greeted by new leis (red and white) and the news that customs takes a minimum of two hours for those boarding in Samoa, because of fumigation against a coconut tree beetle. Fortunately we escaped this and were taken to the Hotel Tahiti, a pleasant establishment of tropical bungalows.

Strolled through Papeete, which is a sordid port town of jerrybuilt shacks, filled with hot dust, stirred by cars, Vespas, and the trucks that are unloading ships bringing in material to be used in constructing the French nuclear test installations. The people of Papeete, regardless of color, seem singularly unattractive. Shops offer tawdry goods at steep prices. A cafe called Vaima is the main afternoon center—overpriced bad goods, customers idling in the heat. At night they gather at Quinn's where drunks play slot machines, get roaring, and dance to disks.

Called on Jean Sicurani, the governor, who says there is virtually no race problem here. The mixed-bloods (called *demis*) are the upper class and look down on the *indigènes*. The *demis* have French, Anglo-Saxon, and German names.

In 1880 a Tahitian king gave the protected islands to France. There is no monarchist movement remaining. French is taught in the schools but Tahitian at home, and there are Tahitian hours on the radio. Tahitian (a Maori language) differs widely from one island to the next.

There is a nationalist movement which didn't want to accept French rule when a choice was offered. It has a party named the Tahitian Democratic Peoples Rally. Its head staged a minor putsch and was sent to France and imprisoned. Recently de Gaulle amnestied him but he has not been permitted to return.

AUCKLAND, *March 15, 1966*

Staying at New Zealand's government house where [Brigadier Sir] Bernard Fergusson is now governor general (as were his father and two grandfathers).

Bernard, moustache bristling and monocle flashing, is admirably suited to the job because, apart from his family connections (which he modestly overstresses) he came here at fourteen because he had bad eyesight and spent a year while his father was governor general. He learned Maori and made several friends who are now well-placed.

The protocol is exactly the same as in Buckingham Palace, Bernard being here as a viceroy. He enters and leaves a room first, then his wife, then the various guests. He is served first. He is attended by various aides, in and out of uniform, and she by a lady-in-waiting. There is a printed memo in our suite labeled "Notes for the Guidance of Guests." Among other things it says:

> (a) When meeting Their Excellencies, a gentleman bows (from the neck only) and a lady curtsies:
>
> (I) On being presented; and
>
> (II) On the first and last occasions of meeting during the day.
>
> (b) The governor general enters and leaves a room first.
>
> (c) Ladies and gentlemen rise when Their Excellencies enter a room, and remain standing until Their Excellencies are seated or guests are requested to be seated.
>
> (d) At dinner all stand for the Loyal Toast, which is proposed by the governor general.

We dined alone with them. After dessert, with the port, butlers went around turning out lights, leaving only candles, and I thought some kind of flaming dessert was to be brought in. Instead, B. arose, lifted his glass, and as we all stood, simply said, "The queen." It was quite moving.

Despite the protocol, they keep it cozy and informal.

Fergusson said New Zealand would have gone into Vietnam sooner except that Cabot Lodge, uninvited, announced his intention of coming to New Zealand at Easter-time 1965. The government had to delay its decision to send a force so as not to appear a U.S. puppet.

AUCKLAND, *March 16, 1966*

This morning, early appointment with Prime Minister Keith J. Holyoake, up from Wellington for the day.

The prime minister received me in his simple hotel room, the icebox covered with beer bottles: a stocky, sunburned man in his early sixties, a farmer by origin, very friendly but not very impressive.

Holyoake said New Zealand felt it was Britain's job to take care of the western end of the south Asian defense task while the United States took care of the eastern end.

CANBERRA, AUSTRALIA, *March 19, 1966*

Edward Clark, the Texas banker Johnson sent here as ambassador, invited us for tea. We were greeted by a Chinese servant who put a yellow rose of Texas in my buttonhole then led us in. Clark had assembled his entire staff and wives (all men wearing Texas roses).

He tells me Australia is booming. A huge petroleum and natural gas deposit has been discovered. There is more iron here than in the U.S.A. and incalculable amounts of bauxite.

Clark says the U.S.A. has been allotted a missile-testing range here of 1,250 by 150 miles. No one else, not even the British, allowed on it.

CANBERRA, AUSTRALIA, *March 20, 1966*

Lunched at Lord Casey's, now governor general. Although he is about seventy-five and she well over seventy they look remarkably agile.

He is sceptical about British determination to continue defense burdens east of Suez, no matter what they say. Says Australia has to rely on the U.S.A.

He made some politely cutting remarks about Senator Fulbright, who admitted to a press conference here that he didn't know Australia had any soldiers in Vietnam.

CANBERRA, AUSTRALIA, *March 21, 1966*

Drinks with Prime Minister Harold Holt in his office at the parliament.

Holt said the British had initially been "too pessimistic" about their ability to hang on in Singapore but the Australians had stiffened them. "We believe the Singapore base will be tenable for some time to come. And this is very important for Australia. We are in a far stronger military position with Singapore held as an allied base than we would be if such a base were south of Indonesia."

During the period right after World War II Americans were for a while regarded as "demigods" here because they had saved Australia. But that attitude had changed. There was a stronger sense of self-reliance now and a growing Australian nationalism.

CANBERRA, AUSTRALIA, *March 22, 1966*

Yesterday evening I spent a couple of hours with Allen Fairhall, minister of defense. Fairhall said that in Australia, "the realists are with America although there are strong psychological roots in Britain. But the British really want to withdraw their commitment east of Suez. They have been overtaken by history. Now they are a third- or fourth-rate power.

"And we know they would sacrifice us if necessary. During World War II Churchill said that Australia was expendable. We don't want to be overrun and then liberated."

SINGAPORE, *March 27, 1966*

Talk with Prime Minister Lee Kuan Yew. Since last August Singapore has been an independent state, having been expelled from the Federation of Malaysia. Lee is an extremely bright man who did very well at Cambridge University and used to be a left-wing socialist. Despite his Marxist background, however, he has done a remarkable job of keeping the communists from gaining influence in Singapore. He said:

> The problem is basically one of finding a balance in this area after an interregnum of two hundred years of European empires. Changes and conflicts were going on among the peoples of this part of the world when it was taken over. Thus, for example, the French arrested the conflicts between Cambodia, the Thais, and the Viets and replaced them by a conflict of those people with France. Now the old problems must resume their place—with very different bits of furniture.

> Of course we hope that if the situation eases up in Indonesia, the result will be to case up the security situation here. Nevertheless the harm has already been done. Now there are deep-seated fears of racial hegemony and Indonesian efforts to encourage a Pan-Indonesian movement. Indonesia has promoted racial disharmony and economic conflicts.

> I am convinced that a British base is very necessary for our survival. But new arrangements must be made—directly between the British and us. This must satisfy the uncommitted world that the base is not for aggressive purposes but for regional defence.

SINGAPORE, *March 28, 1966*

In 1960–61, when Singapore was becoming self-governing, Washington decided we didn't know what was going on and an attempt was made to subvert the Special Branch and get the U.S.A. piped in on security matters. Two Americans came down from Bangkok to fix the job up, after an official in Singapore security had been approached and pretended to play along (although he'd informed his superiors). The two Americans were arrested. Lee proposed to Washington that they would be exchanged against $100 million in economic aid. This suggestion was made in early 1961, just after Kennedy had come in. The administration told Singapore to go to hell, that we would consider economic aid on its merits but not as ransom. This answer appealed to Lee. He released the two men. Rusk sent a letter of apology to Lee. But Lee later claimed we tried, in the middle of this negotiation, to bribe him personally with $3 million.

SINGAPORE, *March 29, 1966*

Air Chief Marshal Sir John Grandy, head of Britain's Far East command, told me: "If South Vietnam goes, everything goes. The small nations are firmly convinced that they must be on the winning side. If the U.S.A. is defeated in Vietnam, this will be seen in Asia as a great victory for China. And there is no second line to fall back upon."

Grandy says that if the U.S.A. had yielded in Vietnam last year, it is very unlikely that there would have been an anticommunist take-over in Indonesia.

BANGKOK, *March 30, 1966*

Went to see Graham Martin, the American ambassador. It is perfectly evident from talking to Martin that Thailand is a military base of great importance for use in any war against China if such a war would come. Incidentally he says that ninety percent of the bombs dropped upon North Vietnam come from here.

Then I went over to see Dick [Major General Richard] Stilwell who is now American commander here. Stilwell says things are going much better from a military point of view in South Vietnam. We are slowly gaining momentum and nothing is able to stop us. But it is still going to take quite a time. We have slowed down the North Vietnamese shipments of supplies and men along the Ho Chi Minh trail and across the seventeenth parallel.

DJAKARTA, *April 3, 1966*

Djakarta is hot and muggy as always, but there is a splendid new hotel with air-conditioning. Sukarno had it built for the Asian games; it has never been full.

The hotel lobby is guarded by an indolent soldier on a chair, with tommy gun and helmet; and all the soldiers you see in the streets are armed, whatever they're doing.

The country is in dire straits. Today [Sunday] there is an open market for rice which has become a form of currency; the soldiers bring their rations in and sell them to the public. The price has multiplied twenty-one times in the past year!

Still everything is done in the name of the Good King, Bung Karno (as Sukarno is often called), a semiprisoner, while his wicked counselor or *durna* (from Indonesian folklore) Subandrio, and others, languish in "protective custody." There will probably be a series of big trials eventually. Subandrio tried to kill himself with sleeping pills but was prevented. They need details from him—including where he has hidden the money he stole.

Went to see Adam Malik, new foreign minister. Malik is a member of the triumvirate that runs the country. The triumvirate: Malik, Sultan of Jogjakarta, General T.N.J. Suharto. Suharto is the most powerful.

Malik received me at his house, very hot, filled with mosquitoes. He is a tiny man (about five feet, five inches, very thin) with gleaming black eyes, plastered-down black hair, protruding teeth, ready smile.

Said past Indonesian neutralism had accentuated China. This was now finished. Indonesia wanted to have a policy of neutrality "like India's—but more positive."

Indonesia definitely wished to rejoin the United Nations: "We would like to do this as soon as possible, but it is not easy for domestic political reasons. Sukarno, in his capacity as prime minister, wants to go slow on this. He is still under the influence of his dreams."

He said Indonesia now wanted coexistence, which meant an end to the formula expressed in the Subandrio-Chen Yi communiqué of January 28, 1965, saying coexistence was "impossible" with the Old Established Forces (OLDEFO in Indonesia's odd Orwellian jargon). Malik hopes the Malaysian confrontation can be ended by secret negotiations.

He said: "We want an independent Vietnam and if the United States can solve that problem by creating a strong South Vietnam, and then go, that is the best solution. The best result would be to have South Vietnam defeat the Vietcong and then be independent."

Malik didn't know just how Indonesia would set about trying to unscramble its economic mess. The first step was clearly to try and reschedule foreign debt payments. Indonesia therefore needed U.S. and Russian help especially.

After Malik's went to dine at Ambassador Marshall Green's: a slight, red-headed man of medium height. He said: On February 21 Sukarno had fired Nasution, the top general, and also announced that the students were in the pay of a foreign power, implying the U.S.A. (CIA). The students were affronted; they felt their honor had been impugned. This was the background for the Courteous Javanese Coup which has now taken over power. Sukarno has only vestigial presidential trappings.

Green says U.S. policy aims to get Indonesia back into UN, favors Indonesian neutrality of the Indian sort, wants better relations between Indonesia and its neighbors. The mere fact that Djakarta-Peking relations are bad is bound to have an effect in Hanoi and cool off relations with Djakarta.

Had the U.S.A. given up on Vietnam it would have had a bad effect here. If we gave up there now, the communists would again become bolder here.

The old nightmare of a Chinese-Indonesian nutcracker in southeast Asia is gone. China wanted Indonesia to be an honorary member of its socialist camp and to develop a Peking-Djakarta axis. The main Chinese weapon is the argument that "We are the wave of the future, the east wind will prevail."

China might have tested an atomic weapon here. The U.S.A. learned from a French scientist that something was in the wind.

Sukarno, no longer really in power but not yet formally ousted, still wants to set up CONEFO (Conference of New Emerging Forces) for which secretariat buildings are rising. It is supposed to meet this summer but probably never will. Sukarno wanted to be *the* Afro-Asian leader. He looked to China for support in this and Peking was delighted. Sukarno's big internal goal was NASAKOM (Nationalism-Religion-Communism). Last summer he was close to declaring Indonesia a NASAKOM state with the communists as the dominant party. That, of course, also pleased China.

The greatest massacres occurred in October. The probable total of people killed since October 1 is 300,000. This has been mainly done by Moslem youth organizations in east and central Java, Sumatra, Bali, the Celebes, and South Borneo, usually with knives; it was done for a combination of reasons; vengeance on the PKI (Indonesian Communist party) for bullying; Moslem fanaticism in a rural setting and local mysticism.

Indonesians don't like communism, but mainly they don't like Chinese —and identified communism with them. The communists nevertheless had made enormous progress here. By summer 1965 they had seemingly taken over. But the abortive coup changed all. People were enraged by the particularly brutal killing of six generals (tortured and mutilated; the army later distributed awful photographs). The gentle Indonesians were shocked when they learned the details and blamed communism. It was a near thing. Had either Nasution or Suharto been killed with the other generals the communist leader D. N. Aidit, might now be boss instead of dead.

DJAKARTA, *April 5, 1966*

This afternoon I visited the Sultan of Jogjakarta, one of three bosses of the New Indonesia, in what used to be the office of Subandrio, now under arrest. It is to be jointly occupied by the triumvirate soon.

The sultan is a civilized, forthright man who speaks quite good English and who studied in Holland. He has a slightly dish-shaped face with prognathous jaw.

He thinks Indonesia will have to borrow $400 million more to get out of the hole. Private enterprise will retain an important role in the economy, which has both private and public sectors as well as joint participation projects. The sultan is chief economic czar at the moment.

BANGKOK, *April 7, 1966*

Talk for an hour and a quarter with Foreign Minister Thanat Khoman. He told me the French in Vientiane, Laos, had plotted with Chinese and North Vietnamese communist agents to kill him and the prime minister, that a mortar plot against the Thai embassy was discovered there last night in Vientiane. Thanat says Cambodia has approached Thailand three times recently to reestablish relations. Sihanouk seems disillusioned with his communist protection and is playing more neutral. He realizes the East isn't winning.

Thanat said: "The only way to resist China's expansion is to develop an independent southeast Asia. There are more than 200 million people loosely connected but if they stay together they can be free and independent. I told the Burmese that the way to get rid of SEATO, since they don't like it, is to stay together in the area. I'd be only too glad to get out of SEATO and the U.S.A. would be happy to give up the pleasure of protecting us."

Long talk with Graham Martin. He says it is true that in March 1966 the French military attaché at Vientiane met with certain North Vietnamese and Chinese representatives to discuss what could be done to spoil the Thai state visit to Laos and that one subject "mentioned" was the assassination of Thanom (the prime minister). M. thinks all through this area France is trying to work against U.S. policy.

Sihanouk has a peculiar personal rule. What he says (in Cambodian) in the provinces doesn't count and shouldn't be taken seriously. What he says in French or is published in French by the *Agence Presse Khmer* is serious. He has recently indicated a swing back our way.

On April 4 Rusk sent a personal message to Thanat asking if he had any suggestions on how we should handle the Buddhist crisis in Saigon. Thanat offered to send distinguished Thai Buddhists (of a different sect) to persuade Thich Tri Quang and his boys in Saigon to calm down.

Among them were the president of the Dika court (supreme court) and a princess. He thought they could go under the guise of discussing a projected international Buddhist conclave scheduled for May.

PHNOM PENH, *April 12, 1966*

Deputy Prime Minister Son Sann, a distinguished, thin, elderly Chinaman, said the three requirements prior to any resumption of diplomatic relations between Cambodia and the United States were that we must: (1) end our aggression (cease incursions across the frontiers from South Vietnam and Thailand); (2) recognize the present territorial frontiers of Cambodia; (3) pay compensation for damages and loss of life caused by American airplanes and other infringements on Cambodian territories.

The Australian ambassador, Deschamps, says the Cambodians regard the Vietnamese minority here as a real danger and not in the same category as the overseas Chinese. The former Cambodian provinces of Champa and Cochin China are now part of Vietnam. Almost all the fishermen and artisans in Cambodia are Vietnamese. They are seen as a real threat to the integrity of the country. The Vietnamese and the Thais are yellow peoples whereas Cambodians are brown. There is a kind of subtle racial feeling.

Prince Norodom Sihanouk, chief of state, works by intuition, is a natural pessimist, and considers that Cambodia's choice is one between bad and worse. He is more afraid of a complete Vietnamese take-over here than of a Chinese take-over. Throughout history both China and Cambodia have been enemies of Vietnam. Above all he fears a reunited Vietnam.

SAIGON, *April 14, 1966*

Rode in yesterday on a Royal Cambodian Airlines DC-3 from Phnom Penh. The first indication anything was wrong came when we were persistently buzzed by a U.S. jet fighter, who came roaring over, under, and around us as if he were trying to convey a message. If he thought a Cambodian could comprehend, he was nuts. Down below we saw long clouds of smoke marking that morning's bombing raids.

When we got to Saigon we circled. There was a huge fire on the airfield, billowing clouds of black smoke and tongues of orange flame. We finally found that the Vietcong had launched a most successful mortar attack early in the morning, wrecked some planes and helicopters, damaged others, set fire to one of the main fuel storage tanks, killed about ten (Americans), and wounded over one hundred. We were the first (and only) plane in. The airfield had been closed to civilian traffic but God bless Cambodian thick-headedness.

Staying with Bill Porter, deputy ambassador. Bill told me Saigon is a far less tough city than Jerusalem during the Arab-Jewish riots or Algiers during the FLN-French or OAS periods. Thousands of GI's walk about unarmed at night between Saigon and Cholon and there are no VC-originated incidents.

In January 1966 we controlled 52 percent of the Vietnam population (all the main cities and towns) and the VC controlled 23 percent. It is our plan that by January 1967 we will control 66 percent of the population.

The Buddhists have benefited from the improved military situation. On the one hand they are prodded by the VC and on the other they can shelter under the umbrella of U.S. protection.

Porter is in charge of pacification and one aspect of this is the Chieu Hoi (open arms) program. This invites back VC's, telling them they will be well treated, exempted from the draft for a year, fed, and taught for a decent job. They are paid extra if they bring their arms. Pacification teams are largely provided by the CIA.

The VC weapon is terror. The U.S.A. must assure the people we are here to stay. Once the population is convinced of this we get backing and intelligence information.

The country lacks leaders—because the VC has deliberately killed the intellectuals, teachers, officials. The French are working against us. They fear we will succeed in Vietnam where they failed. They stress that there is an alternative to our aid—France.

SAIGON, *April 15, 1966*

Drinks with Major-General Edward Lansdale (ret'd), former CIA chief here and now heading a special pacification team brought out by Lodge.

He says one fundamental problem is the disintegrating effect of U.S. society on this simpler social structure. No Vietnamese thinks we will stay on forever or try to be colonialists. They see that our temporary presence, with its complex way of life, is a phenomenon that will pass.

The values of the social structure have changed. The old cultural hierarchy, the university graduate and government worker, are slipping. Unschooled barmen, taxi operators, prostitutes move up the scale as newly rich. They outbid the wives of the old hierarchs in butcher shops, etc.

Also, inflation has hurt—especially the lower-paid like civil servants and NCO's, some officers. This breeds anti-U.S. feeling which the VC soup up. The Vietnamese have a tremendous latent xenophobia, but VC propaganda has been heavy-handed and hasn't increased this much.

The communists put agents among the Buddhists as provocateurs, not to control them. They saw a good thing going and moved in. But there is no evidence that someone like Tri Quang follows the VC line as such. He wants a Buddhist Vietnam and probably has ambitions for power himself. This is a new phenomenon here; there is no tradition of Buddhist political leaders such as the Catholics have had.

The VC follows Mao's line: first the mountains, then the countryside, then the cities. It doesn't surface in towns except in Hué—where it will pay for it. There is probably a good VC organization here in Saigon. These people don't commit themselves prematurely. They keep on just enough terror to maintain their own side's morale; collect taxes; keep food out.

Lansdale said, "I am very concerned about the situation but I don't think they'll get the support of the armed forces or the people and make it stick; they won't be able to invite us out. If they are clever, they'll move slowly, and step by step. But there are many real patriots in this country who are quite pro-American.

"The bulk of the population is in areas we control. We have a clear majority; but we can't tell about the influence of secret organizations."

Long talk with Cabot Lodge, here on his second term as ambassador. He said military success is a prerequisite for a real evolution here; this will need a year or so. But we must do more than win on the battlefield. North Vietnam could be rendered militarily harmless within a year; and yet the war would not necessarily be ended.

Our policy in Vietnam is to achieve and maintain independence, "doing here in 1966 what we didn't do in 1936 [the Rhineland] or in 1938 [Czechoslovakia] to Hitler. Thus we will avoid World War III. There is no safer choice open to us; this limited war is the lesser of obvious dangers. A communist take-over here would be the greatest defeat in American history and the immediate consequences would extend from Japan to Australia."

We must give the Vietnamese a better revolution than that offered by the communists. The communists try and convince the Vietnamese that we are like the French colonialists; but they know we aren't.

The U.S.A. must keep the junta on until a legal turnover. Ky [Air Vice-Marshal Nguyen Cao Ky, Prime Minister of the Republic of Vietnam] is a hard worker and astute; he has learned a lot; he can move things forward. Anyone else would have to start all over again from scratch.

Lodge sheltered Thich Tri Quang, the Buddhist leader, when Diem was hunting him in 1963. He was running down the street in sneakers, disguised as a Catholic priest, when he burst into Lodge's house and the soldier allowed him refuge. Lodge asked Kennedy if he should keep him. The answer was yes. He stayed six weeks.

Tri Quang wants a theocratic state with Buddhism as the official religion. The Buddhists are wreckers, not builders. Their medieval loyalty to their religion is stronger than any to a government. They create opportunities for communism without worrying about it. Last month's crisis was deliberately trumped up. The Buddhists want a quick constitution, a theocratic state, and a one-chamber parliament. The communists are riding along and injecting the anti-U.S. line.

No cement binds this country together, so if anyone pushes a wall, the bricks come out separately. The factions use terror against each other: threaten to maim, torture, kill if they don't gain their way. The Buddhists as well. You can hire a man to kill anyone, right here in Saigon, for five U.S. dollars.

In an election wholly free from intimidation and with a truly secret vote, Lodge doubts if the communists would get ten percent of the vote in South Vietnam. The VC has lost lots of its magic.

There is not enough racism at the moment to interfere with military or personal contacts. But it could flare up and become serious. The Vietnamese is very racist. The cost-of-living rise ignites anti-U.S. feeling. The professional classes can't make ends meet and there is embitterment. Decent people can't afford to rent houses taken over by profiteers and whores.

SAIGON, *April 16, 1966*

Dined last night with Gordon Jorgensen, head of the CIA mission here and a classmate at Harvard. Born in Japan, the son of missionaries, he has been a Far East specialist. An exceptionally nice and thoughtful fellow.

Militarily, the battle had been going our way. Unlike Korea, each U.S. unit coming in did very well as it was engaged. This threw the VC back on a search for new and other means to win; and they were ready to exploit the political crisis. From captured documents we have seen VC exhortations to make trouble for the government by student and religious agitation, neutralism xenophobia, the rising cost of living. The Buddhists know the VC is riding piggyback on them.

The VC wants desperately to establish a "Third State"—apart from both Hanoi and Saigon. Each rainy season it has massed in the western part of the northern two or three provinces. This is their usual spring strategy.

We have evidence that the original "struggle committee" in Danang—Buddhists-military-police—is being superseded from below by a new committee run by the VC that has in effect taken over. Each day Danang and Hué are rotting away more. If a halt isn't soon brought about there will be an Annam neutralist state.

The idea of free elections is pretty abstract. You can't persuade a man who lives in an organized communist village that it is possible to have a free vote; so he'll vote for the communists. And the obverse is true on the GVN [Saigon government] side. You simply can't persuade these people. If we agree to have a vote we will be deceiving both ourselves and our friends. It is a dangerous path.

There is a real danger in rising war-weariness. When the U.S.A. came in it was hoped that we could help end the conflict fairly quickly. But now it is apparent that *we* are preparing for a long war. Five years or more.

The more effective the U.S.A. appears to be in Vietnam the less chance there is of the Chinese coming in. Our impact, on the whole, isn't yet sufficiently tough. And if we try to maneuver our way out of this, the Chinese will surely outbluff us. They will take very big risks—and move in troops—if they detect American weakness.

The main thing China understands is power—combined with the willingness to exercise power. We must not allow them to misunderstand us—and we are fair on the way to doing so, through public expressions of irresolution.

SAIGON, *April 17, 1966*

An interesting point in this war, says Bill [Porter]. The locals say: "There is not a single South Vietnamese hero. Only suckers—those who fight."

SAIGON, *April 20, 1966*

Fascinating day roaming about the countryside by airplane and helicopter with General William C. Westmoreland, commander of American forces here. We lost one plane when an engine and the radio conked out, but were able to make it into Pleiku and commandeer another.

Westmoreland had his left arm in a cast: the general broke a wrist playing tennis. He is husky but lean, about my height, with a pronouncedly square jaw, short, iron hair, and a long scar along his cheek. Not brilliant but glib.

Our first destination was Song Be, near the Cambodian border, headquarters of 173rd Airborne Brigade (U.S.) and an Australian battalion. Westmoreland told me Cambodia was violating neutrality and aiding the VC.

A "Sihanouk Road" has been developed to supply VC troops along the border and to send in rice. It goes from Siem Pang up to Laos. Delta rice is sent to the Cambodians in exchange. This is important in feeding VC troops.

Westmoreland says the ARVN [Army of the Republic of Vietnam] is much better than a year ago when they wouldn't venture out of the towns. The Vietnamese army is now over 300,000 regulars and 400,000 paramilitary. The U.S.A. has 230,000 troops here. We have great strategical and tactical fire power and mobility. This war has escalated far beyond the guerrilla phase.

Song Be. We are eighteen miles from Cambodia in an area mostly inhabited by primitive Montagnard tribes. Half-naked, bare-breasted, ugly little brown Montagnard women stroll by the air strip. On April 18 (two days ago) this outfit captured a North Vietnamese captain. He said his regiment was being shifted through Phuoc Binh province to the south. Headquarters are in tents in a clear area among woods. Helicopters laze overhead.

Later: fly on toward the Special Forces camp of Duc Co, near the Cambodian border, over miles of forested jungle occasionally punctuated by white puffs of phosphorous shell.

The VC is trying to move great tonnages to the south before the rainy season sets in. This is difficult because of our surveillance. North of the border they have to use truck transport because their forces in the south are now so numerous.

Certain strategic targets in the north should surely be destroyed. Militarily it is necessary to block Haiphong port from military materials. Haiphong is more important militarily than Hanoi, as a source of arms and fuel. Westmoreland says the war has now escalated to such a point that ultimately military considerations will override all others—in other words, we will inevitably attack Haiphong, at least.

I told Westmoreland I had heard that Republican bigwigs were trying to get him to make himself available as a GOP nominee in 1968. He said this was the first he had heard of this, but he seemed a bit coy. He has never run for any office but was elected to one—president of his high school class in Spartanburg, South Carolina. He dodged the question of whether, as a citizen, he voted Republican or Democrat, saying he believed in the swing vote. His father had been a great friend of James Byrnes, an extreme conservative Democrat.

Westmoreland says people here are perplexed and disgusted by the dove opinion of people like Fulbright at home. They resent the lack of wholehearted backing as displayed in past conflicts. The average officer and man cannot fathom the lack of support for a national policy which the troops here are trying to apply. Westmoreland thinks the present policy is good—half-way between bombing Hanoi and not bombing at all.

At Duc Co, the Special Forces unit has organized Montagnard tribesmen into what are called CIDG [Civilian Indigenous Defense Group] units. Tough, tiny tribesmen in leopard-spotted jump suits with blue kerchiefs at their necks, a few Vietnamese among their brown faces, line up in two double lines for review, their weapons at the ready. The camp is on a hill and, Westmoreland confided, will be attacked about three weeks from now by two VC regiments. All around the bare hilltop are coils of barbed wire, trenches filled at the bases, sides, and tops with sharp *punji* sticks; the camp buildings are walled with sandbags.

The VC has been shooting from Cambodian territory. Captain Conway, commander of the Special Forces unit, was killed near the border and his body dragged toward it. There are four outposts across the border manned by Cambodians; these support the VC. There is a good truck road inside Cambodia. There is a large concentration of VCs in Cambodia; also some North Vietnamese.

Westmoreland makes a small speech: "I share with you your great loss. Captain Conway was a credit to the Green Berets, one of the best. The advantages will be ours this rainy season. We didn't have these last year. The VC will have more sickness—malaria and pneumonia. They don't like the highlands. They can't move their heavy weapons. If they want to fight they will find us ready."

The tribes here are the Jarai and the Bahnar. An officer gives me a small crossbow and a quiver of arrows such as those the briefers use as pointers. Looks like a toy but is deadly for small game and birds up to thirty-five or forty yards. Larger bows for larger game—including humans.

All the walls of the bunkers are being thickened with logs and dirt to take 120-mm. mortar shells (except delayed fuses which penetrate). We will fly in artillery and howitzers if need be.

On to Dak To, another Special Forces camp. First, we review lines of tough, brown litle Montagnards in jump suits (camouflage uniform). Helicopters are whirling on the landing strip.

The intelligence officer says the VC is "using Cambodia all over the place—right across from us. [We are fourteen miles from Cambodia, seventeen from Laos.] There is a very extensive VC build-up in Cambodia and Laos."

We inspect underground billets where the Montagnards and their families live. The idea is that they are protected in tunnels, beside their firing positions, and will be forced to fight to protect their wives and kids. They are gloomy, smelly, dark underground caverns and trenches, partitioned off, children squatting and women sitting silently.

From here we take a helicopter-gunship, a machine-gunner leaning out of each open portal, Westmoreland, a Special Forces lieutenant-colonel, and I wedged between, strapped to the bench-seat, the wind blowing through. The crews have helmet emblems such as fire-belching dragons, painted above their names—like old-fashioned knights.

Fly on to Dak Pek, Special Forces outpost near the border. W. tells me this is perhaps the most isolated position we hold. We fly by chopper at a pretty high altitude to keep from the hilltops and VC fire. A series of lovely mountains and valleys, with the heights of Laos to the left, fly over a Montagnard village from which last week four hundred women and children were evacuated. Not one woman was pregnant; their men had all been abducted as forced labor by the VC. W. shouts in my ear over the wind: "This is all VC territory. We usually draw fire here."

Westmoreland considered abandoning the Dak Pek outpost a month ago because he doubts if it can be defended, but the Special Forces pleaded to stay and protect the local Montagnards. The only way to reinforce the position is by helicopter, and it is hard to bring them in when there is a serious attack.

We come in amid swirling dust and are greeted by the Special Forces commander, six feet two, two hundred-pound, red-headed Captain Sanford, who leads us once again through two lines of little Montagnards in camouflaged uniforms. He has some 746 of them on his roster. A battery of six 105-mm. howitzers is firing away as we drive a jeep up to his central command post. The 105s were flown in by Chinook helicopters and are supporting a clean-up operation of infantry.

The tribes are the Jeh, Sedang, and Hlang. They have 1,525 Montagnard dependents in camp with them. Around here there are numerous Montagnard hamlets of fifty or more families, which are each controlled by three or four VCs who make them cultivate mountain rice.

Sanford guides us through the deeply-dug fighting-sleeping positions of his handful of Special Forces; machine-gun posts set in apertures right by the officers' beds. We are taken to one building where a room is jammed with little Montagnards (mostly under five feet tall) with secretive brown faces and straight black hair, wearing black pyjamas. They had all been captured by the VC last August when a Special Forces position was overrun and wiped out. They were forced to work on short rations and brutally treated, they tell us through bad interpreters. Finally they were released because the VC had insufficient food, and now they are back.

We rejoin our U-8 plane and take off for Binh Thuan province, far to the southeast on the sea, where we are to go to Phan Thiet, a fishing town which serves as the headquarters for the 101st Airborne Brigade.

We lose an engine and our radio over VC territory. There is a sputter–sputter–sputter and we begin to lose altitude. Our pilot finally brings us in over the mountains to Pleiku.

Not long after our arrival another U-8 comes in, on assignment to pick up two majors. Poor fellows are out of luck. W. commandeers the plane and off we go.

On the flight W. says until May 1965 our policy was to try and win the war by using "advisers." In May a policy decision was taken to employ a sizable number of ground forces. This decision brought a requirement for a logistic structure involving facilities and troops. We had no system capable of supplying deployed forces in May. We have now built up a logistics complex to support a field army on a sustained combat basis.

This is the toughest kind of revolutionary war. The society is fragmented sociologically, ethnically, geographically, politically, religiously. There had been a tradition of years of French divide-and-rule. We have a wide open military flank in Laos and Cambodia. Communist infiltration has penetrated the entire social structure. "If we can solve this one—and we must and can—we can solve any."

At Phan Thiet we come in as helicopters are taking off on an operation. Brigadier General Willard Pearson, a taut, intellectual looking officer who commands the 101st Airborne Brigade, leads us to a hurried briefing. Operations are underway against a network of nearby VC positions.

We then go to take off. Bad luck with us again as the left wing is spewing gasoline like a fountain. Finally a mechanic stops it. The plane stinks of gasoline. W. sternly orders no smoking. Far too late for a cocktail party Porter was giving in my honor, in we came. I struggled home, got out of my uniform, dumped my crossbow, changed, descended, had many drinks.

SAIGON, *April 21, 1966*

Lodge is going to quit this summer and Mac Bundy asked Porter to come up with the name of a successor. Bill asked for my ideas; a tough job to get a man both suited for the job and endowed with renown and political sex appeal.

Bill told me an appalling story. When a Boeing was sent to take the Vietnamese and American parties to Honolulu for the Johnson-Ky conference, there were two lower berths in the front of the plane and a few upper berths in back. The lower berths had been reserved for Mme. Ky and, across the way, for Ky. Lodge had the names switched, grabbing a lower for himself and putting both Prime Minister Ky and the president of the republic [Nguyen Van Thieu] in uppers in the rear. Cabot has, I fear, very much the proconsul's attitude.

SAIGON, *April 22, 1966*

This morning Brigadier General J. A. McChristian, chief of intelligence gave me a briefing on Cambodia.

We are convinced the Cambodian government is providing support to the Vietcong and North Vietnam. Large quantities of Chinese arms, ammunition, and aircraft have been furnished to Cambodia. Sihanouk seems convinced the Vietcong will win in South Vietnam, that China will dominate southeast Asia and is setting his sails accordingly.

Chinese businessmen are purchasing rice in Cambodia on behalf of the Vietcong. A Vietcong nurse we captured said she had received her training in Cambodia. We confirmed all her information through an independent agent. The Fifth U.S. Special Forces Group, during a sixty-day period in late 1965, reported twenty-eight actions against the Vietcong when the VC was using Cambodian territory.

There are communist concentrations opposite Pleiku Province around the Cambodian Chu Phon Mountains. During the first three months of this year there have been numerous incidents involving Vietcong groups ranging in size from 30 to 2,500, coming from Cambodia. Recent reports indicate the presence of three North Vietnamese regiments in Cambodia around Chu Phon. There are seven North Vietnamese regiments just across the border in the same area.

We do not practice hot pursuit into Cambodia. But we have plenty of evidence of Cambodian support of the Vietcong. At least one hundred North Vietnamese prisoners taken in the area have admitted they were previously in Cambodia.

Way south along the coast of the delta in the area of Kampot-Ha Tien there is lots of smuggling of supplies for the Vietcong. There is similar evidence in the delta area of Moun Lo Go. There is a network of roads and sanctuaries in the Cambodian territory extending into Vietnamese Svay Rieng. Vietcong troops in South Vietnam cross this area to go from the Fourth Corps region to war zone C. We have reason to believe that there is a secret agreement under which 30,000 tons of Cambodian rice will be sent annually to the Vietcong and North Vietnamese.

The COSVN (Central Office for South Vietnam) is the central headquarters for the political and military control of the Vietcong. It manipulates the National Liberation Fronts. The COSVN headquarters works directly under Hanoi. It is located about three miles from Cambodia in Tay Ninh province.

SAIGON, *April 24, 1966*

Talk with Air Vice-Marshal Ky, prime minister of South Vietnam, now threatened by a movement to oust him led by a Buddhist political activist. I saw Ky in the prime ministerial palace. This large ugly building is separated from the city by barbed wire and guards.

A helicopter was standing in the courtyard ready for immediate take-off. Guards wearing red berets and armed with tommy guns peeped from the corridors. I was politely received and guided into an antechamber by white uniformed officials. Pretty soon Ky came in, sat down, and we were served strong bitter green tea. Ky smoked steadily.

Ky is a slight, slender, handsome man with bristling military moustache and rather shrewd eyes. He has a bland expression. He is frail but wiry and only thirty-five years old. He was wearing a well-cut blue suit and seemed quite composed. But under his gentle manner he was talking tough.

Ky said he was quite optimistic about the political situation and that he thought the Buddhist agitation had calmed down. He added: "They have no reason to continue their fight. The government and the generals' directorate have signed the electoral decree which satisfies the aspirations not only of the Buddhists but of the majority of the people. Why should they continue to fight? If they do they will only put themselves in a weak and wrong position."

He is very worried about Vietcong agents penetrating in the northern area, especially in Danang. Yesterday he received a communication from the commander of the First Corps, who recognizes that during the last four weeks there has been a serious Vietcong infiltration. This was taking place in the "struggle committee" of the Buddhist movement.

I asked if Ky thought there was a danger of a "peace at any price" movement led by the Buddhists. He thought this was not a real danger. The majority of Vietnamese are very "wary about peace." They want an assurance of their freedom and they know it is impossible to have peace with the communists.

The communists were deliberately working to encourage autonomous movements in Hué and Danang. But he did not think they would succeed.

Ky thought that from this vantage point there seemed to be "warlords" quarreling with each other in the United States but it was less dangerous there than here. We were further removed from the war.

Eventually, once peace had been established, it might be possible to have certain exchanges between South and North Vietnam without recognizing each other diplomatically—as between East and West Germany today. But the "primordial condition" was to have real peace first in the south and to build a strong state with a firm economy.

Ky said it would be an absolute disaster if the United States ceased fighting this war and that the communists would immediately take over. Ky was perfectly pleasant but I find him rather unimpressive—even in this bush league.

HONG KONG, *April 29, 1966*

This morning I had a briefing at the U.S. consulate-general (equivalent to our nonexistent embassy in Peking). China has attempted to rationalize away its setbacks—setbacks in Africa, Indonesia, etc. It tries to do this in terms of revolutionary currents and counter-currents, arguing that setbacks are inevitably bound to occur.

In south Asia, China is still supporting Pakistan against India on Kashmir. The Chinese hope to wean Pakistan from the United States. China has developed a phobia about encirclement during recent months and Pakistan represents an important geographical opening from the Chinese point of view.

The defeat of the U.S.A. in South Vietnam would be such a major victory in weakening U.S. military pressure on China, in shaking the U.S. position in Asia, that it would relieve China of the constant fear of some U.S. move against it.

How far the Chinese will go to support their theories depends on the U.S.A. Even if the Vietcong is defeated in South Vietnam, it is unlikely that there would be a direct Chinese intervention to try and pull victory out of defeat. China is fully aware of the military power and superiority of the U.S. Therefore, it is probable that China will continue to demonstrate prudence.

China would probably feel that U.S. bombing of Hanoi and Haiphong would *not* play a crucial role and would not be worth the risk of a Chinese intervention.

There are something more than 20,000 Chinese now in North Vietnam, primarily in logistical-type units. But these are protected with a certain number of antiaircraft and security troops.

The logistical units are concerned first of all with maintenance of the Y-shaped railroad that goes down to Hanoi from two points in China, Lao Kay to the north west and Ping Siang to the north east. China's interest in the Y-shaped railway to Hanoi is not simply because of North Vietnam. China needs this line to supply its own troops in Yunnan which is the key to Burma as well as to North Vietnam.

If we bomb China there is no doubt that China will go to war with us. If we send troops north of the seventeenth parallel there is little doubt that China would oppose them with "volunteers" in North Vietnam— although Hanoi definitely does not want them in.

MACAO, *May 2, 1966*

Came here for the day. A pleasant hydrofoil ride along the China coast with plenty of sampans and junks fishing or carrying goods. Macao, less than ten percent as populous as Hong Kong, has a Mediterranean air, a Chinatown suburb of Lisbon. Plenty of pastel Portuguese houses, but nothing except Chinese faces, save for a few Portuguese soldiers and officials.

Macao was given to Portugal by China in 1557 for helping squash offshore pirates. It is a funny little enclave and now exists largely by exporting firecrackers and joss sticks, manufactured on a Portuguese island which also contains a leper colony and poor house. During World War II it wasn't occupied by Japan, as Portugal was neutral.

It is a tiny peninsula (five square miles) with green fields on both sides of the narrow inlet which separates the neck leading to China (and Canton seventy-two miles away). There is a sleepy Portuguese police station and, one hundred yards down the dirt road, a yellow gate through a wall —and then China.

In the green field beyond the shallow inlet, across which Chinese refugees flee on rainy, dark nights, one of a series of rather tall, old-fashioned pillboxes in which China stations sentries. There used to be one in each pillbox; now two. Too often before a replacement would come to his pill-box, find his predecessor's rifle and uniform, the predecessor having skipped across to Macao. Refugees are held at the frontier police station, interviewed by a Jesuit priest, finally registered. After six months they can be listed as residents of Macao. Then they usually go off to Hong Kong looking for work.

TOKYO, *May 6, 1966*

This afternoon I had a talk with Prime Minister Eisaku Sato in his official residence. Sato is about sixty-five, moderately tall for a Japanese, with dark brown face like that of an American Indian. He was wearing a grey-black suit, was relaxed, friendly.

He was comforted by the fact that seventy percent of the American people stuck behind Johnson on his Vietnam policy. He professed himself at a loss to understand why the Japanese were largely hostile to the U.S.A. over Vietnam. "I can't run this down," he said. "But certainly the government and the leaders of industry are not against your policy.

"When I was in the United States in [January] 1965, before you started bombing the north, and met President Johnson, I told him I agreed with his position. But I opposed escalation. I don't oppose bombing the north but would oppose bombing Hanoi and Haiphong. It is all right to bomb the north while they are infiltrating the south."

I asked what effect it would have on Japan if the U.S.A. were kicked out of Vietnam. He said: "Japan is sensitive to the threat of communism in Asia. There is no alternative but to strengthen U.S. policy."

Sato believed the "domino theory" in southeast Asia was logically correct and "there is a danger that Chinese influence would extend down to Singapore. We must be alive to the danger of communist expansion." Many Japanese leaders were aware of the threat to Japan of a Chinese grip on the Malacca Straits through which most of Japan's oil comes (from the Middle East).

TOKYO, *May 7, 1966*

Excellent talk with Edwin O. Reischauer, the Harvard professor and student of Japanese affairs who has been ambassador here since 1961. He speaks Japanese and has a well-connected Japanese wife whom he knew as a kid when he was a missionary's son here. Thoughtful, a tall, lean, pro-fessorial-looking man with a kind of agreeable homeliness.

He says the Japanese are decidedly less opposed to U.S. policy in Viet-nam now than a year ago. They are now convinced that we do not want war with China. But emotionally they still oppose our presence in Viet-nam, even if they understand it intellectually. Race issues enter into all this. They see an underdog Asian (North Vietnam) bombed by the white Americans who, after all, destroyed Tokyo. Also, the Japanese oppose our position on China. There is an emotional feeling for China here. Japan feels caught between two intransigent, unreasonable powers, the U.S.A. and China.

If the U.S.A. were driven out of Vietnam, R. thinks it would produce no shift in policy and we would get a lot of sympathy for having tried but simply not knowing enough about Asia. It probably wouldn't damage our relations. But Japan knows it depends on the Malacca Straits for oil and if China extended its influence to Singapore, Japan might react by building its military strength and offering us more help on defense matters.

Nuclear weapons was considered a dirty term until recently. But now they are starting to discuss it openly as a question, even the idea of some day maybe having their own atomic arsenal. The public is still horrified, however, and it is politically touchy.

I asked R. if China, not Russia, wasn't now the main object of the U.S. Security Treaty. He agreed and said, "China has slipped into the lead."

HIROSHIMA, *May 8, 1966*

Rode down here by the excellent sleeper train across Honshu—the smoothest roadbed I've ever slept over—through the mountainous south-west of the island. Clouds, mists, heavily wooded hills, rushing streams, litle Japanese farm houses, and villages bristling with TV antennae . . . . Almost every inch of flatland carefully cultivated for rice.

Our guide claims 240,000 people, or two-thirds of the population, were killed by the August 6, 1945, A-bomb. (I think the figure is about half that.) He lost his son and wife; they seemed all right and then just died a fortnight or so later. Leukemia. There are now over 500,000 in the city, bigger than prewar. The widest street in the city is Peace Avenue.

Drive to the shores of the Inland Sea, filled with islands and rimmed with mountains. Rafts of bamboo shafts, buoyed up by empty barrels, are hung with oysters in specially-trained beds. Ride across to lovely Myajima Shrine, a Shinto holy place, in the rain which glistens on its Torii gates and stone lanterns. Noh plays and sacred dances held here. . . . Buildings roofed in cedar bark. . . . At high tide the entire shrine with its orange pillars seems to float on the sea. Because this is a sacred island, no births or deaths are allowed here. There is no cemetery on the island, although ashes can be brought. A statue to Kanon, goddess of mercy, with a baby appealing to her against atomic war. . . . A sacred Shinto horse (a fat palomino) in his stall happily bowing and eating in his own shrine. . . .

On returning, visit Hiroshima Peace Memorial Museum, recounting the grim events of August 6, 1945, even including pickled keloids and pieces of skin and fingernail torn off by a dying boy. Atomic Bomb Casualty Commission where, with U.S. funds, there is research into the after-effects. . . .

TOKYO, *May 9, 1966*

Foreign Minister Etsusaburo Shiima says the constitution would not allow Japan to contribute to UN peace-keeping because it didn't permit maintenance of a normal military force. Japan is strictly limited to defending itself and can't get involved in disputes abroad, even through UN.

He didn't think the money saved by not spending on defense should be spent in augmenting the defense of others. Japan preferred to spend this on economic and cultural aid to developing nations.

ANCHORAGE, *May 13, 1966*

Arrived here early this morning and was taken to Elmendorf Air Force Base near Anchorage, where I had a talk with Lieutenant General Raymond J. Reeves.

The Siberian Peninsula (and its Chukotski subpeninsula) is fifty-five miles from Alaska. It is a huge wasteland with bad transport problems, dependent on the Trans-Siberian Railroad, the North Sea route and the highway to Magadan. Russia has a large military force in Siberia, including submarines and considerable air, but the principal army concentrations are far from Alaska.

There are two army mechanized brigades at Forts Richardson and Wainwright. In the west and northwest there are small detachments of Eskimo Scouts primarily to report activities. There are two Nike-Hercules battalions at Fairbanks and Anchorage, including nine missile sites.

WASHINGTON, *June 1, 1966*

I had an appointment with President Johnson, arrived early at the White House and was taken (kept discreetly out of sight) to an office near Bill Moyers'.

Walt Rostow came in. He was very voluble. Says Johnson feels we must "lead from the middle," not from the front. Kennedy's reputation in history will, strangely enough, depend on Johnson's success; for one is carrying out the program started by the other. Johnson, despite Vietnam, works constantly on many things: like India-Pakistan peace, aid to India, the whole of Africa, stimulating the Alliance for Progress. Johnson is fascinated (as was Kennedy) by foreign policy.

Fulbright, Rostow says, has become almost nutty on Vietnam. At the West German embassy he said to Rostow (in front of foreign diplomats) that he intended to press for the disappearance of the U.S. presence from all southeast Asia and he thought it might be a good idea for us to get out of Europe also. "Imagine," says R., "what all the diplomats cabled home." R. says Fulbright is deeply embittered because he was never made secretary of state and has set out to wreck the entire foreign-policy program of Johnson.

At this point a secretary opened the door and said: "The president wants you now." I went in to Johnson's office and Secretary of Defense McNamara was standing there.

The president looked better than when I'd last seen him: fitter, thinner. He was suntanned and well-dressed in a dark blue flannel pinstriped suit. He said: "Why don't you come on in and have lunch with me." (By then it was about 2:30 P.M.)

So we trooped down the cloister-hallway that links the offices to the residential quarters and rode up in the elevator, followed Johnson through the foyer where the Eisenhowers (but not the Kennedys) always used to sit, and entered the small dining room off it. A table was set with cover and seven places. I told Johnson I only wanted a cup of coffee and McNamara asked for the same.

The president then, waving me to his right hand, said: "I asked Bob McNamara here to stay on so he could answer any questions you want. Don't hesitate to throw them at him." Soon afterwards Rostow joined us; then eventually Moyers. They ate and drank nothing. The president ate little and kept thumbing through a folder of papers.

Marvin Watson, one of his aides, came in and murmured something about an urgent telephone call. The president picked up an ivory-white receiver beside him and sat listening to it a long time, saying nothing. He seemed preoccupied. In the meantime I talked with McNamara, just as if the president wasn't there.

McNamara, to my surprise, denied that there were some ten thousand North Vietnamese troops in Cambodia. He said the defense intelligence agency had no "confirmed" evidence of the presence of any units inside Cambodia. It was true, as I had reported, that some had been there (near the Chu Phon massif) and some might be basing themselves from there, but there were none there now. I told him of what I'd seen and heard. McNamara said things had apparently "changed" since. I doubt it.

I asked McNamara about the current rumor that Hanoi, through Rumania, had sent out peace feelers. "There's nothing in it," he said. Rostow added that one Rumanian official had expressed as his personal opinion that Hanoi was ready for peace, and this had been "leaked" by "another embassy."

Rostow had told me that everyone, including Couve de Murville, had been surprised by de Gaulle's decision to move now against NATO instead of many months later; that we suspected this was partly to improve his bargaining position before his Moscow trip. But McNamara assured me there had been no "surprise" in the timing and that "all the advance information we had" showed it would come as it did.

I asked McNamara how the U.S.A. could avoid becoming an empire despite itself in southeast Asia, pointing out that we had huge investment in bases and many commitments. He said: "We need more than the U.S. presence when the war is over. We need an international guarantee."

Rostow chimed in, as the president listened, looking sceptical: "First we have to demonstrate to the communists that this kind of game doesn't work. Then we have to negotiate on the basis of the 1954 and 1962 (Laos) Geneva agreements with a more effective international control commission. Under the 1954 agreement we have the right to keep from two to four thousand 'advisers' in South Vietnam. We don't need bases out there. We can go back to the background of the 1954 and 1962 agreements once we have made it plain that subversion doesn't pay. Then we can eventually work out a kind of grand security agreement for the area, perhaps linking ANZUS and SEATO together."

I then got on to NATO, which was the main purpose of my visit. McNamara and Rusk had both told the Allies last December we would have to replace certain specialists and temporarily reduce our forces in Europe. McNamara said there would *not* be a second withdrawal of 15,000 U.S. troops from Europe as the press has predicted. He and Rusk had explained that the U.S.A. would have to build up its Vietnam forces throughout 1966, but that it had *no* intention of withdrawing any major combat units from Europe.

I asked about rumors that the U.S.A. preferred to have penurious Britain concentrate on Europe and abandon its east-of-Suez commitments. McNamara said just the opposite was true. He said: "We took five years to tie the British down on this, on Singapore. President Johnson spoke very strongly and at length about Singapore to Prime Minister Wilson when he was over here."

I said I had encountered doubts in Australia and New Zealand about British intentions to stay. McNamara said: "It is clear that Wilson means what he says on this because of their decision to purchase our F-111. That was a very difficult political decision for him and is the best evidence that they intend to maintain their commitments east of Suez. After all, we didn't recommend the F-111 to them unless they wanted it east of Suez. We told them the F-4 was adequate if Britain intended to stay only in Europe but that it would need the F-111 if they planned to stay on in the East. That's when they had to take the basic decision—which they took—on remaining east of Suez."

(At this point Mrs. Johnson came in. She was pleasant, quiet, efficient. She had a murmured conversation with the president, shook hands with all of us, stayed on to chat briefly, then discreetly, quietly left.)

Rostow made a very interesting observation. He said: "Britain's planners feel they have to hold the line east of Suez until Britain gets into Europe. Then, once they're in Europe, they hope to make Europe accept world-wide responsibilities. Britain doesn't want to abandon its world role but is approaching it in a different way."

Johnson by then seemed to have completed his half-hearted concentration during which he was dividing his time between his folder of papers, occasional telephone-listening (but not conversing), and us. He began to talk, warily at first, and then suddenly, as usual, in great torrents. At around 4:30 P.M. Moyers had to pass him a note and eventually remind the president that he had a very busy schedule remaining.

Johnson said he had "no plans now for any kind of European trip. Of course that doesn't mean I won't make one but I don't have any plans." He continued:

> I want you to know I'm spending most of my time on Europe these days. We are trying to be constructive there and to establish a calm atmosphere. We have no desire to hurt the French people or to insult de Gaulle. But we look forward to the steady evolution of NATO. We would like it very much, were that possible, to have this occur with France. But we are prepared to do without that if necessary— although I hope not for always.

> I am very pleased with the solidarity the fourteen remaining NATO allies have shown. This is important, most important. All our future action will be based on the most complete and intelligent consultation in an atmosphere of harmony.

> Of course we all know that this is 1966 and not 1950. [Meaning that Russia is a very different country.] We intend to pursue our search for a bridge to the East and there is lots of evidence of this in the presidential record. [His own.]

> I don't agree with the French that NATO is no longer important. Its great deterrent value remains and this depends entirely on the speed and certainty with which it can act in any crisis. That relies on peacetime preparations and joint planning; promises of aid (like de Gaulle's) in the event of trouble are not enough.

> We think grave errors are being made by some people who today are misjudging the requirements of present security. The situation would be dangerous if everyone saw it the same way.

> The most difficult problem we face right now is that of French troops in Germany. We are giving our full support to Erhard and we think he wants to keep French troops there—but not with any smell of an occupation force.

Our policy is one of dignified acceptance of de Gaulle's invitation to leave. We will leave in a gentlemanly, efficient, and effective way —in due time, and ahead of schedule. Now I want you to protect me on that. I don't want to seem to be threatening so be careful how you use this. We feel that maybe we and the French might want to come back together some time. But we'll leave in a dignified way—ahead of time. Just the way I expect you'd do if I had invited you here to the White House and then one day I said: "Cy, you have to get out of here by June 30." I expect you'd be dignified but you wouldn't wait 'til the last minute. So handle this carefully, because I trust you. After all, I've seen more of you than any *New York Times* reporters. I wish you'd give up Paris and go to Saigon and send all those reporters of yours there to Paris.

Johnson burbled on, the way he sometimes does, and I took no notes. Then he got back to a main thought train, talking about Ted [Edward] Heath, the British Tory leader he'd seen that morning. He said: "I spent a lot of time with Heath. We have a very good and improving relationship with Britain; I am in continued contact with Wilson. We also have very fine relationships with Germany, with Erhard. And there are much better relations now between Britain and Germany, which is very good, I think."

I remarked that it seemed a propitious moment, since he was so concerned both with improving NATO and bettering relations with Russia, to try and do something on the latter with the former. He said: "We're exploring approaches to the East right now. That's one of the things we discussed this morning and I'm hopeful about making some progress—after things have been straightened out in NATO, maybe in the earlier part of next year. We're now considering the problems of relocating Allied headquarters and strengthening relations among the fourteen. But early next year we may be able to make some moves affecting the East."

At this point Johnson went off on another long ramble. He discussed the way too many people thought he spent all his time on Vietnam and thought of nothing else. Thus, that very morning, he had arranged for reporters to come in and ask questions of those in his cabinet most concerned with Medicare. But then (imitating a whining baby and with exaggerated mimicry): "All they did was keep whining Veetnam, Veetnam, Veetnam."

He admitted expenditures on the Vietnam war constituted a strain but there were many other things going well "and we are pleased by what we see. Take for example this hemisphere. It is going well. Why, even in the Dominican Republic it is going well. Of course there's always trouble there, lots of trouble. There has been in the past and will be in the future. But today, right as I'm talking with you, they are quietly voting there. The people themselves are choosing their government right now.

"And in Africa—we've met with all the African ambassadors and we have given much study to our policy on that continent. Our very best minds are concentrating on the problems there.

"And India and Pakistan. Everything there was going to hell in a hack. But we cut off our aid and showed them that we weren't going to finance them in any war against each other and that had a good deal of influence on both of them. We showed that we aren't going to finance any local wars.

"And we're very happy with the way things are going when we look at Korea, the Philippines, Japan. All these things are receiving our attention —despite Vietnam, despite what the 'intellectuals' and the *New York Times* and those people in Georgetown say. But the press won't believe it and when I bring them in to talk to my cabinet all they say is 'Veetnam.'

"This nation, if it's worthy of its leadership, mustn't concentrate only on Vietnam but on freedom all over the world. But don't you forget that now eighteen-million people [those who benefit under Medicare] have now had the yoke taken off their backs and they don't just have to keep worrying about which of their children is going to help them out. That's what I call progress."

Johnson asked when I was going back and I told him next week. He said: "We love France and look on her with sorrow rather than with anger. We hope the French people will not always feel about us the way they do right now—or maybe they don't. General de Gaulle may even find that there are some things he can work out with us. But right now it would be hypocritical if we thanked or complimented him."

At this point Moyers more or less insisted, firmly but politely, that the president simply had to go about his business. It was well past 4:30 P.M. and we were still at table (except McNamara who had quietly slipped off). Johnson made some more minatory remarks about "those people in Georgetown who don't know what's going on." I suppose Georgetown because the Kennedys lived there and many of their supporters still do. He then started to say goodbye and said: "I suppose I'll have to come over to Paris to see you. You know I still remember that long talk we had in Paris."

Then suddenly (we were all standing) he opened the folder of papers he had been browsing over and started to read a cable sent to him by Lodge in Saigon that very day. He asked Rostow if he'd seen it. Rostow hadn't. Johnson then read: the Ky-Buddhist negotiations had gone well. Westmoreland was very optimistic and said, "it looks too good to be true."

Johnson said to Moyers: "Bill, I want you to get a bottle of aspirin and give it to Cy so he can take it to New York with him and give it to [John] Oakes and [Herbert] Matthews and those other people on the *Times* because this news is sure going to disappoint them." We all wandered out, the president going to his bedroom.

WASHINGTON, *June 2, 1966*

Long talk at the White House with Walt Rostow down in the basement office that used to be tenanted by Mac Bundy.

Rostow's "Plan 6" for Vietnam originated as follows: In 1961 Max Taylor was having a chat with Rostow, who said we would never be able to close the border of Laos and we couldn't win the Vietnamese war without doing so. Rostow recommended that we must bomb North Vietnam. He went to Saigon with Taylor and when they returned reported his belief that the north must be made to pay if the Geneva Laos settlement didn't work out. Since SEATO "Plan 5" was the basic military plan for southeast Asia, President Kennedy always called the idea of bombing North Vietnam Rostow's "Plan 6". It was simply a recommendation to bomb North Vietnam.

On the Middle East I asked if there were any evidence that a real nuclear arms race had started. He said Israel has "the elements for an option to make atomic warheads." I observed that this had been the case for a long time. Did he mean there had been no change? He said yes.

I asked Rostow to amplify his remark in the White House the other day about possibly arranging a Pacific security alliance including ANZUS and SEATO. He started by saying that in 1956 the state department, the defense department, and the White House had prepared a ten-year "China Study" analyzing prospects of developments in China and Chinese policy in terms of our national security and diplomacy.

Our own defense plans ultimately must depend on what happens in Japan. The Japanese constitution still prevents any real defense commitment or valid force for Tokyo. Until this is amended they can't join in any basic defense. Therefore our commitments must remain based on bilateral agreements, plus ANZUS and SEATO, the kind of hodgepodge we have today.

But we reckon that when China gets a medium-range nuclear capability, the Japanese attitude will change and Japan will then want a real self-defense capability of its own. There is already intense discussion of the nuclear military future inside the Japanese Establishment. We are in no hurry on this.

Rostow is convinced that by 1971, "after the death of Mao Tse-tung," Peking will have revised its essential policy. It will no longer be convinced that China will inherit the earth and will accept the fact that it is only one of perhaps five Asian powers.

I then asked what kind of instruction President Johnson had issued to officials not to "hurt" the French people or "insult" de Gaulle. Rostow said Johnson had actually sent out a letter telling officials not to speak up on this, aiming at George Ball and Dean Acheson.

I asked how he proposed we should answer the difficulties of a possible

French ban of NATO over-flights. He said this was a very difficult question but he thought the French had "a powerful interest" in agreement on this issue. Walt contends that "the *force de frappe* is deaf, dumb, and blind without our help; it needs radar, early warning, and intelligence."

The United States was now worried about what any kind of pact with de Gaulle was worth. President Johnson does not trust him and does not want to be in hock to him on anything. We don't rely on him any more. What would he be worth if there were another Berlin crisis? De Gaulle calls the Germans "provincials." He refers to Germany as a "defeated power" and not as a nation.

I remarked that I was puzzled by several things McNamara had said in the White House. I couldn't understand his observations on Cambodian aid to the communists in Vietnam because I had been into this question very carefully and if the theater chief of intelligence and all his subordinates reported one set of facts to Westmoreland, it was peculiar that the secretary of defense flatly contradicted these. Likewise it was rather strange to hear the secretary of defense blandly assure me that he and the government did know in advance of de Gaulle's intention to make his move against NATO in early March. Everybody else, including the prime minister and foreign minister of France, the American ambassador, and the secretary of state had no such advance inkling. I am reluctantly coming to the conclusion that McNamara is either a conscious or an unconscious dissembler.

WASHINGTON, *June 3, 1966*

Long talk with Dean Acheson. Dean has been put in charge of preparing the U.S. position on the NATO crisis precipitated by de Gaulle.

Our conversation was interrupted in a somewhat embarrassing way when an aide came in and said: "Mr. Helms of the Central Intelligence Agency insists on urgently speaking to Mr. Sulzberger." Dean left the office and I talked to Helms, who said there was something he wanted to see me about and could he come and wait for me in Acheson's office. I said yes. Afterwards Acheson said: "This certainly raises your prestige. Are you a spy?"

I started by asking what Dean thought of the report that de Gaulle in Moscow might offer to pull back his two divisions from West Germany if Russia withdrew two divisions from East Germany. Acheson said he had heard such reports but they were pure speculation. "France is now like Russia under Stalin. There is no real source of information prior to the event."

I asked what was the French legal position. It claimed to continue membership in NATO as an alliance. It was also tied into Western European Union until the end of this century. Acheson replied: "The legal position of France does not bother de Gaulle at all. He has an utter disregard for any form of legality. He has agreements with the U.S.A. running for the life of NATO unless both powers are in accord to scrap them."

I asked Acheson to show me the text of the agreement negotiated with Couve which he said had been violated, and he produced a telegram book showing me a secret *aide-mémoire* to all NATO capitals including a "system of communications agreement" signed by France and the United States on December 8, 1958. This stated that if one party wants to modify the terms of the agreement and if the two signatories are unable to agree, the agreement can end in one year. Otherwise it would endure for the length of the treaty.

Acheson says the French position is curious. WEU [Western European Union] has no integration and the French like it because it gives them a legal hold on Germany on the nuclear basis. Now France is *in* NATO to make mischief and *out* of NATO from the viewpoint of obligations.

Acheson says we will have to put a bill in to France for all the expenses involved in moving out but he is certain we will not collect. This is a "shocking" situation.

It will be very difficult to negotiate a new agreement on NATO over-flights across France. He says: "We can't make a deal. De Gaulle won't yield. However, if he says there can be no over-flights that will end any pose of France remaining an ally. Therefore he will probably continue permitting over-flights on a monthly basis. He will restrict things enough to embarrass us but not to wreck us."

Acheson said the French air force fears NATO will cut off French access to its intelligence: radar and early warning systems. Whatever credibility the *force de frappe* has would vanish when "it goes blind." I argued that this does not matter because de Gaulle does not believe there is going to be a war and does not contemplate using his *force de frappe*.

SHAPE headquarters will go to Brussels. We also want the council to move to Brussels. EUCOM [The U.S. European Command Headquarters] must leave France and will go somewhere in the region. The military committee will go to Brussels and the standing group will be abolished.

Acheson scoffs at those who say that NATO will be stronger because de Gaulle has prodded it into necessary action. He quotes General Lemnitzer as saying "one more benefit of this sort and we will be out of business."

P.S. Helms had brought me a memo I had asked for, on a minor matter, en route to his lunch.

WASHINGTON, *June 4, 1966*

This morning I had a long talk with Vice President Humphrey. He seemed full of enthusiasm for his work and was very proud of a series of missile models on a table. He said that in the near future we should catch up with and perhaps surpass the Russians in engine thrust.

Humphrey is convinced the Russians and the French are going to have a combined space shot and that this will be announced as one of the conclusions of de Gaulle's visit to Moscow. France is technically proficient in many aspects but is weak on booster engines.

The implications of all this are uglier than the fact. The United States has actually launched a French satellite in the past and we have helped the French in many respects, although we have admittedly been stuffy about sharing our space technology just the way we have been remiss in some nuclear and computer sharing.

Nevertheless, de Gaulle has been so abrasive in recent actions that he has forced us to do things that we should do. Thus, for example, we are helping to balance our payments by reducing the flow of U.S. investment capital to France. And he has compelled us to come to grips with NATO and its application to the modern world.

Humphrey was in a philosophical mood. Rather to my surprise he said: "The odds are against my ever being president. I reckon the chance is only one in twenty. The way I see my future I shall probably go back to the senate. But I like my job and it is a satisfying feeling to know that you can help to make things good."

Humphrey thinks the United States is not nearly so internationalist as it believes itself to be. The country is "European-oriented." Hitler's outrages were understood but we have never really understood the true meaning of the communist threat and its highly skilled, politically sophisticated force. We have not realized that this is an international menace to us just the way Hitler was.

We even keep South America in a separate mental compartment and somehow assume it is separate from the rest of the world. Americans think "international" means Europe or conceivably South America. The average American has a simplified view of China as a place where there used to be a lot of missionaries and now there are a lot of communists, a place from which lots of laundrymen came. To the average American, Asia has meant Japan and Pearl Harbor and cheap goods flooding our markets—in other words: disagreeable things. India means famine and despicable poverty.

Humphrey agreed that the political rot in the U.S.A. occasioned by Vietnam had become a great deal worse. He added that this "will take a heavy political toll." But he said his own position on Vietnam was not just a Lyndon Johnson position. He had drawn up a paper in August 1964, before he had been elected vice president, in which he recommended a policy on Vietnam very similar to that we are now following.

I 3

THE GOLF-COURSE
THEORY OF SOCIALISM

Lunched with André de Staercke [Belgian ambassador to NATO]. I said to André that he shouldn't reckon indefinitely on American hatred of China. This was a very emotional relationship and we might be back in love with each other again long before anyone believes it possible—and this would worry the hell out of the Europeans. "This is exactly what Kosygin said to Harold Wilson on Wilson's Moscow trip," de Staercke said.

Rocquencourt, *June 21, 1966*

This afternoon I went out to SHAPE headquarters here—perhaps for the last time—to see Lemnitzer.

I said I was struck by the fact that de Gaulle had achieved a victory inside NATO by withdrawing from the organization: imposing French strategy on the Alliance. De Gaulle always wished to stick by the old U.S. strategy of instant, massive retaliation with nuclear weapons. France always opposed attempts by the Kennedy administration to substitute a strategy of flexible response. Now that NATO's conventional forces were weaker, the Alliance, perforce, had to depend more heavily on prompt use of nuclear weapons.

Lemnitzer ruefully agreed. He had about twenty-three divisions at his disposal on the vital central front (as compared with the original target of thirty). During the 1961 Berlin crisis, the U.S.A. had reinforced the Alliance with considerable combat strength, including two armored regiments, but these had subsequently been withdrawn. The Germans were not then up to their full strength, but now have twelve divisions. Nevertheless, the disappearance or restricted assignment of two French divisions would make a difference. The Alliance obviously is not going to reach the goal set for 1966 by its fundamental plan, MC 26/4. Therefore, with fewer divisions, there would be a need to call on reserves sooner, and the chances of bringing nuclear weapons into action were increased.

All French forces in Germany will be removed from commitment to Lemnitzer's command on July 1, come what may. Thus, Lemnitzer doesn't know how to rely upon them even if they remain in Germany. He must therefore plan to do without the two French divisions.

Paradoxically, some of the Americans most irked by de Gaulle want to reduce the U.S. commitment in Europe, which would even further reinforce the massive retaliation strategy France favors.

In 1964, Operation Big Lift moved an armored division from Texas to Germany. This encouraged many people to talk about cutting U.S. forces in Europe because they could be so swiftly replaced in emergency. But this is nonsense. Their heavy equipment has to be stored over here. Secondly, there has to be a strong holding force in Europe to hold the airfields at which reinforcements would arrive. Thirdly, an American pullout would have a disastrous repercussion among the other allies.

Russia could still start an invasion in Europe without any advance warning just the way the North Koreans invaded South Korea. The North Korean attack was camouflaged as a normal exercise in a training area, and the Russians could do the same thing.

Lemnitzer confessed that no matter what the relations between France and NATO, France's geographical location gives it automatic protection in the event of any war in Europe. Obviously, if we defend Germany and Italy we have to defend France.

PARIS, *June 23, 1966*

Lunched with Martial de la Fournière, right hand of [future prime minister] Pierre Messmer. He was sent to Indochina in 1946. [Admiral Thierry] d'Argenlieu, the imperialist-minded French governor, wanted bloodshed to reconquer Indochina for France. And Ho Chi Minh and Giap wanted bloodshed to expel the French.

F. knew both Giap and Ho and has great respect for them as remarkable men but says they are coldblooded, ruthless communists. Ho is a great actor who often weeps publicly (or pretends to) in order to stir the masses.

F. once gave a dinner for Giap and among the guests was an Armenian Frenchman who had taught Giap as a youngster. Giap sat rudely, saying nothing, until the Armenian recalled the days when he had taught the general, and said: "Surely you must have something in common with the

French." For the first time Giap opened his mouth. "Yes," he said, "they killed my father. They killed my brother. They imprisoned my mother. I have much in common with them."

Paris, *July 11, 1966*

Letter today from Walworth Barbour, American ambassador to Israel. This wound up a long episode that started when I wrote a column on my "golf-course theory of socialism."

December 27, 1963. Morfontaine Golf Club, Thiers, France (in part):

> Hitherto there has been no simple rule-of-thumb method to measure the extent of socialism in socialist countries. For this reason I offer my revolutionary discovery. The golf-course theory of socialism may not be a precise economic gauge but it seems to reflect diplomatic truth.
>
> According to the golf-course theory of socialism a nation's political alignment may be judged by the number of golf holes on its territory. Its ideologists aren't Marx or Mao, but Palmer, Nicklaus, and Snead. Let us see how the theory applies.
>
> There is not a single golf hole in the entire Soviet Union, which occupies one-seventh of the earth's surface. Two recent American ambassadors, Charles E. Bohlen and Llewellyn Thompson, were driven to putting on the rug of their official residence. Nor, so far as I know, is there a course in communist China, although it covets three fine links in Hong Kong.
>
> Tito insists his communism is the purest and proved this by plowing under the excellent little course at Koshutniak, outside Belgrade. This was opened a generation ago by Prince Regent Paul who, wearing a derby hat, drove a ball seventeen feet. But Tito is eager to stay uncommitted between the power blocs. He has therefore maintained an excellent links at Bled.
>
> President Nasser wants to socialize Egypt but he also wants good relations with the West. He has commandeered nine holes at Cairo's Gezira Sporting Club while keeping the other nine in first-class playing condition. The Socialist Mapai in Israel started at a disadvantage when it took power fifteen years ago because Israel had no links. This embarrassment has been rectified. Unsocialist Rothschild money built a first-rate eighteen-hole course at Caesarea, insuring Israel's political balance.
>
> One of Caesarea's ardent clients is American Ambassador Walworth Barbour, who learned much of his golf before the war at the Royal Buggeroff course in the little Bulgarian village of Buggeroff, near Sofia. The Royal Buggeroff consisted of nine soup cans sunk into a sheep pasture tenanted by ferocious dogs.

Bulgaria has since become a loyal Soviet satellite and there is no more golf. But nationalism hasn't been entirely squashed in Moscow's East European empire.

Budapest and Bucharest each still has a four-hole course, indicating the permitted degree of independence.

The golf-course theory of socialism provides a significant yardstick—everything from four-hole to eighteen-hole socialism.

> American Embassy,
> Tel Aviv, Israel,
> January 20, 1966.

Dear Cy:

Merry Christmas and all the rest.

We are having slight problems in connection with the golf course here and it occurred to me that that super think piece of yours of a year or so ago called "The Golf-Course Theory of Socialism" might be helpful in the current contest. Could you dig up a copy and send it to me.

> Wally

> July 5, 1966

Dear Cy:

I am happy to report that we have now reached a relatively satisfactory compromise and the golf course is being maintained with little damage. . . .

You might be interested in the comment I received from one avowed, or perhaps I should say professing, high socialist official to whom I spoke and subsequently gave a copy of the article.

"Mr. Sulzberger has, indeed, opened up a new vista for the comparative study of political systems. However, I wonder if Mr. Sulzberger is completely right in considering only the *number* of golf holes on a nation's territory. How about golf holes *per capita* or *per square kilometer*? I am not sure that socialists like me would be very happy with Israel's standing by *such* measures—very very capitalist I would guess."

> Very sincerely,
> Wally

PARIS, *July 21, 1966*

Lunched with Randolph Churchill. Poor fellow, he really looks awful, like an unusually feeble man in his mid-seventies. He had a lung operation a couple of years ago, but he still smokes, can only eat soft things—no meat or anything that has to be chewed. He has lost his taste for every-thing else. He had a most peculiar lunch: beer, snails, and vanilla *pot au crème.* Alex Allegrier, the restaurant owner, came over afterwards and gave us a bottle of champagne. Horrible mixture.

Randolph says his life of his father will be ten volumes long—five vol-umes of text and five "companion" volumes of pictures and documents. The first volume, dealing with Churchill's life up until 1900, will be published shortly. Randolph has finished a good deal of the second volume but he doesn't look strong enough to me to do the whole job.

PARIS, *July 27, 1966*

Lunched with Harlan Cleveland [U.S. ambassador to NATO]. NATO is split by what some officials now refer to as "The Elysian Curtain." This refers to the potential and actual barrier between NATO's Mediterranean allies and the north created by Jugoslavia-Austria-Switzerland-France [the Élysée Palace is where de Gaulle lives]. One can get around this with airplanes, but it is difficult to maintain an efficient communications sys-tem. Right now NATO depends on line-of-sight communications passed on towers or high points that can keep in direct contact and are not blocked by the earth's curvature, but France is too big a space.

The United States is preparing a plan to make communications satellites available to NATO. The idea is that NATO will have its own satellite system in the 1970s, some 22,700 miles up, so that it can kick communi-cations back and forth above the Elysian Curtain.

BONN, *July 29, 1966*

Long talk with Franz-Josef Strauss. Strauss said the U.S.A. was now changing its strategy in Europe for the fifth time. First there was the Lisbon plan for ninety-six divisions. Then there was the Radford plan for massive retaliation, which Radford explained to him as providing for total U.S. response against any enemy if he hadn't retreated to his take-off point by the following dawn. Third was the 1957 Dulles plan which opposed automatic and immediate release of strategic weapons and preferred initial reliance on a broad spectrum of tactical A-weapons. This was adopted in 1958 by NATO as MC-70. It gave West Germany a huge nuclear arsenal through means of delivery. Fourth, there was the McNamara plan—pause, threshold, flexible response. Now there was a fifth—somewhere between (2) and (3).

Strauss said:

> Of course, ultimately the only long-range solution is a European
> nuclear weapons force coordinated with that of the U.S.A. There are

300 million Europeans in NATO and 185 million of them are in the Common Market. Isn't it ridiculous to say we are unable to defend Europe unless 250,000 American soldiers remain here? This can't be a permanent condition. For the long run Europe must be able to establish its own defense organization, responsible for Europe's own security—but tied together with a continued American presence and an American commitment.

I'm not for the dissolution of NATO. But I am for more responsibility on the part of Europe. This would loosen U.S. political and military control in Europe but it would also make the U.S.A. much more mobile.

Look at Vietnam. Supposing there were suddenly some new critical area, in South America or in Africa, crying for American help. We Europeans must be able to replace part of the American strength in Europe. For now it isn't really an alliance but an American military protectorate surrounded and helped by minor supporters. I haven't the slightest anti-American sentiment. I only want to normalize relations and create a permanent alliance between our two continents.

BONN, *August 2, 1966*

Long and agreeable talk with old Dr. Adenauer [the ex-chancellor] today in his office in the Bundesrat. I had been told he tires easily nowadays (at the age of ninety-one). But I was with him from noon until 1:20 P.M.; and it was I who broke off the conversation. He seemed prepared to go on indefinitely. His hearing and eyesight are excellent; no glasses. It is a remarkable physical triumph.

When I finally got up to go, he took my hand in both of his, looked me in the eye, and said: "I am truly grateful that you came. And I mean this from the heart." He said he hoped to see me again. I remarked that I hoped the world would be in better shape. "*Ach*, you are not planning to come for a long, long time?"

Adenauer gets up between 6:00 and 7:00 A.M. At latest he starts reading his papers at 7:00. Then: "If I want to work on my memoirs, calm and undisturbed, I stay home [in the village of Rhoendorf]. Otherwise I go to Bonn. I normally continue like this until 9:00 or 9:30 in the evening. I find I can work more easily at my memoirs when I'm home. You know, your American presidents have a round office in the White House. I had a round pavilion built in my garden. Half the wall is covered with bookshelves, half is windows. I work better in a round room."

Adenauer doesn't have a battery of secretaries "and there is no ghost [writer] in my house." He dictates part of his memoirs and writes part, in pen or pencil. His research assistant who has been with him for years, combs through the material each section will deal with and then "distills" it. A good shorthand stenographer is made available to him by his publisher. Adenauer added: "I like writing—but I hate proofreading."

He was not bowling these days but he hoped to resume soon. The bowling ground had become too soaked and green in the heavy summer rains. Also, he didn't have time now and wanted to wait "until this book is behind me. I am on a tight schedule and you know, publishers can be very tough."

He said his wine cellar was "still there and it is always being replenished with what is required. Unfortunately I just don't have enough time to enjoy it."

I asked if, now that he was an old man, he found himself reflecting often on such nonpolitical subjects as religion and death and afterlife. He answered obliquely: "That interests me very much. For example, I find the history of the Bible fascinating. During my recent trip to Israel I saw many of the biblical places of which I had read all my life and I was deeply moved. Yesterday I was visited by a Jewish scholar and we had a most interesting conversation about the language in which the Bible was first written and about Israel and religious tradition. I was deeply impressed by my trip there.

"And not only was I moved by all the historical and religious associations but I was impressed by the energy and dynamism of the people. But I am concerned for their future. Israel must have good and true friends and it depends greatly on the United States because it is a country that may have overstrained its capacity.

"I attended a meeting of the claims conference [claims against Germany] and there were many Jews there who had come from Germany. I would like to see these people come back here. But they don't want to return—at least not for good. They are only interested perhaps in visiting Germany.

"You know, one of my sons is a Catholic priest and he is living in my house. I often discuss religious questions with him. I am much interested in what effects the ecumenical conference will have on the church. These are things I follow with close attention—but I am completely ignorant on nuclear physics and such matters."

I asked how he envisioned the role of Jews in Germany. He said: "Unfortunately there are only a few Jews here now. I sincerely wish more would return. But it takes time. We will have to wait. I never forget that we Germans owe a great deal to the Jewish people. Especially in the field of science and research."

I asked if he thought Europe was actually entering a new epoch. He said: "Look at the map. Look at the size of the Soviet Union. In Europe alone it is enormous and yet more than half of it is in Asia. The rest of Europe is small compared with Russia.

"Europe must not only stay together but there can be no united Europe without the United States. We need the United States by all means. If you are not with us, Europe will ultimately, in the long run, come under Russia's sway.

"I am convinced the basic political line of Russia is this: if Russia can attract France and Germany into its sphere it will then be stronger even than the United States, both economically and militarily. And this would also enhance Russia's position in its confrontation with China. I have no doubt that this is the object of Russian policy, to gain control of France and Germany.

"When de Gaulle is no longer there—I hope he has a long life, but when he is no longer there—there is a real danger that the communists will take over. And we Germans have simply experienced and borne too much since 1914—two wars, two defeats, changing regimes, Hitler. Now a young generation is coming in that has forgotten all these experiences because it did not personally endure them. They feel no guilt about the Nazis who meant nothing in their own lives. So the country is disrupted and not sufficiently tied to the permanent threads of our past history.

"When de Gaulle came to see me last month I told him I thought his assessment of present-day Russia was too optimistic. I agreed with him that Russia is in the full sway of development. But no one can foresee what they will be doing or trying to do in ten years time. I think de Gaulle understood me.

"Whenever the Russians, by their policy, indicate that they are being reasonable, the whole world cries that they have changed. Of course, in a way they have changed. One instance is the mediation at Tashkent between India and Pakistan. This represented a real change because in the past the Russians have always sought to stir up wars, not peace. The Russians did a great thing at Tashkent, a good thing for peace; and I recognize that.

"Russia is developing fast and it is a very big country. It has many nationalities. But we must await the results and it is still far too early to predict the future. The Russians like people to be friendly to them and we should be friendly, but Russia must still be cautiously, carefully watched."

I asked the old man if he would spell out his views on U.S. policy. He said: "The continued withdrawal of U.S. military forces shows a decreasing U.S. interest in Europe, and I consider this a serious mistake. The German question is a European question and vitally affects world peace. That's why de Gaulle wants German reunification." (An odd belief!)

I observed that de Gaulle had certainly done a good deal to disrupt western unity by his move against NATO. Adenauer said: "I think de Gaulle is in a large degree right in what he criticizes about NATO, although I don't like the way he acted. The problems aren't really new. You know he even spoke to the late President Kennedy about all this. It's an old story.

"NATO was created seventeen years ago and immense changes have occurred, even in weapons, since that date. I don't believe NATO as it now exists is in its best form but I do regret the way de Gaulle acted. Nevertheless, you should not forget that de Gaulle wants to remain allied, he simply doesn't want to be militarily integrated."

I put the following to Adenauer: "If by some magic you were suddenly made president of the United States, what would you do about Vietnam?" He looked at me sadly for a moment, then with a twinkle he said: "First of all, if I were president of the United States I wouldn't compare Wilson with Churchill (as Johnson just did last week). Anyone who can say that doesn't know much about Churchill.

"As for Vietnam, it wasn't Johnson who started it you know, it was Kennedy. Johnson inherited it. Johnson has to eat the soup that Kennedy cooked.

"But you must realize there is nothing humiliating or dishonest if a great nation discovers that a certain course of action is much more difficult than it had expected and therefore, in all sincerity, it tries to get out of it. And you must get out of Vietnam, get out of the problem. That is the only way."

I observed that Johnson was trying as hard as possible to find a way out but it hadn't yet turned up; that we couldn't just suddenly retreat with tail between legs. Adenauer answered:

"Johnson shouldn't listen too much to his military people. This wouldn't be the first war that has been broken off in the middle. Somehow you must find a way to break it off."

I said a German friend of mine had recently commented that if the U.S.A. quit in Vietnam the Germans would fear we wouldn't honor our pledges in Europe. Adenauer said: "Of course no one can be certain that your promises here will be honored. Can there be absolute certainty that an American president would use nuclear weapons against Russia, to protect a piece of Europe, knowing that your own country would suffer terribly for it? I have often had my doubts on this and I made this point to Dulles when he was secretary of state. I said I'd like to see the president on whom I could count absolutely for this. But the Vietnam problem doesn't affect this matter one way or the other.

"Of course I don't think in terms of sudden, total, dishonest withdrawal in Vietnam. But is growing escalation the answer? Where will it lead? And won't there be a very bad effect on the American people as they begin to realize the extent of their own losses?

"President Kennedy once told me that the most significant and dangerous area for the United States was Latin America, that this was of greatest importance to you, and that if communism came there he simply didn't know what would follow. So you can see the difference in outlooks: that was the same President Kennedy who started everything in Vietnam, who didn't heed de Gaulle's warnings not to get embroiled.

"And Johnson's way out is certainly not by getting more and more strongly in. If I take a road and I find that I am going in the wrong direction, certainly I see no purpose in continuing along it. Instead, I seek a new road.

"I'm greatly, gravely worried about the whole world. The United States is so seized by the Vietnam problem that there is a danger it, the greatest world power, will overlook other problems it must face. Europe, after all, is still the most important area for the United States, especially in political terms. This has always been my view. And if you ignore us, if Russia succeeds in gaining control over Germany and France, then we are all lost, you and we together."

PARIS, *August 12, 1966*

Dined last night with Chip Bohlen. He had a long argument with Walt Rostow last time he was in Washington about bombing North Vietnam. Chip argued that if it was militarily desirable we should indeed go ahead and bomb but that it was lunacy if we thought that by bombing we could force Hanoi to parley. Anyone who has analyzed communism knows that you can never bully the communists into negotiation.

To my astonishment, Chip assures me that the French consider me a CIA agent who operates under the facade of being a "Gaullist." He says this is true of Couve, Pompidou, and all the rest. I say Chip is full of you-know-what.

ATHENS, *October 1, 1966*

Yesterday evening I talked for an hour and three-quarters with young King Constantine at his palace at Tatoi; like the country home of a well-heeled gentleman. The house itself is quite modest—stone-built and old-fashioned, but the acres of pine woods which extend for some distance along the whole sides must have tremendous value.

I arrived around twenty past seven, a cool agreeable evening with a strong smell of pine in the air. I was received in the sitting room-study where so many times in the past I had chatted with King Paul. There was a log fire burning. Constantine was wearing grey slacks and a dark blue blazer.

I asked what he thought would be the result of an Andreas Papandreou government if Andreas ever managed to get himself elected prime minister. He said: "Judging from his press statements and from his past history that would probably be just the push that Greece needs to go off the cliff.

"He would certainly, I suspect, swing the country toward the East and neutralism. We always go to the edge of the cliff and then, from the very edge, turn back. But I think with him at the helm we would go right over. Not his father. His father has some good men around him and I rather like the old man. But Andreas would get us over the cliff."

I asked if he thought the policy of the Papandreous now was openly to oust the monarchy. He said: "Perhaps this is the case with Andreas. Of course he sent me a message through some friends of his assuring me that if Greece did not have a monarchy it would be a disaster and he would always support the monarchy. I said to that friend: 'How does this compare with the public statements he makes?' The fact is I do not believe him."

I asked what role Prince Peter was now playing. Constantine said: "You know he issued his first strange statements just after my wedding and that is when the whole thing blew up. I was told ahead of time that he was going to make a statement so I am sure that Prime Minister Papandreou [head of the government at the time] must have known of his intention. I think it is possible that Andreas might be thinking of Peter as a kind of regent once he gets rid of me—and then he would move him out to make way for a republic."

The king said he had found last year's crisis "very exciting" but "I confess I did not enjoy it at all. Looking back I realize that it was really very disagreeable but I feel that I was quite justified in my actions. I could not let Papandreou take over the defense ministry and conduct the ASPIDA [an alleged military plot] investigation which involved his son."

Constantine said he was convinced that the army is quite reliable now and that there is absolutely no danger of political infiltration or a coup.

He had no direct contacts with Caramanlis in Paris. All he knew about him was what he learned from his former ministers, who would visit Caramanlis and come back and report his views—"each man differently." He asked me what I thought of him and I said that he had been Greece's best statesman since Pericles and worst politician since Alcibiades, all white and all black. He should have stayed as leader of the opposition when he was defeated. The king agreed and said that he probably would have been able to save the country from its present situation if he had remained here.

I asked if he thought there was any trace of Gaullism in Greece or any fallout from the known political views of de Gaulle. He answered: "There is more of a shadow of Tito and Nasser than de Gaulle. Of course, Andreas goes around talking about a 'Greek' and 'independent' policy. But this is just a naive appeal to the Left. Nationalism is out of date. Andreas should know we cannot act alone without help and that we are not even nearly as rich or as strong as France."

I said to the king that I was going to ask a very indiscreet question: namely, would he bypass the constitution or install a dictatorship under any circumstances, for example to prevent Greece from "going over the cliff" under Andreas? I recalled how his father had called me in, in 1949, to ask my advice on putting in a dictatorship under [Field Marshal Alexander] Papagos and how I had warned him against it. He answered:

"The best way to answer you is this. I will do my best to see that this country gets back to a peaceful, quiet, prosperous life. But you can be quite sure that if it depends on me to save this country from disaster, I will be ready to bypass one or two paragraphs of the constitution if necessary—that is to say if it is necessary in my opinion I will do it to protect Greece.

"I want to go down in history as willing to save Greece from what I regard as evil, and I know I am not evil myself. The question of the form is difficult. Will one have to act through a political party? Through generals? Through civilians? Would it have to be a real dictatorship or just the suspension of one or two paragraphs of the constitution on a temporary basis? I do not know and I hope it will never come to that, but if necessary I would surely act."

I asked the king whether when people spoke of "Nasserism" here (with reference to the ASPIDA plot), they meant in terms of a conspiracy to oust the king or in terms of socialism. He said he thought they meant it both ways. He then went on to say that he liked Nasser a lot personally.

"I first met Nasser here and then in 1961 in Egypt. I do not trust him but I like him a lot and I will tell you something interesting. Whenever I traveled in Egypt I never saw Nasser's picture alone. He was always with Amr [commander of the armed forces]. I wondered why but I suspect that Nasser told me the answer indirectly and unconsciously. At our dinner party I asked him why, in Algeria, Boumedienne had moved Ben Bella out. Nasser answered that they were both his friends but he knew they were quarrelling and this was a pity. Ben Bella had made the mistake of bypassing Boumedienne who then got fed up." Constantine thought this was why Nasser was always playing up to [Field Marshal Hakim] Amr's vanity and keeping a close eye on him.

Constantine had told Nasser at the dinner that he thought it was uneconomic to do what Egypt was doing in the Yemen. At this Amr roared with laughter and Nasser grumbled to the king: "Those damned [Yemeni] royalists."

Constantine said his friendship with Makarios, which had been enriched on the trip, helped a lot in the difficult Cyprus situation and that "we get on very well."

I asked him if he thought there was much fallout in Greece from the Vietnam war. He said, "There is no fallout. People are not that interested in Vietnam and I believe they see you are really trying to get a settlement there."

I asked how he relaxes nowadays. He said that when he went to Denmark this summer he had not sailed for two years. In his first race, the European Championship, he was only 30th out of 35 boats. But in the last race, the World Championship, he was 6th out of 125.

He also plays squash and he loves to be with his wife and baby and to drive around. He is working hard at karate and has just been awarded his third-degree Black Belt. There were a few instructors in Greece who know karate and judo.

I asked about his reading. He said he had come to the point where he did not like to read serious books any more after a tiring day. (I wonder if he ever did.) Before he used to read history, but now he found it necessary to relax.

BUCHAREST, *October 5, 1966*

Flew up from Athens last night. I could only get into town by black market taxi (a half-ton truck which had no meter and clearly was picking up trade), which I shared with two Belgian chemical salesmen.

I 4

WE FOUGHT ON

ONLY ONE SIDE

IMPRESSIONS: THIS IS NO LONGER A BRUTAL POLICE STATE. THERE are hardly any political prisoners and those held were arrested relatively recently. But the system still produces inefficiency; there is no incentive to work, much lassitude; the cooperative shops are unimpressive. Despite glowing reports I had read abroad, the goods in stores are costly and shabby. There are lots of TV antennae. Some programs are ancient British, U.S., and French movies.

I walked through the central park, filled with people dreaming or chatting on benches. This is still a rural people: flower beds are beautifully tended. Most apartments with little balconies have box gardens with plants and herbs. Citified peasants still hang out strings of peppers to dry. (Note: there is still no pepper on restaurant tables—as in 1956.) One sees no pictures of the present leadership displayed in posters. There is no atmosphere of fear.

There is an essential contradiction in Rumania. Society works to produce producer's goods, invest in capital equipment. But Rumanian society has a consumer's mentality. There has been no economic reform here like in the rest of East Europe, emphasizing production-incentives, because the state doesn't want to give more money to the population but to keep it for capital industrial investment. No need to encourage consumers.

Life is better now but not yet secure. People therefore are impelled to enjoy each moment as best they can, not knowing what tomorrow will bring. There is a vast amount of ambition (worldly) and corruption.

Rumanian writers are obsessed by the form, not the content of their work. They are uninterested in fundamental changes. There is no Rumanian Solzhenitsyn.

BUCHAREST, *October 9, 1966*

I drove to Transylvania in a rather shaky Soviet Volga with a terrible driver named Marinescu and a little government interpreter named Bec. He speaks fluent but only fair English and somewhat better Russian, is a party member, and has a touching innocence in all the wondrous accomplishments of "planification." He thought it was sheer propaganda when I told him America had invented basketball and self-service groceries, both of which he assumed were Russian.

As we entered the Carpathian foothills there were millions of blue cornflowers and purple autumn crocuses; the October sun shone hot. No pictures of the leaders on any walls or buildings (unlike the old days) and many villages had shrines by the roadsides with ugly stencilled Christs therein.

Across the Carpathians with splendid yellow, brown, russet autumn foliage, huge pines and oaks, low mountains but with sharp cliffs and escarpments, beautiful and dramatic, to Brașov, a most lovely town with mountain sides rising almost vertically immediately behind its buildings. Brașov (Kronstadt in German) is almost half-Saxon and has a fine old "Black Church."

We rattle on through the flat Transylvania plateau past vineyards, duck ponds, occasional dovecotes, to Alba Iulia. From before Alba Iulia it is evident big preparations have been made for Nicolae Ceausescu's visit: banners (party and national), peanuts, arches of evergreen, a few slogans: the best blankets and rugs laid out on windowsills along the main streets. Here and there officers in boots and Soviet-type uniforms.

Entire population is urged out, lining streets to wave flags, schools and factories closed. Lots of peasant costumes, men in white homespun or linen tight pants and kilts, embroidered black and white blouses and vests, small round felt hats or lambskin *kalpaks*, tall and curling; women in white and black skirts and blouses and kerchiefs. The highway through A.I. is strewn with flowers and there is a carpet of flowers before the little dais where C. will speak.

Ceausescu, boss of the Communist party, reads his speech from small pages of manuscript, has a good, resonant voice in the microphone. He is short, dark curly hair, slightly florid complexion, fattish, black eyes, cleft chin, wearing a four-button, homespun squire's suit with high button-down breast pockets.

He talks of Rumanians as a mixture of Dacians and the Romans who conquered them. Recites a long list of national heroes such as Michael the Great. Pays tribute to 1918 veterans. Very nationalist. Says the Rumanian Communist party continues the national tradition. Says the Magyars and Germans join in creating Rumania's culture and wealth and wants all communities to live in friendship.

Afterward I was taken to C.'s open American car, over the red carpet (embroidered rug) leading to the dais, by a member of the party "protocol" and an "activist" of the Central Committee who told me Ceausescu would see me. Bec kept saying: "But he has never seen a noncommunist journalist before."

Suddenly C., diminutive and almost invisible, emerged from the throng, shook my hand, looked up with a poker face. I started asking questions right away, making B. translate, and C. looked puzzled but answered. The crowd pressed around. Television cameras ground and two microphones were held before us. First time I've starred on communist TV, but I am sure they'll have to sanitize it first.

Our conversation lasted about forty-five minutes and, although C. looked perplexed and even hostile at times, the others pressing around us, including the two presidium members and officials, smiled and seemed friendly and even approving.

C. said: "We consider the period of military blocs has ended. They prevent cooperation between peoples. But I am not sure how the process of dissolution should be started. I am against the idea of the two alliances meeting. Things should be started by direct, bilateral cooperation and talks between individual countries. This would mean preserving their sovereignty and equal rights. If this principle is established and bilateral explorations are held, then conditions would be created for the liquidation of military blocs."

(All the time he spoke, before translations, I watched C. Despite his plumpness and rather delicate features, glowing eyes, he has a stubborn little chin and could be ruthless.)

C: "We expressed our position on European security at the Warsaw pact conference that was held in Bucharest this summer. Everyone is familiar with our position. Essentially, it is that the European countries should be allowed to solve their own problems without any interference by non-Europeans."

CLS: "I assume by that you mean the U.S.A. Do you?"

C: "Yes, the U.S.A. is not European."

CLS: "Russia?"

C: "Russia is European."

(The atmosphere was getting a bit hostile. The crowd pressed in and the TV men kept complaining we weren't talking loud enough and their pictures were being obscured.)

C: "How would you feel if Europe demanded a right to decide on America's future? What right have you here?"

CLS: "Well, we came over twice to save Europe, including Rumania, to liberate it. I think this gives us some right. And Germany, the biggest problem bequeathed by World War II, remains to be settled. There is no peace there. Many American men were killed to defeat the Nazis, after all."

C: (truculently) "America lost fewer soldiers in World War II than Rumania."

CLS: "Mr. Ceausescu, you must remember that we fought on only one side." (Nudge to Bec.) "Be sure and translate that." (Scarcely disguised smiles in entourage which recalled that until autumn 1944 Rumania was with Nazis.)

C: (irked) "I recognize the contribution America made. But this does not give the United States the right to interfere in Europe's internal affairs. These are for Europe.

"We want to avoid another world war. But there are some forces pushing toward it. We think the American people can do much to prevent World War III. I even read articles in the American press to that effect."

CLS: "I am glad you read the American press. You must realize that, unlike certain other presses, it speaks with many voices."

We parted on a sour note. I stuck out my hand. He seemed to hesitate before shaking it. Then he gave it a firm grip in his small hand. The crowd around us was delighted and most merry.

BUCHAREST, *October 11, 1966*

Last night I invited a group of young intellectuals, to get some idea of the future generation's thoughts and dreams. We dined together after they had had a good deal to drink, then wound up in my room.

The group: L.—about thirty-five, dark, discontented, ambitious to be a great novelist, clearly anticommunist. L.'s wife—thirty-two, black-haired, not pretty but interesting, intelligent face, good figure, speaks no foreign language, essayist and journalist, respected as "brilliant" by her peers. B.—in his early thirties, small, blond, editor of students' literary magazine, speaks rather bad French. R.—twenty-seven, tall, fine-figured, rather dashingly pretty ash blonde (false, she told me), writer of short stories, member of the editorial staff of a literary weekly; she is a member of the Communist Youth League Central Committee.

B. and R. are members of the Communist party. L. and wife are opposed. B. when seventeen (now thirty-three) was student of literature and poet. Friend who was actor was fanatic communist who urged need to sacrifice his life if party asked. Wouldn't now be so absurd but believes party holds the future. It stresses economic equality. It is a natural stage through which society must pass.

R. finds communism a moving, changing concept. Her generation has known no other system. It is no longer the brutal communism of her parents' day. There are no rich and poor now. All R. knows of the past (precommunism) is "out of literature." But she is discontented. Although in the Communist Youth Central Committee: "I write on love yet I must work for my husband, I must make children for him (she has none yet). Everywhere women are under men."

L.'s wife (through translation) says: "I am from a petty bourgeois milieu. Before the war it made great efforts to keep the rank of petty bourgeois. In a talk with my mother, the most interesting person I have ever met, she said that what is best in communist society is that everyone has to work. Before that my mother had to work secretly to keep up the life of a petty bourgeois but now she can do so openly because everyone does the same.

"Personally I find the best thing in communism is that all human energy is harnessed, willynilly, well or badly. I don't mean only the workers but the peasants who have been obliged to enter history. For our generation communism forces the youth to oppose our parents; the revolution pushed youth against their elders who belonged to another society. When we were young we were taken seriously by the government. This was the good side of communism. When we were teen-agers we believed we were writers and leaders and this was very flattering.

"But our parents have been proved right. They asked us to learn and not to make politics, not to be serious. To shout is not sufficient. I believe that knowing what is good, we must avoid what is wrong. For our generation the bad is Stalinist dogmatism. What gives our generation a certain solidarity is the duty to prevent other generations from falling into the same Stalinist trap again. In that we differ from generations before and after us. We have been interested in the older generation without any responsibility for it. We *have* a responsibility for the younger generation."

R.: "The worst people are those who profit from our generation's sacrifice to try and climb the ladder and put themselves on pedestals."

L.'s wife: "I detest those who, when writing, try to pass over the enormous sacrifices of our generation by speaking only of their little sexual problems. [Meaning R., a very sexy number and writer.] I am interested only in truth, not just literary fashions."

R.: "The difference between my generation [twenty-seven] and hers [thirty-four] is that hers saw the building of socialism and mine just read about it and got sick. We have had enough of dull socialist life [R. was getting a bit boiled—as they all eventually did] and need emotion, innovation. But all we writers have changed so far is the style, not the content. I want freedom to live as I want, do what I want, to have no one tell me what to do."

L.'s wife: "My ambition was to be quoted in a speech by Georgiu-Dej and cursed on the Voice of America. My second ambition was to write a second edition of *Don Quixote*."

More and more booze. At 1:00 A.M. we got kicked out of the hotel restaurant, went to the bar, commandeered a bottle of whisky (costly, black market), and piled up to my room. The bartender came along and took an enormous slug from the bottle. Argued incomprehensibly until five. It soon emerged that all of them, pro- and anticommunist, hated it and wanted only to achieve personal triumphs like writing great books. . . .

BELGRADE, *October 13, 1966*

This morning saw Burke Elbrick, U.S. ambassador. He says the Jugoslav motto should be: "We don't know where we're going but we're on our way."

All prices on the Dalmatian coast and many elsewhere are quoted in dollars—real estate, taxis, etc. On the coast several villas are being built by foreign movie stars. Tourism is booming—this year it will bring in about $150 million (vs. a hard-money and gold reserve of only about $120 million).

BELGRADE, *October 14, 1966*

P. says the chances are that when Tito dies a triumvirate will take over temporarily: Kardelj (a Slovene), Bakarić (a Croat), and a Serb. But which Serb? Koča Popović, an arrogant millionaire's son is unpopular. Todorović, who succeeded Ranković, is a *fonctionnaire*. Ranković has gained popularity by being disgraced. But the only Serb with stature (a Montenegrin) is Djilas. In jail, Djilas is the moral reserve of the Communist party here. He might, after Tito's death, some day emerge a popular hero.

PARIS, *October 31, 1966*

Yesterday golfed with Couve de Murville and Bohlen. I asked how Brezhnev was being treated in a protocol sense when he comes to France next year, because he doesn't have any official position apart from being head of the Russian Communist party. Couve said that was "a very embarrassing question" because there was no precedent and France had not yet decided how to handle it.

Couve says that after Tito dies, "there is going to be a lot of throat cutting." He says that only the Serbs speak of "Jugoslavia." The others talk of "Croatia" or "Slovenia," etc.

Couve thinks the next German government is going to be socialist. It is likely to be headed by Willy Brandt, whom he describes as "*un brave type*." He thinks Strauss is ambitious and hard-driving but stands no chance of becoming chancellor until after a socialist government has been tried and failed.

Chip finds Jugoslavia fascinating because he thinks everything that is now happening there, including the gradual withdrawal of the party from the government, will eventually happen in Russia.

PARIS, *November 13, 1966*

Golfed with Bohlen. Chip was rather proud of himself at the recent diplomatic shoot at Rambouillet, because while de Gaulle was standing behind him watching he got seven pheasants with nine shots. Chip mentioned Germany during the subsequent luncheon talk and de Gaulle said: *"Ces Allemands m'agacent"* (the Germans get on my nerves). The Germans didn't seem to realize that they had lost the war. Then the General made an interesting additional remark. He said: "The Germans can't make up their minds. Anyone who can't make up his mind gets on my nerves."

PARIS, *November 22, 1966*

Lunched today with John Bennett, who finished a few weeks ago as British ambassador to Burundi and Rwanda. John says that shortly after communist China and Burundi opened diplomatic relations, one of the Chinese diplomats fled to the American embassy and, after many weeks of hospitality, was dressed up as a white woman, smuggled out of the country. As an eventual consequence, the American ambassador, his deputy chief of mission, and the USIA man were bounced.

Bennett says the Chinaman reported that Peking believes the future of Africa lies in the former Belgian Congo, an area almost as large as India, and is concentrating all its efforts there. He also said Peking sees Burundi, a pimple on the eastern Congo border, as the place from which to launch subversion.

PARIS, *November 25, 1966*

I asked Bohlen about the famous Lenin quote that the Germans would never stage a revolution because they'd form a subway queue first. He said it was Stalin who had said this to Churchill, either at Teheran or Yalta. Stalin had been in Germany around 1907; there was to be a secret meeting, but the German comrades queued for tickets at the subway and didn't show.

PARIS, *November 26, 1966*

Lunched with Manlio Brosio [NATO secretary-general]. Brosio thinks the ultimate policy of the West should be to squeeze China and Russia against each other and exploit their differences. This requires the United

States to hold tight in southeast Asia against China so that it cannot expand southward but therefore to expand northward or westward. Simultaneously NATO must hold firm in Europe and encourage Russian energies eastward.

PARIS, *November 30, 1966*

An hour with Couve de Murville at the *Quai d'Orsay*. I began by asking if it was possible to arrange an agreement with the U.S.A. covering reactivation of American bases in France in case of aggression or a threat of war. He answered: "Of course. Your embassy doesn't understand or pretends not to understand. But we have offered an agreement to put the ports and bases at your disposal if our two countries are at war under article 5 of the North Atlantic Treaty." Then Couve admitted that France would not contemplate any "advance preparations" in moments of crisis or threatened war. He said: "There can be no crisis agreement as such."

He thought the idea of any Spanish admission to NATO had vanished; nor was there any thought of any French-Spanish alliance. "Against whom?" Couve asked. But the question of Spanish admission to the Common Market "is a real problem." This is being negotiated but so far without any conclusion. "It is always the same with Spain," Couve said. "The socialist governments are always opposed."

I said that if France wishes to remain an ally of the United States I wondered if—as an ally—it was willing to try to help find a way to peace in Vietnam by exploring diplomatic possibilities with the FLN, Hanoi, and Peking. He answered: "I don't know. Certainly that would have to be on a basis of which we approve. We don't agree with your policy and therefore we cannot serve as an intermediary on the basis of a policy of which we disapprove."

I asked if it would be necessary for Britain to devalue the pound in order to qualify for admission to the Common Market. He said: "How can I answer that? The problem is theirs. Of course they must put their house in order if they wish to join but how to do so is their responsibility."

Couve said the main effort of French policy in Europe was "to have the Iron Curtain disappear. That is what we really mean—to end the partition of Europe. That is what we are trying to do and it is starting to happen but there is much remaining to accomplish. Were it not for the Vietnam problem you would have long preceded us to Moscow—but more on the basis of a world-wide accommodation than on a European basis. But it is not possible for you to do much while the Vietnam war continues—although the will to do so unquestionably exists on both sides [Moscow and Washington]."

Unless the dollar were devalued, a change in the pound would probably not have a world effect on currency values. But of course France would like to see a change in the price of gold. All the world's problems would be settled if the U.S.A. revalued gold. He continued: "However, you oppose this primarily for reasons of prestige. Actually I think such a move would strengthen the dollar, not hurt it. And we all have the same interest. We don't want a crisis for either the dollar or the pound."

PARIS, *December 2, 1966*

Yesterday evening Don Juan, the Spanish pretender to the throne, dropped in for a drink together with Count Motrico, former Spanish ambassador here. Don Juan is a big bruiser. He looked rugged and healthy with a beaked face like a ship's figurehead.

Motrico, incidentally, always referred to him as "the king," in his presence. It was very informal, indeed cozy: wisecracks, drinks, smokes; but Motrico always quietly made it plain that the guest of honor was already a monarch.

Don Juan confessed there really isn't a thing he can do except wait for Franco to die—since it is obvious Franco never intends to resign. I said Franco came from a very long-lived family. Don Juan laughed sourly. He said Franco's father had died at the age of eighty-seven (Franco is only seventy-four today).

Don Juan said there was no rapport between Franco and the youth of Spain. "Europe" is the catchline for the young Spaniards. To this Motrico added: "They know the king's ideas and they agree with his views on Europe. All the young people—those under thirty-five—felt disappointed in Franco's recent speech and his new constitution. He has no appeal for the future."

Don Juan said: "Franco is trying to perpetuate a period of legitimacy for his own kind of legitimacy." He claims Franco is deliberately avoiding any indication as to which royal candidate he favors for the eventual succession. He said that he and his supporters would have to move very quickly the minute Franco died in order to avoid being out-maneuvered.

I said Don Juan had once told me the army would be the decisive force when the critical moment came, and that he had his greatest backing among the colonels. "They were colonels then," said Don Juan, "but they are all generals now."

Don Juan said undoubtedly one big change had taken place during recent years and this was that the threat of bloodshed following Franco's death has now gone.

Don Juan said Franco has not made any arrangements with Juan Carlos, Don Juan's son. His son "feels the pressure and is concerned but has not made a deal with Franco." But he seemed a little bit skittish on this and I asked him point-blank whether his son would support him or oppose him. "I don't think you can say my son has a feeling against *me* but there are some who may think that he would be more convenient in terms of arranging a Franco-like solution after Franco."

I asked if Sophia, Juan Carlos' Greek wife, was exerting any political influence. He said that her mother, Queen Frederika, "quite obviously wants her daughter to be a queen just as soon as possible and she is pushing my son. She is not a Greek, she is a Prussian." (Frederika is the kaiser's granddaughter.) "It got so bad that I had to tell her not to meddle in our affairs." He then went on somewhat sadly and said: "It all depends on how long Franco lives."

Don Juan said: "The country is getting very restless. It doesn't like the idea that it has to wait for Franco's death as the only solution."

Motrico complained about the stupidity of American generals who come through Spain and praise the military dictatorship saying, "this is the kind of thing we need in Vietnam." The result is that the Spanish generals—upon whom Don Juan is evidently counting—get the impression that what the United States military wants is the kind of situation that is already prevailing in Spain. Even McNamara who, Motrico says, "looks like a general in disguise," gives this kind of impression and it is lamentable. It hurts the effort of Don Juan to build up a more liberal kind of support.

ROCQUENCOURT, *December 2, 1966*

Interesting talk with General Lemnitzer. He got quite emotional when discussing the crosscurrents of pressure. The French government insists on one thing. The NATO council is paralyzed by its own red tape. And U.S. politicians keep urging him to do insane things like cutting off severance pay for French workers in U.S. installations here, or even like removing from cemeteries in France the bodies of American soldiers.

Lemnitzer is determined to do as efficient a job as possible of withdrawing without losing his diplomatic sangfroid and also to try and negotiate with de Gaulle's representative, General Charles Ailleret, the least disagreeable terms for retaining a vestigial alliance.

I asked if it was possible to reckon on ever again using United States bases in France, if they could not be prepared during a crisis period for emergency use. Lemnitzer said the United States had put almost two billion dollars into the line of communications in France. It took a decade to put this in and we were having to get out in a year. This included all kinds of installations. And the French are not allowing us to return prior to their actual involvement in a war.

Likewise, most of NATO's reception airfields for U.S. reinforcements are in France. What will happen to them? Some will be used by the French but others will no longer be used. We cannot henceforth count on the continued availability on such airfields of fuel supplies. The result is "absolute disaster." Lemnitzer says we can't count on French troops or on French airfields. Therefore, we are pulling out all kinds of things from these fixed installations because the U.S.A. is simply not ready to leave behind lots of valuable equipment for the French to look after.

At the time of de Gaulle's edict the U.S.A. had 750,000 tons of equipment in France—everything from vehicles and tanks to spare parts, ammunition, and hospital equipment. All this has to be moved out because we can't keep it here. The only feasible area in which to place it is forward—and there it is too concentrated and vulnerable.

Since July 1, 1966, SHAPE has only given France what is called "need-to-know" intelligence, that is to say the minimum requisite for French planning in a particular field.

PARIS, *December 4, 1966*

Dined last night with Averell and Marie Harriman. Harriman said Roosevelt and Churchill had virtually reached agreement at Casablanca in late 1942 to get rid of de Gaulle by 1943. However, Eden, who was always pro-de Gaulle, blocked this and, on his own initiative, brought de Gaulle to Casablanca. Somewhat regretfully, Averell conjectured how much easier things would now be if Roosevelt and Churchill had succeeded.

He says President Johnson particularly resents the fact that he is not getting any help from Europe on Vietnam. He argues that the United States is not letting down Europe, despite the Vietnam burden, but that it is not getting any help from Europe.

PARIS, *December 5, 1966*

Lunched for two and a quarter hours with André Malraux, a memorable experience. Pale, nervous, with twitching features, sniffing, gesticulating, his luminous eyes staring hypnotically, more than ever he gives the impression of a character from Edgar Allen Poe. His conversation ranges enormously. He referred *en passant* to: de Gaulle, Churchill, Stalin, Kennedy, Jacqueline Kennedy, Bobby Kennedy, Gavin, General Pechkov, Maxim Gorki, Picasso, Mao Tse-tung, Chou En-lai, Mendès-France, Couve de Murville, Debré, Pompidou.

Emerging from a concentrated conversation with Malraux must be like emerging from a Bessemer steel furnace and discovering that one is still intact. He is an incredible man. He has been one of the great novelists of the twentieth century; he is one of the great experts on painting and sculpture; he was a soldier-adventurer of success and courage, having commanded a fighter unit on the Republican side in the Spanish civil war and, having commanded a large Maqui unit in occupied France, holding the equivalent rank of brigadier-general. He has been a cabinet minister for years. Now he says: "It will not be a bad monument if, when I die, I shall have left one hundred new museums in France behind me."

Malraux said, as he sat down, shaking my hand, that it always gave him special pleasure to come to this Lucas Carton corner of Paris because, just fifty meters away, had been La Rue's (the fine restaurant that sold out a decade or so ago) where General Boulanger always used to go and finally made up his mind not to make the attempt to seize control of France.

When it came to choosing our food Malraux said, "but of course we must have the *jambon au Chablis* because this is the only place in Paris that has it." This was hard enough for me to take, after a difficult gustatorial weekend, but then he proposed that we precede this with a terrine of duck so as not to "*changer les vins*" and we had an excellent bottle of Pomerol.

I asked Malraux if it was indeed true that he had said of de Gaulle: "He is the man of the day before yesterday and the day after tomorrow." Unfortunately, it wasn't true at all. He didn't know who had made up the crack but it was a good one. Nor had he said, as legend has it, that it was "de Gaulle who led us to the Rubicon and then told us to take out our fishing rods." That was Léon Delbecque, one-time UNR [Gaullist] deputy.

It was unfair to dismiss de Gaulle in terms of a "day after tomorrow" because de Gaulle was very concerned with *today* and *tomorrow*. De Gaulle realized the basic question facing France was how to change a backward society based upon landed estates into a modern industrial society. He was fully aware that the United States had managed this brilliantly. There are no peasants in the United States and there never have been. Furthermore, landed proprietors have no influence in the United States, if they exist at all. American millionaires like the Kennedys have "*dachas*" in the country but do not depend upon land for their wealth. But at least one hundred members of the French senate are old-fashioned, landed men of wealth. De Gaulle sees the necessity of making the shift from an old, deeply rooted landed society to a modern industrialized society geared to the machine.

Malraux thought there would be no UNR without de Gaulle and it will dissolve when he disappears. And ultimately, it was quite impossible to conjecture on who the real successor of de Gaulle would be. No one had been able to foresee that Stalin would succeed Lenin; everyone imagined it would be Trotsky. Likewise, no one assumed Khrushchev would succeed Stalin. Everybody thought that Suslov would succeed Khrushchev, not Brezhnev.

I said it was absolutely imperative that Malraux write some kind of book about de Gaulle—whether or not it was a biography. He said that in his memoirs he has devoted three chapters to the General—but it would be improper and indiscreet to go into serious matters while de Gaulle was still alive.

He said de Gaulle could never talk to a foreigner without feeling that he was representing France and therefore forced to assume a certain attitude and represent a certain point of view. For example, de Gaulle undoubtedly had an enormous admiration for Churchill, and although he had had a savage argument with him, the two men were really in the position of a divorced couple who wanted to make up and yet were never able to get around to it. Oddly enough—and it was perfectly evident that Malraux was not trying to flatter me because he said this in a haphazard way—he remarked that the General had often told him he had a *"certaine sympathie"* for me but, Malraux added, "he can never really talk to you because you are not French."

I said one of the things that puzzled me about the relationship of France and the United States was that the electrical current of friendship seemed to be short-circuited. He said this was precisely the case. The only American ambassador to France in recent years who had attracted real sympathy was General [James M.] Gavin. Ambassadors really had a very small role nowadays when foreign ministers and chiefs of state could maneuver directly with each other, but Gavin had had a courageous role during the war and he appealed to the French because, though he was a distinguished general, he was also a shy and timid man.

I speculated as to whether it would be a good thing for de Gaulle to meet Johnson next year. He said Johnson was an interesting man in some respects. Then—and only a Frenchman would think of such a thing—Malraux said the royal apartments of Louis XIV in Versailles would be ready for occupancy as a state guest house in about six months—approximately the time of Johnson's probable visit to Europe, Malraux observed—and there can be no better occasion for opening them as a residence for a state visitor.

Malraux asked me: "You, who see all the news, what do you consider the most significant piece of news today?" I had no idea what he was getting at. I said that I thought the crisis between England and Southern Rhodesia was probably the most important event for the U.S.A.—not only because of our close relations to Britain but because of our own excruciating Negro problem and the effect that bloodshed in Africa would have when mirrored in the U.S.A.

Malraux thought the most important event was the naming of Madame Mao Tse-tung [Chiang Ching] as cultural consultant to the general political department of the Chinese army. It was immensely significant that she had been named to this new post, and it showed Mao's determination to take over control of the army and to put an end to the insolence of the Red Guard youth. Mao was very worried about the youth. He had confessed to Malraux during Malraux's visit to Peking in July and August 1965 that he knew the youth of China was against him. They did not seem to have the messianic qualities required.

Malraux said Mao had confided that it was very difficult to lose one's old friends and that almost all the survivors of the Long March were now dead. Malraux said Chou En-lai had not dropped in rank but had no ambition to advance and had earnestly assured Malraux that he was now sixty-five and did not wish to accede to power. He is again being bruited as a possible successor.

Incidentally, Malraux says that one of the survivors of the Long March is General Huang Chen, the present Chinese ambassador to Paris. Malraux says he is really an idiotic choice as an ambassador because he doesn't speak a word of any Western language nor do any of his secretaries. He has no concept of the West. When you go to dinner at his embassy there are two tables—one for the men and one for the women. As Malraux says, not even the most reactionary Mohammedan country behaves like that in the West nowadays.

He said Mao hasn't the remotest idea of what the United States is like and what the power of an industrialized state amounts to. He is building up an extraordinary torrent of hatred for the United States among the young Chinese; but it is a wasted emotion that can lead to nothing. Mao doesn't want to have a war with the United States and it is perfectly obvious that the U.S. is never going to invade China. The Vietnam situation is impossible and nobody can do anything with a man like Ky. But if there is an embroilment between the U.S.A. and China, all the U.S. has to do is destroy ten Chinese cities and it will set back Mao's revolution by fifty years. He cannot afford this.

Mao said one thing of tremendous interest. Malraux quoted him: "We, people like de Gaulle and myself, have no successors." It was perfectly evident that Mao thinks whatever has to be done will have to be done by himself. Malraux told this to de Gaulle when he came back to Paris and de Gaulle was fascinated.

Malraux agrees with Mao and does not think de Gaulle can either form or designate anyone to follow him. But de Gaulle thinks he may yet have some time to carry out the project of transforming French society to the requirements of an industrialized age. Malraux said de Gaulle isn't going to shift France's alliances or make any deal with Russia because "he is not an idiot."

De Gaulle had always had a special personal interest in Adenauer, because of his tendency to seek friendship with older men and because it always gave him comfort to see a man who was so much older continuing to exercise power actively.

Malraux said Kennedy's role in history had been assured by the fact of his assassination and that even lesser men were ennobled by political murder. But, delicately and politely, he hinted a belief that there was far more to the assassination than had been said by the Warren report.

Malraux had met Bobby Kennedy. He thought Bobby was tough and ambitious; he indicated both admiration and doubt. He made a curious observation: President Kennedy was a "dog" but Bobby was a "cat" (by this he meant that JFK was a warm and forthright, open personality and RFK was subtle and feline). He also said he was a "false youth." By this he meant that he cultivated enormous appeal to youngsters although he was far from being a youth himself.

I told him that once when I dined at the White House, Kennedy had said: "I don't understand Malraux. He is Jackie's friend." Malraux said this was correct and he added that he had an enormous admiration for Jackie, that she had a great wisdom about what she could do and what she could not do, where she could interfere with her husband and where she could not interfere. He said she would be a first-class president, a woman of real talent. I suggested that she would also be an excellent ambassador and maybe she could restore the electric current between France and the U.S.A. to which I had referred earlier.

He agreed—but he added: "It all depends for whom you are ambassador. I don't think she would do very well under Johnson." He didn't smile. Malraux was very interesting when he was talking about ambassadors. He told me—which I had never known—that Rubens had served as Spanish ambassador (because Spain then ran Holland) to Richelieu and that Rubens and Richelieu hated each other.

Malraux said de Gaulle was much more a Roman type than a Greek type. He really belonged to the nineteenth century by intellectual formation and all the great nineteenth-century figures like Chateaubriand, who had greatly influenced de Gaulle, were Roman rather than Greek. Malraux often talked to de Gaulle about history, philosophy, etc. De Gaulle had commonplace tastes in such things as music and painting. He only went to art museums—in the old days—to relate himself to the stream of history.

But he was essentially a literary figure and kept contact with literature. In this vein, he was a "Roman" and talked about Caesar much more than he talked about Alexander the Great. In the days before de Gaulle came back to power in 1958, Malraux occasionally loaned the General his flat so he wouldn't have to stay in the Hôtel Lapérouse. In Malraux's study is a picture of Alexander the Great. Sometimes de Gaulle would look at it and talk to Malraux and say that he hoped he could live as long in history as Alexander.

This recollection prodded Malraux to some observations on Alexander. He said: "You know he was a bastard and was fully aware of it. He was not the son of Philip of Macedon—although Philip, of course, knew this and still remained very fond of him. The probability is that Alexander's mother had him with a priest. Alexander never knew whether he was descended from a man or from a god—but he knew his father was not Philip and he preferred to think he was a god."

He said de Gaulle was much influenced by Napoleon and fascinated by the fact that Napoleon had accomplished so much so young.

Malraux said the United States was a remarkable country in many ways, and one of them was the fact that it was the most powerful nation on earth but it had never had a foreign policy—with the exception of the Marshall Plan. This was the sole coordinated approach to global affairs. Roosevelt had been involved in a tremendous internal revolution in an effort to achieve a posture in world affairs but would not have succeeded if war had not been thrust upon him by the Japanese.

We talked about the role of the intellectual in diplomacy. He said the last great artistic figure to serve as a French ambassador was Paul Claudel. There was little role for an ambassador nowadays with instant communications.

Malraux said a curious thing about Stalin whom he had first met when the latter was quite young. He said: "It is extraordinary how much his appearance changed. You know, he used to be about my size and he had a huge shock of hair. But later on he became a very small man [Malraux is almost as big as I am] and his hair became far less abundant."

Malraux knew both General Pechkov, the French Foreign Legion officer and diplomat who has just died, and his stepfather, Maxim Gorki. He said Gorki always showed traces of his impoverished youth, and that he remembers vividly Gorki with an enormous mound of ice cream and being delighted to let the waiter pay for it.

He said Picasso is a very peculiar man who lives in his own private world where he is the absolute emperor. At various times it has included Françoise Gilot, his former mistress, Marie-Laure de Noailles, and Malraux himself. But Picasso doesn't like to come out of his world and, for example, was very frightened when he heard that de Gaulle was going to see his exhibition in Paris. Picasso is very eccentric about letting his own pictures and sculptures—the ones he still possesses—go out on exhibition, and it took a lot of prodding to get him to contribute adequately to the present splendid Paris show.

PARIS, *December 13, 1966*

I had an excellent talk with de Gaulle this afternoon. I knew that this was a terribly busy week for him and right on the heels of Kosygin's visit. Therefore, I didn't think he would give me much time.

The General greeted me with grave friendship, a somewhat flaccid handclasp, and then waved me to the chair across from him beside his desk. He has changed physically again. It seems to me his cheeks were somewhat puffy and that his eyes had shrunken in size. He has certainly put on weight. But he was quite pink and exceedingly alert and active.

This was one of those talks which I am quite sure he enjoyed and, although I had made a list of twenty-four questions covering the whole damn universe, he let me persevere to the end and I was sorry I had no more to go on with. He then kept me with chitchat asking what my travel plans were and we discussed my daughter's wedding, Tito, etc.

I began by asking if he didn't consider that the biggest task remaining to him in France, now that the constitution had been changed, was to push the country from an agrarian society into a modern industrial and technological society. He answered: "That is very true. Until now this [referring to industrialization] has not been France's avocation, but from now on it must increasingly be so. This is quite evident because this is an industrial epoch. We have done much, we have advanced perceptibly, but not by any means enough, and we must proceed in this direction and accomplish such a change in depth. France's population and above all France's youth are most interested and preoccupied with this question. The youth is especially interested in it and insists upon this movement.

"But it will not be excessive, France will not exceed in this direction. France is a country with social and economic traditions and traits that never tend to excess. Furthermore, we lack many raw materials. And our population is not too dense. As a consequence, there is no pressure urging toward excessive industrialization. We are fortunate in this respect."

I said that some time ago in a conversation with me de Gaulle had conjectured aloud as to whether or not it would be advisable to have a vice president in France. I wondered what his views were nowadays. He replied: "I never really wanted this. In France a vice president would produce a bizarre situation. It would be very strange and rather pointless. After all, there is a president here and there is a prime minister also. What would a vice president do? In the United States, the vice president replaces the president in emergency. But in your country the president is also prime minister. It would be artificial to have a vice president here. He would have no role, no function, nothing to do."

Such being his view, did he contemplate any constitutional change in the position of the prime minister with regard to succession of the president? He foresaw no need for such a change. He then went on: "The prime minister's position is very different from that of the president. Of course a prime minister could become president under the constitution but he would not be elected president because he had been prime minister."

I said I had heard conjecture that de Gaulle had definitely decided not to serve out his entire second term. He said: "This could be the case. I could be led to terminate my term before the end—by events or developments. I simply don't know. But for the moment I have no such plan. It is difficult therefore for me to make any prognostications on this. I really can't answer you any more on this point because I just don't know."

I said that when Churchill was still prime minister he had told me Eden was his crown prince ("dauphin") and I wondered who was de Gaulle's "dauphin." He smiled shrewdly and said: "Perhaps I have chosen one, but if I have I couldn't say who he is because that would hurt him in France. I am sure you can see the point." There was an amused glint in his eye.

I asked him if he planned to write volume four of his memoirs. (Of course, if he did plan to do so he would have to plan on some period of retirement.) But he said: "No, I won't do it. I will not write a volume four. The wartime period required full explanation in my memoirs but this is not true of the years after the war." I expressed regret as a reader. He said: "You are very kind, but I shall write no more memoirs." [He did, after retiring.]

I asked whether he thought England could come into the Common Market and whether it could really qualify as a "European" country. He said: "Certainly up until now, until this moment, I frankly don't think that England could qualify for admission. Take England's economic situation, for example, it is not up to France or Germany or Italy. France, Germany, and Italy have analogous economies. They complement each other industrially and agriculturally. The Germans of course have more commerce than France and less agriculture. The Italians have a different balance in agriculture and industry and trade but their basis is rather the same. And the three countries together represent an important economic reality. They go together."

With a sniff and a look of disdain he added: "Of course Holland and Belgium are not important. But Britain is another affair. It doesn't resemble the continental countries economically. Certainly this is the case today and until now. Britain still thinks of itself as a world country and not a continental country. Its economic function is based on transit of goods, on banking and shipping. This is not the same thing as exists in Europe, which has another kind of industrial basis.

"Perhaps the British can change but the British are not great changers and I do not foresee that they will make any fundamental alterations. And yet their present role as a world power is far too much for them. They are more and more impoverished. Their burden has become too great. They cannot carry the load any more.

"Quite frankly, I don't think Britain can qualify to come into the Common Market. Maybe I am wrong. We will see.

"But can she change sufficiently? Britain is very dependent on the United States—above all on money. Europe must be a true partner of the United States as your President Kennedy foresaw. But a true partner must be independent and equal. Otherwise this is not worth it. Take the practical question of pound sterling, which is so attached to the dollar. Or the balance of payments. The balance of payments in Britain continues to be very bad. And nevertheless Britain remains closely linked not only to you but also to the Commonwealth. It gives priority to the purchase of Canadian wheat. It gives priority to the purchase of New Zealand mutton. It gives priority to the purchase of Australian wool. How can Britain separate herself from all of this? I doubt if she can."

I then asked, apropos of this, whether France was not, nevertheless, interested in cooperating with Britain in the development and maintenance of a nuclear weapons force. He said: "Now it is very late, it is too late. Too much has happened since the time of the Nassau Conference [December 1962]. We will have our own weapons systems and any association with Britain in this connection is no longer of interest to us.

"Naturally, if Russia were to attack we would remain allies of Britain and the United States, but I doubt very much if Russia will attack. There has been a big change in the international mood and therefore it is really much less important anyway to develop such extensive weapons systems."

I asked if he foresaw an eventual reunification of Germany or simply a confederation of two German states under separate governments. He replied: "I don't know. It is hard to foresee this. There is, of course, the basic fact that there is only one German people, not several. There is the same German people on one side and on the other side of the Berlin wall, for example, but this fact alone is not enough to make for a single German state.

"You should remember that this has always been the history of Germany. It is very hard to make German unity. Wilhelm I and Wilhelm II managed to do it. And it was reestablished under Hitler. But don't forget, German unity is never necessary. [And there he stressed the word *necessary*.] For a long, long time Germany has consisted of a single people but several states, and this fact remains today. It is an inescapable fact that there is one people but it is divided between the federal government and a communist government in the Eastern zone. This doesn't prevent the existence of one people; but it also does not prevent the exis-tence of two states.

"What will come of this situation? Certainly the fact of one German people will continue to be a fact. And when Europe gradually relaxes, inside that Europe there will be a rapprochement between the two states in economic, cultural, touristic, and commercial affairs. It is possible that the two states will grow more closely together and one does not know where this could lead. It is even possible that some day it might lead to reunification or perhaps to a confederation of the two states.

"But what would all that accomplish? One single German people will continue to live in the same ethnic community anyway, whether it exists as one or two states. And do not forget that even West Germany is divided into the *Länder*, which are separate states with considerable autonomy. So you see it is hard to speculate beyond the fact that the community of

German people will continue. That stays. But anything else must develop gradually as the over-all European situation develops, and the Russians must accept whatever changes come about. This will take a considerable amount of time. So, that is our policy on this. There must first be détente in Europe—and then let the German people find themselves within it."

I said I was struck by the impression that French Indochina policy had switched. De Gaulle had favored neutralism in the past but now, since his Phnom Penh speech, he seemed to be endorsing Hanoi. He said: "These are two different things—to make peace by ending the war and then to preserve peace. Indeed, in my Phnom Penh speech I spoke of a formula for ending the war. But for the future, once there is peace, we still want neutrality for the entire area. There can be no peace there without neutralization. And neutralization means that there shall be no special privileges in southeast Asia for *any* foreign power—France, United States, China, or Russia. That refers of course to the future once peace has been established.

"But first of all a means must be found to achieve peace. The area to be neutralized should include Vietnam—which means both North and South Vietnam—and Cambodia, Laos, and certainly Thailand at least. But I think that North as well as South Vietnam must be neutralized. The North and South will inevitably come together into a single country just as they were under French administration. They are of course not identical. The North is tougher and has less food resources than the South. But the North needs the South and vice versa. They are really one people, one country, and I think in the future Vietnam will be reunited into a single land just as it was under Bao Dai or under France.

"The fact that Ho Chi Minh recognizes this and openly fights for reunification gives him a big advantage. When he was fighting us he was fighting for unity and he is doing the same now. This helps him with the people of course."

(I was rather interested by the contrast in de Gaulle's views on Germany and Vietnam. He is quite obviously prepared to see an indefinite continuation of German political partition and equally obviously he is all out to end political partition in Vietnam.)

I asked him whether he considered France to be anti-American. "Certainly not," he said. "We are not anti-American. But you must remember that you are a big people, a colossal power. You have a huge industry, a gigantic economy and military force which give you enormous political power, the greatest in the world. Inevitably a country like France, wanting its own independence, doesn't want to be dominated, led by or integrated into your system. But this does not make us hostile to you, not at all. We are simply taking precautions to avoid being absorbed because you are so especially powerful.

"Perforce [*forcement*] a country like France must be on the alert to preserve its own personality. But the same thing is true vis-à-vis the Soviets. Without the United States—or with a less powerful United States—we would have to be very much on the alert against the Soviets. Indeed, we are on the alert vis-à-vis the Soviets and we do not wish to be absorbed by them. We are for an equilibrium. We are obliged to be for an equilibrium by the simple geographical and political facts. We oppose any hegemony, either American or Russian. But this does not prevent friendship. There is no instinctive ill will [*malveillance*] against the United States here in France."

I then asked him if he would consider it useful to have a meeting with President Johnson in 1967. De Gaulle's mobile face looked very sceptical. His eyebrows raised, his forehead wrinkled, his nose twitched. "If he wants to come," he said, "we would be very happy. Indeed, I would be both happy and interested to see him—if he wants to come. But I don't really know if he thinks it would be a good idea. This depends entirely on President Johnson. We have not proposed any such meeting and there have been no official communications about it between our governments."

I asked if he contemplated any political accord with Russia. He said: "Certainly there is cooperation in the sense of a concerted viewpoint on big political questions such as Germany and Vietnam. There are no major differences at this moment between us on these big issues. But I don't foresee any kind of a treaty or pact with them. Why? To do what?"

I asked him if France would stay in the North Atlantic Alliance or denounce the treaty when it becomes possible in 1969. He replied categorically: "We will remain in the Alliance. We will not denounce the treaty."

I said that one of the last times I had seen him he gave me the impression he preferred a system of bilateral alliances to a continuation of the North Atlantic Treaty. He said: "Perhaps in the future we might wish to have such alliances with the United States, Britain, and Germany. I could imagine this for the future, but not now, it is not necessary now. And the Russians are much less menacing. They are more peaceful in their words and in their behavior and we all know the reasons—above all China. They are having trouble; they are worried about China.

"But things can change in the future. For this reason the Alliance exists and we should keep it."

(It is interesting that de Gaulle was categorically in favor of the West. He plans to stay in the Alliance and all he thinks of to replace it in the future is other Western alliances, nothing with Russia.)

I asked whether he thought China would be a superpower in the future. Again without any hesitation he said: "Certainly, but in thirty years. And when this happens China will make claims against everybody, against the whole world, but above all against Russia. China will make claims against India. It will insist on expelling United States influence from Formosa, from

South Korea, and it will even insist on removing your protectorate from Japan. But Russia, the Soviets, will feel tremendous pressure."

Was he worried about the chances of a world war exploding out of Vietnam? He said: "There will be no world war because of Vietnam. Nevertheless, without producing a world war, Vietnam prevents a true world détente and continued tension can lead anywhere, but I do not think it will lead to war."

I said I had heard speculation that France and Russia might diplomatically intervene in the Middle East to secure Palestine peace. He observed: "There will be no joint intervention in the 'Orient.' But I discussed this with Kosygin and, like us, he wishes to avoid dramas there. Naturally so do we. Neither the Israelis nor the Arabs should be allowed to exaggerate. We want a status quo; and the Russians do also."

I asked him which personage living or dead had most influenced him. He replied—*tout court*—"My father. My father was a great influence on my formation. He was a modest professor but a very eminent man, very cultivated and a gentleman, very balanced and reasonable, very, very patriotic. His influence on my formation was capital.

"Then, also, there was Pétain. Pétain also had a great influence on my formation when I knew him as a young officer. I learned much from his method and manner of command when I was a lieutenant and he was my colonel. His influence was great but when he ceased to be the same man it ended, of course. Events separated us and turned us against each other. But he ended by moving toward me. Did you know that he sent someone to me, Admiral [Paul] Auphan, when I came to Paris in 1944? Auphan brought me a message from Pétain saying, 'You must take over, you must lead France,' but, of course, that was too late, alas, and you know how things ended."

I asked what he considered his greatest success and his greatest failure in his long and eventful life. He seemed a bit startled and pondered this. He wondered aloud: "How do you define success or failure? Only history itself can define these terms. In reality, life and action are always made up of a series of successes and checks [*échecs*]. Life is a combat and therefore each one of its phases includes both successes and failures. And you cannot really say which event was a success and which event was a failure. Success contains within it the germs of failure and the reverse is also true.

"Certainly France suffered a terrible failure as a nation in 1940. It was catastrophic, but what occurred in 1940 merely reflected what had really happened before inside France. Nevertheless, that was a failure without precedent.

"And now France has been notably reestablished both in its own eyes and in the eyes of the world. How far that will continue into the future of course we cannot foresee. But the comparison between France in 1940 and France in 1966 is very evident, very striking. That was a success for France and I think I have participated in this success, but no one can foresee where it will all lead."

I confess when summing up that, all in all, despite his tantalizing maneuvers with the various communist nations, he strikes me as very much a man of the West, suspicious of the communists and perhaps a bit inclined to look down on them, and wedded to Richelieu's old basic rule of French foreign policy—keep Germany divided; also, beware of the English.

PARIS, *December 17, 1966*

Golf and lunch with Chip Bohlen. Chip claims the Marshall Plan was in no sense stimulated by Dean Acheson's famous Mississippi speech in 1947. After Secretary Marshall saw Stalin in Moscow (during the Council of Foreign Ministers meeting) in the spring of 1947, he concluded that it was imperative that the United States take the lead in acting to save Europe's political and economic health. He gave Bohlen orders to draft a speech along these lines and later on this speech was the famous address given at Harvard by Marshall.

Chip says that George Brown [British foreign minister] last night, at the *Quai d'Orsay* dinner given by Couve, deeply offended Paul Martin, the Canadian foreign minister, by continually mumbling in a very loud voice, "Watch out for him. When you eat with him you need a bloody long spoon."

Chip conceded that Rusk made a mistake to keep harping on the Pacific being NATO's "western flank." He says Rusk was doing this on president's orders because Johnson wanted the record straight. Rusk insisted at this last NATO meeting that Hawaii was not covered by the treaty. I told Chip that when Hawaii became a state, both Spaak and Norstad assured me it was now included in the NATO area.

PARIS, *December 24, 1966*

Golfed and lunched with Chip Bohlen. He had seen Pat Reilly, the British ambassador, four days earlier to ask him about de Gaulle's talk with George Brown. "It was almost an exact paraphrase of Cy's column," Reilly said.

PARIS, *January 12, 1967*

Lunched with Étienne Burin des Roziers, secretary-general of the Élysée. Étienne suggested that I should be the vis-à-vis interviewing de Gaulle on French television during the campaign performance prior to the March elections this year. I explained this would be quite out of the question; I could not possibly mix into the politics of a foreign country. (I doubt if Étienne was very serious but I can certainly see that it might be convenient—in a vote-getting sense—to demonstrate that de Gaulle got on well enough with the Americans to be interrogated on French government television by an American.)

I said that one thing which had struck me during my recent conversation was de Gaulle's lack of interest in Tito. Étienne smiled and said: "You know, for the General Jugoslavia doesn't exist. It is only Serbia. Therefore, for him Tito is merely a Croatian agitator."

PARIS, *January 20, 1967*

Last night at dinner Liliane de Rothschild, who spent October in China, said it was already evident the place was becoming restive. A French scholar who was in their group said sadly: "On arriving I felt as if I were in France in 1790. Now, on leaving, it feels like 1793."

Lunched at Brosio's. René Mayer, the former prime minister, was there. He said he had taught Couve de Murville as a youth at the École Libre des Sciences Politiques. In all his experience that was the only time he ever graded a student perfect—twenty out of twenty.

Couve was the same as a youth as he is today: cold, self-assured, polite, capable of deliberate rudeness, and remarkably brilliant.

Mayer said that in 1935 he went to Moscow with Pierre Laval, a very intelligent, able man and a good speaker. On the way back, Laval, "with his eternal cigarette, me with my eternal pipe," said: "One thing we must make certain of—that we never see in France what we have seen here."

PARIS, *January 24, 1967*

Lunched with Étienne Manac'h, head of the Asian division of the *Quai d' Orsay*. He said that last August (1966) the Cultural Revolution began in China. Even before that, Hanoi had started to show signs of increasing independence of Peking. The North Vietnamese are fearful that if the Chinese troubles continue there may be serious repercussions on their supply lines.

The Chinese, said Manac'h, have been pushing a very hard line in Hanoi. They oppose peace negotiations under any conditions—even if the United States accepts all kinds of humiliations. But many of the principal North Vietnamese leaders are privately against China. And in recent months there has been a steady growth of Soviet influence in Hanoi.

The Russians agree with Hanoi there must be an unconditional cessation of United States bombing of the north before any peace talks can start. The Russians are determined to avoid a precedent which would show a communist country ceding under pressure of bombardment.

The last congress of the Chinese Communist party was in 1956, Manac'h points out. That was a "peace congress" and sponsored the famous "hundred flowers" line. It can be likened to Khrushchev's twentieth congress in Russia where de-Stalinization began. There was no split with Russia and the congress was followed by a deliberate effort by the Chinese to woo support in Asia and Africa. But since then, Mao's policy has swerved dramatically away from that peaceful line and has become increasingly hostile to both the U.S.A. and Russia.

Mao's wife, Madame Chiang Ching (Green River) has no personal importance. She is a former actress, who never before mixed in politics. But for six months she has been climbing up the ladder. She only represents Mao. She is not a personality in herself. It is as if Madame de Gaulle suddenly began to make pronouncements on state affairs.

The *heart* of the problem in China now is symbolized by the wall posters everyone reads instead of the press. Because of his quarrel with the apparatus of the party, Mao has had to create parallel institutions and irregular channels. After all, the party hierarchy still controls the regular apparatus. So there is an irregular kind of guerrilla parallel hierarchy being created by Mao. He is, as it were, using the techniques of revolutionary warfare against the revolution itself.

For the first time in history, says Manac'h, a communist country is employing mechanisms outside the Communist party for political purposes. This is the reason for the Red Guard made up of students. Normally in communist countries, crises are regulated inside the party, which supervises, purges, arrests, tries, confesses, etc. The party is the only channel. Even in Russia, when the secret police took over from the normal party apparatus, they were controlled by Stalin as secretary-general of the party. But in China, Mao has chosen a nonparty device—the students and the Red Guard.

Mao is trying, before his death, to rekindle a revolutionary fervor and to discard the sclerotic party apparatus. This is the internal spark of the present situation and Mao's intention, whether he is sick or not—which we do not know.

Without going into detail on the names of the factional leaders, Manac'h says that the Maoists are led by Mao himself and Lin Piao and the opposition is led by Liu Shao Chi, president of the republic (he succeeded Mao in that post) and Teng Shiao Ping, secretary-general of the Communist party and therefore boss of the party hierarchy.

Chou En-lai falls in between these two groups, but he is a very important man. As prime minister he represents the state and tries to keep the state functioning. He has sought desperately to prevent the Red Guard revolution from engulfing the government ministries and wrecking the national economy, so that both the mechanism of the state and the machinery of the country can keep going. He is probably the man who could produce a synthesis, a compromise.

The Russians, says Manac'h, now openly support Liu and the Chinese Communist party hierarchy against Mao and Lin. Just this month Brezhnev told this to the Poles. What we now have is really a war of succession between Lin Piao and Liu Shao Chi.

Manac'h feels that now is the time for the United States to act dramatically in China. We should do our utmost to bring China into the world. We should even be ready to endorse another communist government there as long as it is less fanatical. During the past decade we lost a great chance to exploit the terrible illness in the communist world dramatized by the Sino-Soviet split. We were too obsessed with Vietnam, the Achilles heel of our policy.

Russia is very worried about the possibility of either an outbreak of trouble between the U.S.A. and China or a settlement between the U.S.A. and China. Russia is perfectly aware that a United States military presence on the Asian continent won't last forever whereas it will eternally confront China along enormously long frontiers.

To achieve an ultimate peace in Vietnam, the U.S.A. must regulate its affairs with China first, because geographically China represents a reality and will always be a neighbor of Vietnam. China has definitely conveyed to the United States that it will not attack the U.S.A. if the U.S.A. does not touch China's borders. This applies to Vietnam, to Formosa, and to Korea. By tacit agreement the U.S.A. and China have joined to isolate the Vietnam problem and prevent it from igniting a world war.

Manac'h feels we are at the threshold of an enormously important historical period. Until October 1, 1965, Vietnam was in a nutcracker between China and a pro-Chinese Indonesia. But the U.S.A. has been given two fantastic presents. The pro-Chinese government of Indonesia collapsed. Now China is collapsing. The nutcracker is gone.

PARIS, *January 27, 1967*

At dinner last night General Lemnitzer said there had been absolutely no agreement on the relationships between French armed forces and NATO in case of war.

Lemnitzer said the way we are proceeding now is "no way to fight in Vietnam." We should not restrict our bombing and we should not be inhibited by the fact that almost all the antiaircraft defense weapons are Russian.

PARIS, *February 21, 1967*

This afternoon I had a talk with Mai Van Bo, head of the North Vietnamese delegation here in Paris and Hanoi's most important diplomat in Europe. I was received in a salon with little furniture, a thick carpet, and a large picture of Ho Chi Minh, and was offered tea, cigarettes, and cigars.

Mai Van Bo is a small, well-dressed man of middle age, smiling and courteous. He speaks passable French which he learned entirely in Vietnam. He was accompanied by a younger man who took notes.

Mai said there could be no conversations until there was first a definite and unconditional end to American bombing in the north. I asked what effect the Sino-Soviet dispute was having on the war and he said it was "only speculating" to discern any effect. He added: "We are more determined than ever to follow our own independent policy. World events do not influence us. We run our own affairs."

I asked him if there were any direct discussions or contacts between Hanoi and Washington at present any place in the world. He answered: "Before Tet, U.S. spokesmen spoke of 'contacts with Hanoi.' Until now, whenever an American individual wanted contact with us at one of our embassies or delegations in order to ascertain our viewpoint or in order to explain your viewpoint, we were ready to talk or to listen. But it is false to say that any negotiations or contacts between our governments have been taking place. Why did the United States launch such an idea? Obviously it was put out as a diversionary plan. Public opinion was pushing for an end to your bombing of North Vietnam and it was only to divert attention from this that the false impression of diplomatic talks was put out."

I then said I wanted to go to Hanoi and showed him my passport with its state department authority to visit North Vietnam. He said, "Your name is well known. Of course, there are many applications for visas at this time but I think that yours requires very special attention."

[I never got it.]

Paris, *February 22, 1967*

I dined at the Eytan's [Walter is Israeli ambassador to Paris] and was lucky enough to sit next to Madame Jean-Jacques Servan-Schreiber, a pretty twenty-six-year-old. Her father and grandfather had both been cavalry officers. Jean-Jacques's grandfather, a German Jew, was Bismarck's secretary for twenty years. One day he went into a restaurant and saw a sign "No Jews Allowed." He immediately packed up and left Germany with his family, settled in Paris, and would allow no one to use a word of German before him. He began *Les Échos* and from it the family fortune again prospered.

Geneva, *February 27, 1967*

Long talk with Bill Foster of the U. S. disarmament agency, here as special ambassador heading the American delegation to the Geneva disarmament talks. We are trying to work out an agreed treaty draft with the Russians and present it to other nations in order to achieve a ban on proliferation of nuclear weapons.

I asked what would happen if no treaty were finally agreed on. He said within the next five years from three to five nations would have moved toward a nuclear weapon and would have tested it underground. If these initial tests prove to be successful, they would then break the atmospheric test ban treaty (the Moscow treaty) and proceed to test above ground.

Foster said a United States of Europe could accede to British or French nuclear weapons and take them over as the treaty is now worded. That is to say, at least a confederated Europe with a single defense or security authority could inherit; but that would be the only formula that could work it out. No intermediate group could take over such a stockpile under the treaty.

LONDON, *March 7, 1967*

Dined tonight with Dick Nixon. He couldn't have been nicer. There is something earnest and rather appealing in him, strangely contrasting with the image he sometimes gives in speeches and on TV as "Tricky Dicky." But beneath the assurance is a kind of lack of self-confidence; I don't quite know what. His gestures are strange (the way he continually moves his hands) and his heavy jaw is puffy. As a man I like him but I simply don't know how he would be as a national leader—in charge.

He talked a lot about himself. His great hero is Churchill and no one else of our time has similarly affected him. He has great respect and affection for the British. Saw Macmillan today and admires him. Thinks Harold Wilson has shown courage and ability although he overplayed his hand on Vietnam indicating things were nearer a settlement (with Kosygin) than was true. Nixon thinks we must keep the British going east of Suez even if we have to finance them, because we need their expertise on China.

Says the state department gave him a good briefing on Europe before he left. CIA won't brief him; only Ike, among nonmembers of congress. Nixon is on the first lap of a two- or three-month series of trips in Europe, Asia, Africa, Latin America. He has two aides at home putting together papers for him. He hopes at the end to arrive at a series of positions—for the 1968 campaign season.

He thinks Bobby Kennedy will make his play in 1968, either for president or vice president. Nineteen seventy-two is too far away. People will have forgotten the magic of his name and he will have suffered from too much exposure then. Johnson hates him (and vice versa) but they still might join on a ticket. Bobby knows there's no point in having a Republican elected in 1968. Nixon strongly disapproves of Bobby's Vietnam attitude and "playing politics" at the country's expense. Nixon admires Humphrey's loyalty. He says Romney has no gift for expression but is a decent man.

Obviously Dick is going to make one more big run for the presidency next year and is going to make foreign policy a big issue. He says Vietnam would be an almost impossible GOP issue; hopes (politically as well as other reasons) the war is over. Thinks we are ignoring Europe too much.

He says the two men who most influenced him are his Whittier College football coach, an Indian former All-American named Chief Newman, and his history professor, named Smith. Dick never made the team after four years of trying but Newman inculcated in him a competitive spirit, the need to keep trying against all odds. Smith taught him to love history. Had he not gone into a political career, he wanted to teach English history. Still loves to read history and biography most. He says writing comes very hard to him, and slow; he likes to outline and compose his thoughts.

I must say he does not give the impression of being immodest or ruthless. When I got him talking about the "greatest man" he had ever met he started out soundly enough with Churchill; then he continued about Khrushchev ("a nice fellow and fine politician who would have done well in America"), Nehru ("he accomplished a lot by holding that great mass together but he was antiwhite—meaning anti-British and anti-American— and a snob"), Menzies ("too bad he hadn't a bigger power base to work from"), Sukarno. He was pleased when I told him Sukarno preferred him to Stevenson.

Nixon said Eisenhower was a very complex, subtle figure, not the simple-minded boob so often advertised. After he had had his heart attack during his first term "he spent a lot of time batting out fungoes to see what reaction he would get. He was no fool."

N. is convinced Bobby [Kennedy] is running for office now. He says: "He's got to make his play. After all, he's a little fellow—not like his brother—and by the time 1972 comes along, he'll not only have lost most of the glamor of his name but he'll be old and insignificant-looking."

LONDON, *March 8, 1967*

This morning I saw Denis Healey, minister of defense. He is a good man to talk with: intimately acquainted with details, thoughtful, quick.

The allied nuclear force, created at the Ottawa NATO meeting, is "moribund." Britain had proposed it "as a better way of achieving the aims of the MLF" (which is to say, as a means of helping to kill MLF). The problem now is how to get governments, nuclear and nonnuclear, to agree in the alliance on common decisions for use of atomic weapons. This is best handled through the NATO planning group.

Healey said he did not think the idea of Britain offering its nuclear cooperation to France in exchange for admission to the Common Market was a "relevant consideration" for France. He added: "De Gaulle will keep us out of the Common Market while he's alive." He said France wants some atomic information from Britain but can't get it under the British arrangements with the U.S.A. Anyway, France is against any kind of nuclear integration. "The British nuclear weapon is not a bargaining counter" in the negotiation, Denis added.

Denis says there has never been any other NATO strategy than massive retaliation because SACEUR [Supreme Allied Commander, Europe] was always short at least a third of the troops he required for flexible response. It was always obvious that in a conflict we would have to go to nuclear war within a few days. No European country wants to change from this. They don't want a long war to be fought on their territory. If the U.S. deterrent were to be withdrawn they would want one of their own.

PARIS, *March 12, 1967*

Played golf with Bohlen and Couve de Murville. When Nixon and Couve met last week he warned Couve that there was a strong revival of isolationism in the U.S. and growing pressure to withdraw from Europe. "But that would mean the end of the alliance," said Couve. Chip snorted later and said: "They might have thought of that earlier. More than one country can break up an alliance."

BONN, *March 15, 1967*

An hour this afternoon with Willy Brandt, head of the Social-Democratic party, vice chancellor, and foreign minister. He received me in his office overlooking the Rhine, a comfortable room, rather austere with bookshelves and maps, rendered gay with spring flowers.

Brandt said that until last year Federal Republic governments had concentrated on reunification, whereas this government saw as the primary issue European and world peace. It has not given up on reunification but is trying to fit the problem into the new search for détente.

I asked why U.S.-German foreign relations were bad. He said he was in Washington last month. Discussions had been frank and good. The trouble was that for some time previously not enough time had been taken out by our two countries to discuss what should be planned jointly for the future; the only serious bilateral talks were when differences arose between us.

I asked if there was a deal between Bonn and Paris: Paris support for Bonn's East Europe policy against Bonn opposition to Britain in the Common Market. He said: "The first part is true. We find in Paris a good broad basis for common discussion of our East European policy. Paris has been very cooperative in this respect. But there is no such 'deal' involving the Common Market."

Brandt said U.S. Vietnam policy was not damaging relations with Bonn. Germany felt its best approach was not to meddle in the problem. Germany was accustomed to *not* being a global power.

BONN, *March 16, 1967*

This morning I met Kurt Georg Kiesinger, the new chancellor of West Germany. I found him most easy to chat with. He spoke English—and very fluently. His French is even better.

Kiesinger is a tall, handsome man with curly silver hair, well-cut features, unusual green eyes, a look of health and vigor. He is sixty-two and carries his years well, although like all Germans he is a bit thick around the middle. He has the same lazy elegance as Harold Macmillan.

After Kiesinger had ordered coffee and we sat down at a table I asked why he thought Russia was so strongly opposed to his East European policies. He answered: "Soviet policy is very complex. On the one hand they agree with our efforts to improve relations with Eastern Europe but then, on the other hand, they want the status quo and a recognition of the Oder-Neisse frontier.

"So long as Moscow hopes that we will give way, Pankow [East Germany] and Warsaw hope we will recognize East Germany and the Oder-Neisse line, and for this reason they try to keep working for those goals. We want to overcome this antagonism indicated by Warsaw's view—but not by accepting Russia's demands."

He said de Gaulle "really favors German unification." I expressed great doubt on this and Kiesinger looked surprised. He said de Gaulle had reassured him on this point both in their tête-à-tête and in plenary sessions of the French and German delegations and in press statements.

I asked if the Germans favored a European nuclear force, and if so, whether it should be based upon the French *force de frappe*, the British deterrent, or both. He answered, "We favor such a force in a united Europe. It should have its own possibilities of defense because any united Europe is meaningless without its own defense and this means nuclear weapons. But German possession or control over such weapons still is a prospect that worries people and we do not aim to renounce our pledge not to manufacture atomic weapons here.

"If we are wise, Germany should never try to give the impression of attempting to get its finger on the trigger of nuclear weapons by the back door."

I asked Kiesinger if he thought that Vietnam was the reason for the evident cooling of U.S.-German relations. He said: "It is more than Vietnam. Ever since the cold war eased and a new situation arose, the people of Europe have been aware of a new order of priorities in the U.S.A. The cold war had been dealt with by NATO but the nuclear problem produced new elements, above all since the Cuba confrontation of 1962. From that date on a new relationship has been developing between Moscow and Washington. This is, of course, necessary, but Moscow and Washington must be very careful because it is a strange and paradoxical relationship.

Washington sees a *raison d'être* for a kind of super-understanding with Moscow, but there is also a *raison d'être* for NATO and the new trend produces a danger of erosion in the alliance."

I asked if he meant that Germany felt the U.S.A. was prepared to sell her down the river to Russia either for Vietnam or for something else. "Precisely," Kiesinger said. "There is a widespread feeling here along those lines."

Kiesinger was convinced the Russians wanted to feel free of worries on Europe in order to face their problem of China. He had discussed this with Khrushchev in Moscow in 1955. Khrushchev pointed out the danger of all those Chinese soldiers who could survive if each day they had a handful of rice. He told Kiesinger he wanted to bring two million Russian troops back to work on farms and factories in Siberia. "I said he should invite in the Chinese," said Kiesinger.

PARIS, *March 21, 1967*

Last night Harlan Cleveland (U.S. ambassador to NATO) gave a farewell dinner party for General Lemnitzer and General Graf von Kielmansegg (commander of Allied Forces Central Europe). It was a very moving occasion. Many toasts were drunk, and one of them was proposed by Pierre de Leusse, French ambassador to NATO, who said quite frankly: "I know it is our fault that you are going, but I can't help it."

PARIS, *March 29, 1967*

Two-hour lunch with [Pierre] Mendès-France. He looks careworn, confessing that six months of steady political campaigning for the recent elections had worn him out.

He says the de Gaulle regime is now crumbling rapidly. He cannot figure out whether de Gaulle will choose to stay in power or resign when things begin to go perceptibly wrong.

The real difficulties will come later. There is an economic and social current of unease. There will be strikes and discontent. Gradually, the system is coming apart although it may take a long time. It is like a pregnant woman; you know that she will end up producing a child, but you don't know exactly when or what sex or how many babies.

In the sense of an alliance among the left-wing parties to defeat de Gaulle a popular front already exists, but Mendès acknowledges this is only a front *against* something and not *for* something of its own. De Gaulle cannot transfer his own personal charisma to parliamentary candidates and, furthermore, the French electoral system is made to order for such a popular front alliance because it virtually imposes upon the leftist parties the need to make a deal.

Mendès says the constitution of the Fifth Republic must go when Gaullism goes. It was designed explicitly for de Gaulle's personal rule. No one else can govern for very long with it—and, besides, everyone will remember that it has already been employed as a vehicle for personal power and it will be regarded as a potential vehicle for that purpose until it is replaced.

Foreign policy had played absolutely no role in the elections. The Frenchman is a xenophobe anyway. He doesn't like America but wants to be sure he will be backed by America in case of trouble with Russia. He doesn't like Russia. He doesn't like England but thinks it might be useful to have English support as a sobering influence in Europe. He detests Germany but wants a reconciliation.

Mendès-France said there was no point in thinking seriously about foreign policy these days because absolutely nothing could be done while the Vietnam impasse continues. This was a disaster. It tied up Europe because it prevented a reconciliation between Russia and the United States and nothing could be done without that. The only people gaining from the continued war were Mao Tse-tung and de Gaulle. The Russians very much wanted peace in Vietnam because they would like to improve relations with the West and because they see that China benefits now. The Russians, Gromyko told Mendès-France, are sending all the equipment North Vietnam wants, but there has not been a single word in the Hanoi press acknowledging this because Hanoi is afraid of offending Peking.

There is a three-way atmosphere of suspicion. America is afraid Russia and China may get together. China is afraid Russia and America are getting together. Russia is afraid China and America may get together. Meanwhile the war goes on and is being slowly escalated.

Mendès-France doesn't see any prospect of ending the war as things are. Meantime de Gaulle is happy to see it continue because it ties up the United States and allows France more room to maneuver in Europe. It is very probable that de Gaulle would not have been able to get away so easily with the expulsion of NATO had it not been for the weakening of American influence produced by Vietnam.

He doesn't think we should get out of Vietnam and he doesn't think we should escalate. We should simply withdraw to the main coastal areas in the Saigon region and prepare to sit there indefinitely, ending all the bombing and terminating antiguerrilla operations in the mountains and forests. We could then stay there for twenty or thirty years if necessary. After all, the British have held Gibraltar for more than two and a half centuries. And the Cubans haven't been able to get us out of Guantanamo.

PARIS, *March 31, 1967*

Yesterday attended the ceremony formally closing down SHAPE headquarters at Rocquencourt. There was a cold spring wind as the flags of fifteen allies were hauled down just before sunset. Only fourteen will be raised at the new headquarters in Casteau, Belgium. The French, although insisting they are still in the alliance, are not participating in the headquarters.

BRUSSELS, *April 12, 1967*

Pleasant lunch and chat with Paul-Henri Spaak.

He says NATO lacks leadership from the U.S.A. now. We are too involved in Asia. France isn't really in the alliance (which is largely meaningless without its NATO organization). Britain is too worried about offending voters on the Common Market. Germany is afraid to offend; so no one takes the helm.

How can a military alliance continue without a common foreign policy? Look at what Vietnam is doing to NATO. All the alliance's main strains have been occasioned by issues outside the Atlantic area—Korea, Suez, Cuba, Vietnam. There was never any split on Berlin or Germany.

There is a great worry—will the U.S.A. and USSR make a deal over Europe's head? Spaak strongly recommends that NATO start multilateral negotiations with the Warsaw pact to put an end to the rival bilateral East-West talks. The NATO allies must formulate policy and stick together vis-à-vis both communisms, Russian and Chinese.

He said Europe's position would be greatly changed by a nuclear nonproliferation treaty. Europe could then never be envisioned as an equal partner of the U.S.A., militarily or politically. But economically it could play a vital role, provided Britain joined. Without Britain it would become an unimportant "Switzerland of the world." Its economic and scientific power would go down the drain after its military and political power.

There is no other policy for us to follow in Vietnam but the one Johnson has taken. The day Truman said the U.S.A. would support the Brussels treaty signatories, taking America out of isolation, the logic of our policy was set. It has been the same—NATO, Berlin, Greece, Vietnam; all are part of the same logic. The U.S.A. has accepted a role as protector against communism. This *is* a policy and follows coherently on the previous policy of protector against Hitlerism. The Greek policy of the U.S.A. was precisely the same as that in Vietnam, except on a lesser scale.

If the U.S.A. got out of Vietnam, Europe would allow itself a sigh of relief—because Europe doesn't understand the problem. It would be like Europe's sigh of relief after Munich. "A policy of sighs is no good. And I say that although I am a man of peace and I abhor war."

CASTEAU, BELGIUM, *April 13, 1967*

This afternoon I went out to the new SHAPE headquarters for the first time, driving down from Brussels. You know you are getting to SHAPE because already in villages just outside you see signs such as "Hi-Way Inn" or "Drink Coca-Cola" or "Bowling." These Belgians are pretty quick businessmen.

The Belgian consortium did a very swift job and it is a huge permanent structure, only two stories high but on a scale almost comparable to that of the Pentagon. The only sad thing is that the French tricolor is not among the flags flapping at the entrance.

I had a long talk with Lemnitzer. He said: "We need to maintain a strong position in order to discourage military adventures by our enemies. But there are bad trends. I am trying desperately to stop the stampede to reduce our forces. The other side is continuing to improve his military capacity."

Lemnitzer now has to make two sets of plans for everything; one based on French participation in NATO defense and one based on French non-participation. The latter is very important, particularly because it assumes that French air space is denied to NATO and also the fuel pipeline.

I asked Lemnitzer if, in reality, he considered France as still an ally, even if it wasn't in the NATO organization. He said no. "France is no longer in the alliance."

Lemnitzer said he thought it was very unlikely that any kind of political conspiracy like the French OAS could ever develop in the U.S. army in Vietnam. The situation in our army was not like that of the French. Besides, Algeria had been considered part of France, and Vietnam is very foreign to the U.S.A.

PARIS, *April 18, 1967*

Breakfasted with Larry [General Lauris] Norstad. General de Gaulle has invited him on this visit. Larry was deeply concerned about Vietnam. We have to find some way of putting an end to the situation. It is not in the nature of the American people to continue this kind of war indefinitely. He had seen various statistics by the Rand Corporation and others, and they all indicate that if things continue at the present rate with the present slow increase of commitment, we would be no nearer a settlement a year or two from now. Even 200,000 more men wouldn't make much difference.

Larry has evolved an idea of his own which he intends to put up to President Johnson. Johnson would announce he was planning to go to Geneva on a fixed date. He hoped that the old Geneva conference on Indochina could be reconvened under the former co-chairmen, Britain and Russia, but this time the United States was prepared to play the role of an active participant and signatory of any agreements. The president would meet with anybody from any country such as North Vietnam or China, and they could bring with them anyone they wished, including the Vietcong.

The president would commit himself to staying in Geneva for a minimum fixed period, let us say five days, whether anyone showed up or not. He would announce creation of special American committees under selected chairmen, who would proceed immediately to Geneva in order to be *sur place* to receive any contacts or communications.

Finally, in order to encourage an atmosphere favorable to some kind of negotiated settlement, the president was ordering immediate cessation of the bombardment of the north. This was not a specified commitment for any fixed duration or a pledge never to resume bombing under any circumstances. The president would add that he hoped North Vietnam would make some kind of similar move to create more favorable negotiations for settlement, by ceasing to take advantage of the cease-bombing through the shipment of more men and supplies to the south.

Larry pointed out that this would not of course avoid the risk that Hanoi would push in more men and material and that we would lose more soldiers, but sometimes greater numbers of men have to be sacrificed for some particular over-all cause.

Johnson would then go to Geneva and just sit, talking with anyone who was there in favor of peace. He would set himself up before the world as a man of peace who had unilaterally taken the initiative. Then, if nothing happened, Johnson would go home after five days—having proven himself to the entire world—and we would begin to blow the place up—Hanoi, Haiphong, and everything.

The basic purpose of the idea is to dislodge things from the paralysis of dead center where one side is saying it will only do something *if* the other side also does something, and to move things along either toward peace or victory.

PARIS, *April 20, 1967*

This afternoon I had a good talk with Waldeck Rochet, secretary-general of the French Communist party, at party headquarters—a squat, strong building.

Rochet is of medium height, bald, with somewhat Russian-looking features although he is a Burgundian peasant. He was wearing a dark blue suit, neat shirt with semistarched collar, and dark red tie. The only wall decorations were a picture of Thorez and another of Lenin.

I asked what kind of government would succeed de Gaulle. He answered: "When the Gaullist power goes, there is bound to be a government of the Left. Perhaps it would be better not to call this a Popular Front like that of 1936, but only a government of the Left. Things are very different today from 1936 and the situation is such that the Left is bound to inherit power.

"There is no future for the other parties because they cannot ever dream of forming a government without participation of the Left. The Center can never gain power. So now our party is seeking to build a common program with the rest of the Left."

Rochet also said there would have to be changes in the electoral law. The communists wanted the system of proportional representation with only one ballot. Under proportional representation the communists would have 105 deputies instead of the 72 they were allotted and the Gaullists would have 177 instead of the 242 they were allotted, according to Rochet's calculations.

He said of the communists: "We are not *a priori* against the Atlantic alliance. We are for a policy of cooperation with the United States of America and the Union of Soviet Socialist Republics and for equal ties for France with the countries of the West and of the East."

Rochet said Chinese communism "goes against common sense and is totally inapplicable to Western countries like France." He thought it had no chance of developing here.

I asked if he still considered the French party "revolutionary." He said that depended on the definition. "If by 'revolutionary' you mean trying to take power by force or violence, then in that sense we are no longer revolutionary, but we wish to struggle to transform society into a just society. Revolution means economic transformation, not violent methods. We want a peaceful road to socialism in France. In this system we want several parties, a plurality of parties—communist, socialist, and other democratic parties."

PARIS, *April 21, 1967*

At dinner last night I sat next to Madame Béthouart, a lively, intelligent lady in her seventies. Her husband, General Béthouart, is the last man alive to *tutoyer* de Gaulle. They were in the same "promotion" at Saint Cyr.

She told me it was absolutely certain that General [Maxime] Weygand had been the son of the Empress Carlotta [Maximilian's wife] and a Mexican doctor. He was adopted by a Belgian family. This was arranged by the Belgian government because Carlotta was the daughter of Leopold I. Weygand was enrolled as a "foreigner" at Saint Cyr. She says when he was asked why he did not fight to the end instead of yielding in 1940, he said: "That is the kind of decision a foreigner can never take for a country."

I 5

LINCOLN, ARISTOTLE,

AND A "REVOLUTION"

EARLY THIS MORNING THERE WAS A *coup d'état* IN GREECE. COM-
munications have been cut off. Shortly before noon I talked to
[Constantine] Caramanlis [former prime minister, now a voluntary exile here] on the telephone. He thinks this is a dead-end street and
on the road to disaster.

PARIS, *April 23, 1967*

Last night I spent hours with Caramanlis discussing his plans. He
looked pale and worn, sitting with a whisky he hardly touched and some
crackers spread with Greek cheese (*fetta*) and roe (*avghotariko*).

He said democracy is finished in Greece. The Greeks are not suited to
it by character. They require a strong leader. But this military coup was a
great mistake. C. conjectures about returning now to "restore democracy"
by replacing the coup. In this sense his job would be easier. But he
doesn't really want to go back. If he returns to politics it is obviously for
life.

He is not at all sure the military can rule very long in unity. It is likely
the army may divide into factions and then there will be real civil war,
bloodshed. Constantine Kollias, the new premier, is a nonentity.

PARIS, *April 25, 1967*

Interesting lunch with Manac'h. France now *knows* from Moscow and
Hanoi that there is a new accord between Russia and China and North
Vietnam concerning overland transshipment of military aid.

The Chinese had been delaying Soviet aid shipments, copying some of the equipment, and feeding it through Hanoi by driblets in order to exert political pressure on North Vietnam. Russian aid was controlled by a Chinese "faucet." Under the new agreement, North Vietnam officers take over supervision of aid shipments on the Chinese-Soviet frontier.

The French [according to Manac'h] are convinced that in bombing North Vietnam we are, in effect, bombing a communist "principle." They cannot admit that any part of the Marxist world should be allowed to suffer from attack. Thus Hanoi is not even free to negotiate so long as it is under attack, because it is part of the communist world.

In 1959, Molotov told Western diplomats during a Berlin crisis that Moscow would never permit one inch of "socialist territory" to be yielded to the West. This same formula applies nowadays to North Vietnam.

There can be no negotiations until the United States agrees to an "unconditional" end to bombing. But Hanoi let it be known that it would be ready to start negotiations three weeks after such an "unconditional" end.

Manac'h concludes that Washington has never understood that the bombing is not just of territories or to establish a military symmetry but is the bombing of a philosophical principle of communism.

In the third week of February 1965—about a fortnight after the U.S. bombing program started—Soviet Ambassador Vinogradov presented a note to General de Gaulle in which he said Moscow agreed that the Vietnam war should end with a diplomatic conference but that this could not happen so long as a socialist country was being bombed.

This spring there has been a very significant change inside China. The importance of both Chou En-lai and the army has increased. Perhaps Chou and the army are working together, or perhaps they are parallel forces. Nobody yet knows. But Chou represents the primordial necessities of the state—assured administration and continued economic production. The army represents Chinese power and an end to any weakening internal disorder.

ATHENS, *April 28, 1967*

Armed sailors and soldiers with helmets are in front of some ministries and armored personnel carriers with machine guns trained on the surrounding streets are parked outside parliament. I saw a police car go by containing a young man shackled between two gendarmes. But it is a nice, sunny day, the tourists are out in droves, and this being Greek Good Friday most people are getting ready for Easter weekend.

Began my peregrinations with Brigadier General Stylianos Pattakos, one of the three prime movers of the military *coup d'état* and a former tank commander. Pattakos speaks some English and has visited the United States where he has a seventy-two-year-old brother who lives in Salt Lake

City and an older sister who lives in Sioux City, Iowa. His daughter's son is a captain in the U.S. army, serving as a dentist in Vietnam.

Pattakos, fifty-four, has brown eyes and long, heavy eyebrows. He is short but strongly made. He stands straight and clearly models himself along the lines of military appearance. He has a simple face with a tough slit of a mouth. His expression is stern although he has a fairly easy smile —that also snaps shut easily. The only pictures on his office walls were a hideous landscape and large official photographs of the king and queen.

I asked when the plot had started, how and by whom. He said this information was "classified" and the leaders were "the Greek army." Everything connected with the plot was classified "because we are still concerned about our security and we do not want to teach people the trade." I asked him what the code name of the operation was and he said "Plan Prometheus."

I asked why the conspirators decided to act now. Pattakos replied that the preelection campaign for the scheduled May elections had been slated to start last weekend (April 22–23). According to the plotters' information the communists had planned to use the occasion to provoke bloodshed. Pattakos continued: "We wanted to avoid harming innocent people."

I asked if the conspirators had studied any other *coups d'état* to see how the techniques had worked in places like Egypt or Turkey. He answered: "We did not have to study anything else. This was entirely Greek." I felt this was slightly excessive national pride.

I then asked who was the real boss today? He answered: "The Greek army is the real boss and we obey General Spandidakis [the lieutenant general who is now defense minister and used to be army chief of staff] because he is our senior officer." He said the conspirators took no oath of loyalty to each other or to the plot, but they were bound by their word of honor as officers.

Did Pattakos call this regime "a dictatorship"? He said no. I asked him then to please define what it could be called. "Freedom under law," was the curious reply. The junta hoped to establish a system somewhere between that of the U.S.A. and Gaullist France.

I asked if there would be widespread restrictions because of people's political beliefs. He said: "Not for an indefinite period but for some time to come—until we feel that our security has been reestablished. Then we will reconsider what to do with members of EDA [far left] and other suspects."

I asked if he expected that there would be any executions such as those in Turkey when the military grabbed power. He replied: "Our policy during the eight days we have been in power is proof of our intentions. We want to avoid spilling any drop of blood."

How long would it take before trials were over in the special courts that had just been set up? That depended on how the situation developed. What possible sentences could the new military courts give? He said the military penal code places no limit on sentences which meant they could go up to and including death.

Was he confident that all armed forces, police and gendarmes were behind the junta? He said: "I am absolutely confident. I will let you call any nomarch (district governor) you want." He took me up to a map and said: "Pick a town and you can call."

I asked if any members of the armed forces had been arrested and also how many had been retired since the coup. At the start, early April 21, some officers had been arrested. Not because of fear they would oppose the coup but because the plotters wanted to prevent any reaction that might have had a harmful influence because of the rank of the officer involved.

Five lieutenant-generals had been retired since April 21 which, I deduce, means they at least objected to the coup. One navy admiral was retired and one resigned.

I asked if both George and Andreas Papandreou would be tried and on what charges. He said Andreas would be tried for treason but that his father, George, would not be tried and was being kept "for his own sake" in a hospital—"the best army hospital in the Athens area."

I asked how many political prisoners there were at this moment. He said at most there were 4,500. The great majority of them in the islands. Only twenty-five politicians were still being held and they were under house arrest, not in prison. Only a handful of those they moved against had managed to escape.

He maintained that "many things proved" the communists were planning an imminent coup. Rifled tubes that could be fitted into 12-gauge shotguns had been discovered in great quantities. Pattakos said seventy truckloads of material had been discovered that contained evidence of an imminent plot. He showed me two crudely printed leaflets. One said approximately: "Organize democratic resistance committees. Down with the coup. Remember 114. Fascism won't be allowed to triumph." (Article 114 of the constitution expresses the people's rights.)

Pattakos said [Panayotis] Canellopoulos had been arrested when the coup began because he was prime minister of the government that the plotters wanted to replace. "But he is now home and in good health although he is guarded—in order to protect him." I do not exactly know against whom.

He said the same about the King's friend, Major Michael Arnaoutis. But he refused to talk more about Arnaoutis saying he did not want to embarrass the king. And he refused to discuss the king's present or future role.

I asked what his own personal ideology was. He said: "I do not believe in anyone's personal cult. I believe in the majesty of my own country. I believe in my obligation to cooperate with my fellow human beings under law and in harmony with them." I then asked whether he had read any political philosophers. He quite solemnly said: "Abraham Lincoln." If it were not also frightening, it would be funny.

I then called on Colonel George Papadopoulos, minister to the prime minister's office. Papadopoulos is even shorter than Pattakos, but has a considerably more intelligent appearance: flat face with shrewd eyes and high forehead. He is a bit tubby, has soft, white hands and a moustache. He does not speak any English and, unlike the clipped, terse, Spartan answers of Pattakos, he tends to the florid, discursive, Athenian speech. In fact he comes from Patras.

I asked which of the three—Pattakos, Papadopoulos, and Col. Nikolaos Makarezos, minister of coordination, was boss. He said: "The chief of the general staff is the boss." He then conceded that Spandidakis had not been kept informed about the conspiracy until it actually broke out—although he joined it promptly. The officers who "took the initiative" operated on the basis of hierarchy. Obviously Pattakos, as a brigadier-general, was the senior of these officers. But my own assumption is that Papadopoulos is *primus inter pares.*

Papadopoulos said: "We enjoy the confidence of the entire officers' corps and we merely initiated what they wanted." He said that when they were ready to strike "the chief of staff was briefed and he accepted." The briefing had been done by "Makarezos, Pattakos, and me."

They had started only two or three months ago—early this year. The tensest moment of the plot was during the few hours when they had to spread word of its existence among other officers. A limited number of officers—about fifteen—had been brought into the picture one day before the actual outbreak on April 21. The rest were only brought in fourteen hours before the plot exploded. In other words they came in at noon on Thursday, April 20 and the coup took place at 2:00 A.M. on Friday, April 21.

Papadopoulos admitted that the real operation had been carried out in Athens and by the Attica Special Command. (There are three army corps in the rest of Greece.) He also acknowledged that the commander of the Attica Command has been retired since the *coup d'état.*

Papadopoulos told me only one important man got away. That was Adonis Brillakis, the EDA deputy and member of the Central Committee of the clandestine Greek Communist party. He thought Brillakis had not been able to flee Greece but was in hiding.

I asked Papadopoulos for his ideas about ideology. He said: "It is a revolution which the Greek army has undertaken with the objective of clearing up the anomalous situation into which the country was being led."

The ideology the plotters wanted for Greece was "similar to all other Western states that are not socialist." The plotters perhaps most wished to emulate France among European countries in the sense of putting the king in an equivalent position to that of General de Gaulle—presumably meaning they wish to give him more executive power. But even Papadopoulos does not give the impression of being very clear on these matters.

Papadopoulos said: "We took charge of the country in order to implement a revolutionary program that would take corruption out of political and social life. Then, when the state is healthy, we wish again to restore democracy. But I cannot forecast how long that will take. It will depend on how long the sickness lasts."

I asked who was the political philosopher of this revolution. He answered: "Aristotle, basically. [An odd mixture with Abraham Lincoln.] Part of Aristotle's theory is that the state intervenes in the regulation of the individual and different public bodies. I would describe our ideology as 'directed liberalism.' No, perhaps 'guided liberalism' is the philosophy we are seeking to bring about. At least, that is as I see it. I would feel at ease under the American system. I would like all Greeks to feel much as American citizens do."

He said the revolution produced only two victims. One was killed resisting and another was killed by a ricocheted bullet the day after the coup. He explained the low casualty list by saying: "The population was in search of a sergeant to save it. But it found an officer instead. And it trusted officers even more, therefore it did not move."

The communists had been taken totally by surprise and all their key leaders had been arrested. Communist radio stations abroad were now broadcasting instructions for the Greek people to resist the coup and they were transmitting exaggerated reports of purges. He estimated there were probably about 300,000 communists in Greece, of one or another sort, but they no longer presented any danger because they were "minus their head."

I asked why the king had initially opposed the coup. He answered: "The king did not oppose it. He was simply displeased because we acted without his knowledge. And the king as head of a constitutional government would naturally oppose our movement."

I said there were reports that the king's proclamation accepting the new situation bore a forged signature. Papadopoulos was most indignant. He said: "This is the greatest lie ever told. The president of the government is the attorney general of the highest court, who has been a judge for forty years. A Greek judge never commits a forgery."

Papadopoulos told me he was forty-eight years old. In his present job his first responsibility is to the prime minister. He deals with administrative, financial, and organizational responsibilities; with radio broadcasting, sports, archeology, tourism, and the press; quite a mixed bag.

I then went down to see the prime minister, Constantine Kollias, previously chief prosecutor of the supreme court. Kollias is sixty-six, a short, plump, little man with black hair, rather pink cheeks, moustache. He told me the civil courts were continuing to handle regular civil cases. The special military courts are only judging offences against national security, such as treason, resistance against state regulations, or disturbances of the peace. He said "seven or eight" articles of the constitution had been suspended.

Kollias hoped that "even if the U.S.A. changes its policy we Greeks will never alter our friendship for the Americans."

He said the king was not opposed to the present government: "The king was unaware of the coup. But after it had stabilized things, he asked me to form a government in order to avoid bloodshed. Therefore, he was obviously not opposed. And he approved of the list of ministers. He himself asked [Economou] Gouras to join as foreign minister."

Kollias hoped a return to normal life would come soon. It was the intention of his government to produce a program of radical reform, but this program was still under study. He was determined to hit tax evasion "which is greatest among the rich. We want to introduce just taxation at all levels."

I concluded my morning with Defense Minister and Vice-Premier (General G.) Spandidakis: a flat-nosed, plump man, dressed in a grey suit and wearing glasses. I am struck by the way most of these fellows can all be described as if they had come out of the same heavenly mold.

I asked Spandidakis how he could be sure the armed forces supported the coup. I pointed out that, after all, only forty-eight hours before the coup took place he did not know anything about it. So how could he be confident there is no plot brewing against him right now?

He said he had been chief of staff for one and a half years and in that position he knew the army. The situation had been "not at all pleasant" when he first took over command. But he had quickly rectified things.

When Papandreou ran the government "the necessary ideological fight against communism had not been carried on and the different armed services began to be infiltrated by leftists. But once I recognized the situation, I tried to eradicate these elements and guide the army on its correct course."

Today, he thought, the army was "completely dedicated to its military duties. But many political leaders in the past were corrupt and the nation's youth was abandoned and without guidance. There was a general feeling in the army of the necessity to intervene. I can say that the coup really represented the initiative of the entire army."

Spandidakis said it was untrue that he had heard of the plot only the day before. He said: "I supported it from the start." At this point he tactfully changed the conversation by producing the shotgun with its rifled tube which I mentioned earlier. The government has information that about 60,000 weapons have been imported to Greece by communist supporters since July 1965; but he does not define what "weapons" are.

Spandidakis said the coup had not weakened NATO; on the contrary it had strengthened it because there was no more reaction from Greece against the allies such as that encouraged by Andreas Papandreou. "This country belongs to the West. Our future is linked to the West."

He said the coup had succeeded in three hours and with total effect because the orders for executing it had been passed on "by the chief of staff." (Himself.) It was done in order to prevent the possibility of a communist coup. The army had drawn up a plan against a communist coup—"the kind of plan any defense staff has in any country. I only had to implement this plan." The particular plan used had been drawn up about eighteen months ago. He seemed startled when I asked him if the code name for the plan was "Prometheus." He said it was.

I asked if the coup plot as well as the long-range plan which enabled the coup to work so well had also been named "Prometheus"—in other words was that the code name for the coup itself as well as for the blueprint on which it functioned? He said yes.

ATHENS, *April 29, 1967*

Last night, Good Friday, there was the usual holy procession in which leading priests bore the Host around Constitution Square and back to the cathedral, accompanied by the nation's military leaders, assembled brass bands, and the clergy in Byzantine robes bearing tapers. Silent groups carrying candles lined the rainy streets. It was a solemn, moving occasion, and not a single incident occurred.

This is the second dictatorship I have seen in Greece. The first, under Metaxas, was also in the king's name. Oddly enough many of the old liberal opponents of dictatorship *one* are now in favor of dictatorship *two*. Perhaps the reason is an emphasis on the adjective "old" as compared with "liberal."

This morning I went to see Colonel Nikolaos Makarezos, minister of economic coordination and third of the triumvirate responsible for the coup. Makarezos proved to be a mild-mannered man with intelligent, humorous face. Dressed in double-breasted grey suit with a conservative dark red necktie, he looked more civilian than military.

I said that as I understood it the coup was to take power in order to prevent a left-wing take-over. What, I asked, was the positive purpose? What did they hope to achieve?

Makarezos said: "Our positive aim was to achieve the goals that had been frustrated by the political bankruptcy of the past. Greece belongs to the Western world and to NATO, and we had to make sure that this would continue. Our primary aim was to develop closer ties with the United States because our government sees the United States as the leader of the free world.

"It is our intention to cut out all unnecessary expenditures for consumption that are now in the budget because they were introduced by political pressures. We want to impose austerity in the public sector. We must strengthen the currency and create a climate favorable to investment. We want to encourage redistribution of wealth and we are studying methods of tax reform.

"Ours is a revolution with a real social program, not just a negative *coup d'état*. It is the intention of the government to restore democracy and there should be no doubt on this. But" (and here is the hitch) "we do not want the old state of affairs. We will restore democracy only when we know there will not be a return to the old state of affairs. We must clean up the rotten parts of the administration. We can only return to constitutionalism when it is in a workable form. Therefore the constitution obviously will have to be amended."

I asked how long the Greek press would remain under censorship. He said he hoped the censorship would be lifted fairly soon but "false criticism" had to be restrained.

He said Aristotle was the "political philosopher" who had most influenced him but he had no particular ideology. He is forty-eight years old and comes from Gravia, not far from Delphi. He claims that the revolutionary movement resulted from "a unanimous opinion among the officers" which decided to use the "Prometheus" plan. But he reluctantly conceded that he, Papadopoulos, and Pattakos had been prime movers "together with Spandidakis." He and Papadopoulos had been classmates at the cadet school and Pattakos, who is older, was three years ahead of them. They had known each other ever since and were good friends but they had not met together alone since April 21, the day of the *coup d'état* because "there is no time for private meetings now." He claimed there was really no triumvirate and that among the three of them they were all equal. He admitted that his last job before the coup was in general staff intelligence—KYP, which is a kind of Greek CIA.

When I was through with Makarezos I got one of his aides to take me downstairs, put me in a taxi, and instruct the driver to take me to the Hotel Pikermi, in Pikermi, where Andreas Papandreou is held. As we drove by the Greek general headquarters, which they rather proudly call "the Pentagon," I noticed three tanks dispersed at the entrance with one armored personnel carrier behind them.

It was a bright, warm, spring day with everything from the olive trees to the late April grass glowing. Even the Pikermi Hotel, despite its present dour assignment, looked merry. The taxi driver had no idea what was going on but both gates of the hotel were locked and he had to stop.

There were helmeted guards with bayoneted rifles all over the place, plus two armored cars and another American armored personnel carrier.

An extremely fat regular-army captain strode down the driveway. The gate was opened, he read my permit, ordered the taxi driver to park outside and waved me in. He offered me a Nescafé and then an unusually tall lieutenant—a handsome fellow about six foot three inches—came down the stairs and joined us. His English was excellent.

The captain asked if I wanted to see any other people incarcerated in the hotel. I said no, only Andreas. They took me upstairs and down a small, narrow hall. Outside each door stood a soldier wearing a helmet and carrying a bayoneted rifle. The captain opened one door and I squeezed by his pot belly to see Andreas stretched out on a bed and another man sitting in an armchair. Greek hotel rooms are small and this was on the small side for a Greek hotel room. There were two narrow twin beds, I eventually sat down on the corner of one of them. The captain and the lieutenant stood in the doorway.

Andreas got up off his bed and greeted me with unusual cordiality and warmth as I entered the room. He was wearing a blue Brooks Brothers shirt (with no necktie), trousers, and socks. He looked extremely well. He made a great effort to be casual, but underneath it I could see he was quite nervous and the bold front did not disguise a certain amount of fear.

He shook hands with a solid grip, grinned widely and said: "You and I have exchanged some pretty hard words in the past and they have been in public. Well, it is all over. Let's forget it. I am glad to see you." Then he introduced me to his roommate, a fat, oily, dark character named Alevras, a Center Union deputy.

Andreas stretched out on the bed and I squatted on the next bed explaining meanwhile: "Andreas, as I understand the ground rules I am not supposed to ask you anything dealing with politics. But you can tell me anything you feel like and before you start I want to tell you that I saw your father this morning and although he did not feel like talking he looked pretty well physically."

Andreas said he had been given similar instructions about nonpolitical talk. He asked a few questions about his father's appearance. We agreed that it is strange to see each other under the present circumstances; and then we chatted.

I told him there had been rumors that he had been wounded in the foot. He explained that his ankle had been injured at the time of his arrest (when he tried to make a getaway) but it was not serious and the doctor told him it would be okay in three or four days.

He admitted the coup had been a total surprise. He had had not the slightest advance suspicion. After a late dinner at the Hilton Hotel, he had come home and had been asleep about an hour when the army arrived for him at the door. He was sleeping heavily when the bell rang and I gather that they busted in when there was not a swift answer.

He told me he was very well treated. He showed me a wall radio in the hotel room which had the regular Athens stations but could not be dialed outside. I told him his father had a television and he seemed surprised and also laughed, knowing what Greek television is. Andreas had a few detective stories in English beside his bed and told me he would like to get a few more plus at least one serious book. He asked me to call his wife and request her to send some. He gave me the telephone number and told me to tell his wife "you and I have made up." Poor fellow, I guess we have in a way but I have not changed my mind about him.

He told me his morale was excellent and that spiritually he felt optimistic. He admitted that this gave him a chance to think but said his intellectual activity was "rather spotty" because of the restricted quarters and lack of exchanges with other people, plus information.

He had not yet been able to receive a visit from his wife. What he specially wanted was more reading matter. That was about all. I did not want to carry on the conversation indefinitely, although Andreas would have enjoyed it—as a break in a pretty dull routine. But I had no more on my mind because it was obvious I could not embarrass Andreas by asking him anything political, considering the rules laid down. He did tell me he was sure he would get a square deal and that he was not deeply concerned about his future. He did not look too convincing when he said this. I said to him, "Well, Andreas, I am sure we will have many more public polemical exchanges together over the years." "I hope so," said Andreas, with a certain amount of vigor.

When I got back to my hotel I called Margaret Papandreou at the number Andreas had given me. Some American woman's voice answered the phone. She was not in the least obliging. Finally Margaret came to the phone and spoke to me in a haughty manner. She told me that if I had a message from her husband I could come around now because the guard had left the door. I said that my message was not secret and I only wanted to tell her how her husband was and what he wanted in the way of books.

She thawed a bit and when I was through describing how Andreas had appeared she thanked me rather coldly and told me if I had any books I wanted to send out I should bring them to the house.

P.S.   I got the following books for Andreas: thrillers: *Judgment on Deltchev* by Eric Ambler, *Dr. No* and *From Russia with Love* by Ian Fleming, *The Masque of the Red Death* by E. A. Poe; serious books: *The Splendor of Greece* by Robert Payne and *Ethics* by Dietrich Bonhoeffer.

After gulping a sandwich I went off to see Eleni Vlachos, owner and publisher of *Kathimerini* and *Messimvrini*, and old friend. She has a wonderful penthouse apartment on the same street as the royal palace.

Eleni claims she is not going to resume publishing either of her papers for as long as the dictatorship lasts. But she hastened to explain that she would lose more money by publishing now than by not publishing. She would get very little advertising as things are, and she has no reserve in cash. On the other hand, she has a large payroll and all kinds of contracts for foreign news services including the *New York Times*. She makes it quite plain that she will probably be less badly off financially by not publishing than by publishing. She will certainly get a lot of credit with public opinion.

Her theory is that the guiding force behind the controlling apparatus [of the revolution] is an organization known as "Zoe" (Life) which publishes a monthly magazine called *Aktinas (Rays)*. She says that "Zoe" is a very orthodox, conservative, old-fashioned religious organization of a sort of free masonic variety that is said to run about one thousand Sunday schools. It is a wealthy, simplified, puritanical type of body. Pattakos is said to be a member. It has existed for at least thirty years and *Aktinas* is a publication much read by people like domestic servants.

Eleni, who is a good conservative millionaire, said the population was strongly anti-king already before this coup and that now he has become a figure of fun by accepting the coup. She said, giving me a glass of cognac: "Where are we? We have no king, no parliament, no Right, no Left." The communists had folded up like a paper tiger when the coup struck. She was appalled that not one single left-wing labor-union member or student had had the guts to get up and throw a rock. It made her in a sense feel ashamed as a Greek.

A little before midnight I looked out of my balcony over Constitution Square and saw the troops lined up on the sides of the street and the patient crowds behind; and I wondered, knowing that the king would shortly be driving along this line, how do they do it? Today is eight days after the *coup d'état*. And yet anyone—on my hotel balcony for example—could drop a bomb or grenade, could even shoot an arrow, and kill the king—or anyone else.

Evidently there is a triumvirate; Papadopoulos is Number One. Pattakos was head of the army tank training center near Athens and had all the tanks near the capital; the rest are up north. He had the power: no tanks, no coup. Papadopoulos was on the general staff in political education. He had formerly been in intelligence. Makarezos was in intelligence at the time of the coup.

The three had been trying to get in touch with the U.S.A. at various levels, seeking support long before the coup. We knew the three were among those believed to be plotting a coup; but we had no idea when and we didn't know they were the bosses. We didn't believe they'd act without the king. But they forced the timing, telling Spandidakis at the very end and adding nine members to a special twelve-man executive committee.

"Prometheus" goes back to the 1950s and has often been amended. This version is perhaps eighteen months old. As a NATO war contingency plan it was designed to cut all communications. This helped it to put out radio announcements implying it was endorsed by the king and the constitutional parties. All the U.S.A. stands for has been hurt by this; but not our national interests. The U.S.A., like the king, has passively accepted the coup.

ATHENS, *April 30, 1967*

I dined with Panayotis Pipinellis, my very old friend, former foreign minister, former prime minister, an extremely decent, although reactionary, old man. He says the entire Greek army today is royalist. The trouble is there was no legal power in the government for many weeks before the coup. The real power was outside the government and parliament. The famous German historian Theodor Mommsen wrote in his *History of Rome*: "The regime that ceases to govern ceases to be legal." This was the case in Greece.

ATHENS, *May 2, 1967*

I took a taxi out to Kifissia where Panayotis Canellopoulos (former prime minister) is staying in the house of his wife's nephew, a comfortable old-fashioned place surrounded by a large wall and with shady trees in the garden. There was a tiny separate building in the garden where Canellopoulos himself works and sleeps. The only policeman I saw insuring the validity of his house arrest was lounging around the corner about ninety yards away. Canellopoulos said that when George Papandreou took power in 1963 it was the first time a party had assumed the responsibility of governing in Greece and at the same time had opposed the state. Papandreou is more irresponsible in his old age. He allowed his party to have contact with the communists and so for the first time in Greek history a loyal national party became a tool of communism.

The coup had come as a total surprise. He was arrested at 2:55 A.M. A group of officers and men burst into his apartment armed with tommy guns. He did not know if they were really army, or disguised communists. He had a revolver but they grabbed it. Canellopoulos explained: "We have to have a revolver here with communism such a threat." He said King Constantine tried to call him, but the telephone was cut. At last he was "obliged" to follow. Outside, where there were more tommy gunners, he told the captain: "Give me back my revolver or you can kill me here."

Many people heard him say this, and the captain returned the revolver. He did this because he was still prime minister of Greece and could not permit any officers to take his gun; also because he calculated that if they were communists they would not return the weapon to him. He wanted the revolver so that if anyone tried to force him to sign a paper against his will, he could kill himself.

He was taken to general headquarters (the "Pentagon") where Pattakos spoke to him very politely. Canellopoulos asked who he was. Pattakos told him the army had taken over. Canellopoulos asked if he was a prisoner and Pattakos said yes. At 11:00 A.M. Friday Constantine came to the "Pentagon" and at 12:30 two officers took Canellopoulos to speak to him.

Saturday, Pattakos and General Spandidakis told Canellopoulos he could go home under house arrest and he requested the same privilege for all other cabinet ministers. It was granted. He is still under house arrest.

Canellopoulos said he felt the way he did in 1940 during the war. "Now we must wait and see if the junta is really willing to restore democratic life to Greece." He adds: "I believe in democracy and I cannot accept what happened here, even as an emergency measure. These people have to prove that they will return the country to democracy. I shall wait."

ATHENS, *May 3, 1967*

I spent two hours this morning with King Constantine in the Athens palace. It was more hush-hush than ever and he asked me not to tell a soul I had seen him. Young Constantine seemed tired and bleary-eyed. In fact, his eyes looked as if he had been crying. But he talked very tough. He was full of energy and at times he even burst into broad smiles.

He gave me a warm handclasp when I came into his study, and we sat down, beside the fireplace. He told me he wanted me to know the facts. Then he started talking a mile a minute. He said:

"I was out at Tatoi [his country place about twenty miles from Athens] and the very first I heard about the coup was around 2:15 Friday morning. I had been reading late and just dozed off when the telephone rang. I was amazed. I had told the telephone center not to disturb me. But it rang again and I picked it up. It was my secretary, Arnaoutis. He is a trusted friend of mine. He shouted into the phone: 'They are smashing my door in with guns.' 'Who?' I asked. 'I don't know,' he shouted.

"I told him: 'Hold on. I am coming to help you.'

"Arnaoutis said, 'For God's sake don't come, call the police. Have they announced anything to you? What's the army doing? I am trying to get reinforcements sent up to Tatoi.'"

Constantine summoned his aide-de-camp immediately and told him to double the guards and to alert everybody on the royal property. He continued: "I grabbed my revolver. My ADC came and the guards took up their positions. Then I rang up another officer, a friend of mine, and told him to help Arnaoutis. Soon after that he reported to me he couldn't help because there were ten soldiers with machine guns outside Arnaoutis's house.

"I called my mother at her house. The telephones hadn't been cut yet. So I asked her to get my sister and her children (who are visiting from Spain) all into the same part of the house and I told her I was trying to send reinforcements. Then the phones were cut.

"My mother told me later that after that two tanks arrived at her house; she was delighted, assuming these were the reinforcements I had promised her. Only too late she realized they were working for the coup. One officer in the group that surrounded her put a machine gun right on top of her house, and when she demanded that they let her come and see me, they refused.

"It is hard for me to remember all this in consecutive order." (The king rubbed his hands over his face and knuckled his eyes.) "I think it was about this time that [Dimitri S.] Bitsios called me up. You know, my counselor. I told him to get hold of the prime minister and tell him to do something. I told him the prime minister should order out the cadets if necessary. I never heard any more from Bitsios until 5:30 that afternoon because they picked him up.

"Bitsios rang up Canellopoulos who was then standing in his apartment with a bunch of coup officers around him, one of them holding a tommy gun in his tummy so Canellopoulos couldn't do anything.

"Then I alerted the air force. You know those fellows are awfully slow and they take a long time to get up. I told them to send some men right away to Arnaoutis's house but it was too late. The air force did send some men over to Tatoi, but by the time they got here the tanks of the coup were starting to roll up and they turned back the air force, so I instructed my guards that they should only shoot if they were shot at.

"I just can't remember the order of all those things. Arnaoutis has one of those old-fashioned houses in Psychiko with great big iron grille doors and the coup people couldn't get in. They kept beating on the door and shooting through it and his poor wife fainted dead away. But Arnaoutis kept his head. They kept shouting to him demanding that he open the door but he kept ringing up various people trying to get help.

"They started machine-gunning the house right into the hall, but he had gone into the basement and had come up again the back way so he was actually sitting quietly in a room off the hall when they finally burst in and started looking for him in the cellar. But the poor fellow couldn't escape. They caught him and manhandled him. They hit him and cursed him. They finally took him to the 'Pentagon' and locked him up.

"Suddenly [George] Rallis [the minister of justice] got through to me on the telephone. By God, that was good news. He has an enormously low deep voice, you know. He said to me: 'I managed to get away. Right now

I am in Maroussi police station.' " (Maroussi is a village between Athens and Tatoi.)

I interrupted the king and said I couldn't understand how he had kept going on the telephone all this time, but he explained that his phones had not been cut for more than an hour after the coup started at 2:00 A.M. Friday, April 21.

He continued: "I told Rallis to mobilize the troops in the north and tell them to come down and take over Athens. A few minutes later Rallis called back as soon as he had finished drafting an order. The order said that the Greek government had been arrested and the only free minister of the government, Rallis, under the direct orders of the king, was commanding all troops in the north to proceed south immediately and to act on behalf of the king."

Constantine chuckled. He said: "You know what I told Rallis? I said, 'You could be arrested for that. Don't let them find that order on you.'

"By now the tanks had taken up their positions outside my house. It was still dark. I sent word to the commander of the coupist tanks ordering him to report to me. He didn't show up.

"At that time I didn't know who was running the coup. I didn't know who they were, Left or Right, or what the hell was going on.

"The air force commander at the little Tatoi airfield rang up and told me he had received an order that no planes were to be allowed to take off. I asked him who signed the order. He didn't know. I said: 'You bloody fool, you read an order and don't even look to see who signed it!' My ADC checked and we found that it was Pattakos. It was only then that I knew that the coup was a right-wing coup.

"I kept telling my wife to calm down. You know she is expecting a baby in three weeks. She was pretty nervous and we were all isolated and there is no doctor on the place. I couldn't go out and I didn't know where to go if I could get out.

"Just before 8:00 in the morning I was informed that three officers were coming to see me. It turned out to be Pattakos, Papadopoulos, and Makarezos. I had been listening to the radio, which was my only source of news after the telephone was cut, and I knew they had made an announcement suspending the constitution and signing it 'The prime minister and the members of his government' without giving any names.

"When the three officers showed up they informed me that they had saved Greece for my sake. They had a letter from General Spandidakis (chief of staff at the time of the coup) which said the coup had been done in my name in order to save the country. When I saw this I blew my top. I have never been so angry in my life.

"I stormed at them. I raged at them. I asked them: 'How could you do a thing like that?' They tried to stand their ground, and Pattakos said the chief of staff would be ready to receive me later. This made me even angrier. 'Where is my prime minister?' I shouted. 'Where is my government?'

"Pattakos then answered: 'You have none. We have arrested them all.' "

The king said Rallis called him again, told him that [Evangelos] Ayeroff (a former foreign minister) was with him, and said: "Don't sign anything, Your Majesty. Don't sign anything until you have had a chance to think about it." The king said he replied: "How can I have time to think about it when they are already walking toward the house?"

Constantine continued: "I told the three officers I would refuse to see anyone—Spandidakis or anyone else—until Arnaoutis was released. They stood at attention like cadets in front of me. I told them the letter from Spandidakis was not good enough. Then they started arguing. Pattakos spoke first, but Papadopoulos was the one who seemed to explain the ideas. Pattakos said the king should know they supported him and he pledged this on his honor as an officer. 'What honor?' I demanded. 'You go back and tell Spandidakis to come here. I want to talk to him.'

"They left. Just as they got outside the house I stuck my head out and yelled to Pattakos as he was walking to his car, 'I give you exactly two hours to come back here with Arnaoutis. It is an absolute disgrace.' "

I asked the king: "Did they?" "No," he said.

He continued his account: "Around 10:00 Spandidakis finally came. I told him what I thought of him. Spandidakis said he had heard about the coup at the last minute and that he only took command in order to prevent junior officers from taking over and plunging the country into chaos.

"I told Spandidakis to remove the tanks from my mother's house and they did. After Spandidakis left, I chased through Athens looking for Bitsios but I couldn't find him. They had grabbed him. I passed by my mother's house and she was all right so I asked her to go out to Tatoi and wait.

"Then I went to the 'Pentagon' around noon. There was a real atmosphere of revolution there. There were tanks all over the place and officers wandering around inside shouting at each other. They were all jabbering. But they put together a kind of guard of honor for me and I went through the main room to the office of the chief of the defense staff. I found him but he didn't know what in hell was going on because he had been arrested and so had the chief of the air force and the chief of the navy.

"When I saw the three officers who made the coup I gave them a direct order to release Arnaoutis at once, now, and to get all the generals to the 'Pentagon' and gather them into one room so I could talk to them, and also to bring my prime minister, Canellopoulos, immediately.

"When Arnaoutis finally showed up he told me they had come for him with tommy guns and pistols. The officer who arrested him when they broke in shifted his pistol from his right hand to his left hand so he could shake hands because he said, 'We are on the same side.' Arnaoutis refused. Then one of the men hit him. Arnaoutis looked him in the eye and said, 'I can see you never fought for your country. No soldier who was ever in combat would hit an unarmed man.' And Arnaoutis said to me: 'Be careful. This is a revolution. Be very careful how you handle them.'

"Then Canellopoulos came in. He was in desperate condition. He was absolutely livid and shaking. Well, I told him my story and he told me his. Then I asked him what he recommended. He suggested there were two possible solutions. I could call the generals together and ask the generals on my side to stand up and then order them to arrest the coup-makers. I told Canellopoulos that the mere fact that the coup-makers had moved without my knowledge and arrested him showed that they meant business. They would shoot all the generals—and everyone else. Canellopoulos agreed. The other solution he suggested was some form of acceptance. I suggested that it might be best to put some civilians into the government to gain time and I thought of Kollias who is a conservative trusted by the army. Canellopoulos said he would stand by me.

"Then I went to the room where all the generals were and I said to them that I was convinced that what the army had done, it had done to save the country, that what had happened had happened. I then said: 'I want to know if you are still with me. My father taught me discipline, the discipline of an officer. I want to know which officers are on my side. Will those on my side please stand up?' They all did. But I realized that this was a gesture that meant nothing. They had no power, all those generals. They didn't even have a pistol among them.

"And the chief of staff kept charging in. He kept saying: 'Stop seeing generals and make a government!'

"So I saw the three leaders of the coup again and I told them: 'You have done all this without my knowledge. But the mere fact that you succeeded was because you used my name. Without the name of the king you would be nowhere. Now, take my orders!'

"I screamed at them. They were slouching. I said: 'The first thing a Greek officer learns is to stand at attention. Now, stand at attention!' They all stood up like ramrods.

"Then I called in the service chiefs. At this moment Arnaoutis stuck his head in and hollered: 'They are going to arrest me again.' I tried to intervene. I told the chief of staff: 'If you don't release him now I will never agree to anything you want.'

"But it was complete anarchy. You can't even imagine what an atmosphere of anarchy there was. Why, I saw a captain roughly pushing a general to one side.

"I had a two-hour struggle to force a civilian government on the three. They wanted Spandidakis as prime minister. I said: 'You must be completely mad. It is bad enough with a military coup, and now you want a military man to head the government.' They said the army must run the show. They said the Americans were on their side.

"I told them: 'Obviously you are mad. Certainly the Americans are not on your side. Remember the case of Argentina? When the army took over there, the United States withdrew its ambassador. The way you are going you are bound to fail and you will isolate Greece from its friends. I tell you you need a respectable judge as a head of government, not a soldier.'

"There were loads of young officers downstairs screaming when they heard the news I was asking for Kollias, shouting, 'We won't take him, we won't take him.' But I had convinced the three. Pattakos went down to the young officers and said: 'We will appoint Kollias or I will shoot myself right here.' They accepted.

"The three named themselves as ministers which I thought was very foolish. I told them they would be wiser to stay out of the light. I refused their first two choices for minister of foreign affairs. And I insisted that the other ministers should also be civilians.

"When I had finally finished these discussions, I was informed I could leave when I wished but that Arnaoutis was staying. I told Spandidakis: 'If I go, Arnaoutis goes. Otherwise you can all go to hell.' They realized I meant business. Then I ordered that a guard of honor be prepared. I wasn't sure whether to shake hands with its commander but at the last minute I decided to, and they all roared approval.

"Just as I was about to get into my car, Kollias arrived. 'What's going on?' he asked. I told him. I said: 'I haven't got time for details. I have just appointed you as prime minister. If you don't accept, there will be chaos. Goodbye.'

"I slammed the door of my car. When I came back to the palace—this house, not Tatoi—it was completely surrounded by tanks. They had thought of everything. You know, they really went into all kinds of details. The commander of the tank battalion at Tatoi was the brother of Papadopoulos."

At this point, Constantine said, he had tried to mobilize the navy from Tatoi in the early morning and ordered all ships to shoot if anyone attempted to board them. But only one destroyer apparently got off to sea.

He then went on: "Later in the day I swore in the government. I told Pattakos, the new minister of the interior: 'I hold you personally responsible that no drop of blood shall be shed and no politician shall be harmed.' "

We then got to the tricky point of whether the king had ever signed the first declaration to the people issued in his name. He said when he was in the "Pentagon," Papadopoulos gave him a paper which he was supposed to broadcast to the nation, but he did not do this; nor has he done so since.

When the three came to Tatoi, they asked him to sign the document legalizing the coup and he told them to go to hell. "I never signed," he said to me. "But they broadcast the declaration." I told him I had heard they forged his signature but Papadopoulos furiously denied this to me. Constantine said: "I doubt if they forged the signature but they used my name. Then next evening they sent me the document. I have still got it. I never signed it and I never will but that is a tremendous secret. If they knew I had told you there would be awful trouble. But I don't want to go down in history as the king who is known for suspending the constitution."

I asked him what he knew about the conspiracy itself. He said he had known of the defense plan (he didn't remember the code name "Prometheus"): He had first heard of it when he became an officer. And the three coup-makers had been in key staff positions. "They knew all the right code words. They moved fast. And they used my name. That is what did it. Pattakos told me: 'If we hadn't used your name we would never have succeeded.' "

Constantine told me that [Phillips] Talbot, the American ambassador, "behaved beautifully—he couldn't have been better." I asked what he thought the U.S.A. could do to help. He said: "What the United States can do depends on what I do. I had only two courses before me, either to leave the country and disassociate myself from everything or perhaps to remain isolated in Tatoi—or to do what I am doing.

"Nobody doubts my disapproval of the coup and everybody realizes that I knew nothing about it, so now I really believe my duty is to make this new government succeed.

"If I denounce them or fail to take a part in events, what happens? Many of the army units would become bitter and try to move against the coup. Even if only some units move it will be a ghastly first-class civil war. To have a nationalist army fight itself would be terrible. The best thing I can do is to influence people and to bring my country back to a parliamentary democracy as soon as I possibly can. Already each of the three coup-makers has come to me and thanked me for insisting on putting Kollias in as prime minister. I hope they will listen to me in the future.

"Those who have criticized me in the past now depend upon me. I can serve my country better by staying and helping.

"I told Pattakos and Papadopoulos: 'No executions. Remember you can't execute politicians.' Pattakos replied: 'Turks we shall never become!' I told them bloodshed would ruin all their efforts."

I told Constantine that Pattakos had informed me Andreas Papandreou would be tried for treason in a special military court, that there was no appeal, and that the maximum sentence possible was death. Constantine was furious. He said: "There is always appeal to the king, and if they sentence anyone to death and he appeals to me I won't confirm the sentence. If I have any power left I will stop it."

Constantine said he set a pattern for cooperation with his cabinet in his first meeting when he sat down with them on Saturday. He said: "I told the cabinet I am not presiding. I am not discussing things with you. I am just here to get things started. Then, privately and unofficially I told them that they have the power to create and to do good for the country. They should not become aggressive and arrogant. I told them it was their duty to become humble and make themselves loved. Otherwise they would fail. I told them to forget their personal role and just to work for the country. Then I said: 'If you do this and if you keep me informed of everything you do, you will have my cooperation.' The strain was terrible."

At this point the king again rubbed his face hard and lit a cigarette. After a moment he said: "The United States should keep emphasizing that this government ought to succeed because they are in control and that they must succeed and can do so if they avoid bloodshed."

The king told me that actually there was a good deal of efficiency in the air. There was a bad earthquake in the northwest, and Easter Day Constantine flew up with Pattakos to visit the area damaged. He said: "I was very impressed. Of all the earthquakes this is the one where there has been the swiftest action and help. And people felt it. I went to Preveza and Arta and Jannina, and I am very sensitive to crowd reactions. That is something you have to learn in this business and I can tell you it was *very* good. Of course everybody was very upset at the disaster and it was terrible to see, but all they wanted to do was to hoist me to their shoulders and tell me I had saved Greece. I turned to Pattakos and said: 'You can't let these people down.' "

The king said: "I told them to get the best people possible into this government and not to worry whether they came from the Left or the Right. I told them they can't fail now because it would be disastrous. They just had to build more schools, to force more doctors, priests, and teachers to come up into the poor areas of the north. They had to listen to the economists and not to try to do things on their own in economics, and Pattakos agrees with me.

"And there is a delicate problem, as I told Pattakos. Everybody in the army knows that this plan on which the coup was carried out existed for a long time. Everybody in the army realizes that the king didn't know anything about the *coup d'état* ahead of time. I told Pattakos: 'I am going to tell the generals to do their best to help the government to succeed. But you three must be careful not to irritate them, not to aggravate them by your bossiness. After all, you are rather junior officers.' Pattakos said to me: 'You couldn't be more right.'

"I said to them you have to hurry up and turn back to the old system— king, government, chief of staff. The army won't accept a clique of officers trying to run things in its own way.'

"I must say they have been fantastically correct toward me despite the fact that I have told them I will sign no documents unless I am kept well-informed. You know, it is a very funny thing. I am in command of the army—and at the same time I control nothing. The people know who the king is and not who Pattakos is. But I have no real power.

"I told Kollias, the new prime minister, that I would sign all decrees of the government but no revolutionary decrees. If they issued any revolutionary decrees, they would have to carry on without my signature."

PARIS, *May 18, 1967*

At dinner last night Chip Bohlen made the interesting observation that de Gaulle conducts foreign policy on a "solar system" basis. Each planet has its own satellites and area of influence, but must keep out of the way of other planets in order not to be attracted into their orbit. Chip thinks the Cuban confrontation in 1962 accelerated de Gaulle's desire to get out of NATO because he feared the possibilities of war coming up between U.S.A. and Russia outside of Europe.

PARIS, *May 22, 1967*

Lunched with Manlio Brosio. He is very worried about the Middle East. He sees U Thant as a small and insignificant man who did a criminal thing in giving Nasser a needless propaganda victory by pulling out the UN emergency force as soon as Cairo demanded it. Brosio doesn't think Cairo wants war, but it may be very difficult to stop, and there is no indication that Russia is doing anything, either publicly or privately, to try to calm things down.

I then shifted the subject. I pointed out that the "Prometheus" coup in Greece was based on a contingency plan for internal security that had been filed with NATO. Other countries must have similar contingency plans—for example, Italy. How was NATO going to assure they were not similarly misused? For example, there had recently been rumors that General Giovanni de Lorenzo had been thinking of a *coup d'état* in Italy a few years ago. What would have prevented him from doing what the Greeks did?

Right after lunch he was going to consult his *directeur du cabinet* and see what they could find out from Lemnitzer's headquarters.

PARIS, *May 23, 1967*

I spent an hour this afternoon with Prime Minister Georges Pompidou. While I was sitting in the antechamber Couve came out looking tired and grey. Obviously Couve had been briefing the prime minister on the Middle East crisis.

Pompidou greeted me and led me to the round table by the window, away from his desk, where we could look out over the Matignon garden. Right away we started talking about the Middle East.

He was very worried. The most disturbing thing was that Russia had not yet shown its hand. There wasn't the slightest evidence Moscow was trying to calm things down. He hoped we would remain wise ("*sage*"). I hoped we, France and the U.S.A., would remain together.

Pompidou said France's policy would be decided tomorrow at a cabinet meeting. In other words, there have not yet been any definitive decisions.

Pompidou thought France still considered the 1950 U.S.-British-French guarantee valid; this was a pledge that the three Western powers would act forcibly if need be to preserve the territorial status quo in the Middle East (in other words, safeguard Israel). (But, I may recall, the 1950 pledge was violated—against Egypt—in 1956 by Britain and France.) I asked P. flatly: "Does it still hold for you?" He thought a moment. "Yes," he said, "I think so."

I asked if France had any kind of alliance with Israel. He said not. Furthermore, since 1956 France had drawn much further away from Israel. It still had friendly relations; but that was all. He admitted that the Israeli government had sent recent urgent messages to Paris. But these had not asked new "aid." They dealt primarily with requests for speeding up delivery of military equipment that had been ordered long ago.

I asked if France would participate in any joint operation with the U.S.A. to keep the peace if necessary. Again he hesitated a long time. Then he finally said he thought so, but I wouldn't really know until tomorrow; the matter would be discussed at the cabinet meeting. He assured me again, however, that France strongly supported the status quo in the Middle East. But he was deeply worried by Moscow's failure to give any indication, public or diplomatic, that it wanted to cool the flames. He thought U Thant had behaved very foolishly in yielding UN's trumps by caving in right away to Nasser's demands.

All this having been said—and it boils down to being worried and waiting for (1) Moscow to give a sign and (2) de Gaulle to speak—we shifted to the French scene. Pompidou relaxed a bit. He smiled and seemed to slump comfortably into his chair when we got on to politics and social reform.

I asked Pompidou how de Gaulle could possibly bequeath a succession, establish a "dauphin." He said (1) If the General retires between now and December 1972, he could announce, "My mandate is over; I am old and must retire; therefore I ask all French voters to support so-and-so." (2) Or, if he dies, he could leave a letter or testament. He added that, "I don't know if he has prepared such a testament but, knowing the General, I am ready to bet he has." He looked at me knowingly and added: "I cannot imagine the General leaving no counsel to France if he dies."

PARIS, *May 24, 1967*

Pompidou was wrong. Today there was a cabinet meeting and obviously de Gaulle decided that France would not stick with the U.S.A. and Britain and does not think the 1950 tripartite declaration applies any more. Also, France is neutral—which means less pro-Israel, more pro-Egypt—in the present argument. Clearly these were the General's own decisions, since I had seen Pompidou after his talk with Couve on the late afternoon prior to today's cabinet meeting.

PARIS, *May 26, 1967*

Brosio called up this afternoon—anent my request for a check on national security plans similar to "Prometheus" in Greece. This morning Brosio saw Lemnitzer and asked him about it. Lemnitzer insists the Greek plan was purely national and had nothing to do with NATO.

PARIS, *May 31, 1967*

Prince Paul and Princess Olga gave us a dinner party last night. Paul, who is half Russian, was talking about Prince Felix Yusupov who murdered Rasputin. He says Yusupov was a vain homosexual; in this way he attracted Rasputin and induced him to come around for the final act of murder. He thinks the only book Yusupov ever read was Oscar Wilde's *The Picture of Dorian Gray*, and that he really seemed to model his life on Wilde's horrible hero.

Olga who is really very lovely told me King Constantine called up Queen Elizabeth of England this month when his first son was born to inform the queen: "It's a boy—and I'm drunk."

WASHINGTON, *June 17, 1967*

Long talk this morning with Dick Helms, head of the CIA. The U.S. appraisal was that Israel could stand an attack on all three fronts (UAR, Syria, Jordan) and throw it back. Dean Rusk was rather sceptical. He said to Helms: "Well, in the words of La Guardia—if this is a mistake it's a beaut." As a result of this CIA appraisal President Johnson decided Israel could go it alone.

The CIA was confident Israel could stand off its enemies and win. It was also certain that at a convenient moment Israel would strike first. No one, of course, will ever know just exactly how the war started, but Israel clearly picked its own moment to push off and that's how it managed to destroy so many Arab aircraft.

If Soviet intelligence appraisals could be so wrong about the Middle East, how bad are they when they assess the United States, or the Vietnam war? Do they have a mechanism capable of producing objective appraisals?

The Soviet bloc has resumed extensive arming of the Arabs, above all Egypt. Possibly the aim is to help Nasser keep office. Moscow has always been interested in supporting the "radical Arabs."

WASHINGTON, *June 18, 1967*

Tommy [Llewellyn] Thompson, ambassador to Russia, who is staying with us at the Wisners', says that this month, during the Palestine war, was the first use of the Washington-Moscow "hot line" teletype—on both the Israeli attack on our ship, the *Liberty* (when we sent off planes) and on the Israeli march toward Damascus, which we sought to prevent.

WASHINGTON, *June 19, 1967*

Had a chat with Mac Bundy this afternoon. He is heading up a special emergency committee on the Middle East (for Johnson). When he left the White House it was understood he would be available for such assignments.

Mac says the Suez Canal will be closed only three or four weeks. The blockage isn't as bad as in 1956. It's primarily a political question. One shipload of food for India is stuck in the canal. But apart from a fortnight's extra delay and added costs, Indian food shipments and Soviet shipments of war material to North Vietnam can go around the cape. We shouldn't exaggerate the difficulties.

He says the crisis got out of Russian control. Moscow urged the Syrians to be tough and then stirred Nasser to help them; but Moscow didn't want war. Now Russia has been "penned into a position" of working for a fourth round of the Palestine war some day. But it will be years before it explodes.

Good talk with Secretary Dean Rusk. I started by asking how he expected to salvage the Middle East from an adverse vote in the UN assembly. He said: "They'll have difficulty in getting two-thirds unless there is a very low vote and lots and lots of abstentions."

Anyway, all the assembly could vote was a "recommendation." He insisted: "No one outside the area can give orders to those inside it—the Russians and the Arabs or us and Israel."

Rusk thought passions were beginning to cool off. Kosygin's speech was the standard Soviet line and not as polemical as some others. The key point now is whether it is a question of withdrawal, alone and by itself, or as a preliminary to other reciprocal moves.

I said it was saddening to see how isolated we were becoming in the world. "Where have *you* been?" he asked. I said he knew perfectly well, and repeated the observation. He claimed we are not getting isolated.

He pointed out that India and Russia would both suffer from the Suez Canal closing. India depended on U.S. food shipments through it. Most of Soviet arms shipments to North Vietnam were from the Black Sea through the canal. Would the Russians want to bunker their ships in South Africa? Dean doubted it (with a wry smile).

Rusk did say one interesting thing: the U.S.A. is convinced de Gaulle personally ordered a stop to the emergency arms shipments taken by Israeli jet transports from France.

The basic reason for the French shift in Middle East policy was to build up France's position with the Arabs; no more, no less. Maybe, however, the French will try to get into the production picture in states where oil has been seized from British or American companies.

Rusk said we don't think Russia wanted any major military hostilities in the Middle East and, after U Thant withdrew the UN emergency force, Moscow sought to restrain Nasser. But Nasser went out ahead of Russia.

He conceded that the *coup d'état* in Greece had been "very distasteful" and we can't stay away from that problem. The king had behaved with much moderation and courage and was slowly improving things. The crunch is likely to come after six months when the constitution is supposed to be adopted.

Rusk said the Egyptians were in bad trouble in Yemen. They had been using a poison gas there which was so deadly that a single drop killed.

WASHINGTON, *June 21, 1967*

Lunched with Bill Bundy, assistant secretary of state for Far East, Mac's older brother, and Dean Acheson's son-in-law. Our conversation was wholly about Vietnam.

He told me one of our problems was getting top-flight high-level men. Bill Porter helped out during Lodge's second term. It's a pity he couldn't have been chief of mission instead.

Westmoreland seems to be a perfectly good military commander but wholly lacking in genius. And his judgment on nonmilitary things is unimpressive.

The situation now is poor; we are going through one of our low periods. The Vietcong is aggressive and our weakness in the north (I Corps) has been exposed. The election campaign isn't proceeding well, with Ky and Thieu, the two top generals, competing for the presidency. Now summer and the monsoon are upon us and we may be in for a tough time militarily. There is no doubt at all that if we decide to reinforce our troops with another big slice (there is press talk of moving from 470,000 to 600,000) the north can send in enough to offset this—and supply them.

The last approach to negotiations for peace started late last year through the Poles, who initiated things through Janusz Lewandowski, their man on the international control commission in Vietnam. On December 1, 1966, he told Lodge (in Saigon) that Hanoi was ready to talk to Washington if the U.S.A. accepted as a basis ten points drawn up by Lewandowski and previously submitted by him to Hanoi.

When Lodge reported this to Washington, Washington authorized U.S. Ambassador [John A.] Gronouski in Warsaw to go to Foreign Minister [Adam] Rapacki and say we would be happy to meet and discuss the "interpretation" of the ten points "during" talks. Rapacki stalled and, after we had bombed Hanoi December 2 and 4, sharply criticized these attacks around the capital.

Then we put a ten-mile circle around Hanoi unconditionally exempting the area inside it from bombing. On that basis—although there had been no *quid pro quo* conditions—we asked the North Vietnamese in Moscow if they wanted to meet us. A series of meetings occurred between John Guthrie of the U.S. embassy and the North Vietnamese chargé d'affaires.

The climax to this phase came in President Johnson's February 8 letter to Ho Chi Minh in which we proposed there would be no future bombing if they simultaneously ceased reinforcing the south. The letter specified that the cut on infiltration should coincide with the halt in bombing.

The Russians had always wanted the formula of peace talks in exchange for a bombing halt. But China opposed this. Hanoi was ready for contacts in early January 1967, probably because we weren't bombing at the time and also because both the military tide and the political tide seemed then to be running quite well for us in the south. Furthermore, China had been on the verge of bubbling over as the Cultural Revolution spread into factories and the countryside in December 1966, and Hanoi was worried about a possible cut-off of aid.

On January 25, 1967, Mao formally asked China's army to take political action. At the time we thought this meant the army was with Mao. It has since become clear the opposite is true and that the army has been brought in to restore stability and to moderate, not exacerbate, the revolution.

WASHINGTON, *June 22, 1967*

Lunched at the White House, a huge state luncheon honoring Prime Minister [Jens Otto] Krag of Denmark, Prime Minister and Foreign Minister [Aldo] Moro and [Amintore] Fanfani of Italy, and Foreign Secretary [George] Brown of Britain.

Fanfani told me he thought the Russians would now step up the cold war. They would try to keep Nasser in but it wouldn't be easy. At all costs they had to prevent China from becoming the Arabs' revolutionary sponsor. We must play things subtly to encourage the Arabs who were pro-Western—like Libya, Saudi Arabia, Lebanon, Tunisia.

Extraordinary evening. It started with a chat with President Johnson in the little "think tank" off his office, moved on to his armored Cadillac down to the presidential yacht, *Honey Fitz*, continued over drinks and then dinner on a slow cruise down the Potomac, and endured until midnight, when the President sent me home in that same monster, bullet-proof Cadillac.

He is a strange, indeed extraordinary, man but I cannot say I either like or admire him. I wish I did because he has always been exceptionally nice to me. But there is something that puts me off. He is almost pathetic in his efforts to please and to build himself up in the visitor's (and his own) mind as a tremendous and fine figure. He is hospitable, generous, incredibly energetic. But he always seems to be aggressively on the defensive.

On the boat trip was a distinguished assemblage of about two dozen people including the executive committee that has been put together on the Middle East crisis and which had just met that late afternoon: Mac Bundy (executive secretary), Clark Clifford (special intelligence adviser), General Earle G. Wheeler (chairman of the joint chiefs of staff), Secretary of Defense McNamara, Dick Helms (head of CIA), and Walt Rostow. Also a few others had been rounded up including mesdames Wheeler and Rostow, Kay Graham (owner of the *Washington Post* and *Newsweek*), etc. They didn't really look as if they enjoyed the undoubtedly great privilege. Some seemed to be unnecessarily toady-like (for example, McNamara) while others sat with a certain quiet, glum dignity.

At the wharf, we boarded the *Honey Fitz* (named for Kennedy's grandfather by Kennedy) as the crew saluted, and went up on the top deck. It is a modest little yacht about the scale of that of a low rank Greek shipowner, certainly no more, except that it has a marvelous set of communications: antennae sticking out in all directions. From time to time a light blue telephone was brought to the president and plugged in so he could accept calls from his wife. He would sit there, a satisfied grin on his face, saying "Lady Bird" this or "Bird" that.

As we swung slowly downstream, followed about forty yards behind by two little protective navy boats, Johnson sat in an olive green leather-covered armchair at the stern, in the center, waved Kay beside him and me beside her. This was difficult enough since he was on my deaf side, his Texas drawl doesn't carry far, and the flight path of the airport was right overhead so every ninety seconds or so a plane roared above us. I craned and almost got a stiff neck, cupping my hand around my good right ear.

There were drinks for all. I had three scotch highballs (which the president, who didn't seem to be looking, commented on). He drank out of a plastic mug-glass which obscured the contents, a kind of diet cola. He gave it to me to sip, saying each glass contained only two calories. It tasted like sarsaparilla.

Then, to my surprise, the crew brought little tray-tables placed in front of everyone, set them and produced a supper of rice, curried shrimp, meat, vegetables, etc., ice water, rolls, and vanilla ice cream. The president made up with food calories what he'd yielded in drink calories, had two heaping platefuls and smothered his ice cream with caramel sauce.

Finally, after coffee, the president said: "How about a little movie?" He sat back while the screen was swiftly set up and the projector produced. Successively we had incredibly boring films (three of them) of the president and how government runs; a long, long series of shorts advertising U.S. savings bonds; and finally a film on the awarding of a Medal of Honor (by the president) to a marine sergeant from Vietnam.

The yacht drifted slowly downstream under a haze-obscured full red moon, then turned and slid slowly back upstream and was pulled beside the wharf a good fifteen minutes before the final reel concluded and we rose, filed off, were driven back to the White House. Everyone seemed to have a car. "Have you got a car?" Johnson asked. I said no and he said: "Take mine." So I gave Kay a hitch home and then was driven in the armored Cadillac up the narrow Georgetown street to the Wisners' house where I'm staying. On the way the Negro chauffeur, who was wearing a straw trilby, not a chauffeur's hat, told me the glass was two inches thick (I pushed the button to lower a window and noted that he only exaggerated a little) and weighed an enormous amount but handled just like an ordinary Cadillac of that model.

On the way back Kay assured me: "Don't think this happens every day. I haven't even seen him [President Johnson] for a couple of years. But if you live here he may sweep you up for two or three days in a row, and then drop you." She was clearly fascinated and, at least for the moment, filled with admiration.

So much for the ambience. I shall now try to recapitulate some of the things Johnson said. By all odds the most important thing was on the subject of Russia and the "hot line."

Apparently we had used the hot line during the incident when Israel attacked the U.S. communications ship *Liberty* and we sent off planes, but Moscow initiated its use later during the last phase of the war— between Israel and Syria—and most ominously.

As the story emerged, Israeli troops were driving into Syria and toward Damascus when a Soviet warning came rattling over the teletype (which is what the hot line is) warning that if we didn't make the Israelis stop, Russia would take action "including military action." Johnson promptly ordered a formation of ships from the Sixth Fleet, including carriers, to turn eastward and head for Israel.

This being done, he started to answer Moscow, but in paragraphs considerably spaced apart in time, so that by the time the second paragraph was on the wire, Soviet vessels and planes in the Mediterranean would be fully aware of the direction our ships were heading. He said in his message that the U.S.A. was trying to curb Israel but explained this was difficult. Then he asked what Moscow was doing to curb Syria, remarking that no indications had been reported to him on any such actions.

Of course, the crisis simmered down and the Israelis never got to Damascus, as they had intended, to oust the regime, which is one of Moscow's favorites. This explains why and also demonstrates how determined Moscow is to keep a toehold in Syria. It confirms my suspicion that they'll get a naval base there.

Johnson went on at length to talk about Russia, about [Russian Premier Aleksei] Kosygin's difficulties both at home and in China, and about Russia's serious miscalculation in the Middle East. He admitted we are disturbed about the implications that Moscow can make so large an error; where else would it miscalculate?

He thought the Russians were in very deep trouble and that was perhaps why Kosygin didn't dare see him. Perhaps Kosygin just didn't have the authority to do so. (He did—soon afterward!)

He then talked about de Gaulle and repeated what he has often said to me, that he didn't want to quarrel with him, that he wasn't picking quarrels with anyone.

He expressed much admiration for Israel's army. He said [Ambassador] Arthur Goldberg had called up from UN when the war started and was deeply worried. Johnson said General Wheeler had given him an estimate that Israel could easily and quickly handle all its enemies. Goldberg objected that the military was too often wrong, we should do something. Johnson asked Wheeler for another estimate and got the same.

Johnson said he had sought to get a naval force into the Aqaba straits, including us, the British, Scandinavians, etc., and had warned Israel not to move, that "they'd be alone if they go alone." He had told this to Abba Eban, whom he admires. However, Israel did in the end move. And it did go alone, successfully.

He said that day the state department had begged him—and he'd yielded—to halt the ban on U.S. visitors to Israel and several Arab states. "And who do you think was the first person to take advantage of this? Richard M. Nixon." (Nixon flew briefly to Israel.) "I mentioned this at EXCOM this afternoon and Bundy said: 'I suggest we proceed to the next item of business—rapidly.'"

Johnson reminisced a lot. He said Lady Bird had been a very shy, poor girl. She lived for a long time on $70 a month, when in college. She was afraid of flying but had helped campaign for him in his early days in a little single-seater plane. He clearly admires and adores her, and he is a most admirably affectionate family man.

Talking about his decision to send the ships toward Israel and call Russia (it wasn't a bluff, he said, because Israel did stop) he admitted it was "the most open-ended, filled-with-dire-consequences decision" he had

had to make (like Kennedy and Cuba) because it might have started World War III, but there was no alternative. It was easier than the decision to intervene in the Dominican Republic where he had to confer with his cabinet while our citizens and embassy were being threatened, but while the meeting was still on (having agreed intervention was needed) the troops landed, because it took only forty-five minutes between the order and its implementation.

The Russia-Syria decision was easy because a man couldn't be bullied. Johnson was opposed to "cowardice" in any form (he pronounces it "ice" not "iss"). He had learned this as a little boy; if you gave way to bullies, they bullied you even more. It was an easy decision. After all, every president did his best and he had done his best. Kennedy, Eisenhower, why even Herbert Hoover had tried to do their best.

Johnson said another very, very tough decision he had had to make was on Cyprus. During the height of the crisis there a Turkish invasion fleet had actually taken off for a military intervention and he had to order them back, warning otherwise of U.S. armed opposition.

He kept reverting to Kosygin, quite naturally, indicating a certain pique that the Soviet premier hadn't taken the initiative in seeking a meeting or, at least, in acknowledging he was in the U.S.A. rather than just UN territory. He said Kosygin was in much greater trouble than he, Johnson, was. Johnson had his share—with senators Fulbright, Morse, and Bobby Kennedy; "but he's got China and his own Central Committee to worry about."

WASHINGTON, June 23, 1967

Long talk with Vice President Humphrey. I started off on today's meeting between Johnson and Kosygin at Glassboro, N.J. By 4:55 P.M. when I left him the vice president had not been told a single thing about what happened in the meeting. However, he said: "The two men simply had to meet. The world expected it. But it is unlikely that there will be any result unless the politburo makes major decisions."

I asked whether he didn't think foreign policy had now become perhaps *the* major issue in American national politics. He said: "I doubt that it is a crucial matter in most instances and in most circumstances as far as local office is concerned, but it has become extremely important for the presidency. The central issues are: (1) fiscal and monetary attitudes, (2) national security and foreign policy, (3) the attitude on economic matters such as unemployment and development.

"Item (2)—national security and foreign policy—is *the* most important issue now for the president since he is commander in chief and principal architect of foreign affairs. During the 1930s item (3)—the economic-unemployment-development—was the most important and during the 1920s it was item (1)—the fiscal and monetary attitude.

"But today people are really concerned by national security and foreign policy as far as the presidency is concerned. For senators I guess the ratio is about half way between the situation of a congressman and the situation of a president. Foreign *aid* is not really a political issue of any importance. All that I am saying of course has to be taken against the backdrop of certain selective constituencies where foreign policy is very important, like New York with its Jews and Milwaukee with its Poles.

"In 1968 foreign policy will probably figure more than ever with arguments about the Middle East and, above all, Vietnam. The trend of political life in this country, except during the depression years, has increased popular consideration on foreign policy and national security. And the issues are becoming more difficult. There are no more solid blocs in the world, no clear-cut black and white. Nor is our own power so much greater than that of others as it once was. Now our foreign policy must generate support from logic, not strength."

I had the impression that Nixon, who is an expert politician, was being very clever by traveling all around the world these days and making himself genuinely familiar with foreign policy issues because he recognized that this is issue number one in the next election. Humphrey agreed emphatically. He said: "Nixon is pushing this. You are quite right. Don't underestimate him—even as a candidate. I wouldn't have a chance to get identified with foreign policy as vice president because all vice presidents are overwhelmed by their president. Don't forget that Jack Kennedy had the solid Catholic vote, the solid Jewish vote, and a lot of other solid strength, and yet Nixon ran so close behind him that a shift of only a county or two would have changed the outcome. He is still very much there. And he has been very responsible in his foreign policy statements.

"As a Republican candidate—and I think he will probably be nominated—he will run against an incumbent of his own age and not against a young nonincumbent as he did in 1960. He will run against an incumbent with scars, just the way he himself has scars, and not against an unscarred young nonincumbent. Nixon will be a very strong contender. He is no fool. And he knows that foreign policy is the issue for our day—more than ever.

"The big issue in 1968 will be Vietnam. This produces grave new pressures because it is a new moral and ethical question and you may recall that Aristotle said that ethics and politics are inseparable."

With this as a background Humphrey went on to discuss Vietnam vis-à-vis Johnson in the 1968 elections. He said: "The president is in a box. If Vietnam goes well, he's made. Otherwise it will be very tough. And I am sure that the north and the Vietcong will do everything in their power to try to hang on until our 1968 elections. They realize Vietnam will be the major issue. This could be a disastrous interpretation for them but it seems to be the way they think."

FISHER'S ISLAND, NEW YORK, *July 2, 1967*

We are spending the weekend at Jock [John Hay] and Betsey Whitney's. Chip Bohlen came for dinner last night.

Chip says there was a roar of French protest against de Gaulle's anti-Israeli policy and that if Israel had lost last month's war he has no doubt the government would have fallen. What de Gaulle simply does not take into account is that this whole Arab-Jewish issue is a question of emotion and not logic and that the conscience of the West is involved.

The Rothschilds put enormous pressure on Pompidou to hold off the embargo on arms shipments to Israel which had been personally set by de Gaulle. Pompidou yielded, delaying its application while the Israelis loaded up. Couve de Murville was appalled by de Gaulle's bitter statement which, Chip says, was actually in the General's own handwriting.

NEW YORK, *July 11, 1967*

Fascinating day yesterday. I had an appointment with Eisenhower down in Gettysburg so, having bummed the *New York Times* company plane, I took my son David along. When we arrived at the little airstrip, there was a car from Eisenhower's establishment which drove us to his office on the campus of Gettysburg College.

Considering what I had heard about his health and that he is now more than seventy-six, Ike looked pretty well. When I said so he grinned rather sadly and said: "Well, you know, there are three ages of man. Youth. Middle age. And 'How well you look.' " He seemed frailer and complained he was fairly weak. He has played nine holes of golf four times this year, and he sadly observed that he can't hit the ball more than 150 yards now, so he is going to buy a new set of light clubs.

He held out his hands and wrists to show how they had shrunk and said he will never regain his strength because of all the time he has had to spend in hospital not exercising. I asked if he played bridge any more and he admitted this was very rare also.

He said the trouble with policy-making today was that there were too many "intellectuals" involved who thought they knew the answers to everything but who had never been up against the "hard knocks" of reality. He specifically mentioned Kenneth Galbraith, Mac Bundy, and Walt Rostow.

I recalled that before he had made up his mind to run for the presidency he often used to say that what he really preferred was to look forward to a period of retirement when, as a kind of elder statesman on a nonparty basis, he would be at the service of his country. Such being the case, what would be his advice concerning the Middle East today. He immediately perked up at this and after he began talking I asked if he would mind if I took notes; he told me to go ahead. This is the essence of what he said.

The United States should take the lead in facing the real issues of the Arab-Jewish problem, which were the shortage of water and the question of the Arab refugees. It required an imaginative plan, especially because diplomacy had shown itself ineffective in recent UN discussions.

Two or three large nuclear plants should be built to desalt water and generate between 750 million and a billion gallons a day of sweet water. There should be really enormous plants because "the bigger the plant, the more economic the operation.

"This water would cost more than the price of New York City water but it is cheap for a country that doesn't have water at all. And Syria, Jordan, Israel, and Egypt would all profit so much from such a plan that the people couldn't permit their governments to refuse participation."

Eisenhower had been struck for the first time in 1942, when his troops landed in Africa, by the enormous hatred prevailing between the Arabs and the Jews. This was something he simply couldn't understand because they were so much alike and had lived together so long that you couldn't tell them apart. Nevertheless it was a fact and it had to be recognized.

The plan he envisioned would meet both requirements in the Middle East because it would not only provide work for the refugees in building and manning the plants. Once they were in production they would recover enormous areas of barren ground in Syria, Jordan, the Israeli Negev, and Sinai.

I expressed great interest in this idea and he then said it originated with [Admiral] Lewis Strauss, (formerly Eisenhower's chief of the atomic energy commission). Eisenhower stressed that something new enough and big enough had to be done to end the present stalemate, because now all that was happening was a name-calling contest among the Arabs and the Jews against each other and against the U.S.A.

But he thought the idea had such obvious material value to both sides that it must be of major interest to them. The idea would be to create a worldwide corporation like the International Atomic Energy Agency established in Vienna as the sole concrete outcome of Ike's own 1953 "atoms for peace" proposal. In this the U.S. government would take up 51 percent of the stock and private investors and traders would take up the rest. Maybe the cost of the program could never be completely amortized but it would certainly produce some income—just the way the cost of the Panama Canal and its operation was never completely amortized but some income was produced.

Ike continued: "Lewis Strauss and I have been great advocates of atomic power and what can be done with it." He recalled that he had tried to get the Arabs and Jews together when he was president by sending Eric Johnston to the Middle East to work up a Jordan River water-sharing program, but this never took. However, the scale of the present scheme was so enormous that one would think it had to attract support. One plant alone would produce as much as the entire water flow of the Jordan and all its tributaries, simply by transforming sea water into fresh water.

Eisenhower said it really was not important whose name was attached to this plan, and that he had even mentioned the idea to President Johnson and also to Ambassador "Tommy" Thompson (our envoy to Moscow who had briefed Ike on the Glassboro talks with Kosygin). He had suggested to Johnson that he should raise the matter with Kosygin.

Ike said one of the difficult diplomatic factors—and why he had kept Strauss's name out of discussions so far—was that Johnson and Strauss hated each other, and Johnson, as a senator, was personally responsible for blocking Strauss's confirmation as secretary of commerce.

He then returned to the project itself and his eyes lit up. Ike has a very special talent for getting excited about the important things, pushing them, developing them, and selling them. He said: "This thing makes the Eric Johnston plan look like a flea against a dog."

He said that if I wanted to go into this more thoroughly I should talk to Strauss. I asked him if he could call up Lewis and he did, reaching him at his farm in Brandy Station, Virginia. I told him to tell Lewis I had a plane and could I come down and have lunch with him together with my son? Ike transmitted the message and the answer was yes. He then called his aide and told him to find out what airfields were in the neighborhood of the Strauss farm, to work out with the pilot of my plane which field it could come in at, and to call Strauss when we took off so he could meet us. There is nothing like military efficiency operating on one's behalf.

Ike then settled back in his swivel chair at the desk in his comfortable, modest office and we resumed our conversation. I asked if he had to play over again the 1956 policy of the U.S.A. and the Suez crisis if he would do it the same way. He chuckled ruefully and said:

"Of course, hindsight is more accurate than foresight. But foresight is more valuable. I suppose, looking back on it, I would have made a greater effort in advance to win over Israel, France, and Britain to my viewpoint. The Suez Canal was owned by a private company and, of course, the British had bought a lot of stock in it. As long as he offered to conform to the provisions of the treaty of 1888 signed in Constantinople, Nasser had every right to nationalize. And the British were damn fools. They claimed it was impossible for the Egyptians to operate the canal, but within weeks of taking over Nasser was getting through more tonnage than ever before.

"We were all bound by the principles of the UN, and I said we should not allow the whole world to retrogress from peaceful efforts and go from the conference table to the battlefield. But I told the British that, for God's sake, if they determined to go to the battlefield—and they certainly knew my views in advance—they should be sure to have the proper basis to go on with the full understanding and support of their public opinion.

"They knew exactly what we were going to do and I talked to Anthony [Eden] time after time, and then the damn fools, when they decided in spite of us to act as they did, they did it very badly. Their operation was a mess. I like Anthony and I still write to him. We have always been friendly. The British attitude then was understandable in terms of their resentment. But they did it all wrong. And I can tell you in confidence that I sent a hell of a message to Ben-Gurion also."

Knowing that now I was going to have to leave in order to keep my date with Strauss, I moved the conversation out of the past and into the present, asking Ike what he thought of the 1967 Middle East war. He scratched his chin and said:

"Well, I was certainly surprised by the speed of the victory. Naturally, when I saw the first claims of Israel I said right away this looks like an Israeli surprise attack. But I don't know what they could have done except that, with all those Arab armies on their borders and Nasser talking of a total war to drive Israel into the sea. Try and make an analogy for this country. Supposing I had been president and some combination of enemies, much bigger than us, had been gathered on the seas and in Canada and Mexico promising our extinction. If I hadn't attacked first while I had the chance I would have been tried for treason.

"I will tell you that as a professional military man I was amazed that the Egyptians could be caught that way after bragging so much about what they were going to do. I was surprised that they could be caught tactically like that with their planes parked all together on airfields and not even any revetments. But that sure was some harvest the Israelis got. I never had a harvest like that in World War II—340 planes in one night."

He talked a bit about de Gaulle, of de Gaulle's "tremendous pride." He said: "He confounds himself with France and thinks anything offending France must be revenged." Ike thought de Gaulle's visit to Cambodia with its anti-American speech and his recognition of Peking stemmed from this. But, he added: "Despite all this I make it a point to keep on good terms with the General. He wrote to me the last time I was in hospital. I am sure that if I ever get back to Paris again I will see him there."

At this moment his telephone rang and some aide asked a question. Ike said: "How the hell should I remember? Call [Harry] Butcher. He was there." When he hung up he said: "They are trying to ask me if when Jodl came in to surrender in 1945 he came in alone. I don't remember that now."

Ike then reminisced a moment about the German surrender. He said all he had told Jodl was: "Do you understand every word of this document and what it signifies?" When Jodl said yes, he dismissed him. "I wasn't one of those fellows in favor of hobnobbing with the Nazis after we licked them," said Ike sternly.

At the end he talked briefly again about the Eric Johnston plan and attributed its failure to the insufficient scope of the project and to the fact that not enough recognition had been made of the terrible Arab-Jewish hatred. He added: "The Arabs would have gotten much more out of it than Israel but when they found out that the Jews would get something they just refused to go along."

Ike said, "I don't want to hurry you but if you are going to get down to Strauss I think you had better be moving," so he gave me a pretty good handshake for an old man and off we went.

We flew across the rolling countryside to Orange County, Virginia, where there was a 2,000-foot airstrip at the Airlie Foundation. A few minutes later Strauss showed up with his car and driver.

About ten days ago Strauss had sent Eisenhower a memorandum on a Middle East water plan. It was obvious from the UN debate that the resources of diplomacy were exhausted and we could not expect peace negotiations in a decent climate. Therefore, he saw the need for something dramatic to change that climate. The two basic issues that had exacerbated the Middle East are water and displaced populations. A single bold stroke by the United States could solve these both. He said:

"My idea is that there should be a corporation with its own charter and that the United States should guarantee to finance 51 percent of the cost. The rest should be taken up in world security markets. I have looked into this and I am confident that $200 million could be underwritten very fast."

Strauss wanted to build three very large nuclear plants, two of them on the Mediterranean coast of Israel and one of them at the head of the Gulf of Aqaba, probably in Israeli territory. These would be dual-purpose plants, to provide electric energy and fresh water. For energy it was necessary for a plant to operate at one temperature and another for water. But the basic objective of the plants would be to produce water with energy as an incidental.

The first plant would produce 400 million gallons of water a day—which is the total water flow of the Jordan River and all its tributaries. The nuclear material to fuel these plants had already been allocated by President Eisenhower in 1956 to the IAEA (International Atomic Energy Agency) in his offer to encourage plants for peaceful purposes.

All principal belligerents in the Middle East were members of IAEA so they have both a forum and the material with which to get going on this project. The IAEA would be responsible to account for the fuel and to see to it that there were no diversions which could be used for atomic weapons.

This vast scheme required thousands of unskilled workers and the Arab refugees were ideal for this. First they could work and then they could be settled on irrigated lands with plenty of electricity available. The method of desalting water originated at the U.S. laboratory at Oak Ridge, Tennessee. The idea sprang from the need to do something with waste material produced by weapons.

16

"THIS IS THE TREE

I EXPECT

TO BE BURIED UNDER"

LUNCH AT THE WHITE HOUSE WITH WALT ROSTOW. HE POURED ME an ice-cold martini out of a bottle, then ordered steaks and Jell-o from the rather touching White House menu.

Walt talked at length about Vietnam. He said: "We are convinced the population is moving our way." One use of bombing and increased pressure on the North Vietnamese was to try to persuade Hanoi that it was really on the wrong track. In the south, the Vietcong was having a more and more difficult time filling its ranks. (I wonder how over-optimistic this belief is.) Manpower was now an obsessive problem for the Vietcong. The war in the field was being won but the real danger was political and centered in Saigon and Washington.

We had decided to hit the buffer zone with China, the Haiphong marshaling yards, and the key bridges, but we are staying away from China itself and from ships in Haiphong. We are not enlarging the war. We are not trying to kill more civilians.

"The target officer" is President Johnson. It is he who makes decisions on what should be hit. He works these matters out with General "Bus" (Earle G.) Wheeler and McNamara.

This evening I had an appointment with the president and I arrived a little before 6:00 P.M., which was the time of our date. Rostow came down and sat with me in one of the consultation rooms.

He told me he had heard Johnson say that one of the motivating forces in his life was the shock of the depression. He had always been deeply distressed that his father, who was not a wealthy man but who had made his way in the hard farming life of Texas, was forced at the age of sixty to go to work on a bus.

His [Johnson's] first job was as a teacher for Mexican children. There were five other teachers, all women, who had been related to minor political figures and who felt put upon by being assigned to impoverished Mexicans. But Johnson felt very emotional about the chance to help these youngsters. During the depression he had been deeply upset when he saw Mexican kids raiding garbage pails, shaking the coffee grounds out of grapefruit peels and devouring them to get the vitamins. The President wanted to do glorious things for his first young charges—like organizing a school band.

Another time Rostow heard Johnson say at his ranch in Texas: "This is the tree I expect to be buried under. And when my grandchildren see this tree I want them to think of me as the man who saved Asia and Vietnam and who did something for the Negroes in this country. Yet I have lost twenty popularity points on Vietnam and ten on the Negro question."

At the Manila conference on South Vietnam Rostow heard Johnson talk to Ky and Thieu about politics in general. He told them the reason he was in politics was because he wanted to do good for humanity and that he thought Asia was probably the area where he could do the most good because two-thirds of humanity lived in Asia. "That's where the people are," the president said, "and for the most part they are poor and under-privileged. So that's where I can do the most good—and you can help me."

A few days after Johnson succeeded the assassinated President Kennedy he was already going around saying: "I don't think this country is ready for a president from Texas. I just don't think the East is going to accept me. I am sure that in this respect I am doomed to fail."

Suddenly [presidential aide] Marvin Watson opened the door and told us the president was waiting. We went through a secretarial office and past the little "think tank" to the Oval Room and Johnson came in from the other door: looking rather tired, not wearing glasses, appearing somewhat greyer in the hair. He seemed preoccupied.

He sat down in the presidential rocking chair (a newer and more padded variety than that Kennedy once used) with Walt on his left and me on his right. He asked if we wanted a drink. Walt took a scotch on the rocks, I a scotch and soda. The President ordered a Fresca, mumbling apologetically: "I have to watch my weight these days." Facing him on the wall was a color picture of Roosevelt; there were color photographs of his family on the two little tables by the sofas on which Walt and I sat. On Walt's sofa were some charts which the president looked at at the end of our conversation. They dealt with casualties in Vietnam.

He said he was behind schedule and that his wife was going to give him hell for being late. He said he was glad to see me, but he also made some of his customary unkind remarks about the *New York Times*. He then put his glasses on and read a sheaf of papers Watson handed to him which dealt with the subjects I wanted to talk about—namely South America and Africa, where I'm going.

He started to read out from the sheaf of documents while Walt doodled on a pad and I scribbled notes. But he was mumbling in a low Texas voice on the side of my deaf ear and I didn't get it all. So finally I asked if I couldn't have the working papers to which he was referring. Somewhat wearily, Johnson tore off the first page (classified) and handed me the papers.

He said I could use whatever I wanted concerning what he said and I could write anything I wished from the papers he was giving me. I should merely say, "I believe President Johnson feels, etc., etc." He then started to muse, not very brilliantly.

He said: "I want to tell you something about what we are trying to do in Latin America and Africa. We spend a lot of time on these things." He murmured on in a rather mixed-up way. He had met seventy-five leaders from different countries during the last twelve months and this was "an all-time record." He had seen all the Latin American leaders except Barrientos [General René Barrientos Ortuño] of Bolivia, who did not go to the OAS meeting in Uruguay and President François (Papa Doc) Duvalier of Haiti.

His administration had substantially increased the U.S. aid program for Latin America and Africa. His administration had virtually doubled Latin American aid as compared with the Kennedy administration. He had sent Under Secretary [Nicholas deB.] Katzenbach to Africa—the highest American official who had ever been there. He himself had gone to Punta del Este for the OAS conference, "and I met all of them there."

His approach to the Latin American leaders was always: "I am glad to meet with you fellows to discuss our common problems because this is helpful to all of us. We have a very big country but we must work in partnership and I think when we get together like this it emphasizes the fact of our partnership. I want to make you fellows into good junior partners."

I don't think the president noticed a conversely jarring note in that adjective.

Patience and understanding were particularly required in Africa where economic and political development simply had to be slow. Our commitment to Africa was to push for self-determination and the political conception of one man, one vote, just as we wished elsewhere in the world. We wanted to press for moderation and good sense in both black and white Africa. And we kept on pressing for regional and subregional development. We wanted Africa to get ahead on this kind of international approach in power, transportation, telecommunications, and other things.

He wandered on like a tired machine that continued to function without any particular coordination. Latin American exports had been rising in the last three years and were up 22 percent. There was a new feeling of confidence in this country about Latin America and U.S. private investment there had gone up from $242 million in 1963 to $457 million now. He said: "Private investment is what will do it in the end. That must be the ultimate answer. But you will have to have confidence in an area before you can get investment there."

He admitted there was a deep connection between our foreign policy in Africa and our internal policy on civil rights. He said: "We know Lincoln had his emancipation proclamation. But that was just a proclamation not a fact. And we are paying the price for this.

"Of course we are a more mature and sophisticated nation than the African countries. Our people have lost their jungle instincts, but we still have terrible national problems. You can't deny that. So obviously what happens here has its effect in Africa and the same thing is true in reverse."

The 1964 and 1965 enactment of civil rights and open housing laws helped to encourage the desire for progress here, but as progress came it increased impatience.

I asked if he thought it might be necessary to enact a race relations act here as the British had done in 1965. He does not think so. Every state has its own laws right now, but the House is studying the possibility of a federal law. Our founding fathers did not want to have a federal police force with the result that, for example, New York City has more police than the FBI and each state has its laws on these issues.

He added: "I would say that it would be a sad country if we couldn't depend on the local citizen following his city or state laws. Certainly it would be a very difficult thing for the federal government to interfere with all local violations. If we can't depend on city and state law, we can't depend on very much. In my speech today in Kansas City I gave my philosophy on this. But I can see that the day may come when a federal law is needed."

Johnson then rambled on. He made scoffing remarks about Stokely Carmichael who he said was now in Algeria. Somewhat bitterly he said the Eastern seaboard of the U.S.A.—"including the *New York Times* and the Harvard intellectuals" is tending to become more isolationist. He said Castroism was making enough headway among Negro extremists here "to concern us," but it is not yet a serious problem on a major scale. He said the 1943 Detroit riots during World War II—"when there was no national guard around" were far worse than any city riots last summer.

He showed me the Vietnam casualty charts that had been turned backwards on the sofa and which demonstrated that our casualties in Vietnam are only 10 percent those of the enemy. He handed me a funny little card on which were typed out twelve major decisions he had taken during the past summer and, "It was a tough, hard summer." Here is the text of the card:

1. Middle East War—Began June 5—Hot Line—Held fast on cease-fire without rollback of Israeli forces. Russians finally conceded.
2. UN debates on Middle East—Russian failure Security Council—June 5–June 14. General Assembly—June 17–July 21.
3. Glassboro—June 23–25.
4. C-130's to the Congo—Three arrived July 10. Two withdrawn August 3.
5. Vietnam Election—September 3. Clifford-Taylor Mission—July 24–August 4. U.S. Troops—45,000—announced August 3. Year-long turmoil in China continues.
6. Rail strike—reversal of the House's "Pepper Amendment" on July 17, 1967.
7. Debt ceiling—reversal of the House on June 27, 1967.
8. Riots—Newark (July 15–16, 1967), Detroit (July 23–25, 1967), Milwaukee (August 4, 1967).
9. Taxes—message on August 3, 1967.
10. Draft Bill—message on March 6, 1967. Law passed on June 20, 1967.
11. Non-proliferation treaty—identical drafts tabled by U.S. and USSR on August 24 in Geneva Conference.
12. British and German troop levels U.S.-UK-German agreement—May 2. Kiesinger signs on August 16.

I figured I'd better get out by this time because the poor man really looked awfully tired. He wandered over to his big desk and was fumbling with papers when I said I thought I would be off. He shook my hand, but his mind was elsewhere—I think it was already focusing on his night's sleep.

When I went off with Rostow, he took me down to his office (although it was already twenty minutes past eight). I remarked that the only really interesting thing the president mentioned was the fact that he had sent a warning to Castro through the Russians. Walt then said:

"Around May 13, when the Russians were sending word to Cairo that Israel was mobilizing against Syria—an untrue maneuver which set off the Middle East War—the president sent a most remarkable message to Kosygin. I think it is one of the most remarkable messages that any president has ever sent.

"In short he made it perfectly plain that we knew what was happening in the Middle East, that we knew the Cubans were expanding communist subversion in Latin America, and that we knew that Russia was not being helpful in Vietnam. But he wanted to point out that, powerful as our two countries were, Russia and the United States, we could not entirely control dangerous spots elsewhere. We were the older children in the family and if we stayed together we could influence the others, but if we did not stay together and exercise some kind of joint control, it was difficult to read the future.

"He suggested that it might be useful if the Russians were to calm down Castro, try to quiet the Middle East, and tell Hanoi to get back to its 1954 attitudes.

"At the Glassboro meeting with Kosygin this message was revived. The Russians had been desperately alarmed by the Middle East outbreak. In fact they initiated the use of the hot line with Washington in their frenzy to avoid a spread of the war, and at Glassboro we helped Russia out in arranging a cease-fire.

"But also at Glassboro we again warned the Russians about Cuba making trouble in this hemisphere. We talked about the need to arrange some kind of agreement on antiballistic missile systems and nuclear disarmament. There isn't any doubt that Kosygin was very impressed by this."

WASHINGTON, *September 16, 1967*

This afternoon I drove out to see Bobby Kennedy at Hickory Hill, his pleasant house near McLean, Virginia. A colored maid showed me into a cozy sitting room where I was immediately besieged by children. (The Kennedys now have ten of them.) Young Max, aged two, and Christopher, not quite four, crawled all over me, aided by a huge wet English sheepdog, while Carey, a pretty little girl of around ten, did startling handsprings on a slippery rug. Bobby was outside playing touch football with his wife and some other kids. He came in wet and tousled in shorts and a jersey. Although he looks very slight in regular clothes, he has massive legs and extremely strong wrists. He was excellent with the children—checked up on their manners, quite firm and yet unusually gentle.

I explained I was going to South America and Africa and wanted to exchange a few ideas. He rambled along about his own African views and experiences. He said it was too bad there were increasing congressional restrictions on aid.

He thought Sekou Touré in Guinea was "pretty good," that he would be opposed to giving money to Guinea but this was one of the points on which "I disagreed with my brother. It now looks as if he had been right." He said Félix Houphouet Boigny, president of the Ivory Coast, was the most stable West African leader.

He acknowledged the attention focused on Africa during the early months of the Kennedy administration had an effect that wore off fairly quickly and then the Africans felt neglected. We got by under the Kennedy administration with relatively little expenditure and effort because that was compared with the Eisenhower administration, but it is tougher for Johnson, who is being compared with the Kennedy administration.

Bobby said there were quite a few differences between the Kennedy and Johnson administrations on Latin American policy. There is a closer relationship now between the South American Establishment and we are more identified with it, less identified with reform. Bobby was not really sure which would prove to be the right approach.

In Latin America everyone on the left is anti-U.S.A. although the Russian communists are rather moderate. The Chinese are the radicals and have strong influence in many universities. Bobby is convinced that Castro is "very dead" and that his revolution in Latin America "has gone nowhere."

CARACAS, VENEZUELA, September 23, 1967

Excellent talk with Dr. Leandro Mora, minister of the interior. He says there are two basic communist groups here, about twelve thousand relative conservatives who follow the Moscow line and about two thousand who follow the Chinese line and include the pro-Castro element. There are only seventy-six guerrillas in the mountains.

The guerrillas have not met with much success among the population. They don't really offer anything that the government hasn't already offered—like education, agrarian reform, or social improvements. Their approach seems to be that "anything you can do we can do better."

A Cuban army captain was captured in Caracas a month ago and Mora offered to allow me to see him. His full name is Captain Manuel Espinoza Diaz. He had been in the mountains for several months but fell ill and needed medical attention.

We went into a room next door and there were two fellows there—both rather short and wearing shirts and trousers. I didn't know who was who but one of them left the room. I suddenly realized the man sitting quietly was the Cuban captain. He was wearing a grey shirt and light grey trousers and ordinary brown shoes but had no necktie, shoelaces, or belt. He kept smiling and seemed completely composed.

Espinoza Diaz told me he was thirty-three and came from Oriente province where he had been a taxi driver. He had been in the "special service" of the army and was given a chance to apply for work overseas. After intensive training he came over by boat to Venezuela where he landed on a beach under the command of Petkoff, a Venezuelan communist who had been training in Cuba.

Nobody was waiting on the beach. It was fourteen days before they met any Venezuelan guerrillas. Espinoza insisted he had no idea he was coming to Venezuela until he got on the boat. He says he spent eleven months in the mountains but wasn't engaged in any military battle.

Mora asked him what would have happened to a Venezuelan guerrilla captured in a similar way in Havana. With a smile, Espinoza replied: "He would have been shot within twenty-four hours."

CARACAS, VENEZUELA, *September 25, 1967*

This morning I saw a couple of left-wing university students at the home of Sabeth Ramirez, the beautiful young *Life* correspondent, whose father is a rich oil man. The principal talker was José Enrique Mieres, a twenty-three-year-old from a small city in Monagas, a state to the east. He and others are professional agitators who stay in Caracas University year after year, studying one subject after another, making a career of spreading political propaganda and organizing students.

He said he was a Marxist-Leninist. He had read "a little Ché Guevara" and described Mao as "the great master." He then dove into clichés: "Instead of reading we live the revolution." "We practice what we preach." "The important thing is agitation and propaganda."

The government hasn't "been able to eliminate" the guerrillas but the PCV (pro-Russians) have hurt them. Moscow is an ideological enemy, although not as bad as Washington. Tito is a rank revisionist, allied to Yankee imperialism.

This afternoon I saw President Raúl Leoni at his new official residence, La Casona, which used to be a great plantation in Spanish days and has been remodeled and refurnished as a colonial mansion. After our talk, Mrs. L. took us around. It is truly lovely, with courtyards containing trees, flowers, and fountains scattered throughout among the various suites, fine old Spanish and French furniture, not-so-fine Venezuelan paintings, etc.

Leoni was "absolutely convinced that any possibility of a coup in Venezuela is out." There would be no more violent overthrows of government by military force.

I then asked why agitators among the youth were permitted to stay on year after year in the universities. He agreed this was bad, that there were adult agitators among the students. The government had ordered the end of this by executive order but this had "provoked great opposition from the student body."

I asked him what were the positive and negative aspects of U.S. policy here. He summed up the negative with one solemn word, *"Petróleo."* As for positive, he said the U.S.A. has been cordial and cooperative. However, oil restrictions hurt.

He said: "In Venezuela there is no racial discrimination. Everyone is equal regardless of color of skin. This was not easy for Venezuela to achieve. Our revolutionary war gained independence for the nation but differences of race and social class continued. The Negroes had no rights. They were virtually on the same level as animals. And the Indians also suffered heavily from discrimination. Slavery was not easy for us to abolish. We had great arguments in congress and in public opinion before achieving emancipation.

"The trouble was that after the initial exuberance following emancipation, the freed slaves found no economic place and many of them returned to the plantations. Former slaves found they could expect nothing from the oligarchic government of the rich. The real problem was social.

"Slowly we achieved integration. You can say that Venezuela or Brazil have created a new American race, the product of integration, what the Mexican philosopher, José Vasconcelos, called a Cosmic Race. Unfortunately, Vasconcelos, who was originally influenced by Marx, became rather fascist in his old age, favoring a kind of superman."

Leoni was optimistic about eventual success of U.S. integration. He cited the marriage a few days ago of Dean Rusk's daughter and a Negro student, saying this had produced a most favorable image here.

LIMA, PERU, *September 28, 1967*

Pedro Beltrán, old friend, publisher of *La Prensa* and former prime minister met us at the airport and put us up at his lovely old house, the last of its kind in Lima.

Pedro is very worried, says Peru is going bust. President (Fernando) Belaúnde (Terry) has no idea of economics, finance, or administration. U.S. Ambassador Johnny Jones says the argument about U.S. planes remains tough. We don't want to sell Peru the supersonic F-5s they wish but France is peddling Mirages and we may have to. Belaúnde depends on the military's political support and they want supersonics. So there it is.

LA PAZ, BOLIVIA, *September 28, 1967*

The jet soars through the permanent fog-belt over Peru's coastal strip, over the barren Andes, above Lake Titicaca and down on this capital's airfield, highest in the world (over 13,000 feet). We were met by a deputation from the U.S. embassy and driven down into the cup where La Paz is perched at different levels, all over two miles high: a strange town, ugly but attractive; stone buildings, curving streets, tremendous snow-covered ranges in the background. Several peaks are around 20,000 feet. Walls are either plastered with slogans or covered with childrens' paintings (the U.S. ambassador's idea). The streets are filled with Indians, impassive Asiatic faces (much like the Tibetans of North India), the women all wearing felt derby hats.

Staying with Ambassador Douglas (and Dorothy) Henderson, a nice Massachusetts couple who have served all around here. He was once vice-consul in Arica, Chile; later consul in Cochabamba, Bolivia; later counselor and chargé in Lima, Peru. Speaks excellent Spanish and a good deal of Quechua, the Inca tongue. In their backyard the children have a zoo including two coatimundis, two monkeys, assorted guinea pigs, rabbits, parrots, macaws, etc.

It is evident the CIA plays an important role here, and the station chief is in personal touch with the president (semi-dictator) Barrientos. We have a sixteen-man Special Forces team at Santa Cruz which has trained a Bolivian battalion in counterinsurgency but which takes no part in the fighting.

Barrientos, an ex-air force general who took part in previous leftist revolutions, is optimistic about the guerrilla war and confident he has Ché Guevara bottled up. The Régis Debray incident is a nuisance. Henderson had to intervene to save Debray's life at the very start. This country has no death penalty but dissidents have been shot (or dropped from airplanes). It's a rough place. H. thinks Havana was making use of Debray who was a contact with Mexico, a main center in the underground link.

H. says the Cuban revolution needs momentum or it will die. It hasn't worked in Venezuela or Colombia and can't in Argentina or Chile; it failed in Peru; so this was the choice (or Ecuador). It doesn't seek a communist state, which would collapse, but wants to arouse people against the government.

We are positive Guevara is here. There is an organized support apparatus in the cities. By accident the Bolivian army (after several mishaps) stumbled on to a guerrilla camp where they got Ché's passports and other papers. They got an undeveloped film from which prisoners and deserters later identified several leaders.

In May 1967, there was a plot to swing the armed tin miners behind the guerrillas but in June Barrientos took over the mines and frustrated this; it would have been dangerous.

La Paz, Bolivia, *September 29, 1967*

Talk with the president, General René Barrientos Ortuño. I saw him in his office in the presidential building (called the Burnt "Quemado" Palace because it had been burned down). This is featured by a lamp-post with plaques marking where another president's wounded body was strung up by a mob. Beside the palace is a church with Indians squatting on the steps. Soldiers in the red and white uniforms of the "Colorados," a regiment that fought Chile unsuccessfully in their war, guarded the palace. Inside the rooms were cold and threadbare. In the anteroom various soldiers and officials were waiting. There were bad paintings of Bolívar and Sucre and a sign: "Important notice. H.E., the Constitutional President of the Republic, confers no audiences in his own home."

Barrientos is a strongly built man who looks as if he might have been a star halfback: handsome, bronze complexion, good features, black hair, young-looking although he is nearing fifty.

He started out talking about the political impact of transistors. Said they were useful for spreading education but Havana was using them against the regime politically. He was doing his best to introduce wide-spread "fundamental" education but more money was needed to finance this. It was a problem that Aymara, Quechua, and Guarani were still spoken by the Indians, and more Spanish had to be taught.

B. thought the communists were focusing on Bolivia for three reasons. It is very poor and backward. Therefore it is easy to make big promises and stir discontent. Secondly, Bolivia is the continent's geographical center and has strategic importance as a base from which revolution could be spread. Thirdly, communism wanted to upset things "because we are making a democratic revolution here."

He thought their strategy was to link guerrilla fighting with agitation in the cities. The guerrillas were doing badly, "and I am sure I will get Ché in a few days at most."

I asked B. his ideology. His lame answer: "My acts describe me. I have been fighting for my country twenty-eight years. I am trying to change the economic and social structure. We have to use some force to push for change. I believe in the doctrine of Christianism. This supplies the moral needed. I am a Democratic-Christian-Revolutionary-Nationalist."

La Paz, Bolivia, *September 30, 1967*

Henderson told me something about Ché Guevara today. When he first left Cuba (1965?) Ché went to the Congo. He found the people there treacherous and lacking in revolutionary fervor so he returned to Havana. He then sent out an agent with the *nom de guerre* Ricardo to scout Latin American prospects. Ricardo told Ché Bolivia offered possibilities but he must move swiftly. In autumn 1966 he decided to come here.

La Paz, Bolivia, *October 2, 1967*

The Hendersons took us on an all-day car trip (by U.S. land-rover) across the high Altiplano and down a steep pass into the valley of the Zongo River and the rain jungle. Within three hours we had gone through a 17,000-foot pass winding beside snow-capped mountains over 20,000 feet, and down a narrow valley beside a trout stream, packed with jungle foliage including orchids at a level of 5,000 feet (when we stopped). It continues right down almost to sea level. All kinds of foliage in the Zongo valley. On top, barren wind-swept plain with occasional herds of llamas, watched by impassive, Tibetan-looking Indians and fierce dogs. On the way back we stopped to fill a bucket with snow for the evening's pisco sours.

There was a big flap preceding de Gaulle's visit. He was received at Cochabamba, the second city, not La Paz because it is too high for him. The Bolivians gave him the baton of a marshal and it was left behind in "Mon Repos," the Patiño house where he was lodged. The ambassador here

The author with President Tito of Jugoslavia, May 16, 1968.

At a farewell lunch for Ambassador Charles E. Bohlen, restaurant Lucas Carton, Paris, February 3, 1968. From left to right: Ambassador Cecil Lyon; Ambassador Bohlen; Alex Allegrier, owner of the restaurant, presenting a special cake to Ambassador Bohlen; the author. (*Keystone*)

With Nicolae Ceausescu, Communist leader of Rumania, October 1968.

The author with President Pompidou of France, February 10, 1970.

With President Nixon, March 8, 1971, on the occasion of the first
exclusive interview given by the President to an American journalist.

Sheikh Mujibur Rahman,
first President of
Bangladesh.

With Chancellor Kurt Kiesinger of the German Federal Republic,
March 16, 1967. (*Bundesbildstelle*)

Author with his friend Benjamin Beagle (wearing his yachting boots),
Spetsais, Greece, 1971.

A .C. L Sulzberger,
fraternalmente,
Fidel [?]
Cuba, Oct. 30, 64

Token of one of many meetings with President Lyndon B. Johnson.

LEFT
Gift from Prime Minister Fidel Castro, chief of Cuba's revolutionary government.

PARIS LE 7 Février 1969

Cher Ami,

Il va de soi qu'une fois de plus les auteurs inventent et que le Général de Gaulle ne m'a jamais appelé Georges.

Mes hommages à Madame Sulzberger et croyez, cher Ami, à mes sentiments très amicaux.

Georges Pompidou

Monsieur C. L. SULZBERGER
The New York Times
37, rue Caumartin
PARIS

The answer to a question I addressed to President Georges Pompidou of France, successor to General de Gaulle.

Meeting with President Anwar el-Sadat of Egypt, successor to Nasser, the first interview he granted to any journalist, October 19, 1970.

Photograph recording a meeting with Prime Minister Il Kwan Chung of South Korea, Seoul, April 23, 1969.

Letter from President Richard Nixon concerning a column I wrote. *(With permission of the Office of the President)*

THE WHITE HOUSE
WASHINGTON

April 7, 1970

Dear Cy:

Your recent column, "Foreign Affairs: The Shield vs. the Sword," has come to my attention and I just wanted you to know how much I enjoyed seeing it. A perceptive account of the facts about Safeguard on the editorial page of The New York Times is, of course, helpful. If the system I have proposed is approved, you can take credit for an important part in making clear its role.

With warm personal regards,

Sincerely,

Mr. C. L. Sulzberger
The New York Times
229 West 43rd Street
New York, New York 10036

Page from a manuscript written by Milovan Djilas when he was in prison in Jugoslavia. Djilas—at one time number two to Tito—was sentenced to jail for opposition. During this period (1962–1966) he translated John Milton's *Paradise Lost* into Serbian on toilet paper, the only material he had at hand.

Conversation with President Salvador Allende of Chile, Santiago, March 23, 1971.

Yasir Arafat

Duke and Duchess of Windsor

Chancellor Willy Brandt

Queen Juliana and Prince Bernhard of Netherlands

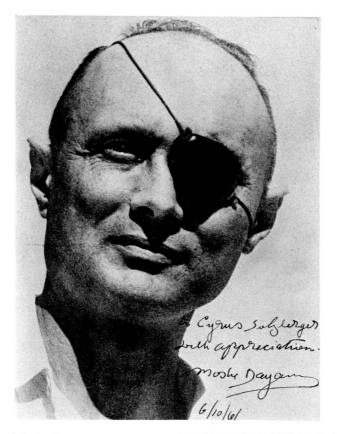

Moshe Dayan

Houari Boumedienne

was in a dither cabling menus back and forth to Paris for his approval. They finally served fish which was bad and everyone fell ill. The French dinner included *truite au bleu*. When they got the trout, the French kept it overnight in the swimming pool and their commercial attaché had to sit by it all night pumping in oxygen and fishing out trout if they turned over on their backs.

Ché Guevara, according to latest government reports (via guerrilla deserters) is surrounded, sick with asthma and rheumatism, in a shrinking band, many wounded all shaving off their beards to make escape easier.

Bustos, the Argentine communist agent and painter, was sent here on a mission by his party which was to tell Ché the Argentine party could offer no help to his guerrilla movement here. Bustos had a row with Ché and has been singing like a canary since the government got a hold of him.

MONTEVIDEO, URUGUAY, *October 8, 1967*

We drove to Punta del Este, where the important summit meetings of the Alliance for Progress have been held. The Rio de la Plata is so broad that you can't see across it, and feel as if you were going by the ocean. Down at Punta Ballena (whale) we saw a school of porpoises playing right off the beach.

The road en route is lined with eucalyptus and pine forests and also fields of absolutely beautiful flowers: the "purple land" of W.H. Hudson.

MONTEVIDEO, URUGUAY, *October 9, 1967*

This afternoon I saw the president, General Oscar Diego Gestido: very modest, unusually decent.

The presidential palace is guarded by grenadiers in the uniform of Meissonier's paintings of Napoleon's army.

The president is a big, ugly man with plain, ruddy, strong face. He has thin, dark hair and an earnest expression like that of a dog trying to please his master, but not quite understanding him.

He thought the Alliance for Progress was "positive and good." But that did not ignore the fact that lots remains to be done. The Alliance should take into account Uruguay's deteriorating economy and help the country.

The president agreed that "every citizen should pay as much attention to his obligation to the state as to his rights under the state." The natural tendency was for people to claim their rights and ignore their obligations.

RIO DE JANEIRO, *October 12, 1967*

Ambassador Jack Tuthill says the military is the most important political force in this country. President (Artur) da Costa e Silva told Tuthill: "Look upon me as the best of a bad situation. The military establishment determines the issues in Brazil today. But my objective is to pave the way for a civilian successor."

Marshal da Costa e Silva has now been in as president for six months. He is determined to get supersonic aircraft for the country. The French offered the Mirage, which is more costly than our F-5, but they have proposed very good credit terms. Tuthill has pointed out that if Brazil gets the Mirage, it will start an orientation of Brazil toward Europe on both military equipment and military liaison.

RIO DE JANEIRO, *October 14, 1967*

Spent yesterday at Brasilia, the brand-new capital constructed on the inland plateau some seven hundred miles from here. We flew up in the military attaché's plane on its way to Panama for overhaul. Herb Okun, political counselor who heads the United States embassy representation in Brasilia, was along, a nice, bright, red-headed fellow.

Herb said that apart from the top ten percent—the snobbish and power elements of Brazil, where there is a strong racist complex—the mixture of white and black and brown had been carried out in a relaxed way. An all-time carnival hit is played every year. The principal verse:

> Your hair gives you away, Mulata [Mulato girl]. Because you are colored. But since your color isn't catching, Mulata, let's make love.

Everybody sings this, white and black, and loves it. It is the favorite samba of Brazil.

Brasilia is a monstrosity. I hated the location, disliked the architecture, and resented the fact that it is built as a series of ghettos. Different people live in what are called "superblocks." People from one ministry live in one ghetto and another in another. All the American diplomats now there, for example, live in the same apartment house—just like Moscow.

In the late afternoon I went to see President da Costa e Silva. He is a pleasant-looking, fattish man with grey hair and moustache and a suspicious gleam in his eye.

I asked him whether Brazil was planning to buy Mirages from France. He would prefer to get U.S. F-5s. Brazil likes to use American material and has no tradition of using French material. But if Brazil cannot get the F-5s, it will have to look elsewhere for the planes it needs.

He said it was necessary for the army to move in in 1964 for national security reasons because the country was drifting faster and faster toward communism. The people were reacting against this drift and the army merely stepped in by going along with public opinion. The president insisted that the military do not want to stay in government.

This morning I read some reports that Sir John Russell, the British ambassador with whom we are staying, let me see. One described the inauguration ceremony for da Costa e Silva in Brasilia. The Spanish chief representative, head of Franco's military household, was dressed in full regalia and white uniform with sash. He mistook the ornamental water in front of the palace for the gleaming wet pavement and stepped into it and disappeared up to his order of the Golden Fleece. Russell murmured as he watched this: "Gibraltar, to you."

Brazil assimilates the mixed stream of humanity well and seems to have "the gastric juices of a python." But it is ridiculous to say it has no colored problem. Sammy Davis, Jr. said, after a visit here: "Sure, I saw niggers riding in Cadillacs; and they were all chauffeurs."

RIO DE JANEIRO, *October 15, 1967*

Yesterday evening we went over to Ambassador Jack Tuthill's for a drink with Roberto Campos, former minister of planning. Tuthill said he thinks the evidence makes it perfectly plain that Ché Guevara was captured by the Bolivian army and later executed.

Campos says that Latin American political behavior in one country is almost always mirrored in another country. He thought that military governments wanted capitalism without profits and perhaps without capitalists. This was because so many South American capitalists wanted development without paying for it.

The army was important in South American politics because Portugal and Spain had bequeathed a political anachronism to this continent. There is no up-to-date democratic or political idea in the Iberian peninsula. Even today they are obsolete in Europe.

De Gaulle asked Marshal (Humberto de Alençar) Castello-Branco what a Latin American military dictator was. Castello-Branco replied: "A man, not necessarily a general, who finds it pleasant to get power and extremely unpleasant to leave it."

RIO DE JANEIRO, *October 17, 1967*

John Mowinckel told me a telegram had been distributed among U.S. embassies from La Paz. In this our spooks described the end of Ché Guevara. Apparently Guevara was captured after being wounded by the Bolivian army. He was executed by the Bolivians after being interrogated. While he was interrogated he was asked: "What do you do to prisoners you capture in Cuba?" Ché replied boldly: "Shoot them." After his interrogation, he was shot by the Bolivians. The telegram said he died bravely.

DAKAR, SENEGAL, *October 19, 1967*

Arrived before dawn from Rio, exhausted and hot; it's like a Turkish bath. This is a fine city built for a huge hinterland of French West Africa that has now split into eight bickering states; Dakar is left stranded and purposeless like Vienna after World War I.

Senegal would swiftly collapse without French economic support on which it depends. Infant mortality is more than fifty percent; venereal disease hits sixty percent of population.

The French hold on the elite is strong. Twelve out of seventeen ministers kept their French passports (dual citizenship) and take holidays in France. Senghor, the president, has a French wife with a place in Normandy, and was a member of various French cabinets, taught in the same *lycée* as Pompidou. The French still run Senegal and their ambassador is like a governor general. They bequeathed a lot, including a bureaucracy and economic system.

The French colonial method was to try and develop a small, selective elite of "black Frenchmen" who became *évolués* and got French passports. The British never tried to develop black Englishmen although they sent aristocrats to English universities. The Belgians boasted their Negroes had a high standard of living but they forgot moral, cultural, and human values. French bureaucrats here accept and mix with the blacks; not the *colons* who won't even let them in their clubs. The French, being cultivated people, tended to encourage culture.

Admiral Édouard Rivière, French commander, told me he keeps a regiment of paratroopers assigned to intervene if need be, anywhere in Francophone Africa where Paris has permissive accords. They went to Gabon for the crisis. It is necessary to move fast—a thirty-man commando can do the job in two hours; a company in twelve hours; three regiments in two days.

DAKAR, SENEGAL, *October 20, 1967*

An hour this afternoon with Léopold Senghor, poet-president of Senegal: pleasant experience. I drove up to the presidential palace guarded by tall black soldiers in high red tarbooshes, red jackets, blue pantaloons, and spurred, black boots. First I was conducted to a waiting room in which the only decoration was a photograph of Senghor in white tie and many decorations.

After a few moments I was conducted to the president's office: big desk, comfortable furniture, and only two decorations on the wall: a photograph of de Gaulle in color (unsigned) and a large painting (hideous) by a modern Senegalese artist. There were some Ivory Coast fertility rite sculptures on a sideboard.

Senghor greeted me in French which, of course, he speaks flawlessly. He is short, trim, younger than his sixty years, dressed in well-tailored striped grey suit. He was wearing dark glasses. In a vase on the table beside him were some roses.

I started by inquiring whether there were any other poet-presidents nowadays. "Mao Tse-tung and Ho Chi Minh," he replied right away, adding that he didn't have many other things in common with them. He thought Mao a better poet, "less political."

He only wrote poetry during his holidays in Europe. "I have to have a certain distance in order to write. All my poems evoke Africa and when I am here I am too close, I have my nose in Africa. Abroad I develop a certain nostalgia that helps."

Senghor said the Francophone legacy was intellectually helpful. "One must forget the spirit of Fashoda, however, and go beyond Europe which is still trapped in its ancient quarrels." French is "a classic language, a useful instrument, logical and clear." But he made English compulsory in school also. It was a more flexible tongue. The two complemented each other.

Senegal had inherited qualities and defects from France. The Anglophone states were better in practical and economic ways. But the French had "gone beyond prejudice. I am a Catholic but we represent not even ten percent of the Moslem population. And my wife is French; but that doesn't count here. In Anglophone countries tribalism is more developed. This human aspect is most important."

He wanted African unification; he had always opposed Balkanization. He had sought to maintain the old French federations of West and Central Africa. Now he was pushing toward a return to confederation. There should be a common market; there lay the future of Africa. He wanted to avoid all divisions: developed and underdeveloped lands, north and south, white and colored.

There was no alliance with France, only a one-way treaty: France was obliged to aid Senegal, not vice versa. A French regiment was here and also several paratrooper formations in South France, earmarked for Africa, ready to intervene wherever necessary under treaties with Paris. From time to time there were combined maneuvers.

ACCRA, GHANA, *October 23, 1967*

Our hosts (U.S. ambassador) Franklin and Shirley Williams are American Negroes. He is a tall, thin, handsome man with strong saturnine face. Williams collects Ashanti gold weights, the little brass figures once used by traders as standard measure for gold dust. He has given many away to museums. He is a lawyer, fought hard for civil rights, and was with the Peace Corps in Ethiopia.

ACCRA, GHANA, *October 24, 1967*

Pleasant talk at the University of Ghana, in Legon, a suburb, with the vice chancellor, Professor A.A. Kwapong, actual head of the university; the chancellor is the chief of state.

Kwapong is a tall, handsome, ebony man, very well dressed in white suit and blue shirt, youthful, entirely at ease, who speaks good English with an Oxbridge accent (and slight Ghanaian intonation). He got both an M.A. and a Ph.D. at Cambridge and spent a year at Princeton as a visiting professor. He is a classicist, Latin and Greek.

I liked him a lot. He seemed to have no complexes, racial, colonial, etc. He said it was a mistake to think American Negroes had any particular bond with Africans. In fact they often did not get on very well because the Americans came over with all their complexes, from a tragic past, and met the Africans who had large happy families, tribal ties, etc. and were therefore psychologically much more content.

The main functions of the university were to prepare teaching cadres, conduct research, and serve the community through its graduates. It was an instrument both for preservation and for change. Ghana was more literate than its neighbors but needed more efficient intelligence resources. The problem was how best to train youngsters for both the immediate and long-term needs of the country.

Computer training must be injected into Ghana's educational system even to ascertain the magnitude of Ghana's problems. "We can't stay with our handicrafts while the rest of the world races to the stars."

ACCRA, GHANA, *October 25, 1967*

This morning I talked with Dr. K.A. Busia in his air-cooled office at the Parliament building. Dr. Busia, a small, frail, soft-voiced man with spectacles, is chairman of the advisory committee of the ruling council. He was an outspoken political opponent of former Ghanaian President Kwame Nkrumah and an exile for a long time.

I asked if [Lieutenant-General J.A.] Ankrah was a kind of "Naguib" for the young officers who staged the coup and whether a "Nasser" like [Brigadier-General A.A.] Afrifa might not now emerge. He smiled and said Ankrah had been in retirement (eased out by Nkrumah) so he couldn't have played an active role in the coup. But when the young officers took over they could only think of a prominent military man to head the show.

Tribalism is a plague here. People are beginning to get the impression more and more that jobs are allotted and contracts awarded on tribalistic prejudices. Western countries don't understand Africa. Generally the structure of an area is dominated by a tribe: common inheritance of traditions, customs, religion, kinship. This persists even under modern communications, with a tribal core remaining dominant. And a feeling for one's area means a feeling for one's tribe.

"In the struggle for democratic rule your sympathies go with the people you know, your tribe. It takes education to feel sympathies outside your area. Very few people have reached a national (much less international) breadth of sympathy. This is the case all over Africa. Of course 'tribe' is a poor word. You see the same regionalism for example among the Welsh in Britain. And tribalism is going too far in Ghana now. Too many appointments and contracts are on a tribal basis."

Accra, Ghana, *October 26, 1967*

This morning, in Christiansborg Castle where Nkrumah once lived (and before him the governors general) and where the national liberation council now makes its headquarters, I saw Brigadier A.A. Afrifa, commissioner for finance. Afrifa is a slender, well-built, trim, soldierly figure with coal black skin, guardsman's moustache, very neat olive-tan uniform, red tabs on his collar, a British accent. He is a Sandhurst graduate (where he studied history and German). Absolutely everything he said was perfect—endorsing civilian rule, democracy, eschewing office himself; yet I had an intuition that here was a power-hungry man who might be the Nasser of the outfit.

He hoped civilian rule could be restored by February 24, 1969, the third anniversary of the anti-Nkrumah coup. He added: "I loathe *coups d'état* but this is part of Africa's history at this time. Nevertheless, we have done our job and the civilians should come back. Soldiers are also human beings and there is no guarantee that they would be good politicians. I don't want to see a protracted period of power in which the military entrench themselves. We did a job civilians couldn't do, and got rid of this man. We have prescribed the right remedies. That's enough."

He told me his proudest moment was a few weeks ago when he wanted to send a telegram congratulating a friend. The corporal to whom he gave it saluted, apologized, and said: "Sir, this is personal and cannot go by government wire."

Accra, Ghana, *October 26, 1967*

Ambassador Frank Williams confirms my intuition about Afrifa. Says he is filled with charm and charisma but is consumed with ambition. Fortunately, he is pro-Western. (I remarked: "So was Nasser at the start.") Once, at a small school in the bush, Afrifa said, almost without knowing it, when he saw a group of kids: "I shall rule over them one day."

ACCRA, GHANA, *October 27, 1967*

I was received at his office in the castle by Lieutenant-General J.A. Ankrah, chairman of the national liberation council and thus chief of state. He is a hefty man with a limp (from an old football injury) and broad brown face. He was wearing a tan uniform with two rows of ribbons.

I asked him to describe Ghana's current ideology. He said: "Before our revolution the communist ideology tried to prevail here with the help of Nkrumah. But nobody can analyze or even attempt to interpret Nkrumahism.

"Nkrumahism is no more and no one in Ghana wants anything to do with communism. We just want to be democratic people governed for ourselves and by ourselves. We follow no particular bloc of powers but we want to be just as democratic as we can be."

I asked if he saw a relationship between the Ghana coup of 1966 and the series of other West African coups around that time (Nigeria, Congo, Dahomey, Upper Volta, Central African Republic). He said: "Ours was a revolution, not a coup. It stands out by itself in the field because we were getting rid of a dictator in order to free a people. Some of the coups in Africa have been different—staged by men ambitious to hold power."

LAGOS, NIGERIA, *October 30, 1967*

Snotty inspection at customs. There's a civil war on and they are looking for weapons and smuggled currency. When Nigeria was recently divided into smaller provinces the oil was taken from the Ibo tribe who, frustrated and angry already, split off. The Portuguese seem to have encouraged this, and São Tomé, an offshore Portuguese-held island, is the rebels' main point of entry. A Fokker Friendship shot down over Lagos one night this month, after rolling out some bombs, had several whites aboard including crew, an arms merchant.

There is growing respect for the Russians (who sold some MIGs at a good price) and now a Moskvitch car has been placed on display in one of the squares.

This coast (Bight of Benin) supplied U.S. and Brazilian slave traders after the British abolished slavery in 1807. Many aristocratic Lagosian families are descended from Brazilian freedmen brought back here by the British.

First sentence of lead story in *Morning Post* of Monday, October 30:

> Encircled by imminent vanquish, the rebels led by monster-looking Odumegwu Ojukwu, have escalated acts of atrocities, indiscriminate arrest of innocent personalities and leading personalities in areas still held by them.

Started off seeing Okoi Arikpo, commissioner for external affairs (foreign minister), a bright young intellectual. I was carefully searched for arms and bombs at the entrance.

Arikpo acknowledged that "tribal factors" were "at the bottom of all our problems, mixed with the struggle for personal power.

"The Hausas, Yorubas, and Ibos are all linguistic groups and large communities so that they are really nationalities. The smaller tribes are not important enough to be so classified."

He said army seizure of power had become inevitable because of "the kind of leadership in most underdeveloped countries and the low standard of public integrity. The army was traditionally the only neutral apolitical factor. But one must hope this is only a temporary phase. After all, it is very rare that armies remain stable. Once they take on political functions they begin to disagree. Then they remove their opponent with a gun, not a vote."

I then drove over to the residence of General Yakubu Gowon, the thirty-three-year-old chief of state. This was well protected by red-capped MPs with sten guns and blue-capped police. Also an armored car. Again searched for weapons, politely but carefully.

Gowon turned out to be a pleasant young man of middle height, lean and athletic, with guardsman's moustache (he went to Sandhurst), dressed in green-tan bushjacket uniform with one ribbon and major-general's tabs. He said:

"I'm not a believer in coups. My upbringing as a soldier teaches that my role is to support the government of the day irrespective of the political party in power. The great countries like the United States and Britain have able soldiers who don't dream of taking power. And they are the most stable governments in the world. That is my hope for this country in the future."

I asked, when did he hope to step down. He said: "At the moment I have a program for 1969 when there should be a turnover. The general public here was fed up with the political situation in the country. There was a lot of corruption. The politicians were corrupt. The place was filled with ten-percenters. People were looking after their own ambitions and interests. The coming in of the military was to clean up that political mess.

"A coup did happen on January 15, 1966, but I had never believed it would happen in this country because of my belief and trust in the army and its role." (At this point Gowon seemed to completely change his argument because the hated Ibos ran the first coup, the people he is now fighting.) "I said if a coup did happen I hope there are a few of us loyal ones who can save the day. I think this is what did happen. Otherwise bloodshed would have been unreckonable. I just escaped myself."

Gowon said [Biafran President Odumegwu-] Ojukwu's regime was effective in propaganda but it had brutally eliminated opposition and people were afraid to ask questions. He said Ojukwu had sent an agent to Paris to negotiate with the Rothschilds and had offered them all the mineral concessions in Biafra ("in inverted commas," said Gowon) in exchange for six million pounds. "He's clever. He can fool the devil himself."

He said: "We have never said we were at war with the Ibo people. Our quarrel is with Ojukwu and his clique who are forcing the rest of the people to follow a lost cause. I promise and will continue to give assurances to the ordinary Iboman, from the heart, that their safety and the part they play in this country is assured if they can throw out this demon and accept to join their brother Nigerians in making a great, happy nation."

He showed me the photo of a corpse (white) in jungle uniform and the identification card from it. Name Henri Block. No nationality given. Signed by the Biafran DMI. He said they'd sighted about ten mercenaries in the Calabar area.

Gowon gave me a copy of the operational code of conduct he had issued his forces and had translated into the main languages from English: Hausa, Ibo, Yoruba, Efik, Ijaw. It says:

> Many soldiers and civilians will surrender. You should treat them fairly and decently in accordance with these instructions.
>
> You must also remember that you are not fighting a war with a foreign enemy. Nor are you fighting a religious war or Jihad. You are only subduing the rebellion of Lt. Col. Odumegwu-Ojukwu and his clique. You must not do anything that will endanger the future unity of the country. We are in honour bound to observe the rules of the Geneva Convention . . .
>
> Soldiers who surrender will not be killed. They are to be disarmed and treated as prisoners of war . . .
>
> No looting of any kind. . . .
>
> Women will be protected against any attack on their person. . . .

LAGOS, NIGERIA, *October 31, 1967*

I called on Chief Obafemi Awolowo, commissioner of finance and leading Yoruba politician who is the great rival of Chief Anthony Enahoro for eventual civilian power. He was infuriated by the "prestige projects" of Mobutu at the recent OAU meeting in Kinshasa because he thinks the luxury quarters provided were wasteful. "We were all blacks, you know." He wants a common economic approach in Africa. Resources should be pooled and imports rationalized. Right now Africa didn't rely enough on itself and "we behave like beggars."

KINSHASA, CONGO, *November 2, 1967*

We arrived here at an interesting moment to stay with Ambassador Bob McBride. Everyone strangely edgy and untalkative.

Some time late last night or early this morning a force (perhaps 150 or more) of white mercenaries invaded from Angola, seized a railway train and are heading east into Katanga. Whites are warned off the streets by the embassy.

Bob sat with me at lunch by his swimming pool and, quite calmly, in his bathing trunks, typed out on his French portable a cable to Washington recommending we bring in some transport planes—either for the Congo army or to get the Americans out. Bob was summoned by President [Joseph] Mobutu who wants help desperately, up to and including the Sixth Fleet.

The Belgians left the best physical and worst intellectual infrastructure in black Africa. Result: a schizophrenia that tears Congo apart. Like training a child to be an athlete but not to read.

The coordinator of the Bukavu mercenaries and the Angolan invasion is probably Bob Denard. Bukavu mercenaries' radio nickname for mercenary is "Napoleon." There they are headed by a man named Jean Schramme—pronounced "scram" which is what he won't do. ·

Country is full of tensions; yet terribly inert. Tribal tensions, internal political conflicts, racial hate. Yet bulk of population is weary and passive. Thousands of blacks killed since 1960; less than five hundred whites. Mulele rebellion deliberately slaughtered all intelligentsia, under Chinese inspiration.

The U.S. defense attaché, a colonel, briefed me on mercenaries. Mercenary is generally straight bar-room type recruited in South Africa, youngster seeking adventure and money. Schramme is a plantation operator, once a Belgian enlisted man. Lots are here on fake passports. They are disciplined by fear. Most are pretty tough specimens who beat up or shoot dissidents. Bob Denard is a former French sergeant who knows all the tricks.

The Congolese army are rapers, not fighters. Only fight if convinced they are protected by sorcery.

KINSHASA, CONGO, *November 3, 1967*

Bob McBride told me that in last July's crisis they rolled barrels out on Kinshasa airport and every landing field in the country was blocked for fear of mercenary landings. I could use an extra fortnight in the Congo like a hole in the head. So we are going on Alitalia; plenty of seats.

The atmosphere remains very calm. Washington has agreed we can use our C-123 to ferry troops so Mobutu is sending off part of his first paracommando battalion to Kamina.

Bob and I called on President Mobutu this afternoon in his residence within the compound of the first paracommando barracks; a sort of pretorian guard where they live with their families, sullen, ugly men in red berets and tiger jump suits. Mobutu and his foreign minister, Justin Bomboko, were standing inside the large house. A record player was grinding out French jazz but there was a volume of Mozart near it.

Mobutu is a big man, thirty-seven, with sullen expression, easy smile, large veins swelling on his temples. I suspect he could blow his top easily. Bomboko is fat, round, short, with a streak of white running through the center of his wooly hair.

Mobutu suggested we go out in the garden where we strolled chatting until we sat down in a flower-surrounded nook near a bar, looking down on the roaring rapids of the Congo. Mobutu ordered beer and coffee.

Mobutu said: "My policy is to prove to the world that the Congo is right and is an innocent victim. My policy is to live on good neighborly terms with all countries. But Portugal is obviously in this affair. It is an aggressor. And we provoked no one."

He said about "250–300" mercenaries had come in from Angola, seized sixteen trucks, then a train, were now back in trucks heading for Kamina.

He said that in 1960–1965 the Congo was in an anarchic condition and "independence was a fiction. Since then (when he came in) we've gained our economic independence (nationalizing Union Minière du Haut Katanga). It is like the United States in the eighteenth century. Your economy required your independence.

"The Congo was an economic colony until 1965. Union Minière and other companies will never pardon us for that. We have now reduced the regionalism and introduced administrative rather than political governors."

Mobutu said the youth and some members of his political bureau wanted him to swing against the U.S.A. He said: "They claim we are too pro-Western. Nasser showed that Russia really helps a friend in trouble. I told Mac here [McBride] this is our dilemma."

He said the mercenary invasion plan was designed to attract Congolese troops to Bukavu, then attack Katanga and Kinshasa. It had been drawn up by a Belgian colonel named Félix Van Dewalle, commander of the infantry school at Arlon, former security chief here. "Certain Belgian officers are mixed in this," said Mobutu.

He said French, German, and Belgian mercenaries had been sent in transit through Portugal to Angola. Their aim was to foist a "white government led by a black" on all the Congo and "Tshombe is the only man who can do this for them." (He's still in an Algerian jail.)

Bomboko said the aim of the whole scheme was to take control of the entire Congo and reconquer the Union Minière properties. (Later McBride said that by dumping independence suddenly on the Congo in 1960, Brussels, which is heavily influenced by U.M., thought a dummy government would be put in, run by permanent Belgian officials.)

We then talked of other things. Mobutu said he had learned to love the "trilogy" of Mozart, Bach, and Beethoven from a "very pretty" music teacher when he went to secondary school in Belgium. He complained several times that "you never hear of mercenaries from the East, only from the West. These people are never Russians or Jugoslavs, only Belgian or French."

KINSHASA, CONGO, *November 4, 1967*

Bob McBride has eaten a few meals with Mobutu and his ministers aboard the president's boat in the Congo river. Among other things served is monkey meat, tough and stringy. They call it "Cousin"!

Yesterday the Soviet ambassador in Brazzaville came across the river to see Bomboko (there are no Soviet-Kinshasa relations). He offered Bomboko MIGs for use against the mercenaries. The ambassador said Russia could provide fifteen Congolese pilots they had been training. Bomboko said: "But these are Gizenga men (leftists). I'd be their first target."

LUANDA, ANGOLA, *November 8, 1967*

Here we are on the edge of the Congo once again. This is a lovely town, very Mediterranean-looking. None of the "Europeans Only" signs that humiliate Negroes and degrade whites in South Africa.

Factories rising all around the suburbs—oil refinery, automobile assembly, cement, etc. Luanda gives no evidence of the nationalist insurrection except for the very fit-looking troops in tiger-suits wandering about town.

I can't help feeling that the Catholic Latins (like French and Portuguese) are more relaxed with other colors because they possess more sexual self-confidence than the Protestant English and Afrikaners.

The U.S. consul general confirms the presence here in Luanda of seven mercenaries (all Belgian) and estimates that 100 to 150 have been here during the past four months. They come from Lisbon. A small group definitely crossed into West Katanga.

When [Portuguese President Antonio de Oliveira] Salazar dies there is bound to be a change. Until then there will be immobilism in Angola. The Portuguese have been brainwashed into a belief that they can't govern themselves; they are politically emasculated, wouldn't know what to do with freedom.

LUANDA, ANGOLA, *November 9, 1967*

I called on the governor general, Lieutenant Colonel Camillo de Miranda Rebocho Vaz, in his palace on a hill near the center of town: a most amiable fellow, good-looking with slightly dark countenance, a thatch of grey on each side, somewhat like an elegant Athenian.

I asked how he explained the fact that Portugal was the last dinosaur, that while all other overseas empires had virtually vanished, this one was almost intact. He said: "Perhaps it is because we see no difference between black and white. This is the truth, it is emotional, not just legal. When I was in Carmona [where he governed the northern province previously] my children played with the servants' children and went to the same school. We have black doctors, black officials. Merit is the only measure for promotion. It is this different psychological feeling we have that is most important."

The greatest danger is "a revolution in the metropole. We can't foresee what influence that might have on us."

The Portuguese have been interfering in Nigeria for Biafra and so have the Rhodesians, who run a charter line called Transafrican Air. São Tomé is the staging point.

An Irish diplomat has just been in Biafra rescuing Catholic missionaries. He flew them out from Port Harcourt to here. Says the Biafrans are getting more and more antiwhite as the pressure on them grows. Says he's going home to Dublin for rest and reassignment. Never wants to lay eyes on Africa again.

SALISBURY, RHODESIA, *November 13, 1967*

Have been here a few days: bored, gouty, and frustrated. When last I was here fourteen years ago there was hope in the air: the Capricorn Society with its concept of racial integration; federation with its idea of linking present day Rhodesia, Zambia, and Malawi. Now this is a stultified village dictatorship of less than 225,000 mediocre whites ruling 4 million restive blacks.

An old Greek friend who settled here years ago, gave a cocktail party assembling all kinds, right, left, and center. They are hard to tell apart, ranging from Goldwater Republicans to John Birchers. A pleasant man described as center, told me Rhodesia had the same problem as the U.S.A. and was handling it better. I pointed out we had a Negro minority of 11 percent, not a white minority of 6 percent; that we were settling our problem by granting equal rights at last. "You don't mean you're going to give them all they want?"

This morning I called on Sir Humphrey Gibbs, the last British governor. The Rhodesians have appointed an acting chief of state and don't recognize Sir Humphrey—but the British do. He is a kind of unperson. He lives in a pleasant-looking governor's palace, Cape Dutch architecture with nice grounds and lovely jacaranda trees.

G. said Europeans simply had to take the Africans along with them, although "not too fast." It was dangerous if no political experience or responsibility is given to the Africans. Their numbers doubled in less than every twenty years while there were very few Europeans. You needed an immigration of about 12,000 a year just to maintain the existing racial balance; and it wasn't coming.

Furthermore, he said, "You need masses of money to develop the country. We could absorb large sums and many people." But unemployment is rising, African employment is down 28,000. At the same time, there are about 40,000 Africans leaving school each year, building a discontented class.

Said he sadly: "We could be an example to the rest of Africa. The countries to the north could follow our example if we made a success of things. But the way the countries to the north of us are now going simply solidifies the people here behind Smith."

Ian Smith's propaganda apparatus had built him up so that "he now gets standing ovations everywhere no matter what he says and how often he contradicts himself."

JOHANNESBURG, SOUTH AFRICA, *November 15, 1967*

Visited Mrs. Helen Suzman, only parliamentary representative of the Progressive party, elected by the prosperous suburban silk-stocking district of Johannesburg, which contains a large number of wealthy Jews. She has an exceptionally attractive house with a fine garden and spacious lawn, tastefully furnished, warm, cozy, and adorned by a small and amiable Tibetan dog. She herself is pretty, trim, blue-eyed, and has just become a grandmother.

I asked whether real communism—as distinct from the bogeyman—was making any headway. She said no. There had been a small group of dedicated communists here but [Prime Minister B.J.] Vorster and the Special Branch had exaggerated its importance out of all reason "to end the rule of law." She then added with a flash of her straight blue eyes: "It is a disgrace that the United party, the official opposition, voted for the government on this."

Mrs. Suzman said there was a certain resemblance between the present indentured labor system from contiguous African countries and that of early America. Furthermore, there was a pool of voluntary labor seeking employment in the cities. But it was more and more difficult for the voluntary African worker to leave his district and to enter an urban area.

Mrs. Suzman told me that nowadays the word "white" was more prevalent than the word "European." Japanese who have invested heavily here, are classified as "honorary whites." Chinese are classified as "other colored." There was a famous pair of incidents popularly known as the "Sing-Song case." An Indian named Singh had a white wife who wanted to be classified as Asian so she could live with him but this was refused by law. At the same time, approximately, there was a Chinese named Song who had been accepted for years as "white." He applied to be reclassified as colored but this was refused.

She said: "This government is firmly entrenched. It is one of the most firmly entrenched governments in the world. The whites, who are the voters, are increasingly convinced that they must maintain their racial integrity. They are terrified by events in the rest of Africa.

"Our Africans are very different from the others. They belong to South Africa and have become used to our society. Despite everything they don't want chaos."

PRETORIA, SOUTH AFRICA, *November 16, 1967*

This morning I had a long talk with Prime Minister B.J. (John) Vorster in his office on a height above the city. Vorster has a rather somber, quiet way about him which belies his reputation as a wit, an orator, and a popular politician. He is stockily built and slightly over-weight, with a red nose, quiet voice, somewhat grim expression. He spoke freely, answering all but one of my questions with apparent frankness. The one he skipped was on the *Broederbond* [a secret society]. He spoke very deliberately, waiting for me to take down all his words even when I did not wish to, and was extremely courteous.

Vorster, who is fifty-two, comes from the Cape Province and graduated from the University of Stellenbosch where he studied sociology under Professor Verwoerd, who preceded him as prime minister. Vorster was a lawyer and during the war he was a member of the pro-Nazi *Ossewabrand-wag*. He was interned from 1942–44. He has never been timid about this experience—nor ashamed.

He entered parliament in 1953 as a National party deputy and was made a cabinet minister by Verwoerd in 1961 (minister of justice). After the Sharpeville massacre when there were many rumors of communist subversion, he handled the government's tough policy of repression.

He said in severe tones: "Economically our future and that of our neighbors are bound up with each other. They know this and we know it. Furthermore we have demonstrated in practice as well as in theory that neighboring states, in spite of differences in domestic policy, can coop-erate to mutual advantage.

"I visualize that this constitutional impasse in Rhodesia must and will come to an end sooner or later and this will eliminate the only stumbling block to South Africa's economic division.

"I don't see the future in terms of federation or confederation, only economic cooperation, no political entity. In general I am thinking along lines like that of the European Common Market. I don't envision any political tie-up with Rhodesia or the rest. I think that the existing political frontiers will remain as they are.

"My party, particularly under Verwoerd, has stated emphatically that it is *not* our policy to incorporate the Protectorates. Even if they were handed over to us we wouldn't take them. They are politically separate entities and it is our policy to assist them.

"Of course we cannot pour millions into a bottomless pit—but we can help them to help themselves. We have gone out of our way to assist them and we will increase this aid."

Verwoerd insisted that the different attitudes on race in South Africa would in no sense be a barrier to regional cooperation. He said: "This will have no effect. From our point of view, domestic policy is not a barrier to cooperation with anyone, black or white.

"Our basic philosophy of separate development is not based on the assumption that we think that we are better than the other man, richer or more learned. It is simply that we are different. We have lived together for generations and we know they are different, they know we are different. We want to maintain an identity as whites and they want to maintain an identity as colored, Indians, Zulus, and so forth.

"Segregation has always been the traditional policy of this country. The difference is that under previous governments it was horizontal segregation to a great extent. Under the separate development policy segregation is vertical. Previously the nonwhite could develop up to a ceiling, no more. That wasn't the intention but it was the fact. Now the sky is the limit.

"When we took over as realists we decided that the only moral and practical thing to do is to create universities for all the various racial groups and to enable students to be students in the full sense of the word; to give those who could qualify an opportunity to become professors and everything else and thus to take over completely.

"Likewise we are building up the black homelands. The Transkei is the Xhosa homeland; Zululand is the Zulu homeland; the Northern Transvaal is the Venda homeland; the Western Transvaal is the Tswana homeland. These are black nations which will be led to complete independence like that of Malawi."

I remarked to Vorster that it seemed to me the aims of his separate development policy and that of Black Power in the U.S.A. were strikingly parallel. He said: "The obvious difference is that these black nations have their own land and have always had it and it is not a question of expelling anyone as would seem to be the case with America's Black Power movement. You must remember our history. The Dutch settlers moved up as the Bantus moved down and each settled portions of the territory. The white man cannot own land in the black areas."

I asked Vorster what were the proportions of territory allotted to blacks and whites. He said, "80 percent of South Africa is settled by whites (including coloreds and Asians in that area); 13 percent is settled by blacks." He added: "If you include the Protectorates then South Africa is roughly divided 50-50 between black and white. We know that people say: 'You have 87 percent and they have 13 percent' but included in our 87 percent is the whole of the Kalahari desert and the arid Karroo region, whereas the blacks have in fact got the best land in South Africa, the most fertile land."

He continued: "We have always looked upon ourselves as part of the free world. We are violently anticommunist. We are the only country I know of that has declared total war on communism. We are even anti-socialist.

"All Southern African countries are anticommunist. We just cannot understand why the U.S.A. takes up this attitude toward us. Our attitude is simply that it's no concern of ours what U.S. racial policy is—and vice versa. Our domestic policy is separate development.

"I am perfectly prepared to learn from any country. Problems of race are the most difficult problems to solve. And I cannot conceive for one moment that the U.S.A. has solved its problem.

"What right has any country got to condemn any other country for following a certain policy—if the country that does the condemning has not even solved its own similar problems. You follow a policy of integration that is your business. I have no quarrel with that. But our policy, South Africa's policy, is separate development.

"It is my firm conviction that the whites, Bantus, colored, and Indians of this country will settle their problems in their own way and to the satisfaction of each racial group. It is my firm belief that whereas all the world is looking for a solution to the race problem, in years to come people will visit South Africa not only to see its beauty but to study our society of different colors, outlooks, languages, and religions, living harmoniously together in one geographical entity.

"We have more whites than all the rest of Africa. We produce 70 percent of the free world's gold. We have more uranium than all Western countries but Canada. We furnish 20 percent of Africa's exports. We buy 18 percent of Africa's imports. We operate 50 percent of Africa's vehicles and have 50 percent of all its telephones. We honestly and sincerely are trying to find a solution to our problems. Disagree with us or condemn our approach—but give us the fair break of recognizing that we are honest and sincere in our attempts."

He insisted: "Our blacks are the best educated in all Africa. Their standard of living is higher. Their facilities are better than anywhere else. Yet we find ourselves the whipping boy of the world." He recalled that he had said to a U.S. diplomat: "We are a small country but we would rather be murdered any day than commit suicide." Then with a slight note of despair he said: "Do you know what the real trouble is with the world today? The real trouble is that the leaders of each country have the solutions for the problems of every country but their own."

I 7

"HE WAS MORE FREE THAN THOSE WHO BANNED HIM"

DROVE UP FROM PRETORIA. AFTER THE BORDER, LOVELY FLAT road through the bush (low veldt) leading to Gaberones and soon thereafter to the Kalahari Desert. Flocks of doves took off; also plenty of slate-colored guinea fowl, partridges, and a turkey-sized bird, like a large grouse, called korhaan.

Gaberones is a tiny town. They say it has 15,000 population now but no one knows. People drift in and out. It is spread all over the place. It was built for independence (September 3, 1966) because Mafeking, in South Africa, used to be Botswana's (Bechuanaland) administrative center.

Botswana will develop fast because copper, nickel, and an enormous diamond find have been discovered here. There is a good meat-packing plant which exports, and large arable areas. Botswana is the size of France —220,000 square miles, and has only 550,000 people (10,000 whites).

Drove across this sprawling hamlet to the office of the president, Sir Seretse Khama. In a few moments I was guided upstairs, past an amiable uniformed policeman with a large black billy, to the president. His office is air-conditioned, dominated by a council table, a nice desk with flowers, phones, a clutter of papers. There is a large bust of his grandfather Khama III, in massive bronze, a large photo of himself behind his desk, and a colored snapshot of his English wife, the red-haired Ruth, and their daughter and three sons.

The president is fairly tall and has a very soft voice. He is getting quite a belly, which he admits with a smile, is very brown, wears glasses, a moustache, speaks good English but with an accent, is forty-six, studied at Fort Hare University College in South Africa and at Oxford (no degree). Met his wife in England and was dethroned by the British for marrying her at a registry (the Church of England refused). He was friendly, modest, and at ease.

He said: "If we want to help the Africans of South Africa, apart from taking in refugees and furnishing them political asylum, we should establish a relationship with South Africa so that we can talk directly with them. Those in authority there should come here and we should go there. There must be contact.

"Here we have a nonracial state and we believe that black and white can live together if an effort is made. As far as I am concerned, this experiment is succeeding. If it succeeds in Botswana, I see no reason why it cannot also succeed in South Africa and Rhodesia, provided good will exists racially on both sides."

But he acknowledged it obviously didn't.

PRETORIA, SOUTH AFRICA, *November 19, 1967*

Drove back by way of Mafeking, site of the famous siege in the Boer war. The country is flat and much of it semi-arid pasture: jackals, guinea fowl, partridge, dove galore. Mafeking is just a place (dingy at that) with no natural military feature, simply the center of a flat area. It was defended only with earthworks and mines. Today it is a country marketing center and railway junction: lots of Indian shops, idle Negroes, grumpy-looking whites; a rather foul and dreary joint.

PRETORIA, SOUTH AFRICA, *November 20, 1967*

This morning I had a talk with Dr. Albert Hertzog, minister for posts and telegraphs and health and renowned as the most right-wing member of a decidedly conservative cabinet. When I arrived in the anteroom outside his office, his secretary got up, shook my hand, and asked me to sit down and wait a minute "because the minister's gone to the toilet." I sat.

A few minutes later Hertzog greeted me: a dapper, small, trim, brisk old man with pointed features, glasses, white hair, and white goatee. He is the son of the famous Afrikaner general and prime minister James Barry Munnik Hertzog; he speaks excellent English.

Hertzog, who looks more like a refugee from the pages of *Trilby* than a right-wing Afrikaner politician and farmer, was extremely courteous, friendly, and indeed cordial. He waved me to a seat and a woman promptly brought in tea and cookies. As we sat munching I said to Hertzog: "I understand that you are charming, highly intelligent, very *verkrampte* (reactionary), and anti-American." He grinned and said: "That depends on what type of American you are."

I asked Hertzog what legacy the Boer war and the quarrels with Britain had left here. "They left a legacy of history," he replied. "They made the Afrikaans-speaking people draw together as a solid mass because they are aware of the dangers they have to face. And they left a psychological legacy, a feeling of guilt on the part of the English-speaking side and on the Afrikaner side a deep suspicion of England in Africa."

Hertzog is clearly anti-British in every respect. He said: "Our history starts in 1806 when the British sent a governor to the Cape to try and make the Boers into Englishmen, to suppress our language and to stir up the blacks against us. Our fight started in 1806 and it is not yet over.

"The English tried to develop a race policy against us and this was partly because the missionaries dictated to London what this native policy in Africa should be. And when we trekked north from the Cape the missionaries egged the British government on to follow us. When wealth came to the Transvaal, foreign financiers then came in and took over where the missionaries had left off, trying to egg the British on. Our history has been a fight through today."

Durban, South Africa, *November 27, 1967*

Last night I dined with U.S. Consul General Red Duggan and his wife, and Alan Paton, author of *Cry, the Beloved Country* and head of South Africa's weak Liberal party. Paton is a short, bitter-looking man of sixty-seven. His wife died a short time ago after a long and painful illness. This broke him up and he now goes out very rarely. Nevertheless he was very talkative.

Now he can travel no more because his passport has been taken away from him. No reason was given. He is quite fearless. On July 30, he gave a speech at the funeral of Chief Albert Luthuli, Nobel Peace Prize winner who died after being hit by a freight train (he was half blind and deaf).

At his funeral Paton said: "I am not allowed by some foolish law to tell you what he said but I will tell you what he did. He did what other heroes did. He stood up for the people, the poor, and the dispossessed. For this he had to choose between his Zulu chieftainship and what he thought was good. He chose the latter. They took away his chieftainship but he never ceased to be chief. They took away his freedom but he never ceased to be free. Indeed, he was more free than those who banned him."

Johannesburg, *December 1, 1967*

Last night we dined at Lawrence Gandar's, the courageous and crusading editor of the *Rand Daily Mail* who made a great name by his exposé of prison conditions (torture, brutality, etc.) in South Africa. He is a small, gentle man of fifty-two.

Also there was Reverend Beyers Naude and his wife. Naude, a vigorous-looking man with pleasant, open face, is a minister (*Predikant*) in the Dutch Reformed Church and was a member of the *Broederbond*. But he became more and more liberal, resigned from the *Bond*, and is now being deliberately persecuted in every way possible.

He thinks the U.S.A. should stop boycotting South Africa and, instead, should make every effort to improve cultural and personal contacts to infect the country with a more worldly spirit. Vorster is a tough guy and reactionary by instinct but he is a realist and pragmatic.

PARIS, *December 9, 1967*

This morning I had a talk for an hour with Governor George Romney, a nice, honest, warm fellow of no great brilliance. He said we shouldn't get out of Vietnam except on terms of an honorable settlement and that all our allies would lose respect for us if we didn't follow this precept. He is a decent man who would be overwhelmed by the presidency.

PARIS, *December 12, 1967*

Lunched with [Costa] Caramanlis. On October 30 a confidential courier from the king saw him in Paris and asked Caramanlis if there was nothing he could do to help the king in his present difficult situation. He wanted to express his support of the king while there was still a chance of saving something. He had heard that the junta was about to fire the thirty to forty remaining promonarchist generals in a purge. If the generals went, the king was finished.

Caramanlis sent word to the king that what he would like is the creation of a government of between twelve and fifteen ministers under Caramanlis empowered to govern by decree for about a year. The idea would be to "make the revolution" that the junta has shown itself unable to make.

Caramanlis would guarantee the colonels' safety and they might be sent as military attachés abroad the way the Turks had done with their 1961 revolutionary officers.

PARIS, *December 13, 1967*

A new *coup d'état* in Greece! Apparently the king has committed himself to overthrow the junta by force.

I called Caramanlis immediately. He sounded nervous, complaining: "I don't know what's going on. I have tried to get word to the king but I have no answer."

I pointed out that communications were cut off. "I have other means," he said. "He should have told me ahead of time—if he wanted my help. I don't know what I am going to do."

PARIS, *December 15, 1967*

Dined last night at Elie de Rothschild's. Before dinner I asked him about the Biafra offer to sell mineral rights to the Rothschild Bank for £ 6 million. He said that indeed this offer had been suggested over the telephone by a notoriously corrupt French agent here on behalf of Biafra, but the Rothschilds had turned it down promptly.

PARIS, *December 17, 1967*

Golfed today with Couve de Murville. Couve thinks the U.S.A. should have revalued the dollar by doubling the price of gold five years ago when America could have gained something from this. Now it is too late—and we are going to have to revalue anyway. The U.S.A. must take drastic steps to curb the balance of payments deficit and still it is inevitable that we will have to devalue. Nor will we have any profit from it when we do because of the decline in U.S. gold reserves.

PARIS, *December 18, 1967*

This morning Caramanlis called up. He has a bad cold which makes his high-pitched voice even more difficult to understand. He complained: "The king knows I am from northern Greece. I could have saved him if he had confided in me. The least they could do is ask my advice. They ask me to pay for their mistakes. The whole trouble with Greece is the mistakes of the palace. The king should have asked me to help. No one asks for my help; they only blame me afterward. I cannot afford to become ridiculous, you know."

PARIS, *December 21, 1967*

Dined last night with General Henri Navarre, who commanded the French army in Indochina at the time of Dienbienphu. We dined *en famille* at the Bordeaux-Groult's. Pierre Bordeaux-Groult was Navarre's aide de camp at Baden-Baden.

Navarre said that like many other people in the French military, he devoutly hoped the United States would win in Vietnam.

The outcome depends on the struggle inside the U.S.A. itself—whether America demonstrates the willpower to stay with it. Of course, one way of winning the war militarily would be to bomb and destroy the Red River dikes, but that would involve killing three or four million people which even Navarre acknowledged might be "excessive." It was odd to hear these thoughts emanating from the lips of a timid-looking little old man who resembled a prosperous small-town *patissier*.

He said Dienbienphu and Vietnam could have been saved even at the last minute if the U.S.A. had followed Admiral [Arthur] Radford's advice and bombed hell out of the Vietminh forces around Dienbienphu for five or six days. General Giap had concentrated practically the entire striking power of his army in that area and the target was perfect.

PARIS, *January 6, 1968*

Intriguing lunch with Victor Dimitriu, the Rumanian ambassador, who is leaving after five years. He is by profession a doctor and hopes to be assigned to the world health organization in Geneva. He says science has made communism and old-fashioned socialism impossible and the future is founded on democracy, perhaps like Sweden's. Russia gave nothing to Rumania, and the Comecon (Soviet Marshall Plan) was useless because Russia is an underdeveloped country itself, except in military terms, and can't help its neighbors.

He said he had gone to say goodbye to Malraux who had told him: "You are all Titos, '*ouverts ou couverts.*' "

PARIS, *January 8, 1968*

Lunched with John Loudon, head of Shell, a charming, civilized man. He says the big change in the European oil picture is that the Suez Canal doesn't mean anything anymore. Western Europe now depends much more heavily on shipments around Cape Horn in huge supertankers of 200,000 tons or more. These are very difficult to handle because it takes them nine miles to stop after the engines are turned off—they have so much momentum.

ROME, *January 13, 1968*

I flew down to see King Constantine. I must have spent at least six hours with him in a little unadorned study in the Greek ambassador's residence where he is staying.

The king was wearing a blue-grey jacket and grey slacks, but he took his jacket off in the overheated room. We had drinks from time to time although he stuck to Coca-Cola. The Queen (Anne Marie) came in three times to ask if we didn't want to eat, but I said no, we wanted to get the job done. She is a tall girl—close to six feet.

I started by asking: "Would you please stipulate your precise conditions for your return to Greece; also, the precise conditions of the junta; and where any gap comes between these?"

He replied: "It is easier to answer by explaining what they did after I arrived in Rome, December 14. That day Papadopoulos sent word to me through Dr. Doxiadis, our personal physician: 'Tell the king not to burn any bridges, not to do anything that might make the situation worse. Tell him I am sending the archbishop with my views.'

"The archbishop sent a telex asking me please not to do anything that might harm the situation and please to wait until he came here. Militarily my action had failed and therefore I decided to wait and see if I could succeed politically. Air Vice-Marshal Potamianos told me Papadopoulos had said: 'The king must come back. You have my full authorization to persuade him to return.'

"I can't come back until I get the things I want for my country.

"The archbishop's mistake was not to come right away, by airplane. He said he wasn't feeling well and came the next day. But he saw Papadopoulos the same evening and Papadopoulos had already changed his mind. He told the archbishop in that second conversation: 'Don't be in too much of a hurry. He shouldn't come back too soon.'

"I told the same thing to all who came to see me. I said I am willing to come back on conditions. Papadopoulos has got to do certain things first:

> He must publish the new constitution. He must announce when there will be a plebiscite. He must indicate what he will do on free elections for parliament. He must form some sort of committee, including judges, which would investigate political prisoners and see who is being kept in prison and for what reasons and to determine who will stay in prison on the islands and for what reasons. The members of the junta should resign their commissions in the army—which they have now done—if they intend to stay in the government. There must be a free press in order to have public discussion of the proposed new constitution.

"Papadopoulos replied: 'We will probably do all these things. But the king can't come back yet. Because if he comes back now the public reaction against him, because of the events of December 13, will be so severe that it will do harm to the crown.'

"I decided to leave open the question of *when* I return. They sent Potamianos back with a paper saying the government had never intended to constitute itself as a permanent regime: 'It fully intended to have a plebiscite and free elections as soon as possible but *not* before it could finish its work.'

"They wanted me to announce this. They had drafted an announcement they wanted me to make to the effect that 'I am very happy to hear of my government's good intentions. My return will be decided between me and my government.'

"The word 'my' was in Papadopoulos' handwriting. I turned this down as ridiculous. It is not up to Papadopoulos to decide when I go back. I'll make that decision.

"The situation hasn't changed much since then. Of course he's done some of the things on which I insist. But not all of them. He announced an amnesty—but he was clearly overruled by the junior officers on his committee. He had to let Andreas Papandreou out because he was also a conspirator—except that he failed."

The king indicated that the real blocks to his return at the present are two of his conditions: committee to investigate political prisoners, and free press. He speculated: "Maybe the top boys want me back—but not the juniors. They hate my guts." I asked him why and he said he thought their feeling was "To hell with the old officers and everything that went before."

He said: "Papadopoulos is keeping the question alive. On the first few days after my action lots of photographs of the royal family were taken down and they stopped saying the customary prayers for the royal family. But this was all resumed very swiftly. And Papadopoulos has gone out of his way to say in public 'Long live the King.' "

I asked why he had chosen December 13 to attempt his coup. Was it because he knew that many of the monarchist senior officers were about to be retired and this might be his last chance? He said: "That was one of the main reasons. But there was another.

"One general—Peridis—made a terrible miscalculation. I had been in touch with him for some time. During the Cyprus crisis he had moved all his troops to the Turkish border from Salonika. He said we should move before the Cyprus crisis eased too much and while his forces were at their greatest strength. I wanted to wait. I argued it was essential to get Salonika and it would be much easier if his forces were back there in strength. But he assured me we would have Salonika by 11:00 A.M. on the day we struck. He was wrong. He said Salonika was in his hands and it just wasn't. I wanted to wait—but he is one of the best generals we have.

"Of course, if we had taken Salonika, there would have been no discussion. Everything would have been finished. There would have been absolutely no further discussion. Did you know that in Larissa people were coming out with Easter eggs to celebrate? I would have had a mass rally. I would have spoken on the Salonika radio and I would have called the ambassadors up there to be with me. And all the generals who were hesitating would have stuck with me."

I asked how important he thought the young officers' group was in the present government. He answered: "For six months I had been telling Papadopoulos to get rid of the committee of officers. There are said to be about thirty-eight of them. I told him he couldn't govern with all of them. But now he has them on his neck."

He added: "The behavior of the archbishop hit me harder than anything else. He swore in a government while I was still in Greece. You know, he was our chaplain for many years. He handled my religious upbringing. Now the people call him either Peter or Judas."

I asked if worse comes to worse whether he plans to establish an emigré government. He said, "I haven't made up my mind yet but I don't think so. It is an expensive operation to run a government abroad and who's going to recognize it?"

Constantine said: "My father gave me certain principles that I can't go against. When my father died in March 1964 I put my hand on the Bible and I swore to protect the constitution and my people, their freedom, and their religion. I intend to honor these promises.

"From a military point of view I have failed bitterly but I did gain the support of my people—except for the Establishment. But they are just a handful ,and they feel happy when they can look around and say there are no politicians, no strikes, no communists. On the morning of December 13 they were saying 'bravo for the king' and on that same evening they were saying I was awful. But they don't represent the people and I don't care what they think."

The king said he was disappointed in the lack of support abroad. He added: "Here you've got all these big politicians in all these big countries talking about democracy. But only one of them, Harold Wilson, a socialist, had the courage to get up in the House and say, 'I pay tribute to a brave man.' What happened to President Johnson? What happened to Fulbright?"

I said it had been reported that one condition for the king's return laid down by the junta was that his mother, Dowager Queen Frederika, should not return to Greece. Constantine said this was "absolutely untrue." He added: "The subject of my mother has never been discussed. This is absurd."

He might be able to return if two basic conditions were met: a satisfactory date for promulgation of the new constitution; and adequate free discussion of its text before any referendum. "Then I will probably decide to go back. Because if I do so I will be in a position to hinder the efforts of the junta, to perpetuate its rule. If there were any trend in the wrong direction I could either speak out against it or I could get out of the country again."

The king then sent for his own private dossier on his negotiations with the junta—a red-covered rather simple notebook jammed with a sloppy assortment of papers. He shuffled through it and then read me the statement Papadopoulos had proposed and Constantine's suggested reply.

The basis for the constitution would be the same as that of the present constitution and the head of the state would continue to be the king. It was desirable to strengthen the monarchy and every effort would be made to base the throne on the "trust of the Greek people" and to take away the bad effect of the misunderstanding of December 13. He commented with a big grin, "Isn't that simply marvelous?"

In the second statement sent him by Papadopoulos, he was supposed to answer that he had "just received the announcement of my government" and that he agreed to its contents. He was to state: "I will decide on my return in conjunction with my government. I am happy that the political crisis has been cleared up for the national good."

PARIS, *January 22, 1968*

Spent yesterday with Chip Bohlen, golfing and lunching.

Before coming back to Paris George Kennan invited him for lunch with Svetlana Stalin. Chip says she is an attractive, warm, wise woman. She has no consuming interest in politics or ideology, but she admitted that her children used to complain bitterly about the boring hours they were forced to waste at school studying communist doctrine. Svetlana was staying at the house of [Lavrenti] Beria on the June night in 1941 when Germany attacked Russia. Stalin telephoned her, ordered her home and grumpily asked: "Why, at such a moment, were you staying with a man I can't trust?"

Good talk with de Gaulle. It is amazing to think he will be seventy-eight on his next birthday. He seemed thin, alert, full of beans. As usual, I whipped out a pencil and notebook, spread a list of typewritten questions before me on the desk and announced that I had many things I wanted to ask but would pursue our usual custom of taking notes but not quoting them. He nodded and set himself with a certain amount of curiosity.

I asked if it was true that he considered the United States had become too powerful in the scale of world power balances and that he considered this was dangerous and was trying to offset this fact by his policy.

He said: "Certainly your country is very, very strong. Maybe it is not too strong but it is extremely strong. It possesses enormous power. This is not the first time in history that one nation has been so formidably strong in relation to others but at any rate now it is evidently the turn of the United States. This makes your policy and your wisdom a matter of especial interest to the whole world. It is inevitable that other countries, especially mine, must adjust to this appearance on the world scene of such a formidable power. Of course we must do everything to seek an equilibrium, to restore a balance. Such is the eternal history of the world."

I then asked what he thought of President Johnson's new economic policy designed to defend the dollar and to curb investment in Western Europe. He answered: "I would not give advice to your president or your government. I have merely pointed out what our own requirements were and what we considered good for France. It is evident that the investments of your country in France, as elsewhere in Europe, had a direct effect on monetary policy. You used all your advantages including the export of dollars and your large gold stocks to further your interests and this had a direct repercussion on the system of the gold exchange standard.

"Now the United States does not want to change its policy on gold. It is lending to other banks and trying to conserve as much gold as is possible in its own stocks. The consequence is that the United States has too many dollars which it doesn't want to keep at home. It wants to send these abroad, to export them as loans and investments, in order to avoid an excess of dollars at home and consequent inflation. This export of dollars is used to buy up European enterprises while protecting you from inflation. Obviously Europe doesn't like to see its enterprises taken over.

"President Johnson has now announced a restriction on the export of capital. But we will have to see if he actually *does* what he *says* he will do. If he actually acts as he has said he will act, that will be good. We would make no objection. But at the same time, he must take great care that his policy will not limit foreign trade. This is what France fears might happen and that of course would be bad for everyone, including the United States.

"You know, I am not an expert on financial matters, but President Johnson has not yet brought about the increase in taxes at home about which he has talked. He has not yet done the necessary things such as restricting consumption in the United States in order to avoid the danger of inflation. Any serious inflation in the United States could have dangerous repercussions in Europe.

"In France we have no desire to see the United States embarrassed. The only thing we want is to see a healthy and normal economic equilibrium. And I must say that I doubt that if the measures so far announced by President Johnson will be enough to achieve the necessary balance of payments—even if all these measures are enacted by your congress."

I asked if de Gaulle thought there was anti-American feeling in France.

"No," he said. "None at all. Anything of that sort you might hear is the result of invented stories. It is simply that there are some anti-American *milieux*, especially in the press.

"What is really at the root of any such impression is the fact that now France follows a policy of independence. We stress what is of interest to us and, because we are independent, this does not always coincide with what is of interest to you. Thus, our policy of independence inside the North Atlantic Alliance and our separation from the NATO organization was not pleasing to you. And, from our point of view, we dislike your Vietnamese policy. All this irritates you—just the way our opposition to your gold exchange standard concepts is disliked by you.

"But this is normal. Often we resent the powerful intrusions of the United States and we do not accept its efforts to lead us where it wishes. But this is not anti-Americanism—the mere fact that on certain issues our viewpoint is politically different."

I asked if he thought a world war were possible nowadays. He looked quizzical, and said: "At the present time I think that is excluded. But this does not mean that such is permanently the case. Perhaps in ten years or fifteen years or twenty years the situation will be different. We cannot know today. For example, we cannot know who will be governing the United States, or Russia, or China, or Germany. Who knows, for example, what will be happening in South America then? You cannot exclude the possibility of world war in the future. But, as for now, it is not an issue."

I asked if he thought the members of the North Atlantic Alliance had been correct in shifting from a strategy of massive retaliation to a strategy of flexible response (*riposte graduée*). Rather wearily, he said, spreading his hands:

"In truth there has been no change by NATO. The United States changed its own strategy. That is all. The United States had a strategy of massive retaliation when it alone had atomic weapons, when it had a monopoly. But when the Russians got the atomic bomb and developed means of delivering it, your attitude changed. When you only had the atomic bomb you could tell the Russians that if they moved on Berlin, you would blow them up.

"But when they were in a position to blow you up, too, you were no longer willing to treat Berlin exactly as if it had been North American territory and part of the United States. That was when you invented the strategy of flexible response. At its last meeting, NATO just echoed what had already been a fact for years. Of course we were not concerned. France did not participate in that decision by the NATO organization.

"The whole question of United States military commitments is extremely complicated. To justify any United States military command over allied troops in Europe, the United States would have to be absolutely certain of using its atomic bombs immediately against any aggressor anywhere in the European area covered by the treaty just as promptly as it would reply to any attack on American soil. But it won't. That's entirely evident."

I asked if the implication of General Ailleret's announced strategy of defending against attack from all directions was not similar in theory to the idea proposed by de Gaulle ten years ago to President Eisenhower and Prime Minister Macmillan. (Ailleret, French chief of staff, recently wrote that France's strategy was aimed at all points of the compass, "*tous azimuts*.")

De Gaulle said: "If the United States and England had accepted the arrangement I suggested to coordinate among the three of us a closer policy and a global strategy, certainly this would have been a strategy of '*tous azimuts*.' It would have been capable of being applied in Asia or in Africa or anywhere. But this wasn't done. My proposal was not accepted.

"For France, therefore, we have had to take into consideration our own position. We are now making our own atomic arms. Naturally, we must be concerned with all points of the compass—just like the United States whose strategy must aim in all directions. For example, its submarines can cover the entire world. Although we are not nearly so strong, we also must devise systems of atomic weapons that are able to act in all directions. Who knows what the world will be like in several years' time?"

I asked point blank whether he had decided if France should stay in the North Atlantic Alliance—pointing out that I did not mean the organization but the alliance—when it became legally possible to opt out. De Gaulle replied cagily:

"Until now I have not decided whether or not to leave. When we left the NATO organization [March 1966] I wrote to President Johnson saying that France would stay in the alliance after 1970, when it becomes possible to denounce the alliance, if East-West relationships had not by then commenced to change very substantially. The decision will be announced in 1969 and we will have until then to judge whether there have been considerable changes in East-West relationships. Certainly until now there have not been sufficient changes in such relationships. If I had to take a decision this evening, France would not leave the alliance."

(In a nutshell he [de Gaulle] thinks the United States is far too strong; he doesn't believe in a world war for some time to come, presumably because of this American strength; but France is changing its strategy and by implication is holding the door open to Russia. If Russia makes some substantial offer to Paris, I suspect this country would respond by getting out of the alliance pact; but it isn't going to make any move in that direction until it has a very solid proposition from Moscow. And it hasn't got one yet.)

I asked de Gaulle if—whatever France's doubts on the Atlantic pact—this country would not remain bound in the Western European Union. WEU was a fifty-year treaty, not twenty years like the Atlantic pact. Therefore, wouldn't France be obligated to WEU for almost thirty more years no matter what it did on the Atlantic treaty?

He agreed; but he said this was a matter of "no importance." France would "stay in WEU," but this didn't matter because WEU had no power. "It takes no decisions. It is only a point of contact. The Treaty of Rome (which governs the Common Market) calls for decisions and therefore has valid importance; but WEU has none."

I asked if France's ultimate policy might conceivably seek to have an alliance with members of the Atlantic pact and, simultaneously, an alliance with Russia. He sniffed. "No," he said categorically. "That is not possible. Against whom would this alliance be? Against China? No. That is out of the question. Of course there could be declarations by both sides that they were opposed to war or opposed to aggression but this sort of thing is meaningless, and is not an alliance."

Should France ultimately withdraw from the Atlantic alliance, would this automatically mean that NATO aircraft could no longer fly over French territory? De Gaulle pondered a moment and then said:

"Probably. I suppose that is probably the case. I haven't studied the matter yet. I don't see the urgency of its consideration at this time. But obviously it would not be easy to justify the privilege of overflying our territory for certain aircraft but not for others if we were not a part of the alliance. Obviously, if we were to leave the alliance, it would be to seek a form of neutrality, something like that of Switzerland. Switzerland does not permit the military aircraft of other countries to overfly its territory."

(Here again I was fascinated by the hinted implications. De Gaulle made it clear that France is not trying to build up a system of dual alliances such as those Turkey maintained during World War II with both sets of belligerents. He doesn't seem to be contemplating any kind of military compact with Russia; but he does at least conjecture about the idea of a form of neutrality like Switzerland—which, of course, would deeply inconvenience NATO and be of enormous help to Moscow.)

I asked if he thought the new reforms announced for Britain by Prime Minister Harold Wilson made it more likely—in his opinion—that Britain would qualify for membership in the Common Market.

He said: "Of course, Mr. Wilson has announced certain measures, above all with respect to Britain's foreign policy and defense commitments. He says Britain will remove its military forces almost entirely from the area east of Suez by 1971. But that is only for 1971 and so far it is only words, not actions. We must see what ultimately happens. And even if he does do what he says he will do, it is not a policy he wishes to follow but one that has been imposed upon him by fact.

"Of course, the more England disengages from its distant obligations and the more it establishes an internal equilibrium by putting its economy in order; the more it establishes its independence of the United States—by all such moves it makes itself more ready for entry into the Common Market. It makes it easier for the Common Market to accept the idea of British admission.

"But you can't tell yet whether Britain will go far enough. After all, Mr. Wilson has spoken but Britain has not yet acted and there are all these other commitments. There is Gibraltar, there is Malta, there is Cyprus, and there is Libya. Why should Britain have commitments in all these places? There is no reason at all.

"I don't see that the program spoken of by Mr. Wilson is big enough, extensive enough. There must be an internal effort by the British to work more, to work harder, and to cut public expenditures. And all this is very difficult. France had to go through strenuous moments and I am the first to see how difficult and how arduous such a program is to carry out—if, indeed, Britain ever does it in the end. It is not easy for a parliamentary government to accomplish such brutal tasks."

I asked if his policy was to encourage an autonomous French Canadian state which would then be confederated with English-speaking Canada.

To my surprise, he went a good deal farther. He said: "I don't know. I have never told the Canadians what to do. But it is very evident that big problems exist there—in Quebec. I have seen this myself and with my own eyes. It is a fact that the French people of Quebec do not govern themselves and are discontented and I cannot tell where this will lead in the end.

"Personally, I think it will lead the French people of Quebec to make their own state which will be independent and sovereign. Such a state would be in charge of its own internal and external policy, its defense, its monetary affairs, and everything else. Maybe it might end up by being confederated with its neighbor or maybe it would be totally independent. I cannot foresee how the French people of Quebec will arrange their future."

I asked if such a deep interest in the fate of the French Canadians implied a similar interest in the French-speaking populations of Belgium and Switzerland.

"No," he replied quite categorically. "There is no connection. The French-speaking people of Canada are French but the Swiss who speak French are Swiss. [I don't wholly follow this logic.] The people of Quebec are French living under foreign rule. England took Canada and the Canadian French when France was preoccupied with other parts of the world. The French people of Canada are under foreign domination. In the whole world this is the only people subjected to foreign domination with the possible exception of the Arabs in Palestine and the Tibetans in China."

Since de Gaulle had mentioned the Arabs in Palestine, I asked if France's new and active Middle Eastern policy was founded on the desire to get into the Arab world so as not to leave it solely exposed to Russian influence. He said:

"Certainly it is not a good idea to leave the Russians alone with the Arabs. The Soviets are very interested in the Arab world with all its petroleum and with the Suez Canal. After all, if the Soviets want to send a ship to India, it must go by way of Suez.

"France can have a useful influence with the Arabs just as it has had in the past. But this is of course not a monopoly. This does not prevent other countries from coming in. We don't want to be the only representative of the West. Nor do the Arabs; and the Arabs certainly don't want to be alone with the Soviets."

I inquired if the special relationship between France and Israel was categorically at an end. "Yes," he said. "It is finished. They exaggerated and they continue to exaggerate. Israel must agree to evacuate all the territory it has taken by force although in some cases there might be negotiations adjusting certain frontiers. But they cannot keep what they have seized by force."

I asked the General was there any chance the embargo placed by France on selling its Mirage jets to Israel would be ended.

"None," the General said. "It must continue. Israel doesn't need any more Mirages. They showed they had more than enough in the war last June. Why, the Israelis took 8,000 Egyptian prisoners and lost only twenty prisoners themselves. They demonstrated a great superiority in armaments. If they had new Mirages what would be the result? The Israelis would go on to Damascus and Cairo."

On the way out he murmured that the press had been quite unfriendly to him and that there had been many hostile articles in my newspaper, although he knew I had not written them. I remarked that obviously he was aware that in an independent newspaper in a free press, various kinds of opinion, often contradictory, were frequently expressed. He took off his glasses and looked down at me with a humorous expression. He said: "You will recall Pasteur, one of our great Frenchmen. Pasteur told one of his colleagues that he felt pleased because the press was treating him in a less hostile fashion. His colleague remarked: 'Perhaps you think this is better for you but it is not. It shows that you are sinking.' "

PARIS, *January 23, 1968*

Chip Bohlen was appalled when I told him de Gaulle said only three peoples are under foreign oppression today—the French in Canada, the Arabs in Israel, and the Tibetans in China. "Really, the old boy is going off his rocker," said Bohlen.

Incidentally, Couve confessed yesterday: *"Le General est devenu un peu dur, n'est-ce pas?"*

Long talk with Georges Pompidou, de Gaulle's prime minister and certainly, at the moment, heir apparent. Pompidou is of medium height but somehow looks larger than he is: stocky, composed, with a most intelligent face. He chain-smoked American filter cigarettes as we chatted. We sat at a table in his office overlooking the Matignon garden.

He said two things were involved in the present state of United States-French economic relationships:

(1) There was a considerable U.S. opinion which wanted to boycott French products and services "for sentimental reasons." So far there was no equivalent movement in France. But Pompidou did not think the U.S. government could let this sentimental boycott movement develop any further. France has a deficit in its annual trade balance with the U.S.A. and in any commercial war America couldn't win because France bought more than it sold.

(2) The Johnson measures to protect the dollar were different. The president was doing what he could under prevailing circumstances. He had three main problems: the costly Vietnam war "always on his back"; the

dislike of congress for enacting heavy taxes; and coming elections, which made 1968 "a bad season for austerity measures."

If the U.S. government had more freedom of maneuver, it should obviously cut expenditures both abroad and at home as well as increasing national revenues through taxes. Furthermore, it was not a good thing for the United States to have a continual excess in its favorable trade balance. International trade must be balanced over-all and not too heavily in favor of one country. If anything, Johnson was trying to make the United States trade balance still more favorable, and this could not be allowed to happen.

Pompidou said France's new Middle East policy was not dictated by a desire to gain petroleum concessions. He acknowledged that "all countries are egoistical and if we can get a deal with Iraq, why so much the better. But the objective is simply that the Arab world and the Mediterranean represent a very important area and we simply cannot leave the Middle East alone to pass over to the Soviet side. France has a definite role in trying to keep the Arab countries really neutral."

Pompidou said France had been convinced last May and June that Israel was not "truly menaced" by the Arabs despite Nasser's threatening troop movements. Nasser was simply exploiting the prevailing situation but his "Arab brothers—as they say in the *métier*"—didn't want a war and Israel knew it. "I confess I congratulate myself in having said Saturday, June 4, two days before the war—that if a conflict came, Israel would win a smashing victory. On that day I saw Alain de Rothschild and a couple of deputies who came to ask for help and argued that Israel would be destroyed. I told them: 'If a war does come, Israel will win it within four days.' "

Pompidou said France knows "more than anyone" about the Israeli army because for ten years our forces and theirs have been in most intimate association—"almost in symbiosis."

I asked if the French Jewish community had tried to exercise pressure on the French government to influence their Middle East policy. He said there had been a reaction. Since the 1956 Suez expedition a habit of thinking had grown up which assumed France was always on the Israeli side against the Arabs. France's Jewish community had been very shocked by de Gaulle's press conference as well as by the arms embargo. This had been a moral shock. But, Pompidou said, "I hope the situation is calmer now. I personally regret the General's historical and philosophical exposé on the Jewish people and I didn't think it was necessary."

But he thought the fundamental in this instance was to retain the best possible relationships with the Mediterranean Arabs. It was silly to consider de Gaulle anti-Semitic. He never has been nor was he today.

I said that some people recalled that [Michel] Debré was an *Algérie Française* man and de Gaulle had used him to separate France from

Algeria; that Pompidou was regarded as pro-American and there was speculation whether he was being used to "distance" France from the United States.

He replied: "Of course, I am very pro-American. I can never imagine France in the Russian camp against America. But you know as well as I do how the General feels about the present state of affairs in the world. He sees Russia on the defensive everywhere. By far the heaviest weight, the greatest power, is that of the United States. We here in Europe—and I especially refer to France—must keep from being absorbed by the U.S.A. As a matter of fact, little by little I think this is bound to come about anyway but you know what we are trying to do.

"What you must remember is that the General thinks that after the Vietnam war is over, there is bound to be an *entente* between Moscow and Washington, and it may come at Europe's expense. Peking *fears* such an *entente*. De Gaulle doesn't fear it but he foresees it. After all, American and Soviet interests coincide on two points: (1) the need to control Chinese dynamism, and (2) neither wants Europe to develop as a rival superpower capable of acting on a scale equal to their own."

Pompidou concluded by saying there were no profound differences except for ideology dividing Moscow and Washington and ideology was losing its importance. "After all, when the Russians have automobiles, what will be the difference?"

PARIS, *February 2, 1968*

Lunched at Dolf [Baron Adolf] Bentinck's (Dutch ambassador). I sat next to Comtesse Josée de Chambrun, [Pierre] Laval's daughter. She hates de Gaulle not only because he had her father executed but because the French government appropriated their property. She and her husband are slowly cataloguing all the Lafayette (his ancestor) papers found in their château but will never hand them over to the *Bibliothèque Nationale* or any other organ of the Gaullist state.

LONDON, *February 5, 1968*

Lunched today with Sam (Sir Charles) Elworthy, chief of the defense staff and marshal of the royal air force. He is worried about Malta's future. He is very suspicious of Dom Mintoff, now leader of the opposition, and fears that Mintoff may gain power and turn Malta into a pro-Soviet base.

LONDON, *February 6, 1968*

Agreeable lunch with Denis Healey, minister of defense. He thinks the position of the U.S.A. in Vietnam is pretty poor. We could certainly lose and there is no chance that we can win. We must reduce our peace terms.

LONDON, *February 8, 1968*

Drink with (Brigadier Sir) Bernard Fergusson, until recently governor general of New Zealand. When President Johnson attended the funeral of (Prime Minister) Harold Holt in Australia he put his arm around young Prince Charles, the principal British mourner, and said, "It was good of you to come. I welcome you." Charles shook off the arm and said, "It's our country, not yours. We welcome you."

Talk with Roy Jenkins, chancellor of the exchequer, and widely regarded as the next leader of the Labor party, a pleasant-looking man with glasses and cultivated manner.

I asked why Britain could not become a western "Japan." Jenkins said Japan's economic position was not solely because of geography. Japan had the curious advantage of having had both its society and its economy destroyed during the war, and therefore rebuilt afresh. Perhaps it was a price of victory that this had not happened in Britain. Rather ruefully he said: "We came out of the war worse than any other country."

Jenkins said it was not a question of the British not working hard enough. Some countries work harder, others less. One cannot form impressionistic ideas. People here do not work an unusually low number of hours.

Likewise, it was difficult to decide what were the right things to produce. There was a certain structural imbalance in Britain that makes people consume too much. Therefore, the British imported too much and exported too little.

I asked him what he thought Britain's role should be, reminding him of Dean Acheson's remark that Britain had lost an empire but had not found a role. He thought it should be a leading component of Europe, but should not lose interest in the world outside. It should continue close relations with the U.S.A. Britain would be the most outward-looking European country. The leadership of Europe would lie with Britain and France and would probably shift from time to time between them. Germany will never have the political leadership equivalent to its economic position.

LONDON, *February 13, 1968*

Long talk at the foreign office with George Brown (foreign secretary). He was very dignified and Palmerstonian, although wearing garish yellow socks and bright brown shoes.

I asked how he thought Britain's policy today differed in aims and methods from the past. He said: "With the development of the world, the evolution from an empire to a commonwealth and then to a looser group of independent states, the centers of commonwealth power moved to other parts. Obviously, there was a substantial change which brought about new policies, more different in method than in aim. Equally, the escalating cost of modern defense charges imposed upon Britain increasing economic obligations. Finally, there was the enormous rise in power of the Soviet Union and the United States, both economic and military. This has changed the capacity of any nation as small as our own to have a decisive influence.

"Added together, all this throws us back to the necessity of looking at the idea of Europe, a clearly integrated Europe in which we would play an important part. This Europe would to some extent assume a comparable importance to that of our U.S. ally or the Soviet Union. But this new situation is not a total change in this sense: one should not assume that Britain no longer feels it has a role to play in the world. It is merely that the role is different. It is no longer the role of an imperial center, the superior controlling point of an empire. But we would not only be in Europe, we would continue our connections with the loose commonwealth, our special connections with the United States, thus giving us a better opportunity to play a role extending in various directions."

I asked him what he personally meant by "Europe." He said: "The largest number of Western European countries that can get together and accept common obligations. I suppose by that I certainly mean the Common Market six, plus the Danes, the Norwegians, the Irish, and ourselves.

"There are, of course, other nations that would have difficulty in accepting all the obligations that must be assumed and especially the so-called neutrals, like Switzerland. Perhaps they can be embraced in some kind of associated status, but obviously they cannot be fully integrated."

Late this afternoon, saw Edward (Ted) Heath. He doesn't give one a feeling of being charismatic; simply an intelligent, agreeable, and cultivated fellow.

He said on Europe that the Tories had committed themselves many years ago, whereas Labor was a very recent convert and no one could tell how deep the conviction went. Europeans have no doubts about the Conservatives, but they do about Labor. After all, the 1966 election was fought partly on the issue that Labor was against Europe.

On the U.S.A. the Labor government was always being hounded by an anti-American left wing which keeps hitting Wilson on the subject of Vietnam. He thinks the Tories had healthier relations with the U.S.A. when they were in power, based on respectable public positions and frank private talks.

The Tories thought it was extremely foolish for the Labor government to pull out of the Middle East and the Far East, as was now being done. British income from the Persian Gulf region was very important, so that it was ridiculous to withdraw from that area for a saving of only £12.5 million a year.

I asked him if it would be possible for a Tory government to reverse recent Labor policy decisions. He said this would depend on how quickly the government runs down the forces that are to be taken out by 1971. When Lee Kuan Yew, prime minister of Singapore, came here, he dined with Heath as soon as he arrived and said the objective of his visit was to get a promise from the Labor government that the last date for a final withdrawal from Singapore would be later than the last date possible for the next general election. A general election must be held by March 31, 1971. Lee managed to get the final withdrawal postponed until December of that year.

Now the big issue would be whether there was anything left in Singapore by that date. Anyway, Heath said, once you announced you are going to withdraw all your influence goes.

Heath kept insisting that nobody believes Harold Wilson is genuine in his efforts to get into Europe. He was also very bitter on the subject of South Africa. He said the refusal to sell arms there was a *quid pro quo* to make peace with Wilson's left wing.

LONDON, *February 17, 1968*

We have been staying at the [David] Bruces (U.S. ambassador) all week. He is a most excellent human being, straight as an arrow, handsome, tall, gracious, alert, and keen. As for Evangeline, she is the only woman I have ever known who has actually become more beautiful and younger-looking over a period of twenty years.

Last night we sat up until midnight gassing. In 1958, when David was still ambassador in Germany, he went to Spandau Prison at the request of Jack McCloy in order to see Albert Speer, one of the three remaining Nuremberg war criminals still incarcerated there. McCloy had never been satisfied with the conviction of Speer, who headed Hitler's armaments industry and ended up as economic czar, because Speer's only crime was that of efficiency. His remarkable efforts had largely negated the success of our bombing campaign. He was finally convicted, like Alfried Krupp von Bohlen und Halbach for using slave labor.

At this point David observed that the conviction and imprisonment of young Krupp had only been because his father (Gustav Krupp von Bohlen und Halbach) was too ill to face the court. This was the first time in history that a son had been allowed to substitute for the crimes of his father, such as they were.

Bruce had been admitted to Spandau. A Russian officer was in charge that day. He was taken to a garden compound. On a bench Rudolph Hess was sitting—in silence—obviously insane. On another bench was Baldur von Schirach, whom David describes as hateful. Near one wall Speer was digging potatoes. Bruce introduced himself as the American ambassador and said he had a message from McCloy.

He took David to his cell because it was easier to talk there. There was no light except a window high on the wall. The wall was covered with pictures and writings. But Speer said these hobbies had cost him dearly because he was allowed no other light and was losing his sight. He said the worst thing about his imprisonment was that it was not solitary. He, Hess, and Schirach hated each other and didn't speak to each other but were forced often to be together, even to go to the toilet and the shower together.

We then talked about Hemingway. Bruce first met Hemingway during the summer of 1944 when David, a colonel in the U.S. army, was head of the OSS detachment then about fifteen miles from Rambouillet, shortly before the liberation of Paris. Hemingway showed up and they established an immediate rapport and made a date to meet the next afternoon in Rambouillet because Hemingway's scouting had indicated it was to be evacuated by the Germans. David was the senior American officer "*sur place*." Finally, General [Jean] Leclerc joined them, arriving with his French armored division.

Bruce and Hemingway each had jeeps and incorporated themselves into Leclerc's column and entered Paris with him. David said Hemingway was always festooned with arms and his room in the Rambouillet Hotel looked like an arsenal, but when there was an investigation by the U.S. army inspector general as to whether Hemingway had violated his war correspondent's status, David was able to swear he had never seen Hemingway "use" arms.

Hemingway hated Leclerc and Bruce thinks this was because of personal vanity. He didn't like to see anybody else get into the limelight. In fact, Carlos Baker, a Princeton professor who is doing a life of Hemingway, sent Bruce an account of the entry into Paris written by Hemingway, and David says it was completely fictional, Ernest of course playing the main role. Bruce sent it back to Baker saying he couldn't really remember the event well. Hemingway was obsessed by vanity.

When David eventually was able to get to the Ritz Hotel, he entered together with Hemingway and Captain Lester Armour, also of the OSS. They were greeted by the manager who was most impressed to see Bruce again, plus one of the famous Chicago millionaire Armours. He didn't know Hemingway who had never stayed there. He asked David if he wanted anything to drink. "Yes," Bruce replied, "seventy martinis." He then waved to the batch of ill-assorted, rough-and-tumble FFIs who had rumbled up in a truck with him, invited them into the garden, and they all sat around while Auzello produced the drinks. To David's astonishment, a long time later he was billed about $1,000 for the Ritz's wartime hospitality.

PARIS, *March 5, 1968*

Lunched today with Étienne Manac'h who has been head of the Asian department of the *Quai d'Orsay* for eight years. Manac'h assured me categorically that if the U.S.A. announces a cease-bombing—or conveys such a guarantee to Hanoi secretly—the north promises *immediate* negotiations.

Unfortunately, the conflict has now become "an American war aided by South Vietnam" instead of a "South Vietnamese war aided by the U.S.A." Washington finds it is unable to de-Americanize the war sufficiently to make Saigon assume enough responsibility and become strong.

Saigon only controls the cities. A mile or two outside of any city the Vietcong *is* the government. The U.S.A. is only supported by a clique of officers, not by the population. The peasants support the Vietcong because there has been no agrarian reform since the Diem regime and Diem's reform was minimal. The Vietcong constantly promises the peasants they can keep the land they till.

The last thing Manac'h said as we parted was, "Be sure and tell your son to be prudent when he goes to Vietnam. You remember when the three of us lunched together and I told him to be prudent and then the Tet offensive came. Now tell him on my behalf to be even more prudent and tell him again."

PARIS, *March 6, 1968*

Lunched with Jean Soutou, *inspecteur général des postes diplomatiques et consulaires*, a brilliant, intense Basque. Soutou is a strong supporter of Mendès-France.

He said that the column I published on Wednesday, December 28, 1966, was the best thing he had ever seen on de Gaulle's policy and that I had grasped reality by intuition. This column said:

> De Gaulle seems to be trying to evolve for France a very complex version of the balance of power policy first practiced by the papal states and later taken over by England. As I see it, France would like, in a series of concentric rings, first to attain ascendancy in Western Europe and then to make Western Europe the leader in a continental bloc between Britain and Russia. Ultimately that bloc would be established as a major peacetime voice in global affairs. Nevertheless, if its influence were shattered by a war, it is conceived, I believe, as aligned with the West.

Soutou says de Gaulle's is the classical French policy of keeping Germany weak and divided and excluding Britain from Europe. This is not because Britain would be a "Trojan horse" for American influence; even an anti-American Britain would diminish France's authority.

Soutou had a very interesting analysis of why the Élysée announced de Gaulle had received me this last time. He said I had always been too discreet in the past so people couldn't be sure if what I wrote had really come from the General. This time de Gaulle wanted to make sure that people knew it was the real stuff. De Gaulle himself always takes such decisions and looks after the smallest minutiae.

Soutou says the tragedy of de Gaulle is that he is unable to fulfill the dreams he seeks. He is an example of what naturalists call "petrified instincts," exemplified by the wasp which, like the bee, continues to manufacture cells but no longer has any honey to put in them.

When de Gaulle visited Moscow, he made his basic policy very plain to Kosygin. He said to him that he was neither "ardent nor in a hurry" for German reunification. If, however, German unification were to come some day, all that France would permit would be a confederation, never another Third Reich. He made it plain that he saw Russia and France as the two nuclear powers in Europe, each controlling the only nuclear armament in the respective halves of Germany.

Soutou then said that in December 1944, de Gaulle had congratulated Stalin on pushing Poland westward into the heart of Germany "because this will guarantee the Poles and Germans can never get together." But when de Gaulle went on and demanded French occupation of the west bank of the Rhine, Stalin hastened to cable Churchill and Roosevelt that he thought the General was a madman.

PARIS, *March 7, 1968*

Long talk with General André Beaufre, who used to be French representative on the NATO standing group and served twice in Indochina. He had returned from a trip to Vietnam. Beaufre thinks the war is a series of anomalies. "The principal objective of the Vietcong during the Tet offensive was psychological. The principal U.S. objective was military." If the U.S. kills 10,000 Vietcong, who knows about it because they are killed in bits and pieces around the country? But if a U.S. strongpoint is lost or there is an attack in the heart of Saigon, it is a heavy blow. After all, at Dienbienphu the French lost only 10,000 men out of an expeditionary force of about a quarter of a million.

The U.S.A. is fascinated with statistics. Beaufre said: "As a young officer I was taught to make the right decisions on the basis of the wrong figures. I fear the U.S.A. makes the wrong decisions on the basis of figures it believes to be right."

CAIRO, *March 17, 1968*

Long chat with Mohamed Heikal, editor of *Al Ahram* and probably Nasser's closest friend, and then took him and his wife, Hedayat, out for dinner. Mohamed is short, wiry with a keen, bright face. She is also small, intelligent, and charming.

Mohamed talked at length with Cairo student leaders after the February riots. They are serious youngsters suffering from psychological shock after the 1967 defeat. They had been reared on the story of how Britain was expelled and were shocked to think Israel could beat Egypt. They'd like to go to war all over again, reasoning that the longer they wait, the more Israel prepares.

I was fascinated by some of Mohamed's tales and urged him to write memoirs which should be a great success. His wife echoed this heartily. He keeps a detailed diary—even of telephone conversations. He said many foreign publishers had asked him to write a biography of Nasser but he felt too committed and biased.

We talked at length about Ché Guevara. Mohamed had come to know him well during his three long visits to Cairo. (His wife said he had a devastating effect on the ladies.) Heikal said he first was convinced Ché was dead when he read my column on him published October 8 in which I honored him as a romantic revolutionary. He assumed I knew Ché had been caught. I told him that oddly enough the column was sent and printed October 7 and Ché actually wasn't captured until the afternoon of the eighth; it was sheer coincidence.

Ché was a genuine romantic, a poetic type, not a professional revolutionary and not an intellectual. His education was not particularly good. He had left Cuba because he had a quarrel with Raúl Castro and Fidel turned cold toward him. He went to Tanzania for a while, where the Cubans have a Negro ambassador who was a union leader. He also went from Cairo to Algiers; and later to the Congo. Mohamed never saw him after the Congo, but the Cuban ambassador in Dar es Salaam later told him Guevara had been deeply disappointed, indeed horrified, by the Congo rebels. Mohamed agreed that it was best that Ché, as a poet, died when and as he did; no one could imagine him a fat man of sixty-five.

CAIRO, *March 21, 1968*

This morning I dropped in on Heikal. He took me to the immensely impressive new fourteen-story office *Al Ahram* has built and will move into this May.

He told me that this morning Israel invaded Jordan with armored columns and helicopters to punish terrorists' bases. (Later in the day this event canceled my scheduled 6:00 P.M. talk with Nasser.)

Heikal says U.S. and Western influence are declining; that in ten years there will be 4 million Israelis against 100 million Arabs who are developing also, as well as the Israelis. If necessary the Arabs were ready to join the Soviet bloc to win, that the U.S.A. has a bad policy and hardly any influence left.

CAIRO, *March 22, 1968*

This evening I went for a drink with Sir Harold Beeley, British ambassador. He has the disturbing theory that if another explosion comes in the Middle East Russia may not stay out. She stayed out in June 1967 because she knew America would not permit Israel's destruction. However, Russia might decide to intervene in Sinai if Egypt were attacked and to move up as far as the old international boundary, announcing in advance that this was its intention. It would be hard for the U.S.A. to intervene on Israel's behalf under such circumstances.

PARIS, *April 1, 1968*

Lunched at the [Costa] Caramanlises (ex-Greek prime minister) in honor of Malraux. Malraux looked very bad. I was struck by how Roman his face looks nowadays; decline and fall epoch.

He talked interestingly about Joan of Arc. He said there is considerable suspicion that she was the bastard daughter of Isabeau de Bavière (who was the queen of Charles VI) and that therefore she was the half sister of the dauphin whom she had crowned as Charles VII. Isabeau was famous as the most lecherous of French queens and she slept around a lot in both Burgundy and Lorraine.

Had Joan been half sister of Charles, it would explain how they recognized each other. Under medieval law witches were burned with a sack over their face, so it never could be proven that Joan was actually the woman who died at the stake. There were many legends afterwards that she had reappeared. Charles VII took the lead in reestablishing her reputation after the burning—by formal procedures. Maybe he first sold her out—from jealousy. The Vatican has always refused to make public its own records on this curious affair. Incidentally, Charles VI went mad with syphilis. The only other French king known to have been syphilitic, says Malraux, was François I who died of it.

PARIS, *April 5, 1968*

Lunched with the Comte and Comtesse de Paris and Prince Michael and Princess Marina of Greece. Young Michael's mother was the sister of the count, and when she died (Michael's father was already dead) the young Greek prince was brought up in the French pretender's family.

The count, who is now nearly sixty, looks like a modern-dress replica of his ancestors: very thin, a death's head face with elegant pencil moustache and light blue eyes staring out of a dead yellow skull. He says de Gaulle is going to stay in power for a long time and just likes playing with various potential successors, moving them around like puppets.

PARIS, *April 11, 1968*

Unusually interesting lunch with Manac'h. The present search for peace really started when Washington leaked the news that Westmoreland had sought reinforcements of 206,000 men and that these had been refused.

Hanoi recognized immediately that this meant a profound change of strategy.

Last month Bill Sullivan, U.S. ambassador to Laos, came through here on a brief trip. Sullivan explained to Manac'h that Clark Clifford's succession to McNamara was entirely consonant with a peace policy. In France it was necessary for a general (de Gaulle) to quell the army in 1958. In the U.S.A. it was necessary for a "hawk" to keep the hawks in our military under control.

PARIS, *April 19, 1968*

Hervé and Nicole Alphand gave a very small, informal lunch today at their lovely and cozy apartment on the Rue de Grenelle for Al [General Alfred M.] Gruenther, who is here on an overnight visit. Present were: General Michel Fourquet, who has succeeded the late General Ailleret as chief of the French armed forces, and Gaston Palewski—plus womenfolk.

Fourquet made the point that North Vietnamese losses were nowhere near as high, proportionately, as those suffered by the French and other nations in World War I, and there was a lot of staying power left.

PARIS, *April 21, 1968*

Golfed and lunched with Couve today. At one point we were discussing superstition and I remarked that (B.J.) Vorster, the prime minister of South Africa, was immensely superstitious and had a blind faith in the number thirteen. Couve was very surprised. He said: "It is incomprehensible for a Protestant to be superstitious."

PARIS, *April 24, 1968*

Pleasant lunch with Walter Eytan, the Israeli ambassador.

He told me Dassault is continuing to make the planes ordered by Israel and storing them. They won't be given to anybody else but the final legal disposition is by no means clear. Pompidou had consulted de Gaulle and had been instructed to tell Eytan that France was maintaining the embargo and therefore wished to give the friendly counsel that there was no point in paying the large final installment on the contract—since the planes would not be delivered.

But Israel did pay. The French government got hold of Dassault's bank and told them to reject receipt of the final installment. But by sheer luck the Israel government's bank had already paid and received its receipt of payment—a half-hour before. So the matter was closed.

In 1961 when Ben-Gurion was received by de Gaulle everyone was startled by the way de Gaulle referred to Israel as a friend and "ally."

Therefore, when Prime Minister [Levi] Eshkol came here in 1966, Eytan was even more startled that de Gaulle started off his conversation with him by once again referring to Israel as an "ally." Yet, during May 1967 there was a profound change. When Foreign Minister [Abba] Eban came through at the end of the month, de Gaulle received him with only four hours' advance notice and warned him that Israel should, on no account, start fighting. De Gaulle indicated France felt no obligation to keep open the Straits of Tiran in the Gulf of Aqaba.

PARIS, *April 30, 1968*

Eleanor Philby, Kim's wife, dropped in and I took her out for a drink. I told her I had only met Kim in 1938 at a time I was in Paris when he was here with his first (Austrian communist) wife. She said: "Oh, they're still trying to find out all about that period. It is a missing period." I deduced that British and American counterespionage are trying to fill in some gaps. (I was best man for Eleanor's previous husband, Sam Brewer.)

PARIS, *May 6, 1968*

(Count) Motrico (ex-Spanish ambassador here and Washington) came for a drink. He says Madrid University is "lost" to the state, another world. The corridors are lined with huge placards attacking Franco, the church, etc. It is Spain five years hence, ignoring Franco, discussing Brecht and Ché Guevara.

General Pierre Gallois gave me lunch. Others present were: General Becam (director of the air war college); Colonel Auffray (in charge of nuclear-missile affairs at the Elysée); Colonel Arrouays (in charge of nuclear-missile affairs at the Matignon); Colonel Chesnais (chief of operations of the French air force); and Colonel Barthelot (an influential voice in national defense affairs).

Gallois is convinced Israel will have workable nuclear weapons within a year. Auffray asked—where will they test them? Becam said: "It is unnecessary. They can know ahead of time they will work."

Both Auffray and Gallois are convinced the Germans will get nuclear weapons of their own. Gallois says he is for this because it will reduce German complexes, and won't make any difference in the world picture because the Germans can never threaten Russia or the United States.

HANOVER, GERMANY, *May 7, 1968*

Lunch with Adolf von Thadden, head of the National Democratic party [NPD], a minority group of right-wing malcontents considered neo-Nazi.

Von Thadden is regarded as a potential poor-man's Hitler. I simply don't think he is intelligent, or fanatical enough. He is a tall forty-six-year-old son of a Junker. His formal education ended with graduation from high school.

His ideas are a half-baked collection of platitudes. My suspicion is that he is just being borne like a ship on the crest of a wave of minority discontent and will some day be discarded.

Von Thadden told me he was the son of a Pomeranian landowner. His mother, from Hanover, was half English. His great-grandfather was David Hume, the English philosopher. He was born in 1921 near Stettin, now Polish.

In the army from September 1, 1939, when Germany attacked Poland, until the last day, he was wounded three times. His half sister was executed by the Gestapo for treason. She had written to a clergyman she knew in Switzerland, enclosing a plan organizing the feeding of starving children in Germany after the war. She envisioned a German defeat and this is what got her in trouble.

I asked him who, in all his years, had most influenced him—people either alive during his lifetime or thinkers already dead. He replied that there had been three people—Bismarck, Stalin, and Hitler. Then he added: "And also, in a degree, Churchill." What a strange stew.

It is within the concept of a "white" unified Europe that Thadden sees the only chance of German reunification. The Russians must see that they require peace in the West because of the threat of China. All Thadden wants the NPD to do is to move step by step to expel from Europe the forces "preventing unification"—by which he means Russia and the United States.

The NPD's aim was to preserve "enough space for the German people to live in."

Thadden admitted he had been in the Hitler youth movement from 1933 to 1939. This was compulsory and every boy in his school was also in it. But a Jewish organization had recently said he joined the Nazi party on September 1, 1939. This was untrue.

Thadden wanted as Germany's borders the 1938 frontiers—minus Austria. Clearly he covets the Sudetenland as well as huge areas of what are now Poland and the Soviet Union.

BONN, *May 14, 1968*

Two hours this afternoon with Chancellor [Kurt] Kiesinger, the Teutonic Harold Macmillan.

I asked what he thought of the Vietnam talks in Paris. He replied: "When the United States is able to arrange a tenable peace it will be able thereafter to devote more attention to European affairs and to its own internal situation. I would like to stress that the greater the internal health of the United States, the better it is for all of us in Europe. Of course the solution of the Vietnam problem must not appear as a mere surrender by the United States. This is most important.

"I don't think a settlement in Vietnam would mean that the United States does not stand by its commitments. Over the years we have all come to know and understand the realities of this Vietnam war and we are aware of the difficulties and the problems involved."

He said his government had great sympathy for developments in Prague, which were bringing more freedom to the Czechs. Bismarck had once said that Bohemia in the hands of the Russians meant a Russian preponderance in Europe while Bohemia in the hands of the Germans meant a ruthless Russo-German war. Today, the problem was similar. Obviously, the greater degree of Czechoslovakian independence the better it would be for Germany's interests.

I asked if he thought U.S. policy toward Europe—and especially toward Germany—had changed during the last few years and if so how. He replied warily: "The two big powers are now more aware of the necessity for crisis management. This has produced more contacts and some cooperation which could create certain difficulties for the allies of the United States—for example, the nonproliferation treaty. Don't misunderstand me. I am convinced of the necessity for more crisis management. But I am just as convinced of the necessity to consult the allies very, very, carefully."

BELGRADE, *May 16, 1968*

American Ambassador Burke Elbrick invited me to lunch. He said what really worries the Jugoslavs about the Middle East is this: Israel showed it could move fast, seize and hold territory, and the world didn't force it out. Belgrade fears Italy (backed by NATO) might do the same some time with Istria. What would isolated Jugoslavia, a member of no alliance, do?

Since the Soviet fleet moved into the Mediterranean in 1967 the Jugoslavs have been calling for *all* foreign fleets to leave that sea. This angers Moscow, which interprets the Belgrade policy as hostile.

Burke talked about Tito's establishment in Brioni. It includes one small island he only uses in the summer, where there is a raft anchored offshore, a desk on the raft, and he has the newspapers and documents rowed out to him. As a youngster he was a metal worker and this is still his hobby. So he has one den with a desk in it, surrounded by metalworking gadgets.

I 8

TITO: "I AM NOT THINKING OF ANY SUCCESSOR"

BELGRADE, *May 16, 1968*

THIS AFTERNOON I SPENT AN HOUR AND A HALF WITH TITO. A YOUNG man from his secretariat called for me in a chauffeured black Mercedes and we drove out to the lovely Dedinje area where Tito lives. Armed guards and a couple of plainsclothesmen patrolled outside. A heavy steel gate slid inward on rollers after a guard surveyed us and pushed an automatic button. We drove up the driveway through the garden, filled with roses, thick lawns, a few pheasants strolling among odd bits of statuary.

Tito's villa is luxurious, but might be that of any small millionaire in Germany or Italy or Austria. I was introduced to a plain young woman who was the interpreter. Unfortunately, she was lousy. Tito might talk four or five minutes and then she would say, "The president thinks peace is the most important thing." Things were complicated further by the fact that Tito now speaks some English but it isn't terribly good.

When I entered the huge study, Tito was sitting on a sofa beside the oval table. General Vlada Popović, my old friend, former ambassador to Moscow, Washington, and Peking and now secretary-general to Tito, was beside him in an armchair. They both rose and greeted me. Tito's dogs, an old Alsatian and a little white poodle, came up to sniff the aroma of my beagle. As we sat down a butler came in with a tray of drinks.

Tito looked astonishingly well for a man of seventy-six. He is much too heavy but his hair is light brown (I looked carefully and am sure he doesn't dye it); his face is vigorous; his hands look no more aged than mine. He was wearing a neat blue suit, black socks and shoes, blue necktie, white shirt, and smoked four cigarillo cigars in an ivory, pipe-shaped cigarette holder during our conversation. I noticed on his left hand a flashy solitaire diamond ring.

I asked if he didn't think present events in Czechoslovakia, like other events in Eastern Europe over recent years, were a direct consequence of what the world calls "Titoism." He answered:

"I call this democratization, not Titoism. People in other countries are trying to democratize and liberalize situations that had previously been stagnant. It doesn't mean that they will follow the same path we have pursued in Jugoslovia. But practice in the past has shown that changes are necessary. We are dialecticians and we know that what is good today, or necessary today, becomes neither as good or necessary tomorrow."

I observed that Jugoslavia, in asserting its freedom to develop its own road to socialism twenty years ago, had made it easier for other Eastern European lands to do so. He said: "It was more difficult for us in 1948 than it has perhaps been for others since. Yet our desire was not to give an example to others but to act because it was a necessity. We haven't yet reached the end.

"We have never said any particular aspect of Marxism is outdated. We still use Marxism as our main inspiration. Marxism remains a dogma, but we apply it to our own special needs and to the international situation as a whole—as it develops. We think the truth of Marxism is more than ever confirmed today." (I noted that Tito never once mentioned Leninism; in the past, he used to talk of Marxism-Leninism.) He continued: "Marxism must be applied according to the conditions prevailing in any country; and these differ everywhere."

To my mind the big ideological shift of the last two decades had been that Moscow had joined the Titoist camp, not vice versa. Tito said: "They see they must change things as a result of their own internal requirements. As soon as Trotsky's idea of the permanent revolution was defeated it became evident that there were different roads to socialism. Nowadays, only China wants one road to socialism."

With special reference to current events in Prague, Tito added elliptically: "I now do not expect exceptional events there. I am sure Czechoslovakia will find a peaceful way of achieving liberalization and democratization. It is a question of putting democracy into practice; there is no need to change theory, only its practice. We here in Jugoslavia have often found the need to change practice. But it is more difficult for them to apply this change because they let their errors accumulate too long.

"As for Poland, the situation there is different and less known. I don't expect anything sensational. The influence of religion is very strong and there is more foreign influence." Plainly implying he meant the U.S.A., he said: "You know what I mean." He continued: "The contradictions are stronger in Poland. No socialist society is immune from contradictions, but that is not an insoluble problem."

He said: "As far as coexistence is concerned—the relations between states—we favor active coexistence. The essential question is European security. As far as security is concerned, obviously contacts between people and between governments are beneficial. For example, we had worse relations with Italy even than with West Germany, but we have now reached an exemplary level of relations despite our differing ideologies."

I asked if he foresaw the day when either a European federation or confederation could be established embracing all countries between the U.S.A. and the USSR, regardless of ideology. He said: "This is a big question. Already we have smaller economic groupings in Europe—like the Common Market—and the results are certainly not yet good. The Common Market, for example, keeps other countries out and this has negative results. As for a federation or a confederation—I would like to see a united group to prevent war. The main element is economic; economic problems prevent political rapprochement. A federation can't solve that contradiction. You must start on the sound basis of equality."

I asked what area Tito envisioned as within Europe. He said: "I don't want to comment on de Gaulle's idea of the Atlantic to the Urals. One must approach things from a wide angle." When I pinned him down, Tito acknowledged that perhaps a fair definition of "Europe" was everything west of the Soviet border, including Britain and Ireland.

When I brought up German reunification within a united Europe he commented: "We have always thought this was up to the German people to decide on how or whether to reunite. We recognize that two German states became a necessity after the war, but how they should be reunited is up to them. West Germany must see the need to cooperate with East Germany as two states and also as one people. But Bonn doesn't have this view yet. Reunification cannot come now. It takes time. And if Germany is reunited some day it can never again be as the policeman of Europe, never again."

I turned to Vietnam and the Paris peace talks. Tito said: "I want military operations there to end. The bombing must end. The Vietnamese people must be given the possibility to decide on their own fate; and the sooner the better, for them and for the world. If this happens the Americans will rid themselves of a certain hatred abroad. I know the people of the United States want peace but there are some Americans who are responsible for this situation."

On China, Tito observed: "They scream against us. They disliked my visit to Asian countries." (He recently came back from Japan and Iran.) "I did nothing against China. I only heard what I was told in those countries. It was plenty.

"But China itself has people who think differently from the government. And of course there is a responsibility on us all for what is happening in China. The fact that it wasn't admitted to the UN is a negative point.

The American government has a responsibility there—as well as other governments. Had China been in the UN it could have taken a more responsible position in the world. But an isolated China feels it must take a harder line. Nevertheless, China will survive—despite everything."

I then asked if he was making any new efforts to arrange a Middle East peace. Tito said: "We think things have moved a bit forward. The situation is now nearer to our proposals of July 1967. But events must move by stages. A political solution must be found, not a military solution. The United Arab Republic and Jordan accept this basis, and the other Arab nations have not opposed it. But time has shown Israel stubbornly holding the territories it captured. Nevertheless, now there are some signs of improvement. It is fundamental that the UAR and other Arab states accept the idea of a political solution. Naturally their situation is not easy with the constant threat of war. It would be better for Russia and America to find an agreed basis for solution. The United States is in a position to exert influence on Israel." I observed Russia could do likewise on the UAR. He replied: "Cairo has accepted on this point."

I told Tito I had asked Churchill, as prime minister, who would be his successor and he had said Eden; who was Tito's Eden? He answered: "I am not thinking of any successor. I don't want that responsibility. It will be up to the people to choose."

I asked if Djilas had a political role to play. Tito said, "He will never play any political role. Of course, he can write what he wants. But usually writers are rather bad politicians. If they are out of politics they can write more and better."

I commented that everyone criticized "blocs" but, in fact, they had prevented World War III for twenty-three years. He said: "The creation of blocs was a mistake. It provoked the cold war which lasted for a long time and its repercussions are still being felt. Questions of war or peace are not settled by blocs but by the nuclear balance between the Soviet Union and the United States. There have been local wars like that in the Middle East and that in Vietnam. These should be settled by agreement between the Soviet Union and the United States. Such agreement and public opinion are more important than blocs."

I asked if the position of the nonaligned leaders had been much changed by the death of Nehru and the fall of Sukarno and Nkrumah. He said: "The idea of nonalignment as adopted by the Belgrade and Cairo conferences has always remained alive. The question is now how to make this idea more active in keeping peace and in preserving the newly independent lands. During the visits I have made to Asian and African countries I have always found a wish to reactivate these ideas. Today the concept of nonalignment is accepted by many countries, even countries inside blocs like NATO."

I asked why, since the Balkan pact was so obviously dead, it had never been formally denounced. He said: "When someone is dead there is no point in mentioning the fact. The pact was buried long ago. We saw early that we could not be tied to countries in NATO like Greece and Turkey, because we are against all blocs."

I asked him, as an atheist, what he considered death and the purpose of life was. Tito said: "Death depends on how one lives. If you have done something useful it will survive you. If someone has played a certain role in life, even then the world won't go downhill when he dies. What he has done for the good will remain. Much depends on what one has contributed to a country or a people. History is a long process. People never forget what was positive in the contribution of any leader. They will always remember what was good in his achievements. There is a proverb: 'Happy is the man who lives forever.' What this means is that he has done something good."

I then asked what person had most influenced his life. He replied: "It is difficult to say. I have met many good and bad persons but I never lost faith in humanity. I have always been influenced by those from whom I could learn—and the greatest master is the people themselves." I recalled that I had asked Nasser the same question and Nasser said: "Tito—because he showed me how to get help from both sides without joining either." Popović laughed when I said this but Tito just gave me a blank look.

I inquired what he considered his greatest success and his greatest failure. He said: "My outstanding success was winning the battle to defeat Hitler here alone and to make of the Jugoslavs, torn by internal conflicts, a sound federation. As for my failures, there have been many both small and big. I remember them still but I prefer to look back on the successes. I try not to think of the failures. There are still problems ahead that we must face."

BELGRADE, *May 17, 1968*

Fascinating day revisiting Milovan Djilas for hours. When Tito first introduced us in the last spring of World War II, Djilas was bigger, huskier, a real Montenegrin, and he looked me up and down, said bluntly: "Ah, you are the man who writes that our Tito is slaughtering Serbian peasants with American guns," then turned his back. "Pay no attention to him," said Tito, patting me on the shoulder.

Djilas was a moody, fanatically brave Montenegrin poet with a bloody war record and was a favorite of Stalin. When I was coming to Jugoslavia in 1946, to drive a jeep down to Athens, Djilas announced on the radio that he would have me hanged as a friend of Draža Mihajlović. But he became my friend. In 1951 when he was Number Two in the hierarchy he asked me (at Tito's request) to take a message to the King of Greece proposing a Balkan alliance. Once when I reminded him of his threat to hang me he said: "Times have changed."

I hadn't seen Milovan in years. When I rang the doorbell to his apartment he answered, shook my hand warmly, and said: "But you have become smaller." "So have you," I answered. Both statements were true. He looked shorter and frailer. He is lean, pale; his hair is greying, but nothing like mine; his eyes are clear; he has a firm grip, a pleasant, smiling face and a tranquil expression, despite all the suffering he has experienced during the past fourteen years, including nine in prison.

Milovan (his communist pals and Stefanija—Stefa, his second wife—call him Djido) was wearing a grey-brown woolen shirt and dark blue jeans. He took me into his book-lined study and gave me a *slivovica* (he didn't join in because, as he explained, he got "pre-ulcers" or hyperacidity in prison). He introduced me to Stefa, whom I had never met: pleasant-faced, earnest Croatian from Zagreb who adores the ground he walks on, does his typing, puts up with his Montenegrin moodiness, suffers the fears and loneliness of his persecution. They have one son, Aleksa, a tall boy with pale face, blond hair, thin big features; Aleksa is best in his class at school and speaks quite good English.

We drank lots of Turkish coffee. It was a splendid day and I found Milovan, gentled by time, one of the finest, most sensitive people I have ever known. He spoke little of his suffering, unless I prodded him, much of his mistakes, tenderly about life and his friends, and tolerantly about everyone, from Tito (who has persecuted him) to Stalin (whom he hates, but still admires).

After showing me huge packets of toilet paper manuscript of his translation (in prison) of Milton's *Paradise Lost,* he gave me a page of manuscript as a souvenir. I asked why he was given such vast supplies of toilet paper without proving he had dysentery; and ink, pens, etc. He said the guards had loosely interpreted the embargo on paper handed down by the authorities and wanted to be kind.

After we had talked a long while I said: "This is too fascinating. I am going to take out my notebook and jot down what you say even if I can't write it." "But why can't you write it?" he asked. "Well, I don't want to get you in trouble all over again. After all, it was my column on your forthcoming book, *Conversations with Stalin,* that got you your last four years in jail."

"Yes, but I had told Bill Jovanovich [the president of Harcourt Brace] to give you the manuscript and let you write about it. I would have been arrested at that time anyway. Now not. You can write whatever you want."

"But I'll be damned if I want to see you behind bars again."

"Go ahead. Things are easier now. And I trust the way you do things. Anyway, what will be, will be."

So, from here on, are the notes I took:

"Prison refined and deepened my thinking, my ideas. Prison for a short period is good—from two to five years. You have the possibility of thinking about life, about destiny. But now I have been there too long; I do not need it again. During those years in prison I changed many of my thoughts on history, on policy. But I did not change my personal thoughts, my personality. I became more and more courageous. I cannot explain this but it was a fact.

"During the first period, from 1956 to 1961, I was in for four years. The second period was from 1962 to the very end of 1966; nine years in all, under this regime. And under the old regime I was there also, from 1933 to 1936. I had only one fear during the first period [1956–61], and that was the fear of being poisoned; not poisoned to kill me but drugged to change my thinking, to change my brain, to break me, to force me to repent. During the second period [1962–66] I had no fear at all, I knew by then that nothing could change me.

"During the first twenty months of my first period I was isolated, all alone. I was in solitary confinement only four months of the second period. All told, I had two years in solitary; but they always let me have books. But for two years I had no paper. I could only have toilet paper. But, using this, I wrote some books and started to translate *Paradise Lost*."

Milovan said he was in very good health (despite pre-war tortures, wartime privations, postwar suffering). He only has hyperacidity and "migraine headaches which I had always and which I inherited from my mother."

During both of his prison terms under Tito "I thought much about politics, although the second time perhaps a bit less. It is a very complex feeling and difficult to understand. I was in a high position when I started to change my opinion and I consciously got out of the seat of power. I deliberately disagreed with the Central Committee of the party [over his theories expressed in the book *The New Class*] and I knew they would overthrow me.

"I never really liked power, but I held it from 1945 to 1954. Power engenders suspicion in a man's psychology. He becomes unable to live without power. It corrupts him. In the end it didn't succeed in corrupting me; but it corrupts.

"I wasn't disappointed, however. I began my new life as an author. As a student I had started in politics, opposing the dictatorship of King Alexander [of Jugoslavia]. The first time I was imprisoned [under Tito] I wasn't guilty, juridically speaking and from a Western viewpoint, but I had really been aggressive toward the party and the government in opposing their views. However, the second time [over *Conversations with Stalin*] I was absolutely innocent.

"The first time I was a rebel and a malcontent. The second time I was not. I was sure of my innocence then and that it would be legally proved. I was arrested the second time only because I didn't capitulate and also because Russia was involved as a matter of state policy when *Conversa-*

tions with Stalin came out. They would have arrested me even without that book—just for seeing the foreign press."

He said he had evolved his "new-class" idea quite alone. But "I find that Bukharin had a similar idea of a new class although he didn't follow it up, he didn't develop it. Nevertheless, my idea was arrived at very independently."

I asked how he described his ideology today. He said: "Today I don't know if I'm a Marxist. I'm surely a democratic-socialist, politically—not a regular social-democrat in the Western sense. I'm an atheist. I'm a materialist. But not in a Marxist sense. Marxism is outdated. It is old-fashioned. The human being and modern society are too complex to be adjusted to Hegelian dialectics.

"I am not a religious man but I know that a human being must have conscience and morality. I agree with religion that a man must believe in something; but not in God. All versions of communism are becoming decadent. They must inevitably change into a new democratic society. This is absolutely inevitable. Communism is a combative warrior's concept and organization, and society cannot bear to live indefinitely in such a tense atmosphere.

"Imprisonment involves moral elements that I could not at first understand. But I knew. I knew from the start that I could not be broken. Now there is much more tolerance. My picture has been removed from museums and records and there are still the restrictions but everything is less rigid."

Milovan had written a long letter to Tito last year on political matters. He said his analysis had been totally negative. Tito never answered; but Djilas could tell from the Marshal's speeches later that he "was developing a polemic with me." He then added: "In the Communist party as in religion, if there is a difference in opinion between two men they sever all relationships."

I asked him about Bill Deakin and Fitzroy Maclean, who headed the first two missions London parachuted to Tito. Djilas smiled. He said: "You know, when the English first came, we communists were curious to watch how the bourgeois Englishmen behaved under shelling and bombardment. And we watched this little Deakin, the first. He had nerves, but he controlled them wonderfully. He was good, absolutely good. He was not cold and nerveless but he was conscious of his duty. But Maclean; Maclean was like stone, like metal; there was nothing that unnerved him. And Maclean was useful to us. He understood the Jugoslavs and he told Churchill the Cetniks were losing. This was very helpful."

Milovan said: "In East Europe, anywhere, there is no communism any more. But what you and some people call Djilasism is synonymous with democracy. Now I am even more convinced that communism must move toward democracy than I ever was before. I have always been fundamentally socialist. Socialism and socialist ownership must be the main force, but unfortunately this form of ownership is allowed to produce bureaucracy and dictatorship.

"I think that small businesses should remain under private ownership and the larger concerns must be publicly owned. But the latter must remain free despite public ownership, free to make their own and competitive deals with some other countries and other firms, just as they wish. And they should give some form of ownership, some participation in their profits to the workers in the enterprise. The present system of public ownership is old-fashioned. Our state-ownership system is rigid, conservative, typical of the revolutionary period.

"Likewise, we are in no way ready for a parliamentary system like that of Britain or France. We cannot allow parliament to control the government. But parliament must have its real voice, and there must be a free press, free speech, free trade unions with the right to strike. There must be a democratization within communism. An essential new force for freedom can be born within communism, inside it."

He continued: "I still think Karl Marx is the greatest man of modern history. He was a prophet, not a scientist. You cannot find in all human history any idea that has taken hold of mankind like Marxism."

I observed that Jugoslavia seemed to be going toward the East, diplomatically, and toward the West, economically, thus producing a strange schizophrenia. He said:

"This is true. But it typifies our history. Before the Turks came, the Serbian kings were tied through religion with Byzantium and traded mostly with the West through Venice. And then the Turks kept the Serbs looking eastward. On the other hand, the Croats are half-Western and the Slovenes totally so. The Serbs, Macedonians, Bosnians, and Montenegrins looked more eastward. This affects the psychology and also the poetry of the country. But, even though we have looked eastward, more eastward than the Croats, the Serbs are different from the Russians; they are more rational, more empirical, and less dark psychologically. The Russian will kill you—and then weep. The Serb will just kill you.

"Today the old split continues. Our modern industry is German but our ideology is Russian."

I remarked that Professor [Hugh] Trevor-Roper had compared events in China now with Stalin's purges in the thirties; what did he think? He said:

"No. Only superficially. Mao, indeed, was treated as a godlike figure, like Stalin. But there were major differences. Mao was the first Marxist to say that the classless society must be educated and developed in a period of centuries, not decades. Practically, of course, this means he is speaking in terms of eternity. He uses Marxism as a religion. He is even more convinced by his own theories than Lenin or Stalin. But his ideas are very simplified; even his Marxism is simplified."

Djilas said Mao was far less brutal in fact than in words. "His methods are not the same as Stalin's. Stalin had cruel methods in the party. Mao has killed no party leaders, even if he disagrees with them. Even Liu Shao Chi still has his party functions. And Mao has understood that what has come about in Russia now is the development of a new privileged class. He is trying to prevent the same thing from happening in China; but he will succeed only during his own lifetime, as long as he lives.

"After he dies, everything will change. Ultimately there must be an understanding between China and the United States. The United States is infinitely the greatest economic power, and the second greatest power is the United States in Europe, the American economic empire in Europe. There is a strange phenomenon today, the expansion of American technology, not of American military force. The only modern empire today is that of the United States. The Russian empire is old-fashioned, continental, not global, world-wide, and modern. America is a great military force, has a great military power, but it is not a military empire, only a technical empire."

I asked Djilas if he thought that the state—as Marxist legend says—can really "wither away." He said: "The state can wither away; the Leninist-Stalinist party doesn't exist here now; there are different currents, not just one current. The ruling government doesn't discuss abstractions like the classless society but practical questions. Dogmatism and its effects must inevitably end, so that Marxism becomes only one of the theories in a broader society."

I remarked that Tito now seemed to talk only of "Marxism," no more of "Marxism-Leninism." He said with a tired smile: "Now he is going back to Marx, to the young Marx. Now he is a Marxist theoretician. The young Marx wasn't a Marxist; he was half Hegelian. And you can't stop there. The thinking Marxists here now believe that Lenin and Stalin were wrong from a *Marxist* point of view. We are going back to Marx from Lenin the way the Protestants went back to the Bible from the Vatican.

"Democratization will occur here in Jugoslavia without any revolution; it won't be quick or easy but it will happen without a civil war. After all, in 1956, the trouble in Hungary wasn't a revolution in the classical sense. It was just one single mass explosion. In several days it was finished. There was never really a civil war. Today in Czechoslovakia a peaceful revolution is going on."

At this point Djilas went out to get a bottle of *šlivovica*. I looked around. Two walls were lined with bookshelves to the top and most shelves had two lines of books, in front and in back. There was a bronze bust of Marx set at the end of one and a plaster bust of Lenin in another. The apartment itself is very nice by Belgrade standards—about five rooms:

entrance, good-sized study, living room-dining room, kitchen, and, I suppose, at least two bedrooms. There are some good Jugoslav modern paintings.

When he came back I asked Milovan whether he considered Marxism really a philosophy or merely an outdated system of historical analysis. He replied: "It is a social theory with religious elements. Marx was a prophet, a scientist, and a fine literary man. He not only saw that society was changing but how it would go. He was the real founder of sociology. Comte was not; he was too influenced by religious philosophy. Nor was Spencer, who came later.

"But Marx is now outmoded, like a scientist, like Newton or Galileo. Yet he was the first to take all society as a subject for scientific investigation; and above all he was a prophet. He felt that all mankind was on the road to industrialization and the automation of his own life. He had tremendous vision."

At this point Djilas ventured into prophesy. He said: "The East and the West [meaning Russia and the U.S.A.] are going toward each other, together, not as societies but as countries: Russia has an old imperial idea but this will be changed and modified in the West as a great China develops and Moscow sees the old-fashioned danger of a yellow threat. You know, there are genuine elements of racism in Maoism.

"I am pro-Europe. Jugoslavia's future is in Europe. But Europe alone can't be a separate force; it must be tied in with America. It can't be a separate power, and Jugoslavia must go with Europe. Europe can no longer be a center of history; history is going to the east and west of Europe. Europe is too small and it is in a bad geographical position. To assault it would only be a single-front operation for the Soviet army, and you know what a 'front' is for them. [*Front* to Moscow means what *sector* means in Washington.] Europe cannot defend itself against Russia. De Gaulle may think it is true that it can, but he is wrong.

"And for one or two centuries the United States will be *the* most important world power, like Britain was in the eighteenth and nineteenth centuries."

We talked about his own personal credo. He said: "I'm a democratic socialist, not a western social-democrat. I don't want to reform capitalism; I want to reform communism. I am fifty-seven now and I don't covet power any more. But my ideas will prevail. If necessary to help them I might assume some responsible position some day, but I don't seek it. And if I do come to power ever, it will only be for three to five years, just to found my ideas.

"My personal possibilities are not great. Fifteen years have already gone by since I started to give shape to my ideas. They are more alive now than at the very beginning but they are in a changing form. You can't speak of Djilasism. There is a wide spectrum of democratic ideas and I am not its origin. I am responsible for only one aspect and I merely formulated part of the picture and what many people already thought."

I asked about his writing plans. He said: "After I have finished the novel I am still working on I will start to write about what I thought about in prison; and I thought much. Maybe it is only in prison that one can think of such things, deep thoughts."

I asked Milovan what people, alive or dead, had most influenced him. He said: "In literature it was Dostoevski and our poet, Njegoš, and our old epic poetry (anonymous bards). In policy it was Marx, Lenin, and Stalin. And as a statesman, a human, I like Churchill.

"I loved Tito in the past. He is a great man, although I don't agree with him. He is historically great and he did two magnificent things—the revolution and victory during the war, and the 1948 victory over the Cominform. In 1948 he was no more resolute than I and the other members of the Central Committee but without him there would have been only confusion.

"Politically he is a fine leader, very courageous. Militarily he was not a good leader during the war. He is more a politician than a military man. After all, our war was only a war of small units without a master strategy. But as a political leader in the army and in the nation during the war he was wonderful. His mistakes were only military, never political. Like Churchill. Churchill made many mistakes when he mixed in military operations. The Central Committee and Tito were really two things. We could have succeeded without him but it would have been harder and taken far longer. He was more important than all the rest of us together and all the major decisions were his."

Milovan explained he was forbidden to take any job, and he could publish nothing in Jugoslavia. He had to live on his royalties from abroad. But Harcourt, Brace allotted him regularly $3,500 a year and he also received his state pension as an old partisan leader of 250,000 (old) dinars a month (about $200). He said: "Maybe I can't buy a villa but we live very well, at a pretty high standard."

He then got on to broader subjects. "I hope," he said, "that we are moving toward the death of all ideologies; not ideas, ideologies. Religion was the first ideology but it lacked a social outlook; it was only moral. The first truly complete ideology was Marxism. But now we are going towards the death of all 'isms.' Hegel produced the last great philosophical *system* but he was not a great philosopher."

As we were winding up, Djilas said: "I learned during my last prison term that a man may fight against reality—and even win. The second time I was sentenced, my wife asked me: 'How can you endure this?' I answered: 'I am used to prison. I am above and beyond fear and difficulties.'

"She understood. For she also is."

BELGRADE, *May 18, 1968*

Today I went back for lunch with Djilas and Stefa: an excellent lunch, served by Mica, their loyal maid.

He said he had decided to translate Milton during his second postwar jail term for two reasons: Milton had vast courage and triumphed over blindness; he also wrote about the contest between good and evil, Satan and God. *Paradise Lost* had never been published in Serbian and he felt as an author's debt the need to rectify this.

Milovan said my 1943 articles on the partisans had not only helped change U.S. policy but had a profound influence in Britain.

Milovan today was wearing a neat blue suit and necktie. He said: "I was reading your book *The Resistentialists* last night and I saw you wrote I never wear a necktie." He grinned.

Milovan is most proud of the large painting of Dušan Silni (called "Victory") given him by the artist, Lazar Vozarević, who recently died at forty-three. It is first-class, massive, dark, menacing; looks part Byzantine and part Aztec.

He disliked writing the first time he was in prison after the war (in the 1950s), but it came easy and he enjoyed it the second time. His only prison mates with whom he could talk were ignorant, illiterate old murderers—plus occasional agents put in by the authorities to spy on him.

Now he doesn't enjoy writing, out of jail, "but I can't avoid it. I'm nervous and afraid of it but have to do it." When he was young he tried painting a bit and adores colors. Maybe some day he'll try again.

In 1951 Djilas went to London as the first Titoist minister to visit England. [Clement] Attlee was prime minister and Tito wanted help among European social-democratic parties. He called on Churchill, then chief of the opposition, in his house one morning, in bed. Churchill asked: "If you were a member of the Russian Politburo would you attack Europe now?" "No," said Djilas.

"I would," said Churchill. "Europe is weak. Russia could go right across, perhaps right up to England. Only the American atomic bomb can stop them." Then he sat up in bed and imitated with his hands the dropping and exploding of A-bombs. He asked if the Jugoslavs had been upset by the attack on them in his Fulton, Missouri, speech. "No," said Djilas. "We were pleased. It was a form of recognition." "No," said Churchill. "It was a mistake. But I have made many mistakes. I didn't think about them."

Djilas says he was a bad military commander. He had known nothing about warfare except he was a good shot, having often swiped his officer father's rifle to practice shooting fish, and he had read a few theorists like Clausewitz. But during the war, he held no regular command; instead he was generally sent to take up especially desperate causes and, "I almost always lost them," he added with a grin.

He says Tito is moving back toward Moscow—but won't go all the way; he will never sacrifice his independence.

PARIS, *May 23, 1968*

Last night Averell Harriman came to dinner with Cyrus Vance, his co-ambassador and deputy in the Vietnam peace negotiations.

Vance said the most interesting thing to him about the meetings with the Vietnamese so far was the contrast between their faces and their feet. They are poker-faced and bland, whatever goes on, but under the table their feet get more and more restless as the situation becomes tense. They smile only when they are angry or nervous; but the smiles are impenetrable. The shuffling feet are the giveaway.

Averell had seen [John F.] Kennedy in Paris in the spring of 1961 just before he went off to Vienna to see Khrushchev. He advised him not to take Khrushchev too seriously but just to enjoy himself. Unfortunately, Kennedy's advisers were urging the president to be tough. This was the wrong approach and the meeting was disastrous.

I recalled to Averell how I had prepared a memorandum on request advising Kennedy how to treat with de Gaulle, to ask his advice and defer to his age, etc. "You were quite right," said Averell. "That's my line with de Gaulle and I hope eventually it will be useful."

Averell agreed with my impression of Ceaucescu and also found him very arrogant. However, the Rumanians had played very straight with us on Vietnam and had sent a special envoy to Hanoi in an effort to help report faithfully and honestly to us. The Poles, on the other hand, had doublecrossed us.

Averell said he had been instrumental in getting Admiral Alan Kirk sent as ambassador to Taipei. Kirk had very cleverly set up a joint planning staff with Chiang Kai-shek to blueprint an invasion of China. In this way he was able to convince Chiang how impossible it was to support units once they were landed on the mainland.

Averell said he had been ordered by Kennedy to "get" a Laos settlement at the Geneva talks. I recalled a "fight" with Averell on this because I had urged partition instead of the settlement we got. Averell looked puzzled. He said, "I never fight with you. I like you too much and have too much respect for you. I don't know why some of these countries keep letting you come back because you always write honestly about them—not like H. who always licks their boots."

PARIS, *May 27, 1968*

Yesterday, while the revolution lurched forward in France, we took Averell Harriman and Cy Vance out to Mouchy. It was more or less like driving out to Versailles on the day the Bastille fell. They were still mopping up the barricades in the Latin Quarter, using army engineers, while we sat down to a pleasant lunch.

Vance told me about his Cyprus mediation. Last November Under-secretary of State Katzenbach called him in New York at his law office and asked him if he could fly right away to Turkey. K. had to know immediately for the president. Within a very short time Vance was in the air in a special Boeing. He had with him a stenographer and a state-department expert each for Greece and Turkey. His first immediate task was to prevent the Turks from invading Cyprus; they were all set to take off. He worked out a formula: Greece to renounce all claims to *enosis* and Turkey to give up partition. Both sides now seem quite pleased.

Chat this afternoon with Sargent Shriver, new U.S. ambassador to France, sleek, modest, and "American." He told me Johnson had offered him any diplomatic job he wanted but had specifically suggested France. Johnson had obviously been trying to get a message through to him: we were going to push hard for peace in Vietnam and Paris might be the center of negotiations. Shriver now realizes the president had already made up his mind not to run again.

I remarked that my French friends speculated whether it would be difficult for Shriver to serve Johnson while Humphrey and Bobby [Kennedy] were fighting for the succession. He said: "I think they should realize that our attitude is, 'The king is dead; long live the king.'" I said it hadn't occurred to me to put it that way.

PARIS, *May 29, 1968*

Lunch today with Étienne Manac'h as the Fifth Republic began visibly to come apart. This morning de Gaulle suddenly called off a cabinet meeting without even advising his ministers and took off for Colombey-les-deux-Églises.

Occasional trucks filled with people carrying the red flag rumbled through the Place de la Madeleine. At the end of our luncheon, Alex Allegrier, owner of the restaurant, came and joined us with a bottle of Marc de Chablis (*age inconnu*) from the private cellar of André Tardieu, who was prime minister of France from 1929–30 and in 1932. He insisted we drink this, saying that he would never sell it and the situation was so uncertain he didn't want to see it wasted.

Manac'h told me the present "revolution" was reaching down to the very roots of the government. This morning Alphand, as secretary-general of the foreign ministry, spent his entire consultation with the principal officials of the *Quai d'Orsay* discussing logistical problems. They have arranged a system whereby many of the people who live far away simply do not come to work, and those who do bring four or five colleagues to and fro each day in their cars. The *Quai* has commandeered emergency army signals corps services to help transmit diplomatic messages.

He said foreigners should not exaggerate the aspect of the "barricades" in Paris today. Frenchmen are brought up on a mystique of the barricades. Schoolboys of his generation had their books filled with pictures of various heroes dying on the barricades. Each generation has its own moment at the barricades. In France, the only way of preventing the sclerosis of the state is by erecting barricades.

Manac'h says that on May 18, when de Gaulle came back from Rumania, Pompidou had a long confrontation with him. De Gaulle insisted the Sorbonne should be kept closed, that the police should break up student demonstrations, and that all students arrested should be kept in jail. Pompidou demanded precisely the opposite policy; otherwise he would resign. De Gaulle yielded. From that moment the mystique of de Gaulle evaporated.

The government cannot get ballots printed for the proposed referendum because the French trade unions refuse to do the job. The government tried to get the ballots printed in Belgium and the Belgian unions refused.

This is a really revolutionary atmosphere—not in terms of violence or rumbling tumbrels—but in terms of rotting garbage and intellectual ferment.

PARIS, *May 30, 1968*

Yesterday in the late afternoon I watched a CGT (procommunist labor federation) mass demonstration against de Gaulle. The demonstrators walked from the Bastille to the Gare St. Lazare demanding de Gaulle's departure and "popular government." Most of the shouts for *"gouvernment populaire"* and *"de Gaulle à l'hospice"* were with exactly the same rhythm as the mass screams of demonstrators ten years ago for *"Algérie française"* and *"de Gaulle au pouvoir."* Here and there were red curly revolutionary caps of 1789. On the whole, they were a smiling group and many of the shouts referred to de Gaulle as *"Charlot."* Their flags were red, not black, indicating that the regular communist movement was in control.

Among the other shouts were *"Adieu Charlot, adieu"* and *"de Gaulle démission."* I could not help but reflect on the cruelty of history. Ten years ago de Gaulle came in with the tanks when armored units were rumbling across the Pont de la Concorde. Now they want to push him out with the garbage festering in uncollected cans.

De Gaulle disappeared from the Élysée yesterday and did not show up in Colombey-les-deux-Églises for seven hours. Nobody knows where he was. It is my guess that he must have been conferring with General [Jacques] Massu and other commanders of the French forces in Germany along the Franco-German border.

The situation is critical. The student "new left" which started this whole thing has now been joined by organized labor in a total assault on the government so that their catalytic role could become similar to that of the students in Korea and Turkey in 1960 when they were joined by the regular army establishments.

PARIS, *May 31, 1968*

Yesterday was moving and important. De Gaulle came back from Colombey, held a cabinet meeting, then went on the radio (television is blocked out by the strike) and announced he was going to fight to keep the communists from taking over.

A demonstration supporting de Gaulle had already been organized on the Place de la Concorde and the Champs-Élysées. More than half a million people took part. The demonstrators proved to be a good-natured, rather relaxed crowd whose mood was very comparable to that of the CGT demonstrators I watched a couple of days ago, although they were on opposite sides of the fence.

Right across the river parked along the quays as usual were the long lines of grey-green beetle-shaped trucks in which the CRS (armed gendarmerie) moves from threatened point to threatened point.

Lunched with Jean-Marie Soutou. He gave me a fine quotation from Chateaubriand: *"Le plus grand effort de l'amitié n'est pas de partager nos infortunes, mais de nous pardonner nos prosperités."*

Soutou has absolutely no use for [François] Mitterand who he thinks has excessive ambitions not warranted by any abilities. I remarked that Mitterand is the only politician I have ever known who has the serious aspiration to be a Kerensky.

Soutou was cynical about his colleagues at the *Quai d'Orsay*. Said he: "Yesterday morning [de Gaulle made his electrical speech yesterday afternoon] everybody in the *Quai* was pro-Mendès-France. This morning they were all Gaullists."

Soutou was absolutely fascinated by Malraux's account of his meeting with Mao Tse-tung in 1965, as recounted in *Antimémoires*.

The essential truth was in Malraux's observation that when he left the old Chinese communist boss, he saw a look in his eye that must have resembled that of the ancient emperor Charlemagne as he saw the boats of the first Norman marauders coming up the Seine. What Malraux meant was that Mao clearly knew that he and all his philosophy were doomed in China.

PARIS, *June 3, 1968*

Went over to the Odéon which has been taken over by students who use the theater as a kind of debating hall. The lobby is filled with scrawled posters and there are others attached to the main curtain hanging above the stage. Dominating these is one huge sign saying: *"L'ex-Odéon est une tribune libre*" and another says "*La Révolution n'est pas seulement celle des comités mais avant tout la vôtre.*"

A continual debate goes on with participants sitting in the armchairs of the orchestra and first balcony. Most were students in their early twenties but there were some middle-aged people present, many reading a student paper called *Le Pavé* which was being sold for the benefit of "our wounded." On the front page is a huge cartoon showing a naked body shitting on de Gaulle. At the door, collection boxes were passed for "our wounded."

PARIS, *June 6, 1968*

Lunched with Harriman on this grim day. The news just came that Bobby Kennedy had died. There is some strange hell taking place in the United States. Harriman and Vance are flying back tomorrow (Friday) for Bobby's funeral.

Bobby's assassination removes from the American political race the one man who could be regarded by Hanoi as a "dove." Harriman said Bobby wasn't really a dove and wanted a genuine compromise settlement without any surrender, but he admitted Hanoi might have misinterpreted it.

Averell described General Maxwell Taylor and Walt Rostow as bitterend hawks who wanted a military victory. He thought Fulbright and McCarthy were extreme doves; Bobby came between them.

Averell had just dictated a statement to the press on Bobby's death and he spoke of Bobby's compassionate championship of the Negroes. Vance asked Averell why he didn't also use the word "compassion" for LBJ. Harriman refused to do this. Johnson was not a compassionate man—any more than Roosevelt.

Bobby made a lot of enemies but this was probably because he insisted on telling the truth. He didn't "glory" in his enemies the way Roosevelt did. Averell remembered when Roosevelt went to Harvard for an honorary degree in 1936 and President Emeritus Lowell quit the platform. The platform where the dignitaries sat was covered by canvas but a summer shower drenched the audience. Roosevelt looked up from the prepared text of his speech and said: "I am glad to see that God has intervened to soak the rich."

Poor Randolph Churchill died today—as always, a footnote.

PARIS, *June 7, 1968*

Long lunch with Wilfred Burchett, the Australian left-winger who acts as a kind of unofficial foreign press attaché for the North Vietnamese government.

Burchett is short, stocky, fifty-five, but filled with vigor and health. He is a third-generation Australian farmer. Wilfred spent five months with the Vietcong wandering around South Vietnam in 1965, so he must be in good shape.

Burchett lived in Moscow for more than five years. He comes from a modest family outside Melbourne.

PARIS, June 10, 1968

Lunched with André Malraux. His hair is still black, his hands are youthful, and his face is pale and expressive, but he seems to be getting old.

He said that old men writing memoirs can always remember their childhood and their youth with far more accuracy than recent years. If a man learns a language—such as Chinese—in childhood, he would forget it once he left the country but it comes back, at least partially, in old age; this is not true of languages learned later in life. In old age a man becomes much more fond of pets like dogs and children. De Gaulle now likes children and dogs far more than when he was forty.

He said Madame de Gaulle was a real "*Tante Yvonne*" who, from the start, had decided to make her life looking after the General. She had limited subjects of conversation apart from children and grandchildren. But she has a striking intuitive sense about people and had often whispered to Malraux when they sat next to each other at dinner, "That man doesn't really like the General."

De Gaulle has few relaxations. In Colombey he likes to play "patience" and plays chess with occasional local adversaries. He adores his grandchildren and dogs and says "they are not afraid of me." He doesn't have a dog now since his last German shepherd died but he was very close to that one. The German shepherd always slept on his bed at night, to the horror of Madame de Gaulle who would complain about it. The General would always say: "There, there, we'll see," but the dog continued to sleep on his bed.

De Gaulle also has a passion for woodworkers. He has a genuine personal interest in the foresters and carpenters around Colombey. Malraux says most men either have an affinity for wood or for metal; that psychologists don't know why. De Gaulle has an immense interest in carpentry but none in locksmiths or plumbers.

Probably the last "*tutoie*" friend de Gaulle had was Marshal (Alphonse) Juin. All his life he tended to have friends older than himself, but practically all of them are gone. Only Catroux remains and he is very old. None of de Gaulle's children call him anything but "*vous*". This formality is partly due to his generation but also partly due to his provincial upbringing, shared by "*Tante Yvonne*" who was raised in Le Havre and Metz.

De Gaulle's relationships with his ministers are entirely those between a boss and technicians—except for Malraux and Pompidou. Couve is a technician *par excellence* but has always had considerable influence on de Gaulle on financial matters. De Gaulle has a genuine affection for Pompidou and a respect, but there is no intimacy. Malraux has a special position because he is the only minister with whom de Gaulle can discuss nonpolitical things.

Malraux was not terribly impressed by the student movement but he thought it might go on for a long time. It had some seeds of the 1848 revolution in it because, internationally, it was so widespread, but the students didn't know what they wanted.

The trouble with the students was that they had no serious philosophy to follow. Ché Guevara and Régis Debray had nothing to impart. In fact, the reason for French intellectual interest in Cuba was that Cuba was so meaningless.

He thought it was possible and would be very wise—if the General wins—for him to retire to Colombey and put Pompidou in the Élysée so that de Gaulle could act as a kind of Oliver Cromwell, giving advice from off-stage. Pompidou will have very little importance once de Gaulle is really dead.

I asked how many more volumes of *antimémoires* there would be. There would be three. But one won't be published until fifty years after his death. I asked why and he said it included such things as a talk with President Kennedy about the advisability of A-bombing China. It would be unfair to Kennedy to mention this for some years to come but in a half a century nobody will care.

Malraux said that after the bombing attempt on de Gaulle at Montfaron in 1964 (a bomb was hidden in a flowerpot but didn't explode) the General had made a point of never being in the same car as the prime minister. There is still a handful of OAS terrorist agents in France.

On this subject, Malraux said Churchill had once told de Gaulle that if ten percent of a crowd wants to kill a man no security precautions can protect him. However, if only two or three percent of a crowd wants to kill a man—even if there are one hundred thousand people in the crowd—they won't be able to succeed. This seems a curious rationale. Incidentally, Malraux says he doesn't believe de Gaulle has any faith in his luck but simply has "geological courage."

PARIS, *June 14, 1968*

One of my few prewar Rumanian friends who still lives in Bucharest called up. De Gaulle's visit was fantastic. There has not been such popular interest for anyone or anything since World War II.

It was fascinating to attend the General's official reception at the French embassy. He and Ceausescu stood side by side and shook hands with everyone—including the Rumanian cabinet, all diplomatic chiefs of mission, and all holders of the *Légion d'Honneur* or the *Croix de Guerre*. The last group contained some of the most savage anticommunists in Rumania —all the old princes. They were gravely introduced as "Mister" or "Mrs." instead of by their titles, and shook hands warmly with Ceausescu—the man they hate most.

For weeks prior to de Gaulle's arrival, wives of Rumanian officials were ordering gowns in Paris. They had never heard of any dressmaker except Dior so the wives of the entire Rumanian cabinet were dressed by Dior.

PARIS, *June 15, 1968*

Lunched with Harriman. When he last saw Kosygin in 1965, Kosygin told Averell that Moscow considers support of Hanoi as vital to its own interests as Washington considers support of Saigon.

Averell says there is not a chance of Hanoi's making any concessions at this time in exchange for us halting the bombing. We must be patient and tough.

LONDON, *June 26, 1968*

Lunch with young Winston Churchill. Winston told me Bobby Kennedy had asked Randolph to write the authorized biography of Jack Kennedy, which touched Randolph deeply.

Randolph died within an hour of Bobby. He was still conscious when told Bobby had been shot and, when told the assassin had been captured, murmured: "But who pushed me?" He collapsed of bad kidneys, liver, heart, all together. For six months he had been unable to work at all on the biography of his father, all energy gone. But he insisted the doctor tell no one how bad he was: he preferred to die alone. As Winston says: "He wasn't the kind of man who needed someone to hold his hand."

LONDON, *June 27, 1968*

This morning I visited J. Enoch Powell, Conservative M.P. for Wolverhampton and the maverick of today's Tory ranks. He was a member of the Tory shadow cabinet but has been forced out as the result of a speech against commonwealth immigrants, which was rightly described as racist.

Many people had told me Powell was brilliant, if eccentric. He impressed me as deeply serious but not too bright. I am astounded he can be talked of seriously in political circles.

He thought the "apocalyptic treatment" of British admission to Europe had been unrealistic. "Europe" didn't mean life or death to Britain.

To get Britain moving Powell wanted to (1) cut the pound loose from gold and the dollar and let it float, at its real value; (2) maximize competition in trade and production, eliminating all artificial barriers; (3) get the government out of business and subsidies (like agriculture).

America was moving into socialism without using the word—getting into industry and national health service. He wanted to go in the other direction here—away from featherbedding and subsidized agriculture.

Paris, *July 7, 1968*

Dined last night at the Harrimans. Averell keeps saying he was behind Kennedy's policy on Vietnam but indicates disagreement with Johnson's policy. I think this shows an unconscious change in his own views, because he was strongly behind Johnson also a year or two ago.

He thought Israel was pursuing a very dangerous and mistaken policy now. It had been a terrible error for Israel to refuse to arrange a peace last year, a peace that surely would have been guaranteed by Russia and the U.S.A.

Paris, *July 8, 1968*

Golfed and lunched yesterday with Couve de Murville. Couve says the French political scene has always been misunderstood by French intellectuals of both the right and the left and these misinterpretations have traditionally been echoed abroad by foreign correspondents and diplomats.

We were talking about the relations between the French and other European peoples. Couve says that the Slavs and, on the whole, the Germans like the French. The British, Spanish, Italians, Belgians, Dutch, and Scandinavians hate them. The Dutch particularly detest them because of Louis XIV (who fought them), because the French are Roman Catholics and the Dutch are afraid of the Catholics (an odd observation from the Protestant Couve), and "because we pay no attention to them."

Couve told me I would find Pompidou "very tired" when I see him.

An hour today with Georges Pompidou, and it was sad. He has just pulled de Gaulle's fat out of the fire and now he is rewarded by having his throat cut. The poor man looks awful. Although a solid, country-built type, he was pale, drawn, and incredibly tired. He had bags under his eyes.

The story is simple: de Gaulle is firing him as prime minister, and he is being succeeded by Couve de Murville. This is likely to be announced the day after tomorrow after the cabinet meeting.

Pompidou told me he would not accept any other official position, but would remain a deputy in the national assembly. De Gaulle had told him he could try to build up his prestige in the assembly. Pompidou didn't say this with any resounding confidence.

I said I assumed Pompidou was still de Gaulle's "dauphin" despite this throat-cutting. He said yes, that de Gaulle had twice told him recently, both before and after the elections, "It is only you." I remarked that it was an odd way of showing confidence. Pompidou grinned wearily.

Couve would be prime minister. "It was my recommendation," he added. I remarked that I had heard some rumors about Chaban-Delmas, but I simply could not believe them because Chaban was not serious. "The General agrees with your impression," he answered.

I asked if Pompidou wouldn't take any other position—for example vice president or president of the assembly. He answered: "I've had enough." He also said de Gaulle was in one of his moods where he didn't want a vice president—an idea he has gone up and down on for years. A vice president of France might be taken by the French people as the "real president" and, at the very least, would imply de Gaulle's imminent departure.

He wanted to take a real rest and to write a political novel on which he has already started work.

I told him I made a habit of asking statesmen with whom I talked who had most influenced them. He said—and under the circumstances I find this particularly interesting: "Obviously, de Gaulle." He went on to add that de Gaulle had brought him into public life, he would have remained an intellectual and university type without him. Also de Gaulle's ideas and his methods had had a powerful influence.

I then asked—since it was now just a historical footnote—had de Gaulle really gone to Taverny, the secret nuclear headquarters on the way to Baden-Baden, during those fateful hours when he disappeared on May 29. Pompidou said he had gone straight to Baden-Baden.

He said there had been no deal then, that de Gaulle had simply made the journey in terms of psychological warfare and its political effect upon the country.

Was it true that de Gaulle had left some written testament (as an insurance against accident) which designated Pompidou as his successor? He was sure there was such a document but admitted he didn't know what or where it was.

He added, "As you know perfectly well, the General has occasional periods when he is in a mood to retire. In one of those moods, not long after the 1965 presidential elections, he said that he intended to quit and he added: 'I have done the necessary for you.' I am sure he meant by that that there is a written text to that effect."

I observed that it was difficult for a prime minister to function properly without having a political machine of his own. Pompidou had a powerful political machine which had been carefully built up over the last six years, but Couve, who was a preeminent *fonctionnaire*, had none. Pompidou pointed out: "I had none either in 1962—and yet I was prime minister."

I then said: "Well, at any rate, I hope you can keep your machine going." He answered with a grim look: "My machine stays. I will see to that."

I asked how he would define the French position in the Middle East. He said: "French foreign policy depends only on General de Gaulle's personality and on his moods. But I would say that in the Middle East we are truly neutral. And also we are not very active. For the present, I don't think foreign policy is going to be a very active field."

PARIS, *July 10, 1968*

Agreeable lunch with (Ambassador) Sarge Shriver. He would be willing to run for the vice presidency if Humphrey asked him, but he thought his brother-in-law, Ted Kennedy, was the obvious choice, provided he was asked and that he had surmounted the psychological shock of Bobby's death.

Jack Kennedy had been the intellectual of the family and, had he lived, undoubtedly would have moved increasingly into purely intellectual work. Bobby was much more moody and up-and-down as could be seen from the way he had shifted from McCarthyism to left-wing liberalism. Teddy was the best political personality of the family—much more like his grandfather, Honey Fitz.

JERUSALEM, *July 19, 1968*

Chat this afternoon with Teddy Kollek, mayor of Jerusalem, in his apartment. Teddy pointed out this is a most peaceful city despite the recent war. He has no police at his door. He drives his own car. He goes without guards into the Arab city.

There are 200,000 Jews and 70,000 Arabs living in combined Jerusalem as equals (although I doubt if the Arabs are citizens). This is comparable to Montreal. It isn't a U.S.-type melting pot. There is no desire for the Arabs to become Jews. It is only hoped that all will dwell together peacefully. This is the only place in the world where Jews and Arabs meet together en masse.

JERUSALEM, *July 20, 1968*

Tour of the occupied area of Jordan (what is called here the West Bank). At the northern end of the Dead Sea, some 1,400 feet below sea-level (the earth's lowest point) I took a dip beside a shabby, dirty little café, equipped with sordid showers.

I burned my feet badly in the thirty-yard walk (two ways) from the café to the water. It was like walking on hot coals. The sea is warm and so buoyant that half one's body sticks out, as if floating on a rubber mat.

Drove south a few miles to the Qumran Caves where the famous Dead Sea scrolls were discovered in 1947. It is a bleak, hot place. On to Jericho, a townlet with modest hotels and villages that used to be an Arab winter resort. The area is largely waste, sandy, dotted with pitiful poor villages.

Then to Nablus, the second (once first) city in Jordan, with good houses, active markets. Hardly any Israeli soldiers to be seen in the city, apart from the military headquarters with its Israeli flag; none visible in the countryside.

Finally drove through impressively twentieth-century Israel to Herzliya, the prosperous beach suburb north of Tel Aviv, where I visited Abba Eban, foreign minister.

Eban said the Eisenhower plan had never been presented to Israel in any official way. He said: "You can't get peace in the Middle East by economic approaches."

I asked whether it was possible for Hussein to make peace for Jordan; wouldn't he be assassinated right away? Eban answered: "That depends on what kind of peace is produced. If a peace is supported by the Palestine Arab leaders, Egypt couldn't oppose it. If the Palestine Arabs accept, Egypt must also. If Jordan makes a peace cutting its losses to the minimum, Hussein's picture in the Arab world will change.

"The key is now Jordan, not Egypt. The Nasser regime today is even weaker than Hussein's. We have had recent visitors such as [McGeorge] Bundy and Gunnar Jarring who say that Nasser now admits he cannot move at all. He cannot recognize Israel as a fact or even talk about peace, even if this means Israel stays on in Sinai. He is tied down by his own rhetoric which commits him not only to liquidate the 1967 war but even the 1948 war.

"Hussein at least talks of peace. He wants to know what the deal would be. He is pragmatic. He maintains contacts with us through Palestinian Arab leaders. The question you put is wrong—can Hussein survive if he makes peace? The real question is can he survive if he does not make peace?"

Jordan knows that if there is a settlement, Jordan will have to recognize Israel's identity as an independent state. For Egypt this ideological issue is the most important. Therefore Israeli diplomacy now aims more at Amman than at Cairo.

Nasser wants to keep rearming so that in a few years he can either try another round of war or attempt to negotiate a settlement from strength. Hussein is much harder-pressed for time.

Soviet rhetoric is now less anti-Israeli than it was in 1967. The Soviet influence on the Arabs is mainly through arms. It would lose this and its propaganda gambit—"Russia is the only power to aid the Arabs"—if a settlement came. But Russia doesn't want to give the Arabs all they ask. Today there is a rough parallel between the Moscow-Cairo relationship and the Washington-Jerusalem relationship. In each case the client is told: "You'll get your arms—but not as much as you want or as quickly as you want."

The U.S.A. and the USSR seem to be disengaging a bit in the Middle East. The U.S.A. certainly won't send soldiers into this area. Therefore it cannot *impose* a solution because it would have to guarantee anything it imposed, and it isn't ready to.

When he saw de Gaulle at the end of May 1967, just before the six-day war, the General "warned" him Israel should not make war. The way he expressed it made Eban feel he meant a "world" war; that he had an "apocalyptic obsession." He dismissed Eban's statement that the war had already been started by Nasser's blockade of the Tiran straits. De Gaulle assured him the Four Powers could look after that; the Soviet Union had to be brought into the picture. He "assured" Eban that Israel was not in ᴜanger, that the blockade could be settled by Four-Power diplomacy. When Israel rejected these assertions he complained—and still does—that Israel had let him down.

Ben-Gurion had visited de Gaulle in 1960, and Eshkol in 1964. De Gaulle told Ben-Gurion France would not let Israel be destroyed, and assured him Eisenhower felt the same way. De Gaulle later told Eshkol that if Israel were attacked France would be "among those" who would not let Israel be destroyed.

My impression of Eban is that he is overconfident. He is a verbalist. He speaks many languages very fluently. He is a fine orator. But his mind is too fascinated by the sound of his voice.

JERUSALEM, *July 21, 1968*

This afternoon I had a talk with Prime Minister [Levi] Eshkol. He is pleasant, moral, and courageous. Yet it is incredibly tedious to try and understand what he is trying to say.

Eshkol's difficulty in communicating is like Erhard's. Moreover, both Erhard and Eshkol had been finance ministers. Both were impossible to understand. And in each case the old boss tried to ruin his successor. Adenauer succeeded, Ben-Gurion failed.

Talking about the future twenty years hence, he said Israel looks more to Europe than to the Middle East. There might then be some joint Israeli-Arab enterprises and some kind of regional defense scheme extending from Morocco to Ethiopia to Turkey. He stressed that relations with Morocco were good but this couldn't be advertised because it would embarrass King Hassan, who's scared of Nasser.

Eshkol thinks the chances of getting the fifty Mirages from France are nil so long as de Gaulle is in power: "It's a lost case." When he visited Paris in 1964 de Gaulle was very friendly and spoke of Israel as a close friend. But now he wants to "get his feet in Arab oil and do the U.S.A. in the eye."

JERUSALEM, *July 22, 1968*

Saw Yigal Allon, minister of absorption (integrating immigrants), at the Knesset, comfortable and well-equipped parliament building, built largely on contributions from the Rothschild family.

Allon is the principal rival of the overwhelmingly popular General Moshe Dayan, whom Eshkol dislikes, who is Ben-Gurion's prodigy, and who is far ahead in all polls. Allon was also a general in the first war (1948–49) and commanded the southern front (against the Egyptians).

I asked him how menacing *Al Fatah* (Arab guerrilla organization) was. He said: "You can't compare them in fighting quality to the Israelis. There are three reasons for the *Fatah*'s failure: the efficiency of the Israeli secret services, police and army; the refusal of the Arab population to cooperate; the full cooperation with our forces of those *Fatah* agents we capture. They talk—and fully—without any pressure at all."

I remarked that it was a danger and a snare to assume that "Arabs can't fight." The same had been said of Jews—and Vietnamese. He said that in 1948 some of the Arabs had fought back very bravely, "But we must not overestimate their ability—or our own. We must maintain qualitative superiority. There's something wrong in their social structure and, as an army, they will be inferior for years to come. They didn't fight better in 1956 or in 1967. Indeed, they really fought best in 1948."

TEL AVIV, *July 23, 1968*

Last night I went out for drinks with Michael Hadow, British ambassador, a very straight fellow who disagrees with his government's policy. He says the foreign office is run by old-fashioned pro-Arabs and anti-Semites. He says George Brown, until recently foreign secretary, has a Jewish wife and used to get up, when attacked for anti-Semitism, and talk about "my Jewish wife."

Hadow was called back for consultation in 1967 and Brown called on Hadow, who had never before seen him, saying: "Now, Michael, you tell us about the picture." When Hadow was through, having said the only way to force Israel to make concessions to Jordan as Brown wanted was by getting the UN to vote sanctions—something he knew Brown didn't dare do—George was furious and said: "Hadow, you're the kind of man who never follows instructions." He made a long speech about "poor Jordan" and "the gallant King Hussein" and said Israel must give up Jerusalem (not just the Old City, which it had just captured, but the whole city, including what it previously held) for the sake of peace. He raged at Hadow: "You follow my instructions, you." Right afterward Hadow went to Sir Paul Gore-Booth, permanent head of the foreign office, and tendered his resignation. Gore-Booth said: "Look here, Michael. You only have to take this sort of thing once a year. I have it almost every day. Don't be a fool."

First-class talk with General Aharon Yariv, Israeli chief of intelligence. Of all the factors in Israel, I find the army most impressive. This citizens' army is producing a new kind of state and relationship between citizen and state.

Yariv looked so young (about thirty-five) that I asked his age. "Forty-seven," he said. "I'm the oldest general."

By its captures last year, Israel got the secrets of almost all items of Soviet equipment in the East European satellites. But the satellites have no MIG 23s or SAM 3s. I asked if the U.S. had been able to get a look at this stuff and he politely said he couldn't answer this.

I asked if Israel had been hampered by de Gaulle's refusal to deliver the Mirages. He said Israel would like more supersonic jets but "even with what we have we can still lick the Arab air forces. The question for us is not only to win—but to do it at a low price. For us the eight hundred killed during the six-day war was a high price. If you translate that into American statistics it would be like the U.S. losing sixty thousand dead in one week."

Yariv said there was only a four-minute warning period against attacks from Egypt before the war; now it was twenty-seven minutes. But if Egyptian planes came in low over the sea, there wouldn't be any twenty-seven minutes; the only warning then would be from "intelligence." It would be hard for Egyptian planes to come in low all the way and still have a sufficient load to strike hard when they got here.

Yariv said that in theory Israel could be satisfied with the demilitarization of sensitive areas like the West Bank and Sinai; but only in theory. The Arabs are simply not ready to change their basic attitude vis-à-vis Israel. They haven't given up the idea of settling final accounts.

The Arabs see things accordingly, says Yariv. They suffered a "severe setback" in 1967. But it was not disastrous. All the neighbors of Israel preserved their political entities and regimes. Time is on the Arabs' side; they have had similar problems in the past. It had taken them seventy years to wipe out the Crusaders. Israel is a small land. It is 2.5 million people now. It might even grow to 4 or 5 million. But they will some day be submerged by 100 million Arabs.

Were the Arabs ready to seek a fundamental solution it would not be difficult to work one out; but they are not. The problem is deeply emotional. The six-day war didn't sober the Arabs up. For many it merely served to exacerbate their emotions.

It seemed to me Israel was condemned by its location to strike first, whenever war threatened; otherwise it might be destroyed. Therefore, in the interest of its own security, it was forced always to sacrifice world popularity. This was a fundamental disadvantage.

Yariv agreed this had been the case but said now, for the first time, it was no longer true. Because of the new map Israel can now afford the military risk and political luxury of a second strike. In its present positions, Israel had sufficient strategic depth and shorter, more easily defended borders.

Israel recognized it could never "win" a definitive war by driving the Arabs away, as the Arabs hope some day to push Israel into the sea. Israel views its future in terms of risks. There can be no gilt-edged guarantees. Israel must be ready to accept some risk in exchange for happiness and freedom. But he thinks the risk is small. Israel must rely upon itself. It didn't wish to belittle world powers or public opinion but the decisive factor was Israel's own will to resist and to exist. The defection of France proved that outside support could be fickle.

I asked if theoretically and technically it was possible to stage a military *coup d'état* in Israel. He said it was; all you needed was intelligence, armor, and planes. This had been shown in Greece and Iraq. But there was a democratic spirit here that was impossible to minimize; the military is by tradition subject to the civilian authority.

TEL AVIV, *July 24, 1968*

Drove down to Sde Boker, the desert kibbutz, to see David Ben-Gurion, Israel's grand old man, former prime minister, and (together with Chaim Weizmann) principal founder of the Zionist state. Sde Boker is an exceptionally simple cluster of houses and huts in the Negev. It survives on orchards and fields carved out of the barren desert; the life is rugged. It is an isolated existence for an octogenarian who was once active on the world stage—especially since last year, when his wife died.

When I walked from the parking place to B.G.'s modest house (only relatively superior to the others) an army guard with a tommy gun was lounging outside. He called an aide and I was taken in. B.G., now eighty-one, was seated at his desk in the book-lined study, wearing simply khaki pants and shirt. He is even shorter than before and certainly fatter, a portly but very active old man, almost totally bald in the center of his head, with wings of thin white hair sticking out above both temples.

He seems to have few teeth left, making his tough jaw even more prominent. But he was pink, alert, and vigorous. His mind and memory are excellent. His fine forehead seemed to gleam with mental energy.

His study was an incredible mess. Behind him in the center of one shelf was a bad plaster bust of Plato. Books and papers littered his desk and cluttered up most of the chairs and the other table. He has a messy filing system of his own, including all kinds of precious documents such as letters from de Gaulle and Kennedy, stashed in simple portfolios. In one bookcase is a set of four volumes, bound in leather, containing all the records, papers and conversations of the 1956 Suez war. He says there are only three sets and they will not be published "until after Eden's death."

In 1960, Ben-Gurion said, Eisenhower told him, during his visit to the U.S.A., that America would help if Israel were attacked. But, he continued: "I said this takes time. You would first have to consult your congress, your government. And we are a small country. Haifa could fall within a day. Anyway, we don't want American boys to die for us.

"I said the same thing to de Gaulle a little later that same year: that we wanted no French boys to die here. It was a very friendly conversation. And the very last time I saw de Gaulle was at Adenauer's funeral, in 1967. He came up to me and we had a long talk. I simply would not have believed it if someone had said to me at that time that we wouldn't get our Mirages from France because de Gaulle prevented it.

"Nevertheless, you must remember that people here don't realize a statesman must consider his own national interests, the interests of his country. The Jewish people spent hundreds of years abroad in other lands and do not fully understand this concept. De Gaulle simply wanted to be friendly with the Arabs in what he considered the interest of France.

"I admit I was very disturbed when he made his statement about Israel and the Jews at a press conference [in 1967]. De Gaulle was very friendly at that last talk we had in Bonn. He has always been. In 1960 he described Israel as France's friend and ally. When I wrote him last year his answer came, by cable to his ambassador, just two days later. He requested me to allow publication of both letters and I agreed.

"I think he misrepresented the Jewish people but of course every Frenchman is a Bonapartist, and he is a great Frenchman. Every Frenchman also, I must say, is against his government."

I asked about his correspondence with Kennedy. He said: "You know, I met Kennedy three times. First he came here, before he was president, with Franklin D. Roosevelt, Jr. He didn't make much of an impression. Then, in 1960, I met him in Washington even before he was nominated as his party's presidential candidate. He was so young-looking that I couldn't seriously think he stood a chance of being nominated, much less elected. Then I met Kennedy the last time in 1961 in New York. He said to me: 'You know, I was elected by the Jews of New York and I would like to do something for the Jewish people.' I was shocked. Why should he say such a thing to a foreigner?

"I could see by then that he was a great man, but I also have always remembered that Eisenhower, as a human, was more likable. Eisenhower is a very lovely person. I was deeply impressed by him. I have never forgotten that just after Germany's defeat I had pointed out to Eisenhower, then commanding the occupation, that there were no Hebrew books or teachers left in Germany and none of the thousands of Jewish displaced persons had the material to learn. Right away he arranged to do something. He sent a plane every week to pick up books and teachers here to work for the D.P.'s. The British government, which still controlled us under the Palestine mandate, didn't like it but they didn't dare do anything against Eisenhower. So they complained to the state department, and the state department got the arrangement stopped."

Referring to the four volumes of the Suez secrets, which he got up and brought over: "There are only three copies," he repeated proudly. "But I won't publish anything until after Eden's death, because he is very much involved. Everything is really now known but still I won't publish—even though Eden was no particular friend of ours and didn't keep his word. He was supposed to send me a very important letter [B.G. didn't specify what, but I imagine confirming their secret alliance] but he didn't do it. He only sent the letter to Guy Mollet, the French premier. But Mollet is a decent fellow and he sent me a photostat.

"Do you know, Eden sent over to Paris after the affair in order to have all the original documents destroyed. But he found that I had copies. And I may note that it was only then that he became friendly to Israel."

He continued: "When I had lunch with de Gaulle in 1960, he asked me: 'Are you satisfied with your present frontiers?' I said: 'If you had asked me this question twenty years ago I would have told you what the boundaries should be. In 1920, three years after the Balfour declaration, I sent a memorandum to the British Labor party outlining my ideas on this point.

" 'Our northern border should some day be,' I said, 'the river Litani in southern Lebanon. In the east the frontier should be a line running south of Damascus along the Awage river and then through the desert east of Jordan. And our southern border should be the Red Sea.'

"These, I felt in 1920, should be the proper boundaries of an eventual state of Israel. But when the UN adopted the 1947 resolution which we accepted—even without Jerusalem—I was prepared to agree on this frontier—yes, even without Jerusalem. If the Arabs had accepted this we would have that border today.

"Had the Arabs agreed in 1947, the borders fixed then by UN in the partition plan would have been final. But the Arabs refused. War came and the entire situation was changed. The boundaries of Israel, after the 1948 war, included five thousand more square kilometers than the 1947 partition plan.

"Now I return to that conversation with de Gaulle. I told de Gaulle that if the Arabs had accepted the UN decision in 1947 we would have stuck to it. The area designated by UN in 1947 was big enough for all the Jews I could imagine coming to Israel, five, six, or seven million of them. They could have fitted in. After all, not all the Jews in the world intended to come."

I asked what he thought should be Israel's boundaries today, after three wars. He said: "I am now a private citizen. I speak only for myself. But look: after the six-day war two groups came into being here. One wanted peace with the Arabs, peace on a reasonable basis. The other wanted the entire area of old Palestine, the area I described in my letter to the British Labor party. My private view, now, is that if the choice lies between peace and the boundaries we obtained as a result of our victory in the six-day war, peace and the boundaries that existed in early 1967, I prefer peace.

"But I don't just mean a signed document. The Arabs don't respect papers. They didn't keep the armistice agreement, after all. I mean a real peace. I mean cooperation between Israel and the Arabs, economic, political, cultural cooperation. For such a peace I would prefer to yield all the territory we took last year."

I asked: "Including East Jerusalem?" His reply was Delphic: "It would be very hard to give up East Jerusalem."

He then continued: "I know there is no real hope for such a peace for years to come. The only real possibility of peace would be if Russia and America decide to work together in this world. Only they can make a real peace. The two great powers could compel the Arabs to make such a peace. And then they would have to underwrite it, guarantee it.

"But talk of a much larger Israel, something like what I mentioned almost fifty years ago, is meaningless without a Jewish population in the whole area included; not just a Jewish population everywhere but a big majority. We have west Palestine and a part of east Palestine. But if we were to hold any more, without Jews inhabiting it that would be sheer nonsense. Now our government, here, could increase immigration of Jews from America and other rich countries.

"Now the only problem is: Will there be enough Jewish immigration? Take the American Jews. I believe I know American Jewry. I lived there for three years—fifty-two years ago—and I have revisited America many, many times since. It is not just a material matter. You know, in 1951 I saw Einstein in the United States and I asked him if he thought American Jewish scientists would come to Israel. He said: 'Yes, they are not trusted here.' That is no longer the case. In 1961 Robert Oppenheimer came here and I told him of my conversation with Einstein. I said that I knew things had changed. But Oppenheimer said: 'They will still come. They will come because there is no meaning in life—in the United States, in Britain, in France.'

"The human race can be divided into two groups: those who want to get and take, and those who want to give and create. This is the meaning of life. And—forgive me—you don't have it in the United States, but we do have it here. Oppenheimer could see that. Remember, he was a non-Zionist, and he had a non-Jewish wife.

"Our ability is to give and to create. Sargent Shriver was here two or three years ago and he asked me why I thought there were proportionately more Jews than non-Jews volunteering for your peace corps. I said: 'Because they are Jews. Because they have ideals. They want moral satisfaction.' If Israel's present government realizes that this question is now their main task, that it is now immigration just as it used to be security, there are plenty of Jews in America, in Britain, in South Africa who will wish to come here."

He continued: "I have a double loyalty—to the Jewish people and to the human race. I understand this quest for moral satisfaction because I am a Jew. The Jewish people have certain original qualities. You can see these qualities in the Bible, in the Old Testament, which has been our Book for more than 2,500 years. It has educated our people.

"You remember in the New Testament, the First Gospel, Matthew, begins with the lineage of Christ, and it traces this way back. But the Old Testament starts with Adam, with the first human being. Thus, all human beings are the direct descendants of Adam and Eve, all humans of all creeds and colors. They were created in the image of God. The entire human race was created in the image of God. But God cannot be seen or heard. God cannot even be conceived. Thus this conception is completely universal.

"The Greeks were the most civilized people of the ancient world and, among them, the most civilized were the Athenians. And the greatest Athenian, I think, was Plato. Plato lived in the midst of the war with Sparta and he exhorted the Greek tribes not to make war against each other. He said war was only permissible against the non-Greeks, the barbarians. But Isaiah taught, in the Bible, that there would be no war at all. This is the essence of the Jewish religion.

"Moses taught the Jews they had to exceed, to be the best, in order to survive, a small people surrounded by mighty Egypt and Babylon. And they learned this lesson; for otherwise how could they have survived? For 1,900 years the Jews dwelled in other lands. Hebrew became a dead language. And yet, after 1,900 years, they had the vitality to rebuild their state. In 1850 there were 10,000 Jews in Palestine. In 1948 there were only 650,000. Yet in 1948 these 650,000 Jews were attacked by 30 million Arabs.

"The real war, in fact, started in 1947 with the *Haganah* [the Jewish Agency's armed force] protecting us. Your General Marshall greatly admired the *Haganah* but he feared every Jew in Palestine would be slaughtered in the Arab invasion. Logically he was right: it was one against forty; and the Arabs had good arms. But our people knew they had to excel. They knew what they were fighting for. I wrote a letter to my son in 1937, long before Israel existed, and I said to him: 'We will have a state one day; and it will have the finest army in the world.'

"It is this moral factor that counts. This is the essence of the question. The question of our survival is whether we will manage to preserve our moral superiority or not. In 1949 I made this point to a group of scientists, scholars, and intellectuals. I told them it was up to them to see that the moral superiority continued.

"I can understand why other countries, for material reasons, find it better to seek friendship with the Arabs. The only way we can balance this is by maintaining respect and admiration for our moral qualities. Look at France. We originally won French friendship despite the traditional anti-Semitism represented by the Dreyfus case, simply because the French army admired our behavior during the 1948 war. And the Americans know that Israel and Japan are the only real democracies in Asia. They see we are creating, in our kibbutzes, a kind of society that doesn't exist anywhere else.

"It is this kind of thing that attracts the best Jews abroad. Jews used to come to Israel because life at home, where they were, was bad for them and because of messianic hopes. Now things are different. If our government does its job properly you will see large numbers of Jews coming here from wealthy, developed lands—at a rate of one or two percent of our population each year—because they are drawn here morally. With these people we can fill up territories like the West Bank, the Golan Heights, East Jerusalem." (I note this is a far cry from B.G.'s antimaximalism and modesty about frontiers, described by him earlier.)

I inquired: "Now that you are an old man who has devoted much time to contemplation, what do you consider the real purpose of human life?" He said: "I am not religious in the Jewish sense. I am not orthodox. I am not even a Reformed Jew. I never go to synagogue here. I only go when I am abroad to show my Jewishness. But Jewishness is different from Christianity or Buddhism. It is less than just a religion. It is national. Our religious holidays are also national holidays. The Holy Land is our national land. Jerusalem is a Holy City that is dear to us nationally.

"The Jews are not merely a religious people. Jewishness is the most universal religious concept in the world, because it goes back to the first two human beings and embraces all their descendants in its thinking. The Greeks were the greatest ancients, the Athenians, but only those born there were eligible to full rights. But our Torah said: 'The stranger among you shall be treated as a citizen and loved like yourself.' "

We talked about death. He said: "The purpose of life is to enjoy it, to make it pleasanter for every human being. We don't know of another world so we must concentrate on this one. People should be just and decent and loving. There is no mention in our Bible of an afterlife. Death is simply the end; there is no word of another world. This is what it seems to be. But I don't know. Nobody knows. Once I talked about this to Einstein and he said: 'The more we progress in science, the more we realize what we don't know. Our ignorance increases; the riddle grows.' I asked him: 'Is there life after death?' He said: 'I wish I knew.' But remember, in his will he left orders that his body should be burned. He didn't think he would come back again. Remember, there is no word in the Torah that concerns any other life."

I recalled that I had seen de Gaulle after Churchill's funeral and asked him if he had prepared his own funeral plans. He said he had, but there would be no "spectacle." Had Ben-Gurion made any posthumous arrangements? He said only: "I have ordered that my remains should stay here at Sde Boker, beside my wife."

He rambled on about various things. He said when he last saw Churchill, very old, Churchill told him he had once written an article on Moses (B.G. called him 'Moshe' the Hebrew version). "I expressed interest and Churchill had a secretary dig it up. He sent it with a letter saying: 'I reread the article and I want you to know I wouldn't have written it now.' I read the piece and at the end were two sentences saying: 'Several centuries later a greater prophet arose.' He was referring to Jesus. I think he said that about not writing it 'now' because he didn't want to offend me. He was a great man."

As he drew breath, I politely excused myself. Very kindly, like a little, plump, old bear, he took me to the door, shook my hand warmly, and stood gazing as the car started off. He was still there, on the threshold, shielding his intense blue eyes, when we swung around into the desert.

P.S. I forgot to mention: Ben-Gurion spoke of three "great" men during our talk: Churchill, de Gaulle, and Adenauer. Very interesting for a Jew to select a German.

TEL AVIV, *July 25, 1968*

Today, before flying off to Cyprus, Wally Barbour, our ambassador, drove me home to a pleasant and interesting lunch. I went from there to the airport.

Wally said U.S. policy is to get peace to the area. We have carefully avoided, however, any thought of having a "U.S. plan" that would link our name and prestige to a certain set of conditions. But there is certainly no chance of imposing a Four-Power solution as the French have often suggested. The Four Powers don't agree at all among themselves.

Wally says it is absolutely untrue that President Kennedy promised Israel we would support it with the Sixth Fleet if, in exchange, Israel foreswore the manufacture of atomic weapons. He doesn't think they are making such weapons.

In May 1967 enormous casualties were anticipated. All big hotels outside Tel Aviv were set up as huge hospitals and Jewish organizations recruited volunteer doctors everywhere in the world.

"What should U.S. policy be?" I asked. Wally said: "It's very simple. The only way we can get into real trouble is if America is forced to fight Russia to defend Israel's existence. We would only get in trouble if it became apparent Israel was going to lose. Therefore, we have to keep Israel strong enough to look after itself. One can worry about the possibility of 100 million Arabs some day fighting 4 million Jews. But numbers are not necessarily an asset . . . and the Arabs just won't unite."

NICOSIA, CYPRUS, *July 26, 1968*

Pleasant talk with Archbishop Makarios, still president of Cyprus. Makarios seemed more worldly and at ease than in the past. His English has improved and no interpreter was present. He is about five foot ten, with his pope's hat off, which it was, of medium build, has astonishingly small, soft hands for a peasant's son. His father was a shepherd in the mountains above Paphos (where Aphrodite emerged from sea foam). But he never came to the sea himself until he was ten. Makarios entered an ecclesiastical school as a boy and later studied theology at Boston University.

Makarios waved me to a seat beside him on a sofa and I studied his face carefully as he talked: a long nose, long face, craggy head with bald central band and curly hair along the sides, hooded eyes, greying beard. His voice is agreeably modulated. He offered me Turkish coffee while he took a half-glass of milk.

I inquired who, alive or dead, had most influenced his life. He said: "First of all the Stoic philosophers of ancient Greece." This was not unexpected since Zeno, the great Stoic, was a Cypriot, born at Citium (now Larnaca). "But from our era, of those alive in my time, I have no doubt it was Gandhi. Especially during my stay in the Seychelles Islands" (where he was exiled by the British during the wind-up of colonial days). "I had the time to read a good deal about him. He was the greatest moral personality of our time, a real prophet.

"You know, people admire two kinds of personalities—the hero and the saint. Most people prefer the hero type but I believe the saint is greater. For me, I will always be a man about whom people will disagree. Some people will say that I didn't care about bloodshed, people outside Cyprus. But people in Cyprus will say that I am too moderate, that I compromise too much. You cannot please everyone."

Makarios acknowledged that he is the only ecclesiastical chief of state except the Pope (Vatican City) but added: "The Pope is there permanently. There is no limit to his term. I am elected." I inquired whether there might not be certain conflicts between the realms of Caesar and God in his dual capacity. He said:

"There would be such a conflict if I was a political leader in the usual meaning of the word. But I have no party. I am not a representative of particular political factions. I have just offered my services to the people of Cyprus because they asked for them. There are certain universal moral principles in Christianity and, since I apply these, I can see no possibility of conflict in my twin roles."

Didn't he think it was difficult for an Orthodox Christian prelate to supervise the lay affairs of a population which included a twenty percent Moslem minority? He said: "There is a complete division between church and state in Cyprus. Despite the fact that an archbishop is chief of state, the state has nothing at all to do with religion. And I want to keep it that way. Cyprus is not like England or Greece where the state is formally interested in church affairs. You may think it unusual but I can look upon Moslems or Christians as equal Cypriot citizens with equal rights."

I asked what he thought of the present junta government in Athens. He said: "My policy is to cooperate with any Greek government, whether I like it or not. I have cooperated with thirteen Athens governments since I came to office in 1960. The present government is honest, in my view, and has good intentions. But I must admit I don't like dictatorship."

KYRENIA, CYPRUS, *July 27, 1968*

I strolled through the barricaded town of Nicosia. Not far from the Ledra Palace Hotel the Turkish quarter starts. It is entirely cut off. UN sentries in blue berets are at their posts or driving their jeeps. At the border is an obstacle built of loaded oil barrels and a checkpoint manned by regular Turkish troops (from the mainland). Above it is a house with the Turkish flag and the windows cemented in, save for machine gun slits. All signs in the Turkish quarter are in Turkish: movies, restaurants, etc. Except for armed men it seemed quite peaceful.

Drinks with Taylor Belcher, the American ambassador, and his wife. They have a beautiful little house by the sea, about a mile east of Kyrenia. He says that in November 1967 war really loomed. The Turks had massed 100,000 men across the way and brought down all the Bosphorus and Marmora ferry boats. Ankara sent an ultimatum: it would attack unless Greek General Grivas and his detachment were withdrawn. (The Greeks had killed and looted a Turkish region, even slaughtering sheep and chickens.) The Turks achieved a diplomatic victory when Athens yielded and agreed to pull out Grivas and his troops.

ANKARA, *August 2, 1968*

This morning with Prime Minister Suleyman Demirel, the forty-four-year-old chief of government (youngest in Turkish history), a fat, bald man with luminous eyes, sensual mouth, fleshy face.

He said: "In this country people are not anti-American. They know about our alliance and our friendship and these are strong facts. We share the same philosophy of life. There is nothing ugly in the background of our relations; we have never been at war.

"Of course, there have been irritations like the recent incident during a U.S. naval visit. Turkey is different from ten years ago. Demonstrations are allowed without any advance permits. We have here a leftist, almost

Marxist party (although communists are legally banned). And they used the same slogans as elsewhere: Vietnam, down with NATO, imperialism. Because we now have more freedom, it is easier for left-wing agitators to act.

"But in reality our friendship and alliance with the U.S.A. are as strong as ever. Your Sixth Fleet has as much access here as ever before. Turkey sticks to its NATO commitments."

I asked how Turkey, for so long a great power, had become an under-developed land. He said: "There is nothing wrong with the Turkish people. They are our greatest resource. But the Ottoman empire was based on several nations with the Turks of Anatolia supplying the manpower and natural resources for our wars. We wasted these resources and our national blood. We tired ourselves out as a nation. We were exhausted. The Ottoman empire was set up in 1299 and lasted over 600 years. We weren't able to keep up with the progress and development of Western Europe during our long decline. Once we had the greatest navy in the Mediterranean; but we lost out to steam and iron.

"It is difficult to make a democracy within twenty-two years. There was almost complete illiteracy when the republic started. There was only one rather old-fashioned university. Now 86 percent of our children are in school and by 1972 it will be 100 percent. We are a young nation: 42 percent of our population is under fifteen."

ISTANBUL, *August 6, 1968*

This afternoon I scrambled across the Golden Horn in old Constantinople and called upon Patriarch Athenagoras in his beat-up, little patriarchate, situated in a lovely garden, opposite an ugly Greek church.

Kittens played among the flowers and pigeons sunned themselves on the wall. Inside flies buzzed, especially when old Athenagoras summoned (with a loud, clanging bell) *mastica* from Chios (a thick white jam, of which I dutifully took a spoonful) and sweet Turkish coffee.

He is now eighty-three and his formerly towering stature has shrunk to a mere six foot two or so, rendered more impressive by his rimless top-hat. Unlike Makarios, he wore his hat as well as black robes inside as well as out. His office is heartbreakingly plain, the main decorations being a picture of Kemal Ataturk opposite his desk, an enlarged photo of himself with Pope Paul VI behind it, and at his left hand an inscribed photo of President Johnson whom he has never met but claims to admire. Athenagoras spoke in glowing terms of almost everyone. The only person he positively disliked was Makarios, saying he had made all the trouble for Greeks in Turkey by igniting the Cyprus problem, and that Athenagoras could have settled Cyprus himself if only the Cypriot church were under him instead of being autocephalous.

On his desk he had two volumes of Harry Truman's memoirs (in English) sermons of Paul VI (in French), what looked to be an old Serbian dictionary, and a set of seven well-worn volumes on "Mental Efficiency" including two bearing the respective titles: *Personality—How to Build It* and *Speech—How to Use It Effectively.* He gave me a tawdry medallion he had had struck (in brass) to commemorate a meeting with Pope Paul. He told me the pope had visited him in this same room and they had had a fine "brotherly" chat in French.

I asked if he thought Pope Paul's encyclical banning birth control to Catholics would set back the cause of ecumenicalism. He didn't. He said, fingering his great beard (of which God the Father would be proud): "The Pope is a great man. A great leader. I respect him. He couldn't do else but issue that encyclical. He had to follow his gospel. I am close to him and I know.

"Pope John opened the window; but Paul VI opened the door. He is destined to translate the doctrine of Paul I, the apostle, into a new and modern age. He is a great and sincere pope.

"When Pope Paul was elected I congratulated him and almost that same day I read in the newspapers of his desire to visit Jerusalem. In a service I praised this decision and I proposed a meeting in Jerusalem of all the heads of the church. But he did not have the time to arrange such a conference with them all.

"Nevertheless, he and I had our meeting in Jerusalem in January 1964. When we saw each other, our arms stretched out and we embraced as brothers. Together we read the gospels and recited the paternoster and expressed the desire to meet one day in the same chalice of the blood of Jesus Christ (communion). As an answer he offered me a chalice. Then he lifted the excommunication that had endured for centuries. Later he visited me here and I visited him in Rome.

"A true personal understanding and agreement has come out of all this. I hope to develop a theological dialogue of a mixed, interfaith committee. I want to push ahead, not toward union for the time being, but toward unity of approach. Already any Roman Catholic can take communion in an Orthodox church and vice versa, if their own clergy is not available. My ultimate hope is to have such an understanding with all Christian churches."

The Orthodox church is split into fourteen autonomous bodies, independent of each other in domestic affairs. But in common matters of faith, morals, and administration "we are united under the spiritual leadership of this patriarchate. And only this patriarch can convoke a synod."

Athenagoras lived eighteen years in the U.S.A. and was an American citizen. "I hope still to go back there some time. America has a secret destiny. Nothing can stop it from fulfilling this secret destiny. Vietnam? Pooh."

ATHENS, *August 13, 1968*

Saw Stylianos Pattakos, first deputy prime minister and minister of the interior. As a brigadier, Pattakos provided the tanks that produced the *coup d'état* on April 21, 1967.

Pattakos's office contains huge pictures of the king and queen and enormous symbols of the April 21 revolution, not only on the walls, but even on the cuff links of the minister.

I asked his opinion of the popular front agreement between Andreas Papandreou and Brillakis, the communist leader who escaped. Pattakos said: "Andreas has committed political suicide by this. Any cooperation between a regular politician and the communists in Greece has always been proven to be fatal."

Pattakos said Andreas had no resistance movement here; nor had anyone else, even the communists. He said even the attack on Prime Minister Papadopoulos today (a botched-up assassination attempt) was probably not organized.

I asked about foreign reports of torture and beating up of political prisoners. He got very indignant. He said: "Such stories are absolutely untrue. Civilized people should be ashamed of themselves for saying such things. Only barbarians would commit such acts."

When I left Pattakos I went to the press direction and was shown in to the office of Byron Stamatopoulos, the boss. It was a complete madhouse. There were about six or seven hysterics who seemed to be cutting out paper dolls, untangling telephone wires, talking to people who were not there and otherwise disporting themselves in strange and inefficient ways.

On the desk of Stamatopoulos there were probably between eighty and one hundred photographs of the man arrested for attempting to assassinate the prime minister. The photographs were all identical. The poor fellow looked like a mouse in a bathing suit. What Stamatopoulos and Co. were doing was scissoring off different sizes and shapes of the same photo and then announcing "this one for Vima," "this one for Acropolis," or "this one for Ethnos." Here was the whole public relations section doubling as censors.

ATHENS, *August 15, 1968*

Pattakos invited me out to Aghios Andreas to see him and Makarezos, there for the holiday (Assumption Day). Aghios Andreas turned out to be one of a series of vacation colonies along the coast opposite Euboea. This particular colony, where Pattakos has a modest bungalow, is owned by the air force. There were several dozen bungalows scattered under the pine trees just above the slate-blue late afternoon sea, the whole enclosure being surrounded by wire and guarded by air force sentries.

Pattakos and Makarezos, dressed in dark civilian suits, were sitting on the porch. Pattakos's elder daughter, there with her husband, brought out some whisky, ice, and soda. Mrs. Pattakos produced a plate of carefully peeled figs.

I asked why on earth they kept the membership—even the number of members—of the committee of the revolutionary council secret. Pattakos said this was "necessary in order to make things more difficult for the communists in case they ever had a plot against the regime."

ATHENS, *August 17, 1968*

This morning I had a talk with Prime Minister George Papadopoulos. He recalled our last meeting just after the *coup d'état*—and made it quite clear that he did not recall it with favor.

He received me in the traditional prime minister's office in the parliament building. On the wall behind him were large pictures of the king and queen and the emblem of the April 21 revolution.

Papadopoulos is small but tough. He is clearly bright and has a massive forehead with heavy veins at the temples showing that he has a passionate temper. He is a rather ugly but intense man with a high, flat voice. Throughout our conversation he smoked long filter cigarettes. On his desk, among other decorations, were a small vase of flowers and a crucifixion scene.

He said there was no change in the foreign policy of this government; it sought the stability and friendship of NATO as well as good relations with all countries. It had agreements with the United States on naval and aircraft access rights, both on a bilateral basis and through NATO.

I asked if Russia had been making any efforts to urge Greece toward a neutralist policy. He said: "From what I understand this is being done by the Americans, not the Russians. So far the Russians have not made any effort at all. They merely maintain the same attitude toward us as the Americans do—and they have never dared to try to ask us to change our policy."

He said: "We have no differences with America, but America does not realize what the situation here is—especially with reference to the Russian fleet in the Mediterranean. And this has its consequence on the sentimental ties of the Greek people vis-à-vis the American people. The Greek people do not understand this cool U.S. policy. And it affects the military preparedness of Greece. The Greek government does not request arms from the United States to impose its own political views, but only in order to be prepared to fulfill its obligations within the alliance."

I pointed out that Americans inherently opposed *coup d'état* and military governments. Papadopoulos said: "We also oppose coups and military governments. We did not make a *coup d'état* in order to establish a regime. We made a revolution. If we had not made our revolution and if you had sent the weapons you are now holding up, they would have been turned against you."

I asked if parliamentary rule would be restored right after next month's referendum on the constitution. He said one could only consider this as "a first step along the road to parliamentary rule." It was evident it is going to be a long, slow walk.

I asked if he planned to bring King Constantine back soon. He said: "As we have provided in the constitution, the king will return at the latest with the proclamation of elections—or even earlier if it is considered opportune." However, he acknowledged that no time had yet been fixed for holding elections.

Concerning his political philosophy, he said: "As long as there is no parliament, the government simply must continue to do its best for society. You could call this guided democracy. After parliament has been brought back the position is described clearly in the constitution—parliamentary democracy with certain safety features neutralizing the weaknesses of the past." Papadopoulos described these as fundamentally "an increase in the freedom of the executive from legislative shackles so that the executive can move more rapidly as is required by modern society."

I asked if it was true the colonels had staged their coup only after learning that the generals did not have the guts to go through with one of their own. He said: "We intervened at zero minus one. We tried to convince everyone from the king to the last competent individual, including Canellopoulos, that it was necessary to take action. But when we saw that we had reached the end and nobody was ready to act, we moved. On this issue I summon anyone to challenge the truth of my statement."

I told him I was appalled by the incompetence of his public relations and press apparatus.

He fixed me with a stern expression and said: "Any difficulties you encountered were not because of a bad press mechanism but because of my own attitude. You remember I saw you a few days after the April 21 revolution and I gave you a good deal of time. You could, of course, believe anything you wished but you did not respect what I had said. I realize it is a great honor to have an interview published by Sulzberger, but you did not accurately repeat my views."

ATHENS, *August 18, 1968*

Tom Pappas, the Greek-American millionaire from Boston, took me to see the famous Colonel Ioannis Ladas, who is supposed to be the right-wing fanatic of the colonels' junta. We went over to his office in the ministry of public security (he is secretary-general, under a minister, but the real boss).

The first thing I noticed about Ladas's office was the total absence of any picture or insignia of the king or queen, confirming his reputation as a strong antimonarchist. The room was decorated with various symbols of the April 21 revolution (the phoenix) and his military insignia as a colonel (now retired) who had served both with the airborne and military police. Ladas ordered Turkish coffee and Tam-Tam, a kind of Greek Coca-Cola.

He is very small, even shorter than Papadopoulos, but strongly made, with jutting chin, slightly beat-up straight features, and a puzzled wild gleam in his eyes. The conversation was rudimentary. It started on the forced jocular level: "So now you see the man who is supposed to drink a glass of blood for breakfast and another for lunch."

He is lonely, bitter, fanatic. He told me eighteen members of his family, including his mother, brothers, etc., had been killed, some of them after torture, on one night of the civil war—by the communists. This explains his savage ideological views; and also his deep attachment to the army. He is not married and has no family at all. His unit was his family, and now he is out, and admits he's too old ever to go back to service.

He is bitter against all communists but also against "parliamentarians" and "professional politicians." He complained America didn't understand the regime or help it. I told him we had been helping Greece since 1944; all they had to do was get their constitution going and start working their way back to respectability.

Ladas is a brutal man. Some weeks ago a picture magazine called *Ikones* published an article on homosexuality through the ages, including all the ancient Greeks. The three main editors were brought to Ladas's office, one by one, and he personally beat them up. One of them has signed a long statement of the incident.

ATHENS, *September 28, 1968*

Drove out to Kifissia to see Panayotis Canellopoulos, prime minister of the government that was upset by the coup on April 21, 1967. We sat on the terrace of his cousin's house looking at a garden filled with late summer roses.

Canellopoulos said that although released from house arrest five days ago, he felt very isolated. A police car was still parked in front of his house and followed him wherever he went. He had been warned not to make any statement or he would be rearrested.

Canellopoulos said it was impossible to do underground work here without collaborating with the communists—and such collaboration was impossible for him. Article 138 of the new constitution authorized the government to continue suppressive rule. It is a contradiction to even ask the people to talk about freedom.

He did not belong to those who demanded foreign intervention (from the U.S.A.) but thought moral pressure was desirable. Washington had the right to press for an end to censorship—which was different from the Russian procedure of entering Prague with tanks to impose censorship. Washington had shown too many courtesies toward the regime.

Under the Metaxas dictatorship, there had not been so much psychological terror as today. Nevertheless, this was not really a totalitarian regime, as was seen by its mild repercussions on economic and social life. In a sense it was fascism without fascist trimmings. Instead of a party, it had the army—or a party within the army.

Canellopoulos said: "All is dark—the mood of the junta and the psychology of the Greek people. I cannot foresee the future as was always possible in past crises. In June 1939, I could write to Metaxas from exile warning that there would be a war and the Nazis would overrun Europe, but freedom would triumph in the end. No predictions are possible now. I am 100 percent against the colonels but I fear they are unable to foresee the future any more clearly than I am."

Dined tonight—the eve of the referendum on Greece's dictatorial constitution—with Panayotis Pipinellis, foreign minister. He used to be very tubby but now he is thin, with a triangular head, pointed chin, and broad brow, looking delicate and both older and younger than before. I kept saying to myself: "I wonder who it is he vaguely reminds me of." And then I remembered who it was—Panayotis Pipinellis. That is how time changes men.

P. said this government was really revolutionary. The officers belonged to a new class; they were almost universally the sons of peasants or workers, honest and intelligent men. When you saw the new leaders standing together you were struck by their simple dignity and honesty, their naiveté and plain patriotism.

P. makes no bones about his own autocratic tendencies. He says you can "do" much more with this kind of regime. Now relations with Turkey are very good. Cyprus peace is imminent. And relations with Jugoslavia have vastly improved.

P. called this a "government of emergency" and said there was no foreseeing what kind of ideology would come: probably rather autocratic. He surely wants that. His conservatism of the past has developed a fascist tinge.

ATHENS, *September 29, 1968*

Today was the referendum on Greece's strait-jacket constitution. Few people understand the document and those who aren't afraid of voting against it are either mesmerized by propaganda or wholly apathetic—save for an educated minority or the traditional far left.

Lunched with an old journalist friend who told me my conversation with Papadopoulos had been taped, copied out, and disseminated among top levels of the committee. A "double agent," who really works for Caramanlis, had picked it up and sent it to C. in Paris.

All this goes to show how confusing things can get in a police state where CIA methods (Papadopoulos was an old KYP man) and eavesdropping feature the scene. Between snoops, spooks, and double agents, everything gets around—but, as usual in Greece, in distorted form.

ATHENS, *October 1, 1968*

Lunched at Prince Michael's lovely house in the country (just beyond Marina's old place). Benjamin, our beagle, misbehaved by tearing up the lawn with his claws; lawns are rare and precious in Attica. Michael (who is thirty-one but mature and cultivated) was charming, as was also his Marina, who is now quite swollen with pregnancy.

He said the junta had given him permission to return to Greece provided he lived incognito and said nothing—which suits him to a tee. He thinks the junta is going to be in power for years. Had Constantine stayed on here he might have had some chance of influencing and softening the junta; no more.

PARIS, *October 3, 1968*

Lunched with Caramanlis. He is very bitter at the U.S.A. Costa is convinced the United States could throw out the junta in no time if it wished. He says only five percent of the people support it. I fear, as the saying goes, exile is a bad counselor.

PARIS, *October 6, 1968*

Dined last night at the Harrimans'. Averell very glum about election prospects. He says Humphrey is doomed. He won't fight, and he has crummy advisors.

It is a disgrace that General [Curtis] Lemay should be named as Wallace's vice presidential choice. When Lemay was air force chief of staff, he was planning to visit Chiang Kai-shek and called on Harriman in his office first. Harriman told him to warn Chiang not to expect help in landing in China.

"I agree," Lemay said to Harriman, chomping a huge cigar. "That's not the way to do it. We must take out China's industry." Harriman asked if he meant China's nuclear installations—something he, too, was prepared to consider. "Nope, all her industry." Harriman asked how many people this would kill. "Oh, a few million. They've got plenty." And what would happen when they rebuilt their industry. "Hit 'em again," said Lemay.

Harriman now obviously detests President Johnson and is quite dovish himself. But he admits he was a hawk two years ago.

He hates Nixon. Claims Nixon won't appoint any of the distinguished men being talked of for cabinet posts but will assemble the peers of Agnew, his vice presidential choice.

Played golf with Couve de Murville, the first time since he became prime minister. André Gros, French judge on the Hague high court, who played with us, kept kidding Couve (who picked his ball up off the fairway to clean some mud off it) saying that now he was changing all the rules because power had gone to his head. (Normally one can only clean a ball when it's on the green.)

Couve had little use for the American electoral candidates but obviously is convinced Nixon will win. One French diplomat thought he was a mediocrity. He lacked education and culture, was *"un primaire."* We were discussing talk about the "new Nixon." Said Couve: "I suppose that means the rich Nixon. He has money now, doesn't he?"

ROME, *October 8, 1968*

Dinner last night with Jozsef (Jozska) and Trudi Szall, the Hungarian ambassador and his wife.

They are profoundly pessimistic about events in East Europe symbolized by the rape of Czechoslovakia. J. blames [Alexander] Dubček for pushing things too far and too fast and says he is a most mediocre man, that the only Czech worth paying the least attention to is President [Ludvik] Svoboda; but he makes no excuses for the Russians.

Since 1966 it has been plain the Russians intended to do something with Czechoslovakia. The 1966 Warsaw pact "Vltava" maneuvers showed a tremendous weakness in Czech defenses opposite Germany and the U.S. army; the Czechs just didn't have the fighting quality and the Soviet army, which now runs things in Moscow, was determined to plug the gap. Even so, the decision to occupy Czechoslovakia was very sudden.

The Soviet government comprises a bunch of third-raters. Kosygin is just a stolid technocrat and knows nothing. Brezhnev is a nonentity put in by the army. He has always been a fairly low-ranking political commissar and has no intellectual importance. The one important man in Russia who opposed the Czech rape was, surprisingly enough [Mikhail] Suslov, generally thought of as a Stalinist.

Now the trend toward liberalization is dead throughout the communist world. Jozska spoke at various times, sadly and seriously, of possible suicide. He and Trudi hinted very strongly at a willingness to defect. J. kept saying his mission now was to write the truth, which he knew, and added that in the capitalist world at least one was free to write as he pleased.

I don't want to get mixed up in any kind of hanky-panky or fall into devious communist traps. I merely urged J. and T. to persevere and see things through for the sake of their ten-year-old son.

J. fears the heat will come very soon in Hungary, an effort to curb the trend to freedom. The press is already under rigid "self-censorship." Today's Hungarian joke: "Which is the most secure country in the world? Israel. It is only surrounded by enemies."

Throughout the world communists are outraged by the immorality of the Soviet act and also by its "illegality" because it is a communist "law" that no party can interfere in the affairs of another without the accord of a majority of the latter's central committee.

Drink and long talk with King Constantine. He looked pale and tired.

He asked what I thought he should do. I said get out of Rome, go either to London, a serious capital, or take a house in Zurich and go to the polytechnical institute. "I'm bad at mathematics," said he.

He thinks Papadopoulos is going to keep things as they are for years. It will be at least three years before there are elections. He arrests people of right and left without any excuse, just to keep them off balance. "It's like judo, political judo."

Constantine had wanted the various political leaders to issue a joint statement urging all Greek citizens to vote yes in the recent plebiscite, saying a referendum is illegal under martial law, therefore vote yes to avoid any risk of trouble. This would have wrecked the effect of the colonels' big majority. But nobody would go along with the idea.

If Washington wanted to bring the regime down it should ban investments, not hold back heavy weapons. That just left Greece weak with no political result.

He was savage on the subject of Pipinellis. When Pipinellis had first been asked to become a foreign minister he asked Constantine's position and had given him a promise to resign whenever the king wished. Constantine said to P.: "Use your own judgment but I warn you, they will squeeze you like a lemon and then, when they're all through with you, they'll throw you away."

The king said Makarios saw Constantine in Rome, invited him to Cyprus, but said publicly: "I don't need to invite him: the king of the Hellenes can always come when he wants."

ROME, *October 10, 1968*

Dined last night with Étienne and Jane Burin des Roziers. He is now French ambassador here. He had a marvelous story about the French embassy in Washington when Henri Bonnet was ambassador. Bonnet was giving an important dinner for Foster Dulles so he had truffles specially flown from France. When they arrived his chef brought them and Bonnet, sniffing them, thought they were too high. The chef assured him they were all right. "Let's try them on the dog," said Henri. They gave a chunk of truffle to his dog who enjoyed it.

The dinner went fine, truffles in the first course. When they were well along toward the cheese a pale butler brought Bonnet a brief note from the chef: "The dog just died." Henri blanched, excused himself, said he had an urgent telephone call. He called his doctor, asked his advice. How could he risk poisoning the secretary of state? The doctor said he would rush right over with emetic pills.

When Henri returned he suavely mentioned, as of little account, that sometimes people were sensitive to truffles. *En passant,* he added that his dog, who had shared this particular truffle, had just died so he had taken the precaution of obtaining some emetic pills. If any guest would feel safer he would be glad to provide a pill. All the guests, headed by Dulles, grabbed them. The various bathroom facilities were shared out among senior ranking guests and the ladies; the rest, including Bonnet, went out into the garden and retched.

Finally, after a disheveled, frantic group had reassembled and Bonnet was tranquilizing them with cognac somebody asked: "Did the dog suffer much? Did it take him long to die?" Bonnet thought this a good question and summoned the chef. Said the chef: "Not at all, M. l'Ambassadeur. It was over in an instant. The truck hit him squarely and broke his neck."

SOFIA, *October 24, 1968*

Lengthy talk with Ivan Bashev, the foreign minister. He insisted the "socialist commonwealth" was not a "new" Soviet doctrine but consistent with the "political line of socialist countries." He acknowledged that "if events compel us" the socialist lands were ready to take "hard steps" against transgressors but "this doesn't mean there is a new doctrine."

In Czechoslovakia the reason for "the assistance we rendered [the Warsaw pact occupation]" was well known. Internal and external forces were ready to "tilt the balance" in favor of counter-revolution and change the equilibrium "between the two blocs."

BUCHAREST, *October 28, 1968*

Spent two days driving across Bulgaria to the Black Sea, revisiting Balchik for the first time since I occupied it with the Bulgarian army twenty-eight years ago, and then driving up here, crossing the long Danube bridge that links Russe (Bulgaria) with Giurgiu (Rumania). I was interested, after the mass of rumors that Russian troops had entered Bulgaria, to see nothing confirming this.

We started on a fine autumnal day through the russet countryside leading to the Balkan range. We had rented an English Cortina Ford with a godawful driver named Sasha, who spoke pidgin French. At Lovetch a soldier in a long greatcoat stood with bayoneted rifle guarding a couple of hundred prisoners working in a marble quarry. "Thieves," said Sasha.

We lunched at Veliko Turnovo, the medieval capital where Assen and Peter, two chieftains, built a huge fortress on Tsarevets hill and stood off first the Byzantine Greeks, then the Turks.

Varna seemed most impressive, with fine looking shops and lighted ships standing off outside the harbor. But the massive hotel was a disappointment, with queues for everything, cold, uncomfortable rooms.

Everything somehow is so arranged that it is mass-produced in the least efficient way. Thus, in Varna, set amid vineyards and a fish-filled sea, it is impossible to get local wine or fresh fish, all of which I suppose are assembled in some central place and exported or distributed, stale. In the casino I noticed Bulgarian couples drinking Bulgarian champagne as white wine and Bulgarian Koka Kola (sic) as red wine.

Yesterday we drove through the rain to Balchik which still has a mixed population, with plenty of gypsies and Turks. We visited some of the old seaside villas (now hotels and restaurants) of Queen Marie of Rumania and her entourage and walked on the beach beside the sad sea.

Drove through Varna port after lunch and visited the war museum where Sasha pointed out the torpedo boat he had served on in World War II—a French vessel built in 1908!

BUCHAREST, *October 29, 1968*

Dined last night with Dick (U.S. ambassador) and Harriet Davis. Harriet said when Nixon was here early this year he stayed with them. (Harriet had decided, when Dick was named ambassador, to get some modern American paintings to take with them to Rumania and had spent her own money to go from Washington to New York to select them.) Nixon: "Hello, honey, where did you get all this crap you've got on the walls?" When she said she'd gotten it herself, not imposed by the state department, he said: "Aw, all you state department folks stick together."

This evening had successive drinks with Elena P. and Bishy Catargi. Elena, who hated what the regime did, is pro-Ceausescu now, as is Bishy. "Even if I had a chance to leave Rumania, I never would. It is me, my country."

Bishy was under arrest four years and worked on the ghastly Danube canal, a project that has now dried up in useless, weedy scars and human skeletons. He is a gallant little fellow; and Mic, his eighty-one-year-old mother, ex-princess, has survived everything. They share an apartment with another family. They have two rooms, each family has a kitchen, one bathroom for all tenants. Says Bishy: "I'd have preferred two bathrooms, one kitchen."

BUCHAREST, *October 30, 1968*

Dick Davis says there is no evidence of real Soviet pressure on Rumania now. There is no such kind of effort as in 1948 in Jugoslavia to build up an opposition force in the party.

Dick doesn't foresee a repetition of the Czech affair here. Rumania's position is different. Moscow claimed that the end of censorship and open criticism inside Czechoslovakia constituted the beginning of a legal internal opposition. But there is nothing like that here. There are no pressures for liberalism inside Rumania. The regime has slowly eased controls but it is still a police state—more implicitly than actually.

The Rumanian leadership is very careful. It would never pull out of the Warsaw pact or go neutral. But Bucharest makes its own foreign policy and differs strongly from Moscow on many issues—such as, for example, the Middle East.

1 9

RUMANIA KNOWS
HOW AND *WHEN*
TO PLAY DEAD

BUCHAREST, *October 30, 1968*

GOOD TALK OF ALMOST AN HOUR AND A HALF WITH NICOLAE Ceausescu, president of the state council (chief of state) and general secretary of the Communist party, total boss of Rumania. He received me in his office in Communist party headquarters.

He was standing with Gheorghe Macavescu, the acting minister of foreign affairs. I came in with an interpreter (Macavescu's secretary) and stenographer. Ceausescu shook my hand quite firmly, smiled, introduced me to Macavescu, and then moved us all over to chairs and sofa. He was wearing a neat, old-fashioned, grey-striped suit, grey-striped socks, white shirt, dark tie. He sat quietly, replying with some deliberation but frequent smiles.

I said I had a message from Harriman, namely that Averell was grateful for the help Rumania had provided in helping arrange the Paris peace talks with Vietnam. Ceausescu said he was disappointed with the talks, that there was no movement, they seemed to be stalemated. He thought it was entirely up to the United States; that if we simply stopped bombing peace could come.

I remarked that Rumania, before the war and revolution, had always been known as a singularly corrupt country. Yet this feature had now largely gone. How had he changed a national characteristic?

He said: "The existence of widespread corruption originated in the fact that private ownership and distribution of the means of production prevailed. Under such circumstances corruption could easily manifest itself.

(469)

But the revolution changed both the ownership and social structure. There was no longer any large private ownership and as a result the basis for widespread corruption was eliminated. Furthermore, during recent years the living standards of the population have been raised. A number of steps have been taken to insure that the national income is distributed according to the contributions of each member of society."

In his speeches Ceausescu always referred to "Marxism-Leninism" whereas Tito, above all in his last talk with me, now seemed to use "Marxism." Did this imply an ideological or philosophical difference? He answered:

"To tell you the truth, I had not noticed such a difference in phraseology. Naturally, if one refers to Marx's own period, to the period before Lenin, one only speaks of Marxism. Certainly no conclusions can be drawn concerning ideological differences. Marxism means not only what Marx wrote but also all the body of its descendants writing on Marxist social science.

"Of course the philosophy created by Marx and later developed by others cannot be claimed as the 'property' of any single man or group. For, as in every other field of activity, social science requires continuous development; it does not remain static. No theoreticians can claim the right to pass final judgments."

He had recently, in a speech, said Rumania sought the "broadest democracy" possible. Were the ultimate implications of this a free press and a permitted political opposition?

"To be quite frank," Ceausescu said, "I did not have such things in mind. Our concept of democracy differs somewhat from that of a society which contains various classes who are ruled by an exploiting class. I believe that in such a society real democracy simply cannot exist. I think one cannot claim that the private owner of the means of production is really on an equal footing with the workers who labor under the conditions that he and his system impose.

"It is obvious, however, that even in the specific sphere of political democracy there is great inequality between the people who possess the material means to impose their will and the people who do not possess such means. When I spoke of the 'broadest democracy' I meant that all of the members of our society possess equal rights and participate directly in the discussion of all problems on both internal and external questions. They can speak their minds and openly criticize such errors and shortcomings as may appear, and which are bound to appear.

"I don't think, however, that in a socialist society where conditions for a permanent partnership of all groups have been created, there is any need for different political parties. Such would have no meaning here. There is no need for more than one party today—and tomorrow, I may say, this is even more true.

"Furthermore, I for one think our press enjoys the broadest freedom." (It is quite state-controlled.) "Of course, if this means the freedom of anyone to write anything—we do not agree. We don't permit people to write unless they take into account the real interests of our society.

"We ask editors to write about things which comply with the interests of the people and the necessities of the country's development. Our censorship is mild—and often nonexistent. Editors understand our requirements. There is a kind of self-censorship which is certainly in step with the development of the people's consciousness and, as this improves, censorship will vanish entirely some day." (In other words, when everyone learns to think and speak alike, there will be no need to curb individualists.)

I inquired whether he still considered Rumania an "active" member of the Warsaw pact despite the Czechoslovakian crisis. "Indeed," said he, "we are active members of the Warsaw alliance and we will stay in it as long as it exists. Two years ago—here in Bucharest—all the socialist countries decided to work for the liquidation of military blocs, but until NATO agrees to dissolve itself, thus allowing the Warsaw pact to dissolve, the Warsaw treaty will continue to exist and we will continue to be members. But from the very start we did not regard such an intervention [Czechoslovakia] as justified from any point of view. And with the passage of time our conviction has become even stronger."

Ceausescu said Rumania had never been notified of the decision as a Warsaw pact decision—because it had not been that; nor had it ever been publicly represented as that. Rumania had never been asked to furnish any troops in the invading contingent; this country's attitude was well known in advance.

I asked: "There have been widespread press reports of Soviet pressure on Rumania—economic, military, political. Is this true?" He hesitated several seconds, rubbing his chin reflectively. Then he said: "That depends on what one considers pressure. Officially, I would not say such things existed. Pressure. Of course, if one has in mind such things as what a newspaper says, that's another matter. Officially, there has been no pressure. But it is different if you take into account the position of the press—the Soviet and other presses."

I asked if he considered President Johnson's August 30 warning to the Russians on laying off Rumania had been helpful. "Yes, it was useful," he said. I asked for permission to quote him on that. "No," he replied, politely but firmly. "But next time you see the president please pass on my message."

I remarked that although there was philosophical similarity between the Soviet and Rumanian ideologies, this country's foreign policy differed on many issues from Moscow's. He commented:

"Such differences are not so much on problems of principle as on concrete approaches to issues. On the fundamental questions our viewpoints are very similar or at any rate very close to each other. On peaceful coexistence. On an active coexistence policy toward the U.S.A. On nuclear matters. On disarmament. Naturally, on such matters as China and Albania there is divergence. But we believe that existing differences between some socialist nations are passing differences.

"And even the Middle East shows no basic difference. We saw no use in breaking diplomatic relations with Israel. Among other things this would be tantamount to a precedent in other circumstances. This could mean that whenever there was a conflict between two countries we would be expected to break relations with one or the other. In such a way we would lose our potential influence as a peacemaker."

He said: "The greatest single influence in my life was the moment when I first made contact with the revolution in Rumania. That was in 1932." (He was born in 1918.)

When I had finished and was tucking my notebook in my pocket, Ceausescu looked at me a bit timidly and asked if he could now ask a question. Who did I think would win the American presidential election next week? I said it looked as if Nixon would win but that in any case I did not think there would be any difference in the foreign policy of a Nixon or a Humphrey. As for Wallace, he was just a sad joke.

"I met Nixon," said Ceausescu. "That was about two years ago. Of course, he wasn't a president then. But neither was I." (Ceausescu became chief of state last December.) I asked what he thought of Nixon.

He was diffident. "I don't want to seem to interfere in your affairs," he kept saying. But I prodded him and he went on: "We had a very good talk. He impressed me. He showed a real understanding of international problems and of our own situation. I found that we agreed very substantially on China. We both thought there could be no solid basis for world peace until China was brought into it. We also agreed on disarmament. He impressed me as being an experienced and knowledgeable man."

BUCHAREST, *November 1, 1968*

Victor Dimitriu, formerly ambassador to France, gave me his views. What is going on here now is a kind of "conspiratorial liberalism." Ceausescu had resolutely made up his mind to liberalize, before the Czech crisis this summer. But the movement has been set back by fear of Russia. Nevertheless, the Rumanians in their long history under Byzantium and Turkey have learned how to feign death, to play possum. That is what they are now doing. They know the Russians have many agents studded about the party, army, and security police, and Ceausescu is playing it very cool because he doesn't want to risk invasion. He believes Moscow wants to push some of its agents into high positions in Rumania's March elections, and he is working to exclude that chance.

True independence became possible here only after the Russian troops left in 1958–59. Moscow now is trying to wreck that independence and this is what Ceausescu is working against. Above all, he is determined to give Russia no excuse to get troops back.

This past April he began a purge, trying to clean out the pro-Russian elements, above all in the police. Things were moving along quite well when the Czech crisis came and spoiled everything. In early September the Soviet ambassador visited Ceausescu and behaved like a gauleiter. They had a very stormy session. He demanded an end to mobilization, to the patriotic guards, to the increasingly free press. Ceausescu backed down— but only tactically. He is determined to pursue his strategic goal of liberalization.

On the whole, the Communist party is with Ceausescu on this but there are some waverers at the top. In the meantime, the Russians have cut their arms deliveries. This puts a big burden on Rumania's budget since this country now has to manufacture much of such material.

Ceausescu is playing down the crisis in what his admirers here call "Byzantine fashion." But he is not yielding. The *big* calculation here is that the Soviet regime is doing very badly, is facing a crisis. The contest in Russia is not between rival elements such as army and party, but between the young and the old in all structures of society.

Dimitriu sees disastrous repercussions for communism as a result of the occupation of Czechoslovakia.

"Czechoslovakia finished communism in the West. Mediocrity and conformity are triumphant." He says Ceausescu is now resolutely determined to work toward democratization but it is a tricky, slow game, based on the need to avoid confrontation with Moscow and on the assumption that if he waits, there will be a Soviet upheaval.

His concluding words: "Throughout history Rumania has known how or when to play dead."

BUCHAREST, *November 4, 1968*

Marvelous weekend in northern Moldavia looking at monasteries and convents with their magnificent painted frescoes, up near the Soviet border. Even at Suceava, a town of about 40,000 some 24 miles from Russia, one saw less uniforms than in Bucharest. And in Radauti, 7 miles from the border, there were none. In terms of incipient crisis, I have confirmed to myself that there is no sign of any.

We picked up a guide in Suceava and took off for a series of fifteenth and sixteenth century monasteries (one, late fourteenth), built when Suceava was the capital of the principality of Moldavia: one more splendid than the next, usually with every inch of the walls of the church within the walled courtyard covered with beautifully colored frescoes, both inside *and* outside. These are jewels worthy of medieval and renaissance Italy.

We spent the night in Moldovita convent, the first time I have ever slept in a convent. A full moon rose out of the Carpathians and we could look from our window and see the central church standing against it.

The nuns were especially charming and quite lovely, especially the sixty-five-year-old mother superior and her right hand, forty-six-year-old Sister Lorenza. Both came from the neighborhood but one had learned a bit of German, the other French. Their black robes and wimples are very chic with little pillbox hats like those of Dalmatian girls, and coifs.

All these churches were surrounded by walled fortresses to beat off Turkish, Polish, Greek, Austrian invaders. The bells rang for services and a nun hammered on a kind of xylophone of wood in the belltower to summon the villagers to Sunday mass, which was read by an old monk because women are forbidden this holy rite. From all around peasants came: the women in sheepskin (fur inside) embroidered jackets and shawls; the men in similar jackets (less embroidery), white kilts, white leggings, black fur hats. They bowed right to the earth (Islamic fashion) as the monk droned, the nuns sang.

We dined on *mamaliga* (Rumanian corn-meal mush, served almost hard with cheese and onions), meatballs, fruit, kümmel (convent-made), and wine; and breakfasted on tea, toast, and marvelous convent butter and honey. There are only eighteen nuns now (there used to be thirty-five before most of their land was taken away by the state) and they work very hard. The mother superior says sometimes they sleep only three or four hours, "but in the summer, when the days are long, occasionally we can take a nap."

The colors of the frescoes (as well as the painting itself) are lovely: greens, blues, lots of gold leaf, and scenes repeated over and over again like the thirty-two steps to heaven (with sinners being dragged off and down to hell by devils), the life of St. Nicholas, the 365 saints for each day, the various royal donors of churches, holding models in their hands, presenting their churches to Christ, attended by their families. At Sunday service peasants left plates of food, from simple sandwiches or cheese to elaborately iced large cakes, to be blessed by the nuns and at least in part eaten by them.

The whole area is not only beautiful but astonishingly peaceful; most people seem to be religious, attending church. There is lots of fat livestock and each house has a well with a multispoked wheel to draw up the bucket. We visited a couple of peasant houses and they overwhelmed us with generosity and gifts of such things as apples, nuts, and pumpkins. Houses with daughters in them have shelters over the gates—so, if it's raining as the girls say goodnight to their swains, they won't get wet.

In one village there was a cemetery filled with leaning stones of Jewish graves. Now all the Jews are gone—to death in concentration camps, or to Israel.

BUDAPEST, *November 6, 1968*

I was received by the boss, [Janos] Kadar, at Communist party head-quarters. Kadar came out to an antechamber and greeted me, then waved me to the end of a large council table, saying "We take our usual places."

I noticed a large painting of Lenin, a few plants, neat stacks of books. There was a bookcase with many Marxist volumes. As we talked, fruit juice and mineral water were served. Kadar offered cigarettes. He smoked, without inhaling.

He seems to have gained weight; his face was more seamy, careworn, making his heavy jaw and puffy lips stand out. His eyes were tired and he spoke with an unusually faint voice. I felt that he was ill or had been deeply depressed.

I am certainly the first Westerner of any sort Kadar has seen since August 21 (Czechoslovakia) and U.S. Ambassador Martin Hillenbrand says no Eastern diplomat has seen him either. We chatted about hunting. He said that this was an unusually fine "Old woman's summer—what you call Indian summer. The sun is still shining and this gives old women new hope; old men too."

I asked if the previous liberalizing trend would continue in police affairs, censorship, travel, economics—despite "recent events" (Czecho-slovakia). He said: "We shall continue our course in every aspect includ-ing what I prefer to call democratization of our own life."

I asked if there had not been a recent recentralization of economics and whether, in line with what he had said, there would be a decentraliza-tion. He replied: "There was no recentralization. The management of our economic life under the present plan has been under study and prepara-tion for a period of two and a half years. Its tendency is definitely toward decentralization."

I remarked that I had been most distressed, after our last meeting, to motor to Austria and see the border fences and mine fields. Why were these necessary?

He said: "That has been changed. The frontier is still guarded—but in other ways. There are many reasons for this guard. The least important is the question of individuals who might wish to go across although, even so, in such personal traffic the orderly way is by the door, not by the back fence. On this kind of border—a frontier between two social systems—not only benevolent tourists cross it but other kinds of people. Nevertheless, since our last talk, most of the mines and other defenses have been removed."

I turned to foreign policy. What was the meaning of the Soviet doctrine of a "socialist commonwealth" described by Gromyko at UN? Kadar said: "The socialist commonwealth is a term that can be used like the commonwealth of NATO" (a term never used). "It is not a new doctrine. After all, since there is no longer only one socialist state, the Soviet Union, but fourteen, we now must call it a commonwealth of socialist states. We use the term not in the sense of a treaty but to identify the socialist system. There are, of course, differences and contradictions among the fourteen, but there are fundamental identities of view."

I asked if the cold war was now reviving because of Czechoslovakia. He was gloomy. He said: "The cold war has revived, first and foremost because of the Vietnamese conflict. To this trend the Czechoslovakian events and clashes have had an additional effect. In my opinion, there are many dangerously sensitive questions in the world—like the Middle East or Germany.

"The cold war trends are plain. First came the extension of the Vietnam war. Then there was the Middle East crisis and war. Then, this year, came the political debate on Czechoslovakia." ("Political debate" is not probably the way history will describe the events of August 21.)

Why, I asked, had Hungary felt it necessary to join in "physical action" against Czechoslovakia? He said: "Because in our judgment the situation there had developed to such a degree that it seriously endangered socialism and there was a real threat that they might end up in taking Czechoslovakia out of the Warsaw pact."

Did this imply, I inquired, that Czechoslovakia in 1968 was comparable to Hungary in 1956, Dubček to Nagy? "In the essence," said Kadar, "there were many similarities, although the form in which they expressed themselves was different.

"Of course, we regard this question as the affair of the five countries that took part in the action and of Czechoslovakia. We all agreed that we would look only forward to the future, not behind to the past. Therefore we no longer discuss the events that preceded August 21. But certainly one motive was to prevent the development in Czechoslovakia of a situation like the last phase of the Hungarian crisis in 1956.

"Czechoslovakia threatened the stability and security of Europe. In this part of the world we take the threat of West German militarism very seriously and, in that same context, it is fair to say that this militarism is supported by important American circles."

I observed that it must have been an especially unhappy personal experience for Kadar to join in the action against Czechoslovakia. (Kadar was the man who rode to power on the backs of Soviet tanks in 1956.) He looked at me sadly, saying:

"I wouldn't say that I was happy. Sometimes it becomes essential that such decisions are taken for the sake of vital interests of the people living in this part of the world. But we all regarded this as a step that had to be taken. We saw it as an unhappy necessity."

I had been told he had seen Dubček at Komárom on the weekend of August 17–18 and had pleaded with him to calm things down or face trouble. He said: "During the process of events since January 1968 there have been many efforts to find a simple, political solution to the Czecho-slovakian problem, both bilateral and multilateral efforts. I saw Dubček several times—including the one you mentioned.

"The aim of these meetings was to find a political solution in the interests of the Czechoslovakian people and the other socialist countries. On the part of those of us who spoke for Hungary on these matters, it was not difficult because from the start we had a clear viewpoint. We always urged that the problems of Czechoslovakia's Communist party could and should be solved by it; and that the problems of Czechoslo-vakia's society could and should be solved by the society."

I asked if Kadar considered Rumania and Jugoslavia "socialist" coun-tries. He answered: "Yes, they are socialist countries—with differences in practice. And, of course, Rumania is in the Warsaw pact; Jugoslavia is not."

I asked if—now that Vietnam peace talks were clearly moving forward —he thought United States-Hungarian relations were likely to improve. He said:

"Hungarian-American relations are fundamentally influenced by mutu-ally antagonistic positions on the most important international problems— Vietnam, the Middle East, European security. But this doesn't preclude the possibility that our two countries can live together within these limita-tions. We certainly have a desire to improve relations; and the United States has told us it also would like this."

A secretary came in quietly and handed Kadar a sheet of paper. He read it and then told me the latest news flash was that Nixon had 264 votes and all radio and television stations were conceding the election to him.

BUDAPEST, *November 10, 1968*

Spent the day in Esztergom, seat of the Roman Catholic primate, with a horrible cathedral but a marvelous museum of Hungarian, Swabian, and Austrian medieval and renaissance masters. We went with Ed and Rose-Ann Alexander and their kids. The Alexanders are the charming, culti-vated American cultural attaché and wife.

Cardinal Mindszenty has been in the U.S. embassy (formerly legation) since November 1956, when he was warned Russian tanks were swarming in and sought haven. He is a dour man who lives in the past. He always refers to "the Bolsheviks" here, not the "communists."

He has been given a radio and TV and is fed regularly (likes his beer and wine) at the expense of Catholic funds sent through the U.S.A. He shows no gratitude, is obdurate and stubborn. He reads American, British, French, and German papers avidly as well as the *Osservatore Romano*.

He frequently talks with members of the embassy staff and irks stenographers by demanding their typing services (often in Latin).

Mindszenty holds regular services and American embassy Catholics attend Sunday and Christmas mass. Mindszenty was furious when Washington decided to exchange ambassadors with Budapest and resolved to leave the embassy, and face rearrest. He thought we should not make concessions to the regime. He started burning his private papers and let his plans be known.

Washington got hold of the Vatican and the Pope passed on instructions to Mindszenty not to move, thus saving immense embarrassment (autumn of 1967).

Another Catholic priest confesses the cardinal. He gets dental and medical aid from American doctors flown in from West Germany. We have a list of emergency Hungarian doctors to be called on in case of mortal danger.

The cardinal's old sister, a peasant woman, comes to see him from time to time. He is shown American movies on our projector, in the chancery hall. He is always brought his food by U.S. staff members.

PARIS, *November 16, 1968*

Averell Harriman had his seventy-seventh birthday party last night. We talked about his sixtieth birthday party here in 1951 when he had all the brass—Eisenhower, Bradley, Gruenther, Admiral Kirk, Acheson, etc.

He was as excited as a youngster by his presents and the candles on his cake, as well as by a claret laid down in the year he was born—and still remarkably good. We gave him a carefully wrapped-up can of Rumanian carp which is spelled crap.

Cy Vance, George Ball and wife, and Congressman William Moorehead and wife were there. Both Ball and Harriman blamed Johnson for not announcing the cease-bombing a few days earlier, because they think this might have won the election for Humphrey.

PARIS, *November 17, 1968*

Dined last night with the Harrimans. Ivo Vejvoda, Jugoslav ambassador, was also there. He said Jugoslavia has written into its constitution a specific clause stating that no official can sign a capitulation or an agreement for the country to be occupied. A new clause is being written into the constitution that anyone who attempts to sign such a document can be charged as a traitor.

Averell said: "I simply can't stand Nixon. I was all ready to quit under Johnson, but I won't stay one second under Nixon. I just don't trust him. There's no use mincing matters."

PARIS, *November 18, 1968*

Y. of the Czech embassy called today and told me this riddle: Which is the most neutral country in the world today? Czechoslovakia—because its government doesn't even dare intervene in its own affairs.

MOSCOW, *November 22, 1968*

This morning I had a talk at the foreign ministry with Ambassador Leonid Zamyatin, head of the press division, pale, cold, courteous.

He said: "We have contacts with the Johnson administration and these could become more active of course (when Nixon comes in). We think it is difficult to solve international problems without a dialogue.

"We have always thought such contacts served U.S. interests, not only ours. But there have been difficulties and complications. And we never considered it possible to maintain these relationships and to have close contacts with a nation that was carrying on a war against a country with which we had very close relations—Vietnam. This has scarred Soviet-American relations."

Z. insisted that in the Middle East the Soviet Union "tries in every way to bring about a settlement on the basis of the UN resolution." In that area "we [referring to the two superpowers] should not play with fire. Israel should withdraw its troops and fulfill the UN resolution. Otherwise, it might happen that war might come again."

I telephoned Yuri Zhukov at *Pravda* and he suggested I come on over. His views, summarized:

The Czechoslovakian occupation demonstrated only that Russia was determined to maintain the status quo, not that it wished to change it. Any change in the status quo is dangerous.

If NATO says it wishes to avoid any alteration in its frontiers or what lies behind them, OK. But there can be no "grey area" as now suggested in the November Brussels communiqué of NATO which spoke of Austria, Jugoslavia, Finland, Albania, and without mentioning it, implied Rumania also.

I said Moscow's new "commonwealth doctrine," as expressed by Gromyko, implied a "right" to interfere in the affairs of any "socialist" state. What were they? Cuba? China? Mali? Egypt? Yuri said such states were "well known." It was sheer "romance" for (Leopold) Senghor, president of Senegal, to consider himself a "socialist."

Russia had no desire to send its forces into other lands. Czechoslovakia was a very special case. First of all it was necessary to "help the Czech people to defend themselves." And secondly, from a strategic viewpoint, it was necessary to keep the status quo.

It was foolish to talk of any threats to Rumania or Jugoslavia. If Stalin didn't invade Jugoslavia in 1948, "why should those who renounced Stalin do so? Of course, we have big differences with Jugoslavia, although I don't understand why they are insisting on a crisis atmosphere now."

Yuri argued that Czechoslovakia had presented a curious, menacing, but subtle situation, quite different from the return of "feudal elements" in Hungary twelve years ago. Czechoslovakia had never had a civil war. First, it had been liberated by the Red army, then it had had a subsequent peaceful change of regime. The regime changed without any bloodshed. And the change was not followed by any mass deportations. "They have no Siberia," said Yuri with a cold smile. "So the people accepted the change in a sly way; they went along with it. The social democrats of Beneš and Masaryk decided to amalgamate with the Communist party." (An odd way of putting it.) "They created a joint party—just like East Germany, Poland, and Hungary.

"But the political forces in Czechoslovakia were different. The social democrats in Hungary had been unimportant. The communists were very strong in Poland and East Germany. But in Czechoslovakia the social democrats had had a long—twenty years—experience of power and of dealing with ideology. So, when the union was achieved, the communists took control of practical things, but the social democrats hung on to theoretical things—like the press and trade unions. Thus, in the structure of the state, the split was maintained.

"You must understand our position. We did not back outmoded, reactionary forces. Indeed, we applauded the new Central Committee chosen in January—Dubček and all those who were against Novotny. But they went too far. They tried to use economic and social reform for their own ends—and they lost control of events."

Yuri said two additional things of interest: (1) "Nobody understands China—or what goes on there." (2) "We want to concentrate on our own internal problems now. We must."

Moscow, *November 23, 1968*

Pleasant chat with [Ambassador Llewellyn] Tommy Thompson. Tommy said Khrushchev was not regarded here as just a chief of the opposition but as an enemy who would have his successors bumped off if he ever were able to scramble back to power. Nixon had made the great mistake of trying to see him on his last trip. This left a bad taste, and the regime still looks on Nixon with scepticism.

Tommy thinks the essence of Soviet foreign policy is now to keep the status quo—in order to concentrate on internal affairs. This was the real meaning of Czechoslovakia whose occupation was a purely defensive move. Russia will probably try and scare Rumania into line and its attitude toward Jugoslavia is unclear. But this is not the forerunner of further expansionist tendencies.

There will very likely be some change in leadership next year. There is evident dissatisfaction with the lack of strong and decisive government. It is now recognized that the regime did not handle the Czechoslovakian crisis well, although, right now, everyone remains united because they are under attack.

The growth rate is slowing down. Russia is trying to keep up a military and space competition with the U.S.A. on about half our economic base. Continued need to support Nasser, Ho Chi Minh, Castro—and now the cost of Czechoslovakia—comprised too large a drain on resources. Russia needs big new investments in agriculture. It is falling behind on housing requirements. To meet these urgent needs it has been using up investment money.

The role of the Communist party these days is anachronistic—and resented. Factory managers want to make their own decisions—but everything is still far too centralized and has to be referred to Moscow. The economic reform is but a drop in the bucket. Prices are still fixed by the government. Decisions to make new models, or how to use the labor force, come from the center.

Furthermore, there is an undoubted generation gap. This is a major problem. Youth is apathetic and only interested in its own welfare. This hurts deeply in an ideologically-based system like this. Even in the military the problem exists. The younger officers resent the great layers of older commanders standing in their own way of promotion.

There is a danger that Russia could go beyond its present status quo attitude if the Czechs provoke stronger Soviet measures—which in turn would be resented by the West. Should that happen there is no doubt that the Russians would further tighten up bloc discipline and force Rumania to fall into line.

As for the Far East, Russia wants the U.S.A. to counterbalance Chinese influence. But there is no serious worry here about a war with China—either about having such a war or about losing it; Russia could clobber China. However, Moscow worries about the ideological fight with Peking.

In some fields, like disarmament and the nuclear nonproliferation treaty, there is close cooperation between Moscow and Washington. But politically there is none. Moscow, furthermore, has found it advantageous to play with de Gaulle. Khrushchev might conceivably have wanted to work out a spheres-of-influence deal with Washington; not Brezhnev and his group.

Moscow has been pushing "progressive" governments wherever it can, hoping to guide them leftward—as in Syria, Algeria, and Mali (now overthrown by a coup). This policy certainly does not accord with any deal on national spheres of influence.

The ideologists are on top. These men are deeply committed communists. The pragmatists of the Khrushchev era have declined in influence.

And the ideologists look at everything with an orthodox view that is out of step with world reality.

He thought Moscow was worried about its position in the Middle East and did not want to get involved in a brinkmanship contest with us, resulting from a new Arab-Israeli war. Therefore, it genuinely wanted a settlement there.

The Mediterranean is much closer to Russia than America and if it wants to play superpower, it must maintain its role there.

Moscow, *November 24, 1968*

Spent the day at the American embassy *dacha* twenty miles from Moscow: a nice, crisp (14 above zero, Fahrenheit) Sunday with the sun shining through a rosy mist and the birch trees sheathed in frost. Tommy and Jane [Thompson] called for me and we took a short, agreeable walk, then lunched with the very bright, thoughtful Canadian ambassador, Robert Ford, and his Brazilian wife.

Ford regards the leadership as a competent, exceedingly well-briefed team. Brezhnev is tough, cold, unsmiling, courteous, humorless. Kosygin is more at ease, smiling. He speaks well on foreign as well as internal matters.

Moscow, *November 25, 1968*

I gave a luncheon in my room for Yuri Zhukov and Georgi Ratiani of *Pravda*. Ratiani said a new movement that had sprung up by itself was now growing in various communities called "one service for ten." Apparently different people in apartment houses or collectives—a plumber, electrician, etc.—would pledge to do all the necessary work in their field in their community, in exchange for similar services, thus obviating wasted time and red tape.

Ratiani was amusing about his experiences in the U.S.A. where people were most helpful, arranged meetings with right- and left-wing whites and blacks, and even a lunch with the Ku Klux Klan boss of Atlanta, who explained how his organization had saved American society so far but now had to take power to prevent integration. Ratiani found that even the most extreme right-wing Americans had nothing against Russia, only sometimes regretted they couldn't handle Negroes the way Hitler had handled Jews.

Moscow, *November 27, 1968*

Dined last night at the British embassy with Ambassador Sir Duncan and Lady Wilson. She told the latest tale of the "Armenian radio" (the joke mart). Alexander the Great, Julius Caesar, and Napoleon come to

Moscow for the army day parade. Says Alexander: "With tanks like that I could have conquered China." Says Caesar: "With missiles like that no city could have withstood my catapults." Says Napoleon: "With newspapers like *Pravda* no one would have heard of Waterloo."

Moscow, *November 28, 1968*

Luncheon in my honor given at the Prague restaurant by Ambassador Leonid Zamyatin. He pointed out in a toast that he had deliberately chosen the Prague!

Present, in addition to Zamyatin and myself: Henry Kamm (*New York Times* correspondent here); Victor Sudriakhov, the big-shot interpreter who translated for me and Khrushchev; Professor Yuri Arbatov, head of the new institute on the United States, started by the academy of science; a former professor of social science and journalist, Tseitlin, a foreign affairs expert of *Izvestia*; and Simonov, an assistant to Zamyatin.

Zamyatin said Russia was Public Enemy Number One in China (way ahead of us) but he thought the people who opposed Mao were pro-Soviet, that the U.S.A. had no friends. When change comes it will be pro-Moscow.

Arbatov denied that Russia was muscling into control of East Europe's economy as we had in West Europe. He claimed that if there were political good will Russia and America had much to exchange—above all technical information.

Zamyatin said he had taken up with Brezhnev's office my request to see him and B. was "too busy." Zamyatin then said he had something unpleasant to raise. The *Times* was devoting too much time to reporting on the activities of an "unimportant minority of oppositionists." Kamm had recently sent an account of a letter of a well-known "felon," who had nothing to do with politics. This was clearly a warning against Kamm—who replied that he appreciated Z.'s frankness.

Kamm says his piece in the *Times* (sent three days ago) has not yet been printed. Therefore, this information obviously comes from the phone-tap.

Warsaw, *December 1, 1968*

Arrived yesterday evening by train: both Moscow and Warsaw airports socked in. At the border the largest Soviet customs guard I've ever seen deprived me of my last sixteen rubles ($17.50), which I'd saved for lunch and a porter's tip, and gave me a receipt instead, guaranteeing me sixteen rubles next time I go to Russia. The usual pair of guards made me leave the compartment so they could search under the berths, a habit Eastern travelers are inured to.

Spent the day with Walt and Mary Anne Stoessel (now U.S. ambassador here), a charming, young couple. He says for the present we aren't inviting any official Poles around (because of Czechoslovakia) but soon may resume. In the meantime, all the intellectuals, artists, etc., we do ask, come happily.

WARSAW, *December 2, 1968*

Talked at length with Henry Krzeczkowski, an editor and translator (of literature) who speaks beautiful English. "I learned it from my nannie," says he. He insisted on talking only in the middle of the room, amid a murmur of voices, or turning on radio music to avoid being bugged.

He foresees trouble in the spring and calls the present regime a "provisional government," not implying who he thinks will succeed. He says the thirty-five-year-old Kociolek, just named as the youngest member of the Politburo and party secretary for Gdansk (Danzig) is regarded as Gomulka's dauphin. But there is an old Polish proverb that "the dauphin (dolphin) never gets to port."

The youth is completely out of tune with the regime but has no ideology or heroes. It is like Pirandello's *Six Characters in Search of an Author*—who has yet to show up. The youth is against Marxist ideas but not the Marxist system, because it knows there has to be some kind of system to make the economy work.

WARSAW, *December 3, 1968*

Lunched with Stash Gajewski, Polish ambassador to France until 1961, now attached to foreign relations work in the *sejm* (parliament). Stash went to Moscow this autumn (with a *sejm* committee) just before the U.S.A. halted bombing of North Vietnam. He was impressed by Kosygin as a reasonable, soft-talking realist. Kosygin told the Poles Russia was so over-extended economically by the arms race and overseas commitments that it had to make a deal of some sort with the U.S.A.

WARSAW, *December 4, 1968*

Long talk with Jozef Winiewicz, acting foreign minister. He was rather right-wing before the war, spent the war years in London with the emigré government.

He hopes Czechoslovakia's role in the Warsaw pact's northern tier grouping will be reestablished. Poland's special position in the communist world ("let's not use the euphemism, socialist," he suggested) resulted largely from Gomulka's personality as "personalities do play a role in politics." Poland was the largest European communist state, outside of Russia, and had a large economic potential.

Gomulka was not opposed to an agreement with Bonn provided this was based on recognition of East Germany and the existing status quo. Poland was most insistent on this "because our experiences with Germany differ from other European countries like Rumania, Hungary, or even Czechoslovakia which was long under German and Austrian cultural and political influences. We are the people most concerned about the German problem. Now for the first time in our history we have a German state (East Germany) cooperating with us, recognizing our borders, redressing the wounds of the past. Therefore, quite apart from our ideological bonds, we support East Germany. But we have close economic, scientific, and cultural links with Bonn. Nevertheless, we can never recognize it until it accepts our frontiers."

W. acknowledged that the northern tier was in large part designed to give Warsaw a position that could help frustrate any conceivable future effort by Moscow and Bonn to make a deal at Poland's expense, and he added that when Khrushchev had sent Adzhubei to Bonn to explore such a deal, there was "horror" here.

WARSAW, *December 5, 1968*

Yesterday evening I had a good stroll through the town and was really impressed by the way it has been reconstructed, especially the old city with all its buildings meticulously rebuilt on former plans, stone by stone. What a durable people. They have dug so many pits for themselves in the past, always falling into them, that they are good at recovering. And they certainly are a better-looking people than the shapeless Russians of brooding Moscow. Women really look like women here.

But this reconstruction according to nationalist traditions has brought back much of the old nationalist thinking, ill-disguised under communism. And General Moczar's appeal to people in his effort (as security boss) to unseat Gomulka is on lines of anti-Semitism, anti-Russianism, and war veteran patriotism that is a kind of neo-fascism under hammer and sickle slogans.

PRAGUE, *December 7, 1968*

Arrived this morning by sleeper train from Warsaw, and after a terrific argument at the frontier, which lasted from 3:00 A.M. to 4:15. The frontier police authorities who went through the train inspecting passports insisted that, although my visa was valid (as they acknowledged) I was not allowed in Czechoslovakia and would have to dress and leave the train. They were tough, stupid cops.

I refused to get out of bed and said they would have to carry me. After, an endless argument, finally, they disappeared with my passport after endlessly repetitious shouts. Then, at 4:15, to my glum surprise, one of them came back with what passed for a smile, handed me my passport, said *"Gut, gut,"* shook my hand, and left. A moment later the train started off. I can only figure that things are so confused under the continuing Soviet occupation that no one knows from whom to accept orders.

Lunched at Jake Beam's (American ambassador). Jake is a tall, grey-haired, shy, good diplomat, Russian-speaker and experienced. I would not be surprised to see him go to Moscow as our envoy soon.

It is fair to say that in 1938 most Czechs (before Munich) preferred to see war as a solution to their crisis with Berlin but in 1968 they want peace as a solution to their crisis with Moscow. It is too soon to say whether they can keep up their stubbornness and survive. It looks as if the battle has been lost, but not necessarily the war. They hope the concatenation of circumstances will produce so many problems for Moscow at home and elsewhere in East Europe that Moscow will have to loosen its grip.

PRAGUE, *December 9, 1968*

Even though Czechoslovakia is occupied, freedom's vestiges are far more impressive than its inhibited practice in Poland or Russia. The Czechs know by experience and instinct what freedom is and what to do with it. In this fettered land, which knows it must remain allied to its enemies because of geopolitical reasons, officials frankly speak of it as "occupied" and talk of the Russians as "them."

Dufek (head of the foreign ministry press section) and Trhlik (chief of the American department at the foreign ministry) gave me a luncheon at the Praha restaurant above the Vltava river.

They have no use for the Poles and East Germans. I said I was probably going to East Germany and Dufek observed: "You'll probably learn much more about us there than here. They can tell you where all the secret arms caches were and who the underground fascists are."

PRAGUE, *December 10, 1968*

Excellent talk this morning with P. of the economic institute, a large man with glasses, uninhibited and nice. A good Communist party member, he thinks communism is going to hell. He is not going to take part in the Soviet-Czech economic talks due to start soon and is glad: "I would have to commit either murder or suicide; suicide is easier."

He is convinced Russia is doomed if there is no change in its economic system, therefore its society. Czechoslovakia's big mistake in the past was to think what was being done—"here, or in Russia, was socialism." In Russia it isn't even state capitalism. It is tsarist bureaucracy mixed with Byzantium. If this continues, at most Russia has two years before a bust.

"In my opinion, the main reason for the Soviet invasion here was that once you alter an economic system that necessarily brings with it changes in the political system—which was happening."

He said it was imperative in Russia that there be more independence of enterprises. This meant elimination of state interference. That in turn would end certain functions of the Soviet Establishment, which would become defunct. In a country like the Soviet Union where the political apparatus has been strong for years, the apparatus is identified with both the society (working class) and state and its strength is far greater than in other lands. It has a greater power to resist change.

"If Czechoslovakia can't reform Russia, it will go down with Russia. And I don't see how we can reform Russia. Two thirds of our trade, approximately, is with the East. This trade is not subject to rational economic conditions and therefore its continuance requires artificial administrative measures.

"This produces a built-in system of self-paralysis. It can work—and did —during an era of industrialization. It is a system of war economy and can work where you can intensify production, with predictable results, in a relatively simple economy. It can concentrate economic means for special targets, at the risk of neglecting other targets. But this demands a kind of consensus of the people, even if they grumble, as during a war.

"But once a country has been essentially industrialized, as in Russia, this must change. The people won't take it any more; either they will passively sabotage things or revolt. Once a certain more sophisticated structure has been established, above all in this era of automation, you can't continue to run along these lines. The interconnection of all the units of an intricate and complicated system is such that the method of central management is impossibly crude."

PRAGUE, *December 11, 1968*

A group of editors received me at their request at the press and information center for foreign journalists. They agreed Czechoslovakia will have economic chaos because nothing was done most of this year. Then there may be a crisis. Things will get tougher and worse because of Soviet pressure.

Russia hopes to turn the clock back—without wrecking Czechoslovakia's economy. Their invasion lacked a collaborationist leader and the mass media unite the nation against them, but it was a near thing. Said one: "Our economic situation was a mess but at least we now have a plan to make it work." Another complained that Moscow has two economic systems, one modern and geared to military and space affairs; another lagging, "to which we unfortunately are attached." The latter operates on the theory that if Russia gets a Czech locomotive below world standards, at least it's better than no locomotive at all. This encourages shabby, sub-standard production here.

Then I went to the prime minister's office to see Peter Colotka, vice premier, a pleasant, well-built Slovak whose healthy appearance was belied by a very nervous eye twitch. At one point he looked up at the ceiling and I am certain it was a subconscious reference to microphones.

He said "normalization" could only be considered as returned when all Soviet troops leave (which I forecast as decades hence). "Our neighbors must understand our problems." He insists the Russians have made no direct political or economic interference. I asked if such was the case, why did they come in the first place. He admitted no Soviet troops were here prior to August 20 and "none were ever invited; we want that situation again." The present troop accord specified it is a "temporary" arrangement.

WEST BERLIN, *December 12, 1968*

Got an East German visa in Prague this morning, after days of bureau-cratic muddle-headedness. As it turned out, the visa was either by malice or stupidity wrongly stamped and did not permit me to leave East Berlin to West Berlin; it required me to drive hundreds of miles to the Czech or Polish borders; but I managed to talk my way past a bored East German guard at Checkpoint Charlie.

I took off with a hired driver in a tinny little Moskvitch (Russian) sedan. Rattled past spreading fields where thousands of crows pecked the frozen earth, while occasional convoys of heavy Soviet road transport lumbered by. An enormously long wait at the border post of Cinovec where everything in the car and our baggage was searched by a lumpish East German Volkspolizei guard in snappy long white leather coat and Soviet-type, ear-lapped fur cap. He even went through my books (although he couldn't read English—if anything). When we were all through, the driver muttered: "It doesn't take me so long on the frontiers of our enemies, West Germany or Austria."

Went through Dresden, which is booming with new apartment houses, shops, roads. Television aerials everywhere. Also, numerous signs with quotations from or pictures of Ulbricht, who thus seems to be the last remaining practitioner of the outmoded cult of personality. The slogans are exceptionally dreary but then the Germans, although they have pro-duced several humorists, are not noted for their national sense of humor.

The autobahns are first-class. Finally arrived at East Berlin where I planned to spend the night. However, not having been able to get accommo-dation (by phone from Prague) because of a world federation of trade unions conference, I had messaged Colin McIntyre, the Reuters corre-spondent, asking him to book me somewhere, and drove in the darkness to the grim area where he lives: a dilapidated apartment house next to a beer hall, ice-cold and pitch-black, not a flicker of light. I felt my way through the hall by the Braille system, up a flight of stairs, and saw a faint glimmer under the crack of a door. Beat on the door and McIntyre appeared, small, skinny, long-haired, Australian, son of a diplomat; very nice and most helpful.

In East Berlin he is the only resident noncommunist Westerner. His office was freezing cold. He was most apologetic but, having spent the entire day at it, had been unable (with the help of the foreign ministry) to unearth a room for me in any hotel; there are too many communist trade unionists. But he kindly offered to drive me to West Berlin where he was going to jollify for the evening (he has a special pass), and I accepted with alacrity. This proved lucky because he helped me talk my way past the visa contretemps which I discovered while working my way through the Wall. I must say, when I arrived at the Kempinski and found they had room, warmth, luxury, and good food, I was delighted.

WEST BERLIN, *December 13, 1968*

Message via the Reuters bureau that Joachim Wittwer of the [East German] foreign ministry press section wished to see me.

I scrambled over by taxi to Checkpoint Charlie, registered with the American booth (which is supposed to institute a search if you don't come back), went over to the east side, registered again, paid a five westmark tax (changed into eastmarks), then strolled through the various barriers and found the solitary, battered taxi waiting which took me to the foreign ministry.

The foreign ministry is a large impressive building on the Spree River across from the shell of the old Reichstag. I waddled through the red tape, filling out forms, waiting, and finally Wittwer came down, cold, impolite, looking rather like Marlon Brando. He took me to an anteroom where he carefully locked us in and then sat down.

He had a peculiar habit of waiting literally two or three minutes before the simplest question, brooding or looking coldly hostile. In this strained mood he asked severely why I hadn't arrived at 10:00 A.M. yesterday by plane as he'd expected. Why? I asked. That's what his Prague embassy had advised him. I told him they should fire the whole Prague embassy, a rude bunch of idiots who had given me a wrong visa anyway and who couldn't have expected me to take a plane landing at 10:00 when they'd only granted the visa at 9:30.

He asked why I hadn't stayed last night in East Berlin in the suite assigned me—yes, a suite—at the Unter den Linden. For the simple reason, I replied, that his foreign ministry and the hotel—and all other hotels —had said there was no room in East Berlin. Would I move in now?

Damned well not; I was comfortable at the Kempinski, had unpacked, and sent my laundry out.

This went on until he asked why I hadn't given earlier notice of my desire to see Ulbricht. I had, five days ago. Why didn't he know of it, he asked. Because, said I, of his inefficient bureaucracy. In the end he said he would contact U.'s office and let me know.

McIntyre came by in his beat-up old Wartburg car (while I stood shivering in the sub-zero weather on the Spree) and took me sightseeing. McIntyre says there were many demonstrations against the Czech invasion, and sympathizers swarmed around the Czech embassy in East Berlin to register regret. There were trials of protesters underway throughout East Germany. The psychological situation is grim and disquieting.

We lunched at the Ganymede restaurant where John Peet, an English renegade, joined us for a fairly expensive and poor meal. Peet is tall, thin, with long sideburns, about fifty, rather distinguished-looking, said to be of a good family, with a Bulgarian wife (whom he met in Berlin). His story is that he was a pacifist and then moved to the East. He ekes out a living in the communist world.

PARIS, *December 19, 1968*

Last night we went to a bash at the Rothschilds' and dined first with the Harrimans. Averell was absolutely furious with [Nguyen Cao] Ky, the South Vietnamese vice president and coordinator of the delegation here. At a reception the South Vietnamese people gave yesterday, Ky talked very critically about the Americans.

Although he acknowledges that Colonel Lau, Number Two on the communist delegation, is known as "the Butcher of Hué," and although he says "you can never trust the communists on anything," he adds that they are behaving with dignity, unlike the "cheap Ky."

He feels enraged at the thought that some two hundred American boys are being killed each week while arguments continue here about the shape of the table eventual negotiators will sit around. The importance of this point, of course, is that Saigon doesn't want to acknowledge the equal status of the Vietcong's FLN. I suggested to Averell that while arguing this ridiculous point we should cease to think in two dimensions but work it up to three and have higher and lower tables and chairs. I proposed that Ky be given a baby's highchair. Averell was delighted with the idea.

He doesn't think much of [Nguyen Van] Thieu, the president, either, although Thieu remains in Saigon. He says that Thieu has twice double-crossed Johnson. "The first time you are doublecrossed, it is a matter of bad luck," says Averell; "the second time it is bad judgment and if it happens a third time you're an idiot."

Incidentally, he doesn't approve of [Ellsworth] Bunker's diplomatic activity in Saigon, which surprises me, because I think Bunker has been very patient. It is extraordinary when I think back over the last three years to see how Averell has shifted from a rather hawkish to an extremely dovish position.

He told me that when he was home he had a good talk with Nixon. [William] Rogers, the secretary of state-elect, and Henry Kissinger were there. Averell admires Kissinger greatly and he admitted with much frankness that Nixon had made a good impression and "handled me very skillfully."

He told me the first serious painting he ever bought was when he was a young man. It was a Renoir—which he still has—and he and his mother paid fifty-fifty for it "because it was so expensive. Of course, it has multiplied in value ten times since then," he said happily.

PARIS, *December 23, 1968*

Lunched with Manac'h. He is going to be France's next ambassador to Peking. He invited me to come and stay with him "*à la Gascogne*"—that is to say, if I get a visa, which is doubtful.

He says it is perfectly obvious the strategy of Hanoi now is to use military threats in the south in order to shift American diplomatic attention to the FLN from Hanoi. In other words, Hanoi threatens a new offensive in the south and tells Washington if it wants to avoid this it should deal directly with the FLN, as it forced us to negotiate with Hanoi originally by this year's costly Tet offensive.

Just before Vance went home for Christmas late last week, he saw Colonel Lau and warned him directly that if there was a new offensive against Saigon or another city, the U.S. would have to consider a military *riposte*—by implication this might include anything—including bombing the north. Lau objected that this was a threat which he could not accept. Vance said it was not a threat but a statement of fact.

There has been a series of secret conversations between Vance and Colonel Lau—occasionally attended by Harriman—at Sceaux in a mutually acceptable house and through an interpreter. These are so secret that Vance sometimes wants his French security contingent to leave him and takes a taxi to the meetings.

PARIS, *December 25, 1968*

Lunched and played bridge yesterday with the Harrimans. Averell told me that he had congratulated Stalin at Potsdam for being in Berlin. Stalin's only reply was "Tsar Alexander got to Paris."

PARIS, *December 27, 1968*

Lunched with Harriman and Jean-Marie Soutou. Harriman said there had been continual secret contacts with the Hanoi people since June, but at one point he said he had not personally seen Le Duc Tho, the Hanoi Politburo representative here, since the cease-bombing announcement last October.

Soutou thought there were three peace solutions for the Vietnam war: (1) an American withdrawal with a bare saving of face; (2) a more complex mechanism in which Washington sought to establish a strong enough South Vietnamese regime to have a chance of standing on its own feet and preventing a communist take-over; (3) a deal with China recognizing an independent southeast Asia.

Soutou stressed the importance of China much more than Harriman. Harriman thought we must prevail on Russia to bring about a settlement because Russia wanted, in its own interest, to neutralize southeast Asia and keep it out of China's clutches. And the North Vietnamese had indicated that, just as they had dropped their hostility to France after 1954 and become friendly, they were likewise preparing to drop their hostility to the United States and work together for an independent southeast Asia after peace.

Harriman made a particular point of saying that the Russians had played a role in getting the secret Sceaux contacts going in Paris because Russia was so eager to get peace.

Soutou said the only way to bring the Russians to their senses, encourage liberal elements in the Soviet communist hierarchy, and get the Russians to really work for a settlement in the Middle East, was to threaten them with the nightmare of a Chinese-American rapprochement. Peking had very carefully chosen to say that its objective in the next (February 20) Warsaw talks was coexistence with the U.S.A.

Soutou said the Soviet Union is entering a critical period. Stalin had been succeeded by a "college" of people so that power was dissipated. He had bequeathed an empire in Eastern Europe which was a poisonous cancer rotting the Soviet system. And he had just managed before his death to introduce basic heavy industry. Russia had never managed to develop the subtler and more delicate industry required by a really modern society. Now they were going to pay for these three weaknesses.

Incidentally, Averell arrived a few moments early and I asked what he considered the greatest mistake and the greatest achievement of his career. He said his greatest mistake had been the usual one of Englishmen and Americans—feeling that by charm he could break through Soviet reserve and get things accomplished with Moscow. "But I learned quickly," he added. His greatest achievement had been the refusal—without even asking Washington—to let Soviet troops take part in the occupation of Japan.

PARIS, *January 1, 1969*

Quiet New Year's Eve. The Harrimans came over. We dined and then bridged until past midnight.

Marie adored Bobby Kennedy. She still weeps a bit when she talks about him. She describes him as shy, modest, and with only one passion—the elimination of poverty and injustice.

She told me Ethel takes the children for romps by their father's grave. They play naturally and then ask heartbreaking questions such as: "Is Daddy really with Uncle Jack? Are they really happy there?"

Averill is fed up with the negotiations here and his dislike of President Johnson, Rusk, and Ambassador Bunker (in Saigon) becomes more evident each day. I have a feeling Averell almost has more sympathy for Hanoi than the Saigon government at this stage.

2 0

MALRAUX:

"THE CHINESE ARE

THE FRENCH OF ASIA"

PARIS, *January 9, 1969*

LAST NIGHT WE GAVE A FAREWELL PARTY FOR AVERELL AND MARIE
Harriman. Among others there were Prince Paul and Princess Olga,
and Fred Warner (who is staying with us and who is now assistant
undersecretary of state for Asian affairs at the foreign office). Averell
thinks Bunker wrongly conceives of his mission in Saigon as a device for
propping up the government of Thieu. Averell as much as admitted that
Washington would be just as happy to see "Big Minh" form a peace
government.

Prince Paul considers Tito a real savior of Jugoslavia and a man who
in the name of communism has driven out the worst features of communism such as secret police dictatorship.

PARIS, *January 11, 1969*

I saw four papers from the *Quai d'Orsay* file. These were respectively:
the official account of the meeting between André Malraux and Ch'en yi,
Chinese foreign minister, July 23, 1965; between Malraux and Prime
Minister Chou En-lai, August 2, 1965, and between Malraux and Mao
Tse-tung, August 3, 1965; the fourth was Malraux's own account of his
meeting with Mao together with Malraux's observations and recommendations (as sent to General de Gaulle).

It was clear from their versions that Malraux and French Ambassador
Lucien Paye adulated Mao personally as a "hero." Malraux in his own
account says he told Mao "the Chinese are the French of Asia." I doubt
if Mao was enormously impressed.

Mao himself denied Malraux's observation that Mao was a "hero" in the Chinese tradition. When Malraux drew a comparison between Russia's hold on Siberia and American "rule" of Taiwan, Mao observed that after all the Russians had been legally in Siberia for some time.

Malraux, in his summary, said that Mao viewed the "external enemy" as the U.S.A. and the "internal enemy" as revisionism, meaning the Soviet version of communism.

The first three reports were made by Yakovlievitch, the French embassy interpreter in Peking. The last is Malraux's own summary. It is fascinating to compare Yakovlievitch's version of the Mao talk with Malraux's paper for de Gaulle and, finally, with Malraux's account of the whole thing in his recently published *Antimémoires*.

> *Paper 1.* July 23, 1965: Conversation between Malraux and Chinese foreign minister.
>
> Ch'en yi said that, since Khrushchev, Soviet policy had been to divide the world between the two superpowers, Russia and America. China wanted to halt the aggressive policy of the U.S.A., not to destroy capitalism or to promote a big war.
>
> If the U.S.A. extended its Vietnamese operations, China would have to participate in the war there. But not otherwise. (This was before Johnson's bombing decision of November 1, 1968—when the Chinese did nothing.)
>
> Ch'en yi said reunification of Vietnam was necessary after the U.S.A. was driven out, but the struggle might last five, ten, or twenty years. Nevertheless, Ch'en yi spoke of the "traditional friendship" of the U.S.A. and China. He said "the friendship between their peoples" surpassed both disagreement and propaganda. He spoke of a possible eventual "neutralization" of Vietnam.
>
> He said the United States must leave Taiwan. When Malraux compared Siberia with Taiwan, Ch'en yi said Taiwan (Formosa) is not a part of the U.S.A.
>
> *Paper 2.* August 2, 1965: Conversation between Malraux and Prime Minister Chou En-lai.
>
> Chou En-lai recalled that bilateral conversations between China and the U.S.A. started August 1, 1955. China had often since then stated its desire for an accord based on the five principles of coexistence.
>
> Chou En-lai added that the U.S.A. must quit Taiwan but Washington refuses to do this. Chou said the U.S.A. must leave all of Asia and, furthermore, all countries where it now had troops, such as the Dominican Republic, Cuba, and the Congo.
>
> He told Malraux that China values French opposition to the Soviet-U.S. "monopoly."

He complained that Taiwan had China's United Nations seat and this was a "major insult." Malraux suggested that maybe it would be a good idea to have a new kind of UN to replace the old body and to move its seat to Geneva.

Chou said that perhaps UN should be reformed and radically improved, even moving to Geneva. This would taken ten, twenty, or thirty years. But he did not seem to accept Malraux's idea of scrapping UN by setting up a rival organization.

He thought it would be nice to have common action with France for the reform of UN in cooperation with the countries of Africa and Asia.

Paper 3. August 3, 1965: Conversation between Malraux and Mao Tse-tung.
Mao praised France's independent attitude toward the U.S.A. He suggested France and China should oppose the U.S.A. and Russia and their "double hegemony."

Malraux went on to say that many French communists and intellectuals were "pro-Chinese." The meeting, even with translation, lasted little more than a half-hour.

Malraux's paper presented to de Gaulle started off talking about "the nature of my mission" which he described as of the "highest level." He then talked of an "orchestra of information." He spoke of his hosts—"the Chinese are the French of Asia." He said he had told this to Mao and that he had proposed sending French technicians and mathematicians to China.

PARIS, *January 13, 1969*

Lunched with Edgar Faure and his wife in their apartment. He thinks that while de Gaulle may have lost some popularity because of his Middle East policy, it isn't permanent.

His wife, who is Jewish, was much more steamed up. She reminded him that for three years he said he had been on the point of resigning but never did. She was furious with de Gaulle and his embargo of arms to Israel.

Faure said there was no leader of the opposition. The only real opposition was inside the Gaullist party and he supposed he was its chief. Giscard d'Estaing still had a potential political position and Mendès-France was stronger than people thought. Then there were always the communists who remained fairly strong. But there was no united opposition.

Faure sniffed at Servan-Schreiber's political ambitions. He made a caustic observation: "Nobody in France likes politicians, but they are the only people anybody has heard of."

BELFAST, *January 19, 1969*

Flew to Dublin yesterday on an Aer Lingus jet loaded with hunters and shotguns plus a cargo of Irish priests and nuns. Hugh Smith, our correspondent, a diminutive Irishman with white hair and an Abbey Theater voice, met me and took me off to the Russell Hotel where we dined on Galway oysters, steak, draft Guinness, and Irish coffee.

This morning I drove off for troubled northern Ireland via Drogheda and Dundalk. My chauffeur earnestly crossed himself each time we passed a Catholic church (all Protestant edifices ignored). After the frontier (virtually wide open and no passport required despite riots in the north) signs were in just English—instead of English and Gaelic.

BELFAST, *January 21, 1969*

Yesterday I went to Stormont, the parliament, where Prime Minister O'Neill gave me lunch. O'Neill (Captain Terence) comes from an old family of loyal aristocrats (taking over the ancient royal name from distant maternal relatives) and is thoroughly anglicized: Protestant, World War II, Eton, etc. He is pleasant, not very tough. I could imagine some of the tough monkeys on the right-wing of his party gobbling him up for breakfast.

O'Neill said: "Partition bought peace for Ireland. It ended the war and murder that had continued to feature here since Norman times. The reformation had only made things worse by introducing the religious element—Catholic versus Protestant."

The "plantation" system, under which Ulster was colonized by Scotch Presbyterians, took place mostly in the seventeenth century, at the "same time as the Virginia plantations." I pointed out that the Virginia plantations were more interested in vegetable than human crops.

He thought that rather than foreseeing an end to partition inside a United Europe one could imagine a day when "regional governments" were set up in Wales, Scotland, south England, north England, etc.—"a kind of U.S.A. in which southern Ireland could join as an associated member."

O'Neill said the original "Irish" were treated as "natives" by conquerors and were treated like "your Red Indians." Even in the 1920s Catholics here were seen as a kind of lower class; but no longer.

O'Neill said a Pennsylvanian had told him once (a man of Scotch-Irish antecedents): "You know, we north Irelanders own the United States. But the south Irelanders run it."

I then drove on a terrible, sleety day to Armagh, site of St. Patrick's best-known church and uniquely the see of both the Catholic primate and the Church of Ireland primate. I was shown into Cardinal William Conway's residence by a pleasant servant who turned on the electric fire, took my coat, and invited me into the cold, unattractive sitting room, featured by a photograph of the cardinal with Pope Paul VI. A moment later he came in, a sturdy, tall agreeable man with a clear, strong face and courteous manner. He offered me cigarettes, took out a pipe, and summoned a tray with deliciously creamed coffee and Irish cookies. He was wearing his red-fringed black robe and I noticed his socks were flaming red. He has short-cut grey hair (fairly bald) and intelligent blue eyes. Might have been a fine tackle at Notre Dame.

He said Armagh (which has only 7,000 people although it looks ten times larger) was founded by St. Patrick in 432. It was Patrick's principal church in Ireland.

He said that in northern Ireland politics and religion were inextricably mixed. The Protestants were descended from English conquerors and Scottish colonists, from garrison soldiers and from postreformation settlers. "The presumption here is that if you know a man's religion you know his politics."

In Ireland, he said, there was too much myth and not enough reality. There was no established church here and the Church of Ireland had no legal advantage over other faiths. As a matter of fact, the Catholics (with over one-third of the population) were the largest single denomination. The extremist Paisleyites are not recognized by the orthodox Presbyterian synod.

The cardinal said that Armagh, with its 7,000 people, had one Catholic, two Protestant high schools. Yet among the almost fifty employees of the Armagh education office there was no Catholic. The Armagh population was about half and half but there were no Catholics in city hall. There was "real segregation" in local government.

In housing, there were three Protestant, two Catholic wards. A Catholic can't get a house in a Protestant ward. He said in the south of Ireland (and "half of my diocese is there") people were "generous to Protestants."

LONDON, *January 23, 1969*

Drinks with (U.S. ambassador) David Bruce. I asked if he thought the British character had changed as a consequence of the psychological shock of losing an empire. Had the lack of world responsibility made the people of England grow soft? He said: "Their character hasn't fundamentally changed. Because of the change in their international position, while they are still interested in outside events, they have become more concerned with their own. They are questioning the policies of their government more than ever before in modern English history.

"The British used to have large numbers of their people working in various capacities around the empire and they continuously journeyed back and forth between distant points and home. This continual cross-fertilization, intellectually, perhaps has stopped. But now there is the greatest concentration of expertise at home that Britain has ever known."

He thinks the only future role of Britain is in Europe and that it simply must get into the continent. It has an enormous amount to contribute, including a great knowledge of foreign affairs. But there is no outlet for this vast expertise which is now confined to Britain itself where the accent is on domestic policies.

Britain had a certain role to play as a bridge between Europe and the U.S.A. But this role will diminish because of the relative size and the still-increasing power of the U.S.A. and the USSR—with China becoming more important off-stage.

Certainly Britain cannot be useful as a middleman between Washington and Moscow because neither the Americans nor the Russians need or wish this.

But the real future will be a commanding British position within the European complex and we should be prepared to deal with such an arrangement on the basis of equality. Of course, there are some areas in which we can never permit other nations to control our actions—like the atom. No nations will entirely yield their sovereignties. There must always be reserved powers.

Thinking back about the U.S.-British relationship, David said: "There are very few areas where British policy can't be adjusted easily to our own and vice versa. This is not true for either of us with any other country." David thought the "Drake Spirit" still exists in England, but the people have adjusted to a slower tempo of life and their working habits have become sluggish because there are no incentives for overtime or working weekends, and taxation is punitive. Too much money has been invested in unprofitable nationalized industries. There is no psychological incentive. What adventure can be offered during times of peace?

David thought the big problem right now was the need to get true efficiency which doesn't, at present, exist. The trade unions have no authority over their own members. Greater incentive is needed in the managerial class. After anyone reaches the £5,000 a year income level, because of taxes, there is little incentive to rise any higher and there is no widespread existence of stock options in England. The participation of the people in shares is too limited. The American gambles in Wall Street and thus provides money for industrial development. The Englishman gambles on racing and pools which provide no capital for the building up of the economy. Summing up, David thinks that, despite their hippy exterior, the young people in England are skilled, talented, and courageous, but they tend to be lazy.

PARIS, *January 28, 1969*

Agreeable talk with (former prime minister) Georges Pompidou, center of a recent political storm. Before going to Rome this month to be received by Italian political leaders and the Pope, he called on de Gaulle. When he was in Rome, he had a press conference in which he said he was a candidate for the presidency of the Fifth Republic in the next elections (de Gaulle is due to retire in December 1972).

This created a tremendous furor in France. The impression was built up that Pompidou was trying to ease de Gaulle out of office prematurely. At a cabinet meeting de Gaulle made a very precise statement of his intention to remain in office until the very end of this, his second, term. This statement was interpreted as a deliberate slap in the face for Pompidou.

I saw Pompidou (ousted as prime minister last June) in his small rented office. He was cheerful, seemed at ease, and I noticed that now he smokes filter cigarettes and seems to be trying to cut down.

He admitted his relations with the General were a bit strained. He had gone to see the Pope in line with the General's counsel last spring that he should "prepare yourself and travel and see people," the obvious inference being that this was the way to get ready for the presidency.

In Rome he issued no official statement of his candidacy. He only had a very small conference—a handful of people—in his hotel room and among the questions asked was whether he would be a candidate in the next elections. He said, of course.

Three developments changed the situation. (1) The *Agence France Presse* sent a dispatch in which it abruptly stated that Pompidou had "declared his candidacy." (2) This stimulated great excitement in Paris and Couve de Murville got irked. (3) Couve told de Gaulle the "announcement" of candidacy was embarrassing to the General because it weakened his position.

All this happened on January 17. On January 18 he was dressing for his visit the Pope when the telephone rang and it was Pierre Charpy of France-Soir. Charpy said: "Your declaration has upset everyone." Pompidou replied "What declaration?" He swears he didn't know what Charpy was talking about. Nevertheless, Charpy went on—on the basis of this conversation plus a few more banalities—to write a banner headline dispatch called "*Déclaration Exclusive*" in which he said Pompidou had told him he would be a candidate. Pompidou says the dispatch was "one hundred percent a lie." Shortly after his return to Paris he told Charpy "You should spend a month with the *New York Times* to learn professional ethics." De Gaulle's reaction gave the affair too much importance and also gave the impression that Pompidou was threatening the General's position. The fat was in the fire. Pompidou admitted he had not seen the General since returning.

Pompidou says editors know French public opinion is becoming increasingly eager for a change in administration and therefore the editors were ready to snatch any available straw.

De Gaulle's fundamental attitude is that "there can be no successor to General de Gaulle." Nevertheless, he acknowledges that there must be a president of France and he feels Pompidou is the "least bad" choice.

Pompidou himself does not think his position has been dangerously hurt. He acknowledges that Couve aspires to the job and "he is bitter against me." Pompidou does not think Giscard d'Estaing is in the race because he prefers to play the role of being a young man and a brilliant second (by inference to Pompidou). I doubt this. Edgar Faure doesn't want the job "although his wife is pushing him more and more and maybe he will try." Chaban-Delmas doesn't want the position and, as a matter of fact, he is the best of all of them in his relationships with me. As for Debré, he is finished.

He then said: "I am convinced that de Gaulle won't urge the French people to vote for any candidate. In other words, nobody will have his positive backing. But I have made up my mind, come what may, to be a candidate. Either de Gaulle will put up someone against me or he will accept my candidacy. I think the latter is far more likely."

Pompidou said pro-Israeli sentiment is very widespread in France. It goes back to resentment at the treatment of Jews during the Nazi occupation; to the anti-Arab feeling engendered by the Algerian war and to the alliance with Israel in the 1956 Suez war. Above all, he says, there is hostility for the Arabs. There is really a "profound" pro-Israel and anti-Arab sentiment.

Nevertheless, the clamor on the Israeli arms embargo was relatively superficial. The big reaction was against the methods of de Gaulle. There was a feeling that here was an old man acting alone and the persistent question was: "Where is he leading us?" There was a feeling of insecurity in the future.

Pompidou said Couve was the only important cabinet member who supported this move because Couve is pro-Arab.

But Pompidou said de Gaulle's popularity has sunk and he is really on bad ground for the proposed national referendum, if it is this year, on doing away with the senate and regionalizing administration.

PARIS, *January 30, 1969*

This afternoon I paid my first visit on Michel Debré since he was named foreign minister.

He is a small, nervous man with a petulant, impatient face and manner but is very bright.

I had the impression that relations between France and the U.S.A. were definitely better now and I wondered why. He answered: "There is one small reason and one big reason. The small reason is that certain problems such as the urgency of the international monetary problem have left us for the moment.

"The big reason is that the American leadership has at last recognized that friendship doesn't necessarily mean alignment. Likewise, nonalignment doesn't necessarily mean opposition. All great powers have gone through this experience. They have all had to learn their lesson. They have to learn that just because another nation doesn't embrace *all* the ideas of that particular great power, it does not mean that it is automatically an adversary.

Debré said before Nixon was inaugurated he had sent indirect word to the French government that he hoped to visit Paris. I asked if there were any special Franco-American problems that would be useful for the two men to discuss. He answered: "Certainly. Very serious problems. The two most important are these: (1) What will be the nature of our discussions with the Soviet Union? (2) And then there is the matter of the future of Western economy. We are very worried about the protectionist trend inside the U.S."

Debré added: "There should be long and serious discussion, not just a perfunctory exchange of positions. After all, we both need to look at the forthcoming years in the broadest possible sense."

I asked how the special friendship treaty with Germany was going. Debré said:

"The monetary crisis in November showed that Bonn has become giddy with power. Relations are continuing to be good but Germany has become so strong economically that many people were awakened to that fact with a start last autumn."

I turned to the Middle East. He said: "It is urgent that something be done. I am very pessimistic. Each month, each week that passes makes the situation worse. If anyone were to propose another formula than ours to try and stabilize the situation, I would be pleased. But no one has come forth with another proposal."

Debré feared disaster brought about by three separate steps: (1) Arab anarchy would slowly spread and *all* moderate elements in the Arab world would disappear into it; (2) then, without even wishing it, the great powers would be drawn in by being forced to support their own extremists on each side; (3) with this background, a particular incident could blow things up.

Debré didn't think the terrible public hangings that have been going on in Baghdad could in themselves bring about such a crisis. "Horrible, savage as this is, it is probably not critical," he said. "Unfortunately, the world has become used to the barbarity of Iraq."

PARIS, *February 1, 1969*

Went to a most unusual dinner party last night at the Shrivers' in honor of Madame and Michel Debré. The guests, apart from the Debrés, included: Julie Christie, Peter Ustinov, Warren Beatty, Princess Elizabeth of Jugoslavia, Ambassador and Mrs. Cy Vance, Jacques Duhamel, plus a few others.

Ustinov was the star of the evening, immensely funny. He told me he was now domiciled in Switzerland (for tax purposes), still had a French passport, was born in Jaffa (now Tel Aviv) when it was part of the Turkish empire, is the son of a German army officer from Würtemberg, and the grandson of a Russian refugee.

One story: he had witnessed a Swiss military maneuver recently in which a car containing four colonels rumbled by drawn by a team of plow horses. "Why?" Ustinov asked the senior colonel. "The assumption is," replied the officer, "that all gasoline stocks in the confederation have been destroyed."

He visited Albania a couple of years ago. Ustinov said the most impressive political slogan he saw plastered all over was: "Long live our potatoes."

Debré joined us and puzzled me by saying to Ustinov as he put his arm around me: "I like our friend Sulzberger despite his opposition to our policies." I said "You know, I am accused of being the only remaining American Gaullist."

P.S.

> *Translation from the Paris newspaper, L'Aurore, February 7, 1969*
> Mr. Debré, accompanied by the sweet Mrs. Debré, dined the other evening at the American embassy. Debré aimed for the American journalist Sulzberger, who for twenty years has reported on the French scene wisely and courteously for the *New York Times*. He is also, by the way, the favorite golfing partner of Mr. Couve de Murville.
>
> "Mr. Sulzberger, I don't like your articles, they make France look so bad," said Debré in a pinched tone.
>
> Sulzberger commented gently for all to hear that he had always had a fine opinion of the French. A journalist is not expected to laud; he writes to explain and to inform. He hears, he observes, he analyzes, and then he reports. No one asks him to dip his writing pen in acid. Nor should he dip it in holy water.

PARIS, *February 3, 1969*

Lunched with Cabot Lodge. When we talked about Vietnam he indicated that the Nixon administration is keeping a tight line on things but has not yet really decided on a precise policy. It hasn't been decided yet in any precise way other than a desire for peace without paying too steep a price for it.

Cabot thinks the South Vietnamese have done a fair job of working out a system of government but argues it is quite ridiculous to expect them to have a democratic system equivalent to our own.

He has no doubt that South Vietnam is strong enough to be able to stand up and defeat the Vietcong if only the North Vietnamese can be gotten out of the country. But the latter is still pretty doubtful.

Cabot speaks good French and went to school here (in 1912, 1913, 1914) after the death of his father. He still remembers the outbreak of World War I. He was in Normandy that summer and vividly recalls the way all the farmers' horses were mobilized and branded on the feet so they could be returned at the end of hostilities. "Not one came back," he says grimly.

PARIS, *February 7, 1969*

Last night we gave a dinner party for Edgar and Lucie Faure. Faure is now minister of education. Among those present were the Shrivers.

Shriver had taken Colonel [Frank] Borman, one of the three astronauts who circled the moon, to see de Gaulle in the afternoon. De Gaulle asked what happened in the space cabin if the three-man crew disagreed on anything. Borman replied that, as on any vessel, there was a commander. De Gaulle also asked how the earth differed from other planets in appearance. Borman said it was the only one that had color—a vivid blue-green. All the rest of the universe seemed to be black and white, but the clouds around the earth gave it a special sheen.

PARIS, *February 14, 1969*

This afternoon I spent almost an hour with de Gaulle and it was exceedingly interesting. I arrived early at the Élysée and sat for ten minutes with air and naval aides. Suddenly the door opened and out came General de Guillebon, chief of military intelligence, and, several minutes ahead of schedule, I was ushered in.

As usual, de Gaulle was standing with his hand outstretched, greeted me courteously, and waved me to the chair opposite him at his Louis Quinze desk. As usual, I hauled out my notebook, pencils, and list of questions, spread them out on my side of the desk.

The old man (he will be seventy-nine) looked remarkably fit although several times he had small spasms of coughing. His eyes had a piercing, wicked, shrewd look. He took his glasses off and I know he couldn't see, but his eyes bored right into me. He is less turnip-shaped around the middle.

He talked with immense self-assurance, although some of the things he said, when all the implications are examined, scared me.

He took no trouble to disguise his growing anti-German feelings—and I mean West German. He is clearly frightened about the increase in German power and he thought it had been a mistake for France to join the Americans and British in supporting Bonn's desire to hold its present elections in West Berlin.

De Gaulle talked swiftly, with great concentration, persuasively, and with a complete mastery of what he had in mind. I think that at times he was more indiscreet than he intended to be.

I asked if he felt that because there was now a new administration in Washington it would be easier to improve Franco-U.S. relationships. He said: "I think this process had already begun before President Johnson left office. Our relations were starting to get better during the last months of his administration. But now it is even easier to further this tendency because of developments. It is not a question of presidents, of Johnson or Nixon, but of the problems posed.

"For us the principal question between our countries was NATO. Now that is all over. It is no longer a subject for discussion as far as we are concerned. There is no NATO for us French so there is no reason to have a problem on this with Washington.

"Then there was Vietnam. But President Johnson started negotiations while he was still in office. The negotiations are bound to go on for a very long time. That is inevitable. But it has started and, in the end, it will lead to peace.

"There is no reason for major differences between us now. Our problems are on the road to regulation. Of course, there is the question of the Middle East. We have not been in accord with you on this since 1967 [the six-day war]. But you should remember that this is merely a reverse of the previous situation. With the Fourth Republic, there was also disagreement. You were against France and Israel in 1956 at the time of the Suez invasion for reasons that are just the contrary of our differences now. Now the United States is with Israel, which wishes to take the Suez Canal. The United States has changed its policy—and so has France. In 1956 the Fourth Republic backed Israel. But the Fifth Republic doesn't want Israel to exaggerate. We agree that Israel should exist and should be a state— but not in an exaggerated way. The situation in the Middle East is not good today and it is not soluble along the lines Israel wishes. On this subject, perhaps Nixon can draw closer to our policy.

"Then there is the monetary affair. We question the worth of the present system, the gold exchange standard. The United States has kept saying that it is the fault of the French that there is a gold leak and that currencies are not solid, above all the dollar. This is not true. Since 1966, we have not been buying gold from you. But we dislike the system. It gives false preference to the dollar and to the pound. There is no reason for the dollar to have such preference. Now the mark, the franc, and the lira are holding firm. It is even bad for the United States that this artificial system of preference should continue, because people purchase gold in order to abuse the dollar.

"We must have an impartial international monetary system. But this is an eventual matter and it is not acute at this moment. The dollar holds, the franc holds; as for the pound, I don't know, but that is not very important. The question of the ultimate reform is not a burning subject today even if it has great significance.

"For all these reasons, I think we can hope to further the rapprochement between Washington and Paris. And there is another aspect to the whole problem—namely relationships with Russia. Little by little, you are becoming more like us in your view of this problem. Like us, you don't want to have them submerge Europe. But you are beginning to see that it is useful to develop practical contacts such as those we started. You will follow the same path that we have been following because that is the practical approach."

I asked if he thought it would be useful, with Nixon now coming, to discuss the possibility of coordinating U.S. and French military strategy. The General was dubious. He said: "Not by NATO. It can't be done by NATO. That's the point. Yes, eventual coordination perhaps. But we don't want NATO. NATO is an integration and we don't want an alliance structure within which the United States integrates all the others.

"Without NATO it would be easy to coordinate things between the U.S. and French general staffs. They could arrange cooperation and coordination of forces in case of war. But that is not possible now. You use NATO as the basis for your European defense. And you cannot make special arrangements with France outside of NATO because of the obvious resentment this would provoke among other NATO members."

I asked if his 1958 concept—the so-called *directoire* idea about which he wrote to President Eisenhower—was philosophically still valid. Categorically, he replied: "No, that is over. It is ended. It was possible in 1958 because there was a big Soviet danger at the time but there is no reason for it now. After all," said the General, "nobody thinks the Russians will move west any more, do they?" I did not mention the word "Czechoslovakia."

I observed that in the past he had told me no country in the long run could avoid being drawn into the orbit of influence of one or the other superpowers, Russia and America. Was he worried about this possibility now? He answered: "That is not quite precisely what I told you. Let me explain. Since always, we have favored the United States. Historically, we have always been friends. This has been for various reasons. World reasons, the nature of the country, ideology. Also, we have never been rivals before. Remember, in the past, you were never in Africa, in Asia, or even in Europe.

"Also, you should remember that we have old reasons for being friends of Russia. For us, in Europe, this Russian friendship has always been necessary as a counterweight to Germany. Constantly in history, we have sought to be on good terms with Russia, with the tsars, with the Soviets, as a counterweight to Germany. We have been old friends with America and old allies of Russia. And the Franco-Russian feeling is a natural event. Today we have no reason to renounce friendship with the United States. Neither, especially now that Germany reemerges, have we any reason to break off with Russia.

"And another thing, something we should never forget, is that one must always remember what France was, historically, just after the war and what it is today. France is as it is and the French are as they are. If the French don't think of France, it disappears. But you cannot think of France if you lose a sense of independence. The friendship of the French for the United States requires no American hegemony. The same is true with Russia. It is for that reason that the communists have never succeeded here, for national reasons, not for social reasons.

"Germany has been demolished, has been cut in two. And we must remember that Germany has only been one country for a relatively short period of time. Germany's history is not the same as that of France. The Germans are readier to accept a United States hegemony—and anyway" (here de Gaulle flashed a malevolent quick smile) "they can't avoid it. As for Britain, Britain has renounced its independence. It has sold it off for advantages of all sorts. And Italy counts for very little. It knows less than one century as a united, independent country."

I interrupted and asked if the ultimate aim of his present policy was to neutralize the Mediterranean, expelling both the American and Soviet fleets. He said: "The Mediterranean is a sea. But we think that the concentration of a big United States fleet and the appearance of a big Soviet fleet do not constitute anything good for peace. However, if an international *détente* can be brought about, there will no longer be a reason for a permanent U.S. fleet stationed in the Mediterranean. And, at the point, that would reduce the reason for the presence of a Soviet fleet. Naturally, American and Russian vessels could continue to pass through the Mediterranean but they would no longer have reason for stationing large, permanent, naval concentrations there."

I asked how long he thought American troops should remain stationed in Europe. He replied: "Until there is a real East-West *détente*, it is obviously normal to keep American troops in Germany. But if there is a *real* [and he stressed this] *détente*, there would be no more reason for such detachments except for symbolic units. But the fact that you have troops in Germany now doesn't irritate us; so have we."

I reminded de Gaulle that the last time I saw him he said France had no intention of denouncing the North Atlantic treaty when this became legally possible this year—unless basic changes occurred in East-West relationships. Would France denounce the treaty?

He said: "Obviously, there has been no real improvement in East-West relationships. Therefore, clearly, the question does not arise. The alliance exists. But you must remember that this is a declaration of principle. That means we go together if attacked."

I inquired whether he had any suggestions about how the recurring Berlin crises such as the one now shaping up could be avoided. He said: "Unfortunately, this situation cannot end soon. The situation is entirely abnormal. The Bonn government wants to consider West Berlin as entirely a part of West Germany. But this is not true. And West Berlin is not East German either. It is a 'Western' area in the sense of what its people wish. The real sovereignty of Berlin was awarded to the victors of World War II. But the Russians abandoned their position and went over to their own side of Berlin. Therefore the only good sense would be to maintain the situation as it is until the German question can be settled.

"I must confess that the West German government tends to exaggerate. It is not worth the trouble involved to provoke an Eastern reaction by holding presidential elections in West Berlin. The allies—you, we, and the British—have the responsibility of sovereignty. We (France) gave a reluctant yes when the question was put to us. This was really a mistake. We should have looked at the question squarely and said no. That would have avoided the present crisis."

I told de Gaulle that in Moscow I had read the official Soviet account of his conversations with Stalin in December 1944. He was quoted as saying: "French policy compels Frenchmen to desire first of all a mutual assistance pact with the Soviet Union." Was this still true, I inquired? He answered:

"When Germany is a danger—yes. If there is a German danger, we would have to have an alliance. You must remember how much both Russia and France suffered from Germany. If Germany were to become a big power militarily, economically—and in a nuclear sense—then we would have to have an alliance. Neither of us can accept a dangerous Germany."

I asked if he thought it was feasible to work out a compromise revision of the world monetary system. Said he: "You mean, should we have a new Bretton Woods? Should there be a new international monetary system? If so, it should certainly be done in the most secret way, not by a large, public conference. That would only start off a wave of speculation. Something like this must be discussed discreetly and tranquilly.

"It would certainly be good sense to have a monetary system under which gold would be the criterion. The criterion of exchange would be gold. And gold is not a money like the dollar which is now serving as the criterion.

"You must remember that credit has an immense importance. Credit is what is necessary for international commerce and you cannot always move gold around in order to pick up the credit. You must work a system of credit and also international banks must apply its regulation. Capital should only be used for real trade, never for mere speculation. Thus, if speculatory funds were to enter Germany, the Bundesbank would have to force them out."

I had a feeling de Gaulle was getting just a bit beyond his depth on this and he confessed rather disarmingly: "Of course, you know, I am not a great expert on these things."

Nevertheless, he plunged ahead. "Gold would be the world criterion for the balance of payments between states. And we must agree among us on a common value for gold. Obviously, it has to be increased from its present value. Gold is worth more than the value accorded to it now under the gold exchange standard. It is worth at least $40 an ounce. Not $35. This must be readjusted. And that would increase the value of gold against both the dollar and the franc."

I asked the General if it was true that France intended to send troops to the Lebanon. He replied in the negative—but then added: "If Israel were to attack the Lebanon, we would not let it fall. We would take action. We insist that it stand."

I asked if France considered itself neutral as between Israelis and Arabs, in the sense that it would support either side if it were attacked by the other. He said, "Yes. In 1967 I told Israel not to attack. I also told the same to the Arabs. We told both sides that we would hold either one responsible if it attacked the other."

I asked what was the ultimate goal of his policy in Nigeria. Did he favor complete independence for Biafra or a federation of two autonomous countries, or what? He said: "We always want each country to decide on its own fate. But this must be decided by the people of a country. Biafra is one people." (This betrays de Gaulle's ignorance of the ethnography of West Africa.) "It must be allowed to choose its own destiny. If it doesn't want to stay in Nigeria, no one can force it to do so. Good sense argues that it should become a state itself. Then it could form a union with Nigeria; but it would be an independent Biafra."

"It is just the same in Canada, there is a French people there. They don't want to be anything else. There is also an English people; and in the West there is a people that is almost American. They must make their own union on the basis of reciprocal engagements on such things as defense or currency. But to pretend to make English law on the backs of the French in Quebec can not work. It is not just. It would be better to accept a state of Quebec in a union of Canada."

I observed that on the basis of what he had been saying concerning West Germany, I had a distinct impression the special friendship pact wasn't working well. Was this true? De Gaulle shrugged his shoulders very high.

An expression that was half whimsical and half disagreeable came over his white face. "It is not a big thing now. I suppose that is the least one can say," he observed.

I asked if France would be willing to take part in any conference of nonaligned countries, such as the usual confabulation of India, Jugoslavia, and Egypt. With some hauteur, he replied: "No, not that. Of course, we are against blocs. We don't want to be in a bloc or in anyone's hegemony. But that is not the same as being neutralist or neutral."

I remarked that he had known all the American presidents from Roosevelt to Nixon and he knew Nixon as an individual. How did he compare them? He said: "Their personalities are very different. Each had his own particular difference from the other and different conditions were playing their role. This was true for Roosevelt, Truman, and also for poor Kennedy. It is the same for Johnson and Nixon. I suppose one should leave this matter to the historians.

"Each had or has a strong personality and that is definitely good. I include Nixon. Certainly. But now we will see how he is as a president. He is just beginning his mandate. He has all that is needed in his personality to be a strong president."

I asked him to analyze his own career. He said: "Because of events, I started from a very, very low beginning. It was a very terrible situation, a desperate situation from which I began. This was not true for the others. It wasn't true at all for Roosevelt. Churchill was in a dangerous situation, but not a desperate one. The same may be said for Stalin. But my beginning was desperate."

As we were getting up to go, I asked if there were any chance at all of his writing his fourth volume of memoirs, and he said none. He would merely leave his papers for history.

We rose and, as we were walking toward the door, he asked me if I was traveling much. I said I was leaving shortly for Cairo, where I had an appointment with Nasser. He had never met Nasser, but thought it was better than he should stay there than to have somebody worse come in. On that note we parted.

By way of summary, I would like to recollect my impressions and intuitions. I found de Gaulle overconfident and possibly in a dangerous mood. I suspect he was fully aware of his weakening position, although he spoke with great assurance and sought to give an impression of his strength, even to the degree of indicating that Washington was coming over to his viewpoint.

I know de Gaulle quite well and I never forget that he is at his most dangerous when he is in a weak position. I cannot prove this by any particular phrases he used, but I have a feeling that he is going to dangerously embroil things during the almost three years that remain to him during his second term as president.

He is trying to practice a kind of judo diplomacy in which he uses the weight of the two superpowers against each other and against themselves. It is clear to me that if he cannot reassert his ascendancy over West Germany—which is now perceptibly fading—and make the United States eat some Gaullist dirt, he is going to play the last great trump—alliance with Russia.

The French people are political babes in the wood, although they are always the last to see this—and de Gaulle may manage to lead them around by the nose. Furthermore, he can always look to the communists and the Left for necessary support if the Right tries to throw him out on the Soviet issue.

De Gaulle's policy toward the U.S.A. is in no sense based on malice. Indeed, were he able to get France back to the top of the heap (patently impossible) he would regard us with an amused, kindly disdain if not affection, plus a certain admiration for our energy. But he is a visionary and deals with the world not as it is but as he sees it could be—or should be. And a principal element in frustrating the realization of this dream is the size and power of America—overshadowing the reduced circumstances of France.

If he could only get us to an isolationist shell he could go back to the old Maurrassien game of playing Germany and Russia against each other. He plays it now but today's roles and players are different and Maurras did not have the answer to the modern version. De Gaulle tries to move the pieces with brilliant panache and he seeks to use the Russian castle audaciously as a pawn. He is unaware, I fear, that Moscow is meanwhile using him—not as a piece in its own version of the same game, but to smash the board itself.

PARIS, *February 22, 1969*

Lunched with (Count) Motrico, former Spanish ambassador to Washington and Paris, now principal aide for Don Juan, pretender to the Spanish throne.

Motrico talks about Franco and his boys as the "Spanish John Birchers." He says Opus Dei and Fraga Ibirarne, Franco's information minister, put the heat on young Juan Carlos, Don Juan's son, to run for the succession himself as a stooge of the Right, headed by Admiral Carrero Blanco. Queen Frederika, his mother-in-law, and Princess Irene, his wife, played along with this. As a result he abandoned his previous promise of prior loyalty to his father's wishes and is ready.

Don Juan is trying to head this off. Motrico plays him up as a middle-of-the-roader who is a respectable liberal. He claims Juan Carlos is a puppet.

M. says that the day French Foreign Minister Debré arrived in Madrid on this month's official visit was the same day André Malraux's books were removed from Spanish libraries as too left-wing!

CAIRO, *February 25, 1969*

Lunched at the cafeteria of *Al Ahram* with the [Mohamed] Heikals. The food was excellent. I was enormously impressed with the modernity, cleanliness, and apparent efficiency of their new building. After lunch they took us out to Gizeh to see the huge boat of King Cheops which had been discovered near the Great Pyramid and has been reassembled during the past fourteen years. It is 130 feet long and looks almost exactly like an enormous Venetian gondola. It is made of Lebanese (Phoenician) cedar wood held together by tightly-lashed rope—no nails or pegs.

An archaeology professor speaking elegant English and French conducted us around, aided by his expert in restoring ancient objects, a stocky little man with grey spade beard, who is so devout a Moslem that he takes a clean handkerchief and encloses his hand inside it in order to shake hands with a woman; he could not otherwise touch her.

CAIRO, *February 26, 1969*

Spent two hours with Nasser in his residence in eastern Cairo. Mohamed Heikal took me out. This is the eve of the annual big holiday, Bairam, but despite this, Nasser chose the time and seemed fully at ease, unrushed. After being held up by tommy gun-carrying guards at the gate while we were checked, we went in, were greeted by an aide, sat around waiting in the same antechamber I have often seen before. This time Nasser joined us and had the interview here instead of in his office.

Nasser came in breezily, wearing grey trousers and a short-sleeved, summer-weight shirt with open collar. He had just had a "throat treatment" from a Soviet doctor. Later in the conversation he said he had gained fourteen kilos last year, when he had been seriously ill, had lost them all, was now gaining them back again. He has given up smoking, which is one reason, of course, and can't play tennis any more because he apparently has rheumatism in his left leg. He now walks before lunch every day and tries to cut down on his food. (Heikal says it's no trouble dieting around Nasser's house because he has an abominable cook.)

Once Mohammed Fawzi (then foreign minister) and Heikal were on the presidential yacht with Nasser, bound for Morocco, and they complained bitterly about the food at Nasser's table. They said they were eating in the "second-class dining room" because they got the same as Nasser while all the aides ate splendidly at their mess. Nasser seemed puzzled and told Mohammed he could arrange with the cook to have whatever he thought desirable.

Nasser said: "We are ready to resume relations with the United States, but as long as the United States supports the Israeli occupation of our territory and as long as the United States supplies Israel with planes while it is occupying our territory, there will be difficulties.

"Of course we hope for more from the Nixon administration than its predecessor. After the June [six-day] war we faced a situation where the United States supported completely the views of Israel. We want from the United States not to take sides. Not to take our side, but not to support the occupation of our territory by Israel.

"We have great admiration for President Eisenhower and for Nixon. When Nixon visited us in 1963 he was finished with politics but we received him as Eisenhower's vice president."

I asked if he foresaw a fourth round of war. He said: "This is a very simple question. We are striving to end the occupation of Arab territory in Egypt, Jordan, and Syria by a political solution—by peaceful means. If we don't achieve it by peaceful means, what result? We must strive by other means to achieve it. One could not accept occupation of his country. One has to fight."

I then asked if there was danger of a nuclear explosion in the Middle East. He answered: "As long as the Israelis don't sign the nonproliferation treaty, there is danger. We have signed it, but if they begin there will be a race. If they tried to build nuclear weapons we would try to have our own. We have the capacity but what we need is the investment money required. I do not believe the Israelis have such weapons now."

I asked him to spell out his short-range and long-range terms for peace. He said:

"When I speak of a settlement I don't mean short-term and long-term. If we solve the problem of the occupied territory and of the refugees from Palestine, this will result in a peaceful settlement in spite of what took place during the last twenty or more years. But if we solve only the problem of the occupied territory, and neglect the other part, there will be no peace.

"The Israelis have expelled more than one million Arabs, Christians, and Moslems. They wanted a country based on Judaism. If they accept refugees and evacuate conquered areas there will be lasting peace.

"After the war of 1948, there were resolutions in the United Nations according to Arab refugees, expelled by Israeli terrorists, the right to return to their land. Now they are outside because Israel refused. This is the reason for the *Fedayeen* movement. They are mostly the children of those expelled in 1948 and who wish to return. This is the main problem—the right of the Palestinians in their own land.

"I don't mean that Israel should gain part of our Arab territory and then say in exchange it would accept Arabs. Nobody will accept the expansion of Israel. If this is permitted, it would merely be a step to achieve the dreams of some of the leaders of Israel to have Israeli territory expand between the Nile and the Euphrates. We would take the June 1, 1967 frontiers."

I wondered what he thought of Eisenhower's formula for installing large nuclear plants in the general area of Palestine in order to desalt water for irrigation and provide power for industry in settlements which could be developed by Palestinian refugees. He said:

"We gave great attention to these statements by General Eisenhower and those by President Johnson and we tried to have contact between American officials and our government to put these ideas into effect in our country. All were without any result. The last contact took place two months ago. But what happened after the ideas of General Eisenhower were only statements. We need water for our deserts, but there is no attempt to put that into effect. We could not neglect the rest of the problem and deal with it from this point of view only. The idea of nationalism, the Palestine problem, the people who want to return to their homeland. This is our character and our inheritance and we cannot separate it from other approaches."

I asked about the position of Jews now residing in Arab states. He said: "We have here about 5,000 Jews. We have about 100 under arrest because they are Zionists and in contact with Israel. Those who want to leave the country can leave and many got permission to leave the country. The rest live as Egyptians and have all rights.

"The Jews are our cousins. Moses was born in Egypt. Don't stress this. I don't want it to be an Israeli claim. They say we are anti-Semitic, which is nonsense. We are Semites ourselves. We look upon Jews in our country as Egyptians. The Jews who live in the Arab countries feel it will be always more suitable for them to live in Arab countries rather than to go to other countries. Their fathers and grandfathers lived here for thousands of years without any discrimination."

Did he still feel there should ultimately be one single Arab state, a kind of federation of pan-Arabism?

"I think," he said, "that when the Arabs realize that unity and federation will be in their own interests and strength, this will help to achieve the object of Arab unity. It is not an easy question because of the contradictions politically and socially. People of all Arab countries want unity, but how to fulfill it is not an easy question."

He said there were no Soviet naval bases here, adding: "We don't have any base in our country for any foreign country. Of course the Soviets were visiting our ports before the aggression against our country and they visit our ports also now. We welcome visits because the Soviet Union helped us after the aggression, they supplied us with arms after we lost our arms."

I asked: "How many Soviet military training personnel and technicians are there today in the UAR?" He said: "Really, I don't know the figure, but I am asking for more technicians.

"It is less than five thousand. You know, it is probably even less than one thousand." (Of course not true.)

"We are trying to rebuild our armed forces and, of course, we have new arms now instead of the older arms which were lost during 1967. But I could not say we have exceeded what there was in 1967. That is why we are particularly worried about statements in Western countries that they want to ban arms entering this area. The meaning of an arms ban would be that Israel will have superiority in both army and air force, while we won't get the opportunity to replace what we lost."

I asked if he could describe his ideology. He answered: "We don't describe ours as socialist democracy, but as a 'socialist community.' People base their lives on socialism. Democracy, according to the charter, is freedom for the community and freedom of the individual, but it ends exploitation of the individual."

I observed: "It seems to me that you have an unusual talent for turning defeat into victory and for climbing out of pits. What is the secret?" He said:

"You know, I believe that I am a lucky man in spite of the catastrophe we face now. On the other hand, I don't plan it. It is natural. After the defeat, I was willing to leave. But, you know, when I said that I was selfish. I was trying to escape, but I was not able to. Nobody was informed of my intention except three men. I was really intending to leave. I was very tired and sick. But now it is over. When I went to Khartoum, all the people came to the streets and I could not forget what was said in one of the magazines: Hail the conquered. To be conquered is not a determined issue, but to surrender is. I am not going to surrender. I believe in God. I am a fatalistic man. I believe in his will."

I asked who had most influenced his life. He replied: "Of course, I was influenced by Mohammed and also by Jesus. I believe in both of them. Did you know that we believe in Christ also? Of contemporaries, I think the most effective man was General Aziz el Masri. I admired him when I was a young officer. He fought for independence. I met him many times. He was in Turkey during the First World War and then he came to Egypt. He was not in our army except for a period during the Second World War."

Nasser told me he had been very ill. "Last year I was not able to read a lot, but now I am regaining my capacity to work as before, so I read more. In the last few days I have been reading a book about Mao Tse-tung. I have a real hobby of airplanes and I read all books and magazines I can get on them. I don't read detective stories any more. Sometimes I ask Heikal to give me *House and Garden*—just to change things."

I asked what he dreamed Egypt will be in twenty-five years' time. He said:

"My main dream is to develop this country. To have electricity in each village and have work for every man. We have work for every man in spite of many problems—the increase of the population by one million per year. We must have an increase in order to have jobs for one half a million every year. This year we will have electricity in three hundred villages. We have surplus electricity and water because now we have the water of the High Dam which will help in land reform. We don't have money for investment.

"This is, of course, my dream. I want to see this country without servants before my death. Now it is difficult for people to find servants. And this always-increasing problem about getting servants means an increasing standard of living.

"I have no personal dreams. I have no personal life. I have nothing personal. Many people may not believe that, but this is the truth."

At the very end we chatted several minutes. Nasser told me he now had two grandchildren, a girl two and a half and a boy one and a half, and one comes for lunch every day. (Heikal tells me he spoils the hell out of them.) Even the baby can now say "Hello, Grandpa." Furthermore, since he gave up smoking Nasser has taken to chewing Chiclets as a substitute and the kids are mad for them. Incidentally, Nasser says mournfully he still desperately misses smoking cigarettes, almost a year after quitting.

He told me that all last year, when he clearly was suffering a physical crisis, he used sleeping pills but now he has broken the habit and sleeps about six hours nightly, going off easily, retiring at 2:00 A.M. and rising at 9:00. Later in the car, Heikal told me he had had a bad nervous depression, especially after the treason and suicide of his old friend Field Marshal Amr.

RAWALPINDI, PAKISTAN, *March 3, 1969*

Flew up to Rawalpindi. It is slightly disconcerting when the captain announces that "*Inshallah*, we shall soon be landing."

A gentleman from the information department greeted us.

General Rafi, Ayub's military secretary, told me my appointment was for 10:00 A.M., March 6. I objected that I wouldn't be in Pakistan then. This didn't impress Rafi who said the president [Ayub Khan] couldn't change his schedule "to suit the press." I decided to leave tomorrow.

Trouble is obviously coming here. This time the power may leave the elite. The future is murky. Will the constitution be changed? Will the East get autonomy?

LAHORE, PAKISTAN, *March 5, 1969*

Drove here from Rawalpindi. The road is crowded with bullock carts and two-wheeled tongas drawn by plumed horses. Islamabad, the new capital being built outside Rawalpindi just below the mountains, is hideous and looks like an enormous boondoggle.

Too bad, Lahore is such a much more lovely city and eminently suited for a capital—save that it is almost within artillery range of the border.

Drove around today to the old Moghul Palace-Fort, the Badshahi Mosque (it must be almost the world's largest), Shalimar gardens. None of the listed sightseeing tours even mention the Sikh temple, one of their holy of holies, where Ranjit Singh is buried, and the museum guide carefully tries to steer you past the room with Sikh mementos.

What a military history these people have had: Greeks, Mongols, Moghuls, Afghans, Sikhs, and British have all fought here. Almost each type of artillery piece has its name: the Tiger's Whelp, Zamzamah, the batterer of citadels. And the Punjabis and Pathans of the west show their martial past: handsome, lean men, an enormous number of slender, beautiful women.

2 1

MRS. GANDHI:

"I CAN'T TELL, NEVER

HAVING BEEN A MAN"

PAKISTANI CARS AREN'T ALLOWED IN INDIA. AT THE BORDER (Huseiniwala—Firozepore) we went through endless filling-out of papers and then four porters (called coolie-wallahs) carried our baggage over, through customs, handed on to Indian coolies, and finally these loaded it into a car sent from Delhi.

It is interesting to contrast the enormous, flat, fertile Punjab on both sides of the border. The people are much better looking on the Moslem side but even worse off. On the Indian side they are moving slowly but perceptibly from the tonga level of society to the bicycle age; and they are inching slowly from the buffalo and camel to the tractor.

New Delhi, *March 7, 1969*

Lunched and had a long, pleasant talk with Ambassador [Chester] Chet Bowles, sitting under a tree in his garden. The poor fellow has Parkinson's disease. He's a courageous and idealistic man but he is clearly declining.

He started out saying China was aiming southward from Yunan and Tibet through the hill states to Calcutta (via Nagaland). India could not allow West Bengal to break away and form a state with East Bengal (East Pakistan). Chet foresees a serious crisis in Calcutta (with China behind it) within six months. There are plenty of Moslems still in West Bengal and they are preaching the line—join with East Pakistan and form a Bengali state. But India can't agree to this; anyway, it would be a sitting duck for China.

Chet says the U.S.A. has *no* policy in Asia, "only a series of reactions to different crises, and the reactions always differ." He thinks the weakness of our position is that we try to develop a counterweight to China from the little states like Taiwan and Thailand, only eight percent of the population of noncommunist Asia. We should try to build a grouping of India-Japan-Australia, etc., which we could "support but not control."

India was humiliated in the 1962 war with China. In early 1963, it came to us and asked us to modernize its military forces. Washington was afraid of irking the Pakistanis. Kennedy wanted to consider a basic policy change but was buried the day before a scheduled national security council meeting on the issue. We had a chance, says Chet, to "get close to the Indian army," but we muffed it. He argues that India is the only source we have for large ground forces against China, with its army of one million volunteer soldiers and good training, high morale.

Allen Dulles asked him in 1953 what chance he thought India had of surviving as a democracy. Fifty-fifty was his answer. Now he would say it was a seventy-thirty chance; the odds are much better.

He says our new Vietnam policy is paying off here. Mrs. Gandhi wanted bombing stopped at all costs and had an indiscriminate, emotional view. But the Indian people as a whole are worried about what would happen to them if the U.S. got out of Asia. Chet thinks if we smacked Hanoi for two days we could live with it here, after a big initial fuss.

NEW DELHI, *March 8, 1969*

W. tells me we are convinced China's policy is to sterilize its frontiers and weaken India. And, because Moscow and Washington work so hard in India, this also weakens Russia and America. The method used is classical Han policy. To this, communist ideology and world revolutionary dogma have been added. We must remember that China does not *like* to see communism established through elections; this is the Soviet method. China prefers power through violence to the parliamentary road to power.

Russia is arming India heavily. Moreover, the Russians are pushing a new definition of nonalignment. It used to be a balance, midway in the world political equilibrium. Now it is held that a nonaligned country must move toward a socialist economy. The Russians are insisting that India prove itself in this respect. The Soviets are pushing the "public sector" hard.

There is no real indication yet of whether India will decide to make atomic weapons. It is pushing its peaceful nuclear program hard to get it in shape for a switch-over—if it decides to later. If it makes the decision it could probably get warheads in twelve to eighteen months.

Chet Bowles gave me some papers to read. Two were cables on Kashmir, both sent January 31, 1969, saying in substance:

> No Indian government could allow the Pakistanis to get Kashmir and retain office. The Kashmir Valley is essential to the defense of Ladakh against the Chinese because supplies for two Indian frontier divisions go through Srinagar. The Indians argue that if Pakistan is allowed a voice in the fate of Kashmir's 2 million Moslems it will claim the right to interfere in the fate of India's 55 millon Moslems elsewhere.

NEW DELHI, *March 10, 1969*

This afternoon I spent an hour with Mrs. Indira Gandhi, the prime minister, and enjoyed it a great deal. As far as I am concerned, she has more charm than the legendary appeal of her father, Nehru.

She is a small woman with dark brown eyes, black, greying hair. She was seated behind a large desk, remained in her chair as she shook hands, but produced a pleasant smile. She was wearing a white blouse under a blue sari. I remarked that there must be both advantages and disadvantages to being a female chief of government. She said:

"I don't think it really makes any difference. Obviously every person has some advantages and some disadvantages in a job like this. For India you can have pluses and minuses in terms of the region you come from or the caste to which your family belongs. Some people say that a woman hasn't as much stamina as a man. Of course, I can't tell, never having been a man. But I certainly have more physical stamina than anyone else around here."

I observed that, in any case, a woman prime minister might benefit because men were more polite to her. "Certainly not," said she with only half a smile. "They surely are no more polite. Don't think that."

I said her father's ideology had been described frequently as Fabian socialism although I personally thought that a rather fuzzy label. How would she describe her own ideology? She answered:

"I don't think I can be said to have any ideology at all in this vague sense. After all, I have to face specific problems and specific situations. You just have to find the best way of doing things as they arise. Sometimes you just have to compromise with what you would prefer. For example, we didn't want to import food. But we had to; it was a matter of life and death.

"Our party wants to use the tool of socialism to raise living standards, but this obviously isn't necessarily the socialism of other countries. Our methods must be fitted to the minds and the backgrounds of our people.

"Essentially, there are no two ways open to us. Ours is such a large mass, so poor and so backward economically that you can't afford just to let tnings take their course. The people won't wait that long. The state must take things upon itself. It would just create more problems were we to leave everything to private enterprise. Private enterprise always seeks to make a profit and you can't have a profit in all the aspects of the problems facing us, above all with the enormous need for social justice and for welfare. We must be pragmatic.

"It's hard to say just what our ideology is. We use the word socialism as the nearest thing. But there is no particular prophet of our socialism. We are really seeking a new and middle path. We believe in a mixed economy."

Apropos of ideological trends, I asked her what writers or persons had had the greatest influence in shaping her ideology and personality. She replied:

"I suppose the influences were mostly Indian. I was a very voracious reader and when I was a child I simply devoured books. I could name Tagore as one influence, but I know Americans would never have heard of the others. My father, of course, exerted an influence, but my mother quite as much.

"And you must remember that my childhood was right in the middle of our freedom struggle. Therefore, I was impressed at the time by any stories having to do with freedom anywhere. As a small girl I was told about Joan of Arc, about Garibaldi in Italy, and about many others."

I got the impression from these remarks and from a later aside on her grandfather that she wasn't quite as influenced by her father as many people make out. She wanted to stand on her own feet, to be accepted by and as herself.

I said her father had once suggested to me that the next generation of India's political leadership would suffer the disadvantage of not having been heroes of the revolution and the freedom struggle. She commented:

"This is no longer the case. For our younger generation, the years of the freedom struggle no longer have any meaning. They don't harp on it. It's not that they are bored; they simply accept the fact that freedom is here."

I asked if her late husband's family had any connection with Mahatma Gandhi. She said. "My husband's family was Parsee, originally from Persia. There was no relationship with the Hindu Gandhis. And the voters aren't in the least concerned with the fact that I'm Nehru's daughter. After all, I established my own political life. I entered the working committee of the Congress party in 1955 and I had been working at the villages level long before. I became president of the party in 1959. And don't forget, my husband was very well known at the village level before his death."

I asked whether the essential policy of nonalignment was practical any more in a world where "imperialism" and "colonialism" no longer played a prominent role. She answered that nonalignment remained valid. There was nothing "dogmatic" about it. "It just means that we do not wish to belong to any alliance or political bloc. In fact, nonalignment is very valid as a concept now because more and more countries are subscribing to it.

"The world was very sharply divided between Eastern and Western blocs, involved in a cold war, when we started this policy. Only later a period began in which the outlines of this cleavage were more blurred. The cold war is still on in a way but many people are crossing the barriers of alignment into each other's camp—on such matters as trade, culture, and other relations. They work more and more with the people of the other bloc to their own. Therefore it is really the concept of alignment that has changed, not the concept of nonalignment.

"India never wanted to be part of a special bloc for two obvious reasons. First of all there is our geographical position, our neighbors. And then, if you are aligned, you irritate those who are not in the same bloc. Certainly that's not worthwhile."

I observed that some people thought India—and her government— were over-dependent on Russia because it was so heavily the source of the country's military equipment nowadays. She said: "That's the argument of the Swatantra and the Jan Sangh (the extreme right-wing parties). But, in fact, we don't wish to be dependent on any country or any group. We are now seeking and will always seek more diversification in the sources of material and to get things where we can. We want to stand on our own feet and we try our hardest to be self-sufficient. And remember this—just because we get equipment from a country doesn't mean we'll do what they want. We won't do what anyone wants simply because we get hardware there."

I asked if ideology represented any barrier between India and the United States. "Not for us," she said. "What does come up is this sort of thing. When we learned that the CIA was indirectly financing institutions that were helping us there was a wave of anger at getting any such help. That's upsetting. But we have no ideological divisions; I have none and I hope the majority of us don't.

"Some people in the United States say that we are too close to Russia and that we vote too often on the Soviet side in UN. But this really isn't so; it is only true on such issues as those involving colonialism and racism, and here it is not a question of us following the Russians but a question of the Russians taking the stand that happens to agree with ours. The Russians have simply shown a greater understanding of the needs and mentality of newly-freed peoples. And when you are so close to preindependence times and attitudes as we still are, you remember these things very well. You are a little touchy on some of these matters. It takes time to adjust and to get used to being a country."

I asked how she felt about the "Brezhnev doctrine" that Moscow had the right to interfere in other "socialist" lands. She said: "We stand firmly for the right of all other states to independence. Each country must be free. The only thing in UN, during the debate on Czechoslovakia, was that we didn't want to 'condemn' Russia because we had never used the word 'condemn' before. But we made every point stressed in the UN debate right here in our own parliament and before these points were made in UN. I wish to be very clear about that."

I then asked if she could tell me a bit about her private life. Did she have any? What did she do with her spare time? She said:

"I try to squeeze private things in when I can. Of course, I have no rigid schedule, but I like to see my family when I can [she has two sons, one married—to an Italian]. Normally I take meals with the family. And if I have a moment I like to go to exhibitions—sculpture, painting, manuscripts, tapestries, all kinds of things—on Sundays. I like music but that I hear mostly at home. I rather like classical music—Bach, but also folk music, also Indian music.

"I do my reading mostly while traveling or on weekends." I asked if she could remember the last three or four books she had read. "*The Naked Ape* was the last," said she. "On the whole, I prefer reading something that retains my interest. You know, with detective stories I either guess who did it or I look at the end to see. So that doesn't really do."

She said the family owned a small plot of land outside Delhi on which they had intended to build a house, but this was declared a "Green Area" and it was forbidden to construct. But she has planted some citrus trees and likes to go out and look at them sometimes.

I asked if she actually liked being prime minister. She smiled and said:

"You know, I had a very strict training. My grandfather, who died when I was thirteen, brought us up in a most Spartan way. There wasn't even any heating for us young people during the winter in Allahabad where we lived. My grandfather told us: 'You can't ever do anything well unless you enjoy it. If you think a job is boring or a drudgery you will never succeed in it.' I guess that is your answer."

I asked about her grandfather, to whom she clearly paid more regard in our talk than to her far more famous father. He was Motilal Nehru, one of the early Congress party members. "He started with very little; it was the kind of story you Americans like. Our family has had many ups and downs and also we have always had a very close-knit family system in which a young man may have to support everyone. My father started poor but he was a very good lawyer and became rich. He saw that even all his nephews were educated in Europe.

"And although we had a Spartan upbringing, he was fond of the good life. He got on very well with the British, but he was always keenly conscious of India's situation and he fought hard for greater rights. He joined the Congress party early when it was a small middle-class party, and saw Gandhi make it into a mass party. This was partly through the influence of my father and my mother as well as Gandhi; he gave up everything and joined the movement."

NAINITAL, INDIA, *March 16, 1969*

We have been up here for two days in the mountains below the main Himalaya range. To drive some 250 miles across the steaming plain from Delhi—through a tangle of oxcarts, horse-drawn tongas, obviously drugged pedestrians, buses jammed with three times their load of passengers and driven by madmen, bicycles, rickshaws, motorcycles with as many as three Sikhs holding on at once, camel wagons, herds of goats, buffalo, and Brahma cattle—is as much as the nerves can stand—on dusty, narrow roads. But finally, after Hanlawi, a small garrison station, the road leads upward past oak woods and bright red rhododendron trees (not bushes) to Nainital, a hill resort "discovered" according to the sign, in 1839, now with 16,000 inhabitants. It is a seedy town by a rank, fetid "lake" (really a pond) and contains six of India's best boarding schools. It is about 6,000 feet high and pleasantly cool at evening time, cold at night.

We had a good ride and walk to a peak from which we could look across the high, snow-covered ranges to Tibet, getting a magnificent view before a sudden haze and cloud cover obscured it all. The horses are tiny, with delicate little feet, but quite spry. Marina was delighted with rhododendrons, violets, fruit blossoms, and numerous other flowers. Incidentally, when looking back over the plain from the edge of the peak, you feel you are staring at a sea because the haze completely obscures the great, flat, baking pancake that is India.

NEW DELHI, *March 20, 1969*

This, our last afternoon, we visited a Sikh temple on the Chandni Chowk. A stern, bearded, old man in turban, with white hair and a sharp spear, guarded the doorway, but a charming member of the temple staff took us through a side door into a little room where we left our shoes and socks. He tied kerchiefs over our heads (in lieu of turban for me) and led us in where men and women together were holding a very cheerful, moving service in the main hall, while a small orchestra played accordion-like instruments and sang hymns. It is a touching religion: monotheistic combination of Hinduism and Islam (perhaps), tolerant, believes in equality of sexes and no caste, in courage and truth. The farewell salutation is "Eternal truth!" Each temple has a kitchen where poor members of the congregation are fed, and they can also sleep in a temple dormitory. Courage is the big requirement, emphasized by the last of the ten gurus, Gobind Singh, who turned them into a warrior sect and gave them the name of lions (*Singhs*).

BANGKOK, *March 22, 1969*

Pleasant talk with [U.S.] Ambassador Leonard Unger in the garden pavilion of his expansive, old-fashioned embassy residence.

Our bases here are under the Thais and we would only withdraw with Thai agreement. The probability is that after a Vietnam settlement our military establishment here will be somewhere between a maximum of 40,000 and a minimum of 5,000. This estimate does not include the two unlikely extremes of an outright invasion of Thailand or a U.S. decision to withdraw totally from Asia. We are here under SEATO and also the Rusk-Thant communiqué concerning Vietnam, and the Thais want us to stay on, even with peace in Vietnam, as long as there is any trouble in Laos. They are very afraid that peace in South Vietnam might unleash the north against this country.

China is always Problem Number One here and there is wary hope that Russia may yet be helpful in this respect.

SAIGON, *March 25, 1969*

Lunched today at the home of Sam Berger, deputy ambassador (and now chargé d'affaires because Bunker is home reporting to Nixon). Sam criticized McNamara as "always thinking any problem can be solved in a quantified sense." He didn't have the faintest idea what revolutionary warfare was about.

Long talk with President Nguyen Van Thieu in the presidential palace, right in the middle of Saigon and especially hideous.

It certainly is well-protected, surrounded by a coil of barbed wire in which a gap is opened by guards for vehicles or pedestrians. Inside, I saw two helicopters poised in a state of readiness and several tanks and armored personnel carriers. On the roof I noticed two machine guns manned, presumably against a possible airborne attack.

Thieu was sitting at his desk and arose with a smile and a handshake. He is small, delicately made, and has an alert but hooded intelligent face with a slightly Chinese cast of features. The president started off in English and handled it extremely well.

I asked if he thought relations between Washington and Saigon had changed at all as a consequence of Nixon's election and the substitution of Lodge for Harriman at the Paris talks. Thieu replied that the relations between our two governments had not changed, but there was better collaboration now between our two delegations at the Paris negotiations.

Were there any fundamental differences between the ultimate peace aims of Saigon and Washington? Thieu assured me there were none. Both governments were in agreement on objectives. They would not accept "a false solution" although they intended patiently to settle the war by negotiation. They would insist upon an "honorable peace."

I asked if any kind of nonalignment for South Vietnam was possible in the eventual postwar situation. He replied: "No. That would clearly not be realistic. South Vietnam must belong to the free world. We should work within that framework.

"Neutralism or nonalignment or whatever you may call it gives a confused meaning. Everybody would think this meant we were going to the Left and toward the communists. The Vietnamese people are obsessed by such an interpretation of these words."

He added: "There can't be any form of neutralism that does not result in our being dominated by the communists. Any other interpretation is simply an illusion. I don't believe in all this talk about Ho Chi Minh as a kind of Tito. You can't compare Vietnam and Jugoslavia. We know perfectly well that the Chinese simply would not permit that kind of development, even if the communists tried it, because we know what the Chinese intend to do."

He didn't think SEATO had been very efficient in protecting Vietnam. The United States had not really operated within a SEATO frame here but had committed its forces as an independent action. He continued: "America is the defender of the free world. Really, if you look at it carefully, SEATO has been neutralized,"—he meant, by France and Pakistan. However, he concluded that some kind of international guarantee would be necessary after a peace.

I asked if he thought any kind of unification—economic unity or even a political move by loose confederation—would be feasible to bring together north and south after the war. He didn't believe any kind of confederation was practical. It was impossible to conceive of confederation between a free country and a communist country. Furthermore, the communists of North Vietnam would never permit such an idea. But an economic approach might work.

On Cambodia he said: "I understand the attitude of Prince Sihanouk. He knows what not to ask for. He knows he can't be anticommunist. Cambodia is too small and too weak to fight Hanoi. Sihanouk's whole policy is based upon the simple desire to survive. He helps the communists in order to avoid an invasion. Nevertheless, I think he is beginning to shift. He seems to believe increasingly that the free world is clearly ready and determined to stick by its goals."

Thieu concluded: "The problem can be settled. We are ready to reopen the record." He said France still had a good deal of influence in Cambodia and that de Gaulle was very much listened to by Sihanouk. He wondered if perhaps de Gaulle would not be able to help. I asked Thieu if Saigon was prepared to take the initiative in improving French relations. The answer: "We are certainly ready to take the initiative for an improvement."

SAIGON, *March 26, 1969*

This afternoon I met General Creighton W. Abrams, commander of our forces here, and I came away well impressed. He is a very tough-looking man of about five feet ten inches, stockily built with slightly reddish complexion, balding brown hair and a quiet, firm aura about him. He has a gentleness to him that sometimes very strong men have, a soft look in his blue eyes and a low, soft voice. I am told he is extremely fond of music. He was wearing fatigues and smoking a cigar when he received me in the headquarters complex near Tan Son Nhut.

I asked what was the strategic goal of the present communist offensive? He answered: "It is too early to assess this with any high degree of confidence. Certainly I think one objective of this offensive is its effect on the American people. But then, don't forget the communists *do* want to overthrow this government and that is the number one objective—to get Thieu, Ky, and Huong out of there.

"And don't think that this isn't a pretty big operation. They've got almost 50 percent—I estimate 47 or 48 percent of their combat strength —in here in the Third Corps area of the adjacent border region. They've moved eight regiments down from the Second Corps since last summer and five of these regiments were moved in preparation for this current effort.

"This objective of getting rid of the government or seriously weakening it doesn't tie in directly with the question of American public opinion. Increasingly the American kill is tangential. That's picked up as gravy from their viewpoint. But what they are trying to do is to bring military pressure on the government from the outside and political ferment from the inside in order to topple the government. That's the number one objective.

"The main pressure is right here. In the highlands and the southern First Corps the pressure has been put on primarily to prevent us from shifting many troops around. The same is true of the DMZ (Demilitarized Zone). They want to keep alive a threat in those areas, but this is a diversion."

Abrams then asked his aide to bring in a paper and he read from it statistics in order to prove to me that "this has been a big effort" on the part of the communists.

Abrams said that it was impossible to rely on the absolute exact accuracy of figures because they were totaled from the battle reports of units, but he concluded that the present offensive has "now almost run its course." He is convinced that the position of President Thieu and also of his Vietnamese corps commanders has remained strong.

The enemy had "realistically sought to accomplish his objectives in the most effective way." But Abrams disagreed with his own staff which argued that the communists were trying to conserve manpower in their present tactics. "Look at those figures," said Abrams. "I say that's a hell of a way to conserve manpower. I think we got into his machinery more than we ever did before. And we need a good understanding of this before we can really understand what his strategy was—whether it was to weaken American public opinion, to change the situation at the Paris talks, or to knock down this government."

The general said our program of bombing the north had the tendency of pulling all the people there together "because it gave them something real to fight against." He did not think that the complete bombing halt against the north had "adversely affected what we are doing here in South Vietnam."

I asked him about Cambodia. He said, "I can tell you that all the munitions used by them in the Third and Fourth Corps areas, all of the food they eat that is not in-country by origin, the medical supplies and their weapons—all of these come through Sihanoukville and Cambodia. It goes by ship from East Europe and China—mostly China—it is not trans-shipped via Hanoi." He also said that a substantial part of the munitions used in the Second Corps area came through Sihanoukville.

I had a feeling that the greatest U.S. strategic success in our Vietnam commitment had been saving Indonesia from Chinese communist control. He agreed and said: "That's the idea I came out here with." He thought the United States was now gaining time as a result of the continued war and the enemy was losing time; that, therefore, we were benefiting in a relative sense during the protracted peace talks. He especially thought that Thailand, South Korea, and the Philippines were benefiting from this gain in time. By sending troops here, those three countries were training their manpower in all the techniques of this kind of warfare and strengthening their defenses back home. He commented: "This is really buying something for the area as a whole. All of these countries are fighting for their national existence against one system combining political, military, and guerrilla action. All of our allies are gaining experience in the necessary techniques to counter this—police, intelligence, etc. That's what Vietnam is doing for them."

I observed that I felt the United States had not yet managed to learn how to fight and triumph over the strategy of revolutionary warfare, but that now in Vietnam we might have learned how to prevent revolutionary warfare by frustrating its efforts to get going. He added: "Hopefully, we have learned how to get at this kind of thing in its earliest stages. I am not thinking so much about the fighting itself but about the political aspect. You have to reform many things in this part of the world. We have had to see a revolution brought about in what was the South Vietnamese government and in the relationship that formerly existed between the people and the government. You cannot have extreme poverty in the masses and just a few very rich people. This government now realizes that and that is what keeps the communists back."

I asked if he didn't think we were building up in this country a South Vietnamese army so complicated, mechanized, and expensive that Saigon could not hope to man, equip, or support it after our withdrawal. He replied: "There is no question but that the force we are putting together is substantially more than they can maintain for any extended period. But they must peak it with our help in order to get on top. Then, as the whole infrastructure in the country strengthens itself, they can adjust this force downward. Eventually such an adjustment will have to be made."

I asked him if he thought there was any way in which a new sag in American public opinion could be prevented.

He said: "If we can realistically get the Vietnamese more in front, at least in some places, that would help. It would help if we could arrange on the basis of a sound program to reduce the number of U.S. troops in actual combat. But, of course, this is all fraught with the possibility of a boomerang. It's difficult for us to get the American people to sufficiently acknowledge some of the good performances of the Vietnamese forces. And then there's the risk that if you ballyhoo this too much, the enemy will set out a program to prove that you're wrong" (by concentrating attacks against the South Vietnamese).

I dropped in today to see Sam Berger in his office. Berger says this is the most effective Vietnamese government since independence. Starting in the autumn of 1968, Thieu accelerated the pacification program in the countryside.

The communists have now recognized that the U.S.A. is not going for an all-out military victory. The big change in the south has been Saigon's readiness for a negotiated settlement to end the war. Thieu's government has more confidence in the nation's ability to survive and the logical conclusion of this is a readiness to talk with both Hanoi and the FLN. As a matter of fact, there may be a negotiated settlement—even this year.

The communists are trying hard to make the Americans replace the French as a symbol of hatred and to a degree this has been succeeding. The apprehension that there might be a U.S. abandonment of South Vietnam helped, however, to counteract anti-American feeling. The communists never really had very much mass support—perhaps 20 percent of the population, and Thieu is confident that the 20 percent minority cannot take over from the majority.

Russia is trying to keep the communists here strong but also wants negotiations—from a position of strength. China is still supporting a hard line and opposes negotiations.

SAIGON, *March 27, 1969*

I was walking down one of the main streets when I heard a sound like small firecrackers. Suddenly I noticed several people lying flat on the ground and others cowering along walls. I watched a bunch of military policemen overhaul a young man on a bicycle and then another a few yards away. The cops were already around with rifles and slightly battered the second young man with the butts, before frisking them both. The crowd closed in to watch. What fascinated me was to see the mask drop from the faces of two elderly ladies as they regarded these proceedings. Their eyes mirrored nothing but sympathy for the two youngsters—whoever they were, VC suspects or draft dodgers, etc.

SAIGON, *March 30, 1969*

Especially interesting lunch with Wallace H. Terry, II, one of the *Time* correspondents here in Saigon, a bright young Negro. He is thirty, and graduated from Brown University. He is forthright, uninhibited, and in some cases justifiably bitter.

Vietnam presents an entirely new problem: how do you adjust black-white relationships here to the black-white relationships prevailing back home? Here the blacks and whites are brothers in the field—although off the battlefield there is residual discrimination on both sides.

How do the black and white soldiers here react to events back home? A white soldier will get a letter saying "Daddy was mugged by niggers" or a black will get a letter saying "You are fighting for racist pigs. Come home and fight for us." GIs in World War II never got such letters. At that time the black and white communities back home stayed away from each other. Negro leaders like Roy Wilkins and Walter White kept telling the black man they were fighting for the opportunity to serve their country on a basis of equality. But now there are black troops who wonder if they should fight for their country at all.

The military establishment is creating more potential black leadership than any other institution in the United States. Senator Ed Brooke, who was trained in Howard University, became a lawyer, was an officer in Italy during World War II. His war effort represented a responsibility to the whole fabric of U.S. society and now he is in the senate.

There are now three different kinds of black GIs: (1) the career soldier; (2) the draftee; (3) the reject from a society that has not encouraged his ambition. This last type came into the army as a draftee but stayed in its womb for protection. Group one is very small. Group two wants to rejoin the civilian world. Group three reenlists because of lack of encouragement to rejoin civilian life.

Two years ago none of the Negro soldiers in Vietnam identified with the real Negro militants back home such as the Black Panthers. Now there are some but only about one percent. There are some very violent characters in this small minority who go around saying things like "If I don't get what I want, I'll blow up the barracks." There are also sympathizers with the Negro extremist movement who are not actually extremists themselves. Many give the Black Panther clenched-fist salute when they pass each other in the streets.

Wally used to agree with Roy Wilkins that the civil rights movement should be kept separate from foreign policy. Wilkins felt that Martin Luther King had hurt the civil rights movement by involving it in attitudes on the Vietnam war.

Terry said the average black soldier sees no end to the Vietnam struggle and considers things like the election of Agnew as vice president an affront to the black community. Furthermore, he considers the present stress on law and order is really at the Negro's expense. He feels that in a sense he himself was murdered with King and Bobby Kennedy, the most popular white man in recent black history.

The army is faced with a bigger racial problem. Soldiers used to be only volunteers or career men, but now they are primarily draftees. As a result, discussion and argument are on the increase here in both the black and white communities. Greater forces are at work to trigger these arguments. The war for some blacks has become less of a crusade to defend democracy than a holding action "until we can get out."

We have had military successes and, strangely enough, these have allowed more blacks and whites to relax together. There is less foxhole activity and more sitting around. This makes for trouble. Blacks and whites are really brothers when they face death together, but they get into scraps on leave.

When a black boy comes half way around the world to Vietnam he thinks, "If I'm ever going to be free, I'll have to be free here." As a result, we have a more thinking black soldier now. He is not thinking about survival, but about why he is here and what he is going to do when he returns home.

The military is going to have to go through an experience similar to that of college campuses. There can't be black sit-ins in the army because that's mutiny, but the military must continue its forward thrust and stay ahead of American society as a whole. The military asks more of a man— his life, which is quite a freedom to give up. Therefore, the military should reprogram its training of officers and enlisted personnel and make a serious attack on civil rights problems. Especially it should consider why the blacks are participating in this war and where they are going when it ends. It cannot afford to have its black soldiers feel like mercenaries rather than full participants in the conflict.

The American heritage is not just white; it is also black. It must teach the whites as well as the blacks and cannot afford to have either feel that it is getting a worse deal than the other.

There must be a national program to integrate the returning black soldier into an equal society. Each local community must appreciate that here is a black soldier who went away and got shot at for his country.

How many towns in the U.S.A. have gone out to meet a train for a returning black GI? Has a city like Columbus, Ohio, told a returning Negro veteran, "We're happy to have you here and we'll do all we can to make you happy?"

White Americans should be aware that many a black man is now beginning to say "Why should I defend someone else's freedom if no one defends mine?"

SAIGON, *March 31, 1969*

Yesterday I flew up to see Dick Stilwell, now a lieutenant general in command of Twenty-fourth Corps at Phu Bai, the airport and military complex out of Hué. A lieutenant colonel was waiting for me in a jeep. A moment after my arrival Dick came in from a helicopter tour and we sat down and chatted for a long time in his frighteningly air-conditioned office. As we talked I heard outgoing artillery rounds. The VC rocketed the headquarters a few days ago blowing up his officers' bar.

Stilwell, who is fifty-two, comes from Buffalo and is a stocky man with thinning reddish hair. He is tough, bright, and thoughtful. During the war he served a bit with the OSS and he was also with the CIA a while.

He says it is quite possible to arm a country like South Vietnam sufficiently to care for itself and when the war is over, reduce the economic and military effort so it can sustain itself. Thus, South Korea (where Stilwell was [General James A.] Van Fleet's chief of staff) had twenty divisions in 1954, but this was brought down to ten in 1956. Reserve units with cadres were maintained for possible emergencies.

He made the point that no single South Vietnamese group had a national organization except for the communists. However, he thought that if you could promise the majority of the present extreme Left fair representation in a postwar government, a large proportion would accept.

I asked Dick if he could summarize the lessons learned here that might apply in other revolutionary wars. Here are his offhand answers:

(1) The first thing you must be sure of is that you can develop political viability in the government you intend to aid.

(2) There must be a consistent theme of U.S. policy.

(3) If "another Vietnam" were to break out elsewhere during the next couple of years, it would be hard to determine how Congress and U.S. public opinion might go. But in ten years, if the same imperatives existed as those which brought about our intervention here, we would do the same kind of thing because there are certain fundamental national interests.

Dick says that what we are fighting for principally here is time and that Indonesia has been our greatest strategic triumph. We have now reached the point where time is on our side and the longer Hanoi refuses to make peace the more we gain. The Saigon government is improving and the army is more and more capable each passing day.

We had a quick steak sandwich and raced off to his Huey helicopter. This was manned by a pilot and copilot and two gunners. Once strapped in, Stilwell handed me earphones and mouthpiece so that we could carry on our conversation despite the noise of the chopper.

We started along the coast, inspected one after another village, rode around Hué at low level, then took off for the mountains, the A Shau Valley and the Laotian border where fighting is going on. The mountains are beautiful, covered with thick forests of high trees. Stilwell has uncovered one after another secret trail, hidden under the trees, that the Vietcong had been using for fifteen years. He has seized enormous caches of rice, ammunition, and weapons.

Our chopper flew us over flat lands near the coast. One Catholic village had been heavily VC, but Dick surrounded its three land sides with troops, leaving the seaward side open. The VC all rushed into the water with underwater breathing tubes to hide when the village was about to be searched; at that moment Stilwell sent in helicopters and hovercraft and clobbered them.

In the fighting area, over which clouds and fog were lowering, time after time we had to get out of the way of gunships or Chinook helicopters hauling loads to isolated hilltop points of American or South Vietnamese forces. We put in at one fire base of a unit of the 101st Airborne Division where artillery trains in on the Laotian border area. A young major was briefing us when a Chinook came down with a load of ammunition and knocked down the briefing board as well as ourselves with its tremendous wind-blast.

The A Shau Valley is a key point for infiltration of material from Laos. Every now and then Dick pointed to slashes in the jungle where VC grow manioc in order to alleviate their food problem.

We landed at his headquarters so he could show me a VC hole he had had dug in the lawn right by the entrance and plugged by a regular plug taken from a real VC hole. Although everyone knew exactly where it was, it took two officers about four minutes to find the top, so skillfully was it camouflaged and set into the ground. When the plug was pulled up it disclosed an entrance into a cave about eight feet deep.

SAIGON, *April 1, 1969*

Most interesting evening yesterday, dining alone with Ted Shackley, local CIA boss. Shackley is an American Michael Caine: about my height, looks relatively slender, but when he sat down and his trouser leg crept up I could see he has very muscular calves. He is pale, thin featured, with blond hair, and wears glasses. He looks rather like a high school teacher.

He ran the immensely complicated CIA operation in Laos for two and a half years.

He picked me up in his air-conditioned, chauffeur-driven car. When we drove off I noticed that all windows were closed and there was a communications set-up (telephone and aerial protruding through the roof).

Ted carried a rectangular flat leather dispatch case with which he fumbled when we got held up in a dense, immobile traffic jam that seemed to make him fidgety. Later he told me that the favorite assassination method is for the VC to get someone tied up in an artificial traffic jam. Because of closed windows, they couldn't do their usual of chucking a grenade into the car and shooting was too chancy. Their method against his type of set-up was to toss a plastic under the car. If anyone hurled a package under the car the only thing to do was immediately open the door and dive out as the blast came right up from the bottom.

I found that his dispatch case contained a beeper (an instrument that made a small noise if his office urgently needed him) and spare batteries for it, as well as a .38 revolver and extra ammunition. We were followed by a security car containing armed guards. Ted kept the dispatch case beside him in his house as we talked and even took it in to the dining room when we ate. He is a weapons expert, he told me, and keeps a Swedish automatic machine pistol in his bedroom. A radio played very softly to drown out our words and there were guards in the back yard of his walled-in, wire-fringed house.

He said the objective of the present communist offensive seems to be to test Nixon, to make him act, to end his honeymoon with Congress. The idea is quite simply to reopen old wounds in the U.S.A. and to get word across to Washington: "You won't have an indefinite amount of time to make up your minds." The idea is to persuade American opinion and also to convince the South Vietnamese public that their government and army are weak. The enemy has not chosen to move against the much more vulnerable pacification effort because this would offend the population.

General Ed Black, deputy commander of the 25th Division, lunched with me today. Ed's division is stationed northwest of Saigon and covers that approach to the capital as well as the provincial capital and Cao Dai seat of Tay Ninh, just off the Cambodian border. He says the Vietcong is under orders (COSVN Order No. 8 and an order by General Giap, both orders taken off dead VC bodies) to keep pushing with the ultimate goal of slamming Saigon. This is going to be a long offensive and we know that communist replacements for June are already on the march down the Ho Chi Minh trail in Laos. Hanoi has promised the troops that there will be an all-out strike in June, aimed at a big effect on the Paris peace talks, and that this will be heavily supported by Soviet materiel.

HONG KONG, *April 4, 1969*

On our last night in Saigon, our son David gave us a farewell dinner party at which I had an excellent talk with Colonel Montague, now in charge of the pacification program. The Chieu Hoi program, which attracts defectors over to our side has produced a surprisingly large number of volunteers for South Vietnam's provincial and regional forces (PF and RF). They have proved to be tough and dedicated soldiers and their kill-rate is the highest of any units on the allied side.

Incidentally, David made a very good point: this is the first war in history where an army's supply lines are ahead of the troops, not behind them. He was referring to the prepositioning of community ordnance and food stocks in hidden caches which become available to the troops as they move forward.

HONG KONG, *April 10, 1969*

Lunched with Bert Levin, Number Two in the "China-watching" section of the consulate general. He is persuaded that relations between the U.S.A. and communist China will surely improve, but it may still take some time. Both Mao and his ideology might make a sudden shift and reconcile themselves to a new look at the U.S.A. After all, we can't forget such things as the Hitler-Stalin pact which swept away ideological prejudices.

America is the *known* enemy for China, whereas Russia is the unknown enemy. Over the years, Peking has come to realize that we are not as aggressive or as determined to destroy communist China as it has feared. In 1965, we made it very plain through the Warsaw talks that we had no intention of invading China from Vietnam. We responded calmly when the Chinese sent labor troops into North Vietnam. The Chinese have gotten used to the idea that we are not going to blow them up and we are getting used to the idea that they are less aggressive than they seem. But this is not the case between China and Russia. They don't have a long tradition of shared mutual hostility—at least under communist rule, and they don't know how far one or the other will go. China has not officially made any claim to Soviet territory except for islands on the Chinese side of the Ussuri River's main channel. All the other "claims" to Siberia are inferential. The Chinese merely imply that if Russia does not behave, they will denounce the nineteenth-century treaties awarding great chunks of east Asia to Russia. In fact, all those regions were taken by both Russian and Chinese imperialism and originally belonged to differing nomadic tribes.

Another fascinating development is the new flirtation between Chiang Kai-shek and the Kremlin. Since 1927, when Chiang turned against the communists and his own Soviet advisers, he has been violently anti-Soviet. But, now that he is an octogenarian, he says that he is willing either to forget ideology or to revert to the ideology of his youth. Taiwan has begun to acknowledge for the first time that there are different types of communism and that it is not all the same hateful disease. When Victor Louis, a Soviet literary agent, journalist, and undoubtedly a representative of the intelligence apparatus, was in Tokyo earlier this year, he applied for admission to Taiwan. Unquestionably the desire was referred up to Chiang Kai-shek and the visa was granted. Louis saw General Chiang Ching-kuo, son of the generalissimo and his heir apparent. The flirtation has proceeded since then. Anti-Soviet propaganda has almost ceased in the efficiently controlled Taiwan propaganda apparatus.

Tokyo, *April 15, 1969*

The Japanese point out that they have never been attacked by China; they always did the attacking. The Chinese can't even take Quemoy and Matsu so it is absurd to think of them as a threat to Japan. And China can only encourage a guerrilla-type movement in a rotten society like Burma or the Philippines, not in blooming Japan.

Nor, despite China's nuclear arsenal, would it ever atomize Japan. Japan is more valuable to China as it is and anyway it is ready to give China anything it wants. Finally, Japan is protected against China by the U.S. defense umbrella. Japan is therefore not worried about China in its direct relations, but only in third countries where it has interests—like Burma, Thailand, and the Philippines.

The number one policy of Japan is good relations with the U.S.A., which is its principal trading partner and nuclear protector. In the Liberal Democratic party platform there is talk about amending the constitution in order to permit a proper military establishment, but there is really no substantial desire for such a change. Nor is there any wish here to take on a role in an Asian alliance or to expand national military forces.

The Japanese are not particularly perturbed by the Sino-Soviet dispute. They have an old proverb—"To look at a fire from the other side of the river." This means they can watch without being affected by the argument. And Russia remains *the* unpopular country for Japan.

Tokyo, *April 17, 1969*

Saw Prime Minister Eisaku Sato at his official residence, a singularly hideous building.

The prime minister is a friendly, dark-complected man with hoarse voice, large ears, and somber expression. Sato started off by saying how pleased he was to be reassured that the U.S.A. is exercising great caution and restraint in the present crisis brought about by the shooting down (two days ago) of a U.S. reconnaissance plane, far out at sea, by the

North Koreans. It was easy to understand U.S. anger, but he counted on the wisdom of our leadership to restrain it.

I observed that Japan still had no proper military force and asked whether Sato favored eventual constitutional amendment to allow this. Sato said he thought it was a tribute to the "extreme wisdom of the Japanese people" that the present constitution had been established. As far as war was concerned, three wars had already occurred during his childhood—with China, Russia and War I—long before World War II. "The truth is we are tired of war."

The possibility of localized wars continued and this required a limited armament such as Japan's. There was criticism of Japan for the smallness of its effort but "we are not selfish."

I asked if he believed Herman Kahn's prediction that by 2000 Japan would be ahead of all European and Asian states. He said he used Kahn's analysis in the election campaign and it helped him win, but one shouldn't exaggerate. If Japan was now number two industrial power in the free world, there was a huge gap between number one and number two, and as Japan advanced, so did the U.S.A.

I inquired about the status of a peace treaty with Moscow, ending the last vestiges of World War II. All that exists is a 1956 declaration stating the war was over and opening diplomatic relations. Sato said there could be no peace treaty while Moscow controls the northern territories. Japan is not prepared to accept the return by Russia of only the two islands of Habomai and Shikotan, which Tokyo simply considers part of the home island of Hokkaido. It also wants Etorofu and Kunashiri, which are much larger and which were never occupied by Russia before.

Sato then remarked: "I am glad that you are interested in this question of our northern territories. You are the first visitor I have had who has raised this matter."

SEOUL, *April 19, 1969*

Flew in yesterday amid a crisis. The North Koreans shot down an unarmed U.S. snoop plane miles outside territorial limits and everyone is waiting to see what Nixon will do. Early this morning (local time) he decided—nothing. Makes him look a bit foolish after his campaign boasts that he wouldn't let a "fourth-rate power" push us around, as on the *Pueblo* case.

Staying with Ambassador Bill Porter. Porter says the U.S. was correct to restrain the South Koreans from warlike reactions to the Blue House raid of January 21, 1968, when thirty-one infiltrators came across the line and tried to assassinate President [Chung Hee] Park. (The alternate target was Porter.) Two days later the *Pueblo* incident came. There was a borderline question there as to whether it was in international waters or not, although now it seems certain it was. But this plane incident is different. There was no violation of North Korean territory.

Bill, who was previously deputy ambassador in Saigon, admits he was a real hawk there. He is convinced the U.S.A. could have moved fast to end the war by extensive bombing of the north (including the dikes) and mines, a naval blockade, and amphibious invasions far enough to the south so that China would not have been frightened.

SEOUL, *April 20, 1969*

Last night the Porters had two Korean couples for dinner. One man, a large gentleman named Lee Bum Suk is foreign ministry chief of protocol. His wife comes from a very distinguished North Korean family. He, too, is from the north—Pyongyang—and claims that northerners are much tougher as well as larger than southerners.

Lee said he had met Kim Il Sung, the dictator of the north, when the latter arrived in August 1945 as a major in the Soviet army. He had a different name: Kim Il Sung was a real historic figure, about a generation older, who had been a Korean guerrilla leader against the Japs in Manchuria. The new Kim went to Russia, adopted his new name (plus the pretense that he was actually the famous guerrilla leader himself) and came back as Stalin's satrap. When Lee first knew Kim, he was quite jovial, easy-going, and pretended to be a genuine democrat, not a communist. The Russian commander allowed a democratic government to be formed (in order to find out who the anti-Russian leaders were) and then arrested them all the next day. Most were murdered; some were imprisoned. Lee's father-in-law, a vice president, got away.

SEOUL, *April 21, 1969*

Talked for over an hour with General Charles H. Bonesteel III: commander of UN, U.S., and ROK forces here. Bonesteel is a tall, blond, lanky, intellectual-looking man with glasses and one blind eye (over which he wears a black lens).

He said North Korea is in a strong position. It has almost twice as many jets as South Korea-plus-the-U.S.A. The army is smaller but has a higher proportion of combat troops. Kim is a dedicated zealot who tried one war here already and is now determined to check southern economic progress.

Since 1967 Kim has been sending fast boats to deliver agents off the South Korean coast. These are PT boats disguised topside as fishing vessels. Hundreds of seven-or-eight-man teams have been dispatched from the coast into the mountainous hinterland, but almost all of them have been spotted, starved, and turned in by the South Koreans, who have a real hatred for communism as a result of their war.

Bonesteel guesses that the Russians are probably trying to ration North Korea's ammunition and restrain Kim; but we can't know. Kim is hard to restrain.

SEOUL, *April 23, 1969*

Last night Prime Minister Chung Il Kwon invited us to a *Kaesang* party ("us" being only the males, including my son David). Bill Porter brought us and there we met George Ball, former U.S. undersecretary of state, who had just come in on a mission for his banking firm. Present, in addition to our host, were about ten of South Korea's big shots, including the wealthiest man, several cabinet ministers, and the ambassador to Washington, who is home to report. Each of us was furnished with his private *Kaesang* girl, the Korean equivalent of Japanese geishas, dressed in the flowing, high-waisted silk dresses of the country. Mine was a lovely little dish named Hopeful Angel, who sang beautifully, danced very well, and spoke a little English.

Chung is a rotund man with glasses, a forty-nine-year-old ex-general, who adores leading orchestras. He firmly gripped a wooden chopstick and stood up before our little jazz combo, leading it like some fervent Asian Toscanini. When Chung tired of orchestral antics, he danced a mean tango. Everyone was in stockinged feet and the floor was slippery.

We ate innumerable courses which Hopeful Angel delicately chopsticked to me, every now and then sharing my drink. Her only deficiency was that she stank so heavily of garlic that every time she returned my drink (and I had to sip before and after her, as dictated by custom) it smelled pretty awful.

Porter pleased and astonished me when the party got going, by letting himself be persuaded to get up and join the combo, singing some Korean folk songs—and very well, with much aplomb. He takes Korean lessons every day.

SEOUL, *April 24, 1969*

Long talk with Prime Minister Chung Il Kwon; he made a far more sedate impression than at the party. In his office, I was much taken by an old-fashioned telephone in three colors—ivory, gold, and ebony.

He started off by asking, anent the crisis: "Why should we be patient? How should the U.S.A. and Korea prevent a major war here? If war does start, we will have to sacrifice many lives and much prosperity and the world will be miserable. Nevertheless, Kim Il Sung should not be allowed to miscalculate the strength and intentions of the U.S.A. and the Republic of Korea.

"We want no repetition of the situation caused when your secretary of state Acheson excluded Korea from the American defense perimeter in

Asia and a few months later North Korea attacked us. Kim is getting over-confident again.

"He thinks you are just fooling. Your naval and air forces in this area were increased after the *Pueblo* incident, but this was nothing but a demonstration. He reckons that nothing will happen this time either and that eventually you will again withdraw the new forces."

Chung had been commander-in-chief of the South Korean forces under MacArthur when he was only thirty-two. He comes from North Korea himself. He insisted: "Kim will get stronger if we show any signs of weakness. Kim is fifty-eight years old now and in Korea we have a tradition that whatever a man accomplished must be done before he is sixty-one; that leaves him three more years.

"I think you must be stern with him. You should insist that Kim apologizes for the EC 121 incident and pays damages. You should not be too patient. You should give the north a date by which they must apologize—and then retaliate if they don't."

HONOLULU, *May 3, 1969*

This island is not the interracial paradise depicted, but is carefully split up into racial minorities of which the whites are a relatively small one, the Japanese political top-men, the Chinese big in banking and business. There is much race snobbery. The two snootiest clubs still don't admit Asians to the dining room. Negroes are few because the Asians are more prejudiced even than the whites.

NEW YORK, *May 7, 1969*

Talked to Max Frankel, [*New York Times*] Washington bureau chief and he told me that nobody from the *Times*, including the publisher, has seen Nixon since he was inaugurated—and they have all been trying. This is quite a change from the Johnson days.

NEW YORK, *May 14, 1969*

Dined last night at Marcia Davenport's. She is a charming author, a daughter of the famous singer Alma Gluck, a great friend of Toscanini, and the romantic adoration of Jan Masaryk for years.

The Norstads and the Yosts were there. Charlie Yost is ambassador to the UN. He is very pessimistic about the Middle East situation and fears another outbreak of the Arab-Israeli war.

Norstad, now heading Owens-Corning Fiberglas after years in uniform, said with touching patriotic pride: "You know, I have already paid back to the government in taxes more money than it paid me throughout my entire career."

WASHINGTON, *May 15, 1969*

This morning Chip Bohlen said that recently when Acheson met Nixon and Nixon said they hadn't always agreed with each other but, he said, he greatly respected A., Dean replied: "Dr. Johnson, when addressing George II, said: 'I never bandy words with my sovereign.'"

Chip has been going through his old papers and found the account of Pierre Salinger's talk with Khrushchev (on behalf of Kennedy). Khrushchev didn't like Nixon and said he reminded him of the kind of grocer who puts sand in the sugar.

WASHINGTON, *May 16, 1969*

Have been here a couple of days now, staying with the Bohlens. Chip is now retired, writing a book of memoirs.

Yesterday I had successive talks with two cabinet members whom I had never met, Melvin Laird, secretary of defense, and David Kennedy, secretary of the treasury.

Laird is a bald, fairly heavy-set man with pale face, strong jaw, and a hint of sneakiness in his eyes. We started off, sitting in a corner of his huge Pentagon office, discussing the problem of rebuilding public trust in the judgment and intentions of the military establishment. He said the credibility of the Pentagon had been open to serious questioning and there had been a sharp downward trend ever since it was "decided that this department had the right to lie."

Regrettably, said Laird, "the impression has been given that the military is running wild and controlling the civilian authorities. I know better. For example, I know that McNamara was a strong civilian secretary of defense. But the impression had gained credence that the military was running over him."

At present we were spending on defense at the rate of 9.7 percent of the GNP per annum. This was less than the 1960–64 period although we were not then at war. But defense effort should not be fixed by the budget. The necessity was to revise some of our commitments. Laird contended that (in terms of dollars—not rubles) the Russians were now out-spending us three to two in strategic offensive weapons and two to one in strategic defensive weapons. "The Russian effort is much greater than ours."

I then rushed over to the treasury and Kennedy, a short, chunky, white-haired man with the quick smile of a leprechaun. I asked if Kennedy thought it possible to carry out a successful fight against inflation without endangering our defense or foreign policy positions.

He said: "There is a lot of leeway there. The budgeting end is so large that there is ample room to maneuver. Costs are escalating on defense also because of inflation. The same thing is true with respect to our foreign policy commitments. Some change would certainly be all to the good."

Kennedy said we were now spending $30 billion a year on the Vietnam war and ultimately fifty percent of this could be saved. However, during the first fiscal year after peace is restored the cut will be only $1 to $2 billion. There are huge costs of transportation for returning soldiers.

I inquired what was the basic requirement to restore a U.S. trade surplus. He said: "If we can get price escalations stopped and slow down the economy so as to reduce imports, we could get back to a $1 to $3 billion annual trade surplus within one to three years.

Pleasant lunch with Dick Helms, head of the CIA, an intelligent, civilized man.

I thought the two most important things in Nixon's speech the evening before last were: (1) his insistence that Hanoi's troops evacuate not only South Vietnam but also Cambodia and Laos; (2) his warning that if Hanoi lunched a new offensive, as expected, we would reply by hitting back. Helms agreed and said he was puzzled that no paper or commentator had seen this.

Dick says the Russians have now doubled their troop strength on the Chinese border. They are scared of the Chinese starting something simply because they regard them as crazy. The island (Damyansky) in the Ussuri over which they squabble is a worthless mud flat. Furthermore, the Chinese have a legal right to it because it's on their side of the river channel.

For the Middle East he is very gloomy. He foresees a fourth round of war unless there is first an arms freeze and an imposed settlement, and there is scant hope of that.

2 2

NIXON:

"A GREAT NATION

SOMETIMES HAS TO ACT

IN A GREAT WAY"

I HAD NEVER BEFORE MET SENATOR EUGENE McCARTHY (DEM., Minn.) so this afternoon I went up to the senate office building for a chat and enjoyed myself considerably. He is a tall, well-built man with grey hair, pale face, rather nice-looking, a somewhat tired expression, agreeable voice. He is thoughtful, earnest (and I am told very religious —Roman Catholic).

He feels that many of the processes of our society are in need of change. For example, the political process. There has to be a change in this, opening it up more freely to individual participation. Labor unions used to be willing to be represented politically by a boss. Now not even the Negroes are content to be represented by a spokesman. Caucuses and conventions are still run by old-fashioned guidelines. Stockholders in corporations feel they have no adequate way in which to exert influence on decisions. "Even in the Catholic church you see this," he added as an afterthought.

We discussed the background of secretaries of state. The last three before Rogers (excluding Herter), said McCarthy, were sons of ministers, Rusk and Dulles of Presbyterians. "The state department is the last established church in the western world. Calvinism runs strong in it. It is the one department where that tradition lives on. And there is a Cromwellian approach in the effort to force it on the rest of the world."

WASHINGTON, *May 18, 1969*

Lunched with Bill Leonhart who is going in June as our next ambassador to Jugoslavia. Bill said one of the reasons for delay in filling many important ambassadorial posts was the reluctance of distinguished Republicans to accept such assignments. Among these who had turned down posts were: for Bonn—Governor Scranton, General Norstad, Neal McElroy, George Champion, Tom Gates; for Tokyo—John D. Rockefeller, Scranton, Bill Burden, Rudy Peterson (Bank of America).

Early in the Nixon administration word was passed around that no career men would be sent to Western European posts, generally considered the most agreeable. Since then one of these has been filled by a career man—Lisbon—where Ridgway Knight is going largely because John Eisenhower felt embarrassed at dislodging him from Brussels and felt Knight should be given the equivalent.

WASHINGTON, *May 19, 1969*

Good talk with President Nixon (the first as president) and then lunch (in latter's office) with Henry Kissinger, Nixon's special assistant for national security and foreign policy matters.

I was taken to wait for my appointment in the room opposite the presidential office, which was called the fish room in Franklin Roosevelt days (the president kept some angling trophies there including a large blue marlin) and is now known as the Roosevelt room, featuring bronze plaques with profiles of Theodore and Franklin Roosevelt on walls facing each other and including, among other decorations, a Remington painting of the charge of Teddy Roosevelt's Rough Riders in the battle of San Juan Hill. T.R.'s plaque bore this inscription: "Aggressive fighting for the right is the noblest sport the world affords." F.D.R.'s plaque bore Seneca's words: "I shall hold my rudder true."

While I was musing, Kissinger suddenly came out, shook hands and shoved me in ahead of him to the president's office. Nixon was sitting at his massive desk. Behind was a table stacked with folders of classified documents. There was scarcely anything on the desk save a copy of my latest book, *A Long Row of Candles.*

The president looked well: lean, sun-tanned, no grey in his hair, no bulge in his jaw. He seemed relaxed and at ease. He asked me how my golf was—I said miserable and virtually nonexistent—and he told me he has given up the game altogether.

Kissinger sat in a chair opposite the president and I took one by his desk. We had a long, rambling conversation.

I felt Nixon was a much-changed, much-improved man since his vice-presidential days. He looked me straight in the eye. His eyes are very black and penetrating. He expressed himself well and without hesitation, never fumbling for a word. Kissinger told me later that he writes far more of his own speeches than any other political figure Kissinger has known; for example, he wrote the entire last part of his speech on Vietnam five days ago; there was no first draft by a White House ghost. Nixon has slightly odd gestures with his hands as he talks, seeming to shape ideas or to embrace them with both rather small, unimpressive hands, in a slightly feminine gesture. But he exudes strength and self-confidence.

He complimented me on my columns and said he thought my analysis of the Vietnam problem was accurate and profound, even if it disagreed with that of my newspaper. He spoke briefly but with keen disappointment of *New York Times* editorial policy and said it gave considerable comfort to Hanoi.

He recalled his visit to Paris last February and his talks with de Gaulle. He thought de Gaulle very wise to choose to fall on a referendum that didn't openly pose the issue of himself. Thus, he would assume a better place in history than otherwise.

De Gaulle had told him it was easier for the United States to leave Vietnam than it had been for France to leave Algeria. After all, there had been "two million Frenchmen" (the real figure is one million) in Algeria when the decision was taken. Had Nixon been in his place, "I would probably have done the same thing. He saw the way history was going and knew withdrawal was inevitable. He carried it out with vision and courage."

De Gaulle had been wise in his African policy and the fact that France now had good relations with all its former west African possessions was part of the heritage he had left behind. He thought de Gaulle a great man who had achieved an eminence far beyond France's real capacity, thanks to his will power and personality. But that was over now. He didn't know who would succeed—and he asked: "Henry, what do you think?" Kissinger said he thought the odds were definitely in favor of [Alain] Poher. (Pompidou won . . . later note!)

Nixon said de Gaulle had known all along he couldn't achieve certain things such as the unification of Europe. The time for that had gone. There wasn't any chance of unifying Europe today "and we all know that. Of course, I'll go on making the proper noises—but it isn't going to happen. Things are moving in another direction. Just as with NATO. It isn't possible any more to return to the military emphasis on NATO. The Left would simply object too much."

The present trend was one of disintegration rather than unity, and this was true all over the world, in Europe, in Asia, in the free world and in the communist world. The stress was now on national states and national policies working for national interests. We had to look at reality and base our policy on it, not on inherited dreams. France was more nationalistic and so was West Germany. And inside each country there was less unity, more fragmentation.

This, he said, was the particular problem of the United States. He agreed with what I had written of the need for unity here if we are to persist in Vietnam. And he meant everything he had said in his television speech Wednesday about our determination "not to fold" and to adhere resolutely to "our very modest objectives." This was not simply a case of "prestige," he added.

"We can't fold. A great nation sometimes has to act in a great way. Otherwise it destroys its own moral fiber. The British knew that. There is more to this war than just prestige and I am not speaking only of the thousands of people who would be slaughtered if we just pulled out. I don't know what you think of the dominoes theory, but it is obvious that if we pulled out other countries would crumble. Thailand would come first. Malaysia is already in the throes of new troubles. And Lee Kwan Yew [prime minister of Singapore] was here recently and told me the effects, in such a case, would inevitably reach down to him. And south of there, Indonesia is a very weak reed although we are now trying to help them get stronger.

"And think of Europe. No matter what some of the politicians say about hoping the 'dirty war' will end and that then America can pay more attention to Europe, they really know this wouldn't happen. They fear this would be the start of isolationism and a weakening, not a strengthening, of the American position there. We would be forced by isolationism to go home from there too.

"A great power like ours sometimes has to meet challenges elsewhere in the world. The British knew that and there was something valid in the *Pax Brittanica*. It worked. Well, some people talk of a *Pax Americana*. But we have to stay with it.

"And we would destroy ourselves if we pulled out in a way that really wasn't honorable. It might take our people a year or two to realize what had happened but they would know in the end. And the reaction would be terrible. I hate to think of it. It would be destructive to our own morale.

"You know our objectives in this war are very limited. We only want to establish a real peace. The true objective of this war is peace. It is a war for peace."

I told Nixon I thought his primordial problem was to organize enough public support in time to carry out his objectives; but I wondered if he had the time.

I had been struck by his insistence that Cambodia and Laos, as well as South Vietnam, must be evacuated by Hanoi's troops. Also by his warning of retribution if Hanoi launched new attacks. He nodded but said the response to his speech had been encouraging.

He said the real moral crisis in this country was a "leadership crisis." He continued: "The trouble is that the leaders, not the country as a whole, are weak and divided. By the leaders I mean the leaders of industry, the bankers, the newspapers. They are irresolute and lack understanding. The people as a whole can be led back to some kind of consensus if only the leaders can take hold of themselves."

Briefly, he touched on China and Russia. He said China clearly had no intention of leaving Russia alone. At this point Kissinger looked at me and I realized from the clock on the wall that it was almost twenty minutes of two and well past presidential lunch hours (he usually eats with his family). So I made as if to rise and he did likewise. There was a bit more badinage about golf and about how he liked my column and would read my book, then we shook hands—he has a firm grip and dry palms—and off I went with Kissinger.

Kissinger, who is forty-six and looks younger, is a stocky, brisk man with spectacles and a shock of brown hair. As we walked downstairs to his office (the same one Mac Bundy and Walt Rostow used to occupy) he told me he had never been a Nixon man but had been for [Nelson] Rockefeller. Yet he admired Nixon greatly and was impressed by the cool, relaxed way he approached problems.

He said Vietnam was politically tricky. For example, when Senator Jacob Javits got wind of the fact that the administration had certain plans to get the question off dead center in May and June, he immediately made a speech urging this—so he could claim later on that the president had acted in response to his (Javits's) prompting.

When we got downstairs I sat in an armchair while Kissinger glanced at some papers and told his secretary: "See if someone can bring us some lunch." I noticed that the bank of television sets Walt Rostow used to have to the right of the door was gone. The plain wall was hung with the framed certificate, signed by Nixon, in which he designated Kissinger an assistant.

After he had finished with his papers Kissinger plunked himself in a chair across from me, and started talking about the *Times* again. I am certainly getting used to having presidents and their aides beef about the paper to me. Once again I heard the old story that my columns are the "only sane spot" on the editorial page. But Kissinger went further. He insisted the news is played to suit policy and that criticisms of our Vietnam attitudes are played on the front page but that when, for example, the AFL-CIO backs the administration, this is buried way inside.

He claimed the editorials twist facts and state demonstrable untruths. When the president made his speech, which brought support from all quarters of the nation, the *Times* only complained that he hadn't ordered immediate withdrawal of 50,000 troops. How could the *Times* prove that Hanoi would be made more malleable by this? It is almost certain the opposite would be true. The *Times* seemed deliberately to go out of its way to help the nation's adversaries.

I remarked that it did not behove me to comment. Kissinger then went on to Nixon's speech. Just as he began, two waiters came in with trays so he waved me over to a small, low table and we continued.

We munched, he talked, I scribbled notes. He said: "This president always promises a little less than he can actually deliver. He wants to know what all the possibilities are before he moves. And this was the basis for his Wednesday speech. I can't tell you what we might feel necessary to do if Hanoi pushes its offensive."

He went on to say Johnson had been a patriotic man but he had simply not applied policy well in Vietnam. He had not told the people straight out what our aims were and he had always increased the degree of our intervention too slowly and too late; this vitiated its effect.

At this point I observed that in Vietnam I felt the basic problem was to relate internal and external U.S. capabilities and policies more tidily. "Precisely," said Kissinger. He went on: "We've run out of the policy concepts of the thirties, the liberal theories that we had no inherent conflict with any people, that economic action can solve political problems. In this respect Kennedy wasn't the great innovator; he was the sunset on an era."

Kissinger then went on rather grimly, after stating the urgent need to reexamine the world and our role in it, saying: "I've often said, when I present our choices on any particular issue to the president, that if we have a failure in carrying out our policy because we didn't weigh all the considerations well, it would be unforgivable. He feels very strongly that he must avoid being surprised by something he could have foreseen. All the possible results of any given line must be examined.

"We must decide where the world is going and how we can develop our own interests in this atmosphere. Then we must seek to get a national consensus on such an approach. In former days there were certain ideas that received automatic support. For a time any kind of intervention anywhere was automatically endorsed because it was believed good. Now the exact opposite is true."

I asked Kissinger how long it would take to complete a reexamination of world realities and policy goals and to obtain sufficient public support to set out on a coherent new policy. He thought it could be done in eighteen months; but everything depended on Vietnam. If we were to pull out from there pell-mell, no matter how this was disguised, no one would believe us in any other policy commitments.

Nixon was being very courageous about this, he added. "He could have said in his speech on Wednesday that Johnson had screwed up the war and therefore we now had to get out, that the Democrats were the party of war but the Republicans brought peace. This would have been the cheap and easy thing to do. But he is going to travel a lonely course instead."

I said I thought the most disturbing thing that had struck me on returning was the moral decline of the United States; even distinguished Americans were declining official jobs offered to them by the president; the old idea of serving the nation was dead. Kissinger said: "This is our biggest challenge, the loss of moral fiber. This is why Nixon worries so much about what he calls the leadership problem. There is a real crisis of authority. The leadership class has lost its will. To restore it we need some sort of success—preferably on something they disagree with. I don't mean that we should look for an artificial field in which to achieve this.

"I have been struck by the Harvard riots. You heard about the students who rifled university files and found a telegram from Harriman praising me for my peace efforts a few years ago. They stole this and published it without comment. But the mere fact that I had done something for my government was considered damning."

I asked if he'd mind roving about the map a bit since my time was drawing to a close. He thought it was silly to talk of making India into an anti-Chinese bastion of democracy in Asia. All this talk had done was to incite China to "clobber the Indians."

He spoke admiringly of de Gaulle and said he had been present during Nixon's private conversations with him. He described the General as "a great man with a conception of history." He said de Gaulle had spoken nonstop for an hour and a half on all the countries of Europe and concluded: "Every European country lost the war—and two were defeated."

When German chancellor Kiesinger visited Washington he said de Gaulle had told him: "You and we have gone through much together. We have gone through jungles swarming with wild beasts and through heavy storms, looking for hidden treasure. Now we realize that there is no treasure—and all that remains is friendship."

I asked if, as a result of our global policy review, he thought it would be possible to inter unsuccessful alliance commitments such as SEATO and CENTO. He said: "First we must know what we are really committed to. After all, nations are not defended primarily by formal obligations. We must find out where our national interests lie. Then you don't have to formally bury any pacts. You simply tone down the rhetoric. The first thing is that we must know what we are able to do and then what should be done. If it were not for Vietnam we could bring about a conceptual revolution in foreign policy."

Kissinger said one significant thing. While we are on record as demanding that Hanoi evacuate its troops from both Cambodia and Laos, in fact we are ready to agree that they remain in the two northeastern provinces of Laos: "We could live with that."

WASHINGTON, *May 20, 1969*

Long talk in his office with General Earle G. ("Bus") Wheeler, chairman of the joint chiefs of staff. Wheeler is tall, well above six feet, with a scholarly appearance.

I asked if he thought it technically possible for the United States to meet its foreign obligations—even if they were reduced to a minimum, and defend itself without some form of draft. Wheeler replied:

"No. It would be impossible. We made some examination of this, but the soft area is how many people enlist in the navy, air force, and marines because the draft is breathing down their necks. Some people estimate this amount to be 50 percent of all volunteers although I don't think so."

Was it technically possible to have a professional military service? He said: "It is technically possible if you are talking about creating a long-term, truly professional force. Except for the officer corps you would depend on long service men. But you would have to accept undesirable short-falls in skills and intelligence.

"The draft gives a cross section of young American society. You would lose this with a professional army. And also there is not the slightest doubt that this would present the theoretical danger someday of a praetorian guard. One of the great virtues of our armed forces has been that they really are representative of American society.

"It is my feeling that over a period of years you could get a dangerously detached military force—that is to say, detached from normal American society. One of the strongest bulwarks of the republic is that the armed forces are largely drawn from the civilian side."

Wheeler said: "The professional army would cost more. Of course, there would be some offsets. You wouldn't have to have the same training load. We lose 25 percent of our military population each year and it costs a great deal to train their replacements. But if you 'hired' an army there would be a large increase in pay and fringe benefits that would more than offset any savings on training. But money is not the final determinant on this. Right now there is a great desire among many young men to serve and they are attracted by various things such as quarters, food, opportunities to learn a trade."

Inflation was a tremendous problem. General [John P.] McConnell, chief of staff of the air force, pointed out to him a few days ago that the air force budget for 1964 was $19 billion. Today it is $26 billion. But this does not buy any greater air strength and amounts to exactly the same kind of air force without even allowing for the expense of the Vietnam war. Our growing military budgets are not buying any more defense.

Wheeler said the Soviets did not have a substantial force in the Far East prior to this year's confrontation with China on the Ussuri River, but now it was substantial. Russia had expanded its ground and air strength and had built a great many more airfields but the concentration opposite China was nowhere near so strong as that in Eastern Europe. The Chinese forces facing them were not as large as the Soviet forces, and China hadn't moved as many troops to the border.

Incidentally, Wheeler said that China today wasn't a military danger to either Russia or America, but that the Russians have a phobia on the Chinese and something in their nature doesn't permit them to forget the old Mongolian hordes.

Wheeler was reasonably sure that the departure of de Gaulle would make it possible to establish a modus operandi between France and the other NATO forces.

NEW YORK, *May 23, 1969*

Last night Julian Bach gave us a dinner party. After dinner Commander Lloyd Bucher, skipper of the ill-fated spy ship *Pueblo*, came in and we sat up very late talking.

Bucher intends to stay in the navy although he knows his career there is finished.

The tale he told was substantially as follows: A decision was taken at the highest governmental levels to go into the surface ship electronic espionage business in order to catch up with the Russians' electronically equipped trawlers. The program was begun in 1966. It would have been sensible to have used trawlers also. But probably because of the objection of the very few American trawlers working for private enterprise in the fishing industry, this was not done. Instead very unseaworthy, lumbering army coastal vessels were assigned to the task. They were particularly unseaworthy, Bucher said, "because the army had designed them."

The great value of the trawler is that it can sit off a shoreline or a group of ships and just wait and maybe during two or three seconds over a period of a month someone may get careless, there will be a lapse in security, and invaluable information can be picked up. Aerial espionage moves too fast and cannot handle this kind of job.

Originally it was decided to send these ships out unarmed. Then some brass hat with no seagoing experience suggested they should have three-inch guns but, as Bucher said, these would have sunk the ship right away as soon as they used them. Ultimately the lunatic decision was taken to put a couple of machine guns on board but keep them under canvas.

Contrary to all naval tradition, he was not fully in command of his ship. Various spooks of the national security agency were cleared for subjects of such enormously high classification that they were not allowed to mention anything to him. Thus part of his personnel was automatically shut off from the rest of his personnel.

They had been specifically promised immediate "deterrence" in case of necessity. When they were overhauled by the North Koreans they expected American aircraft to show up. It took a long time before these hopes subsided.

Some problems posed are quite insoluble. For example, is the commanding officer in such a situation morally obligated to protect his crew against torture and death, or to protect the papers and equipment he is unable to keep from an enemy's hands?

PARIS, *June 30, 1969*

Lunched with Jean-Marie Soutou, as always, intelligent and provocative. He remains inspector-general of the French diplomatic corps. He says the basic shift in French foreign policy antedated the Pompidou government and even the referendum. On January 4, just a few days after de Gaulle's return to Paris from his Christmas holiday at Colombey-les-Deux-Églises, he told Debré (then foreign minister) it was clear Europe would be formed and that England would be admitted.

Unfortunately, Christopher Soames, the British ambassador, misunderstood de Gaulle's message when he talked with him in February, and misplayed his hand. De Gaulle wanted to approach the problem bilaterally with England, and the English should have insisted that France and the other five members of the Common Market agree among themselves on a joint approach to negotiate.

When I saw de Gaulle in February, Soutou says, he was already playing his last card—the blackmail threat of a private deal with Russia.

It is noteworthy that Pompidou has brought back into power the three men who hold real feudal fiefdoms—Jacques Foccart, the secret service boss; Olivier Guichard, the political apparatus boss; and Raymond Marcellin, who runs the network of interior police.

PARIS, *July 1, 1969*

As usual, I came back fascinated and delighted from a luncheon (two and a quarter hours) with André Malraux. He is increasingly difficult to understand as he murmurs along with machine-gun rapidity, often mumbling, often gesticulating, and frequently contorting his features as the meticulousness and speed of his speech strive to keep up with the dazzling pace of his thoughts. I have developed an affection for him as the years have gone by. Incidentally, he said quite blandly during the middle of our conversation "You know, I am now living with Louise de Vilmorin." I had indeed known about Louise and I find it hard to imagine the intellectual tournaments that must take place between the two.

It is extraordinary how elegant his French is in actuality, although so obfuscated in presentation. I really think his main problem is that he just thinks too much and too fast for even the swiftest Parisian tongue.

We started off talking politics. I don't know what to believe, but it didn't lack in fascination. He admitted he hasn't seen de Gaulle since he quit on April 28, but he expects to see him soon. De Gaulle is now working on his fourth volume of memoirs—despite all his assurances that he would never do this—and also on a kind of political testament in the form of an analytical essay. Malraux said that sudden disappearance from power was quite a shock and it was fortunate that de Gaulle was now simultaneously engaged on two books that fully absorbed his energies because "writing comes just as hard to him as it does to me."

De Gaulle made it very plain that he does not support Pompidou by carefully refraining from any statement indicating such support, although he was courteous and sent him his congratulations when he won the elections. "Obviously he could never want Poher in the Élysée," Malraux added, with a sneer. But Malraux indicated that de Gaulle intends to continue exercising a rather active "blackmail veto power" on the Pompidou government. Furthermore, he implied that if the opportunity presents itself —presumably a communist threat—that the Gaullists might once again consider a *coup d'état* by force. I observed that the General was going to be seventy-nine on his next birthday, but Malraux said he was younger now physically than a decade ago and that, after all, he was younger than Clemenceau at the height of the latter's authority.

He went on to compare the Pompidou government with that of André Tardieu who later on attempted to carry on Clemenceau's policies. He said Tardieu's was a traditional, right-wing government and Pompidou's was going to be the same thing. It would base itself more and more on parliament and political parties—just the things Gaullism opposed.

De Gaulle himself did not think there would be any serious troubles ("*pagailles*") this autumn when the schools and universities open up again, but Pompidou is much more pessimistic on this subject. Troubles here can immediately become serious, as was shown in May 1968, because student unrest is always directly connected with labor unions seeking to exploit their advantage. This is not the case in the United States where no matter how bad things become on a campus like Berkeley, the students act alone and there is no serious sundering of the social fabric.

The new cabinet is already well along toward being a cabinet of politicians dependent upon parliamentary factions instead of the kind of technicians' cabinet of independents invisioned by Gaullism. Malraux said that Pompidou had begged him to stay in the cabinet, but he refused. Somewhat startled, I heard Malraux say that de Gaulle had sent word to him he was free to accept any position under Pompidou "except minister of foreign affairs." Personally I could not imagine Pompidou naming Malraux minister of foreign affairs. (But Malraux said, "After all, I could speak with much more effect than Maurice Schumann in the United States or before the United Nations.")

He made a very interesting point—namely that the only two positions of real power in terms of a *coup d'état* are held by the most ardent of the Gaullist "*fidèles*." The first is Michel Debré, now minister of defense; there are some fifty of the highest French officers corps who are one hundred per-cent Gaullist and would back Debré in any test or showdown. "It is a matter of the tanks," said Malraux, "and Debré can rest assured that the tanks are with him, come what may." The other "*fidèle*" in power is Jacques Foccart, who has been restored to his official position as secretary-general for African and Malgache affairs which, of course, says Malraux, is unimportant but it is "the police aspect that counts." He adds that he doesn't think "the police" would really matter much in any conceivable test, that would remain for the tanks. But he conceded there was no harm having a good intelligence apparatus loyal to the General. This whole con-cept stuns and horrifies me.

He specifically excluded Couve de Murville from the "*fidèles.*" He said Couve had behaved with great dignity and competence as prime minister. Nevertheless, he had no roots going back to the resistance and no human contact with the other "*fidèles.*" After all, he only arrived in Algiers in 1943 as secretary to General Henri Giraud. He was a com-petent "eighteenth-century type" for whom the General had respect "but no serious intimacy."

Malraux speculates that de Gaulle deliberately used the referendum as a means of getting off the stage. After all it was perfectly possible for him either to avoid having the referendum at all or not to stick the tenure of his office on its outcome. But de Gaulle chose to regard the referendum as a popular sampling on the May 1968 events. He saw in the outcome—although he was defeated only by a small fraction—discontent with the government's program of the spring of 1968.

He didn't think the government would dare to make any serious changes in foreign policy because it was too afraid of de Gaulle and there were 300 Gaullist deputies in parliament who were in a position to reverse any trends they did not like. And neither Pompidou nor Chaban-Delmas (also an adroit maneuverer but not the man for a showdown) were ready to risk a confrontation with the assembly.

Malraux said the Nixon visit here had been extraordinarily successful. He himself had talked at length with both Nixon and Kissinger. Both he and the General had found that Nixon had grown enormously in stature, and was well-informed. De Gaulle had an odd personal sympathy for Nixon which was probably based upon the fact that Nixon also had had his period of exile and de Gaulle knew what he had suffered. He had made a point of keeping in touch with him occasionally during the Nixon exile and undoubtedly Nixon was deeply grateful.

We then moved into an entirely different set of ideas. I remarked that in Carlos Baker's biography of Hemingway, Malraux is mentioned from time to time and not always favorably (from Hemingway's viewpoint). Malraux said he had known Ernest quite well but there had never been any genuine intimacy, although in Spain there had been no trouble between them "because I was going on operations eight times a day while he was just a journalist amusing himself." Although Hemingway was a writer of immense talent, he was not at all as "solid" a personality as the image he cared to cultivate; and he was devoured by jealousy. After the liberation of Paris, Malraux ran into Hemingway in the Ritz Hotel, but not at all in the manner described by Hemingway, although there is some similarity between the two stories. He said Hemingway was carousing when he (Malraux) came into the room. "He was disporting himself ridiculously while I stood before him dressed in a tank officer's uniform. I asked him how many men he had commanded and he said perhaps twenty. It was disgusting. I turned and left the room."

He said it was a curious thing about American writers that they had never been either "*engagés*" or truly mature politically. In this respect, they are like French painters, not like French writers, who since the time of Montesquieu and Voltaire have been politically committed. In America one could only find intellectuals who could help the government in the university, never among the writers. This was not true of French writers, but it was true of French painters. There was a very valid comparison between Hemingway and Picasso in this respect. Both were emotional and neither was serious.

Malraux said that Picasso was not really a great "painter" although he was a fine artist. He was not like Goya or Vermeer because he did not really have the genius of colors. He was now in his latest phase experimenting only with colors and this, of course, was interesting. But a truly great painter knew exactly which blue he wished to put on the canvas and which grey to place beside it, and then did so. Picasso was simply unable to paint with that degree of perfection.

Categorically Malraux said, "There has been only one great painter in modern times—Braque. And then, but far, far below him, there is Poliakoff. That is all."

He said the United States was a strange country because it was the only great power in history that became an international force quite unconsciously and by accident. It was only because of a dazzling industrial and economic system that this had happened. But the United States had never wanted to be an international power until it stumbled into the position. It was not like Rome or Britain or even Russia. The British had a real idea of what they wanted and how to attain it in a country like Egypt, for example. But the Americans had no idea what they wanted to do in Egypt and they don't really care if they have influence there or not.

Malraux said there were only two aspects of policy which de Gaulle was watching like a hawk in the new Pompidou set-up: foreign policy and *participation*. I said I didn't think there was a Chinaman's chance of getting anything done on *participation* because I was sure Pompidou opposed it. "That's the trouble," said Malraux. "This is a very conservative regime. It is almost quasi-fascist. It is going to move more and more to the right."

PARIS, *July 3, 1969*

Dined last night at Pierre Salinger's. There was a charming half-French, half-Bolivian girl there—the granddaughter of Antonio R. Patiño, the Bolivian tin billionaire. Patiño was a thirty-year-old mixed blood (*cholo*) from a small town named Oruro, not far from Cochabamba. He ran a shop somewhat like a smithy. Nobody ever knew who his father was. At the age of thirty he married a fifteen-year-old Quechua Indian girl whose father also was unknown.

Patiño was owed a small debt by a man who paid him off in the title to some mining land in the Alto Plano which had already been explored and condemned as barren. Without any scientific knowledge and by sheer luck he struck a thick layer of tin that was easily accessible and near the surface. Encouraged by his frugal Indian wife, he invested more and more in mining property and invariably was able to find tin where others had passed it by. He became incredibly rich and finally moved to Europe.

The girl knew her grandmother very well until the latter's death. She always remained a secretive and isolated Indian with impassive poker face, like an old Tibetan lady with withered features, "exactly like the Indians in felt bowler hats you see in the market place of La Paz." The grandmother died in Europe, but the family flew her remains back to be buried in Bolivia, "according to a custom that is more atavistic than religious."

Agreeable talk with Christopher Soames, the British ambassador, and then had drinks with him, his wife (the former Mary Churchill) and Nicko Henderson, now British ambassador in Warsaw.

Soames doesn't think de Gaulle will manage to keep an active influence in French politics, despite the efforts of the Gaullist die-hards to use his shadow for political purposes. He said: "I know about this. Nobody can last long as a political influence once they are out of power. I saw that with Churchill" (his father-in-law).

He said that after drafting his telegram to London on his famous talk with de Gaulle, he excised from it his personal recommendations and comments and took a copy of the cut-down version to the Élysée and personally gave it to Bernard Tricot, secretary-general of the Élysée. He asked Tricot if he would please read it and also asked him what de Gaulle had told Tricot about the conversation. Tricot said all he knew was that de Gaulle had proposed talks with Britain. He had not seen any other record (and there was nobody present at the dialogue except Soames and the General). Soames then asked him if he would read his account and Tricot promised to do this. Soames had an appointment with Foreign Minister Debré on Saturday (February 22) and Tricot would tell Debré if there was anything wrong with Soames's "*compte rendu.*" When Soames saw

Debré, he saw a letter in Tricot's handwriting and Debré told him that the Élysée didn't seem to have any objection to his version.

He then shrugged his shoulders and said: "Of course I have absolutely nothing to say about the way my government—or the French government —handled things afterwards."

The British government leaked the substance of Soames's secret telegram and then the French—in a rage—attacked, criticized, and distorted it, creating a crisis. Soames indicated that, of course, the British government had to keep its European friends advised, but he also indicated he thought it would have been wise to pursue the idea of secret bilateral talks for a while.

PARIS, *July 4, 1969*

Lunched today with Henri Froment-Meurice now Manac'h's successor as chief of the Asian division of the *Quai d'Orsay*. I asked him why he thought the South Vietnamese communists had now established a "provisional revolutionary government." He saw this as an initial step toward a coalition government in Saigon. He personally takes the view that the Vietcong really wants a neutralist separate South Vietnamese state that is not part of a communist super-Vietnam run from Hanoi.

PARIS, *July 5, 1969*

I went over to see Jean Monnet and had a long talk but I don't find him brilliant or stimulating.

Nevertheless, by dogged persistence, he has had a big effect on postwar Europe, by arranging France's first economic plan and then by giving the impetus to launching European unity ideas such as the coal and steel plan (which succeeded), the European army (which failed), Euratom (which is neither a success nor a failure), and the Common Market. He has been steadily trying to get England into the Common Market for the last decade or so. Monnet is a stocky, unusually fit man of eighty who speaks with great precision. He has a humorless, solemn face.

Monnet said: "If you want to put industry on an efficient international basis, competition does this. You don't have to take special steps. But agriculture must be organized and competition will not succeed in that. There is no country in the world except Canada whose agriculture is not fed by subsidies or by export.

"For industry, it's just a question of competition and avoiding discrimination. But industry is supported by an export demand whereas agriculture is not. An agreement on subsidies and on each nation's contribution to the common agricultural fund is a necessity."

He pointed out that the Common Market requires the delegation of national sovereignty on specific points to European institutions and the acceptance of decisions by them on the basis of majority vote—not unanimity. Europe, including France, has to a great extent accepted this method. Britain has accepted the principles of the Common Market but it has not yet made fully plain that it will go along with this system of majority vote and the yielding of sovereignty.

PARIS, *July 11, 1969*

Drove out to the gloomy Château de Verrières, where Louise de Vilmorin lives with André Malraux. It was a small dinner party. Both the setting and the characters made me feel as if I were playing a bit part in Sartre's *Les Sequestrés d'Altona*—and I wondered whether some nut was incarcerated in the attic upstairs.

The large sitting room in which we gathered was lit almost entirely by candles. Louise said, "We haven't got enough money for more electricity." Only one servant was in evidence—a totally silent butler. I noticed that neither Louise nor the niece ate a single thing. But Louise drank champagne.

As for Malraux, he looked like an unhappy Poe character with deep pockets under his luminous eyes and such a pale face that he might have been buried for a couple of days and then exhumed.

Louise started off in a pessimistic way by discussing the advantages of cancer over a bad heart as a means of dying. After all, she said, you could be pumped full of pain killers and would have plenty of time to assemble your family and domestics around you before the end, thus dying in a properly theatrical way. She thought the greatest tragedy of her time was the disappearance of the army and the church as dominant influences —which provoked spirited response from the doctor who is a Protestant.

Malraux described Pompidou as a Louis-Philippe and said that his program was simply another version of "*enrichissez-vous.*" He described the present government in France as "a triumph of mediocrity." He thought Pompidou's press conference had been boring but he was sure de Gaulle had watched it on the TV "because he cannot restrain his curiosity."

Malraux swears that at the time of the Kennedy visit to Paris in 1961 de Gaulle told him that Jackie Kennedy was obviously the type of woman who would end up as the wife of an oil millionaire.

CAPE KENNEDY, *July 16, 1969*

Arrived here at 4:45 A.M. aboard a special Boeing that *Paris-Match* had hired on a brilliantly organized promotional and goodwill trip. The passengers included Ambassador Sargent Shriver, Prince Jean of Luxembourg, Prime Minister Werner of Luxembourg, and a large assortment of top-level French businessmen. Charles Lucet, French ambassador in Washington, joined us here.

Breakfasted in Melbourne, a village near Cape Kennedy, with Shriver, Wernher von Braun, the head of the rocket building program for space, and Jacqueline Auriol, the aviatrix. Von Braun is a big, strong man with resolute face that reminded me of the portrait of Alexander the Great. He was very calm and relaxed, considering the events that were about to take place. He said it was already evident from the "slow trajectory" of the Soviet *Luna* rocket that there was no human passenger on board, although it was possible it might swoop down to the moon to scoop up earth samples and bring them back ahead of *Apollo* XI's crew. "But," said von Braun, "that cannot disturb the purpose or success of our mission. We need human beings there—men—to know the effect of the moon atmosphere, its gravity, and other factors as far as human lives are concerned."

After breakfast we loaded into air-conditioned buses and inched our way through traffic jams to Cape Kennedy. Among the very few thousand people allowed into the actual vicinity, the luminaries were gathered in four small grandstands like bleachers set up for a high-school football game. We were in the stand near former President Johnson and Vice President Agnew, plus the ambassadors in Washington. We stood waiting for a couple of hours in the blazing sun. Fortunately the thoughtful *Paris-Match* organizers provided each of us with an imitation Texas-type hat made of white plastic.

The countdown was announced on loudspeakers and then, at the precise scheduled second of 9:32 A.M. there was a huge ferocious orange blaze. For several seconds the rocket seemed to be hung in suspension, struggling to get away, then there was a thunderous noise like a great artillery barrage and slowly it moved upward, accelerating with enormous rapidity until its smoke cut a great scar into the sky. We were able to watch this very accurately because here again the excellent *Paris-Match* organization had provided us each with binoculars (I noticed that they were stamped in Portuguese as made in Macao—so that I am sure they were actually of communist Chinese origin).

HOUSTON, TEXAS, *July 17, 1969*

We flew in here yesterday afternoon and today we had a fascinating briefing all morning at the "manned space center" run by NASA. Then we were flown in smaller planes from the NASA airport to Houston airport where we climbed wearily aboard our chartered Boeing.

Visited a laboratory and medical section which will study moon samples when material is brought back by *Apollo* XI. The astronauts will live in this building, quarantined entirely for twenty-one days to prevent any chance of an epidemic starting from some strange moon germ.

The staff we saw were wearing hospital uniforms. We looked at them through huge glass windows. All moon samples brought back will be doubly isolated so that if the first isolation container breaks, they are still cut off.

In space itself, all waste material from the mission will either be sterilized before it is left on the moon or will be released to burn up in the sun's orbit. It was pointed out that *all* earth organisms die if they are left on the lunar surface—even if they are in a sealed tin can. They would have to be deposited below the surface to survive.

While we were in the control center, the Houston ground team, in coordination with the astronauts, corrected the course of *Apollo* XI by a very short burn of the rocket engines, and we heard the calm soft voices of the astronauts and the ground team talking to each other gently in the matter-of-fact tones of friends discussing a chess game.

We looked through a huge glass window at dozens of technicians in serried rows with televisions and charts in front of them checking on computer information and changing dials. Above them was a huge world map with the course of *Apollo* charted in a very slowly moving line. Above this was a series of large dials like speedometers giving time, distances, etc. The entire course change was actually handled and ordered by computers in Houston, but the commander of the space capsule had the authority to countermand the orders if he thought necessary. He didn't.

Then we attended a conference given by Lieutenant General Sam C. Phillips, commander of the *Apollo* project, a clean-cut, thin, well-built, balding man with glasses. With him were Colonel Bill Anders, pilot of the *Gemini* XI mission, and two scientists.

Anders said NASA is already thinking of possibly going to Mars, or going into space-station activities (manned "platforms"). One program under study is the possibility of establishing a station on the moon which can be inhabited by humans. Within ten years he hopes the first spatial station can be put up with international crews. We want scientists and technicians of various countries to participate—including all nations of the world without regard to ideology.

Anders said members of the public will someday be taken to the moon and the date will be sooner then we now think because of the dazzling rate of technical progress. Phillips added that within a few years transportation to the moon can be placed on a commercial level and anyone in good health who is able to afford it will be able to make the trip. Two years ago he made a bet that by 1987 commercial travel in space will be available.

Anders said it is impossible to imagine that there is not another planet —indeed several planets—with the possibility of life on them, although he was talking in terms that might extend beyond our galaxy.

The French were enormously impressed by the democratic simplicity both of the moon-shot and the space center. The idea of General Westmoreland's having to find a seat for himself on a bus tickled them almost as much as *Apollo* XI. "If we had been able to have an event like this, each general would have had six aides de camp with him, covered with decorations and fourragères, and his own transportation."

PARIS, *July 21, 1969*

Lunched with General E. Ben Arzi, a diminutive, stocky, intelligent, amusing Israeli officer who is now in retirement. During the Israeli war of independence he became chief of logistics (G-4). Later, he was named head of El Al (the Israeli airline) and is now in charge of water projects.

He told me that when the French slapped an embargo on the export of arms to the Middle East (above all Israel) in June 1967, Air France and other organizations helped Israel materially to violate the embargo. Emergency shipments of spare parts were either transferred by Air France to El Al planes or to Holland, where Israeli aircraft picked them up. South Africa was also of enormous help. South Africa permitted the Israelis to pick up arms shipments scheduled under bills of lading for South Africa and to send them to Israel. Likewise, South Africa made available to volunteers for the Israeli cause numerous airline seats (presumably for technicians and experts). Said Ben Arzi: "After all, their interest and our interests are common—to crush Nasser."

PARIS, *July 29, 1969*

Exceptionally good talk this afternoon with Georges Pompidou, the first since he became president of the French Republic last month. It was odd finding him in the same chair behind the same desk, where I have been seeing de Gaulle for the past decade. Somehow it made him look smaller, although he is not a little man. His manner was extremely cordial. He rose to greet me and, at the end of our one-hour conversation, conducted me to the door.

I started out by saying I had heard there was agreement in principle that he would go to the United States on an official visit in January 1970. He said: "Some time during the first three or four months. The date has not yet been fixed."

I observed that relationships between France and the United States had warmed up. He commented: "Two things have been fundamental. (1) The United States position on Vietnam has made a big difference, the manifestation of a desire to end the war, and (2) the visit of President Nixon to General de Gaulle, which showed a new U.S. conception of general strategy. This seems to demonstrate that the Nixon government admits the position of France as an ally—but an ally that is not integrated into NATO.

"Of course, this is due to the fact that the problem of war in Europe is much less immediate. There is no longer the former attitude that conflict is possible at any time and that all units must be ready. There is a much more supple attitude and this allows an easier relationship toward France and its objection to integration. Of course, you don't want our example to be contagious. You certainly don't want Germany to take its liberty. Or even England, for that matter. But our attitude is less troubling to you now. And I must confess that there is really a third point which is namely that there is no chance of France's making war by itself—without its allies."

Was it safe to assume that France has no intention of denouncing the North Atlantic treaty for the next few years or the predictable future? He said this was a safe assumption. Certainly France would not denounce the treaty for the predictable future. France was perfectly prepared to discuss joint strategy planning with its allies. But it preferred to talk directly with the United States rather than with NATO, which was virtually the same thing since it was under an American military commander. Among the things France was prepared to discuss were joint targeting and a common understanding on the use of the French nuclear force—in line with allied objectives and NATO's nuclear strength. (This is a big change since de Gaulle.)

Did he think Britain was prepared to enter the Common Market by accepting all conditions of the Rome treaty? He grinned, regarded me shrewdly and asked: "What do you think?" I did not think Britain was willing to do this, that it couldn't afford it. He said he thoroughly agreed with me. He did not think Britain was prepared to pay the price of admission—above all for agriculture. The day Britain came into the Common Market it would cause a profound change in that organization, which would have to become far more supple. The agricultural community, above all, would have to be profoundly changed.

If Britain were admitted, it would mean that in a very short time the community would contain ten countries instead of six. Norway, Denmark, and Ireland would have to be admitted almost immediately. And there would also be the problems of Sweden, Switzerland, and Austria. Before this process had ended, you would have a market covering a massive area and including some 320 million people. As a real Common Market, this community would have such strength that it would be bound to exasperate the United States.

American policy would then be forced for economic reasons to compete in every way with the Common Market. Already, one could see the rivalry between the U.S.A. and the Common Market of six over European grain exports, which were creating a serious problem for America.

Pompidou did not believe that Britain could accept the conditions of entry. Furthermore, he did not believe it was desirable to have a large rival bloc in Europe competing with the United States.

He was now engaged in preparing a speech for the two hundredth anniversary of Napoleon's birth and he was doing a lot of reading on the subject. He had been struck repeatedly by the fact that the Europe of Six —the existing Common Market—was almost exactly the same Europe as that run by Napoleon—even including the division of Germany.

Probably, he thought, the Common Market of six members would continue as it is and Britain would probably continue as it is—outside of the European community. Otherwise, the Common Market would in fact become a loose free trade area permitting special agricultural agreements among its members. But it would be an open and looser group in order to avoid confrontation with the United States.

I asked—should he prove wrong about Britain and should Britain be admitted to the community—did he think it would be wise to form a joint Anglo-French nuclear force to be placed at the disposition of Europe? He answered obliquely: "Could Europe have a policy, including a defense policy? There is the German problem, after all. Perhaps there could be a small Anglo-French umbrella under the much larger American nuclear umbrella. But Britain doesn't really want a nuclear accord with France. And anyway, there really isn't much chance that Britain will come into the Common Market."

I wanted to move to another sensitive area. What was the position of France on delivering to Israel the fifty Mirage jets which had been paid for by the Israelis in 1967? He said there had been no change in French policy on this. "The door is closed" for a long time to come. Government "policy" was not to release the planes to Israel. But "if Israel claims its money back, we must discuss that claim." This was up to Israel and Israel could take the initiative. France was perfectly prepared to negotiate.

France had lost a great deal of gold during the past year; did he think devaluation of the franc was becoming a possibility? He said monetary questions must face the whole world one of these days. The German mark was a big problem.

France could wait before contemplating action of the franc. Since Pompidou's election, French losses in devises had come to approximate existing trade balances. This showed speculation against the franc had ended. By the end of the year, the trade balance would be restored. From then on, any action on the franc would depend on how the world monetary situation developed.

Did he share de Gaulle's belief that French Canada is suffering foreign rule and domination? He smiled and said: "Of course that is not my opinion. But I must admit that General de Gaulle sowed a seed. He has accelerated the development of Canada."

I asked if he thought it possible for France to play a more active role in trying to break the existing deadlock in the Vietnamese peace negotiations.

He said this was a very complicated affair. "The Asiatics" were very complicated people. But Russia was in contact with the United States on this. Furthermore, if it seemed needed, France might, at a chosen time, try on its own to help move things along. But France did not want in any way to irritate the United States. "After all," he added, "we know how difficult this kind of negotiation can be." (He was referring to the tedious Algerian talks that preceded settlement of that war.)

I turned to internal affairs. Was de Gaulle's old idea of "*participation*" still policy? He asked me: "Do you really know what '*participation*' is?" I confessed that I didn't. He then said with a grin: "I don't know what it is either. It really isn't anything at all. It is a word, a word that has now entered our political vocabulary.

"Of course, we must have a *cadre* in every enterprise. But it is certainly desirable to have better information—better labor-capital consultation and over-all relationships just as exist already in the U.S.A. and Germany. Unfortunately, the tradition of family enterprises is still strong in France and the idea that the boss can speak alone. Workers should be able to understand why they work and they should have a greater share in profits. But modern capitalism develops this far better than we do in France.

"But as for '*participation*,' the only question that faces me is whether I should keep the word '*participation*' in order to attract political support —or not. The future will guide me on this."

Could he tell me how his administrative and policy-making methods differed from General de Gaulle's. He replied: "I would say that the prime minister and the assembly must have more freedom. Certainly the prime minister now is much freer in a political sense than he was under de Gaulle. De Gaulle had a kind of hold on all the Gaullists—both in the cabinet and in the assembly—and worked things in such a way that all questions ultimately had to be settled by his word, by the news getting around that the General wanted things done in such and such a way. I leave much more liberty to Chaban and political freedom to maneuver in the assembly. I refuse to take a personal position on such questions as, for example, the elections of the president of the assembly. This is for the assembly itself to decide. Under de Gaulle the deputies would have asked 'Who does the General want?' I say to them: 'That is your affair.' But I am more *présent* [on the scene] than de Gaulle. He concerned himself primarily only with diplomatic and military affairs except for the really major decisions. But I operate on a day-to-day basis in all domains. Nor do I keep my reserved domains to be run only by the presidency. Of course, for foreign policy, it must be *me*. But this is the case in all countries."

I asked him about his personal relations with de Gaulle. He said he had had no letters or telephone conversations since the General's resignation. Last February he had lunched at Chaban's with Couve, and when he told

Couve that de Gaulle would never designate a successor, "Couve was stupified." He added: "I told Couve that de Gaulle of course hoped the next president would be one of his supporters, but he didn't want to take any responsibility for what happened after him. If he did that, people might be in a position to say that things went wrong because de Gaulle had chosen badly."

As for today, he said: "I don't think de Gaulle will play any part in French politics. Of course, on vital questions I would ask his advice. And I am sure that if he saw something that he considered terrible, he would say so. But the odds are nine out of ten that he will do nothing."

He did not think de Gaulle cherished any hostility toward him but he was equally certain "that he is not happy—for human reasons you know well."

I asked if he could tell me a little bit about himself, what he was reading these days, what his preferences were in music, painting, etc. He said he didn't get much time to read. Right now he had been concentrating on Napoleon's writings—his letters, diaries. He tried to keep up with painting and, until three or four years ago, he was "a fanatic for the abstract." But this phase in his taste was now finished. He was now more interested in neorealism: Martial Raysse and Yves Klein. In books he was more interested in modern novels. He liked the writing of Marguerite Duras. His musical taste was classical. He was very fond of Yannis Xenakis. He didn't really have much time for music; he couldn't put a stereo set in his office, but he could always grab a few minutes to read.

I asked if he and his wife had done much to change the *décor* and protocol of the Élysée. He admitted the desk and armchairs were the same as under de Gaulle but the French museums had unloaded some 1890 furniture on the General which he (Pompidou) couldn't stand. He pointed out two magnificent eighteenth-century small black lacquer cabinets and a superb eighteenth-century chest of drawers. He had obtained these from the museums. But on the top of the chest of drawers was a Cambodian head which belonged to Pompidou himself.

PARIS, *August 1, 1969*

Cabot Lodge had me up for lunch in his suite at the Crillon today. He is bored silly by the negotiations and makes no pretense that they are moving at all, but we cannot be the people to break them off.

The only discernible military objective of the communists in Vietnam now is to keep up the figure of U.S. casualties while occasionally shelling Saigon. This does not require a very high commitment in troops and reinforcements. It is possible that the war is gradually beginning to fade away but one certainly can't prove it.

Hanoi obviously looks forward to the day when it can be the capital of a united Vietnam containing forty million inhabitants, which would put it virtually on the same level of strength as France or England. It wants to dominate Laos and Cambodia and this whole concept frightens to death Thailand, the Philippines, and Malaysia. But the procedure had already cost the seventeen million people of North Vietnam 500,000 dead soldiers, which is a massive price.

Hanoi is interested in the method of our withdrawal. They don't like to see us going out slowly as South Vietnamese troops come in. They want to see a disorganized helter-skelter bug-out. What Hanoi fears most of all is the development of a kind of stalemate that the U.S. feels it can live with.

There have been absolutely no "negotiations" of any sort here since Cabot arrived in January. Hanoi's position is simply: "You Americans get out, unilaterally, all by yourselves and, as you go, we want you to bust the Saigon government."

PARIS, *August 5, 1969*

Agreeable conversation with Maurice Schumann, the new minister for foreign affairs, a large man, slightly stooped, with an earnest, intellectual face.

Every kind of contact between France and the United States was now once again within the range of possibility, he said. There were no more taboos. When he goes to Washington in September (at the time the foreign ministers participate in the UN assembly) he will see Nixon and Rogers and discuss this. So will Pompidou when he goes to Washington next year. Everything is now open to discussion—military, political, and monetary problems.

I understood France had no intention of delivering the fifty Mirage jets Israel had bought. Schumann said that was correct but I should be very careful to distinguish between the various kinds of embargo. From June 1967 until just after the December 28, 1968, Israeli raid on Beirut airport, the embargo had been on heavy weapons and aircraft, but France was still sending spare parts and defensive weapons including helicopters and small patrol boats. Then, from January 1969 until now, there had been a total embargo. Today France was prepared to go back essentially to the pre-January 1969 situation and to let spare parts go to Israel—on condition that Israel did not make any more difficult the Four-Power efforts to establish peace in the Middle East.

Schumann could not imagine a Soviet-Chinese war in the foreseeable future, at least from the Chinese side. As for the Russians, they could not launch such a conflict without having the guarantee of a quiet situation in Europe. The Russians could never forget that their revolution started more or less in consequence of their weakness in Asia through the Japanese war of 1905. He was sure the Russians did not want to touch off any conflict without some sort of gentlemen's agreement ahead of time with the U.S.A.—and that was wholly unlikely.

PARIS, *August 6, 1969*

Last night dinner with Costa and Amalia Caramanlis. He claims that the Greek people, while disliking the regime, are incapable of upsetting it. The only way to do this is for the United States to expel Greece from NATO and for Europe to expel it from the Council of Europe and association with the Common Market. I argue that the time has ended for direct United States interference and that we are certainly not going to expel Greece, with its favorable geography, from NATO, an alliance which has included dictatorial Portugal from the very start. He claims that if we were to make such a tough move against Greece the army would rise up and chuck out the junta, because the army knows neutralism is impossible, given Greece's position on the map.

He says that in October 1967, the king sent his personal aide, Major Arnaoutis, to see him and to ask him to come back and take over as prime minister. He said he replied that he could not accept power from either the king or the Americans—only from the people. But he recommended to the king that he should start to apply "peaceful pressure" for change, turning the heat on but seeking to avoid a solution by force. He said that Constantine never answered him and the next move was the king's pathetically unsuccessful counter-coup in December 1967.

Lunched with Walt Rostow, who is just winding up a round-the-world tour. I recalled the lunch I had with him, Johnson, and McNamara in 1966, in which I asked why on earth the Pentagon was denying that the Vietnamese communists were being reinforced and supplied from Cambodia and McNamara insisted that this was not true. Rostow said he remembered this well and that after lunch Johnson had asked him to assemble a report on the problem; that Rostow had strongly endorsed my viewpoint.

JERUSALEM, *August 14, 1969*

This evening I had a long talk with Mrs. Golda Meir, the seventy-one-year-old grandmother who runs Israel as prime minister. She is a homely but pleasant-looking woman whose face contains a warmth that rarely appears in her photographs, humorous blue eyes, wrinkled brow, long nose and chin, a bun of greying hair. She was neatly dressed in an unpretentious dress. Whenever she talked of her grandchildren, a soft look crept over her features. She smoked several cigarettes and said she didn't dare ask me how I had stopped (since I last saw her) because she wouldn't be able to do so.

Mrs. Meir says internal politics are exceedingly important to Arab military postures. The Arabs have been fed with dreams of victory by their rulers—in order to compensate for bad conditions at home. There is no democracy among the neighboring Arabs (except in Lebanon). The voice of the people is simply not known. Nasser made many promises when he first came in but nothing, in reality, has happened: the Nile farmers are still starving; babies are dying; and per capita income remains very low.

"When Nasser says he wants peace and development," she said, "he always adds: 'But I can't; I would be assassinated if I stopped the liberation struggle.' If so, it's his own doing. Look what he reports about the Suez fighting: he claims they have knocked out 60 percent of our so-called Bar Lev line. This is sheer nonsense. Nothing has been knocked out. And when we shoot down his planes, he claims they are our planes.

"As for Hussein, had he taken a stand at the start, preventing the *Al Fatah* and other *Fedayeen* guerrillas from acting there, things would have been different. Now they are getting out of hand. At least Nasser doesn't let other organizations operate from his territory. He has his infiltrators— but they are all from the Egyptian forces."

She admitted: "Security as it is now is an extreme burden for Israel. And if we have to do more the burden will increase. But there is no limit to what we can take. How do you know how much pain you can suffer before you die? This people won't commit suicide. We know we suffer and we have other dreams. But if this is our fate—war can be made by one side but peace must be made by two—we are prepared to endure. There is no alternative."

She said the U.S. F-4 planes are not a substitute for the Mirages Israel bought from France. The F-4s had always been reckoned on. She says there is no change in policy on the Mirages. Israel regards them as her planes; France simply won't deliver. Israel has no intention of negotiating a return on the purchase price.

I asked if she had approved the Beirut airport helicopter commando raid last December. She said she hadn't been in the government then and when she heard how destructive it had been at first she thought it excessive. Since then she had concluded it was a correct measure and had helped restrict activities of the *Fedayeen* in Lebanon.

She continued: "I am convinced the only solution for this complicated problem is for us and our neighbors to make peace. But negotiations must be direct, not through mediators. When this will happen, I don't know. But in December 1967 and again last year we told Jarring (the UN mediator) we were ready to meet the Arabs any place."

She said Israel was even prepared to have secret negotiations at the start. It didn't wish to insist on negotiations as a means of blocking peace, but as the only sure way of getting it. However, "This time it must be the real thing." Israel wanted "agreed frontiers" which meant not "imposed." There are no preconditions, no maps outlining Israel's demands. But first there had to be someone to negotiate with. Now there were only armistice lines, not frontiers. And after each war the Arabs wanted the borders they had lost in the previous war.

It was unbelievable, she thought, that Russia would risk entering the conflict, announcing it would only go so far as the 1967 Sinai border, then quit, merely getting the canal open. Of course, having seen what happened to Czechoslovakia, anything could happen, but the Russians hadn't come in in June 1967.

Some years ago, she said, Israel had suspected when German scientists were in Egypt that an attempt had been made to make a nuclear weapon, but it failed. Israel had no plans on what it would do in such an event but didn't think it probable.

She admitted that war was "unwinnable" here because Israel couldn't conquer and occupy the Arabs. "The only solution is peace. We didn't initiate the last war—but we won it. Yet we say, come and negotiate with no preconditions. We see that we must live together. We even dare to dream dreams now of doing some day in Jordan what we already do in Africa, helping a country to improve its life. Regional economic development would be so simple. We have everything to contribute. Look, for example, at the great increase in the agricultural output already in the Arab areas under our control since June 1967."

She thought the day would come when something like the Eisenhower plan for water sharing and industry would be possible. There had even been a Hammarskjöld plan for regional development, in order to care for the refugees, but "we said yes and the Arabs were enraged. The difficulty is that the Arab leaders don't care enough for their people. I don't know the date of the peace that must come. But I know the principal condition; that is when Nasser begins to worry about the infant mortality rate in Egypt instead of how to destroy Israel."

She said she was astonished by the indestructible spirit of Israel. Men who had just come here four or five years ago from Morocco, where they cowered in the ghettos, were wholly unafraid here. There was no legal way of forcing people to live in border villages or kibbutzim where they suffered, and if one folded up, the others would, and the state would collapse. Yet no one dreamed for a moment of quitting. Just before the six-day war she went to the Negev to see her grandchildren (then eleven and fifteen). (She now has two more.) She was confident Israel would win the war but not confident that everyone would survive. At their kibbutz, only children twelve or under were allowed in the shelters; there wasn't room for the others, except in shallow trenches. Her granddaughter, fifteen, had the job of getting the kids to their shelters. She made a brief speech to the colony and everyone was so tense and silent you could hear each breath. All she said was, in effect: "We will have a war but we will win it. And we will have to fight it alone; no one will help us."

I remarked that Israel was often criticized for its over-reaction policy of two eyes for one eye. She said: "None of these acts are acts of revenge. That has to be excluded absolutely as a thought. These acts are taken only to prevent further activity from the other side. Revenge never enters into our planning."

Then I left this kindly Grant Wood figure with the Milwaukee accent, the most unlikely looking Amazon of history.

HERZLIYA, ISRAEL, *August 16, 1969*

Two conversations in Tel Aviv with General Aharon Yariv, chief of intelligence, and Abba Eban, foreign minister. Yariv says Egypt has lost forty planes since the June 1967 war (about ten percent of its present air strength).

The Russians in Egypt are playing only an advisory role. They give current operational advice but the decision is Egyptian. The Russians do sit in the command posts. Israel has *no* news concerning Russian casualties in Suez operations.

Yariv says King Hussein didn't originally invite the Iraqi forces (now stationed there); they just came in on the eve of the six-day war and never left. Now the Syrians have moved in under the eastern-front arrangements supervised by Nasser. Both eastern and western fronts are under the Egyptian chief of staff and Egypt wants pressure also on Israel's eastern border. But Jordan didn't want the Syrians so only artillery has come in there; artillery can't make a revolution.

Yariv insists a revolutionary war against Israel is not possible. *Fatah* and other guerrillas can maintain terrorist cells in Israel but not guerrilla bases (in occupied areas). It can't work. They will not be able to pass from the first phase (terrorism) to the second phase (guerrilla warfare). Even topographically this area is too difficult.

But there is cause to worry about eventual development abroad of a "code-word" possibility for *Fedayeen* or *Fatah* or Arab; a symbol, pressed by Russia on the world's youth, hippies, students, discontented. *Fatah* itself hasn't masterminded things to this degree but they *are* using the new Left, even Jews. A small Jewish group in London supports *Al Fatah*.

It would be very difficult for Egypt to put a force over the canal to hit Israel. They could get across but not stay very long. They would have enough armor and artillery but they are weak in the air—and they know this. A large-scale operation designed to drive the Israelis back from the canal requires air superiority to hit Israel's air bases.

Unlike others, Yariv says Israel should "not rule out" the possibility that Russia might some day intervene to force Israel back from the canal, announcing limited objectives. But so far there is no evidence of this. The Russians are being very careful. They discourage the Egyptians from acting offensively except in limited attacks to build morale. Moscow doesn't want to get involved directly in *any* kind of war. It can't tolerate another setback. And there is no sign of a Soviet troop or materiel build-up. The Soviet Union has *never* mounted a war with a country with which it has no common frontier.

The biggest gain of the 1967 war was that Israel now has a second-strike capability, doesn't have to hit first. The greatest danger to Israel today would be an inability to keep up its end of the arms balance—should the U.S.A. ration its supplies too tight and France maintain the blockade. This would "invite heavy pressure on us—and also could push Israel into taking another initiative."

He was most interesting in terms of the relative Israeli-Arab strength in coming years, saying: "We have really studied the Egyptian officers we captured. We gave all kinds of psycho-technical tests to the new generation of junior officers and found that the average of quality in 1967 was even lower than in 1956. The reason was because there has been a bigger intake from the population, therefore less rigorous selection.

"Our educators say that unless there is a total change in the Egyptian and Arab societies, there will be no chance for their military weaknesses to change. And if there is no such basic alteration soon, the gap will widen even further—because of technology.

"But I always say—do not underestimate quantity. Their armor, to protect their qualitative weakness, is quantity. You cannot underestimate the importance of that armor shielding their weakness."

Afterward, I had tea and a chat with Foreign Minister Abba Eban at the Dan Hotel suite made available to him: a large, brilliant man, fascinated by words; a sort of plump Israeli George Kennan. We started talking about Jordan's King Hussein. Eban said:

"He thinks Israel's mere existence is a disaster. He regards himself as king of the Palestinians as well as Jordan. Therefore, he figures he must explore Israel's peace terms because he knows he can recover a great deal through them. He could cut his losses—in exchange for peace.

"Hussein used to say that Nasser had given him a green light to explore peace conditions; but no longer. Now we hear that he feels he must be supported by the Palestinian community in anything he does, not that this community should merely acquiesce. And Hussein just can't deliver the goods; his country isn't a real country and it is occupied by three foreign armies plus guerrilla groups.

"The center of political influence in this affair is Egypt. But the people and territory involved—as apart from politics—are not in Egypt; they are in Jordan. Hardly any Egyptians are involved at all."

Eban didn't think there was any substantial difference in policy between the Johnson and Nixon administrations "and the Arabs also understand this now. The Nixon administration has shown continuity from the Johnson administration, not disconnection. The Russians and the Egyptians feel no change in Washington.

"The Nixon administration *did* decide that Russia is the power behind the Middle East problem and that the Russian gambit must be played. But Washington finds the Russians are curiously the slaves of Cairo. Nowadays a big power doesn't always call the tune. If the great powers disassociate the Middle East from their own problems, it would eventually become extraneous, like Kashmir or Cyprus. In March 1969 I was told in Washington that this was a powder-keg. But now we are told that while the problem is serious it won't blow up the world."

The important thing for the U.S.A. is that Israel should be able to look after itself. This suits the Nixon doctrine. Give Israel enough arms to fight so America doesn't have to.

TEL AVIV, *August 17, 1969*

General Ben Arzi, the diminutive former G-4 of Israel's army, took me out for lunch.

He told of his adventures when heading El Al Airlines. An atomic spy, wanted by the U.S.A., came here via Air France on a fake passport. Bobby Kennedy, then attorney general, got in touch with Israel, and it was arranged to ship him out by El Al to London. Ben wanted to send him by Air France, as he had come, but the government insisted and he was sent with a doctor to look after him and a U.S. marshal. Despite this, he tried to kill himself with a knife, was hospitalized in a London prison, but the Russians smuggled poison to him and he finished the job. Says Ben, it wasn't even the right man—but his brother.

Ben participated in the Eichmann kidnapping. Many weeks ahead the security services confided in him and one other El Al official what was required and why. Special El Al agents were placed in Buenos Aires and also Recife, Brazil, and instructed to cajole the authorities. Finally, Abba Eban was sent to Buenos Aires to represent Israel at a centennial celebration. As soon as he and his official party had left the airfield, Eichmann and his security kidnappers were smuggled aboard the plane, including a large box into which Eichmann was to be crammed if he resisted. But he was well-doped and didn't come to for hours, although he could walk (like a somnambulist). They refueled at Recife in order to fly from there nonstop to Israel, right across Africa. The Brazilian authorities started red tape proceedings to hold up the plane, but Ben called up their envoy (a woman) and had her instruct the Brazilians to release the plane, which was "diplomatic." He said Eichmann "was yellow" and looked scared silly when he got off here.

The role of an airline in a war is interesting. Ben says the most important thing is the "scramble plan"—how to keep planes from possible destruction. Only two El Al Boeings were held at Lydda when the six-day war started. All the rest were in Athens or other nearby foreign airports. Ambassador Barbour asked if a plane could be assigned for possible emergency evacuation of American families. Yes, said Ben, but he wouldn't say where the plane was—only that it would be ready in twenty-four hours. (Actually it was in Athens.)

Planes were used during the alert period ahead of time to fly in emergency equipment. Above all, huge loads of gasmasks were flown from the U.S.A. and France—because Egypt had mustard gas and nerve gas, which it has used in the Yemen, and was itself taking antigas precautions.

SPETSAIS, GREECE, *September 18, 1969*

Pleasant and interesting holiday interlude this morning. Stavros Niarchos invited me to shoot before breakfast at Spetsopoula, his island across the channel from here. The shooting was lousy (no dove today), but it was lovely and afterward we breakfasted. He showed me his new Picasso (bought three months ago, a fine harlequin), and we had a long chat.

Stravos thinks the junta is in for years provided it doesn't fight within itself. [Stylianos] Pattakos is gaining in strength. He keeps showing himself around the country. He represented Greece at Eisenhower's funeral this year. King Constantine also went and was furious at being given the brush-off by Nixon. He told Stravos that when he shook hands with Nixon he murmured that he hoped to see him afterward. Nixon pretended not to understand. But he received all chiefs of state and heads of mourning missions—including Pattakos.

ATHENS, *September 27, 1969*

This evening I had a chat with Panayotis Canellopoulos (prime minister at the moment of the *coup d'état* in April 1967). Canellopoulos said Papadopoulos made the decision to try and seek power as long ago as 1958.

When General Spandidakis was chief of the army staff, he appointed several people from the junta group to positions around Athens on the assumption that they would be working for his "generals'" coup. They used Spandidakis and merely decided to do themselves what Spandidakis would have done had the king given approval to the plan for a generals' coup.

He thought the U.S.A. begrudgingly supported the junta not because it liked it, but because U.S. policy everywhere is now in a passive phase which prefers to let things lie. He thought Washington should *do* something even at the risk of it proving wrong, in order to give the impression of activity. But the U.S.A. was in an historical phase where it got dragged into things like Vietnam and did not make its own policy decisions. We should be more like the Russians who moved into Hungary and Czechoslovakia brutally but forcibly and faced up to consequences. After all, the

U.S.A. is the head of the free world. It should not intervene in Greece, but it should cut off *all* military aid to this regime which negates democracy.

He said that if the two parties asked Caramanlis to head a transition government to run an election and change the constitution, Greece could be brought back to normal. If the U.S. announced an arms embargo and its readiness to help such an enterprise, both parties would act together.

ATHENS, *September 28, 1969*

This morning I had long talks with two of Greece's best known retired military chieftains. I first went to the humble, little office of Lieutenant General Solon Ghikas, chief of the army general staff until he retired in 1956. His principal importance is as the founder of IDEA, an officers' associaton that dominated the army from the middle of World War II, until the *coup d'état*. IDEA stands for *Ieros* (Holy) *Desmos* (Band) *Ellinon* (Greek) *Axiomatikon* (Officers). Ghikas headed this secret officers' society throughout its existence.

Ghikas said the leading generals had planned their own *coup d'état*. The army feared the communists would gradually take over if the Center Union won the elections scheduled for May 1967. He himself had become convinced of this when he heard a toast to Andreas Papandreou (who was present) at a dinner party to the effect that the Greeks should leave NATO and the Americans would leave Greece. He added: "The danger was great and Andreas was on the verge of taking over."

As a result, the senior officers of the Greek army decided to "interfere" in 1967. The supreme military council, made up of lieutenant generals (highest rank in Greece except for the king) met under the presidency of General Spandidakis in April. Four weeks prior to the May election Andreas Papandreou had announced a preelection mass meeting in Salonika. It was feared a violent demonstration was scheduled to arise from this as an excuse for a leftist take-over. The supreme military council met shortly before the Salonika meeting and discussed the timing of their proposed coup, which would have been on behalf of the king and the conservatives. Opinion was divided. Some generals wanted to act before the Salonika meeting and some afterwards. Lieutenant General George Zoitakis (now regent) insisted they should move before the Salonika meeting. However, the council decided by a majority to interfere only after the meeting. Zoitakis, who at that time commanded the Third Army Corps in Salonika, immediately tipped off the secret colonels' junta of this decision. They struck on April 21. Ghikas said Zoitakis was offered his job as regent as a pay-off. But he told me this job was first offered to him (Ghikas) on the evening of December 13, 1967, after the king had led an unsuccessful counter-coup. Ghikas refused.

I asked how it happened that all the top generals were involved in their own plot and did not know anything about the colonels' plot taking place in their shadow. He said Zoitakis and Spandidakis both knew about the colonels' group, which at one stage was actually conspiring jointly with the generals. Had the generals moved fast enough there would never have been a separate colonels' coup.

He said the main power of the junta plot was the fact that it was protected by Spandidakis and orders were issued in his name which gave the colonels the appearance of authority.

He did not think that divisions inside the junta would influence the situation now. Papadopoulos exaggerates such differences for his own reasons—so he does not have to call elections or ask the king to come back. The slogan of the junior officers in the junta (known as "the captains") is: "No king, no elections, no parties."

He thought any American interference would be ineffective. He did not think it wise for the U.S.A. to cut military aid. Instead, we should give aid and say that we would give still more if Greece became democratic.

I went on to the apartment of Lieutenant General Athanassios Frondistis, former chief of the joint chiefs of staff (therefore outranking the army chief), a position that has now been canceled. Frondistis retired in 1963: a white-haired man with a hearing aid in his left ear. He has an extraordinary kind of lisp and is the only man I ever heard speaking Greek and making it sound like Hungarian.

Frondistis said in 1956, General Nicolopoulos, head of the council, told the other members that he had learned of a group of officers organizing a political plot in the army "along Nasserist lines."

The members of the council, however, were not convinced. Nevertheless, Nicolopoulos named certain officers specifically and Frondistis still remembers that these were headed by Papadopoulos, Makarezos, and Ladas (now prime minister, minister of economic coordination, and one of the chief security bosses).

Two years later Nicolopoulos called a special meeting of the supreme military council, solely to discuss the question of this same group of officers "trying to mix the army into a conspiracy." Nicolopoulos asked the council to retire them. Again the council refused, claiming they had excellent records, and that the evidence was inconclusive. This was one of the main reasons for Nicolopoulos's own resignation in September 1958.

He was succeeded by General Siridakis who dropped the issue entirely. Siridakis was succeeded in 1959 by General Kardamakis who actually promoted the suspects to key positions.

Kardamakis has been rewarded for sheltering the junta during this critical phase and is now head of the national power authority—a cushy job.

At the very beginning the plot's original leader was General Balas. He was succeeded by General Patilis. But, even under these two, Papadopoulos was the guiding genius.

Frondistis says that the junta is disunited now and there are considerable differences among its members. But Papadopoulos is a very subtle operator, manages to reconcile controversies and to keep the confidence of all factions. The army is in bad shape. A junta man is assigned to every important unit commander and has enough power to reverse the commander's decisions. A system almost equivalent to political commissars exists.

ATHENS, *September 29, 1969*

Lunched with Ambassador Sir Michael and Lady Stewart at the British embassy. Torture, he says, is not a systematic instrument of the government, but the use of police is. There is continual arbitrary arrest and intimidation. There are occasional proven cases of torture by electricity but this seems to be the kind of thing done by local, tough policemen who are simply modernizing the old bastinado.

One cannot forget that political prisons and internal exile have long been the custom here. Even under the Papandreou government there were from 900 to 1,000 political prisoners, and today the number has perhaps just about doubled.

He thinks the king's influence has dwindled immensely and that Andreas Papandreou's is about nil. Costa Caramanlis has more influence than any other *émigré* but even he is probably supported by only one-third of the people. The opposition is divided and fragmented both inside Greece and abroad. This is a very effective police regime and the security people probably know what is going on in America, England, France, and Italy among the Greeks just as much as they do here.

U.S. policy should give the Greeks the arms they have been promised, including the heavy equipment that is now being held up, but at the same time we should continue to make plain to the regime that we dislike its ideology and methods. Yet we have to arm it as an ally. After all, it now depends on obsolete M-47 tanks whereas Turkey has 300 M-48s.

The whole eastern Mediterranean area has virtually abandoned parliamentary democracy (except for Israel) so that Greece is not the only sore thumb sticking out. Furthermore, there has been a long tradition here of dictatorship and military *coups d'état*. Now these two trends—the Greek heritage and the eastern Mediterranean tendency—jibe.

2 3

THE KING WHO COOKS

FOR THE FAMILY

YESTERDAY EVENING I WENT OVER FOR A TALK WITH STYLIANOS Pattakos, deputy prime minister, minister of the interior, and one of the three members of the triumvirate at the head of the officers' junta which now runs Greece. When I asked about torture he said: "Both the prime minister and I assert that if anyone can prove that he has been tortured the man who tortured him will be shot in Constitution Square. I told the prime minister that if anyone can prove to me he was violently tortured, I will commit suicide."

AMMAN, *October 6, 1969*

This morning I drove to Jerash with Rafet Ramzi, a Palestinian from Jerusalem. On the way to Jerash we stopped at a Palestinian refugee camp at Bazaa where some 40,000 Palestinian Arabs have been settled since the June 1967 war. They live a dismal life in tin huts and tents with barely adequate food and absolutely no entertainment. The population is made up almost entirely of women, children, and old men. The young men are either on jobs or signed up with the guerrillas.

There were a few guerrillas in battle dress with red berets or in tiger suits carrying their weapons and presumably calling on their families. There are guerrillas all over the place in Jordan: they even have their own representatives at Jordan army road blocks and their own MPs heavily armed and patroling the streets in Amman.

U.S. Ambassador Harrison Symmes told me that since September, because of growing incidents of violence against us, he has been followed by a Land Rover filled with armed Jordanian guards.

The king's writ doesn't run down certain *wadis* and in some regions near the border. The guerrillas levy taxes and many of the villages resent this.

AMMAN, October 7, 1969

Talk with King Hussein in the Basman palace. Just three days ago there had been an attempted coup against Hussein by right-wing Moslem fanatics. The air of anxiety this engendered has not yet fully subsided.

He was wearing a light tan summer battle dress with no decoration except for his pilot wings and with the shoulder insignia of commander-in-chief of Jordan's army. His office is square, with dark walls and several photographs including one of his grandfather, Emir Abdullah.

I started by asking Hussein whether he thought there would be a fourth round of the Palestinian war. He said: "If the situation continues in this area without any real progress brought about by the help of the big powers—on a basis of justice—another explosion is inevitable.

"Our position must remain defensive for a long time. Our army has to build up its strength to avoid the risk of a future disaster. Therefore it will take a considerable period of time in order to reach a military balance between the Arab side and the Israelis."

I asked if his policy remained the same as in 1963 when he preferred not to accept Soviet military equipment. He said: "If I cannot get some material in the West I will have to look for it in the Soviet Union."

I asked, could not an Islamic "Vatican City" be established within the walls of Jerusalem under a religious ruler or committee which would at the same time have temporal authority the way the Pope does inside Rome? Its security, in a police sense, might be arranged by a Turkish guard hired in exactly the same way that the Vatican hires its Swiss guards.

Hussein had no interest in new thoughts. He said the Arab part of Jerusalem—both Moslem and Christian—must continue on the same political basis of administration as the last 1,300 years. He asked: "How far can we go to establish peace? Everything hinges on the 1967 Security Council resolution. Jerusalem is covered by the UN demands for an Israeli withdrawal. Our political and other rights must be recognized in the old city, the Arab city.

"Israel says the issue is security, not annexation. But Jerusalem has been annexed. We insist on freedom of access to the holy places of all who are concerned with their holiness; but politically our rights must be recognized."

I asked if Jordan was interested in trying to gain an outlet to the sea through Gaza, and a corridor across Israel. He was very enthusiastic about this. He said it would have great economic value to Jordan and also "in any future settlement I would like all the Arab Palestinian people to be grouped together under one administration—either Jordanian or Palestinian."

I asked about the relations of his own forces with the guerrillas. He said: "As far as we are concerned, in terms of the West Bank it is Jordan and will be Jordan until it is liberated." (In other words, he does not accept the *Fatah* arguments that the West Bank is "Palestine.") He continued: "But we have a very open mind on what its future will be. Once it is liberated I have every intention of allowing the people living there complete freedom of choice. I intend to offer them a plebiscite on whether they wish to be administered as Jordanians or Palestinians."

I asked if he had any secret contacts with Israel now. Hussein said he had tried secret direct contacts but they had failed.

I told him I felt the only way to imagine peace in the Middle East was by having a compromise settlement imposed by the great powers. Nobody would like the results, which would be bound to be based on concessions, but everybody could use the excuse that there was no choice because the great powers had insisted on it. What did he think?

He said: "We cannot deny that the great powers have the right to do this, because the peace of the world is important. And we would have to accept."

I said I had regretfully noticed a tendency toward the rotting of political structures throughout the Middle East as the extremists assumed more power. He said: "That is right. Things are rotting all over, even in Egypt. Despite our efforts to obtain peace things here are clearly getting worse. This can lead to a blow-up at any time if something is not done. But nobody listens to talk of peace now."

I moved the talk along to his personal life. He told me he often cooked breakfast for his wife and children in the morning. His principal hobbies were swimming, water skiing, and flying. He likes go-carting. He still hopes to go into parachuting. "But I have not gotten into this yet because I cannot afford to break a leg at this stage." He prefers to read political books. He also likes to read detective stories. He is fond of popular music and played the piano as a youngster, but has given it up.

As a final note, he said to me gloomily: "The way things look, I cannot be optimistic. It should be obvious that Israel might have military power now and for some years to come, but it can never become as strong as Nazi Germany and if it follows the same tactics it will eventually wind up in the same way."

BEIRUT, *October 10, 1969*

Spent the day on a trip across Lebanon and into Syria to Krak des Chevaliers, the magnificent castle built by the crusaders north of Tripoli after 1110 and held until the Arabs captured it in 1271: an enormous fortress on a peak, occupying six acres, housing a garrison of 4,000 men and 300 horses. It existed on rain water accumulated in cisterns and it is tragic to see an endless procession of women and girls climbing up nowadays from the village below, bearing jugs or fuel tins on their shoulders, to fill them with dirty water from the castle cisterns and bear them home; there is no water in the village itself.

MOKHTARA, LEBANON, *October 11, 1969*

Lunched today with Kamal Junblatt, the socialist yet feudal Druze chieftain, who is one of Lebanon's best-known politicians. He received me in his manor house just above this little fruit-growing village tucked up in the mountains near Syria. It is a large stone manor (which everyone calls a "castle") the foundations of which were built in the eighteenth century.

Junblatt is a tall, thin, intense man, with long nose, weary eyes, a moustache, brown hair, pale skin. He is cultivated and rather elegant, speaks excellent French, good English. His family came here 250 years ago from Dyarbekir in Turkey, was Kurdish and originated in the Caucasus. They were converted from Islam when they arrived. He said the Druze religion is "the religion of everyday life, not faith." It has no church, is not Islamic, believes in gnostic wisdom, and worships holy or wise men from Pythagoras to Vishnu.

Junblatt told me it is custom (both tribal and family) to give hospitality to any passerby. My chauffeur, who ate in the kitchen, said there were many other strangers at table.

He has the reputation of being far-out left and anti-American. He said the war in Palestine was idiotic and would some day be settled by negotiation; Nasser simply required a small victory first to salvage his pride. He thought the obvious solution was to apply the Lebanese formula in Palestine and establish a binational state of Jews and Arabs, even possibly with a Jewish majority, as Ben-Gurion had once proposed to Abdullah, suggesting that Abdullah should be king.

As for his socialism, he said: "There is a general family of socialism; it seeks to integrate the individual into society. But there are variations in the Middle East. Thus Nasser, as a nationalist, goes back to Hegel. Certainly I am a Marxist. Who cannot be? The first book of Marx was on Heraclitus and his theory that everything in this world is generated by antagonisms, like protons and electrons. Socrates was a Marxist because he used the science of dialectics. Jesus was a Marxist in that sense. Our Socialist party is perhaps nearer to those of India and Burma than any others.

"You Americans lack a comprehensive view of the problems of this part of the world—the Arab problem *and* the Israeli problem. We ask you only to study these problems objectively and make up your own views. But no American has dared to do this since Franklin Roosevelt. The Russians have an objective view. The Soviets like to help all nationalisms and cultures to succeed. They accept the principle of neutralism. Russia doesn't wish Israel wiped out. It accepts its presence. It simply wants to solve the Arab refugee problem, not to wipe out Israel. Your CIA is more powerful than your president. It always seeks to back strong men, meaning the military. It is not helping the people to create democratic conditions. It always goes with the military—even here in Lebanon.

"The United States has lost all its influence in this area, but Soviet influence remains high. Chinese influence is growing, especially with the young. There is no more hope placed here in the United States. People believe that you are governed by the Jews of New York, the CIA, and Caesarist imperial complexes. You regard the whole world as your satellites.

"We don't want to be aligned. But the trend is going toward the Soviets. Even Nasser doesn't want to be aligned. But you are obliging the Arab world to be aligned. Our youngsters are all studying Mao and Guevara."

PARIS, *October 19, 1969*

We dined last night at the Windsors. The poor old duke, who is now seventy-two, is terribly frail. His bad left eye seems to half close and he has such arthritis in his left hip that he limps heavily and uses a cane. Nevertheless, he said he had played nine holes of golf today and was very proud of the fact. He is a tragic little man and I feel much compassion for him and a bit embarrassed to think that I have been so indignant at him, because he clearly doesn't mean any harm. The duchess seems increasingly nervous and sad. She kept telling me during the evening, as she looked across at him: "He had everything—and he gave it all up for me."

When we were smoking a cigar together after dinner, the duke asked me about Greece. He criticized King Constantine and said: "He never should have listened so much to his mother. When I made my big decision I told my brother, my mother, and even my prime minister not to come near me because I didn't want them involved in this. It was my decision. I made it and that's the way it should have been."

The duchess said they had been in Portugal a bit last summer and one thing had struck her, that there were no pansies around. "The whole Mediterranean is filled with fairies nowadays," she said. "Of course, they cluster around rich women because they like a good life and no problems are involved. They are good extra men at dinner and they're almost always intelligent. When the duke complains to me about them, I tell him: 'Don't worry. They'll fly away. And you should listen to them, because they're much brighter than you are!' "

BONN, *October 23, 1969*

Talk with Walter Scheel, the new foreign minister and head of the Free-Democratic faction which stuck by the socialists and allowed Brandt to form a government. Scheel is a fifty-year-old Rhinelander who was a fighter pilot during the war.

I started off by asking Scheel if he didn't in fact think the only solution to the present impasse on German unification was to propose some new version of the old Metternich confederation idea which would allow for cultural relations, a common assembly, a customs union, but separate governments, foreign, and defense policies. I pointed out that in such a loose confederation you could have a NATO West Germany, a Warsaw pact East Germany, and a neutral Austria.

Scheel said today's reality was really not so far from this. There are no customs or trade barriers between East and West. Commerce between them is considered as domestic, not foreign, trade. But the two parts of Germany, while organically one nation, were completely separate societies. It was impossible to recognize the East German state under international law. Both social and foreign policy were wholly different in the two Germanies. Nevertheless, the ultimate result of the long process of normalization might in the end develop toward something like confederation.

BONN, *October 24, 1969*

Breakfast with Herbert Wehner, the tough, sixty-three-year-old Social-Democratic theorist who is generally given credit for the tactics that have finally brought the chancellorship to Brandt. Wehner was a communist and a refugee in Moscow during the Hitler days. He worked with Walter Ulbricht, now the boss of East Germany. During the war Ulbricht, whom Wehner always disliked, sent him on a secret assignment to Germany via Sweden. In Stockholm somebody peached on him and he was arrested and thrown in jail. By the time he came out he was no longer a communist. Wehner has a modest but comfortable bungalow-type house with a little garden. His study was lined with books, including many on painters (like Chagall). He speaks in a deep voice, is extremely verbose. I like him, but had a feeling that here was a man whose heart was more disciplined than his mind.

I asked Wehner if he thought Marxism was *"demodé."* He said: "I'm in politics, not museums. I'm not engaged in ideologies. Ever since the 1959 Godesberg program [when the socialists began to eschew Marxism] my work has been pragmatic. But we must never forget that one-third of the world is Marxist and accepts one or another form of Marxism as a substitute for religion."

His approach to Europe was completely nonideological and "it is not a question of a socialist Europe, only a united Europe. I want a united Europe for its value in itself. But Adenauer wanted Europe to prevent Europe from becoming communist or social-democratic. That approach is nonsense and anyone who thinks that way today belongs in a museum."

It was up to the Germans to devise a policy regulating their relationships with their neighbors without force and based on realities. To do this required a broad consensus. For a long time the "hallucination" remained in Germany that something could be achieved by "one big solution" instead of a series of smaller steps. But he thought a big-solution approach really involved German nationalism—the very thing the Allies were trying to defeat. The Social Democrats—and he kept stressing that they were Social Democrats and not "socialists"—didn't have any ideological approach on this matter.

Wehner said with some satisfaction that Brandt has obtained the support to become chancellor ninety-one years to the day after Bismarck had outlawed socialism in Germany. He expressed confidence that during the next four years (before scheduled elections) the Social Democrats will achieve a broader majority than they now have.

Wehner said: "It is in our interest to get East Germany out of the Soviet empire, but it is in the Soviet interest to keep it in because of its industrial value. Other East European countries, like Ireland, have their own national personality, but East Germany has none. That's why the East Germans have such a hysterical desire for recognition."

BONN, *October 25, 1969*

Had a good talk with Willy Brandt, the new West German chancellor. Brandt is a massive fellow, about six foot one, about 215 pounds, handsome, possessed, standing very straight. He has a very "chancellorial" manner, speaks earnestly and well, but does not give me any impression of brilliance, rather of decency and dignity.

He said there will be no change in relations with NATO, the United States, or closeness to Western Europe.

I told him I was confused by his own recent foreign policy book on the subject of the Oder-Neisse line because this says that frontier doesn't concern West Germany and has been accepted with the East; so therefore, by implication, it has nothing to do with reunification, one way or the other. He said: "We are in no position to move independently of our major partners [U.S.A., Britain, France] on this. Our accord of 1954 with the three powers says a final settlement must await a peace settlement, juridically speaking. Therefore, when I present the case to the Bundestag next week, I shall avoid details on this. I will say that we will respect the territorial integrity of all our neighbors."

On internal reform, he said Germany has the same problems of any industrial society: education, housing, cities, new initiatives in social security. There was the need to improve the efficiency of government administration; also tax reform. He said: "We have much less of a problem with the youthful rebels among students than we had expected. We have a basically critical young generation, especially in the universities. But the extremist influences among them have been greatly reduced."

At this point, Brandt said the philosophical importance of his regime was a major matter. He added: "I want, in a peaceful and understanding way, to make it clear that Hitler has been conquered not only by external military power but by his own people. I want to make the foundations of parliamentary democracy still safer."

He talked a bit about democratization, saying that one of Adenauer's great achievements was his "willingness to gain time" by allowing tensions to subside and sifting out the genuine non-Nazis from Nazis in a dominantly Nazi Germany. He continued: "We have gained time. So many new people have come on to the scene that you don't risk dealing with the 1933–45 events and have them feel they were personally involved."

Brandt said his goal was a United States of Europe but this couldn't develop in the same way as a United States of America. It couldn't be a "melting pot," but had to be based on "Europe's existing nations."

He had no intention of asking for a truce from his CDU [Christian Democratic Union] opponents. He thought their most important leader would probably be Rainer Barzel because he had been elected by both the CDU and CSU [Christian Socialist Union–Strauss' faction] as chief of the parliamentary opposition for the next four years. The opposition would probably start out by being belligerent and nationalistic.

Paris, *November 5, 1969*

We dined last night in the Bank of France at the invitation of Olivier Wormser, now governor of the bank. The governor's private quarters are in the early eighteenth-century building (the palace of the Comte de Toulouse, bastard son of Louis XIV by Madame de Montespan), which contain a long, high, Baroque gallery, one of the most famous rooms in Europe. The brass doorknobs bear the royal seal of three *fleur-de-lis* with the bar sinister of bastardy stamped between them. The building was taken over by the bank in 1806, when its first governor was named.

Paris, *November 12, 1969*

Yesterday Chip and Avis Bohlen flew in for a brief visit and we dined *à quatre*. When we were talking about American foreign policy, Chip said Korea was the big point of change. When we agreed to accept a stalemate solution there, Europe immediately understood that America was shifting and that its firmness in overseas commitments was declining.

He says Averell Harriman is now saying that he had "peace in my grasp" toward the end of the period while he was head of our delegation to the Paris Vietnam talks. When Mac Bundy heard about it, he telephoned Lyndon Johnson, who blew up and said: "If the son-of-a-bitch had peace in his grasp, he never told me about it."

PARIS, *November 13, 1969*

Spent two hours with Foreign Minister Maurice Schumann, lunching with him *en tête-à-tête* in his private apartment at the *Quai d'Orsay*. I was taken immediately to a small waiting room and a butler gave me a whisky and soda.

Schumann came in as I was looking at an icon of three saints with old Slavonic writing describing it as the Holy Trinity. "I was given that when I visited Zagorsk last month," Schumann said proudly.

After lunch we returned to the little salon for coffee and cigars.

I asked Schumann what was the exact role of Jean Sainteny as a go-between from Nixon to Ho Chi Minh. He said: "I appointed Sainteny to represent France. And I suggested to Nixon that he would be a good man to carry any messages. This was entirely done at my initiative. I saw Sainteny both before and after he went to Hanoi and he reported to me. He went as the official envoy of France."

"Well," I asked, "if he was your envoy, he surely told you all about the Nixon–Ho exchange."

"No, he told me nothing. But this merely proves he is an honorable man who can keep a secret. And I can assure you I saw him right after he came back from the funeral."

"But," I remonstrated, "I knew that Sainteny had represented France at Ho's funeral, but I assumed he had gone to Hanoi before the funeral also because President Nixon obviously can't carry on a correspondence with a dead man, and Ho's letter to him was dated before Ho died." Schumann looked puzzled.

I asked if France was eager to join with Britain in creation of a European nuclear force. He said Britain seemed uninterested. The position of France foresaw the possibility of "cooperation" between two national nuclear forces, French and British. But there was no thought of joining them. He went on to say that not a single nuclear weapon in the whole world was "integrated."

The British had made no approach to France on this subject since just before the Nassau talks in 1962. It had been discussed between Macmillan and de Gaulle at that time, although there has been some disagreement since as to whether Macmillan did or did not promise to report to de Gaulle on the Nassau decisions.

I asked if he thought Britain would be prepared to pay the full price of

Common Market entry by accepting all the necessary conditions. He said: "I have no doubt that Britain will want to get in as Britain realizes increasingly that the United States wishes to disentangle from Europe— not from its commitments here but from Europe [whatever that means]. Once Britain realizes that, it will recognize that it must bridge the .gap, but that is a long process."

He confirmed that Israel had presented a shopping list to France trying to get spare parts and weapons other than the embargoed Mirages. He added: "I am surprised that you know about this, because it is supposed to be very secret." The only condition attached by France was that Israel should take a "positive" attitude to four-power negotiations.

He was confident Israel was not manufacturing atomic weapons but "if the Jews decide to do this, I would be the last person they would tell." He then went on to say that the "large size" of Israel today jeopardizes its security instead of helping it. Once Israel recognizes that it cannot occupy the conquered territories forever but that it can perhaps leave with a deal guaranteeing its borders, the outlines of peace can be arranged.

Ben-Gurion was the only figure of public stature in Israel who recognized this. He then went on to draw comparisons between the politically exiled Ben-Gurion and the politically exiled de Gaulle.

PARIS, *November 14, 1969*

Long luncheon with Michel Jobert, secretary-general of the Élysée. Jobert is a frail, short, thin, intense-looking man of forty-eight.

He thought de Gaulle had been completely square with Soames early this year when the famous incident arose in which the British put out the story that the General was trying to negotiate with London behind the backs of his Common Market partners. Jobert thought Soames was simply unused to the vague and elliptical language habitual to de Gaulle.

He told me Pompidou had completely written the manuscript of a book on how the French people could be governed in modern days with the idea of publishing it this year, but now the project had been shelved. The book was especially interesting on the events of May 1968.

Seven years ago, Pompidou was a terrible speaker—so bad that it was a joke with his staff. But now he enjoys speaking. He does not employ ghosts and writes original drafts himself. Then the draft goes out for criticism, which he is happy to receive so long as there are positive suggestions.

The president really enjoys shooting now. He took it up late in life and was very bad at first, but has definitely improved. Incidentally, Pompidou had to give up smoking his favorite cigarettes, Winstons, because they are American-made and for political reasons he was advised to smoke French cigarettes.

PARIS, *November 15, 1969*

We gave a large dinner party for eighteen people, among them the Couve de Murvilles, André Malraux, the Bohlens, the Bentincks (Dutch ambassador), the Clermont-Tonnerres, the Van der Kemps (he is curator of Versailles), etc. The guests were startled to see armed guards patroling outside our house. It happened to be a day when violent anti-American demonstrations (because of Vietnam) were expected throughout Paris.

Malraux told me now that de Gaulle is writing two books. One is volume four of his memoirs and one is called *History and Policy* and deals with the contemporary art of governance. Malraux has given me so many versions of what de Gaulle is up to and how many books he's writing that I am a bit sceptical. Malraux observed that great painters and sculptors can continue to work well and with originality until they are eighty or ninety years old but writers age much more rapidly because the brain is unable to create words well after a certain time.

Couve said he didn't feel democracy is a workable system any longer because of the impact and frequent misuse of radio and television. These had taken over the old "town-meeting" functions of democracy and distorted it.

Malraux made some interesting comments about Alexander the Great. He said he was a born myth-maker He was a great warrior and he died young (something Malraux considered desirable forty years ago when he observed that he had no fear of death, but was frightened of reaching the age of fifty). The only thing lacking in Alexander's life was a great love, an Iseult.

PARIS, *November 20, 1969*

I attended a luncheon given by Wilfrid Baumgartner, former governor of the Bank of France.

I sat across from General Beaufre and remarked to him that he has gotten a new neighbor since I last saw him (he lives across the street from the Élysée Palace). "Yes," said he. "Louis Philippe instead of Louis XIV."

Antediluvian but highly agreeable dinner at the [Carl Henrik] von Platens'. He is the energetic and pleasant Swedish ambassador to the OECD [Organization for Economic Cooperation and Development] and his wife is a really striking black-haired beauty with exquisitely chiseled features.

The dinner was in honor of the Duke and Duchess of Windsor and included Princess Bismarck and her lovely blonde daughter, and assorted bankers. Marina told me she overheard Windsor turn to his neighbor at table and ask: "Do you know her husband? He is one of the most brilliant men of our generation."

Windsor was very worried about the moratorium demonstrations against Vietnam in the United States and compared American unpopularity on the Vietnam war with British unpopularity during the Boer war. He went on with the curious statement: "You know we fought the Boer war for the Jews—not the Jewish people but the Jewish industrialists." He said the dislike for Britain engendered by the Boer war had put off for some years the achievement of the *entente cordiale* between London and Paris. He added: "You know, my grandfather [King Edward VII] did a great deal to help things along when he came to Paris on his famous visit and he signed his name 'Edouard' instead of 'Edward'."

Before World War I the Duke used to like shooting a good deal, but did it very rarely after the war "because I saw what killing is." He continues to shoot birds "but only social shooting; I don't really like it any more and I prefer to take pictures of game."

He was indignant with the Duke of Edinburgh for his statement (over American television) about the bad condition of the royal finances. It was a mistake to talk about this in the United States and it was tactless to say he feared he might have to give up polo. "Who cares?" asked Windsor. "Nobody plays polo any more. If he had said he might have to give up golf—that would be different."

PARIS, *November 21, 1969*

Lunched with Wilfred Burchett today. Burchett, an Australian communist, came back to Paris last month from a visit to North Korea and China. He is here on some kind of unofficial but definite connection with the North Vietnamese delegation.

He said that the Chinese have a suspicion Russia started its negotiations with China on frontier questions in order to improve its own negotiating position vis-à-vis the United States at the SALT talks.

STOCKHOLM, *November 24, 1969*

This morning was gleamy, bright winter: cobalt blue sky, snow-lace on the trees, and snow lying clean on the ground. The girls stride smartly in short furs and long woolly stockings; occasionally a man glides through the drifts on skis; the policemen look more like commandos than cops.

There have been 360 U.S. deserters admitted here; some have given themselves up to U.S. authorities afterwards. Of the remainder, some are draft dodgers and about 200 are real deserters. A local "American deserters committee" speaks for them in propaganda and the Swedish government has designated an official to oversee their welfare. They come in on "humanitarian grounds," but most refuse to learn Swedish and can't support themselves.

I spent two hours with Olaf Palme, the astonishingly young looking new prime minister of Sweden. He is forty-two but looks twenty-eight: small, frail, with pale face, sensual mouth, somewhat fishy eyes.

I asked Palme why relations between the U.S.A. and Sweden were so bad. He said: "On a per capita basis we are the largest customer of the United States. It is only on Vietnam that we haven't agreed."

Palme said Sweden began to take a sharper view on Vietnam after the U.S. bombings of the north began in February 1965. It was felt Sweden should speak up on the attitude to be taken toward small nations. There has been hardly anything said since the bombing stopped. But certain "issues" were developed since then.

The first was that of the deserters. "According to our laws and traditions we must accept them—as we took in French deserters from the Algerian war during the fifties."

The second issue was the recognition of Hanoi. But, he said: "This was done according to our principle of recognizing any regime which controls the territory it rules."

Palme said: "The wish of the United States was to go to Vietnam to promote democracy and social progress. But the fate of the United States has been to become a remnant of the old colonial system. That is the tragedy.

"We have been careful about giving concrete advice but you can't expect us to say: 'War in Vietnam is all right; we're for it.' What kind of friendship does the United States want? Is it a token of friendship to agree with all American foreign policy just because it is an enormously powerful country?"

Palme said of ideology: "Sweden is far from being a socialist country. But in important aspects we have changed society. We have built up welfare, housing, labor unions, education. We don't do things for the sake of power but in order to achieve certain social ends.

"The old dream was that everything could be solved by increasing production but experience has shown it is the other way round. High production brings greater gaps in wealth and the social problems of slums and ghettos. This fate is now coming to all industrial countries. It will be the great issue of the 1970s everywhere. We must see to it that there is greater equality in wages, housing, education. We must steer technological development, not be its victim. One way to do this is to activate people. You can't argue with a computer."

I pushed through the snow on a late, dark afternoon past the opera house, surrounded by glittering torches, to the Enskilda Bank, a handsome

Florentine building which has the ultimate chic for a bank—no name on the door. There I had an appointment with Marcus Wallenberg, the seventy-year-old former managing director and one of the biggest business-men in Sweden.

Wallenberg is a massive fellow, healthy and brisk for his age He came from a conservative, wealthy background, but turned "leftward" while he was in the United States during a year in college. He knew Olaf (the prime minister) as a boy and recognized him as a "political animal." Olaf himself married a girl from the old Swedish nobility—but she is very radical.

He says there is undoubted dissatisfaction in the country. There is a tradition of jealousy over unequal pay. But his family was an example of a self-made family and what should be accomplished in Sweden. He comes from the third generation. All sixteen boards on which he is a member are businesses which his family either started or reorganized. His grand-father was a sailor (the son of a poor fisherman) who was in New York in 1837 during the bank crash. This had interested him and so he (the grandfather) bought books on banking and read them aboard ship. He became a banker.

STOCKHOLM, *November 25, 1969*

Useful talk with Arne Geijer, head of the LO (national trade-union federation) for thirteen years.

Geijer is irked by the government's tactlessness to the U.S.A. on North Vietnam and said he could understand why American stevedores wished to boycott Swedish ships, because nobody wanted others poking their noses into private affairs.

One secret of Sweden's success was that the people had learned they must work if they are to improve their condition. They built their own organizations—like labor unions—early. From the start the unions were critical of society because there was too much poverty. But this criticism helped direct the national effort.

There had been much criticism of Swedish capitalists from youth groups, also from radical intellectuals among the social democrats. But there was less of such criticism inside the unions. "We can't solve our problems by socializing the Wallenbergs," he said. "We have to work together.

"The capitalists have evolved a lot during my time. There is a more liberal and reasonable attitude among company heads. Both capitalists and labor leaders can be tough and hard. But we both know we need each other and have to negotiate agreements."

Long talk with Jacob Wallenberg, the elder of Sweden's famous brothers. He is seventy-seven and must have been a huge man once: a handsome, tough, confident man who is chairman of the Enskilda Bank, central point of the family's immense holdings.

The most interesting part of our talk dealt with Germany. Common legend has it that Jacob kept up the contacts with the Germans and Marcus with the Allies, during World War II. In any case, Jacob represented Sweden on economic negotiations with Germany until the end of 1943.

He went to Germany often. He was a special friend of Karl Goerdeler, former mayor of Leipzig, one of the main anti-Hitler conspirators, finally hanged for his role in the July 20, 1944, plot. Goerdeler argued that only the army could take action and so long as it was winning it wouldn't. The trouble was, says Wallenberg, the army had no conspiratorial talents and even the July 20 plotters forgot to cut the main telephone lines.

In 1943 in Germany he was visited by a man he knew and they carefully chatted in the middle of a hotel lobby to avoid police bugs. His visitor inquired discreetly whether W. thought the Allies would be prepared to negotiate a peace with Himmler if Hitler were dead. W. says: "I knew then immediately that Himmler was ready to murder Hitler." He told the agent the Allies detested Himmler almost as much as Hitler.

Late in 1944, it was suggested he go to Germany and see Himmler. It was hinted he might save the life of Goerdeler, who had by then been imprisoned but had not yet been hanged. A German he knew hinted that Himmler was ready for a deal: Goerdeler's life would be spared if, after Himmler put Hitler out of the way, the Allies would deal with him. W. felt he couldn't pass on such a proposal.

His last wartime contact was just before the war ended, when a Hamburg friend asked him to urge the British and Americans to move speedily into Hamburg because Kaufmann, the gauleiter, had promised there would be no resistance and was afraid the Russians would move in otherwise. W. did pass on this message. The English commanding general moved too slowly to test the nonresistance pledge.

HELSINKI, *November 27, 1969*

Pleasant lunch with Tommy [Ambassador Llewellyn] Thompson, who is here as a kind of ex officio expert adviser to the U.S. delegation at SALT (Strategic Arms Limitation Talks) with Russia.

The Russians in the past have always negotiated for victory rather than agreement, and we hope that here they will show more sophistication. The start has been good. But Semyonov, the Soviet delegation chief, has little experience in this field.

Slowly most communist states are learning they cannot deal with economic problems without facing ultimate political consequences. This is one of the influences inside the Soviet Union and is indirectly mirrored in the attitude to SALT. Internal forces in both Russia and the United States call for an agreement here. Russia's growth rate is slowing. There are internal economic pressures to save money on both sides.

To date, in the arms race, each side exaggerates the other's progress and then over-reacts. Russia, furthermore, is sensitive to suggestions that it can't afford to continue the arms race. On both sides there are military cliques that want to keep arming levels up and economic cliques who want to cut them.

Ultimately these negotiations are really condemned to succeed. There is no "linkage" here to problems in other, nonweapons fields. However, if you solve one world question it naturally affects others. If there were a Middle East or Vietnam settlement, things would be easier for SALT.

Tommy doesn't think the Russians have done anything to help us on Vietnam since the early days of getting agreement on the shape of the negotiating table—despite Harriman's insistence that the only way to end the war was by Soviet assistance diplomatically.

HELSINKI, *November 28, 1969*

President Urho Kaleva Kekkonen received me this afternoon out at his suburban residence on an arm of the Gulf of Finland, a modest villa left to the state in 1940 by a wealthy publisher. There are pleasant grounds filled with pheasants, a sauna and swimming pool, and only a small dining room, small sitting room, and large reception room downstairs.

Kekkonen, who is in his third term, is sixty-nine, about six feet tall, strongly built, with bald (and totally shaven) head, and pink complexion. He wears thick glasses behind which gleam shrewd eyes. He is a lawyer, comes from a poor family (lumberjack foreman's son) in Pielavasi, well north of here.

I inquired if he thought it possible that the existing kind of relationship between Finland and Russia might some day extend southwards into East Europe; that is to say close relationships but a noncommunist social system. He considered it difficult to imagine how the "East European socialist countries" could develop social and economic systems like Finland's, which was, after all, essentially Western.

He couldn't believe free enterprise could return to East Europe. Nevertheless, it was clear that if military blocs did disappear it would become less important for the Soviet Union to worry about the security of Czechoslovakia or East Germany, for example.

Competition between the "socialist" and capitalist systems would continue. But it would no longer be flavored by military fear and therefore would develop more peaceful forms.

The methods of capitalism and communism differ on who should own the means of production—private sources or the state. It was impossible to think of the existing communist system being changed by the reestablishment of private industry. But we already see how the communist countries have been trying out a free market economy.

To sum up Kekkonen said: "It is possible to have communism and capitalism coexist peacefully and effectively yet without either changing its system—along the same lines which developed over the centuries between Christianity and Islam."

I remarked that some people called Finnish policy "neutral in peace but not in war," referring to the bilateral consultation treaty with Moscow. He said Finland wanted neutrality in both peacetime and wartime.

I asked if he thought that in some respects Finland's position might be compared with Austria's. He said rather stiffly that there was a big difference: Finland's neutrality was by national wish and desired by all Finns; Austria's had been imposed by the peace treaty.

He observed that "Western circles" say Finland is now working for Soviet interests. Here Kekkonen is indeed right because he has been designated by some as a Soviet "agent of influence." But, he said, "If we pursue a policy in our own national interests we cannot abandon it just because others complain that it might be in Soviet interests."

He didn't want to create the impression that Finland was urging Norway and Denmark to leave NATO. After all, that was their business.

I reminded him that President Paasikivi had told me in 1949: "Our position has always been and of course remains pro-Western despite our geographic proximity to Russia." Was that still the case? It hasn't changed, he said.

PARIS, *December 5, 1969*

Lunched with Henri Froment-Meurice, chief of the Asian section of the *Quai d'Orsay*.

The Chinese feel they could improve relationships with the United States by offering us in China a role somewhat comparable to that now played by Japan. In other words, there would be no question of diplomatic relations but there would be de facto recognition, exchange of cultural, business, and journalistic visits, and the opening up of Chinese markets to American enterprise—the way that they have already been opened up for some years to Japanese enterprise.

The Chinese do not pose as a necessary precondition that America "de-recognize" or hand over Taiwan (Formosa). What they do wish is the removal from Taiwan of the very small number of American army ground forces and the declaration by both Washington and Peking of the intent that force will not be used by either side to settle the Taiwan-Formosa question.

The Chinese have a deep suspicion that what the SALT talks seek is an implicit accord by which Russia and the United States of America will stop aiming long-range missiles at each other across the Atlantic and Europe, but will both continue to aim long-range missiles at China.

Incidentally, I asked how the story started that Sainteny had been Nixon's go-between with Ho. He said the word got around that the contact was someone who had known Ho for almost a quarter of a century. Froment-Meurice personally thought it was probably Herbert Marcović, a French scientist who has been playing a leading role in the Pugwash conferences where intellectuals of East and West meet regularly under the auspices of Cyrus Eaton.

PARIS, *December 6, 1969*

On November 10, I wrote to President Truman because of my increasing concern with the revolt against President Nixon by both Congress and the people, which, I think, would frustrate the president's constitutional powers as chief executive. I attach herewith quotes from his reply.

> The framers of the Constitution were clearly circumspect in being too definitive about the role of the President. In the critical and sensitive area of foreign policy the President had the responsibility. In the matter of national security he was designated as Commander-in-chief. The provision for advice and consent, I believe, is concerned with keeping the Congress fully informed on all decisions and commitments of the Chief Executive.

> Even under our carefully guarded system of power vested rather than imposed, as a practical matter, someone has to be in charge. Someone has to make decisions—and that someone is the President.

> It goes without saying, that under our system the President must keep the people fully informed in all matters that touch on their lives, and he must schedule regular press conferences to give a continuing account of his stewardship—as well as to learn of what is troubling them by the questions put to him by the press.

> A President who fails to communicate with the people forthrightly and courageously, runs the risk of fostering a public detachment or, what could be even worse, a loss of public confidence.

> Presidents from the time of George Washington have been subjected to attacks and abuse. It is a way that a free and open society keeps its government institutions on the alert. It is a small price to pay for an aroused and active public opinion.

PARIS, *December 10, 1969*

Yesterday in the late afternoon, I went over to see Jean Monnet, elated because this month's Common Market meeting finally prevailed upon the French to agree to negotiations for Britain's entry.

He said: "Europe needs Britain and Britain needs Europe. We would not be working so toward unity were we not pressed by necessity. The best partner of Europe is necessity."

LONDON, *December 11, 1969*

Lunched with Denis Healey, defense minister and an excellent fellow. Denis thinks it's a mistake to mix up alliance and friendship with Greece. It would be all right to bounce it from the Council of Europe but inside NATO it should receive all modern arms it needs—as an ally—that is, all arms except what could patently be used against civilian opposition.

Denis is impressed by Laird, says Laird is clearly committed to withdrawal from Vietnam. He also liked Clark Clifford a lot: "Your best equivalent of a Whig gentleman." Clifford has a heart. The trouble with Bob McNamara was that he didn't have a heart ("at least not a human one") and mechanically quantified everything. As for Nixon, Healey spoke of him with respect and added wrily, "You know, he just isn't as bad as many Americans think he is."

Denis feels it would be useful to have some kind of European nuclear force. But this is very tricky. Healey has worked hard to build military confidence in Germany. The political aspects of this project—especially in Germany—are very delicate. One would want German "encouragement" for such a project and not just German "acquiescence." It would also require U S. "acquiescence."

This afternoon I called on Edward (Ted) Heath, leader of the Conservative party, chief of the opposition. We started by chatting about Britain and the Common Market in the light of the recent Hague summit meeting which decided to negotiate on British admission. Heath said he wasn't yet "at all convinced" that it was going to be smooth sailing. "Things are on the move," he said, "but it will take a long time."

The big thing is that "French policy has opened up." Britain will have to accept not only the Rome treaty terms but later actions on economic and monetary questions.

Public opinion here had been getting negative because things took so long and Britain was twice rebuffed. There were things on the Continent the British had disliked—French student riots in 1968; Italy's government crisis of 1969. Also, the British feared the impact of the Market on their cost of living. Britain's currency devaluation had made for a greater gap in prices.

Heath didn't think joining the Market would affect Britain's basic foreign policy. He quipped that "This government hasn't much of a foreign policy anyway as far as the United States is concerned." He added: "For us, Europe depends on the U.S. deterrent."

He thought British membership of EEC would be a "fulfillment" of Britain's interests, which have changed in recent years. "The modern way to deal with a large power next door to you is by a new grouping." He also thought that in EEC Britain would come into closer contact with a larger element of the developing world—Francophone and Belgian Africa, above all.

If membership in EEC resulted in strengthening Britain's economy, Britain would have a better chance (as the Tories have promised) to keep a position in Singapore and Malaysia. It would help maintain a "concrete presence" east of Suez, which would in turn "tighten relations" with the U.S.A.

PARIS, *December 19, 1969*

Last night at Bob Blake's (U.S. minister) where we dined, there was much interest in the report that France is selling $400 million of armaments to Libya, including 50 Mirages and 200 heavy tanks; also that France is going to move into Wheelus Field when the Americans evacuate.

I told Jacques de Beaumarchais that I thought this might, if true, seriously tarnish President Pompidou's visit to the United States in February.

PARIS, *December 25, 1969*

We went to a midnight mass Ambassador Shriver had arranged for about three hundred people in the Sainte Chapelle and then some twenty of us went on to his house for a late caviar supper. The mass was absolutely beautiful—above all the glowing Sainte Chapelle. It had been specially fixed up with search lights outside shining in so that all the windows were glowing simultaneously.

Père Raymond Bruckberger was one of the two officiating priests and afterward at supper he said the Sainte Chapelle had not been used for a mass since before the French revolution. The last king who had worshipped there was Louis XIV because his successors—until the revolution—went to church in Versailles. It was undoubtedly the first mass at Sainte Chapelle in all history that was partially in English.

The fifteen-year-old Shriver boy who had been an altar boy during the service helped the servants at supper and got all flustered with the champagne, pouring it all over Marcellin (interior minister). He was so embarrassed that he said "*merde*."

Lunch with Sargent Shriver. He hopes to win the Democratic nomination for governor of Maryland, to win the election, and to go on in 1972 to win the Democratic nomination for the presidency and move into the White House. He says his ambition is not for power itself, but in order to assume direction of government policy and channel its principal emphasis along internal lines, particularly social reform to eliminate poverty and hunger.

He points out that his luck here has been extraordinary. No ambassador has had the distinction of receiving a United States president in Paris and then going back to Washington to help in the reception of a French president there. Once Pompidou's visit (commencing next month) has ended, he will have accomplished the basic purpose of his mission—to improve relationships.

Shriver was born in 1915. If he is going to move forward into national politics, he must make his move now. Had [John F.] Kennedy (his brother-in-law) not run for president in 1960, he might have stayed on in Illinois to run for governor. Instead, he took time off to organize Illinois and Wisconsin for Kennedy. His real home state is Maryland.

He says that he first went to Washington with the intention of working for the United States government and not for Kennedy, Johnson, or Nixon. Some of the Kennedy people are hostile to him because he stayed on to work for Johnson and then for Nixon but he says they are primarily people he wouldn't want to have around him anyway if he achieves his goal.

PARIS, *January 19, 1970*

Lunch with General Pierre Gallois. His mind always strikes up sparks.

The French recognized that despite the enormous superiority in the Mediterranean of the United States Sixth Fleet, American policy was unable to prevent Russian penetration, and the landlocked sea is now shared by Moscow and Washington. This is the basic consequence of the six-day war. The Russians have steadily increased their importance in the Mediterranean and, moreover, they have been invited in by the Arabs. The United States can do nothing about this.

A concomitant is the following. The more aggressive the Israelis are, the more frightened the Arabs become and the more they request weapons from Moscow. And the more weapons Moscow supplies, the more concessions it asks and the greater Soviet presence in the Mediterranean becomes. If they send out arms to the Arabs, the Russians also send out more and more training missions, technicians, and propagandists, therefore increasing their role in the Mediterranean littoral.

Russian penetration of the Mediterranean increases steadily and all the Arab world is slowly being infiltrated. Thus, for example, there are even Soviet teachers in certain Algerian schools. The Arabs don't really like the Russians very much but they feel the need of their weapons.

Commercially Moscow is gaining a stranglehold on the principal source of petroleum for all Western Europe. Eventually, the Russians will be able to control marketing of the principal fuel for European industry. Europe cannot escape its dependence on Arab oil and the Kremlin is gaining control of the spigot which turns it on and off.

For twenty years the French had been told that the power of the Sixth Fleet would safeguard the Mediterranean against the Russians. But this has proven meaningless. After all, when Washington still dominated the Mediterranean and Israel had smashed the Arabs, the Russians moved in undisturbed. This showed that the problem is political and not military, and that military assets cannot be relied upon to achieve political objectives.

French policy is quite clearly that alternatives to total reliance on Russia must be offered to the most strategically placed Arab countries. As things are now, the Mediterranean is politically virtually lost. When Tito dies, the Russians are going to exploit centrifugal forces in Jugoslavia and may very well attempt a coup in Albania in order to establish a naval base and harbor on the eastern Mediterranean.

The United States has consistently made the mistake of warning the Arabs that the only alternative to American military help is Russian military help. Now France is really moving into Libya. Its real mission goes far beyond the Mirages; it is to create a Libyan air force and army which will be trained by the French who will provide the technicians to man radar installations and keep the planes flying. The Mirages Libya is buying won't arrive for a long time. Dassault's production runs at a maximum of ten planes a month.

PARIS, *January 20, 1970*

It had been quite a while since I saw Jean-Marie Soutou, so I arranged lunch with him today and, as always, it was agreeable and stimulating. He is one of the last men in the upper echelons in the *Quai d'Orsay* with serious intellectual value.

The *Quai* had recommended that not more than ten to fifteen Mirages should be sold to Libya and Schumann endorsed this. The *Quai* was overruled by Pompidou.

Soutou thinks that ultimately Moscow and Washington must agree on an imposed Palestine settlement along the following lines: Israel's return to the 1967 frontiers; internationalization of the Gaza strip under the U.N.; a demilitarized Cis-Jordan; minor frontier rectifications; demilitarization of the entire Golan area. This would be accompanied by a temporary,

makeshift formula on Jerusalem and the pretense of a refugee resettle-
ment formula which would be only gradually applied and never fully
carried out, but which would allow the Arabs to announce success on this
point.

Soutou made a most profound remark at the end. He said that the
French people had shown enormous wisdom by choosing a Gaullist to
liquidate Gaullism. Had Poher been elected president instead of Pompidou, there would already be chaos and he would be opposed on everything by the great majority, including the communists and the Gaullists.

PARIS, *January 21, 1970*

I lunched with Walter Eytan, the Israeli ambassador. He told me more
than 100 Mirages will be going to Libya—more than double the 50
originally announced by the French. Clearly, they will all come under
Nasser. If the French can't control the departure of [Israeli] torpedo boats
from Cherbourg, how can they control the dispatch of planes not in their
hands and 1,500 miles away?

ROME, *January 31, 1970*

Graham Martin, U S. ambassador reminded me that Italy is a nation
only one hundred years old, patched together from regions with varying
conditions of tradition. There is also a tradition of maneuver and a real
influence of Byzantium. There is a great heritage of individualism, which
also facilitates this instinct for maneuver. All these things have left their
mark.

To the outsider there appears to be enormous confusion; but, in fact, it
is surprising how solidly democratic Italy remains. In a sense, one might
make a parallel with Rome's automobile traffic. There is a rhythm to the
apparent chaos. All drivers obey the same ultimate basic rules, and there
is no final disaster despite the widespread minor infractions, such as illegal
blowing of horns and double-parking. When it comes to the point of colli-
sion, the Italian drivers refrain. Their instinct for survival avoids the final
confrontation.

One must never forget that during the last one hundred years we have
seen the only period when modern Italy has even remotely resembled a
unitary state, bringing together such contrasting regions as Lombardy and
Sicily.

Despite the absence of government, there has been a fantastic economic
performance. At times during the 1960s, the growth rate here increased
to a degree second only to that of Japan. Of course, the south still lags.
But Italy has handled a massive internal migration remarkably well.
Approximately three million people have moved from the agricultural
south to the industrial north.

ROME, *February 2, 1970*

Luigi Barzini gave a dinner party tonight including Franco Restivo, the minister of the interior.

Restivo, a plump bespectacled little Sicilian, has a reputation for being effective and tough. He says there is no reason to worry about a possible *coup d'état* or paramilitary attempt in Italy. There is neither a man to lead this nor a public opinion prepared to tolerate it. He told me documents purporting to link some Italians with the Greek colonels were forged.

Dined last night with the Jozsef Szalls (Hungarian ambassador). Jozsef is a disappointed revolutionist. He says Kadar is a decent but weak man. Things are going downhill, and the Russians are destroying all vestiges of liberalism. He observed ruefully: "You know, we were under the Turks for 150 years. A new Turkish period is starting."

He sees his ultimate choice as prison or defection. I warned him strongly against defection, pointing out how *déraciné* all exiles get.

2 4

COMMUNISM CHANGES

ITS TAILOR IN ITALY

WENT OUT FOR DRINKS WITH KING CONSTANTINE IN HIS comfortable villa just beyond Rome. He looked pale and nervous.

He is browned off with the United States, and felt slighted by President Nixon when he was in Washington for Eisenhower's funeral. He is told by his friends in Greece that there is a growing conviction the United States no longer "supports democracy" and, when I objected, he said, "Well, I don't agree but even I have a mini-suspicion." He doesn't think the U.S. should embargo arms to Greece and has told us so twice. His view is that Greece merits heavy weapons as an ally for the defense of the West, but we should be careful, in sending them, not to imply approval of the regime and also not to send light weapons that might be used in civil action.

The U.S.A. could exert moral and economic pressure and, although the colonels try to blackmail us with the idea, it is most unlikely they would dare any serious flirtation with the communists because too many serving officers fought the communists in the civil war and remember the savagery.

He thinks there should be a political committee abroad to indicate the existence of some kind of alternative; but not a "government in exile." He can do nothing himself because he is king of all Greeks and must not actively interfere.

He would like very much to go to the U.S.A. and have informal talks with leaders like Nixon, Rogers, and Kissinger but doesn't know how to arrange such a trip and fears he would be ignored. The colonels are trying to stay on indefinitely and he hasn't even begun any negotiations on his own return. He clearly hasn't made up his mind just what to do if things reach that state—as he disapproves of their ideas but wants to go back and would like to help restore "legality."

He thought it had been a mistake for Caramanlis to call for a military uprising, which clearly wasn't going to happen, although many Greeks suspected for a short while there had been a deal with or signal from the U.S.A. The king opposed violence and bloodshed and had no desire to be vindictive toward the colonels if and when he got back.

I observed there was a danger Papadopoulos would take a leaf from Franco's book and delay action on the royal question until the crown prince was of age. Constantine nodded sadly. At the very best he thought there couldn't even be a start to any solution—not even tentative negotiations—for from two to five more years.

He is a nice fellow and a decent one with lots of common sense. But I fear he is not a lucky man and in his business luck counts even more than in mine.

ROME, *February 4, 1970*

This morning I saw President Giuseppe Saragat in the Quirinale. I am always interested to proceed through that gloomy palace, where I saw Italy's last king and all the presidents who have succeeded him. It is still featured by long, hostile corridors, and huge guards wearing nineteenth-century Hussar helmets.

Although almost seventy-two, Saragat is a big, healthy-looking Piedmontese. Since he became president six years ago he has taken up bird shooting, and spends most of his free time at the presidential country estate near Ostia. He is an agreeable man, with spectacles and informal manner, who converses easily in French.

He said there was no doubt that Italy continues to move gradually leftward, but the problem is to carry on with this trend while at the same time avoiding the danger of communist bureaucratic dictatorship.

The communists, he said, represent about one-third of Italy's population. It is necessary to avoid the danger of being engulfed by their power, in order to keep national liberty. This has been the basic problem since the republic began after World War II.

For the present there is no alternative to the governing center-left coalition, if freedom is to be saved. Of course it is theoretically possible—although not probable—to envision an evolution by the communists toward democracy, which would enable them to participate genuinely in a democratic government.

"However," said Saragat, "when I consider the Italian Communist party objectively, I do not think it is possible to foresee in it a democratic evolution. Maybe within a decade there could be a change; I don't know. I think the communists are too allied to Soviet bureaucracy.

"The country wants concrete reform. But if that means moving so far that the communists can take over, it means nothing. The necessary thing is to demonstrate to the people that genuine left-wing reforms and communism are not the same."

I asked the president if he had the legal right to dissolve parliament. This was indeed the case. He sent one of his aides for a copy of the constitution, showing the document to me and saying, "I swore loyalty to this." He pointed out article 88 as giving him the right to dissolve either or both houses of parliament when the legislature was unable to agree upon the formation of a government. But he said this provision had never been used so far, and he hoped it would not become necessary to do so.

There was absolutely no danger in Italy of any *coup d'état* from the Right. Anybody who thought along such lines was thinking of South America, not Italy. Never in Italian history—since the days of the Roman empire—had the army intervened in politics.

Moreover, he added, "There is not even a danger of a communist coup. They will never seek power by force, because they know how deeply democracy is respected here. What they want to do is to get a majority by legal means, either alone or by political alliance with other parties, which will give them authority." The real problem is whether the Communist party is able to exploit the failings and weaknesses of the democratic parties. This is Italy's Number One problem.

The divisions inside the Christian-Democratic party are much worse than those inside the Communist party. The Communist party was created by "a genius," Gramsci, and is still very solid, even today.

Saragat remains doubtful about Soviet intentions. He thinks it is foolish and exaggerated speculation that Russia is ready to make concessions in the West because of its fears of China in the East, and to confirm his scepticism he says that Czechoslovakia (in 1968) was the first victim of the mutual suspicions of Russia and China. He added: "I fear frightened people. It is very dangerous to have a frightened nation. It would be a great mistake to found a policy on the idea of provoking trouble between Russia and China. Anyone who thinks this is a useful card for the West to play, is terribly wrong."

ROME, *February 5, 1970*

Pietro Nenni is certainly the grand old man of Italian politics today: former boss of the socialists, an old antifascist who fought Mussolini from exile, and an erstwhile collaborator with the communists; but he has given that one up.

I went to see him this morning, now eighty, egg-shaped, with thick glasses, brown withered skin, and only a slight fringe of vestigial white hair remaining on his bald head. But he is remarkably full of energy, despite illness and accidents.

Nenni said there is no alternative to any Center-Left coalition to head this stage of Italy's political development. This comes from the existing balance of forces among the parties and in parliament.

For some years he had thought in good faith that there could be a serious collaboration with the communists, and that a democratic Italy could be run accordingly. But he no longer felt so.

Nenni said sadly: "One is obliged to recognize that in the struggle between orthodoxy and dogmatism on one side and heresy and revisionism on the other side, orthodoxy and dogmatism have won. This, of course, makes it quite impossible to have a coalition with the communists, because this tendency in Soviet communism is unhappily reflected in the Italian party."

The embourgeoisement of communism only represented a change of tailor, not of the real body of communism. He had been optimistic after the Kennedy-Khrushchev confrontation in 1962 that the basis for a permanent compromise was truly coming about and that this would change the nature of communism, but it never happened. Nor was Titoism an important factor outside Jugoslavia.

Basically the Italian Communist party remains under Soviet discipline and what they call "internationalism." There has been no great Soviet leader since Stalin. Nevertheless, the Italian party obeys and acknowledges Moscow as the leading force. Had it genuinely adhered to ideals the Italian party should have been much more Czechoslovakian than the Czechs.

If there were a vote right now it would reflect an increased popular mood favoring "law and order" similar to the movement in America, but potentially dangerous because it might become exaggerated. This would produce an opening to the Right which would not endure but which, while it lasted, could bring about an atmosphere of fear. That must be avoided at all costs.

PARIS, *February 10, 1970*

Interesting talk with President Pompidou. I said I didn't want to waste any time and would dive right in because I had many questions to ask. He looked a tiny bit alarmed and lit a cigarette. From then on he had one cigarette after another hanging down from the corner of his mouth in the approved Parisian way.

He said: "Anyone can see that France is seeking ways to reconcile the assertion that Israel has an absolute right to exist, to function freely, and to live in peace within safe, recognized borders, with our refusal to recognize Israel's rights of military conquest. France has not forgotten the Nazi martyrdom of European Jews, including French Jews, whose courage during the ordeal earned the admiration of all our people. However, France also intends to maintain and develop its ancient ties with most of the Moslem world and more particularly with the Arab countries.

"In the Middle East crisis, France wants and seeks only peace—a peace which I believe is indispensable to everyone and first of all to Israel. This is why we have placed the embargo on the shipment of arms to all the countries in the field of battle. The fact that at first this affected Israel in particular is correct. But since then, all these countries have received increasingly powerful arms sometimes from one nation, sometimes from another, but never from France.

"As far as the Libyan affair is concerned, we do not consider Libya directly involved in the conflict between Israel and a certain number of countries including Egypt. Naturally, Libya is Egypt's neighbor, and an Arab nation. The Libyan leaders have made declarations of solidarity with the other Arab countries. All this is true.

"But France has treated this affair separately for two reasons: first, our ties with the countries of north Africa and the Maghreb, of which Libya is not an integral part but to which it is far from foreign. Because of French interests in the Maghreb, our economic, cultural, and intellectual position in that region, we cannot disassociate ourselves from Libya. As long as she was tied to the Anglo-Saxon countries under the regime of King Idriss, we never tried to make our presence particularly felt in Libya. But the day she offered and requested more cooperation, our north African policy obliged us to reply favorably.

"It is France's duty to herself and also to all the western Mediterranean, to look after those interests common to European and Mediterranean countries. We are not going to seek Libyan oil; we buy oil from Libya, of course, but we are not seeking to extend our control of oil reserves in Libya in particular. It is a country located at our very door and at the door of the Maghreb; it is a country whose oil resources are important for Europe as a whole, not only for France. It is a country whose strategic position is important."

I asked: "Do you believe that the Four Powers can impose peace in the Middle East?" He said: "It is conceivable that the Four Powers might agree on a plan and decide to impose it. This would be possible physically, but psychologically it would be a bad formula. A peace imposed outright would have built-in weaknesses, since neither the Israelis nor the Arabs would give it their wholehearted consent.

"I do think that if they want to, the Four Powers can agree on a plan for the settlement. It should be possible, thanks particularly to the Jarring mission, that the peace achieved be accepted and not imposed. But this is becoming increasingly difficult."

I then asked if there was a possibility that France may one day denounce the North Atlantic treaty. He said: "Absolutely not. As far as we are concerned, we have no plans to resume membership of the integrated NATO organization. We do, on the other hand, intend to pursue our relationship as allies.

"As for bilateral cooperation between France and the United States, I personally doubt that the United States wants this. For the moment, happily, I do not think that either of us will have to use our nuclear forces. Consultations on targeting are obviously feasible, but I want to emphasize that France built a national striking force with the precise intention of enjoying full freedom of decision."

On the Common Market, he said: "I am working on the hypothesis that Britain will come in. I think that Britain and Europe both stand to gain."

I inquired about differences between his foreign policy and that of General de Gaulle. He said: "France being France, our basic needs remain necessarily the same. But there are differences.

"There is what de Gaulle has called the personal coefficient which by his prestige he himself contributed to French policy. All of this creates differences. There is a tendency to say that I am more accommodating. However, I would not like to be less firm in insisting upon what I consider our national interest, the interests of Europe, and the interests of peace. I cannot act differently with regard to these fundamental points.

"You must know that we have often encouraged the German government to seek a *détente* with the East, emphasizing that it was in such an Eastern *détente* that one could hope to find a solution to the German problem."

On his powers, Pompidou said: "I have always maintained that there was no reserved area and that the president's authority extends to all domains. However, foreign affairs are a larger part of the president's activities than those of the prime minister."

PARIS, *February 18, 1970*

Last night Jessie (de Vilmorin) Wood invited us to a small dinner with André Malraux, her mother's tragic lover during the last couple of years —and also many years ago. He was interesting but very sad, with a skin like the letters on a radium watch dial.

When we arrived, he was talking about cats—a subject stimulated by Jessie's little black cat with an astonishing affection for human beings. Malraux said the first cat to appear in European history was in the seventh century when Pope Gregory was given such a pet by Ethiopia, a congregation he especially adored. Not long afterward the church council issued a proclamation saying it would be better if the Pope spent more time seeing to his pontifical duties and less time caressing his cat.

Malraux adduced a new theory for the incomprehensible defeat of the heavily armed French contingent at Agincourt which outnumbered the British by five to one. He claims that the British had a "captainry" of cats who drove the rats toward the French camp where they promptly set about eating the bowstrings of France's archers so they were not in a position to shoot back at the English.

We talked about de Gaulle and his lunch with the General last autumn —the only time he has seen him since he left the *Élysée*. He said de Gaulle really hates the somber forest of Colombey-les-Deux-Églises, although he never says so. It is a huge and all-embracing mass of trees and the General's house, set in a clearing among them, is quite small. In a strange way this smallness is emphasized by the fact that at lunch they talked only about picayune and little things.

He said one third of de Gaulle's first volume of postwar memoirs has now been written. But he very much doubts if he will ever get around to writing a second. The General's interest is primarily focused on this first volume, and all his energy will be spent when he is finished.

De Gaulle is interested only in "historic decisions and not in episodes." He thought he had achieved one extraordinary thing: for eleven long years he had kept alive one of history's great fictions, the power of France. De Gaulle believes that when the French are "*avec la France*," then France becomes something, but when they turn against France, France vanishes. De Gaulle believes he took the dead France in his arms and nursed her back into greatness, that now she is going to her grave again.

It was his feeling that Madame de Gaulle ("Tante Yvonne") is now so happy that she is radiant, and this is very comforting for the General because a sad woman around that little house would make his own personal sadness even greater. Moreover, her pleasure and happiness at being back in real life and out of the concentration-camp existence of the Élysée unquestionably made him happy also.

WASHINGTON, *February 23, 1970*

Lunched in his White House office with Henry Kissinger, President Nixon's national security adviser. We ate off trays and during the first five minutes a French television crew cranked away. Danielle Hunebelle is doing a thirty-minute take-out on Henry.

We spent most of our time talking about the Middle East, a gloomy subject and much in the news because of Jewish protests against Pompidou's current visit—because of his sale of Mirage planes to Libya. Kissinger thinks protests are counter-productive, likely to stimulate anti-Semitism here rather than any anti-French feeling. He says Nixon has gone out of his way to reassure Pompidou, by sending Agnew to greet his plane.

The Middle East crisis is very difficult. Apart from its political and sentimental interest in Israel, the U.S.A. cannot allow Soviet military support to win a victory there by triumphing over an American client. This would have grave worldwide repercussions. Right now the Russians keep trying to maneuver America into the position of initiating all peace offers in the Middle East and demanding of its client all concessions. But, after all, it was a Soviet client state that started the 1967 war.

The United States is fully aware that once Egypt possesses Sinai again, it will immediately resume working against American interests as hard as possible in the Persian Gulf. If Moscow is truly willing to impose some sacrifices on its clients we on our part can press Israel to be more reasonable. The problem is really dual: (1) there is the Arab-Israeli quarrel and (2) the Soviet-Western relationship.

The U.S.A. simply cannot permit Soviet domination in the Middle East. This would, among other things, make Western Europe depend on Russia for all its petroleum. Right now time is working against us and Israel. But the Soviets will inevitably find themselves in difficulty. Someday the Arabs are bound to realize that the only power in a position to really deliver help is the U.S.A. After all, we can force Israel to get out of Sinai; Russia can't.

Our long-range objective is to make the Russians gradually realize they risk losing more in the Middle East by not settling than by settling. And the Russians can't basically change things with anything less than a large intervention of Soviet manpower. If they just send in better planes or SAM-2 and -3 missiles the Egyptians can't run them. If they send in Soviet crews they run the risk that Israel's excellent air force will work over the missile sites as they put them in, preventing their effective use. After all, in North Vietnam, the Hanoi-Haiphong quadrangle where SAM sites were laid down was not really bombed until mid-1967, so there was a chance to get them set well before they had to be used. Even then, the combination of SAMs and conventional flak never knocked down more than 5 percent of our planes on any raid (with one of two brief exceptions going up to 8 percent). This wouldn't ruin Israel.

Thus Soviet options are not really good. Moscow could certainly hurt Israel by massive intrusion of SAMs and MIG pilots plus large ground staffs. But Israeli tactics are good and their air force brilliant. The only danger to Israel is attrition. If its aircraft and pilot losses exceed a certain rate they cannot be replaced; and this would change the balance of power which depends so heavily on air strength.

The Russians, however, are not entirely rational on Israel. There is a hysterical edge. They are basically anti-Semitic and hate being licked by Jews. When Kissinger was in Moscow in 1968 he found he could talk to the Russians rationally on all subjects, even including Vietnam—except for Israel.

The French sale of planes to Libya is not a tangible or valid political factor; it is simply a commercial transaction. France doesn't have the "fire-power," the muscle, the importance to change the course of events in the Middle East. Europe as a unit would, not France alone.

We then shifted to China. Kissinger said there is a very slow but perceptible progress toward eventual normalization of relations. Moreover, they know we aren't going to give up Formosa. We are not going to turn in an ally.

At the very end I asked Kissinger if it wasn't actually imperative to install an ABM system here simply to insure we could stick by our pledges to NATO. After all, we are going to reduce our forces in Europe and the Europeans aren't going to fill the gap. If we are to stand up and defend Europe in a crunch, we must be sure our entire striking power and nation aren't wiped out. Only ABM can do this. "Precisely," said Henry. "That is exactly the situation. That and SALT. We can't give up something (an ABM system) for nothing. And there is nothing sacrosanct. We are not bound not to put in ABM."

WASHINGTON, *February 24, 1970*

This morning I called on Clark Clifford, former secretary of defense who split with Johnson after his own dramatic shift on Vietnam. Clifford is now retired, a busy and successful Washington lawyer, with easy, intelligent manner.

He made the point that our governmental machinery had become archaic. "It had been adequate for thirteen small agricultural communities called states and even then was the result of a good deal of compromise among our founding fathers. For example, one original concept was that in a presidential election, the candidate obtaining the largest vote would be president and the one with the next largest vote would be vice president. The party concept simply didn't exist. This really illustrates how unmodern and unrealistic the founding fathers were.

"We should not permit ourselves to be fascinated by the magic of our forefathers and forget the need for practical reform. It is really remarkable how few constitutional changes there have been. One of the most archaic of our inherited institutions is that of the presidency. He wears five hats: (1) chief executive, (2) commander-in-chief of our armed forces, (3) chief ceremonial officer, (4) responsible for the offering and innovation of legislation, (5) head of his political party. No real machinery is provided for the president to conduct his office efficiently along these lines. We should draw lessons from modern corporate development and benefit our government.

"There should be a constitutional amendment to change the function of the vice president. Today he still represents an antiquated anachronism who is supposed to be part of both the legislative and executive branches of the government. He should be placed solely in the executive branch to serve the president in the same way that a senior vice president or executive vice president serves the chief executive of a corporation. Someone else should be designated to preside over the senate—which the vice president rarely does anyway. The vice president should move into the White House and have an office and a staff next to the president in order to relieve the president of some of his burden. He should be properly used as an executive vice president and not just as a spare tire.

"He could take over most of the ceremonial duties, for example, receiving a great many of the visitors and even sharing the burden with foreign statesmen, brought in to see him by the president. Most other modern governments, after all, divide such ceremonial duties already—in England between the queen and the prime minister, in France between the president and the prime minister, in Germany between the president and the chancellor.

"We already have the titular office. We don't need a prime minister. We have a vice president. But the office is not being properly used. To make this alteration is not a matter of any impropriety. The office exists but its functions should be changed to accord with the times. Certainly most of the president's ceremonial and political party functions could be shifted to the vice president."

A president's own personal relationships with his vice president always seemed to change once they had won office. Thus, Truman and Alben Barkley had been close friends with similar backgrounds. Yet when Barkley became vice president a curious wall arose between him and Truman. After his first term there was grave doubt as to whether Eisenhower wanted Nixon in a second term. Eisenhower once admitted he couldn't think of a single serious policy decision in which Nixon had been a factor.

"And there was a simply terrible relationship between Kennedy and Johnson. I happen to know that the night after Kennedy won the nomination a delegation of southern politicians called on Kennedy and told him he just couldn't win without the south, above all Texas, and he therefore had to take Johnson. He would have much preferred Stu Symington, and I know this. But the deal was made. And for three years it was just awful to watch Kennedy and Johnson, above all the relationship between Bobby and Johnson.

"Now, what do we see now? Well, you know what they say: Agnew has become the Richard Nixon of this administration. The vice president has no real function except to sit and wait for something to happen to the president."

WASHINGTON, *February 25, 1970*

Last night we and the Bohlens, with whom we are staying, went to the White House where President Nixon gave a state dinner for Pompidou.

I sat near former Governor [John] Connally of Texas, a former navy secretary, who was in the car when President Kennedy was murdered. He is a handsome, soft-spoken, intelligent man, and talked quite fascinatingly about such subjects as pollution, segregation by nationality (not race —Germans, Czechs, etc.) in Texas, and the raising, marketing, and insuring of beef cattle.

Fairly good French food with fairly good French wine. I somehow thought it silly to give French cuisine to a Frenchman instead of things like Maryland crabs and Virginia ham. But it was very well served on the White House's 1968, American-made (I looked under the plates) Tiffany china.

After dinner we stood around in various rooms and halls drinking coffee and liqueurs, smoking cigars, when I felt a hand on my shoulder. Turned around, and it was Nixon. "Come over here, Cy," he said. "You know these people." The "people" were President and Mrs. Pompidou and Mrs. Nixon. I stood with the two presidents for fifteen minutes (their wives moved a yard or so away). General Walters and Prince Andronikov, the two interpreters, rushed up and an odd conversation ensued.

Nixon patted my back and said to Pompidou (Andronikov murmuring away like a machine gun) "You know, Cy is an old friend of mine. All the years I was out of office he kept in touch with me. Whenever I went to Paris or London we'd see each other. We used to golf together. You know, Mr. President, when a newspaperman keeps in touch with you when you are out of office it is a proof that he is both a good newspaperman and a good friend." Pompidou smiled and said, *"Monsieur le Président*, I know what you mean because Mr. Sulzberger also kept in touch with me when I was out of office."

I can't say all this displeased me. Apart from the fact that quite a few fellow guests were standing awed and respectful in the distance, too far away to measure the inconsequentiality of our talk, this clearly must help my prestige in the Élysée.

Pompidou said he had been pleased that my interview with him had been widely printed around the world but expressed disappointment that the *New York Times* had published a similarly long interview with Nasser on the same day. I said this was a haphazard coincidence, but he didn't appear convinced. He is remarkably thin-skinned. He said his lunch at the National Press Club had gone off well. "Wasn't it a lions' den?" I inquired. "Well, if so," he said, "the lions' fangs had all been drawn."

Nixon told me that he had had a very good talk for two hours with Pompidou that morning and it had been most useful. "We stuck to the big picture," he said. "But it was useful and we basically agree." Here Pompidou nodded sagely.

Suddenly Tricia Nixon, a small, pretty blonde, was brought up by her mother and the president introduced her, saying: "She speaks a little French, you know. And she's going to France this summer. After all, they like pretty girls in France, don't they?" "*Je ne sais plus,*" said Pompidou.

The presidents then led everyone to a large room where we were to be entertained.

It was, alas, at the level of a college glee club session, and for an intellectually swinging French president and wife who consider Giacometti as archaic as Rembrandt and don't speak any English, it must have hurt.

Charles Lucet (French ambassador) came up to Marty Hillenbrand (assistant secretary of state for Europe) and, almost sobbing, told us appalling news, swearing me to secrecy. All day the phone had been ringing and American Jews like Arthur Goldberg had been calling up and warning that Pompidou should not go to New York. There might be violence. Pompidou is on the verge of canceling the rest of his trip "because he doesn't want to embarrass President Nixon." I said this would be an absolute disaster, exactly what the Russians wanted. Lucet had to use all his influence to persuade Pompidou to carry on.

WASHINGTON, *February 26, 1970*

Stimulating lunch with Dick Helms, head of the CIA, an intelligent realist. Dick said the United States had been incredibly lucky during the postwar years because it depended for its power on an overwhelming military superiority and a constantly expanding economy. Now both of these special advantages were coming to an end. The Russians were carefully preparing for a military machine by around 1975 which would undoubtedly be ahead of us in virtually all respects and, given existing sentiments and political conditions, there was absolutely nothing we could do about this. Moreover, we ourselves were deliberately braking our own expanding economy. So the two primordial factors were coming to an almost simultaneous and predictable end.

On the Middle East, Helms said Israel still has a definite military advantage over the Arabs but this cannot endure forever. There is an attrition rate on plane losses, etc., and the only ultimate replacement source is the U.S.A. The day must come when Israel—while it has its advantage—must somehow start or provoke round four in the Palestine war. Otherwise it will lose its edge.

And the Israelis foolishly don't understand the mood in the United States and the deep distaste for any kind of foreign adventure. We don't know what the Russians will do. They could send in SAM-3s to knock down low-flying planes and it is even possible to train Egyptian crews.

There is no doubt the Israelis could blow up the High Aswan Dam if they become desperate, and no doubt that they have been experimenting with military devices at the Dimona reactor. Some six months ago they floated some mines down the Nile toward the old Aswan Dam, but they caught up on the sides of the river and the project failed. Nevertheless, Egypt is in a sense even more vulnerable than Israel.

What would the United States do in a disaster? Probably, after fulminating, nothing. If Egypt were destroyed, we would be horrified but most unlikely to go to war. If Israel were destroyed, ditto. One must separate the emotional and political reactions from the national and governmental reactions. It is very difficult to calculate just what the Israeli government will do.

As for the Sino-Soviet situation, there is equal confusion. The United States has cards but we don't know which way to play the hand. We know that the Peking talks have been going very badly since they started last autumn. The Chinese pulled troops back from frontier areas but the Russians refused. There is no advance. The Russians have approximately the same kind of choice that on a mini-scale faces Israel. Today they could wipe China out. But in a certain amount of time the Chinese will have a missile arsenal as well as warheads, and the Russians will no longer have an overwhelming, knock-out, first-strike capacity. Should they hit now— or not? There is, as a result, a triangular relationship in which we are inextricably involved.

I went over to the White House at 4:15 and sat in Kissinger's office where we chatted. Henry, who is a German Jew from near Munich, was deeply disturbed about the emotionalism of the American-Jewish community during this Pompidou visit.

He went on to describe the irrationality of the American Jews. Rockefeller, for whom Henry worked prior to Nixon's election, was enormously pro-Jewish, said Henry—"Genuinely and emotionally so, not intellectually or politically or as a disguised anti-Semite. And before the nominating convention he received a letter from Jewish organizations demanding his views on the sale to Israel of fifty American Phantom Jets. Rockefeller replied that he wanted to insure that Israel always had enough arms to defend itself but simply wasn't in a position personally to say about the Phantoms. The result was that Rockefeller received letters attacking him as unsympathetic and saying the Jews would oppose him."

Henry is worried about the repercussions in the United States of organized Jewish opinion. He foresees a wave of anti-Semitism—"and I speak as a Jew"—and a further rise in the extreme Right. "And, furthermore, I very much wonder what the President's own repercussions and reactions will be."

We talked about the Pompidou visit. The two presidents had gotten on well together and achieved some important common ground. The results would become evident during the next few months. I mentioned then my hope that our next ambassador to France (Shriver is leaving) would be good. Henry indicated great doubt.

Henry said the president required a complete spectrum of analyses and recommendations on any subject—and then he would make his decision. This was his operational system. Nixon wanted to be sure that every option was covered and fully explained—he would study them and choose. He saw his job as that of making the final choice after every possible view had been heard. Kissinger was not expected to favor one or another line, merely to present them all with approximately equal impartiality; and there had to be a full, written record of the process. Those who saw him as "a Machiavelli" were silly. His function was to present equally the opinions he favored and disfavored.

At this point we got word to go in to the president. There were sturdy secret service guards stationed along the hall. Despite the fact that Kissinger's must be the second-best-known face in the White House the door to the Oval Room remained shut until the guard reached over, then pulled a secret slide. There was Nixon, standing beside his desk.

He leaned over, shook hands warmly and waved me to an armchair, seated himself, and apologized for having kept me waiting. Then we started chatting. We began about Pompidou and he said it had been a good visit. He had been impressed by the fact that Pompidou was a sturdy country type, not the "Paris intellectual" he had been told about, and a tough, intelligent, solid man. They had talked openly and honestly and it had been "most successful." They had gone over the Middle East, NATO, Russia, Vietnam, and there had been a great deal of agreement.

After about a quarter of an hour, Nixon rose and said: "Henry, you know the last time Cy was here he was in this room and he gave me his book. I think it might be fun to show him where I write, don't you? Let's take him over to my EOB [Executive Office Building] office across the way and have a coffee." He led the way and off we went.

We walked through the west gate where I had entered; it was very cold, well below freezing, and none of us had coats. Nixon looked lean and well. His face was more lined and his hair had a couple of tiny hints of grey in the black (but he still looks much younger than I, although we are the same age). We crossed the street and climbed the stairs where he opened the door and led the way to a two-room suite. The outer room, its walls covered with framed cartoons ("almost all of them from my days as vice president") was spacious, high-ceilinged; the inner room even more so, with comfortable armchairs and sofa, a large desk, various knickknacks on it (an eagle, a model missile, etc.), a few historical paintings, a bracket with hinged family photographs, a thick carpet. He picked up a phone and asked for coffee.

Nixon started talking about the way he organized his life. He had learned from Eisenhower that it was silly to read through and amend every single document presented to him for signature. He signed the unimportant ones and didn't worry about whether they were in good or bad English. He accepted, without pondering, all recommendations for appointments to judgeships or embassies except for a handful. He signed routine proclamations, like one that had come before him today on declaring many institutions obsolescent or others declaring minor disaster areas. One could not waste time on such things.

On the other hand, he made it a point to carefully study important documents or contemplate important appointments. He carefully prepared his press conference statements in advance and worked hard on addresses like that on the State of the Nation. "Anything I have to say or write I want to be said or written by me," he added. It was in this comfortable room with its cheerful cream-colored walls that he did this: "Here is where I write."

He tried to assign Vice President Agnew to as much ceremonial and political work as possible, and he also tried to delegate the organizational preparation of policy analyses to Kissinger.

He considered his job to be to take a look at the long-term implications of problems and also at the broad-scale geographical areas. He got up, to illustrate what he meant, and went to a small world map on the wall behind him and said: "Here is the Mediterranean. You can see how small it is compared to the rest of the earth. And then think of all the problems. There is Spain—isolated from the rest of Europe by Franco. And Italy—with its Opening to the Left and unrest. And Greece—with its colonels. And Israel—fighting the Arabs. And Libya—with its revolution. And Tunisia and Algeria—worried about Nasser. And Morocco—with its nervous king. What do you do? Do you worry about each one as it comes up? Do you worry about the colonels as against Constantine in Greece? Or do you try and see a broad future pattern for the area? And, if you can work that out, doesn't it become easier to get a relatively quicker answer to each local aspect of the problem as it arises?"

He went back to his Pompidou talks and said they had agreed on the same basic approach. They both felt Israel had to be insured as a state but this didn't mean taking a precise line on borders. They both recognized that Russia had justifiable interests in the area. "And I," said Nixon, "if I ran Russia, would insist on a right to a voice there." But also, the United States could not sacrifice its own justifiable rights and interests. Nor could France—or Europe.

Nixon said: "From here we moved on to the subject of NATO. Of course I didn't speak about NATO as an 'organization' but of the North Atlantic treaty as an alliance. I told Pompidou it had been started for three reasons: (1) Europe was weak and destitute; (2) Russia was threatening from the East; and (3) a pattern had to be devised into which Germany could be fitted.

"I then said that Europe was unquestionably prosperous now and could probably become militarily strong. I acknowledged that many people thought Russia was now less threatening—although we weren't always sure of this. But, I said, in any case it was obvious we still had to have an arrangement, a pattern, into which Germany could be fitted. He agreed with this analysis."

Nixon mentioned the danger of West Germany moving too fast toward new arrangements with Russia and East Europe. They hadn't discussed a European (Franco-British) nuclear force—the matter never came up. But a lot of old shibboleths were removed and the atmosphere was realistically cleared for future cooperation.

He started talking about the need for a president to plan far ahead in a "conceptual" way, both for national and international policy. He wanted to look ahead and lay the groundwork for a period long after he himself would be out of office. For example, he was now working hard on a genuine project for establishing a national minimum wage and eliminating poverty. He was working with a special committee against pollution. The birth control problem had to be faced squarely; it was idiotic to keep exporting millions of tons of grain to India to feed a growing population.

Incidentally, he talked at some length about international monetary policy. He said he was giving much attention to this, although people didn't realize it, "and, confidentially, I am working very hard on the subject. I am dissatisfied with the existing system. We can't go on having currency crises every few years. But this is a long-range, conceptual problem and we must work out a fundamental new approach."

As he was sipping his coffee I interrupted by saying I had one special question which linked both his national and international concerns—namely, ABM. It seemed to me that if we didn't have a decent anti-ballistic-missile system we would not be in a valid position to support our alliance commitments abroad. We would be scared to react if an enemy attacked one of our allies. It was that simple; we wouldn't trade off New York for Frankfurt or Manila.

He agreed enthusiastically. He said this was a vital point in both Asia and Europe—and also in terms of the SALT disarmament talks. There was a lot of "theological" argument against the ABM system he had posed, mainly in the "scientific community." But it failed to analyze the facts.

To start with, the ABM system being discussed now was a question of budgeting between $900 million and $1 billion next year. But just to continue with the previous rate of development would cost about $800 million. In fact, not much more than $130 million was involved in any development.

Yet all our allies must be made to realize that the Russians were swiftly catching up to us in missile strength. They now had about 1,250 land-based ICBMs compared to 1,000 for us, although we are still two-to-one ahead on submarine (sea-based) missiles. Before long they would have a 30 percent advantage over us on ICBMs, be even with us on sea-based missiles, and be way ahead in IRBMs aimed at our allies. If we weren't able to "take out" Soviet ICBMs alone, there wasn't a chance of taking out IRBMs to protect our friends. When he had explained that to NATO ministers last year [Joseph] Luns, the Dutch foreign minister, had been horrified.

All we wanted vis-à-vis Russia was "sufficiency." But we had to have that. It was evident that pressures were mounting to withdraw our troops, and in the end, slowly, they would have to be responded to. But we couldn't knuckle under in weapons. The minute our allies realized we were a second-rate power militarily, the political effect would be enormous.

The president had to retain his options. "Right now," Nixon said, arising and going over to the desk, "wherever I am, at this desk or in the Oval Room or at Camp David or in California, I am in direct contact. If the 'line' rings I can give the answer. I am not worried about this. I can sleep. It is part of the job. But it is a fact.

"If the line rang right now, telling me that unknown missiles were on the way, I would have fifteen minutes to make up my mind. The only thing to do, if it appeared that unknown missiles were coming at us, would be to order a reply. That might kill seventy million people. What president is willing to kill seventy million people?

"We can build a system at an annual rate of about $900 million that would be able to defend the North American continent against up to a hundred enemy missiles. In other words, they would have to make an advance decision to let go with everything. If there were a mistake, if there were a stray missile—and we mustn't ignore the fact that other, smaller countries are getting into a position where they can build them— a president could at least push an 'alarm' for ABM defense. We could knock down the incoming missiles without millions of deaths—like the reply of ICBMs.

"Of course this isn't total defense. It is only against a maximum of 100 ICBMs. It isn't a thick defense. But we know the Russians have got it, that they are moving in this direction. We can't afford to let them suddenly become the only protected power. And our allies know this. This thin defense—which would take time to install—might protect North America ten years, into the mid-eighties, against anything China might develop. And China's policy might evolve during that time. And also, it would force the Russians to make the decision that any attack had to be deliberate and all out. Finally, it would allow a U.S. president to avoid ordering that retaliatory ICBMs be fired but only put ABMs on 'alarm.'

"At the SALT talks the only precise indications we have had is on this subject. The Russians have clearly intimated they want to exchange ideas on ABM systems."

I said it seemed silly to me to think in terms of "escalation" when discussing ABM. It was the same difference as that between two men with a sword and shield each. If one began lengthening his sword that was escalation. If he thickened his shield it was not.

Nixon said that was precisely it. He went on to discuss the implications vis-à-vis China. He wanted very much "to bring China back into the normal international community." But meanwhile it took time. There was no chance that China could develop a nuclear-ICBM system with more than 100 missiles in the next decade or so. But we would be remiss to do nothing about getting ready now. After all, if we had nothing, the Chinese might some day threaten Manila—or San Francisco. Or move into territory allied to us (perhaps Japan) with purely conventional means. They might reckon in Peking that with a population of more than 700 million people they could afford enormous casualties to conquer adjacent areas. But we couldn't figure that way.

There were people in our "scientific community" who talked about there not being adequate reason to "provoke" the Russians, that we would only save about "40 million lives" with a "thin" ABM system. But what were 40 million lives after all? That was something.

Beyond that, the president had to have options. He wasn't talking about his own term. He would be out of office long before the results of these decisions. "And there would be a lot of political sex appeal if I said I was going to save $900 million to spend on social improvement."

But he thought his job was primarily "conceptual" and long-range and that he had to think of our diplomatic as well as our strategic position. If our European or Asian allies suddenly realized we had become a second-class power instead of a power at least on parity with the other top powers, they would fall off immediately. We would no longer have options of war and peace. We wouldn't even have decent options on such things as the SALT negotiations.

In some senses, he said, the most important implication of the whole ABM decision was diplomatic, political—not military. We could never afford to give our allies the feeling that they were hostages, that we were in so weak a position that we simply had to sacrifice them.

I was impressed by the decency, modesty, calm, and—above all— orderliness of the president. He has a system, he is experienced, and he has no enormous delusions of grandeur. Moreover, he seems determined, as he says, to stick by his "conceptual" view of both national and foreign affairs.

He and Kissinger discussed an emergency situation in Laos and Nixon turned to me and said, in the middle: "Cy, please not a word of this to anyone. It is very, very confidential." It involved a meeting tomorrow (which Nixon asked Kissinger to summon) of just a few members of the national security council, including Secretary of State Rogers, CIA boss Helms, Nixon, and only three or four others.

We moved out, looking at the family pictures in the wall-hinged bracket, and I noticed someone had brought Nixon's modest grey overcoat when we got into the hall. We walked across the street through the bitter February freeze as the president once again recalled that he was really spending most of his time working on programs for someone who would be in his office a decade or so hence. When we got into the White House he bade me a merry farewell.

Before going back to the Bohlens' for dinner I had a drink with Averell Harriman at his house. He looked old (for him—after all, he's nearly eighty and energetic as can be) and told me in confidence he had bought the house next door as a repository for his papers, was planning to spend "our declining years here." He was warm and friendly, but, as usual, disagreed on Vietnam. He referred to "that awful man Nixon."

WASHINGTON, *February 27, 1970*

Lunched with Kim (Kermit) Roosevelt, for many years one of the CIA's ablest representatives in the Middle East. Kim says he first met Nasser in October 1952, although Nasser had seized power by his revolution in July of that year.

Nasser had been told by a friend just who Kim was and had sent him a message in Iran, where Roosevelt at the time was working on our anti-Mossadegh plot. Nasser asked him to come to Cairo. Kim asked Washington for instructions and was ordered to go.

When he arrived, he attended a dinner in which General Mohammed Naguib, the original front man of the revolution, acted as host. Kim sat on his right and Nasser sat on Kim's right. Naguib got very drunk at the dinner. Nasser had a drink or two, although he showed no effect and only sipped. I didn't think he would even let alcohol touch his lips.

Kim told me Naguib was in no sense a "nice" man, as legend has it. Not even then was he of any importance, and Nasser whispered to him at that first dinner party that Roosevelt shouldn't pay any attention to what his host said.

Nasser would like to escalate the Palestine war because it is his last chance. He might be able to force the Russians to save him, but if he does not get the fighting going again the army may very well dump him. The army does not want to escalate.

Kim is convinced Moscow does not want war in the Middle East. But the Russians are on the spot. They feel that if there is another round of war, they will once again lose a vast investment in equipment sent to the Arabs and once again their prestige will take a beating.

But Israel now also probably wants to escalate, in order to compensate for its stupid diplomacy since the 1967 victory, when wise policy might have achieved a settlement. What Israel really needs now is another victory followed swiftly by a generous offer of peace on terms the Arabs could not refuse. The trouble is it is hard for Israel to figure just where to escalate. Where could it trap and destroy a sufficiently large amount of Soviet equipment now that Israel itself holds the Sinai Peninsula?

Pleasant talk this afternoon with Secretary of State Rogers, a nice man, very decent, no Talleyrand. Rogers certainly is no expert on foreign policy. I am told he is not unusually hardworking, and that the old days of intense and long hours, as typified by Rusk and Dulles, are over.

I had particularly wanted to talk with him about Africa. He just returned from a trip to that continent—the first ever made by a U.S. secretary of state.

He said: "One reason I went to Africa was to familiarize myself with that continent because of the special relationship of race questions there and here in our country. Eleven percent of our population has a strong emotional attachment to black Africa. And this will become more apparent as they learn more about the continent from which they came. Their emigration was a forced emigration and this occasions a particular emotional feeling. I don't think the emotional involvement between American Negroes and the countries of black Africa has yet become fully apparent, but I think it has begun to increase.

"There is a black-white problem both here and in Africa and each relates to the other. Therefore one might say this is a double-barrelled attachment. We can already see the beginning of this feeling in the United States in our own black youth, as it changes its customs and emphasizes Africanness in things like hairdos, music, etc.

"One must go to Africa to find out how closely our culture is related to that of Africa. Take 'blues' music, for example. I was astonished to find how close a resemblance there was between local tribal music that was played for me and the modern American blues such as *Mood Indigo*. They are almost the same thing.

"The long-range interests of the United States clearly require a more active interest in Africa and a genuine spirit of black African aspirations. But I found a good deal of sympathy for us as I talked with their political scientists, professors at law schools, students, etc.

"I explained that African criticism of the United States is often counterproductive. We are not a colonial power. Indeed, we frequently supported independence movements against our own allies. We did not create the problems of Africa today—such as its artifically contrived frontiers, which were fixed in Europe. We oppose apartheid. We are against South African control of southwest Africa. We do not recognize Rhodesia. We support an arms embargo against South Africa.

"But our Congress gets irked by continual criticism and increasingly takes the view: 'why bother to do these things if we are always being scolded by those we would like to help?' There is a constant barrage of violent criticism and I made it very clear that I thought this was not useful. We are not the villain of the piece. *We* aren't Portugal."

He thought it would make sense if a black-white frontier were established from the Atlantic to the Indian Ocean by partitioning southwest Africa and linking the northern part to the northern part of Botswana in order to give it a seaport. There were the same tribal groupings in each state. And in each case there was a considerable white population in the south but a heavy black majority in the north. He felt strongly that we should give more support to Botswana, especially because Zambia is so interested in it.

Rogers thought that two basic things had resulted from the Nigerian war. It may have diminished tribal feeling throughout Africa by reducing the thought of successful secession. Furthermore, it probably made it less likely that other tribal groupings would seek a secession, having watched the defeat of Biafra.

There was some similarity to American history. After the civil war all the little half-baked secessionist movements which had at one or another time existed in the United States vanished.

NEW YORK, *March 3, 1970*

Last night I attended a large dinner for Pompidou given by the various Franco-American societies in New York. The American Jewish community is so enraged by Pompidou's policy of maintaining the arms embargo on Israel while selling Mirage jets to Libya that it organized vigorous anti-French demonstrations in the cities he visited.

Two days previous to the dinner the Chicago demonstration broke, and apparently it was pretty uncouth. Simone Servais, whom I saw at the dinner, told me some of the demonstrators had actually spat on both Pompidou and his wife. He was in a white rage and intended to cancel his New York engagements and send Madame Pompidou straight back to Paris. However, Nixon called up to apologize and substituted himself for Vice President Agnew at the New York dinner. This mollified the extremely sensitive Pompidou and the dinner went off splendidly.

Nixon had just the right touch in the little speech he made to toast his guest, saying he had especially wanted him [Pompidou] to see the country just the way an American president saw it—but unfortunately, as usual, things had been overdone. Pompidou joined in a roar of laughter. Nixon then went on to say that this was an historic occasion. The vice president of the United States was often called upon to substitute at public occasions for the president, but he was confident this was the first time in American history that the president had been called upon to substitute for the vice president.

PARIS, *March 13, 1970*

Jozsef Szall, Hungarian ambassador in Rome and special representative to the Vatican, had sent word asking if he could see me in Paris. I invited him for lunch. With little ado he told me that he has decided in principle to defect.

Early this year he returned to Budapest on leave and was even refused permission to see Kadar with whom he had previously been on close terms.

They had offered Jozsef a job as head of a foreign ministry section dealing with the plans for a European security conference, but even this offer was withdrawn. Szall, who used to assure me what a fine man Janos Peter, the foreign minister, is, now sneers at him as a gutless wonder. He says the only job offered to him is that of director of the state radio broadcasting system, and his sole function would be to put out propaganda —most of which everybody knows he disbelieves. The last man to hold the job committed suicide. His predecessor was arrested and spent five years in jail. Szall says the whole operation is a trap.

Jozsef has written to the government turning down the job. If he is not offered something else that is not merely a device to get him home in order to arrest him, he is going to defect.

He wants to do this in the quietest way possible and without publicity. He doesn't want to denounce his country publicly. He would like eventually to get some job at a college in America or some kind of foundation grant.

I told him I was inexperienced in these matters and in no position to give him any assurances that he could get a job. Furthermore, I warned him there is an economic recession in the U.S.A. But if there was no future except ultimate prison, he had no choice. Nevertheless, I suggested he should try and remain in Italy for about a year before moving to the U.S.A., so that all the fuss would die down and so that he could cushion the psychological shock by staying in a country with which he was by now wholly familiar.

I suggested he should see Ambassador Graham Martin and lay his cards very openly on the table. I told him Martin was a realistic and reliable veteran who would stick by his word.

It is sad to see a man who has suffered for a dream and now finds it was nothing but a nightmare. He told me that even Mrs. Rajk, widow of the foreign minister, who was executed on false charges during the Stalinist period, has refused to rejoin the party because she says: "I will not spit on my husband's tomb."

LONDON, *March 16, 1970*

Interesting lunch with Denis Healey, defense minister. Denis thinks Henry Kissinger the best, most intelligent, and nicest of all the presidential assistants he has known in Washington. Mac Bundy had a fine mind but was arrogant, a bit "too British—mixed with Boston Brahmin." Walt Rostow was not quite up to it.

President Johnson, he thought, was unfortunate. Had he been lucky he would have been assassinated in 1967—a year before he was forced to announce he wouldn't run again. Then history might have said that he had achieved everything in which Kennedy failed (his internal legislation). Denis personally was repelled by him. "He never listened, simply spoke all the time."

Nixon, on the other hand, had done amazingly well. Healey was surprised to find himself acknowledging this, as he had been strongly antipathetic. Nevertheless, on the things that concerned Denis, foreign policy and defense, Nixon hadn't made a single false step.

He said Harold Wilson was a brilliant politician and party leader but only did things in terms of what their political effect might be, not their value. Nevertheless, Wilson didn't know how to make decisions or to delegate authority to his cabinet. He was a sloppy and ineffectual chief of government: nothing like Lincoln, who would say, "Very well, the majority decision is one to twelve; I am the one and we will do it."

Denis thought it would be possible for the United States—after withdrawing from Vietnam—to defend itself and maintain its overseas commitments by a volunteer military force. This would have to be worked out on the British system—paying a salary based on civilian equivalent jobs. The British evaluated the equivalent job—then paid 5 percent more. Nevertheless, although it was possible for America to do this, we would lose the flexibility we now have to expand commitments at will. Only conscription provides that option.

Manpower rationing for the services is as useful as newsprint rationing for newspapers; you make do more with less. No country wants to call everybody up. But if you use *selective* service, too much responsibility is placed on certain qualified groups and this brings about a situation like that today in West Germany, where there is far too high a percentage of conscientious objectors.

Healey doesn't think Europe can ever take up the slack left by any excessive American withdrawal of troops from the NATO area, but he does think that if the U.S. is careful and limits its withdrawals (he indicated a maximum figure of far less than 100,000 taken out), something can be done. But it is silly that we can muster only five divisions from the 310,000 men we maintain on the Continent. There is much fat to be pared away.

Britain, he said, is not interested in any idea of combining its nuclear force with France's in order to provide the basis for a "European" force. The Wilson government has never been ready for this. Britain could gain nothing from such a merger and would lose much, in terms of American aid.

BRUSSELS, *March 24, 1970*

Dined with André de Staercke [Belgian ambassador to NATO] and Vicomte Étienne Davignon, political director of the Belgian foreign ministry and head of a new study group of the Common Market and Britain to consider "European" foreign policy.

André said that at the SALT talks in Helsinki the Russians had defined as a strategic weapon anything capable of hitting the Soviet Union. Thus, depending where it is placed or based, this would include almost every tactical weapon NATO has.

André thinks Spain should come into NATO as soon as Franco dies, and that its contribution would be very helpful. This would end the Gibraltar question once and for all. And it would finish the reviving French idea of a Mediterranean pact (which, says A., would finish NATO by starting to split it up).

His big worry is that if NATO loses its cohesion, we will end up with the "Finlandization of Europe"—a kind of semineutralization, semisatellization.

We discussed the grim implications of the philosophy of war—in terms of ecology, rising birth rate, pollution, overpopulation. André got from his library Euripides' *Oreste* in which Apollo says (verses 1639–1642): *"La beauté d'Hélène servit aux dieux à lancer les Grecs contre les Phrygiens et à entamer les morts pour purger la terre d'une insolente surabondance d'hommes."* Even then, the same problem!

De Staercke made the gloomy remark: "We have made the dangerous gift of peace to our youth," adding that this was one of the sources of trouble with the younger generation.

CASTEAU, BELGIUM, *March 26, 1970*

Drove to SHAPE headquarters for a talk with the commander, Andrew Goodpaster, a four-star general, aged fifty-five, tall, bespectacled, grey-haired.

I asked if he didn't think Europe had to stay more or less divided in two because Russia would never let Eastern Europe go and Western Europe would ultimately succumb to Moscow if it quit its alliance with the United States. He thought this was unquestionably correct. A security system had been evolved in the existing divided Europe which maintained a valid independence for the western half. Since Eastern Europe could never be free of Soviet supervision, the only way Europe could reunite under existing conditions would be by accepting Moscow's terms.

In the defense of NATO Europe, tactical U.S. nuclear weapons are of primary importance. This fact is at the back of SALT discussions and at the back of all our own programs including those for ABM [antiballistic missiles] and MIRV. The thing we have to consider is whether the "nuclear sufficiency" we are now working for would or could allow "superiority" to the Russians.

The present nuclear guidelines of NATO are related to all three of the existing types of forces—conventional forces, tactical nuclear weapons, and strategic nuclear weapons. In the tragic event that our deterrents should ever fail and we find ourselves in a war, a war which we cannot handle just by using conventional forces, the existence of tactical nuclear weapons gives us an intermediate option, a chance to defend ourselves without resorting to all-out strategic weapons.

Soviet thinking matured during the 1962 Cuba confrontation, when Kennedy told Moscow that if there were an explosion in Cuba our own response would not be limited to that island but would hit Russia. The Russians found themselves looking down the barrel of a gun.

The Soviet definition of strategic nuclear weapons put forth at the Helsinki SALT negotiations claimed that anything that could hit the USSR would be "strategic." That would eliminate many of the tactical nuclear weapons that NATO has in Europe. It would exclude all our MRBMs and IRBMs [medium-range ballistic missiles and intermediate-range ballistic missiles]. At the same time the Russians claim their own MRBMs and IRBMs would not have to be defined as "strategic" since they would not be capable of hitting the U.S.A. This is obviously just a bargaining position.

THE HAGUE, *April 8, 1970*

Called on Joseph Luns, the veteran Dutch foreign minister, a charming man, about six foot five, lean, strong, and healthy looking. He has been in this job since the summer of 1952 (eighteen years now) and says: "I am the dean of them all."

Most of our talk was about the Middle East. Luns has just returned from a tour of Lebanon, Jordan, and Egypt. He is deeply pessimistic about the chances of settlement. The only thing is to impose a peace, starting with an arms embargo, so Israel can complain it had no choice and the Arabs can assure the *Fedayeen* guerrillas there was no alternative.

The moderates both in the Arab world and Israel are steadily losing ground to the extremists. He is fond of Mrs. Meir, has known her for years, and has been strongly pro-Israel because of the emotional pro-Jewish feeling of the Dutch since World War II, but doesn't think anyone can force Israel's coalition government to accept the 1949 frontiers as the basis for security and peace.

The only country to gain from the existing "controlled tension" was Russia; not the Arab countries, Israel, the United States, Europe. Russia was taking over more and more. Nasser assured Luns: "I shall remain master in my own house." But Luns told him Russia wasn't really interested in seeing Egypt recover its territories in a fourth round. There were three alternative outcomes to such a war:

> (1) An Arab victory. But this is not in Soviet interest. The Arabs would need Russia less and Moscow's influence would diminish.

> (2) A "highly successful" Arab victory. In that event, human nature must come into play. The United States, should the Arabs achieve this, would doubtless be forced to take the agonizing decision to save Israel from extinction. In that event, the Russians would either have to accept defeat—as in Cuba—or court the risk of all-out war.

> (3) An Arab defeat. The Russians would again have lost face and would again be faced with the vastly expensive burden of reequipping the Arabs.

Luns was worried that Israel was condemning itself to become the Prussia of the Middle East. It should make concessions for real peace. It could really run Jerusalem if it let Jordan's flag fly over the old city. Customs posts could be kept beyond it. The Left Bank would be demilitarized by Jordan and Jordan was even ready for a kind of "Benelux" economic link with Israel.

The Israelis must look at history. In 1786 Prussia was unbeatable. Yet, twenty years later, its armies were smashed at Jena and Auerstadt. He has told this to the Israelis more than once. He also warned that even the Arabs might some day produce their own Napoleon.

PARIS, *April 17, 1970*

Dined last night at the Duhamels'. He is minister of agriculture and the dinner was in the ministry. Madame Duhamel told me her husband and Jean-Jacques Servan-Schreiber have been intimate friends since school. Jean-Jacques was groomed by his mother from the age of four to aspire to the presidency of the republic; this is the original source for his present political ambitions.

PARIS, April 23, 1970

Jacques Chaban-Delmas is handsome, athletic, and cultivated. He had a splendid war record and ended as a general in the resistance. His political career has been a notable success. He has been mayor of Bordeaux, held various ministries under the Fourth Republic, was president of the national assembly during the period of General de Gaulle, and is now prime minister.

Yesterday afternoon I called on him over at the Hôtel de Matignon. We started off discussing the role of the prime minister in foreign policy. He said the president gave the political orientation on these matters. The prime minister's function was to see that these policies were effectively applied by the foreign minister and others involved.

I told Chaban I had heard he opposed the Libyan arms deal. He admitted that, at the start, he had been "mistrustful" but after the guarantees were given by Libya that the Mirages would not be used against Israel, "I gave my accord." He said Paris had the necessary means to check up on this guarantee.

He told me the Greek government had already promised Paris to release the left-wing composer Mikis Theodorakis and that this had been agreed some time before the much advertised trip to Athens of Jean-Jacques Servan-Schreiber, an opposition politician. He brought back Theodorakis and said he had "liberated" him. Chaban said the deal made between Paris and Athens was for release in exchange for France's promise not to vote to condemn Greece in the council of Europe session at Strasbourg, simply to abstain. In other words, the prime minister insisted, Servan-Schreiber was trying to cash in on something already arranged by the government.

He also said that Paris was working very discreetly to try and obtain the release of Régis Debray from prison in Bolivia.

PARIS, May 2, 1970

I went to see Foreign Minister Maurice Schumann this morning. He said that after Nixon's announcement of the dispatch of American troops into Cambodia to strike at Vietcong sanctuaries, there was no prospect in the near future of the over-all Indochina peace conference France had been working for. But France won't forget it and will continue to repeat the suggestion.

He said with regard to the American entry: "The official reaction we announced was moderate, but in fact we feel much more strongly. However, we respect President Nixon and we wish to do no more to embarrass him.

"Last year we had decided—and again this was emphasized when President Pompidou went to Washington—that there would be regular bilateral consultations on all major issues. But this was ignored in the case of Cambodia."

Schumann said that in recent weeks China has been taking the lead in southeast Asia and Russia doesn't like that. This gave us all an opportunity to involve Russia in international attempts to compose things at a peace conference. There was a kind of "objective" solidarity, to use a communist term.

But from now on, things will change out of all recognition as a result of the American invasion of Cambodia. The Russians are bound to speak louder in order to regain their lost influence. It is very likely that they will try to help their Asian friends—although they don't really want to do this—in order to keep China from gaining a political battle. And the most logical way for them to try and ease pressure in the Far East would be to try and create a diversion elsewhere—namely the Middle East.

MADRID, *May 8, 1970*

Dined last night with José María de Areilza, Count of Motrico, former ambassador to Washington and Paris. Only his wife, daughter Cristina, two sons, and a daughter-in-law were present. Motrico was both brilliant and funny.

Motrico was perhaps the staunchest and brightest supporter of Don Juan, Count of Barcelona, now eased out of the succession since Franco, last year, specifically designated his son, Don Juan Carlos, Prince of Asturias. M. says Juan was irked and relations between father and son cooled, but things have eased up now. Don Juan realizes he has no more chance and accepts that at any rate the dynasty will be revived.

Some 65 percent of the Spanish people are under forty and 50 percent are under thirty, so all the old shibboleths dating back to the civil war are archaic and inapplicable. The majority don't even know what is being talked about—or care.

The vice premier and right hand of Franco, Admiral Carrero Blanco, is reactionary and *dépassé*. M. calls him "our Spiro Agnew." He says he is "a great hollow tree, filled with bees." The "bees" are the industrious secret society, Opus Dei, which has filled the government and the economic structure with its members. M. says fourteen of the eighteen cabinet ministers are in it. The organization only has about 50,000 members; a mere 1,000 are all-out devotees who take the three oaths of poverty, chastity, and obedience. The key ministers are all in. Opus Dei has immense power but no popularity, and its head, the Aragonese priest

Escriva de Balaguer, lives in Rome. It has dominated the political scene after the political coalition of 1958–68 fell apart, and it is detested by the Falange, conservative monarchists, and the Left.

Opus Dei has shown remarkable financial acumen. It founded the Bank of Andorra (in Andorra, to escape red tape) to benefit from the great need for foreign currency during stifling restrictions. It seems to be linked with the MATESA scandal (a vast textile firm now accused of fraudulently filching vast funds from the public).

MADRID, *May 9, 1970*

Cristina Areilza took me yesterday evening to see a most interesting play about Goya called *El Sueño de la Razon* (The Dream of Reason), which has caused a sensation here. Working backwards:

The Goya is by Antonio Buero Vallejo and was written recently. It shows Goya in his old age (seventy-six) when he was producing his mad, grotesque paintings and fighting the king's political regime, the inquisition, and all oppression, but refusing to leave Spain for his personal safety. In the end, he is abandoned by all but his loving housekeeper-mistress; his house is stoned and marked with the label of Freemason; he is bullied and mocked by royal soldiers who rape his housekeeper; and at last he agrees to leave his home but never to abandon his ideas.

The political symbolism strikes every Spaniard today. King Fernando VII is depicted as a malicious, frightened old dodo (whom everyone associates with Franco). His prime minister, Calomarde, is seen as Carrero Blanco (vice premier). Goya is taken as the Spanish people, liberty, the spirit of Spain, fighting a decaying dictatorship and all its apparatus. The theater was jam-packed.

Today three young men from Madrid University came to my room and spent a couple of hours: all in their early twenties, of bourgeois antecedents, well-educated, and hoping to lead normal lives. They represented the committee of Madrid University which coordinates student movements. Only one said he was an avowed Marxist. What they wanted was a nonviolent take-over as soon as Franco dies, if not before. They spoke sadly and bitterly of U.S. policy.

One said: "In Vietnam and Cambodia you are not helping the people's needs, and you obey the dictates of the Pentagon, not your Congress.

"Another important thing that bothers us is that your executive ignores your legislature" (one of the complaints in Spain). "Our students are disturbed that your long democratic tradition is being overcome by fascist tendencies, a trend toward totalitarianism. And this is reflected by your relations with Spain.

"The agreements already existing and now being renegotiated between Washington and Madrid show this right-wing trend in America. Opposition to them in your Congress is not reflected in the Pentagon which insists you must have Spain to help your strategic position against Russia in the Mediterranean."

All three objected to the "penetration" here of any form of imperialism and named as "imperialist" states the U.S.A., Russia, Germany, China. They wanted a "European" type of democracy but recognized that a two-party system like Britain's was impractical, that Italy and France might be better models.

They were confident they represented "most Spaniards." They strongly opposed Juan Carlos and forecast he would simply strive to continue Francoism when he becomes king and wouldn't last "because the great majority opposes him." Don Juan might have made a constitutional monarchy possible but he was now finished. The only solution was a republic.

MADRID, *May 11, 1970*

Gregorio López Bravo, minister of foreign affairs since last October, received me this afternoon. He is modern and intelligent, a sophisticated elegant man, unlike some of his colleagues. He has a dark, somewhat Moorish face, speaks English easily, and knows the outer world.

Spain is most eager to join the Common Market. It is now engaged in trying to arrange a preferential agreement as the first step toward final admission. But Spain is not eager to join NATO. It "never asked for this." It is not just a question of opposition from some of the smaller NATO allies, but Madrid thinks NATO is "no longer up-to-date and polarizes attention toward the northeast whereas the biggest danger to Europe comes from the south. The Soviet fleet is in the Mediterranean and the Soviets are in Cairo."

He said Spain definitely considers itself an ally of the United States, which was its most important foreign friend. Current negotiations dealt not only with military matters but with friendship and cooperation in education, science, environment, information. These matters were "infinitely more important" than defense.

We discussed the drawn-out Spanish-Soviet contacts that have gone on intermittently for sixteen years. He said he himself had had personal talks in Moscow, during a lay-over at the airport there which lasted for several hours on a recent Philippines flight. Then the Russians had made contact through "a foreign capital" but they wished to keep this secret. There would be more such contacts "in the future."

Spain still insisted on settlement of its claim to $530 million in gold deposited in Moscow by the former Spanish republic. But the Russians, while not agreeing to end this problem, were taking a new initiative for talks. They have recently opened a merchant marine office in Madrid.

They want to exchange press agency correspondents and airline rights.

The next phase will be discussion of exchanges of consulates and a trade agreement. There are already consulates with Poland, Hungary, and Rumania, and negotiations for consulates with Bulgaria and Czechoslovakia. I asked if Victor Louis, the mysterious Soviet "journalist" and suspected secret police agent had been up to anything unusual on his recent visit here. López Bravo said he had only sought to have a *Novosti* (Soviet news agency) office opened here on the assumption that this might be "easier" for Spain than a TASS office.

López Bravo said Alborán is a small uninhabited rock spit off the coast near Cartagena, shaped like an aircraft carrier. The Russians have shown an unusual interest in it and the surrounding region, sending submarines there and using it as a rest area. As a result Spain has put a small garrison on Alborán and supplies it by helicopter.

We talked about de Gaulle's old idea of a Mediterranean pact. López Bravo said he was trying to revive the concept in a relatively limited form. It would be useful to have a large number of Mediterranean countries sitting around the table together. He thought of Italy, France, Spain, Morocco, Tunisia, Algeria, and Libya and considered it a western Mediterranean rather than a Mediterranean grouping. However, unless Algeria and Libya participated the idea would make no sense.

I inquired how much importance Opus Dei has. (López Bravo is said to be a member.) He assured me "it is only concerned with spiritual or religious things. It has no influence in other fields. There would be no possibility for Opus Dei to get involved in foreign policy matters, for example, not even such subjects as Russia."

Two workers, representatives of the underground national commission of workers, came to see me later on. One was a communist, an intellectual, from a very good family, married to an Italian, has often been arrested and beaten up by the police. Both are printers and up to the ears in secret activities against the regime. They continually linked "capitalism" with "dictatorship" as evils that had to be cleared away.

They said their organization represented both workers and peasants. These people had no valid representation in the state-directed syndicates. The underground had its organization in factories; the latter were then represented regionally; and there was a central headquarters to which both belong. The factory committees manage, during rest periods or the lunch hour, to have secret discussions on such things as strike plans. The organization also prints and distributes underground leaflets.

They were strongly in favor of a republic and opposed to Juan Carlos as king under any circumstances. They had called a protest strike as soon as he was designated Franco's heir because "the masses want a republic."

They admitted it would be a step forward if even a conservative liberal like Ruiz Jiménez were named prime minister, but they excluded the possibility. No gradual change was possible in Spain; it had to be total. Said N.: "This isn't a question of choice; it is a question of the objective forces involved. The regime is now at a dead end. Of course, it would attempt to react violently against us but violence can be controlled and civil war avoided. The great majority of students, intellectuals, and workers oppose the dictatorship."

Still later, I had a fascinating conversation with three members of the liberal clergy. Two, Father G. and Father C., were Jesuit priests. The third P., had been a Jesuit but left the order to become a layman and is now very active in various fields, ranging from film production to politics.

G. and C. were wearing regular black priestly suits with turn-around collar.

G. and many other liberal priests had "acknowledged" the regime until the second Vatican council (1962–65) whose liberal deliberations echoed through Spain like a shock wave and stimulated independent, antiregime thought. The younger clergy swiftly turned against Franco. No country in Europe had more priests in prison today (45 or 46—as against about 100 two years ago).

C. interjected that another profound influence had been the public protest of 140 Catalan priests in the streets of Barcelona against the torture of a communist student. "That," he said, "was the first time people could see with their own eyes how many priests opposed the regime." All agreed that the heaviest proportion of opposition came among priests under forty and that young men now leaving theological seminaries were more and more anti. Indeed, some actually quit the church and became "Maoist-extremists."

G. conceded that the majority of Spaniards were still proregime because of Franco's great personal prestige, because the police split up opposition, and because the government brainwashed them with TV. He thought that in a free vote today more than 75 percent would vote for Franco. But the people have no real idea what they want. Oddly enough, the important Maoist and anarchist faction came largely from sons of the middle class.

P. spoke about an eccentric far-right group called "Warriors of Christ the King" which struck at all even vaguely moderate elements, including the clergy. He himself had been wounded by them. C. added: "For them religion is politics," and P. said: "They are like the people who admired Charles Maurras in France earlier this century."

G. said Opus Dei was "very important." He described it as a kind of "sect" which acts in the name of God and regards Christ as a sort of caudillo. It had a totalitarian conception of the regime. It was semisecret, since no one knew exactly who were members, and was a sort of Catholic freemasonry. Opus Dei represented the first time a homogenous group had taken charge in the Franco government.

They all agreed that no real governmental reorganization can start until Franco dies and Juan Carlos takes over. It is impossible here to have "Francoism without Franco." There are no valid institutions in Spain. The monarchy has been forgotten. The Cortes is discredited. Franco is the *only* institution and most of those who back him today would not back Juan Carlos tomorrow. The only power factor that Juan Carlos can inherit is the army's loyalty.

The church is in a crisis. It has no organized political influence. G. commented: "We are heading toward a clash with the government and a separation of church and state. The bishops are beginning to take positions against the government ever more clearly, for example, on trade unions."

G. said the United States is regarded today as an unpopular right-wing country, especially because of the American bases here. The students and workers are especially anti-U.S. Nor is there much American effort to offset this. Our radio programs here never mention Spain while the communist broadcasts do.

MADRID, *May 12, 1970*

This morning I drove out to Zarzuela Palace a few miles from Madrid to see Juan Carlos de Borbón, the thirty-two-year-old Prince of Asturias who has been designated as Franco's official heir and next king of Spain (the first to sit on the throne since his grandfather, Alfonso XIII, left in 1931). Still unknown as a political figure and overshadowed by the bleak heritage of Francoism, he is widely called "Juan Carlos the Brief" because many people believe it will be impossible for him and a monarchy to survive very long. The old-fashioned conservative and liberal monarchists strongly preferred his father, Don Juan, Count of Barcelona, who has been cast aside. The present young generation is quite republican.

Zarzuela is a small palace inside a huge estate, rolling land studded with oak trees and containing considerable game. It is well-protected by military guards. The prince has an officer as his aide and a small staff, but the atmosphere is pleasantly informal. First, I waited in a study featured by a three-volume set on *Los Toros en España*, a signed photograph of Santana, the great Spanish tennis player, some bad old paintings and one indifferent modern, family photographs, silver cigarette boxes from service academies he had attended, a silver-plate trophy from a sailing race.

Then I was taken to another sitting room where he was standing, a grin on his sad, handsome face. He is about six feet two, slender but well set-up, with reddish fair hair. I had met him years before in Corfu and he greeted me as an old friend. I sat on a sofa facing color snapshots of his three youngsters, on a mantlepiece, and he sat in an armchair beside me, smoking several filtered cigarettes. I looked around: bookshelves, a model of a U.S. missile, knickknacks.

I started things off by asking if he automatically assumed power the moment Franco died; was there any ceremony; could Franco retire before then, or what? He said: "As I understand the law, within eight days there must be a special session of parliament and once I swear an oath there, it is done. Of course there will probably be some kind of *Te Deum* or religious ceremony. And as I understand it, General Franco can choose either to stay on or, if he wants, to resign. Moreover, I think that if he became physically incapacitated a crown council could decide if he was no longer competent to rule. But that is unlikely, I personally think it would be much easier for his family if he were to decide to retire."

I asked if he felt legally obligated to carry on the present ideology imposed by Franco? Wouldn't that place him in the position of the old Spaniards who rallied to battle behind the corpse of El Cid strapped to his horse?

He said: "I am not obliged to continue the ideology. The idea is continuity but not continuation. The basic theory will be carried on symbolically until a new generation takes over. We don't want to risk a big dramatic shift, a kind of revolution."

He acknowledged that he was lucky to be only thirty-two, because today more than half the country was thirty or less. This would help him to establish a bond with the nation. He thought a king in Spain, which was not only European but also Mediterranean, could never be only a symbol, as in Scandinavia or England. He had to rule through a government and prime minister, not to try and rule himself, but in a sense he had to influence events within the reigning formula. The best technique would be to show "that I am strong but not to use my strength except on very important occasions." It would be possible to do this, to exert pressure when need be, but tactfully and behind the scenes, more or less the way King Paul had done in Greece. "Not Constantine," he added, laughing. Constantine, his brother-in-law, is now an *émigré* in Rome as a result of an unsuccessful counter-coup attempt against the colonels.

Juan Carlos was certain the Spanish people would not like another military man at the head of the government (meaning the prime minister). The law provided that the crown council (about a dozen members) would nominate three names and he would choose the premier from among them. The council was supposed to represent a "quintessence" of parliament's opinion.

I asked whether he thought there was much chance that he would run into immediate opposition and deliberately engineered trouble as soon as he took over. He suggested that things would be a great deal easier for him "if Franco opens the doors a bit first, while he is still in power."

Was there any way of insuring against a "colonels' conspiracy" here in Spain? He said the only thing to do was to keep a sharp eye on "the national requirements and interest" so that the army, among other elements, would feel reassured. Military people are nationalists, he added, and loyal to their duties and vows. "They want no break in either unity or command." I remarked that no one could say the Greek colonels had not been "nationalists" but they had certainly broken army unity and the chain of command. He added elliptically that the army must see that the king doesn't meddle in political things.

I then inquired whether it was possible for him to have any serious contacts with anti-Franco elements so as to know the real mood of the nation. He assured me he did so, that anyone could come and see him, that he also could send for politicians and others he wished to see. He added: "Many think I don't see the variety of people I actually do see in fact, because this isn't reported in the press. The public doesn't know."

He wanted to be king of "all the Spaniards—that is to say, the Spaniards in Spain itself" (underscoring disinterest in Spanish-speaking areas abroad)—so I asked how he could guarantee that "all Spaniards" would be represented in a government under him, or at any rate its parliament. He said vaguely:

"One has to create the value of existing institutions—the municipality, the family, the labor syndicates. And from this point one has to proceed very carefully, step by step. You must remember we are walking along the edge of a precipice and we must above all avoid the risk of falling over."

I asked how his relations were today with his father, Don Juan, and the latter's supporters who still refer to Don Juan as "the king" and think of Juan Carlos as almost a usurper who sold out to Franco. He replied: "In a family sense our relations are very good. I speak to him often by telephone, but I do see him less than before because now I am in an official position. You know, he really did a wonderful thing in accepting this change. Politically, he says nothing, even when he talks with me. He wants to wait and see how things go. No one, not even myself, knows for certain whether he 'politically' accepts the change. But I think he does. Nevertheless, it is morally difficult for him to acknowledge this openly as he and his supporters have always been against Franco.

"He obviously didn't like the situation created when Franco named me, but for the good of the family he accepted it, at least in the sense of doing nothing but watch and wait. And his old supporters are still loyal to him but they accept reality for the sake of Spain. Now I want to show them and everyone that I am above ideology, above personal friendships, that I am ready to hear all viewpoints and talk with anyone."

I asked if he thought that monarchy was an efficient, viable system of government in the contemporary world. He thought it could be "very modern" if properly handled. He had given much thought to this but he couldn't give any public indications of how he intended to handle or modernize the role before he was actually in it; this would be tactless and embarrassing. Certainly television was very important nowadays and had to be used to advertize his symbolic role. Also state visits abroad were important to give a new image of Spain and establish better human and commercial relations.

He considered it most important to give his children a strong sense of family as he had had when a youngster and also to see that they mixed with other kids and had a regular school education, not private tutoring. We talked a bit about his personal life. He said his favorite sports were sailing (which his father adored) and shooting. He used to practice karate with Constantine "but you can hardly call that a sport." He does physical exercises and walks a lot. His preferred reading was history, memoirs, and detective stories.

He said Franco could make things infinitely easier for him if he used the excuse of the MATESA scandal to change the government and make it more democratic. He acknowledged that there was much more of a middle class in Spain today but cautioned me that there is an immense gap still between the educated city people and the backward country peasants.

He wanted to know my opinion of Greece. He thought Constantine should go back to Athens under any circumstances. I remarked that he had set conditions and made himself a symbol of opposition to dictatorship. "People will forget easily," said Juan Carlos. "He should go home." A rather cynical approach!

Above all, whatever he does, he should get out of Rome, Juan Carlos added. It is a bad place and filled with bad people.

MADRID, *May 13, 1970*

Last night Motrico invited a group of opposition leaders and intellectuals (all middle-of-the-road or conservative) for drinks and a chat. Apart from M. himself the following were there: Joaquin Ruiz Jiménez, former ambassador to the Holy See, university professor and lawyer, former minister of national education, a Christian Democrat, and the most important of the non-leftist leaders, the best-known oppositionist in Spain. Also Professor Enrique Tierno Galván of the University of Madrid (Law and Philosophy) a Social Democrat. Also Joaquin Satrustegui, a Basque intellectual, a liberal monarchist.

These four (including Motrico) are the leaders of the Center-Right opposition and were received by German Foreign Minister Walter Scheel when he was here last month. They hope Rogers will see them when he comes May 28–29.

Also there were: Professor Pedro Laín Entralgo, in charge of experimental psychology at Madrid University, member of the academy of medicine and history, author, anthropologist, a disciple of Marañón and a liberal. Also Don Antonio Menchaca, Basque businessman and writer, former army officer, a liberal monarchist. Also Dr. Miguel Ortega, an intellectual physician, a liberal monarchist, son of the famous philosopher, José Ortega y Gasset. Also Julián Marías, professor, author, academician, liberal monarchist (former Republican who fought in the Republican army during the civil war—unlike the others). Also Josefina Carabias, editor of the morning paper *Ya*, former foreign correspondent, an avowed Republican.

It was a pleasant and stimulating conversation in which the Spaniards often disagreed with each other—except on the primordial point: the need to change the regime. Ruiz Jiménez dominated the proceedings: a tall, good-looking, energetic man who speaks fine English.

All agreed that the United States now had an unfortunate image here of authoritarian imperialism; that it was a mistake to renegotiate the base arrangement; that Rogers should listen to opposition views during his visit; that Hill, the present ambassador, was a disaster and both he and his staff were outright regime supporters with whom these people could no longer maintain contact. They said Opus Dei controlled the government, that Franco was going slowly gaga, that Carrero Blanco was a tough, fanatically loyal (to Franco) fool. They disagreed on whether it would be wise to work with the communists and accept them as an open party when freedom comes, in order to keep an eye on them or to ban them. They admitted the communists were the best organized and disciplined opposition group.

PARIS, *May 27, 1970*

George Mylonas is a member of the Greek political emigration and long-time backer of Papandreou, now living in Geneva—having been arrested and exiled to a barren island by the colonels and escaping under dramatic circumstances. I lunched with him today, a charming, short, pleasant man of fifty-one who looks extremely healthy—although he has a bad heart—and makes no complaints that he was beaten up or maltreated. His escape was accomplished by a group of amateur Italian boat enthusiasts.

Although they are from the same party, he savagely denounced Andreas Papandreou. George says Andreas only seeks to further his own fortunes and forgets those of his country. He admires Theodorakis, the composer, a great deal.

2 5

THE CARE AND FEEDING

OF TOURISTS IS

NO SOVIET SCIENCE

Moscow, *June 2, 1970*

F LEW IN HERE YESTERDAY ON A COMFORTABLE FOUR-JET ILYUSHIN
62, the newest Russian passenger plane. It did the flight from Paris
in three and a half hours.

But the care and feeding of tourists is not yet an exact science. I had
been relieved of some $2,300 (all hard money) in advance by the In-
tourist subagent in Paris and given a clutch of tickets good for everything.
I was met by an officious dyed blonde from Intourist (name Smirnov—
"like in the vodka," said she) with the news that there had been some
confusion and my room in the National Hotel had been canceled. I was
going to the Russia, largest hotel in the world.

Every nation, I suppose, gets the tourists it deserves and has its own
way of treating them. The French clip them; the Italians pinch them; the
British disdain them; the Japanese kowtow to them; and the Americans
regard them as curiosities. Only the Russians wholeheartedly make them
at home (Soviet style) by according them the treatment of Soviet citizens.

Within two hours of arriving, I had a tic in my writing hand from filling
out papers and was automatically ready to join any queue of more than
twenty people. I was prepared to acknowledge as impressive a traffic
"jam" that would seem sparse on Sunday in Keokuk, Iowa, and to accept
as beautiful a hotel room with a view of the brown, polluted Moskva
river across from a power station with ten immense, grim chimneys and
a sign recalling Lenin's slogan: "Communism is Soviet power plus electrification of the land."

The Hotel Russia is about the size of the Pentagon. It might have been built and staffed by Ramses II. It would certainly exceed the combined administrative talents of the best Swiss, Japanese, and French hotel schools—none of whose graduates are on its staff—and one can get lost for three hours en route to the dining room. Its operational system combines Parkinson's Law and the Peter Principle. Payment for everything is issued in the special scrip of Intourist, the only travel agency in the world's largest (acreage) country, and every piece of scrip even on the way from waitress to kitchen seems to require a countersignature.

It is probably a compliment to be accepted as one of them by this remarkably durable people, but one does feel like a sheep in sheep's clothing as one is pushed around by the lowest-scale functionaries who have no incentive to be helpful, efficient, or polite.

And yet it is awe-inspiring to see the gaping admiration of tourists arriving for the first time in the free land of socialism with its cities banned to foreigners, its discomforts, its appalling effrontery in making you pay in advance for what you are likely never to get, and its cumbersome method of manufacturing the hugest mountains of difficulty where even a molehill isn't necessary.

The system here is inefficient and costly but it does function—with the large manpower and considerable national wealth available.

Scientists are now so important they are less liable to be purged. One reason for the isolated scientific cities like Dubno and Akademgorodok is to keep them from "infecting" other people.

There is no major dope problem among the youth. However, in Georgia signs have been reported warning against the dangers of hashish. The narcotic of Russia is vodka.

Many cities are still officially closed, including over 15 percent of the country and Sverdlovsk, Gorki, Vladivostok.

The number of arrested dissidents is not enormous. Their underground "Chronicle of Events" lists under 200 as confirmed arrests. This is a small-scale persecution of intellectual dissidents, no neo-Stalinism.

There are no hippies to speak of. One sees long-haired boys fairly frequently but it's frowned on.

The generation gap exists, mildly. Youngsters complain about old-fashioned doctrines. They find inherited dogmas irrelevant. They think more for and about themselves. But they don't feel "rejected" by society as in the West. There *is* something for them to do. The situation here is much healthier than in America.

In the last few months Brezhnev has moved increasingly to the fore. Collective leadership remains, but he is *primus inter pares*. In 1964 he became first secretary of the party. In 1966 this was changed to general secretary. It is inevitable that power accrues to the man in that post; everything is geared to the party. He is now taking a greater "public" role. In April he published a two-volume set of speeches in 500,000 copies; Lenin's last official biography sold only 100,000. Brezhnev couldn't move forward like this without army support but the army is not "engaged" in politics.

Dined with Angelo Vlachos, Greek ambassador. There are some 30,-000 Greeks from the Crimea now living in (transported to) West Uzbekistan (with Greek passports but unable to leave the country or travel in it) and another 10,000 to 15,000 Greek civil war refugees in East Uzbekistan (Soviet citizens). If a Greek diplomat asks to visit either group he is requested to leave.

The Greek military attaché drove to Tbilisi and Yerevan and on the way he picked up a Georgian hitch-hiker. The Georgian said he'd like to buy his car—black market. He explained: "There are wonderful places here to hide it." Seems they pay a huge ruble price, hide the car some weeks in a canyon, then remove the plates and sell it.

Moscow, *June 3, 1970*

Called on Jake Beam, U.S ambassador. Jake thinks there is no such thing as a "Brezhnev policy" but rather a group or collegial foreign policy in which Brezhnev is the leading figure but not solely boss, as Khrushchev had become before he was ousted. The policy is now designed to isolate the U.S.A. slowly but immutably—but at the same time to remain in contact with the U.S.A. on vital matters: to keep the Red Line to Washington handy, to negotiate at SALT, to discuss trade. But the Russians are trying to prise our friends away wherever they can, to slowly isolate us in Europe, to help eject us from southeast Asia, to take over from our vestigial influence in the Middle East.

There is no sign of a thaw on China. Russia is really worried about China preempting Sihanouk, who might have been Moscow's point of entry in Indochina. Russia still has relations with the Lon Nol government and doesn't deal with Sihanouk's ambassador.

Russia helped bring Vietnam to the table in Paris but not to talk, despite our bombing halt. It has now raised the ante and wants us to withdraw before there are negotiatons.

Signs of the current freeze: Beam told me he had told the head of the foreign ministry American department that I wanted to see Kosygin ("and he only grunted"); the acting chief of the press department said he was "too busy" to see me; Arbatov, head of the American studies institute (whom I know) was "unavailable"; and [Georgi] Ratiani, a *Pravda* editor whom I've known for years, had agreed to come with his wife for lunch today, then his secretary called up and canceled—after I'd ordered the lunch.

Lovely, hot, sunny day. Moscow looks soft and different under the lilac bushes than under snow. Very clean and quite gay. Old women sell little bunches of roses on the curbs.

Called on Leonid Zamyatin, head of TASS, former head of the foreign ministry press department. He was extremely cordial. Asked me to promise to call him on return and he will give me lunch with Arbatov (of the American affairs institute).

I was taken in by Ivan Ianchenko, head of foreign relations for TASS, a burly dark Ukrainian. He turned out to be an old friend from Cairo, where he was stationed from 1944 (when I was president of the war correspondents association) until 1951.

Zamyatin said the SALT talks were going very well. Said Mao had attacked Russia as heavily as the U.S.A. in his speech last week. China is trying to divert attention from internal problems by its external quarrels.

MOSCOW, *June 4, 1970*

Six days ago a well-known scientist, Zhores Medvedev, was detained and has since been held in a mental asylum in Kaluga. Major Soviet scientists have protested this, as well as other detentions of intellectual "dissidents." Medvedev is a leading biologist. Professor Andrei Sakharov and Dr. Pyotr Kapitsa, the physicist, have led the protest at his detention. Sakharov has also protested the detention of Major-General Pyotr Grigorenko, another dissident declared mentally incompetent last year. Sakharov called for democratization of the Soviet system last year. Medvedev, for his part, wrote a book published in the West which attacks the officially imposed genetic theories of the Stalin era and other repressive aspects of the state. Sakharov is associated with Roy Medvedev, brother of the detained man, a historian.

Yesterday evening I had drinks with Professor David Joravsky, a historian at Northwestern University, visiting here for a conference. He has known the Medvedevs for years. He told me Zhores M. was picked up six days ago, subjected to medical diagnosis two days later, declared not mentally ill but "very nervous" and is still being held in the Kaluga city psychiatric hospital.

Zhores M.'s story is directly related to the savage political quarrels over fake genetics during the Stalin era, involving Trofim D. Lysenko and the late I.V. Michurin, rather phony "scientists" who dealt with crops. Agriculture is the basic problem of the Soviet system. "Michurinism" and "Lysenkoism" had no application to human beings because it was for years dogma here that only "racists" were interested in genetics. The theory here is that men are developed by social laws, not biology.

In 1948 a political decision was made to give Lysenko a monopoly over all biology in the USSR, education and research.

In 1962, Medvedev wrote a book on the Lysenko affair. At the time Lysenko had reasserted himself as a Khrushchev favorite. Medvedev's book wasn't published but it circulated widely in the *Samizdat* (underground) literary circuit. Lysenko was and is an agronomist, not a classical geneticist. He was a Stalin political colt because he pretended to quack ways of quickly and cheaply increasing crops.

In 1964 both [Nikita] Khrushchev and Lysenko fell from favor and Medvedev's book was about to be published. Then Podgorny stepped in and again banned it. At this point Medvedev decided to have it published abroad and it was issued last year by the Columbia University Press.

Medvedev, who is half Jewish, feels strongly that he must stand up for truth and justice. His father, a professor of philosophy, disappeared in the Stalin purges of the 1930s, and Medvedev wishes to honor his memory.

Zhores M.'s book was frowned on because the bosses today don't want the past of Stalinism once more to be exhumed and criticized. They want what is dead to remain dead. But Medvedev wants to honor his father by proclaiming the truth.

Moscow, *June 5, 1970*

After work this morning I managed to find one of the rare taxis and drove to the house of Edmund Stevens, an old-time American newspaperman here. The taxi driver, when he discovered I was American, promptly offered to change any dollars I had for three rubles to the dollar. (Official rate—$1.10 equals one ruble!) I declined.

Ed's wife, Nina, has a magnificent collection of seventeenth-century Russian furniture, seventeenth- and eighteenth-century icons, and ultramodern Soviet paintings. She is a kind of mother-superior and agent for painters and has arranged exhibits abroad in New York's Museum of Modern Art and other collections.

Moscow, *June 6, 1970*

Lunched *chez* Henry and Ludmilla Shapiro. Henry, the UP bureau manager, is now in his sixties, first came in the 1930s as a young lawyer, married Ludmilla, his secretary. He says Stalin has been rehabilitated as a war leader only. This movement started with Marshal [Georgi] Zhukov who, although demoted by Stalin, described him in his memoirs as an effective wartime leader. All recent military memoirs have confirmed this. But the personality cult is still condemned. Stalin's brutality and authoritarianism are disapproved. He has not been resurrected as a god-like image. Monuments are being built to some of his most prominent purge victims.

Khrushchev has been made into a rather ridiculous figure: a hair-brained schemer, a boorish show-off, a clown. But Stalin hasn't risen because of this. There is no statue on his grave behind Lenin's tomb, although he has been there since 1962.

What runs the country now is less a strong repressive reaction than controlled conservatism. There are no arbitrary arrests (or very few); no midnight knocks on the door from the police. And the reaction from Khrushchev's era is not violent.

Of course, under Stalin, there could never have been a *Samizdat* literature. There is a group of fairly well-known young dissenters many of whom have operated for a considerable time. People don't "disappear" anymore.

There *is* a retrogression. But the extent of "liberalization" under Khrushchev has been exaggerated in the West. It contrasted sharply with the Stalinist past but was far from complete.

Brezhnev is the boss. He was always *primus inter pares* as head of the party and now serves as chairman of the board. But he is not the absolute, unchallenged top man as was Khrushchev. He is a rather colorless, faceless man.

The party is building up Brezhnev, but he is still colorless and it is still collective. Kosygin is brighter than Brezhnev but he also has little personality. He is a small provincial-leader type when compared to the witty, sharp, original Khrushchev, who liked to quote "Russian peasant slogans" he invented himself at the spur of the moment.

The top marshals are all members of the Central Committee—or alternate members. After all, they couldn't even have become colonels without party backing. But Zhukov committed political suicide when, on behalf of the armed forces, he supported Khrushchev against Molotov in 1957. This party will *not* tolerate any voice speaking on behalf of anything except the party.

Stalin never let the army develop any independent policy. Nor did Khrushchev. Nor will Brezhnev. Military policy is made by the party. But now, if Marshal Andrei Grechko thinks Russia is endangered by a liberal Czechoslovakia, he says so. Brezhnev listens with more respect to military opinions than did Khrushchev—on China, Czechoslovakia, etc. But if any marshal shows himself too independent or plays politics, he will be fired.

There is real anti-Semitism today. A very bad writer named Ivan Shevtsov published two very anti-Jewish novels. He is a naval officer and such a lousy author that he was blackballed by the writers' union. He talks in his books of an "international Zionist conspiracy" which backed Trotsky here and grabbed power in many countries. In his last novel, *Love and Hatred*, a Jew kills his mother, wraps her guts around his head, seduces nice blonde Russian girls, and introduces them to hashish. When this was published, he was bitterly criticized; but it was published—and in 300,000 copies, by the armed services publication house.

There is both political and social prejudice and being Jewish is a real disadvantage in public life. And one hears of persecutions, or at least discriminations, reported from local provincial functionaries. Moreover, there is religious prejudice. There is no Jewish religious seminary so the present crop of rabbis is the last. There is no publishing in Hebrew. But Christian Orthodoxy still has seminaries and publishes; its priests travel.

Relations with China are very bad, potentially more explosive than with the United States. The division is basic and will probably continue even after Mao dies. But there is unlikely to be any war. China won't attack Russia; it is fairly cautious and realizes its relative weakness. And Russia won't attack China, thus creating a super-Vietnam. There will be a long period of neither war nor peace.

Sochi, USSR, *June 8, 1970*

Sochi, which was warm, sunny, and lovely today, is a perfect example of "where every prospect pleases and only man is vile." Magnificent trees and flowers, some early ripening figs, the Black Sea rolling up to pebbled beaches, banks of high mountains climbing up behind. Even, one might add, splendid trains, huge hydrofoil sightseeing craft, helicopters whirling tourists into the hills. But heaven forbid that anyone should ever dream of advertising communism by its holiday set on the beaches. I say communism, not Russia, because during the day I walked several miles along the sea front and saw not only our little Intourist Hotel beach (crowded with Finns and East Germans) but many other Russians-only *plages*, all filled with great puddings and barrel-molds of women and men, hideously taking the sun or playing cards with rakish hats atilt and pieces of paper on their noses to fend off the burn. Aesthetics is not the great *forte* of the system.

Sukhumi, USSR, *June 9, 1970*

A pleasant drive to Sukhumi, capital of the Abkhazian Autonomous Republic of the Georgian Republic. The Intourist Hotel Abkhazia proved to be drab and dirty but pleasant, with a friendly staff. My room, best in the place and, I suspect, the only one with a bath, had three beds in it. It had a wide porch overlooking the smooth Black Sea. The bathroom was coming apart, crumbling, with soldered pipes and cracks. As always, you can't tell the hot water by the label or color of the taps, as these are indiscriminately marked hot and cold. At lunch I ordered red wine. "There isn't any," said the waitress, blissfully ignoring the fact that the people two tables down were drinking some. At the next table were three young Russian men who had already consumed four bottles of Soviet champagne.

TBILISI, USSR, *June 11, 1970*

Judging from its benign aspect in Georgia, I know that while I would never make a revolution *for* communism I am not sure I would ever make a revolution *against* it. When I think of the poverty, beggars, and corruption to the south in Iran and Turkey—as well as the elegant intelligence on the tiny top layer and the glitter of their booming new bourgeoisies—I wonder if they are healthier as nations than this pleasantly sluggish haven of the Marxist malformation.

This system eliminates the top and brings everything and everyone down to the lowest common denominator in order to start upwards afresh. Of course, the bureaucrats, technocrats, and a few intellectuals rise like yeast from its depths. They are the most needed. However, half-baked capitalism to the south aspires to hoist the impoverished masses upwards, but it is too greedy to make a serious effort.

TBILISI, USSR, *June 13, 1970*

Drove to Gori on the Liakhvi river in a broad valley with peaks to the west. Tris is Stalin's birthplace and the one city in the USSR where he is still openly admired with a Stalin museum, his original house, a Stalin square with a large bronze statue, and a Stalin avenue running into it.

The cottage in which he was born is tiny (two rooms and basement) and he, his mother, and his shoemaker father lived in one small rented room with a single, not very wide bed. The other two children died as infants. The cottage is sheltered with a large marble roof and walls.

The museum is very large and also marble. At the head of the main stairway is a large statue of Stalin with a quotation from him, in Georgian and Russian, saying: "As far as I am concerned I am just a pupil of Lenin and my aim is to be his worthy pupil."

There are no pictures in the museum of that unperson, [Leon] Trotsky, although all other early Bolshevik and Soviet leaders are shown. Nor is there any of Svetlana [Stalin] although there are letters from Stalin to his daughter (from the 1930s). There is one photo of his first wife, one of his second, one of his air-pilot son, several of Jacob, another son, who died a Nazi prisoner of war. In the section on World War II there are statements praising Stalin from various Soviet marshals. Also pictures of the wartime Big Three conferences. There is a white plaster death mask showing a heavy-lidded, sensual face.

YEREVAN, USSR, *June 16, 1970*

In the afternoon we drive over the Hrazdan river toward Echmiadzin along a flat plain past vineyards, orchards, and mulberry trees (for silkworms). Echmiadzin was built in the second century A.D. and was capital for four centuries.

Visit the austere and beautiful St. Rhipsime Church. She was an early Christian proselytizer who was slain after spurning the king's offer of his hand. Then drive to the cathedral, originally built between 301 and 303 but substantially modified since. It is inside a large, walled enclosure where the Catholicos (patriarch) has theoretically sovereign powers.

YEREVAN, USSR, *June 17, 1970*

Everything is tawdry, for example the clothing they buy and the gimcracks they sell, and there is stifling bureaucracy, inefficiency, with even the Intourist guides skipping off as early as possible or passing the buck to their local colleagues in museums, etc., because there is simply no incentive to do better. But there it is. The patient, durable Soviet people (primarily the Russians) have made it work by making themselves amenable to the system. And by its own priorities—for example making vast numbers of trucks, as compared with automobiles, trucks that can be used to carry soldiers as well as goods, they get more out of their system than more wasteful luxury societies get for the same expenditure.

MOSCOW, *June 19, 1970*

Useful talk with Sherrod McCall, a secretary of the U.S. embassy who specializes in China affairs, concerning Sinkiang (Chinese Turkestan, which had once been a Sino-Soviet condominium). He said that Victor Louis told him last February that China was stirring up a pan-Turkmenian movement aimed at Soviet Central Asia and that Moscow would not take this lying down. McCall interpreted this as advance warning that the Russians were promoting a similar movement for Sinkiang. Within days this was confirmed and since then Isa Yusuf Alptekin, a Sinkiang *émigré* and agent for this movement, has been traveling around the world spreading the free-Sinkiang idea.

Marshal Ivan Yakubovsky's warning last February that China was preparing for war is typical of the feeling in Russia's military-industrial complex which wants an excuse to keep a high level of defense expenditures. On May 8, Marshal Grechko said this country's defenses in the East had to be as strong as in the West.

The best guess is that a decade of preparation is now underway in both China and Russia in which to get ready for a possible showdown. The key will be whether one side or the other uses the decade more effectively than the other. China might make a weapons breakthrough; or Russia might make a deal with West Germany, pacifying its European frontier. Either could make a deal with the U.S.A. If any one of these things happens it could throw off the timing of a showdown.

Moscow's policy in Indochina is now to fulminate against us but to wait watchfully, doing nothing. It hopes Hanoi will come to its senses and see that it is over-extended and also needs to free itself of too much control by the traditionally distrusted Chinese. Russia privately prays for a U.S. success in Cambodia and spreads reports of Chinese armed troops in North Vietnam (which can't be confirmed).

Both China and Russia have strong military dispositions along their enormous border. China's real weight is back from the frontier, ready for a people's war from rear positions. But it has a communications construction program under way. Russia maintains an extensive and costly deployment which includes tactical nuclear weapons in the Eastern USSR and Mongolia.

Moscow has established a new command area—the central Asian military district which includes 1,200 miles of border in Kazakhstan, Kirghizia, and Tadjikistan. Last summer, when there was a tense period, the headquarters previously in Tashkent were sent to Alma Ata and that is where the new district's center is.

On both sides the need for defense is used as an excuse for slowing down of economic programs. Moreover, the military-industrial complex of the USSR uses the Chinese danger as an excuse for asking more funds.

Second only to Soviet fascination with China is Soviet fascination with Japan. And the latter is growing at an even faster rate. There is a substantial Japanese investment now in east Asia. Of the foreign business representatives listed in the information directory for Moscow prepared by a Soviet editor, twenty-four of fifty are Japanese.

A large Japanese involvement is being considered in Tokyo for the natural gas of Yakutia, an East Siberian region near Yakutsk. Linked to this—also under consideration—is a new railway system in the Pacific Maritime Province that would connect with Yakutia—but that would also give the Soviets a new means of outflanking China.

LONDON, *June 30, 1970*

Lunched with young Winston Churchill who is being sworn in as a member of the House. I was interested in doing a column on four generations of successive Churchills in the Commons. Lord Randolph, his great-grandfather, was a member from Woodstock although he was a duke's son (peer's younger sons are allowed in Commons). Woodstock is next to Blenheim, seat of the Marlboroughs. He had a brilliant career and was chancellor of the exchequer at thirty-six, coming within an ace of the prime ministry, his evident ambition. He was well under forty when he died.

The great Winston Churchill always used to say: "I am a child of the House of Commons." He was twenty-six when he was first elected.

(Young Winston is twenty-nine; his father, Randolph, was thirty or thirty-one; his great-grandfather, Lord Randolph, was in his late twenties.) Randolph (young Winston's father) was born in 1911. At twenty-one having read a life of Pitt (who became prime minister at twenty-four) he was convinced he would do likewise. Yet, when Randolph was nineteen (he later told his son) he was walking at Chartwell with his father, who said: "I don't know what I should have done had my father not died when I was nineteen." What he meant was that "two Churchills are a crowd."

LONDON, *July 1, 1970*

Lunched with George (Earl) Jellicoe, leader of the House of Lords and lord privy seal in the new Heath government.

He predicts the new Tory government will be "a less loyal satellite to you people on Vietnam; we believe that a real friend should speak out frankly." This may come as a bit of a shock to Nixon as events proceed. The U.S. president was plainly pleased by Heath's surprise victory.

Afterwards I saw Lord Carrington, the new defense minister. Carrington is a middle-sized, wiry man with spectacles, large nose, taut mouth, intelligent expression.

He said the British people tended to underestimate the efficiency of the South Vietnamese army. Nevertheless, it is clear the U.S.A. will have to review its commitments. One result was that "we shall have to take a new look at SEATO which is becoming unreal quite now, with the special Pakistani and French attitudes." The Philippines and other Asian allies will be less interested in SEATO when the U S. leaves Vietnam.

Carrington said Britain wished to keep some forces in the Persian Gulf area "if we are wanted." It is an uneasy region and with the uncertainty of previous Labor policy too many claims and counterclaims had been advanced by the little states in that region. He thought Britain should try and settle some of these arguments and also get the Persian Gulf federation going before it withdraws.

Britain still depended on that region for more than 50 percent of its oil, despite new exploitation in Nigeria and new discoveries in the North Sea. Moreover, when the British do get out, there is absolutely no doubt that the Russians will move in—in order to make trouble "as they always do." And Kuwait remains exceedingly important to Britain. "We will depend on Middle-Eastern oil for years to come."

We discussed possible nuclear sharing, for Europe, between Britain and France. As an intellectual exercise, he said, this would be wholly sensible. Europe would have to be in a position of looking after itself more as America cut its forces, which seemed likely. And a united (not federal) Europe should favor a nuclear-defense arrangement on a modest scale. But there were immense practical difficulties. It would have to be done with the good will and approval of the U.S.A., on which Britain had depended for secrets and aid. However, once Britain was ultimately in Europe, there must be an effort to do this.

LONDON, *July 2, 1970*

Agreeable chat with Sir Alec Douglas-Home, back as foreign secretary in the new Tory government. Home was his usual polished, unruffled self. With reference to UK-U.S. relationships, now that London's government has changed, he said: "One thing, of course, is that we understand power perhaps better than Labor. For a long, long time the Tory party has been involved in the power politics of the world. We understand the burden of the United States, both instinctively and sympathetically. We understand what your involvement in Vietnam and Cambodia is about. We know that there is a place in world stability for the discreet application of power. We sympathize with the United States in the difficult position you have assumed. It is a lonely business to have to do some of these things alone—as only your president can really know. We ourselves can only do modest things to help out; we don't have the strength to do more.

"But one of the factors that influences our attitude on southeast Asia is the effect of our policy there on the United States. We know that it is helpful if we can share a Commonwealth responsibility in Malaysia and Singapore even if we cannot go into Vietnam.

"Moreover, both of us, your country and ours, understand the role of the sea. We know the need to keep the sea routes open and we want to help on this. We can't do much but we know there is a job to be done for the free world and we would like to do what we can."

Home said Washington was pleased by the Tory government's commitment to keep a small force east of Suez. There was a big problem in the Persian Gulf because all the sheikhs were now busily making claims and counterclaims. And the Shah of Iran wanted control of some of the small Gulf islands (not Bahrain) to keep himself from being bottled up by the Russians.

Russia couldn't very well assert its position in Aden and Somalia until the Suez Canal is opened but that when this happens, the continuation of some British presence east of Suez will be a stabilizing factor. After all, the Russians have greatly strengthened their fleet and one can't be sure just how they intend to use it. We must be certain that our trade routes are not interrupted, and both Britain and America are accustomed to this kind of maritime approach.

DUBLIN, *July 5, 1970*

Flew to Dublin and spent the night with John Moore, now American ambassador here, who has a lovely residence in Phoenix Park, across the way from President [Eamon] de Valera: spacious grounds filled with vast trees, green lawns, and pheasants picking their elegant way across the grass.

Yesterday we flew to Shannon where John's car had driven early to pick us up and then drove on through Limerick and Adare to the coast where John Mulcahy, an Irish-born American who has made a fortune in engineering, has bought a salmon stretch of the Waterville River called Butler's Pool and remodeled a large house beside it. I managed to kill one salmon.

Drove back to Dublin, through the beautiful Killarney lakes. On the way John told me some magnificent Irish titles still in use (although a republic, Ireland still honors as "courtesy titles" the old peerages). Among those in use today: The McGillicuddy of the Reeks; the Knight of Glin; the O'Conor Don.

DUBLIN, *July 6, 1970*

Moore invited me to lunch with Hugh McCann permanent secretary of the ministry of external affairs and former ambassador in London. We ate at the Kildare Street Club, Dublin's last citadel of the old Anglo-Irish aristocracy, where I was much fascinated to examine the weighing chair, a heavy, leather-covered armchair on a scale with weights beside it, on which the club members would weigh themselves.

McCann is a blue-eyed, friendly man who was clearly in a high state of excitement because of the riots, burnings, and stonings in northern Ireland during the past two weeks since Bernadette Devlin (Ulster Catholic woman member of the British House of Commons) was jailed for inciting violence in Londonderry last year.

McCann said Dublin is disappointed that the violence and British military actions of two days ago came right on the heels of the British elections, installment of a Tory government, and the visit to Belfast of [Reginald] Maudling, the new home secretary.

He says that since the Stormont government was formed in Belfast in 1922, after the Irish Republic's creation, there has been no change of government—only the Unionist party. Apart from the Soviet Union it is the only European government that has been consistently run by the same party for forty-eight years.

The Orange Order, the extremist Protestant group in north Ireland, stages 1,400 parades a year, most of them designed to exhort bigots and threaten Catholics. The Orangemen oppose all reform, want the status quo, and blackmail any political leaders who wish tolerance or change. They fear that the larger Catholic birth-rate will menace their favored position unless the Catholics are kept in a legally disfavored position.

This afternoon I had an extensive conversation with the *Taoiseach*, John Lynch. *Taoiseach* (which means approximately "leader") is the title of the prime minister. (*Uachtaran*, which means approximately "top man," is the title of the president.)

Lynch, who is fifty, comes from Cork. He has no independence-war or civil-war record, is an athlete, a lawyer, married, with no children. He is regarded as a low-key moderate.

I started by asking if this was not an age of partition—Ireland, India, Palestine, Germany, . . . Korea, Vietnam? This being so, why and how should these situations be ended?

He said: "Partition is the easy way out of insoluble problems. But it is devised as a temporary solution. No partition is imposed with the idea of permanence. [He is wrong—viz India and Palestine.] This is especially the case for Ireland which was always united until 1922. Lloyd George offered a choice between immediate partition or a terrible war and King George V agreed, but everyone thought of this as a short-term solution."

Lynch said he had become prime minister in 1966. "We hoped admission to the Common Market would make the border between ourselves and the Six Counties (northern Ireland) virtually irrelevant. But this all came to naught when the hardline extremists gained control in Belfast" (and anyway Britain and Ireland never got into the Market).

Lynch said that although the concept of bringing things together inside a larger framework hadn't worked yet he had not abandoned it. Sooner or later he was confident the nations of the world were bound to draw closer together. Dublin was behind the "European" idea for two reasons: (1) Ireland regarded itself as a European country; (2) economically it was too dependent upon Britain and wanted to change that pattern.

He said the prospect of a population transfer of Protestants to England from Ulster (with financial aid) some day was "not on." The Irish, north and south, are now a homogeneous nation. Even the Scottish stock, "planted" in the north, had been there three centuries. Dublin guaranteed full and equal rights to all citizens of all faiths under its rule. "We want no population exchange."

He admitted that "some people" want to intervene with arms, but they are a "very small minority. We haven't got the military strength. And, anyway, we want a peaceful settlement for its own sake."

He said the IRA is regarded as an illegal organization under the "Offences Against the State Act." It is a small minority and, between its traditional and its left-wing (procommunist) factions, doesn't contain more than 1,000 active members.

Later I also called on Eamon de Valera (Dev, as he is popularly known), grand old man of Ireland, eighty-seven, president of the republic and president of the first *Dail* (parliament) in 1919. I saw him in his residence at Phoenix Park, where the English lord-lieutenants used to live, a splendid house in a magnificent setting of lawns, trees, ponds, which the poor man can barely see. I had thought him quite blind and he told me during our talk "seventeen years ago I lost my sight" but his military aide told me he can actually see television programs very dimly.

He is tall (still well over six feet) and has large, thin features, rimless glasses, an austere look, rather humorless. When I entered, I found him sitting erect at the desk of his study dressed in a neat grey suit with some kind of red buttonhole decoration. He arose courteously, shook my hand, and asked me to sit down beside him, I facing the window (so he could at least see a dim outline of my shape). He was polite but remote.

He told me he had been reared in a political atmosphere from his earliest days. His father died and at the age of two and a half his mother brought him home to Ireland (from America, where he was born) to live with an uncle who, although a laborer, was keenly interested in politics. He remembered from his earliest days arguments, talk of shootings, and violence.

He did well at arithmetic when he was at a Catholic school and much to his surprise passed as Number One in the mathematics examination. When he decided to be a teacher he chose math as his field. Catholic priests always taught the classics extremely well, but the Protestants were traditionally better at math because their best teachers were all educated at Trinity College, which was famous for mathematics during the nineteenth century.

As time went on, de Valera conceded that he had developed a passion for the subject—so much so, indeed, that he kept up with it until just five years ago. Seventeen years ago, he had lost his vision, but he asked his secretary to learn the Greek alphabet "so she could read mathematics to me. She kept this up until five years ago. But now some people are writing a book about me. I do not want to write an autobiography myself but I want to be sure the details are accurate, so I set aside a certain amount of time almost every day in order to help out. Therefore I no longer have other time to spare and have been forced to give up mathematics."

The greatest disappointment in his whole life, his greatest failure, had been "the treaty" that was negotiated between Irish representatives and the British in 1921. (This was the cause of the Irish civil war when de Valera's backers fought those of Michael Collins.) De Valera said this treaty, which acknowledged the sovereignty of the English king, had been imposed by the British and did not regard Ireland as a sovereign state although the independence war had just been won. Nor had Ireland's negotiators even reported a word of its contents to Dublin. The first he learned about it was from the afternoon newspapers reporting its text. He had been appalled and furious. "That was my greatest disappointment," he added. "I never recovered from that."

The only subject that clearly ignited his mind and awoke his interest was Ireland—and, apart from the fact that he is constitutionally forbidden to make public statements, this is far too hot and delicate a subject right now to permit presidential views. Just last weekend (and today is Monday) there have been savage riots, killings, woundings in Belfast, and British troops have disarmed the city's most belligerent Catholic quarter without taking similar action against Protestant extremists. There is an air of crisis.

DUBLIN, *July 7, 1970*

Last night the Moores had Todd Andrews and his new young wife over for dinner. Andrews, a very tall man with ugly, intelligent face, is in the inner circle of the Establishment here.

Andrews sneered at the "voodooism" of northern Ireland and the terrible, frightening drum-beating parades of the Orange Order with their broad orange sashes, gloves, and hard derby hats, doing their best to scare out Catholics.

He said with Irish glee: "What damned fools the English are to provoke us into a propaganda contest. Now we are just beginning. We are the greatest propagandists in the world because we are the greatest liars in the world."

This afternoon I visited Foreign Minister Patrick Hillery in the *Dail*, where he has an office. Hillery proved to be a handsome, trim, fit-looking man of forty-three.

He said the trouble with British policy was, as the old Irish proverb says: "You are easily led where you want to go." If a bloodbath starts on July 13, it will be impossible to stop a tragic course of events.

"If the extremists' idea of being British were applied elsewhere in the British isles, those who tried to apply it would be ridden out of town. They have an outdated concept. Being British is a changing thing, not a seventeenth-century thing."

Hillery said Prime Minister Lynch might fairly be called a "dove." He has enormous personal prestige and is a new type of revolutionary who doesn't reach for a gun. But he is using up his prestige and he will perhaps be thrown on the scrap heap if London caters to northern extremism. Hillery made it clear that he was consciously appealing to the "hawk" element himself.

He said he had "loved" his day yesterday, secretly visiting Belfast, and hoped to dictate a private memo on the experience. "They are all Irish people, after all—even Paisley."

Hillery is an attractive, slick fellow who loves acting and action. He is playing a dangerous game, trying to cut the throat of his friend, Lynch. The smell of power attracts him. He has moved to the center of the stage, above the orchestral pit, and would rather fall into the latter than abandon the former.

WASHINGTON, *September 16, 1970*

Started the day with an eight o'clock breakfast at the White House with Henry Kissinger (trays in his office). His office has moved upstairs, acquiring the space once used for press rooms, which have been moved to the old swimming pool area. H. still also retains the former downstairs space for his staff.

Nixon is visiting Tito. Kissinger said Tito had "very useful credentials with Nasser" and we did not; therefore Tito could be effective if he wished. I asked if Tito would also be asked to help in Hanoi. Kissinger answered: "We don't need him on Hanoi. We have our own direct contacts. But he can be useful on Nasser where we have very bad communications right now."

I asked if there was a conscious "linkage" between the Soviet-U.S. talks on SALT, Europe, the Middle East, etc. He said that linkage is "a fact of life" which must be accepted although it was not created as an idea by Washington nor is it consciously pushed as such. But SALT is conditioned upon a reliance on national means of inspection and the assumption that the other side won't frivolously violate agreements. The fact that the Middle East cease-fire has been violated from the start is obviously bound to affect SALT. This has been diplomatically pointed out to Moscow.

The Russians had no interest in destroying Israel—unless the price for its preservation changed, which could occasion second thoughts. But pro-Chinese guerrilla groups were indeed seeking to sabotage peace. The Russians were concerned because they are quite "psychopathic" on the subject of China. (I doubt this. The Russians don't really get psychopathic. I have heard Henry use this word about Moscow on Israel before.)

We really don't know why Moscow itself and through Cairo has so blatantly violated the cease-fire conditions. Had Russia let the cease-fire negotiations get established it could have used the pretext of Israeli violations as an excuse for its own violations. Now we wonder, however. Are the Russians headed for a showdown?

I asked about reports that Egypt had asked for some kind of U.S. security guarantee that Israel wouldn't violate the cease-fire. Henry said this wasn't true and, anyway, commented sadly that nobody was convinced anymore that any kind of U.S. guarantee is any good. It is plain to the world that the U.S. doesn't keep the promises it makes. De Gaulle's 1963 prediction that isolationism is mounting in the U.S. is now coming true.

The UN could serve as a nominal buffer in the Middle East. But it is weak. Right now UN is supposedly "observing" the cease-fire. But it is less able than the big powers (whether the Two or the Four) to obtain observance of its conditions. It can, however, help out on air piracy. A great many countries share an interest in this even though they have *no* special interest in vague problems like the Middle East. Skyjacking affects all lands which use the air and they would support an international agreement of a multilateral sort. Even Cuba.

Henry was "very worried" that anti-Semitism will develop from this crisis in the U.S.A. Many Jews here prefer their Marxist orientation to their Jewish heritage. There are signs of this already. Moreover, many of those most vocal in their opposition to our Vietnam commitment want to fight for Israel. And a great many Americans object to the latter attitude. Both China and Russia will seek to fan this flame and split opinion in the U.S.

At the time of Pompidou's visit this year, the argument over French planes for Libya made differences between Washington and Paris on the Middle East appear more acute. Now they seem less acute. But France is less inclined to support what we want in negotiations, even though it is useful for the West to have one friend among the Arabs. We think there is no real "grand design" in French policy; just an effort to promote French commercial interests and support this with big theoretical arguments.

On the Common Market, Kissinger said we strongly support British membership on the expectation it would lead to a political community that would benefit the West by assuming more of the burden and taking in the German question. This would compensate for the economic disadvantage to us of a competing bloc. But we are certainly not eager to see the Market expand if it remains *only* an economic bloc.

Right now we wonder about German policy. Either Brandt really means what he says about Western unity—which will get him in trouble with the East—or he doesn't—which will get him in trouble with the West. This is a problem to be faced. Yet the illusion of modern statesmen is that a problem doesn't exist if they claim it is solved.

Henry says there is no evidence that the Soviet-Chinese crisis is easing. Soviet military strength on the Chinese border is increasing. There are today more Soviet divisions facing China than Europe. I asked if Henry was sure. "Positive," he said. "And they're smack on the border."

Until the cease-fire violations in Egypt and "Soviet horsing around in Cuba these days" we had thought this indicated a desire for *détente* with the West. Now we are not so sure. The Soviet movement of their own SAM-3 units (six battalions) into the Suez zone worries us. And they continue the build-up each week.

U.S. credibility is involved: both promises to Israel and [Secretary of State] Rogers' statement that SAM missiles are not considered "defensive" weapons by us in the Suez zone.

The problem is how to substitute for old-fashioned gunboat diplomacy, and no contingency papers have found the answer. Gunboats used to be harbingers of more power—if needed. But things are different. And it is nonsense to say, as many do, that wherever the Russians move brutally they are defeated in the eyes of the world. Look at Czechoslovakia.

We have certain hard ideas on precise Israel peace terms—Jerusalem, etc. Also ideas on military problems on that basis. But 2.5 million Israelis against 80 million Arabs makes a difficulty.

We must remember that wars start between countries at peace. The best we can hope for in the Middle East is the kind of situation prevailing between India and Pakistan. Even Arab "moderates" want to regain territory from Israel. And even if the U.S. gives guarantees, the problem will continue. No U.S. guarantee can substitute for Israeli military strength. The U.S. "intends" to do something about the present crisis. But the degree and timing of our action hasn't been fixed.

Frank talk with General Yitzhak Rabin, the Israeli ambassador, a young-looking man of slight, short, but strong build. He has a nice, open face, blond hair, earnest expression. He received me on this abysmally hot day in his shirtsleeves.

He says any acceptable settlement must be based on an agreement between Israel and the Arab states. Such a settlement should include: territorial changes and permitted military deployments making it possible for Israel to defend itself against the total strength of the Arab world without reliance on other countries except for military hardware.

Israel recognizes that it is not realistic to rely on outside guarantees for its survival. The basic consequence of the six-day war was to demonstrate that Israel must rely upon itself.

The two superpowers are involved in the Middle East crisis. But it is a "Vietnam in reverse." Soviet forces are directly involved in a regional war but U.S. forces are not. Israel would prefer a situation in which both superpowers would refrain from involvement of their own forces in any actual Middle East fighting. Israel above all wants Washington to secure such a commitment from Moscow.

Israel *does* want the U.S. to deter Moscow from involving its forces in the area, that is to say, its combat forces, not technicians or supply experts. Israel wants hardware access in the U.S., good credit terms, a deterrence of Soviet forces. It asks no U.S. involvement so long as any war is local.

No political settlement is possible now. Large parts of the Arab world simply aren't ripe for it. But if the military situation is quieted, this helps create an eventually better atmosphere. A year or two of a freeze on the Suez area will help.

However, the only incentive to Moscow for peace is the fear of risk of escalated war. There is *no* other incentive. The U.S. peace initiative was good and well-timed. But Moscow believes Washington will swallow whatever it does and press Israel to continue the cease-fire. The Russians base this calculation on the lack of U.S. reaction when Soviet forces and missiles were first introduced into Egypt last March. The failure of the U.S. to compensate for this was interpreted by Moscow as weakness.

The number of Soviet pilots in Egypt available to fly advanced MIGs exceeds Israel's total force of supersonic planes. If Israel could face Arab aircraft on a one-to-four ratio basis, it could manage. But not also Soviet pilots on operational missions.

In September 1969, when Mrs. Meir was last here, Israel asked the U.S.A. for 100 Skyhawks and 25 F-4s. The stress has now shifted to the F-4s which are supersonic (unlike the Skyhawks). The 50 F-4s sent by Johnson have been reduced by 6 to 7 lost in combat. The U.S. is now meeting some of Israel's request.

Lunched with Averell Harriman. He doesn't think it is very easy to do anything in the Middle East because we have already started to backtrack, before the skyjackings, by not reacting to Soviet cease-fire violations. He is very bitter but says Nixon is quite right to do everything possible to save the lives of American hostages and do nothing to jeopardize them.

He is depressed by the mood of the country and the rise of the "hard-hat" Right.

WASHINGTON, *September 17, 1970*

I spent most of today with Dean Acheson out at his farm in Sandy Spring, Maryland. It is a pleasant, comfortable building set in rolling corn country. I talked with Dean for an hour and a half in the little former print shop which he uses as his study and as a guest house. Then he and Alice drove me to the Olney Inn in a nearby village, where we lunched because today the Achesons' servants were off. I was amused to notice that Alice, who is both lovely and frisky as a septuagenarian, ordered a whisky sour before her lunch. She is charming, quietly mischievous, and feminine.

His print shop office features a huge old stamping press. It was here that the seal of the secretary of state was first designed and printed a century and a half ago, and he has a framed print of it on the wall. He was exceptionally friendly, an erect, distinguished, and elegant figure in a white suit Mark Twain might have envied.

He had a minor stroke earlier this year and is under doctor's orders to take life very easy. His physician misdiagnosed a thyroid condition, and this has had a very bad effect on his eyesight. He has to alternate among three sets of heavy, prism-lensed spectacles.

I told Dean I had only one question to ask him. Was there any way of substituting for the old "gunboat diplomacy," which has become too dangerous in the nuclear age, some other means of applying restrained threats of force for diplomatic purposes? He answered:

"We are in a big fix. The essential difference between our problems and those of Russia is that ours are almost entirely in the field of being constructive and theirs are in the field of letting things go to pot and then picking up the pieces.

"Russia wins by everyone else losing. The Russians don't give a damn about the Arabs or the Israelis. They only want to establish a suzerainty over the Middle East. Israel cannot win any more great victories and the Arabs are too weak. But the United States will be the big loser if the Russians move in and take over.

"Part of our problem is that you cannot make terrible mistakes without in the end paying for them." (Here he was referring to his opposition to the creation of the State of Israel and its support by the U.S.A.) "And the tremendous advances the Soviets have made in the military would make gunboat diplomacy too difficult and too dangerous."

He went on: "Europe is the area where the lesson of power can be learned. One discovers about power that it is a subjective as well as an objective problem. Certain people can do more than others with physical force. Take the example of the Russians and ourselves.

"Even the Russians were weaker after the ruthlessness of their role in Eastern Europe, but they don't have much of a problem with public opinion at home. We can't win even next door in a place like Cuba. Our institutions and our culture inhibit us and break down our effectiveness. Force is useful if you get into a row with another force you want to destroy, but even that is not always desirable. Force is a dangerous thing. When we can and do apply it, we perhaps accomplish more than we wish, as when we totally destroyed Germany and Japan in World War II and upset the entire world balance.

"We have had in the past to deal with fallible and often foolish people. We discovered our terrific weapons. Dulles's great mistake in 1954 was to talk of instant retaliation in places of our own choosing. But we and our allies had been talking about developing conventional forces so that the Russians could not advance without the risk of nuclear attack. When Dulles advanced his cheap formula for atomic protection, all our allies decided that they, too, would defend themselves on the cheap and not raise the necessary conventional forces. And the Russians were smarter than we thought. They developed their own thermonuclear weapons. And all this was worsened when we made the mistake of joining the Russians in 1956 against Britain and France (Suez).

"Now there is stagnation. We can't even deal with Castro. When I was called back during the Cuban crisis in 1962 I found the Kennedy brothers in a terrible flap. If Khrushchev hadn't been crazy he could have won. What would President Kennedy have done if Khrushchev had just paid no attention? We announced a blockade in order to get Soviet missiles out. But you don't blockade things in when you want them out.

"When I talked with Adenauer at the time, after Kennedy had sent me abroad to explain our position, Adenauer said he couldn't understand our policy and asked me to explain it. I only told the chancellor: 'Faith moves mountains.' "

Acheson continued: "What is the answer when one side has a positive program and the other side has a negative program? We are now in a period where there are mediocre men everywhere. People have opinions but no knowledge, and leaders are made in the image of the masses. Democracy is only tolerable because no other governmental system is.

"There is no substitute for gunboat diplomacy. I think it was Elihu Root who said that when governments were run by tyrants the danger of war came from deliberate purposes. But when governments are run by democracies the dangers of war come from faulty premises. Of course both tyrants and democracies can suffer from both weaknesses. It is often possible in this world to have fools and rascals together."

He said we were still besotted with nineteenth-century beliefs, like the idea of world government as expressed in Tennyson's *Locksley Hall.* Franklin Roosevelt, and above all Cordell Hull, had believed this "even after almost everyone in the world had come to consider this impossible." He talked about "that awful UN" which he described as "a curse to mankind." It was ridiculous to think that you could apply the democratic system for all mankind in some kind of a democratic world government. He said that Truman's decision to go into Korea had been right and that it would have been successful if MacArthur had not been in charge of applying it.

He then said that force must always be applied "in a proper way." He added: "Unless one is prepared to act quite wisely and with a great deal of restraint, however, it can get out of hand. But force does not exclude other approaches to a problem. If you are using force you can still negotiate. You can take a military action in an area while still keeping Moscow informed on the hot line to explain your limited goals and methods and avoid escalation."

He said one of the troubles of the 1956 Suez disaster was that the British and French had told Washington nothing "because they didn't trust Foster. I don't blame them. I didn't trust him either."

Dean told me Nixon had called him in once for his advice and he had told the president that the only way to end the Indochina war was to start removing our troops. We had in Vietnam too small a force to crush the opposition and too large a force to be accepted by the patience of the American people.

He added: "We must remind ourselves and the world that we have force and are prepared to use it wisely. But it is hard to convince people that we will use it wisely when it is being unwisely used in Vietnam."

He recalled sourly that Averell Harriman from 1966 to 1968 had been a complete hawk on Vietnam although, he said, Averell simply does not remember this at all nowadays.

WASHINGTON, *September 18, 1970*

Pleasant lunch with Dick Helms (head of the CIA). He is pessimistic about peace between Russia and China although Moscow may have deferred action because of the Middle East problem. The Russians now have about thirty-five divisions—over 300,000 men—facing China, between the Maritime Province and Turkestan. They used to keep only 50,000 men there. The great increase has been since 1965. The troops are very well equipped. Why are they there?

We are now investigating reports that Russia is building a submarine base at Cienfuegos, on the southern coast of Cuba. This, in a sense, is like putting missiles in there although, of course, Soviet submarines could launch a surprise attack from the high seas. It is said the base is designed to shelter Y-class Russian subs, their equivalent of our Polaris-launchers. This is *not* yet confirmed.

WASHINGTON, *September 20, 1970*

This Sunday afternoon I went out to McLean, Virginia, for a drink with Senator Edward (Teddy) Kennedy at his lovely house on a bluff above the Potomac.

Teddy took me around, first showing me the view and then displaying some mementos, including President Kennedy's statement on the Cuban missiles as amended in his own handwriting, and also his completely re-edited (in his own handwriting) statement on Teddy's decision to run for the senate while Jack was president. He also showed me several paintings he had done, including one of the family house at Hyannisport. They were somewhat better than Eisenhower's. He uses the new quick-drying paints.

Teddy is a massive, handsome young man (thirty-eight). He is about six foot one and looks as if he weighs about 210 pounds. He is strongly and heavily built rather than fat, although he may well have trouble with his weight in another decade. He has broad shoulders, huge arms, and great square hands. His features are conventional, his complexion clear, and his eyes frank, open, and blue. He talks glibly but his intelligence is neither profound nor quick.

I asked what kind of secretary of state he would choose if he were ever elected president. He hemmed and hawed and said that of course this was not a subject he could give serious consideration to, but when I pressed he continued:

"Frank Church [Democratic senator from Idaho] would certainly be a good man. He is extraordinarily perceptive and realistic. He might today be very qualified for that job. Of course, in connection with the question you pose, I think of younger people I know well. Don Fraser [Democrat-Farm-Labor, Minnesota] in the House of Representatives is the kind of man I mean. Or John Culver [Democrat, Iowa] of the House foreign relations committee. I think of men whose performance I know. And with whom I have had to deal."

I asked if he could describe his own basic aspirations in foreign policy. He said the objectives outlined by President Kennedy were really valid today—above all "to make the world safe for diversity." He wanted to see a world in which different ideas could exist and be freely expressed. He recognized that the problems of the next ten or fifteen years were enormous, but this was good. He wanted to see other states embrace the concept of frankly expressed diversity of opinion.

I asked when he thought it was valid for a nation to use force in international relations. He said, "The best you can do is to work out a formula to handle situations as they are presented. If we in the United States can do this and establish fundamental agreement on such things between the executive and the legislative, this has the value of making clear our attitudes on other countries and avoids accidental involvements." He said that undoubtedly any movement of Soviet troops into Western Europe would bring a forcible response from the United States. Likewise the Cuban missile crisis could have brought a U.S. employment of force. "Clear situations" demand such a response. But there are other less clear situations where U.S. intentions must be understood even if they are not openly expressed.

"There *are* limitations," he continued. "I would never get involved in a country that is ill-conceived and has no sense of integrity or doesn't have a clear role in terms of our national interest" (he was obviously referring to southeast Asia).

He said we should redefine our alliances and commitments as time passes and should not regard these as static or permanent. When I asked him to be more precise about what he considered a "well-conceived" country with a national tradition of "integrity" he said that Jordan and King Hussein should be regarded in line with his idea of a nation state and were "a great deal different from Laos—or West Africa." I found these observations confusing.

I asked how he discerned any difference between the foreign-policy attitudes of the Democrats and the Republicans. He said both parties have their liberals and their conservatives, but there was quite a difference between the political backgrounds of the parties. Many more of the constituents of the Republican party advocated the use of force than was the case with the Democrats, who had a "more moral and restrained attitude."

He went on to say that foreign policy as such was still an important political factor in Massachusetts and it came up often in his present campaign. Vietnam was still the Number One topic in this respect. He cited a great many figures which certainly are catchy although I don't know how valid or accurate. For example, he said it costs $178,000 to kill each Vietcong where as only $55 was spent per annum to educate each American child.

Kennedy said on more specific matters that he wanted to withdraw two and a half of the five and a half U.S. divisions now in Germany and to do it as soon as possible. He wants to pull all American forces out of South Korea. He wants us to get out of Okinawa as soon as possible to avoid being "pushed out." He wants to see Western Europe defend itself and thinks that if we pull out two and a half divisions unilaterally this will stimulate an interest in European self-defense. He wants the U.S. to be more accommodating to the Soviet Union and Eastern Europe. He wants to see all of Europe develop as an "independent factor" between Russia and the United States.

He continued: "The challenge we ought to bring to the Soviet Union is one of competition on such things as education or pollution. And we should develop in this country a constituency for nation building and development. Foreign aid should not be seen as an anticommunist factor as in the past. We should back national development in other countries and not simply frighten people into nation development.

"And as for West Germany, we certainly shouldn't keep American troops there while they are making a deal with Russia.

"In the 1970s and the 1980s the big crisis will be between the haves and the have-nots. In the world at large it will be like in this country where there are pockets of poverty and American cities are exploding. There are flash fires in the world just as there are here.

"Furthermore I think the Chinese should be in the United Nations and on the security council. It is important that we make our resources available to China's huge population. But unfortunately the United States is becoming more protectionist. I can see this with Massachusetts industries like textiles and shoes. This country is moving into a period of constriction and protection.

"There is a difference between the use of military power and bases and the effort to help other lands improve themselves. But I recognize the need for national defense. We must always have one more missile than the Russians have."

I asked if he thought we should do anything to prevent communism from taking over Latin American countries providing this was done by legal means such as elections. He said the United States had "no right" to intervene in such circumstances and "we should get our CIA and military advisers out." Furthermore, he thought we should reexamine the relationship with Cuba and eventually end our efforts to isolate that country.

He thought foreign policy would remain an important issue in the 1972 presidential election. Moreover he thought the American people saw the special responsibilities of the senate in this connection "and that is why political leadership is now in the senate" rather than among the governors of the different states. Quite obviously Kennedy was talking with at least an unconscious reference to himself as a presidential candidate in two years, regardless of what he says in formal speeches.

Indeed, he said that if he won the presidency in 1972 he would try to pull a Mendès-France policy in Indochina and get all American troops out of there within a specified length of time.

WASHINGTON, *September 21, 1970*

I spent an hour and a half at the Pentagon with Defense Secretary Melvin Laird. There is a riproaring crisis over the civil war in Jordan between King Hussein's army and Palestine guerrilla forces aided by the Syrians.

Our conversation was almost entirely about the Middle East. He was convinced the Syrians in Jordan were "surely there with the knowledge of the Russians." Laird said Egypt was the only Arab country in which there were actual Soviet combat units.

But he did not think there was any chance the Russians would participate directly in the Arab-Israeli war at this stage by joining in an assault on Israeli forces over the Suez Canal. They stood to lose too much in such a direct participation.

Laird said we are still convinced the existing balance between Israel and the Arab forces on its border remains favorable to Israel—if there is no direct participation by Soviet combat units. He insisted there had been no significant decline in the Israeli advantage because of the movement into the cease-fire zone of Egyptian SAM-2s and Soviet SAM-3s.

It was natural Israel should want more weapons from us; all armies always wished more equipment just as all generals did. He said the Israelis had over $40 million in their budget on annual arms purchases in the United States—but the United States has already committed ten times that amount to Israel and "we are satisfied that they will get enough materiel and that they will get it fast enough."

It would be very difficult to supply any emergency materiel to King Hussein, who is now fighting for his life. From the U.S.A. to Jordan was a very long logistical supply route.

The Russians are obviously interested in keeping us tied up in Vietnam while the Middle East crisis goes on. There is no doubt that Soviet strategy has changed and Moscow is intensifying pressures in the Mediterranean and on NATOs southern flank. "Our position there is even worse than a year ago," he said.

There had been quite an argument in the administration at the time of the air hijackings as to whether it was practical to contemplate an airborne operation to seize and liberate the foreign hostages. But as soon as we learned that all the planes had been wired for immediate detonation, we dropped such thoughts because it was absolutely evident that all the hostages would be killed in such an attempt.

NEW YORK, *September 24, 1970*

Sir Alec Douglas-Home told me that when he saw Tito last March the Jugoslav leader said Russia's greatest weakness was technological. The Soviets did not have enough modern technological output to satisfy their own requirements, and had absolutely nothing left over to satisfy the requirements of the satellites. As a consequence the satellites were increasingly restive and eager to have access to Western productive facilities and closer contacts with the West. The Russians wanted to keep their satellites happy, but at the same time they did not fancy the thought of taking the political risk of permitting an expansion of their contacts with the West. This was a dilemma without solution, Tito thought.

The second point made by Home was that ultimately—if there is to be an Arab-Israeli settlement—there must be some kind of arrangement to prevent a new outbreak between them. Either you could place a serious four-power force between the adversaries, or it might be better just to establish a no-man's-land so that it would be clear who violated it if there were any infringements. Should there be a four-power force (with Russian, American, British, and French contingents), it would have to receive specific advance instructions that no state could attack it without being counterattacked, and that no state could bypass it.

Sir Alec is convinced the Russians cautioned Syria not to invade Jordan, but were disregarded. However, he doesn't think Moscow urged Syria to pull its tanks out. That action, he believes, was decided upon by Damascus only after the Syrians "received a bloody nose."

NEW YORK, *September 29, 1970*

I had an unusually interesting lunch today with Allen Ginsberg, the forty-three-year-old poet, purported drug addict, and acknowledged homosexual, who is the idol of the hippies. He has been writing to me for months—long, confused letters decorated with peculiar scribbles which are politically hostile to me and attack me for my views on Greece and other areas, but which have also indicated an undertone of friendliness. I had contacted him in upper New York state, where he is a member of a kind of communal farm of his philosophical brethren, and when he came to New York this week we agreed on a luncheon date.

I met him in Dinty Moore's restaurant, which has suddenly become very jazzy, and I think the headwaiter and his colleagues were a bit startled. Allen had arrived before me and was sitting at our table, sipping a ginger ale, when I showed up. He is a slight fellow of middle height (perhaps five feet nine) with long, shaggy hair and beard, glasses, kindly, glittering eyes, and was dressed in a dark assortment of motley quasi-hippie clothes featuring a chain around his neck. He smelled a bit high but was friendly, disarmingly innocent, and certainly intelligent. When the bill came he touchingly reached into his pocket and came up with a fistful of dollars, offering to pay it.

He is convinced the CIA is up to the ears in dope peddling and that, in this respect, it is in cahoots with the FBI and the treasury customs agents. He thinks J. Edgar Hoover is a frightful man "who is not even a homosexual like me, but doesn't do it with anybody." Moreover, he insists that Hoover blackmailed Martin Luther King by getting evidence on him when he was spending the night with a white woman.

He regards Timothy Leary, the Harvard faculty member who was sent to prison for openly advocating the use of LSD and other hallucinogenic drugs, as a great hero and a martyr to the Establishment represented by the CIA and the FBI. He says that Leary in fact was the first man to advocate a sensible, controlled, and moderate use of such drugs to avoid excess.

Allen claims he himself is not an addict, although he has used all kinds of drugs; he is afraid of the effects of both LSD and heroin. But he is convinced police agents are trying to plant marijuana or other drugs on him in order to railroad him to prison.

He says he only began to write poetry at around the age of twenty. His mother died in an insane asylum and he was brought up in Paterson, New Jersey, by a father who was a rather timid socialist of the kind who "even thought the Vietnam war was OK until two years ago." He was a homosexual from boyhood, and because society refused to accept this he felt so repressed that he was unable to express himself by pouring out his soul in what later became his poetry. It was only when he was studying at Columbia that he got to know Jack Kerouac and William Burroughs and found people who accepted his homosexuality without trying to ostracize him, that he at least felt free enough to embark on his career as a poet.

He says William Blake is his great source of inspiration and he almost feels as if he had had a mystical message from him. Walt Whitman is much less so. I see a great resemblance between the poetry of Ginsberg and Whitman and, moreover, Whitman was a homosexual from New Jersey.

He has a refreshing view of the importance of news, which he says is entirely ignored by the American press. Thus, for example, he claims that the fact that the blue whale ("an animal probably more intelligent than man") is on the verge of becoming extinct is a much more significant bit of news than anything the press carries on its front page each week. He says that 40 percent of the living matter in the world's oceans—primarily plankton—has now been destroyed, and that this is more significant than, for example, the Vietnam war.

NEW YORK, *September 30, 1970*

Abba Eban said that during the brief but bloody Jordanian civil war, after Syria intervened on the side of the guerrillas, King Hussein was in such desperate straits that he conveyed word to the Israelis directly and also through the United States asking for help. He wanted the Israelis either to stage a ground strike against Syria or an air strike against the Syrian tanks in northern Jordan. By good fortune he managed to save his own bacon.

NEW YORK, *October 2, 1970*

Late this afternoon we went over to have drinks with Frank and Shirley Williams at their apartment. Frank used to be U.S. ambassador to Ghana, but quit in the late spring of 1968 because he felt that as a Negro he should know more about what is going on in American race relations, and he felt out of touch.

He now saw that the primary educational need of our time is to educate those who most need it, rather than the middle class, which can afford to pay for it. Obviously this requires an entirely different set of standards. In this day and age a college degree is as necessary to achievement in later life as a high school degree was in our generation. And the poor, under-privileged, and intellectually backward black must be given a chance to catch up even if he does not qualify for the admission standards fixed with the white middle class in mind.

The real need for the black man today was equality more than freedom. It is obvious that the whole "black is beautiful" concept and "Afro" hair styles, etc., are asseverations that have come to be accepted in order to over-compensate for past inferiority. Only after a generation of this overcom-pensation can there be a gradual return to the aspirations for a mixed society that Frank worked for as a young man.

PARIS, *October 8, 1970*

Telephone call from Jozsef Szall in Rome. The poor fellow has skipped.

Jozsef had, in the end, decided to go back to Budapest, following his recall as Hungarian ambassador in Italy, to take a job as head of state broadcasting—much as he disliked the idea. But I gathered from a hysterical and almost incomprehensible call that he couldn't take it any more, "an accident" occurred, and he had suddenly fled to Rome (Lord knows how). He wanted help—badly and immediately.

On my previous advice,* he had called on Graham Martin, the U.S. ambassador, and Martin told him he could give him no answer before Monday (four days from now) and Monday is a long way off. I explained to Jozsef that I was going to Cairo tomorrow, but that I would try and do all I could.

When I finally got him to hang up, I called Martin, who said that he had already contacted Washington and, much to his surprise, was told to lay off.

CAIRO, *October 10, 1970*

Breakfasting *chez* Donald Bergus, the American chargé d'affaires in this anomalous situation where we have no official diplomatic relations but carry on as normal, using the Spanish embassy as a cloak, and even sending a high-level delegation headed by a cabinet member to Nasser's funeral.

He said Anwar el Sadat, the new president-elect, is more impressive than he had believed. The present regime takes about the same view of the United States as Nasser's. We were headed for a showdown on SAM missiles in the cease-fire zone with Nasser—and we still are. It is hard to imagine Washington getting the Israelis to negotiate with the missiles there —and Cairo won't pull them out.

This cease-fire, he continued, is the best there has been since the Israeli war started in 1948. It has been scrupulously maintained. Both sides accuse each other of violating the standstill terms but the cease-fire is kept because both want it. Cairo, however, demands a time limit and doesn't want an open-ended cease-fire. But the Egyptian military are all for it now since it allows them to complete their air-defense system while taking no casualties.

CAIRO, *October 11, 1970*

Cairo looks peaceful and relaxed and there is no hint of emotional hysteria such as was so manifestly demonstrated in the remarkable mass

* See page 622.

funeral demonstrations for Nasser, which everyone says were without parallel. At night the capital is in a semiblackout.

I went over yesterday evening to see [Mohamed] Heikal at *Al Ahram*. He hopes soon to shed his job as minister of national guidance. In 1955 Nasser had asked him to be minister of national guidance but he'd declined. In 1961 he offered him the foreign ministry. Finally, in April 1970 he announced publicly that Heikal had been named minister of national guidance—before telling Mohamed; then he insisted Mohamed accept.

Mohamed is an emotional man and felt the death of his friend Nasser deeply. Also he is overworking, took no holiday. He now wants to write a book about Nasser; I hope he does. It should be very good.

He spoke of the "unimaginable grief" expressed after Nasser died. He had had an "unbelievable" rapport with the people of both Egypt and the Arab world. After his death there was such hysteria that waves of suicide were feared.

On the day of the funeral Heikal breakfasted with Kosygin and then accompanied him to the ceremony. He was struck by the fact that even this emotionless man was moved. "To see tears in the eyes of that man was very strange," he said.

Not one of the heads of the foreign delegations to the funeral was able to move more than ten yards with the cortège. There was really no control. Three army divisions had been called in to help the police but they were simply brushed aside by the immense mob. The mosques and parks were jammed with people sleeping overnight, visitors to Cairo.

CAIRO, *October 12, 1970*

Valuable talk this afternoon with François Puaux, the French ambassador, a tall, thin, pale man. Since June 1967, he says, the Russians have been very clever. Their military help has been unchallengeable as only defensive. They haven't interfered. But they aren't popular. People still rush to see American films, ignore the Soviet cinema. Egypt remains oriented toward the West. It is only interested in the West. The Russians, who are poor, thrifty, hold modest jobs, are looked down on as "poor whites" and not respected. In the army they behave arrogantly and show that they despise the Egyptians. Moreover, nowadays no nation can be popular in a foreign land if it maintains forces there; even the 12,000 to 14,000 Russians here to help Egypt aren't liked.

Nasser never wanted to be left alone in a tête-à-tête with Russia. He constantly hoped for good relations with the U.S.A. He had great hopes after Nixon was elected.

Now a dangerous period begins and Washington should take care not to repeat its 1955 mistakes when we told Nasser he could only have arms if he joined the Baghdad pact and Foster Dulles stopped the Aswan Dam credits. The situation is somewhat similar to 1955. Everyone here says they wish to respect Nasser's desires—which wanted military aid from Russia *and* good relations with America. His successors could stress either line.

Nasser told Puaux in April 1970: "I will never allow a Sovietization of Egypt."

This evening I called on Sir Richard Beaumont, the British ambassador. Lee Kwan Yew, the Singapore prime minister, was recently here and received the impression that Anwar el Sadat had privately felt Nasser was too pro-Soviet. El Sadat was anti-British by prejudice but Beaumont feels he is less pro-Russian than Nasser.

The U.S. and Russia tend more and more to regard the Middle East in terms of each other, not the Arabs and Israelis. The Russians are linked to Egypt's strategy which is in essence defensive. The U.S. is linked to Israel's strategy which is in essence offensive, to punish the other fellow's lines of communications and supplies, etc., if not to strike first in preemptive war. This forces Washington unconsciously into an aggressive diplomatic position.

2 6

EL SADAT–THE PRINCE

OF THE ISLAND

CAIRO, *October 13, 1970*

VISITED THE ANTIQUITIES MUSEUM THIS MORNING. STRIPS OF paper are pasted over the glass cases to reduce shattering in air raids. The stacks of painted mummy cases are both frightening and funny, something like an Egyptian mob. And the idea that the big shots, like pharaohs, were inserted in series of ever-larger cases must have been the origin of the famous Russian babushka dolls.

In the mummy room itself it is ghastly to see the withered remnants of pharaohs dead between 3,500 and 4,000 years, with high-bridged noses, tiny, scrawny necks and curling, agonized feet. Ramses II looks like a pickled Nehru, instead of a massive Nasser with big hips and broad shoulders as in the colossi of the Nile Valley.

Saddest of all is Nefertari, the beautiful queen whose fresco with two handmaidens, at Abu Simbel, is the loveliest portrait of three women in the whole world. Even her parchment-covered skull is still beautiful with a delicate haughty nose, jaw-line, bone structure, and a lilt to the remnants of her hair, despite the dreadful death on her face.

CAIRO, *October 16, 1970*

I spent the day in the Suez Canal area, the famous cease-fire zone which starts around forty miles from Cairo and runs to the Red Sea and northwestward and about which there is so much clamor these days. To be precise, I spent it at Port Suez and Port Taufiq, at the extreme eastern entry of the canal, which begins at Port Taufiq leaving the Red Sea, and runs on to the Mediterranean at Port Said.

No journalist of any nationality has been taken on a solitary trip like this before. The Egyptians are very security-minded.

When I asked the general who was my host at lunch if I could visit a SAM missile site, he said: "What sites? We have never admitted there are any." "But," I protested, "your foreign minister says you won't withdraw a single missile from the zone. If you won't withdraw, it means you are there." He said nothing.

I then asked if I could at least visit an artillery position. He said it was forbidden for any civilian, even an Egyptian, to do so; not even Russian journalists were permitted. Then I asked to be taken to Soviet troops. "In my area there are none," he said. "Nor are there any missiles in my area."

My conducting officer assured me not even Soviet correspondents were allowed to visit Russian troops "because on Egyptian soil they are treated under our law and like our units."

Kamal Bakr, director of foreign press for the information ministry, called for me in a station wagon with driver. We then picked up Major Wafik el Messiri of the defense ministry's security division, a regular army officer.

Bakr told me that for the most part English served as the *lingua franca* between Russian and Egyptian officers. English is the number one compulsory language in Egyptian schools, even today; French is number two.

Port Suez seemed deserted except for rare soldiers and even rarer civilians. We went by block after block of empty apartment houses. Most of them showed no sign of damage—much to my astonishment. I couldn't help thinking the British, Germans, or Russians would have stood up to it much easier and would have done something about repairing what has been wrecked, above all the vital oil refineries, which look hardly touched.

I was then escorted to the underground command post of the security administration, well protected with blast-proof doors. Here I met and talked with a group headed by Lieutenant General Mohiedin el Khafaqa, a friendly fifty-two-year-old with greying, close-cut hair. He is, in fact, a police officer. He said there "was more work now since the cease-fire" than before because of the need to remain on permanent alert against surprise attack, but I must confess I saw no signs at all of any kind of work during my entire visit.

The general said refugees were sent all around the country according to their abilities (fishermen to seaports, farmers inland, etc.) and haven't started to come back. He made a conventional little speech on policy as we sipped *mazbout* coffee: "We hope for peace because a fight would be tragic, but if necessary we must take that way."

I then bade farewell and went off on tour. First we waited at the waterfront while the car gassed up. It was strange to stand in the brilliant sunshine by the blue Gulf of Suez, looking down at schools of little fish, with slit trenches zigzagging at our feet but momentarily unoccupied although a couple of clean Russian-style helmets were laid at the edge of one trench.

We drove across the causeway to Taufiq, passed repaired craters and lengths of rail, climbed up an earth parapet covered with pebbles, and looked down at the canal on the left—still, grey water.

Port Taufiq, a small town, used to be the eastern headquarters of the canal company and was also a prosperous resort filled with middle-class seaside villas. It is now badly chewed up although the only total damage is right up by the canal.

We climbed a rampart of sandbags and there, just below us, ran the canal. Two Egyptian soldiers, one with binoculars, were in a foxhole in front. Then the water, less than 500 yards wide, and then the Israelis, three or four of them staring at us out of their wired, mined positions.

Then we drove past the three oil refineries outside town, silent and motionless but showing slight visible damage. Port Suez, from which a pipeline runs to Cairo, was Egypt's main oil port.

CAIRO, *October 20, 1970*

Yesterday, just after 7:00 P.M., I went to Al Tahira palace with Mohamed Heikal to see President Anwar el Sadat, Nasser's successor.

Mohamed hopes now to spend a major amount of time writing a book on Nasser. He has a formidable collection of notes, including the manuscript of Nasser's only attempt at writing, an uncompleted novel about the first British invasion of Egypt at Rashid (Rosetta) before the era of Mohammed Ali, when they were opposed by a popular resistance. Heikal says that although incomplete the book showed a surprising amount of talent. (Incidentally, he also possesses the manuscript of el Sadat's only novel, *The Prince of the Island*, which el Sadat gave him to look at during the Palestine campaign before the 1952 revolution.)

Mohamed is very bright and astonishingly urbane for the son of a modest village family. His mother could read and write but his father was illiterate. His mother got her brother to take Mohamed to Cairo and a secular school, as a boy, although his father had wanted to keep him in the village to become a religious sheikh. His father died only in 1965. In 1957, when Mohamed went home to see him, the old man refused to greet him. He was furious because Mohamed had been writing "lies"— that the Russians had sent men into space (Sputnik). The village *mullah* had told his father this was impossible because it intruded on God's domain. His father used to say during his last years: "I don't want to live any longer. Everyone tells lies. The Americans. The Russians. Even my son."

The Al Tahira palace, originally built by an aunt of King Farouk, is a large, ornate building furnished with bad gilt furniture and large bad paintings. It was previously used as a residence for distinguished state guests but el Sadat has made it his temporary office. He still resides with his family (including an English mother-in-law) in his old home.

With no formality we were taken outside where he was sitting in an armchair on a small terrace overlooking the garden. He arose to greet us: a well set-up man with very dark skin, retreating black hair, black eyes, black moustache, and gleaming white teeth: not handsome but agreeable-looking, with a far more military bearing and appearance than the much larger Nasser. He wore a black suit, socks, tie, shoes, in mourning for Nasser. He smoked a pipe, which he occasionally refilled and tamped, and we were served tea and Turkish coffee. The conversation was in English which he speaks quite well, explaining that he uses it regularly with his mother-in-law.

El Sadat is not used to interviews (this was the first he has given anyone, Egyptian or foreign, since becoming president) and is not good at grabbing abstract thoughts or playing with ideas. I had a feeling his mind is pragmatic and certainly conspiratorial. He is a disciplined officer, but clearly has a temper under that controlled surface.

We talked for about an hour and a half and although the substance was pretty tough, the means of expression couldn't have been chummier. The more interesting part was that dealing with his personality and ideas as he is a virtually unknown man. He is the subject of a certain amount of gossip, but Heikal says he was divorced from his first wife before he married the second, who is as blond as he is dark, and that he is a plain, unassuming man.

He told me he loved walking and "nature in all its phases." His ambition had always been to be an officer. He had educated himself substantially after graduating from military academy in 1938. He sent out to a "library" for books and got a collection of miscellany, largely history which he most enjoys. From 1942 to 1948 he spent four years in concentration camp and two in prison (solitary confinement) for plotting against the British-dominated regime (with the Germans, during the war). He had "ample time" there and studied German, read "lots of books of every type." He was most influenced by Lloyd Douglas, the American writer, and on an official visit to the U.S.A. in 1966 he bought a complete secondhand collection of his works.

He especially liked *The Robe* and *Magnificent Obsession*. He told me earnestly: "This man started as a doctor and then became a priest. He only began to write after the age of forty. He has great power. He gives faith and confidence. He influenced me greatly, especially while I was in prison and confined in solitary for more than two years."

El Sadat said the other major influence on his formation was Caliph

Omar, second in succession to Mohammed (after Abu Bakr) who was "a just and strict man."

While in prison he kept a notebook of quotations that appealed to him in his reading. He also wrote a novel, a political novel on the subject of revolution versus reform. It was called *The Prince of the Island*. It was never published. (Heikal has the manuscript and says it is more of a tract than a novel.)

He was once a journalist, an editor of *Goumouriya*, and wrote daily articles during the 1956 Suez campaign, bitterly attacking Dulles. He still dreams of writing.

He used to play tennis and swim, but since 1967 "I live twenty-four hours a day with the crisis" (caused by the six-day war). However, he still finds time to walk. He eats lightly, mostly boiled or grilled food. And he reads. He is now reading a book on the U.S.-Japanese battle of Tarawa and before that read one on Guadalcanal. These days he is reading as much as he can on the American campaign in the Pacific; also Churchill's memoirs.

He had always dreamed as a small boy of becoming an officer. His father was a civilian in the army medical corps. Then, a year after he graduated from officers' academy, he met Nasser (1939) and began political action. He hopes some day to retire but "first comes the battle, the liberation of our territory. After that, when I have put everything in shape, I would like to retire and live my own life in my village at the mouth of the Delta, Mit Abu El Kon."

He has seven children, six girls and a boy, ranging from nine up to twenty-nine. He would like to travel and has never had a chance to do so except on official trips "which isn't traveling."

I asked about his health. He said in 1960 he suffered a "heart attack." However, in 1966 when he was in the U.S. he had a complete checkup at the "New York navy hospital" and "Dr. Kemp," who was in charge, told him there was no sign that he had ever had a cardiac condition.

He told me of his policy: "Nonalignment in our view is not passive. On the contrary it is a positive policy. We are not aligned except when it comes to questions of to be or not to be. But we cannot stand passively at such moments. When our people were being bombed for seventeen hours a day and we could bring missiles from any part of the world to help them, we could not stand with our arms folded and do nothing. But our position is an independent one and we will always state our opinion on all important world issues."

On relations with the U.S.A., he said: "Many things could be done. But I should start out by mentioning my meeting with Secretary of State Rusk which took place in the state department in 1966 when I was on a goodwill visit. He asked me the direct question: Do you think we are taking the side of Israel? I told him yes, and moreover you are using Israel as your instrument in the area. Israel always waits for a green light from Washington.

"To my mind this was conclusively demonstrated by the February 28, 1955, Gaza incident when we refused to enter the Baghdad pact and the green light was given to Israel. The Israelis staged a big raid on the Gaza sector and we suffered forty-three casualties.

"We had no arms. The United States and Britain refused to sell us arms. That's why later in 1955, in September, we made an arms deal with Czechoslovakia and the Soviet Union. That was the beginning of the whole thing. From that time on I felt that Israel was planted here for this kind of purpose.

"In spite of the fact that our revolution is eighteen years old the United States does not understand the revolution or the Egyptian people even now. The Baghdad pact represented part of this material and psychological misunderstanding. We are a simple, modest people but we are fierce and stubborn if a big power tries to apply pressure on us. And you lack understanding of this fact.

"It is nonsense to think that you can make a nation like ours succumb to Israel, especially a nation that is 7,000 years old and that gave civilization to the whole world. Attempts to force a settlement by terror and blackmail do not work with us.

"The United States is a big power. Why should the United States as a big power take sides in a problem where the issues are quite clear? Why should it help Israel occupy our territories and give money and aid to the country whose forces do the occupying?

"We once calculated that between $500,000 and $1 million worth of bombs were dropped by the Israelis each day in the Suez area alone. Sometimes these raids lasted seventeen hours and as many as 180 planes would take part during the day. Some of the aviators taking part in the raids were of dual nationality (Israeli and American). We have one of them in custody here right now. How can Israel, a country living on charity, afford to spend this much money on bombing one area alone, the Suez area, which is only part of the whole Arab territory involved?"

I asked if he wanted a political settlement with Israel. He said: "Yesterday President Yahya Khan of Pakistan talked here with me on his way to the United States. I told him that he could tell President Nixon that if the United States were not behind the Israeli expansion drive, the whole question of the Arab-Israeli conflict would be solved by the [Gunnar] Jarring mission within twenty-four hours.

"Israel has already declared quite clearly its determination not to give up Jerusalem, the Golan Heights, Gaza, or Sharm el Sheikh. It would certainly not be a minor adjustment of the 1967 borders if these remain under Israel. Let the Israelis tell Jarring if they want any minor rectifications. All we want is simple and precise.

"And where is the American peace initiative that Rogers proposed? Where is it, I ask? We accepted it unconditionally.

"We agreed on free passage through the Suez Canal and recognition of Israel as a state, of Israel's existence. But this was on the condition that Israel should agree completely with the resolution and fulfill all its commitments under it. Our policy remains unchanged, but I do not see any chance of Israel carrying out its obligations as things stand.

"If Israel rejoins the Jarring talks we would agree to renew the cease-fire for one more period of ninety days—also providing that American initiative starts to work again as proposed originally by Rogers. Don't forget that this initiative stated that Israel would agree to the withdrawal of its troops.

"Rogers also proposed that the United States would not provide any further arms to Israel during the cease-fire period except for fulfilling pledges made under President Johnson's administration such as the Phantom and Skyhawk planes. This provision is not being carried out.

"Who shot fifteen Phantoms down before the cease-fire came into effect? It was the missiles Russia supplied us. They were already there. Nobody can question this. How could I agree or how could I explain to my people any dismantling of the missiles? After all, the land on both sides of the canal is our land. And they have dropped thousands of tons of bombs.

"We put the missiles in before the cease-fire in order to defend ourselves. If Israel really wants peace, why does it raise all this hell on the SAMs?"

Egyptian story, typifying the wonderful national sense of humor: Some years hence an aging man goes to a brain bank, like today's blood or eye banks. He wants a replacement for his tired thinking machine. The superintendent shows him his wares. "Now here I have a first class brain that used to belong to a German nuclear physicist. Only $5,000." "Too expensive," says the customer. "Well, how about this. Here's the brain of an Italian composer. Marked down to $4,500." "No, that's still too much." "Well, I don't know what we've got in stock that's any better. Of course, here's a $10,000 brain. Used to belong to an Egyptian general." "Naturally that's much too much. I couldn't even afford half that price. But please tell me, why is an Egyptian general's brain worth so much more than a German nuclear physicist's or an Italian composer's?" "Sir, this brain has never been used."

AMMAN, *October 22, 1970*

Early this afternoon I had a talk with King Hussein. The yard was filled with heavily armed jeeps and command cars. The flag above the palace was at half-staff in mourning for Nasser's death. I was whisked in to Hussein's office past the colorful Circassian personal guards in long black tunics, black fur hats, and slung cartridge bandoliers.

Hussein was wearing a khaki uniform with his pilot's wings and a bank of ribbon decorations. He sat, a tiny bit nervous, smoking cigarettes and answering questions bravely in his deep voice, striking for a man of his very short stature. I started by asking him how the pact with the *Fedayeen* was working. I said it gave me the impression, judging from the texts I had read, of formally recognizing the existence of two governments in Jordan—his and the *Fedayeen's*. He answered:

"The pact, as far as it goes, appears to be working. I have every confidence that the end result will be the establishment of law and order in Jordan. We have actually started to make a basic turning point. Now we have begun to build a more united, dynamic, forward-moving Jordan. This is a period of great activity.

"The full text of our agreement has not as yet been published. The negotiations are continuing. We are in a constant dialogue to close every loophole and each threat to unity and security. There is a general desire to create a strong, united Jordan.

"We have always supported the right of the Palestinians to oppose the occupation of their territory by *any* means they choose. There is *no* complete agreement yet. We are still searching for a means of achieving unity."

Not from his words but from the innuendo, it was clear, despite his courteous reference to the *Fedayeen*, that Hussein had no particular love for them. I asked if the guerrillas seemed to be working as a unified group. He replied:

"They appear to be unified. That is about all I can say. We are dealing mainly with the PLO [Palestine Liberation Organization] and the PLA [Palestine Liberation Army] as well as with Al Fatah [which is the principal voice in both of the other organizations mentioned]. We are anxious that those who may be under the banner of Palestine should be genuinely united in their Palestinian feelings. We want them to avoid the contradictions of the Arab world as a whole."

I asked him what kind of role Russia and China had played in Jordan's tragic troubles last month when an undeclared civil war was fought. He said Russia had behaved correctly and "throughout the crisis I approached them in precisely the same way as I approached the other members of the Big Four. I kept them in constant contact with realities and with the threats both to ourselves and, on a larger scale, to world peace. And I must say they played the game. The Chinese might have had a different attitude. It looks as if they are trying to get a foothold in the Arab world and to exploit differences."

I said I was struck by a basic difference in policy between his government and the *Fedayeen*; he had pledged, like Egypt, to seek a political settlement of the Palestine question but the *Fedayeen* refused this.

He said: "You are right in saying that Jordan and the UAR have the same basic policy and accepted the security council resolution of 1967. This divides into two essential points. First of all there must be complete withdrawal from the occupied territories seized in the six-day war. Secondly, the UN resolution grants specific rights to the Palestinian Arabs. I would say the *Fedayeen* interpret this second part as granting them more rights than perhaps our interpretation accords.

"If there is a wave of despair and extremism right now in the Arab world, it is an indirect result of the lack of implementation of the 1967 resolution. And the longer this situation continues the more the danger grows, both to this area itself and also to the world community. There is no way out except to implement the resolution."

I asked him if he excluded the idea that a third state might be formed of the Palestinian area, pointing out that the former mandated territory was now shared by Israel and Jordan (although Jordan has lost most of what it held) and that some Palestinian Arabs were talking about creating a separate Palestine based in the West Bank area of Jordan. He said:

"I do not *exclude* anything. The people can choose what they want. But I do not think there is any strong desire among the people of the West Bank to leave Jordan. During the recent crisis in our nation, Jordanian-Palestinian unity was at its best in the armed forces. The officers stuck together whether they were Palestinian or from the East Bank.

"But the people have the right to self-determination—after liberation. At this time the question is not posed. But after a settlement, the people will be free to choose. They can join Jordan or not, as they desire. They can have whatever kind of government they prefer, but it is my belief that they will choose to remain with Jordan."

He continued: "One must look back on the Palestine problem before the partition ever took place a generation ago. Somehow I can sense something, an attempt to solve the problem at *our* expense and to the detriment of Jordan and the Palestinians.

"If the situation in Jordan got bad the Israelis might want to move in and occupy large portions, more territory. And you must remember that Jordan is the only country involved in this war which lacks considerable backing from other and greater powers."

I said I was struck by the fact that his own courage was the greatest asset the king had in the difficult problem of ruling his impoverished and not very well-defined country. He observed:

"I don't think it is a matter of courage but of conviction. If I am convinced of my course, I am committed to it. And once I am committed to a course, the question of odds doesn't enter into the matter. After my commitment, it doesn't matter if the odds appear to be unfavorable. After all, the basic thing is that one has to live with oneself."

I then asked him if he thought that, in the latter part of the twentieth century, kingship was still a viable profession. He said:

"As I see the future of this area kings must fit into it. And if we are to fit into it we must retain the best of our traditions and heritage.

"My own measure of success or failure will be whether I can create a system that works and is not simply dependent on a single individual. I am not happy as yet that I have achieved this. My greatest challenge is to create a system that will endure long after I have gone. But I think the profession of kingship as such is viable. It simply must adjust and meet the changing requirements of time."

Hussein told me he naturally always wears a gun when he is in uniform and most of the time when he is in civilian clothes. However, he said that it gave him great pleasure and pride when on occasions, in civilian clothes, he didn't have to put on his holster.

That afternoon, drove off with Abu Omar, a member of the central committee of Al Fatah, the guerrillas. En route, Abu Omar explained that Arafat himself is known as Abu Amar and is now recognized as head of the PLO [Palestine Liberation Organization], chief of Al Fatah and commander of the PLA [Palestine Liberation Army], that all the smaller *Fedayeen* forces and the militia were under his unified command.

He took me on a tour around beat-up areas of Amman on our way to the command post, assuring me that a minimum of 7,000 had been killed during the civil war and 13,000 wounded. These estimates, while much larger than those of the palace or the American embassy, are way down from the absurd exaggerations being put out by the guerrillas a fortnight ago.

We finally got to Arafat's command post, a shabby building outside which guerrillas were striding about covered with hand grenades and carelessly brandishing Kalashnikov tommy guns. I am not impressed by their military appearance. I felt they might be better in a bar fight than a serious operation.

I followed Abu Omar into a bare, cube-shaped room lit by one naked bulb hanging from the ceiling and furnished with a wooden desk and four plain wooden chairs. A moment later Arafat came in. He also is a decidedly unimpressive-looking man: rather short, much too fat, sensuous heavy features, glittering eyes, and a somewhat evil face. He was wearing a black and white *kafiyya*, khaki pants, khaki sweater, and had a three-day growth of beard. He was carrying a Kalashnikov automatic rifle and also had a pistol and clip of bullets strapped to his side. He is out of condition and overweight for a guerrilla leader.

He was most friendly but wholly useless to talk to since he refuses to answer any question in a straight, factual way, and is enormously pleased with his orotund, meaningless responses. Although he seems to speak quite a lot of English, Abu Omar interpreted most of our talk which went on interminably as we drank sweet tea. Various characters kept coming in and out to interrupt with bits of news or to receive scribbled orders. It was an untidy, amateurish-looking headquarters to me. I have seen guerrillas in southeast Asia, Jugoslavia, Cyprus, and Algeria, and these are by far the crummiest-looking lot.

I started off by asking Arafat what was the present strength of the various movements under his command. The reply wasn't aimed at the question. He said: "We suffered a ferocious attack by the imperialist, Zionist forces. This attack was carried out by the Jordanian army. It was a great conspiracy against our nation."

I asked what his rank as commander was. He said: "I have no rank. I am only Abu Amar, president of the PLO." I asked what ranks existed in his forces and he refused to answer. (This is idiotic because they themselves refer to their "brigadiers" and "colonels.") He said only that he had a "complete military staff." I asked him about his experience in guerrilla warfare. He said:

"I was an officer in the Egyptian army." After this not very proud boast I asked what his rank was. He refused to answer on the grounds that this was a personal question. (Actually, he was a lieutenant.) He only said: "Please, no personal questions. Is it important what rank I had?" He began to fiddle nervously with his Kalashnikov.

I asked him what the real position of the PLA was today vis-à-vis the royal Jordanian army. He said: "We have signed an agreement to define our relationships, so it is not merely a cease-fire." But then he went on in a long denunciation of the brutality and treachery of the Jordanian army and King Hussein. I asked him why there was still fighting between the army and the *Fedayeen* in the north. He said:

"There are two reasons. Certain elements in the regime and the army are still endeavoring to upset the recent agreement. And there have been continuing incidents because the crisis had been so bad that bitter emotions continue." I asked him if he meant the civil war when he referred to the "crisis." He clearly disliked the term "civil war" and said that even the conference of Arab leaders had denounced it as an "act of genocide."

I observed that no matter what agreement the guerrillas had signed with Hussein, it was obvious they had a fundamental difference because Hussein favored a political settlement of the conflict with Israel and they spurned a political settlement. He said:

"Our aim is to liberate our homeland, Palestine, from the river [Jordan] to the sea [Mediterranean] and to create there a democratic society with no discrimination in race or creed. We are Palestinians. We are not concerned with Transjordan although we believe in the unity of our people on both sides of the Jordan." (This is a self-contradictory statement.) "We want to create a Palestinian democratic state for whoever desires to live there."

I asked if this meant including all the Jews now in Israel, all the

Arab refugees and their descendants, and all the Arabs who want to go there. It seemed to me that the area involved was too small to hold them. He said it would not be any more crowded than under the Zionist dream of bringing together in Israel four or five million more Jews from the outside world. He added: "There will be room enough for all. The population density in Palestine will be less than the population density in India today or in the Nile Valley.

"We have always rejected the 1967 UN resolution and we still reject it. Our people were unjustly expelled from their country, the land where we and our ancestors have lived for thousands of years. The power that expelled us from our homeland was Zionism allied with imperialism.

"We have waited many years to see various UN resolutions applied but what has been the result? The only result has been more occupation, more bloodshed, more expulsion, more losses. It was our incontestable right to bear arms in an attempt to return to our country."

I asked about his political ideology. He said: "We are only seekers of national liberation. We consider ourselves a progressive revolution. We benefited from the experiences of all revolutions in the world."

I asked him what military strategists had influenced Al Fatah. He said bombastically: "We benefit from the experience of everybody—Mao, Lenin, Castro, Ben Bella, Tito. Our staff studies the experience of revolutionary warfare. We have sent our men to be trained in Algeria, Cuba, Vietnam, and China."

Arafat said he was certain that the United States had a contingency plan to intervene in Jordan and "only parts of it were executed." He then resumed his attacks on the Jordanian government and army. He talked wildly and said 120,000 tons of explosives had been fired at the *Fedayeen* by Hussein's forces: "Six times the amount of Hiroshima." This is, of course, baloney.

At this point Egyptian Brigadier Ahmed Abdel-Hamid Hilmi with British-type red tabs on his collar and red band around his officer's hat came in and joined us, together with a Tunisian captain. The brigadier is head of the military part of the Arab cease-fire observer mission here (ACOM) and the captain is a member. Arafat kissed them each on both cheeks, which must have been a rather unpleasant experience. Suddenly a guerrilla carrying the ever-present Kalashnikov rushed in and muttered something. They all got up and went out.

Abu Omar explained that two truckloads of Palestinians who had been imprisoned by Hussein's authorities had just been released. We walked down the street in front of the command post and when they saw Arafat, hugging the Egyptian and the Tunisian, they jumped up and down in their trucks screaming, "As long as we live we will continue the war." It seemed odd to me that the Egyptian and the Tunisian who are here to bring peace cheered happily when they heard this. I felt sorry for the poor Palestinians in their trucks: tattered, hungry, and tired.

PARIS, *October 30, 1970*

What a nice fellow David Bruce is! And what a first-class public servant. I just lunched with him, first time since he came over as head of our negotiating mission at the Vietnam peace talks. I have been away since his arrival.

David knows that little dramatic kudos can be expected from his assignment. Yet, at the age of seventy-two, and with little chance of adding to an enormous reputation, there he is, doing his job.

As he sees it, the issue has boiled down to two basic points and the first is totally unimportant: (1) complete evacuation of South Vietnam by United States troops within a fixed period of time; (2) a change of government in Saigon.

Point one isn't worth discussing because it is clear that the U.S. is pulling out its forces and this is irrevocable. Hanoi knows this fact perfectly well. The interesting thing is, however, that the South Vietnamese are proving to be very efficient with the equipment we are giving them, helicopter gun-ships, etc. and they may turn out in the end to be just as unconquerable as the South Koreans proved to be in northeast Asia.

Nevertheless, it is David's guess that Hanoi is going to continue to stall here until it takes one more military crack at the structure in South Vietnam in the hope that it can force a decision elsewhere which only needs to be ratified at the Paris peace conference.

Point two is the crux. We are *not* going to try to oust a government in Saigon and impose a new government. We have tried that before (Diem) and it didn't work. We now know this is impossible. Furthermore, we don't intend to do the dirty work for Hanoi. Hanoi would like to crumble the existing administration in Saigon by forcing out Thieu and Ky and by getting the United States to agree to a kind of proportional representation in the succeeding government (the executive structure) of the communists —the old communist formula of getting for its party the minister of defense, interior, justice, and propaganda. Last night he [Bruce] saw Froment-Meurice at a dinner party and Froment-Meurice brought up the subject of yielding by agreeing to dismiss Thieu and Ky. Bruce said this was impossible and pointed out why. To his astonishment, Froment-Meurice then said: "I think you are right."

He thinks the Cambodian change has been enormously helpful. Hanoi's strength is much less there now than it was. And Sihanouk has sacrificed his popularity to an astonishing degree by going to Peking where he has become a puppet. The Cambodians detest China more than any other country.

He talked quite admiringly of Nixon. He says he doesn't particularly like him as a man, but has enormous respect for him as a machine. Then he even modified the first statement and said he had had a four-hour lunch with him before he was president, and never once talked politics; that Nixon really has considerable qualities. Bruce also expressed admiration for Lyndon Johnson, saying he was an overpowering personality and adding that his decision to give up the presidency was extraordinarily courageous.

PARIS, *November 1, 1970*

I played golf and lunched with Couve de Murville, who had returned two days previously from a trip to China.

Couve has no use for the UN at all. He says it is completely "finished." To his mind, if there is a Middle East settlement, big-power troops must be stationed in demilitarized zones to prevent a new outbreak of war. These should be Russians and Americans, not Irish and Swedes.

He said the United States must get out of Vietnam entirely and he doesn't believe we intend to do this. He is convinced the Pentagon will insist in the end on maintaining a considerable force and a naval base at Camranh Bay. He says the United States has no policy in southeast Asia yet. We should pledge a total withdrawal by a fixed date—even if that is ten years hence.

Couve said someday the U.S. would make a deal with China against Russia. He was convinced of this and "that will be a policy. You don't have a policy now." The fate of Taiwan was increasingly a matter of Japanese rather than American decision, as they were beginning to realize in Peking. He thought from his talks with Mao, Chou, and others, that China was more worried about Japan than Russia is worried about Germany.

The big thing is for everybody to learn the realities of China and forget old superstitions. For 150 years, China was a colony of the worst sort. Europe began its real colonization through Britain, which fought the opium war to force China's sale of opium. Then the T'ai P̈'ing rebellion was fought to squash any efforts to modernize China and make it more independent.

PARIS, *November 3, 1970*

Lunched with the new Israeli ambassador, Asher Ben-Natan, previously his country's first envoy to Germany. He is a big, handsome, blond (now grey-haired) Aryan type, intelligent and tough. He was born in Vienna, left at the age of eighteen when the *Anschluss* came, worked in underground prewar and wartime operations for the Zionists, was then in the Israeli army.

He admitted that the star-boat ("Vedette") episode last December was pretty stupid because it was rubbing salt in French wounds. He has great respect for Maurice Bourgès-Manoury, former Prime Minister, and recalls that in 1958 Bourgès told him: "Never have any trust in de Gaulle. He will betray Israel just the way he has betrayed everybody else."

PARIS, *November 4, 1970*

Lunched with Ambassador Arthur Watson. He asked whether it would be wise to attempt personally to see de Gaulle. My reply was negative.

Watson told me he is trying to build up a personal wine cellar while he is here in Paris. He added: "Naturally everybody around here cheats you if they can; so therefore we only have two keys to this private *cave*, my wife's and mine."

PARIS, *November 6, 1970*

Last night Gheorgi and Nina Ratiani came to dinner. Gheorgi is a political observer of *Pravda* and its expert on Western hemisphere relationships.

He was taken by some official to visit the NASA space installation at Houston. When you are admitted, in order to get a card which you wear on your lapel so you can circulate freely, you provide information at the entrance desk and this is sent directly to a computer which comes out with permission or refusal. He answered all the questions: name: Gheorgi Ratiani; nationality: USSR; profession: journalist; employer: *Pravda*; political affiliation: Communist. To his astonishment, the machine clanked out an immediate permission to enter. He says he has wondered ever since just who the machine is geared to keep out.

I asked how crime was reported in the Soviet press. He assured me *Pravda* always carried very brief reports, but the local papers had regular police reporters who published accounts of local crime. I doubt if these accounts are very extensive, because the Soviet system likes to depict its society as pretty crime-proof. Incidentally, Gheorgi told me everybody on *Pravda* uses the couple of police reporters attached to it to fix traffic tickets.

Nina said there was undoubtedly a drug problem now with Soviet youth, although it was far less serious than in the West. She thought it had been abetted by increasing tourism because many young foreign tourists brought the stuff in. She also acknowledged readily that the present young generation in Russia is bored by its elders and doesn't think it has anything to fight for or against—like the revolution or Nazi Germany. This makes it relatively rootless, although there isn't any really extensive public rootlessness like the American hippie movement.

PARIS, *November 8, 1970*

Last night we gave a small dinner party for Maurice and Katy Macmillan. Macmillan, the former prime minister's son, is now a junior member of the government. Christopher and Mary Soames and David and Vangie Bruce were there.

Mary Soames (Churchill's youngest and favorite daughter) has a warm English countrywoman's way about her. For some years she has been writing a biography of her mother, which should be absolutely dandy. Her mother gave her eight large trunks filled with letters she and Winston had exchanged since the very start. These are priceless—and Mary is fully aware of it.

Her brother, Randolph, when he was doing his four-volume life of his father, wanted the letters, but she had not made them available. She said they had reached "what you might call a brother and sister agreement; not a gentlemen's agreement," governing which of the letters she would make available.

PARIS, *November 10, 1970*

General de Gaulle's death was announced this morning. Actually, he died yesterday evening while playing a solitary game of patience in his somber home at Colombey-les-Deux-Églises. I am glad for the old man's sake that death was swift. He had a horror of the gradual decline which struck so many people before they succumbed. "Old age is a shipwreck," he said.

There is a peculiar hollowness in France this afternoon. Funeral services will be very simple at Colombey, where he will be interred next to his poor little half-witted daughter Anne. But the government is making a big display, as well it must, with a memorial service in Notre Dame Thursday—the same day as the interment.

PARIS, *November 12, 1970*

De Gaulle was buried with maximum solemnity, and French newspapers boasted that on this day Colombey-les-Deux-Églises was the capital of France while Paris was the capital of the world. It is interesting to think that this great man who had so rigidly prescribed, eighteen years ago, after the funeral of General de Lattre de Tassigny, that his own interment should be marked by no honors and no great visitors but only by simple obsequies at his own village, should, in fact, have benefited simultaneously from both more panoply and also more simplicity than anyone in French history. For while on the one hand the stark and simple village ceremony was held and he was finally laid to rest beside his retarded daughter Anne in a cheap wooden coffin, on the other hand, a commemorative service was also held today in the Cathedral of Notre Dame in Paris.

Cardinal Marty, of Paris, officiated, speaking in a heavy Auvergnat accent while his fellow Auvergnat, President Pompidou, sat all alone in advance of the remaining participants. The latter included more chiefs of state than have probably attended any other funeral in history.

As might be expected of the French, both ceremonies were beautifully organized—respectively maximizing simplicity and pomp.

I am struck by the enormous chord of emotion that has echoed throughout the world following de Gaulle's death. Obviously, everybody recognized that this is, indeed, the end of an era, the era of World War II and the subsequent quarter century, so that people personally feel that they have suddenly become one generation older. Everywhere people feel that de Gaulle was, indeed, The Last of the Giants.

PARIS, *November 14, 1970*

Last night I was on a television program with Jean Morin, head of AFP (the French news agency).

Morin said Sergei Vinogradov had gone to see de Gaulle during his political exile in the 1950s after the Soviet ambassador arrived in Paris. He explained that his visit was unofficial and personal, but that his government knew about it. "I know why you have come," said the General. "You do?" said Vinogradov, puzzled. "Why?" "Because you are afraid of China," answered de Gaulle.

ROME, *November 18, 1970*

A sad evening (yesterday). I had invited poor little Jozsef and Trudi Szall for dinner. They have skipped from Hungary, as political refugees, and are here with their ten-year-old son, near the end of the tether. They keep talking of suicide.

Jozsef is the senior Hungarian diplomat. Although only forty-nine, he has been in the career service of the People's Republic longer than any other. He had been ambassador in Rome for years (with unofficial accreditation to the Vatican) and was ordered home last summer after many months of stalling.

Once back in Budapest last July, he says his friends all kept away from them, indicating he was on a blacklist. He was advised by the foreign ministry not to try and see Kadar (the boss) or other leaders. Janos Peter, the foreign minister (an ex-Calvinist bishop) told him he would take him on as a personal counselor. But he received no office or secretary—or any work.

A vice minister of foreign affairs, who had once been a pupil of his, called him in as a friendly gesture and showed him a paper marked confidential but circulated among top Hungarians. This was a translation of a bulletin by Radio Free Europe, all about Szall. It said he had been mixed up in various shady business deals in Italy.

Szall insisted it was all lies. Clearly the information must have been put out to RFE by one of his party enemies in Budapest; otherwise how would they have all the data, whether right or wrong? But he claimed this had ruined him and therefore the United States which sponsored RFE, "*owed*" him sanctuary.

Jozsef went to see U.S. Ambassador Graham Martin. Martin advised him to talk with the Hungarians and also to ask asylum from the Italians. Budapest sent a vice minister and wife to meet the Szalls. They were afraid to meet anywhere but in St. Peter's, in Vatican City. Trudi had been writing a book on "ministates" and had a special pass to the Vatican library, which got them in the back way.

They argued three and one-half hours with the vice minister and his wife but they saw people all around them—Hungarian, Russian, Italian, and American security agents, they thought. The American ambassador had given Jozsef a small tape recorder to tape the conversation and offers made by the Hungarians (who undoubtedly had their own recorder).

Jozsef says he offered to exchange his diplomatic passport for an ordinary Hungarian one if they let him stay abroad and helped get him a job in some international agency. They said he would have to discuss this in Budapest. When he refused, they said he could leave his family in Rome. Then they offered to meet him in Vienna. Szall told me he knew about seven Hungarian police kidnappings in Vienna ("although I never had a hand in them") and he said he wouldn't fall for that one. Then they suggested he at least take a ride around Rome in a car in order to discuss matters in more private circumstances than St. Peter's. He refused.

Both he and Trudi kept clamoring they "must" go to America. Italy was unsafe. It was too close to Hungary and its government was riddled with agents. The security people now in charge of him sneered at the "politicians" in the government. They knew everything he had told the American embassy and they even knew he was dining with me last night. "Obviously they tap the telephones," I observed.

At noon today I called on Welles Stabler, U.S. minister. Ambassador Martin is away. He said a government decision had been taken in Washington [not to bring Szall back].

We had been in touch with the Italians, who knew about his return the minute he and Trudi crossed the border. He was naive. He was followed all the time and the Italian security had saved him from being kidnapped by Hungarian agents on the steps of St. Peter's. That was how they first openly got hold of him, when he sought their aid.

There were reports that some of Moscow's financing of Italian communism had come through the Hungarians. Obviously Szall could tell them. But he was trying to clam up. The Italians had offered him asylum but had not yet signed the papers. He would be foolish to try and bluff them because they could halt proceedings at the last minute. He had to know this was a cold world and he had to earn his safety and support. The Italians had offered Trudi a $500-a-month job in a jewelry shop.

Szall was foolish to think he could both have his cake and eat it. It was widely known he was a refugee in Rome. All the communist countries knew it so obviously the Italian communists also did. The *Agence France Presse* had called the embassy last week to ask if it was true Szall had sought asylum in the U.S.A.

This evening I invited poor Jozsef around (without Trudi) and told him the U.S. had decided not to give him a defector's welcome.

Poor Jozsef kept saying he was ready to tell "all" to the U.S.A. but not to the Italians. (In other words, the issue wasn't strictly moral.) I told him he had better solve that himself.

ROME, *November 19, 1970*

Lengthy talk with Emilio Colombo, the fifty-year-old bachelor monetary expert, who is now prime minister of Italy. He has a weak, thoughtful, agreeable face.

He said: "Communism in Italy knows that it cannot come to power in Italy through its own electoral strength. Therefore, its policy is to seek alliance with other political parties. Furthermore, the Communist party has chosen a more moderate and less violent approach here in order to give the impression to public opinion that it is a constitutional and democratically operated party. Its moderate powers also gives an impression abroad of moderation which is inexact.

"But in our Democratic parties, above all on the left-wing of each party in the government coalition, there admittedly remains a hope or illusion that communism is on the way to being converted to democracy. However, the government itself does not really believe this. We know it is impossible to make a coalition with the communists."

PARIS, *November 24, 1970*

Last night dined *chez* André and Andrée de Vilmorin at the Château de Verrières. André is the brother of Louise de Vilmorin who was Malraux's great love. Malraux, who was present, still lives there—his only home.

Andrée, the hostess, told me after Malraux had gone up to bed that he was the saddest man she had ever known. His whole life has been marked by death and violence. The second woman he loved had died in "a very bloody way." His two sons were killed simultaneously in a brutal automobile accident a few years ago and he rarely even ventures to talk about them. Louise died quietly this year, but it shook him deeply, and de Gaulle's death finished the job.

Malraux still works three hours every afternoon (3:00–6:00 P.M.) writing. He had recently read to Andrée and her son an account of his last talk with de Gaulle (autumn of 1969) and it was brilliant. He plans to have these last reminiscences published after his death.

PARIS, *November 25, 1970*

Long, pleasant lunch with Hervé Alphand, secretary-general of the foreign ministry. He said that after Eisenhower's death on March 28, 1969, he had gone to the funeral with de Gaulle and had a long talk with the General just a month before the referendum which caused his sudden resignation on April 28, 1969. De Gaulle had predicted to him that he was going to lose the referendum and resign. He felt the people of France had reaffirmed their support of him in 1968 at the time of the famous spring *événements* but this was only because they were afraid and he did not wish to govern by fear.

PARIS, *December 1, 1970*

Good talk this afternoon with President Pompidou. He looked well and relaxed. He now has an inscribed photograph of a rather youthful-looking de Gaulle on a table that is very prominent.

He said the president of France made foreign policy just as the president of the United States did. I referred to his visit to the Soviet Union and asked if he thought Russia was genuinely working for a *détente*.

He had received a twin impression. He is confident Russia is now territorially satisfied with its domain. It is not expansionist. Therefore, it wants to see the status quo established everywhere. It wants Germany to sign agreements delimiting its border in the east and it hopes that China will accept the frontiers in Asia. In this policy Moscow has been more or less successful.

But basically, it is an illusory policy. China does not recognize the Soviet border. Germany does recognize the Oder-Neisse line but only because of the prevailing balance of forces. Were Germany ever to become great and powerful, it would again move east; but this is highly improbable. To sum up, Russia now wants a status quo and consequently favors both coexistence and *détente*.

There is another aspect, however. Russia is aware of its strength and it knows it has become a world power. This is a relatively new experience. It is just like the United States, which was never a world power before World War I. France and Britain were world powers. Germany was not. It was only a European power and German was never an international language.

"As Russia expands in terms of world power—above all through its fleet and air force, it penetrates everywhere. As a result, this penetration creates frictions and this is part of the second aspect to which I referred. Nevertheless, I am profoundly convinced that despite such frictions, Russia will halt such penetrations whenever they cause trouble because it definitely wants peace.

"The third phase concerns Russian relations with the other great powers. Moscow realizes that China is a problem for tomorrow; but the United States is still, for Moscow, a problem for today. The Russians want a kind of equality with America, a partition of power. But at the same time, they are not prepared to retreat or withdraw in any sense on the ideological front.

"And yet these contradictions, in the end, are subordinate to the overall desire for peace. Above all, Russia wants to avoid conflict, but its expanding strength is bound to create continuing friction."

I asked if he thought there were still fundamental problems remaining between the U.S.A. and France, or whether they were being more or less pushed together by the Soviet danger he had mentioned. He said: "The basis of my thinking on this is that France becomes closer to the United States as U.S. superiority over Russia diminishes. My foreign policy, therefore, is less anti-American in its expression than de Gaulle's, because he strongly felt American superiority over the Soviet Union and other countries and believed he had to oppose this.

"Of course, certain divergences remain between Washington and Paris on such subjects as the Middle East or Vietnam, but we stress them less. Also, the American position in the Middle East has clearly become closer to our own and it is obvious that you are trying to disengage in Vietnam. I don't approve of American bombing there. How can I? But I think now it is more a problem of patience than of any political disagreement on policy.

"Furthermore, for France, the question of Europe becomes paramount. There is Russia. There is the new Germany. There is Britain. There is the Common Market.

"Also, the Mediterranean-African problem is primordial. As a result of these two basic preoccupations it is evident that we have no profound reasons for disagreement with the United States. There are no fundamental areas of cleavage.

"Additionally, I believe that the Common Market is going to be enlarged by the inclusion of England, and this will help greatly to wind up problems between the United States and Europe."

Pompidou did not think that at this time it would be useful to consider revising the North Atlantic treaty so that, for example, the role of France in it would be less different from that of the other allies. It was better to keep the treaty as it is. At the same time he was determined to build up

French military strength—above all nuclear strength, and this would be "significant" in five or six years, even if it would never be comparable to that of America or Russia.

I noticed a considerable change in Pompidou's view. He is both in favor of British Common Market entry and optimistic that this will be achieved. He said: "I am sure Britain will come in. Its political leaders have taken a position too openly and have assumed too much of a commitment not to fulfill it. The British government is not only firm about wanting to get into the Common Market but it is a prisoner of its own statements and cannot escape this fact, although 65 percent of the British people oppose the move. I am convinced the British will come in."

I asked if he favored nuclear sharing between France and Britain on behalf of this enlarged "Europe." He said this was theoretically possible "under the alliance"—not the NATO "organization"—but he did not believe Britain was free to take part in such sharing because of its binding obligations to the United States. He added: "As for France, we are not asking for such sharing. We are truly building up our own French nuclear force. Nevertheless, in the long run, I believe the probable future trend will be toward such sharing."

He said France had absolutely no interest in fostering any kind of Mediterranean pact. It was good to have agreements with the different Mediterranean countries, but these could not be tied together in an alliance.

I asked him if he thought the Anglo-French Concorde project would go through or whether Britain might have to pull out for economic or ecological reasons. Pompidou said: "The Russians have actually produced a supersonic transport. Therefore, the West *must* do this also. We can't tell yet if it will pay for itself, but it is extremely important because it has become a symbol. To abandon the project would be a national defeat."

Pompidou didn't think the project for federation between Libya and Egypt would affect the French program of selling Mirages to Libya. With a smile he added: "I don't believe much in the strength of that federation. It is more of a club than a federation. I don't think it has any binding military ties." He said there would be no change in the French embargo on arms sales to Israel, which is a total boycott and will remain total.

I asked what effect General de Gaulle's death had had on the French political picture. He said there had always been speculation by some people and some journalists who imagined that de Gaulle might interfere or "make brutal declarations in his memoirs" that could affect the political picture. "But that was always absurd," he added. "It was not at all like the General. Therefore, in reality, nothing changed. The first volume of his memoirs showed that he never intended to interfere.

"The second aspect of the question regards the balance of political forces. De Gaulle personally excited the sentiment of the extremes—his supporters and his opponents. But his death has produced a very strong sentimental shock for all Frenchman. Naturally, this will lead the Gaullist movement to return to its spiritual origins and this may provoke a kind of opening.

"Conversely, on the other hand, the national symbol of the General now that he is dead removes from the adversaries of Gaullism a personal element. There is that much less of a difference, a division between pro- and anti-Gaullists who used to think in terms of personality. And all French citizens acknowledge the greatness of de Gaulle as a figure today."

He said that "Gaullism without de Gaulle" was in no sense changed by the General's death, because the continuity that had been established after de Gaulle left the Élysée would simply continue.

I asked if he thought de Gaulle had deliberately chosen the complicated referendum formula in 1969 as a means of insuring his retirement. Pompidou denied this. He said: "No, he took a risk. Then, at the end, he saw what a risk it was. But he definitely wanted a renewal of his mandate. He was not seeking retirement and that was not the reason for the referendum."

I asked Pompidou if it was true that he had written a book called *Réflexions* and distributed a tiny edition of only twenty or thirty copies. He said he had started to write it in the fall of 1968 when he was still prime minister. He had written about 150 pages but it was unfinished and after he became president in 1969 he completely stopped work on it. It is a political book and he did have twenty-odd copies printed for circulation among his family and close friends of the period involved, but he could not write a book or have a book published when he was president.

I asked him why de Gaulle had not helped him in his presidential cam- paign. He said: "I always believed that de Gaulle considered me as the logical candidate after he left the Élysée. Furthermore, he was convinced that I would be elected. But also I was always sure that he would not give his personal support to any successor and thus incur the responsibility for his successor's actions. He did not wish to place himself in a position where history might blame him for any stupidity caused by those who fol- lowed him."

I inquired about his personal life. He said it was undoubtedly "the life of a hermit" because in France it was impossible for a president to lead the normal existence to which he had been accustomed. He did derive great solace from "family Sundays."

Even his reading was affected by his position because he kept re- ceiving books, some of which he felt he had to read, and that limited his choice. I asked him what he was reading now and he said he had recently read a book by the philosopher Jean Guiton, who had sent him his recent work. He was now reading the latest by Alain Robbe-Grillet, *Projet pour une Révolution à New York*.

One tiring aspect of his job was official travel. In February he was going to five Francophone countries in Africa and he would also visit Belgium next year. He would have gone to Belgium before, but he didn't want to place himself in the position of having someone yell *"Vive la Wallonie libre"* when he was there.

He needed sleep and took pains to insure eight hours a night, and he also watched his weight because he didn't feel well when he gained too much weight and he cut a poor figure on television if he got fat.

As we strolled to the door together when we said farewell, he asked me where I was going and I said to London, where I would see Heath. He said Heath was having his difficulties on the Common Market because of public opposition. Nevertheless, the English were much more governable than the French and even if two-thirds of them opposed a policy they would accept it if their government told them to. He added: "Better Heath than me."

PARIS, *December 5, 1970*

Lunched today with Sargent and Eunice Shriver who just flew in. Eunice says Teddy, her brother, prefers not to run until 1976. She admits to being fascinated by politics herself. Her whole family, she says, is political. They all love power and the chance to do something. And they love people. All of these things are mixed up in politics.

Sarge says that Spiro Agnew *is* Nixon, that he really represents his master. And Nixon and Agnew appoint others like themselves.

LONDON, *December 8, 1970*

Had a drink and first-rate talk with Prime Minister Ted Heath in his study at 10 Downing Street this afternoon.

Donald Maitland the friendly little ambassador who is Heath's press man, took me upstairs to the prime minister's study, a pleasant room with light wood-paneled walls, comfortable furniture, several paintings, and a drinks table behind Heath's desk. Maitland mixed, served, and, as we were standing there chatting, Heath came in, grabbed a drink, sat and talked in an amiable, direct way.

He said he expected to cover a wide field in his forthcoming talks with Nixon. A major topic will be the Middle East.

Heath saw no signs of worry about dollar devaluation—in terms of gold prices. He didn't think there was any reason to change NATO's strategy from "flexible response." "Change to what?" he asked. He said one could rationalize a withdrawal of forces by talk of other methods of defense such as tactical nuclear weapons. But we *could* continue with existing strategic concepts; after all, there was more and more rapid transportation being developed and the United States had lots of this available.

Britain was taking steps to do as much as it can for NATO and sympathizes with Washington's desire to see the allies do more. "We are carrying a proportionately bigger burden than anyone else," he said.

It was silly for people to argue that Britain should contribute more to NATO's infrastructure program, as Bonn proposed. "We make our contribution through teeth, not infrastructure. We can't be expected to do both. President Nixon understands this and he prefers teeth."

Heath is worried about the Mediterranean situation, where Russian strength continues to increase. Only a few days ago Mrs. Meir, the Israeli prime minister, had assured him there was no chance of a military confrontation between Russia and America. "I told her I was more worried," he said, "that the Soviet Union might get its way without a confrontation." He said the Russians now had a base at Alexandria, lots of troops in Egypt, and were gaining positions in Aden, Somalia, and the Sudan. Their submarine fleet and electronic vessels were roaming the Indian Ocean.

There are two aspects to the problem: Western relations with the Arab world; and an Israeli-Arab settlement. Perhaps Britain would now contribute more diplomatic help. After Nasser's death it has become easier for Britain to "get over our schizophrenia" on Egypt and build up reasonable relationships. Britain might now get into a position of relationships with both sides, Arabs and Israelis.

I told Heath of Pompidou's statements on Britain and the Common Market. He seemed enormously pleased, smiled, took a drink, and a slight flush came over his ruddy face. He said he had detected a change in France's "approach" and this had improved the "spirit" of the negotiations. He gave Pompidou full credit for this. On taking steps to improve British public opinion on entry, he said: "You can't push that until the results of negotiations begin to emerge. If you try to change public opinion too soon you get a great many questions raised before you have the answers ready."

He thought the old bugbear of Britain as an American Trojan horse had gone and Pompidou had done much to reestablish a proper approach. When the Common Market is enlarged "we shall all have a reasonable relationship with the States. In the end it will warm up the U.S.-European relationship, although first there will be individual problems and hard bargaining with America." He thought in the end a Europe including Britain would much more represent the Kennedy twin-pillar approach on NATO.

He hoped at the start of the 1960s that the Irish "partition" question would be absorbed and vanish inside "Europe" as both Britain and Ireland joined. But now the Irish have gotten themselves into "a new jam." If the standard of living in the south could be raised it would help to reduce the pressure to stream northward. But all this will take time. "And I only wish the Irish could keep their mouths shut."

He thought the United States was behaving very foolishly about its supersonic transport. Concorde would be sold abroad everywhere except the U.S.A. Then, after two or three years while the U.S. kept Concorde out, it would have to let it in. Later it would reverse itself and start building its own SST—much too late.

I asked who had most influenced him? He thought a while, finally said: "I guess everyone, from Jesus Christ on." He then added: "Of course there are many. For example Winston [Churchill], Anthony [Eden], and Harold [Macmillan]. I like to think I am an all-around character and therefore subject to many influences—mountains, music, people, the sea."

In his spare time he liked to read, walk, occasionally play golf. He enjoyed wine, watching ballet, attending the opera. He liked the theater. Also conducting (orchestras). "I like to drive fast cars—but I'm not allowed to now. I like to travel a lot. I have a great interest in architecture."

I asked about music. He had "very catholic tastes." One should judge the individual works of composers, not the composers as such. But obviously, since he was an organist and pianist, he had "a foundation" of Bach. Also he liked Beethoven, Brahms, Brückner, Mahler, and the moderns, such as Vaughan Williams.

He seems to have gained personality, psychological stature, and ease as prime minister. I found him cool, calm, strong, determined, sure of himself. I think he will do well.

LONDON, *December 10, 1970*

Last night Oliver Hoare came to dinner with David (my son). Oliver works at Christie's, the famous art auction house. They recently had a sale of some of Napoleon's effects. Among the articles sold were the dried-up private parts of the emperor, snipped off his corpse by his doctor. They brought £17,000 pounds, says Oliver, and were rather undersized.

PARIS, *December 16, 1970*

Mohamed Heikal dropped in for a drink. He and Hedayat have been visiting Europe. He is convinced the Khrushchev memoirs are phony. He thinks much of the material is genuine but much is also false. "It doesn't ring true." Maybe Alexei Adzhubei, Khrushchev's son-in-law and former editor of *Izvestia*, had someting to do with putting together a manuscript. The secret police may be involved but he cannot understand why.

Heikal was present during all K.'s conversations with Nasser. He flew to Moscow and then traveled to Yalta with Khrushchev and on by sea to Egypt when he visited Nasser. He was with him day and night and the memoirs don't sound straight.

Heikal said he has taken a cue from my recent book [*The Last of the*

Giants] (which he serialized in *Al Ahram*) and is planning to write his book on Nasser in a similar way. He will start with a section of "Nasser on Nasser" and then go on into a series of confrontations—Nasser and Dulles, Nasser and Tito, Nasser and Nehru, Nasser and Khrushchev, etc.

Mohamed told me that he had roared with laughter when he read my column on Yasir Arafat, which I had headlined "The Kalashnikov Kid." He took it home to Hedayat, who also laughed. Hedayat cannot stand Arafat and Mohamed himself is rather sceptical. But he said the Palestinian Arabs "needed a hero" and therefore made one out of Arafat.

PARIS, *December 19, 1970*

Dined last night with Prince Paul and Princess Olga: a quiet dinner *en famille*—excellent food and wine, fascinating gossip. All of this was enhanced by their lovely pictures, including the famous Titian of the Duke of Mantua, a Vigée Lebrun of one of Paul's ancestors, and a Winterhalter of the Tsarina Marie, wife of Alexander II, and Olga's ancestor.

Paul told very proudly how his beautiful thirty-two-year-old daughter, Princess Elizabeth (now married to a young Englishman named Balfour), invited the English Queen Mother to dine with him and Olga last week and cooked the turkey herself.

Paul said that while he was still regent of Jugoslavia he warned the British during the summer of 1939 that Bulgaria would let the Germans have free passage across their country if war came. He said that he personally gave permission to smuggle Gheorgi Dimitrov (the "good" one, a democrat) out of Bulgaria and across Jugoslavia in a coffin. He says Tito is "the best of all the dictators" and is doing a good job in Jugoslavia.

Both Paul and Olga talked at length about their luncheon with Hitler in early 1941. At luncheon Hitler had made an effort to be quite charming but it was a curious meal. The protocol problem was solved by having the three of them (there were no other guests) served simultaneously by butlers who sprang out at the same instant as if in a ballet. Since no plates were passed, in order to avoid the problem of precedence, they were each served a huge salmon—although Hitler, a vegetarian, didn't eat his. Behind each chair stood a grim officer in the SS, looking like an assassin.

They were convinced Hitler was a homosexual. He talked of the tragedy of seeing beautiful young English and German boys lying dead beside each other on the battlefield. Olga said she rushed to tell this to Princess Bonaparte, Freud's most distinguished pupil, who said Freud would have been fascinated.

Hitler also assured Prince Paul that his [Hitler's] speeches were the only immortal prose being produced in Germany and would live as long as Luther's *Theses*.

Olga asked Hitler if he didn't get lonely without a wife. Hitler replied: "No, no woman could be comfortable here."

They were also entertained by [Hermann] Goering, who gave a luncheon at his Prussian hunting lodge. Said Paul: "He was dressed like Wilhelm Tell with a dagger in his belt and jewels hanging around his neck. He was clearly mad—but also very intelligent. And I thought his wife genuinely nice."

Paul said Goering had told him: "Of course, I know I am greedy. That is why I'm so fat. Every night I have a tray with cheese and cold cuts placed on the table by my bedside so if I wake up I can turn over and eat it and go to sleep again."

Paul had been absolutely positive that war was coming in 1939 so he personally arranged for the secret dispatch of Jugoslavia's gold reserves to the United States that summer. The gold was taken over by Jugoslavia's only naval training ship. Paul was attending a naval review of the Italian fleet and was on the bridge of a battleship with Mussolini and King Victor Emmanuel when a message saluting him was brought as the Jugoslav vessel sailed by. Nobody knew how precious its cargo was.

They both spoke of their sad exile to Kenya after Paul was ousted on March 27, 1941, by the *coup d'état* which put King Peter II on the throne and touched off the German invasion. They had a desperately unhappy time under the supervision of a certain English officer who used to steal from the funds allotted for their monthly upkeep. Finally, they were sent on to South Africa where Field Marshal [Jan] Smuts gave them a warm welcome.

Paul also talked about a curious dinner that took place in Paris a few days ago given by Louis Aragon, the communist poet. Princess Irene of Greece (who is a pianist) was there as well as Mstislav Rostropovich, the Russian cellist, and Amalia Caramanlis. To everyone's surprise, Rostropovich raised his glass and said, "I drink to the King of Greece" (an exile in Rome).

The main part of the conversation had to do with poor King Peter II, who replaced Prince Paul in 1941 at the age of seventeen and who died in the United States last November 3. Paul gave me copies of Peter's will and death certificate. He died after a liver transplant operation in Denver, Colorado, and the causes are listed as "cardio-respiratory arrest (ten minutes), chronic brain injury (three months), chronic liver cirrhosis (six months)."

Paul says Peter had become a hopeless drunk and fell into the hands of a woman who was close to a splinter faction of the Serbian Orthodox Church headed by two monks. Apparently they cooked up a will—and got him to sign it—in which he left a quarter of his estate to "Liberty Eastern Serbian Orthodox Monastery, Liberty, Illinois" and added, "Notwithstanding any other desires of my family, it is my desire that I be

buried in the United States of America at Liberty Eastern Serbian Orthodox Monastery, Liberty, Illinois."

There are many curious questions raised. The will says "my wife's
name is Alexandria Karageorgevic." Her real name, of course, is
Alexandra. He refers to "Liberty, Illinois," but the death certificate orders
the body removed to "Libertyville, Illinois." He calls himself "Peter
Karageorgevic" in the will but the death certificate is made out in the
name of Peter Petrovich. The death certificate says he never married and
has no surviving spouse, although the will names his wife and says she
resides in Venice.

According to Paul his body was held by the Capitol Mortuaries, Inc.
in Denver, Colorado, after Peter died in Colorado General Hospital—until
several days later when it was released for a funeral in Los Angeles. He
claims it is evident from the text of the will and Peter's illegible signature
that the brain damage had already taken hold in June when he signed his
will.

He thinks the whole thing a plot by a splinter faction of the church to
gain recognition through possession of the king's body, to become a center
for pilgrimages by *émigré* Serbs, and to get money from his estate. Paul
said that during recent years Peter created himself chancellor of the
Knights of Malta, an organization in which he had no claim to membership
because, among other things, it is Roman Catholic. As self-proclaimed
"chancellor," he sold titles of nobility to gullible Americans. He said
Peter had spent large sums from the gold reserves which he, Paul, had
sent to the U.S.A. This, of course, was before the reserves were returned
to Jugoslavia after the war.

PARIS, *January 6, 1971*

Last night Nelly de Vögué gave a small dinner for Jim Gavin, former
general and former ambassador to France. His is a remarkable American
success story: the poor son of a Pennsylvania coal miner who entered the
army as a private, finally got to West Point, was one of the most glamorous
World War II paratroop commanders, and became a forceful intellect in
the military establishment.

He is convinced that if Nixon is re-elected in 1972 there will be a
nonviolent but profound revolution in the United States by 1976—a
kind of souped-up New Deal. American youth demands this. He doesn't
know what the revolution will be and calls it an "X factor." When he was a
kid the Model T Ford was the fastest vehicle but now there is the
supersonic Concorde. There was TNT and now there is the H-bomb.
The "X factor" will bear the same relationship to the New Deal.

As U.S. ambassador to France he once was back in Washington to
consult with President Kennedy and Kennedy was furious with de Gaulle's

doubts vis-à-vis the U.S.A. "Ask him if he doubts our promise to stand by our pledges in Europe," Kennedy said. Gavin wrote the words down on a piece of paper. "But you are not going to ask him that bluntly, are you?" Mac Bundy asked. "Of course I am," Gavin replied. When he returned to Paris he did. De Gaulle acknowledged the U.S.A. would honor its word—"but at your convenience and suiting your own national interests, like in 1917 and 1941."

PARIS, *January 8, 1971*

Lunched with Ivo Vejvoda, the Jugoslav ambassador, a most agreeable and civilized man, a good communist but not in the least pro-Russian. His young son (then sixteen) wanted to demonstrate with French students during the May 1968 uprising. He told his boy not to: he was a foreigner and a diplomat's son; but if he wished to demonstrate for more freedom he should go back to university in Jugoslavia and do so there. The boy is now in Belgrade University and up to the ears in youth demonstrations.

Ivo told Frenchmen here when the Pompidou regime took over that there was no sense in worrying about more troubles with the university students. As a Marxist he knew there could be no repetition of the May 1968 "events" for several years; at present it was a burnt-out case. Revolutions never repeated themselves quickly. It was twelve years between the Russian revolutions of 1905 and 1917.

Vejvoda wondered about what was going on in Russia. Probably Brezhnev still was Number One because, after all, he has the army's backing. He made the profound remark: "Today the Soviet army is not only a state within a state but a party within a party."

BRUSSELS, *January 11, 1971*

Interesting dinner with André de Staercke, Belgian ambassador to NATO and dean of the allied envoys. André said "A.D. '70," the basic NATO planning paper for the coming decade, stands for Atlantic Defense 1970. This postulates defense based upon continuing *détente*. De Staercke thought it a mistake to call it "A.D. '70" because that was the year the Romans conquered Jerusalem and might be taken as a bad-luck omen.

PARIS, *January 13, 1971*

Dined at the Windsors'. The poor old Duke looks terrible. His arthritis makes him use a cane all the time and his left eye is almost completely closed. He must have had some kind of stroke. Nevertheless, he hopped around gallantly like a slightly crippled old bird.

Incidentally, I received a letter from Chester Bowles, former U.S. ambassador to India, about his negotiations with Prince Sihanouk of Cambodia in January 1968.

He wrote: "Sihanouk admitted to me privately that he could not really control the border situation; indeed he also made it clear that while he felt that U.S. policies in southeast Asia were inept, he primarily feared the Chinese; certainly he had no use for the North Vietnamese or, indeed, *any* Vietnamese."

PARIS, *January 15, 1971*

Lunched with Jean Monnet in his office flat. He ate like a bird. Rather to my surprise, as we were chatting, he remarked: "You know, for many years we didn't get on very well together. I'm glad to see there is a change." I said I strongly endorsed his policy of European federation, but until recently was bearish about its chances. During 1970 three events had occurred which altered my analysis: Pompidou changed French policy on British admission; Heath was elected prime minister of Britain; and de Gaulle died, terminating the possibility of any implied blackmail against Pompidou if he backed London. Monnet added there was a fourth event— Brandt's election as chancellor of Germany (in 1969).

BONN, *January 19, 1971*

Very long lunch with Chancellor Willy Brandt in his Schaumburg Palais office. He certainly looks the part of a chancellor: an imposing, big, handsome man. But on rereading what he said, it seems devoid of content. Here is a condensed version:

> The Soviet Union is interested in better relations with the Federal Republic and Western Europe. And their leaders must know that better relations between these two states can't coincide with a worsening of the situation in Berlin.

> We learned a bitter lesson in '61 in spite of all theories about the four-power status of Berlin; the reality was that the dividing line became clear where the interests of the United States and the Soviet Union met. This was precisely the middle of the city of Berlin.

> I am convinced that only as the conditions and relations between the parts of Europe change will there be a chance to change conditions for divided Germany. But this does not exclude that the character of the wall may be altered, may be changed, just as the character of the dividing line between the Federal Republic and East Germany might be changed.

> The United States, being the leading Western power and one of the two world powers, has to take a more global look upon things and to

look on how this fits together—the Middle East, Vietnam, SALT, German moves vis-à-vis Eastern Europe, Berlin, and so on. I understand this. But I understand also that as a loyal member of the Western family, one has to take care of one's own interests.

He continued: "My majority is not very convincing. On the other hand, fifteen months have gone and my government has not lost any vote even on minor things. Under the German constitution, to lose votes would not have any consequence as long as the opposition would not be able to elect another chancellor.

"I am very much interested in cooperation with East Germany. But I do not believe in a mishmash, in just mixing. This is impossible. Yet I still think since it is one nation in the feeling of the people, since there are all these family links, since there is only one language and many other aspects of common culture, there could be instead of the situation we have now, that the distance between West Germany and East Germany is greater than the distance between West Germany and Japan (it is easier for me to go to Japan or Kenya or I don't know where than to East Germany)—I think it should be possible to move in the direction based upon common history, common language, common culture, and an economy that also originally belonged together. A good deal of cooperation could be worked out.

"I would not call it a confederation. I cannot see how a confederation could work between a state economy on the one side and a market economy on the other side. What we do not like to recognize is the split of Germany. We have to live with it, but one should not expect that we make this part of our own position. Now we are aiming at good relations with East Germany, because we know these two states exist. We hope one day they will not exist in the same way. They either will be closer together or perhaps even under one roof.

"I hope to make my contribution to a Germany, which now for me is the Federal Republic, which is a good neighbor, which plays an active role in the European family and in making peace safer. I regard this as being one of the prerequisites for also getting closer to a solution of the German problem."

I asked: "Have you ever considered who most influenced the development of your character?" He said: "When I was young, an editor and member of parliament in Lübeck impressed me very much. His name was Julius Leber. He was one of those who later tried to bring an end to the war and he was executed as one of the plotters of July 20. He was a remarkable moderate social democrat in the Weimar period.

"And during my first Berlin years, Mayor Ernst Reuter not only impressed me much but influenced me. I learned a great deal from him. If I had to mention two names I would name these two."

BONN, *January 20, 1971*

Drinks with Franz-Josef Strauss, former defense minister, Bavarian boss (Christian-Socialists), and implacable enemy of Willy Brandt. He is quite a contrast to the statuesque, handsome Brandt with his gift for vague generalities. Strauss is mean, savage, bright.

Strauss said: "If I were an American I would be strongly against Brandt's new *Ostpolitik*. The U.S. shouldn't allow itself to become involved in inter-German arguments. It shouldn't accept the risk of military involvement over the two Germanies. And it should try on its own to secure normal relations with Russia. But it should not watch with approval while Bonn yields the political and military positions of the West. I told this to Henry Kissinger and he agreed.

"Bismarck used to say you don't make things move faster just by setting your watch ahead. That is what Bonn is doing now. The ability to wait is an indispensable prerequisite for a pragmatic policy. What was the reason anyway to start a sudden new *Ostpolitik* here? Brandt argues that the U.S.A. is getting weaker; that it is obsessed with internal problems; that it will lose its position of world power in ten or twenty years and thereby yield its say in policy; that the Soviet star is rising. That because of all these reasons we Germans must settle our problems with Russia now and on the best possible terms.

"Some Americans see what is happening. Kissinger is against Brandt's *Ostpolitik*. So are Clay, McCloy, Acheson, George Ball. You know, I told Kissinger: 'We don't expect you to attack our government and thereby make a hero of Brandt. But America's friends can't defend America's own interests against America's own statements.'

"We can't keep U.S. troops in Europe if we ourselves make a deal with the Russians and virtually get married to them, showing they aren't a threat. The only opponent America has at all the points it is committed in the world—Europe, Vietnam, SALT, Middle East, Cuba—is Russia, now a global and naval power. But this power costs the Russians enormously. Why should we West Germans help Russia overcome the economic problems? It is our *Osthandel*, our trade with the East, that benefits them."

PARIS, *January 29, 1971*

Lunched with Prince Paul of Jugoslavia. Paul told me Prince Tomislav, King Peter's brother, had telephoned from London to ask if he had read my column on the king's sordid death. "Yes," said Paul. "What did you think of it?" "Very accurate." "Where do you think he got all his information." "I have no idea," said Paul, who gave it to me. Incidentally, he says Peter's family is now suing to break the will filed by the late sovereign and bequeathing large sums to a nonrecognized branch of the Serbian Orthodox Church.

Paul recalled that it would be thirty years this March since he had last seen his country, having been ousted by a *coup d'état.* "I didn't know what the British were up to because I told my chief of police to watch only the Germans and the Italians, to leave the British and Americans alone."

He still admires Tito for having preserved the country's unity but thinks it will fall apart when Tito dies.

PARIS, January 30, 1971

The poor little Szall family is safe and sound in America. They are staying somewhere near Washington (in a "safe house" of the CIA). And so at last this sad story—which began over a year ago when Jozska first confessed to me in Rome he was thinking of defecting—has now come to an end. I do hope they get off to a decent start in life in the U.S.A.

PARIS, February 2, 1971

Jean-Marie Soutou, inspector-general of the French foreign service, came for lunch. Jean-Marie thought it was tragic to see a German chancellor (Brandt) today whose internal future depends wholly on the success of his foreign policy vis-à-vis Russia. This puts Germany in Soviet hands. The implication of Brandt's policy is that the West must make concessions to Moscow on Berlin in order to produce a European security conference—in which new and further concessions would be made.

The Russians are convinced things are going their own way. The Soviet leadership believes that for the first time the United States is so divided internally that it won't stand up on any major issue of foreign policy. Never before have these internal divisions so weakened the U.S.A. and the Russians are reckoning on a decomposition in the American view. As a result they see a disarray in Western society.

PARIS, February 8, 1971

Good talk this afternoon with Georges Marchais, French Communist party boss. Marchais, a fifty-year-old Norman worker, is solidly-built with strong face, black hair, blue eyes, and a friendly manner. He told me the party now claims 400,000 members although right after the liberation in 1945 it claimed 700,000. The party reckons it would get a minimum of 5 million votes in a national election today.

He says it is wrong to consider the French party more "national" than in the past. It has always been "national." However, in previous years it had taken pains to be very precise about its socialistic program. There were certain questions in the international field in which the French party disagreed with the Soviet party—like the occupation of Czechoslovakia and the sentencing of Leningrad Jews. But these were not "contradictions." Since the war the party had rejected Stalin's thesis of the "unique party" and was now working as strongly as ever for unity and an electoral alliance with other left-wing parties.

He thought that if a proper left-wing coalition could be worked out and agreed on a "democratic program" it would gain more than 50 percent of the French vote. When I mentioned de Gaulle's theory that there were only two parties in France—his own and the communists—Marchais disagreed. He said the communists were the strongest party on the Left but there were many men and women in the noncommunist Left, neither communist nor Gaullist.

He insisted that despite the differences with Moscow on Czechoslovakia and the Leningrad trial, there was no basic change in the warm friendship between his party and Moscow. He said: "We are for solidarity and friendship with all parties—even with China, despite ideological differences."

BRUSSELS, *February 10, 1971*

I talked for an hour and a half this morning with King Baudouin, whom I had not seen since the late 1940s when I sometimes dined at his father's house outside Geneva and sat around while King Leopold corrected Baudouin's homework. He has become a painfully shy man of forty-one, tall, thin, with pale face and sad eyes. We sat across from each other in the huge hideous study of his palace and, in an odd reversal of roles, he hauled out a notebook and jotted things down.

He said he had been delighted by the way Alan Shepard had hit two golf balls during his moon voyage. He was impressed by the entire U.S. moon program and the astonishing coordination of all its elements. It should help the U.S. image abroad but unfortunately people were getting blasé. It was silly to say men should not go to the moon because it costs so much money which might otherwise be spent on the poor. There was no relationship. One had to do both.

Baudouin is hopeful about European federation and Britain's ultimate entry into the Common Market. He thinks de Gaulle's European policy actually helped the Market because it prevented it from moving too rapidly too far. Now it was progressing at the correct pace.

He didn't think there would be the slightest difficulty as between monarchies and republics when the member countries are eventually confederated with one supranational assembly. He hoped the Walloon-Fleming language problem would ultimately dissolve inside Europe and likewise that Irish partition would fade away as an issue.

Relations between Europe and the Third World were vital. Europe must help backward countries and this is its proper role in history. He certainly hoped the Congo (formerly Belgium's sole colony) would be aided through Europe. There has been excellent progress in the Congo and Baudouin finds [Joseph] Mobutu a very impressive man. He is the first Congolese to give a sense of nationhood to the multiplicity of tribes that previously depended on Belgium.

It was hard to keep the Belgian public interested in paying for national defense and the support of NATO during a period of *détente*. Baudouin hopes the U.S.A. will continue to maintain its forces here. This is good not only for Europe but also for the U.S. Incidentally, he fears that when we do away with the draft, we are going to find a volunteer army extremely expensive.

He and Queen Fabiola are going to Germany soon and this will test whether the Belgian public has now forgotten all that it suffered from the Germans in two world wars. The younger generation is completely at ease with the Germans now.

He asked if I thought Russia would permit the establishment of liberty in Eastern Europe before some profound change inside the Soviet Union. I said if we thought so we were kidding ourselves. The king asked if we had to accept the extinction of freedom in East Europe. I said regrettably that although it was immoral there was nothing else we could do. There had been less of an international ruckus over Czechoslovakia '68 than Hungary '56, and the biggest problem was still to come. "You mean Jugoslavia after Tito's death?" Baudouin inquired intelligently. "Precisely," I said. Baudouin agreed the West would do nothing if Russia takes over control of Jugoslavia and Rumania.

PARIS, *February 11, 1971*

On February 11, 1945, Roosevelt, Churchill, and Stalin signed the Yalta agreements. Today I had lunch with Chip Bohlen, who was Roosevelt's interpreter at the conference. Chip said Yalta represented the best possible deal under the circumstances. But it had to be split into three points:

(1) The areas under Soviet military control—everything up to the German borders which the Red Army was just reaching, and where the issue was simply that Washington and London were trying to produce free elections—above all for the Poles—and the right to select their own form of government.

(2) The voting procedure in the UN security council. On this [Edward] Stettinius made a very clear presentation of the issues.

(3) The Far East and military arrangements there.

Chip acknowledges the agreement on Poland was ambiguously worded. The Russians were able to use holes in the text to advance their pretensions but the *realpolitik* of the situation would not have changed. Had the agreement signed by the three powers been applied, things would have been somewhat better. But the map of Europe today would look the same whether or not there had been a Yalta conference.

From the U.S. viewpoint, the most important thing was the agreement on the UN voting formula. The Russians finally accepted that the veto power would not be applied to procedural matters.

Russian agreement on the UN voting formula made UN possible. And one important fact—frequently misinterpreted—is that France was given a seat on the allied control commission for Germany in the Yalta conference. This is worth contemplating since Stalin showed himself at Yalta to be very anti-French. He argued that France had opened the front to German victory and it would be just to give more credit to Jugoslavia and Poland.

On point 3, the Far East, Chip recalled that the joint chiefs of staff had wanted Russia to join in the assault on Japan before the United States invasion operations started. Roosevelt had been informed by his military advisers that Japan would last for eighteen months following the Nazi surrender. The only thing wrong with Yalta in this respect was that the Far Eastern arrangements were made behind the backs of the Chinese.

By the time of Yalta in February 1945, it was too late to do anything that might substantially change the facts in Eastern Europe. And the Far Eastern agreement has to be viewed in a very special way. Nobody yet knew whether the A-bomb was going to work.

Bohlen says Yalta must be viewed as "the conference at which the illusions of the United States were subsequently destroyed. Perhaps it would be better to say it was the conference at which the illusion was destroyed that Russia would behave like a country and not like a cause."

27

HEMINGWAY DRUNK

WAS "HELL"

LUNCH WITH DAVID BRUCE. IT IS ALWAYS A PLEASURE TO PARTAKE OF his wisdom and infinite courtesy.

Bruce thinks Nixon means what he says about getting U.S. forces out and believes that at least some weeks before the Republican nominating convention next year, all American troops will be gone—except for a handful of officers and technicians. Even the air force will be based outside Vietnam (primarily Thailand, I assume).

He believes we have built a very powerful South Vietnamese force that should be able to take care of itself; "and if it doesn't, that's just too bad." The south may very well even invade the north.

He says there is absolutely nothing to do about the Paris talks. It isn't a negotiation. The north just uses it as a propaganda exercise designed to influence U.S. political opinion. No one on the communist side has the slightest authority to take any diplomatic action at all.

We reminisced. David, who headed OSS in Europe during World War II, said Hemingway was a delight on an operation but absolute hell when he got drunk. Bruce had great admiration for de Gaulle and his integrity and said it was tragic how Roosevelt disliked and misunderstood him. It was ridiculous to think U.S. and British authorities could govern a liberated France and de Gaulle exposed this fallacy right off. Our pro-Vichy policy was idiotic and the later attempt to build up General Giraud was doomed from the start.

Eisenhower made a mistake in agreeing to the creation of an isolated island of Berlin. Bruce once asked Ike about this when he was president. Ike replied that he had only been asked for his "military opinion" by Roosevelt. Now, as president, he thought it undignified to be critical. But "some day" he would publish his viewpoint. He never did. Bruce had favored a frontier between the Soviet, U.S., and British occupation zones established at some point like Magdeburg, which might then have been developed into a German capital, temporary or otherwise. The idea of access corridors to Berlin was insane.

ALGIERS, *February 22, 1971*

Bill Eagleton, the bright young head of our U.S. affairs mission (we have no diplomatic relations—since the 1967 Palestine War), met me at the airport and took me to his house to stay. Bill and his wife, Kay, a long-haired, ivory-skinned beauty, gave a dinner party last night.

Present were M'hamed Yazid, former Algerian ambassador to UN and his American wife, Olive; Abdel Kader Chanderli, president of CAMEL (Algerian gas liquefaction company) and his wife, and some embassy (mission) staff. Yazid, Chanderli, and I recalled how the three of us arranged at a New York restaurant, ten years ago, for me to be "kidnapped" from the St. Georges hotel here, during the French occupation, and taken off across country by the FLN to demonstrate how well the partisans controlled it.

Unfortunately the deal never came off. Yazid, who canceled when the underground in Algiers decided they couldn't risk it, told me that last time I had been here he tried to get me in touch with the FLN [National Liberation Front] partisan who had been assigned to bring off the aborted operation; but he was away.

Chanderli insists that despite dogmatic window-dressing the Algerian revolution is pragmatic and concerned only with economic development and mass education. Already a new generation of youngsters is coming to high positions and is bored with ideology and their parents' reminiscences about what they did in the war against France.

Before leaving, M'hamed said he still had the pictures I had furnished him a decade ago (of myself) by which FLN agents were to identify me to be sure they kidnapped the right man!

ALGIERS, *February 23, 1971*

Talked for an hour and forty-five minutes with Houari Boumedienne, president of Algeria, in his residence-office, a low white building cordoned off and protected by armed guards. The doorway is watched over by two members of the presidential guard in grey cloaks, white turbans, and carrying scimitars.

Boumedienne is a thin man with heavy, reddish-brown moustache, very dark brown hair, pale white skin, unusually bright small eyes, a somewhat stern expression. He was wearing a black *djellaba* over a grey business suit and let the robe fall to his hips after sitting himself on a sofa beside my armchair. He was smoking a long, thick cigar. A servant brought tea, coffee, and fruit juice.

Boumedienne is believed to have been born Mohamed Ben Brahim Boukharouba on August 23, 1932, in Clauzel, near Guelma, East Algeria, the son of a peasant. The story is that, rather than be called up in the French army, he fled to Tunis, later to Cairo, where he studied at the Al Azhar theological university. During the war against the French, he became head of the FLN general staff west and, in 1960, head of the unified general staff at Gardimaou, Tunisia.

I asked if his policy favored a Maghreb federation (Tunisia, Algeria, and Morocco, and perhaps Libya). He started uneasily: "Of course this has always been our aim. It is a fundamental objective of our policy. But one requires time, patience, and clairvoyance to achieve such a program. There is unquestionably an inexorable thrust toward regional unification and the creation of a single Maghreb entity linked to both the Arab world and Africa."

Did Algeria consider itself both neutral and nonaligned? "Exactly," he said. "We are nonaligned. But I must explain. We are very jealous of our own national independence. And we sincerely think the only sound policy for Algeria, given its history and the terrible price we paid for our freedom, given its geographical position, is to insist on non-alignment, avoiding entanglement with the power blocs. We will defend this position with all our force. We need continuity and stability and must avoid being entangled in the quarrels of others.

"We don't want our future to depend on any foreign country—France or the Soviet Union or the United States. We must depend upon ourselves. Of course, this does not mean that we are neutral as between just and unjust causes. We are independent and we support all just causes."

Ideologically, I inquired, how did Algerian socialism differ from others —from Swedish, Russian, Jugoslav, or Egyptian socialism? He said, while indicating that he certainly was no Marxist: "Socialism in its essence is the same. It means avoiding the exploitation of one class by another class. But conditions differ in different lands.

"One of our aims is to completely free the Algerian people from any vestigial exploitation from abroad or any remnants of the exploitation system that existed here. We want to bring about a just distribution of wealth. We want every child to have the chance to be educated. We want everyone to have a job. And we want to insure that no class or category can exploit any other. But we must be realistic. We have chosen realism as our method and progress requires time.

"Although we press for economic advance, we want no forced marches. We are not at all dogmatic. The world goes too fast for theories. We can't take the risk of tying ourselves to theories that will be bypassed soon by events. This is no longer 1917 (the year of the Soviet revolution). This is a time when men are going to other planets."

He said: "Let us not forget that petroleum is in Algerian earth. It belongs to the Algerian people. It must be used for the Algerian national economy and not for the benefit of other, richer lands. We have never hidden our intentions on this. We wish to end the present anachronistic situation" (meaning the 1965 French petroleum concession). Such a situation only exists in formerly colonial lands. The underdeveloped countries have been forced to stagnate as a consequence of what colonialism did.

"The Algerian state, according to international law, has the right to nationalize any foreign concessions; but it must also respect their legal rights. Thus we will indemnify the concessionaires on a just basis. We already have the example of the U.S. and British companies here. They were indemnified for what was taken over; and the basis was accepted."

Boumedienne then drifted on to the natural gas deal now being worked out with the U.S. company, El Paso Gas. Boumedienne said: "This will be the largest gas contract in history." I wondered whether, in view of our developing business, financial, and commercial relationships, it was not time to restore diplomatic relations. He said:

"There are two aspects. I agree that the nonexistence of formal diplomatic relationships shouldn't be an obstacle to the development of economic and commercial relations. Enormous perspectives are opening and I favor this. But with respect to diplomatic relations, you must recall how they were broken in the middle of a dramatic situation for the Arab world. Israel had launched an aggression successively against Egypt, Jordan, and Syria. And the U.S. did nothing to prevent the catastrophe and the resulting humiliation for the Arab masses. All governments, including yours, should have understood the profound sentiment of the Arab people. But the question of our diplomatic relations must not forever be bound by this event."

I asked him about his desire to neutralize the Mediterranean. He said: "We have no precise program. But, in the long term, we would like to see the Mediterranean demilitarized. We don't want to see this region transformed into a zone of tension between the superpowers. But this is not merely a question for the Arab states of the Mediterranean; it is a question for all the riparian powers. They could all work together for a policy of *détente* and cooperation. After all, we are not a cake to be sliced up by the superpowers. We want no one to partition our area, to divide us up."

At this point I interrupted: "Has Moscow ever asked for base facilities in Algeria?" He replied: "No. They never did. They knew the answer would be negative." He admitted that Algeria depends heavily on Soviet arms supplies. But he said these were purchased, although under favorable conditions. "When other conditions are offered by other nations on a more favorable basis, we will buy from them."

I asked if he favored getting the Soviet fleet out more than the U.S. fleet or vice versa. "We want them both out," he answered. "I see no interest for us in having either of them here. But I admit this is a long-range idea. The situation is obviously not yet ripe for change."

When I asked about his personal life, he very firmly but politely said he didn't want to talk about it, the time "had not yet come." He said he read a great deal—but only "for my work." He never took a day off and hadn't since he came to power.

Paris, *February 26, 1971*

Last night we went to a dinner given by Gerald and Florence Van der Kemp. Gerald is curator of Versailles and lives in a splendid apartment in one wing of the palace. Olivier Guichard, minister of education and Pompidou's best political boss, was there.

Guichard had just come back from his first visit to the Soviet Union where he saw [Aleksei] Kosygin and other top officials. He found it depressing. France has nothing to learn from Russia in the education field. They just turn out assembly line cadres. If 1,800 engineers are required in next year's plan, 1,800 youngsters are graduated whether they are qualified or not.

New York, *March 4, 1971*

Delightful evening with George and Ruth Ball. George, sixty-one and head of Lehman Brothers, the investment banking firm, was for several years undersecretary of state.

His hair is now white and he is a bit overweight, but he is a big bull of a man. Some twenty years ago he had a cancerous kidney removed. The next day Ruth smuggled a bottle of Scotch into the hospital and the doctor caught them having a drink. He wrote in George's medical chart that he should be allowed a highball before meals.

He is honest, forceful, decent, and generous in his estimates. Although he disagreed strongly with President Johnson over his Vietnam policy he is still loyal to him and thinks he was a good president with that exception. He speaks highly of Dean Rusk, although they also differed strongly on Vietnam. He said that whereas most secretaries of state would have attempted to block direct communications between the undersecretary and the president when Number One and Number Two in the state department disagreed on an issue, Dean urged Ball to make maximum use of direct contacts.

He thinks McNamara was an intellectually efficient but heartless machine, that he changed his mind drastically on Vietnam in a way that really was illogical.

George had been a member of the jury of the National Book Award which, the day before yesterday, selected James McGregor Burns's Roosevelt biography over my book (*The Last of the Giants*) for an award. I gathered mine was runner-up.

After dinner, George said, "I have something to show you." He rushed upstairs (they have a duplex apartment) and brought down an official state department "briefing book" with the department of state seal on it and marked "Vietnam Papers" and "Master Copy." He told me to take it home and write what I wanted from it.

Among other things that struck me were the following.

> October 5, 1964 (Memo to Secretary Rusk, Secretary McNamara, McGeorge Bundy)
>
> In spite of the strategic importance of the real estate involved, our primary motive in supporting the government of South Vietnam is unquestionably political. It is to make clear to the whole free world that we will assist any nation that asks us our help in defending itself against communist aggression. . . .
>
> It is the nature of escalation that each move passes the option to the other side, while at the same time the party which seems to be losing will be tempted to keep raising the ante. . . . Once on the tiger's back we cannot be sure of picking the place to dismount. . . .
>
> April 21, 1965 (Memo to the president)
>
> We cannot continue to bomb the north and use napalm against South Vietnam villages without a progressive erosion of our world position. This erosion will be limited if we appear to be moving toward some kind of political solution. But that will take more than words.
>
> June 18, 1965 (Memo to the president)
>
> Before we commit an endless flow of forces to South Vietnam we must have more evidence than we now have that our troops will not bog down in the jungles and rice paddies—while we slowly blow the country to pieces.
>
> February 12, 1966 (Memo to secretaries of state and defense)
>
> *There is no assurance that we can achieve our objectives by substantially expanding American forces in South Vietnam and committing*

them to direct combat. On the contrary, we would run grave risks of bogging down an indeterminate number of American troops in a protracted and bloody conflict of uncertain outcome. . . . Politically, South Vietnam is a lost cause. The country is bled white from twenty years of war and the people are sick of it.

We cannot ignore the fact that the war is vastly unpopular and that our role in it is perceptibly eroding the respect and confidence with which other nations regard us. We have not persuaded either our friends or allies that our further involvement is essential to the defense of freedom in the cold war.

March 21, 1966 (Memo to the president)

An effective strategy to cut our losses must be so designed as to make it clear (1) that the United States has fully met its obligations to the South Vietnamese people and to the world, and (2) that it is the South Vietnamese people who have failed, not us.

WASHINGTON, *March 8, 1971*

Agreeable lunch in the White House with Henry Kissinger. We were served in his office, now a nice sunny room upstairs in the area that used to be occupied by the White House press. Henry remarked with glee: "It is only when I get a distinguished visitor like you that I get a decent lunch." We had excellent steaks and red wine.

Henry, no slouch in the art of flattery, assured me that both he and the president thought my column was the best being written. I suspect that similar words have been spoken to others but it rings pleasantly in the ear.

I had a feeling there is something personal about the rivalry between Kissinger and Secretary of State Rogers. He told me that he himself had handled the negotiations with the Russians about cooling the crisis over Soviet construction of a submarine base in Cienfuegos, Cuba—in the interest of preserving security.

He said the state department was very angry that he had been given this role. I have a feeling Henry may go the way of all his predecessors—overworked, underexercised, but I confess I like him and think he has a fine mind.

The White House has not yet made up its mind about Salvador Allende in Chile, but he is an extremely shrewd man and has yet to make a false step. Nevertheless Henry indicated deep suspicion, saying that a man who had been in politics for so long, and who had gone out of his way to receive all of Ché Guevara's colleagues when they were released from Bolivian prison, was fundamentally against us. But he is playing the game so cleverly that it is hard to prove anything.

He said el Sadat of Egypt had shown great skill in taking over the diplomatic charting of the Middle East contest. His appointment of Fawzi as prime minister was most intelligent. There was a "less bad" opportunity to arrange an Israeli-Arab settlement now than at any time since the 1967 war. But the Russians simply had to withdraw their military presence from Egypt.

Henry was puzzled about how the first step toward a settlement could be arranged. I suggested that something should be done about proposing the old (1906) frontier between Egypt and Ottoman Turkey as an initial line of demarcation to which the Israelis could withdraw from the Suez Canal. Kissinger was fascinated by the idea. He had never heard of that border (God knows our policy is curiously fashioned) and said he intended to look into it immediately. I also asked if he had seen my column proposing the creation of a Moslem "Vatican City" inside Jerusalem. He had not seen it and was equally fascinated. Right away he saw the point, envisioned how the Wailing Wall could be left out of the Islamic enclave, and said that in fact Jerusalem lent itself better to a "Vatican City" than did Rome.

Henry confessed he was worried about the degree of anti-Semitism in this country. I think he tends to exaggerate this and for comprehensible human reasons. One must remember that he arrived here as a young refugee boy from Fuerth in Hitler's Germany, and unquestionably has deep-seated complexes. He was astonished at how many people in the Establishment told him of their own feelings, which were evidently although unconsciously anti-Semitic. Because of his high White House position they seem to forget that he is Jewish. One very important man had most recently said to him in confidence that he was convinced there was a Jewish-communist plot. Henry was appalled. Many of these Establishment figures said that undoubtedly the United States had more national interest in a hundred million Arabs with their oil and geographical position than in less than three million Jews in Israel.

He talked optimistically about the situation in southeast Asia, but he did admit it was by no means certain that China might not—quite illogically from his point of view—intervene in Laos. He made the point that after all it would require only thirty or forty thousand troops, which is a mere drop in the bucket from their point of view. However he didn't "think" this was going to happen and he believed the Laotian campaign was going very well.

Henry confessed he had to agree that ultimately new small tactical weapons were going to have to be placed in Europe to make up for the short-fall in conventional NATO troops. He felt that within two or three years the alliance was going to have to face up to this fact—although it hadn't yet done so.

We talked about the SALT conversations. He had been rather optimistic in 1970 but was now less hopeful. He could see some reason to the Soviet argument that U.S. tactical weapons based in Western Europe—which could actually hit targets inside the USSR—should be classified as "strategic" rather than "tactical." There was a fundamental intellectual similarity between the status of such weapons and that of Soviet IRBMs in Cuba in 1962. The only solution would be that this question must be dealt with as part of an overall accommodation.

At the end of our conversation Henry asked me if I would please write him a personal letter as soon as I left Chile giving my forthright opinions of the situation there. He wants this letter for the president.

This afternoon I had an interview of about an hour and twenty minutes with President Nixon. I say "interview" deliberately because he agreed to let me take notes with the express purpose of quoting our conversation. It is the first such interview he has granted. I saw him in the President's suite in the executive office building. He greeted me warmly at the door of his study, sat me down on a sofa, and eased back in an armchair. To my surprise, he summoned a photographer who took several pictures. "You might want one of these," said Nixon with a friendly grin, "just in case you are planning to write another book."

He looked relaxed, sunburned. When I remarked on this he said: "If I didn't know how to stand up under the heat I'd have no business being here." He gave the impression of being self-confident, contained. He was wearing grey-blue slacks and a darker blue jacket. He ordered a cup of tea for himself and coffee for me.

I laid out the case for an interview on the record, which I certainly didn't expect. As usual I anticipated a background or off-the-record chat but to my astonishment he agreed right away. He said I could print it whenever and however I wished and quote him directly. I didn't have to send him any text. He had absolute faith in me. "After all, if I felt I had to edit what you wrote, I wouldn't have agreed to see you in the first place. I know you are a good reporter and will write the truth. However, I think some of your editors won't be happy with what you write."

I said I understood what he implied, but that no word I wrote was ever changed by the *Times*, which was an honorable newspaper, even if it disagreed with his policies. He readily admitted this and said: "Don't worry. Of course I understand that."

At the end he asked where I was bound and I told him Chile. "You lucky fellow," he commented. "I wish I could go there." I told him Kissinger had asked me to write him a letter after my trip—to show the president. "Yes, I wish you would help me by doing that," he said. "Tell me straight what you think." He added that he had circulated many of my columns in the government to clarify understanding of the world situation. He grinned to himself when he foresaw the complaints he would get from the White House and Washington correspondents when my interview was published.

To start his summation, the president said: "I would strongly commend to you my second foreign policy report which I think you should read carefully. I have noticed in some quarters a tendency to discuss this rather condescendingly, saying there is nothing new in it.

> But that isn't so. It sets forth new policy directions and outlines the goals we hope to achieve—the goals not only for this administration but for subsequent administrations. This is a long-range effort. It doesn't get into a country-by-country analysis except in connection with the Soviet Union.

> However, everything you see there is a new philosophy of United States policy. It is the most complete and accurate description of the Nixon doctrine. This doctrine is designed for the specific purpose of maintaining a U.S. policy role in the world rather than a withdrawal from the world and international responsibilites.

> The irony today, for those who look at the Washington scene, is that the great internationalists of the post-World War II period have become the neo-isolationists of the Vietnam War period and especially of the period accompanying the ending of that war. And it is ending.

> This is also true of the attitude of those former internationalists with respect to our defense posture and defense spending. And, for some, it is even true of our foreign trade policy.

> There, of course, it depends on individuals. For example, Senator Javits is an all-out free-trader and a "European," but he takes a dim view of the United States role in Asia. He would also be for a lower defense budget. I merely cite him as an example of what I mean and the varying attitudes I mention.

> The point is, why has this happened? Why have many former internationalists developed neo-isolationist tendencies, at least in some degree? Part of the answer is simply that Americans, like all idealists, are very impatient people. They feel that if a good thing is going to happen it should happen immediately.

> And a great many of these people are very disillusioned with the United Nations. I am not, personally, because I never expected it could settle all problems involving major powers but could nevertheless play a useful role in development and in peace-keeping in areas where the superpowers were not directly involved.

> The older a nation and a people become, the more they become conscious of history and also of what is possible. Now I will explain to

you what I mean. I rate myself as a deeply committed pacifist, perhaps because of my Quaker heritage from my mother. But I must deal with how peace can be achieved and how it must be preserved.

I know that some national leaders and some countries want to expand by conquest and are committed to expansion and this obviously creates the danger of war. Moreover, some peoples have hated each other for years and years.

Look at the divided peoples of India and Pakistan. Look at the situation in the Middle East. You can't suddenly eliminate these differences, these hatreds, just because some political leaders get together. All you can hope for is to bring about a live-and-let-live situation.

With this in mind, I am deeply devoted to a desire that the United States should make the greatest possible contribution it can make to developing such a peaceful world.

It is not enough just to be for peace. The point is, what can we do about it?

Through an accident of history, we find ourselves today in a situation where no one who is really for peace in this country can reject an American role in the rest of the world. Of course, we had our own period of colonial expansion, as typified by Theodore Roosevelt and the idea of manifest destiny. But that period is fortunately gone.

Since then this country has fought in four wars which we didn't start, and really what they have in common is the effort to bring about a better chance for a peaceful world.

And this applies for the Vietnam war as well as the two world wars and Korea. Obviously it was a political temptation when I started office to state simply that we would get out right away without any responsibility for what came next.

But I knew too much about history, about Asia, about the basic feeling in the United States. If we failed to achieve our limited goal—to let a small country exercise the right to choose its own way of life, without having a communist government imposed upon it by force— if we failed to achieve this, we would not help the cause of peace.

For a time, perhaps, we would be seen as a kind of hero. But soon it would be seen that we had left behind a legacy of even greater dangers for southeast Asia and for the Pacific region. And, after all, we are a Pacific power.

In 1966 and 1967—culminating in 1968—the American people began to tire of playing a role in the world. We had fought four wars, selflessly and for no gain. We had provided some $100 billion in foreign aid, much of it to former enemies who are now our competitors, like Japan.

And we found ourselves committed in Vietnam, in a war where there are no heroes, only goats. Our people became sick of Vietnam and supported our men there only in order to get them out—after this period of change in mood. Somewhere a great change had taken place.

We had used our power for peace in four wars but this new attitude gained force: "If we can't handle this one, to hell with it."

We got caught up in a vicious crossfire and it became increasingly difficult to make people understand. I must say that without television it might have been difficult for me to get people to understand a thing.

The crossfire I referred to was this. The superdoves opposed our commitment in Vietnam and all world responsibilities—Korea, the Philippines, the Middle East, Europe. This was the kind of isolationism of those who felt the United States shouldn't have played any role at all in southeast Asia from the very start. For these people, Vietnam was a distant, small, foreign country in just the terms Chamberlain mentioned concerning Czechoslovakia at the time of Munich [1938]. These were the superdoves.

But on the other side, the opposite crossfire came from the superhawks. This group stood by their commander-in-chief, the president, but became fed up with the war for their own reasons. They felt that if the United States can't handle a stinking little war, why then let's just pull out and build up our strength at home. Their logic also favored isolationism but from another angle. And they want to develop a fortress America at home and cram it full of missiles, while the superdoves want us to pull out of the world also, but reducing our strength at home.

In between there are those of us who stand in the middle of the crossfire. The superhawk feels it is his duty to support the president even if that same superhawk isn't sure he wants to see us do what we are doing. The superdove has a different attitude.

He is a good-hearted fellow, but, when he looks around and sees the problems of the poor, the blacks, the Indians, the poor whites, the pot-smoking kids, crime in the cities, urban slums, the environment, he says: "We must get out of the war right away and concern ourselves only with problems at home."

The fact is, however, that there has never been so great a challenge to U.S. leadership. This war is ending. In fact, I seriously doubt we will ever have another war. This is probably the very last one.

In any theoretical question of a war on the basis of "either them or us" I am sure everyone in the country would join in behind, but this is not the case in a small country so far away involved in a situation so difficult to explain.

I am certain a Gallup poll would show that the great majority of the people would want to pull out of Vietnam. But a Gallup poll would also show that a great majority of the people would want to pull three or more divisions out of Europe. And it would also show that a great majority of the people would cut our defense budget.

Polls are not the answer. You must look at the facts. The Soviets now have three times the missile strength (ICBM) of ourselves. By 1974 they will pass us in submarines carrying nuclear missiles.

All of these things are very directly related. For example, when Mrs. Meir, the Israeli prime minister, visited me she understood me right away when I said that if America winds up the war in Vietnam in failure and an image is developed that the war was fought only by stupid scoundrels, there would be a wave of isolationism. This would embrace the U.S. role everywhere—including the Middle East. Mrs. Meir saw the point immediately.

As I see it, we have to take certain specific steps. First of all, what we now have to do is end the war—as we are now doing—in a way that gives South Vietnam a reasonable chance to survive without our help. But this doesn't mean we would withdraw all our responsibilities everywhere.

As I stated in first explaining the Nixon doctrine, our idea is to create a situation in which those lands to which we have obligations or in which we have interests, if they are ready to fight a fire, should be able to count on us to furnish the hose and water.

Meanwhile, in Europe, we can't cut down our forces until there is a mutual agreement with the other side. We must stand with our European friends if they will only do a bit more themselves in NATO —as they have indicated they will do.

And we cannot foolishly fall behind in the arms competition. In the United States we remain ahead in the navy and in the air but the Soviets are ahead in ICBMs and soon will pass us in modern submarine strength.

But each has a kind of sufficiency. The Soviets are a great land power opposite China as well as having far-reaching interests elsewhere. We are a great sea power and we must keep our strength. I am a strong navy man myself. I believe in a strong conventional navy, which helps us to play a peacekeeping role in such areas, for example, as Latin America.

These are all elements that must be considered with respect to each other. The main thing is that I'd like to see us not end the Vietnamese war foolishly and find ourselves all alone in the world. I could have chosen that course my very first day in office. But I want the American people to be able to be led by me, or by my successor, along a course that allows us to do what is needed to help keep the peace in this world.

We used to look to other nations to do this job, once upon a time. But now only the United States plays a major role of this sort in the world. Our responsibilities are not limited to this great continent but include Europe, the Middle East, southeast Asia, east Asia, many areas whose fate affects the peace of the world.

We must above all tend to our national obligations. We must not forget our alliances or our interests. Other nations must know that the United States has both the capability and the will to defend these allies and protect these interests.

Unless people understand this and understand it well, the United States will simply retreat into isolationism, both politically and diplomatically. We would, of course, continue to be an economic giant, but that is not enough.

Let us look at the world today. There are two great powers facing us, Russia and China. They are great powers and great people. Certainly neither of them wants war. But both are motivated by a philosophy which announces itself as expansionist in character. This they will admit themselves.

And only the United States has sufficient strength to be able to help maintain a balance in Europe and other areas that might otherwise be affected.

What I am saying is not a cold-war philosophy. I hope that we can further develop our negotiations with the Soviet Union. For, although we recognize that their ideology is expansionist, they know what it means if the genie comes out of the bottle and that their interest in survival requires that they avoid a conflict with the United States. This means that we must find a way of cooperating.

For obviously pragmatic reasons, therefore, we can see peace slowly shaping up. First, as we are doing, we must end the war in Vietnam. We must continue our Soviet negotiations and open the door of cooperation to China. And in this way there will be a chance of building a world that is relatively peaceful.

I deliberately say relatively peaceful. That doesn't mean everyone will be disarmed, safe, and loving everyone else. The kind of relative peace I envision is not the dream of my Quaker youth. But it is realistic and I am convinced we can bring it about.

Yet, to do this, we can't heed either our superhawks whose policy would ultimately lead to war or our superdoves who believe that only they are capable of achieving peace and that everyone else is a heretic. The trouble is that their policy of weakness would also quickly lead to war.

The day the United States quits playing a responsible role in the world —in Europe or Asia or the Middle East—or gives up or recedes from its efforts to maintain an adequate defense force—on that day this will become a very unsafe world to live in.

I can assure you that my words are those of a devoted pacifist. My very hardest job is to give out posthumous medals of honor.

I don't question the motives of those who oppose me. But I know this world. I have traveled about and talked to many leaders and I know we have a chance to play a role in this world.

Another thing: people should be under no illusion that you can play a role in one area but wholly ignore another. Of course we're not going to get into every little fire-fight everywhere. The Nixon doctrine says only that we will help those who help themselves.

Sometimes people tend to forget the real situation prevailing today. When considering Asia, the great problem is that everyone overlooks the fact that noncommunist Asia—excluding India and Pakistan— produces three times as much as China. Why, Japan alone produces twice as much as China.

What is going to happen if we ignore such basic facts? The United States, as I said earlier, is a Pacific power. And the SST [supersonic transport] will be built—if not by us, by someone else. And then we will be only three hours flight from Japan.

There will be 400 million people in noncommunist Asia relying ever more upon us. Why, Prime Minister Eisaku Sato said not so long ago that Japan depends on the U.S. nuclear field.

In past times, the Number One nation was always in that position because of military conquests. But the mantle of leadership fell on American shoulders not by our desire and not for the purposes of conquest. But we have that position today and how we handle ourselves will determine the chances of world peace.

Do you know, in all my travels, not one leader I have talked to ever said to me in private that he feared the United States as a nation bent on conquest. And I have met many communist leaders, as you know. Whatever some of them may pretend in public, they understand our true troubles and they are also thankful that the United States wants nothing—nothing but the right for everyone to live and let live.

The big question to my mind is: will our Establishment and our people meet their responsibilities. Frankly, I have far more confidence in our people than in the Establishment. The people seem to see the problem in simple terms: "By golly, we have to do the right thing."

But the real problem that worries me most is: will our Establishment see it that way? I am not talking about my critics but about a basic, strange sickness that appears to have spread among those who usually, in this country, can be expected to see clearly ahead into the future.

These are the people who, after World War II, supported the Greek-Turkish aid program, the Marshall Plan, NATO. But today they are in disarray because of two things. They are terribly disillusioned about Vietnam, which is so hard a problem to understand. And they have an enormous concern with home problems of a sort and a degree that did not face us a generation earlier.

I understand these factors. There is a vast need for reforms, for improvements in health, education, and environment. But we have to assume our responsibilities both abroad and at home. We have to do both. After all, if we manage to improve the environment and living conditions in this country we must also assure that we will be around to enjoy those improvements.

When I asked the president if he could give any precise indication as to how many American troops he expected would be in South Vietnam by mid-1972, he grinned and replied: "Well, you know I can't disclose the withdrawal figures. But let me say this: those who think Vietnam is going to be a good political issue next year are making a grave miscalculation.

"Now I am not applying our policy there for political reasons but for reasons of national security. Nevertheless, those who are counting on Vietnam as a political issue in this country next year are going to have the rug jerked from under them.

"Certainly the way the Laotian battle is going is helping our withdrawal program. And I can tell you that if I were running as a political candidate I wouldn't select as an issue something that is likely to become a nonissue."

At this point I asked if he felt it essential to his long-range policy plans that he should be re-elected to a second term. Again he smiled relaxedly and said:

"I work here as if every day was going to be my last day. My theory is that you should never leave undone something that you will regret not having done when you had the power to do it.

"The fact of the matter is that for the next twenty-five years the United States is destined to play this superpower role as both an economic and a nuclear giant. We just have to do this. We cannot dodge our responsibilities.

"If I lived in another country that wanted to be sure and retain its right to self-determination I would say: 'Thank God that the United States exists at this moment in history.'

"We are not bent on conquest or on threatening others. But we do have a nuclear umbrella that can protect others, above all the states to which we are allied or in which we have great national interest.

"This is the moral force behind our position. We could be a terrible threat to the world if we were to lose that restraint or if we were to sacrifice our own power and allow ourselves to become too weak to uphold the weak."

WASHINGTON, *March 9, 1971*

Talk with Secretary of State Rogers at the state department. I am sure he is a good lawyer but he doesn't impress me as a secretary of state, amiable as he is.

We started on the Middle East. He said: "The United States is ready to play a responsible and cooperative role in peacekeeping in that area and to provide all necessary guarantees. That is a major decision of our government. It provides a method in effect for guaranteeing that any agreement will be kept. We will have the security council guarantee a settlement, and this of course permits the exercise of the U.S. veto power."

Rogers thought we are getting near the verge of a settlement. Egypt is now going along. Cairo's telegrams to us are very well worded and the Egyptians at least seem to understand our own problems vis-à-vis them. Rogers is convinced Prime Minister Mohammed Fawzi genuinely wants peace.

U.S. policy hasn't deviated from the position taken by him in his December 9, 1969, speech which outlined the so-called Rogers plan. He added: "We have *never* varied from this despite false stories saying that we had.

"We never insisted on total withdrawal by the Israelis. However, for the Sinai Peninsula we want the 1967 boundary restored. This would exclude the Gaza Strip. Furthermore, there must be adequate security guarantees or arrangements around Sharm el-Sheikh and fixed demilitarized zones in the Sinai area."

I then turned to Chile. He said the U.S. is not pursuing a policy of hostility of the sort we developed against Castro in Cuba. We are trying to maintain proper and friendly relations and to take no action detrimental to the Chilean government.

"We will frame our future policies in accord with Chile's policy toward us. Obviously we don't want to look as if we are rewarding anti-U.S. policies in other countries. We do not wish to appear hostile simply because Chile has a different form of government from ours—like Jugoslavia, for example, a country with which we have good relationships. But if the Chileans develop an anti-U.S. policy we will adjust our own policy in reply."

Rogers said that Admiral [Elmo] Zumwalt "got beyond himself" when offering a visit by the carrier *Enterprise*. "He wanted to use the navy for political purposes. This was naive."

He said Chile is still run by a minority government, stressing that Allende and his coalition are in the legislative minority. He claimed the Chilean revolt does not seem to be spreading among its neighbors, and that our relations with Peru have improved as a result of the new regime in Chile. Other South American countries were worried about a communist takeover. Chile is so far from us and from Russia that it is less likely to become a superpower battleground like Cuba; and we shouldn't forget that trouble-making in Cuba is costing the Russians a lot.

I told him I was going to South Africa and wondered about our policy there. He said the U.S. has no strong feeling about Heath's decision to send some arms to Pretoria. We are perfectly prepared to let the British take their own positions but we are continuing our own arms embargo. Practically there is a limit to what the U.S.A. can do and we feel that it is better to try to influence the situation from inside rather than to attempt pressures from outside. [South African Prime Minister B.J.] Vorster is waking up to the facts and sees the difficulties of maintaining economic growth under an apartheid system. The U.S.A. condemns apartheid and continues its arms embargo but does not believe in total ostracism of South Africa.

Moving to the Indian Ocean, he said we are not greatly concerned about Soviet penetration there. Nevertheless this is important as "handwriting on the wall." Part of Soviet policy is to expand its sea power. Because this is a new development it has demonstrated new implications in the Indian Ocean, whose sea coast nations are worried about the effect on them. The political implications are important but there is no immediate security problem involved.

Rogers said the U.S.A. remains "very much in favor" of Britain's admission to the Common Market. "This is very important to Europe's future," he added. It would have costly short-term effects for the U.S.A. but the long run effects would be beneficial.

When we talked about China, Rogers said there was definitely a hint of change in our policy, which has hitherto sought to exclude Peking from UN, but so far it is more of a hint than a reality.

Lunched with Dick Helms, boss of the CIA. I told him I had seen Rogers who said he didn't think any wave of revolution was going to spread out from Chile among its neighbors and that the situation in Peru had definitely improved since Allende came in in Chile; that U.S.-Peruvian relations were better. "If that is so," Dick replied, "it has entirely escaped me. Nobody has brought any such information to my attention."

I asked what the situation was in Cienfuegos. He said that we and the Russians were playing a kind of cat-and-mouse game. Whenever they moved a ship in there we got a bit tougher and then they would move it out and things would relax. It is hard to know just what they are up to, but right now it is relatively calm.

The Sino-Soviet situation remains unchanged. The Russians have pulled out some of the short-range tactical missiles that were too close to the Chinese border and replaced them further back with longer range missiles. They are continuing to build up both the quantity and quality of their forces opposite China. This does not, of course, necessarily mean war, but it sure as hell doesn't mean peace.

WASHINGTON, *March 10, 1971*

My interview with President Nixon was published today and has caused a stir in intellectually incestuous Washington, whose business is politics and whose relaxation is gossip. We have been staying with Chip and Avis Bohlen and the phone rang steadily with inquiries about whether I would appear on TV, radio, or grant interviews, etc. To Marina's irritation I replied to all of them that I worked for the *New York Times* and could not accommodate them.

This is odd for the simple reason that the only reaction I have so far had from the *New York Times* was one of rage that I wrote the interview. Yesterday while typing out my dispatch and column, I was sitting in a small office next to that of Max Frankel, the *Times* Washington bureau manager.

I was in the middle of typing my news story, some thousands of words of which had already moved on the Washington bureau's line to New York, when Abe Rosenthal, managing editor, burst in, white as a sheet and as close as anyone I have ever seen to foaming at the mouth.

The burden of what he had to say was: "Who the hell did I think I was working for, myself or the *New York Times*, etc.," laced with cursing. I told him it was a nuisance for me to write news stories of this sort but I was always requested in the most urgent way by the publisher to do so.

What goddamned right did I have to see the president without telling him first? Wryly I said I saw no reason to tell him. When did I know I was going to see him? About three weeks ago. That sent him. I then explained that the appointment had been made three weeks ago, but I didn't have a clue that it was going to turn into an interview until I was actually with the president.

Well, I still goddamn well should tell him when I was going to see anybody. How would I feel if someone came to Paris to see the French president and didn't tell me? It had already happened, I said, but I couldn't care less.

I had no right to see people on a secret basis, said Abe. I did not agree and I refused to change my methods. I had seen six presidents of the U.S.A. and many other world leaders, and when they wanted to talk on a confidential basis I respected their wishes; this is what kept open my access to them. I refused to tell him; in fact I never even told my wife. Eventually he stormed out with a face like a festering pear that had been left in a dark cellar all winter.

[In 1972 Rosenthal gave a lavish and cordial dinner party at his home for Marina and myself. He apologized for his behavior in the above incident and said he had been emotionally upset by the funeral of a friend that day and by drinks served subsequently to the mourners. The apology, which I accepted, was gracious.]

Another incident: the *Times* has always begged me not only to see people for news interviews, but to provide them with question-and-answer texts and photographs of myself with the man I am talking to. The White House had sent over by special messenger a couple of photographs and the Washington bureau dutifully transmitted them to New York by wire.

The *Times* cut me out of the photograph published, leaving only Nixon who, because of the artificial amputation, looked something like a stunned character out of a comic strip—since we had been smiling side by side. This reminds me of the way, during Stalin's day, Russian unpersons were painted out of official photographs and paintings as they were successively purged or demoted—like Trotsky, for example.

They also took out of my dispatch the quotation from Nixon in which he said that I didn't have to send him a text from my notes because he trusted me, and didn't have to edit any such text because he knew I was an accurate reporter, and if he didn't trust me he wouldn't be talking with me in the first place.

Frankel was impeccably courteous, friendly, and warm. Old Arthur Krock, who comes to the office every day although retired, said, "It is only a matter of jealousy." Joe Alsop called up to congratulate me and said it was the best statement of Nixon's intentions and personality that he had ever read. And Averell Harriman, at the other end of the political spectrum, called Marina to tell her how delighted he was and how proud —much as he hated Nixon.

Incidentally, I ended Tuesday night at a dinner party which Tom and Joan Braden gave for us, where Stew and Tish Alsop and the Bohlens were present. Both Tom and Stew were fulsome in their comments. The best part of the day was that we played bridge and in the final hand, vulnerable, Tish and I made a grand slam in no trumps—redoubled.

Today we lunched at Harriman's. Bohlen said a certain Dr. Harvey or Garvey (in Russian *H* is represented by a *G*) had gone to Moscow last year from Baltimore to treat Khrushchev's daughter. Harvey (Garvey) is a specialist in internal medicine and she was very ill.

When they returned to their hotel, they were visited by the secret police and given a six-hour search including a complete medical search of their bodies. The secret police only found a letter from Khrushchev thanking him for his courtesy in coming. When they left, the Soviet customs authorities took away from them gifts of silver which Khrushchev had sent.

Obviously, says Chip, the police had heard that some of Khrushchev's tape recordings or diaries had been smuggled out already and were looking for more. Chip thinks the Khrushchev book is genuine. He thinks that when Victor Louis got into the act in Copenhagen last summer he was merely sent out as an MVD agent with false material trying to distort and gum up what the *Time-Life* people already had. It was a "spoiling operation."

Averell talked a bit about my interview with Nixon but couldn't restrain himself from a few savage remarks about the president and Vietnam. When we left he congratulated me and touched me on the shoulder saying, "I want to touch you for good luck."

To my surprise, he was pretty right-wing on Chile. He strongly mistrusts the Allende government. He sees the imminent danger of a left-wing dictatorship.

NEW YORK, *March 16, 1971*

Larry Norstad telephoned this afternoon and told me about his secret visit to King Constantine (in Rome) last year. He had called at 11:30 A.M., stayed on to lunch with him and the queen, then talked until 3:30. Constantine is very bitter; he has been rebuffed too often by the United States. Larry, who had been asked by the state department to make the visit, reported to state afterward and suggested establishment of a continuing contact with the Greek king. No one advises him nowadays and he is most open to suggestions.

BOGOTÁ, *March 18, 1971*

This morning to the presidential palace (also known as *Casa de Bolívar* —after the liberator, who lived there). On the way, saw helmeted, rifle-armed police with tear-gas guns, some with shields. A state of siege was declared early this month when students threatened to riot.

The entrance of the palace is romantic. One walks by the window, above a narrow street, from which Bolívar escaped while his mistress talked would-be assassins off at the doorway of their bedroom above. The main portal is guarded by Indian and *mestizo* troops with spiked Prussian-type helmets shipped here as obsolete by Germany after World War I.

The president received me in a council chamber, long and rectangular with parquet floor and an eighteenth-century crucifixion painted by a Colombian artist. The furniture was heavy, Spanish, and the ceiling magnificent—white with gold inlays.

President Misael Pastrana Borrero is a youthful (forty-eight), elegant man with intelligent face and courteous manner. Lawyer, politician, and diplomat, he served briefly as ambassador in Washington. He spoke English but frequently lapsed into Spanish translated by Ambassador Mauricio Obregón, now in charge of Choco Corporation developing jungle lands.

Pastrana is a Conservative, the party with the strongest pro-church tradition. Under a pact which followed (and ousted) the Rojas Pinilla military dictatorship, the Conservatives and Liberals agreed to alternate the presidency every four years and to share other jobs—until 1974.

Pastrana began warily: "I have always felt that the main population problem is not its size today but the rate of increase in its growth. Every twenty-two years we double our population. This causes increasing problems in education and food. If the increase of growth continues, it will be felt more and more strongly in social repercussions.

"In the case of Colombia the problem is complicated by a rapid change in the distribution of the population. More people tend to move into big cities which are growing at fantastic rates. Bogotá doubles in size every ten years.

"The solution is not simply birth control, an approach that is complicated by religious and social traditions. A large percentage of population increase comes from illegitimate births. The whole problem must be directly attacked by education. Deep religious attachments are involved. But Marxists preach here that the developed countries—above all the United States—demand a limitation of population growth as a means of exerting their control over a smaller nation."

I asked what he thought was wrong with our Latin American policy. He said: "Even though the Alliance for Progress didn't have the quantitative effects expected, it did create a new atmosphere in inter-American relationships. In fact, although the framework has not been substantially modified, there is now a new feeling that the United States priority interest in solving social problems has faded.

"The greatest failure is in the field of trade between the U.S.A. and Colombia. In the specific case of coffee—the basis of economic vigor in fourteen Latin American countries—the U.S. Congress has been faltering and ratifying temporary agreements on a year to year or half-year to half-year basis. What we receive in aid—loans that, after all, must be repaid even if they are granted on favorable terms—we often lose in a single year by falling prices and deteriorating rates of exchange."

On Chile, Pastrana observed: "About 150 years ago, around 1830, Bolívar said that Chile would be the last country in Latin America that would cease to be a republic. I wonder if he was right." I recalled Lenin's prediction that Germany would be the first Marxist state in Europe. "Yes," said Pastrana, "it is the prophets who are most often wrong." He added: "Here in Latin America there is a true old saying: 'In the minds of our grandfathers we are all radicals.'"

From the presidential palace, rushed off to Ambassador Leonard Saccio's residence where he had assembled a distinguished group of Colombians for luncheon. These included ex-President Alberto Lleras Camargo and General Alberto Hauzeur, secretary of the minister of defense.

Lleras, an aging but sprightly liberal, was the most talkative. He said: "Even as things are we don't have enough money to build the necessary schools today. And the population will double in twenty-five years. It is rising at 3.6 percent a year. It is a frightening problem. And religion is a complicating factor. Priests can help out on birth control only unofficially; the hierarchy opposes them and the government doesn't dare intercede against the church hierarchy. The problem of unemployment will be awful. In ten years' time we will have one million new applicants hitting the labor force each year."

General Hauzeur said: "I think all armies tend to be conservative, even in Russia and China, because they are designed to keep a regime. Now that we are in an age of social upheavals and problems, both Colombian parties are in a race with each other to do more and it is hard to draw a line between them."

BOGOTÁ, *March 20, 1971*

One is impressed all over again by certain broad aspects of South America: the enormous development possibilities—like the chance to develop, with chemical fertilizers, the uninhabited and endless prairies to the east of the Andean cordillera; the huge amount of unharnessed water power. All one needs is determination and manpower. Yet the area remains dominated by the same forces that prevailed just after the conquistadors: the Indian population (now largely *mestizo* or *zambo*—half-black, half-Indian), the army, the church.

One feels the colonial heritage in endless paintings (portraits and battles), uniforms, formal regalia, some lovely buildings such as Bolívar's *quinta* (country house) with its rooms, furniture, and garden, dripping camellias and cypresses, but only a few braziers to heat a cold damp house; or the Casa del Florero, a colonial mansion with a store in its ground floor where indignant Creoles broke a flower pot they wanted for a dinner party because the Spanish storekeeper charged too much— and the independence war sprang from this.

The gold museum, with its pre-Colombian collection of artifacts that helped give rise to the legend of El Dorado, the Golden Man, who walked into a lake regularly, covered in gold dust and wearing a golden headdress, is impressive. One can understand how the greedy conquerors were stirred by these endless necklaces, pendants, head pieces, bracelets, idols, etc., gleaming among feathers from the lowland Indians or re- covered from the funerary urns of mummies.

BOGOTÁ, *March 21, 1971*

Near town is a considerable mountain covered with grass and great eucalyptus trees, which is filled with salt. The Chipchas used to mine near the surface. Now great tunnels have been dug deep inside and one of them has been hollowed out into a wide, high chamber that was turned into a cathedral (1951–54). There are pews, an altar, shrines at the side, vast chunky square-hewn columns of rock salt serving as pillars along a lengthy, gloomy apse.

At the end of the long savannah (prairie) on which Bogotá lies in an Andean valley, you come to a village and artificial lake called Guatavita. The lake was formed a few years ago by a dam for a hydroelectric project. The old village was drowned and a charming new one has been built—not too far (over the hill) from the little lake where El Dorado was supposed to have walked into the water at sunset covered in gold dust.

Marijuana is natural here but was used only by prostitutes and criminals to alleviate their sorrow. When prosperous youngsters brought back the habit from the U.S.A., the price shot up so high that the whores and crooks couldn't afford their only solace any more.

SANTIAGO, *March 22, 1971*

Dined at the Korry's. Ed has been ambassador here for several years. He said:

The Tacna regiment in Santiago started off a plot called the *"Tacnazo."* It went into quasi-revolt led by the popular General Roberto Viaux Marambio. When the regiment arose the presidential palace was ringed by garbage trucks as a precaution (rather an odd one) and the revolt collapsed. Although Viaux had tried to get in touch with the U.S.A. before the revolt, Korry decided he was an indiscreet fool and his movement was infiltrated by both left and right; therefore he warned against any contacts.

Viaux was allegedly involved in the plot to keep Allende out. The *Miristas* of the extreme left obviously had *agents provocateurs* in the operation. Now Viaux is locked up.

SANTIAGO, *March 23, 1971*

Two and a half hours this evening with President Salvador Allende in his office, called La Moneda. With me as interpreter was Ambassador Hernán Santa Cruz, Allende's special roving envoy. We were served scotch and soda and, later on, a butler brought in nuts, white cheese, and other tidbits.

Allende, who is sixty-two, is vigorous and youthful: a small, stocky, quick-moving man with grey moustache, ruddy face (he likes sailing), and wavy brown hair, untouched by white. He wears thick, heavily rimmed spectacles. He has a determined, obstinate face with small cleft chin. He preferred to walk up and down, gesticulating as we talked, referring all the time to our discussion as "a dialogue," not an interview. He resembles a slightly overweight, agitated fox.

Allende said: "The Catholic church is clearly convinced our government is doing nothing to interfere with religious beliefs. You might be interested to know that our custom is to have a president installed in office by a *Te Deum* ceremony. In my case I asked that for the first time this should be ecumenical. The service was attended by the Catholic primate and the heads of every faith, and each took part."

I asked about his coalition. He said, "Essentially there are different types of popular front. There were three popular front governments in the world during the 1930s: those of Spain, France, and Chile. In France the experiment disappeared into limbo because Léon Blum, the premier, was a good intellectual but a bad politician. The Spanish popular front government disappeared in the civil war.

"But the Chilean popular front lasted from 1938 into 1941 when World War II came to this hemisphere. And it certainly didn't fail although it was different in its formation and aims from our UP (Popular Unity) government today. The popular front of that period for the first time brought the middle class and workers' parties into active collaboration. I was minister of health in that government and I was just as much of a socialist then as I am today.

"The popular front government succeeded in creating, thanks to state initiative, Chile's oil, electrical, and steel industries. It started Chile's initial industrialization, and the trade unions participated in all these decisions and endeavors. It also saw the beginning of our social legislation. It was, in fact, a government of great significance.

"That popular front regime was on the left of the capitalistic system. But the Popular Unity government now wants to transform the capitalistic system entirely. At that time the leading role in the popular front government was taken by the radical party, representing the small bourgeoisie. Now the leading role is not bourgeois at all. This time the president, myself, is a socialist and not a radical.

"Today, in our Popular Unity government, the socialists, communists and other left-wing groups hold equal roles.

The Chilean communists are a very serious party, known for its political honesty, which has taken an engagement to fulfill our announced governmental program. And the Chilean Communist party is sufficiently realistic to know any policy that might subject Chilean interests to those of another country would have disastrous effects here.

"Furthermore, even if they have very skillful people in the Chilean Communist party, I assure you they don't have any monopoly of intelligence. Don't forget, I am the president, and I run things, a socialist. I have no need to import strength from outside.

"In thirty years' political life, I never failed to do what I said I would do. It could be possible that the dynamic of events might eventually create a revolutionary party, one party of the revolution. The dynamic I refer to—which certainly does not exist now—would be a profound harmony of thinking in Chile and a homogeneity of views on the best tactical approach to our problems.

"But this is not possible for the imminent future. After all, the socialists don't want to be changed and the radicals, who in Chile have had a party for 110 years, surely won't commit suicide. Don't forget that Karl Marx foresaw a time when there would be no governments at all. But when? It hasn't come yet.

"The strategy of socialism must depend on the realities of any country where it is attempted. To be a socialist is obviously not the same thing as being a communist.

"There are different roads to socialism. Jugoslavia is a socialist country. So is Rumania. So are China, Cuba, the Soviet Union, and many others. But all of them have followed different paths. I think capital must be placed at the service of man. I think that man must come before everything and anything else. Our existing constitution was drafted in such a way that we had to reform it even in order to pass the necessary legislation to nationalize our mines. I hope, for the time being, to utilize the existing constitution and our present laws in order to achieve the reforms we urgently need. But as a second step—some time later on—I envisage proposing an entirely new constitution.

"If I were to die tomorrow, no one in Chile would ever dare to abolish the system I instituted of giving every child free milk. No one would ever attempt to end our system of social security. No one would dream of taking away from illiterate citizens the right to vote which they have been legally granted. Nevertheless, if we are defeated another party would certainly take over. I can assure you, however, that we don't think we will be defeated."

Allende said: "My word is formally engaged to respect all the fundamental rights of man. No matter how extensive our economic and social reform will be, we will not only respect human rights but actually increase them. So far they exist only for a minority. Human rights are not merely political; they are also social and economic. Freedom alone is just a fiction for the poor.

"Not the slightest violation of freedom of the press exists. Such allegations are unfounded. How can we be accused of an unfree press when only two days ago the most reactionary party in Chile started its own new paper called *La Tribuna?*"

I asked: "Do you foresee the possibility of any violent confrontation in Chile as a consequence of opposition to your program?"

He said: "Sadly, very sadly, I admit this possibility exists. That is the lesson of history. There is no doubt at all on this point. It would come from the Right. I know it would come from the Right because it has already done something that never before occurred in Chilean history— namely assassinated the army commander, General Schneider. What they really wanted to do was to kill me. There have already been two attempts on my life."

Allende said: "Certain groups in the United States, groups including the copper mine owners who have always been influential in your policy, are trying to upset my government, to interfere with our program. What I mean is that there are local plots, inside Chile, supported or encouraged by certain interests in the United States. Obviously I do not think that the United States government would lend itself to such efforts, to a policy that would clearly violate the principle of self-determination."

He promised to give financial compensation to foreign companies with interests in Chile that are being nationalized, adding: "This is not a process of confiscation. We fully accept the principle of compensation."

He said Chile intends to stand by its existing international commitments. "We will honor every single commitment Chile had undertaken. We are, indeed, very active in the Organization of American States. And we have not changed any of our relationships with the United States.

"We want respect for our policy and understanding of our aims which seek to make of Chile a country progressing along the paths opened up by science and technology. We want respect and understanding of our insistence that a Chilean citizen has the right to work, the right to improve and educate himself, the right to rest and recreation.

"Furthermore, the United States should recognize and accept that the dignity of man is not in any sense related to his per capita annual production rate. In this world small countries should be respected quite as much as big countries. Big countries should never try to use their power at the expense of small countries.

"There is a strange and paradoxical relationship between imperialism and underdevelopment. Underdevelopment is primarily due to imperialism which prevented the full use by a subjected land of its potential wealth and abilities. Imperialism in fact exists as a phenomenon in some countries because of underdevelopment in others.

"But the paradox is that the underdeveloped countries are traditionally forced, despite their relative poverty, to sell their products at a cheap price and to buy abroad the products they need at an expensive price. This paradox is one of the things we are trying to solve.

"The United States should recognize that our democracy here is authentic democracy and that we will never do anything against the United States or contribute to injuring its sovereignty. For example, we will never provide a military base that might be used against the United States. Chile will never permit its territory to be used for a military base by any foreign power, by anybody.

"What we are doing in terms of our internal reform is simply to improve our own country and our own society and standard of living. The United States should understand that if we nationalize copper installations in which there have been U.S. interests and U.S. investment, it is because we need to do so because it is vital in the interests of the Chilean nation and the Chilean people.

"I simply cannot imagine that the United States government would make common cause with private enterprise on an issue like this and frame its policy accordingly. Unfortunately, history does teach that on occasion in the past this has been the case."

Allende said he was married, had three children and two grandchildren. He had always, since student days, intended to go into politics, although he initially started as a doctor. He is not a practicing Catholic and is a Freemason which, Santa Cruz murmured to me, is unusual for a Marxist.

When he had any spare time, which was rare, he liked to amuse himself by playing checkers with friends and also he enjoyed seeing detective movies. He likes small-boat sailing. He has a Snipe and gets lots of fun sailing it. He also rides when he can. The president added: "One hobby I like a good deal is talking to women."

SANTIAGO, *March 25, 1971*

Saw Foreign Minister Clodomiro Almeyda, a small cigarette smoker with glasses, a bald head, and an earnest expression, a lawyer, a professor of Marxist dialectics, and politically a Maoist socialist.

He said the ultimate goal of the government was a classless society and no more private property but couldn't begin to predict when. "Even Mao speaks of one thousand years. This has to be spoken of only as a gradual process."

BUENOS AIRES, *March 29, 1971*

Pleasant chat with Michael Hadow, British ambassador. He points out that Argentina, unlike other South American lands, has a large middle class (both lower and upper) and a high standard of living.

The cycle here runs like this: a democratic and freely elected government gradually becomes more crooked and inefficient, bringing on an economic decline. Then a military take-over, which eventually hands over to civilian administration. Then a repetition of step one. Democratic governments here are democratic but inefficient. Military governments are efficient but undemocratic.

Lanusse is a good man, honest, direct, with probity and stature. He preferred to be a king-maker and was reluctant to be king. He is a gentleman and has democratic, liberal views. The army here is the only cohesive and disciplined group.

There is *no* political volcano bubbling here. The army will keep the lid on. But the political parties are useless. The church is in an anomalous position, trying to ride two horses at once. It says you can't blame the people for trying to aright social injustice, but it also condemns violence.

BUENOS AIRES, *March 30, 1971*

Last week Argentina had another military *coup d'état*. General Roberto Levingston, then president, was chucked out and the army commander, General (Alejandro Agustin) Lanusse, took over. Life in lackadaisical Buenos Aires didn't falter for a moment.

Today I had a long talk with Lanusse. It was his second day in office and I am the first non-Argentinian to see him since he took over. I was enjoined to the strictest secrecy, not even to tell our ambassador.

The president took part in the abortive 1951 coup against Perón and was sent south to a military prison where he was forced to wear ordinary convict's clothes and treated severely for four years.

He is a tough-looking man with white hair, sallow color, youthful hands, kindly brown eyes, but a tough, thin mouth and resolute jaw. When he smiles his face is warm but in repose it is grim. He was wearing full uniform without decorations. He is about six foot one and weighs around 200 pounds.

Before I could ask a question he said: "We want every Argentinian to trust us and in just that way I trust you and know you will respect my confidence. I am fully aware of my own abilities and my own limitations.

And the solution I hope to give our people must be made and framed by them, not simply imposed by a man who happens to find himself on top at this moment."

I asked why he thought Argentina had had recourse to military government so many times during the century since its last war in 1870. He said: "The army has always played an important role in building an Argentine nation. This is a particular Argentinian characteristic.

"Looking back on our history, at crucial moments military men appeared on the scene to solve the most difficult crises. This doesn't mean that military men are any better than other Argentine citizens, simply that they were suited to the needs of the nation at critical times."

I asked what he considered the necessary preconditions for a return to normal civilian rule and when. He said, "My view is that we must do all that is necessary to revitalize obsolete institutions as a first step toward democratic government. After all, why was our revolution [the coup] made? It was made in order to make democracy possible."

I wondered if it would be possible to recreate representative political parties without their being drowned by the Peronistas and neo-Peronistas. It became evident he is ready to make a deal with them, even with Perón himself.

"It would be unwise and foolish," Lanusse said, "to try and ignore that section of the population which follows the ideas represented by Perón from 1944 to 1955. Many people believe Perón is the symbol of these ideas. I spent four years in prison for my opposition to Perón. But I share the concepts of social improvement and the principles of reform being sought. The theories underlined in the plans of Perón don't contradict my own thoughts—neither then nor now. But I have been in the past and still am ready to oppose his procedures—which do not coincide with our democratic traditions.

"But I want to stress, I don't like looking backward [to his own troubles with Perón]. We don't have much time and none of it should be wasted by looking backward. When I am in a true position to know how the Argentinian people want to solve their problems I am ready to talk with the Peronistas and even with Perón himself to hear his ideas, if he approaches problems in a constructive way. The only precondition is that whoever comes to talk with me as president of the republic must come in order to construct the future. On that basis, I would not even exclude Perón."

I asked if he was worried about Chile. He said: "I am very respectful of each country's freedom of action in solving its own problems. If you really knew me you wouldn't need an answer. I'd like to know you better as a friend. But you know, they sometimes call me Doberman as a nickname. A Doberman is a fine dog but it isn't kind to its friends."

I was mystified by these elliptical allusions. But I said I'd talked at length with Allende, that he was a good talker, but revolutions had a way of getting out of hand and this worried me.

"I think your way of thought is similar to mine," was Lanusse's comment.

RIO DE JANEIRO, *April 2, 1971*

Lunched with former President Juscelino Kubitschek de Oliveira at his office. He is now president of an investment bank. Kubitschek was president from 1956–61, a modernizer and one of Brazil's great men. He really began national industrial development. By building Brasilia, he thrust the country's dynamism inland.

He was and is tremendously popular. He was educated as a physician, has much charisma, and is considered extremely "Brazilian." His party was the PSD (social democrats). In 1964, when the military "revolution" came, he was deprived of political rights for ten years. He went to Portugal but returned in 1965.

He is a small, dapper, sallow-complected man of sixty-eight with black hair and an unusually spry and youthful manner.

I asked why there were leftist governments to the west of the Andes and rightist governments to the east. He said this came from misery and underdevelopment in the west (like Bolivia and Peru) and a high percentage of Indians who are badly prepared for democracy. "There are three Americas: North, South—and Brazil, which is very different and special. Bolívar's genius was unable to maintain unity in Spanish America, but Brazil remained united with its mass internal market growing every day."

I asked why he thought Christian democracy had failed. He said there was a tendency of the noncommunist world to move right, and the word "Christian" has lost its meaning in Christian democracy. The church had lived by serving those in power.

In Latin America a popular reaction to this had begun. Bishops and priests in Brazil had been arrested. The church, as an organization, had been serving the Establishment and lost influence with the people. Now the majority of more than 200 bishops were in revolt against oppression.

"When I was president," he said, "I invited Cardinal Montini [now Pope Paul] to visit Brazil. At that time Archbishop Helder [the principal leftist priest] was auxiliary archbishop of Rio and I attached him as an aide to Montini. During a period of five days the three of us met several times and we found much common ground in support of liberalization. When Paul was elected Pope, he invited me to Rome and I noticed his first speech followed the same lines. It was clear Helder's influence was continuing, although Helder is considered a devil by this government."

Kubitschek said Peru, Ecuador, Bolivia, Chile, Argentina, and Uruguay were all on the brink of the unknown and no one could see where they were heading either in the short or long run. There was little chance for a centralist form of democracy.

He thought Allende and his movement in Chile "represent a real danger that Chile is going communist. I believe Allende is trying to bring about democratic socialism, but the pressure of his political allies and of communism abroad is tremendous. If Chile goes communist there will be a threatening situation in Latin America. In Brazil we suffer rightist oppression but we would prefer to return to democracy; not try communism. But if Chile becomes communist, no one else in Latin America will return from right-wing systems to democracy. We would lose all hope of liberty. And even the hope of liberty is worth keeping."

He said military governments in Latin America were composed of officers trained in the U.S. to fight communist efforts to take power. Their tendency, when in power, is toward nationalism, as in Peru or Bolivia. As it seeks to develop an internal market and industry this nationalism tends toward socialism. But the military, like the church, is changing and finds it can move to the Left. It is a small step from socialist nationalism (or vice versa) to communism. The great danger to Latin America is the move from military governments to nationalism to leftist totalitarianism to communism. Signs of this trend are advanced in Bolivia, beginning to work in Peru, and there are initial hints in Brazil.

Kubitschek said there was "an unholy alliance" between the communists and the church in Brazil and other Latin American countries. "A priest must make leftist noises to get the people on his side."

Only the army and the church have widely spread, centrally controlled organizations in Brazil. "The pulpit remains the only outlet for free expression. The government permits this for the sake of international public relations."

RIO DE JANEIRO, *April 4, 1971*

We went to a "samba school"—a demonstration along the Copacabana sea-front where the winning "samba school" of this year's carnival was dancing, singing, and drumming, watched by vast crowds. There were hundreds of men and women dancers in extraordinarily lavish costumes, red, white, silver, long feathers: a kind of pageant of the arrival of an African king. The samba dancers, who pay for their own costumes and the buses that bring them here, were at least 95 percent black (or mulatto). They all come from the very poor districts. It was both lovely and profoundly disturbing.

JOHANNESBURG, *April 7, 1971*

South Africa is facing a shortage of skilled labor because of its apartheid policy which excludes most blacks from the opportunity, according to Harry Oppenheimer, richest magnate in South Africa, king of gold, diamonds, and uranium, and boss of Anglo-American Corporation. He is short, stocky, middle-aged, with a smooth appearance and quiet, agreeable voice.

Oppenheimer says the GNP rise and boom simply cannot be continued under rigid apartheid and "we are now running up against this fact. You just can't prevent 80 percent of the people from doing what they are capable of doing. This government says it won't ease up; nor does Prime Minister [B. J.] Vorster give any sign of change in his attitude. Therefore, we will stagnate eventually—unless there is change."

The black labor pool is not being adequately educated for skilled jobs. It would take a considerable time to create the trained labor force needed. But it can be done; Zambia has shown how well a crash training program can work.

JOHANNESBURG, *April 8, 1971*

Dinner this evening with Tertius Myburgh, editor of the Argus Newspapers' Pretoria paper (English language). Myburgh is an intelligent young man with a charming wife. Both are Afrikaners and cultivated, frank, easy, liberals without the slightest racist tint.

Myburgh said the old Afrikaner-Germanic efficiency is disappearing. Incapable poor whites get jobs that any competitive society would award to better qualified blacks. Now there is the highest train accident rate in the world and one often has to wait two years to get a telephone installed.

Japanese here are treated as "white" under some laws but not under others. For example, they can only sleep with women listed as "other Asiatics"—(non-Indian, Malay, etc.). White children get free education, said Mrs. M.; blacks must pay (on grounds they aren't taxed). A foreign black like [Hastings] Banda can come and be entertained by Vorster but a white foreman can't entertain a black worker.

I asked Myburgh if the Boer war hadn't been Britain's "Vietnam." He agreed. The British had even tried Vietnamization by recruiting Boers into the English forces, the *Hens Oppers* (hand-uppers). The majority came from the British colony on the cape where most of the farmers were Afrikaners.

MASERU, LESOTHO, *April 9, 1971*

Flew to Maseru, capital of the little black country of Lesotho (formerly the British Protectorate of Basutoland). The South African Republic surrounds Lesotho the way Italy surrounds San Marino.

This land received its independence in 1966. A large, handsome Holiday Inn was opened last October in Maseru and is packed with tourists from South Africa enjoying the Easter weekend.

Drove to the residence of Chief Leabua Jonathan, the prime minister—
a round structure guarded by a policeman in battledress from the mobile
police unit (British-trained and the only "armed force").

Chief Jonathan's office is wood-paneled. On the walls were a picture
of an ancestor in an antiquated top hat, a picture of himself in a Panama
hat, several decorations in a glass cabinet, two shelves of books, and a
wooden plaque with the motto: "Lesotho. The impossible we shall do
right away. Only miracles will take a little longer."

The prime minister is fat, short, with friendly face, rimless spectacles,
close-cut kinky hair. He said: "I favor a nonracial society with equal
opportunity for all, regardless of color. A guarantee of this was written
into our constitution which was recently suspended, but the new constitution, which is now being drafted, will contain exactly the same guarantee."

I asked if he thought South Africa's racial policy could work. "No," he
replied. "It cannot possibly work. I am certain it will fail, both for moral
reasons and for practical reasons. It is morally wrong, of course, and it
just cannot work in practice. The effort to bridge the gap to equality by
creating Bantustans also won't work. It just doesn't go nearly far enough."

CAPETOWN, *April 15, 1971*

Today B. J. (John) Vorster, the prime minister, received me in his
simple, long office hung with pictures of the republic's presidents and
prime ministers and those of the Transvaal and Orange Free States, stern,
forbidding men like Vorster himself.

Vorster is not a warm fellow. He is of medium height, solidly built
with grey thatches at the temples, a thin, almost lipless mouth and
watery, slightly blood-shot eyes. But he was very friendly and took pains
to thank me for trying to treat himself and his country objectively when
I last talked to him in 1967. Not that he agreed with what I wrote.

Vorster said his doctrine was to "fight terrorism, not only in our own
country, but also in any other country in Africa where the government
requests us to do so." When I asked if such a request had ever been
made, he said: "No. Never. But it is still our fixed policy although I
can't imagine anyone in the north asking us to do this."

Likewise, although he had offered nonaggression pacts to all African
states, none had taken up the offer. "We have had talks with some countries, but no pacts: Swaziland, Botswana, and Lesotho, for example.
These are fortunate lands. They have no armies and they don't have to
spend a dollar on defense. They know they have nothing to fear from us.
And they could only be attacked from the republic. As for Rhodesia,
we are friends but we don't need pacts.

"We have established a customs union with Botswana, Lesotho, and
Swaziland. And we have firm trade relations with Malawi. We have a

tourist agreement with Madagascar and Rhodesia. And other ties will be established. It is a question of independent nations working together where their foreign interests are similar."

I inquired whether the logical aim of apartheid, or "separate development" as he calls it, wasn't extensive partition and creation of more and larger black states, so that it was possible to envision a day for a smaller South Africa with a white majority. He said: "That is our aim and objective.

"Now you have workers in South Africa from all the different black homelands, their number running into millions; plus the Swazis, Lesothos, Botswanas, and Malawians. For generations the chief export of these black states will be labor because they are not industrialized and can't use their own labor, can't employ their own people. This is a problem of all Africa.

"But as they industrialize they will naturally employ more of their own people and that will decrease the export of labor. Their policy is to develop and it is also our policy to develop people who are not yet independent. But this can't happen in too much of a hurry.

"And as elements of our African population become independent, the time might eventually come when the whites are actually a majority here. That is the ideal. We have stated on the issue of one-man-one-vote that we subscribe to it fully, but each in his own country.

"My aim is to create new African countries based on a system of one-man-one-vote." But when I asked if that would apply here for all offices he said curtly, "According to color. Each people will vote for the officials of its people."

He added the United States and others should understand this. He said that when the United States was colonized there were more red Indians there than blacks in Africa when it was colonized.

I asked if he seriously thought Russia was trying to cut across Africa and split it ideologically. "I'm more concerned about China," he replied. "Tanzania can rightly today be called a vassal state of red China. I am terribly worried that they will ultimately take over Tanzania and Zambia. Those countries are playing with fire. Thousands of Chinese are being sent to help build the Tan-Zam railway. If they decide to remain, they can take over."

Vorster said there was ample evidence that the Russians and Chinese were helping guerrilla movements aimed at South Africa. Their weapons were all of communist origin. They were trained in China, Russia, or East Europe. "There are volumes of evidence to that effect."

I asked if demands of industrialization wouldn't force him to allow more nonwhites in skilled jobs. He said: "It is not a question of forcing us. It is our policy to teach skills to the nonwhites and then incorporate them at a higher level. As they acquire more skills they are given more responsible jobs. We can already employ all that have the necessary qualifications."

I observed that he had been interned as a member of the pro-Nazi *Ossewabrandwag* during World War II and wondered if, looking back on history, he would today have preferred a British defeat. He said: "That never entered my mind or our minds. Our attitude was simply that it wasn't our war. It was simply a question of neutrality. The official reason for my internment wasn't that I was pro-Nazi but that I was anti-British.

"But there is no doubt where we would stand if there were a World War III. We are anticommunist. And apart from our general anticommunist line we know that South Africa is one of the targets. Our own interests demand that we take a stand—for the first time."

CAPETOWN, *April 16, 1971*

Mrs. Helen Suzman, only Progressive party member of parliament, gave a luncheon for Marina and myself in the dining hall of the chamber.

Mrs. Suzman, who is pretty, charming, and youthful-looking for a grandmother, deplored the huge wage gap between white and black workers, the ridiculous obsession with pigmentation, and said nonwhites were getting more and more angry and suspicious of any contact even with their white friends. She feels trouble is simmering. The country is going broke for lack of skilled labor because of the color bar.

CAPETOWN, *April 18, 1971*

A long sleek black American limousine called for us and the chauffeur drove us out to dinner with Mr. and Mrs. Anton Rupert. He is South Africa's tobacco king and the first Afrikaner millionaire, a thin, pale man, quietly polite, rather old-fashioned, and exceedingly intelligent. He is an Afrikaner liberal and does much to ease the lot of the poor blacks, having taken Lesotho under his wing.

Mrs. Rupert, a tall, strong woman with her hair in an old-fashioned bun, has great quality and must once have been lovely. She is clearly a tough Afrikaner, was brought up on a large back-country farm in the Transvaal, and believes natives should be well treated in the most courteous but paternalistic way, like a southern patrician of the antebellum period.

The ambiance was superb. I had a feeling we were sitting in the great hall of an old-fashioned Boer estate of the pre-World War I days. It was graceful, warm, friendly, and religious. When we sat down, Mrs. Rupert waited a moment and then asked across the long oaken table: "Anton, aren't you going to say grace?" Which he did with simple devotion.

I loved everything about it—except the deep gap in philosophical views I felt yawning between me and these warm, decent people.

CAPETOWN, *April 19, 1971*

This morning, before flying to Johnannesburg, we spent three hours in Stellenbosch, second oldest town on the cape, settled at the very start of the eighteenth century.

I can't help feeling that while the Afrikaners produce the most bigoted and reactionary people in South Africa, they also produce the best. They are neither *fin du race* nor third-rate remittance men or petty bourgeois snobs like the English-speakers; even the worst of them have quality and I often wonder if the British hadn't turned New Amsterdam into New York what the U.S.A. might have become under Dutch Puritan rather than English Puritan sponsorship.

We were taken around town and shown some marvelous restored Cape Dutch houses. With their white walls, thatched roofs, Dutch Renaissance facades, they are lovely against the background of green fields, huge trees, and distant mountains—some of the best architecture I've ever seen.

LE MORNE, MAURITIUS, *April 24, 1971*

Long ride to this southwestern tip of the island, winding along narrow roads past largely Indian villages (with a few Chinese shops) and dense fields of high-growing sugar cane. There are lovely, jagged, volcanic mountains inland, covered with green, and a dull sea lapping the shores with lazy breakers. The island is tropical, moist, warm, famous for many varieties of shells, heavy-petaled flowers, and the last dodo bird known to man. It was originally colonized by the Dutch and named for Prince Maurice of Nassau. Then the French took it and the capital, Port Louis, is named for Louis XIV. Bernardin de Saint Pierre lived here and wrote *Paul et Virginie*, his renowned novel, about the gardens at Pamplemousses.

The British took Mauritius (then called Île de France) as part of the settlement of the Napoleonic war, having first conquered it. They returned Réunion to France because it had no decent harbor but kept this because of Port Louis. It is inhabited by about 850,000 people, mainly mixed bloods, some Indian-European, some Indian-black, some Indian-Chinese, some a more general mixture, with a very few pure whites. The British retain a naval communications station on land called H.M.S. Mauritius. The Russians have started increasingly to send ships.

2 8

THE DUSK COMES

DOWN LIKE THUNDER

GAETAN DUVAL, THE FOREIGN MINISTER, INVITED ME TO DINNER AT a little restaurant. Duval is a handsome mulatto with unrefined but not Negroid features, tan skin, rings of long curly hair. He was wearing a flowered open shirt, velvet trousers, and patent leather boots of calf length. He fancies himself as a kind of hippie and has been told he looks like the young Dumas (which is probably true; Dumas was a quadroon) and boasts that he has been asked to take movie parts. He has plastered the island with "Black is Beautiful" signs to muster political support for his Social Democratic party and argues that he favors Black Power.

The government is a coalition, and Duval says his is the largest of the parties in it but is strongly anticommunist whereas the prime minister's Labor party is more neutral. Duval said he had made it a rule never to receive or speak to any Soviet diplomat which, if true, is a singular position for a foreign minister.

He said that he (not the P.M.) had offered the British a full naval base here, largely to offset exaggerated rumors that the Russians were moving in.

He added: "We must have good relations with South Africa. These would produce a boom in tourism and help ward off the threat of Soviet penetration among our unemployed. I am going to South Africa on a private visit next week. France and the United States won't intervene on our behalf so we need South Africa's help and its investments.

"I'm not white, I'm black. But I know we will have to find a way through South Africa's race policy because this is absolutely essential to the Indian Ocean. Together the important points, in that order, are South Africa, Mauritius, Réunion, and Madagascar. And France has been helpful. If the French were not both tough and generous, half of Africa would be under communist control today."

PORT LOUIS, MAURITIUS, *April 26, 1971*

Drove to this humid capital, known around the Indian Ocean as Port Lousy, to see the prime minister, Sir Seewoosagur Ramgoolam. We bumped past endless cane-fields rimmed by jagged mountain peaks, flowering century plants, palms, casuarina trees, and huge, many-trunked banyans, slung with tendrils.

Port Louis is a jerrybuilt town of shacks except for the main square, at one end of which stands a statue of the greatest French governor, La Bourdonnais, and at the other, Queen Victoria.

Ramgoolam proved to be a friendly grey-haired old Indian: short, stocky, dark, with glasses, neat grey suit, and soft, modulated voice. He said: "Russia has never asked for a Mauritius base, only trawler facilities." He admitted that Soviet cultural centers had been opened here but didn't know what they were up to. Maoists were active and had been attacking both the government and the idea of democracy.

Mauritius had been independent just over three years, but a national feeling had been developing for some years. There were several creeds and languages in the country: English, French, Hindi, Urdu, Tamil, Telugu, Marathi, Chinese, and of course Creole, which was the *lingua franca.*

He said the British had kowtowed to the French after taking over the island in the Napoleonic wars because they wanted peace and quiet here. Moreover, French culture was very much admired, which had left Mauritius a Francophone country attending meetings of the Francophone bloc.

He wasn't afraid of Soviet external pressures but of internal disquiet. "If I go down as a democratic leader, anti-Western elements will come up. We are trying to contain them. The more unemployed there are, the more Maoists there are. Naturally I am against that because I was educated in England in a liberal and democratic tradition."

TANANARIVE, MADAGASCAR, *April 28, 1971*

This is a lovely, romantic town with indigenous, terraced, gabled buildings, to which the architecture of a small French provincial capital is added. It is set on a series of hills atop the inland plateau, 4,500 feet above sea level. The climate is superb.

Local customs are quaint, including the removal (every July) from their tombs of ancestors' bodies or bones which are dressed up, driven around to see the sights, presented to friends and family, honored with drinks, and then returned to their cemeteries.

Jack Hasey of the embassy had drinks with me today. He and Eisenhower were the only American members of de Gaulle's *Compagnons de la Libération*. He attended de Gaulle's funeral at Colombey.

He told me China (Peking) is the big problem. He said: "The Chicoms are all over the place. Official figures show a colony of 9,000 Chinese but actually there are from 20,000 to 25,000, mostly Cantonese. They frequently go back to communist China and also send remittances. Many of them have married Malgaches and remain on here as 'sleepers' for long-range penetration. Their main effort seems to be to try and neutralize the Soviets."

The Monima, a southern-based pro-Chinese opposition party, is linked to Peking. While there were only forty-seven listed dead in last month's Monima uprising in southern Tulear province, over 1,000 prisoners were taken. They had been told to expect reinforcements from China, that they would get Peking's help. Monja Jaona, their sixty-three-year-old leader, was captured April 23. He had been in China in October 1970.

Monja Jaona, an old rebel against the French, has hitched his wagon to Peking's star. Stage one is verbal propaganda. Stage two is a peasant revolt designed to produce martyrs for a future mass uprising.

The French made every effort to stay out but secretly flew FRS (security police) reinforcements south at night to the menaced area. Only armed gendarmerie were involved. Some guerrilla pockets are now left, armed with captured gendarmerie arms. Malgache broadcasts from Peking (by Sino-Malgache *métisses*) are inciting opposition to the government.

Diego-Suarez here is an important French naval base in the Indian Ocean and the Third Regiment of the Foreign Legion is also stationed there. The British have an RAF squadron at Majunga, for UN use in the embargo on Rhodesia.

Called on Vice President Jacques Rabemananjara, who is also foreign minister. He received me in a plum-colored dressing gown. He is a diminutive but slightly plump man with dark complexion. His French is very fluent; he attended the Sorbonne. We sat side by side in his study while his wife, a tiny, frail, and homely white woman, jabbered on the telephone.

I inquired about the Narinda Bay project. He said the idea was to provide drydock and repair facilities for the enormous tankers that now ply the Indian Ocean. There was no yard in this part of the world that could handle them. But Narinda, where nothing now exists, has a deep harbor (about 100 feet).

Madagascar is inviting several countries to participate. France, South

Africa, West Germany, and Portugal (because of Mozambique) have already signified an interest. The project would cost "billions of dollars" and it would be about ten years before the port got started.

He said: "China tries to interfere here and we will not recognize Peking no matter what you do. We don't want them messing around."

TANANARIVE, MADAGASCAR, *April 30, 1971*

Accompanied by Ambassador Tony Marshall, I called on President Philibert Tsiranana this morning. The president's office proved to be confusingly cluttered up. His large desk was piled with papers, pamphlets, flags, model automobiles. Behind was a calendar with a colored picture of a butterfly, a party flag, a map, and a banner honoring the fourth African judo competition. There were two glass-topped cases beside his desk, one filled with watches, another filled with key rings. On the other side was a box containing replicas of cats in glass, cloth, wood. There were two model ships on a bookcase and beside it an enlarged letter to Tsiranana sent in December 1963 by Lyndon Johnson.

The president is strange-looking. He is said to be in his late sixties (although Tony claims he doesn't know himself how old he is) and an official stamp was printed last year honoring his "sixtieth" birthday. He was wearing a straw hat shaped like an army overseas cap, colored tan, red, yellow, and blue; also a grey suit and bedroom slippers. He opened his coat to display an assortment of objects chained to his belt, including key rings and two German miniature cameras. He proceeded at one point to haul one of these out and gravely take our pictures. He is small, dark-complected, with a slight Asian angle around the cheekbones, and a smiling face that nevertheless looks capable of sudden and violent furies. He speaks French but is hard to understand because of his accent and because he has had a stroke which partly affected his tongue.

The president said that this week a South African general came here to confer with a Malgache general on means of stopping communism. The two were in the same "promotion" at the French *École Supérieure de Guerre*.

He said the Chinese had big ambitions here, "but they won't succeed." He kept referring to the link of this country with both Africa and Indonesia and said Sukarno hadn't realized that Mao wanted to gobble up his country. Mao was also looking here because the Malagasy have similar appearance and languages to the Javanese (an odd *non sequitur*).

Afterward Marshall told me the French remain strongly entrenched. In addition to the Foreign Legion regiment and naval base at Diego-Suarez there was one French paratroop battalion and two regiments on the island. A French general commanding French interests in the Indian Ocean is stationed in Tananarive.

Moroni, Grande Comore, *May 8, 1971*

A large island with several small, seeping, semiactive volcanoes, whose chocolate-colored lava has worked itself slowly down over the jungles to the sea, where it forms steep escarpments. The main products are copra, bananas, ylang ylang (for perfumes), vanilla, and a little tobacco, manioc, and pepper. The population is filthy, small, lazy, black, and speaks a weird mixture-language, part Swahili, part French, part Portuguese. The colonial French are almost as lazy and quite unimpressive. A Foreign Legion detachment trains here but the old naval base on the smaller island of Mayotte has long since closed down.

We took long walks. The dusk comes down like thunder and we saw huge fruit bats with wings more than two and a half feet in span and bodies as large as rabbits, wheeling in the sky and then coming in to hang upside down from branches by their claws. Little bright red birds, maroon-headed birds, and mynah birds flitted among the dense shrubs: thick-leaved vanilla leaves, manioc plants, numberless bananas, and coconut palms. The jungle was dense and still with the sea lapping beyond as the sun slid into Africa across the way.

Moroni has lovely carved wooden doors like Zanzibar and a mosque of the Shafei sect of Islam, who came from Iran. The island population is made up of a mixture of black slave descendants, Arab aristocrats, and French bosses.

At Mitsamiouli we went deep-sea fishing. We took off from a little bay behind a lava formation called the Prophet's Hole where slave ships used to hide against British naval patrols. We were pushed out half a mile through shallow water by two blacks, one of whom stayed aboard, the other swam back, and then our young French skipper (a forester and hunter from the Ivory Coast) took off past enormous flying fish, schools of porpoises playing with the boat. We cruised along the blue-green sea and boated one barracuda and four good-sized Wahoo.

Nairobi, *May 10, 1971*

Last night the (U.S. Ambassador Bob and Alice) McIlvaines, with whom I'm staying, gave a small dinner. Joe Murumbi and his white wife were there; both charming. I had met Murumbi some years ago when he was foreign minister. (Marina had to fly on to our sick grandson in London.)

Murumbi doesn't see any obvious successor to Kenyatta and says this is the fault of the old man; he has groomed no one. He says: "We have learned democracy well enough to know how to get people into power but not well enough to curtail them once they are there."

EN ROUTE TO CAIRO, *May 13, 1971*

Long talk before leaving with Kenya's Foreign Minister Njoroge Mungai, a medical doctor, graduated from Stanford and then Columbia Medical School. He stands a chance of succeeding to the presidency when Kenyatta dies.

He said the east African federation was essential despite the political differences among its members, Kenya, Uganda, and Tanzania. They all benefited economically from it and from the common services (such as East African Airways) they pooled. Nevertheless, right now there was a problem. General Idi Amin had staged a coup in Uganda ousting Milton Obote as president. Tanzania refused to recognize Amin, and Obote was Julius Nyerere's guest (Tanzania's president) in Dar es Salaam.

Kenya had a pragmatic policy on such matters. There had already been twenty-seven *coups d'état* in Africa and it was foolish to get into a dither over recognition every time. Kenya therefore made it a practice to recognize each government that accepted its country's existing international obligations and demonstrated that it was in effective control.

Mungai felt it most important to strengthen west-east African links. The two halves of the continent should be more closely tied together and not always pass through Europe to contact each other.

CAIRO, *May 16, 1971*

There has been a big crisis, placing under various forms of arrest Vice President Aly Sabry, Interior Minister (and police boss) Gomaa, Minister of the Presidency Sami Sharaf. I had been promised an interview but Mohamed Heikal told me el Sadat now feels it would be a tactical maneuver, playing into his enemies' hands, if the first journalist he sees after the crisis is American. They will label him an American stooge.

CAIRO, *May 17, 1971*

Heikal told me the story of the coup. It should have succeeded because the minister of the interior (police), the head of intelligence, the main official of the Arab Socialist Union (only party), and the minister of war were all in it together. President el Sadat simply couldn't believe it when the plot began to unfold Tuesday night, May 11.

Officers of the security police in the telephone tapping set-up were under the direct supervision of Interior Minister Gomaa. He had his own private archive of tapped tapes, distinct from the regular storage library, and was so suspicious that he was even tapping the lines of his fellow-conspirators.

A police major in these archives was given some special tapes to be put in Gomaa's library. But the note labeling one tape was unclear and he didn't know in which archive it should be stored. So he played it and found it was a conversation between two of the principal leaders and very hostile to el Sadat.

He decided to inform the president. Although only a major, he insisted to the guard that he be allowed to see el Sadat. The guards called el Sadat's principal secretary. The major told the secretary he had convincing information of a conspiracy and had to return the tapes before dawn when his work shift ended. He agreed to give the secretary two tapes for el Sadat to play right away. At 3:00 A.M. Wednesday, May 12, el Sadat woke up and sent for a recorder. When he listened he really woke up.

He heard one leader describe how the broadcasting station could be sealed off so el Sadat would be unable to make a radio speech. Then he heard his own voice in a taped telephone conversation. He summoned the major, who told him all he knew. Then the major said he had to take the tapes back to his office before 6:00 A.M. or he would be fired. El Sadat said: "As president I order you to leave these tapes with me."

The plotters planned to oust him Thursday, May 20. The plan was that only a handful would seize el Sadat because about half of the presidential guard was already won over and wouldn't protect him. El Sadat decided to play it cool. He had a scheduled appointment to speak to commanding officers of the Second Army that Wednesday, May 12. At 11:00 A.M. he carried on and spoke with the war minister beside him on the platform. He told Second Army commanders that centers of anti-regime conspiracy existed in the country but that he was determined not to accept a police state. General Mohammed Fawzi, the war minister, sat unhappily behind him.

When el Sadat got back to his office he alerted the presidential guard and dismissed Interior Minister Gomaa, secretly ordering the governor of Alexandria to take over and seize the rooms in which tapped recordings were stored. El Sadat told Sami Sharaf, minister of the presidency (and one of the plotters) that he was dismissing Gomaa but permitting him to let it appear in public as a "resignation." This "resignation" was immediately announced on the radio.

At that moment the main conspirators were meeting in the minister of war's office. When they heard the news on Gomaa announced, they decided to resign together in order to create panic and confusion. They thought this would precipitate such chaos that both the ASU party (Arab Socialist Union) and people would rise; if the people were shot at by the police, General Fawzi could use the army "to maintain order."

The minister of information promptly broadcast this mass resignation and they waited for el Sadat to collapse and quit. Thursday night el Sadat called Heikal, who rushed over to the president's house.

At this time the war minister was asking the air, navy, and army commanders to join in the plot, but all three refused. The chief of staff heard about the meeting, entered, and told General Fawzi: "You have resigned.

Therefore you have no right to be here now. We do not tolerate political meetings in the ministry."

Late Thursday night, when Heikal rushed over to el Sadat, he was sitting on a balcony over the Nile (connected with his bedroom) in pyjamas and dressing gown. He said: "Thank God they've done it." He had instructed the new minister of interior: "Arrest those people." They were all placed under house arrest shortly before midnight. Then the chief of staff called for orders. El Sadat said: "I have decided to name you minister of war." The chief, a general, replied: "The army has no interest in politics. We only await orders in one battle [Israel]. Everything is secure."

Heikal said the Russians weren't involved in any way. They are simply worried about maintaining a united internal front. They weren't very pro-Sabry although Sabry pretended he was their great friend. Sabry was only interested in seeking personal power.

I invited my old friend Abdul Kader Hatem ("Abou Tarik") for lunch. For the past twenty-four hours he has been deputy premier and minister of information, a comeback after years on the shelf. He told me Mohamed Fawzi, the prime minister, is old and feeble, a symbol without influence. He begged that the U.S.A. do something now to help el Sadat get a real settlement with Israel; otherwise it will be too late.

Hatem says there is a communist underground that has infiltrated everywhere. He is now rooting it out of the information ministry, newspapers, radio, and TV. He is appalled at how far it has gone. Hatem proclaims his strong anticommunism and sympathies for the West.

Before lunch I had a useful talk with Don Bergus, U.S. chargé d'affaires. He said the Egyptians had had an airlift of new weapons from Russia this spring. These included a late type MIG which isn't really the MIG-23. It is a fighter that was produced in limited quantities at a time Moscow thought the U.S.A. was building a new generation of bombers. Now it apparently has no useful mission and has been sent here (less than a dozen planes) where it has had a wonderful effect on morale. It has lots of electrical equipment and special weapons to strike at planes flying below its level.

In March el Sadat visited Moscow and got promises of new weapons. The airlift flew in mostly SAMs, including the very modern SAM-6 which is mobile (on tracked vehicles). These have been placed in upper Egypt to deter attacks on the Nile dams.

Bergus said el Sadat used Heikal as his channel to the U.S.A. The Rogers mission here had been a success because Rogers became convinced el Sadat really wants peace and can make it stick, even though there still are significant differences on an interim canal solution. Now the U.S.A. is talking specifics with Cairo and not just arguing over nitpicks. [Joseph] Sisco came back after the Israel visit to report on our (and Israeli) ideas for an interim canal settlement. No new terms were offered but there are specific discussions.

Bergus thinks there is a three-to-one chance in favor of peace in the long run rather than renewed war—"always provided the factor of a crazy sergeant touching things off doesn't come into play." U.S. interests are clearly in favor of an over-all settlement between Israel, Egypt, and Jordan. Syria, of course, can join in if it wants.

The chances are U.S.-Egyptian relations will be improved by this month's success in crushing the coup. But there won't be a change in Russia's position. The Russians are here to stay. They are committed to defend the Egyptian heartland and realize this can't be assured just by sending arms, that men are needed. But if an interim agreement on the canal produces an extended cease-fire, the Russians will reduce their combat role here. Yet they will continue to train the Egyptian forces and push for economic improvement. The best the U.S.A. can hope for is competitive coexistence here with Russia—what Cairo hopes for.

As of July 1, 1970, there were about 500 Soviet SAMs. Now this is more than doubled. There are about 13,000–15,000 Soviet armed forces here, both operational and advisers.

HERZLIYA, *May 21, 1971*

Staying with Wally Barbour, our ambassador. Wally told me that in 1970 the Russians put their own pilots in MIGs over Egypt for the first time. In one startling encounter, the Israelis shot down four Soviet planes (with pilots) over Egypt. Laird told Barbour that Israel was still powerful enough to knock out the Soviet SAMs in Egypt (including SAM-4s and -6s) although the losses would be heavy.

Saw Foreign Minister Abba Eban. He said it was easy to define U.S. policy: (1) The U.S. has a definite view of a peace settlement, based on the 1969 Rogers plan (despite Israel's objections). This foresaw minimal change from the 1967 prewar Israeli frontiers. (2) The U.S. attitude on the Golan Heights and East Jerusalem is approximately the same as Israel's, although Washington wants a stronger Arab presence in Jerusalem. (3) The U.S. insists that any settlement on Sharm El Sheikh and Sinai should not include any change in (Egyptian) sovereignty. Rogers suggested that Israel study the U.S.-Guantanamo agreement with Cuba (an odd idea, considering our current relations with Havana). In the Guantanamo agreement, sovereignty of the base remains Cuban, but for the duration of the treaty's validity the jurisdiction remains American. The U.S.A. wants any Sinai formula that does not include change of Egyptian sovereignty; this would permit Cairo to stress that the map of Egypt hasn't changed, that no bit of Egyptian territory is negotiable.

I asked why the old Rafa-Suez Egyptian-Ottoman border wouldn't be a good frontier for the interim settlement. Eban said any frontier would do if it was a valid agreement. He also acknowledged that an interim accord could have good psychological and political effects in achieving a final settlement.

However, Eban believes el Sadat is convinced an interim settlement would induce the Israelis to treat it as final, doing nothing further about a permanent peace, once the canal is opened. Eban regretted that Rogers is so ignorant in his knowledge of the area and its history; thus, even when he was flying about, he thought the Dead Sea was Galilee.

Rogers asked the Israelis how far they would withdraw for an interim settlement. Their answer was that it depended on the duration and apparent validity of a cease-fire. They certainly would not put themselves in a position where they might subsequently have to fight their way back into the Bar Lev line.

In the past the U.S. had supported the Israeli concept that there could be no military withdrawal until a full peace. But now Israel was being asked to give up its water-line, its Bar Lev defenses, and the prestige involved in such a basic shift. Israel could not be expected also to give up on the issue of letting the Egyptian army cross the canal.

Russia wants to get the canal opened as soon as possible but dislikes the idea that this might appear to be a U.S. diplomatic success. Russia feels it is losing prestige: first the Rogers plan initiative, then the U.S. restarting of the Jarring talks, then the initiative for an interim solution to open the canal; all are American. The impression is therefore getting around the Middle East that the USSR is a good supplier but the political key is in Washington.

Israel told Rogers that for an interim settlement it would agree to all terms except the return of the Egyptian army to the East Bank. Also, it wants an assurance that the cease-fire would last. The U.S. argues it cannot force Egypt to accept a "permanent" cease-fire but Israel wants an assurance that there will be no agreed deadline by which time the truce would end. In return, Israel would commit itself to a pledge that the withdrawal line for Israeli troops (in the interim settlement) would not be final; and that the interim settlement would not be used by Israel to paralyze the Jarring talks. Finally, it wants precise guarantees that Egypt wouldn't blow up the Bar Lev line.

Israel believes el Sadat is really moving into a post-Nasser period and no longer tying himself to the past. He is beginning to attach greater importance to the problems of Egypt and less to pan-Arabism.

There is no kind of valid guarantee the U.S. can give for any settlement. Israel has (sadly) found this out. Washington would let its enforcement stay with the security council. But whenever there is fighting the council runs for cover. The council inevitably sinks to its lowest common denominator, which in this case is Russia, wholly backing the Arabs. Israel reckons the function of the U.S. is to deter Russia, if a settlement is violated, while Israel deters Egypt.

HERZLIYA, *May 22, 1971*

Stayed up late with Wally Barbour, as able a diplomat as he is devoted, and a balanced, wise man. He said the U.S. has also commended to Israeli study (as a Sharm El Sheikh formula) the Panama Canal treaty which awards sovereignty of the Canal Zone to Panama but allows the U.S. to "act as if it were sovereign" for "perpetuity." I opined that it was bound to throw Arab opinion against us if we ever mentioned either Guantanamo or the Canal Zone which are favorite Third World slogan subjects.

Barbour told me that when Moscow deliberately spread the rumor in mid-May 1967 (just before the six-day war) that Israel was mobilizing against Syria (which had been launching nasty guerrilla forays through Jordan and Lebanon), Prime Minister [Levi] Eshkol summoned the Soviet ambassador. He told him: "I will ride with you in my car or in your car any place you want to go in the neighborhood of the Syrian border and you can ascertain for yourself whether there is the slightest truth to these reports. I can arrange for you to go anywhere; I will get the permits because I am prime minister." The ambassador said he had "no instructions" from his government.

Wally feels it is a plain statement of fact that the U.S.A. couldn't sell Israel down the river or blackmail it, even if it wanted to (which it doesn't) because of the influence and wealth of its Jewish minority of about 6 million. Nor is there anything shameful in this. Our system has always been based upon minorities and heeding their wishes on major issues.

Last time Barbour saw President Nixon, Wally said to him: "You know Israel may be a small horse but it's the only horse we are riding that has four sound legs."

TEL AVIV, *May 23, 1971*

Spent an hour and a half with Major-General Aharon Yariv, chief of intelligence. Yariv said el Sadat is moving on internal Egyptian affairs. He knows the machine and who he must still take care of. Also he knows how to exploit popular feelings. He wants to reduce the tension of a police state (before installing his own quiet apparatus) and to avoid war, which the people don't want. His major problem, however, is not internal. To stay in the saddle he must either deliver a concrete diplomatic settlement or resort to war. Therefore he depends far more on the army now than when he first succeeded Nasser. He found he couldn't rely on the police, the ASU party or intelligence.

He won the allegiance of the army on the thesis that there *is* a chance for a peaceful settlement and this chance must be exploited, but if it fails, he will fight. The army agrees. El Sadat's freedom of internal maneuver is restrained by that same army, which won't agree to any settlement that hurts its own prestige.

Yariv said the Soviet military build-up in Egypt stressed an expensive air defense but included a heavy build-up in fighter strength that could be used offensively, above all the advanced MIG-21 strike aircraft. But there was no major build-up in the strength of bombers, which are rather outmoded. There was a perceptible offensive build-up in equipment, especially in amphibious and bridge-building materiel.

The spring airlift was Moscow's way of reminding the U.S.A. (as well as Egypt and Israel) that Russia could bring in new weapons rapidly and escalate any potential conflict. This was the inference of the new souped-up MIGs brought in in small numbers but potentially menacing to the U.S. Sixth Fleet. And Russia took pains that everyone should know about both the new SAMs and the new MIGs.

The Russians were shocked to realize last September that they would have been helpless to do anything had Israel moved into Jordan against the Syrians. Meanwhile, the U.S.A. was demonstrating that it remained a big power and had more political influence among the Arabs than Moscow had realized. He said there wasn't any real Soviet combat force in Egypt, only SAM crews, radar men, and some air crews, plus guards for installations. There are about 200 Soviet pilots but half of these are instructors.

From a purely strategic viewpoint Israel's present *de facto* borders were very good. The canal is a good obstacle. The Jordan is a good line. The Golan Heights present a better frontier than before. But Israel realizes the Suez Canal cannot be the border. Also, it would like the Jordan as a security line, not sovereignty. And Israel can envision a sufficient strategic depth in Sinai without Suez, developing a better deterrent position than the old (pre-June 1967) line. He then said:

"It is impossible for us to have peace now. No Arab ruler would let us have real peace. All we can do is get an agreement for an improved armistice. Egypt can't give us peace; but we can start the process toward peace. And we are prepared to give up territory and talk of refugees and other problems.

"If there is real peace, we will base our security on that. But if not, we must base our security on strategic advantages. We are not strong enough to initiate aggression. But we are strong enough to discourage those on the other side who want war."

PARIS, *June 5, 1971*

Just returned after two days of quiet fishing in Normandy accompanied by my ecstatic beagle, Benjamin, who has the effect of a Pied Piper on all cows and steers munching in the lush green fields. Whenever they see him their eyes turn red and they bumble angrily toward him while he nervously climbs right up my heels. It is a lovely, bucolic contrast to my normal life: quiet rushing chalk streams, fields with fat brown hares, busy muskrats swimming the river, wild geese flying off in a furious clatter, great fat white fantail pigeons and frail white doves in the farmers' cotes.

In this morning's mail I received a letter from President Nixon. He referred to a paper I prepared for him with recommendations on policy toward Chile. I am glad the president says that the approach being followed conforms with my recommendations. My memorandum said in part:

> Every country has the right to reform or revolutionize its social system if this is the desire of its citizens. There can be no valid U.S. objection if the Chilean people wish to revise their economy and society without bloodshed and by electoral means.
>
> But the United States has a legitimate right to see that such changes are not produced at our expense. We have a fair claim to compensation for property sufficient to cover insurance commitments otherwise chargeable to the U.S. taxpayer. And we must try and safeguard against the spread across South America of an obviously anti-U.S. movement deliberately encroaching on our legitimate interests— especially if (as in Cuba) hostile military installations are permitted. We cannot tolerate a Monroe Doctrine in reverse. . . .
>
> My impression of Allende is that of a clever but not profound man, energetic but undisciplined, intuitive but not intellectual; a man being rendered giddy with success. He is bound to face serious economic and political problems.
>
> There will be inflation, declining production in key sectors, sizeable unemployment. Although the anti-Allende parties have displayed timidity and an inability to unite, those leaders who don't flee the country are destined to coalesce in an opposition to the right of the President. . . . I would recommend:
>
> (1) That Washington should never allow any development to precipitate a break in relations with Santiago, thus sacrificing the ultimate potential of being able, some day, to influence developments from within. The error of Cuba should not be repeated in Chile, even if humble pie features the menu.
>
> (2) That a single individual, directly responsible to the President's staff, be assigned to coordinate all Chilean affairs (diplomatic, economic, propagandistic, military, financial, commercial, and intelligence —including the private sector). Thereby, policy can be directed effectively from the top on both a long-range basis and, should such be needed, an immediate *ad noc* basis.

(3) That the U.S. ambassador and his entire staff be rigidly en-joined to assume an unruffled, infallibly courteous, low-profile pos-ture, regardless of what develops. They should never lose their cool when attempts are made to affront the United States, damage its property, or even menace its representatives.

(4) That this attitude should be coordinated with a deliberate, subtle policy of isolating Chile—at this moment—from its normal commercial and financial contacts with our allies in Western Europe and Japan. . . .

(5) Ultimately it will be in our interest to see our friends expand their contacts and influence in Chile. The long-range political effect would be benign as today the flag follows trade. But during the im-mediate future our friends must be dissuaded from rash moves and postpone efforts to move in before Santiago negotiates satisfactory accords with us to move out. . . .

(6) Until such accords, U.S. diplomacy must persuade our friends to freeze the ball; not to rush into a Chilean vacuum and ease Allende's problem with us. . . .

(7) In the long run we should seek to take advantage of Chile's isolated geographic position (the Pacific, the desert, the Andes) and deter other South American nations from trying to follow Allende's example—at our expense. . . .

PARIS, *June 8, 1971*

Ivo Vejvoda, the Jugoslav ambassador, told me at lunch that he rarely takes alcohol. I remarked that this was an un-Jugoslav habit. He smiled and said sadly: "You know, when I first went to the mountains in 1941 to organize partisan resistance in the area of Croatia between Zagreb and Rijeka, I was met by the peasant group of about 200 who had already moved into the woods away from the Germans.

"I was a young man and was dressed exactly as I am now. [Today he was wearing a most elegant, well-cut suit, with white shirt and con-servative necktie.] I didn't want to make any pretense of looking like too much of a woodsman. The peasants assured me that they were the key to the whole future of Jugoslavia because nobody could pretend to run the country without having bread to give to the people and they, the peasants, produced the bread. It was like something out of literature, out of Tolstoy.

"I told them they were wrong. They had to learn to fight for something and also against something. There they were, standing with their long, drooping moustaches and armed with shotguns, hunting rifles, and scythes. One of them offered me a cigarette. 'I don't smoke, I said. Then one of them offered me a drink. 'I don't drink,' I said. Then I suddenly realized that just as you have said, this was very un-Jugoslav. So I changed my mind and I told them, 'Certainly, I will have a drink. Give me a drink.' That's how my partisan experience started."

PARIS, *June 17, 1971*

Foreign Minister Maurice Schumann received me in his office at the *Quai* for about an hour.

Schumann is a big man with solemn, sallow face. He asked: "Is it right for us, before a European security conference, to back and perpetuate the Soviet military occupation of Eastern Europe? If you reduce Soviet forces (under MBFR) [Mutual and Balanced Force Reductions] in East Germany, Hungary, Czechoslovakia, and Poland, it means that those forces are there with your full consent. From every angle, such an acknowledgment would be wrong."

I wondered in what capacity Brezhnev would be visiting Paris this autumn. Schumann looked startled and said: "But is he visiting Paris?" He then got a little less cute and said: "Yes, Brezhnev does wish to visit Paris. But the trip has not yet been confirmed. If he comes, he will be received as if he were a chief of state."

He said: "The Rogers idea of an interim solution for Suez is a good idea. Once Rogers has put pressure on Israel to accept workable terms, something can budge. But so far Israel doesn't wish a peaceful agreement which includes a full withdrawal from the areas it seized. Only U.S. pressure on Israel can bring about the necessary conditions.

"We are prepared to play a part in helping a settlement—when the time comes—and we have told this to Washington. We are even ready to help man an international force for the UN. But we are certainly not begging for such a role."

Schumann said the Russians didn't like U.S.-Chinese developments, but Moscow simply had to face it. Moreover, the Russians probably recognized that it was better to include China in an international framework and thus ease tensions. Schumann thought the changed atmosphere between Washington and Peking certainly will have an effect on the Paris peace talks concerning Vietnam. He added: "It is the only thing that might have an impact on these talks.

"If both Russia and China can be interested in ending the Vietnam problem, it would give United States diplomacy a chance to apply the whole balance of power policy to the communist world at large. And that might easily prove to be the best thing. Certainly China is essential to any satisfactory settlement of the Vietnam peace talks here."

PARIS, *June 21, 1971*

Called on Jacques Foccart, secretary-general of African and Malgache affairs in the presidency, very important in the governmental structure. He was one of de Gaulle's closest collaborators and was deeply involved in counter-espionage, internal security, and espionage. During the period when OAS conspirators were trying to take control of Algeria, capture France, and assassinate the General, Foccart played a key role at the helm of the so-called *barbouzes* or "bearded ones," who were thugs hired by section 5 ("Action") of SDECE (*Service de Documentation Étrangère et de Contre-espionnage*), the French combination of CIA and FBI.

I asked about the recent reports of a plot in Madagascar and why it was that the United States was referred to as the "foreign power" involved in the whole affair. I couldn't understand why Washington would want to get mixed up in anything in Madagascar.

Foccart said the revolt was largely provoked by economic difficulties and a drought in the impoverished area. The Malgache *Sûreté* (which works hand-in-hand with the French) had seized a document which indicated that the United States ambassador, Anthony Marshall, and some of his aides were involved. He continued: "We sought to tranquilize the situation and we argued, 'why bring trouble with the United States?'"

I smell something fishy about the whole Malgache affair.

Foccart then went on to say the east African coast, above all Tanzania, was attracting Chinese penetration. But this was also evident on the west coast in Mauritania and Congo-Brazzaville. The Chinese have sent a mission to develop a port at Nouakchott in Mauritania and also to build a railroad in Congo-Brazzaville. This made the presence of large numbers of Chinese inevitable.

PARIS, *June 23, 1971*

Lunched today with Ambassador [Arthur] Watson at a small table in the study at his residence. We talked about Madagascar, and Watson professes to be completely puzzled by what is going on. An apparently forged document was unearthed by the Malgache authorities, in which Ambassador Anthony Marshall allegedly gave specific instructions on what to do in connection with a coup the United States seemed to be mounting. President Tsiranana was furious and was ready to declare Marshall and several members of his staff, including Jack Hasey, *persona non grata*.

Yesterday Watson called on Pompidou to present him with a memento of the U.S. moon astronauts. Pompidou assured Watson that France had not been involved in the affair. Nevertheless, there is still a suspicion that

Foccart was in it—either in an attempt to besmirch the American name for reasons unknown, or to mount his own coup—which backfired and is now being covered up.

PARIS, *June 28, 1971*

Manlio Brosio, who will retire at the end of this year as NATO's secretary-general, dropped in for coffee. He says Moscow wants to neutralize the West as a possible help to China by obtaining a formal treaty between NATO and the Warsaw pact. This would isolate the U.S.A. (by nonaggression pledges) from any possible role in a Sino-Soviet conflict.

PARIS, *July 10, 1971*

Late yesterday afternoon Régis Debray dropped in for a beer. He promised to take a message to Fidel Castro, whom he is visiting at the end of this month, reminding Castro of his long-pending invitation to go fishing.

Debray is thirty but looks younger. He has golden brown hair and a droopy oriental-type moustache; he is small and finely made, about five feet seven inches in height. He came swinging in nervously, dressed in light trousers and open shirt and carrying over his shoulder the kind of strapped handbag that is now fashionable with the young man of Paris. He was very nervous, gulping his beer and then striding round my office looking at pictures of friendly (communist) and inimical (Franco, Chiang Kai-shek) subjects.

Debray told me that at the age of twenty he first became interested in Latin America as a consequence of an interest in Spanish revolutionary thought which he had acquired from his reading on the Spanish civil war and above all through Alejo Carpentier, the Cuban writer.

He spent a great deal of time in Cuba and became an intimate of Castro and Ché Guevara. Later he joined Guevara's dead-end guerrilla uprising in Bolivia and was captured by the Bolivian authorities, tried, and sentenced to prison. He was released last year. He said de Gaulle had saved his life by sending a cable to President Barrientos of Bolivia just a day or two after Debray was picked up, urging Barrientos to give him full legal protection. Subsequently, Pompidou, as president, helped facilitate his release.

Debray is frail-looking to have been tramping around the rugged Bolivian jungles with a bunch of professional gun-fighters. But he is obviously courageous. He considers that Guevara, despite his premature death, had already made an important mark on history and was a significant figure. He admits it was terribly disappointing to arrive in Bolivia and find oneself faced with the bleakly hostile stares of the Tibetan-looking Quechua Indians, who mistrusted all white men regardless of their politics.

But Debray says that after Guevara's death and the collapse of his uprising, the Indians have created a genuine revolutionary movement.

Debray described Guevara as perhaps romantic in his strategic vision and the broadness of his scope, but added that he was a cold, hard man in his tactical actions. I am sure this is true. There was evidence in captured code messages between Guevara and Castro that Ché was giving Debray a rough time.

Several times Debray referred to the fact that we were on "opposite sides of the barricade." I said of course this was true, but it shouldn't preclude human contact. He agreed.

He confessed he had moments of great fear when he was in prison. These were more serious than trepidation in the jungle. It was the easiest thing on earth for the Bolivian authorities to murder him and then claim it had been an accident—for example "by the bite of a snake."

We talked at length about Chile and Allende. Debray had gone to Santiago when released by the Bolivians. He seemed surprised when, in response to one of his questions, I told him I thought it most unlikely the United States would ever seriously consider a military intervention in Chile. The only thing that might provoke us into outright action would be the grant of a base to the Russians or the Chinese, and Allende had no intention of this.

He insisted the Brazilian regime (a brutal military dictatorship) represented a brilliant U.S. victory. It had established full control over the largest country in Latin America, even though Washington was now urging the Brazilians to ease up and cease torturing.

Debray is far more interested in experimenting with his revolutionary ideas in Latin America than in Europe. He still has rather youthful and cliché ideas of the United States as a classical capitalist imperialist force and spoke of the immense American investments in Latin America. I pointed out to him that U.S. investments in Western Europe were more enormous.

When I escorted him to the door he remarked with a smile: "I see you have your office in a bank [the Royal Bank of Canada]. That's correct for a capitalist institution."

ROME, *July 15, 1971*

Talk with Ambassador Graham Martin. As a reserve officer he studied military intelligence, under General Fox Connor, Eisenhower's mentor. After the war, he came into the diplomatic service through FSS (Foreign Service Staff) in Paris.

In Italy the emergency of (neo-fascist) Giorgio Almirante's surprising new strength has set back the hitherto unchecked leftward swing. The center faction of the Christian Democrats is scared. From 1955 to 1969 the

communists had managed to steadily increase their gains in various elections, even if each time the increase was relatively small. But in the three
elections since 1969, the communists registered small losses.

The chances of a Chilean formula, bringing the communists to power
by legal elections, have receded a great deal in recent months. My column
entitled "Spaghetti with Chile Sauce" hit the wobblers where it hurt. Business men like Agnelli and many politicians suddenly began to get alarmed
about what might lie in wait for them at the end of the road. There is no
more chance today of a Christian Democratic-communist coalition that
would take over power.

There was almost a military coup during the last nine months, but this
would have been ridiculous. An unsuccessful coup would have absolutely
wrecked any sensible hope of restoring stability. Nevertheless, the military
today is increasingly urging the Christian Democrats to stiffen the central
position and it may still be reckoned probably that if things were to disintegrate the army would move in, but this is much less likely now than a
year ago.

Martin has told the Christian Democrats he will use all the influence
of the U.S.A. to help push for a centralized and reorganized Christian
Democrat party prior to the 1973 elections. Such a party can gain enough
support to form a stable Centralist government which would not have to
discard the Social Democratic Left.

He hinted without saying as much, that it was Washington which had
been behind a potential coup here in case the situation rotted further,
and that the army was its instrument. I asked if he referred to the talk of
a coup by General di Lorenzo in 1964. "Oh, no," he said, "I mean within
the last nine months."

I suspect that Martin, a hard-nosed discreet man who almost never
talks with journalists and who has much experience in handling CIA and
military matters, was sent here (end of 1969) with the basic assignment
of reversing the leftward trend in Italy by any means possible.

ROME, *July 16, 1971*

Two hours this afternoon in the unattractive Quirinale palace with
President Giuseppe Saragat. Although he is seventy-three, he had a
prostate operation a few months ago and apparently this has livened him
up.

We spoke French. During the latter part of the conversation, Saragat's
son joined us. At one point Saragat remarked it was a hot day and we
should have something cool to drink. He ordered champagne which came in
promptly.

Saragat started by asking: "Why all this melodrama about China? Why
did Nixon have to announce this thing and plan this trip in such a melo-

dramatic way? We are a country of melodrama, but even we were startled." (Very late last night Nixon announced he would visit Peking before May 1972.)

"Of course, we agree with what Nixon is doing." Saragat added. "Months ago we recognized China ourselves. We think this a good thing— just so long as it is not taken as a move directed against Russia."

We then talked about Italy. Saragat smiled when he recalled the column of mine called "Spaghetti with Chile Sauce." He said that the drift toward an increasing communist importance had ended. He continued: "In order to understand what is going on here you must recognize that a very swift industrial revolution has taken place in which ten million people, about one-fifth of the population, have been transferred from the country to the city, mostly moving up from the south. This includes some four million peasants and their families. An enormous change has occurred in a few years' time, accomplishing in Italy what it required one century for England to do.

"Today, Italy is the seventh industrial power in the world. In terms of purchasing power the average income has tripled in twenty years. But still there is a great gap in terms of the internal wealth within the country, the difference in the level of life between north and south. Progress is what makes for discontent now. And these people are learning their rights and becoming politicized.

"One result of uneasiness has been that the protest vote, instead of always casting its lot with the extreme Left, has in many cases now started to vote with the extreme Right. But I don't think that this represents a danger to the state. Fundamentally, I see a trend toward serenity.

"There is absolutely no chance of a fascist coup. But if a fascist-type party managed to get 100 deputies in Parliament, this could greatly weaken the Center-Left and make it virtually impossible to govern."

I asked about Giorgio Almirante. Did he think Almirante was a fascist? He replied: "He is no democrat. He has a different view of politics. He is honest and he is brave. His ideas are not clear, but it is obvious he is opposed to democratic liberties.

"And he works against the tide of history in contemporary Europe. Above all, this is true in a Europe which Britain is about to enter. Europe needs the moral and political wisdom of Britain and will greatly benefit from it. In such a Europe the MSI [Italian Social Movement—a neo-fascist party] is ridiculous."

He said he regarded the imminent entry of Britain into the Common Market as a positive feature. Likewise the prospective friendship between the U.S.A. and China was a positive factor in favor of peace—provided it was not allowed to develop into an anti-Soviet move. These two external factors help to create an international atmosphere that favored peace and democracy—in Italy as well as elsewhere.

I asked what he thought the U.S.A. was up to in Italy now. He answered: "We don't see much U.S. influence. Your government is very prudent. It doesn't do idiotic things, like Brezhnev who congratulated the communists on the number of strikes here. As a matter of fact you are at a disadvantage here. Italian TV is very anti-American. It has been infiltrated by the left-wing Christian Democrats, who are clearly pro-Russian and hate democracy. They try to give a negative and absurd picture of the United States."

ROME, *July 17, 1971*

Long lunch with Giorgio Almirante, latest *enfant terrible* in Italy's political kindergarten. I was more impressed by his straightforward character than by his intellect. He is lean, short, fifty-seven, tanned, growing bald. The back of his head is covered with dark brown hair; he has grey patches on the temples and a grey moustache. His eyes are grey-green. He received me in his modest bourgeois apartment, filled with unattractive furniture, rubber plants, a few shelves of books in Italian and French, and an air of middle-class quiet. His wife (the second) looked after us: a young, attractive Calabrian. She supervised the kitchen and the table service of the timid waitress.

Almirante comes from a Sicilian family of actors and is the first of four generations who has not made his livelihood in the theater. His only stage effort was when he wrote a play at the age of twenty-two. It was terrible.

We spoke in French, which he knows well despite his Italian accent. By profession he had been a high school professor of Italian literature. His favorite authors are Dante, Pirandello, and Verga. Two years ago he became secretary of the MSI party when Arturo Michelini, its high-handed boss, died.

When party unity was achieved, he sought to give it "a modern political language" replacing its old-fashioned jargon. The MSI, he contends, was looking to the past, not the future. "We often gave the impression of being stupid and outmoded fascists," he added. "We had to shake off orthodox formalism." The third point in his program was to seek a big electoral success and thus attract public backing. "Now I've done this," he says. He hopes to transform this electoral triumph into a "nationalist Right."

Almirante says the Italian situation has been increasingly dominated by the Left. Article 138 of the constitution provides that it can be amended by two-thirds vote. Almirante wants it changed to create a presidential republic with more executive powers for the president and a single corporative chamber. Also he would like to outlaw the Communist party. It is a "foreign" party and poses ideological problems.

He favors a system of management collaboration, joint participation of industrial management rather than ownership. He claims something like this is already provided in the existing constitution, but it is not followed.

I asked whether he would favor a *coup d'état* if a leftist government took over. He shrugged and said: "One would have to defend oneself but the hypothesis is all wrong. There will be no major changes before the 1973 elections."

I asked if he approved of the present government in Greece. He replied: "Greece saved itself from great danger and I think it did well."

I said it was well known he had been a fascist and even stayed with Mussolini's Salo Republic. Where did he think Mussolini had gone wrong? He said it was easy to answer this: the 1940 declaration of war. But at that time, as a twenty-six-year-old officer, "I was convinced it was a good idea and everyone shared my sentiments. The great mistake was going to war without being ready. Mussolini had bad collaborators. And a bad German strategy was imposed upon him, to attack Russia instead of the Mediterranean."

He had stayed on with the Salo Republic as a simple question of loyalty. "This was the first time that I myself had the opportunity to make a choice in my life." He became *chef de cabinet* of the republic's minister of propaganda. Of these days, he says:

"I renounce nothing. I still respect the memory of Mussolini. I respect my own memory. But I am not a fascist today. I don't want totalitarianism. I don't want a one-party state or a dictatorship. I want freedom of the press, freedom of organization, and freedom of choice for everyone."

I asked him if he had written, as reported, in January 1958: "The MSI is a fascist party which fights in the streets for the honor of fascism." He said he couldn't remember this "but I probably wrote it—and I haven't changed."

He said he was most influenced in his political thinking by the Italian philosophers Gianbattisto Vico and Giovanni Gentile. Without them it was impossible to understand Italian politics. He also had a sentimental interest in Pascal.

LONDON, *July 29, 1971*

Talk with Roy Jenkins, deputy leader of the Labor Party. I asked if there was any danger that Britain would withdraw from the Common Market if and when Labor forms a government again. He said this was out of the question. The Labor party conference might try to reach a decision favoring such a commitment, but Harold Wilson himself would certainly oppose it. Moreover, even if such a position was agreed to at a party conference, it would not be binding on the Labor government.

Opinion is swinging fast. The effects of the international position make it plain that Britain cannot renege on membership once it is in. The outer world should not be worried. It is only an argument involving internal politics of the Labor party. If Britain joins the Market, Labor will accept the fact just as the Social Democrats in Germany, who had opposed the Coal and Steel Community, are now thoroughgoing Europeans.

LONDON, *July 30, 1971*

Saw Colonel Demetrios Opropoulos, the crippled officer who is supposed to direct Greece's external opposition. He broke his neck diving and is in a wheelchair, a fine-looking man with an El Greco face, dark brown hair and beard barely salted with grey, slate-colored eyes, pale skin.

O. was born in Istanbul in 1919. In 1937, he went to the Athens cadet school and graduated in 1940, entering service as a young officer in the Albanian war. He was in the same class as two of the leading colonels. O. was Number One in the class, Makarezos Number Two, and Papadopoulos Number Four.

After Greece fell to the Axis, O. stayed in Salonika, where he organized the first partisan unit, an independent group. Then he went to Athens and was distressed to find that all senior officers he met had no interest in going to the mountains. He escaped to the Middle East and joined the famous Ieros Lochos, later worked with the British commando Special Boat Service. In 1946, he became a captain and fought throughout the civil war. O. had the best record for combat gallantry of anyone in the army. He was awarded eight medals for valor, never before done. "I was lucky," he says. "I missed no battles."

In 1965, he was named a professor at the national defense college. This was to keep him away from troops because the "colonels' conspiracy" was already getting ready. "I was known as an opponent of political organizations in the army."

He realized Papadopolous was conspiring as early as 1956–57. "We knew Papadopoulos and his friends were staff officers, not combat officers. But at first we thought their organization was merely designed to help each other obtain better jobs and promotions, nothing else."

In 1965, he was made a professor at the staff college, where he was when the coup came. The generals thought the Colonels were working under and for their own conspiracy, not realizing they were being used as cover. The colonels succeeded when they got Spandidakis, chief of staff, over on their side the night of the coup, and then used the king's name falsely to fool everyone they were acting against a communist plot.

Not long before the king's abortive countercoup (December 1967) O. went to Salonika, where he heard much rumor about that plan. He sent word to the king through a general that it would fail if it were tried as then outlined. He was the first officer sent to exile on an island after the countercoup.

In Lesbos he broke his neck when he dove on a rock in unfamiliar waters in June 1969. The government thought he would die and because of his prestige they didn't want this to happen in exile, so they sent a plane. He was taken to an Athens hospital for ten days, then his wife obtained permission for him to go abroad for treatment.

O. thinks all factions can be brought into a united opposition, even communists, except those loyal to Kolliyannis (in Moscow). "We can't forget there *is* a Left in Greece, but we must get it away from foreign control." In the "free" communist group he includes Andreas Papandreou's friend, Brillakis. He wants to get him and his followers into a democratic front. However, Andreas, who has visited O., refuses to go along unless it is first decided to oust the monarchy. O. refuses, and says after all the king is also an exile working for freedom.

O. says Papadopoulos is very intelligent but a little crazy. "You can see it in his eyes. He always schemed—and not just for the good. And now they are pushing the Greek people to extremes. This increases the chance of a real revolution and no one knows where that will stop. Moreover, the new generation is being destroyed. It has no idea of the free world; how can it be asked to fight for it?"

REYKJAVIK, *August 1, 1971*

Iceland is covered with low mountains, white with snow, and then a flat expanse of gloom, with great grey flows of frozen, striated lava, utterly treeless. A brown peninsula shelters Keflavik base and airfield, with huge globes and fans of electronic installations standing out against the featureless pastel background.

Was met by the U.S. ambassador, Luther Replogle, a sixty-eight-year-old Chicago businessman. He is a pleasant white-haired fellow with a slow-spoken Middle-Western drawl and a hearing aid. He was a widower (a grandfather) who just a year ago married a pretty Chicago widow.

They had arranged a salmon fishing party and, garbed in warm Replogle clothes, drove out to the Laxa i Kjos, a salmon river an hour from the capital. There we joined Admiral John K. Beling (base commander) and General David Burchinall, U.S. air force, deputy U.S. commander in Europe.

It was a beautiful day although by no means hot. I caught nothing but a modest brown trout but I refused to use anything but flies. The admiral caught one small salmon and the general three, all on worms. I kept my dignity but no fish; on the other hand it was a splendid sight to see hundreds of salmon leaping upstream. In one long stretch of pools below a waterfall they jumped all around me, almost like schools of porpoise.

The ladies (Mrs. Replogle and Mrs. Burchinall) visited a whaling station on the coast, watched a flensing, and returned with a box of huge, heavy whale teeth and the bony inner ears which look like distorted human heads.

REYKJAVIK, August 2, 1971

Called on Kristjan Eldjarn, fifty-four-year-old president of the republic, a pink-faced man with brick-red hair, an archaeologist and museum curator who was elected in 1968 after a strictly nonpolitical career. His position is symbolic and virtually without power.

He cannot dissolve parliament but can recommend legislation tactfully. He can delay enactment of laws of which he disapproves, but within a fortnight parliament can, if it wishes, override his temporary veto by repassing the law. Were the president then to refuse to sign it he could be impeached. He can initiate policy only by informal suggestion to his ministers. His principal political function is tact—to remain on friendly terms with the political leaders.

Most Icelanders, he said, are now used to the NATO alliance and four of the five political parties, a big majority, favor it.

I then went to the U.S. embassy, where I was told the U.S. base contains about 3,500 men and 12,000 acres, made available free for the duration of NATO (with Iceland in it). In 1956 there was a crisis when a new government demanded renegotiation of its terms, and this process actually began, only to be terminated some months later when Russia invaded Hungary. The new government is divided on the issue.

Iceland is considered crucial to the defense and supply of Norway in the first twenty-four hours of any war with Russia and therefore the base can't be "mothballed." Theoretically, the U.S.A. might be able to afford leaving Iceland, but it could never allow it in Soviet hands. We have never told the Icelanders precisely what the base is used for.

REYKJAVIK, August 3, 1971

The Replogles yesterday gave me a large dinner. Among those there were Admiral Beling, and Halldor Laxness, Iceland's Nobel Prize novelist.

Laxness is a charming man with a bluff, hearty manner and open face. He holds contemporary writers everywhere in low esteem. It was easy for the great nineteenth-century authors to produce huge books quickly; the need now is to condense much into short space; for this he values journalism.

Beling, an electronics expert, says the Russians keep their greatest naval strength at the Kola Peninsula area (around Murmansk), where they have an estimated 168 submarines including 60 nuclear subs, plus ample air support. It is necessary to show the new Iceland government what the real threat is.

We must disabuse the Icelanders of any thought that they can "mothball" the U.S. base. The risk is too great that the Russians could then seize it and gain an invaluable asset. We would prefer to see the base crumble into bad condition if we have to go.

I walked home at midnight. It was still light, with the remnants of sunset rosy in the sky. Ducks were sleeping on the pond in the center of town, their heads tucked by their necks, floating in rows by the edge of the water. The modest, clean houses looked appealing in their quiet simplicity. There is something like nineteenth-century American small-town life here. But the two big problems are drink and uninhibited sex.

REYKJAVIK, *August 4, 1971*

Lunched with Foreign Minister Einar Agustsson, a solid lawyer and banker, who is vice president of the Progressive party which dominates the new coalition cabinet.

He said: "An agreement on fishing limitations has priority. We will go very slowly on other questions until this is settled. I'll take my time studying the base problem. Then friendly talks will be held with NATO and the United States. We will do nothing definite prior to those."

REYKJAVIK, *August 5, 1971*

Drove to Thingvellir, where the Althing (parliament) used to meet after the tenth century. It was an assembly of chieftains and the forerunner of the government that still exists. The chiefs set out their "booths," huts of skins or turf, on a hillside beneath a canyon, tethered their horses in the canyon, dueled on a small island in a river when they disagreed, exiled each other for crimes, and drowned their erring women in a rushing trout pool.

I am impressed by the way 200,000 people here can maintain a civilization with two airlines, ships, telephones, road building, etc. But in the end, I don't think they'll have enough people to keep it up. The only place they could go to join or seek sponsorship would be England, not Scandinavia. They are nearer Glasgow than Oslo or Copenhagen, and English is the first language in schools, even if they still must learn Danish, which is very foreign now. The kids like English—language of the movies and TV.

2 9

NEITHER SOUND NOR

FURY IN GREECE

ATHENS, *August 11, 1971*

I SPENT AN HOUR AND A HALF THIS AFTERNOON WITH HENRY TASCA, the much-discussed U.S. ambassador, sharply criticized for being too procolonel.

He said the procommunist faction of the 1947–49 civil war resented and disliked America, which had prevented them from seizing Greece. They perhaps represented 10 to 20 percent of the population. The ex-politicians resented a lack of American support. They had had a stake, a political fief, until disenfranchised by the military. They feel a personal loss as well as a loss of democracy. Like most Greeks, they blame someone else, not themselves.

The rural areas are habitually used to bad government in Athens. They have traditionally felt disenfranchised. Therefore, they tolerate this regime better. This regime has been lucky in inheriting the start of an expanding economy from the Caramanlis years, and it distributes the fruits to rural areas.

Tasca argues the U.S. has to work through existing government. Nobody here wants violence, except perhaps the far Left. The question therefore becomes: How do we induce them to move peacefully toward change? We can't make the colonels disappear by tough talk.

The king's position is slowly weakening, but he is still a symbol of normality. The armed forces oppose him as the man who sought to divide them and turn them against each other. There is not much deep proking feeling anywhere. As for Caramanlis, he is gradually slipping. His 1969 appeal for an uprising, which drew a blank, and his divorce hurt him.

Yet, he still has a big name here that could dramatically revive if he came back.

ATHENS, *August 12, 1971*

Chat with Bernard Durand, French ambassador, a calm, intelligent man. He says Papadopoulos may be aiming at a presidential republic eventually. It is doubtful if he will bring the king back. He is now dividing the army opposition by promoting the hardliners out of sight and dividing the political opposition by playing with lesser-known old regime politicians.

The Russians clearly prefer this regime to its predecessors because it is more independent. But they are keeping close touch with the left-wing underground, which probably represents 30 percent of the people and is more formidable than the old party set-up. They weren't parties anyway, just Balkan political cliques grouped around individuals.

ATHENS, *August 13, 1971*

Invited for coffee with Prime Minister Papadopoulos. At fifty-one, he showed few signs of strain. He has lost weight, is thin, spry, with only a touch of grey at the thatches and in his moustache. He drinks lots of coffee and is a cigarette chain-smoker. He was nattily dressed, in well-cut grey suit, grey shirt with cuff-links, flamboyant striped tie. His new office is much nicer than the old one, large, well-furnished with conference table and desk, plus many chairs, oriental tiled walls covered with birds of paradise. Behind his desk were large pictures (on either side) of the king and the queen. At the end, I remarked on his office, and that it was much more attractive than his old one. "Too many birds of paradise," he said.

He got up, after inquiring what I wanted, and ordered Turkish coffee, lit a cigarette, and relaxed. He was far friendlier and more a man of the world than in the past.

I asked if he still felt as he had said last time when I asked if Moscow was attempting to turn Greece toward neutralism, that: "From what I understand, this is being done by the Americans and not the Russians. So far the Russians have not made any effort at all. They have never dared to ask us to change our policy. The Greek government does not request arms from the United States to impose its own political views, but only in order to be prepared to fulfill its obligations within the alliance."

He said: "Absolutely no change. That's what I still feel. In fact, I could repeat to you that Russia has behaved no differently since I said that and tries to look even friendlier toward us than our real friends. But it has never crossed our minds to change our political attitudes and alliances."

I expressed the opinion that perhaps, on both sides of the debate, there was "more sound than fury." He replied pompously: "On our side there is neither sound nor fury." He continued: "Sometimes I find it amazing to see an expression of a kind of Brezhnev doctrine coming from the Western world which so criticizes Brezhnev's own policy."

I asked about the French desire to expell both superpower fleets from the Mediterranean. He said: "I know this is French policy. However, now when all the free world faces the Iron Curtain countries and the mass of Russian power, we shouldn't confine areas of interest to the nationalities they contain. That may meet the desires of France which, as the greatest Mediterranean power, would end up running this sea because it is the strongest of the coastal states. But it would not serve the interests of NATO.

"I know you are a good strategist and I therefore want to stress two points to you concerning the joint presence in the Mediterranean of the Soviet and U.S. fleets. (1) Up to now, the Sixth Fleet has been present with the aim of deterring an attack or defending land regions and land forces in case of such an attack in either southern or southeastern Europe. But now, if ever an attack came, the Sixth Fleet would have to face the Soviet fleet first. Therefore, this has lessened its possibility of defending positions on land. (2) By its presence, furthermore, the Soviet fleet has created strategic problems in all Mediterranean countries."

I asked how he happened to consider me a "good strategist." He said: "I don't read all your articles on Greece, but I regularly read you on other subjects." I said that as he well knew I disagreed with him on Greece and disliked this government, but thought Greece should be fairly treated as an ally. "Sometimes you are too hard on Greece and not sufficiently informed," he said. He added: "I believe in noninterference as a policy. Moreover, you should know that we don't react to pressure."

I then asked why, for the sake of common U.S.-Greek interests, he didn't make some gesture in the direction of democratic freedoms along lines he had already pledged? Up he stood, quite abruptly if politely, saying merely: "I will do everything I have pledged to do. But not under pressure."

ATHENS, *August 14, 1971*

I drove out to Kifissia and spent two hours in a pleasant garden talking with Panayotis Canellopoulos, former prime minister, head of the ERE (center) party, writer, philosopher, historian, and my old friend. He is rewriting a history of human thought that he published many years ago in 1,000 pages. The new edition will be 4,500 pages.

He said Tasca is rightly criticized for inadequate contacts with the opposition. Tasca saw Canellopoulos and other party leaders soon after he arrived in early 1970. Then there was silence. Last April (months after House foreign affairs committee investigators came here) Tasca called and they had a talk. Tasca then saw other leaders.

C. thinks the army will get fed up and throw the dictators out, giving them a peaceful exile. The only man strong enough to do this would be General Odysseus Anghelis. He thinks A. would take over, invite the king back, and Constantine would perform his constitutional duties. I said I would bet that Papadopoulos gets rid of Anghelis long before he has a chance to move.

He thinks the U.S.A. is mistaken to give weapons to Greece because this allows Papadopoulos to exploit the fact to strengthen his position. But, he says, he understands the U.S. dilemma as an ally with responsibilities.

ANKARA, *August 16, 1971*

Talk for about an hour and a half with Foreign Minister Osman Olcay, a career diplomat and highly intelligent. He is forty-seven and looks younger: pleasant, cultivated, intellectual. After our conversation he gave a lunch in my honor.

I asked Olcay what effect there had been on Turkey—socially, politically, and economically—from the huge number of Turks who had returned here after working several years in Europe, primarily in Common Market countries where there is a real shortage of labor. He said there had been an enormous influence. One "generation" of Turks abroad must have come back by now and this should involve a few hundred thousand people. This might be the most important Europeanizing force in Turkey since the days of Ataturk.

I asked him what had gone sour in U.S.-Turkish relations? He said the process had begun in 1964 when President Johnson wrote his harsh letter warning the Turks not to go to war on Cyprus. But the unnecessarily high profile of the American presence in Turkey was the real reason for the decline in friendship. Now, thanks to martial law (he admitted), "we are in a position to say more broadly that we are pro-NATO, and we can say this without any fear of being stoned in the streets. Likewise we can invite the U.S. fleet to visit Turkish ports without fear of incidents."

A sign of the developing new era of good relations with the U.S.A. was the agreement at the end of June 1971 that Turkey would get out of the opium-growing business.

ANKARA, *August 18, 1971*

Long talk with Prime Minister Nihat Erim, a law professor brought in after the military demicoup this spring. He is sturdy, totally bald, has a ruddy complexion, and wears rimless spectacles.

Erim—who speaks meticulous French—said that before the presentation of an army memorandum to President General Cevdet Sunay last March, everyone was extremely anxious about the possibility of a disastrous explosion. He continued:

"When the army presented its memorandum, there was a sigh of relief. Then from the moment of the resignation of the previous government, there was a cascade of events. On March 19, I was summoned by the president to form a government.

"I had two principal tasks: to reestablish order and end the anarchic situation brought about by left-wing activists; and to carry out the reforms originally foreseen in the 1961 constitution. But law and order was a necessary prerequisite.

"After three weeks in office, I saw the existing constitution wasn't adequate to halt terrorist activities. At that moment (April 26) I found it necessary to proclaim martial law. And the Labor party has been dissolved for fomenting Kurdish separatism. It is frankly Marxist.

"The two extremes on the political spectrum have been banned here from the days of Ataturk. We wish to preserve our democracy from extremists both on the far Left and the far Right. The far Left means communism or Maoism seeking to pull down the democratic structure. The far Right means those who would like to restore the sultanate or to give priority to Islamic law."

ISTANBUL, *August 19, 1971*

Flew here to see President Sunay at his summer residence at Floriya, on the beach of the Sea of Marmora.

Sunay received me in his pleasantly ugly office, a comfortable room with a large desk, blue-covered chairs, blue curtains, blowing in with the gentle sea breeze. The house is built on stilts right out in the water, and is agreeable but not impressively luxurious.

The president is moderately large and must have been quite strongly built in his youth. He was wearing a grey suit and a cheery striped blue tie. His bald head has a certain amount of thin brown hair, and a bulbous nose, tough expression, and almost cruel mouth. His face is brutal and strong; he is quite humorless and almost without emotion, wearing thick-lensed spectacles. Behind his desk was a large picture of Ataturk.

He said, "Turkey has a special position and is a special case, both historically and philosophically. During the war of independence the country was in a shambles. The Ottoman empire lay in ruins after World War I and the only force in the nation that stood up to correct the lamentable situation was the army.

"Only Ataturk and the officers serving under him unleashed the necessary struggle against the great powers and many odds. Turkey had a huge casualty roster during this war and the officer losses were the heaviest of all. This sacrifice permitted Ataturk to save the country.

"As a consequence, I would say that intervention of the armed forces in the country's political life is unlike that in any other country. It was due to the army's effort that the republic came into being. Therefore, the army regards the republic as its own creation and is as solicitous about its health as a mother is about her child's.

"After the country was saved, Turkey was very backward and required modernization. In this effort we were hampered by two main forces of resistance. The first was the ignorant religious opposition and the second was communism, based on neighboring Russia.

"After Ataturk's death, it was natural for the army to continue the fight against religious reaction and against communism and to prevent either from gaining an upper hand in an attempt to upset the republic. This was the spirit of the army's intervention this year; it was in no sense a search for political power."

I then asked how important the left-wing underground was today, now that it had really been driven out of public sight by the events of March. He said:

"I can tell you that the situation in Turkey is such that there is a group of bold, intelligent, and audacious extreme-leftists who are ready to sacrifice themselves for their cause. Furthermore, there is a larger and amorphous group of opportunists used by the leftists to gain their own ends.

"The real leftists are relatively few. The mass of citizens are law-abiding and these were the ones who expected the government to move in. Today the militant left has not been crushed but large numbers have been apprehended and their dupes have been gotten out of the way, thus removing the danger to the state."

He said: "There is no doubt that the Turkish nation is very much in favor of the government's pro-U.S. policy. One would have had to be blind and ungrateful not to appreciate the benefits Turkey received from the United States. Of course, our relationships are based on mutual interests. But in times of peril we can count on U.S. support and U.S. aid."

PARIS, *October 6, 1971*

Lunched with Caramanlis. He said Tasca was a small man, as a diplomat, and was merely trying to put himself in a position vis-à-vis the U.S. Congress of having been in contact with the principal opposition leaders.

He thinks there are only three solutions in Greece: either the junta changes its mind and calls for elections, or there is a *coup d'état* which overthrows the junta, or foreign pressure ousts the colonels. All are highly improbable.

I asked why he didn't just get into an airplane and go home, since he claims 70 percent of the people are for him and it would start a general reaction if the government arrested him. He said he didn't want to gamble his last trump card.

PARIS, *October 8, 1971*

Lunched with Bill Porter, now United States ambassador heading our delegation at the Vietnam peace talks, having replaced David Bruce. He is a very bright, original career diplomat. As a young vice-consul in Syria-Lebanon, he was the official witness who made our wedding in Beirut legal. We have stayed close friends over the years.

He is determined we should no longer take things lying down, leaving the propaganda game free for the communists to play. Much of the Western press has been available as patsies to the communists, signing up on application lists for interviews with various Vietcong or North Vietnamese delegation chiefs and then awarded the plum when it suits Hanoi's convenience.

He has berated the communists and said they stole the initials "FLN" from the Algerians, but this was a shameful travesty. The FLN represented the great majority of the Algerian people, while the Vietnamese FLN represented nothing. No single provincial capital is under their control. In the years since the Vietcong was formed, it has never been joined by one single prominent or distinguished South Vietnamese figure.

He has been hammering away on the theme that East and West Germany and North and South Korea are now moving gradually toward *détente* and accommodation, and it is high time Hanoi should make a similar approach to Saigon and seriously consider the proposals submitted at these meetings by Saigon.

PARIS, *October 22, 1971*

Dined last night at the Windsors'. I asked the duke about his visit from Emperor Hirohito and the empress during their trip to Paris earlier this month. He said it was tough going. They had to talk through an interpreter who was lousy. Out of desperation, he got out some old photograph albums of his own journey to Japan fifty years ago when he was Prince of Wales, and they sat on a sofa simpering at the pictures. There were several of the emperor playing golf with Hirohito, who was then crown prince. In fact, Hirohito really didn't play golf; he only had his picture taken.

Windsor is much tougher on the Japanese than on the Germans. He fully sympathizes with the demonstrations against Hirohito in England and Holland and said: "After all, our soldiers suffered terribly in those Jap prisons. Hirohito must have a pretty bad public relations man to send him on a trip like this. I think it was damned stupid."

Lunched with X of the *Quai d'Orsay*. I dove right into Topic A: What was Brezhnev up to on his visit next week? He said since 1941 France has been useful to Soviet policy as a pawn in two games only: (1) Germany; (2) the United States.

Point (1), Brezhnev is trying to play with France and show his warm friendship in order to get the Germans to react. The primary document he will bring along is a photostatic copy of Soviet records of the Brezhnev-Brandt conversations in the Crimea last summer. This will allow the French to go through them with a microscope to see if there is anything the Germans haven't told him (as they should do under their treaty of special relationships).

Point (2) will be to try again to use France to weaken the position of Europe. Then, if the U.S.A. shows declining faith in Europe it will be more inclined to push its dialogue with Russia.

If French policy results in pushing the Germans toward Russia, that will accelerate the loss of U.S. faith in Western Europe's strength and, in turn, push the U.S.A. toward Russia.

In this connection, the award of the Nobel Peace Prize to Chancellor Willy Brandt is enormously important as a symbol and greatly facilitates Brezhnev's task. It enhances Bonn's importance and encourages jealousy in Paris.

Probably the most important single fact in the world today is that the United States is engaged in the process of changing its myths. In this sense, the myth of "China" in the U.S.A. totally distorted American world views during past decades and, its sudden revision, is about to totally distort U.S. views during future decades.

All of us in the Western world are engaged in a curious operation. We are doing all we can to confirm the truth of the Marxist analysis of international politics and the world revolution—although at the same time, we know it is wrong.

PARIS, *October 23, 1971*

Golfed and lunched with Caramanlis today. To my great surprise, he confided that he's getting so fed-up that he might return to Greece in six to twelve months. That, of course, would mean the end of his political career, because he could only return as a private person.

He is convinced the colonels will never let the king back under any circumstances, so long as they are in power. Moreover, he suspects Papadopoulos intends to create a republic.

PARIS, *October 24, 1971*

Bill and Pussy Deakin came to spend a few days with us. He saw Tito in July and was impressed by the Churchillian manner Tito now affects. At

11:30 in the morning, he was sitting with a large cigar and a whisky and soda.

Tito is absolutely fascinated by the movie being made of the 1943 partisan battle against the Nazis around the Montenegrin mountain of Sutjeska. The marshal regards this as his own last great romantic epic. Richard Burton is playing him in the picture. Burton demanded a huge sum, and Tito ordered that this should be paid for by the Jugoslav treasury. Burton is living in a fancy villa near Dubrovnik, where he is afforded all kinds of luxuries that are rare in Jugoslavia—including plenty of scotch.

PARIS, *October 25, 1971*

Lunched with Deakin. He said that at the very end of his conversation with Tito in July he asked the marshal: "What, if anything, did you learn from Churchill?"

"*Vlast, vlast, vlast,*" Tito replied: "power, power power—and how to keep it."

PARIS, *October 28, 1971*

Lunched with Henri Froment-Meurice, head of the Far Eastern division of the *Quai d'Orsay*. He worries that Washington may be under an illusion that together with Peking it can impose a settlement on Hanoi. The North Vietnamese will never accept this. Any such attempt will play into Moscow's hands by giving the Russians the opportunity to warn the North Vietnamese against a Sino-American conspiracy and to help them to fight on with Soviet backing.

At this point, Froment-Meurice began to talk about recent events in China. He believes Chou has now succeeded in establishing his own personal power and policy and runs China at this moment.

Three chains of events can be traced back to the end of the second week of September 1971. Probably at night, on either September 12 or 13, a Trident jet of the Chinese civil aviation company crashed deep inside Outer Mongolia. The crash appears to have been accidental. It is said that bodies of nine people were found on board—all of them relatively young —and one a woman. It was not a regular airline flight and nine bodies are nothing on a Trident, which can carry well over 100 passengers and crew.

The fact that China has very few Tridents indicates the people aboard were extremely influential—whether they had hijacked or otherwise commandeered the plane or were seeking to escape from China after the failure of a plot.

At the same time, there had been a suspicion of internal fighting in China. Moreover, the chiefs of staff of the three armed services disappeared from the public eye at that time and have not reemerged.

The Communist party had been slowly trying to reestablish itself in power after five years of the Cultural Revolution and its consequences. The army had been Mao's instrument against the party in the Cultural Revolution. All this together, says Froment-Meurice, can be called the military chain of events.

The second chain is that of Maoism. This also seems to have begun in September. Just at the period of the air crash, news came out that the regular October parade in Peking, the biggest national display, had been canceled. Flags and other preliminary preparations were taken down. Pictures of Mao began to become less and less evident.

It seemed the cult of Maoism had gone into a decline. We know that Mao himself favored this, because in December 1970 he told Edgar Snow he thought the Maoist cult had gone too far. But the events starting in September were curious. In early October, a Chinese trade delegation came to Paris. Not a single member of the delegation wore the usual Mao badge or even mentioned him in any conversations.

The third element among these chains is Lin Piao, commander-in-chief of the army and official heir to Mao. He is still missing from the public eye. The Chinese had gone out of their way to play down the story of the plane crash in Mongolia, after it was first revealed by a Tass dispatch, at the end of September.

There has been no public list designating members of the existing politburo since the crash. Chou appears to be running the show alone. Everyone has been awaiting a scheduled meeting of the people's national assembly that was originally to be held at the end of September and was expected to announce the members of the new politburo. But nothing has happened.

All this must be added to previous factors we know about. Mao told Snow in December 1970 that there had been fights between leftists and other groups. It is evident the leftists have been pushed out of power positions.

The Nixon trip is directly concerned with these mysterious developments. Peking's acceptance of his visit may have revived old quarrels. Perhaps the leftists protested that China was now giving an appearance of ending its battle against imperialism, ceasing to support North Vietnam, and abandoning its revolutionary line.

If Chou decided on the Nixon invitation—which must have been the case—he must now prove China is getting something out of it. His future depends on this. But already he can demonstrate factually that since announcement of the Nixon trip, China has gotten into UN. Indeed, as the news broke, Chou appeared before guests at an Iranian embassy reception smiling and toasting everyone in sight. This represented a great victory for Chou and strengthened his position in the internal power struggle. One can assume it weakened the position of leftists opposing the Nixon visit.

Froment-Meurice is very concerned about fundamental U.S. foreign policy and recent developments. He says that we have lost enormously during the past year in both India and Japan. Washington seems to have abandoned the traditional American policy of bolstering India as a democratic socialist force in Asia and the underdeveloped world. At the same time, we seem to have gone out of our way to kick around the faithful Sato government of Japan. In July we announced the Nixon Peking visit without advising Tokyo. In August we imposed a surtax on imports which desperately hit Japan. In October we persuaded the Japanese to cosponsor a UN resolution supporting a two-China policy and preventing expulsion of Taiwan—and the resolution was defeated in a vote that caused tremendous loss of face to Japan and the U.S.A.

PARIS, *October 31, 1971*

The American embassy called up in a flap. They got an urgent telegram from Washington saying there were rumors that Couve de Murville was going to be put forward as a candidate for secretary-general of UN to replace U Thant. He has an appointment with Secretary Rogers the day after tomorrow. Rogers asked the embassy to send urgent word on what they know about this. The embassy knows nothing and Couve is in America. They asked for help. I told them I could do nothing for twenty-four hours.

PARIS, *November 1, 1971*

Today I had one of the most interesting lunches of my life. André Malraux and Régis Debray and his wife came to our house together with Clem and Jessie Wood. Jessie is the daughter of Louise de Vilmorin, and Malraux regards her as a member of his own family.

It was a moving occasion. Malraux is seventy, still illuminating a feverish and brilliant mind, but expressing his ideas with considerable confusion because of his sniffs, whistles, twitches, and frequently failing voice. He is extremely hard to understand, but his mind races along.

On the other hand, Debray is a handsome young man with blond hair and drooping moustache, small, composed. He has a calm soft voice and a cold, ideological, unromantic Cartesian mind.

I felt that I was introducing to each other—across a gap of two generations (forty years)—two French literary revolutionists. And for their own part, they were both clearly aware that such was the case. It is a strange thing that they should have met first in the house of an American journalist since both of them are leary of Americans and of journalists.

I knew from Jessie's cousin, who acts as Malraux's secretary, that he had written in his diary *"déjeuner très important."*

Régis was prepared for an "occasion" and very well-dressed, like a true member of the Parisian *haute-bourgeoisie* to which he belongs by birth. So was his wife, a Venezuelan girl (and fanatical communist) with glowing eyes of black and the little sharp beak nose of a parrot.

It was a great success. Malraux arrived early. I detected a slight note of nervousness. I have a feeling that he was afraid to meet the ghost of his own youth. I offered him the choice between a Bloody Mary and a whisky and soda.

"Whisky," he said. *"Il ne faut pas changer."* It was evident that he had had at least one before arriving at one o'clock.

He had more before lunch, and drank sufficient wine (Mouton-Rothschild 1956). He talked brilliantly about his recent trip to Malta and the role played by Cervantes as a galley slave in the Turkish fleet during the famous siege.

Malraux said he had not made up his mind as to whether he would go to East Pakistan (Bangladesh) until after Mrs. Gandhi, the Indian prime minister, comes to Paris on an official visit next week. Debray took me in a corner for a minute after lunch and asked me what I thought Malraux could possibly do in East Bengal.

I asked Debray (who has recently come back from Cuba) if he had transmitted my message to Fidel Castro. He said that he had—one day when they were off on a spearfishing expedition. Castro said he did not intend to give an interview at this time, but that he would later on.

He thought I had been very fair to Allende in what I had written about him. I must say both Debrays were very friendly when they left, and his original nervous attitude had clearly evaporated. He told me he had heard I often used to see de Gaulle. I said this was true. He said, "But you seem to know most of the French leaders."

As soon as Debray came in, Malraux shot at him, "What were your objectives in Bolivia?"

"The establishment of revolutionary centers as a base for all Latin America," Debray replied.

But he was not able to enlarge; Malraux immediately interrupted, bringing up Bengal.

Malraux, when questioned by Debray on his reasons for choosing Bangladesh as his special cause, answered in difficult fashion. The gist was that he had been asked to adopt Bangladesh.

His aim, he said, was to become a kind of center or rallying point for volunteers. "If I succeed," he added, "then so much for the cause of national freedom. If I fail, what better way to die."

He made some contradictory remarks when talking about Bengal. He first said he loved the cause because it was so desperate. He then stated that the earlier Biafra cause held no interest even from the start because, completely surrounded as the country was by enemy territory, there was no hope.

Malraux enlarged on the objectives of Bangladesh. He wants to form cadres of cadets. "We form four hundred, and they form four thousand," he said.

He warned, "Don't forget that we assume people know everything—but they don't. They either don't have guns, or they do and don't know how to use them.

"Their cause is desperate," he said. And he added, "No cause can survive without a leader with a name. They need a de Gaulle. *Il leur faut un de Gaulle. Il faut un de Gaulle à tout le monde*."

And then he stated, "It is important to know that one must fight not just for a specific objective, but for a long time—for twenty years, for a hundred . . . for as long a time as it will take to convince Pakistan not to occupy Bengal."

When asked whether a class conflict would not develop in the Bengal situation, Malraux bristled. His view is that class is "*antérieur*"; it comes after national liberation. And national freedom, he insisted, is always the strongest force of all, and is a force which unites all. Over and over he repeated, "One thing at a time; one problem at a time."

Debray wanted to know about the international brigade's role in Spain. Malraux told him it had indeed saved Madrid, but that—above all else—it had answered the dream element of republican Spain. "If they are on our side, then we know we are not so pathetic," he said.

Malraux also explained that the brigade's value was enhanced by its temporary nature. No replacement was created after its disbandment.

The conversation moved on to other topics. The resistance was brought up. Malraux said he had not really liked the film, *Le Chagrin et la Pitié*. "The resistance was not really like that," he said.

Malraux commented: "One day I may write the book about *la résistance Française*," and then he went on to tell a resistance story. A group of maquis were ordered to capture a convoy of trucks transporting German sugar. The group attacked, failing to see that machine guns flanked the convoy. All the group's members were killed.

In the Corèze, the group's region, all the women put on black clothing when going to their respective family tombs. The following day the Germans threw the dead bodies into a collective grave while every woman of the Corèze stood by, dressed in black. The next day a cross was found on the collective tomb. And what is more, in a town which had nothing, every day a kilo of sugar was hung from the tomb's cross.

Malraux later talked about the Right and the Left. "The Right no longer exists, and today everybody is on the Left, which means the Left no longer exists."

Debray asked him whom—or what—he considered to be the primordial enemy. Again Malraux bristled. "There is no enemy, there is no single enemy. There are just many, and these are all symbolic."

When the subject of capitalism came up, Malraux said, "The matter is no longer important. One asks oneself if one is good or bad, charitable or egoist, brave or cowardly—but not: am I a capitalist?"

He asked Debray if treason had not played a larger part in his failure in Bolivia with Ché Guevara than had the lack of arms. Debray half-agreed.

Debray pointed out that Tania was in no way the "movie star" that Malraux had made her out to be. Debray also explained that Tania's parents had been German communists, and that she had lived a while in East Germany.

Malraux courteously acceded that he might well have been misinformed about Tania. "I have not been minister for eleven years without knowing that one can be misinformed by the '*services spéciaux*,'" he admitted.

Then he said that the facts were not so important and he dwelled at length on the importance of "*la légende.*"

"What is important in legend is that legendary aspect. One must never overlook the 'Jeanne d'Arc' side of things."

Nevertheless, Malraux then requested to hear the real version. "From time to time it's not bad to know the truth as well."

Malraux gave a long monologue on the "mysterious relationship between great men, simple men, and women." During it, he presented his differentiation between great and not-great men. Alexander and Napoleon were great, the Maréchal de Saxe (who never lost a battle) and Turenne were not. In heaven, Saxe could say "You lost a battle," but Napoleon would answer, "*Vous n'avez jamais fait rêver les femmes.*"

At coffee, we got back to the subject of Bangladesh. Malraux insisted that in order to fight, one must have a chance of surviving; otherwise fighting was "*faire les idiots.*" He said it was obvious that the Bangladesh cause would not succeed during his lifetime, whatever he did personally, but that he hoped to die there.

Earlier, when the Bolivian situation was being discussed, Malraux said it was a mistake to try and form peasant cadres. He said only worker cadres work, and these most of all in countries like Greece or Latin America, countries with heads and no bodies. Debray agreed with his point.

On his way out, Malraux shook Debray's hand. He wished him good luck. Debray was obviously impressed. He said he felt rather uncomfortable with his polemic writings on Malraux's work, after having met the man. "He is more human than the heroes in his novels," he avowed.

Debray was rather bemused by the list of great men adduced by Malraux—ranging from Alexander to Napoleon. "Why doesn't he include himself?" he asked. "Maybe he is the greatest."

PARIS, *November 1, 1971*

Jessie [Wood] called this evening to tell me her cousin said Malraux had enormously enjoyed the luncheon and liked Debray. Nevertheless he added: "But that young man has a lot to learn."

I told Jessie: "So did Malraux when he was the same age."

PARIS, *November 2, 1971*

Lunched today with Jacques de Beaumarchais, political director and Number Three man of the foreign ministry. He will go next year as ambassador to London. Jacques told me he has never heard a word about any project of Couve de Murville's being nominated for secretary-general of UN. For a job of that sort the nomination had to be made by the government, and was not a private selection like the Nobel Prize.

He said Brezhnev obviously had a very good time on his trip to Paris. Riding down to Marseilles on Pompidou's Caravelle, Beaumarchais sat next to Alexandrov of Brezhnev's staff, who speaks French. Several times Brezhnev came back from the private presidential cabin and leaned over Beaumarchais chatting with Alexandrov, saying what fun he was having.

Jacques said the French are strongly opposed to MBFR (Mutual and Balanced Force Reductions). The French think this would unbalance the situation in Europe. They were very interested to find from Brezhnev that he does not want France to reduce its armed forces—only Germany. In other words, he wants the French to be in a stronger position inside NATO and the Common Market than the West Germans. Beaumarchais is convinced the Russians are putting arms reduction at the top of their present schedule because they find it is simply too expensive to continue the arms race while financing Cuba, Egypt, India, and North Vietnam.

He bemoaned the fact that contacts between the *Quai* and the American embassy had dwindled to almost nothing. He said: "I used to see Chip Bohlen once a week. I saw Shriver twice a month. I don't think I have seen Watson in three months."

VIENNA, *November 8, 1971*

This afternoon I met Simon Wiesenthal, head of the Jewish documentation center. He is about sixty-three, with a lively, animated face, moustache, bright eyes, pointed ears, looking younger than his age although he had the grim experience of incarceration in the Nazi concentration camp of Mauthausen. He lost almost his entire family. When he emerged he had no desire to go back to his profession of architecture. "Who could I build houses for?" he asks. "They were all dead."

He devoted his first postwar years to hunting Nazis. He is still at it, working on small contributions from supporters in a modest office with a secretary. He found his wife miraculously after the war, has a daughter who lives in Utrecht, Holland.

I asked his opinion of General Reinhard Gehlen, Hitler's head of Soviet intelligence who was hired by the CIA in 1947 and later headed West German intelligence. Gehlen has just written a book claiming Martin Bormann, Hitler's deputy, was secretly a Soviet agent and fled to Russia where he lived until his death two or three years ago.

W. says Gehlen is a respectable man, not an SS or Gestapo type. However, the Bormann story is a lot of crap. Gehlen says he knows that since 1941 Bormann was a Soviet agent, that he learned this from the Abwehr chief, Admiral Canaris. But Canaris was a member of the July 20, 1944, anti-Hitler plot. Had he known Bormann was a Soviet agent he would have told others. But *nobody* in the July 20 group possessed this information.

Gehlen says that in the 1950s he received information from persons who had seen Bormann in the Soviet Union. If so, why didn't he tell his immediate superior, Globke, or Chancellor Adenauer, Globke's great friend? What would have happened had Adenauer demanded Bormann's extradition? It would have shattered world communism. But the German government and Globke both claim they knew no such thing. Gehlen couldn't have held on to such knowledge, merely saving it for his memoirs.

[Weisenthal continued.] Bormann was in the reichschancellery until May 2, 1945. Had he wished to escape to the Russians he would not have taken off from the chancellery—and with twenty other people, which was the case. Moreover, W. gave me photostats of pages from Bormann's notebook, found on a Berlin bridge near the chancellery, showing how he had drawn a map working out how he could ascertain where the north lay, night or day, in order to escape. He would not have needed such plans if it were only a question of slipping 300 yards to the Russians.

Gehlen says Bormann died two or three years ago in Russia. But it would have been inconceivably dangerous for the Russians to keep him after November 1, 1946, and the Nuremberg death sentence in absentia. Gehlen says Bormann was held in a "special camp." All such camps were under NKVD supervision. At least fifty people—plus those who would have interrogated Bormann—would have known this. But none of the high-ranking defectors from Soviet intelligence knew of this—and surely they would have told.

Wiesenthal has been working for years on the Bormann case. In 1965, he got a letter from a respectable British lawyer, representing a client who offered to sell Bormann's last alias for 15,000 pounds. The lawyer's client had been in South America and learned that Bormann had been there also for surgery. Wiesenthal also received an offer from a Chilean official wanting to sell a copy of Bormann's 1948 identity card.

After the war, a German SS underground movement, ODESSA, was formed. From their documents, later seized, we learned that Bormann in 1946 went to Italy and stayed in a Franciscan monastery on the Via Sicilia, Rome. Through the help of Monsignor Draganović, a Croatian monk who had been ambassador to the Vatican from the pro-Nazi Ustashi regime in Zagreb, Bormann was sent off to South America. Draganović, who headed the *émigré* organization Ustashi after the war, was sentenced to twenty years in prison in absentia by Tito's regime. But he later was allowed to return, a free man, most mysteriously. W. thinks he bought his way back with information.

Wiesenthal spoke with a woman who had known Bormann personally and who spotted him by chance on a bus in São Paulo, Brazil, in 1956 and addressed him by name. He fled. It is known Bormann was in Chile from 1948–52, living with a woman who worked for a German firm. W. also has a statement from a bar owner (now in Haiti) who used to run a bar in Asunción where Bormann and Mengele, chief doctor at Auschwitz, used to drink.

It is definite that Bormann was in South America from 1946 on, not in Russia. The last believable information about him comes from 1969 from a village called Ibiruba, a German settlement in the Brazilian state of Rio Grande do Sul, near the Paraguayan border. The source of this information is a highly reliable former German judge.

VIENNA, *November 9, 1971*

This morning I had a long talk with Chancellor Bruno Kreisky in the famous chancellery on the Ballhausplatz where Dollfuss was murdered. Kreisky, a cultivated, civilized man, is the first Jew to head the government of a German-speaking state. He is a Social Democrat but an intellectual bourgeois, not a workingman.

Kreisky said: "A united Europe can only function well if it becomes possible to create a welfare state in the modern sense. That is not just a matter of social security but also of a special economic life. I don't refer to a planned economy as in the communist countries, something that has proven to be a myth that failed. I refer to the need for regional planning and a framework that shows we know what we want to achieve."

What happened in 1968 in Czechoslovakia "totally convinced" him that "there is only a little room for political development in the communist world" of East Europe. There was always "some chance" of more "national identification" as in Hungary and Poland. But there would never be more real freedom in those countries than in the Soviet Union.

He spoke of talk of "blocs" ending as "an illusion." In 1968 he had warned the Czechs that Moscow would never tolerate a new Social-Democratic development in Prague. "I said: 'I favor it. But you must understand what the Soviets will and will not tolerate.'

"Blocs will continue—the communist bloc and the democratic countries.

And the idea of political or ideological convergence, an idea many people discuss, is also an illusion. It means nothing. Nevertheless, it is possible to encourage a lessening of tension between the systems.

"And nobody today knows just what practical coexistence will lead to because we haven't had it yet. Certainly things are bound at any rate not to get worse. Only peace is politically creative. War, even cold war, petrifies political systems."

Kreisky confessed he was most anxious about what may happen in Jugoslavia after Tito dies. It would be very serious if the country were to disintegrate. Yet Jugoslavia had inherited many of the nationality problems of the old Austro-Hungarian empire and had only managed to solve some of them. Everything depended on what the Russians would do.

Kreisky opposed any concept of reviving the Metternich-type system of a customs union of German-speaking states—West Germany, East Germany, Austria, Switzerland. "It wouldn't help us. It would only create opposition to pan-Germanism. We must accept the fact that there are English-speaking people everywhere and yet they are not linked in any empire system. And French-speakers and Spanish-speakers. Why should German-speakers want such a thing? Anyway, Moscow would never agree to it. Finally, if we can create a Europe, why do we need to create a bigger Germany?"

PARIS, *November 12, 1971*

Lunched with Bill Porter. He told me that Cyrus Eaton had been through here a fortnight ago and had called on him. Eaton told him that the North Vietnamese, whose mission here he visited, advised him that their basic indicator on whether to be hard or soft on American policy was looking at the Dow Jones index of the New York stock market.

Bill told me Prince Sihanouk of Cambodia is having a very rough time in Peking. The Chinese are fed-up with his approach to life—which demands a lot of sex and playing around. He is in their bad books. Moreover, the French tried very hard to get him moved from Peking to Paris which he wanted. The Chinese vetoed this project.

The Chinese mission here last month wholly confounded the French snooping services because whenever they had consultations in their hotel, they would proceed from room to room, moving around and often pausing in the hallways, and switching their talks from one dialect to another. As a result, the French don't yet know what they were talking about.

LONDON, *November 15, 1971*

Good talk with Lord Carrington, the defense minister. He said that if the northern Ireland crisis goes on it is bound to disrupt Britain's troop training program for NATO.

Two or three years ago there were various "foreign" groups stirring the Irish pie, but there is much less of this now and no indication of Moscow meddling. The trouble is genuinely Irish as in 1916 or 1921, even though the communists may be tempted to fish in troubled waters.

The crisis with Malta continues and will surely flame up again. Mintoff wants 18 million pounds a year for continued use of the base. Britain and NATO together (half and half) have offered 10 million pounds. Mintoff is a patriot but unbalanced. He'd like to raise local living standards and so change Malta's economy that five years hence it won't need a base. Britain sees no point in paying through the nose in order to get squeezed out. Malta doesn't mean much strategically, but politically is most important in the sense of keeping Russia out.`

As of now, the prospect of a French-British nuclear force for Europe can be discounted. France isn't willing and Britain is not able or prepared for the move. The French still insist on their sovereign rights of command decision. They would be unwilling to subordinate such a force to NATO control as Britain—and also Germany—would insist. At Nassau Britain pledged to the U.S.A. it would reveal no secrets received. The U.S.A. would have to release Britain from this agreement.

Carrington says the existing north Ireland situation means the two-thirds Protestant majority will always prevent the one-third Catholic minority from sharing the rule. A sensible solution would be a united Ireland with a national parliament in Dublin and a provincial parliament in Belfast and constitutional guarantees to the Protestant minority.

LONDON, *November 16, 1971*

Good talk over tea with Prime Minister Heath—in his study at 10 Downing Street. He looked fine: composed, bronzed with sun and sea winds.

He said that after the 1959–61 troubles, he had shared the view of Eire's then prime minister, Sean Lemass, that when both Irelands and the United Kingdom were in the Common Market a settlement between the two states (Irelands) could be worked out in a European framework. At that time Heath was handling Britain's Common Market negotiations. But the 1959–61 troubles were less serious than today's.

He still hoped the two communities of Ireland could be brought together some day. After all, when Heath had managed to bring [John] Lynch and [A. B. D.] Faulkner, prime ministers of Eire and north Ireland, together with him at Chequers this year, it was the first time the three prime ministers of those states had met in fifty years. Faulkner had been educated in Dublin and he and Lynch talked freely together, almost as if Heath had not been present. "But if I hadn't been there," he added with a rueful grin, "they wouldn't have been either."

The idea of a "European" settlement doesn't "go to the root of things at this moment," he continued. The "root" now is that the urban guerrillas aren't interested in a political solution. "They want to bring about a united Ireland—by violence." Lynch would be the first to disappear if the IRA solution were achieved. One "wing" of the IRA is Maoist and not in the least interested in the kind of solution Lynch wants. It is very difficult at this moment to contemplate, intellectually, any kind of political solution.

Lynch and the Eire government just haven't thought the matter through yet. They complain that in northern Ireland the Unionists (favoring union with Britain and representing the Protestants) are always in power. But they are in power because they represent a two-thirds majority of the northern Ireland population and don't want to abolish the border with Eire. Since the majority doesn't want to abolish the border it must always vote unionist; no one else favors that stand.

This is the reason why the Unionists maintain power against the non-Unionists. The Unionists see that Eire is far behind the United Kingdom in living standards and economic conditions, and the Unionists have the support of the Protestant one million two-thirds against the Catholic 500,000 one-third (approximate).

"That poses the question: how is it possible to form a satisfactory kind of government? The most recent attempt at a patchwork solution between two antipathetic peoples is Cyprus; and that hasn't worked. When Maurice Schumann was here last week he was sitting right in the chair you're sitting in and we discussed this. He mentioned the New Hebrides. But that's a condominium between Britain and France. And it isn't satisfactory.

"Lynch also suggests a coalition government. But that would mean Nationalists and Paisleyites and the National Labor party and even the Social Democratic Labor party would each have some portfolios. Therefore such an arrangement would become nonsensical. Where in the world has a compulsory coalition ever worked?"

I said I felt that the traditional intimacy of relationships between Washington and London was doomed to fade, now that Britain was joining Europe, and, indeed, had already faded as a result of Nixon's abrupt announcement of his Peking trip and equally abrupt monetary moves.

Heath said: "My relations with Nixon have been and remain perfectly all right. It is not so much a question of Britain as of U.S.-world relationships. Once Nixon had announced his intention to go to Peking, many countries felt they must make their own immediate policy adjustments. People thought the U.S.A. would adjust to the new China reality but most thought the adjustment would be gradual. Nobody thought that in one jump you would go from pingpong to major league baseball.

"And the economic package has produced world repercussions because of the way it's been handled. Treasury Secretary [John B.] Connally has been very rough. After all, the U.S. is the biggest economic country in the world and for twenty-five years it has built up a certain pattern of trade and currency stability. Suddenly and overnight all this has been changed. And it is so out of character with what we had been led to expect over a twenty-five-year period.

"Nor have things been helped by Connally's view that the U.S.A. is a free trading nation while Europe is protectionist. The U.S. has a 25 percent defense purchase levy; we don't. The U.S. puts a tariff of 125 percent on British chemicals. U.S. agriculture is protectionist. And when you add to all this a 10 percent surcharge plus special tax arrangements to help your industry competitively, it makes it hard for us to sell. And you still won't tell us what you are going to do in the long run."

I asked if he thought British military dependence on the U.S. would now be lessened by membership in Europe. He pointed out that the U.S. doesn't work out joint arms projects with Britain as do some European countries. This was the hard fact of a nation of 200 million dealing with one of 50 million. But America did buy some of "the stuff" Britain produces. The existing arrangements of Britain regarding nuclear submarines and Polaris missiles from the U.S. would continue.

I asked if the growing Anglo-French *entente* wouldn't obviously offset the newly powerful strength of Germany. He commented: "We have very good relations with the Germans and have had so for ten or fifteen years. On the other hand, following 1963 (de Gaulle's EEC veto), we had a difficult period with France.

"When Nixon finished his European trip last year he stopped off in London on the way home and came to lunch at Chequers. And the queen joined us. I hope we can have the same sort of easy relationship with France now."

I asked if, now that Britain was virtually in EEC, the pace—even if still long-range—of development of an Anglo-French nuclear force for Europe might not be hastened. He said: "If we were not in EEC such a project would certainly be decades off. Now the possibility is obviously somewhat nearer. But when I saw Pompidou this year we agreed the topic was not yet ready to be discussed."

Heath did not think today's would be "less" of a superpower world but thought China had a very long way to go, above all militarily. Europe, on the other hand, would have *half* the world's trade. Thus, in a sense, it was becoming *the* superpower. Russia and China were far behind on trade. And this European position had strong diplomatic implications. It gave Europe a major voice.

I asked if he thought the channel tunnel had become a more likely project with Britain joining EEC. "I have my own very special views on this," he said with a grin. "I live twelve miles from where the tunnel would be. I'd just like to see the sort of tunnel built that would allow me, if I felt like it, to get in my car and drive over to France or Holland for dinner. But this isn't what the experts want. They want a complicated kind of system where you would have to book weeks ahead and then arrange to put your car on a train. I want a big, wide tunnel that you can drive through easily. And if I can't have that, I'd like to see a bridge. But the experts warn you can't have a bridge, it is too risky, too many things might hit it.

"Maybe there's another answer. The channel is quite shallow on both the English and French sides, but there's a slight trough in the middle. Maybe we could build a bridge at each side and have a tunnel in between, making it much shorter. But no one will give me that kind of plan. So I suppose it isn't a very imminent project. But I can tell you Pompidou and Schumann feel quite differently. They want a tunnel."

We chatted about the mysterious disappearance of China's Lin Piao. He said he'd only read the flamboyant account saying Lin had fled and was shot down in an airplane after being betrayed by his daughter. "I suppose it's perfectly reasonable to think that a daughter might betray her father," he said. "But then, of course, I don't know, not having any daughters." (Heath is unmarried.)

PARIS, *November 24, 1971*

Dined last night with the Watsons. The ambassador was giving a dinner for the Duke and Duchess of Windsor. They did not arrive—for a tragic reason. The poor fellow is dying of cancer of the throat. He is such a frail little man that, at seventy-five, one would have hoped he could have died by having a stroke or a heart attack. Apparently the cancer is very near the jugular vein, so that he might go at any time or might survive painfully for months.

PARIS, *November 25, 1971*

Drink with Watson. He didn't think Rogers cut much ice as secretary of state. It would be a very good thing if he were kicked upstairs to the supreme court and Nelson Rockefeller became secretary.

Watson told me Nixon was meeting Pompidou on December 13 and 14 in the Azores. Forty-eight hours later it would be revealed he was going to see Heath in Bermuda on December 20 and Brandt in Florida after Christmas. Treasury Secretary Connally is going to the Azores, as well as Rogers and Kissinger. The most urgent subject is the monetary crisis. Connally has to face up to the fact that if we get too rough with the Europeans, they may turn around and nationalize American companies over here. Those in France alone are worth $12 billion and employ 280,000 workers.

Nixon has done all negotiations on the Nixon-Pompidou meeting directly with the Élysée—[Michel] Jobert [secretary-general of the Élysée]—and not the *Quai* [the foreign office]. Schumann learned about it only yesterday. Nixon wanted to avoid any kind of state visit in France. Martinique or Guadeloupe were suggested. But Pompidou is taking an official trip there next year and didn't want to have two visits so close together. French Guiana was discussed. Ireland was considered, but the troubles in Ulster plus the need to avoid embarrassing Heath ruled that out. At last, they agreed on Portuguese soil.

Oslo, *November 30, 1971*

Flew up yesterday. It was like groping inside a milk bottle. A fellow from the embassy escorted me to the house of Phil Crowe, our ambassador.

During World War II, Phil says, it is often forgotten that not only did the Norwegians "contribute" Quisling, but there were about 100,000 open pro-Nazis who set up an effective government and even sent 5,000 Norwegian volunteers to fight beside the Germans on the Russian front.

Nevertheless, they had a fine resistance, which built up slowly because the country had previously had a neutral tradition. Last night Phil gave a dance for eighty members of the Linge Club (named for Captain Martin Linge, killed in an S.O.E.-[British]-sponsored raid on the Lofoten Islands). The Linge Club seems to include both British-trained-and-based active saboteurs and the local "Milorg" resistance which built up a communications network and kind of militia that took over from the Germans when they surrendered.

At the party was Knut Haugland, twice captured by the Germans. He escaped to England, parachuted back to sabotage the heavy water plant at Rjukan, spent weeks living in the wintry mountains on reindeer, rabbits, and moss, finally blew up the plant and shot his way to freedom. He was radio operator on Thor Heyerdahl's raft expedition across the Pacific and now divides his time between the resistance museum and the Kon-Tiki museum.

Oslo, *December 1, 1971*

Trygve Bratteli, prime minister of Norway, received me this morning: a handsome, small man of sixty-one. He talks slowly and thoughtfully in good, if accented, English.

The big current issue is the Common Market. I asked what Norway's alternative policy would be if it failed to get in. He said: "We haven't discussed an alternative."

He said Norway would prefer to see the Keflavik base in Iceland continue operative. He added: "In a war—which I hope we will never see again—it would make things very difficult for Norway not to see a base in

Keflavik. But during a prolonged period of peace such as that we are now in there are few people in Norway, apart from the political and military leaders, who have any interest in strategical problems."

I remarked that King Haakon had told me in 1949 he was eager to have Norway in NATO "to make it clear to everyone who their real friends are now so they can never be fooled in a war" which would again have "a fifth column" (meaning the communists). Did Bratteli share this view?

"Basically yes," he replied. "But it is more difficult to measure these things after a very long period of peace such as now exists. I don't think you'll meet people here who say 'our friends are in the East and our enemies are in the West.' But you will find many who will say 'we have no enemies on either side.' Today the feeling of a divided Europe is far less strong than it was. But this has not produced a widespread mood of neutralism. So far, NATO remains generally accepted."

BRUSSELS, *December 2, 1971*

Drove out to NATO headquarters, a shambling building on the edge of the city, looking like a concentration camp, for a talk with Joseph Luns, the enormous Dutchman who has replaced Brosio as NATO's secretary-general. He is a charming man, about six foot six, with a long, horsy face and an excellent sense of humor.

He is browned-off that there has been no U.S. ambassador to NATO for almost seven months. He lunched with Pompidou last April and expressed gratitude for France's increased cooperation with NATO. Pompidou said he was glad this had been noticed, but begged Luns not to talk about it "and increase my troubles."

Luns said monetary and economic crises comprise his biggest current worry because "so much depends on the outcome. If recession develops into a real crisis, the implications for the alliance are extremely serious.

"And we must move rapidly. In at the very least one country, the United States, national elections are coming next year. There will be little time left for discussion of matters like this."

I asked if he thought European members of the alliance would meet the American demands that they assume a larger share of the defense burden. He answered: "There is no chance of this unless the currency question is settled first. But don't forget that 80 percent of the allied troops now in Europe are Europeans.

"If there is a real recession Soviet interest in a mutual and balanced force reduction will simply disappear. They would rather get something for nothing, a Western unilateral reduction, in such a circumstance."

There is likely to be another crisis over Malta. Prime Minister Mintoff is being very arrogant. When Willy Brandt, a fellow socialist, offered him a special bilateral West German contribution of 150,000 pounds a year, Mintoff sent him back a message: "I don't like bad jokes." Brandt was furious.

Luns said the NATO position vis-à-vis Russia in Europe was slowly deteriorating. Some new weapons, such as the MIRV warheads of U.S. Poseidon submarines, still gave the West a real edge. But an unbalancing process has been going on and accentuated during the last four years. Soviet naval power is growing by leaps and bounds.

Over the past twelve or thirteen years, the Russians managed to build a huge fleet while at the same time increasing the military threat in Europe and organizing a massive and menacing force along the Chinese border. It is an impressive accomplishment.

CAIRO, *December 9, 1971*

Saw President Anwar el Sadat at noon. I drove to el Sadat's house with Mohamed Heikal in his Mercedes and limped out with my crippling gout.

El Sadat is a trim man with pleasant face, moustache, white teeth, dark skin, balding forehead, and a strange spot in the center just above his brow, like a dull bruise. He smoked a pipe and served glasses of tea. He was friendly, but as the conversation rolled he became more and more emotional and at certain points, when he indicated deception by the U.S.A., I could see his eyes mist over.

El Sadat said: "I think the United States, as a big power, should be keen for peace in the area, if there are diplomatic relations or not. We have severed our diplomatic relations with the U.S. because of its complete alignment with Israel, before the aggression in 1967 and after the aggression. But I told [Secretary of State] Rogers when he was here we are ready, if the first-phase withdrawal of Israeli troops is completed, to restore diplomatic relations and create a new atmosphere in the whole area."

I asked if he considered India justified in invading East Pakistan. He said: "I am not for invading any country because of any cause at all. I have suffered from this here, and still am suffering from this, but it appears that the problem there has many dimensions. I think the key of the whole problem is the problem in East Pakistan and the sort of autonomy they should have, but not a secession at all.

"On India we remark something very funny about the American position. They voted for the cease-fire and everyone to return to his boundaries. In 1967 the position of America was completely contradictory to this and contradictory to all that the UN has taken as tradition since it started. The U.S. is now voting for a cease-fire and everyone to return back to his boundaries.

"In the last eight months we have had contacts with the U.S. and my conclusion is this: I and your state department and your administration were playing hide-and-seek. They told me, in the first place please put confidence in us. I said, very well, I am quite ready to put confidence in you.

"I took my initiative upon the fourth of February (to reopen the Suez Canal), and they said, very well, this is a marvelous thing, we shall be working on it and so on. Then it ended in the same position of the U.S. that was taken during the Johnson administration in the UN—contradictory to that they have taken regarding the India-Pakistan problem.

"The U.S. wants Israel to use the occupation of my land and Arab land as an instrument of pressure to impose all that she wants. I am awfully sorry to say I have lost confidence completely in your administration.

"I am dead sure something was cooked up between Johnson's administration and Israel, and we shall know about it in years to come—as we have learned about the aggression in 1956 (the Suez campaign) afterwards. The U.S. has come to the same starting point taken by the American administration under Johnson: that Israel must impose whatever she wants. I mean using the occupation of our land, the Arab land, as an instrument for this.

"This will be the year of decision; 1971 must be decisive because as I told you, after eight months of contacts with the U.S., they are still in the same position as Johnson's administration—alignment 100 percent with Israel.

"We have done our best for a peaceful solution. We have gone to the utmost. Even [Secretary of State] Rogers when he was here and [Assistant Secretary] Sisco said we have nothing to ask of you. Israel must move, and make the next move. Then suddenly the U.S. retreats completely and we find ourselves still at the same starting point.

"Well, we say this. It is a matter of our pride, our dignity, and our honor to liberate our land. We don't say, what does Israel have? The military men say this.

"But as the man to take the decision here I must say this, I am in a fix now. The U.S. gives Israel everything to put pressure on me, and to impose its conditions on me. We shall do whatever is possible to avoid this situation and to prove to the U.S. and to the whole world that we shall not accept what they want.

"You are giving Israel Skyhawks today instead of Phantoms, and then promising to give them Phantoms later. The problem for me is this: Is the U.S., as a big power, willing for a peaceful solution, an honorable solution, or not? It has been proven to me that they are not.

"I don't want the U.S. to be on my side. I don't ask this. I just want the U.S. to be like a big power—responsible for world peace, to be just neutral, to see the facts as they are.

"I would like to make your administration remember that I have lost a battle but I did not lose a war. I am quite ready for a peaceful solution, an honorable one—that will last. But not at the cost of my dignity nor at the cost of my land.

"Yet, as I told you, we have played hide-and-seek for eight months. I have always felt the Americans were playing this game—until they showed quite clearly that they can't put pressure on Israel. Israel would not survive without the help of the United States.

"I told the Americans that we are speaking of peace and when we speak of peace let us not speak of the strategic values of Sinai, Sinai is my land. On Israeli withdrawal, they say that a withdrawal from the Bar Lev line would cause strategic inequalities and would put Israel in a bad position. I told them when we are speaking of peace let us drop all these strategic problems. The Bar Lev line is in my land. I am dead sure something was cooked up during the Johnson administration between Israel and the U.S. Nixon, it appears, cannot get himself loose from it."

I asked if he meant something like a treaty, some kind of written alliance? He said: "Written alliance, secret agreement.

"The U.S. has its aims combined with the aims of Israel in the area here. I had a two-and-a-half-hour talk with Rogers in this house. He told me that Golda Meir at some time called the American ambassador in Israel and told him to send this message to President Nixon and to Mr. Rogers: 'I defy the whole world that President Sadat will never agree to the words "peace agreement." If he agrees, I am ready to put my cards on the table.' That's what Rogers told me and he told me, 'I am going to Israel from here to ask Mrs. Meir to put her cards on the table because you have already agreed upon a peace agreement.'

"I had confidence at that time. But they have returned again to the policy of hide-and-seek; to give Israel time to prolong the whole thing, and then we come to the year 1972, the year of elections. They will say 'Oh, we are busy with the elections. Let us postpone it until the new president comes in in January 1973. Then in January 1973, he will have six months, according to tradition.' The president takes six months to shape his policy. Then after that it will bring me to 1974 and it will be a de facto situation here in the area.

"There are no Soviet soldiers in the canal zone. Even Rogers said, 'Yes, I know there are no Soviet soldiers or officers there. They are in the depth of the country at the missile sites, the SAM-3 sites.'

"I told him I have officers and soldiers from the Red army. Do you know where they are stationed? Are they on the canal? He said, 'No, they are not on the canal.' They are at the SAM sites in the depth of the country. I am not asking anyone to fight my battle for me, neither Soviet soldiers nor American soldiers nor anyone.

"I know the Pentagon is 100 percent with Israel. For example, they are mixing all this into global strategy and power politics of the two powers.

On December 24, 1970, in my first contact with Nixon I told him, in my first direct message: 'Please, I do not want to be involved in all this. I just want to free my occupied territories.'

"I have here, as I told Rogers, officers and soldiers from the Red army at the missile sites and not at the canal. I am paying their salaries in hard currency. The Soviets themselves, I must be fair, don't want their soldiers to stay here in Egypt, believe me. And every time I try to prolong their stay I must use all my efforts to convince them. You know quite well we are an independent country, and our main problem with you [the United States] was that we did not want to enter into the sphere of influence of anyone.

"This was our problem with the late Mr. Dulles. We are an independent country and we shall always do what is necessary for our security. But we shall never sell out to anyone. This is the first thing. For the second, I have written to President Nixon telling him quite frankly, 'I am giving the Soviet fleet facilities in the Mediterranean because they stood with us in our black days. And I shall continue to give the Soviet fleet these facilities.'

"At the same time I shall be keeping advisers here for my army because war is a science now. It is not, as before, just bravery and so forth. It is a science. I also told President Nixon that I shall be keeping advisers in my country.

"But regarding the Soviet soldiers and officers who are at the SAM sites, well, every time I need all the persuasiveness I have to get the Soviets to keep them here—because they don't want to. My Egyptian crews that they have trained are on the canal. On the canal there are no Soviet soldiers.

"The term Soviet 'presence' here is misunderstood by you. The Soviets themselves don't want their people to stay here at the SAM sites. I myself try to convince them to keep them here."

Mohamed afterward took me home to lunch (although I should much rather have gone to bed with my bad gout). Hedayat, his charming wife, was there, and his little boy (the youngest), whose fifth birthday it was. It was a moving occasion because the radio was announcing sentences of the conspirators who sought to overthrow the regime last May and Mohamed kept it playing, forgetting everything as he stood beside the loudspeaker. Four were sentenced to death but commuted. Several of the leaders, Heikal said, came to his apartment to discuss things. But none were good friends and none had ever been to his farm near Mena House where only friends go.

CAIRO, *December 10, 1971*

Spent day in bed with bad case of gout.

While awaiting the final record, I pondered on my conversation with the president [el Sadat]. He is not charismatic, not another Nasser. I wonder if he'll be able to last. There was one conspiracy against him already (in May). If he can't get action on liberating Israeli-held territory, the pressures may become too much.

PARIS, *December 17, 1971*

I limped goutily over to the Élysée—for an appointment with President Pompidou. I was sitting in the waiting room outside his office when Maurice Schumann, the foreign minister, came briskly out. He strode over for a warm handshake and said: "I just finished your book. An excellent book. I can hardly wait for the next volume."

Pompidou looked well and energetic, although he is slowly losing the battle of the waistline. He seemed suntanned and I asked if it came from the Azores, where he saw President Nixon earlier this week. He said: "We didn't have much time for that."

I asked whether the agreement reached with Nixon at the Azores could provide the beginning of a new monetary balance that might endure a quarter of a century as the Bretton Woods accord had. He answered: "I hope so. Nevertheless, the accord we made was only to thaw out the situation.

"We admitted the principle that we must quickly unblock the impasse in order to force a durable international situation. But difficulties still remain. What will be the role of reserve currency? Is the dollar still to be considered a reserve currency? What will be the role of gold? And how will international liquidity be controlled?

"Nixon was not ready with the answer on these questions. This is not his speciality. Some people call me an expert on these problems, but I never forget that the experts often end up as the victims. Much still awaits the future. The general problems have not yet been settled."

I observed that one implication of the Azores accord seemed to base currency relationships more firmly than before on the gold standard.

"Let us say that it is true theoretically that the dollar has been devalued and the franc remains steady," Pompidou replied. "But although this may be the same thing commercially, it is not the same thing in a monetary sense. I was very struck that the American negotiators did not talk of a devaluation of the dollar but of revaluing gold. This certainly indicates a change of attitude in Washington. But we cannot ever go back to the gold standard as such, although the role of gold is the only ultimate way to avoid inflation while at the same time avoiding domination of world trade by individual great powers.

"The French attitude has led the United States to reconsider its policy. But it wasn't my intention to [*rouler Nixon dans la farine*] take Nixon for a ride. He came with his ideas and I came with mine. But soon we found that they were really quite close together. It was a realistic talk."

I asked if the Azores agreement had eliminated the chances of a trade war and a serious depression. He answered: "The chance of a depression has been virtually ended. But a trade war cannot yet be excluded. After all, there are political aspects to be considered."

I expressed the belief that Pompidou was able to speak in the Azores with the voice of Europe and that France's position in Europe had been strengthened because of the reduction of French diplomatic activities in distant areas and its concentration on Europe. Pompidou nodded. He said: "You are right. Of course, we don't renounce a French world role but there is no doubt that it is limited.

"One must admit that although France does not renounce a kind of moral position in a global sense, we don't have the strength to insist on what is right and what is wrong in many areas. We don't have the means to act everywhere. I prefer to concentrate our action elsewhere—in Europe and in terms of Europe vis-à-vis Africa and in terms of East-West relationships as they affect Europe. There we have the power to act."

I asked how he foresaw the relationship between an expanded Common Market including Britain, and the U.S. He said: "I foresee plenty of friction at many points where we irritate each other. But no real friction on basic problems. Globally speaking, the Common Market wants to develop its living standards and its consumer requirements. All this is understandable, but there are bound to be plenty of small problems of a political nature.

"The big difficulty comes with Japan. I don't think there can be a trade equilibrium if the Japanese pursue a permanent policy of expansion. They cannot have an eternal annual growth rate of 7 or 8 percent."

I asked him if he thought that, after a new Berlin agreement, a European security conference would be called and would *formally* acknowledge all existing frontiers on this continent—and also admit both East and West Germany to UN. He nodded and said with emphasis:

"Certainly. Even Chancellor Brandt spoke of this when he was in Oslo a few days ago. It is impossible to imagine anything else. But this is quite independent of a European security conference. Ultimately two Germanys will be recognized and this will probably take place before a security conference. We will probably get East Germany into UN in 1972. That is, of course, speculation, but I am sure it will come quickly. The West Germans prefer to have the East Germans in UN first before a European security conference, so they can sit next to them more easily at such a conference."

I recalled that he had often talked to me conjecturally about the possibility of a Franco-British nuclear force for Europe. How did he feel now, with Britain on the verge of Common Market membership? "I can't say anything on this yet," he said. "The Nassau agreement between the U.S.A. and Britain was a ten-year agreement, so it is valid until 1973. While Britain is limited by this agreement, no one can speculate on what the U.S. attitude will be concerning such a force. But if the agreement is allowed to lapse in 1973, would Britain decide to choose a strictly European attitude on defense, thus forgoing U.S. atomic aid? Who knows? Of course, if the U.S.A. does not renew the Nassau agreement, the way to such a force may be opened."

I said NATO leaders had told me cooperation between France and the alliance military structure has improved. Was it French policy to work for greater cooperation? He said:

"Of course, there is no question of integration. When the rupture between France and NATO started there was a period of coolness. But even in the last years of General de Gaulle an improvement had started. We don't have common exercises with NATO, but there is good cooperation and good understanding. This does not represent a policy change. But perhaps we say more often that we are in the alliance than was true under de Gaulle. We certainly stressed it to the Russians and they recognize this because they are realists."

Pompidou doesn't think the time has come for a new Big Four initiative to seek a permanent Middle East settlement. I asked him if he thought the Big Four framework hadn't been outmoded anyway by China's admission to the security council. He answered: "We'll see. Anyway you can't have agreements of the four powers unless the U.S.A. and Russia agree."

I asked if France has cautioned Libya, now that it was in a federation with Egypt, that the Mirage planes it had bought from this country must not be used against Israel. He said France's attitude on this was perfectly clear, but he added that "from time to time we repeat our view." In other words we remind the Libyans that they are not supposed to use the planes except at home. To conclude, Pompidou added: "I don't think much of that federation anyway, do you?"

I asked if France would loosen its embargo on arms for Israel now that Israel has agreed to give up its claim to the Mirages it had bought but which France has refused to export since 1967. He answered: "The two questions aren't linked. We decided to use the Mirages for our own armed forces. We told Israel we were ready to pay for the planes and we are discussing the terms right now. We have always been ready to make an agreement on this basis."

"As for the rest, we haven't changed our attitude. But I can tell you strictly between us that we allow certain things to pass from time to time in the form of spare parts and so on. The Israelis are very intelligent and they know perfectly well that we don't want to see any deterioration in the equipment they have already bought from us. We want to see it maintained."

Did he feel U.S. Vietnamization policy was slowly bringing the war to a standstill, and was the moment approaching for serious peace negotiations? He answered: "I think we will have peace. I think the moment is approaching. Of course, it will have to end with your complete evacuation. But this is what I think is coming."

PARIS, *December 20, 1971*

Lunched with Asher Ben-Natan, Israeli ambassador.

He said Israel figured el Sadat cannot make peace and therefore there is no use rushing into negotiations. It would be easy for Israel to make a permanent settlement with el Sadat. The only question is Sharm El Sheikh. And Israel doesn't want sovereignty, only a twenty-five-year lease to insure its own protection in the Aqaba Gulf. But el Sadat doesn't dare make a peace without taking into account Jerusalem and other Arab claims. Therefore, B.N. foresees during the next five years a form of temporary armistice with Egypt, including an Israeli pull-back, but no formal peace. Israel will be on the Golan Heights of Syria for years.

He told me the famous Vedettes (star-boats) "kidnapped" by Israel in December 1969 weren't even French. They were German-planned. The Israelis had gotten blueprints for the boats and engines from the Germans as part of their over-all reparations and armaments agreement. Israel could have had them manufactured in Italian shipyards, but in 1965 the French asked that they be made here because there was unemployment in French shipyards. Therefore, Israel felt outraged when their delivery was embargoed—and swiped them.

He says the Russians want very much to have a diplomatic agent of their own in the Finnish embassy in Israel (now handling Soviet affairs). The reason is so they can have someone on the scene to warn and threaten Israel when necessary, as Soviet ambassadors used to do. They can't envision regular diplomatic relations yet. But they would send a high-level agent.

Israel isn't anxious to go along. Israel knows the limit has been reached about what a nuclear superpower can do about threatening a small power. The Russians have made it clear they intend to stay in the Arab world and to support it in another war, to prevent an Israeli victory. [Ambassador Anatoli] Dobrynin has three times cabled Nahum Goldman and asked him to Washington to convey this message.

PARIS, *December 23, 1971*

Interesting lunch with Michel Jobert, secretary-general of the Élysée, and Pompidou's right-hand man. Jobert is a short, very thin man of fifty. He is intensely intelligent, sensitive, and has a good sense of humor. He looks tired and admits that the work is extremely hard. He never goes to the country and on Sundays, his normal day off, he likes just to sit on his terrace in Paris, regarding the nearby trees.

He joined Pompidou more or less accidentally in 1962. He had been at ENA (*École Nationale d'Administration*) with Pompidou's brother-in-law and was also a classmate of Ortoli, Pompidou's *directeur de cabinet* when he was prime minister. Ortoli asked him to join the present cabinet, and he has been with Pompidou ever since, now running the Élysée for him. He is certainly one of three or four key men in France today.

To my astonishment, he told me that he has only two full-time members of his staff (apart from stenographers), and there are only fifteen of them, including experts on such things as monetary matters, internal taxes, and foreign policy. He compared this with Kissinger, who handles only foreign and security policy and has more than 200 members on his staff. Jobert said he is in charge of everything. Foreign policy only occupies 30 percent of his time. His job is to coordinate things and get the right experts to move immediately whenever required. He has his finger in every pie.

I asked if he had his equivalent in any other government. He said a man named Armstrong had practically the same job in England for Heath. But Kissinger only dealt with foreign and security matters. In Russia there was a position similar to Kissinger's filled by a man named Alexandrov. Alexandrov is attached to Brezhnev's office. He is a very quiet, cautious man who speaks good English and quite adequate French.

He said Pompidou's primary virtue is common sense. From there, he went on to a long analysis. Pompidou is a highly cultivated and intellectual man who knows a great deal about literature, painting, and music. But he doesn't like to read foreign books.

His taste in paintings is excellent. Several moderns he originally bought for a song are now very valuable. But despite his intellectuality and broad cultivation, his literary style is not dazzling. It is much like his conversation —a string of reasoned clauses. The short book he distributed among friends and family which he began to write as a memoir after he was put in political exile by de Gaulle is not elegant. It deals entirely with the crisis of May 1968. The memoir was never finished because Pompidou came back into active life too soon. Perhaps some day he will write his memoirs. And Jobert hopes his style will improve. Nevertheless, Pompidou writes all his speeches himself. He never uses a ghost. When the text is finished, he gives it to Jobert, who then edits it and suggests corrections. Rather grumpily, Pompidou accepts most of them.

Pompidou has extraordinarily good health and is very strong and resilient. This is astonishing since he likes to eat, drink, and smoke, and detests exercise. But he is very solid and sleeps extremely well. He knows how to rest. His one physical weakness is that he is a sucker for any pills suggested to him by any doctor. He often takes these, but thanks to his physical resistance, he doesn't suffer for it. He is a bear for work. He likes to work on airplanes when he travels.

I thought it strange that Nixon and Pompidou got on so well together because they were so different. He said Nixon was very sly (*malin*) but was a reasonable man who had a lot of horse sense. Nixon had used Connally cleverly to play a kind of rough role like a bull during the monetary crisis. But Connally was obviously very subtle. Nixon would keep saying to Pompidou that he didn't understand such and such a technical point and would refer it on to Kissinger or Connally. Kissinger knows nothing about monetary matters. Jobert is convinced Connally will be the American vice presidential candidate with Nixon next year.

He said Heath was strong, but tough. In some ways he was more difficult to do business with than Nixon because he was less flexible and subtle than Pompidou. But he was an effective British leader. Brandt was more of a facade. One could talk with him at great length and later on one would find through the remarks of Brandt or Scheel (foreign minister) or [Conrad] Ahlers (official spokesman) that Brandt really hadn't understood. He said Brandt's "Kissinger" or "Jobert" on Europe was Frau Dr. Katarina Focke who is a member of parliament.

Jobert says Brezhnev is a rough, strong man and that you can see in his behavior to his Soviet associates and their reactions that he is rather a tsar. They are scared of him. Jobert had the good fortune of riding with Brezhnev to and from Versailles during his visit here when he talked with Pompidou. Thus, all told, he had about two and one-half hours of direct conversation with him. Brezhnev posed lots of problems of a protocol nature. He kept wanting to see "Gay Paree." Jobert said he would be glad to take him around in his own car incognito, shaking the security forces in charge, that that was the only way and it violated all protocol. It never happened. Brezhnev's indiscretions were astonishing. He would point out this or that Russian to Pompidou or Jobert and say, "His wife didn't come with him but he wears horns." He would say this in the presence of these unfortunate men who just looked downcast.

Brezhnev has a lot of gusto, and is far from stupid. He is obviously the boss. "When are you going to see him?" Jobert asked. He thought it would be a good idea if I sent him a telegram. He added: "You know, I think he would very much like to be interviewed by you. He has a craving to be exposed to Western newspapermen; and yet another side of him cautions against this. Why don't you try?"

I asked what he thought we could do about the mess in south Asia now. He said it was clear that all the Western powers must support Pakistan and help it to get on its feet again. India was going to have its own troubles and Bangladesh is going to end up either as a Chinese or a Soviet satellite, not an Indian satellite. American policy has been disastrous. The Soviets now have everything between the Suez Canal and the Bay of Bengal—a strategic area they dominate today.

When [Valerian] Zorin, the Soviet ambassador who recently departed, said farewell to him, Jobert remarked: "You know, Mr. Ambassador, your position in Indochina is like ours. Neither Peking nor Washington is going to listen to either of us. But unlike France, Russia is going to have to pay."

PARIS, *December 28, 1971*

Bill Porter says all U.S. policy is now pointing toward Nixon's China visit. Although Moscow has been screaming about our resumption of bombing of North Vietnam, there hasn't been one solitary peep out of Peking. He says the Russians can indeed supply arms to North Vietnam by sea, even if China blocks overland routes. But the North Vietnamese depend upon China for a considerable amount of their food. Since they lost control by the Vietcong of the South Vietnamese delta and access via Sihanoukville of rice through lower Cambodia, they have been on short rations. The Russians have sent some rice shipments by sea to North Vietnam but Hanoi has depended for about 10 to 15 percent of its grain on China. Moreover, this only feeds people in North Vietnam; North Vietnamese troops in Laos and Cambodia must forage for themselves in order to eat. The situation has been seriously aggravated by this year's heavy floods in North Vietnam. The North Vietnamese need even more food than they are getting to maintain any momentum for military operations outside Vietnam, and Peking is not complying.

Bill said the new American tactic is that we are refusing to sit down and negotiate with the communist side here until they are ready to discuss and negotiate in a meaningful way and not merely use the meetings as a propaganda sounding-board. We are going to go on week after week politely declining, by weekly notes, each scheduled session until the communist side sits down for real negotiations.

We reckon they are terrified we might call off the whole conference, because it is an invaluable sounding-board for their propaganda. Therefore, we merely tell them we are waiting for them to get new instructions telling them to negotiate seriously.

PARIS, *December 31, 1971*

Lunch with Jim Jones. He is a short powerful man with high forehead, massive jutting jaw, a quiet voice, and a deeply serious manner. He has himself well under control, but you can easily see that he could blow into a monumental rage.

These days Jim told me he weighs only 165 pounds as compared to about 190 a few years ago. He has been very ill, but is now much better. He has sworn off drink, except for an occasional glass of wine.

Jim is a hard-working writer. He has an office in the same apartment house as his home on the Île de la Cité, and is at his desk by 9:00 every morning. He stays until lunch (when he only has a hamburger) and is then back for about three hours each afternoon. He is now working on a long serious novel and occasionally on a leitmotif, a detective story about Spetsais (where he rented a house last summer) to amuse himself.

Jim comes from simple origins in Illinois where, as a boy, he occasionally shot and fished with his grandpa. I gather he is a first-class shot, both bird and rifle; he says he learned most about it in the army.

He went through the Pacific, emerged as a youngster still, went to NYU to get an education. He wrote a novel and took it to Max Perkins, the famous editor at Scribners, because Jones admired Thomas Wolfe who adulated Perkins. Perkins told him what was wrong with the book, but encouraged him and used to buy him drinks. He took a job on a fishing boat in Florida and rewrote his work. When he brought it back, Perkins rejected it but showed interest in another idea Jim had, a story of World War II with the heroes GIs, a kind of *What Price Glory* but not about officers. Jim wrote it—*From Here to Eternity*—in four years. It was a smashing success.

POSTSCRIPT

In concluding this, the third volume of diaries and memoirs compiled over the decades and finished at the age of sixty, I can only hope to reassure readers that there will be no more of this sort. I can think of easier and more pleasant ways of relaxing over the years remaining to me, years spent perhaps with the gentle noise of grandchildren, trout, and birds substituting for a typewriter's abrasive harshness. Roving journalism takes its toll and I look forward to talking to my wife and friends instead of statesmen, to traveling no farther than I can swim or walk instead of winging the world from pole to pole. So, recalling events described in these pages and in two earlier tomes of equal size, I repeat lines of Cavafy, the Greek poet, cited at the very start of my first volume:

> The days gone by remain behind us,
> a mournful line of burnt-out candles . . .
> I do not want to look at them; their form saddens me,
> and it saddens me to recall their first light.

Index